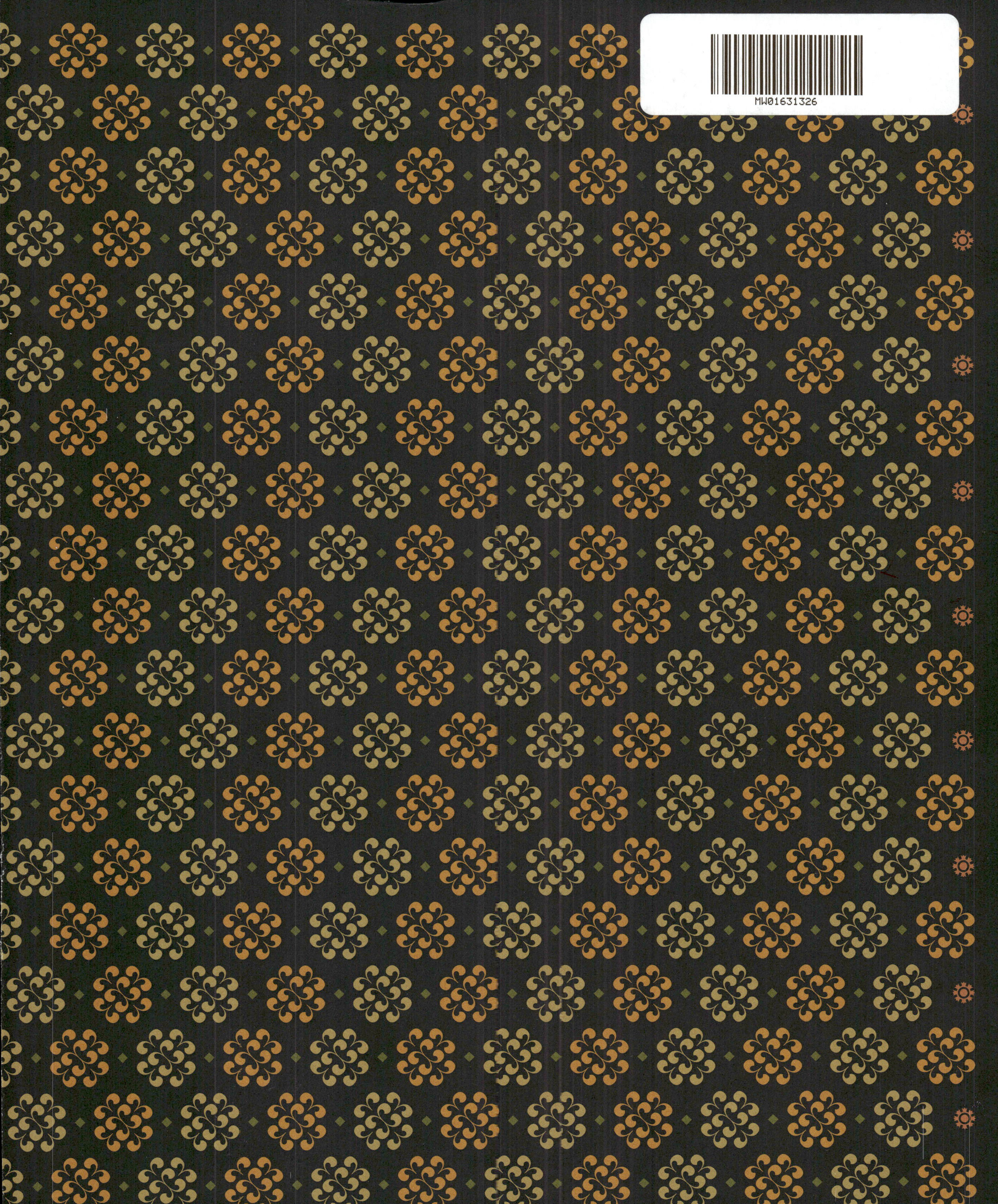

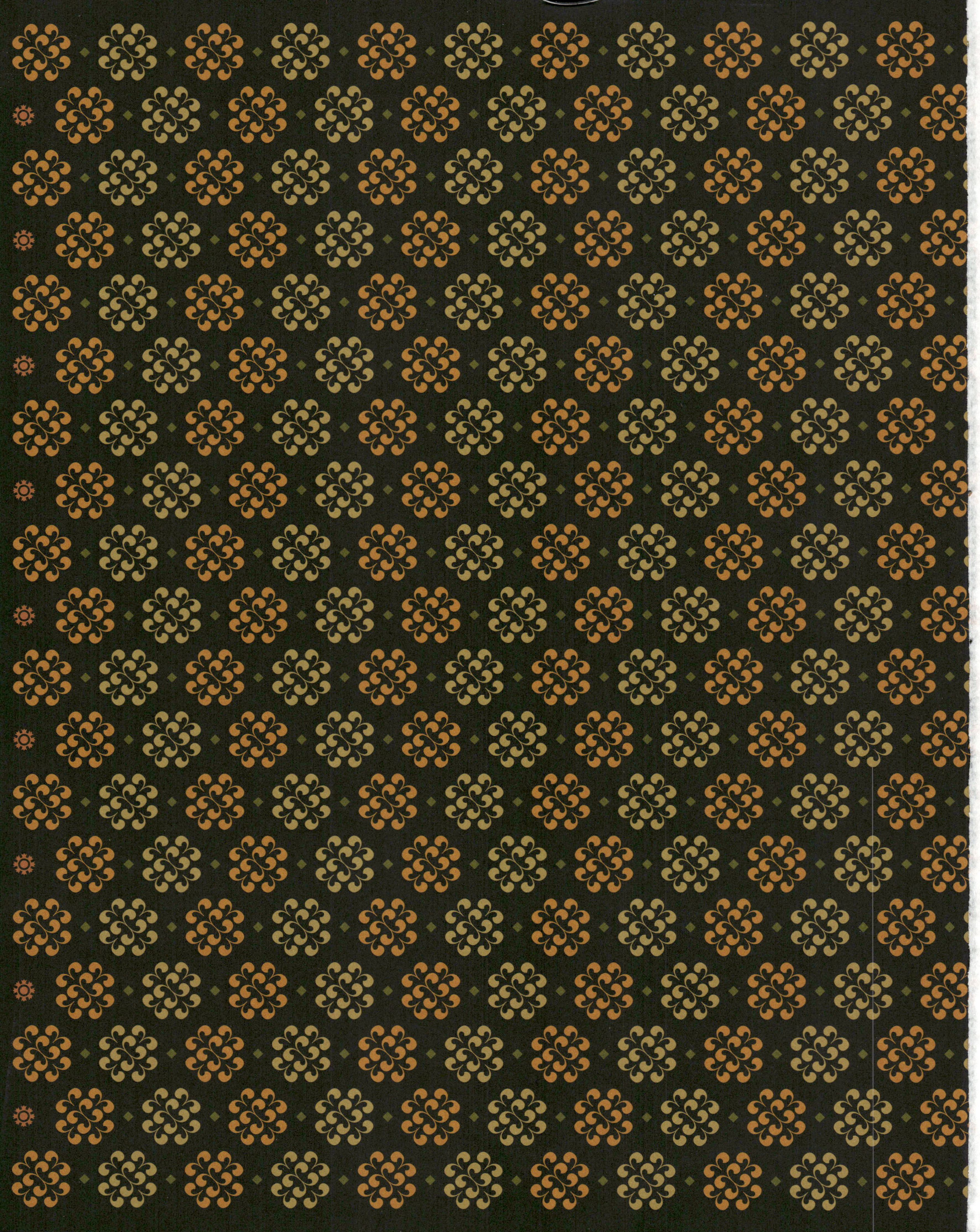

JAMES TISSOT

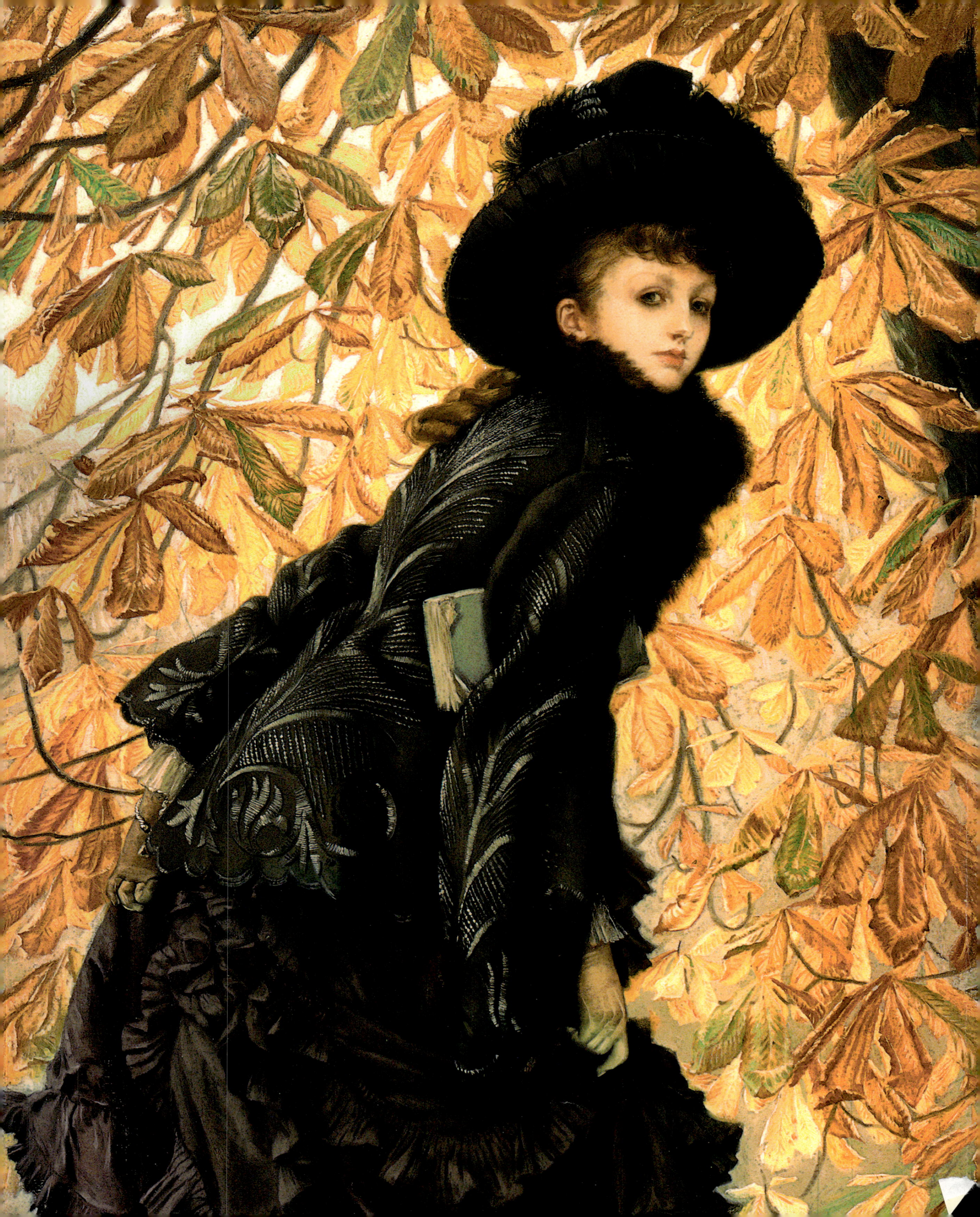

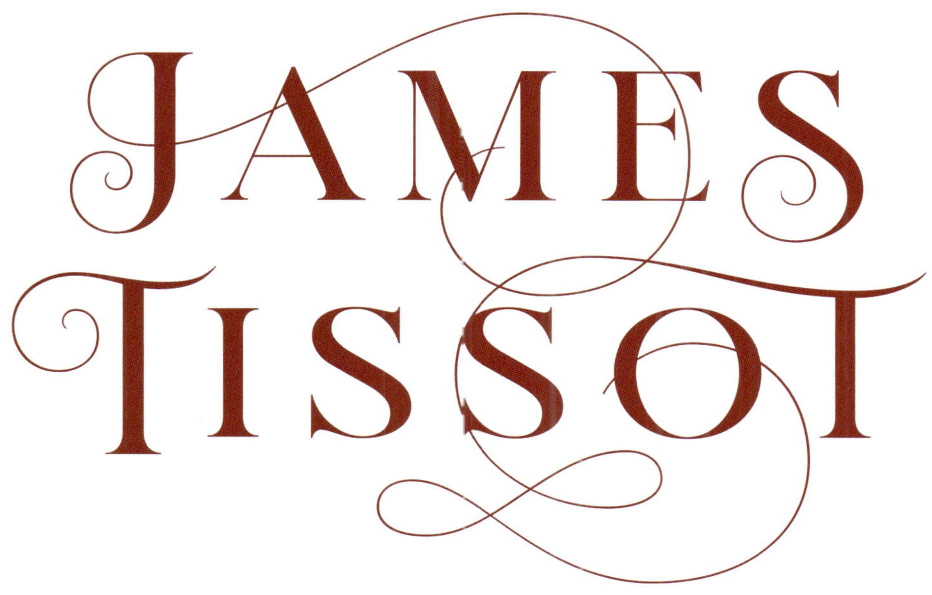

James Tissot

MELISSA E. BURON

WITH

KRYSTYNA MATYJASZKIEWICZ

AND

DONATO ESPOSITO, MARINE KISIEL, SARAH KLEINER, NANCY ROSE MARSHALL,
PAUL PERRIN, CYRILLE SCIAMA, BERTRAND TILLIER

AND

JAN DIRK BAETENS, JUSTINE DE YOUNG, MARGARETTA S. FREDERICK,
CHARLOTTE GERE, FRÉDÉRIC MANTION, VALENTINE ROBERT,
LÉA SAINT-RAYMOND, FRANÇOISE TÉTART-VITTU,
PETER TRIPPI

de Young \
\ Legion of Honor
fine arts museums
of san francisco

DELMONICO BOOKS • PRESTEL
Munich London New York

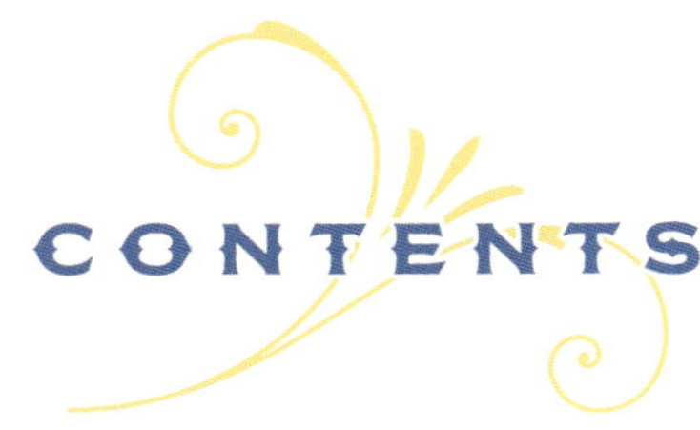

CONTENTS

ESSAYS

CATALOGUE

APPENDICES

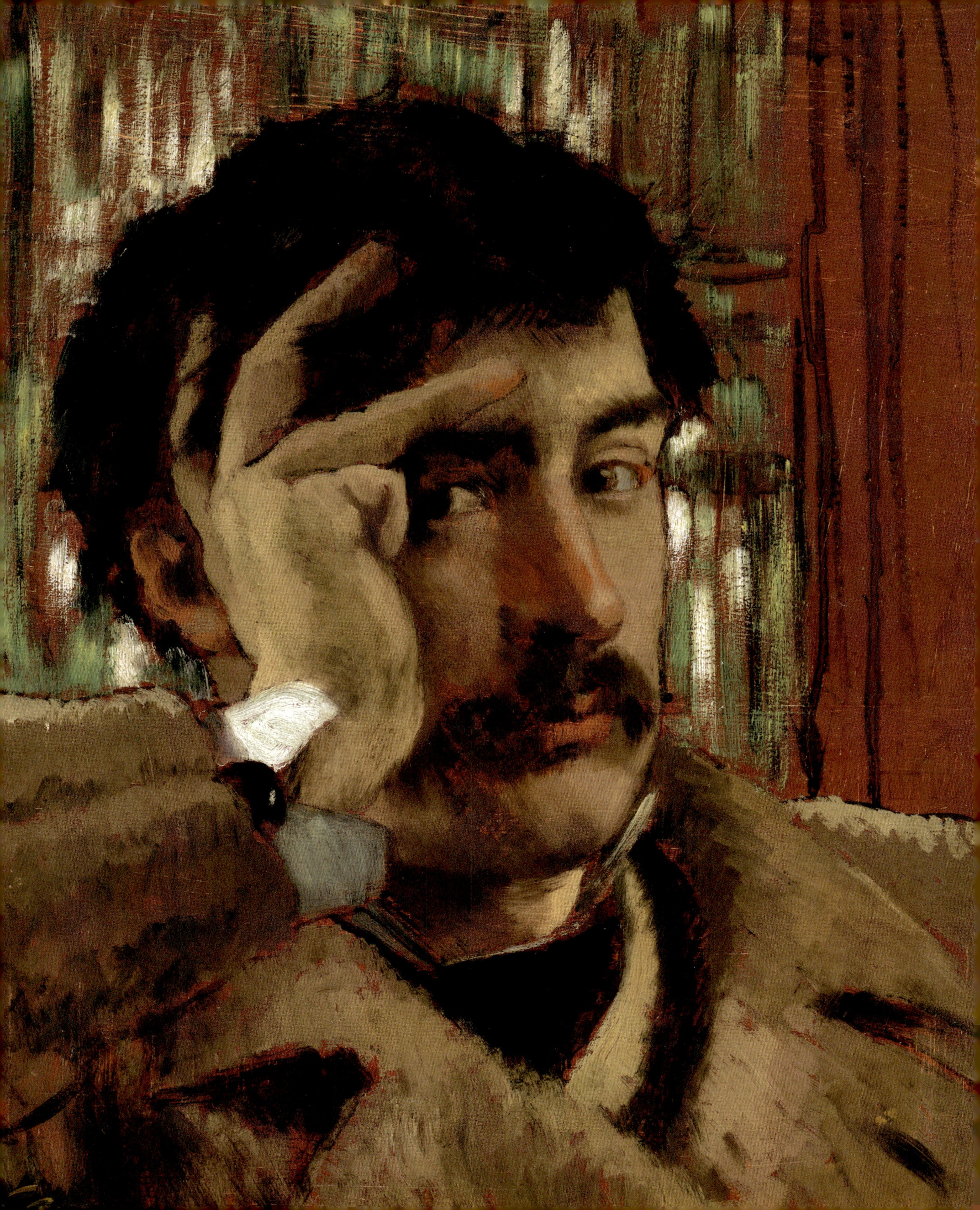

DIRECTORS' FOREWORD

"Our industrial and artistic creations may perish, our customs and our costumes may fall into oblivion, a painting by Mr. Tissot will be enough for the archaeologists of the future to reconstruct our era."

—ÉLIE ROY

JAMES TISSOT has long been recognized as a keen observer of contemporary life, but the exhibition *James Tissot: Fashion and Faith* brings new light to his virtuosity in employing meticulous detail to convey profound narratives about his social surroundings. Upon close study, even the artist's most lively society pictures reveal complex commentary on contemporary culture, religion, fashion, and politics. This presentation delivers original scholarship, as well as copies of such recently discovered documents as Tissot's personal sales notebook and selections from one of his unpublished photograph albums of paintings, to reveal an artist worthy of reconsideration in the twenty-first century.

Tissot garnered commercial and critical success in both London and Paris. For his subject matter, he often turned to social events, such as balls and boating expeditions, to paint cosmopolitan life with his characteristic attention to detail, humor, and emotion. He also depicted a number of domestic scenes centered around his luxurious London home and gardens, where he lived with his companion, Kathleen Newton. After Newton's tragic death, the artist returned to Paris and spent long periods of retreat at his family estate in the French countryside, nurturing a deep commitment to his art and also a renewed interest in religion.

James Tissot: Fashion and Faith, which debuts at the Legion of Honor, is the first major international collaboration on the artist in the twenty-first century, the first in the United States in nearly two decades, and the first ever on the North American West Coast. Co-organized by the Fine Arts Museums of San Francisco and the Musées d'Orsay et de l'Orangerie, Paris, this will also be the first monographic exhibition on Tissot presented in the galleries of the Orsay; it has been more than three decades since the last show devoted to the artist was mounted in the French capital. Both venues will feature approximately seventy paintings alongside watercolors, prints, photographs, and cloisonné enamels to demonstrate the breadth of the artist's technical and aesthetic ability.

Numerous colleagues at both institutions have worked to bring this important undertaking to fruition. At the Fine Arts Museums, we recognize Melissa E. Buron, director of the art division, for conceptualizing the project and shepherding its numerous aspects. At the Orsay, we are grateful to Marine Kisiel and Paul Perrin, curators, for guiding the project for the French venue along with Cyrille Sciama, directeur général, Musée des Impressionnismes Giverny. Beyond the museums, we give particular and heartfelt thanks to Tissot specialist Krystyna Matyjaszkiewicz, who offered tremendous support and guidance on this book. The aforementioned contributors were joined by a superb team of authors to create this volume: Donato Esposito, Sarah Kleiner, Nancy Rose Marshall, and Bertrand Tillier, along with Jan Dirk Baetens, Justine De Young, Margaretta S. Frederick, Charlotte Gere, Frédéric Mantion, Valentine Robert, Léa Saint-Raymond, Françoise Tétart-Vittu, and Peter Trippi.

We are indebted to our many generous lenders, who have graciously shared treasured masterpieces from their collections with us. The extraordinary support of our donors made the presentations possible. In San Francisco, we express our immense gratitude to: John A. and Cynthia Fry Gunn, Robert G. and Sue Douthit O'Donnell, Barbro and Bernard Osher, Denise Littlefield Sobel, Diane B. Wilsey, Gladyne Kenderdine Mitchell, Barbara A. Wolfe, The Diana Dollar Knowles Fund, Carole McNeil, Lucy Young Hamilton, and David A. Wollenberg. Additional support is provided by Sandra and Paul Bessières, Marion Moore Cope, George and Leslie Hume, Michael and Dorothy Leung, and Christina and Barry Ongerth. The San Francisco exhibition is further supported by an indemnity from the Federal Council on the Arts and the Humanities, and this catalogue is published with the assistance of the Andrew W. Mellon Foundation Endowment for Publications. Additional research support is provided by the Paul Mellon Centre for Studies in British Art. Scientific analyses were performed by the Northwestern University / Art Institute of Chicago Center for Scientific Studies in the Arts and made possible by the generous support of the Andrew W. Mellon Foundation.

One hundred twenty-five years ago, in July 1894, Tissot was awarded France's most prestigious recognition, the Légion d'honneur. San Francisco's Legion of Honor museum was conceived as a memorial to Franco-American relations, and it has a deep history of presenting exhibitions on important French art and artists. It is fitting that the original building, the Palais de la Légion d'Honneur in Paris, which served as the architectural inspiration for San Francisco's museum, is situated on the banks of the Seine River, next to the Musée d'Orsay. We are delighted that, through our permanent collections and this ambitious collaborative endeavor, our two museums can share the legacy of James Tissot with audiences in both the United States and France.

THOMAS P. CAMPBELL
Director and CEO
Fine Arts Museums of San Francisco

LAURENCE DES CARS
President
Musées d'Orsay et de l'Orangerie, Paris

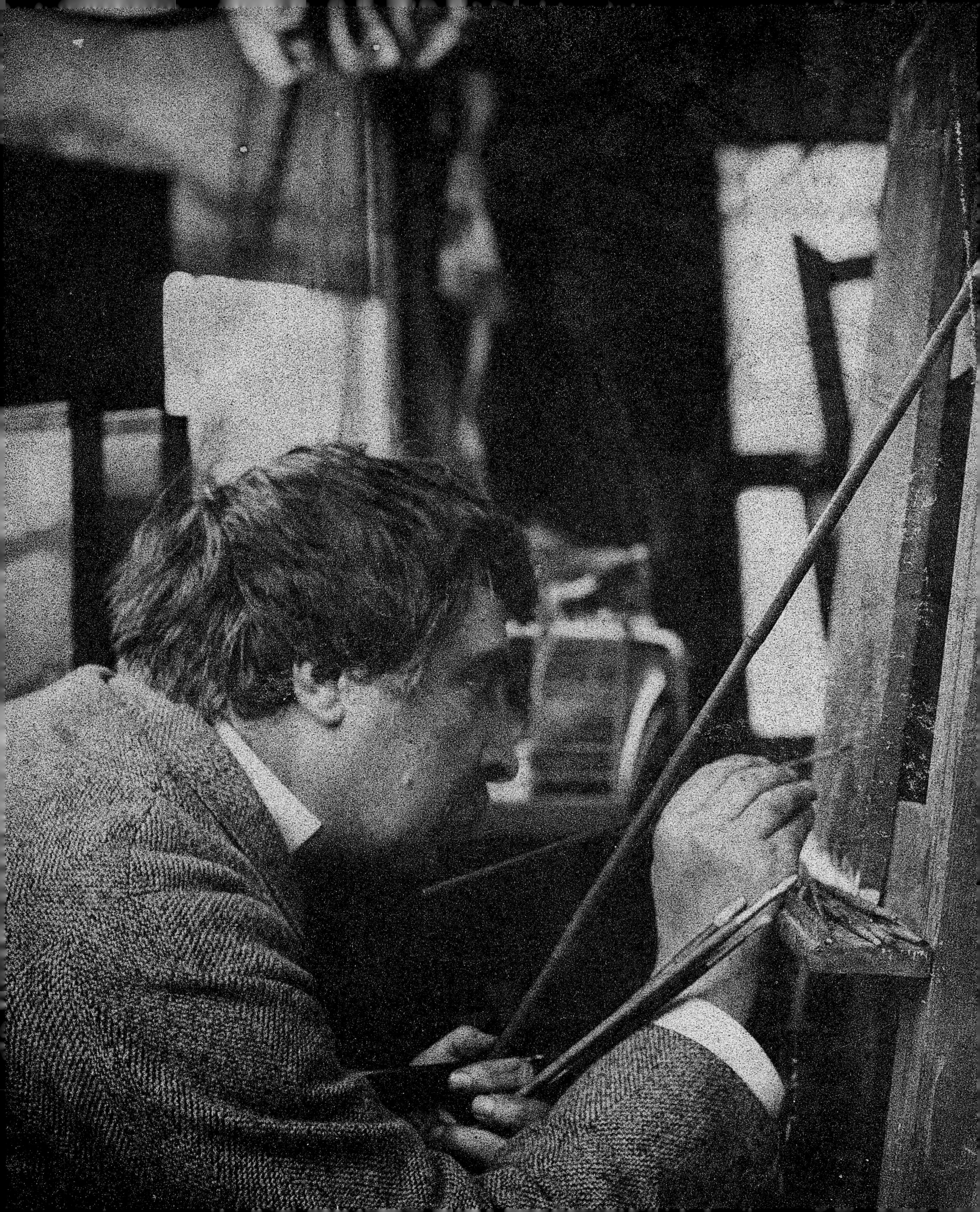

DONORS AND LENDERS

This exhibition is organized by the Fine Arts Museums of San Francisco and the Musées d'Orsay et de l'Orangerie, Paris.

DONORS

PRESENTING SPONSORS

John A. and Cynthia Fry Gunn
Robert G. and Sue Douthit O'Donnell
Barbro and Bernard Osher
Denise Littlefield Sobel
Diane B. Wilsey

MAJOR SUPPORT

Gladyne Kenderdine Mitchell
Barbara A. Wolfe

SIGNIFICANT SUPPORT

The Diana Dollar Knowles Fund
Carole McNeil

GENEROUS SUPPORT

Lucy Young Hamilton
David A. Wollenberg

Additional support is provided by Sandra and Paul Bessières, Marion Moore Cope, George and Leslie Hume, Michael and Dorothy Leung, and Christina and Barry Ongerth.

Scientific analyses were performed by the Northwestern University / Art Institute of Chicago Center for Scientific Studies in the Arts and made possible by the generous support of the Andrew W. Mellon Foundation.

The exhibition is supported by an indemnity from the Federal Council on the Arts and the Humanities.

This catalogue is published with the assistance of the Andrew W. Mellon Foundation Endowment for Publications. Additional research support is provided by the Paul Mellon Centre for Studies in British Art.

LENDERS

Art Gallery of Hamilton, Ontario
Art Gallery of Ontario, Toronto
Brooklyn Museum
Cantor Arts Center, Stanford University, California
Chrysler Museum of Art, Norfolk, Virginia
Cincinnati Art Museum
Colección Pérez Simón, Mexico City
Collection of Ann and Gordon Getty
Guildhall Art Gallery, London
The Hepworth Wakefield, England
The Jewish Museum, New York
The J. Paul Getty Museum, Los Angeles
Collection of Ralph and Terry Kovel
Leeds Museums and Galleries
Collection Frédéric Mantion
The Montreal Museum of Fine Arts
Musée Baron Martin, Gray, France
Musée d'Arts de Nantes
Musée des Arts Décoratifs, Paris
Musée des Beaux-Arts et d'Archéologie de Besançon, France
Musée d'Orsay, Paris
Museum of Art, Rhode Island School of Design, Providence
Museums Sheffield, England
National Gallery of Art, Washington, DC
National Gallery of Canada, Ottawa
National Gallery of Ireland, Dublin
National Portrait Gallery, London
Petit Palais, Musée des Beaux-Arts de la Ville de Paris
The Royal Pavilion, Art Gallery and Museums, Brighton, England
Santa Barbara Museum of Art
Southampton City Art Gallery, England
Staatliche Kunsthalle Karlsruhe, Germany
Sterling and Francine Clark Art Institute, Williamstown, Massachusetts
Tate, London
Toledo Museum of Art, Ohio
Wadsworth Atheneum Museum of Art, Hartford, Connecticut
Collection of Diane B. Wilsey, San Francisco
Wimpole Hall, Cambridgeshire, England
Private Collections

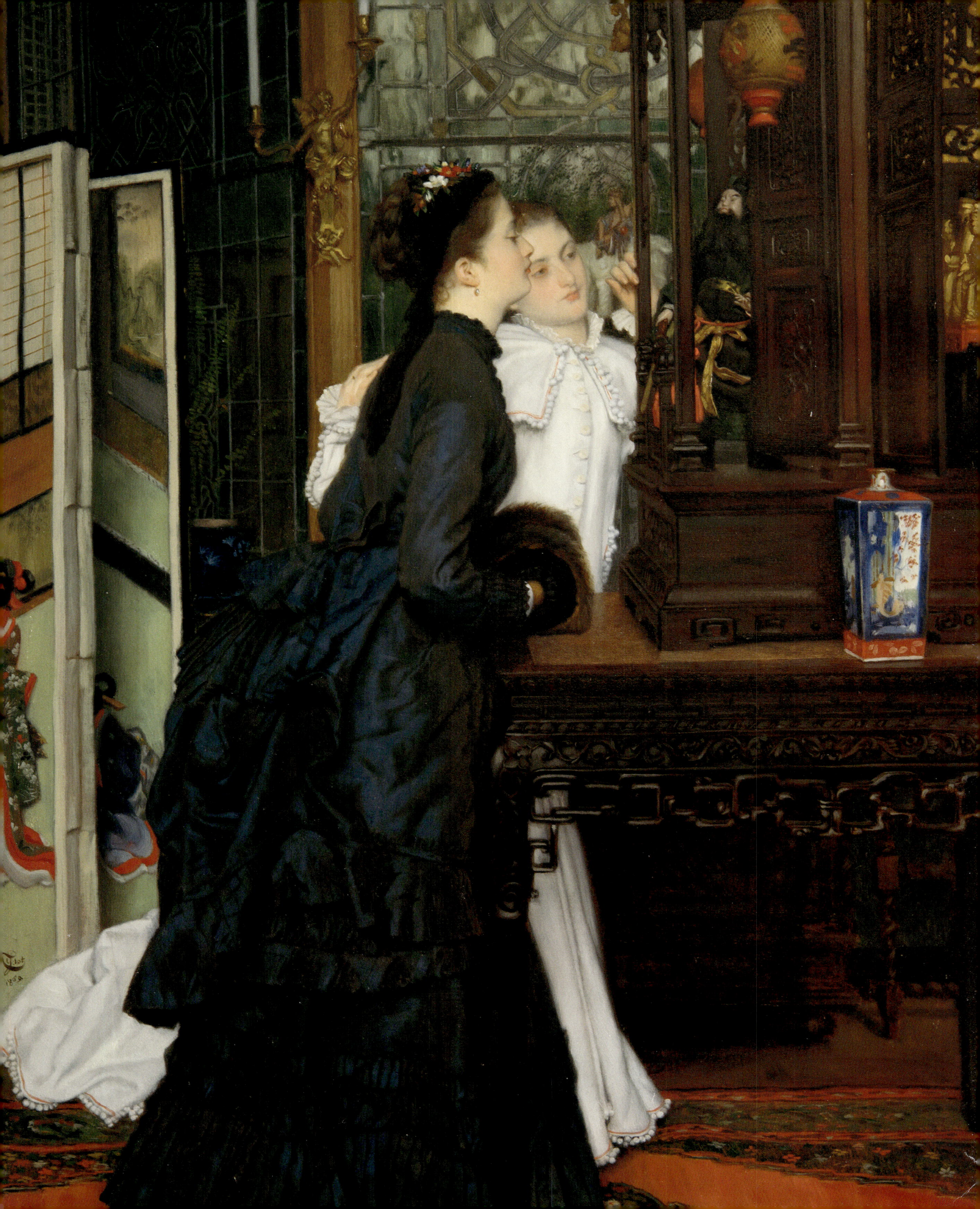

MELISSA E. BURON

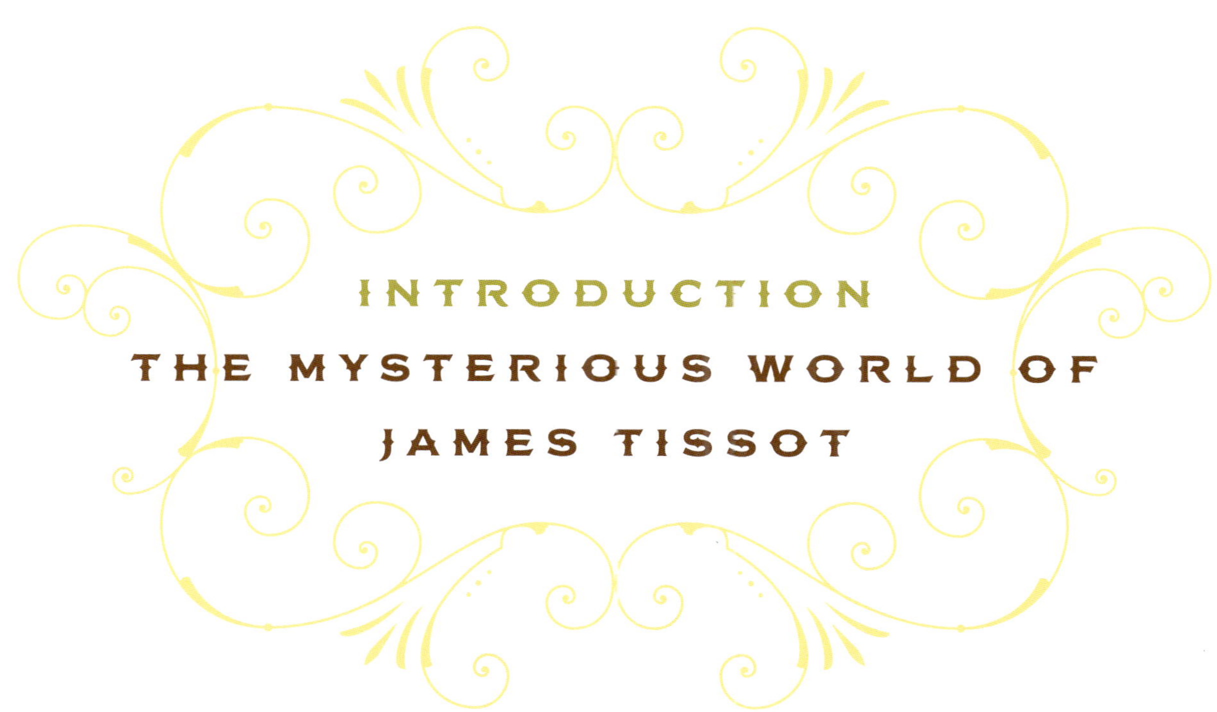

INTRODUCTION
THE MYSTERIOUS WORLD OF JAMES TISSOT

"Tissot, that mysterious forgotten figure, ill-judged for complex reasons."
—JACQUES-ÉMILE BLANCHE

IN HIS LIFETIME, James Tissot (French, 1836–1902) was a widely renowned artist whose mature career spanned both sides of the English Channel.[1] He was firmly of—and ahead of—his time: his observations on the nuances of modern life reflected the social mores of the Belle Époque in Paris and Victorian London, while his late-career religious watercolors anticipated the narratives and modes of visual sequencing that inform modern and contemporary cinema. Tissot was a highly skilled painter, able to record the world around him in rigorous detail—an exactitude that often served as a conduit for depicting the subtext of a scene. *James Tissot* demonstrates how even the artist's most ebullient society paintings offer a rich and complex commentary on the culture, religion, fashion, and politics of the nineteenth century, particularly by hinting at the emotional and spiritual undercurrents that lie just below surface appearances.

Given Tissot's celebrity during his lifetime, why is he not as well known in the twenty-first century as his more famous French contemporaries, such as Edgar Degas, Édouard Manet, and Claude Monet? Perhaps it is because, while Tissot experimented with major trends in the art of his day, including Aestheticism and Japonisme, his work resists classification and traditional labels—he was neither an Impressionist nor a Realist, for example. Nonetheless, his work regularly features alongside these artists in thematic exhibitions. Although Tissot socialized with Impressionists, and was in fact invited by Degas to participate in their first exhibition, he consciously did not participate in their aesthetic agenda, and he chose not to exhibit with them, possibly because of the success he had already achieved by himself.[2] The paradox of Tissot's celebrity is part of what makes him a captivating subject for a monographic exhibition, as these pages will show, through previously unpublished archival materials and essays that provide new perspectives on the artist.

I. EARLY YEARS AND FIRST PARIS PERIOD (1836–1871)

Jacques-Joseph Tissot (he later used the Anglicized "James") was born in Nantes on October 15, 1836, to parents whose textiles business augmented the family's wealth and may have inspired his entrepreneurial spirit as well as his interest in depicting fashion. Cyrille Sciama's essay describes the impact that the city of Nantes—and especially its art—had on the young Tissot (see Sciama, this volume). He moved to Paris in 1855, and in the late 1850s he trained in the Academic tradition of Jean-Auguste-Dominique Ingres at the École des Beaux-Arts, under the direction of Hippolyte Flandrin and Louis Lamothe. Just over a decade after his arrival in the French capital, he was elected *hors concours* following the Paris Salon in 1866. This distinction meant that he could avoid the Salon's jury process and exhibit any painting at subsequent Salon exhibitions. Such recognition caused prices for his paintings to surge and, at the age of thirty, he purchased a plot of land where he built a luxurious home (fig. 110) on

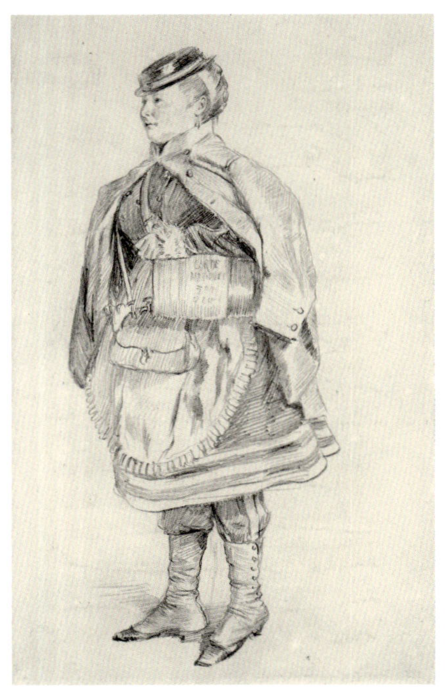

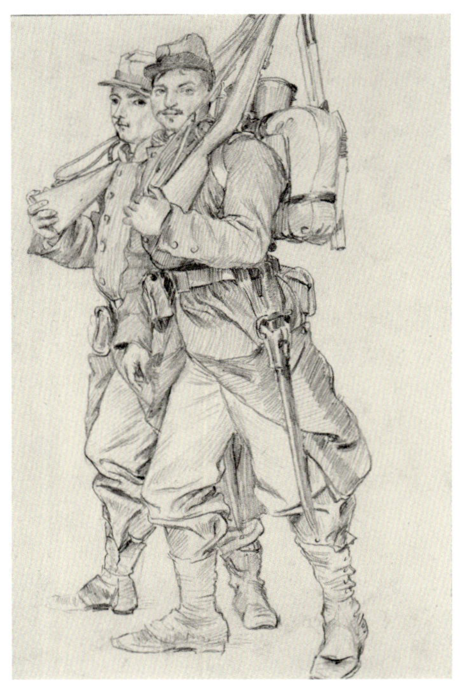

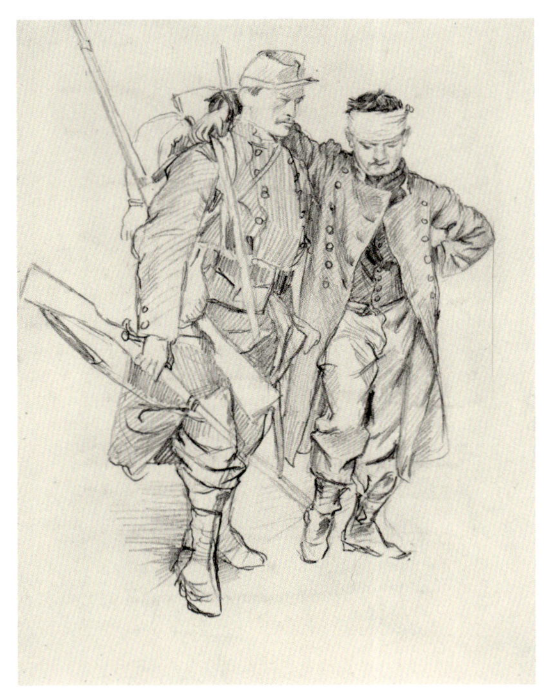

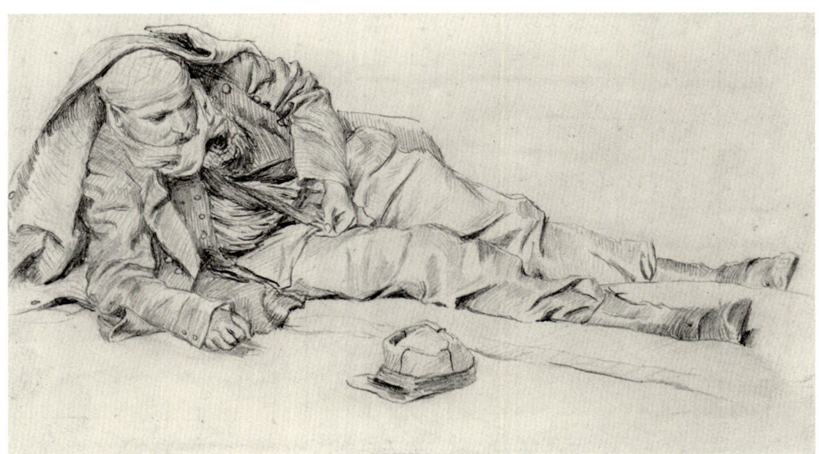

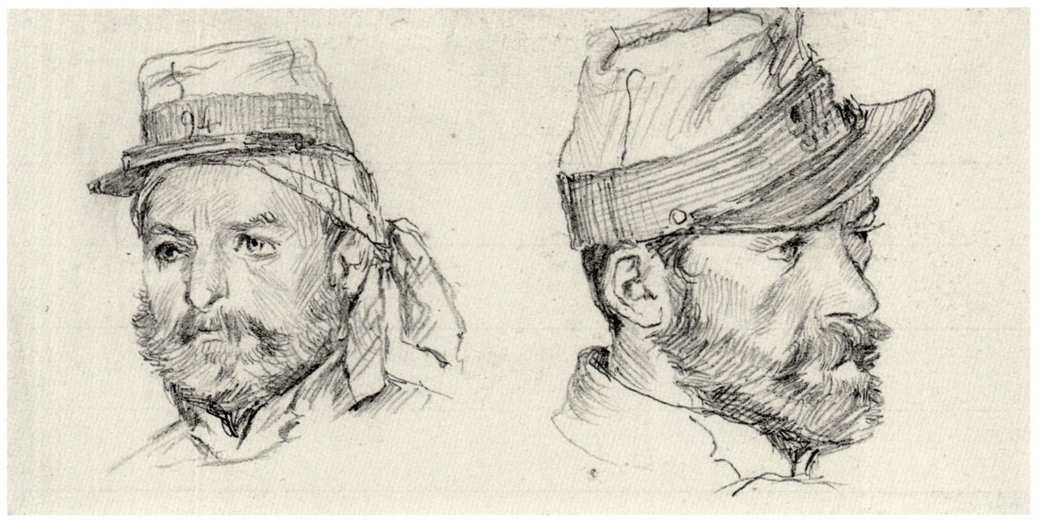

James Tissot, *Drawings of the Siege of Paris*, 1870. Black pencil on paper. Malingue S.A., Paris

(clockwise from top left)

FIGURE 1
7⅞ × 4¾ in. (19.9 × 12.2 cm)

FIGURE 2
6¾ × 4⅜ in. (17.1 × 11 cm)

FIGURE 3
6⅝ × 5 in. (16.9 × 12.8 cm)

FIGURE 4
1⅞ × 3⅝ in. (4.8 × 9.3 cm)

FIGURE 5
4 × 7⅛ in. (10.3 × 18.2 cm)

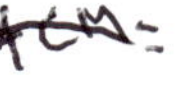

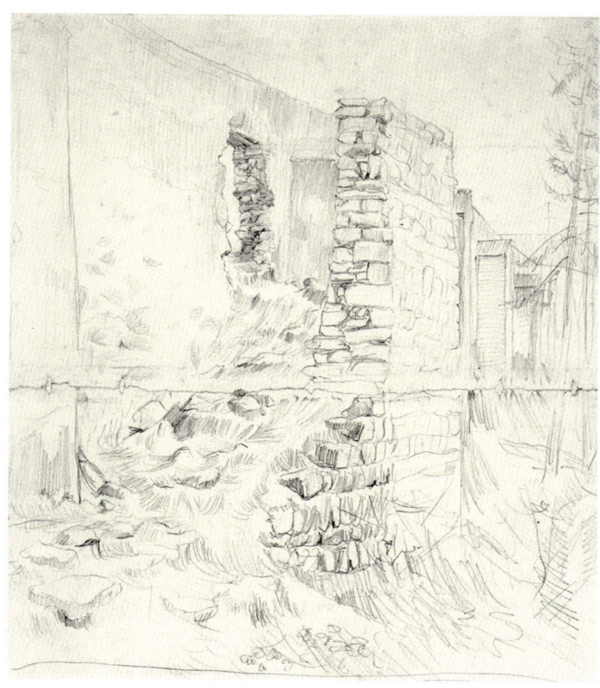

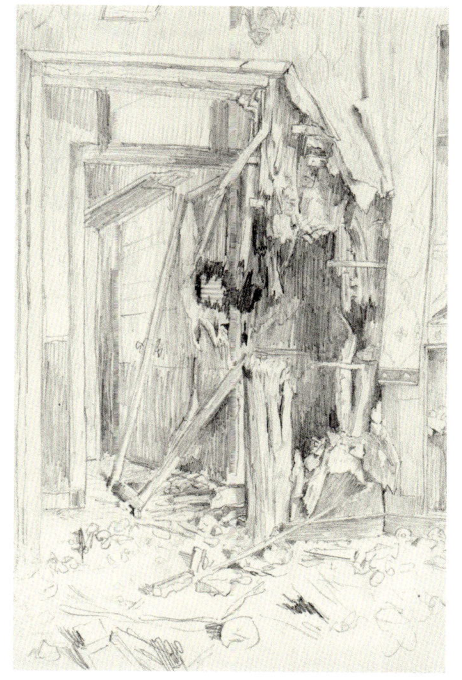

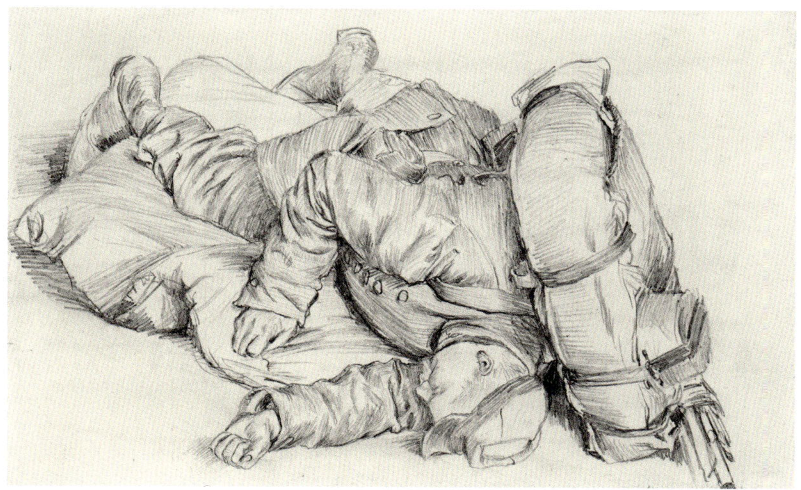

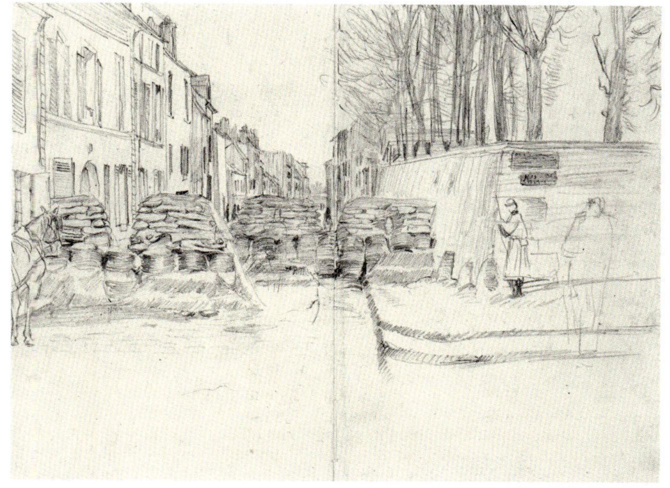

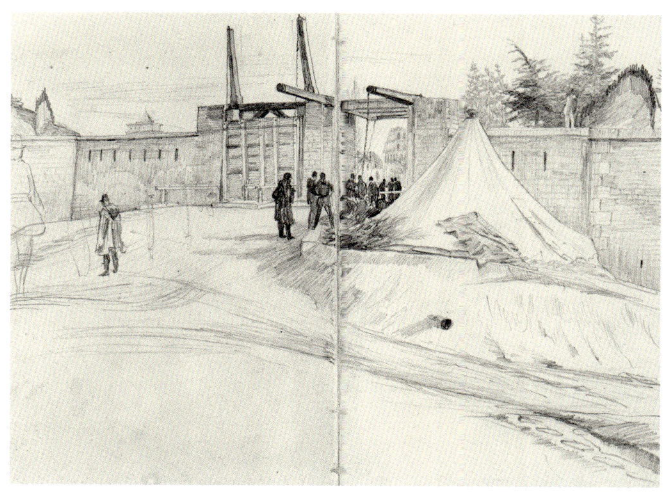

(clockwise from top left)

FIGURE 6
8¼ × 7 in. (20.8 × 17.9 cm)

FIGURE 7
8 × 5⅛ in. (20.4 × 13 cm)

FIGURE 8
7 × 9⅛ in. (17.8 × 23.2 cm)

FIGURE 9
7 × 9⅜ in. (17.8 × 23.7 cm)

FIGURE 10
4⅝ × 7⅛ in. (11.6 × 18.2 cm)

8" = 20 CM

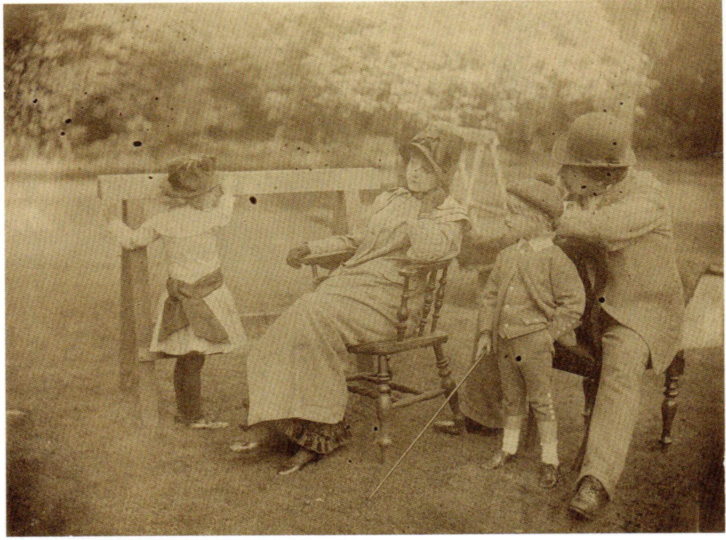

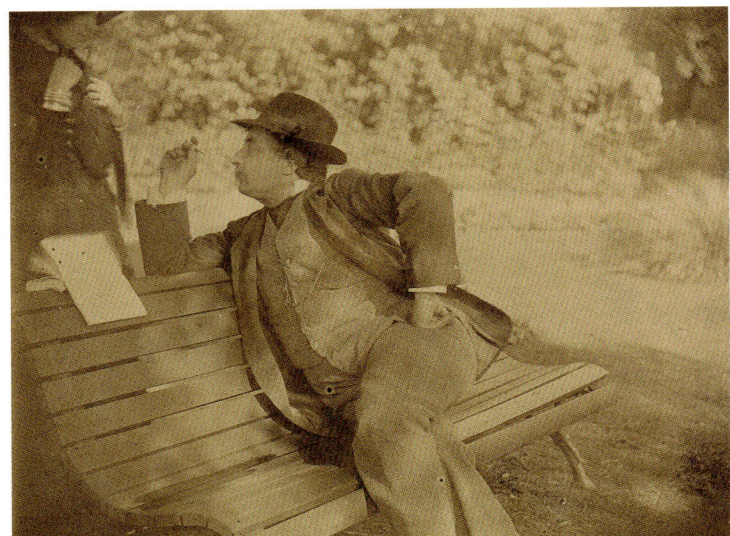

the avenue de l'Impératrice (known today as avenue Foch), then considered the most prestigious new thoroughfare in Paris.[3]

Tissot traveled to Antwerp in 1859, where he met the Belgian artist Henri Leys, known for his historical paintings. Jan Dirk Baetens considers this formative time and sets the stage for Tissot's ongoing interest in the subject of costume, social satire, and experimenting with composition (see Baetens, this volume). Margaretta S. Frederick analyzes the cultural context, drama, and psychological power of Tissot's early—and very Leysian—Faust and Marguerite works, which effectively marked his professional initiation into the Paris art market (see Frederick, this volume).

II. COMMERCIAL SUCCESS AND THE FRANCO-PRUSSIAN WAR (1855–1871)

Unlike many of his contemporaries, such as Monet and Camille Pissarro, who fled France during the Franco-Prussian War (1870–1871), Tissot enlisted in the campaign along with other artists, including Degas and Manet. He served as a sharpshooter, and documented the atrocities of his experiences in notebooks, producing many sketches (figs. 1–10), some of which he later drew upon to make prints (see fig. 36 and pls. 18 and 20). Even during tumultuous times, Tissot could not resist the call to create—perhaps as a means to process the horrors that he witnessed. His impulse angered some, including Degas, who chastised Tissot for drawing one of their dead friends rather than immediately moving his body.[4] Bertrand Tillier navigates the intricacies of this period and examines Tissot's activities during the "Terrible Year" (see Tillier, this volume).

Tissot consistently—though never entirely—defied convention throughout his career, yet he was also critically and commercially successful. His contributions to the Academy and the avant-garde are documented by his participation at diverse venues such as the Paris Salon and London's Royal Academy of Arts, and, later, at the more progressive Grosvenor and Dudley Galleries in London. Léa Saint-Raymond addresses Tissot's rise to fame in the French art market, especially as influenced by his appearances at the Salon, and the eminent patrons—including Americans—who collected his work (see Saint-Raymond, this volume). Peter Trippi expands on the theme of Tissot's internationalism during the 1860s by exploring the works that he exhibited in London before he moved there in the following decade (see Trippi, this volume).

III. LONDON (1871–1882)

When Tissot left the chaos of postwar Paris and moved to London, he found even greater commercial success. As Nancy Rose Marshall explains, Tissot's "deceptively complex endeavor" involved new works that contained elaborate narratives with multiple layers of meaning, which drew parallels to his British contemporaries, including William Powell Frith and Edward Burne-Jones (see Marshall, this volume). Krystyna Matyjaszkiewicz further analyzes the triumphs that Tissot achieved as an expatriate artist living in London, selling in the local art market and to dealers in the United States (see Matyjaszkiewicz, "Tissot's 'Genius' Picture-Selling in Britain," this volume).

During this period, Tissot's companion and muse—and the subject of numerous works (see pls. 73–85 and 95–106)—was a young divorcée named Kathleen Newton, née Kelly.[5] Charlotte Gere describes the idyllic domestic world the couple created at their London home and its gardens (figs. 11–12) in the bohemian artists' enclave of Saint John's Wood (see Gere, this volume). When, in 1882, Newton died of tuberculosis at the age of twenty-eight, Tissot abandoned his London mansion, which was subsequently purchased by the artist Lawrence Alma-Tadema.

IV. FASHION AND FASHIONABILITY

Throughout his career in both Paris and London, Tissot was consistently in demand as a portrait painter, and Paul Perrin explores the elements that made the artist so successful in this genre (see Perrin, this volume). One theme that recurs in his portraits is the depiction of women and men in elegant clothing. Justine De Young follows the evolution of Tissot's fashions, particularly in his portraits and later society paintings, to highlight his repetition of certain noteworthy styles (see De Young, this volume). Françoise Tétart-Vittu's essay discusses a particular white dress with yellow ribbons (see fig. 58 and pls. 48, 58, 64, and 78),

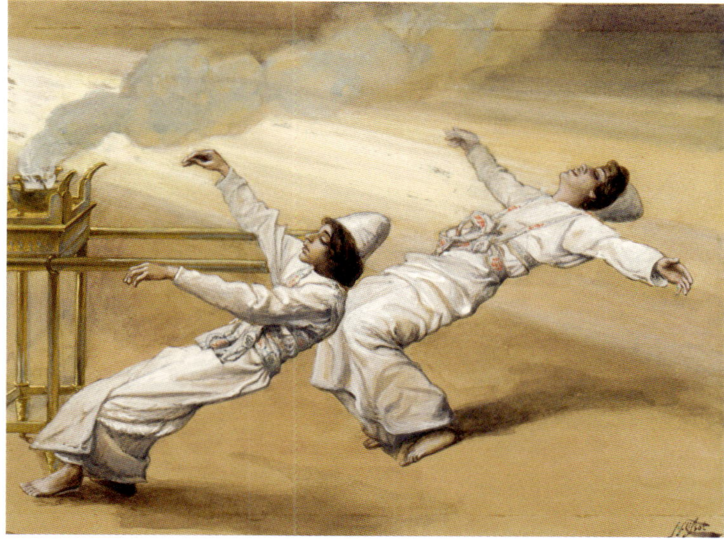

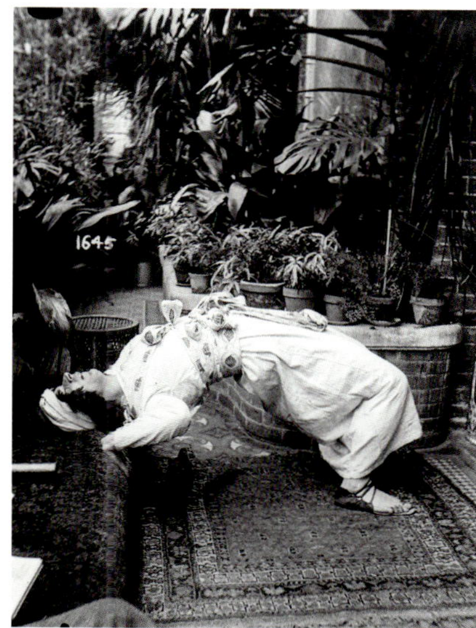

perhaps the most iconic dress in Tissot's repertoire (see Tétart-Vittu, this volume). Tissot never abandoned fashionable portraiture, and he adeptly bridged both sartorial and spiritual subject matter throughout his oeuvre.

V. SPIRITUALITY AND SPIRITUALISM (1882–1902)

Tissot returned to Paris after Newton's funeral and embarked on an ambitious enterprise to reenter the French art world with a series of fifteen large-scale paintings representing *La Femme à Paris* (pls. 117–128), which he intended to reproduce and disseminate as prints with accompanying short stories written by famous contemporary authors. It was during the research for one of these compositions, in the Church of Saint-Sulpice, Paris, that Tissot first described having a religious vision. The experience was transformative. The final two decades of his life were subsequently consumed by the creation of hundreds of sketches and watercolors of the Bible, which were made in tandem with three trips to the Holy Land in 1886–1887, 1888–1889, and 1896.[6] All the while, the painter fostered a fascination with the occult philosophy of Spiritualism—in vogue at the time—and he even attempted to contact Newton's spirit through séances. This publication is the first to include an essay that deeply examines Tissot's concurrent fascination with séances and Spiritualism during his work on the biblical illustrations (see Buron, this volume).

Tissot made a fortune from the exhibition, sale, and reproduction of these biblical illustrations, which appealed to American audiences and even inspired filmmakers working in the relatively new medium. Valentine Robert offers further connections between Tissot and religious cinema—from the films of the pioneering director Alice Guy-Blaché to more modern movies, such as those by William Wyler and Franco Zeffirelli (see Robert, this volume). Tissot dedicated the final years of his life to working on the biblical watercolors, often at his estate in the east of France, the Château de Buillon, which he also spent time lovingly restoring. Here, the artist surrounded himself with nature near the remains of a Cistercian abbey and a private chapel built by his mother, where she was buried and where he was later interred near her. The estate's current owner, Frédéric Mantion, poetically describes the property and its surroundings (see Mantion, this volume), which stands today much as Tissot left it. Rumors once held that Tissot had joined a monastery, and although this was not the case, the transcendent atmosphere of his estate is not far removed from such speculation.[7]

VI. ARTISTIC FRIENDSHIPS AND NETWORKS

After cultivating close relationships with artists in both France and England, Tissot ultimately developed a body of work that was uniquely his own. His commercial success inspired envy in some of his contemporaries, including Degas, who sometimes accused Tissot of hypocrisy while also seeking his career advice. Marine Kisiel explores the nuances of this friendship and professional rivalry through the lens of Degas's magnificent

FIGURE 11
Kathleen Newton with her niece Lilian Hervey (left), her son Cecil George, and possibly Tissot on the right, in the garden of Tissot's Grove End Road property, London, ca. 1878–1882. Albumen silver print, 6 × 7⅝ in. (15.1 × 19.5 cm). Fine Arts Museums of San Francisco, Achenbach Foundation for Graphic Arts, Museum purchase, Mrs. Milton S. Latham Fund, 1988.3.6

FIGURE 12
Tissot and Kathleen Newton in the garden of Tissot's Grove End Road property, London, ca. 1878–1882. Albumen silver print, 6 × 8 in. (15.4 × 20.3 cm). Fine Arts Museums of San Francisco, Achenbach Foundation for Graphic Arts, Museum purchase, Mrs. Milton S. Latham Fund, 1988.3.5

FIGURE 13
James Tissot, *The Two Priests Are Destroyed*, ca. 1896–1902 (pl. 139). Opaque watercolor on board, 7⅜ × 10¾ in. (18.7 × 27.3 cm). The Jewish Museum, New York, Gift of the heirs of Jacob Schiff, X1952-191

FIGURE 14
James Tissot, figure study for Old Testament watercolor, ca. 1896. Black-and-white photograph. Collection Frédéric Mantion

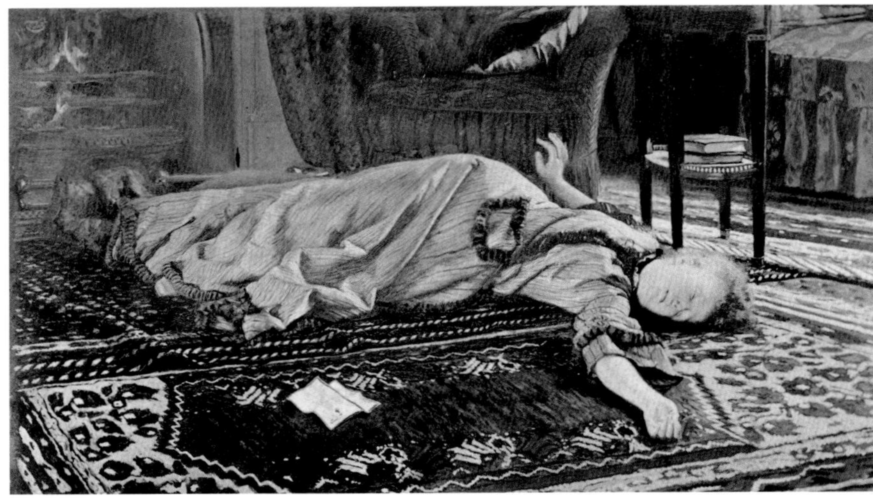

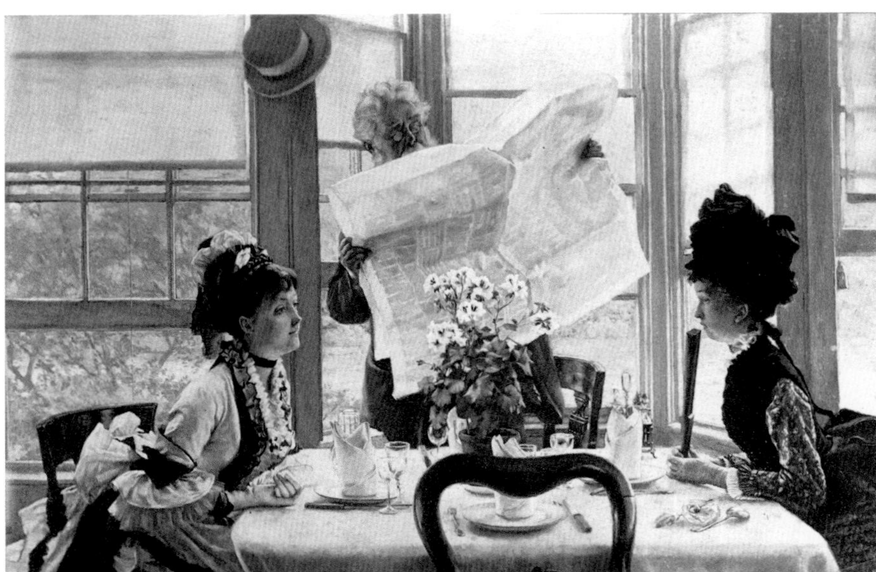

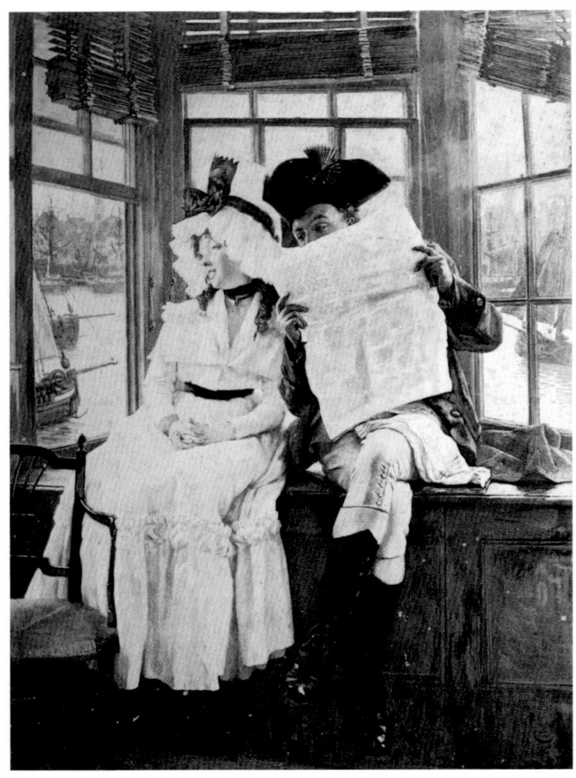

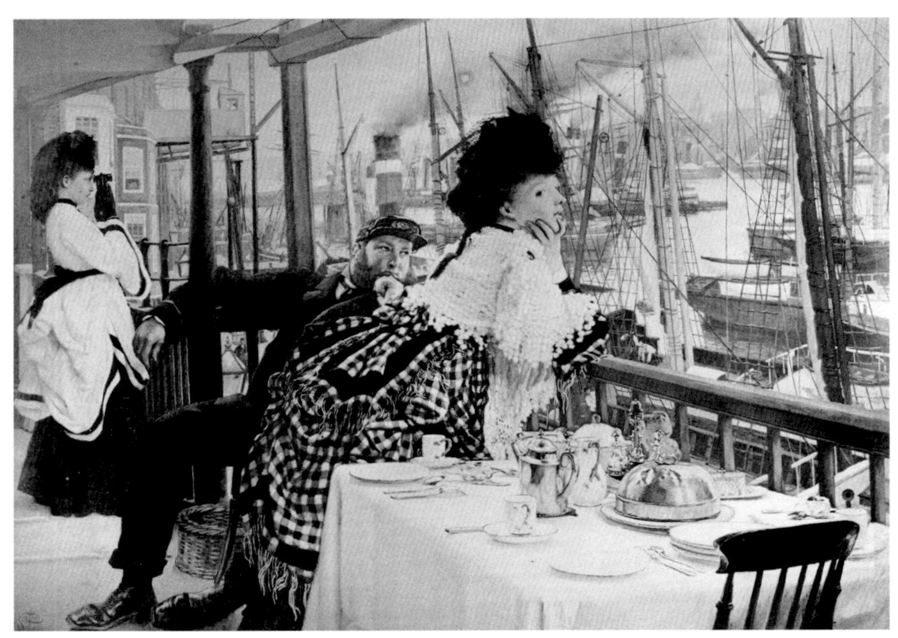

Images from Tissot's London photograph album, 1871–1878. Courtesy Frédéric Mantion

(clockwise from top left)

FIGURE 15
Bad News or *The Swoon* (also known as *The Letter*), ca. 1872; location unknown

FIGURE 16
News of Our Marriage, 1872; location unknown

FIGURE 17
The Thames or *Greenwich*, 1872; location unknown

FIGURE 18
Waiting for the Fourth or *The Last Guest*, ca. 1875; location unknown

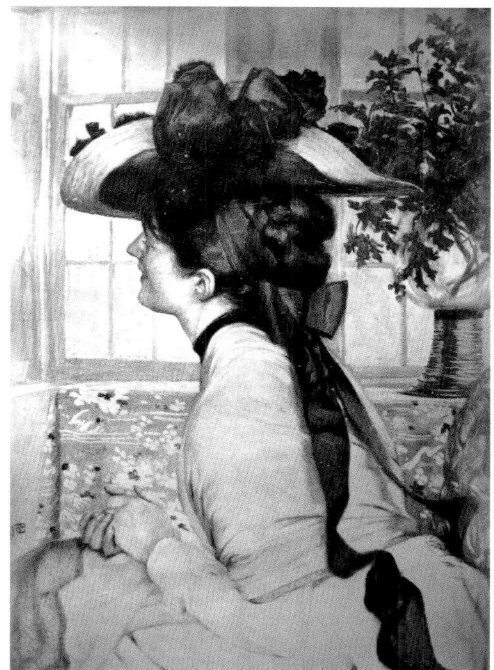
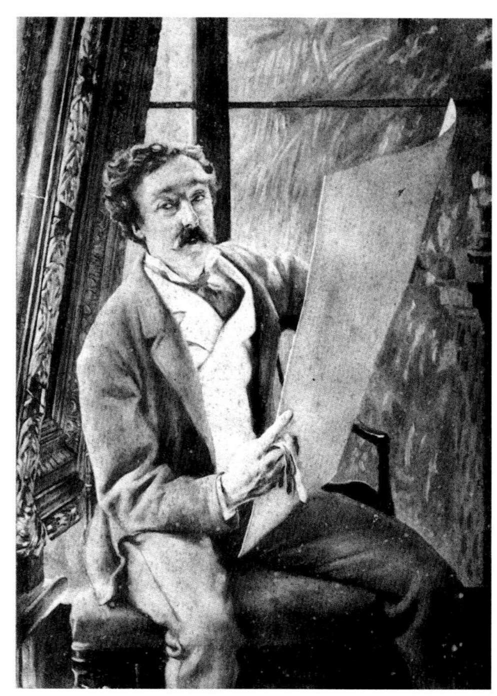
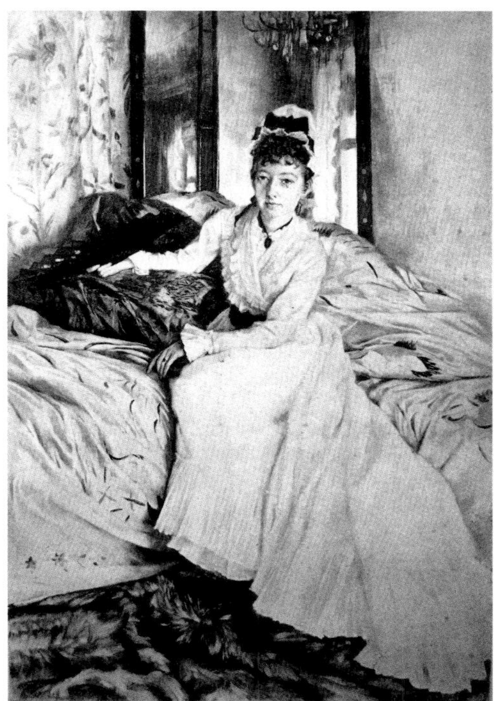
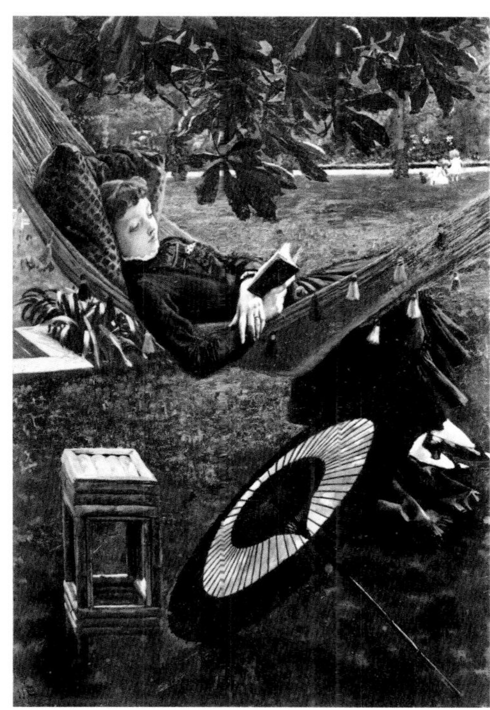

(clockwise from top left)

FIGURE 19
The Rubens Hat, ca. 1875; location unknown

FIGURE 20
Portrait of Edward Fox White, ca. 1876–1877; location unknown

FIGURE 21
Under the Chestnut Tree or *The Hammock*, ca. 1878; location unknown

FIGURE 22
Portrait of Mrs. McLaren (later Lady Aberconway), 1878; location unknown

portrait of Tissot, which may represent, Kisiel says, "a moment of equilibrium in the two artists' trajectories" (see Kisiel, this volume).

VII. TECHNIQUES

One element of Tissot's career that is less of a mystery is his technical ability, which can readily be seen in the works of art themselves. Though heralded primarily as a painter, Tissot experimented with various materials, and was prolific across media. Along with his paintings in oil and watercolor, he created numerous pastels (see pls. 33–34). He was also a talented printmaker (see Esposito, this volume), and he made cloisonné enamel panels and objects (see Matyjaszkiewicz, "'Always in Search of the Exquisite in Art': Tissot's Cloisonné Enamels," this volume). Tissot used photography regularly to prepare for compositions (figs. 13–14) and he made photograph albums to document his own paintings.[8] He created incessantly throughout his life, generating a vast body of work that, perhaps because of its breadth, has yet to receive a complete catalogue raisonné.[9] An important feature of the current project is an investigation into Tissot's painting techniques and materials (see Kleiner, this volume, and "Pigment Analysis," this volume), aspects that previously have been considered to only a limited extent.

This technical study also prompted the reexamination of a lingering mystery about the attribution of a painting in the Fine Arts Museums of San Francisco's collection, which is now being readdressed. *The Impresario* (fig. 101) was acquired in 1957 as a work by Degas. In 1984, on the occasion of the 150th anniversary of Degas's birth, the scholar Richard Thomson proposed that it was Tissot who created *The Impresario*.[10] Compositional comparisons with other works by Tissot include the forward-leaning pose of the man that appears in *Evening* (also known as *The Ball*, pl. 79), and the placement of the man's hand in the tails of his evening coat seen in *Political Woman* (pl. 124). It is also possible that the dashes of paint in the lower-left corner of *The Impresario* may correspond to the folds in the women's dresses in the other two works.[11] Furthermore, many sketches by Tissot demonstrate the same manner of paint handling (see fig. 102), particularly an overall toning layer applied in broad strokes of semitransparent reddish-brown paint, and the dark outlines around the figures. This reattribution will continue to be investigated in future scholarly undertakings on *The Impresario*.[12]

VIII. TISSOT IN THE TWENTY-FIRST CENTURY

A magnificent repository of primary source material was revealed to the curators of this project. Documents, photographs, letters, paintings, furniture, and even Tissot's boots and paint box, are all currently held in a private collection in Buillon, France. Photographs from his personal albums (see "Photo Album," this volume) reveal a previously unexplored window into Tissot's private world. The images also show that Tissot emblazoned his monogram across the grounds of the Château de Buillon—on building façades, metal gates, riding saddles, and silverware—demonstrating that he was keenly aware of what might be referred to today as the power of his personal brand.[13]

A critical resource made available to the curators of this project and published here for the first time is a copy of Tissot's sales notebook (*carnet de ventes*), a ledger recording his art sales from 1857 to 1890, which reveals the extent of his commercial success (see "Tissot's Sales Notebook," this volume). The documentation illuminates the author and critic Edmond de Goncourt's somewhat snarky observation in 1874 that Tissot could afford a refined lifestyle featuring "a studio with a waiting room where, at all times, there is iced champagne at the disposal of visitors, and . . . a garden, where, all day long, one can see a footman in silk stockings brushing and shining the shrubbery leaves."[14] In the notebook, Tissot documented the sales of individual works by year, including each piece's title, buyer, and price. This resource has allowed for more precise dating and, in some cases, new title identifications for the works in Tissot's oeuvre. These adjustments are outlined in new apparatuses prepared by Krystyna Matyjaszkiewicz (see "Catalogue Checklist," this volume). The sales notebook has long been considered the "Holy Grail" of research on Tissot, and its revelations will undoubtedly generate myriad opportunities for interpretation in future scholarship.

Another archival item that has provided new information about Tissot's career is a photograph album of works from the artist's London period, preserved as a digital copy. A selection of the less familiar compositions from the newly discovered album is reproduced here (figs. 15–22). This volume was missing at the time of Willard Misfeldt's 1982 publication of three other albums.[15] Similar to its counterparts, this album contained black-and-white photos of Tissot's paintings, some of which were previously unknown to contemporary scholars and never before published—including one painting, *Two Figures at the Door (The Proposal)*, that has since been located and is printed here for the first time in color (fig. 23). The number of Tissot paintings that remain to be revealed is certainly fewer after this endeavor, yet there are likely still more discoveries about Tissot waiting to be made for the next scholarly project on the artist.

Much of the narrative surrounding Tissot throughout the course of his career focuses on his virtuosic skill; he was variously lauded and criticized for his near-photographic precision. Although his highly detailed works came close to replicating reality, it was through paint that the mysterious power of his scenes emerged. Tissot was a confident but not a brash artist. He took great care to meticulously depict the folds of a dress or the grooves of a column, but not at the expense of emotional content. His impressions of modern life, often tinged with amusement, are never disrespectful. And although he stayed keenly attuned to his subjects, his deliberate eye shielded him from sentimentality. These careful balances allowed for a subtle commentary on his social surroundings that comes across as insightful and empathetic but never heavy-handed—a complex perspective that makes James Tissot an artist perfectly prime for reexamination in the twenty-first century.

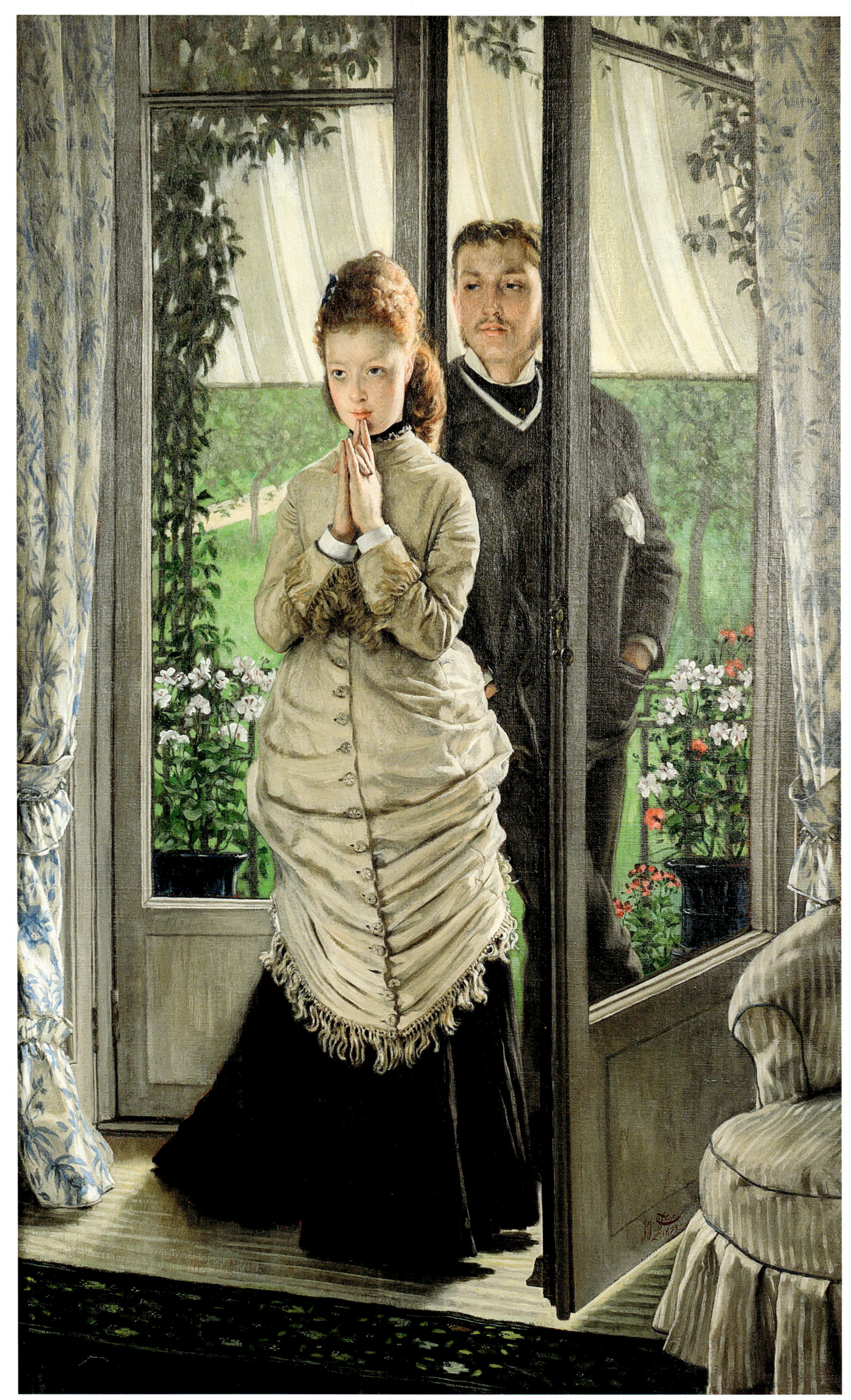

FIGURE 23
James Tissot, *Two Figures at the Door (The Proposal)*, 1872. Oil on canvas, 33 × 22½ in. (83.8 × 57.2 cm). Collection of Ralph and Terry Kovel

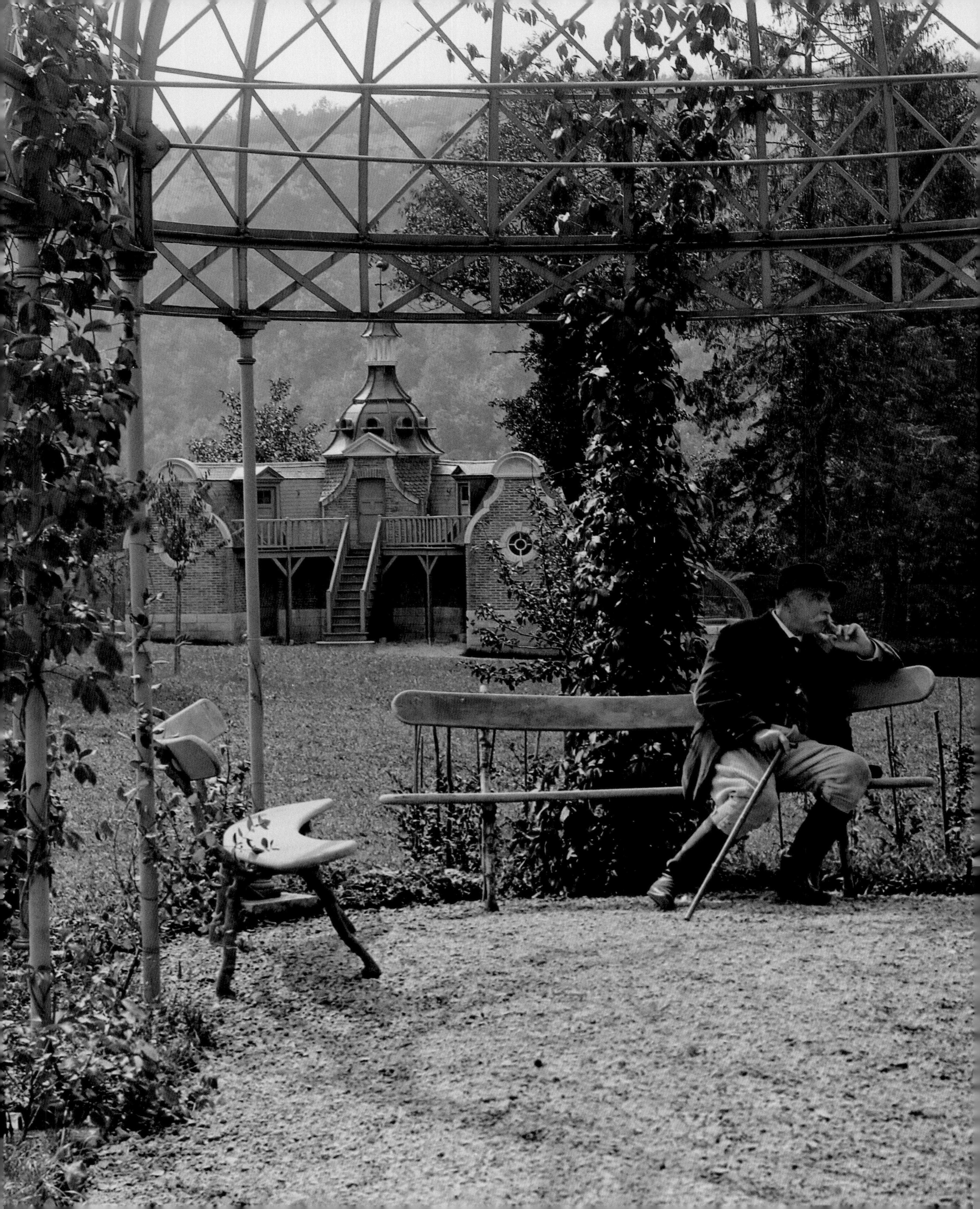

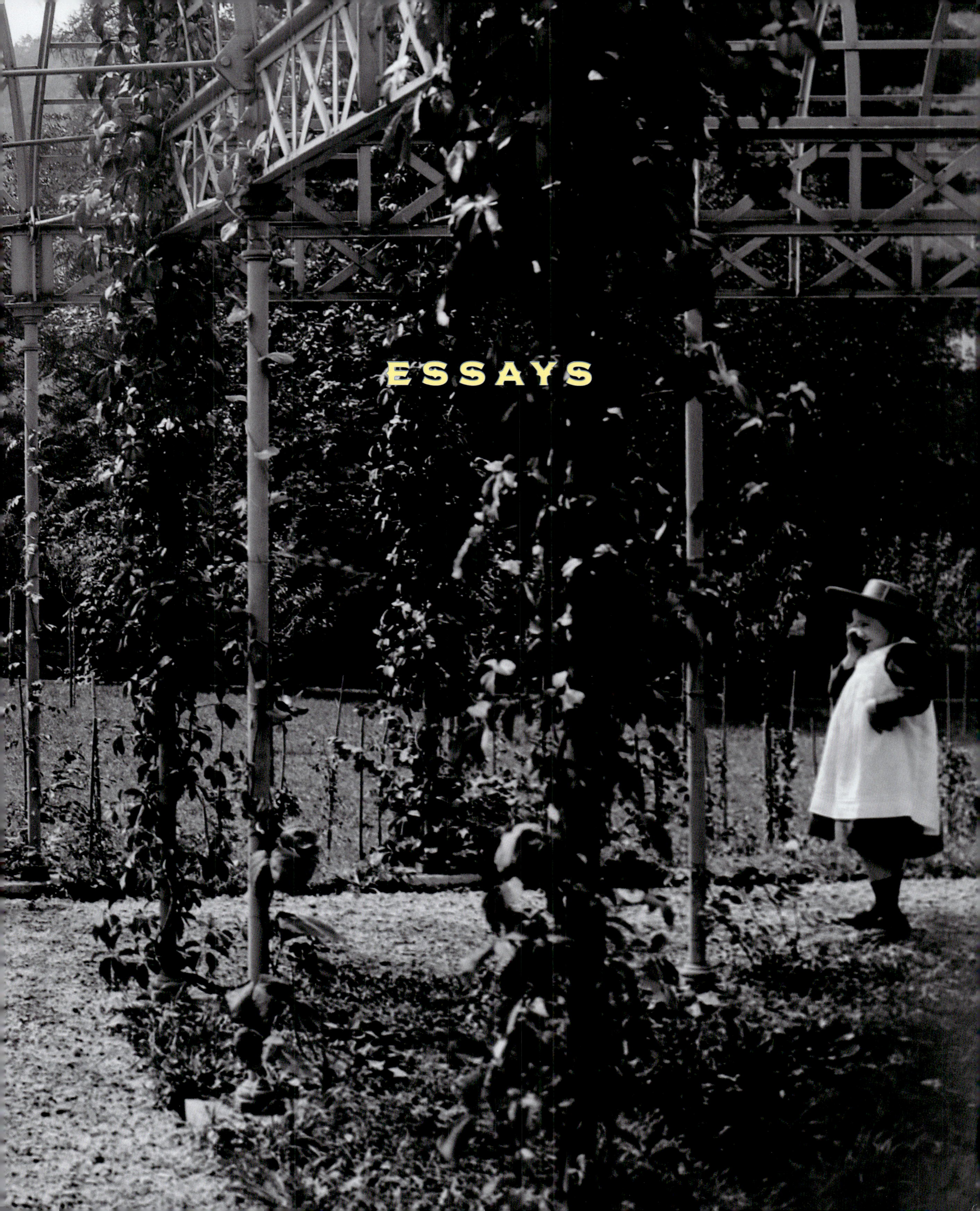

ESSAYS

CYRILLE SCIAMA

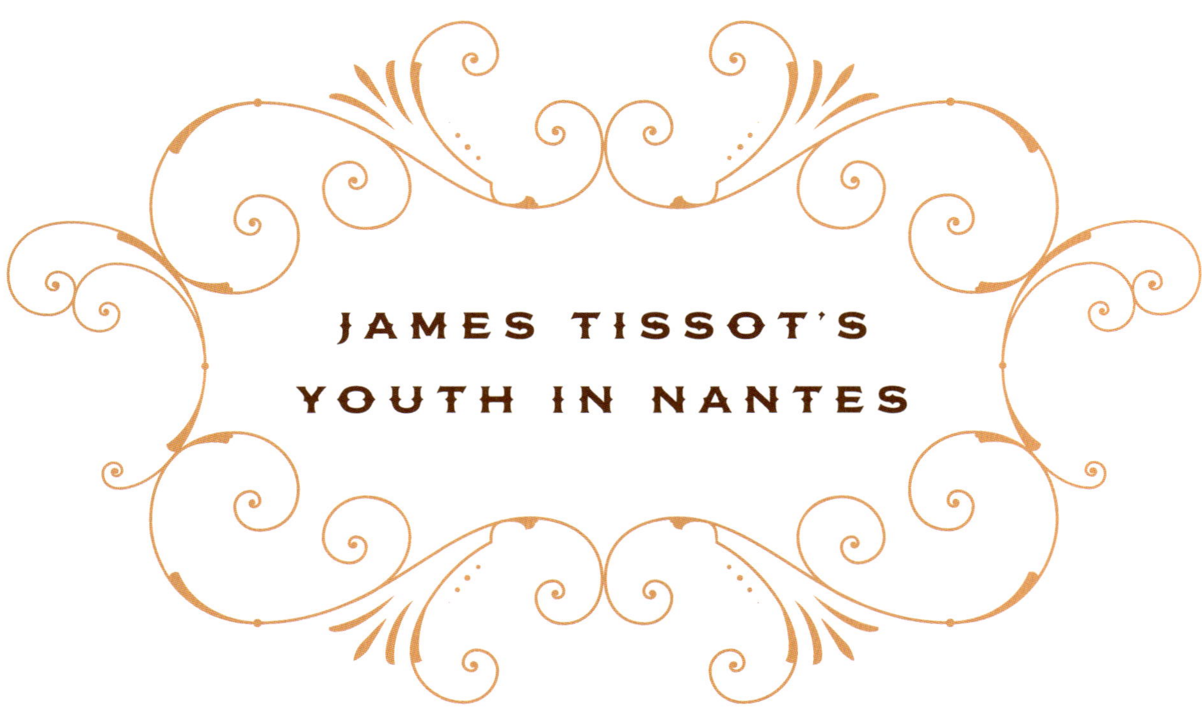

JAMES TISSOT'S YOUTH IN NANTES

BORN IN NANTES, Jacques-Joseph Tissot, later known as James Tissot, presented himself as an independent artist; a traveler, uprooted and exiled in England; and a dandy everywhere.[1] But despite his great fame, which came early, the painter proves difficult to pin down. Obscured by the veil of success, he eludes our grasp. An astute entrepreneur, brilliant portrait artist, and friend of the Impressionists as well as the literary and aristocratic elite, Tissot seldom publicly reflected on episodes from his youth in Nantes. Still, it was in this city of the dukes of Brittany that his taste for travel, his attraction to medievalism and to seafaring life, and his keen interest in fashion came to be.[2] A study of Tissot's life in Nantes—from his birth, in 1836, to his departure for Paris twenty years later[3]—reveals the profound effect the city had on his life and work, an influence that endured up to his death, in 1902.

TISSOT'S FAMILY CIRCLE

Few journalists were able to probe Tissot about his youth. Not until two short biographical pieces, by Alfred de Lostalot (1883) and Georges Bastard (1906), would such information become available to the public.[4] It is difficult to know whether to take at face value all of Tissot's proclamations at the height of his fame, when he is attentive to shaping his legacy. Nonetheless, Nantes's archives do provide important details of the artist's early years in that city.[5]

The marriage certificate of Tissot's parents, Marcel-Théodore Tissot (1807–1888) and Marie Durand (1802–1861), signed in Nantes on November 18, 1832, lists Marcel-Théodore as a merchant.[6] He was the son of Joseph-Marie Tissot (1768–1842), a landlord, and Marie Catherine Beck (1784–1862). Marcel-Théodore was not from Nantes; he was born on February 15, 1807, in Trévillers, near the Swiss border, in the department of Doubs in the Franche-Comté region. At the time of his marriage, James Tissot's father lived on Basse-Grande-Rue (now rue de la Marne) in the center of Nantes, near the Castle of the Dukes of Brittany and Nantes Cathedral, also known as the Cathedral of Saint Peter and Saint Paul. James Tissot's mother was the daughter of Mathurin Durand, a landlord, and Catherine-Angélique Mensch. She was born in Nantes on September 6, 1802, and raised on Basse-Grande-Rue, not far from her future husband.

The witnesses to Marcel-Théodore and Marie's wedding were people who lived or worked on the same street—among them, François Bellangé, a retired artillery squadron leader; Edmond Detreilles Sainte-Croix, a retired officer and engineer; and Jacques Royné, a grain merchant with a shop on Basse-Grande-Rue. These details place the Tissots within the petite bourgeoisie of Nantes, far from the brilliant milieus of Paris and London, where their painter son would later find fame.

Jacques-Joseph Tissot was born in Nantes on October 15, 1836, at his parents' home, the Maison du Guiny, on Basse-Grande-Rue. He was the second of Marcel-Théodore and Marie's four sons.[7] He had two godfathers:

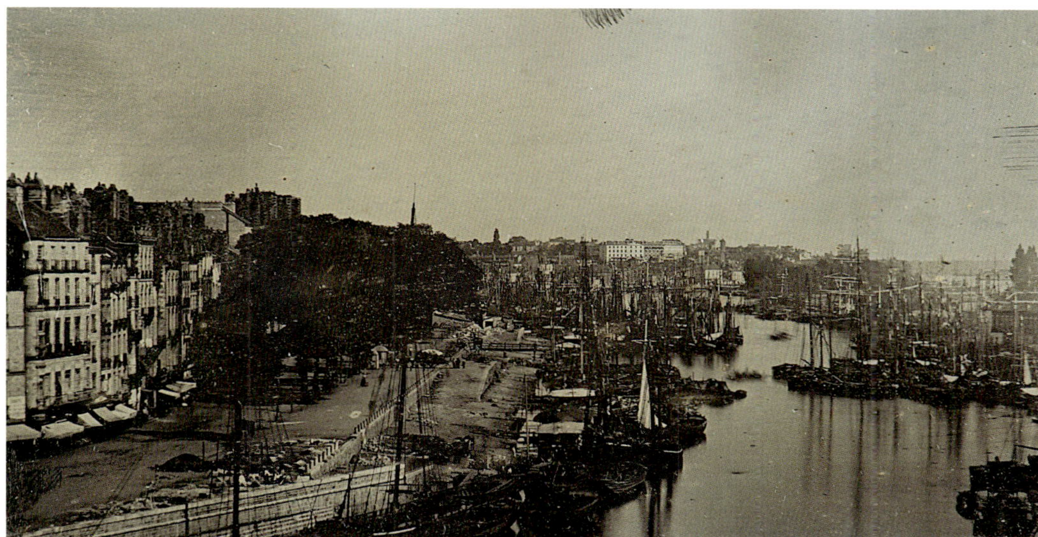

FIGURE 24
Henri Lamoré-Forest, *The Quais of Nantes*, ca. 1839–1840. Daguerreotype, 3¾ × 7⅛ in. (9.6 × 18 cm). Musée d'Histoire de Nantes

his maternal grandfather and Gabriel Gautier, a tailor. Although Marcel-Théodore is still listed as a merchant on his son's birth certificate, his name is not found under that category in the official directories from that period.[8] Likewise, there is some ambiguity regarding the professional life of Tissot's mother. Her marriage certificate lists her as having no profession. But from 1823 to 1835, the *Étrennes nantaises*, the annual commercial directory of Nantes, lists a Durand hat shop, later attributed to Durand-Tissot.[9] First named "Hats and Novelties" and then "Hat Shop," this novelty shop (*marchand de nouveautés*) most likely sold hats, clothing, and smaller decorative objects, such as porcelain.[10] It was housed on Basse-Grande-Rue and owned by "Mlles Durand." Thus, it seems that Marie Durand learned her trade with family members before running a business under her own name beginning around 1836. When James Tissot was born, "Hat Shop," owned by "Madame Tissot-Durand," already existed on Basse-Grande-Rue, and it would be listed at that address until 1839. The store appears to have relocated between 1840 and 1852, when it is listed as being on quai d'Orléans (now quai Lamartine). Between 1853 and 1858, the *Étrennes nantaises* still lists a "hat shop of Madame Durand-Tissot" at the address 1, quai d'Orléans. It was Tissot's mother, therefore, who owned the business with which his father, noted as a "hat seller" on electoral rolls, was associated.[11] Young Tissot grew up in this environment of lace, silk, satin, and frills. It was no doubt here that he first developed the fascination with fashion that is so manifest throughout his work.

FORMATIVE INFLUENCES

What did young Tissot see in Nantes? He lived in the middle-class neighborhood, between the cathedral and the castle, but also near the port. In those days, the city, close to the Atlantic Ocean (some twenty-five miles away), was traversed by dozens of channels; two rivers, the Erdre and the Loire, traced its topography (fig. 24). Twenty-eight bridges punctuated Nantes, which lived with the vagaries of its flooding rivers until the twentieth century, when some of their branches were filled in by the city. Two famous writers came to town during Tissot's youth: Stendhal stayed there from June 2 to 9, 1837, and Gustave Flaubert, accompanied by Maxime Du Camp, explored his 1847 visit in an account that remained unpublished for many years, *Over Strand and Field: A Record of Travel Through Brittany* (*Par les champs et par les grèves: voyage en Bretagne*, 1881). Perched in the cathedral tower, Flaubert described the city in glowing terms:

> From atop the cathedral . . . you discover a horizon that rewards your breathless climb up the stairs: sharply below, the houses squeeze together, their roofs crammed like pointed hats in a packed crowd; to the left, a vast prairie is watered at the banks of the wide, gray river that divides and bends, while the two streams of the Erdre and the Sèvre, their branches and islands multiplying, carve the countryside in large gray lines.[12]

In his *Memoirs of a Tourist* (*Mémoires d'un touriste*, 1838), Stendhal remarked on the spirit of the "big city" more than on the details of its monuments:

> It is Nantes's good fortune to be situated partly on a hill that, emerging from the shores of the Loire, on the right bank and to the north, increasingly draws back from the river, forming perhaps a thirty-degree angle with it. The shipyards where I am occupy the first little plain that lies between the Loire and the hill. But this Loire is not as wide as the Rhône in Lyon; Nantes is located on a very narrow branch: this river, there as elsewhere, is continually broken up by islands. Opposite the shipyards, this branch of the Loire is joined by another, much wider, one.[13]

Stendhal's formal account of Nantes demonstrates a certain snobbery but also a strong sensitivity to the originality of a lively city—one turned toward the ocean and in the process of developing its burgeoning trade. During that period, and up to at least 1860, Nantes was France's fourth-largest port; its wealth came from the growth in trade of products such as clothing, coffee, and sugar, drawing on earlier resources the city derived from the transatlantic slave trade.[14] Urban development helped liberate Nantes from its old medieval walls, many of which were razed in the eighteenth century. The city began to industrialize in the 1850s, with biscuit factories, breweries, canneries, distilleries, and sugar refineries. New neighborhoods emerged, particularly on the east and west sides of the city. Cours Cambronne, the neighborhood near the opera house, expanded; it was graced with beautiful mansions, thanks to the architect Mathurin Crucy, and what is now one of the most famous French arcades, Passage Pommeraye, was inaugurated in 1843. The passage brought the lower part

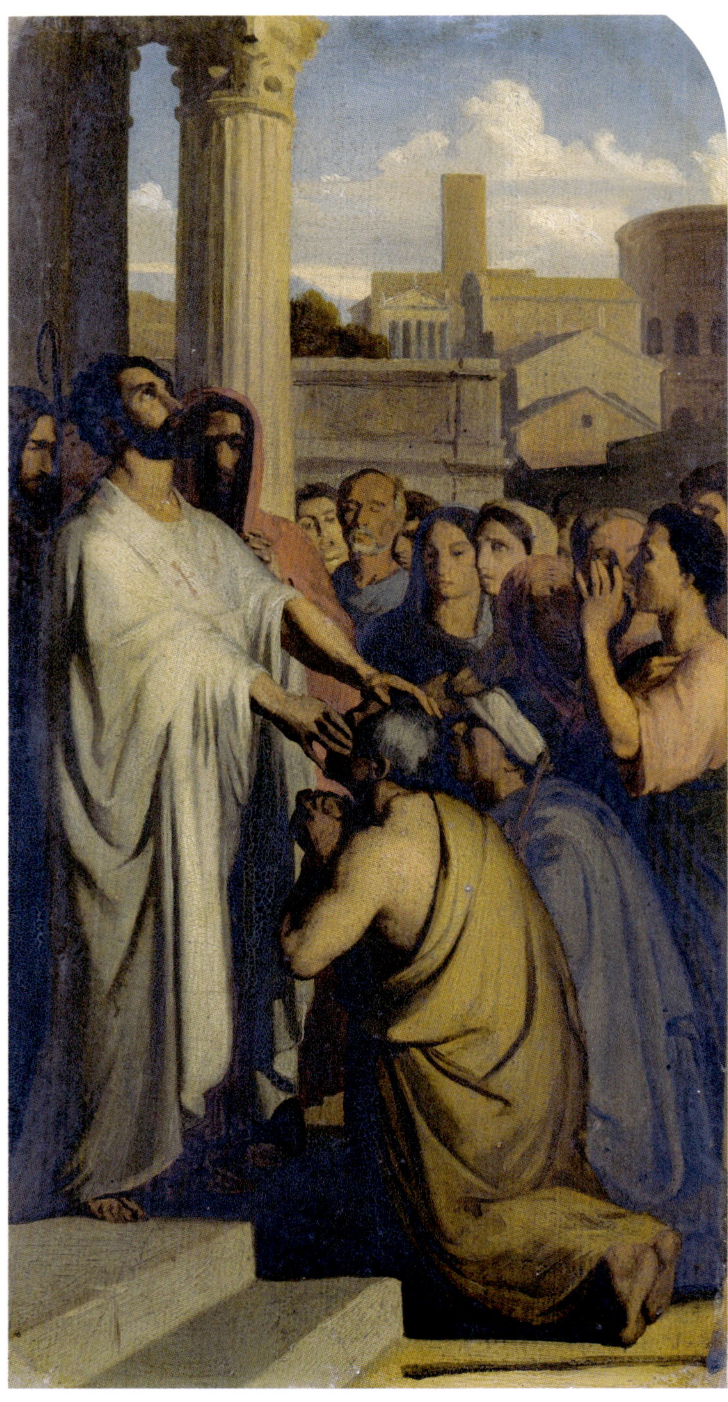

FIGURE 25
Paul Jean Flandrin (French, 1811–1902) after Hippolyte Flandrin (French, 1809–1864), *Saint Clair Healing the Blind*, 1836. Oil on cardboard, 13⅜ × 7½ in. (34 × 19 cm). Musée du Louvre, Paris, RF1987-19

of the city, home to the working class, into contact with the aristocratic upper city. A diverse society mingled along the quays: dockers, merchants, shipowners, and workers.

Tissot, then, grew up among the ships, channels, and floods of the Loire but also amid the city's urban upheavals. He was gifted in art and drew from a very young age. He dreamed of becoming an architect, but his father wanted him to be a well-educated bourgeois.[15] Tissot was sent off to study at Brugelette, in Flanders, around 1848, and then at Vannes (Brittany) and Dole (Franche-Comté), in Jesuit schools.[16] In 1845, Marcel-Théodore acquired the Château de Buillon, a large estate in the east of France, thus cementing his family's dual attachment to the Franche-Comté of his birth and Nantes (see Mantion, this volume). Later in life, Tissot recalled that his father wanted to send him away from home to study so that he could train to be a merchant.[17] For high school, however, Tissot remained in Nantes, studying rhetoric at the Lycée Impérial (now the Lycée Georges Clemenceau), an institution renowned for its arts instruction and whose later alumni would include many writers, artists, and politicians, such as the poet Tristan Corbière; the artists Jules Grandjouan and Maxime Maufra; and Georges Clemenceau, the future prime minister of France during World War I.[18] It was in this fertile environment that the artist James Tissot was formed.

TRAINING IN THE ARTS

No commercial art galleries existed in Nantes before 1868, when the Mignon-Massart Gallery was founded.[19] Thus, Tissot would have developed his artistic eye on the city's medieval monuments, in particular Nantes Cathedral. There, one of the most beautiful tombs of the Renaissance holds a prominent place: that of François II, duke of Brittany, and his wife, Marguerite de Foix.[20] No doubt this extraordinary funerary sculpture with its allegorical figures made an impression on Tissot, as did Nantes's medieval past. He maintained a lifelong interest in architecture and medieval objects, and, in fact, began his artistic career by painting medieval compositions (see Baetens, this volume, and Frederick, this volume). Right next to the great monument to François II and his wife, in the transept, is Hippolyte Flandrin's painting of Saint Clair (fig. 25); perhaps it was not simply by chance that Tissot would later join Flandrin's studio in Paris.

The Musée des Beaux-Arts (now the Musée d'arts de Nantes) was also central to Tissot's artistic education. Founded in 1801 by Napoleon Bonaparte, the museum occupied the former *halle aux toiles* (the covered market where textiles were sold) at the heart of the city as of 1830. A succession of eight galleries housed the exceptional collection of the brothers François and Pierre Cacault (1,155 paintings and 64 sculptures). Acquired by the city in 1810, this collection assembled Italian "primitive" masterpieces as well as superb paintings and sculptures from the seventeenth and eighteenth centuries, most notably three paintings by the French artist Georges de La Tour.[21] During their respective visits to the museum, Stendhal and Flaubert both commented on La Tour's work but also on the beautiful Italian paintings, including the exquisite *Christ Carrying the Cross* (1513; Musée d'arts de Nantes) by Andrea Solario. Tissot later jested that he did not visit the galleries much; he "spent most of his time trying

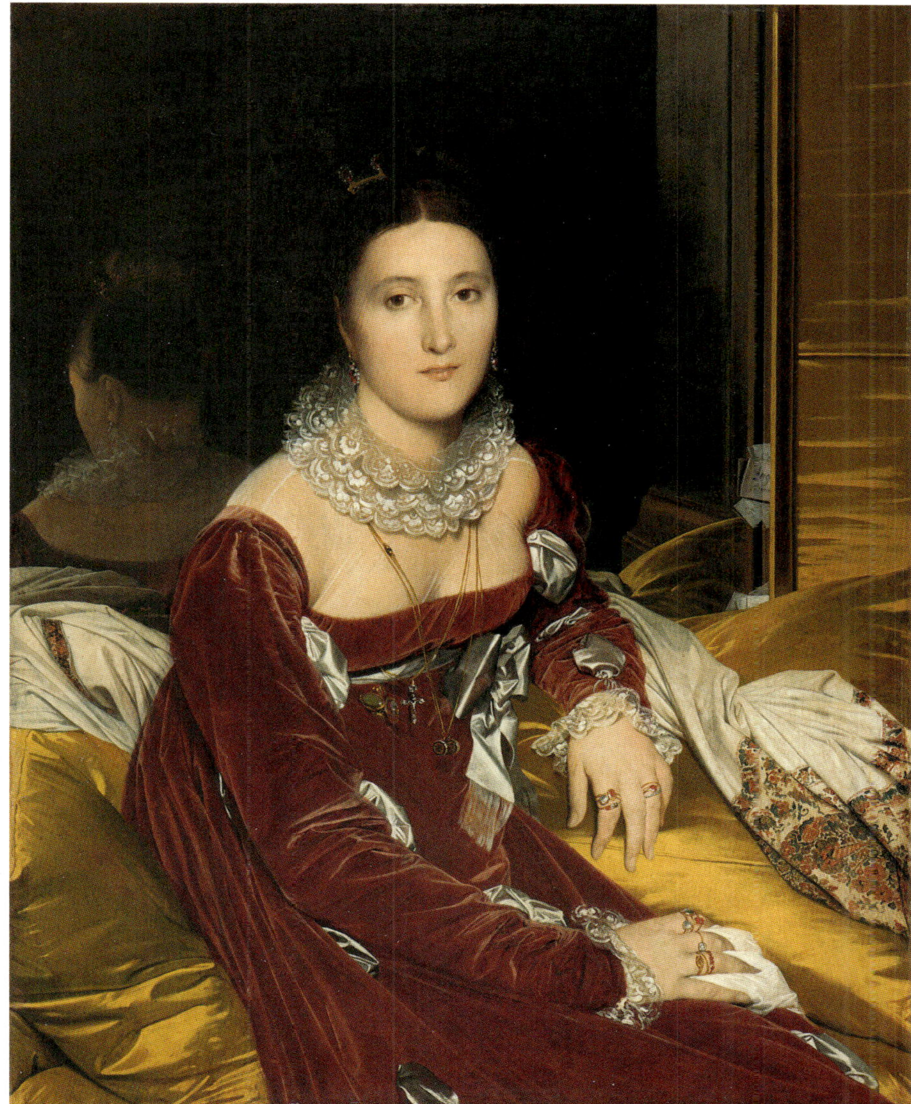

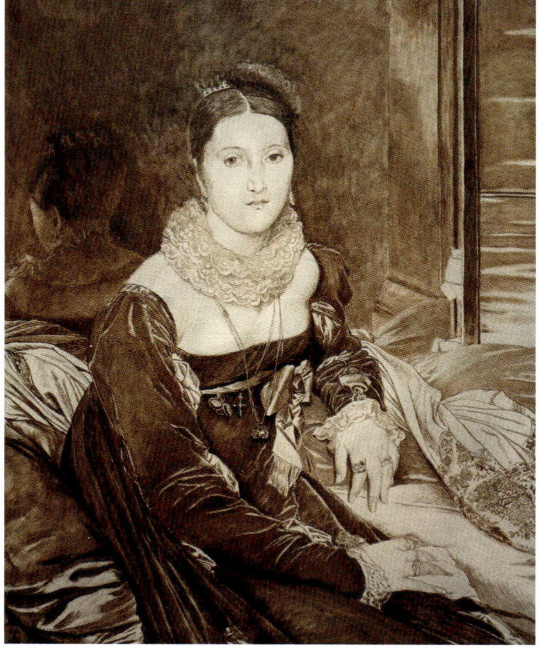

FIGURE 26
Jean-Auguste-Dominique Ingres (French, 1780–1867), *Portrait of Madame de Senonnes*, 1814. Oil on canvas, 41 3/4 × 33 1/8 in. (106 × 84 cm). Musée d'Arts de Nantes, Purchased from M. Bonnin in 1853, Inv. 1028

FIGURE 27
James Tissot, *Portrait of Madame de Senonnes: Copy in Grisaille after Ingres*, 1899. Oil on canvas, 40 1/8 × 31 7/8 in. (102 × 81.3 cm). Musée d'Arts de Nantes, Inv. 04.10.1.P

out roller skates on the museum's waxed parquet floor."[22]

One thing is clear: Tissot must have been deeply impressed by the extraordinary *Portrait of Madame de Senonnes*, by Jean-Auguste-Dominique Ingres (fig. 26). Acquired by the Musée des Beaux-Arts in 1853, the painting was hung immediately and created a sensation.[23] Ingres would continue to have a powerful influence on Tissot. A taste for fashion, the use of wide curves, and a knack for depicting portrait subjects with enigmatic, inscrutable expressions are all traits that the two artists share. Tissot would return to that portrait at the end of his life, when he made a grisaille copy of it in 1899, from a photograph he had requested from the museum's curator (fig. 27).[24]

When Tissot announced his wish to pursue an artistic path, his father cut him off financially. He wanted his son to embark on a commercial career. Bastard recounts that Tissot made it to Paris thanks to his mother's support; around 1856, she wrote to Jules-Élie Delaunay, the celebrated artist from Nantes, who recommended Tissot to the studios of Louis Lamothe and Flandrin, Delaunay's own teacher. Although Tissot did study with Lamothe, where he may have met Edgar Degas, this story seems a bit fanciful. It is hard to imagine that Delaunay, who had left Nantes in 1848 and won the Prix de Rome in 1856, would reply to the Tissot family and offer such introductions. Was it a matter of solidarity with his native city? Or merely an invention of Bastard's? Or, perhaps, Tissot's?

Tissot's mother died in 1861, leaving her son a comfortable inheritance that helped him pay off his debts. Little is known about the beginnings of his life in Paris. He first lived on rue Féron and then rue Bonaparte, in the same building as the writer Alphonse Daudet, who became a friend.[25] Having left Nantes penniless, Tissot overspent his inheritance; by around 1863 he was 70,000 francs in debt. By 1865, however, he had become well established and reports earning 70,000 francs.[26] The wheel of fortune had turned, initiating the young artist's illustrious ascent.

"ONE GRAM OF HENRI LEYS, TWO GRAMS OF TALENT, ZERO GRAMS OF GENIUS": TISSOT'S EARLY PAINTINGS

JAN DIRK BAETENS

In 1860, a year after his first passage at the Paris Salon, James Tissot made his debut at the triannual Brussels Salon.[1] His submission, a painting titled *Marguerite in Church*,[2] was largely ignored by the press, but the graphic artist Félicien Rops referred to it in his satirical survey of the exhibition. Accompanying an exaggeratedly archaic depiction of a medieval cortège, Rops published two recipes for the type of historicist painting that was popular at the Salon (fig. 28). The second of these recipes proposed to mix twelve grams each of the Old Masters Hans Memling, Jan van Eyck, and Bernard van Orley, with one gram of Henri Leys, two grams of talent, zero grams of genius, and one hundred grams of tin shreds, and to sign the result with the name of (Joseph) Ducaju, (Guillaume) Koller, (Joseph) Lies, (André-Joseph) Minguet, or Tissot.

Rops was poking fun at the slavish imitation by Tissot and many others of the work of celebrated Belgian painter Henri Leys, who had been catapulted to international fame after showing his fifteenth- and sixteenth-century-style paintings at the 1855 Exposition Universelle in Paris. Tissot met Leys in 1859, when he traveled to the latter's native city of Antwerp, a vibrant artistic center and a magnet for foreign art students at the time.[3] Ford Madox Brown studied in Antwerp in the late 1830s, and so did—in the 1850s and 1860s, respectively—Lawrence Alma-Tadema and Charles Napier Hemy, who had both come under Leys's spell and were two of Tissot's closest friends during his later London years.[4] Tissot's early paintings—most markedly those dealing with Johann Wolfgang von Goethe's *Faust* (see Frederick, this volume)—clearly depend on Leys's example. In these paintings, Tissot not only imitates the older artist's consciously primitive style but also directly borrows visual motifs and details.[5] Tissot's 1860 work *Meeting of Faust and Marguerite* (pl. 3), for instance, combines Leys's *The Promenade Outside the City-Walls* (fig. 29), painted in 1854 and shown a year later at the Exposition Universelle, with Leys's *Faust and Marguerite* (1856; Philadelphia Museum of Art). The background in Tissot's painting is borrowed from the latter, while the foreground figures of Faust and Marguerite seem to have been derived from the courting couple central to the former. The family group on the left-hand side of Tissot's painting is also clearly related to the group on the right in *The Promenade Outside the City-Walls*, and the little child's quaint medieval toy is taken from yet another Leys painting, *New Year's Day in Flanders* (1853; private collection), which was also on view at the 1855 Exposition.

Tissot was almost universally criticized for these early works.[6] Leys, who studied the remains of the past and in fact lived among them—in the sixteenth-century city of Antwerp—was often described as an old soul who had simply been born too late, rather than as an imitator.[7] He was thus pardoned for his learned historicism. Tissot's work, however, was too obviously secondhand (or, to be more precise, thirdhand) to sustain any such claim. This led to the characterization of Tissot by some of his contemporaries as a commercial plagiarist of artistic fashions, an opinion most famously delivered in the diary of the French writer Edmond de Goncourt, who observed that Tissot found "a new passion every two or three years, with which he could get another little lease on life."[8] As a result, Tissot's early, derivative work is often treated separately from his later, more original modern-life paintings. In this view, the artist's enduring interest in costume and anthropological attention to the minor details of everyday life are generally seen as the only features that bind his later work to his historical scenes, as well as to Leys's work.[9] This hardly does justice, however, to the continuity throughout Tissot's oeuvre and to the significant role that Leys's art played not only as a model for the early pictures but also as a catalyst for Tissot's further artistic maturation.

Tissot built his reputation on his astute observations of middle-class social mores, regularly delivered with a mild form of social satire.[10] In *Too Early* (pl. 46), for instance, he shows the embarrassment of guests who have arrived before the start of a party. The same type of satire, albeit with a historical twist, can also be seen in Leys's work. In their review of the 1855 Exposition Universelle, the Goncourt brothers—Edmond and his brother Jules—who would later become well acquainted with Tissot, presented Leys as the great chronicler of social life in the Middle Ages, drawing special attention to his Rabelaisian satire of religion, courtship, and other features of medieval social life.[11] Many reviewers agreed. In discussions of *The Promenade Outside the City-Walls*, critics especially noted the family group on the right, describing the conceited, rich family patriarch, his jealously sideways-glancing wife, and their all-too-fashionably-dressed,

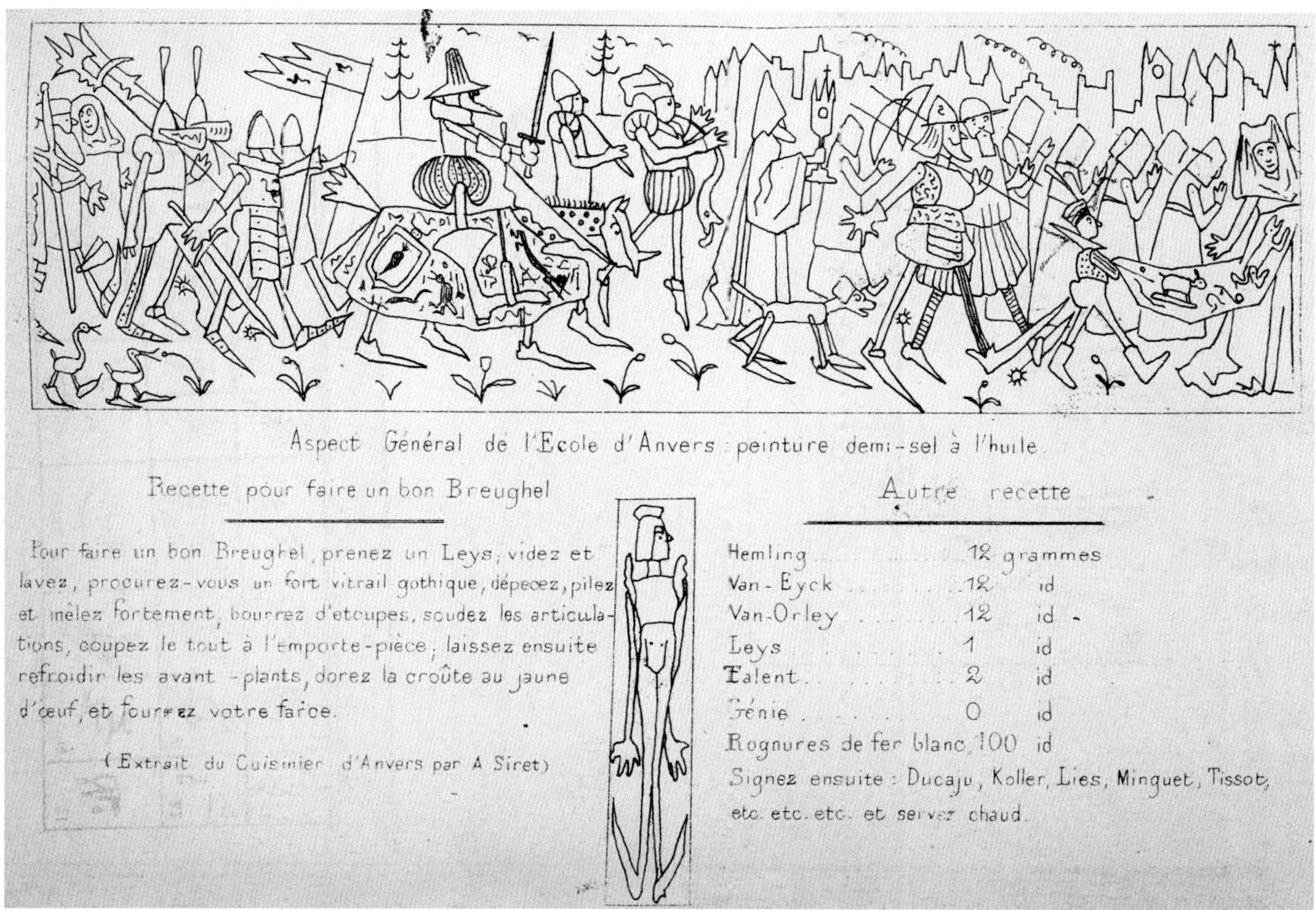

FIGURE 28
Félicien Rops (Belgian, 1833–1898), *Aspect général de l'école d'Anvers peinture demi-sel à l'huile*, from *Uylenspiegel au salon: revue de l'Exposition de 1860*, 1860. Lithograph, 5 × 7¼ in. (12.7 × 18.7 cm). Published by Parent et Fils, Brussels. Royal Library of Belgium, Brussels

arrogant son as typical of the gossiping, resentful, and spiteful burghers of the Middle Ages.[12] Some critics even suggested that times had not really changed. One observed that Leys's provincial medieval shopkeepers "have passed, if not their clothing, then certainly their scoffing and envious characters to ours."[13]

If this shared penchant for social comedy brings Tissot's modern-life works closer to Leys's painted history of social mores than is usually acknowledged, the same is true of some of the innovative compositional strategies that Tissot developed. In the 1870s, Tissot's interest in Japanese prints led him to experiment, cautiously but unmistakably, with composing and framing his scenes in unconventional ways—such as adopting an unusually high point of view or boldly juxtaposing contrasting elements on a shallow plane—that are clearly indebted to Japanese art.[14] This tendency was further reinforced by his interest in photography, which stimulated him, for instance, to cut off his scenes in a seemingly haphazard way, reminiscent of a snapshot (see pls. 100, 118, and 120).[15] Similar features can be seen in many paintings by Leys, although he borrowed his unconventional compositional features mostly from fifteenth- and sixteenth-century northern European prints, which share a number of formal properties with the Japanese prints that inspired Tissot. Leys, too, combined his sources with an interest in photography, resulting in a tendency to include effects such as unexpected juxtapositions and abrupt framing in his paintings. These features are most clearly noticeable in Leys's works of the 1860s, but they can already be detected in *The Promenade Outside the City-Walls*, and

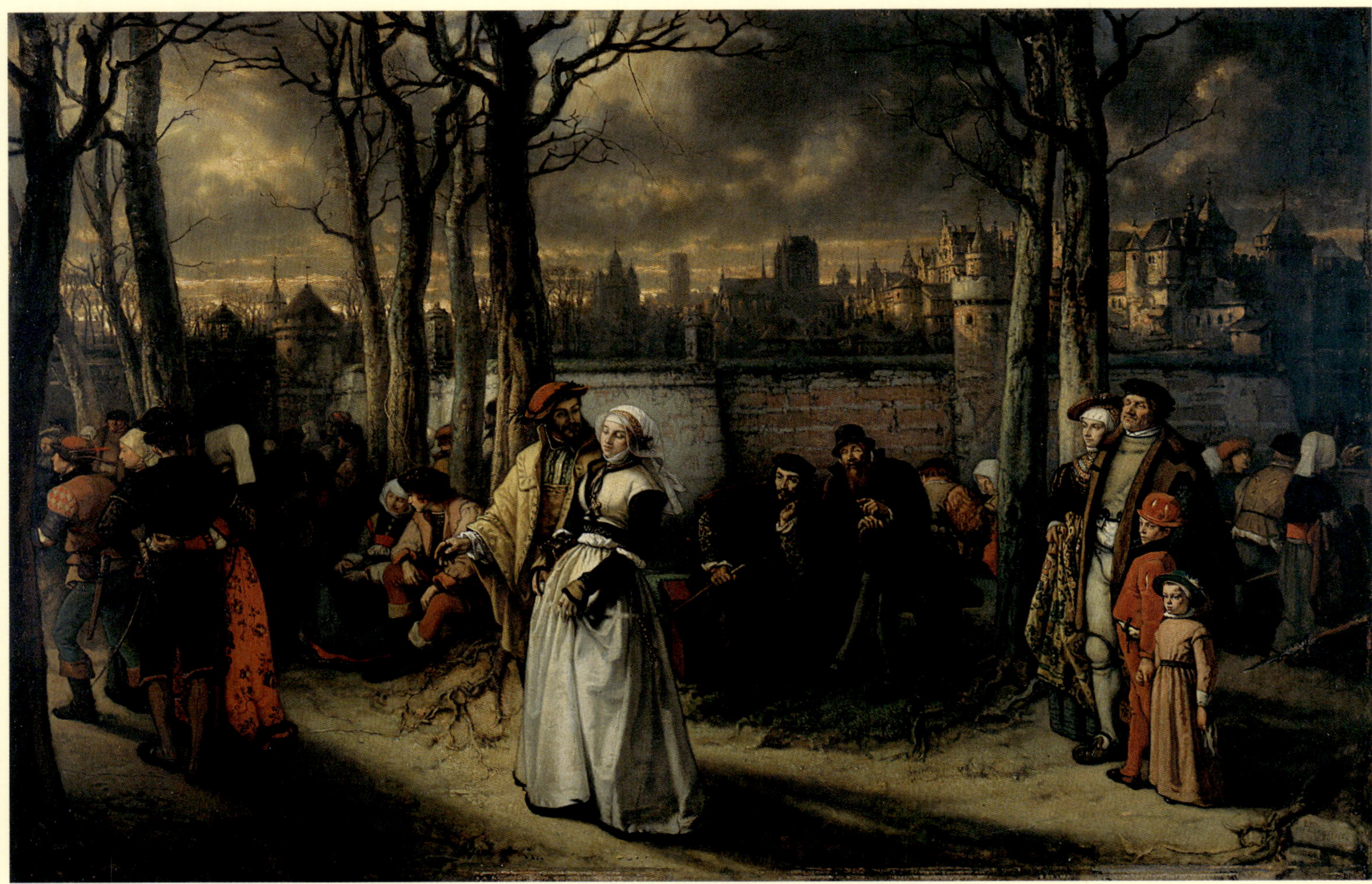

are certainly hinted at in Rops's caricature, which depicts people walking radically outside the frame. One of the results of these techniques is that many of both Tissot's and Leys's scenes seem to show the viewer not an artifical reconstruction of reality but life itself, as if caught by surprise.

FIGURE 29
Henri Leys (Belgian, 1815–1869), *The Promenade Outside the City-Walls*, 1854. Oil on wood panel, 27¾ × 42 in. (70.4 × 106.6 cm). The Museum of Fine Arts Ghent, Belgium, Belgian Royal Collection, 1998-D

Tissot's and Leys's use of unconventional compositional schemes—borrowed from different but nevertheless commensurable sources—and their mutual interest in social satire suggest a continuity that has rarely been recognized between the former's modern-life paintings and the latter's historical work, as well as between Tissot's modern-life pieces and his own earlier historical scenes. The portrait of Tissot by his friend Edgar Degas seems to recognize this continuum (fig. 103).[16] It shows the artist in a slightly comical fashion, casually draped over his chair like a true dandy but also in a position that refers to the pose of the sitter in *Portrait of Mlle L. L…* (pl. 22), Tissot's breakthrough modern-life painting of 1864, while simultaneously inverting the position of Marguerite in *Marguerite in Church* (see pl. 4), that pose itself derived from an earlier painting by Leys, *Luther as a Child Singing Christmas Carols in the Streets of Eisenach* (1859; location unknown). Behind Tissot is a copy or imitation of a Japanese print and under it, almost like a repetition of the painter's face, a little portrait by Lucas Cranach the Elder, one of the chief sources of inspiration for both Leys's and Tissot's historical scenes. Satire, modern life, Japonisme, and historicism are thus not at odds in Degas's synthesis of Tissot's artistic persona. On the contrary, they seem to converge in the painter himself.

"LOVE, ERROR, AND REPENTANCE": THE FAUST AND MARGUERITE PAINTINGS

MARGARETTA S. FREDERICK

Between 1860 and 1861, having been in Paris only a few years, James Tissot created a series of oil paintings illustrating part one of Johann Wolfgang von Goethe's *Faust*. Three of these were exhibited at the Paris Salon of 1861: *Faust and Marguerite in the Garden* (fig. 30), *Marguerite at the Service* (1861; location unknown), and *Meeting of Faust and Marguerite* (pl. 3).[1] The historic style and thematic content of these paintings reveal the strong influence on Tissot's early work of the Belgian artist Henri Leys, who was renowned for his highly detailed medieval works and who had also treated scenes from *Faust* (see Baetens, this volume).[2] But Tissot's choice of subject matter for this exhibition—only his second Salon appearance—can also be viewed within the context of a broader cultural response to Goethe's drama across French literature, theater, and music.

Goethe's two-part tragic play was first published in Germany in 1808, and distributed more broadly in an 1816 illustrated edition with images by the German painter Moritz Retzsch. A French translation by Albert Stapfer appeared in 1824, with seventeen lithographs by Eugène Delacroix. The drama recounts a deal made between God and the devil (in the guise of the demon Mephistopheles) in which the latter attempts to corrupt the morally upright character of the scholar Faust. An innocent young woman, Marguerite, is caught up in this web of devilry and deceit. *Faust* was lauded by leaders of the French Romantic movement in literature, whose fascination with its dark, psychological narrative in turn stimulated the interest of the French public. The text quickly became a common subject within the fine arts including, most notably, in work by Delacroix, Leys, and Ary Scheffer.[3]

The popularity of Goethe's drama in France was also reflected in numerous musical, dramatic, and poetic interpretations. In 1846, Hector Berlioz's *The Damnation of Faust* premiered at the Opéra Comique in Paris. Franz Liszt composed *A Faust Symphony* in 1854, performed in several incomplete presentations before publication in 1861. But perhaps the most important musical composition in relation to Tissot's paintings was Charles Gounod's opera *Faust*, with a libretto by Michel Carré and Jules Barbier, first performed at the Théâtre Lyrique on March 19, 1859.[4] In this adaptation, Parisians were presented with one of the earliest appearances of the lyric soprano in the part of Marguerite. Gounod accentuated the character's innocence and emotion through the warm and full-timbre voice of this novel part. As in Gounod's opera, the focus of Tissot's *Faust* paintings is the love of Faust and Marguerite. Together, the renderings form a kind of Hogarthian moral narrative series centering on the life of Marguerite—the victimized female, rather than the angst-driven male of the title—and, more specifically, as Théophile Gautier perceptively noted, "love, error, and repentance."[5]

Within the visual arts, Tissot's contributions fit contextually in a direct line of descent from those of Delacroix, Leys, and Scheffer, as is reflected in the critical responses to his work, both positive and negative. The French photographer and writer Maxime Du Camp, for instance, fell in the latter category, perceiving Tissot's finely painted realism as pastiche and mere imitation of Leys.[6] At the heart of the criticism was a sense of the intrinsic impracticability of translating Goethe's tumultuous drama onto the static canvas.[7] Arguably, however, Tissot comes closest among all of the *Faust* painters to capturing the treatment of Marguerite as a pawn in a cavalier wager between the forces of good and evil.

The superabundance of detail in Tissot's images—a device inherited from Leys—provides the means for repeated motifs through which the scenes are linked in a contiguous narrative. The earliest episode that Tissot treats, *Meeting of Faust and Marguerite*, was accompanied in the Salon catalogue by Faust's unsolicited initial greeting, "My fairest lady, may I dare to offer you my arm and company?"[8] A number of ancillary details are included in the composition that reference events preceding or following this scene in Goethe's drama. The setting, outside the doors of a religious building, conveys Marguerite's devout and chaste character.[9] Additional elements, such as the Crucifixion depicted at left, reference Easter, the day on which Faust first engaged with Mephistopheles, and symbolically foreshadow Marguerite's fall. The flower on the pillar to the left of the couple prefigures Marguerite's childish plucking of a daisy, which we are shown in *Faust and Marguerite in the Garden*. In that scene, an overly large Faust looms over Marguerite, seated next to him on the bench, as she murmurs, "He loves me . . . loves me not."[10] The link between the two paintings is strengthened by the repeated motif of the Crucifixion. The idea of sacrifice

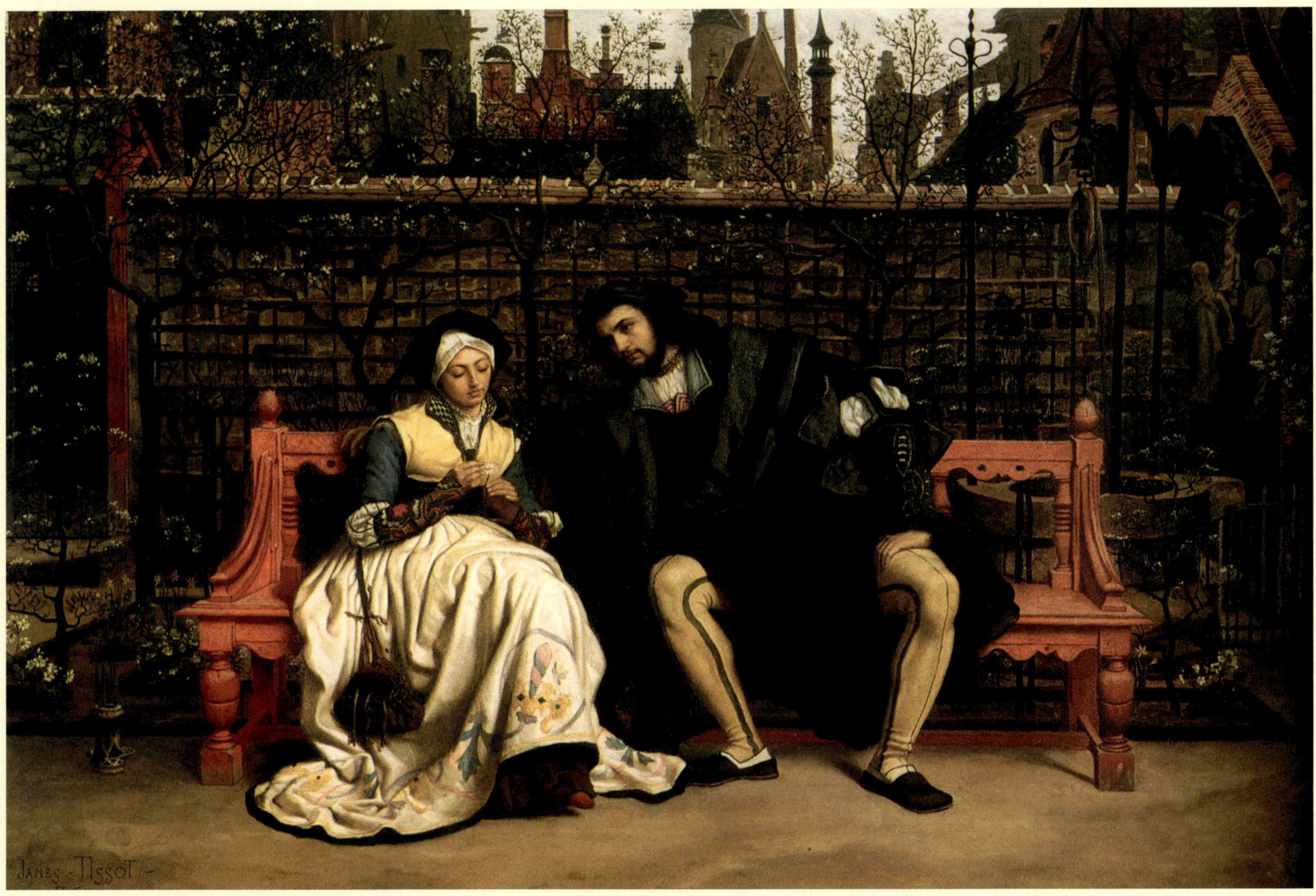

plays out further in *Marguerite at the Fountain* (fig. 31), which depicts a pivotal scene in *Faust*: recalling her own censure of others' unchaste behavior, Marguerite begins to reflect on the consequences of her actions.[11]

Tissot devoted at least five of his *Faust* works to the scene of Marguerite's remorse—her last appearance in the drama—which takes place during a funeral mass inside a church. It is in this setting that she comes to fully understand her disgrace in acceding to sexual compromise. In these images, the artist departs from the text, the discrepancies serving to accentuate the emotional content of the drama. Marguerite is removed from Goethe's designated placement for her within the congregation to a position of isolation behind the choir screen. Tissot dispenses with imagery of the evil spirit, a staple detail commonly used by other artists before him.[12] Instead, Marguerite's tormentor is her own conscience, as shown in *Marguerite in Church* (pl. 4), in which she is surrounded by nightmarish symbols of her fall from grace. She sits, desolate, a scene of purgatory—a sea of souls awaiting judgment—depicted on the wall behind her. Beneath the frieze, a painted decoration suggests the dragon of the Apocalypse. At left, two young children bury their faces in prayer—a skillful contrast of innocence and sin. At center, in a recessed alcove, a prone Christlike body awaits, like Marguerite, his spiritual fate.

The interrelated construction of Tissot's *Faust* paintings emulates a rhetorical device similar to the *chroniques* of Tissot's close friend, the writer Alphonse Daudet.[13] These prose pieces rejected an overtly continuous narrative in favor of successive stand-alone vignettes, each of which nonetheless advanced a plot or scenario.[14] This technique provided an ideal format for Tissot to show off his technical prowess and demonstrate his embrace of Leys's highly detailed, bric-a-brac–filled historical compositions. In addition, by emphasizing the psychological impact of the events that so drastically altered Marguerite's character, Tissot's series advanced the dark, emotional component embraced by contemporary Romanticism. The overlapping narrative of the compositions, depicted with such precise definition, both reflected and captured the widespread cultural preoccupation and fascination with Goethe's tragedy of human nature. But Tissot's attraction to the drama seems to have been deeper than simply the savvy positioning of a young artist, gainfully adopting au courant subject matter. In Goethe's *Faust*, he had found the themes of womanhood and the human struggle to maintain one's faith in a rapidly modernizing world that would play out in much of his mature work. In many ways, Tissot's multicanvas interpretation of *Faust*—focused on a woman's desire for love, her vulnerability, and the eventual betrayal of her faith—sets the tone for other series to come, such as *La Femme à Paris* (pls. 117–130), and culminating in the volumes of *The Life of Christ* (pls. 144–156) (see Buron, this volume).

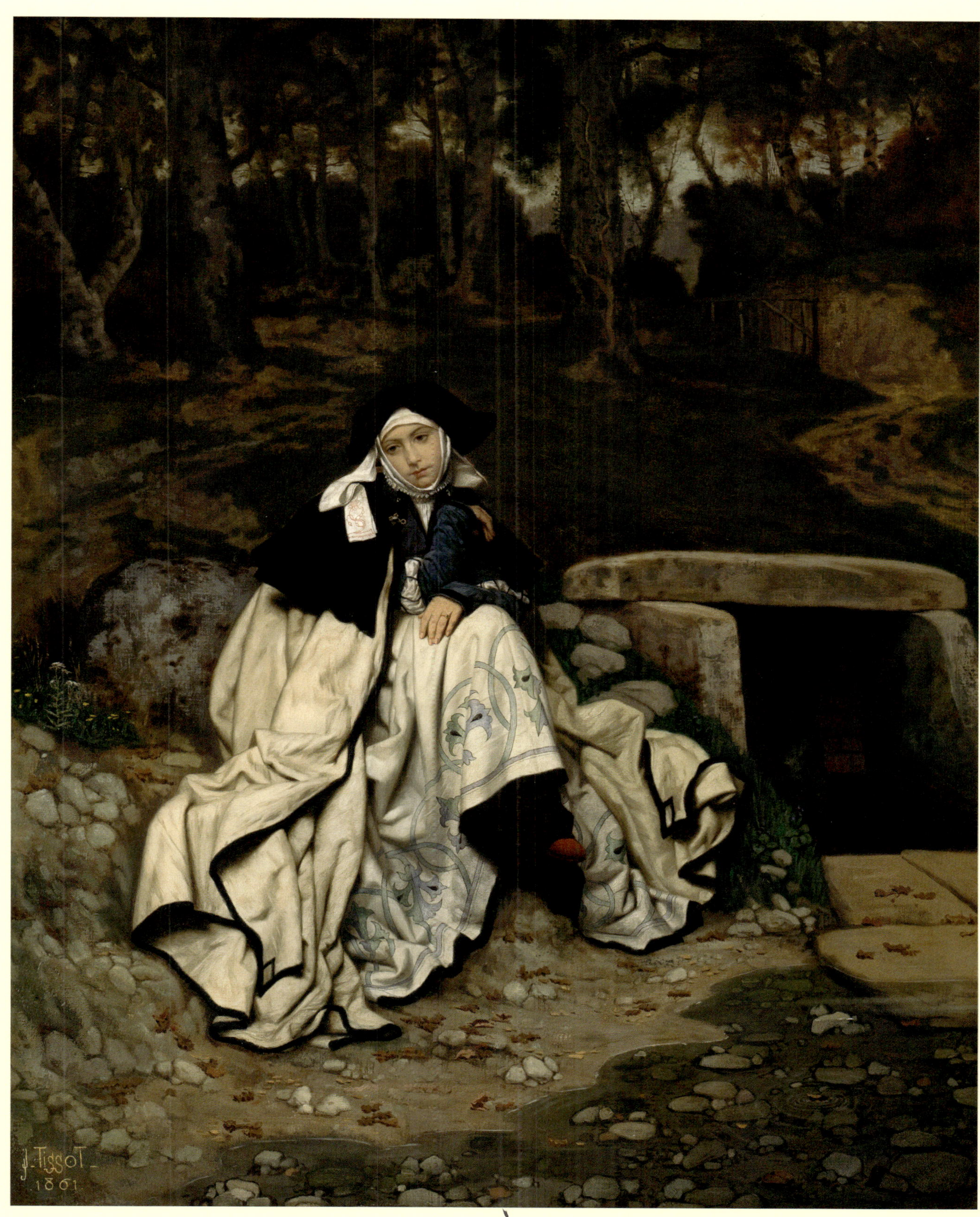

FIGURE 30
James Tissot, *Faust and Marguerite in the Garden*, 1861. Oil on wood panel, 25 × 35 in. (63.5 × 88.9 cm). Private collection

FIGURE 31
James Tissot, *Marguerite at the Fountain*, 1861. Oil on canvas, 50 × 40 in. (127 × 101.6 cm). Private collection

BERTRAND TILLIER

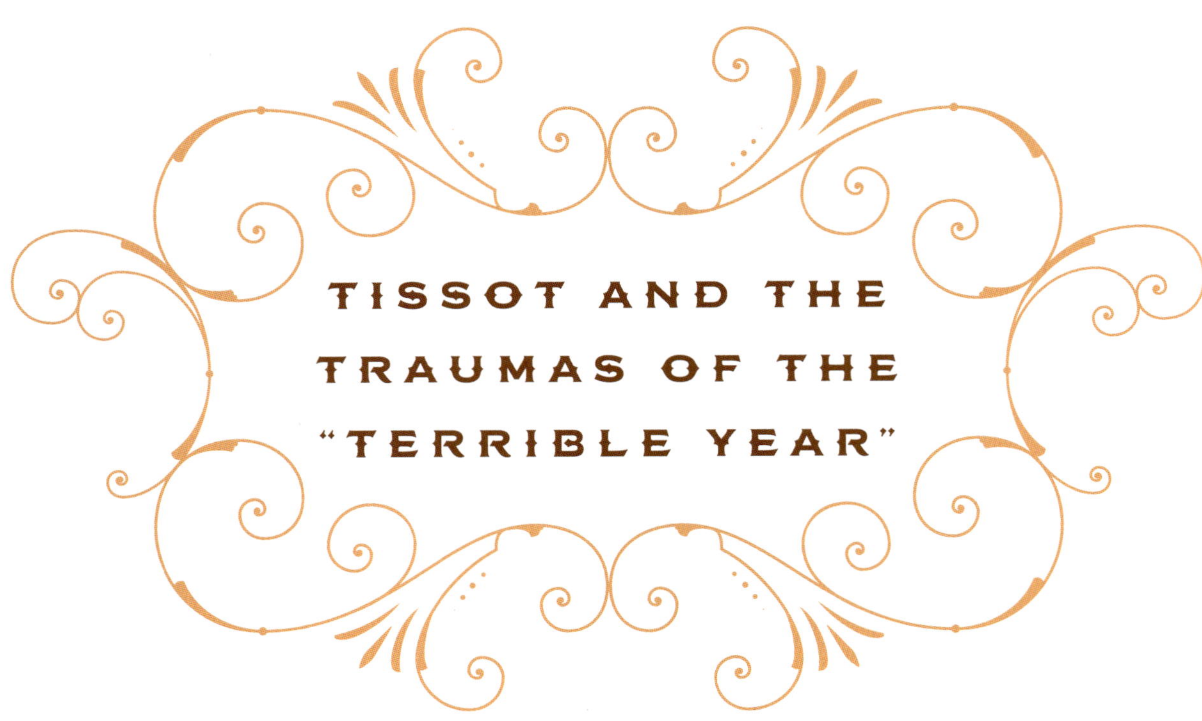

TISSOT AND THE TRAUMAS OF THE "TERRIBLE YEAR"

JAMES TISSOT CAME TO PARIS from Nantes in the mid-1850s to train as a painter, and within a few years developed a paradoxical body of work composed of historical genre scenes tinged with archaism, paintings of Parisian life imbued with modernity, and society portraits—the most spectacular of which is *The Circle of the Rue Royale* (pl. 27), an emblem of the painter's artistic and social success. With the outbreak of the Franco-Prussian War, in 1870, Tissot was probably swept up by the general atmosphere of patriotism, his engagement further inspired by a desire for adventure. The sequence of events of what Victor Hugo called the "Terrible Year" (*L'année terrible*), culminating in the proclamation of the Paris Commune as a refusal of France's defeat by Prussia, offered Tissot a panoply of experiences that likewise mark work by other contemporary painters—such as Edgar Degas, Édouard Manet, and Ernest Meissonier—who, confronted with the violent reality of the years 1870–1871, wanted to see, to know, and to act.[1]

❦ ❦ ❦

In 1897, biographer Octave Gréard reprinted in his monograph on Ernest Meissonier a series of reflections by the artist entitled *Recollections and Conversations* (*Ses souvenirs, ses entretiens*), in which are written these lines about James Tissot:

> I find his painting of the *Ruines de la Cour des Comptes* striking. Two unfortunates, almost mad with sorrow and misery, are there, the man and the woman. The invisible Christ has come over to them; he is gloriously covered in a golden cloak, but he draws it slightly open before these wretches . . . and as if to console them, to encourage them to suffer and endure, he shows them the bloodied body of a divine martyr.[2]

Late in life, Tissot related the circumstances under which the subject of this 1885 painting, also known as *Inner Voices* or *Christ the Comforter* (fig. 32), came to him.[3] Having returned to Paris after more than a decade spent in London, where he had moved in the immediate wake of the 1871 Paris Commune, he went to the Church of Saint-Sulpice "more to catch the atmosphere for my painting than to worship. But I found myself joining in the devotions, and as the Host was elevated and I bowed my head and closed my eyes, I saw a strange and thrilling picture."[4] This vision, and the work engendered by it, has historically been credited as the impetus for the artist's return to religious painting—largely abandoned while in London—and the inspiration for his illustrated Bible, *The Life of Christ*, on account of which he traveled to the Holy Land for the first time on his fiftieth birthday (see Buron, this volume). Meissonier was not unaware of this correlation; he prefaced his comments by declaring: "*Tissot* has noble dreams, he is in love with the ideal. He is entirely taken with religious subjects now; he travels back and forth to Palestine, to the actual sites of the memorable events."[5]

But it is possible to form a different reading of this episode—one that Meissonier's comments implicitly invite. Meissonier had also explored the effects of the war in his own work, including in *The Ruins of the Tuileries*

(May 1871) (ca. 1871, completed 1883; Musée national du Château de Compiègne, France), which he began in 1871 but did not return to and finish until 1883. A confrontational depiction of the destruction of the Commune, the piece presents the devastation of the palace as an allegory of a "colossal downfall," both political and moral.[6] The artist was haunted by the memory of the Terrible Year, during which the defeat of France brought about the end of the war, the decay of Napoleon III, and the advent of a provisional republic, followed by the proclamation of the Paris Commune and its bloody repression in 1871. Indeed, Meissonier had also planned to dedicate an ambitious large-scale painting to that ordeal. In 1871, he began sketching *The Siege of Paris (1870–1871)* (fig. 33), which he discontinued then returned to in 1884. The painting, which ultimately remained unfinished, was intended to provide a retrospective view of the war as a memorial to the dead, famous and unknown, and to be, Meisonnier declared, "a sort of heroic symphony of France."[7]

In light of these two works, Meissonier's response to Tissot's desolate scene in the ruins of the Cour des Comptes takes on a special significance. Along with the Palace of the Tuileries, the Ministry of Finance, the Palace of the Legion of Honor, the Royal Palace, the Louvre, and City Hall—the Cour des Comptes figured among the most emblematic of those structures the Commune had methodically planned to burn down in protest.[8] Although most of the laws governing the reconstruction of buildings destroyed during the Commune had been passed as early as April 1873, the structures' ruins had crystallized symbolic readings and ideological debates.[9] The ruins of the Cour des Comptes—more durably inscribed in the Parisian landscape because they would not be razed until 1898, for construction of the Orsay railway station (now the Musée d'Orsay)—had been abundantly photographed owing to their picturesque character. They had even become a destination for bucolic strolls; botanists discovered previously unknown flora there, and painters came to the site to work in nature, as seen in a late series by Georges Rouard.[10] Poets such as Théophile Gautier effervesced over the ruins' romantic nature:

> These ruins, so suddenly wrought, strangely impress the beholder. It is as if two thousand years had passed away in the course of a single night; as if the poet's dream were realised, who saw Paris a dead city, recognisable only by a few remains scattered on the banks of the Seine: the Column prone in the grass and like 'the monstrous clarion of a vanished Titan.'"[11]

By using this symbolically charged place as the setting for his hallucinatory twilight vision, Tissot may also have been expressing his grief over the loss of his companion, Kathleen Newton, with whom he had lived in London from 1876 until her premature death from tuberculosis, in 1882. Painted three years later, *Inner Voices* can be viewed as a sort of Assumption, marking the end of Newton's earthly life; Tissot had recently tried, with the help of the famous British medium William Eglinton (see pl. 131), to make contact with his lost love. Like Meissonier's works, *Inner Voices* is polysemous; the choice of the place itself can also be interpreted as a means by which the bereaved artist confronted his memories of the Terrible Year. Thus, two funereal registers are fused; the death of Newton quite likely rekindled, upon Tissot's return to Paris, painful visions of the Commune.

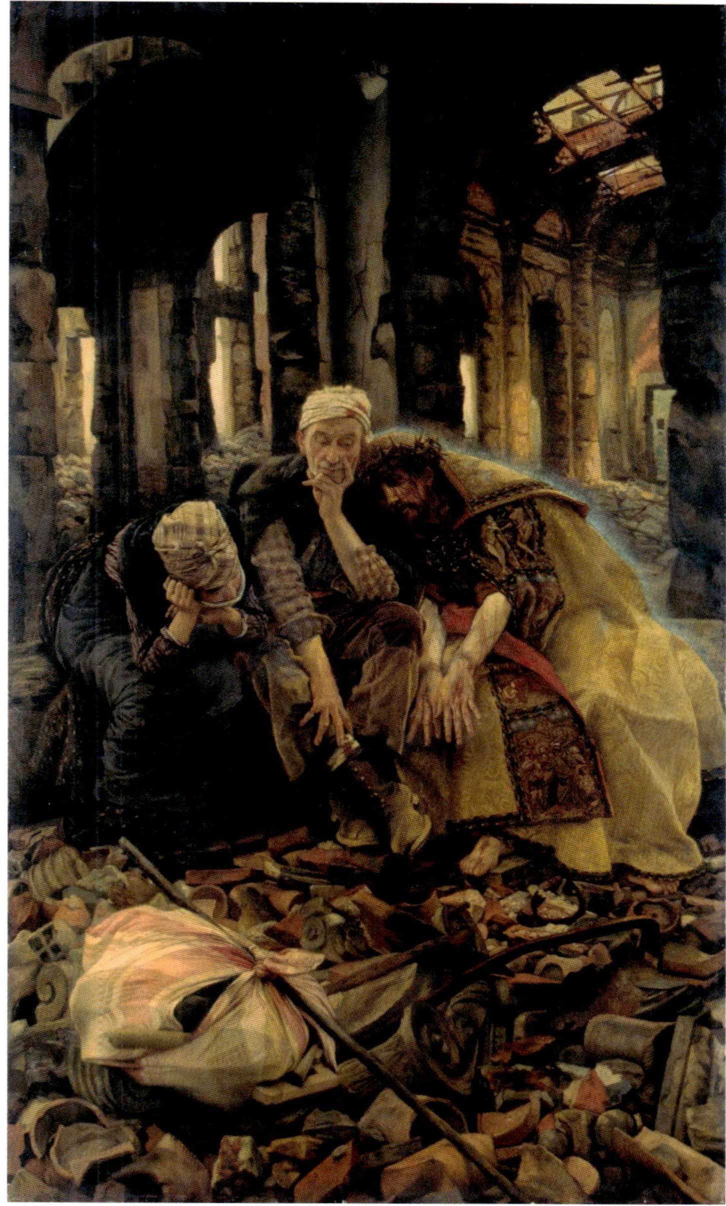

FIGURE 32
James Tissot, *Inner Voices* or *Christ the Comforter* (also known as *The Ruins*), 1885. Oil on canvas, 84¼ × 48⅞ in. (214 × 124 cm). The State Hermitage Museum, Saint Petersburg, Entered the Hermitage in 1922; handed over from the State Museum Fund; originally in the Auer collection, GÈ-4692

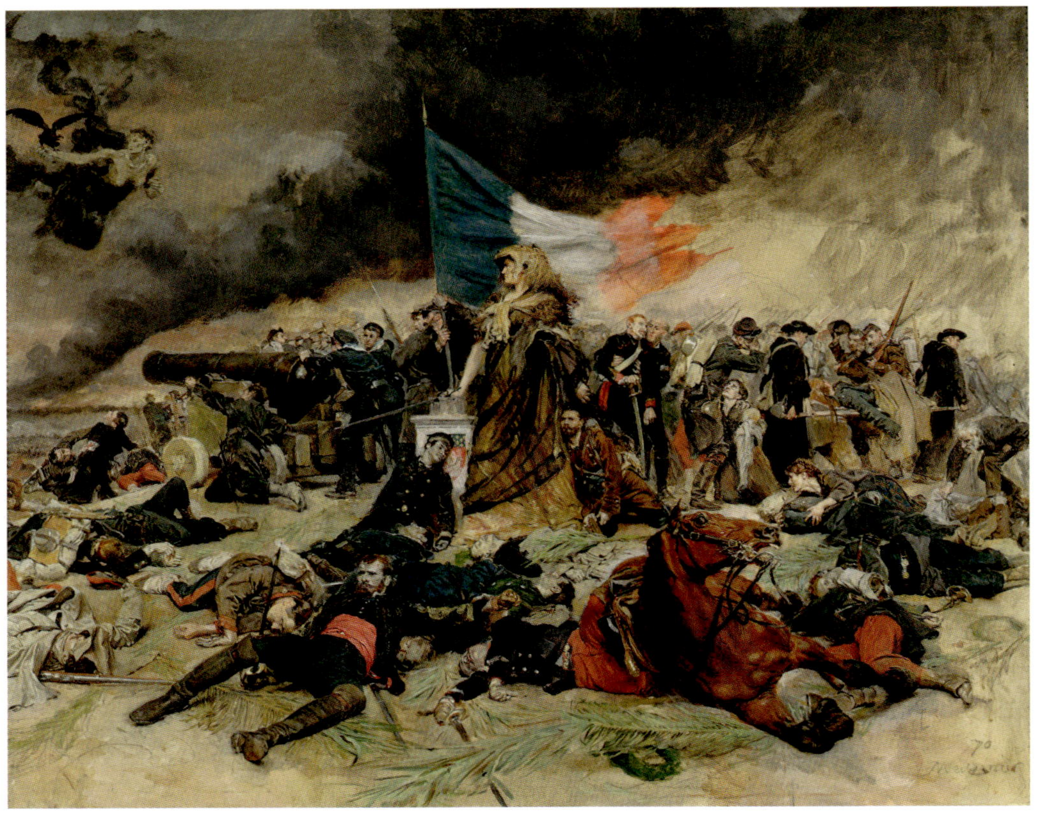

FIGURE 33
Ernest Meissonier (French, 1815–1891), *The Siege of Paris (1870–1871)*, ca. 1884 (first sketched 1871; reworked in 1884). Oil on canvas, 21 × 27¾ in. (53.5 × 70.5 cm). Musée d'Orsay, Paris, RF 1249

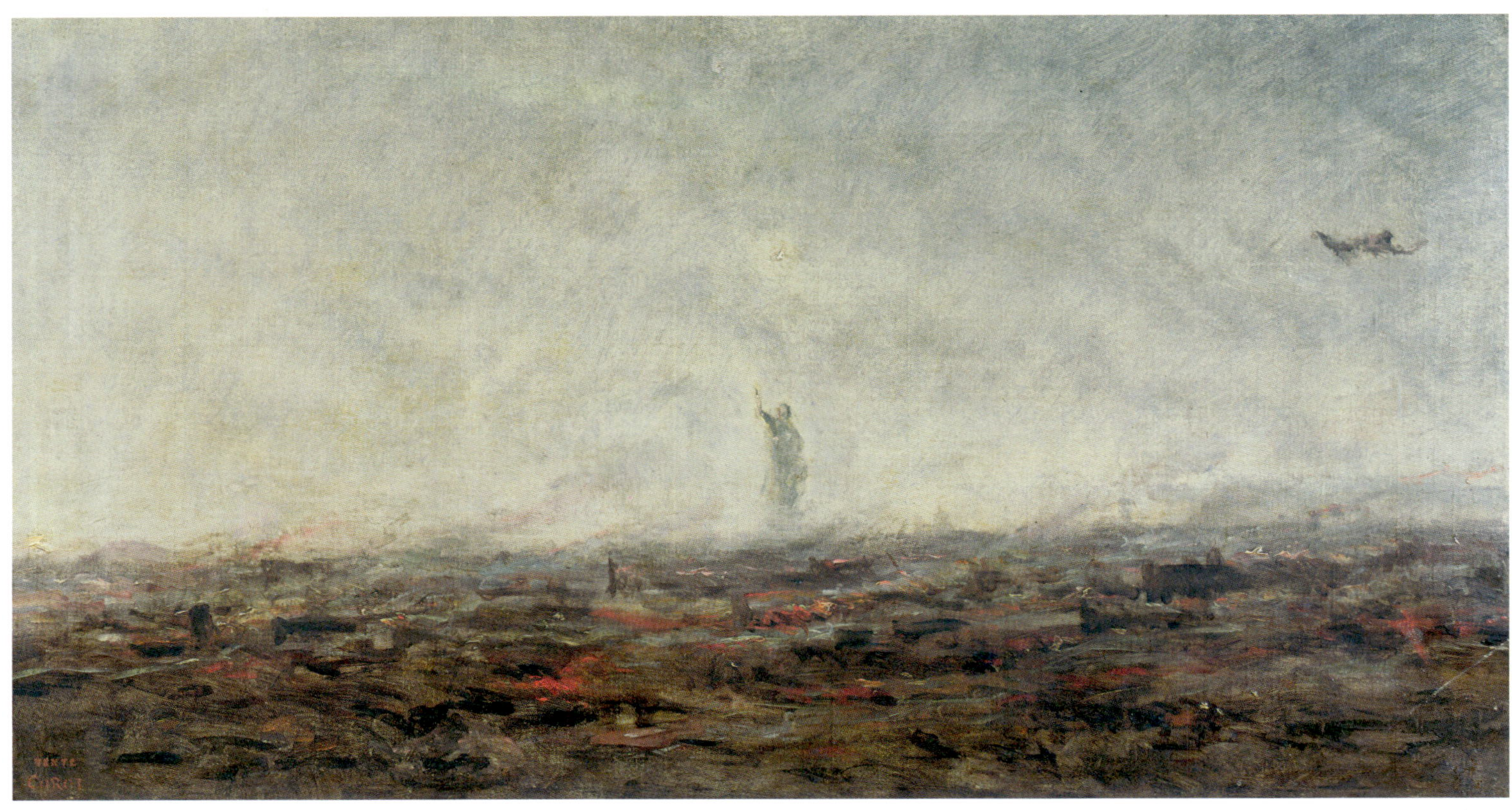

FIGURE 34
Camille Corot (French, 1796–1875), *The Dream: Paris Burning*, 1870. Oil on canvas, 12 × 21½ in. (30.5 × 54.5 cm). Musée Carnavalet–Histoire de Paris, P1628

Meissonier and Tissot were not the only artists to be haunted by specters of the Franco-Prussian War, the Siege of Paris, and the Commune, with their train of violence and destruction. In 1870, on the night of September 9, as Prussian troops were advancing toward Paris, the French painter Camille Corot had a nightmare in which the enemy entered the capital to set it on fire. The next day, in a painting that he titled *The Dream: Paris Burning* (fig. 34), Corot feverishly rendered his terrifying vision of the capital engulfed in flames, as if to liberate himself from it.[12] Some months later, he would see in his own work a premonition of the destruction wrought by the Commune. Up to his death, Corot kept this painting in his studio, almost secretly—a memorial, perhaps, to his traumas stemming from the Terrible Year.[13]

Shortly after the horrific events in Paris, in anticipation of the Salon of 1872, Gustave Moreau likewise sought to explore the traumatic effects of the war through a monumental polyptych, half painted and half sculpted, to be called *France Defeated*. Moreau envisioned the project as an expiatory work dedicated to "defeated France," alluding to the political and military events of 1870–1871—the French defeat opposite a victorious Germany, and the civil war that followed—in which the painter saw signs of the "great modern disintegration."[14] In the end, Moreau abandoned his project, leaving only a series of sketches and a heavily annotated drawing, and he produced few works until 1876—the ordeals of the Terrible Year having driven him to a depression of sorts.[15] Gustave Flaubert wrote, in a letter to his niece, "I learned in Paris that several people (among them Gustave Moreau, the painter) were afflicted by the same malady as I, that is, the *intoleration* of crowds; it is a common ailment since our disasters, it seems."[16]

Although Tissot did not return to Paris until November 14, 1882,[17] the resurgence of the memory of the Terrible Year evoked in *Inner Voices* is in keeping with the climate of an era in which the tragedies of the war were still likened to a "frightful bad dream," to use Émile Zola's phrase.[18] This effect persisted even as reconstruction was in full swing and general amnesty for actions connected to the Commune had been announced in 1880—after heated debates.[19]

Before relocating to London, Tissot had not kept his distance from what Maxime Du Camp would call the "convulsions of Paris,"[20] unlike some of his colleagues who had sequestered themselves in the capital—for example, Henri Fantin-Latour, who holed up in a cellar, where he spent most of his time painting still lifes and studying the Old Masters as he waited for the Louvre to reopen.[21] Nor was Tissot among the multitude of artists who had left Paris in successive waves in response to the declaration of war against Prussia, the Siege of Paris, and, finally, the Commune and its violent repression by the French Army during what was known as the Bloody Week.[22] In the fall of 1870, so many people fled to the provinces or abroad that by the end of May 1871, Théodore Duret wrote to Camille Pissarro, in a half-bitter, half-ironic tone: "Paris is empty and will get still emptier. . . . As for painters and artists, one might think there had never been any in Paris."[23]

Tissot, however, not only remained in Paris but was actively involved in defending the capital.[24] Like the artists Léon Bonnat, Gustave Caillebotte, Eugène Carrière, Georges Clairin, Edgar Degas, and Édouard Manet, Tissot enlisted in the National Guard, joining the National Defense Volunteer Corps on September 30, 1870.[25] Several sources attest that Tissot belonged to the First Company of the Tirailleurs de la Seine,[26] that he was requisitioned to stand guard at the outposts,[27] and that he participated in the sortie of Buzenval on October 21, 1870,[28] where he distinguished himself in the battles of La Malmaison alongside other artists who were wounded—among them, the painters Eugène Leroux and Georges Vibert, and the sculptor Joseph Cuvelier, who lost his life.[29] Degas was quite shaken by this death, as recounted in an October 1870 letter from the painter Berthe Morisot to one of her daughters: "Monsieur Degas was so affected by the death of one of his friends, the sculptor Cuvelier, that he was impossible. He and Manet almost came to blows arguing over the methods of defence and the use of the National Guard, although each of them was ready to die to save the country."[30] Later, Jean-Louis Forain would recount a sharp altercation between Degas and Tissot, which Forain found indicative of Tissot's "austere, severe sensibility for art":

> It was during the war . . . 1870 . . . Tissot, James Tissot, he who illustrated the Gospels for Hachette, met with him and told him that Cuvelier [. . .] had been gravely wounded at Bourget [*sic*], that he had seen him. And Tissot added: "I made a drawing—here, look . . ." Degas held out his arm, his hand, pushed his paper away, refused to see it. "You would have done better to gather him up."[31]

Tissot's political stance and his activities during the Commune are not as easy to chronicle, but several recently uncovered documents demonstrate his involvement, in particular, a letter from January 1872, in which one of Tissot's close friends, Captain Adolphe de Serionne, replies to a letter from the artist exiled in London, telling him he had "read with great pleasure the details that you were kind enough to give me on what your goal had been during the Commune."[32]

Thus, we know that unlike Degas, Alexandre Falguière, Manet, Meissonier, and Alfred Stevens, who were demobilized after the armistice of January 28, 1871, Tissot remained in the National Guard until the end of the Commune, May 28, 1871, despite the antigovernment uprising on March 18 and the government's deadly attack on April 3, and that he provided "ambulance service during the second siege" ("the second siege" meaning the Commune).[33] Given these details, many art historians today consider Tissot to have been a Communard; the National Guard, increasingly independent and politicized, had taken control of the events of March 18 and provided its "army" of insurgent soldiers to the Commune. For that reason, Adolphe Thiers, upon assuming his post as president of the Third Republic, swiftly dissolved the National Guard by law on August 30, 1871.[34]

Documents dated shortly after this reveal that rumors were circulating in Paris about Tissot's involvement with the Commune, an association that some artists harshly judged. Cases of individuals having the same name ultimately sowed confusion, as indiscriminate denunciations fueled repression by the government in Versailles.[35] In October 1871, just a few months after Tissot left for London, Serionne wrote to notify him that in the Circle of the Mirlitons (Cercle des Mirlitons), of which Tissot was a

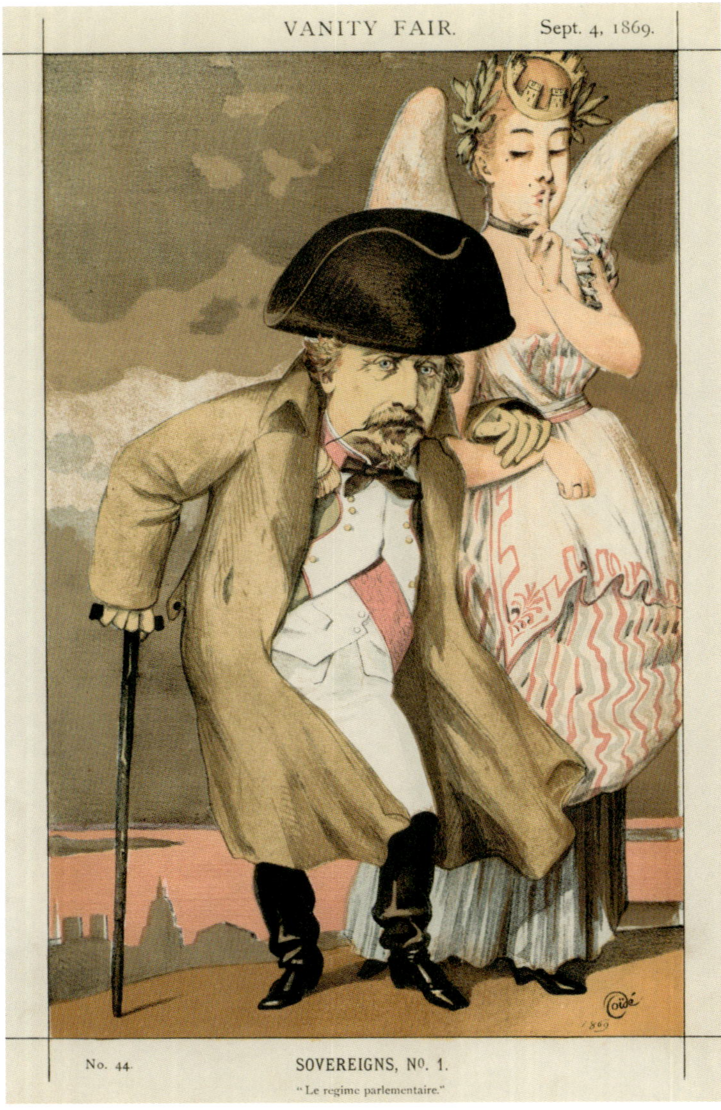

FIGURE 35
James Tissot, *Sovereigns No. 1*: *"Le regime parlementaire,"* from *Vanity Fair*, September 4, 1869. Color lithograph, 11⅞ × 7½ in. (30.3 × 18.9 cm). The Cleveland Museum of Art, Bequest of John Bonebrake, 2014.254

member, Tissot was said to be "absent from Paris for fear of being incriminated for participation in the Commune."[36] Serionne added:

> They say that an engraver in Paris had received a letter from you inviting him to join a committee established by the Commune to designate the objects that should either be destroyed or conserved as artistic. The engraver displayed this letter, signed Tis . . . President of the Committee. In short, certain friends or colleagues did not refrain from accusing you of participation and agreement with the Communards, and I could cite names of those who were not indulgent toward you.[37]

The allegations reported in this letter are bizarre. It is hard to determine which committee Serionne refers to, and there were many sorts of these groups under the Commune. Tissot was not one of the painters in the Fédération des artistes—an association founded on April 13, 1871, and presided over by Gustave Courbet, with the intent of establishing an arts administration run by the artists themselves.[38] He did not even appear among the artists the *Journal officiel de la Commune* named as being enlisted in the Commune; several other artists, unbeknownst to them, were in fact listed, including Corot, Honoré Daumier, Manet, and Jean-François Millet. Moreover, the duties that this gossip attributes to Tissot would more likely have fallen to Courbet, who, as president of the federation, would be expected to decide on which objects were to be protected or destroyed under the Commune's administration. As deliberations recorded in the *Journal officiel de la Commune* show, Tissot was not even part of the committee charged with inspecting the art collections, library, and archives that had been seized from Thiers's private mansion.[39]

In any event, Tissot was well aware that the functions he had performed under the Commune could prove incriminating once the Versaillais repression descended on Paris and the Communards. It may have been another letter from Serionne, informing him that he had been dropped from the Circle of the Artistic Union (Cercle de l'union artistique)[40]—officially because he had not paid his dues for 1871, but every argument was used, after the Commune, to justify the expulsion of those who were said to have belonged to its ranks—that prompted Tissot to reach out from London to correspondents at police headquarters in Paris and the Office of Military Justice at the War Ministry so that they could look into his situation.[41] These inquiries, conducted as early as 1872, determined that the departments had no file on Tissot and that he was thus free to return to Paris.

But Tissot remained in London, where the Communard Prosper-Olivier Lissagaray would often visit him. Lissagaray mentions Tissot—along with the sculptor Jules Dalou, the caricaturist Montbard, and the writer Jules Vallès—in his *History of the 1871 Commune* (*Histoire de la Commune de 1871*, 1876) as a member of the exile community, which, he emphasizes, was the "most heavily spied on" in Europe.[42] As Lissagaray explains it, "Tissot got adopted by the English."[43] A longtime Anglophile, Tissot saw in England the opportunity to start anew and the prospect of gaining recognition as a painter of the highest order, whereas the doubts that surrounded him in Paris over his involvement with the Commune threatened to alarm his clientele and hinder his career. In 1874, perhaps in an effort to improve his reputation by demonstrating Bonapartist allegiance, he even

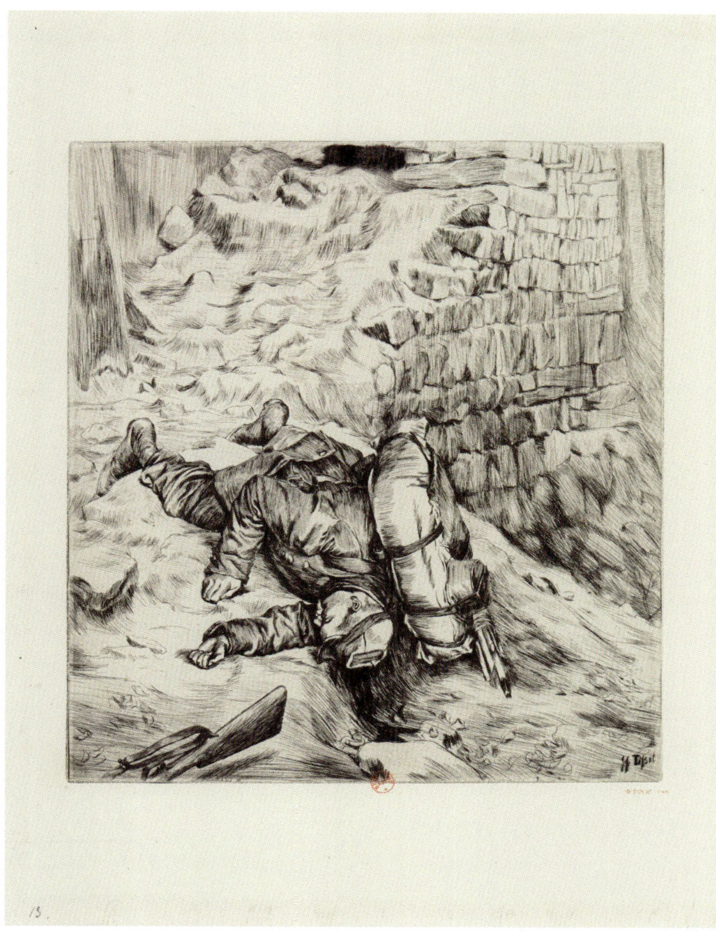

FIGURE 36
James Tissot, *The First Killed I Saw*, 1870.
Etching, 9¾ × 8¼ in. (24.8 × 20.9 cm).
Bibliothèque Nationale de France, Paris

began painting a portrait of Napoleon III's wife, the Empress Eugénie, and her son in exile in Chislehurst (pl. 28). Tissot thus became part of the "new generation of painters earning money between Paris and London," as Edmond de Goncourt described Giuseppe de Nittis.[44] On September 30, 1871, Degas wrote to Tissot from Paris: "Tissot, why the devil did you not send me a line? They tell me you are earning a lot of money. Do give me some figures."[45]

Indeed, upon his arrival in London, Tissot was welcomed by Thomas Gibson Bowles, the founder of the British weekly *Vanity Fair*, to which Tissot had been contributing political caricatures for several years—including a particularly vicious one of Napoleon III he had drawn in 1869 (fig. 35). The two men had become friends during the Siege of Paris, when Bowles was in the city as the correspondent for the *Morning Post*. After their reunion in London, Bowles introduced Tissot to members of the English upper class, where his art found many devotees. Bowles did not judge Tissot's involvement with the Commune, even asking him to illustrate his book *The Defence of Paris: Narrated as It Was Seen* (1871) with his meticulous Naturalist drawings, dated and reported as direct testimonies of "things seen" (*choses vues*), à la Victor Hugo.[46]

Tissot eventually took up these same subjects in his drypoints and in a series of etchings titled *Memory of the Siege of Paris* (pls. 18 and 20), which he worked on from 1875 to 1878. As was customary in the military art of Tissot's day, these compositions depict encampment scenes and portraits of soldiers. One is in a particularly macabre vein, reflecting the violence of the artist's trauma during the Terrible Year. Titled *The First Killed I Saw*, this etching depicts, with unsettling topographical and clinical precision, a soldier's cadaver curled up at the bottom of a collapsed embankment.[47] With the tight framing of the etching's second state (fig. 36), Tissot produces a metonymy of the part for the whole, in which the body and the ruins are complementary distillations of the war as a reign of death and destruction. The composition's concentrated structure and the precise execution of the image function almost like reportage, implying a detachment from the work's disturbing subject, one that also put its artist in a difficult moral position.

Even far from Paris, Tissot tried in vain to rid himself of the specters that haunted him. Degas understood this; in a letter from March 1874, he invited Tissot to return and participate in the first exhibition of the soon-to-be-named Impressionists: "Look here, my dear Tissot, no hesitations, no escape. You positively must exhibit at the Boulevard. It will do you good, you (for it is a means of showing yourself in Paris from which people said you were running away) and us too." Near the end of the letter, Degas adds, "Exhibit. Be of your country and with your friends."[48] Might he also have been inviting Tissot, between the lines, to confront the phantoms of the Terrible Year?

TISSOT AND THE FRENCH MARKET

LÉA SAINT-RAYMOND

After moving to Paris around 1855, James Tissot found almost immediate success as an artist. He exhibited frequently at the illustrious Paris Salon, and his regular presence in those exhibitions coincided with his financial success—from sales to collectors and some of the city's most influential art dealers—as well as higher prices for his work sold at Parisian auctions.[1] In 1871, he moved to London, where his fame reached even greater heights. But upon returning to Paris in 1882, Tissot found himself to be somewhat of a fallen star in the Parisian market. Some reviewers found his work too "British," and his decreased visibility in France had affected his sales.[2] Quantitative evidence analyzing the performance of Tissot's artworks at auctions sheds new light on these stages of the artist's reception in the French market.[3]

THE RISE OF A SALON STAR IN PARIS (1860S)

Tissot first participated in the Paris Salon in 1859, at the age of twenty-three. The Salon, controlled by a jury, was considered to be a valuable gateway to artistic recognition and market success.[4] For many artists, the exhibition served as a token of recognition; the jury decided on admissions and then rewarded the artworks deemed most successful with first-, second-, and third-class medals. The Salon captured the attention of the art world, caused ink to flow in the press, and was a lucrative commercial opportunity—both the state and private collectors could buy the works on display. One of Tissot's works shown in his Salon debut, *Walk in the Snow* (1858; private collection), was bought by the Parisian financier Émile Péreire.[5]

Tissot exhibited at the Salon every year between 1861 and 1870,[6] and this period corresponded with both a rise in the prices of his work sold at Parisian auctions (see fig. 37) and his stable business relationship with Adolphe Goupil, one of the city's most important art dealers (see fig. 38).[7] A work titled *Marguerite in Church* (1860; location unknown),[8] for example, bought by Goupil in 1860, was sold at auction in 1866 for 2,604 francs.[9] Five years later, the painting's purchaser, the London-based art dealer Asher Wertheimer, sold it at another Parisian auction to the art dealer Nicolas Malinet for 5,145 francs, nearly double the original price.[10]

Very quickly, thanks to Tissot's success at the Salon—he won a medal in 1866 and was exempt from jury trial in 1867[11]—Goupil increased the prices of his work, from 2,400 francs per painting in 1864 to 4,000 francs in 1865.[12] At an 1875 auction, one of Tissot's historical scenes, *Promenade on the Ramparts* (1864; formerly Fine Art Society, London, location unknown), sold for 7,000 francs to the Parisian dealer Hector Brame.[13] Thanks to this hammer price, Tissot became the ninth most valued living artist at Parisian auction in 1875.[14]

As further evidence of Tissot's fame in the 1860s and early 1870s, his artworks also entered the prestigious collections of the bankers Adolphe-Ernest Fould[15] and Hermann Oppenheim.[16] Tissot's genre scenes were right in line with the tastes of Péreire and these other financiers, who also collected similar anecdotal and academic history paintings by Paul Delaroche, Jean-Léon Gérôme, Ernest Meissonier, Joseph-Nicolas Robert-Fleury, Ferdinand Roybet, Ary Scheffer, Florent Willems, and—one of Tissot's greatest influences—Henri Leys.[17]

OUT OF SIGHT, OUT OF MIND (1870S TO 1902)

Tissot's success in the French art market began to decline when he moved to London and stopped exhibiting at the Salon.[18] The reasons for this fall are speculative, but one hypothesis would be the key role that the Salon played in the art market until the late nineteenth century: out of sight at the Salon meant out of mind in the Parisian art market.[19] Support for this idea can be found by assessing Goupil's activity with Tissot's work, which underwent a net slowdown in the 1870s, due to Tissot selling almost all of his new output to collectors or dealers in Britain.[20] As figure 38 shows, while Goupil sold twenty Tissot paintings between 1864 and 1871, he only sold three from 1873 through 1880. At auction, too, the sales of Tissot's works became scarcer. Ten artworks were sold at auction between 1873 and 1889, and thirteen from 1890 until his death, in 1902.[21]

In addition to Tissot's decreasing visibility at Parisian auctions, the prices of his works during this period also went down. When Brame decided to sell *Promenade on the Ramparts* at auction in 1877, just two years after purchasing it, the painting's price did not reach the same heights. Unable to overrun the initial price, Brame had to repurchase the work for 2,000 francs, a 71 percent loss.[22] Another repurchase happened one

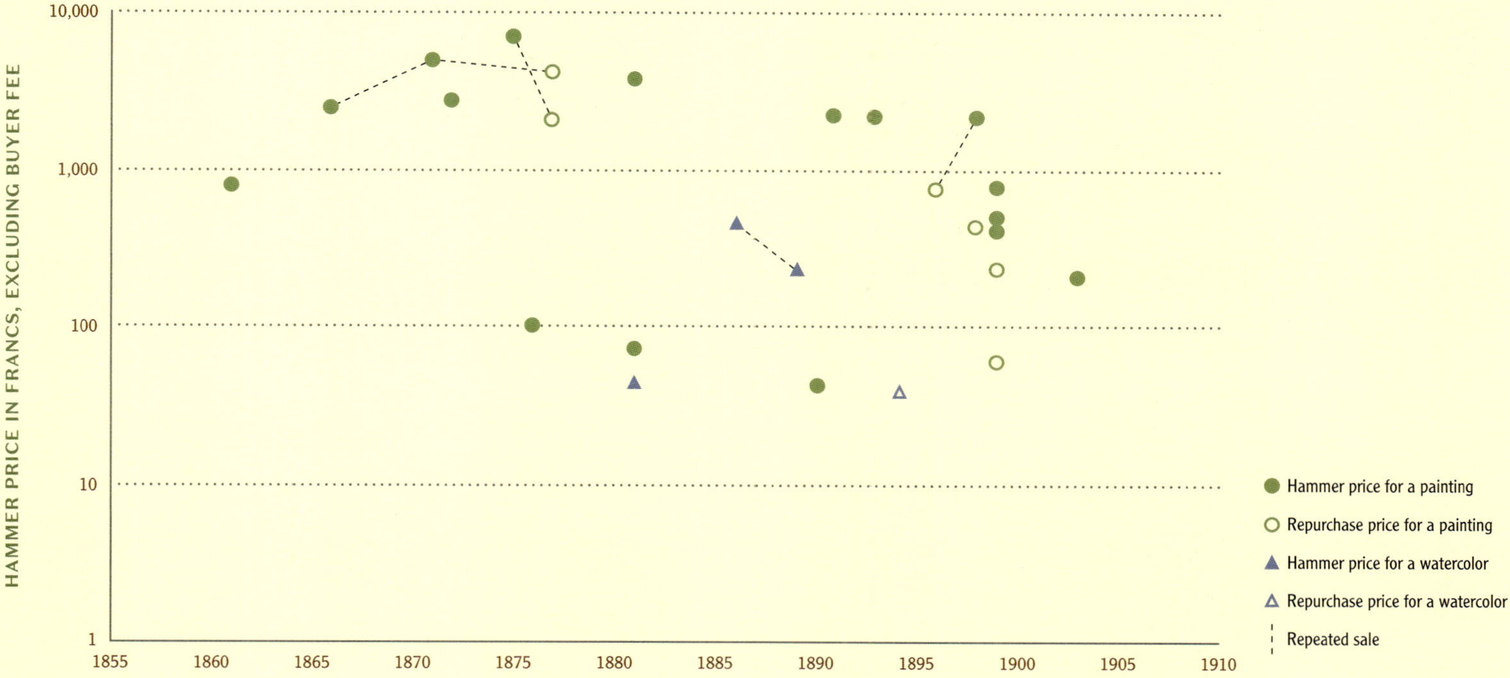

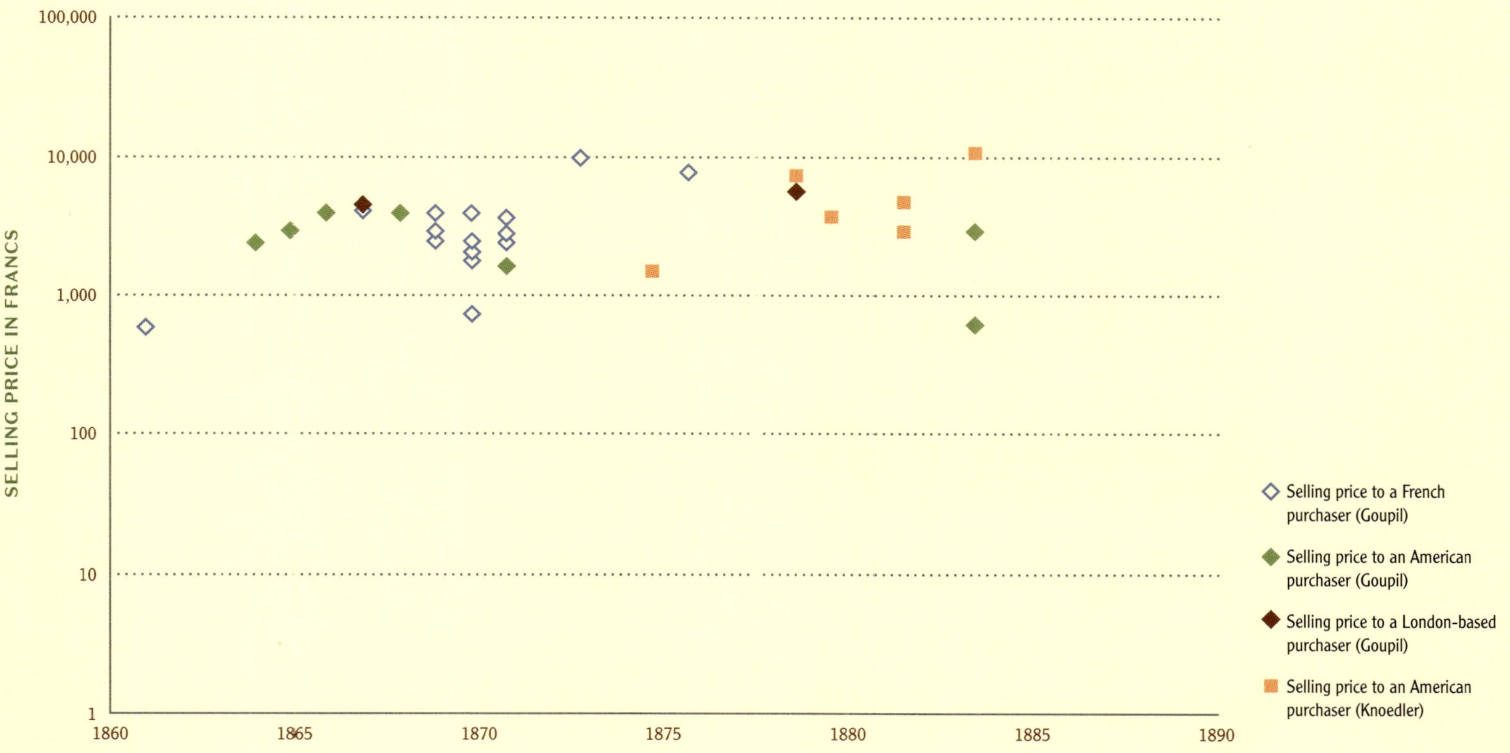

FIGURE 37
Hammer prices of Tissot's paintings sold at Parisian auction during his lifetime

FIGURE 38
Selling prices of Tissot's artworks sold by Goupil and Knoedler, depending on year of sale and nationality of purchaser

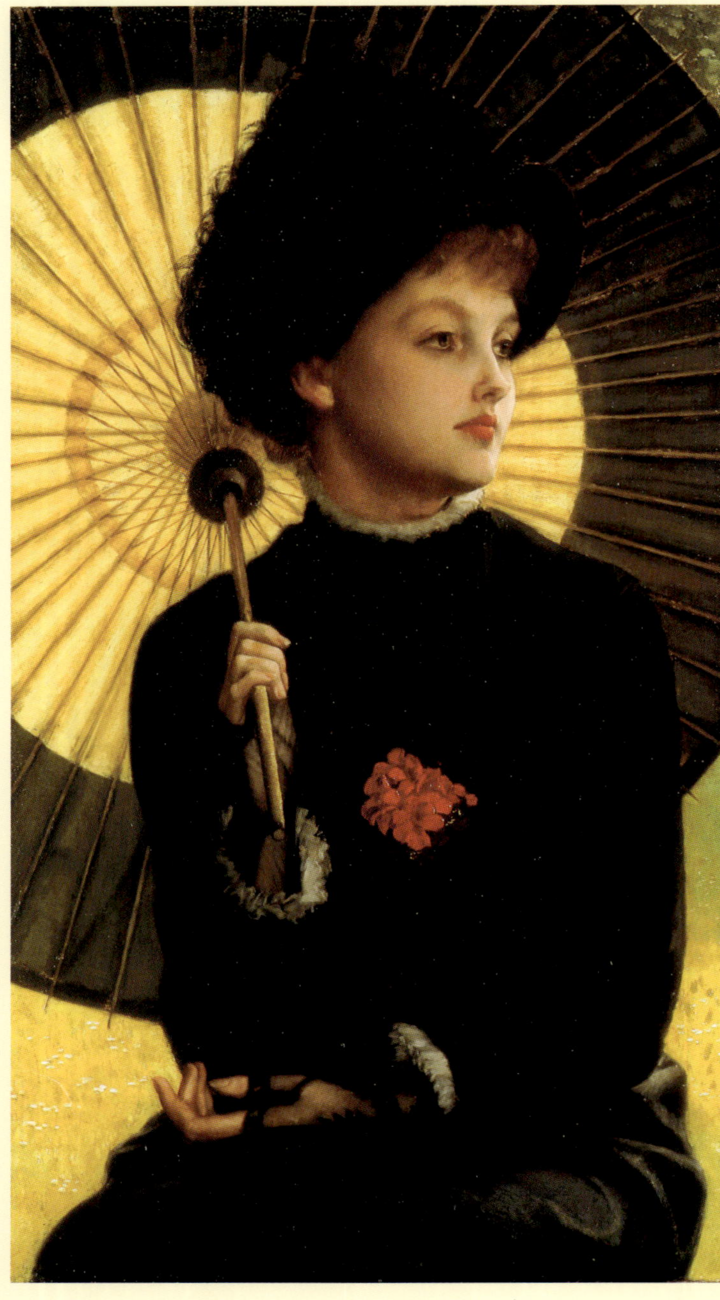

FIGURE 39
James Tissot, *Summer*, 1878. Oil on canvas, 36¼ × 20¼ in. (92.1 × 51.4 cm). Private collection

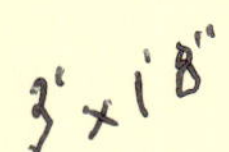

month later, in April 1877, when Oppenheim's widow paid 4,150 francs for *Marguerite in Church*, which had reached 5,145 francs six years earlier.[23]

From the 1880s until his death, ten of Tissot's paintings failed to exceed the threshold of 1,000 francs at Parisian auctions, and three did not even reach 100 francs (see fig. 37). Even *Departure of the Prodigal Son* (pl. 9) and *Return of the Prodigal Son* (pl. 10), two large canvases that Tissot exhibited at the Salon in 1863, failed to meet their reserves. In 1896, the Parisian notary Louis Paul Delondre—who had bought the pair from Tissot in 1868 for 2,000 and 4,000 francs, respectively (see "Tissot's Sales Notebook," this volume)—decided to sell them; unfortunately, *Departure* remained unsold, and Delondre had to repurchase *Return* for 750 francs.[24] After Delondre's death, these two paintings appeared again at auction, in May 1898. *Departure* was repurchased by the Delondre family for 430 francs, and the picture dealer Bernheim-Jeune bought *Return* for only 2,150 francs.[25] One contributing factor to Tissot's decline in the Parisian market might be that from 1886 onward, Tissot exhibited few works in Paris and was creating very little new work for sale as he focused on his great project to illustrate the Bible, *The Life of Christ* (see Buron, this volume).[26]

SUCCESS ABROAD

Even as Tissot fell out of favor with French collectors, his paintings continued to succeed in Britain and the United States. The previously mentioned *Marguerite in Church*, for example, was sold to Goupil by Oppenheim's widow in 1879, and immediately found a buyer in the London-based collector Henry Martin Gibbs, who paid 6,125 francs.[27] In 1884, Goupil sold two Tissot paintings, *The Confessional*[28] and *Summer* (fig. 39), to an art dealer from Philadelphia, Charles Field Haseltine.[29] This period corresponded with purchases by the elite American art dealer Roland Knoedler, who bought six Tissot paintings from 1879 through 1883, five of which he very quickly sold to American collectors living in New York, Providence, and Buffalo.[30] Figures 37 and 38 show that the prices the American collectors were paying for Tissot's works were higher than those seen in the Parisian market during the same time period. In 1884, Knoedler sold Tissot's *Visiting the Louvre* (also known as *Foreign Visitors at the Louvre*, pl. 100) for 2,000 dollars, the equivalent of 10,460 francs,[31] whereas in Paris in 1881, *A Luncheon* (fig. 48) was sold at auction for 3,700 francs.[32] The falling star had traveled to other skies, to glow more brightly across the English Channel and over the Atlantic Ocean.

LOOKING BEYOND PARIS: TISSOT'S RECEPTION IN ENGLAND DURING THE 1860s

PETER TRIPPI

From Paris, James Tissot submitted paintings to exhibitions in Britain throughout the 1860s because the vigor of its contemporary art market enticed him. Though usually brief and frequently unfavorable, critical mentions of his exhibits in London, Paris, Brussels, and elsewhere appeared in Britain often enough to make his name familiar by the time he relocated there from France, in 1871.[1] One of Tissot's earliest inspirations, Henri Leys, was already renowned in England for his sober themes, archaic lack of perspective, and quaint bric-a-brac also associated with the Pre-Raphaelites.[2] In 1860, a review by *The Athenaeum* of a Brussels exhibition noted the abundance of Leysian scenes inspired by Johann Wolfgang von Goethe's *Faust*, and that Tissot's highlighted "Margaret's coming maternity with Pre-Raphaelite mercilessness."[3]

At the 1862 International Exhibition, Tissot made his first official appearance in England with *Walk in the Snow* (1858; private collection).[4] It impressed Tom Taylor of *The Times*, who the following year commissioned Tissot to create two illustrations for his translation of *Ballads and Songs of Brittany* (fig. 108). Appearing in 1865, this volume positioned Tissot among such leading illustrators as Charles Keene, John Everett Millais, and John Tenniel.[5] Just as the text underscored the connection between Breton legend and Arthurian romance, so Tissot's drawings epitomized the kinship of Leysian quaintness with Pre-Raphaelite eccentricity.[6] Dante Gabriel Rossetti thought them "admirable things" and asked the publisher for copies of proofs.[7]

Another outcome of Tissot's British debut was the commencement of regular appearances in the annual French and Flemish Exhibition, mounted by the Belgian art dealer Ernest Gambart and his aides at the French Gallery in central London.[8] This began in 1863, with three Leysian scenes that aligned with Gambart's lucrative promotion of aesthetically conservative, well-crafted historical genre scenes, especially to newly rich merchants and industrialists.[9] Gambart handled the medievalizing scenes of Tissot, Victor Lagye, and other Belgians, and in 1864, he began addressing the growing British taste for classical genre scenes by offering those of Joseph Coomans as well.[10] The future of Tissot's exact contemporary, the Brussels-based painter Lawrence Alma-Tadema, was essentially secured in 1865, when Gambart commissioned twenty-four pictures on the strength of his Leysian works. In 1866, however, Alma-Tadema shifted toward classical subjects, and Gambart raised his profile by generating long articles in British periodicals, a benefit he did not extend to Tissot, who worked with other dealers as well.[11] In 1864, Tissot sent to the French Gallery the medieval work *Departure of the Betrothed* (1862–1863; location unknown); the fact that it was exhibited next at the Royal Manchester Institution suggests that both gallery and artist recognized the buying power and the more traditional tastes of northern English collectors.[12]

It is revealing that in 1864—the year that Tissot debuted at the Royal Academy's annual exhibition—he showed only medievalizing scenes in London, while presenting more daring modern ones at the Paris Salon. The two works shown at the latter, *Portrait of Mlle L. L...* (pl. 22) and *The Two Sisters; Portrait* (pl. 21), were genre-like portraits that owed more to Gustave Courbet and James McNeill Whistler than to Leys. Tissot's Academy exhibit that year, *At the Break of Day* (ca. 1861; location unknown), was overshadowed by one of his two submissions to the less prestigious Society of British Artists.[13] Attention focused on the expensive (320 pounds) *Return of the Prodigal Son* (pl. 10), Tissot's largest canvas to date.[14] After noting its "angularity, stiffness, and awkwardness" while also acknowledging that its "school" was "earnest, sincere, solemn, and conscientious," the *Art Journal* insisted that "such pictures cannot escape the condemnation of being anachronisms, if not indeed monstrosities."[15]

This stridence echoed that directed at the early Pre-Raphaelites; in 1850 a critic had described that group as "practitioners of 'Early Christian Art' . . . who . . . devote their energies to the reproduction of saints squeezed out perfectly flat."[16] William Holman Hunt, Millais, and Rossetti had moved on stylistically, and apparently Tissot needed to as well. Leys was going out of fashion; in 1867, the *Illustrated London News* observed that Alma-Tadema's "classical archaeology" was "far outdone by the more-than-ever grotesque mediaevalism of Baron Leys and his followers (Tissot, Lagye, and others)."[17]

Just as Alma-Tadema's classical scenes succeeded his Leysian ones, so Tissot began to shift toward modern-life subjects.[18] At the French Gallery in 1866, his *Spring* (pl. 15) attracted scant critical attention, but it was

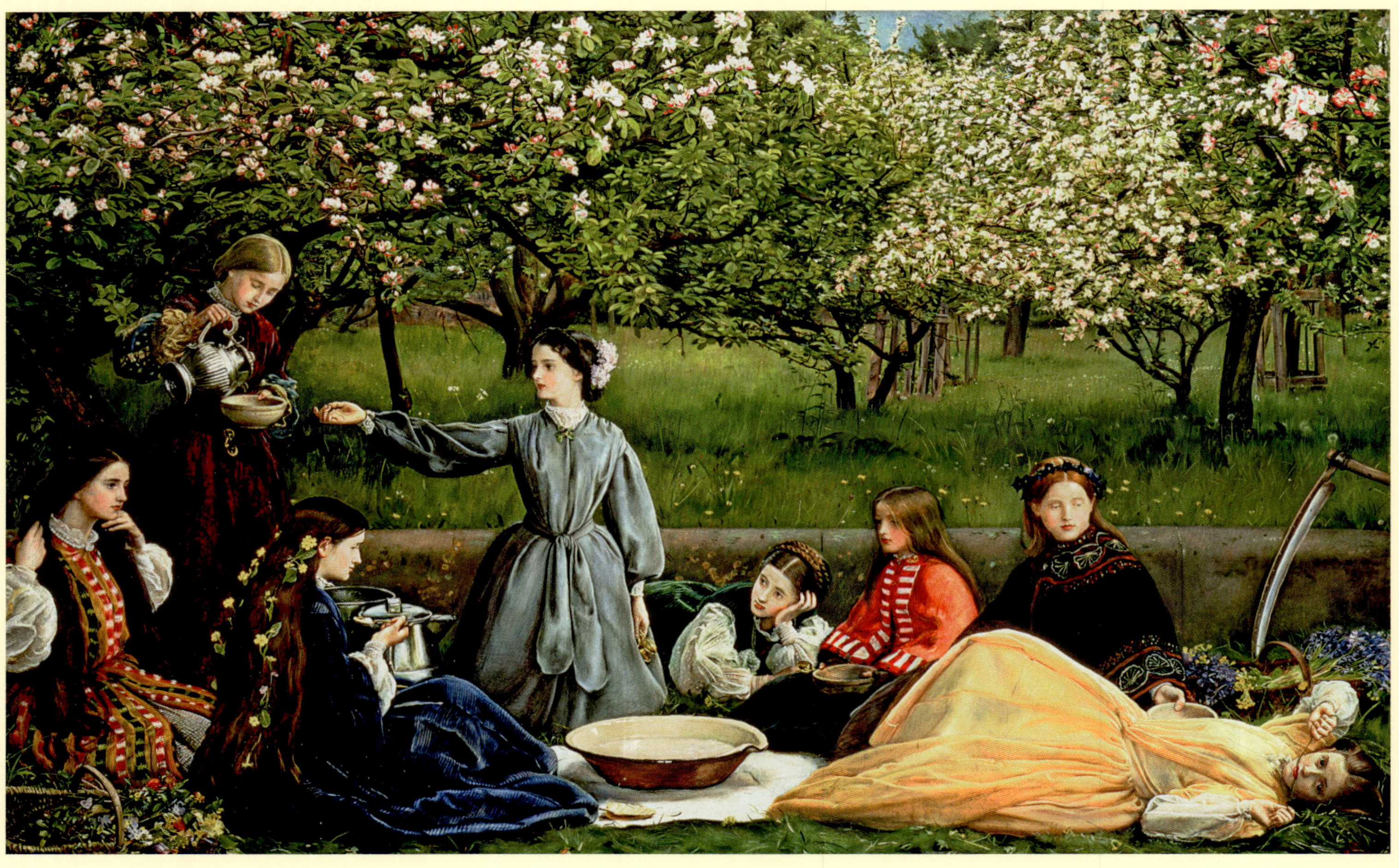

FIGURE 40
John Everett Millais (British, 1829–1896), *Spring (Apple Blossoms)*, 1859. Oil on canvas, 44½ × 69⅜ in. (113 × 176.3 cm). Liverpool Museums, Lady Lever Art Gallery, LL3624

clear Tissot was now admiring the elaborately dressed ladies painted by Belgium's rising star Alfred Stevens, and also Millais's glamorous portraiture. Hugely successful, both painters used unconventional compositions and expressions to depict enticing figures whose situations were ambiguous. An apposite example of this effect is Millais's *Spring (Apple Blossoms)* (fig. 40), which Gambart handled for the artist after it failed to sell at the Academy in 1859.[19]

Tissot's submission to the 1866 Paris Salon, *The Confessional* (1865; Southampton City Art Gallery, England), drew attention on both sides of the Channel.[20] The *Saturday Review* remarked that its elegant lady "may perhaps needlessly excite the pity of her Protestant sisters, for the fact is that ladies are very fond of going to confession."[21] Viewers surely wondered what this "mysterious, graceful lady in black," as one reviewer described her, needed to confess, just as they might have speculated on the topic the two young ladies whisper about in Tissot's *The Secret* (also known as *The Confession*, fig. 41).[22] Enigmatic pictures such as these fared so well that Philip Gilbert Hamerton included *The Secret* as one of just fourteen works featured in his 1869 publication *Painting in France, after the Decline of Classicism*.[23] After assessing such luminaries as Courbet and Édouard Manet—as well as artists now forgotten—Hamerton focused on this "picture of petticoats and parasols," deftly linking Tissot's Leysian density to the can't-look-away oddness of his modern-life scenes:

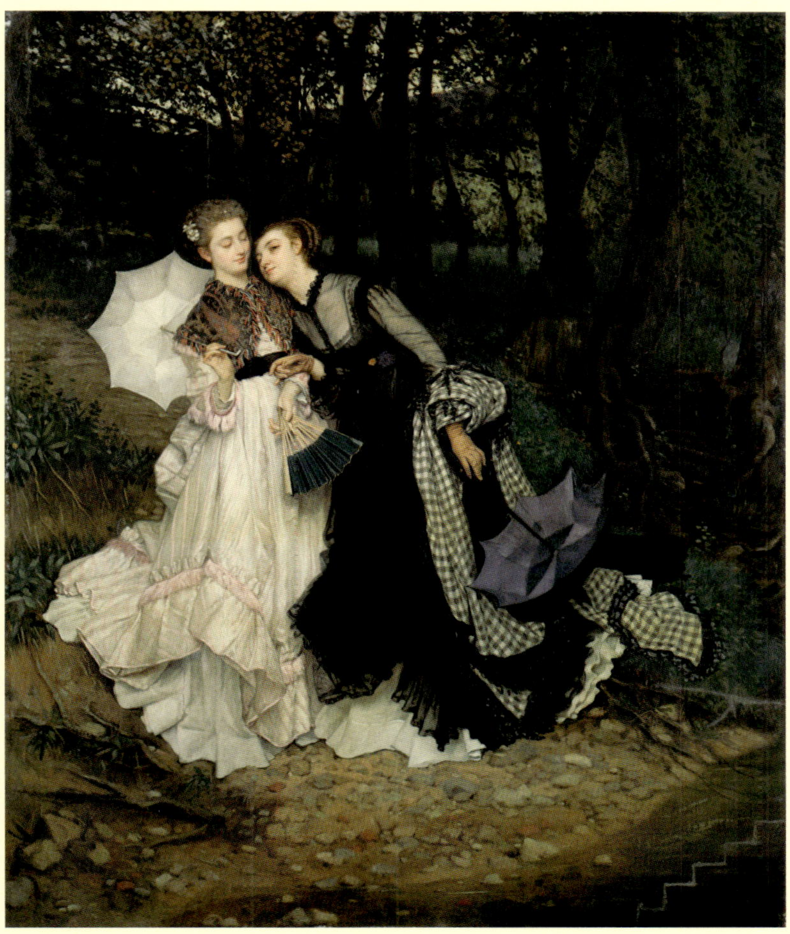

FIGURE 41
James Tissot, *The Secret* (also known as *The Confession*), 1866–1867. Location unknown

> [T]he spirit of Classicism . . . sought . . . simplicity; but in this picture . . . the artist . . . arranges these entangled folds of drapery, and sets his figures in this all but impossible attitude . . . in order to satisfy some taste or craving in the modern mind. . . . A taste for intricacy, for quaintness, for quantity, suddenly developed itself in Romanticism. . . . Romanticism is now dead; but Modernism, in taking its place, has inherited these predilections.[24]

Michael Wentworth notes that *The Secret* looks to Courbet "for its narrative impetus, modified again for social propriety, and to Millais for its poetic vagueness of mood."[25] He argues convincingly that such pictures "represent Tissot's Pre-Raphaelitism at its height, but it is clear that Pre-Raphaelite vision had not been taken over wholesale in the way Leys' archaism had been. What Tissot discovered in the Pre-Raphaelites of estrangement and brooding disjunction can only have reinforced what he had already found in Leys."[26] The "entangled" aspect was equally visible in Tissot's *A Duet at High Mass* (1866–1867; location unknown), exhibited at the French Gallery in 1867.[27] The *Art Journal* noted that the work's "composition had been intentionally made complex, in order that the artist might prove his power of bringing conflicting elements into pictorial keeping and unity."[28] Tissot could show off, and get away with it.

Tissot's reputation for draftsmanship was remarkably high in Britain; as early as 1865, the *London Quarterly Review* had described Taylor's *Ballads and Songs of Brittany* as "full of engravings by Millais, Tenniel, Tissot—the French Millais."[29] To equate the Frenchman with so revered and prolific a draftsman as Millais was noteworthy, considering that few Britons had even seen the four etchings Tissot had made to date.[30] In 1870, the British Museum completed its "arrangement of modern French prints in eight volumes, including the works of [Eugène] Delacroix, [Alexandre-Gabriel] Decamps, [François] Flameng, [Jean-Léon] Gérôme, [Anne-Louis] Girodet, Tissot, [Alphonse] Legros, [Ernest] Meissonier, [Ary] Scheffer, and [Pierre-Paul] Prud'hon."[31] This, too, was heady company, considering that the museum owned only one Tissot print, *Louise* (1861; Wentworth 3).[32] Given this high esteem, it is remarkable that the British readers of *Vanity Fair* did not even realize that sixteen of the magazine's irreverent caricatures published between 1869 and 1870 were actually drawn by Tissot under the pseudonym "Coïdé."[33]

The variability of Tissot's reception in Britain reflects the ambivalence the art establishment felt about foreign influences, a leitmotif in British culture across time. In 1863, the London-based magazine *Fraser's* fretted that the "considerable tincture of foreign, and especially French, views and method of art is now to be traced among us."[34] Tissot's talent was undisputed in Britain, but it was only in the 1870s that he found the spotlight there he both craved and deserved.

NANCY ROSE MARSHALL

TISSOT'S BRITISH MODERN-LIFE PAINTINGS

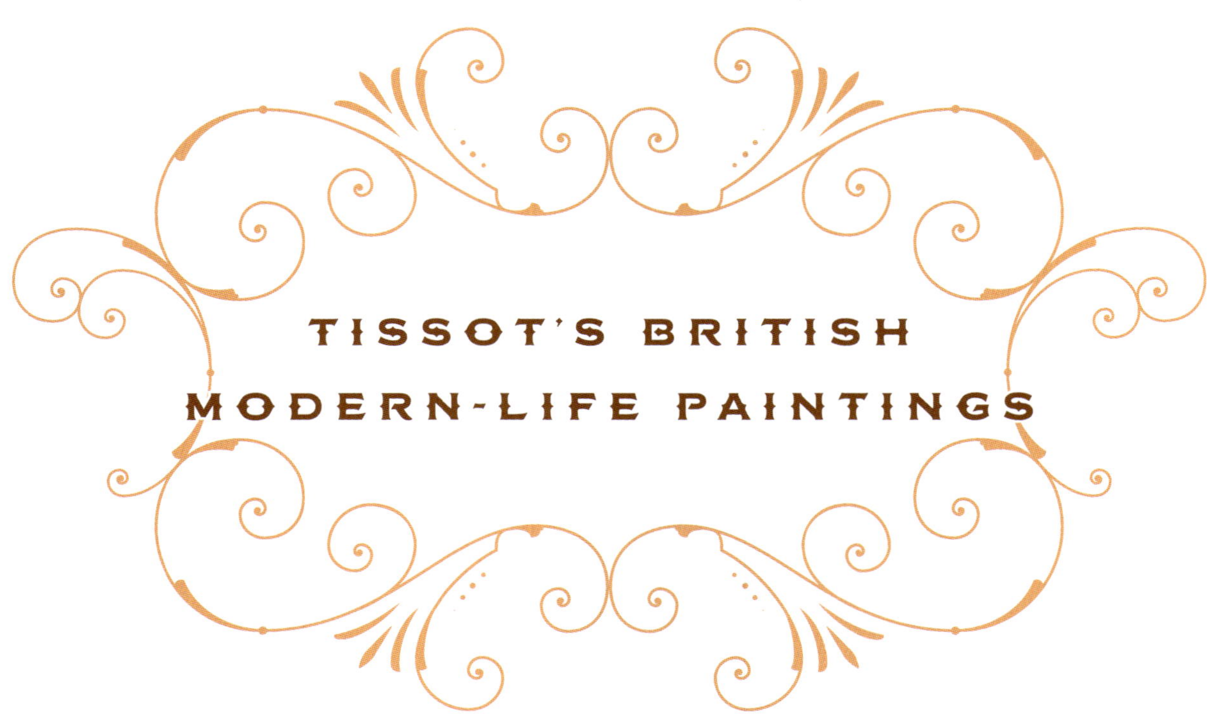

UPON THE 1882 PUBLICATION of the etchings from his series *The Prodigal Son in Modern Life* (pls. 91–94), James Tissot somewhat mysteriously declared: "I strive to produce compositions that reveal the hidden meanings of our everyday life. I would select subjects that others shrink from handling; it is as if I planted a pioneer standard upon lands hitherto undiscovered."[1] To modern viewers, Tissot's paintings of elegant London society and contemporary Thames-side life might seem like little more than aesthetically pleasing documents of that era. It is difficult to grasp how the artist could have perceived his subjects as daring or pioneering. Yet, Tissot's statement is key to a true understanding of his deceptively complex endeavor: he did not transcribe reality so much as depict surface appearances of the age in such a way as to provoke greater questions.

This achievement, the rendering of a plausible version of the world that at the same time pushed viewers to see more than what was superficially represented, is at the heart of Tissot's enduring impact. Under the guise of being a lighthearted recorder of trivial details, the artist was—like other artists of the nineteenth-century French avant-garde, with whom he associated—portraying modern life as a means of considering the nature of the material world. Following a popular dictum of the influential French poet and art critic Charles Baudelaire, Tissot sought to "extract from fashion whatever element it might contain of poetry within history, to distill the eternal from the transitory."[2] To fully engage with Tissot's oeuvre, then, it is necessary to look for its eternal, poetic qualities.

During the eleven years that Tissot lived and painted in London, 1871 to 1882, he focused largely on subjects drawn from contemporary middle- and upper-class British society. After his first introduction to the city by *Vanity Fair* editor Thomas Gibson Bowles and the hostess of an established artistic and political salon, Frances, Countess Waldegrave, Tissot quickly established himself as a prominent figure, earning nearly 5,000 pounds a year by 1875.[3] He entertained lavishly at his home in Saint John's Wood and in turn was invited to social events, such as the banquet at the London mayor's residence, Mansion House. There, Tissot mingled with painters from the Aesthetic circle, such as Albert Moore and James McNeill Whistler; Royal Academicians, such as William Powell Frith and Edward Poynter; and other art world celebrities, including Elizabeth Thompson (later Lady Butler) and Lawrence Alma-Tadema, to whom Tissot would eventually sell his large London house when he returned to Paris.[4]

While living in Paris in the 1860s, Tissot had been an active participant in debates concerning the nature and purpose of art.[5] He shared a number of techniques with his friend Edgar Degas that rendered his work startling to British viewers. In the early 1870s, in fact, Degas invited Tissot to exhibit with the as-yet-unnamed Impressionists,[6] and although he declined, throughout his career Tissot remained attuned to this avant-garde movement, signaling his allegiance in both obvious and subtle ways.[7] Like the Impressionists, he rendered light naturalistically. As one British reviewer noted of the paintings *Croquet* (pl. 50) and *Spring (Specimen of a Portrait)* (pl. 78), Tissot "carried study of light so far that he aims at nothing less than abolition of the studio with its artificial chiaroscuro. He paints either in the diffused and general open-air light or the gentle and natural shadows of a room."[8]

In his invitation to Tissot to exhibit with the Impressionists, Degas referred to the planned exhibition as a "salon of realists." While today it might seem surprising that Impressionism and Realism were at one point conflated, the term "realism" then referred to the close observation and portrayal of everyday life. Like their literary contemporaries Gustave Flaubert and Émile Zola, the early Impressionists scrutinized the nuances of the material world and human behavior with an astute gaze that aspired to objectivity. These qualities imbued Tissot's work and were vividly apparent to his new British audience; as one reviewer noted, Tissot was "looked upon over here as a kind of artistic Zola."[9] Describing Tissot's *Rivals* (pl. 83), this same critic continued with another literary comparison, to the society novelist Anthony Trollope, renowned for his richly detailed descriptions of Victorian life and behavior.[10] Indeed, *Rivals* meticulously captures the body language, dress, and facial expressions of the two gentlemen competing for the reclining woman's affection, as well as the fine details of the tea setting and the luxurious conservatory environment.

As *Rivals* demonstrates, one feature of Tissot's realism was his virtuosic ability to replicate details of the world around him. Even the most critical reviewers had to acknowledge that the artist was an astonishing master of his medium. Declared the British journal *New Quarterly*, *Rivals* was "painted in the most dexterous way, without exaggeration, and with amazing truth and observation."[11] Tissot seemed to revel in his ability to solve the most challenging technical problems; as another British critic stated in 1877, he had an "uncommon propensity for doing something peculiar and startling, for selecting a singular point of view. . . . He seems to have a rather perverse pleasure in disconcerting the spectator; he does injudicious things judiciously or sensible straightforward things curiously." Tissot was a show-off, selecting and framing subjects in order to promiscuously display his pure painterly skills, "bantering himself and his public on what he can do, and how he can do it."[12]

Works like *The Gallery of HMS "Calcutta" (Portsmouth)* (pl. 64), painted around 1876, exemplify what the novelist Henry James characterized as Tissot's tendency to choose "a subject which it takes a kind of *tour de force* to render."[13] The work portrays a complicated spatial arrangement and expends extravagant effort on details of the women's costumes, including the titillating pink fabric panels on the backs of their dresses, which imply bare skin just under the filmy material. The painter's flamboyant technique could produce disquieting effects, as in the gaze of the woman on the steps of the National Gallery in *London Visitors* (pl. 56). One reviewer commented, "Wherever you walk or turn she is looking at you, and you of all people seem to be the favored object. It is wonderful how this handsome lady irresistibly catches your eye."[14]

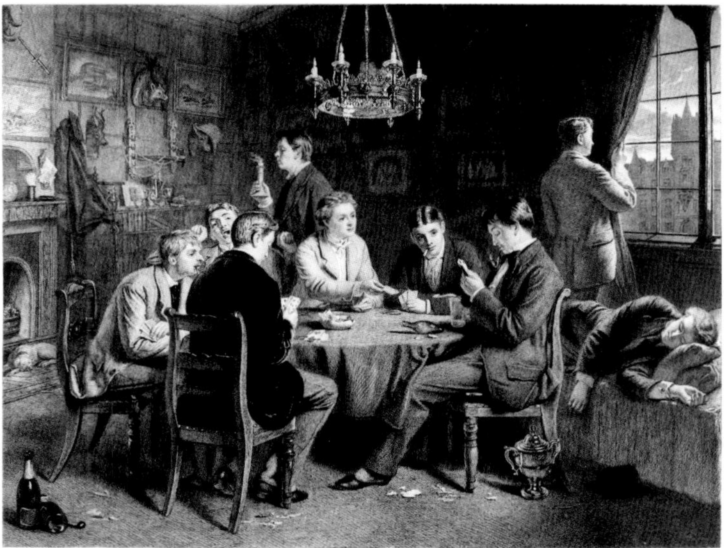

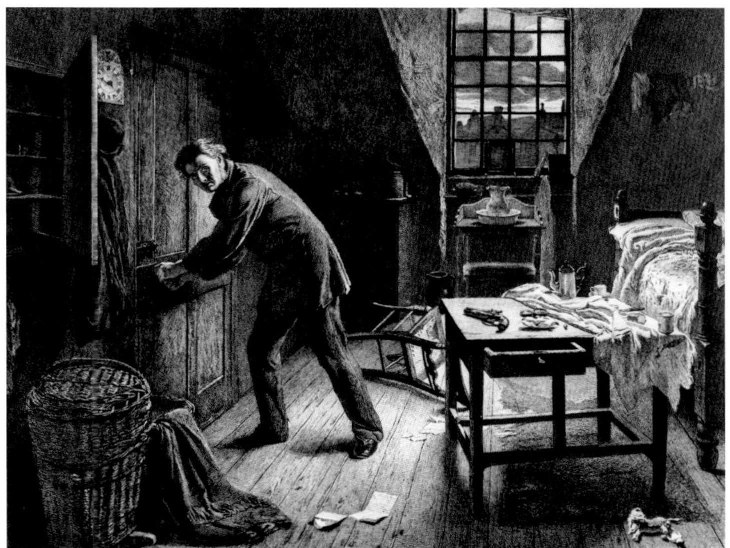

FIGURE 42
Léopold Flameng (British, 1831–1911) after William Powell Frith (British, 1819–1909), *The Road to Ruin: College*, 1878. Etching and engraving, 17¾ × 21 in. (45.2 × 53.5 cm), 1882. British Museum, London, 1913,0213.18

FIGURE 43
Léopold Flameng (British, 1831–1911) after William Powell Frith (British, 1819–1909), *The Road to Ruin: The End*, 1878. Etching and engraving, 17⅜ × 20⅞ in. (44 × 53 cm), 1882. British Museum, London, 1913,0213.22

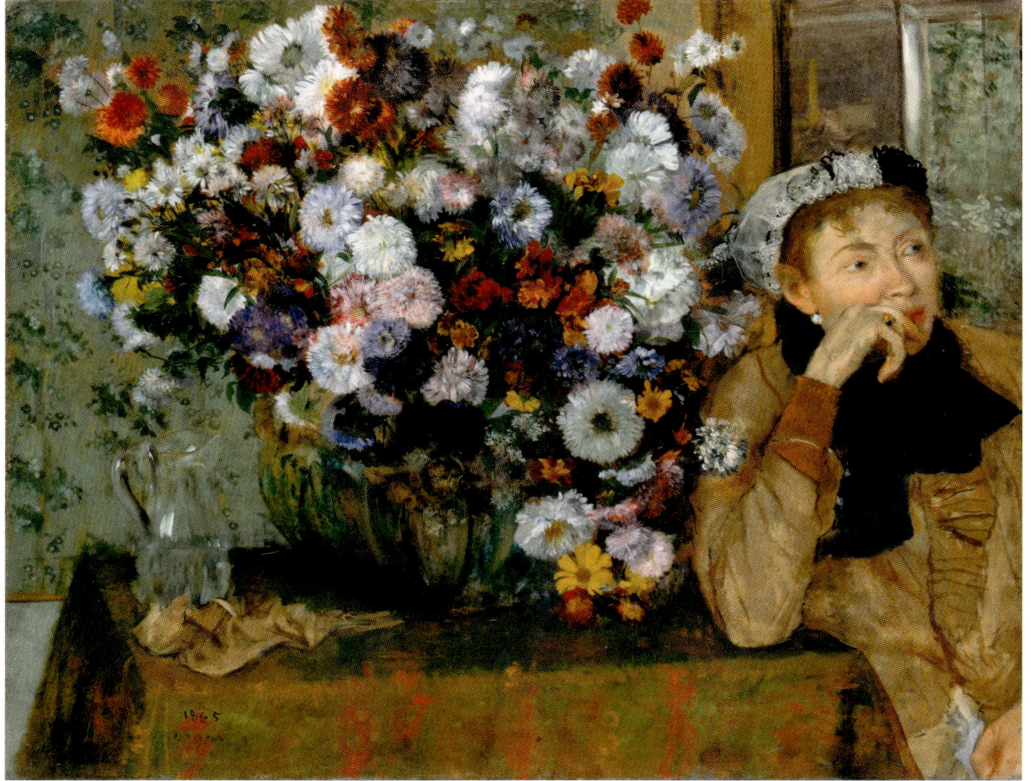

FIGURE 44
Edgar Degas (French, 1834–1917), *A Woman Seated Beside a Vase of Flowers*, 1865. Oil on canvas, 29 × 36½ in. (73.7 × 92.7 cm). The Metropolitan Museum of Art, New York, H. O. Havemeyer Collection, Bequest of Mrs. H. O. Havemeyer, 1929, 29.100.128

FIGURE 45
Edward Burne-Jones (British, 1833–1898), *Autumn*, 1869. Watercolor, 48¼ × 17¾ in. (122.5 × 45 cm). Private collection

To fully comprehend Tissot's artistic trajectory and his strategies in response to his new British context, it is helpful to consider him alongside artists with whom he was in dialogue. One such figure was Frith, a popular painter of contemporary genre pictures at the time of Tissot's London sojourn. In works such as his five-part series *The Road to Ruin* (figs. 42–43), with which Tissot's *The Prodigal Son in Modern Life* was directly compared, Frith explored how best to integrate narrative and visual imagery.[15] Like *The Road to Ruin*, which treats the perils of gambling and which Tissot would have seen at the Royal Academy in 1878, *The Prodigal Son in Modern Life* tells a story across several scenes, comprising both painted—in oil (1880) and watercolor (ca. 1880)—and engraved versions (1881), in which one critic saw "far more *finesse* and far wider introspection" than in Frith's works.[16] Tissot's series updates the biblical parable about two brothers who come into their inheritance—one who selflessly stays at home in diligent employment to support the family, and the prodigal, who embarks on a career of pleasure that lands him in ruin. The series opens with *The Departure* (pl. 86), in which the prodigal leaves his father's Thames-side warehouse to travel abroad—specifically, to the pleasure quarters of a Japanese city, where he is seen in *In Foreign Climes* (pl. 87) enjoying the singing and dancing of local beauties. Ragged, penniless, and penitent in *The Return* (pl. 88), the son stumbles onto a British commercial dock to receive his father's blessing. The final canvas, *The Fatted Calf* (pl. 89), depicts the prodigal as he prepares to carve the eponymous roast represented by the silver-domed platter on the alfresco dining table. Coming full circle back to a Thames-side setting—here downriver in the pastoral English countryside—the series emphasizes the importance of forgiveness through the fall and redemption of a family member.

In *The Fatted Calf*, however, the good brother looks perplexed and irate as he happens upon the celebratory meal while rowing with his companions, all of whom wear striped caps, which contemporary viewers may have identified as those of the Bullingdon Club of Oxford.[17] By referencing the dissolute reputation of this club, Tissot blurs the moral positions between the two brothers, suggesting that the concepts of good and evil may not be so clear-cut. Some critics commented that in the last panel, the two men appear almost visually interchangeable.[18] In setting up an apparently straightforward moralizing tale only to subvert its certainties, the work implies that in the modern era, things are not necessarily what they seem, and that truth is unstable rather than fixed.[19] Frith's series, by contrast, retains an obvious moral clarity in which bad behavior is indeed the "road to ruin."

Despite this avant-garde version of Frith-like storytelling, Tissot more often shied away from narrative art, like his fellow French painters Degas and Édouard Manet. But while Degas twinned this move with an overtly modernist style that emphasized brushwork and the surface of the canvas, as in *A Woman Seated Beside a Vase of Flowers* (fig. 44), Tissot chose to render subject matter that was similarly enigmatic but that showed a polished, highly detailed technique. For British audiences, the use of excessive detail in paintings signaled the lurking presence of a story that would eventually emerge from a diligent tallying of pictorial cues.[20] Tissot's compositions frustrated such detective work because his clues did not easily add up to a semantic revelation or sometimes even conflicted with one another. One critic commented on Tissot's *Evening* (also known as *The Ball*, pl. 79): "It is not funny, it is not pretty, there is no story. It is very like what it is intended to represent. . . . We can see the reality of the flounces any day in Russell & Allen's windows in

Bond Street, and there is nothing in the painting of them that makes them more valuable painted than real."[21]

Not only did Tissot often provide proliferating, seemingly gratuitous details that remained indecipherable, he also upset conventions of compositional hierarchy by giving equal emphasis to his renderings of the inanimate and the human. One reviewer complained of *The Captain's Daughter* (pl. 63): "Her dress has received as much attention as her face.... In nature there could be no mistake as to the relative values of the girl's head and the sky behind it, but here the one is nearly as solid and rich as the other." Another objected to *The Ball on Shipboard* (pl. 71), "M. Tissot seems to have no perception of pictorial values, and will paint a ship's rigging with as much precision and zest as a young lady's countenance."[22] Tissot's works, then, lacked clear signposts as to how the viewer should evaluate the depicted subject. As with other French art of this period, this resistance to conventional artistic codes unsettlingly suggested the overturning of other normative hierarchies, threatening traditional social as well as artistic values with modern ideas and ways.[23]

Although their high prices suggest that Tissot took pride in his painstakingly rendered scenes that invited but then resisted narrative closure,[24] in the late 1870s, the artist seems to have felt that something was lacking in his work. He had developed his version of Baudelaire's call for a "painting of modern life"—but how might he be seen as distilling "the eternal from the transitory"? Exposed to new types of art in Britain, Tissot was inspired to produce richer, more resonant pictures. In a letter to Edward Burne-Jones's widow, he spoke tellingly of his response to the painter's oeuvre: "I sensed the heights to which he had soared in comparison with the material world in which I was then struggling more and more."[25] Provoked by what he saw as the second-generation Pre-Raphaelite artist's ability to suggest higher realms of meaning while still retaining a detailed style, Tissot sought ways to make his own materiality more profound.

One early effort was the allegorical oddity *The Triumph of Will (Poem in Five Parts): I. The Challenge* (pl. 99), which appeared in 1877 at the Grosvenor Gallery, and which the critic Joseph Comyns Carr identified as having been motivated by the example of Burne-Jones.[26] Intended to be the first panel of a series (which was never completed), this grandiose image of a female knight, representing Will, vanquishing a writhing Vice, depicted in the shape of a chimeric beast that combines the torso of a bare-chested woman with the hindquarters of a wildcat, was not a critical success.[27] It was gently mocked even by Tissot's friend and fellow painter of fashionable society Ferdinand Heilbuth, who pretended that Tissot's printed description of the work was the menu for the gallery's artists' dinner, declaiming, "Soup of lady with serpent!" to the uproarious laughter of the assembled party.[28]

Following this unsuccessful experiment with allegory, Tissot altered his tone for his 1878 Grosvenor submissions, seeking instead to make modern subjects resonate more subtly with deeper meanings. That year, both Tissot and Burne-Jones exhibited figures of women representing the seasons. But while Burne-Jones's works featured his usual classically draped forms, such as seen in *Autumn* (fig. 45), the subjects in Tissot's

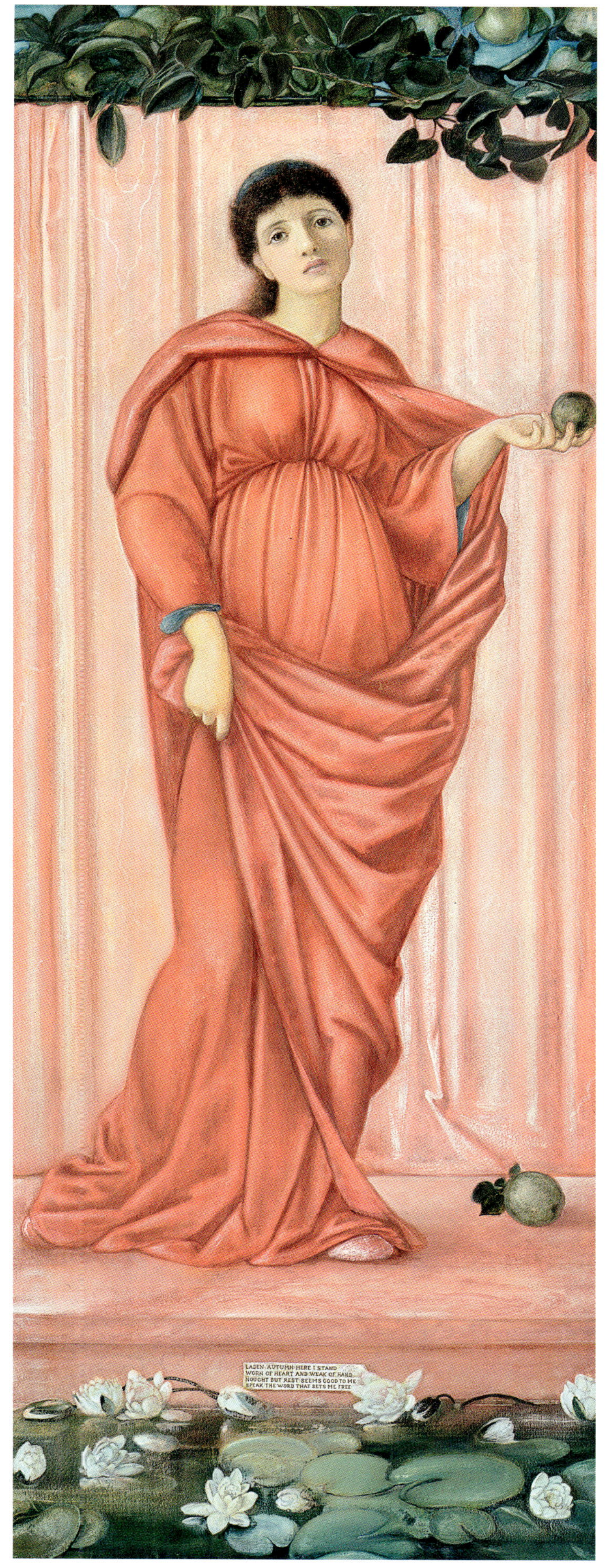

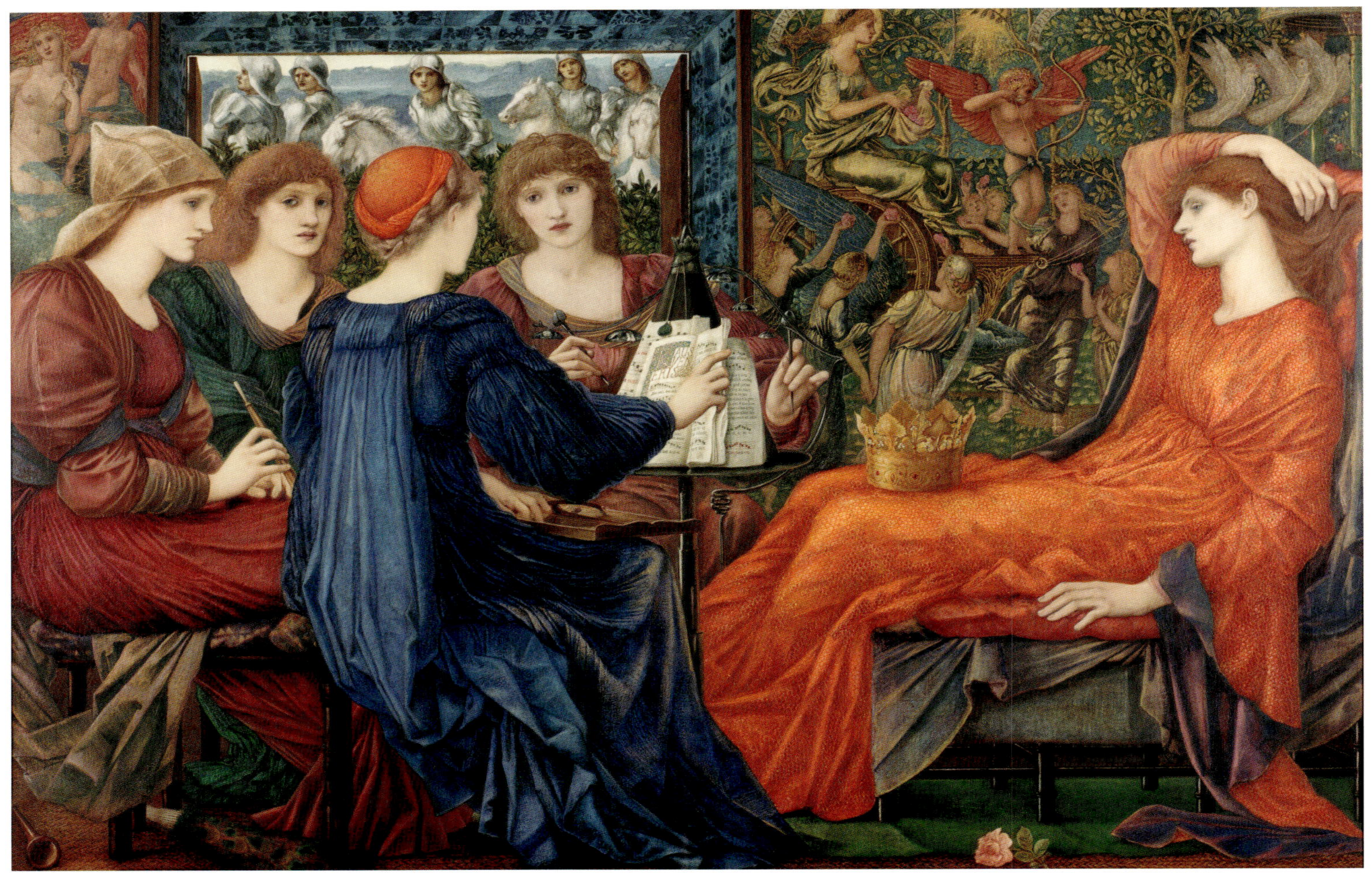

FIGURE 46
Edward Burne-Jones (British, 1833–1898), *Laus Veneris*, 1873–1875. Oil on canvas, 48¼ × 72⅛ in. (122.5 × 183.3 cm). Laing Art Gallery, Newcastle upon Tyne, England, TWCMS: B8145

October (pl. 84) (exhibited as an etching at the Grosvenor, under the title *Autumn*) and *Spring (Specimen of a Portrait)* wore cutting-edge fashions. In this way, Tissot suggested that fashion plates were the modern allegory of the seasons, provocatively declaring that a new era demands a new form of representation—one with the potential to make Burne-Jones's work seem labored and old-fashioned.

At the same time, however, Tissot also began emulating Burne-Jones's Aestheticist qualities. An artistic movement and way of life that emerged in Britain in the 1860s, Aestheticism privileged beauty over the expression of conventional moral values. Aesthetic artists produced pieces characterized by an interest in "art for art's sake," the idea that artworks should center on the beautiful arrangement of color, line, and form in lieu of an edifying narrative. In its blatant appeal to the senses, Aesthetic painting was associated with luxury and pleasure. Exhibited at the Grosvenor in 1878, Burne-Jones's sensuous *Laus Veneris* (fig. 46)—a depiction of the seductive, lovesick Venus and the court in which she entraps the German knight Tannhäuser—exemplified Aesthetic art with its mesmerizing harmonies of color and intricate surface patterns.

Tissot's work was, in fact, directly compared to Burne-Jones's. As one critic observed of his 1878 Grosvenor submissions *Evening, July (Specimen of a Portrait)* (fig. 58), and *Spring (Specimen of a Portrait)*: "Tissot is simply Burne-Jones modernised. He says in the careless slang of the day what the other says with his fastidious archaisms." Citing the "voluptuous languor" of these figures, this writer continued: "Look in her eyes—can you find a thought in them of anything beyond her own pleasure, or perhaps a fretfulness that she is too weary to be pleased?" Reviewers found these same qualities in Burne-Jones's Venus, who displayed "the weariness of satisfied love, and the pain of unsatisfied longing."[29] In this light, the elegant lady attending the ball in *Evening* was viewed as a contemporary Venus—a woman of the world, or perhaps of the *demimonde*, jaded and listless from overindulgence. Similarly, in Tissot's *Rivals*, exhibited at the Grosvenor in 1879, the reclining woman resembles the enervated goddess of *Laus Veneris*, presiding over her mystical erotic kingdom. Tissot was clearly finding his stride, creating a new type of art that drew on subject matter from the world around him to produce the same sorts of effects that other artists found in classical or historical subjects.

Rivals and other works from the late 1870s, such as *Orphans* (pl. 85), take up what came to be an increasingly dominant focus for Tissot until his departure from London; during this phase, he moved from portraying professional models in tableaux of society events to limiting himself almost exclusively to scenes peopled by a few personally dear individuals set in the domestic spaces of his own house and garden. Many scholars have attributed this shift to the artist's new need for privacy due to his relationship with the model for *Orphans*, the Irish divorcée Kathleen Newton, a dominating presence in his work from around 1877 until her death from tuberculosis, in 1882.[30] However, Tissot could easily have painted Newton into the vignettes of sailors with their ladyloves and London high society that he had already been producing. By refocusing his subject matter to nonnarrative scenes of women and children in gardens or luxurious Aestheticist interiors, he was demonstrating his growing acknowledgment of both the centrality of domesticity to British taste and the ways in which such apparently simple subjects might bear profound implications. Known as a canny chameleon who changed his style based on what would sell, Tissot had hit upon a new mode that, like Trollope's novels, drew on detailed observation of individual narratives to probe greater questions about human life and society.[31]

Unlike Trollope's fiction or more straightforward moralizing British genre painting, however, Tissot's works from the late 1870s to the early 1880s cleverly balanced multiple interpretive contexts, starting with his inner circle, who could easily identify the intimate biographical elements of the pictures; extending outward to viewers who simply admired the finely painted domestic scenes; and finally, appealing to those who—like Tissot himself—understood the works to be suggestive of deeper meanings.[32] His project was, ultimately, to suggest that the details of the material world could act as a vehicle for contemplating invisible spiritual realms—indeed, that it was *only* through attending to our perception of mundane reality that we limited human beings might access any intimation of something beyond.

This belief echoes contemporary ideals informing Aestheticism and, eventually, Symbolism, the poetic and artistic movement invested in the notion that visible forms are only a thin veil over an infinite, unknowable universe. It also helps to explain Tissot's easy adoption of Spiritualism in the next phase of his career (see Buron, this volume). In the wake of unsettling new scientific discoveries based on analyses of the material world, such as Charles Darwin's theory of evolution, a fierce debate between the philosophies of idealism and materialism had emerged; idealists argued that the goal of both life and art was to seek inner mystic significance over mere human perception. Only in the invisible realm of the spirit did the true nature of all things become evident.[33] Tissot, remarkably, refused this binary and instead emphasized a world in which the ordinary details that he observed around him could, in fact, resonate with profound meaning. While the mourning young woman in *Orphans* may be as stylishly dressed as a fashion plate, for example, her haunted gaze at the viewer implies that she, brushed by death, has seen other realities. With its mesh of chestnut leaves and reeds producing abstract decorative patterns against an unearthly golden glow, the work provokes an Aestheticist contemplation of another world. The stylish young woman stands in a liminal space between realms; she is neither fashion plate nor heavenly figure, but rather both at once.

TISSOT'S "GENIUS"
PICTURE-SELLING IN BRITAIN

KRYSTYNA MATYJASZKIEWICZ

"A wonderful businessman" is how James Tissot was described by his compatriot Jacques-Émile Blanche, "almost a dealer—of genius, said [John Singer] Sargent. . . . In the eighties, young artists, my fellow students . . . liked Tissot's genre paintings, his dry-points, and loved the Lady . . . known as a sitter to Tissot. John Sargent, [Paul] Helleu, [Giovanni] Boldini insisted that I introduced them."[1] What these younger artists so admired was not only the way Tissot captured modern life and female beauty, but also his ability to make a good income.

Almost from the outset of his career, Tissot had aimed high. In an 1860 letter to a potential buyer, Tissot offered to "go down to" prices that in some cases were more than triple what he eventually received, asking 9,000 francs for *During the Service* (also known as *Martin Luther's Doubts*, pl. 5) (sold in 1870 for 2,000); 6,500 for *Meeting of Faust and Marguerite* (pl. 3) (bought by the French state in 1860 for 5,000); and 5,000 for *Way of Flowers, Way of Tears* or *Dance of Death* (pl. 7) (sold in 1870 for 2,000).[2] A *Marguerite in Church* was priced by Tissot at 5,500 francs, but he was bargained down to 1,500 for one bought by the art dealers Maison Goupil in 1860, and to 2,500 for another version that he sold directly to the French economist Léon Say in 1861.[3] At this early stage, purchasers remained few (other than portrait commissioners), but Tissot held out against compromise on price and continued to focus on subjects in "medieval" (actually German/Flemish sixteenth-century-style) dress.

Beginning in 1863, Tissot changed tactics; his subject matter was taken increasingly from modern life, often centered on attractive and fashionably dressed young women (see pls. 13, 15, 22, and 38). Such pictures were popular with American collectors and with the dealers who sold to them, such as Goupil.[4] Tissot also increased his output—though without compromising high quality—so that there were more works available at prices attractive to dealers, who had profit to consider. Furthermore, the modest size of Tissot's paintings made them easy to accommodate in large or small spaces, yet still their visual richness was stunning.[5]

Tissot's supreme advantage was his fluent paint handling; his rapid, fine strokes of color give the appearance, from a distance, of precise detail (although seen close-up, they are rather fluid and loose). Nineteenth-century collectors liked to feel they were getting value for their money, and careful execution was seen as evidence of labor expended. John Ruskin's famously libelous criticism of James McNeill Whistler's painting centered on Whistler having asked "two hundred guineas for flinging a pot of paint in the public's face." By contrast, of Tissot's works in the same exhibition—the opening of London's new Grosvenor Gallery in 1877—Ruskin said they required "especial notice, because their dexterity and brilliance is apt to make the spectator forget their conscientiousness."[6] Whistler's speed was evident in his painting, but not Tissot's. Edgar Degas, who had seen and admired Tissot's Parisian output in the late 1860s, wrote to him from New Orleans in 1872: "You, with your terrific activity, would be capable of drawing out money from this mob of cotton brokers, cotton dealers, etc."[7] Whereas Degas tended to agonize over his pictures, frequently dissatisfied and making changes,[8] Tissot was a confident finisher.

Upon arriving to work in England in 1871, Tissot used the knowledge he had acquired of current British painting, and therefore taste, from printed reproductions as well as exhibitions he had seen in London and Paris. Tissot had long admired—and been influenced by—British eighteenth-century art, for which there was a revival in taste.[9] To the 1872 Royal Academy exhibition, he sent *The Farewells* (pl. 43) and *An Interesting Story* (fig. 47), both employing figures in eighteenth-century costume. A variant of the latter painting, *Before the Departure* or *The Parting* (pl. 42), was bought—through the art dealers Thomas Agnew & Sons—by Lord Dunmore, who became lord-in-waiting to Queen Victoria in 1874. Agnew also probably commissioned *Tea* (1872; Metropolitan Museum of Art, New York), a replica of the left-hand figure in *Before the Departure*, and sold it in November 1872 to John Kynaston Cross, an owner of cotton mills in Bolton.[10] Perhaps in joking reference to the letter Degas had sent, Tissot gave his friend a pencil study of the model whose image was bought by a "cotton dealer."[11] At 15,000 and 10,000 francs, respectively, *Before the Departure* and *An Interesting Story* had achieved—indeed exceeded—the level of price Tissot had sought in 1860.

The eighteenth-century-dress compositions Tissot had made in Paris were based on French paintings and fashions. In *A Luncheon* (fig. 48), ankles with patterned stockings are revealed, and in *The Partie Carrée* (pl. 41), there is décolletage too—elements that American collectors would recognize as "French." His London works took a more restrained cue from mezzotint reproductions of paintings by artists such as Thomas Gainsborough, Joshua Reynolds, and George Romney. Instead of revealing striped gowns and lacy petticoats, the subjects of these pictures wear white dresses, black or white shawls, eighteenth-century-style hats or mobcaps, and symbolic British-army red coats.

Tissot's eighteenth-century pictures are easy to read: for example, in the center of *Before the Departure*, just beyond a boat of redcoats on the river, is a black-and-white-striped warship, which the young man in the foreground must shortly be joining. In *The Farewells*, railings separate the subjects, and the dressmaker's scissors allude to the couple's imminent parting. Capitalizing on British audiences' attraction to such storytelling, Tissot also incorporated clues into many of his modern-life pictures. In *Waiting* (also known as *In the Shallows*, pl. 60), a young woman faces the viewer, the glove removed from her right hand, expecting, perhaps, a proposal. An iron column divides the couple and hides the man's face in *Quarrelling* (pl. 51). Guests who have come to a domestic ball in *Too Early* (pl. 46) are captured in the awkward discomfort familiar to anyone who has arrived before the host is quite ready. *The Graphic* reported, "No more humorous and yet strictly truthful picture is to be seen in the [Royal Academy] Exhibition."[12] The painting recalled "the novels of Jane Austen, the great painter of the humour of 'polite society,'" said *The Builder*.[13]

All of these London works found immediate buyers at increasingly high prices. Most collectors used dealers to make transactions with Tissot, and dealers bought work when they were certain of onward sale. Tissot's paintings were especially popular with industrialists and entrepreneurs in northern England and Scotland, such as Hilton Philipson of Tynemouth, who bought, through Agnew, *The Ball on Shipboard* (pl. 71) and *London Visitors* (pl. 56), and John Polson, Scottish cofounder of cornflour manufacturers Brown and Polson, who owned *Rivals* (pl. 83) and *Summer* (pl. 58).[14] Northerners were "outside" London society and responded to the way Tissot viewed it as a foreigner. The *Illustrated London News*, for example, described Tissot's works as made "possibly with caricature, something smacking . . . of a Gallic sneer."[15] The painter's fresh take, stylish women, and beautiful detail attracted buyers so readily that some British artists considered Tissot to be a threat to their livelihoods. According to art critic Alfred de Lostalot, they "closed their ranks."[16] In a crowded market, an artist who could readily sell all the paintings he produced was unwelcome.[17]

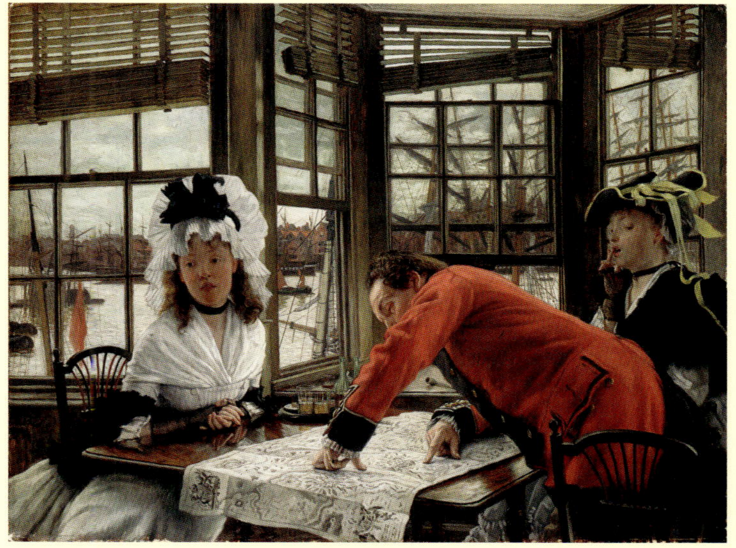

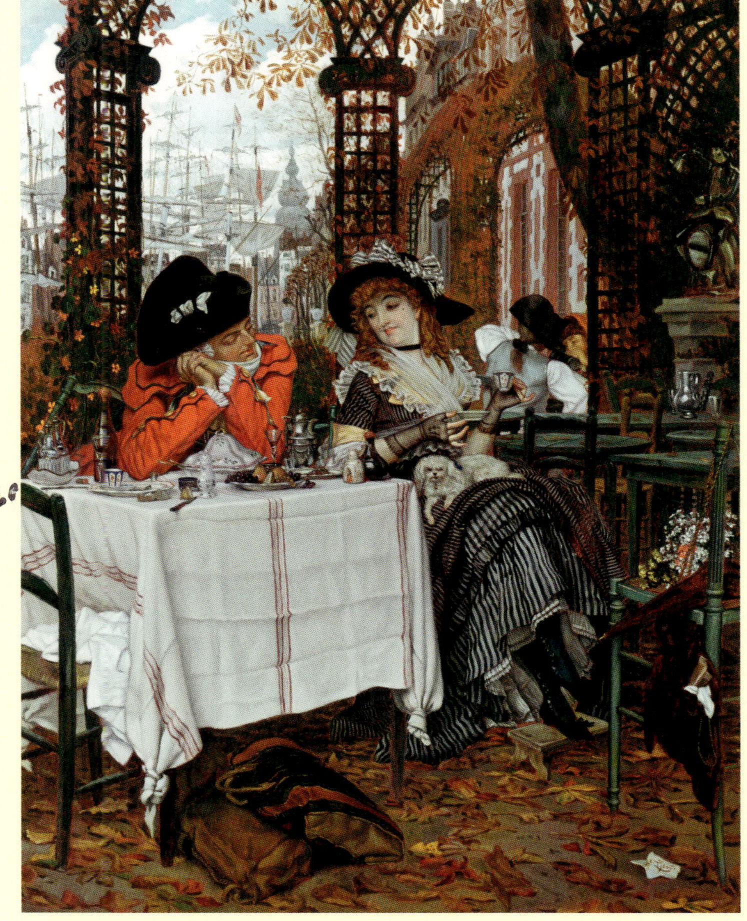

FIGURE 47
James Tissot, *An Interesting Story*, 1872. Oil on wood panel, 23½ × 30⅛ in. (59.7 × 76.6 cm). National Gallery of Victoria, Melbourne, Felton Bequest, 1938

FIGURE 48
James Tissot, *A Luncheon*, ca. 1868. Oil on canvas, 22 × 16½ in. (55.9 × 41.9 cm). Private collection

TISSOT'S HOUSES IN SAINT JOHN'S WOOD, LONDON

CHARLOTTE GERE

Late in 1871, confident of his future earnings and potential for success in England, James Tissot left his Paris house—eventually letting it to the Italian painter Giuseppe de Nittis—and began to look for a place to live in London.[1] He had come as a guest of Thomas Gibson Bowles, editor of the London-based weekly *Vanity Fair*, who had employed Tissot as a caricaturist for his magazine. Drawn to the Thames and its riverside and shipboard life, Tissot might have joined his old friend from Paris, James McNeill Whistler, in Chelsea, but ultimately he chose the neighborhood of Saint John's Wood, leasing a modest terrace house at 73 Springfield Road. Away from the polluted city center and on higher ground, suburban Saint John's Wood, a long-established artistic quarter, was known for its healthier air. More importantly, the light was better.[2] Tissot's London dealer, Ernest Gambart, lived nearby, as did other artist friends. The names of Tissot's closest London friends are inset into a cloisonné enamel plaque made by him around 1882, including Lawrence Alma-Tadema, also a Gambart protégé; the British painters Charles Napier Hemy, Robert Walker Macbeth, and Philip Morris; and the satirical cartoonist George du Maurier. Similarities between Tissot's London socialites and du Maurier's satirical caricatures in the British weekly *Punch* cannot be coincidental.[3]

In London, Tissot resumed his Parisian practice of setting his costume pictures and modern-society conversation pieces in his own house and garden. He continued to add to his impressive collection of Japanese items and Oriental rugs, probably advised by Whistler, who patronized Farmer & Rogers's Oriental Warehouse in Regent Street.[4] Tissot also began acquiring antique and modern furniture, china and silver, and other decorative items. An eighteenth-century gate-legged mahogany table and a Victorian dropleaf table appear in pictures exhibited in 1872, when he was still at Springfield Road.[5] Other items, such as ebonized chairs (purchased from William Morris's decorating company) and a bentwood rocking chair—the latter seen in *The Last Evening* (pl. 69)—reveal a taste for convenience, modern design, and simplicity.[6]

Early in 1873, Tissot moved into 17 Grove End Road, a detached 1825 villa with an ilex and a chestnut tree in nearly an acre of garden.[7] He would remain there until he returned to Paris, in 1882. Two domestics lived in the house, and the gardener and his wife resided in a newly built red-brick lodge by the coach house and stables. Here, in 1876, Tissot was joined by his companion and muse, the Irish divorcée Kathleen Newton, and embarked on a series of transparently autobiographical subjects set on the property and featuring Newton as the model (see pls. 96–98). Since Tissot's eleven years in London predate the trend of dedicating extensive press coverage to elegant show studios, these paintings and prints serve as primary sources for gauging his taste in decoration and furnishing.[8] The work reveals a contemporary and eclectic but not pretentious style; Parisian eighteenth-century brocaded and gilded furniture exchanged for solid English comfort.

THE STUDIO AND CONSERVATORY

Additions made by Tissot to the Grove End Road house consisted of a large studio and a conservatory, or palm house, designed by the young Scottish architect John McKean Brydon.[9] Featured in *Building News* in 1874 (see fig. 114), the property is described as:

> a large apartment, amply lighted, principally from the north and east. The whole of one side (the right in the view) is open to a large conservatory, from which it is separated by an arrangement of glass screens and curtains. The floor is laid with oak parquet, and the walls are hung with a kind of tapestry cloth of greenish blue colour.[10]

In the studio, a bow window—a replica of one facing the river at the Trafalgar Tavern in Greenwich—enabled work on Thames-side subjects, to be continued away from the Greenwich waterfront.[11] A larger bow window and a French door overlooked the garden, reached by a flight of brick-and-stone steps, with the conservatory, entered via a lobby, on the right.

Tissot's *Hide and Seek* (pl. 82) is set in this studio.[12] A screen obscures the large bow window; the conservatory is just visible on the right. The presence of an easel identifies this as a studio, but in all other respects it functions as a living room. A woman, modeled by Newton, is reading while children play. But even a game of hide-and-seek encourages interpretation. On this sunny day, the family is confined within a dark room, hinting at a secret behind the façade of bourgeois comfort.

The curved, iron-and-glass conservatory at Grove End Road added a tropical dimension to Tissot's subject matter: a blending of inside and out, a show of wealth as well as horticultural expertise. In *Afternoon Tea* (also known as *In the Conservatory*, pl. 54), for example, elegantly dressed women take tea in the lobby. The conservatory also served as a forcing house for Tissot's chrysanthemums (see pl. 57).[13] Conservatories were associated in Victorian lore with ambiguous messages of assignation and seduction. Critics accused the painter of "staging modern life" in the *demimonde*, the world of hidden mistresses and irregular partnerships,[14] and of reveling in the "exotic growth of splendid conservatories," where "graceful ladies in irreproachable costume, keep a brace of rivals in play at five o'clock tea" (see pl. 83).[15]

THE GARDEN

Tissot set scenes of romance and emotional tension in the Grove End Road garden: a couple quarrelling; a young woman thinking of her admirer, whose hat and stick lie on a nearby chair; a picnic on the grass.[16] After Tissot met Newton, these became idylls of family life.[17] The garden's most distinctive feature was the ironwork colonnade surrounding the ornamental pool, a smaller model of the stone version in the Parc Monceau in Paris (see fig. 49). The planting was designed in the French taste: dense drifts of brightly colored flowers with an emphasis on geraniums, enclosed by panels of climbing ivy (see pl. 104). Behind the garden bench, Tissot introduced trellis pillars covered with climbing nasturtiums, reminiscent of his Paris garden.[18] Nearer to the house, a fan of irregularly shaped beds filled with embroidery or carpet bedding was a mark of labor-intensive horticulture.[19] In *Croquet* (pl. 50), the terra-cotta flowerpots seen in the foreground are for the bedding plants raised in the lean-to glasshouse. The bulrushes, flag irises, and flowering rhubarb by the pool also filled large flower vases in the house.

The garden was thought to be healthy for Newton, who suffered from consumption, but in the paintings it could also be viewed as a seductive element. Reviewing an exhibition at the Grosvenor Gallery in 1879, which featured *The Hammock* (fig. 118) and *A Quiet Afternoon* (ca. 1879; private collection), the *Daily Telegraph* described the garden as "Armida's garden full of hammocks,[20] rocking-chairs, Japanese knick-knacks, bulrushes and slim sirens in black stockings and high-heeled shoes."[21] The Chinese rattan armchair, hammock, and croquet lawn were all recently introduced novelties. Rugs and furs were laid on the grass and garden bench; elegant teaware, both antique and modern, served for picnics (see pl. 52).[22] In several works, such as the two exhibited at the Grosvenor in 1879, Newton reclines in the hammock, another call for outrage. As *The Spectator* remarked, "These ladies in hammocks, showing a very unnecessary amount of petticoat and stocking, and remarkable for little save luxurious indolence, are hardly fit subjects for such an elaborate painting."[23]

Following Newton's death, Tissot abandoned the house and everything in it. It remained empty for two years, until Alma-Tadema took over as its new owner in 1884. The villa in which Tissot set his record of this idyllic love affair all but disappeared in a rebuild, which left nothing but the conservatory, much reduced in size, and the cast-iron colonnade.

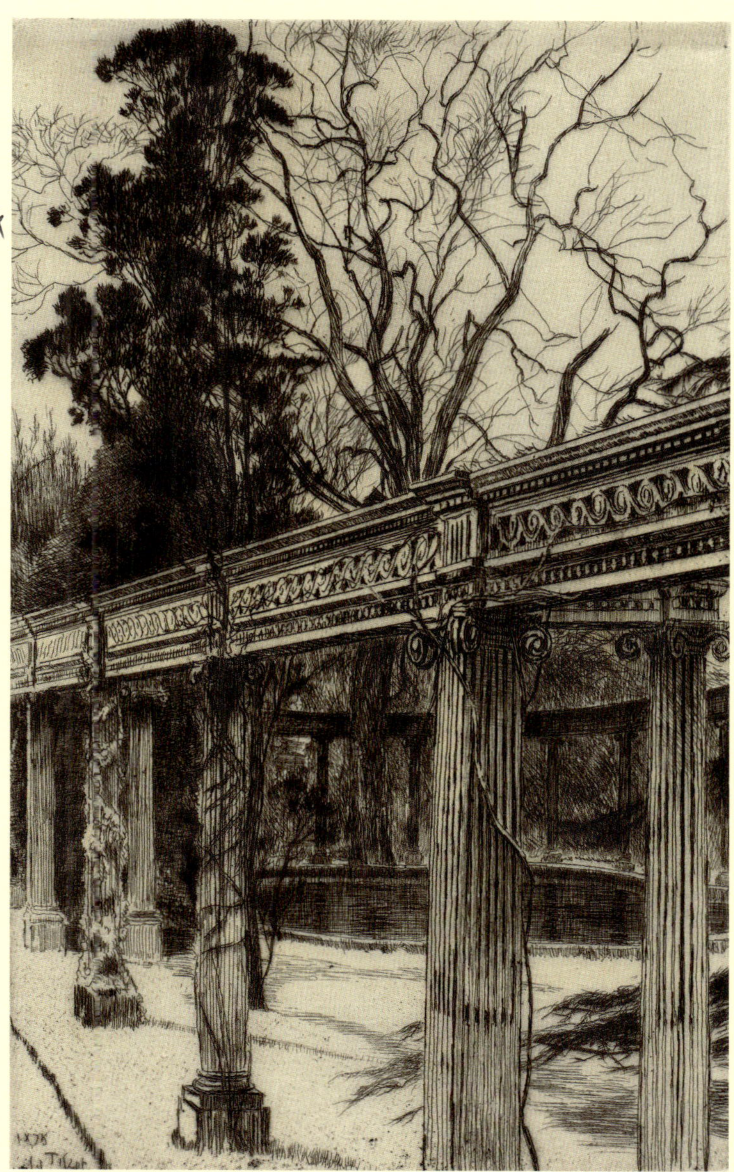

FIGURE 49
James Tissot, *My Garden at Saint John's Wood*, 1878. Etching, 7⅜ × 4½ in. (18.7 × 11.3 cm). Fine Arts Museums of San Francisco, Museum purchase, Achenbach Foundation for Graphic Arts Endowment Fund, 1981.1.63

PAUL PERRIN

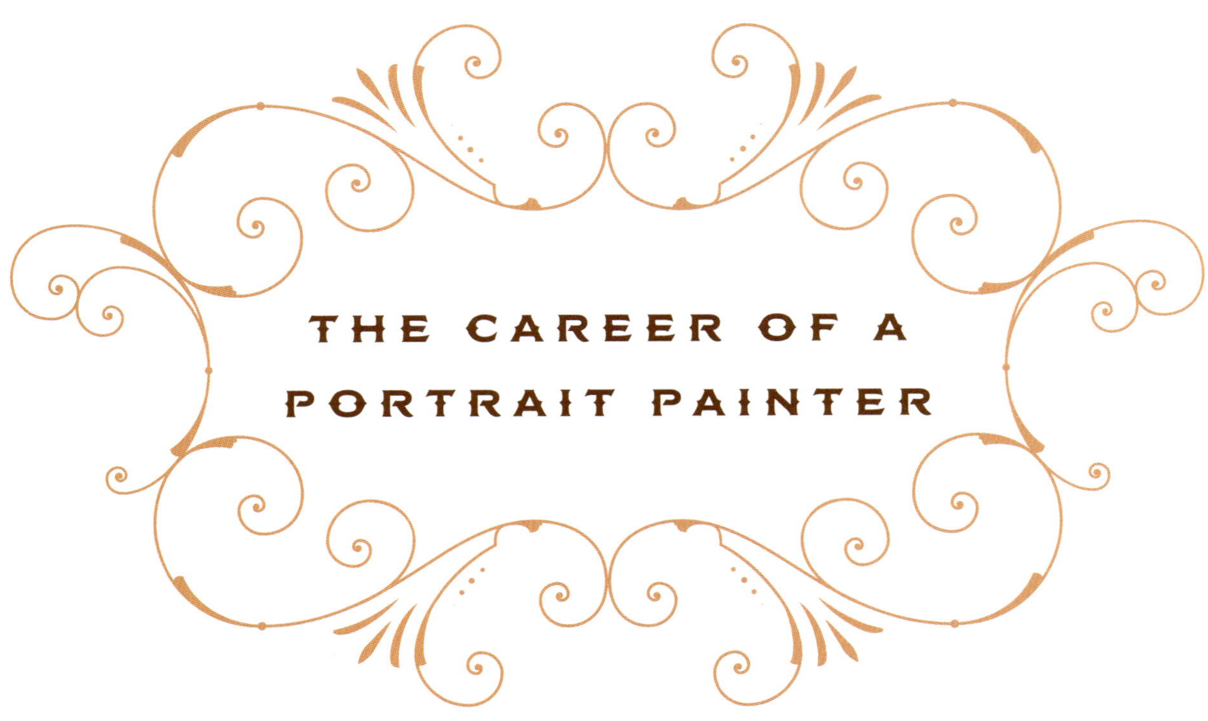

THE CAREER OF A PORTRAIT PAINTER

JAMES TISSOT WAS MOST FAMOUS as a master of genre painting, though he painted portraits throughout his career. Upon his death, in 1902, few recalled that, in addition to genre scenes and biblical illustrations, he had also painted *The Circle of the Rue Royale* (pl. 27) as well as a portrait of the soldier and adventurer Frederick Burnaby (pl. 29). Because they are less well represented in museums, Tissot's portraits are, for the most part, still little known.[1] Recently, two unpublished archival documents have come to light: an album of photographs of the artist's works made in London (see figs. 15–22),[2] and an account book he used to record sales from 1857 to 1890 (see "Tissot's Sales Notebook," this volume).[3] These discoveries contribute to a better understanding of Tissot as a portraitist and offer a greater sense of the artistic and social circles in which he moved. In addition, for some of the major paintings, they make it possible to propose identifications of models who have thus far remained nameless.

Tissot compiled several photograph albums of his work. Four of these reflect his career into the 1890s and comprise 276 paintings and pastels, of which some sixty-two are portraits, amounting to a little more than one-fifth of this number. In his account book, Tissot noted the names of sixty-five sitters as well as the amount charged for each portrait.[4] Overall, portrait commissions represented about 10 percent of the artist's income from the sale of paintings, pastels, watercolors, and prints between 1857 and 1890.[5] Although he practiced the genre irregularly, three key periods of Tissot's portraiture emerge: 1857–1859, 1864–1868, and 1883–mid-1890s.

❦ ❦ ❦

Like many young painters starting out in Paris during the Second Empire, Tissot benefited from the strong demand for portraits from the bourgeoisie. According to Georges Bastard, who penned a short biographical essay on Tissot, the artist, having just arrived from his hometown of Nantes in the mid-1850s, initially lived on "portraits of *maidservants* and *housekeepers*," selling them at 40 francs apiece.[6] In 1857, Tissot recorded in his sales notebook the execution and sale of four portraits and a copy of a "Louis XV–era" portrait. In the late 1850s, the first commissions came from "Madame Maton" and "Monsieur and Madame Bourgeois," but also from Anatole de Ségur, Catholic and Royalist, and son of the famous countess and author Sophie Rostopchine. Tissot composed two portraits of Rostopchine's grandchildren, Pierre-Marie and Henri de Ségur, for which he charged 400 francs total.[7] In 1858, the children's uncle Gaston de Ségur, a priest, commissioned from Tissot a "copy of the Child Jesus" and a "Saint Francis de Sales."[8] That year, Tissot recorded selling to date a total of six paintings, "all portraits."[9] In 1859, for his first works in the Paris Salon, Tissot, seeking commissions, showed two portraits—*Portrait of Mlle H. de S...* and *Portrait of Mme T...*—out of five canvases.[10] Some critics disparaged this debut, including Zacharie Astruc, who observed severely:

"M. Tissot finds it amusing to make student paintings and then frame them as masterworks. His two small portraits of a woman and a girl are nothing special. They are derivative—It is immediately obvious—of MM. [Hippolyte] Flandrin and Joseph Nicolas Robert-Fleury."[11]

Tissot would finally break through at the Salon in 1864, with two paintings that he exhibited as portraits but that anonymous models had posed for: *Portrait of Mlle L. L...* (pl. 22) and *The Two Sisters; Portrait* (pl. 21). The two full-length portraits, featuring modern dress and settings, departed from the smaller, more traditional portraits he had previously submitted, and even more so from his medieval scenes and Flemish-inspired works (see Baetens, this volume, and Frederick, this volume). They established him as a painter of his time and a great portraitist in the making. "The two portraits exhibited by M. Tissot are genuine paintings, and they are good paintings, whose greatest merit consists in the sincerity of their modern feeling," wrote Léon Lagrange.[12] The critic was alluding to a debate of the period—the elevation of portraits to the status of *paintings*. Tissot's works stood out among the dark bust-length portraits set against monochrome backgrounds that predominated in the Salon at that time. While these aimed above all to achieve a resemblance to the model, Tissot's portraits had the substance of genre scenes, a quality noted by Charles Clément: "M. Tissot . . . has executed this year two paintings that we will categorize as portraits, although we could just as well, because of the importance given the props, classify them as genre subjects."[13] These two portraits served as templates for those to come. *Mlle L. L...* prefigures the portraits set in interiors, reduced to the smaller size of genre paintings, while *The Two Sisters* announces the more monumental outdoor portraits, composed at the larger scale of history paintings. All of Tissot's portraits follow one of these two seemingly opposing formulas, but in both, the figure's role transcends that of mere model.

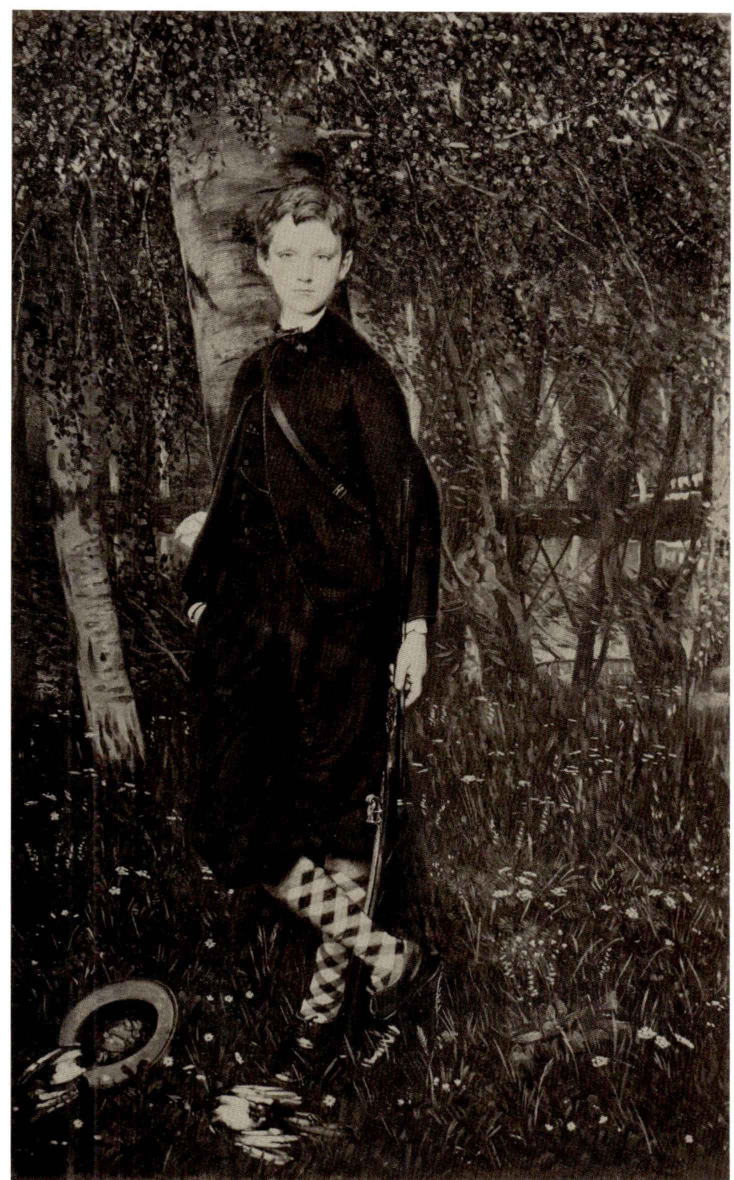

FIGURE 50
James Tissot, *Portrait of Jacques de Monbrison*, 1866. Location unknown

In the wake of this success, Tissot received a commission for his first large group portrait—of the Marquis de Miramon, his wife, and their children (pl. 23)—delivered in 1865 for the significant sum of 5,000 francs, that is, ten times what Tissot had hitherto charged his clients. Like de Ségur, René de Cassagne de Beaufort was from a conservative aristocratic milieu, nevertheless tempered by his Anglophilia and dandyism. Tissot, likewise influenced by the British—he regularly spent time in London—devised a novel conversation piece in the French style, with the family posed on the terrace of the Château de Paulhac, on the family estate in the Auvergne. No doubt pleased with the final product, the marquis commissioned an equally original portrait of his wife, Thérèse Feuillant, heiress to a northern French mining fortune, in interior dress in her room (pl. 24). For this piece, Tissot mixed genres, electing to execute the standing portrait in a medium format and emphasizing the stylish dress, décor, and accessories. There is little difference between this intimate painting and the contemporary genre scenes that accounted for Tissot's success at the time. Fashion and décor are rendered in great detail in his male portraits as well, such as the one of the wealthy industrialist Aimé Seillière (pl. 25).

In 1866, no doubt recommended by the Marquis de Miramon, Tissot received another prestigious commission: a group portrait of the members of the Circle of the Rue Royale, an aristocratic club founded a decade

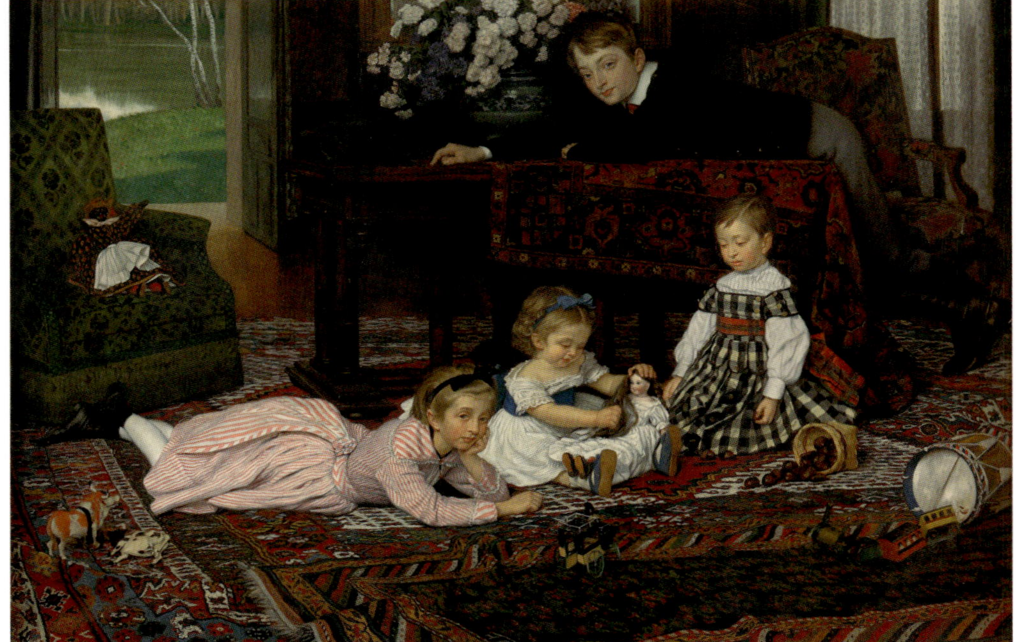

FIGURE 51
James Tissot, *Portraits of the Children of Émile Gaillard: Marie, Jeanne, Eugène, and Joseph Gaillard* (also known as *Children in an Interior*), 1868. Oil on canvas, 55¼ × 83 in. (140.3 × 210.8 cm). Private collection

FIGURE 52
James Tissot, *Portrait of Sydney Milner-Gibson*, ca. 1872. Oil on canvas, 50 × 39 in. (127 × 99.1 cm). Moyse's Hall Museum, West Suffolk Council, Bury Saint Edmunds, England

earlier, located in place de la Concorde. With this monumental "painting of twelve portraits," as the artist describes it in his sales notebook, Tissot brilliantly met the challenge of representing in a great variety of poses and outfits blue-blooded dandies such as the Marquis de Galliffet, future opponent of the Commune, and the Prince de Polignac, seen musing over a biography of Louis XVII, as well as new-money industrialists and financiers, such as Rodolphe Hottinguer, who won the painting by lot.[14]

That same year, through her brother Rodolphe, Amélie Hottinguer commissioned Tissot to portray her ten-year-old son, Jacques de Monbrison, as a hunter (fig. 50).[15] As in *Spring* (pl. 15) and *The Two Sisters; Portrait*, the painter deftly integrated the modern figure with the landscape. In the mid-1860s, Tissot seems to have developed a reputation for his portraits of children. In 1868, he executed an astonishing double portrait, listed in his sales notebook as "a portrait of Monsieur Kanh's 2 boys," posing on the threshold of their home.[16] He also composed a painting that was until recently titled *Children in an Interior* (fig. 51), in which he plays with a mix of interior and exterior spaces; a door opens to a landscape in the upper-left corner, an opulent bouquet of flowers has been brought inside. Research has made it possible to now identify this as the portrait of (from left to right) Marie, Jeanne, Eugène, and Joseph Gaillard, the children of Émile Gaillard, a powerful banker close to the Comte de Chambord, an investor in railroads and a collector of medieval and Renaissance art.[17] Tissot's innovation in this work was to align the viewer with the children's point of view, close to the ground, further emphasized by Eugène bending over to fit within the frame. The younger children appear unselfconsciously absorbed in their game, while the elder two, nearing the age of reason, hold more melancholy poses and seem aware of being observed. In late 1867, Tissot recorded in his notebook that in ten working years he had sold thirty-nine paintings, thirty-two of them portraits.

After 1868, Tissot applied his portrait-making skills toward a new form: caricature.[18] Thomas Gibson Bowles, owner and publisher of the British satirical weekly *Vanity Fair*, commissioned from the artist—now renowned for his great society portraits—eleven caricatures of European royalty and other public figures (see figs. 35 and 112). The two men became close friends, and soon thereafter Bowles asked Tissot to paint his portrait[19] and, several years later, Tissot created an etched portrait of Bowles's wife, Jessica.[20] In 1870, Tissot painted the portrait of Bowles's close friend Captain Frederick Burnaby, a work Bowles subsequently owned. In 1872, Tissot also painted Bowles's half sister, Sydney Milner-Gibson (fig. 52).

After moving to London in the summer of 1871, Tissot continued to contribute caricatures to *Vanity Fair*. His production of these drawings—more flattering to their models than it might seem—gave the artist entrée to the English elite. In 1871, Frances, Countess Waldegrave, commissioned—as a gift to her from Parliamentarians, peers, and bishops—the wonderful standing portrait of her husband, the politician Chichester Samuel Parkinson-Fortescue (fig. 113).[21] For this painting, as well as that of Milner-Gibson, Tissot still emphasized the décor and objects surrounding the model but altered his palette, now favoring darker, less vivid tones. This color scale is evident in *Portrait of Colonel **** (also known as *Gentleman in a Railway Carriage*, pl. 31), which was displayed along with the portrait of Burnaby at the International Exhibition in 1872, introducing Tissot as a portraitist to the London public. The long-anonymous train passenger can today be identified as the "L[ieutenant] Colonel Longley" whose portrait Tissot recorded painting in 1872 (see "Tissot's Sales Notebook," this volume). George Longley (fig. 53), a British officer of the Royal Engineers, was the son of Charles Thomas Longley, Archbishop of Canterbury. He served in Crimea and China before retiring in January 1872 with the rank of lieutenant colonel, hence his depiction in civilian clothing. The railroad car may refer to his extensive travels.[22]

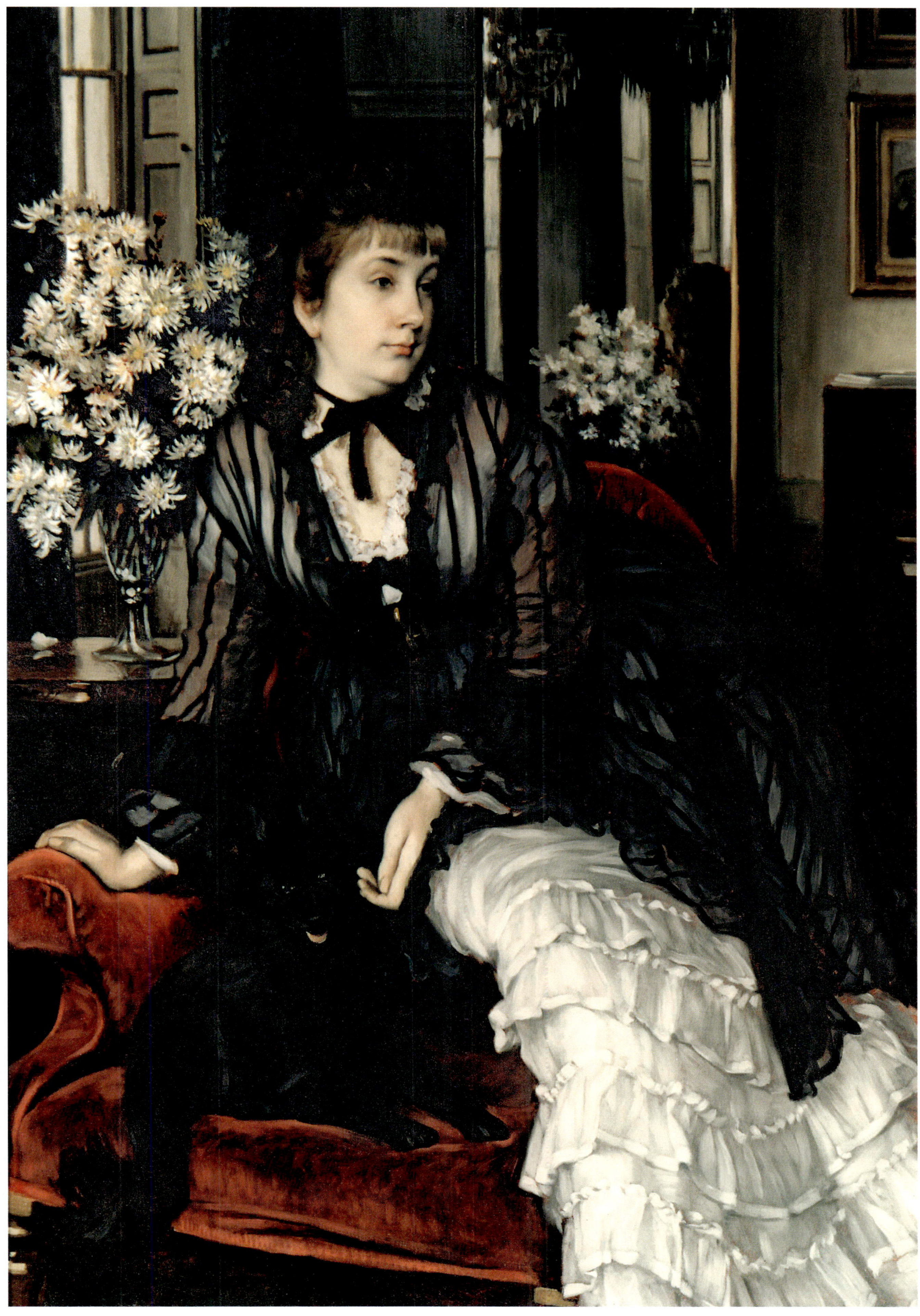

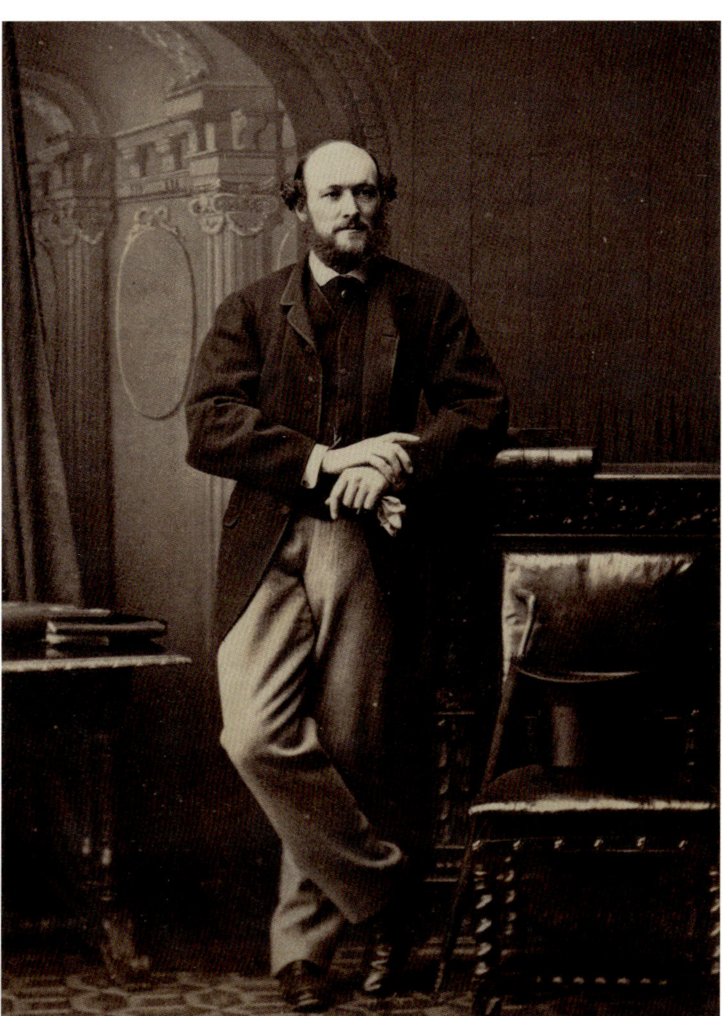

FIGURE 53
Camille Silvy (French, 1834–1910), *George Longley*, 1860s. Albumen print, 3¼ × 2¼ in. (8.3 × 5.7 cm). National Portrait Gallery, London, Given by John Webster, 2007, NPG Ax137924

FIGURE 54
James Tissot, *Portrait of Laure Hayman*, 1883. Location unknown

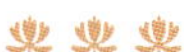

Before his return to Paris, Tissot executed some ten more portraits along these lines. An exception was that of Empress Eugénie and the Prince Imperial (pl. 28), begun in 1874[23] and sold in 1875 for 17,500 francs, making it Tissot's greatest portrait sale thus far.[24] With the portrait of the empress and the prince, Tissot explored, as he had in the portraits of the Miramons and the Circle of the Rue Royale, how a portrait might be introduced naturally into a landscape. A very fine series of autumn garden scenes followed this painting (see pls. 48 and 52). Conversely, Tissot sometimes inserted portrait-like figures—often recognizable to contemporary viewers—into his scenes of modern life, as Krystyna Matyjaszkiewicz demonstrated in the cases of *The Ball on Shipboard* (pl. 71), *The Concert* or *Hush!* (pl. 45), and *The Last Evening* (pl. 69).[25]

The end of the decade brought a turning point, with Tissot receiving fewer requests for portraits and instead using his lover, Kathleen Newton, and her children as his only models. Independently of any commissioned work, Tissot began freely painting very large figures. These works' monumental size, associated with the format of history paintings, was accompanied by a new formulation of allegorical language. Works like *October* (pl. 84), *Spring (Specimen of a Portrait)* (pl. 78), *Summer* (pl. 58), and *Winter* or *Mavourneen* (pl. 73), followed by the compositions *Quiet* (ca. 1881; private collection) and *The Garden Bench* (pl. 104), are as much homages to Newton's beauty as they are meditations on the seasons, innocence, and time—this last would soon take the young woman's life. With these paintings, Tissot returned to his truly modern ambition of the 1860s: to make portraits that were unarguably *paintings*.

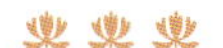

Tissot's move back to Paris, in late 1882, inaugurated his last and particularly fortunate period as a portraitist. Over the next ten years, he would execute nearly thirty portraits, most in pastel. The genre must have allowed the painter—forgotten by the French after ten years in England—to reestablish himself. In 1883, for example, one of the first portraits Tissot made after his return was one of a famous courtesan, Laure Hayman (fig. 54).[26] Easily navigating both the *demimonde* and the high society to which he now belonged, and well regarded as a painter of women after his much-publicized series *La Femme à Paris* (pls. 117–130), Tissot began attracting commissions for portraits of rich Parisiennes. These included portraits of Madame Robert de Bonnières (née Henriette Arnaud-Jeanti), whose literary salon was attended by the writer and Tissot's friend Alphonse Daudet;[27] Madame Ernest May (née Marie Ferré), wife of the collector of Impressionist canvases;[28] and the Comtesse Pillet-Will (née Clotilde Briatte) (pl. 34), wife of the director of the Bank of France.

Around 1890, Tissot reconnected with his youth when he made two portraits of the Marquis de Miramon's daughter, Geneviève, now Vicomtesse de Montmorand,[29] as well as portraits of Aimé Seillière's niece and nephew, Christine Bordères-Seillière and her brother René.[30] The French public now regularly saw Tissot's portraits at the Salon of the Société nationale des Beaux-Arts and at the gallery of his art dealer, Georges Petit, as well as at exhibitions of the Société des aquarellistes français and, later, the Société des pastellistes, of which Tissot was a founder-member. The most

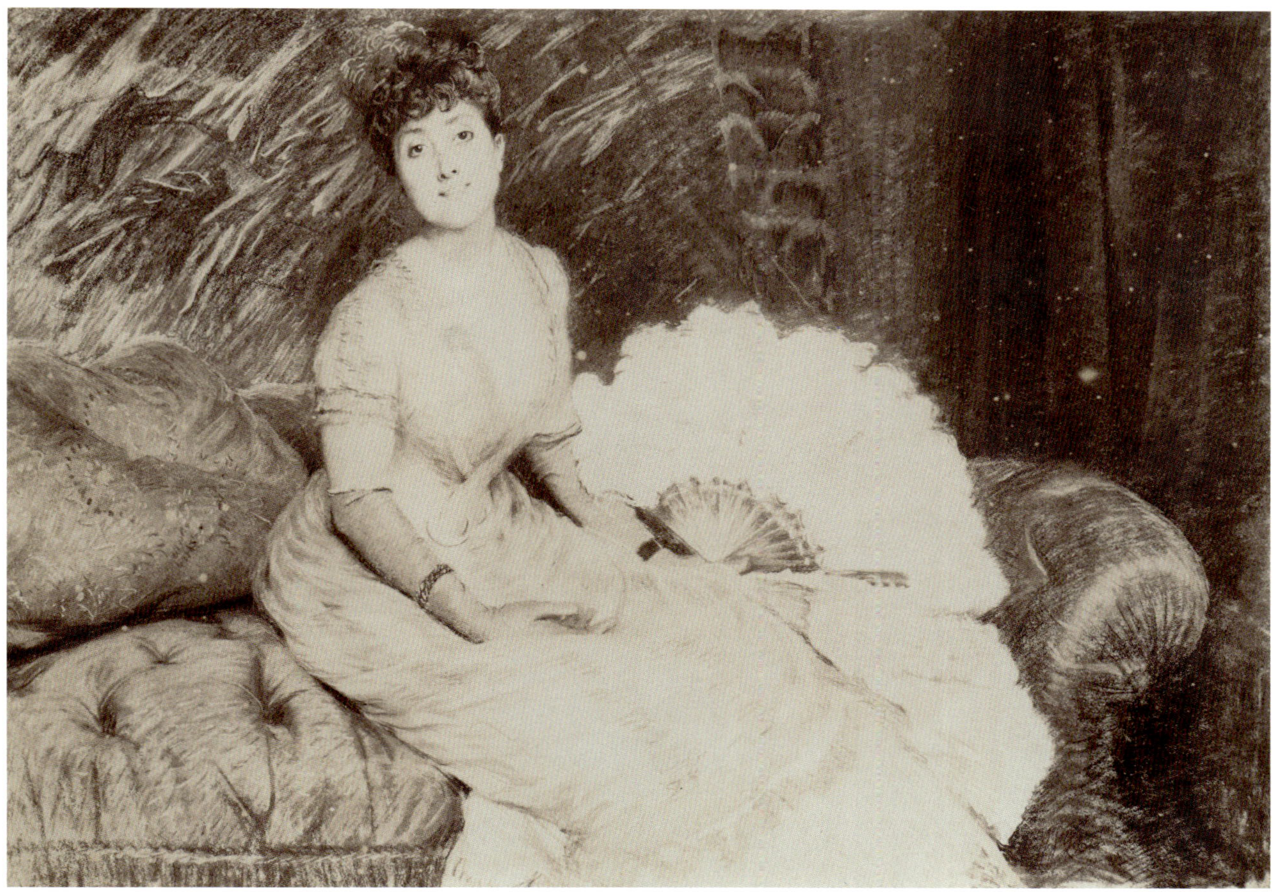

successful of these late portraits is perhaps that of the flamboyant Marie Say, Princesse de Broglie, heiress to a sugar fortune (pl. 33).[31] Using a Japonisme-style vertical format, Tissot organized around the princess's elegant and subtly off-center contours a play of full and empty spaces, geometric and organic shapes, lively colors and pastel tones. A far cry from the atmospheric effects, mannerist deformations, and graphic stylizations dominating French portraiture at the end of the century, Tissot's strong drawing and mastery of rendering textures was a form of Ingresque classicism. That reference, from his year at the École des Beaux-Arts as a student of Jean-Auguste-Dominique Ingres's pupil Louis Lamothe, would endure. In the evening of his life, Tissot painted a grisaille copy of Ingres's *Portrait of Madame de Senonnes* (see figs. 26–27), which he admired in his youth at Nantes's Musée des Beaux-Arts. The artist's last public appearance as a portraitist was at the Salon of 1893, with the portraits of Madame Robert de Bonnières and the Comtesse d'Yanville and her children.[32] The exhibition at the next year's Salon, of a first series of illustrations for Tissot's *The Life of Christ* (see Buron, this volume), would mark a new phase in the painter's late life and signal the end of his public career in portraiture.

TISSOT AND FASHION

JUSTINE DE YOUNG

The son of a milliner and a *marchand de nouveautés*, or "seller of the latest dress items," James Tissot grew up in a household attuned to fashion.[1] His portraits, which he painted throughout most of his career, consistently depicted sitters in fashionable dress. In both his portraits and his genre paintings, he became renowned for his highly detailed depictions of clothing. Yet, while the paintings might appear to be superficial renderings of contemporary fashion, Tissot did not merely translate detail into paint. Indeed, when they were first exhibited, many of his paintings caused controversy due to their divergence from bourgeois conventions, thus dramatizing how fashion influenced the ways in which women of the period were perceived. Nineteenth-century critics were quick to conflate dress with character, using any sartorial deviations to cast doubt on a woman's class and respectability.[2] Moreover, Tissot's repetition of dresses and accessories—and also models—suggests an artistic fascination with perfecting the familiar rather than the fashionable. Through this repetition, the paintings illustrate how the same dress or even the same woman could be perceived differently, depending on context.

❧ ❧ ❧

Tissot began his career in the mid-1850s, painting not contemporary life and dress but costumes for imagined scenes set in the past, inspired by the highly detailed medievalist compositions of painters such as Henri Leys and Ary Scheffer (see Baetens, this volume, and Frederick, this volume).[3] From about 1868 to 1875, he also created works depicting eighteenth-century life. But whatever the period, Tissot seemed to glory in meticulously transcribing details of dress and setting. His technical mastery is equally evident in his modern-life works. About the painting *The Last Evening* (pl. 69), for example, the critic for the *Illustrated London News* remarked, "He will paint a ship's rigging with as much mechanical precision and zest as a young lady's countenance."[4]

At the 1864 Paris Salon, Tissot exhibited *The Two Sisters; Portrait* (pl. 21), which features a young woman in a white muslin gown with sheer sleeves standing alongside her younger sister. The French art critic Théophile Thoré praised the portrait for its realism but also for its departure from convention, deeming the young woman "a model of elegance, nobility and simplicity . . . in a modest and dignified pose. . . . We are far from fashionable portraits, with their pretentious airs and their brilliant attire!"[5] Tissot's other Salon work that year—a portrait of the unknown Mademoiselle L. L., wearing a red Zouave jacket and black taffeta skirt—received a far less glowing assessment, though her look was extremely fashionable for the day (pl. 22).[6] The messy yet luxurious room and informal posture of Mademoiselle L. L., perched "negligently"[7] on the edge of her table, made her morally suspect, with one critic remarking that "these expertly rendered accessories, this fancy furniture, this elegant interior, no longer exude the healthy scent of the family."[8] Audiences were evaluating not only fashionability but also respectability and class. Wearing fashionable clothes was not enough to win acceptance or approval; the character of the setting and the comportment of the sitter also mattered.

Many of Tissot's modern-life paintings subtly evoke the frisson of the forbidden, hinting at the allure of the mistress more than of the wife or mother. Between 1868 and 1869, he created at least four genre scenes featuring a white-caped peignoir with fashionable ball fringe, including *Melancholy* (pl. 13), *The Staircase* (pl. 14), *Young Women Looking at Japanese Objects* (pl. 38), and *Young Women Looking at the Chinese Temple* (pl. 37). The intimacy of the setting as well as the sensual allure of the peignoir invited critics to imagine the body beneath it—the accuracy of its rendering became an alibi for close inspection and delectation. The details of both dress and décor in these works were so precise that a critic for *L'Artiste* declared: "Our industrial and artistic creations may perish, our customs and our costumes may fall into oblivion, a painting by Mr. Tissot will be enough for the archaeologists of the future to reconstruct our era."[9]

❧ ❧ ❧

In 1871, after his move to London, Tissot began to repeat himself with greater frequency, developing a repertoire of favorite looks. He seems to have fixated on a set of dresses not for their fashionability but for their formal characteristics—he especially favored stripes, ruffles, and sheer muslin, which were challenging to paint and showcased his talent. This is perhaps most obviously demonstrated by his repetition of a white muslin dress with yellow silk ribbons, seen in *July (Specimen of a Portrait)* (fig. 58), *Spring (Specimen of a Portrait)* (pl. 78), and a half-dozen other works (see Tétart-Vittu, this volume).

Tissot's tendency to repeat dresses is dramatically on display in *The Ball on Shipboard* (pl. 71), which is remarkable for its repetitions both *within* the piece and for its overlap with other works; every dress represented in the painting appears in at least one other work by Tissot. While these dresses were fashionable for the time, their repetition in other works suggests that Tissot enjoyed the technical challenge perhaps even more than the trends themselves. One example is the gray-and-white-striped dress with a black velvet bodice seen in the left foreground of *The Ball on Shipboard*. A very similar look, in blue, appeared in the pages of a Societé des journaux modes réunis publication that same year, proof of its fashionability (fig. 55). The same dress also appears in Tissot's *London Visitors* (pl. 56) and *Gravesend* (also known as *Waiting for the Ferry at the Falcon Tavern*, pl. 62). The pallid blue muslin dresses in the background of *The Ball on Shipboard* reappear in *Afternoon Tea* (also known as *In the Conservatory*, pl. 54), also painted in 1874.

Diverging from social conventions around dress could provoke harsh condemnation by critics, as Tissot discovered when *The Ball on Shipboard* was exhibited at the Royal Academy. The low neckline of the blue muslin dress made it inappropriate for an afternoon event (an error Tissot corrects in *Afternoon Tea*). This daring daytime exposure of décolletage likely prompted the critic for *The Athenaeum* to write that Tissot "has given us no pretty women, but a set of rather showy than elegant costumes, some few graceful, but more ungraceful attitudes, and not a lady in a score of female figures."[10] The *Illustrated London News* deemed the work "garish and almost repellant."[11] The critic for *Tablet* was perhaps the most scathing, writing, "The girls who are spread about in every attitude are evidently the 'high life below stairs' of the port, who have borrowed their mistresses' dresses for the nonce."[12]

Notably, the aspect of *The Ball on Shipboard* that most disturbs and attracts viewers today—what some scholars have referred to as the "decidedly unrealistic" and "strange repetition" of women in identical costumes—is never mentioned by Victorian critics.[13] Many theories have been proposed to explain the repetition, from attributing it to an ironic commentary on conformity, an imitation of fashion plates, or a kind of stop-motion photographic effect.[14] In fact, it simply was not considered strange in the nineteenth century for women to dress alike. Sisters often dressed identically, as can be seen in hundreds of surviving *carte de visite* photos as well as Berthe Morisot's portrait *The Sisters* (fig. 56). Indeed, British fashion trendsetter Princess Alexandra (later Queen Alexandra of England) and her sister, Dagmar (later Tsarina Maria Feodorovna of Russia), had dressed identically for six weeks in 1873.[15] Critics often lamented Tissot's repetition of models and settings; if his repetition of dresses within the same work was similarly remarkable, they doubtless would have pointed it out.[16]

Around 1876, Tissot began a relationship with Irish divorcée Kathleen Newton and began to paint her repeatedly. In these compositions, Newton occasionally wears dresses previously worn by studio models, but Tissot mostly seems to paint her in her own clothes, with the same pieces

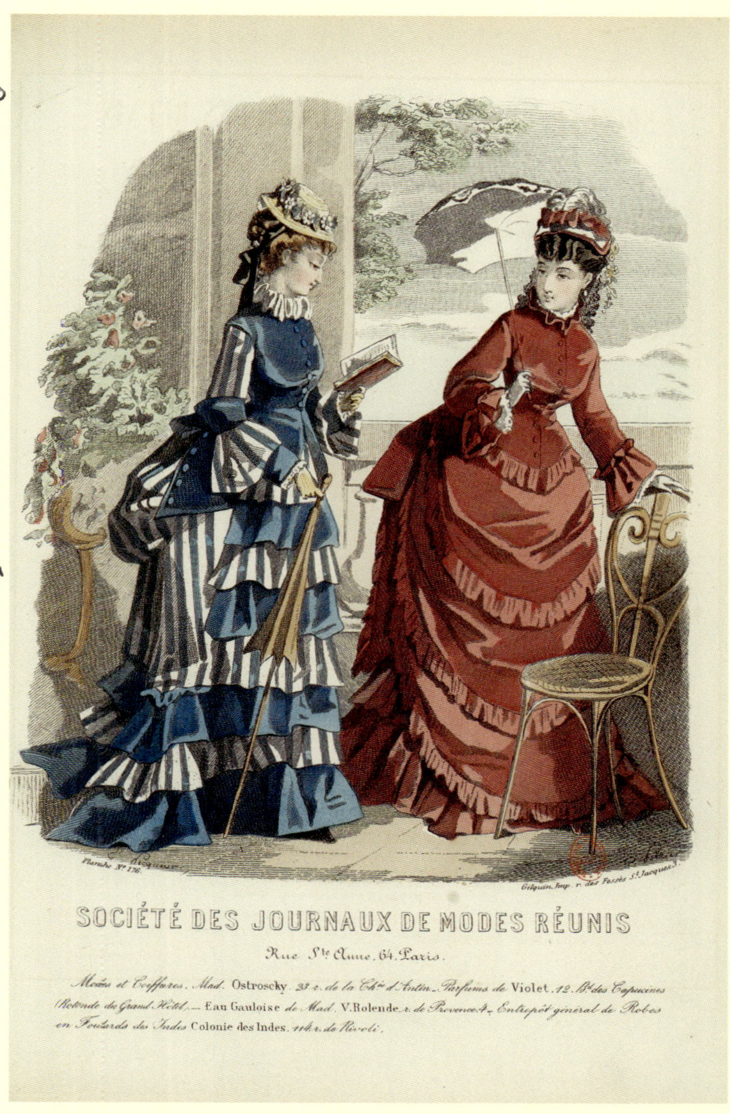

FIGURE 55
Fashion plate published by the Société des journaux de modes réunis, no. 176, May 9, 1874. Bibliothèque Nationale de France, Paris

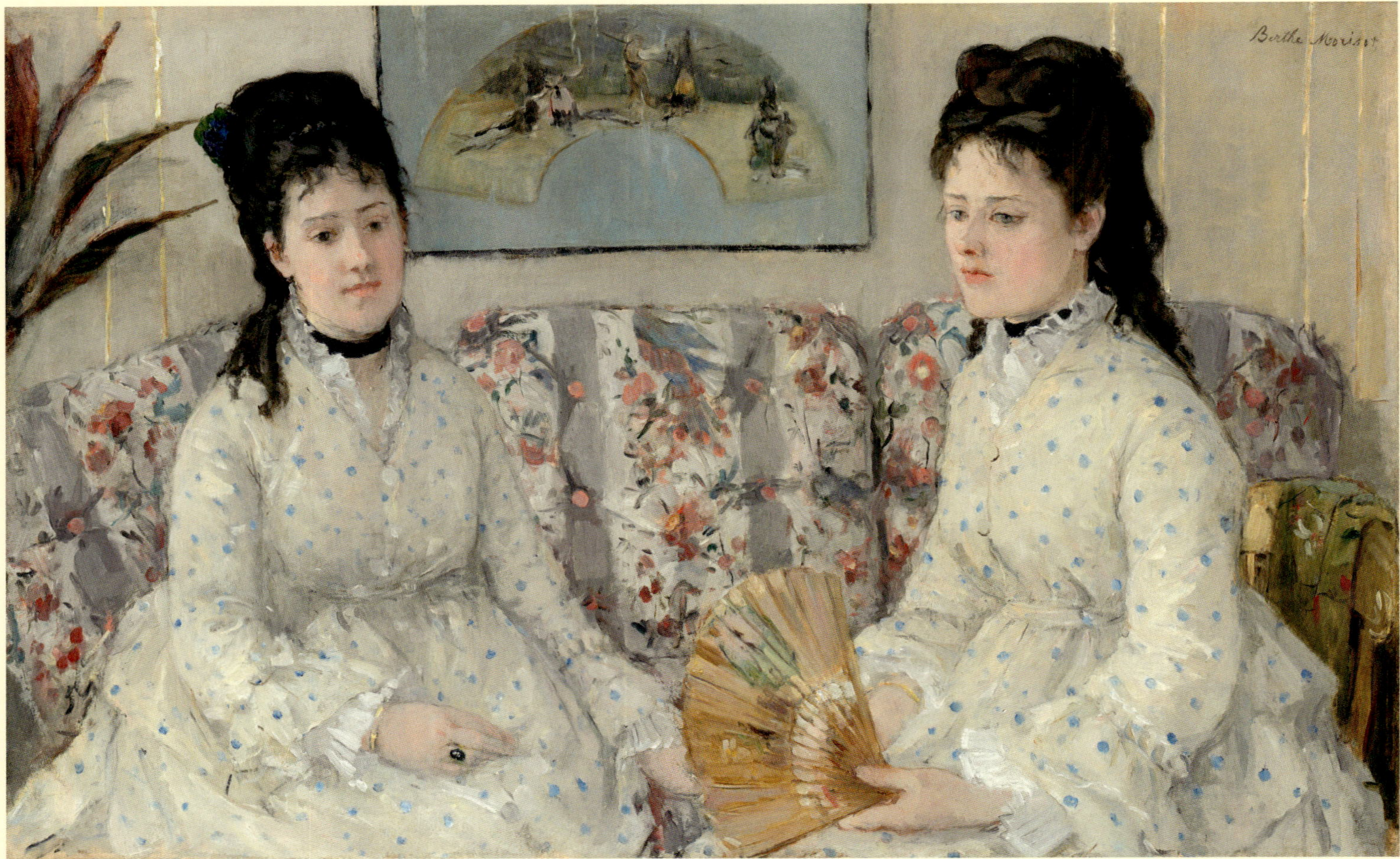

recurring frequently; a carrick coat, green plaid dress, and black princess-line dress—featured in *The Hammock* (fig. 118) and *Orphans* (pl. 85)—appear most often. Even though Newton's clothes in general conform to the predominant silhouette of the period, the painter's interest is clearly more in the model, the setting, and the storytelling than in the details of her dress. Reviewers interpreted the "'smart' vulgarity" of works like *The Hammock*—with its languid, sensual, and sunlit protagonist—as intended to "satirize the British plutocracy," and constructed imagined narratives of the illicit *demimonde* connoted by the canvases.[17]

Tissot's *La Femme à Paris* series (pls. 117–130), painted between 1883 and 1885, after Newton's death and the painter's return to Paris, was meant to depict various types of French women; French critics, however, nearly uniformly perceived the women as English rather than French. One critic wrote, "The woman he paints is a woman from the banks of the Thames. She has not yet the grace and elegance of the real Parisienne."[18] The pink dress in one painting from the series, *Political Woman* (pl. 124), was particularly singled out as completely unfashionable.[19] Punning on the French title for the work, *L'ambitieuse*, a critic for the fashion-savvy illustrated paper *La Vie Parisienne* outlined the dress's deficiencies: "She clearly does not have the ambition to be described as elegant, wearing one of those pink gowns that you wish would finish but never do, of antiquated cut, without any bustle, but with a pointed black belt like those worn twenty years ago."[20] *La Femme à Paris* marks the end of Tissot's depiction of fashionable life in his genre paintings. His almost devotional manner of rendering, enthusiasm for historic costume, and love of repetition would find their ultimate fulfillment in the biblical watercolors that consumed the final decades of his life (see Buron, this volume).

FIGURE 56
Berthe Morisot (French, 1841–1895), *The Sisters*, 1869. Oil on canvas, 20½ × 32 in. (52.1 × 81.3 cm). National Gallery of Art, Washington, DC, Gift of Mrs. Charles S. Carstairs, 1952.9.2

A SUMMER DRESS WITH YELLOW RIBBONS

FRANÇOISE TÉTART-VITTU

In spite of the success that James Tissot garnered among the social elite of his day, some critics still denigrated his fastidiously detailed work as being more akin to a photographic reality than to a creative vision. But, in fact, Tissot, a friend of Edgar Degas, Claude Monet, and Alfred Stevens, was precisely in step with contemporary painters who were fascinated by modern life—especially by women, with their finery and fashions. This tendency conformed to the ideas of Théophile Gautier, who in 1858 was already extolling a modern vision of feminine apparel,[1] and to the concept of modernity famously championed by Charles Baudelaire, who wrote that

> it is much easier to decide outright that everything about the garb of an age is absolutely ugly than to devote oneself to the task of distilling from it the mysterious element of beauty that it may contain, however slight or minimal that element may be. By "modernity" I mean the ephemeral, the fugitive, the contingent, the half of art whose other half is the eternal and the immutable.[2]

The painters of the 1863 Salon des refusés, including those later called the Impressionists, offered up their takes on the modern Parisian woman in works such as Monet's *Camille (The Woman in the Green Dress)* (1866; Kunsthalle Bremen, Germany), which exhibited at the 1866 Paris Salon; Pierre-Auguste Renoir's *The Parisian* (1874; National Museum Wales, Cardiff), shown at the Salon in 1874; and Édouard Manet's *The Parisian* (1875; Nationalmuseum, Stockholm), displayed at the Salon in 1875.[3] Like these Impressionist works, Tissot's modern-dress paintings remain essential references for fashion historians as well as for exhibitions on nineteenth-century fashion, Impressionism, and, of course, the painter himself.[4]

The son of merchants who sold clothing and hats, Tissot was intimately familiar with fabrics (see Sciama, this volume). His move to Paris in the mid-1850s and his work in the studios of Hippolyte Flandrin and Louis Lamothe (where he may have met Degas) placed him in contact with decorative painting and acquainted him with genres finding success at the Salon, including historical paintings inspired by seventeenth-century Flemish or German works, where precision in costumery was a major element.[5] As part of an elite artistic crowd, Tissot was also introduced into aristocratic circles by the Marquis de Miramon. He painted the marquis's family in 1865 (pl. 23), and the marquise in a dressing gown in 1866 (pl. 24), which led to a commission to paint the group portrait *The Circle of the Rue Royale* (pl. 27) that same year. Tissot, a painter in vogue, now seemed to be following the example of Stevens, who was finding great success painting young women dressed in the latest styles. Unlike contemporaries such as Charles-Édouard Boutibonne or Auguste Toulmouche, whose familiar compositions simply recalled the fashion plates of the period, Stevens evoked an implicit reality that the viewer could interpret.

At the 1867 Exposition Universelle, at which Tissot showed *Portrait of the Marquise de Miramon, née Thérèse Feuillant*, Stevens presented eighteen paintings with as many variations on dresses, each used for its color on essentially interchangeable women. So central was the role of the dress that Stevens repeatedly used the same attire for different compositions. It is easy to spot these repetitions. For instance, in works dating from the mid- to late 1860s, a certain yellow silk dress with a low neckline and little cap sleeves is used as an outer dress or covered by a gauzy white muslin dress, which the model is shown removing in *The Studio* (1869; Musées royaux des Beaux-Arts de Belgique, Brussels), and which Stevens had also used in *In the Country* (fig. 57) and *Ophelia: The Tattered Bouquet* (ca. 1865–1867; Musées royaux des Beaux-Arts de Belgique, Brussels).[6] In Paris, Tissot moved in the same circles as the Stevens brothers—Alfred, the artist; and Arthur, an art dealer in Paris and Brussels—and surely admired the Belgian painter's use of clothing and repetition, as we can infer from Tissot's similar compositions at that time, such as *Young Women Looking at Japanese Objects* (pl. 38).[7]

In 1871, in the wake of the Franco-Prussian War, Tissot moved to London, where he focused on painting outdoor city and contemporary genre scenes that featured modern fashion. Ascribing to Baudelaire's concept of fleeting modernity, Tissot seemed to be heeding the poet's call to extract the "hidden beauty" from modern dress. Perhaps also inspired by the commercial practices of the fashion industry, which used drawing and, later, photography in order to document multiple angles of a piece of clothing, Tissot often showed the same dress in different contexts in his work. Identical dresses are seen repeatedly in many of his paintings dating from the 1870s. For instance, a black-and-white dress appears in both *The Ball on Shipboard* (pl. 71) and *Reading the News* (1874; private collection), and the same pink ball gown, with different bodices, can be seen in both *Afternoon Tea* (also known as *In the Conservatory*, pl. 54) and *Too Early* (pl. 46).

From 1874 to 1878, Tissot particularly favored variations of a summer dress in white muslin with yellow silk bows. A morning-gown version is worn by the lovesick women in *The Coming Storm* (1874; Beaverbrook Art Gallery, Fredericton, New Brunswick) and *The Convalescent* (pl. 48), and an elegant afternoon-dress version, with a hat, features in *The Gallery of HMS "Calcutta" (Portsmouth)* (pl. 64) and *Summer* (pl. 58). The afternoon dress was also chosen for two *intimiste* portraits of Tissot's companion, the divorcée Kathleen Newton: *July (Specimen of a Portrait)* (fig. 58) and *Spring (Specimen of a Portrait)* (pl. 78). This dress, composed of a tunic with pleated tails and a straight skirt garnished with a cascade of flounces, was typical of contemporary style. In these works, the delicacy of the semitransparent fabric, the abundance of frills and pleats, and the undone ribbons allowed Tissot to showcase his unique ability to depict challenging details. The bright yellow, reserved for the ribbons, recalls effects achieved by Stevens, who skillfully used vibrant color as a way to differentiate similar scenes. The choice of color was significant: yellow was a feminine color, a bit provocative, and above all hugely fashionable at the time. Had not the couturier Charles Frederick Worth imposed yellow ball gowns even on Empress Eugénie?[8]

In 1859, Charles Blanc, an art critic and professor of aesthetics, published his reflections on fashion in the *Gazette des Beaux-Arts*, in which he remarked on the evocative power of dress: "It is natural, in fact, that man, after having become accustomed to attaching certain ideas to a garment, can no longer revive it without being penetrated by the ideas that this garment represents." Blanc's work was well known by artists, and the topic of ancient and modern costume was of current interest for portraitists and theater designers.[9] Tissot demonstrates the concept by using similar dresses to different effect in various paintings. In 1878, a yellow satin dress covered in flounces, modeled by Newton, appears in *Evening* (also known as *The Ball*, pl. 79). Here, Tissot's choice of yellow symbolizes the triumph of life, the radiance of a beautiful woman as she joins a festive gathering, rather than the yellow synonymous with frailty or a fallen woman. Further playing on color symbolism, Tissot presented another version of this dress in *Political Woman* (pl. 124), this time choosing a brilliant pink that evokes an ambitious cocotte, a risqué impression underscored by the addition of a wide black belt that resembles a corset.

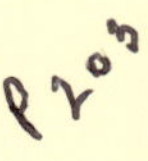

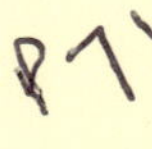

This technique is employed again by Tissot when he reuses a version of the ribboned summer outfit in *The Gala Day–Seaside* (also known as *A Fête Day at Brighton*, pl. 81), dated ca. 1877–1878. Here, the dress is transparent white with blue ribbons, and is worn by a joyous young woman walking down the street and carrying a large bouquet. This painting, too, may be a depiction of Kathleen Newton; Tissot and Newton visited Brighton in the spring of 1877, and blue was said to be her favorite color.[10] The blue contributes to the gaiety of the scene, and is a marker of happy days. The reappearance of the ribbons draws a common thread between this intimate portrait and the others, allowing the painter to anchor the fleeting moments of the daily life of his beloved, thus capturing the ephemeral nature of beauty.

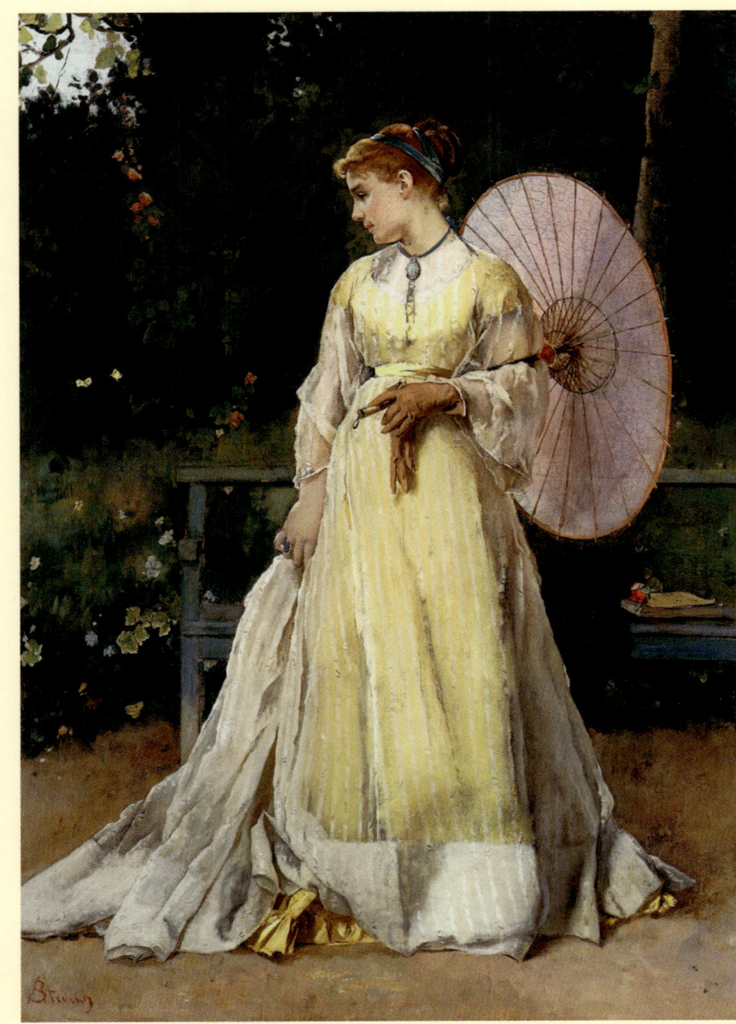

FIGURE 57
Alfred Stevens (Belgian, 1823–1906), *In the Country*, ca. 1867. Oil on canvas, 30¾ × 22 in. (78 × 56 cm). Private collection

FIGURE 58
James Tissot, *July (Specimen of a Portrait)*, 1878. Oil on canvas, 34 × 23⅝ in. (86.2 × 60 cm). Private collection

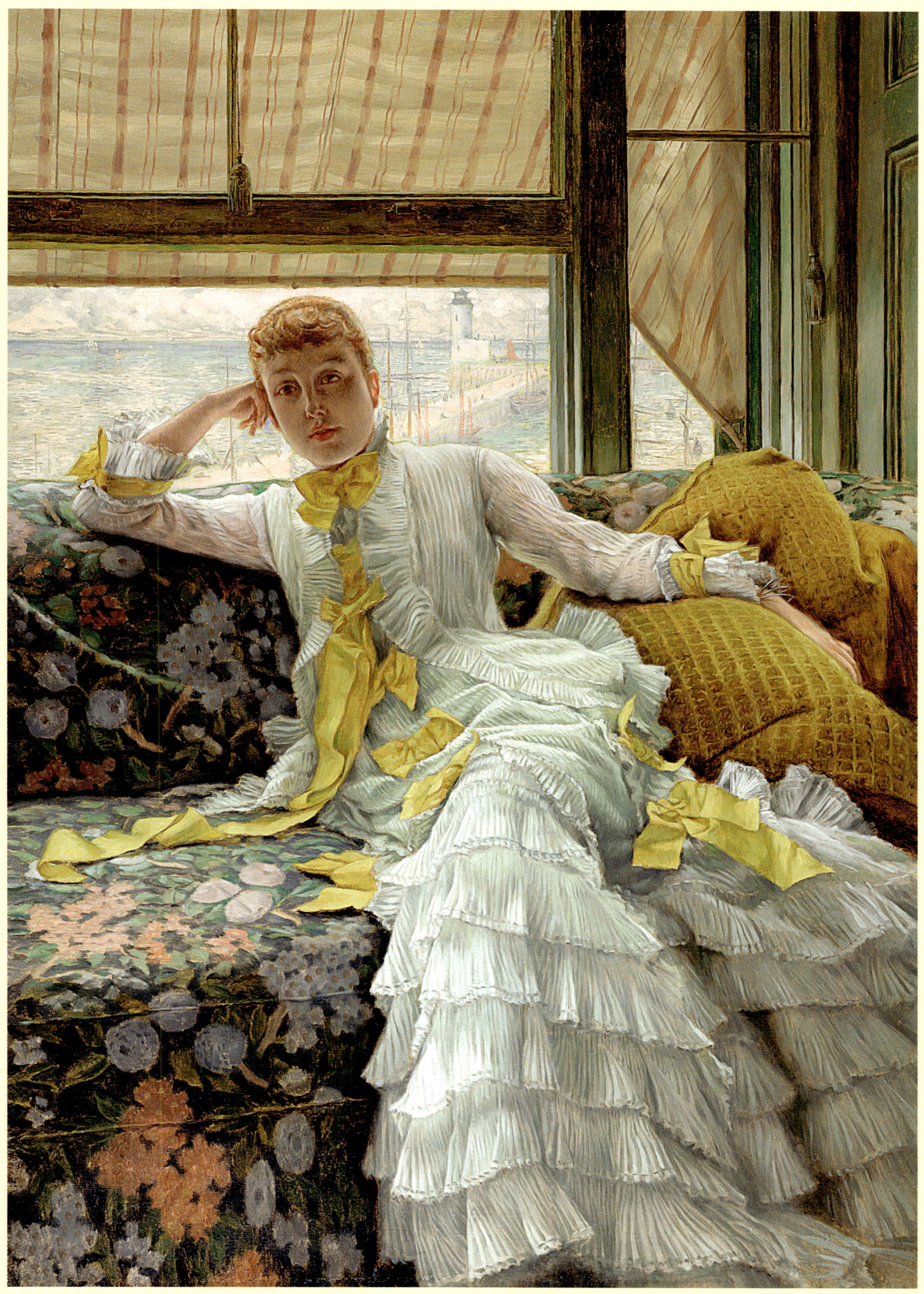

3x2

A SUMMER DRESS WITH YELLOW RIBBONS

MELISSA E. BURON

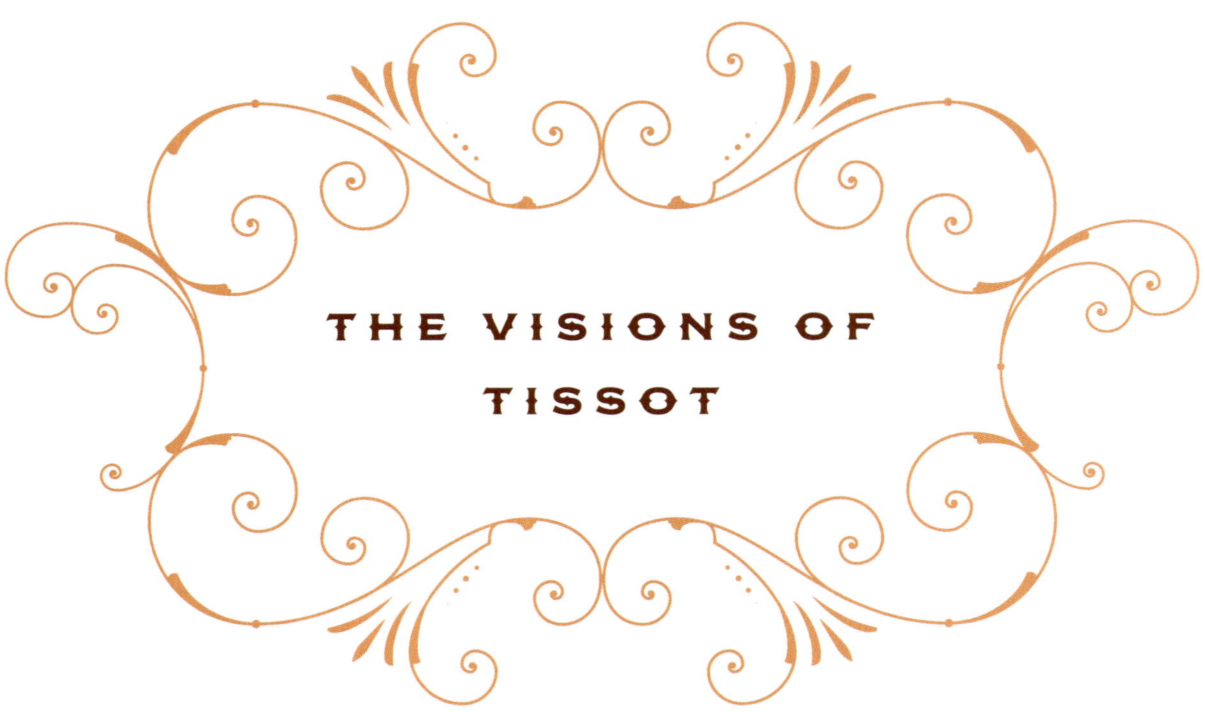

THE VISIONS OF TISSOT

THE NAME JAMES TISSOT evokes depictions of fashionably dressed women and debonair men, images that seem to celebrate materiality over spirituality, yet Tissot's most personally meaningful work was as a visionary religious artist. From 1885 until his death, in 1902, he was consumed by an extraordinary campaign to meticulously research and illustrate the Bible, ultimately creating hundreds of watercolors depicting scenes from the Old Testament (pls. 134–139) and the New Testament, the latter under the series title *The Life of Our Saviour Jesus Christ* or *The Life of Christ* (pls. 144–156).[1] Today, the colloquially named "Tissot Bible" illustrations are among the artist's least-known creations, although they brought him more fame and commercial success than any other work during his lifetime. Despite their underestimation, their legacy endures in popular culture, most notably in film (see Robert, this volume). This deeply personal magnum opus was Tissot's most ambitious artistic effort. A greater appreciation of its historical context, meaning, and influence can be attained by interpreting it through the lenses of nineteenth-century European trends such as Spiritualism and the French Catholic revival.

Raised and educated in the Roman Catholic tradition, Tissot expressed a renewed interest in the religion as well as in Spiritualism following the death of his companion and muse, Kathleen Newton, in 1882.[2] Spiritualism and its French counterpart, Spiritism, were complex socioreligious belief systems popular in the late nineteenth century that attempted to scientifically prove the existence of the afterlife.[3] Spiritualism looked beyond Judeo-Christian concepts of the hereafter by conducting rituals such as séances and presenting "evidence" of direct communication between the living and the dead, such as table rapping and slate writing.[4] After Newton's funeral, Tissot abandoned the London home they shared together, returned to Paris, and began attending Spiritualist séances in an attempt to make contact with her. Around this time, while attending mass at Paris's Church of Saint-Sulpice, Tissot also experienced a transformative religious vision, which inspired the painting *Inner Voices* or *Christ the Comforter* (also known as *The Ruins*, fig. 32) and, soon thereafter, his series of biblical watercolors. He publicly declared his Catholic faith in interviews and through his art while also continuing to explore the occult philosophy of Spiritualism.[5]

Ever the savvy businessman, Tissot quickly capitalized on how his personal narrative and his religious and spiritual convictions dovetailed with the zeitgeist of his time, resulting in a spectacular body of work that combines both Catholic- and Spiritualist-inspired visions. The merging of traditional religious imagery with the late nineteenth-century themes of Spiritualism, especially on such an ambitious scale, was particularly unique to Tissot. Although later art-historical evaluations have dismissed the significance of the "Tissot Bible," this work preoccupied the artist in the final years of his life, and it is more important to a thorough understanding of his career than previous scholarship has claimed.[6]

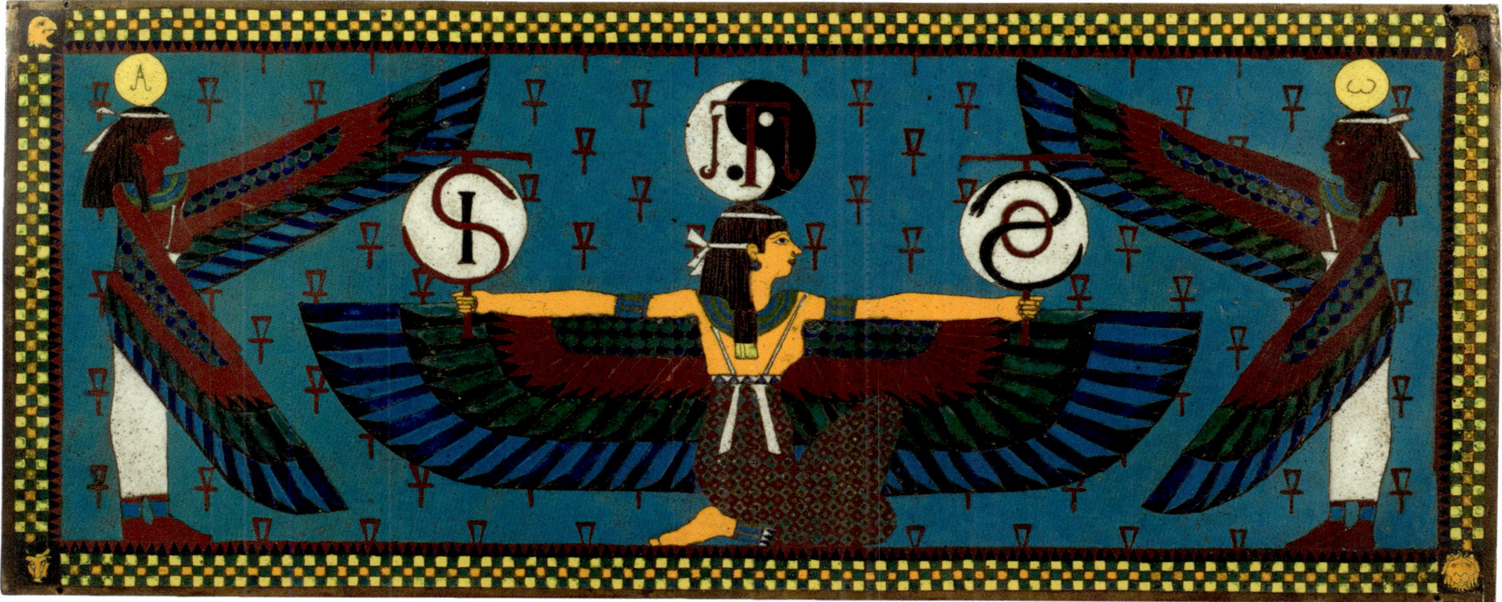

SPIRITUALIST VISIONS

Kathleen Newton died in London on November 9, 1882. Her niece Lilian Hervey recalled that afterward, a bereaved Tissot "draped her coffin in purple velvet and prayed beside it for hours."[7] In his journal, Edmond de Goncourt documented that a grieving Tissot left London and returned to Paris, visiting him on November 15.[8] It is not clear how long Newton had suffered from tuberculosis—also called consumption because it seemed to consume the invalid's body—but witnessing her decline surely distressed Tissot.[9] According to the artist Louise Jopling, it was Newton's death that stimulated Tissot's Spiritualist interests:

> At one time James Tissot was very hospitable, and delightful were the dinners he gave. But these ceased when he became absorbed in a *grande passion*. . . . After her death, he came across some spiritualists, who easily persuaded him that he could get into communication with his *chère amie*. . . He used to hold séances every afternoon, after his day's work was over.[10]

On May 20, 1885, Tissot attended a private séance in London, facilitated by the British medium William Eglinton.[11] At this séance, Eglinton purportedly materialized the deceased Newton along with the medium's spirit guide.[12] According to Eglinton:

> The figure of the One, lost and loved, appearing so distinctly as to be recognised not only by all the sitters present from her portraits . . . but by M. Tissot himself; and so much was this beyond question that he instantly transferred the whole scene to canvas, that he might retain it in his memory. In the "Apparition Médiunimique" . . . there are two figures, one the ascended friend of the eminent artist, the other being my guide "Ernest." As a portrayal of what actually took place, it is perfect in the extreme, no idealism of the painter being used to embellish it—all is shown as it happened, neither more nor less . . . a monument to the abiding truths of Spiritualism, and of the genius of one of its latest converts.[13]

The work that Eglinton refers to, the 1885 oil painting *The Apparition* (also known as *The Mediumistic Apparition*, pl. 133), re-creates this mysterious event. The representation of glowing spirits wrapped in shroud-like garments anticipates the mystical themes and motifs of Tissot's forthcoming biblical illustrations.[14] That same year, Tissot made an etching of Eglinton (pl. 131), which appeared as the frontispiece to the medium's biography, *'Twixt Two Worlds* (1886).[15] In this portrait, Eglinton's relaxed pose suggests a level of familiarity between artist and subject that indicates Tissot's confidence in the medium's abilities.

Volumes documenting the proceedings of the Society for Psychical Research found after Tissot's death at his estate, the Château de Buillon, confirm his sustained curiosity about Spiritualism and the occult.[16] A newspaper report covering the 1964 sale of Tissot's possessions described a collection of five thousand books, including publications demonstrating that Tissot

> had a weakness for ectoplasms, turntables, esotericism and spiritualism. Several hundreds of volumes are collected dealing with these subjects . . . the Empire-style tripod pedestal tables . . . may have been used for the invocation of spirits. One feels that James Tissot had brought back from his long stay in England a taste . . . for . . . ghosts haunting the romantic castles.[17]

THE MEDIUM'S MESSAGE

Contemporary accounts reveal that Tissot eagerly shared *The Apparition* with visitors, including Georges Bastard, one of his earliest biographers. Bastard describes "electric rays" emitting from the composition's figures; this effect is echoed later in Tissot's biblical watercolor *The Resurrection* (pl. 154), a depiction of the resurrected Messiah with incandescent stigmata.[18] Goncourt also reported seeing the work in a room where Tissot performed rituals:

> In the dusk, refusing to look for candles, with a voice which he made mysterious and a vague gaze, he showed us a crystal bowl and an enamel panel, which served at his conjurings. . . . He took up a convenient notebook, where he showed us entire pages containing the history of his conjurings, and he finally showed us a picture representing a woman with luminous hands, whom he said had come to embrace him.[19]

The panel that Goncourt describes may be a recently rediscovered cloisonné enamel made by Tissot that conflates Egyptian, Christian, and

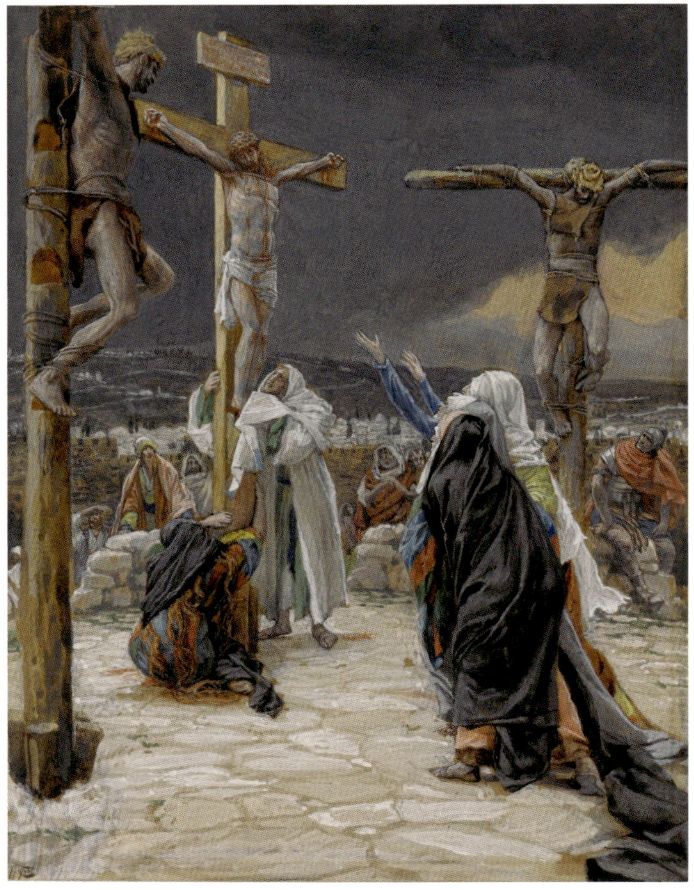

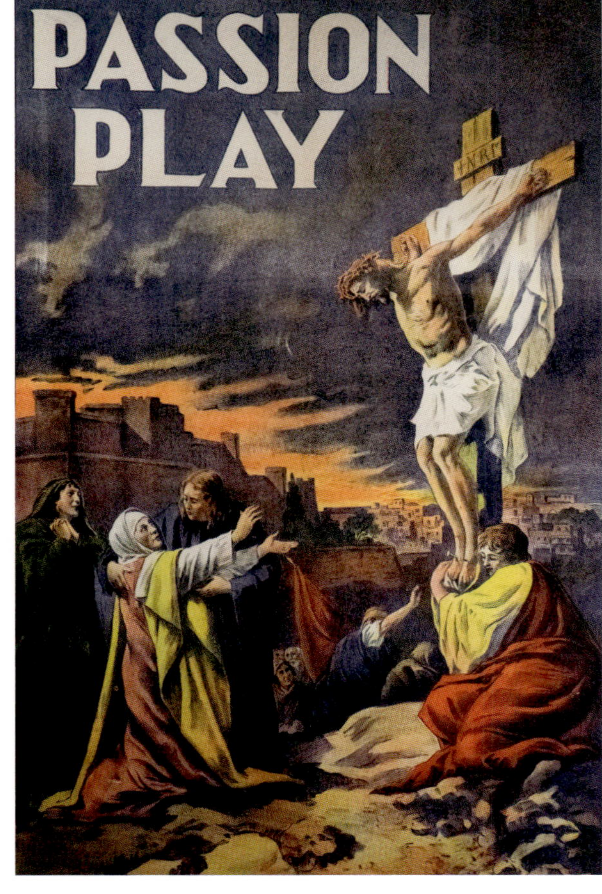

PREVIOUS PAGE, FIGURE 59
James Tissot, panel with theosophical symbols, 1888. Cloisonné enamel on copper, 6¾ × 16½ in. (17 × 42 cm). Private collection

FIGURE 60
James Tissot, *The Death of Jesus*, 1886–1894. Opaque watercolor over graphite on gray wove paper, 9⅝ × 7¼ in. (24.3 × 18.4 cm). Brooklyn Museum, Purchased by public subscription, 00.159.305

FIGURE 61
Poster for Henry C. Vincent's *Passion Play*, 1908. Lithograph, 48 × 30¾ in. (122 × 78 cm). Blackfriars Gallery, Dominican School of Philosophy & Theology, Berkeley

Chinese symbolism relating to the afterlife (fig. 59), demonstrating Tissot's knowledge of international and historical spiritual iconography.[20] Each of the panel's corners features the symbol of one of the four Christian Evangelists. The standing winged protectors of the dead are the Egyptian goddesses Nephthys and Isis, sisters of Osiris; the central figure is their mother, Nut, goddess of the sky, who often appeared on Egyptian coffins.[21] Tissot rendered the disk above Nut's head as the ancient Chinese yin and yang symbol, enhanced with his own monogram, "JTJ." In the background, stylized ankh signs represent both mortal existence and the afterlife.[22] This combination of diverse symbols reflects the late nineteenth-century European interest in alternative spiritualities, which borrowed concepts as well as iconography from a variety of belief systems.

Tissot also created a mezzotint version of *The Apparition* (pl. 132) that was described somewhat hyperbolically by Eglinton's biographer, John Farmer, as "the wonder and talk of the artistic world . . . a lasting monument of the artist's appreciation of the blessing bestowed by spirit communion."[23] Like the painting, Tissot's mezzotint depicts ethereal, luminescent spirits who seem to emerge from the darkness.[24] To create a mezzotint, an artist works from dark to light, coaxing images out from the background, much like a medium conjures illuminated materializations at a séance.[25] This overlap between the art-making process and the séance experience foreshadows Tissot's later claim of entering a trancelike state to compose his biblical compositions. In his introduction to *The Life of Christ*, he mused, "Is not the artist, indeed, a kind of sensitive plant . . . and through a kind of hyperaesthesia, is powerfully affected by contact with objects outside of itself; this contact producing vivid images on the brain?"[26] A disclaimer follows this reflection: "I will not enter here into the details of the brilliant light, almost amounting to divination . . . to do so would be to risk being accused of mysticism."[27] Despite his attempts to deflect allegations of mysticism, Tissot's characterization of his working method suggests that he felt empowered to manifest visions through his artistic compositions, just as mediums such as Eglinton reputedly made apparitions and spirit writing visible.

RELIGIOUS VISIONS

In 1885, Tissot described a profound religious experience in the Church of Saint-Sulpice that he credited with triggering his biblical illustration campaign.[28] Second in size only to Notre-Dame, Saint-Sulpice was famous for its enormous organ and for being one of Paris's "richest and . . . most important [churches] on the left bank of the Seine."[29] The church was also associated with fashionable contemporary society,[30] scientific inquiry,[31] and even—according to rumors in literary circles—occultism.[32] Tissot went there to research *Sacred Music* or *The Choir Singer*, a painting to be included in his *La Femme à Paris* series (pls. 117–130).[33]

According to Tissot, he went to Saint-Sulpice "more to catch the atmosphere for my picture than to worship," when, at the moment of transubstantiation—a sacred point in the Catholic mass when it is believed that bread and wine become Christ's body and blood—he witnessed a vision of Christ consoling a couple huddled together:

> It came about in a mysterious way—one that I do not pretend to understand . . . as the Host was elevated and I bowed my head and closed my eyes, I saw a strange and thrilling picture. . . . The vision pursued me even after I had left the church. . . . I tried to brush it away, but it returned insistently. Finally I was attacked by fever, and when I was well again I painted my vision.[34]

This vision, which Tissot depicted in *Inner Voices*, was not an anomaly; experiences of this sort belonged to a wider cultural context of reported spiritual visions that became popular as part of the nineteenth-century French Catholic revival, including the mystical visions of the eighteenth-century nun Anne Catherine Emmerich, which were published in the 1830s,[35] and the 1858 Marian apparitions at Lourdes to the peasant girl Bernadette Soubirous.[36] It is significant that *Inner Voices* may be Tissot's earliest depiction of Christ, who subsequently became a primary focus of the painter's work.

BIBLICAL WATERCOLORS

Tissot traveled through the Holy Land between October 1886 and March 1887, and returned there in 1888–1889. In 1894, he exhibited 270 watercolors and sketches from *The Life of Christ* at the Salon du Champ-de-Mars in Paris. All 365 New Testament watercolors were exhibited at the Lemercier Gallery, London, from 1896 to 1897, where they caused a public sensation. The Lemercier Gallery, at 35 New Bond Street, had been previously known as the Doré Gallery, after Gustave Doré exhibited twenty large-scale New Testament canvases there from 1868 to 1892. Tissot surely knew that placing his exhibition at this site would strategically position him as another prominent illustrator of the Bible.

The fervor over *The Life of Christ* watercolors increased as they toured from city to city. Accounts described that "people were seen to go away weeping; women made the tour of the rooms on their knees. . . . It partook, indeed, towards the end . . . the character of a pilgrimage."[37] Similar reports posited that

> rarely has any artistic exhibit created so profound an impression on the public. . . . Even the callous and the skeptical were observed to remove their hats as . . . they passed from one picture to the other . . . women were seen to sink down on their knees as though impelled by a superior force, and literally crawl round the rooms in this position, as though in adoration.[38]

This success coincided with the popularity of events such as the Oberammergau Passion Play in Bavaria, Germany, which had begun to attract "pilgrims" from other European countries as well as the United States.[39] Inaugurated in 1634, these performances featured spoken text, music, and tableaux vivants reenacting the Passion of Jesus—the period from his entry into Jerusalem up to his crucifixion. Tissot's biblical illustrations were even emulated by Passion Play advertisements, linking the two forms of religious spectacle (figs. 60–61).

The fame of Tissot's biblical works flourished after their 1898 arrival in the United States, as the series toured major cities such as Brooklyn, Philadelphia, Boston, Chicago, and Saint Louis.[40] In 1900, the Brooklyn Museum acquired *The Life of Christ* series (watercolors, plus pen-and-ink drawings and five oil sketches) by public subscription for 60,000 dollars.[41] The success of these New Testament subjects encouraged Tissot to return to the Holy Land in 1896 to prepare illustrations for the Old Testament, a series left incomplete when he died.[42] Previously unpublished glass-plate negatives and photographs discovered at the Château de Buillon reveal that he incorporated photography into his practice, asking models to pose for his subjects and using landscape photos as *aide-mémoires* so that he could later reproduce the scenes in watercolor (see figs. 13 and 14).[43]

Unrealized architectural designs by the French architect Henri Paul Nénot suggest that Tissot may also have planned to exhibit his biblical illustrations at the 1900 Exposition Universelle in Paris (figs. 62–63).[44] The title on the designs, "Musée des œuvres de James Tissot," indicates that a museum dedicated to the artist's work was possibly conceived to display *The Life of Christ* and the Old Testament watercolors together. Hundreds of biblical illustrations on display side by side would have been spectacular, but the sale of *The Life of Christ* to the Brooklyn Museum likely terminated these plans.

Tissot's religious works were popular with orthodox viewers, but Jopling observed that also "*The Life of Christ* was treated from a spiritualist's point of view, and very remarkable the drawings were . . . one picture of the dead Christ surrounded by a multitude of hands, with their fingers extended towards the Holy Body . . . had a weird, mystical effect, haunting in its beauty."[45] Indeed, this work, titled *Jesus Ministered to by Angels* (pl. 148), derives from a biblical narrative, but the otherworldly intercessors who reach for Christ's body with outstretched arms recall participants at a séance. A similar blend of orthodox and mystical symbolism occurs in *The Annunciation* (pl. 144), in which the Archangel Gabriel is depicted as a disembodied glowing face encased by semitransparent wings,

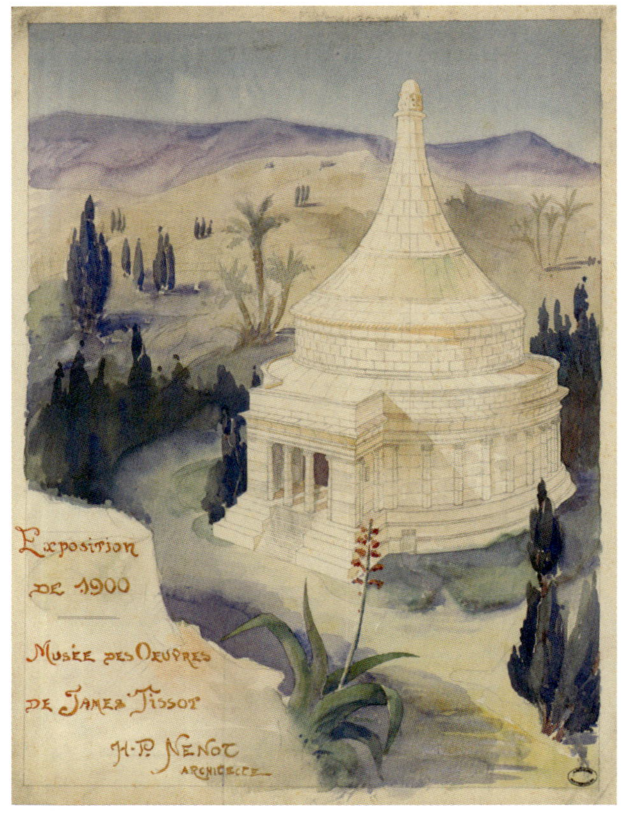

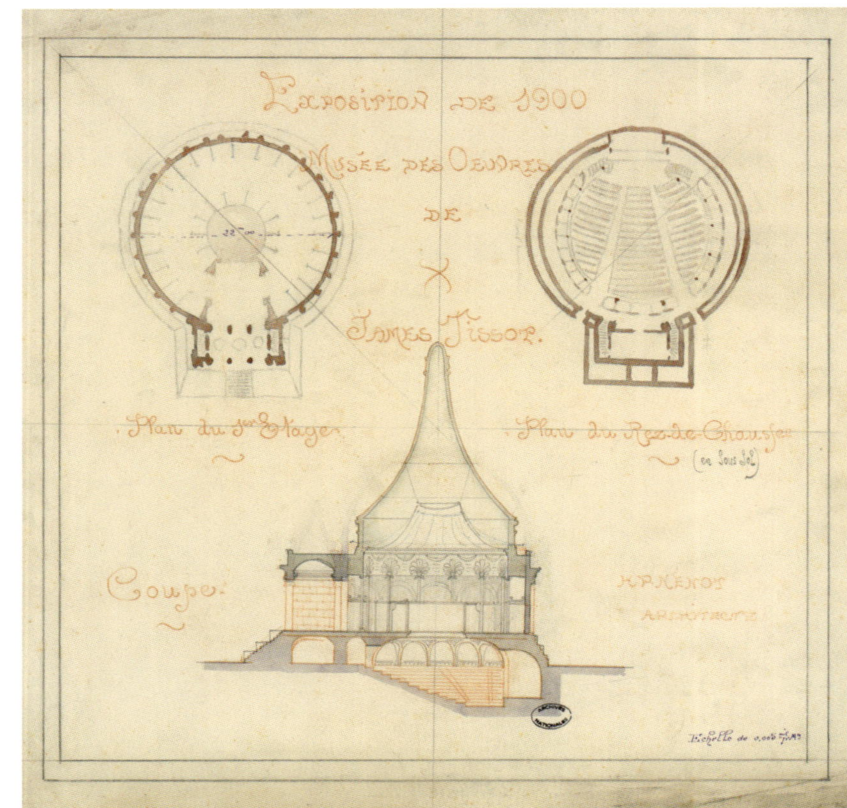

FIGURE 62
"Exposition de 1900. Musée des œuvres de James Tissot," perspective view, ca. 1895–1897. Pencil and watercolor on drawing paper, 25⅝ × 18⅞ in. (65 × 48 cm). Archives Nationales, Pierrefitte-sur-Seine, France, CP/F/12/4446/D/28

FIGURE 63
"Exposition de 1900. Musée des œuvres de James Tissot," plan for the first and ground floors, ca. 1895–1897. Pencil, orange pencil, and wash on drawing paper, 19¼ × 19⅞ in. (49 × 50.5 cm). Archives Nationales, Pierrefitte-sur-Seine, France, CP/F/12/4446/D/28

a departure from the traditional depiction of the Annunciation angel as a winged human form. The luminous aura surrounding the shrouded figure in *Jesus Walks on the Sea* (fig. 64) recalls *The Apparition* and anticipates Christ's glowing stigmata in *The Resurrection*. Although he borrowed tropes from centuries of religious art before him, Tissot was able to effectively fuse his traditional religious background and his esoteric occult interests into a unique visual vocabulary, resulting in powerful, highly original works imbued with multiple layers of meaning.

A self-portrait of Tissot, *Portrait of the Pilgrim* (pl. 157), appears as the final illustration in the published volumes of *The Life of Christ*, accompanied by a plea for the reader to pray for him.[46] Set in a dark, mysterious setting, the artist stands between a prominently displayed crucifix and a large wreath bearing his own monogram, surrounded by funereal religious articles, including two tall tapers, a draped coffin, and a silver aspersorium. His hand is lifted in a signal of blessing—a Christlike gesture typically used by religious officials.[47] Tissot, the artist—"a mystic and seer of visions"—thus rendered himself both an agent of benediction and a subject of prayer.[48]

CONCLUSION

Some descriptions of Tissot in his final years characterize him as "a man whose actions are not fully explainable in rational terms."[49] This period has been derided as ruinous and guilt-fueled; the writer Arnold Bennett claimed that Tissot considered himself to be Newton's murderer, leading to "the origin of his journey to Palestine and the ruin of his art."[50] The perception that Tissot's talent had collapsed, an impression that persisted after his death, rests largely on changing aesthetic views toward nineteenth-century religious art, and assessments that Tissot's works "are least worthy when he contrives to convey mysticism and supernatural power."[51] Perhaps the most scathing evaluation came from the preeminent twentieth-century Tissot scholar, Michael Wentworth:

> Tissot's religious pictures proved detrimental in their effect on his posthumous standing as an artist. . . . With their mediocrity looming monolithically in the immediate historical background, they continued to exert a baleful influence. . . . Their sanctimonious dullness antagonized the admirers of his earlier work beyond all patience, and their only lasting effect was to create a confusion about Tissot's aims and qualities as an artist which has persisted to this day, resulting in an aesthetic disrepute and diminished historical standing which is undeserved.[52]

The features of these works that have been most derided, however—particularly the exceptional combination of mysticism, Spiritualism, and piety—are ultimately what make the works so effective.

❀ ❀ ❀

On his final trip to the Holy Land, in 1896, Tissot wrote to Maurice de Brunhoff from Jerusalem, reiterating the deep emotional conviction, mysticism, and devout belief behind his biblical illustrations: "I was moved in Jerusalem . . . the old remembrances, everything based on faith, one is in a special state of mind. . . . I feel a certain presence around me, intuition is developed, one dematerializes oneself, one is constantly moved."[53] Using this intuition, Tissot created an ambitious and innovative series of works that deftly articulates his unique syncretism of established religious iconography and motifs from Spiritualism. A reconsideration of these illustrations reveals a complex artist who transcends the characterization of being a mere chronicler of fashionable society. Tissot combined his own convictions with the zeitgeist of his era to create a body of work that is more important—both to his oeuvre and to subsequent artists—than has previously been considered.

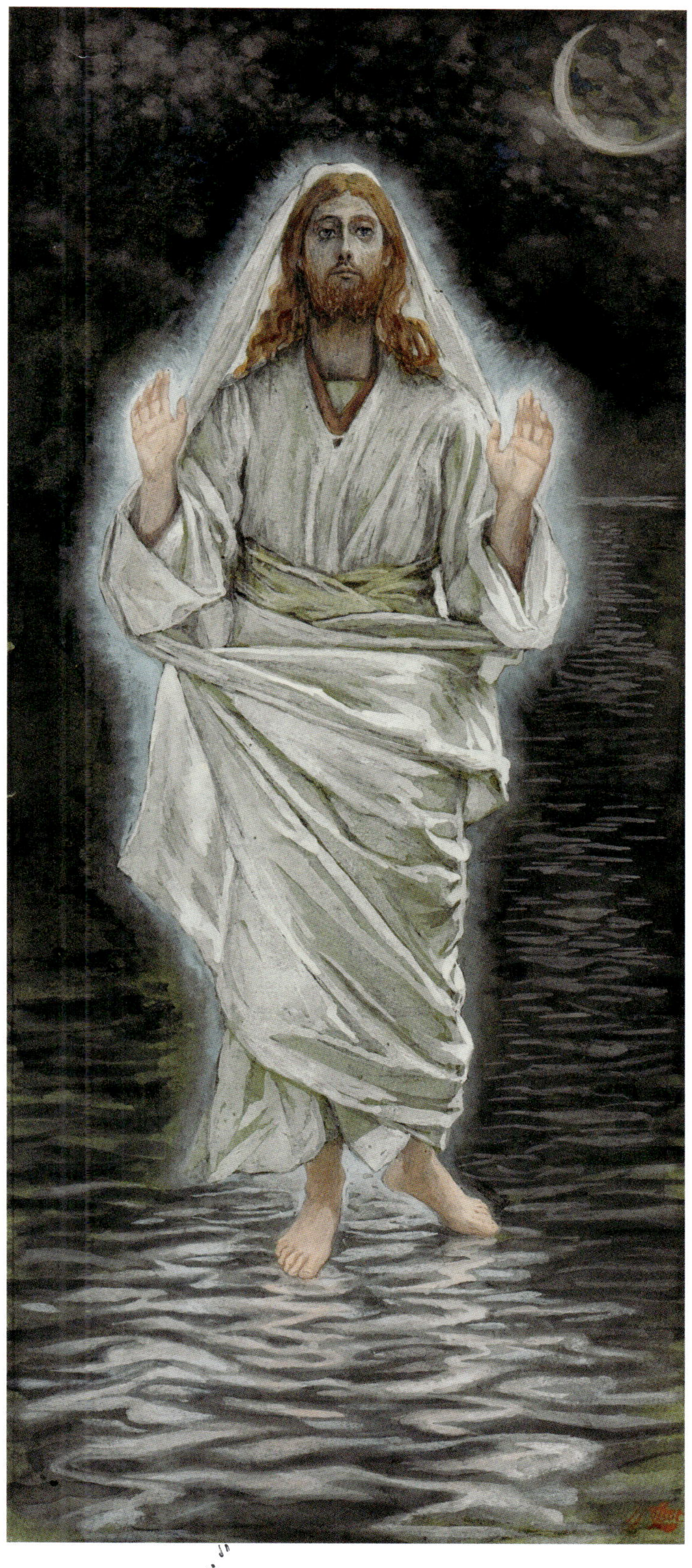

1 × 4"

FIGURE 64
James Tissot, *Jesus Walks on the Sea*, ca. 1886–1894. Opaque watercolor over graphite on gray wove paper, 11⅛ × 4¾ in. (28.4 × 12.2 cm). Brooklyn Museum, Purchased by public subscription, 00.159.138

THE RESURRECTION OF PAINTING: TISSOT AND CINEMA

VALENTINE ROBERT

Known for their innovative framing, documentary detail, and spectacular appeal, the works of James Tissot have had a profound impact on cinema. *The Life of Christ*, Tissot's series of 350 watercolors illustrating the New Testament, has been of particular interest to filmmakers. Begun in 1886 with extensive campaigns of study, sketching, and photography in the Holy Land, Tissot's biblical illustrations were both exhibited as a pictorial cycle—at first in 1894 in Paris, then in London, the United States, and Canada—and published as a book (see Buron, this volume). Commonly referred to as the "Tissot Bible," the published edition of *The Life of Christ*—which initially appeared in French in 1897, and in English in 1898—combines images with excerpts of the Gospels (selected and harmonized into one continuous narrative), historical and artistic commentary, and plot developments added by Tissot based on sources such as apocryphal texts, Jewish writings and testimonials, and archaeological and ethnographical research.[1] But it was cinema that perhaps offered Tissot's illustrations their richest "remediation."[2] Not only have the compositions given rise to numerous film reenactments, faithful even to the tableau vivant, but also Tissot's artistic approach as a whole has been a source of inspiration for generations of filmmakers who have depicted the Passion of Christ.

TABLEAUX

Since the medium of film emerged, at the turn of the twentieth century, many of the movies dedicated to the life of Christ have explicitly acknowledged the influence of Tissot's religious illustrations.[3] The early film *From the Manger to the Cross* (Sidney Olcott, 1912) was so closely based on the painter's work that the art historian Cyrille Sciama claimed to "have the sense that Tissot himself was behind the camera."[4] Indeed, the film includes nearly twenty tableaux vivants—exact reenactments, down to the smallest detail—of Tissot's biblical compositions.[5] The Annunciation scene illustrates the precision with which Olcott re-creates Tissot's sets, props, and costumes: the blind arcades and their checkered cladding, the carpets, the cushions and drapes—all materialize in front of the camera (figs. 65–66; pl. 144). This tableau vivant also demonstrates how the mystical aspect of Tissot's iconography—in this instance, the supernatural effect of the angel—is finely translated into a cinematic play of lighting and special effects using the technique of superimposition.

Olcott's experimentation with lighting also led to "improved" tableaux vivants—for example, in the reenactment of Tissot's *The Youth of Jesus* (ca. 1886–1894; Brooklyn Museum), enhanced by the addition of cast shadows. In the filmmaker's version, young Jesus carries a wooden board that projects the shadow of the cross at his feet, making the prefiguration of the crucifixion even more striking. Olcott even more drastically appropriated some of Tissot's other illustrations, such as *The Vision of Saint Joseph* (ca. 1886–1894; Brooklyn Museum), where the angel is transposed into a dazzling light beam. Nevertheless, the filmmaker's fidelity to the painter remained consistent and is apparent from the opening scene of *From the Manger to the Cross*, which restages Tissot's *The Holy Virgin in Her Youth* (ca. 1886–1894; Brooklyn Museum) so faithfully that the tableau vivant has been considered a primer for considering Olcott's film as "almost like a motion picture version of Tissot's *The Life of Christ*."[6] Olcott's film is not an isolated case; Alice Guy-Blaché's *The Birth, the Life, and the Death of Christ* (*La vie du Christ*, 1906) and Giulio Antamoro's *Christus* (1916) also contain many scenes modeled on works by Tissot.[7] And from *Intolerance* (D. W. Griffith, 1916) to *Redemption* (*Redenzione*, Carmine Gallone, 1919) to *Ben-Hur* (William Wyler, 1959), numerous biblical films have imitated at least one of Tissot's compositions for a scene.[8]

In addition to inspiring direct reenactments, Tissot's biblical illustrations may also have played a less comprehensive but nonetheless substantial referential role for specific filmic images. The raising of Lazarus in *The Life and Passion of Jesus Christ* (*La vie et la passion de Jésus-Christ*, Alexandre Promio, 1898) features the same frontal staging as Tissot's raising of Jarius's daughter. The painter's complex architectural setting of the third denial of Saint Peter, featuring interweaving arcades and colonnades, can be recognized in Ferdinand Zecca and Lucien Nonguet's *The Life and Passion of Jesus Christ* (*Vie et passion de Notre Seigneur Jésus-Christ*, 1907); his depictions of the rocky depths of Lazarus's tomb are reflected in *The Raising of Lazarus* (*La résurrection de Lazare*, Honoré Le Sablais, 1910) and *The King of Kings* (Cecil B. DeMille, 1927); and his solemn portrayal of the face-to-face encounter between Pilate and the Man of Sorrows is echoed in Franco Zeffirelli's *Jesus of Nazareth* (1977).

FRAMES

The prime feature—often called "protocinematic"[9]—of Tissot's Bible is the sequential nature of the illustrations, which depict the book's events in an almost continuous temporal flow, using various points of view. Traditionally subdivided into the fourteen Stations of the Cross, the Passion of Christ as depicted by Tissot develops over more than three hundred compositions, resulting in a work that unfolds, like a film, "frame by frame."[10]

In 1906, films were typically broken down not by shots but rather by tableaux, since each set was traditionally filmed in one take, with a wide, static frame. Tissot's Bible, however, inspired Alice Guy-Blaché to re-frame her sets.[11] Twice—both times influenced by Tissot's use of multiple points of view of the same scene—the shots in *The Birth, the Life, and the Death of Christ* change within the same tableau. The miracle of the veil of Veronica is thus augmented by a precursory "cut-in shot" that isolates Saint Veronica's frontal display of the holy face of Jesus, an effect found in Tissot's two-frame depiction of the same scene.[12] And while the flagellation of Christ and the *Ecce Homo* take place successively in a common décor—scrupulously modeled on Tissot, who depicts the setting from a half-dozen viewpoints—Guy-Blaché also varies their framing, changing the shot size.

It is no accident that Olcott's *From the Manger to the Cross*, the film most influenced by Tissot's *The Life of Christ*, was the first film about Jesus that broke with the cinematic form of individual tableaux, varying the angles and presenting all of the scenes in a continuous fashion. This way of filming Evangelical events—one reviewer described the movie as "linked together in one chain . . . from the 'Manger to the Cross'"—was immediately hailed as an effective means of matching the ambition of Tissot, who, in seeking to "link together those great occasions which earlier artists had only depicted separately," was said to have been "waiting for the advent of the wonders of the cinematograph."[13]

Still, the painter's "editing" and "framing" remain richer than that of Olcott's—particularly in the treatment of the Crucifixion, which in Tissot's work marks the culmination of his use of multiple points of view. For that scene, Tissot covers all viewing angles over the course of twenty pictures, revolving around the cross, cropping it, and even adopting the perspective of Jesus himself (see pls. 151–152). To attain such diversity, cinema would have to wait for the virtuosic editing of *The King of Kings*, *The Last Temptation of Christ* (Martin Scorsese, 1988), or *The Passion of the Christ* (Mel Gibson, 2004). Nonetheless, Olcott's method of depicting the crucified Christ with shots taken below, behind, and very far from the cross was groundbreaking and would have great cinematic impact.[14] Even the intertitles that punctuate these shifts in framing were directly inspired by the texts of Tissot's Bible, which Olcott truly considered as "a kind of preliminary script, a storyboard."[15]

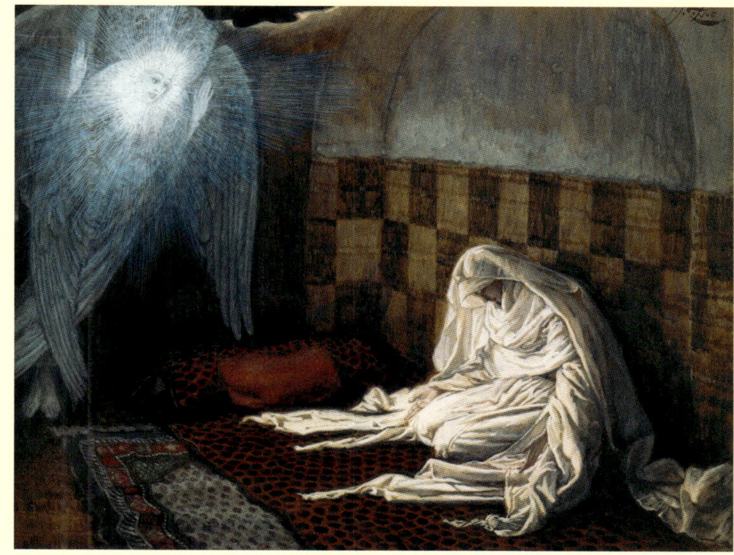

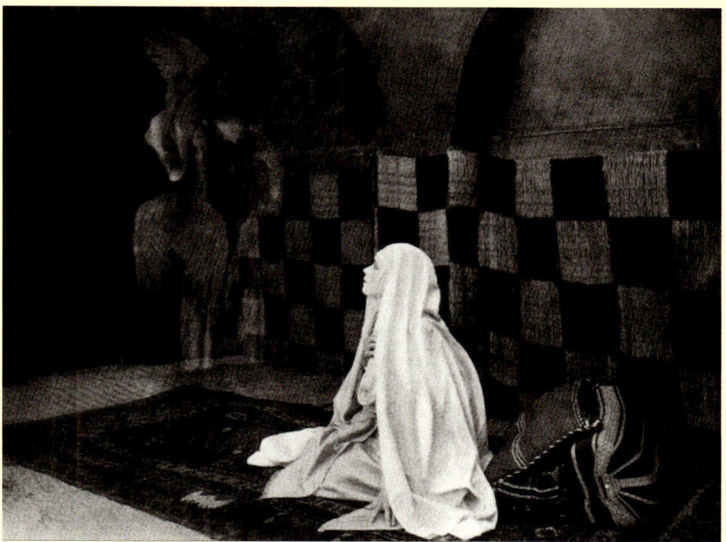

FIGURE 65
James Tissot, *The Annunciation*, ca. 1886–1894 (pl. 144). Opaque watercolor over graphite on paper, 6¾ × 8½ in. (17 × 21.7 cm). Brooklyn Museum, Purchased by public subscription, 00.159.16

FIGURE 66
Promotional photograph of Sidney Olcott's *From the Manger to the Cross*, 1912. Private collection

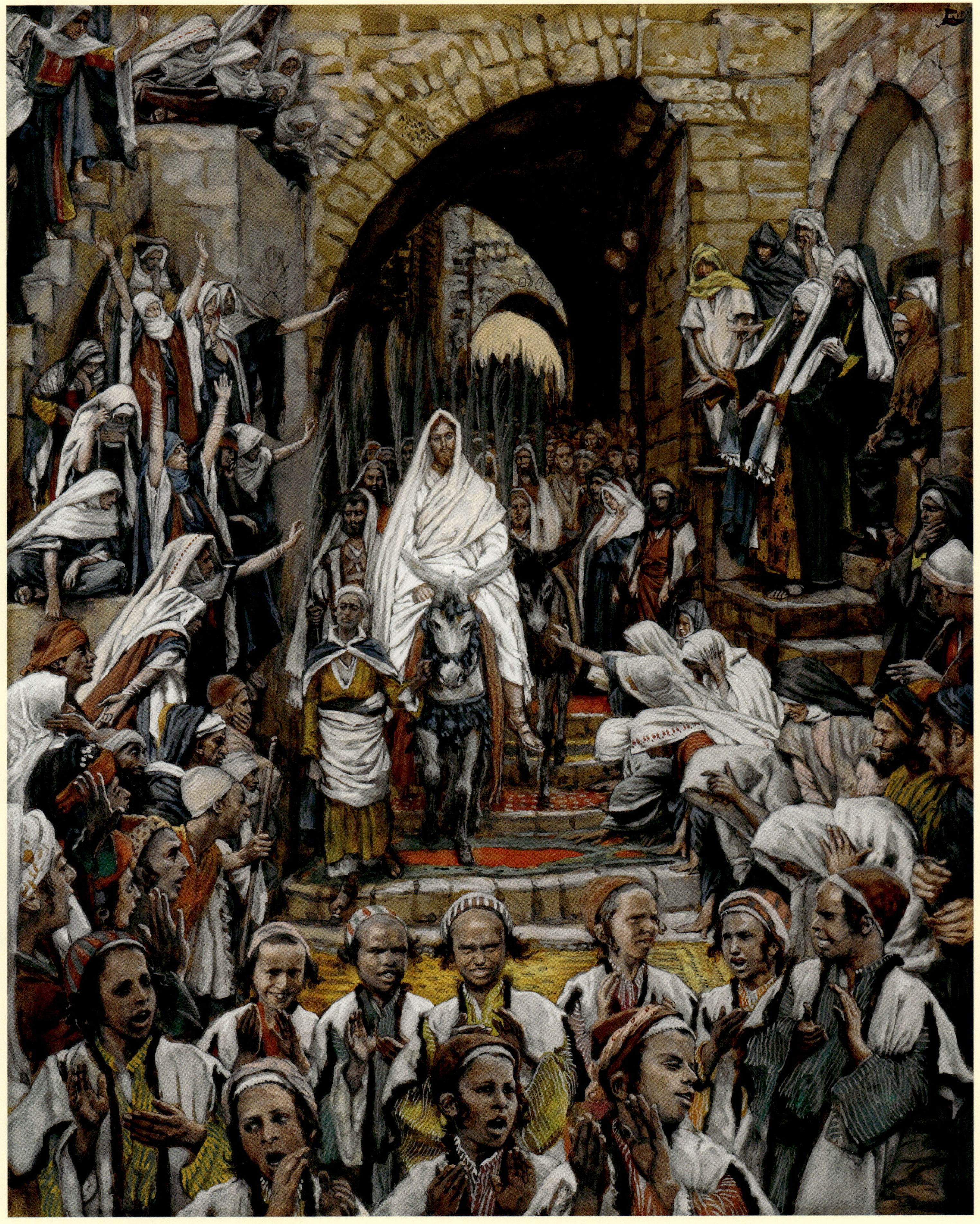

FIGURE 67
James Tissot, *The Procession in the Streets of Jerusalem*, ca. 1886–1894. Opaque watercolor over graphite on gray wove paper, 8⅞ × 6⅞ in. (22.5 × 17.6 cm). Brooklyn Museum, Purchased by public subscription, 00.159.194

FIGURE 68
Film still from D. W. Griffith's *Intolerance*, 1916

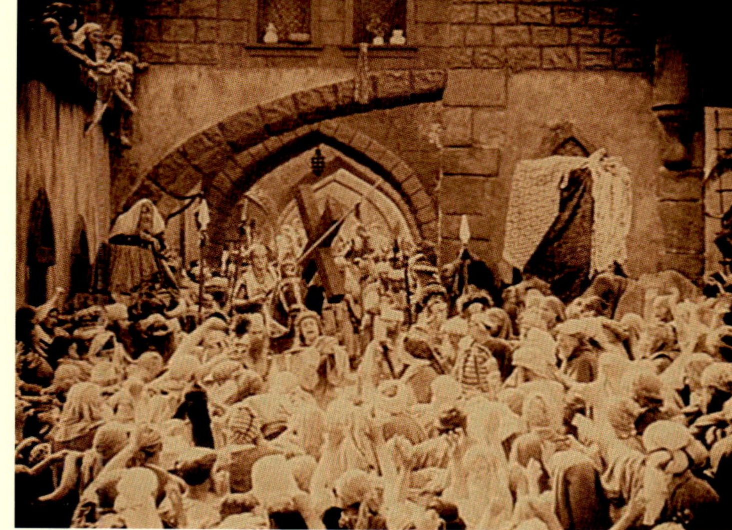

DOCUMENTS

Filmmakers not only used Tissot as an artistic reference they also saw in him "a way of attaining the authentic imprimatur of history."[16] One defining attribute of Tissot's religious works was his travel to the Holy Land, which permeated the images with an exoticism seen as authentically biblical.[17] In addition, his compositions were accompanied by "notes and explanatory drawings" presented in a scientific manner.[18] Whereas Olcott followed Tissot's example by going so far as to shoot his own story of Christ in the Holy Land—an approach that was deemed an extraordinary sign of historical authenticity—Guy-Blaché made use of Tissot's *The Life of Christ* as "ideal documentation."[19] For *Intolerance*, Griffith referred to it in a similar way, listing Tissot in his intertitles as an authority on a par with the greatest scholars of biblical history.[20]

Not all films about Jesus enact proper tableaux vivants of Tissot's illustrations, but many of them include one or more visual details from the Tissot Bible—long considered a veritable encyclopedia for representations of the era, and used as an iconographic repertory in film production since its beginnings. Whether recognized in a film's settings (such as the enfilade of the arches in *Intolerance* [figs. 67–68]), the costumes and accessories (such as specific earthenware jars, lamps, or flower garlands), the ropes used to raise the cross, the trilingual titulus, or the hat-like crown of thorns that covers Jesus's head, it is hard to verify the historical accuracy of these details. But through Tissot, who itemized and popularized them in his Bible, these features have become referential in film history.

SPECTACLE

If the film world immediately seized on Tissot's images, it is because the artist himself had intended them for reproduction and spectacle. When he first exhibited *The Life of Christ* in 1894 at the Salon du Champ-de-Mars in Paris, Tissot had not even yet finished the series. As soon as he had, he converted it into an international sensation, propagating his work in a myriad of books, using the most sophisticated lithographic processes.[21] Tissot went so far as to display the pages of his Bible side by side with the original watercolors, pioneering a new type of exhibition, dedicated less to the paintings themselves and more to the spectacular quality of their reproduction.[22]

Tissot's compositions even spawned by-products such as postcards, prayer cards, catechism pictures, and stained-glass windows,[23] with the magic lantern becoming a favored means of dissemination.[24] Indeed, as early as 1898, *The Life of Christ* had become an onscreen phenomenon in which the paintings were projected, enlarged, and illuminated, enhanced by added commentary, dialogue, and music.[25] In the magic-lantern slides format, the works' immersive power was magnified and their sequential logic perfected: the images flowed in succession, almost filmic. Although no current research has uncovered a concrete link between Tissot and the emerging cinematograph, he is known to have been involved with at least one of these numerous lantern-slide screenings of his works.[26]

Moreover, it is no exaggeration to consider Tissot's display practices as akin to that of an early cinema exhibitor. Already in 1890, when he unveiled the first compositions of his *Christ* series at home to a circle of friends, he did not hesitate to present a full spectacle. He successively presented 125 paintings while playing with great intensity the role of the narrator—a key figure in lantern-slide shows who would become essential to early film screenings.[27] Finally, right after having published them, Tissot took his images on tour. *The Life of Christ* became a traveling paid public exhibition, reaching mass audiences throughout North America in the years 1898–1900. These exhibitions filled the same halls as many nascent film shows, which likewise toured at that time.[28] The tableaux vivants by Guy-Blaché and Olcott may thus have been projected on the very same walls where Tissot's original paintings had once hung, almost as if the paintings themselves had come to life. Having followed the artist's compositions line for line, his pictorial narrative frame by frame, and his production and promotional itineraries step by step—from the Holy Land to the New World—cinema, ultimately, would grant Tissot's work its most perfect resurrection.

FINAL YEARS AT THE BUILLON ESTATE

FRÉDÉRIC MANTION

Located in eastern France, next to the village of Chenecey-Buillon, some 20 miles from the city of Besançon, the site of the Buillon estate lies at an altitude of about 920 feet, at the bottom of the valley, on a fluvial terrace that forms at the right bank of the Loue River. The site is remarkable: it faces south, bordered to the west by a limestone cliff about 230 feet high, and protected to the north by hills. There is rich botanical diversity, with numerous varieties of conifers, catalpas, ginkgos, pines, plane trees, silver lindens, and Virginia tulip trees. It is also a true refuge for fauna, with numerous species found there. James Tissot's father, Marcel-Théodore Tissot, who purchased the estate on July 11, 1845, wrote: "Everything on these premises inspires the greatest tranquility and the sweetest, most irresistible melancholy. This residence is buried, as it were, in the depths of a desert, where a ring of immense, steep rocks forms a barrier against the ravages of time, against the gazes, and perhaps even the passions, of men."[1] It was here, on this tranquil property, that James Tissot spent much of his time during the final years of his life.

HISTORY OF THE ESTATE

The abbey of Buillon, originally called Notre-Dame de Billon, or also *Buillon le pauvre* (Buillon the poor), was founded in 1128 by Abbot Burchard from the abbey of Balerne, with the advice and assistance of Bernard de Clairvaux, his teacher. Clairvaux, who would become Saint Bernard in 1174, was a French monk and reformer of Catholic religious life. An important promoter of the Cistercian order, he also brought recognition to the Templar Order (the Knights Templar), whose statutes he drafted and for whom he helped develop the Latin Rule.[2]

The lords and knights of Chenecey-Buillon offered the monks a piece of land on the banks of the Loue River. Richard, Lord of Montfaucon, agreed to pay for all of the construction costs. Some of the structures were built with materials taken from a Roman house near the estate. In 1135, the abbey of Buillon was consecrated by Humbert de Scey, archbishop of Besançon.[3] In the wake of the French Revolution of 1789, the French government abolished religious orders, and more than four hundred abbeys, including that of Buillon, were sold as national properties. After passing through six consecutive owners in nearly sixty years, Marcel-Théodore acquired the estate.[4]

Following the untimely death of his companion, Kathleen Newton, in November 1882, James Tissot left England and thereafter divided his time between Paris and his father's property at Buillon. Upon his father's death, on March 13, 1888, Tissot—Marcel-Théodore's sole surviving son—inherited the estate and moved there permanently, while still keeping his Paris home and studio. On August 8, 1902, the artist died at Buillon. He was buried beside his mother, Marie Tissot, née Durand, in the vault of the estate's private chapel. His two nieces, Louise and Jeanne, inherited the estate and lived there until their deaths—in 1949 and 1964, respectively.[5]

THE STRUCTURES

The present estate of Buillon is much as it was when James Tissot occupied it. It comprises numerous buildings. Several elements dating from the monastic period remain, such as the abbatial residence and the ruins of the magnificent church, nearly 175 feet long, with its almost intact chevet, the chapels of the transept, the pillars of the nave, and the capitals. At the center of the estate stands an imposing château, which was originally a large manor house built on the foundations of the old monastic buildings (fig. 69). The structure is an amalgam of three distinct periods. The central part of the structure to the left of the front steps dates to the end of the sixteenth century, and to the right of the steps, including the south wing, to the mid-eighteenth. The north wing was completed in 1829. After relocating there, Tissot made major modifications, adding wings, arcades, and many other elements, thus transforming the residence into a château.[6]

Adjacent to the château, on the north side, is the stately home of the monastery's abbots. Around the fourteenth century, the Cistercians built a tall octagonal tower that is attached to this building. The watchtower holds a splendid staircase of finely carved stone, which fills the whole interior of the tower's thick walls. Beneath the monastic buildings, a vaulted cellar gives access to a wide underground passage, the function of which remains unknown.

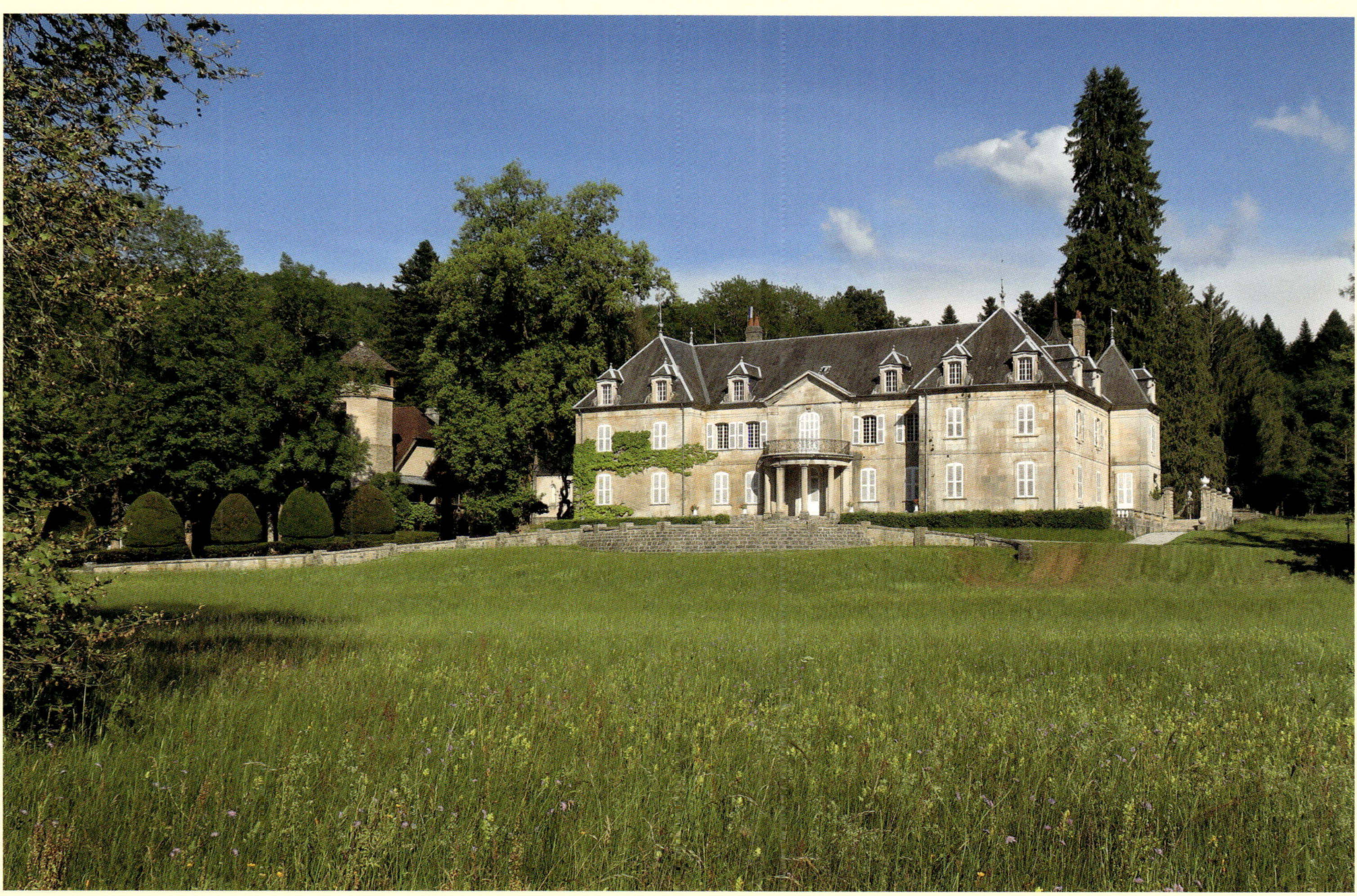

Within this abbatial residence and its tower, Tissot chose to set up his large working studio as well as his bedroom, his photo laboratory, and his enameling kiln. In front of the building, he constructed an expansive, magnificent hothouse that overlooks a vast garden. A dozen yards away, on the north side of the property, stands the large chapel in which Tissot is buried. Built in 1848, at his mother's behest, the chapel is of ogival style, with a porch, apse, and bell tower surmounting the gable of the façade. Behind the choir, looking down on the altar, is a beautiful sculpture of the Madonna and Child by Jean-Baptiste-Joseph de Bay.

An extensive farm at the entrance to the Buillon estate originally formed the main entrance to the monastery. The farm is made up of numerous buildings, including a huge barn with an imposing Cistercian frame, stables that can hold eleven horses, a cowshed dating to the time of the monastery, and several dwellings for the estate's staff. On the banks of the river, the mill originally used for grinding grain would later furnish electricity to the château. Tissot converted the structure that houses the mill into a luxurious abode, a sort of second residence, where he enjoyed moments of relaxation and entertained friends.[7] Throughout the estate, he made significant changes to existing structures and also built new ones. Although he seemed to have been little concerned with historical accuracy, he exposed vestiges of the past through a décor born of his imagination. He infused the estate with a charm that only an artist could offer, mixing styles in ways that were sometimes surprising but always refined. With the aid of his inventive vision and discerning taste, Tissot revived the soul of the old estate, which stands to this day as a testament not only to its medieval past but also to the creative inspirations of an artist.

A MEMORY PRESERVED

Today, the estate of Buillon is in many ways unchanged, a monument to Tissot's final years, which were spent working on his great series of biblical watercolors (see Buron, this volume). The current owners have labored to sustain and preserve the site, which brims with history, and to passionately conserve the memory of Tissot. His studio is still there, untouched, tubes of paint laid out on a small red table, almost as if the great artist might at any moment appear to add a few subtle brushstrokes to a work in progress. So profound was the mark that Tissot made on the estate, fashioning it with as much care and style as he did his beautiful paintings, that he still seems present there—so much so that one might expect to pass him, quite naturally, at the bend of a path.

FIGURE 69
Château de Buillon, France, 2018

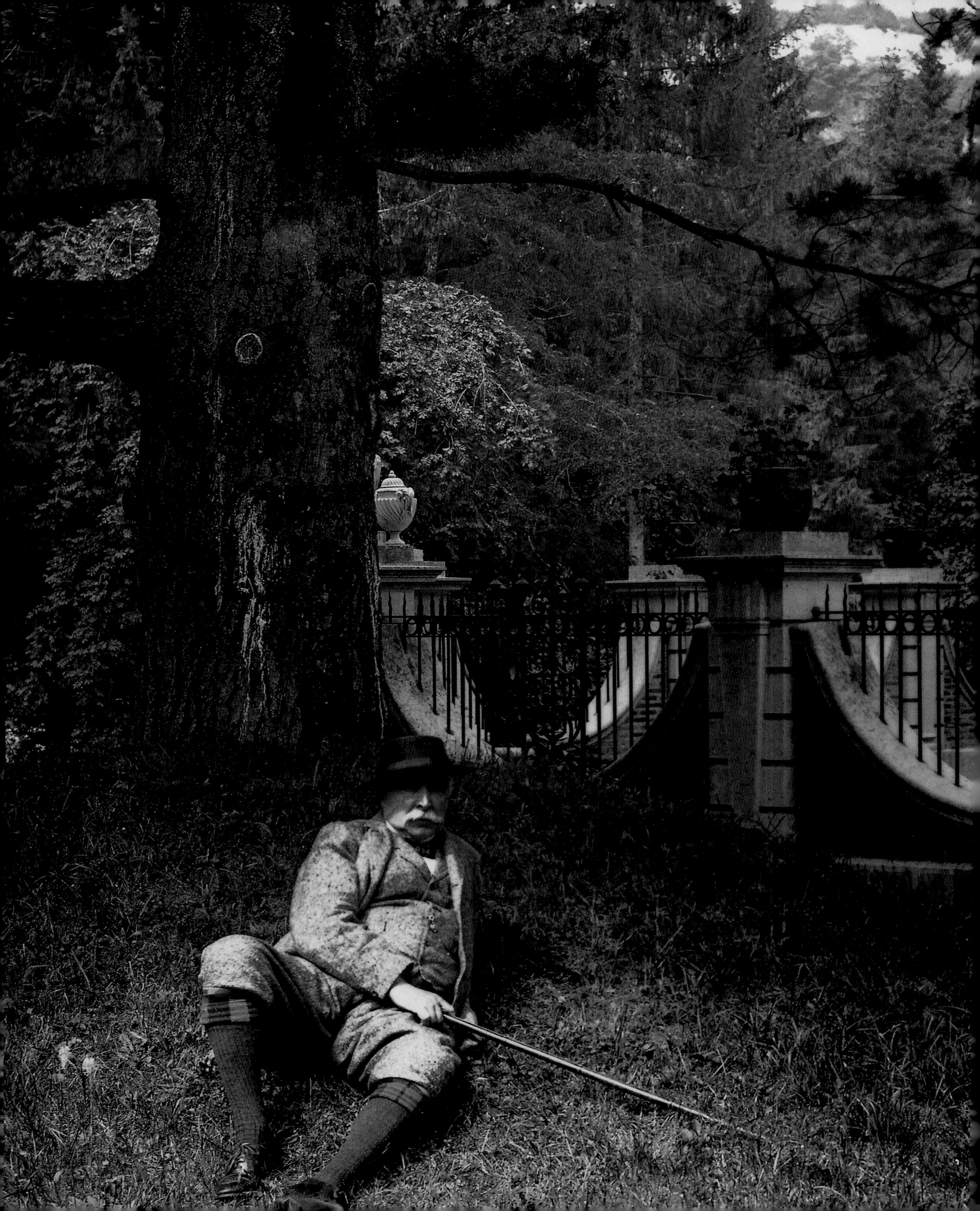

CATALOGUE

A NOTE TO THE READER:

The titles used in this catalogue are the ones used for each artwork upon first exhibition, recorded sale, or publication. When two titles were originally used interchangeably, both are given. Original French titles have been translated into English. If the work is now widely known by a different title, that title is also included. See "Catalogue Checklist," this volume, for the original French titles and other alternate titles, as well as detailed apparatuses for each work.

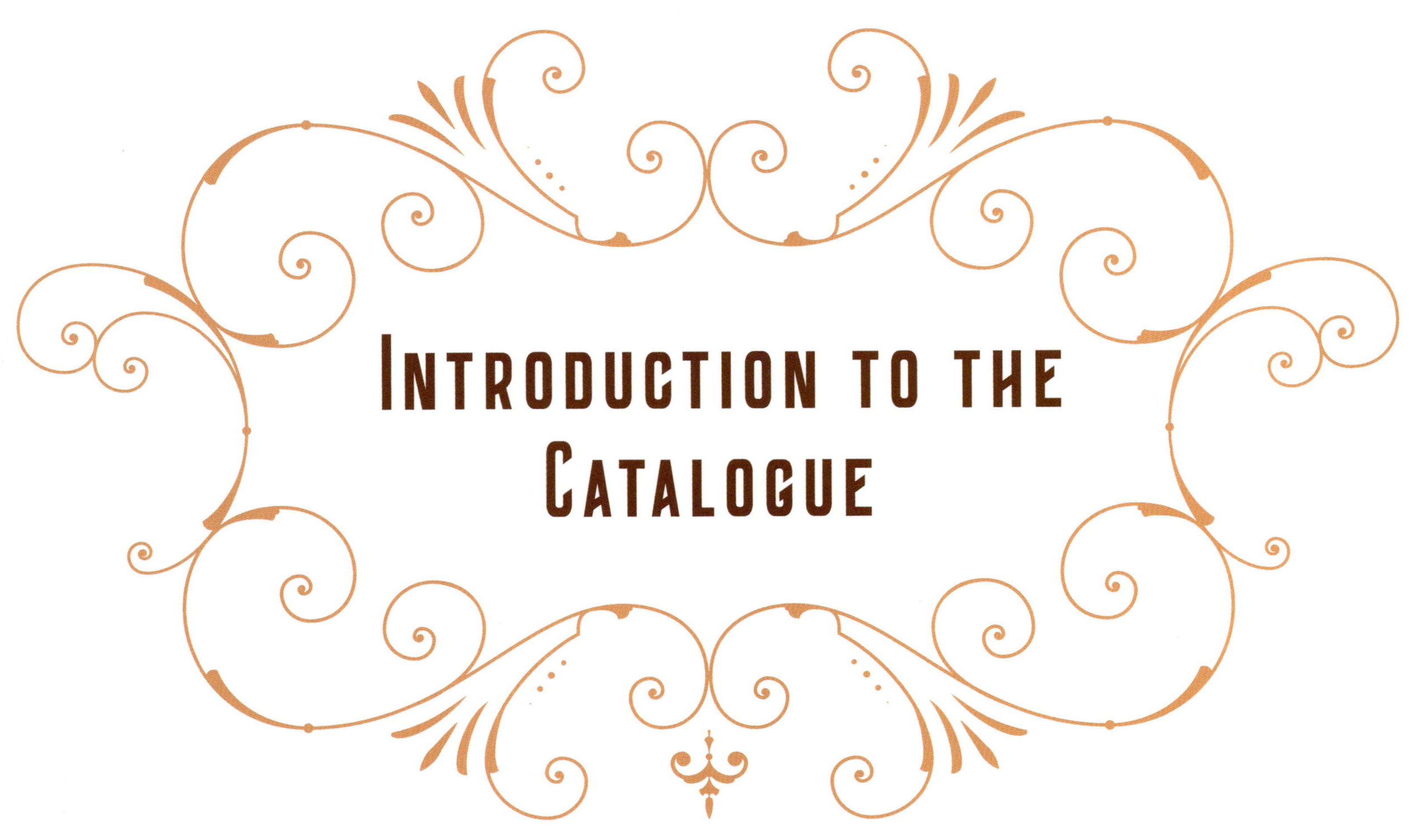

Introduction to the Catalogue

Melissa E. Buron
with
Krystyna Matyjaszkiewicz

THE SELECTION OF PLATES in this catalogue illustrates the variety and depth of James Tissot's work across the span of his prolific career. The plates are organized thematically; they adhere to a rough, but not strict, chronology. Almost immediately, the artist's most enduring traits and styles emerge, some of which traverse his oeuvre from beginning to end—most notably, his use of meticulous detail, which served rather than detracted from the complexity of his scenes.

Tissot debuted in Paris in the late 1850s painting medievalist pictures, a trend in Europe at the time, embodied by the success of the Belgian artist Henri Leys, whose work had a strong influence on Tissot's early career. "Medieval and Modern Life" opens with paintings that are clearly indebted to Leys, including compositions based on Johann Wolfgang von Goethe's *Faust* and the biblical parable of the prodigal son. Soon thereafter, Tissot began painting the modern depictions of women that he is best known for today. Already, the artist's interest in dresses as works of art as well as his subjects' psychological states is apparent. Tissot's time in Paris came to a close when in 1871 he moved to London after the Franco-Prussian War, a topic he treated through a variety of mediums, including in a series of etchings titled *Memory of the Siege of Paris*.

In Paris, Tissot developed a reputation for his striking large-scale portraits of fashionable sitters. "Portraits," a survey of these arresting works, reveals a painter perfecting his signature techniques: a scrupulous attention to detail, especially of clothing, and a knack for capturing enigmatic, ambiguous facial expressions. The artist's fascination with Asian art and artifacts is briefly addressed in "Japonisme and Chinoiserie." This interest reflected the wider European trend of Aestheticism, a movement that championed "art for art's sake." Indeed, Tissot's precision demonstrates a devotion to beauty, for which he was both criticized and praised.

The "Vanity Fair" of London in the 1870s inspired Tissot to compose numerous variations of *fêtes galantes*, suggestive scenes of flirtation and leisure. Whether depicting eighteenth-century or modern dress, Tissot continued to delight in painting sartorial details, especially flounces, pleats, and ruffles. Several of these works are set at Tissot's house in Saint John's Wood, London—in its lush conservatory or in the luxurious garden, with its pond ringed by a colonnade based on the one that graces Paris's Parc Monceau.

Born in the port city of Nantes, where the Loire River is joined by the Erdre and the Sèvre, Tissot maintained a lifelong fascination with riverside and nautical settings. In "By the Water," the paintings' subjects gaze contemplatively across the sea, socialize on ships, or float languorously along rivers, often as part of mysterious, sometimes provocative, scenarios. A series of works on the Thames recalls similar themes by fellow artist and friend James McNeill Whistler. Tissot's commanding execution is on full display in his skillful depictions of intricate ship rigging and deck furniture.

Around 1877, Tissot's companion, the Irish divorcée Kathleen Newton, moved into his London home. Though her name was not widely known to the public, "*La Mystérieuse*" began appearing in many Tissot paintings, whether in tranquil scenes of domestic bliss—oftentimes set at the Saint John's Wood property—or as a woman about town. Newton also features as a model for the artist's *The Prodigal Son in Modern Life* series and his illustrations to Edmond and Jules de Goncourt's novel *Renée Mauperin*. Tissot was deeply affected by Newton's premature death from tuberculosis in 1882, which precipitated his return to Paris and the next arc of his career.

After a decade in London, Tissot planned to announce his triumphant return to France with a series of large-scale pictures representing the modern woman in Paris, many of which feature in "*La Femme à Paris*." Exhibited first in Paris as *Fifteen Paintings on the Woman in Paris* (*Quinze tableaux sur la Femme à Paris*), these works received a mixed critical reception, though they continued to showcase Tissot's flair for fine detail and enigmatic scenes. While preparing to compose a painting for this series, Tissot experienced a transformative religious vision inside the Church of Saint-Sulpice in Paris, and once again the predominant theme of his work shifted.

The year after Newton's death, the painter began attending séances in an attempt to make contact with her. At one of these, led by the British medium William Eglinton, Tissot claimed that Newton's spirit appeared to him. He subsequently recorded this event in an oil painting and a mezzotint, both titled *The Apparition*. These two profound experiences—in the church and at the séance—heralded the themes that dominate the final phase of Tissot's career, explored in "'Twixt Two Worlds." During these years, the artist committed to making hundreds of watercolors illustrating the Bible scene by scene. He started with the New Testament, which was published as *The Life of Christ*, before moving on to the Old Testament, a project left incomplete when he died. Although today they rank among the painter's lesser-known works, these biblical illustrations made him famous and were familiar worldwide into the early twentieth century.

Tissot is himself an enigmatic subject. Readers of this volume will meet a private artist, one who achieved renown over the course of his career but had a reserved public persona, who smoothly navigated between artistic movements and countries without declaring a firm allegiance, and whose wry, sometimes satirical observations were at once rigorously astute and somewhat detached. Possibly, what speaks most intimately about him is his work, found in the pages that follow.

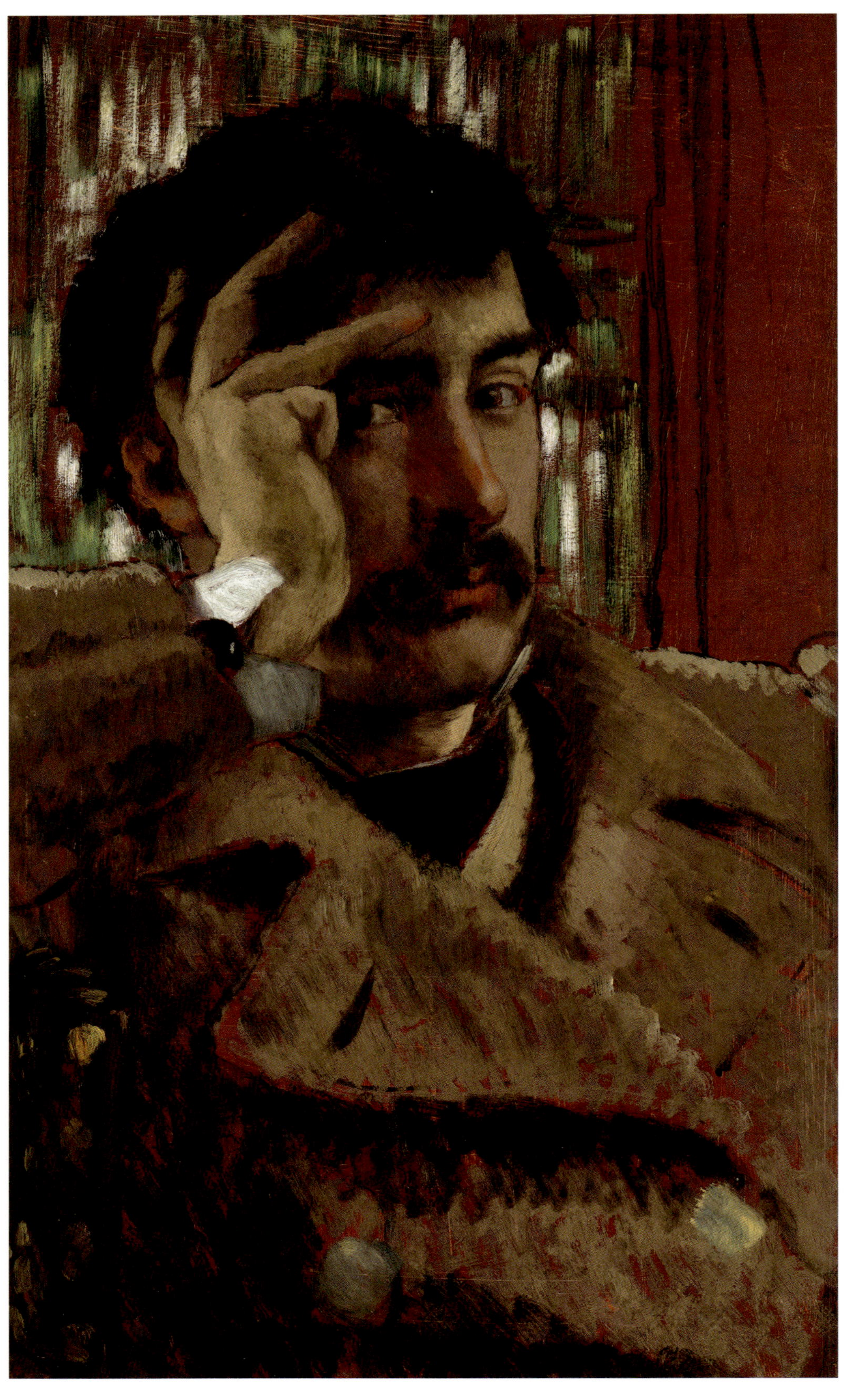

1

Self-Portrait, ca. 1865

Oil on wood panel, 19⅝ × 11⅞ in. (49.8 × 30.2 cm)
Fine Arts Museums of San Francisco, Museum purchase, Mildred Anna Williams Collection, 1961.16

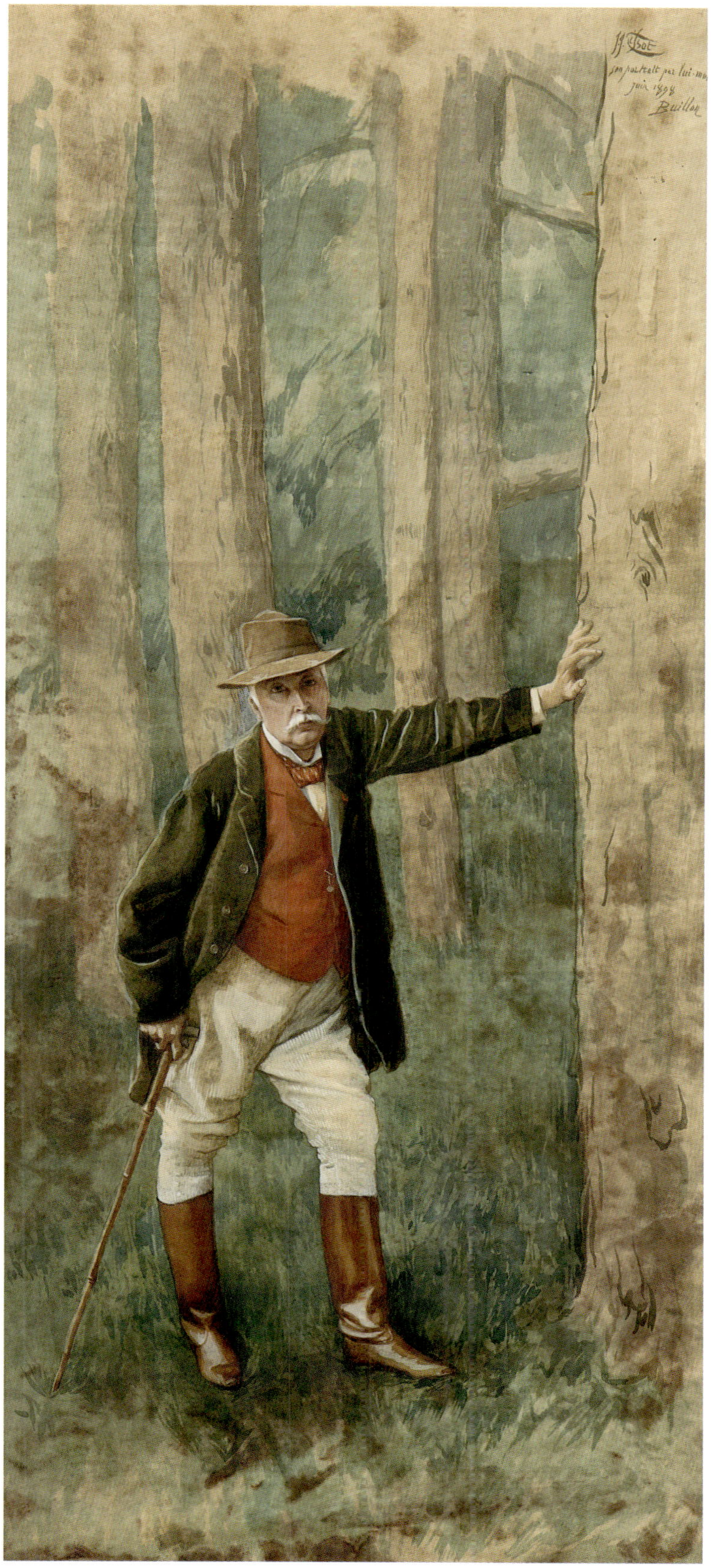

2

Self-Portrait, June 1898, Buillon, 1898

Opaque watercolor on silk, 44⅛ × 20⅛ in. (112 × 51 cm)

Collection Frédéric Mantion

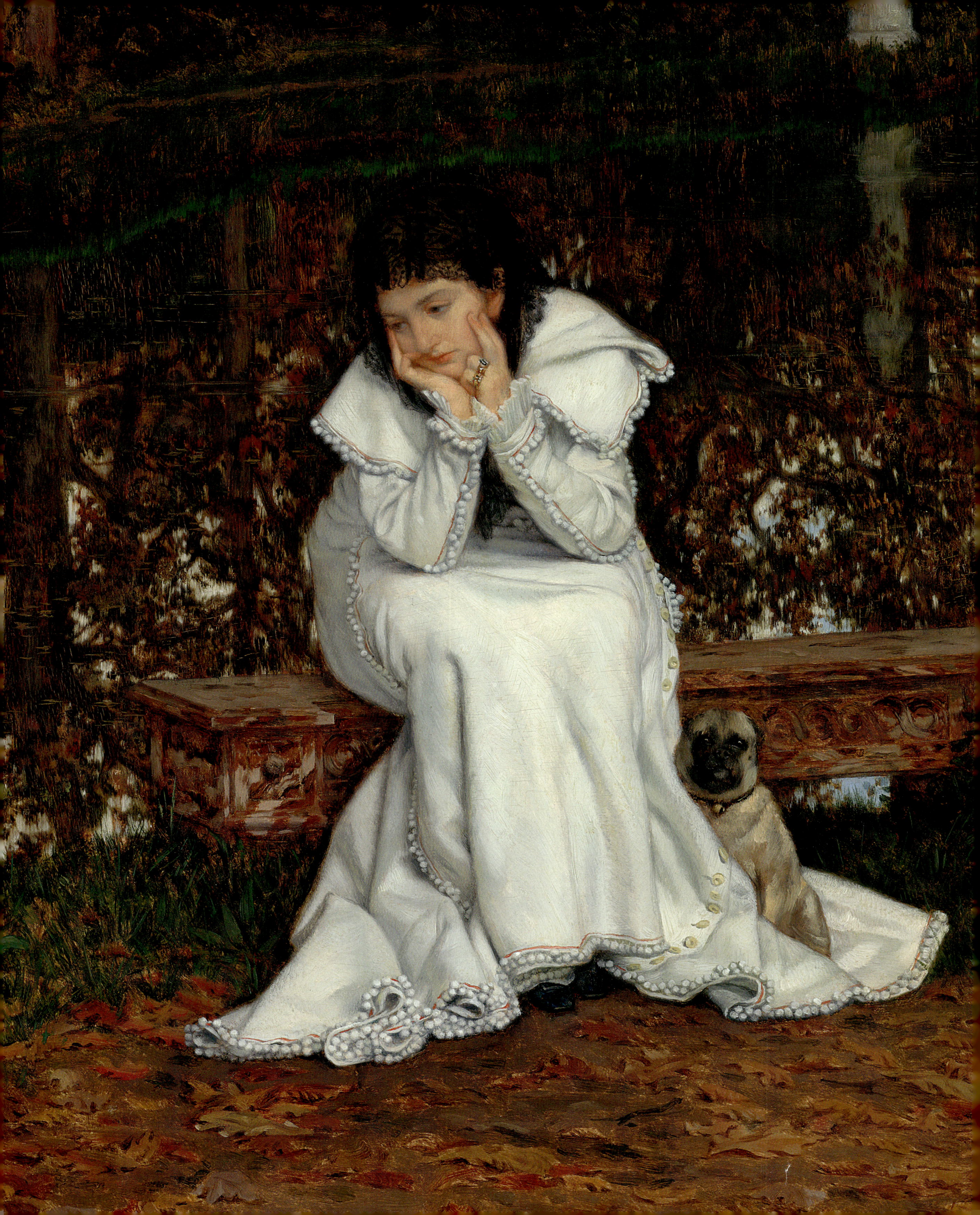

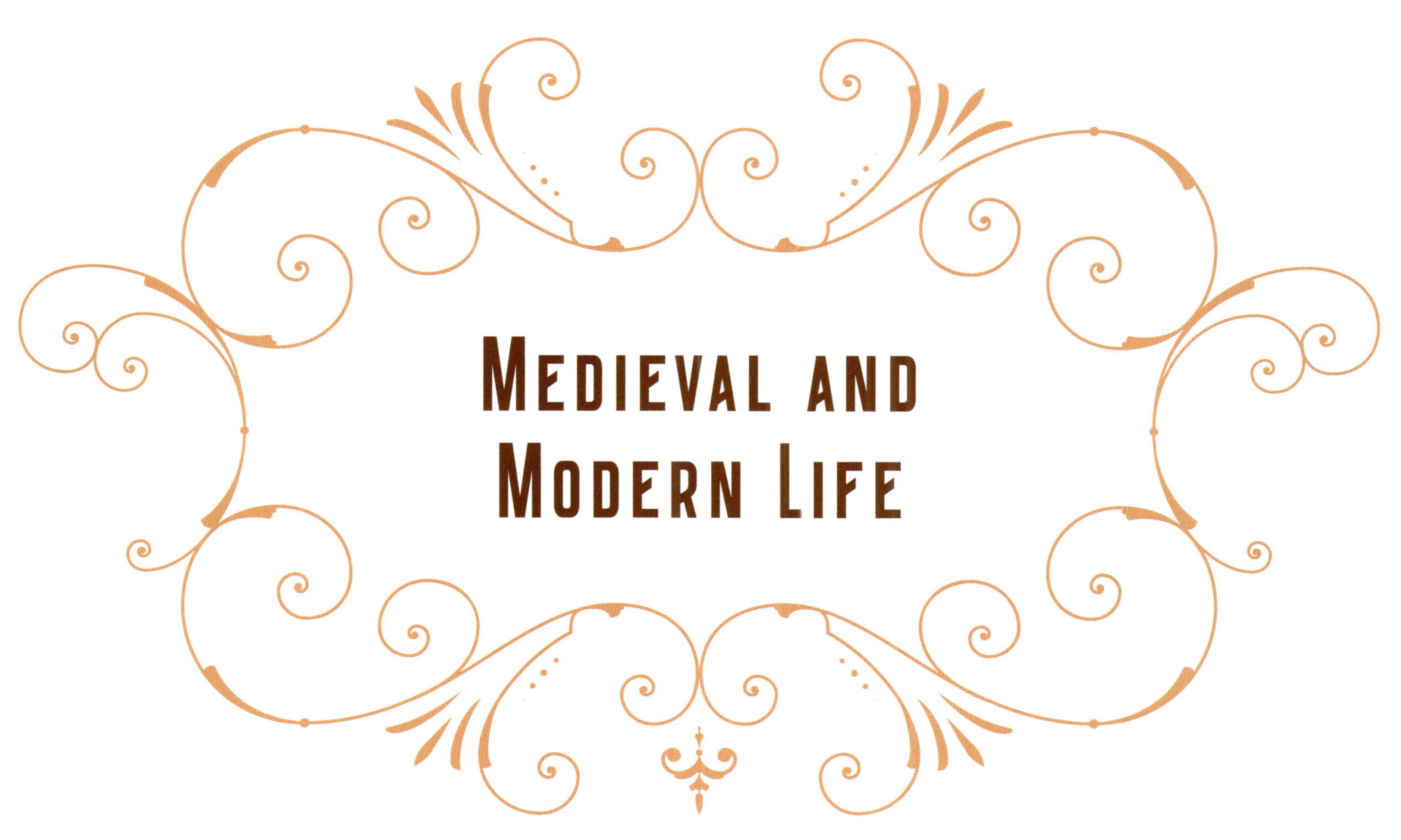

Medieval and Modern Life

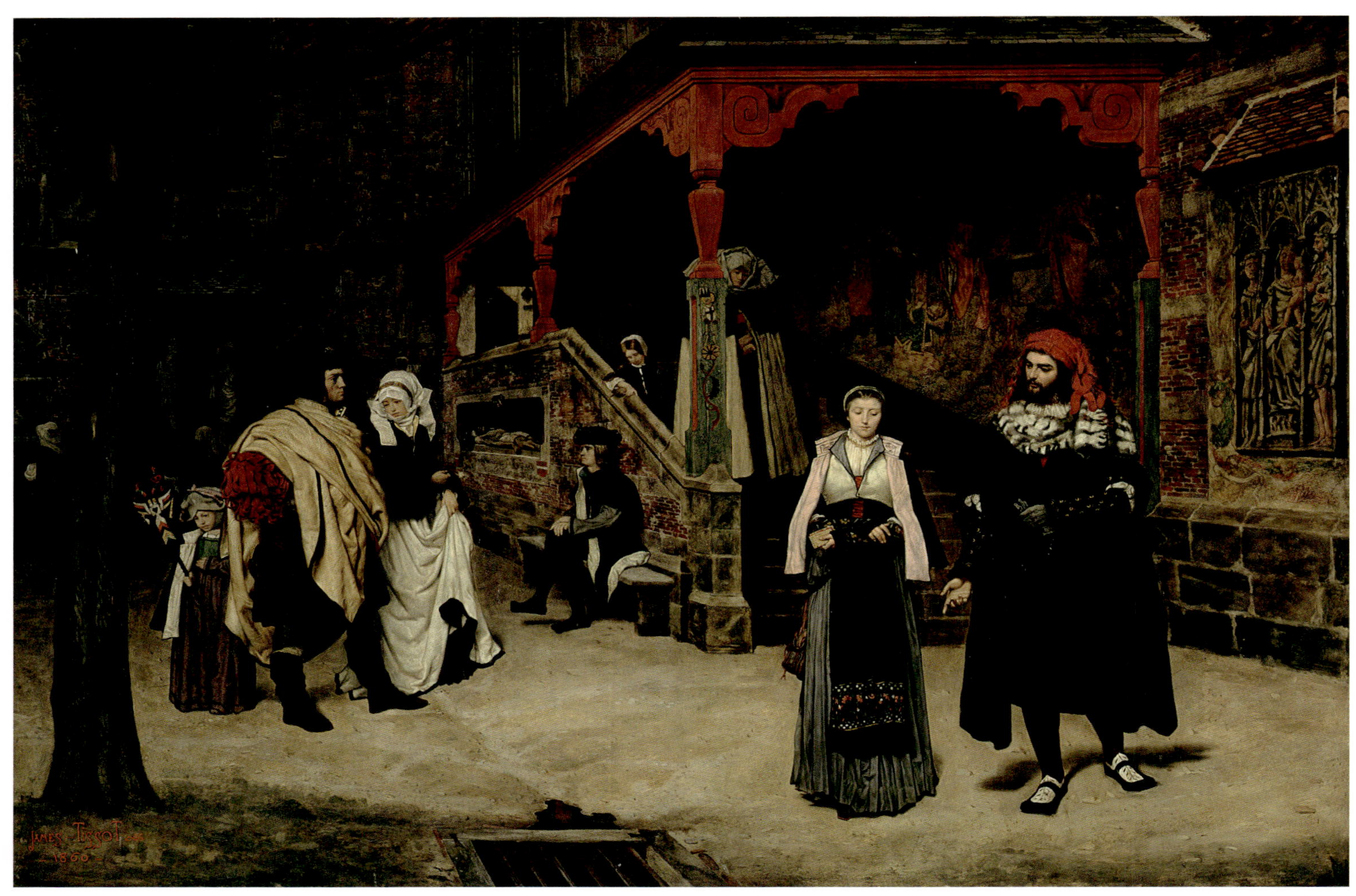

3

Meeting of Faust and Marguerite, 1860

Oil on wood panel, 30¾ × 46⅛ in. (78 × 117 cm)
Musée d'Orsay, Paris, Acquired in 1860, RF 1983.93

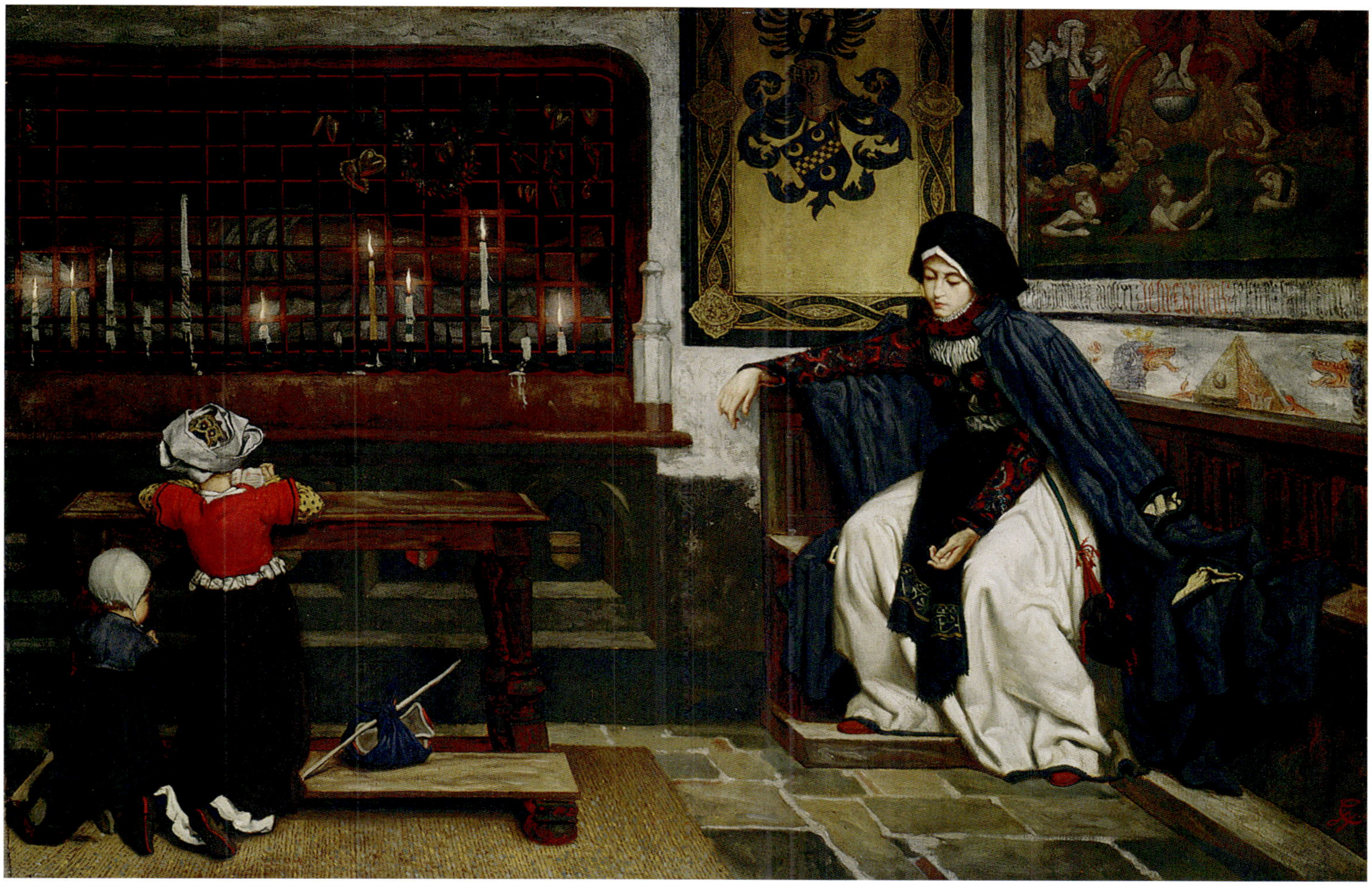

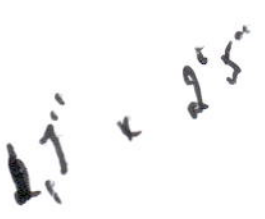

4

Marguerite in Church, ca. 1860–1865

Oil on canvas, 19¾ × 29½ in. (50 × 75 cm)
National Gallery of Ireland, Dublin, Presented, Sir Alfred Chester Beatty, 1950, NGI.4280

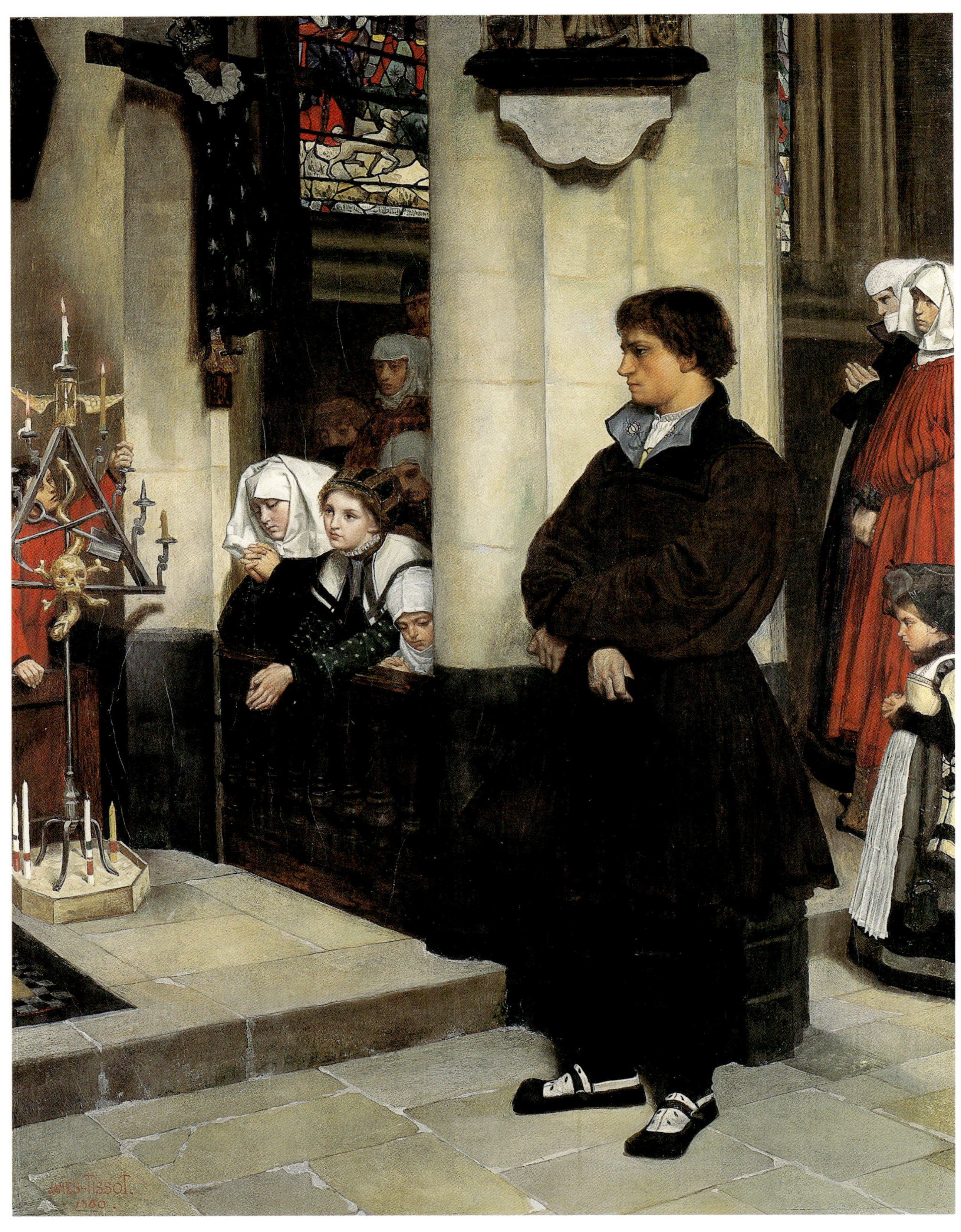

5

DURING THE SERVICE, 1860
also known as MARTIN LUTHER'S DOUBTS
Oil on wood panel, 34¾ × 26¾ in. (88.3 × 68 cm)
Colección Pérez Simón, Mexico City

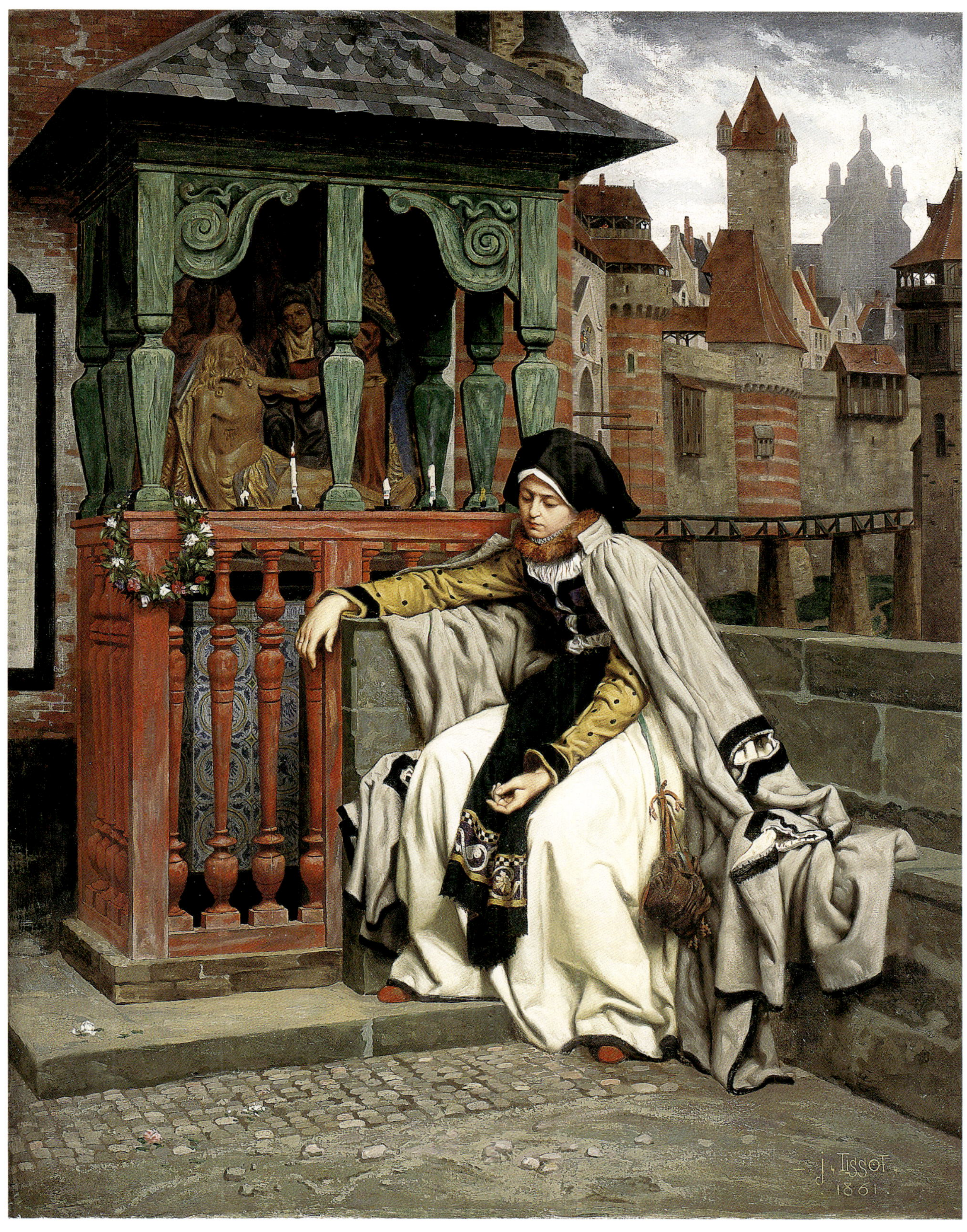

6

Marguerite on the Ramparts, 1861

Oil on canvas, 43¼ × 34 in. (109.9 × 86.4 cm)
Colección Pérez Simón, Mexico City

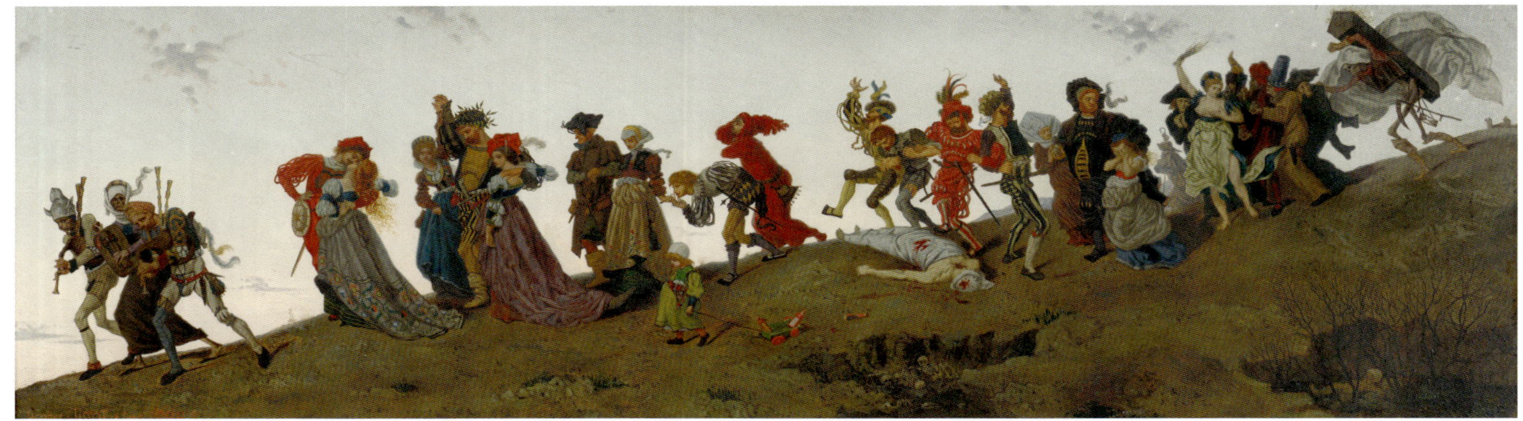

7

Way of Flowers, Way of Tears
or Dance of Death, 1860

Oil on canvas, 14⅝ × 48¼ in. (37.2 × 122.4 cm)
Museum of Art, Rhode Island School of Design, Providence,
Jesse Metcalf Fund, Georgianna Sayles Aldrich Fund, Mary B. Jackson
Fund and Edgar J. Lownes Fund, 54.172

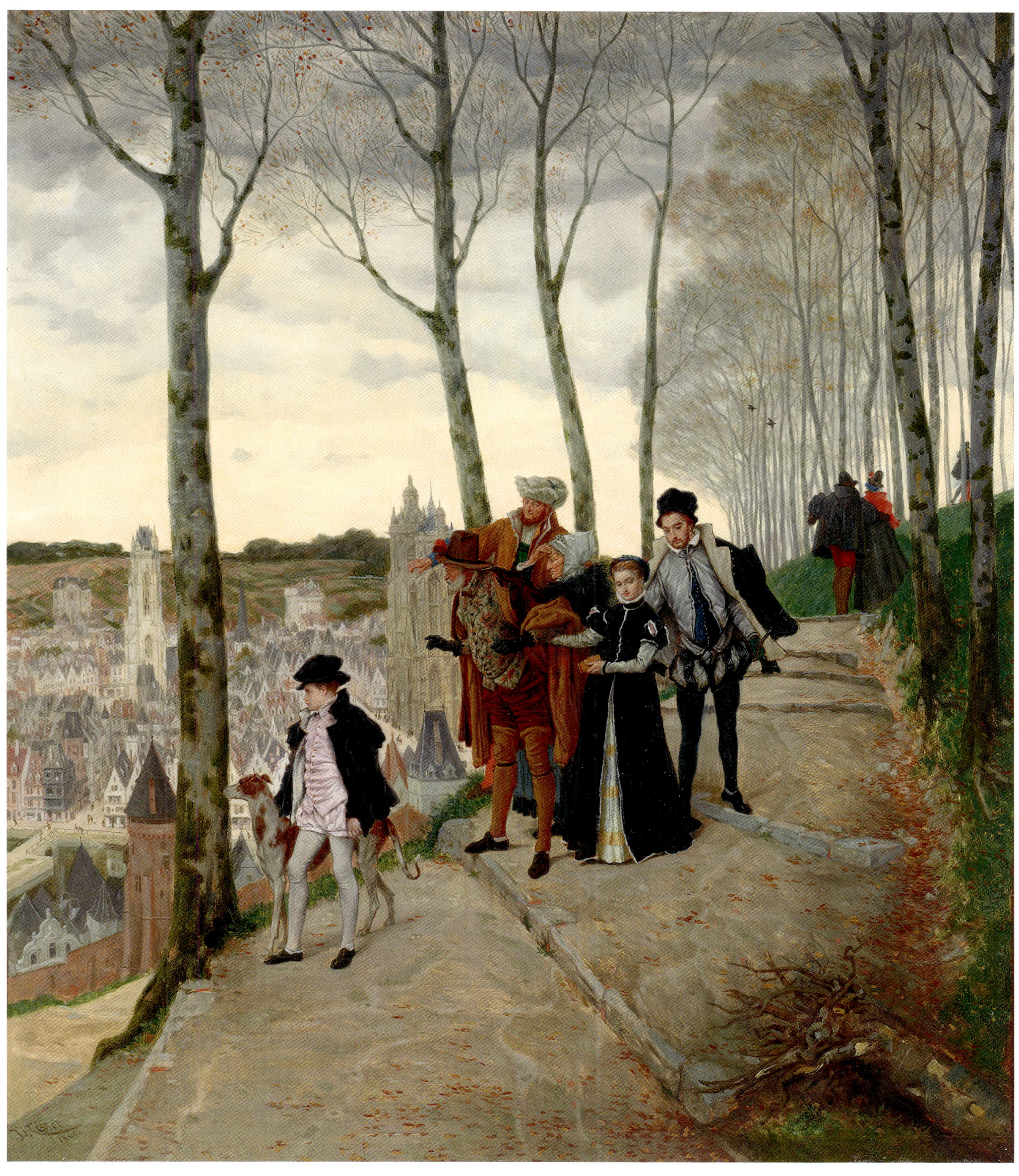

8

PROMENADE ON THE RAMPARTS, 1864

Oil on wood panel, 20½ × :7½ in. (52.1 × 44.5 cm)

Cantor Arts Center, Stanford University, California, Gift of Mr. Robert Sumpf, 1968.107

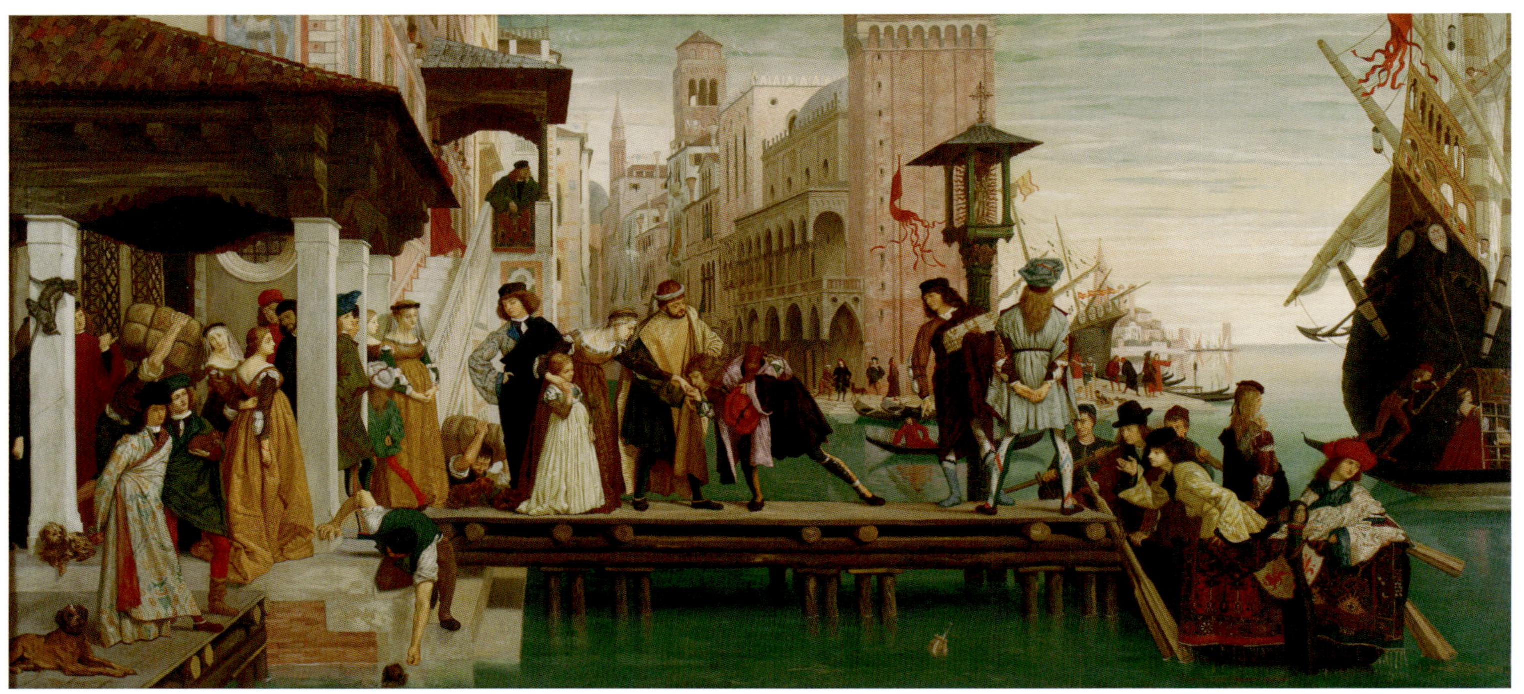

9

Departure of the Prodigal Son, 1863

Oil on canvas, 42⅛ × 89 in. (107 × 226 cm)

Petit Palais, Musée des Beaux-Arts de la Ville de Paris, Purchased, 1985, PDUT1453

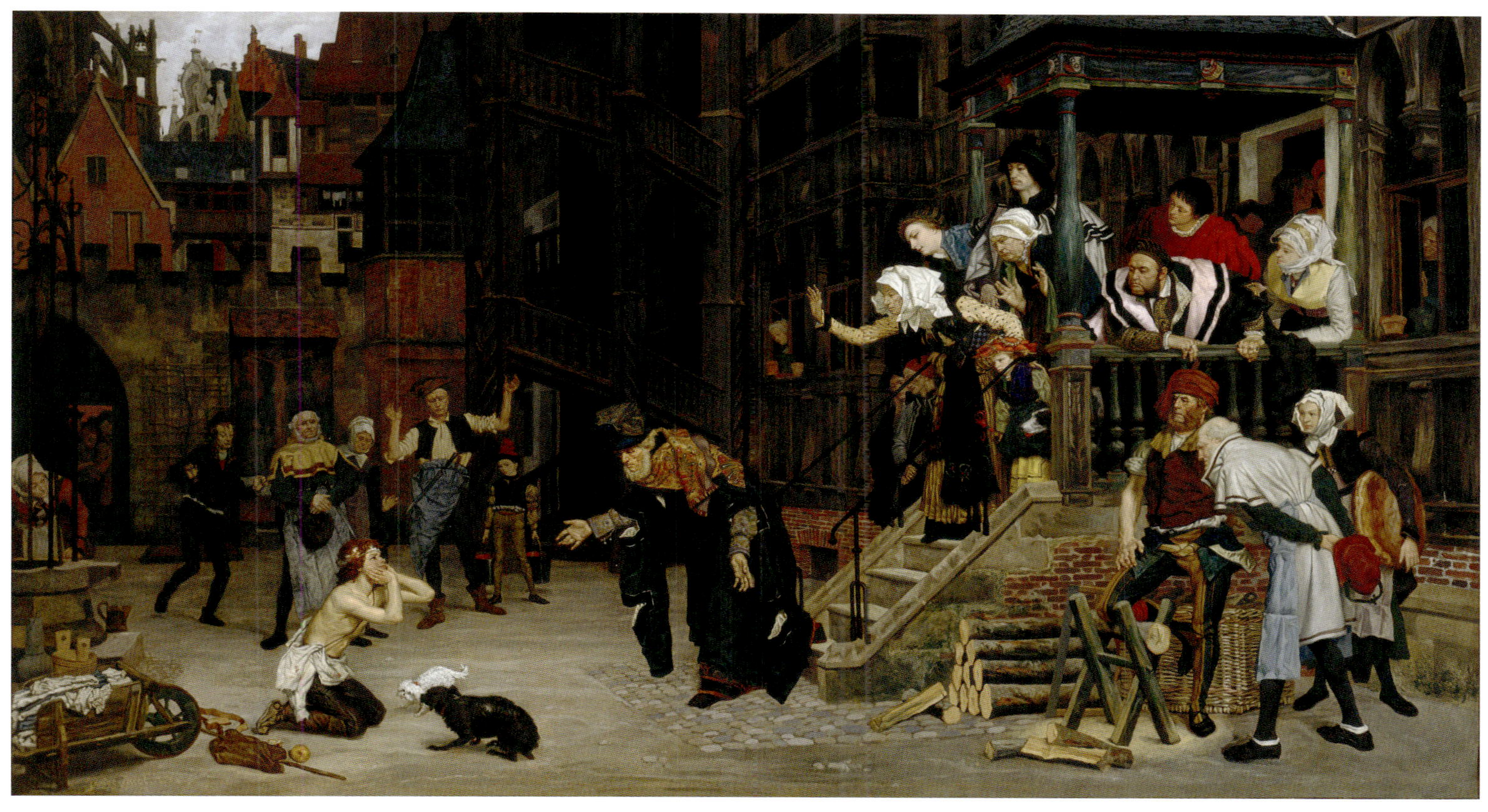

10

Return of the Prodigal Son, 1862

Oil on canvas, 45¼ × 81⅛ in. (115 × 206 cm)
Petit Palais, Musée des Beaux-Arts de la Ville de Paris, Purchased, 1992, PPP4856

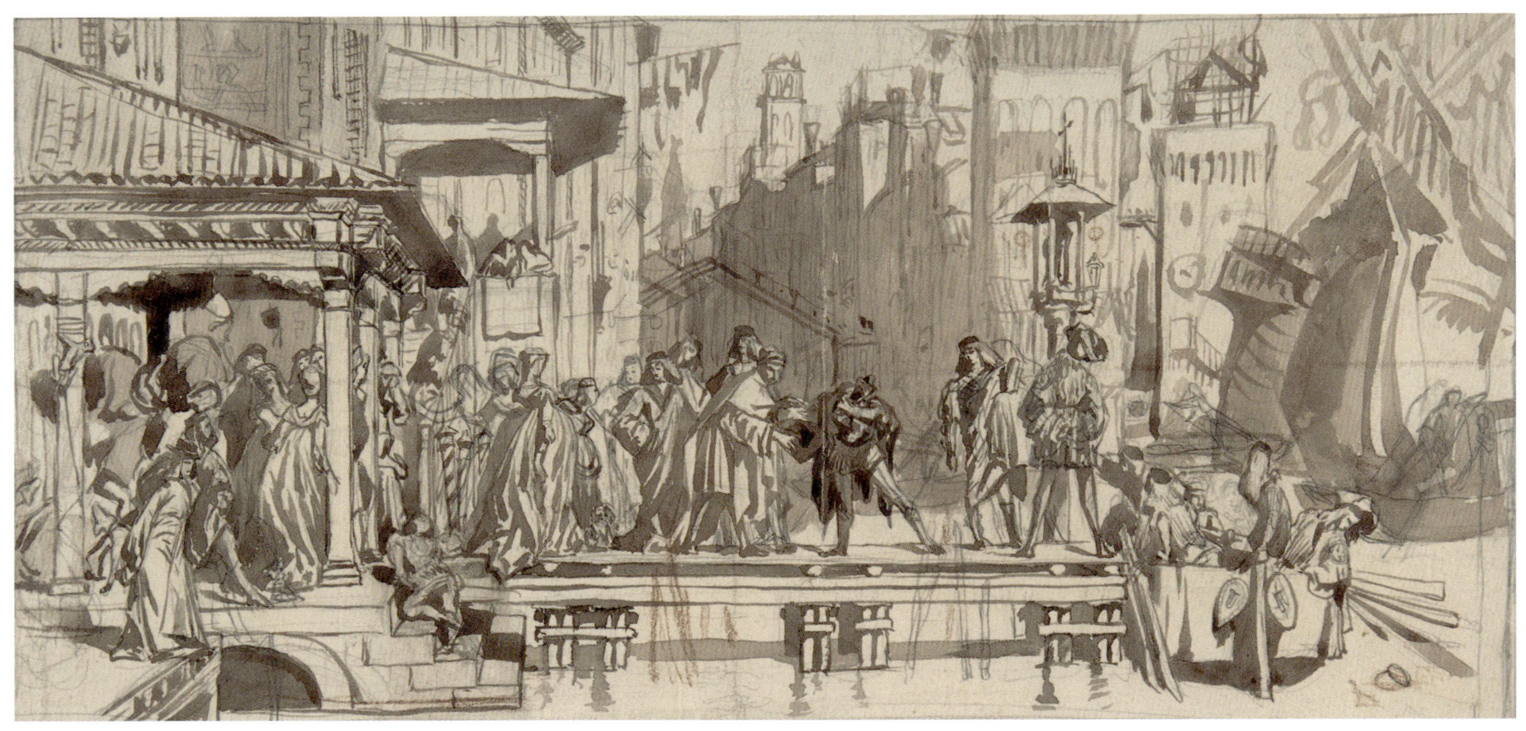

11

Study for "Departure of the Prodigal Son," 1862–1863

Brush and brown ink, brush and brown wash, over graphite (recto); graphite (verso), 6 × 13 in. (15.2 × 32.9 cm)
The Metropolitan Museum of Art, New York, Rogers Fund, 1970, 1970.114.2

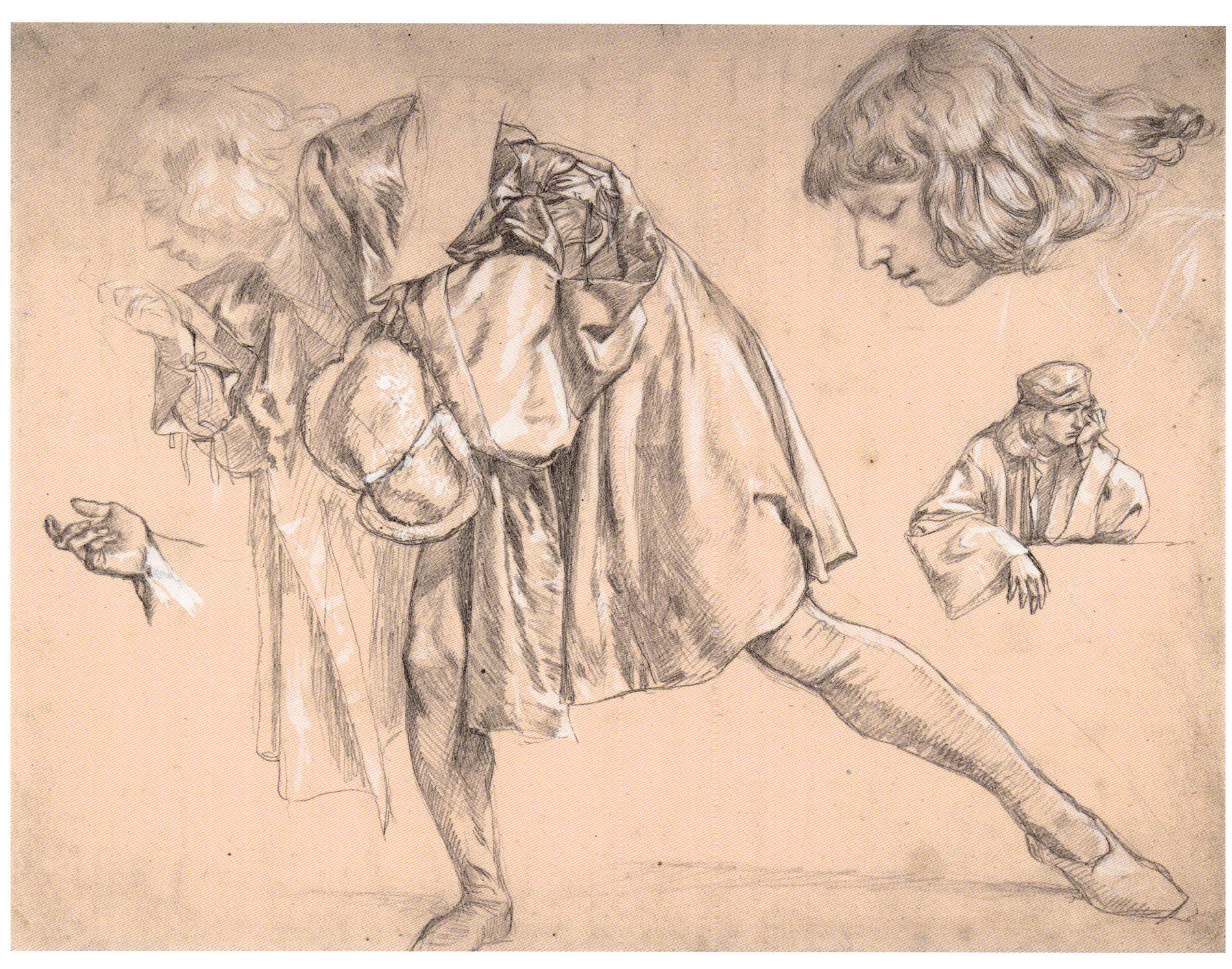

12

Studies for "Departure of the Prodigal Son," 1862–1863

Graphite, heightened with white, on pink paper, 9½ × 12 in. (24.1 × 30.6 cm)
The Metropolitan Museum of Art, New York, Rogers Fund, 1970, 1970.114.1

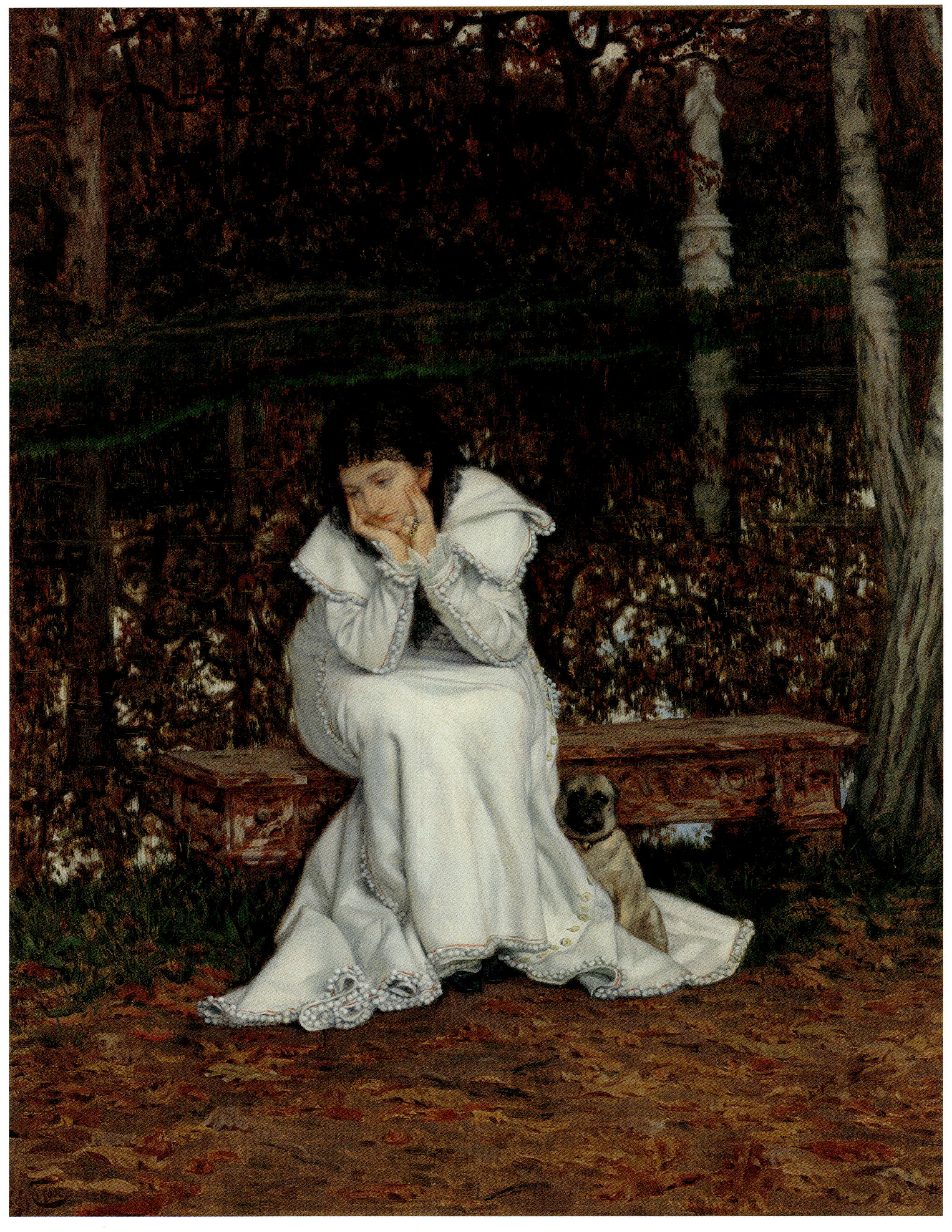

13

MELANCHOLY, CA. 1869

Oil on wood panel, 19½ × 14¾ in. (49.5 × 37.5 cm)
Collection of Ann and Gordon Getty

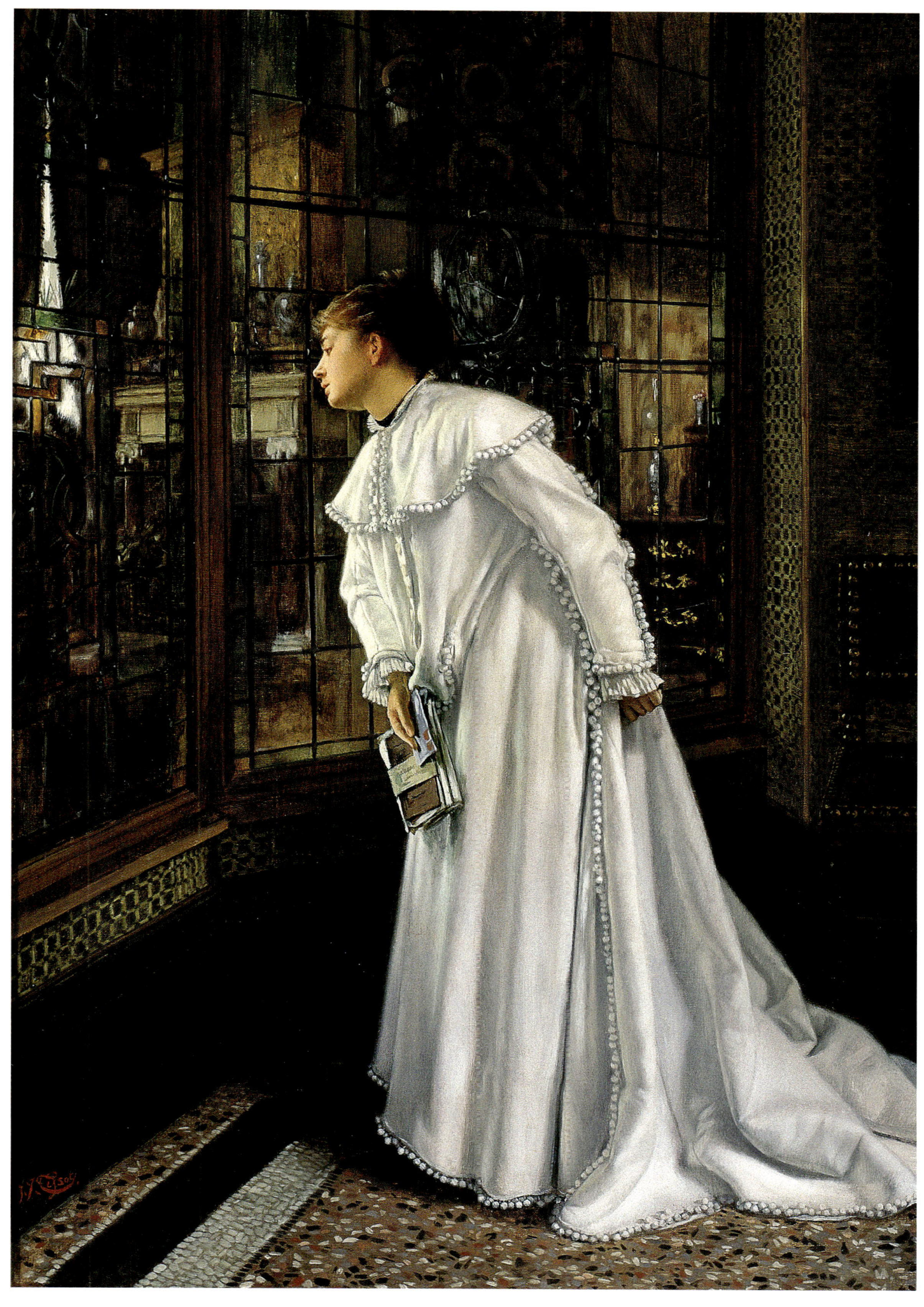

14

THE STAIRCASE, 1869

Oil on canvas, 22 × 15 in. (55.9 × 38.1 cm)

Colección Pérez Simón, Mexico City

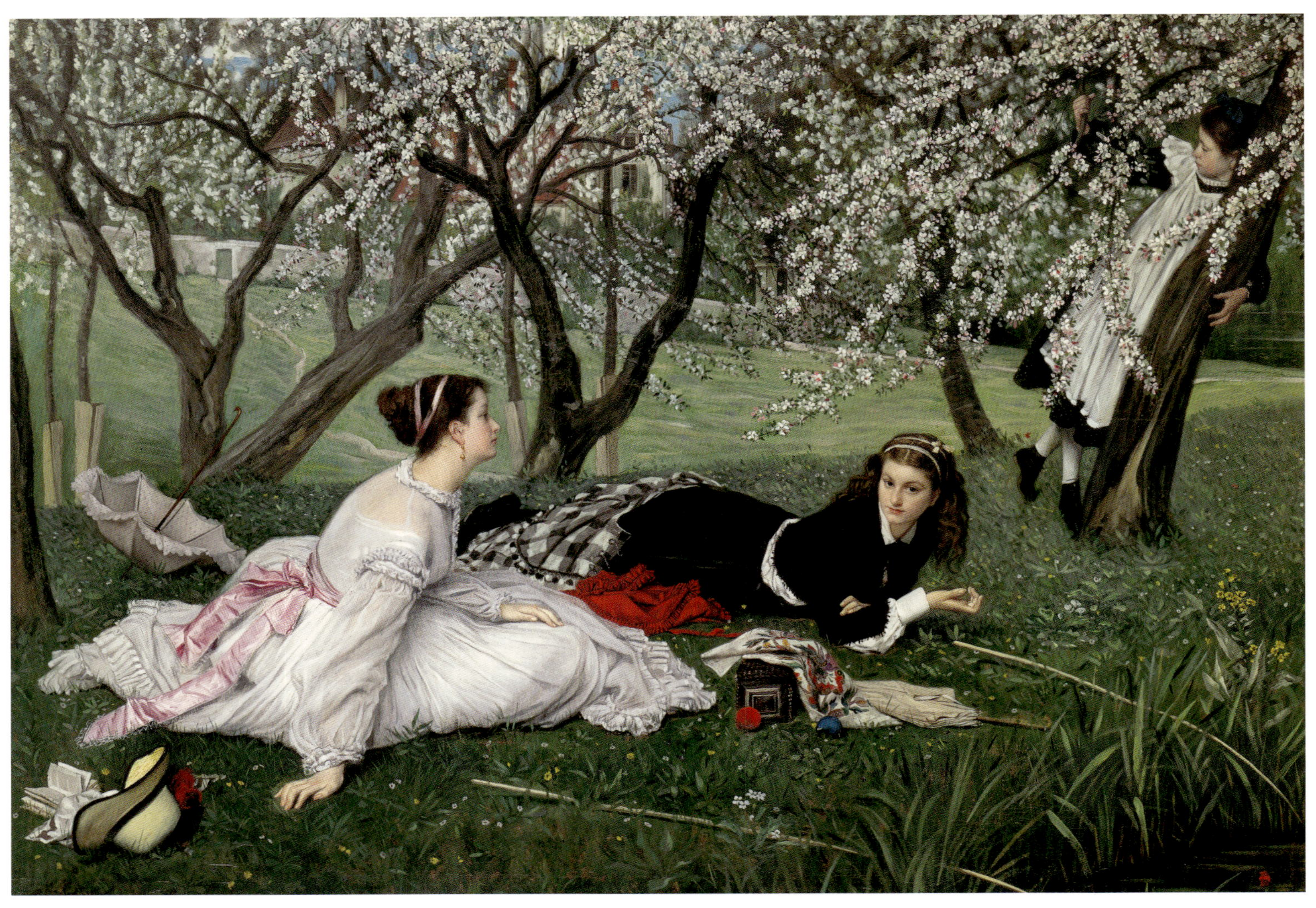

15

Spring, 1865

Oil on canvas, 36 × 50 in. (91.4 × 127 cm)
Colección Pérez Simón, Mexico City

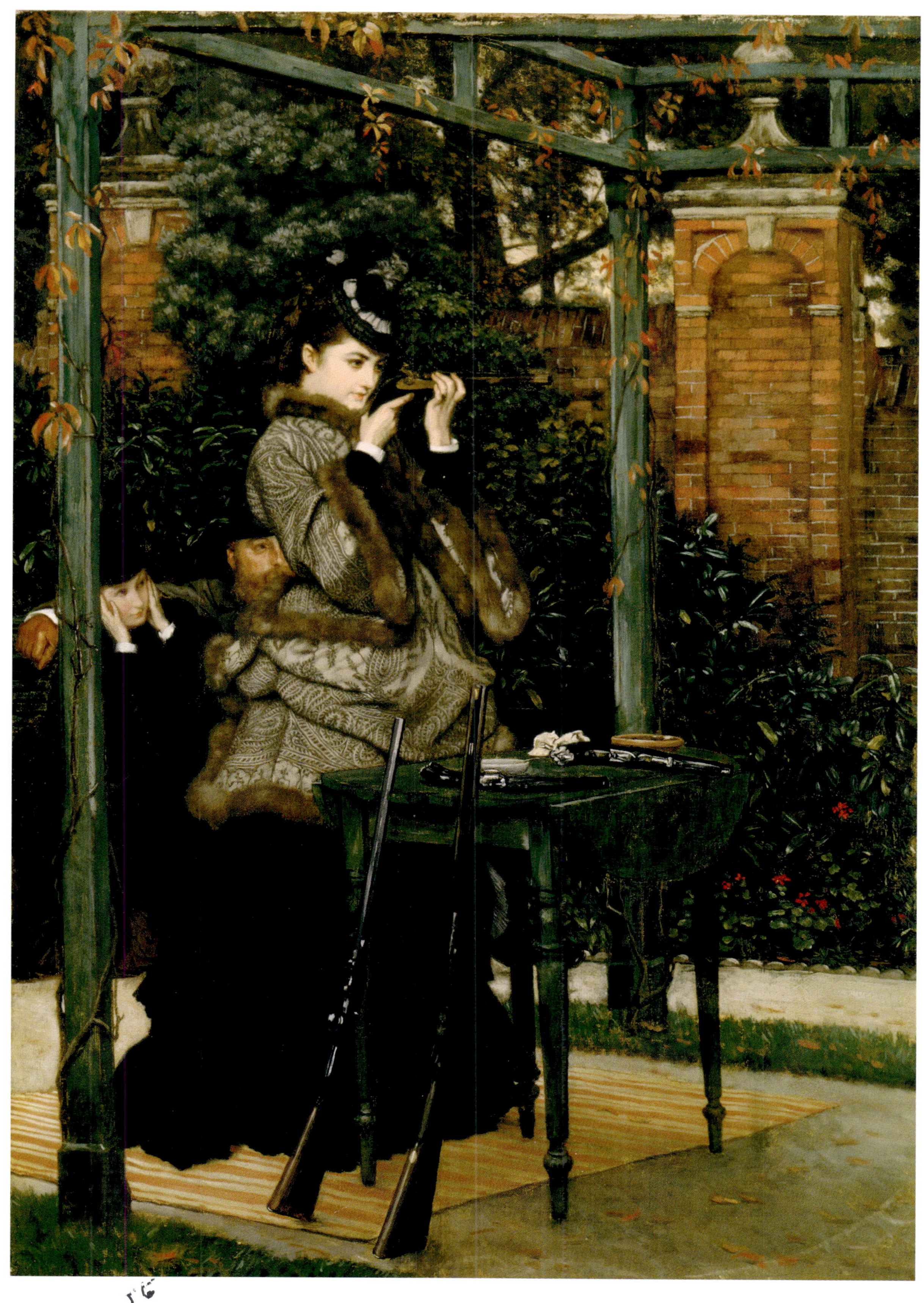

16

Safe to Win, 1869

also known as **The Crack Shot** or **At the Rifle Range**

Oil on canvas, 26⅝ × 18¼ in. (67.3 × 46 4 cm)

Wimpole Hall, Cambridgeshire, England, National Trust Collections (The Bambridge Collection), NT 207841

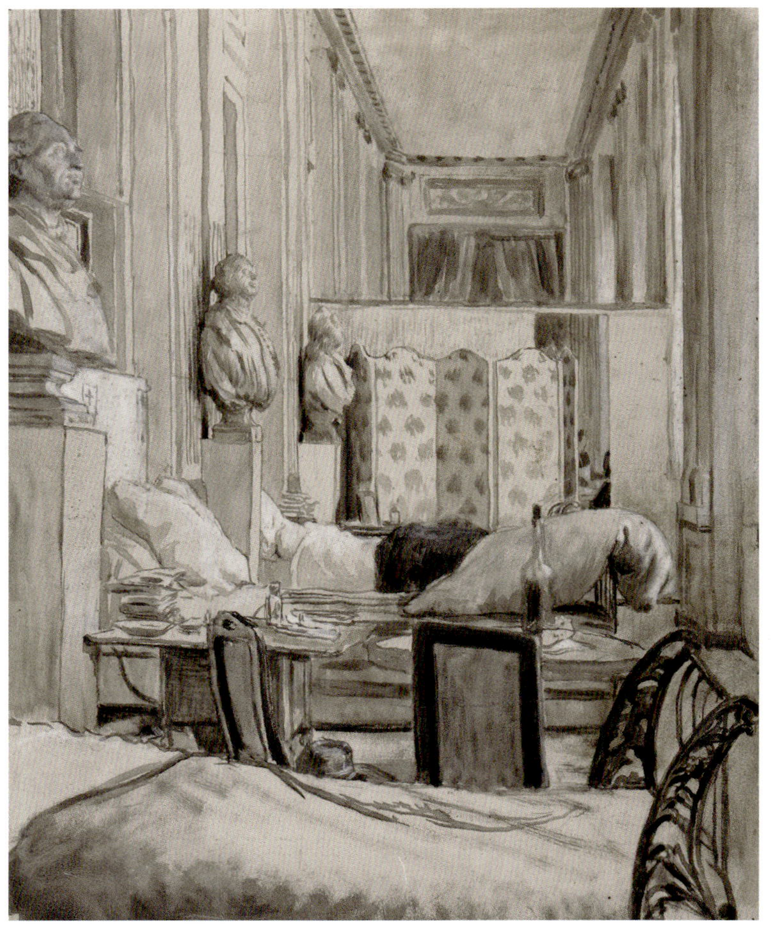

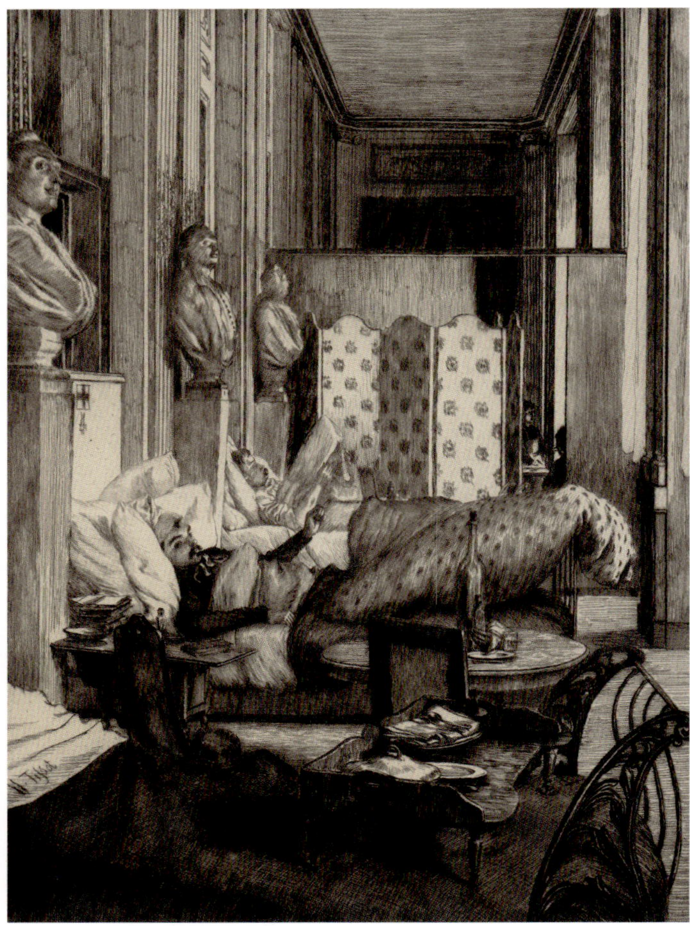

17

Study for "Foyer of the Comédie-Française during the Siege of Paris," 1870

Graphite, heightened white opaque watercolor, and wash on paper laminated on cardboard, 19½ × 12½ in. (49.6 × 31.6 cm)
Musée d'Arts de Nantes, Bought in 2014, 14.2.1.D

18

Foyer of the Comédie-Française during the Siege of Paris, 1877

Etching, 15 × 10⅞ in. (38.1 × 27.6 cm)
Fine Arts Museums of San Francisco, Museum purchase, Achenbach Foundation for Graphic Arts Endowment Fund, 1978.1.32

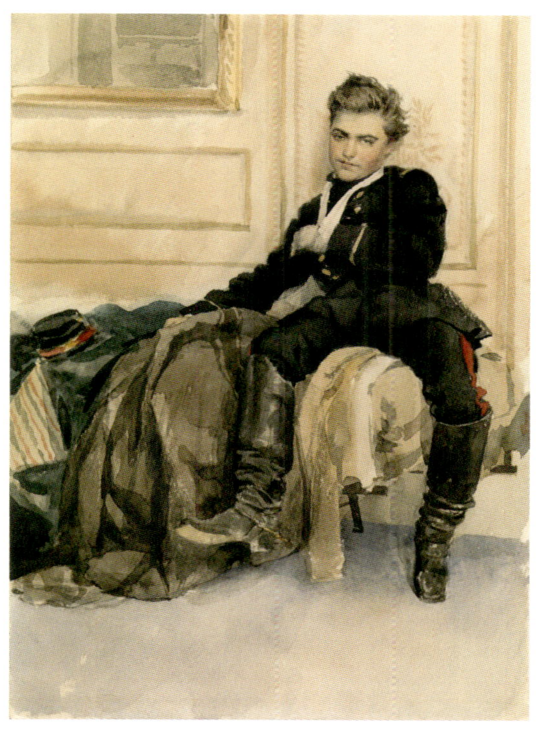

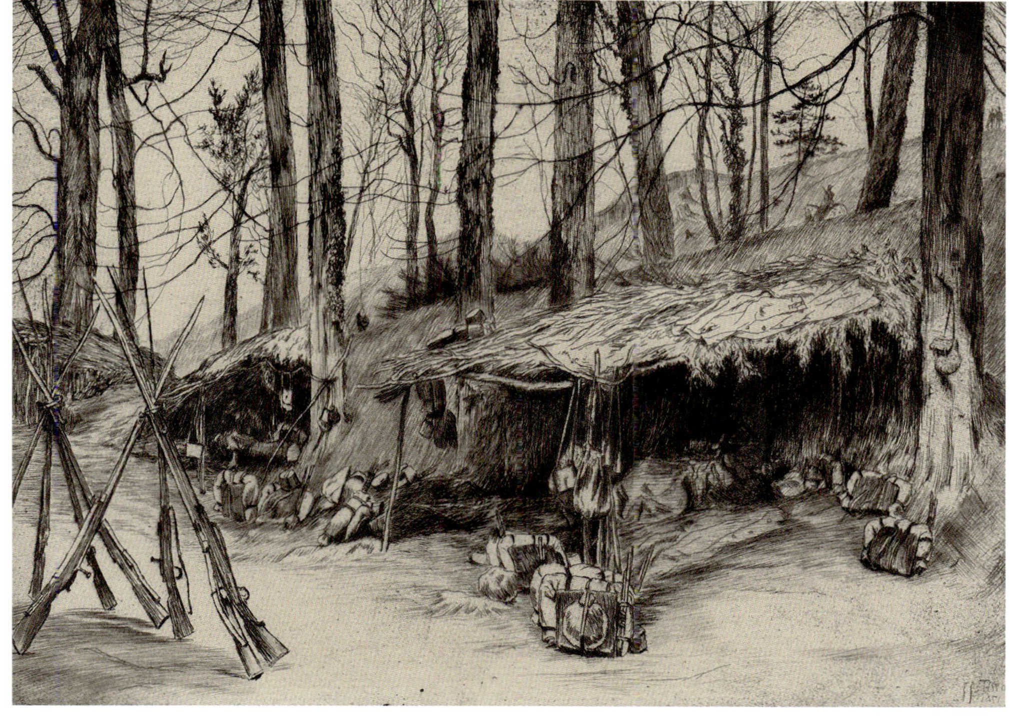

19

The Wounded Soldier, ca. 1870

Watercolor on paper, 13⅞ × 9⅞ in. (35.3 × 25.2 cm)
Tate, London, Purchased 2016, T14636

20

An Encampment—Siege of Paris—Parc d'Issy, 1878

Etching and drypoint, 6⅝ × 9⅛ in. (16.8 × 23.2 cm)
Fine Arts Museums of San Francisco, Museum purchase, Achenbach Foundation for Graphic Arts Endowment Fund, 1980.1.26

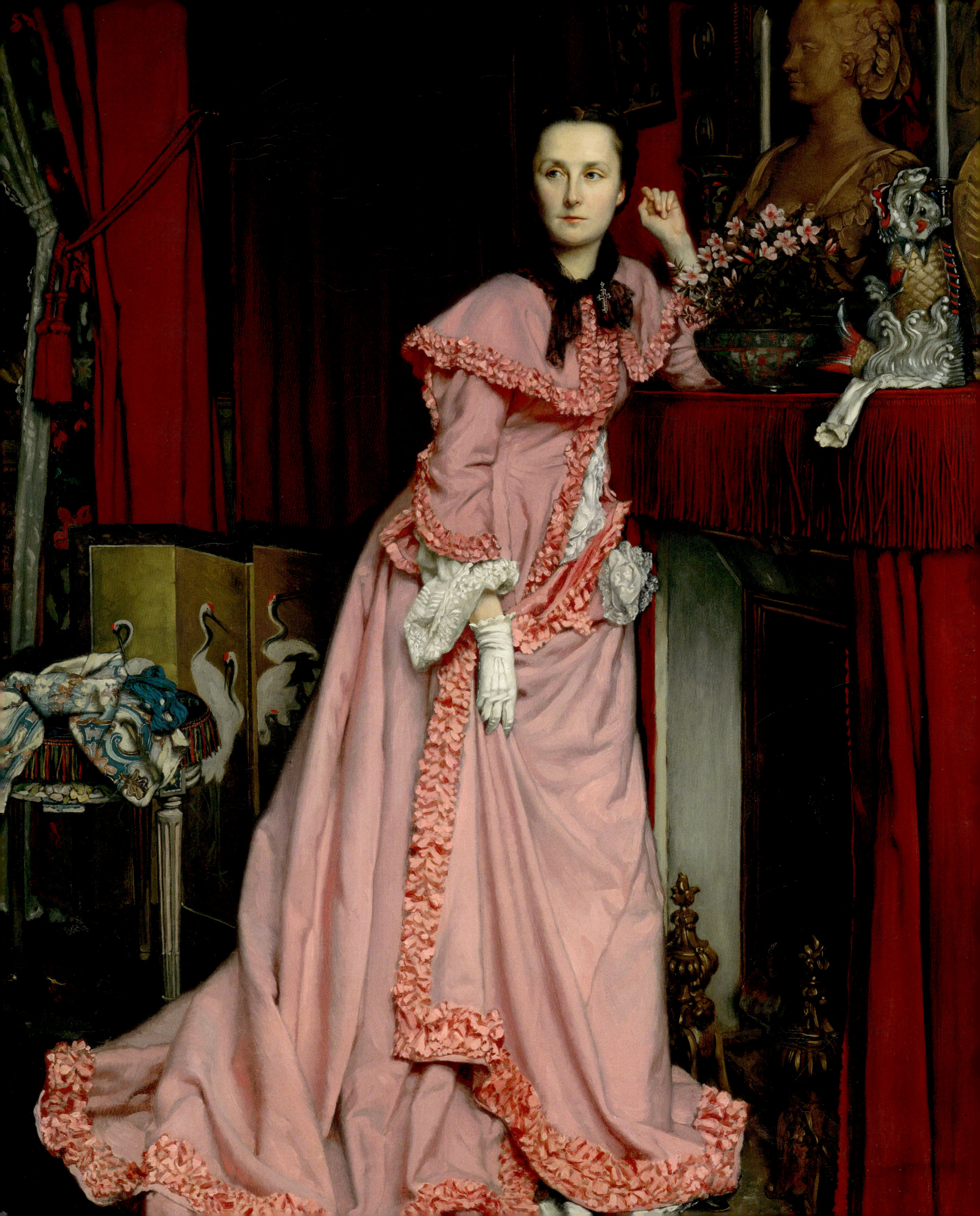

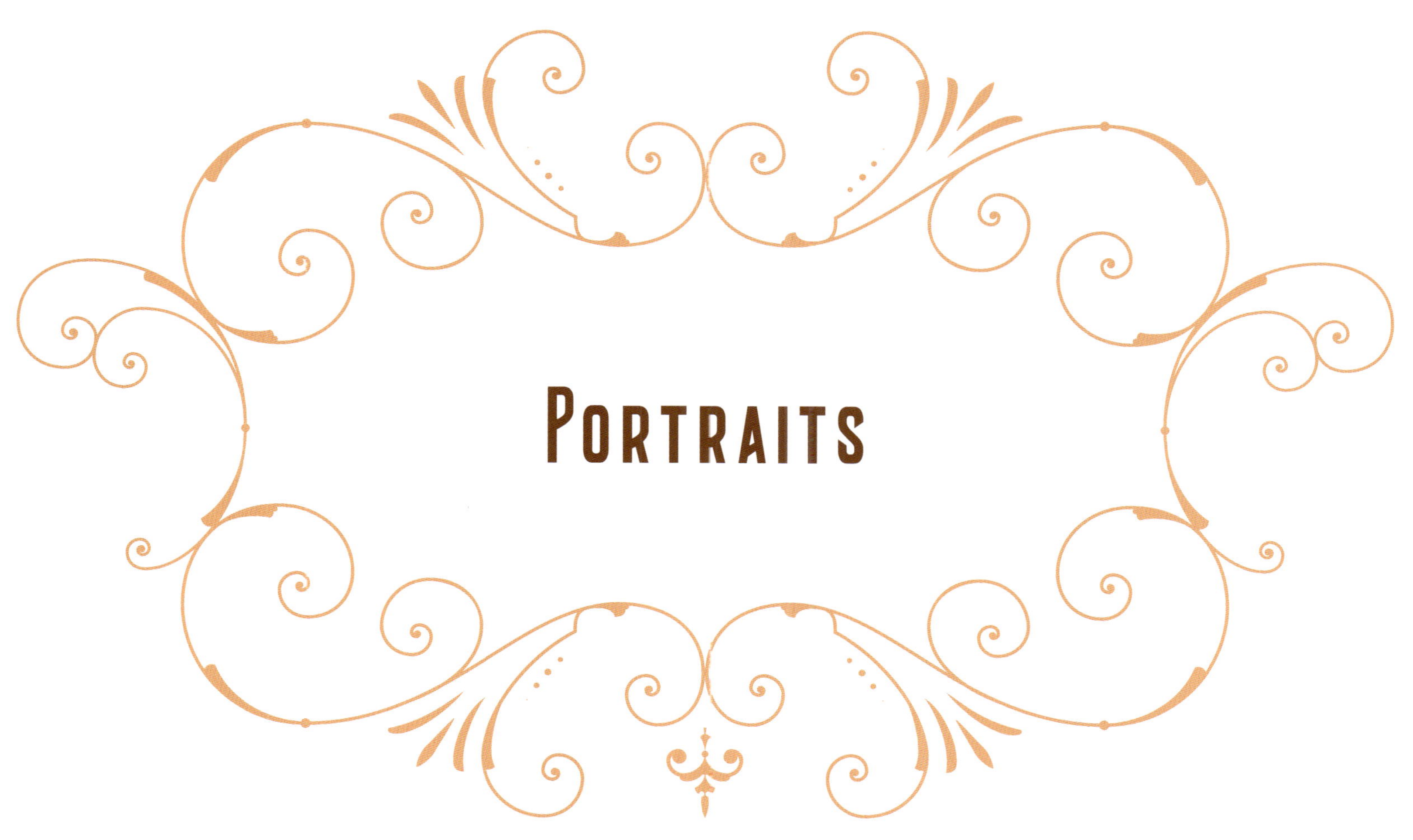

Portraits

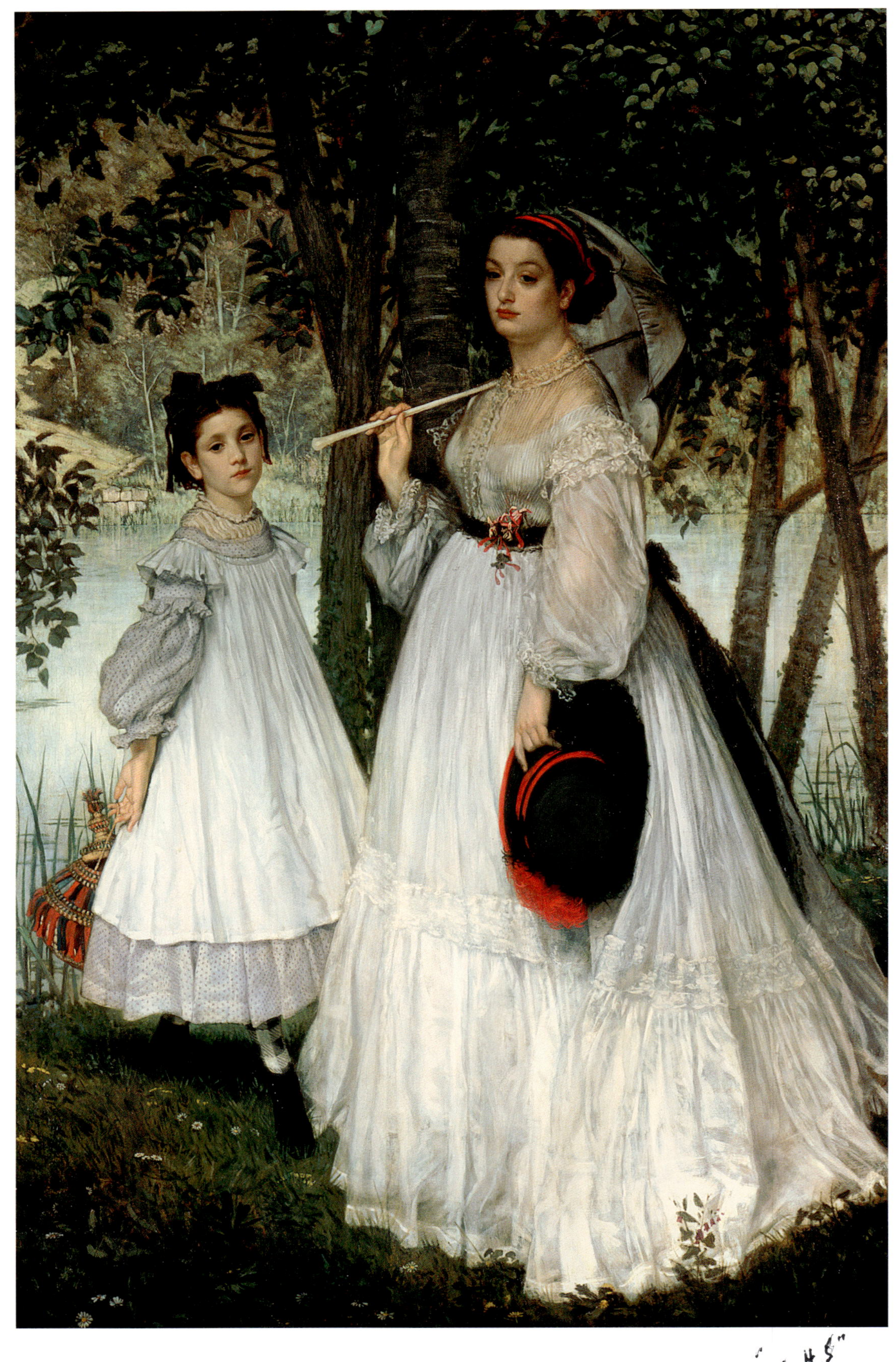

21

THE TWO SISTERS: PORTRAIT, 1863

Oil on canvas, 82⅝ × 53½ in. (210 × 135.5 cm)
Musée d'Orsay, Paris, Gift of Albert Bichet, RF 2788

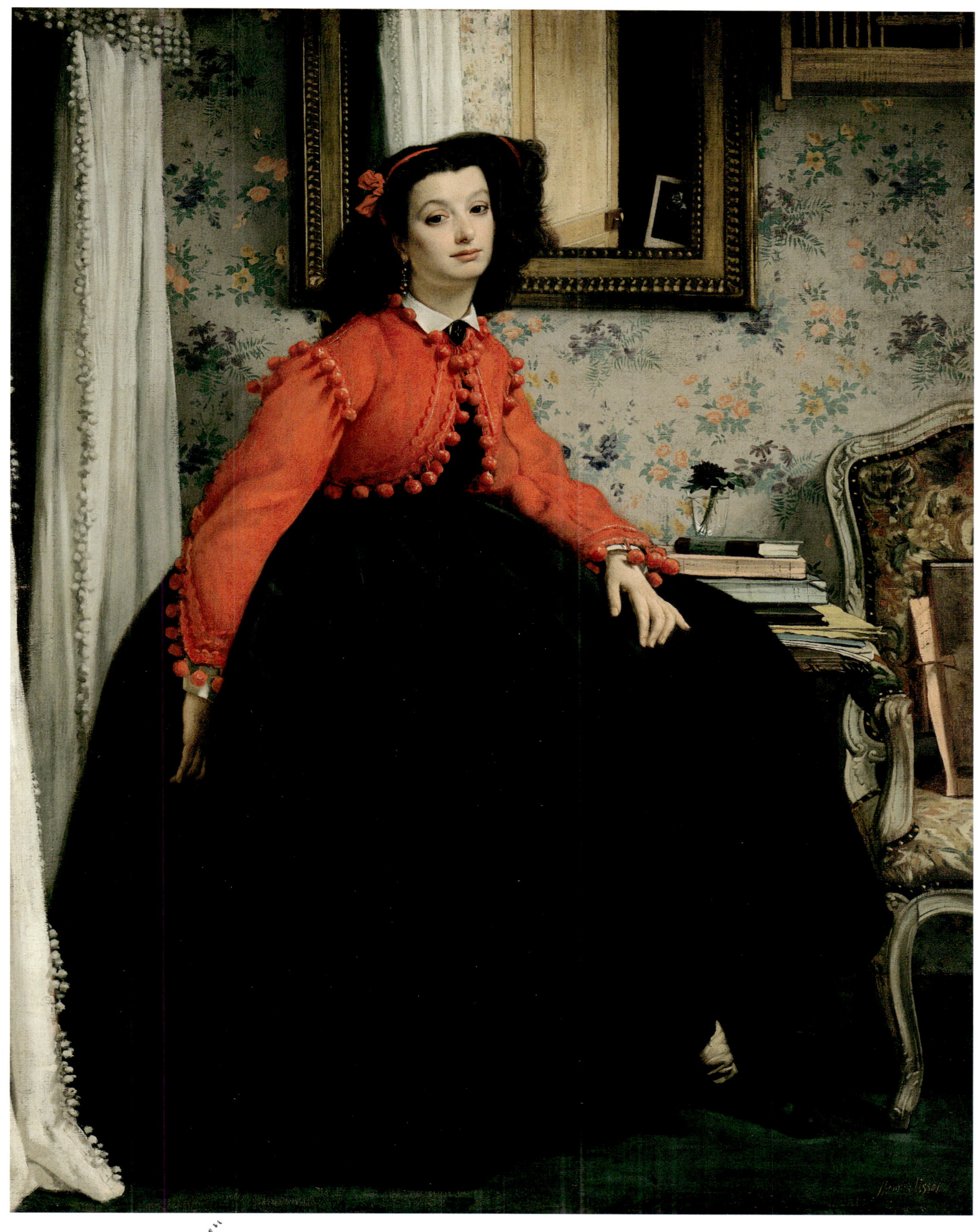

4' x 3'5"

22

Portrait of Mlle L. L..., 1864

Oil on canvas, 48⅝ × 39⅛ in. (123.5 × 99 cm)

Musée d'Orsay, Paris, Acquired at the Thiébault-Sisson Sale, 1907, RF 2698

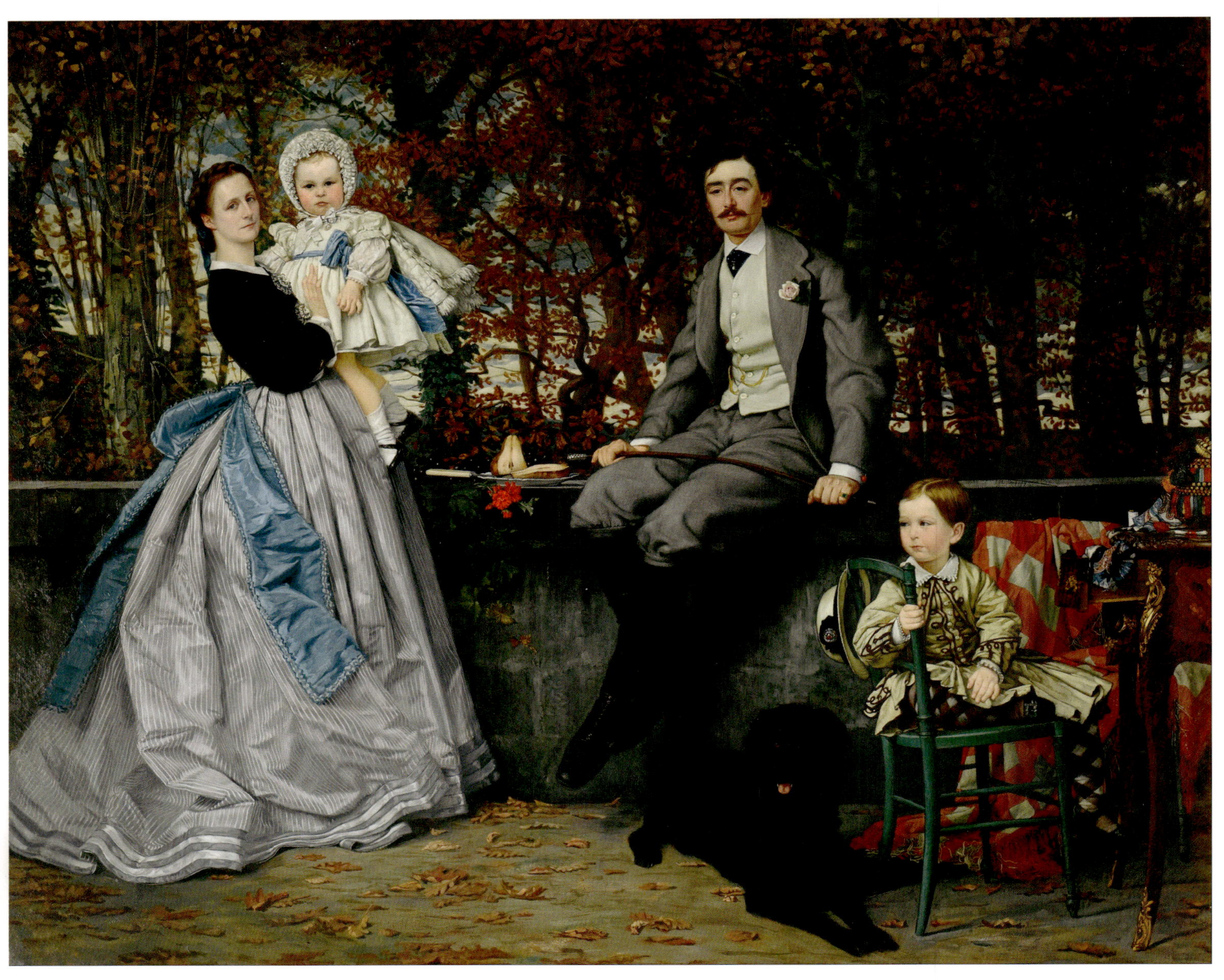

23

PORTRAIT OF THE MARQUIS AND MARQUISE DE MIRAMON AND THEIR CHILDREN, 1865

Oil on canvas, 69 3/4 × 85 3/8 in. (177 × 217 cm)

Musée d'Orsay, Paris, Acquired in 2006, RF 2006.22

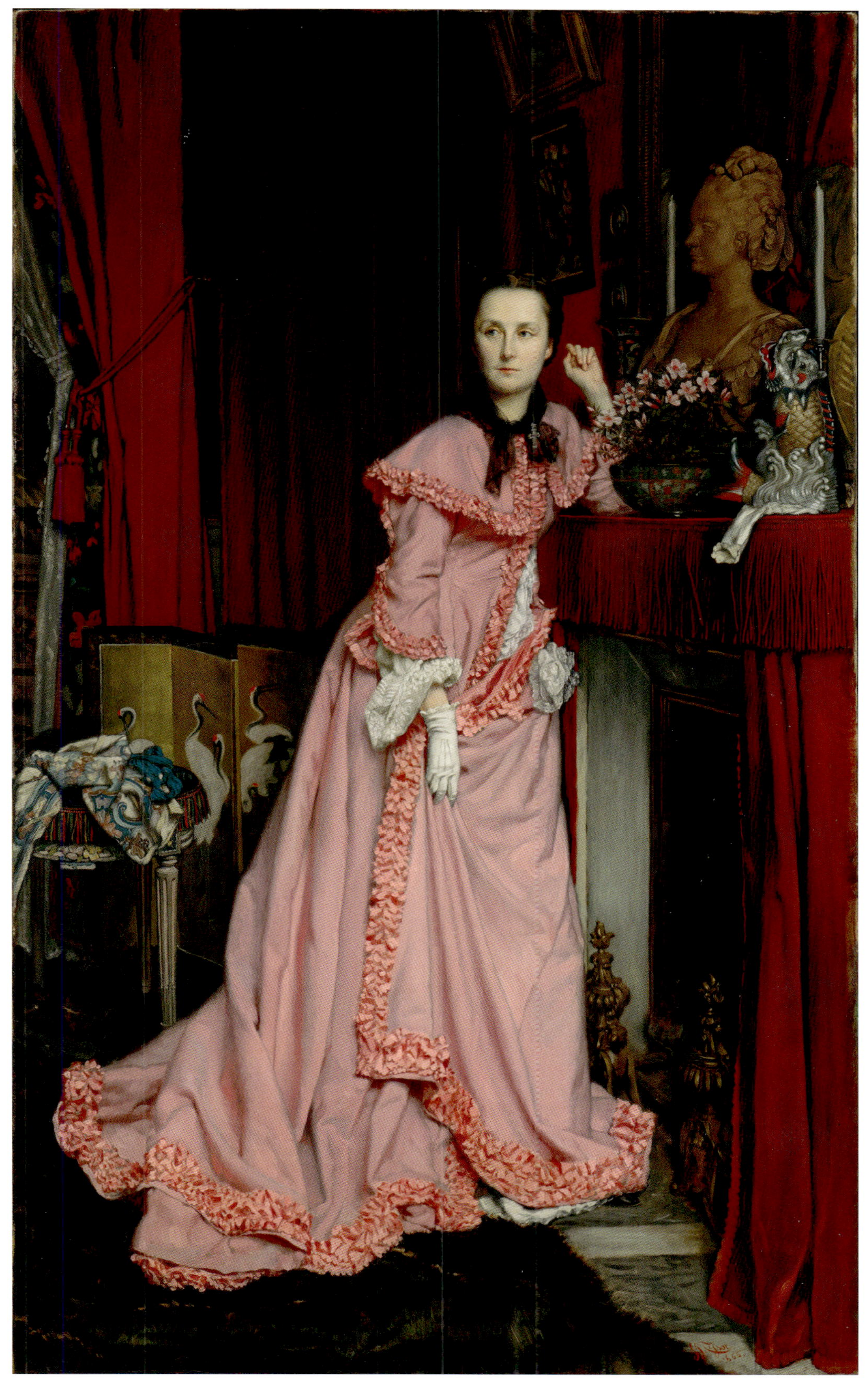

24

PORTRAIT OF THE MARQUISE DE MIRAMON,
NÉE THÉRÈSE FEUILLANT, 1866

Oil on canvas, 50½ × 30⅜ in. (128.3 × 77.2 cm)
The J. Paul Getty Museum, Los Angeles, 2007.7

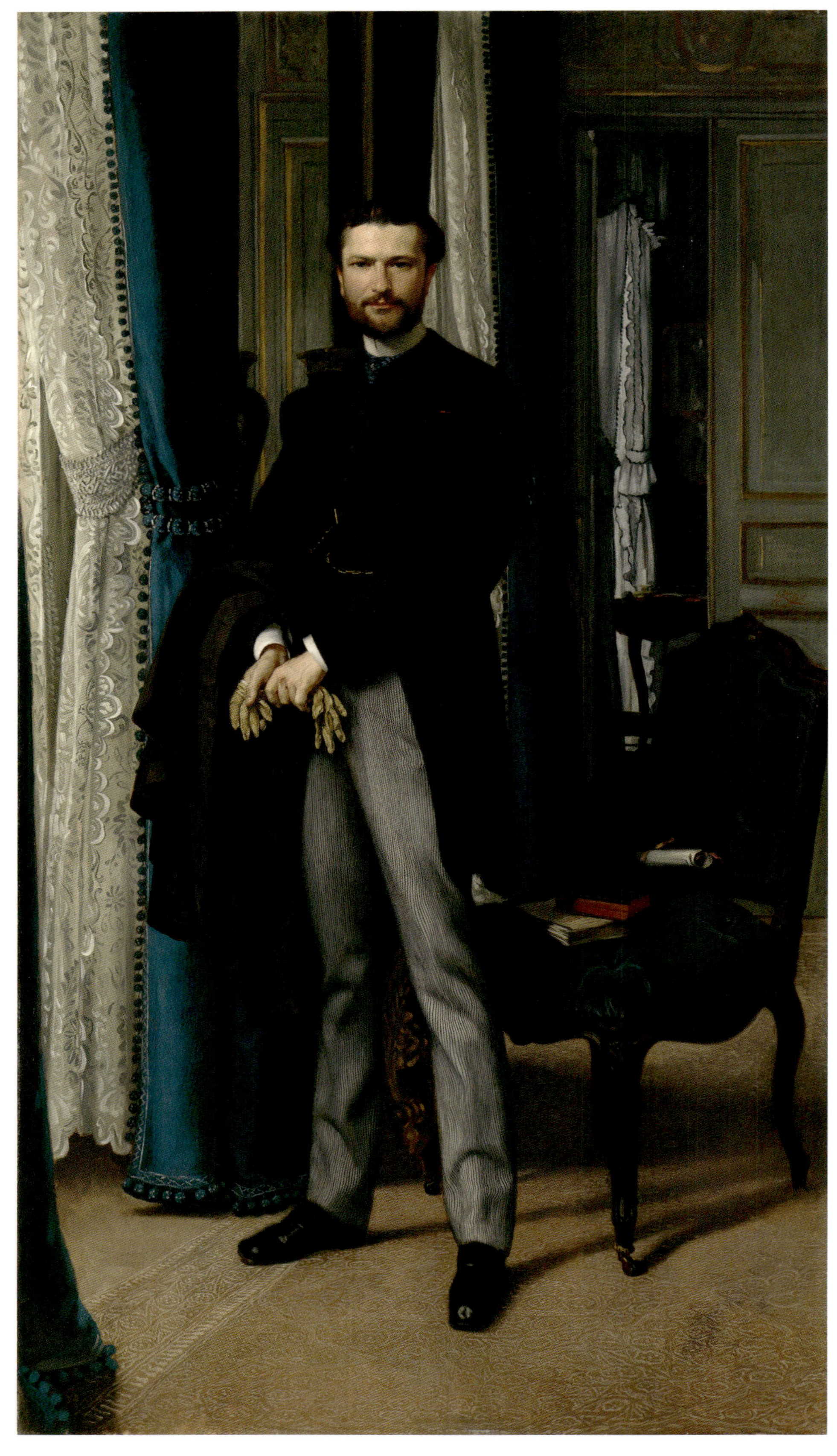

25

Portrait of Aimé Seillière, 1866

Oil on canvas, 50⅜ × 28 in. (128 × 71 cm)
Staatliche Kunsthalle Karlsruhe, Germany, Inv. 2826

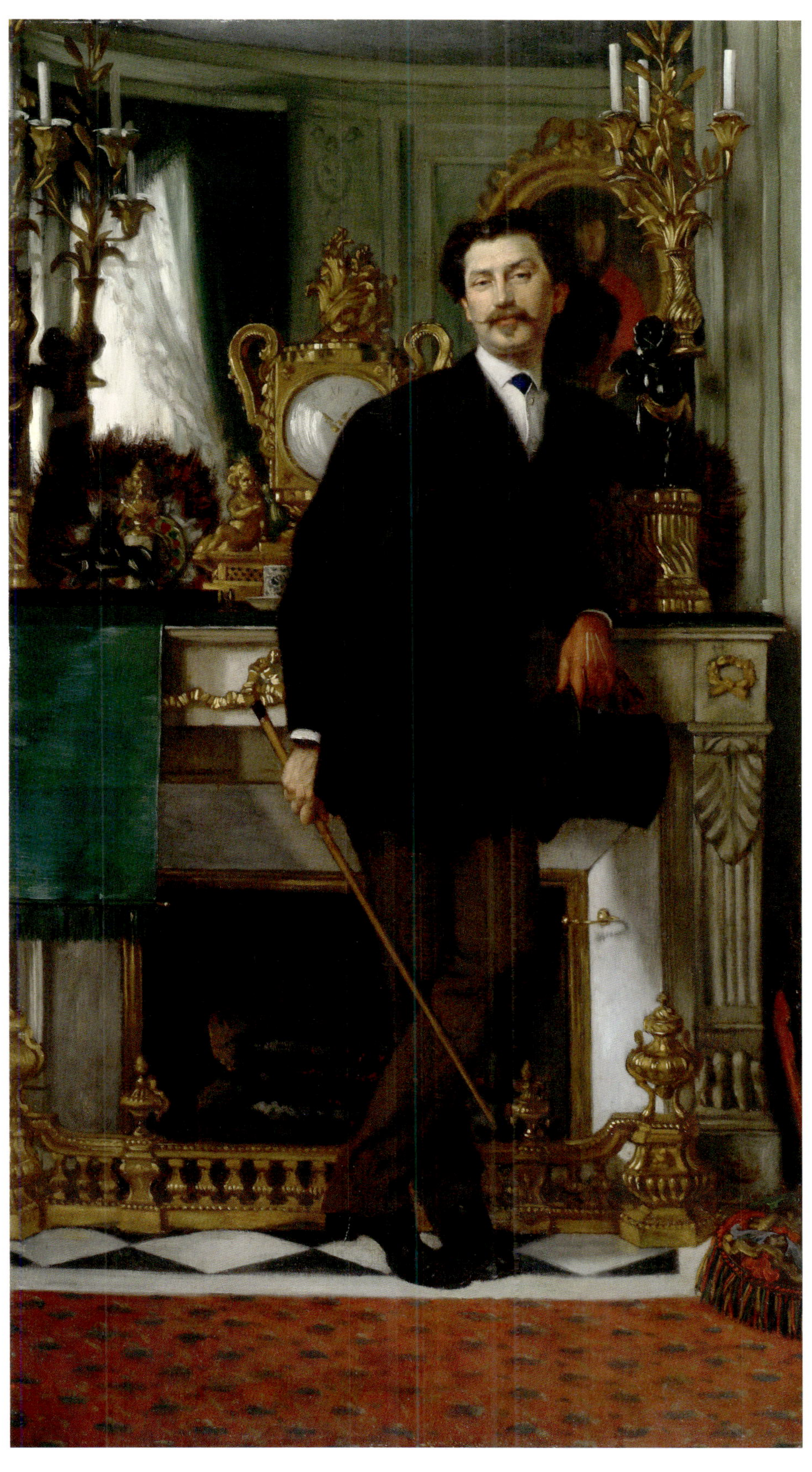

26

PORTRAIT OF EUGÈNE COPPENS DE FONTENAY, 1867

Oil on canvas, $27\frac{1}{2} \times 15\frac{3}{8}$ in. (69.8 × 39.1 cm)

Philadelphia Museum of Art, Purchased with the W.P. Wilstach Fund, 1972, W1972-2-1

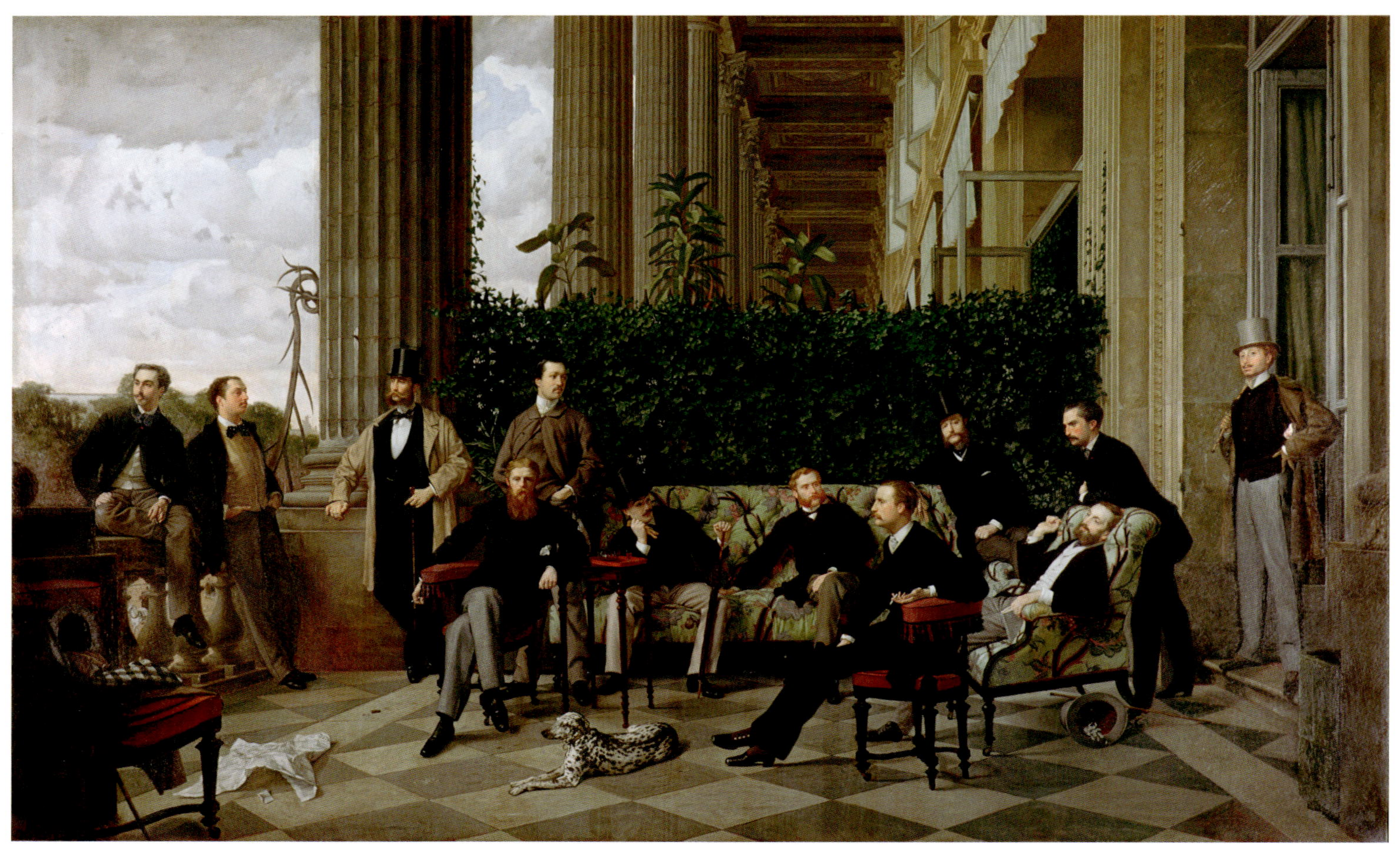

27

The Circle of the Rue Royale, 1866–1868

Oil on canvas, 68⅞ × 110⅝ in. (175 × 281 cm)
Musée d'Orsay, Paris, Purchased, 2011, RF 2011.53

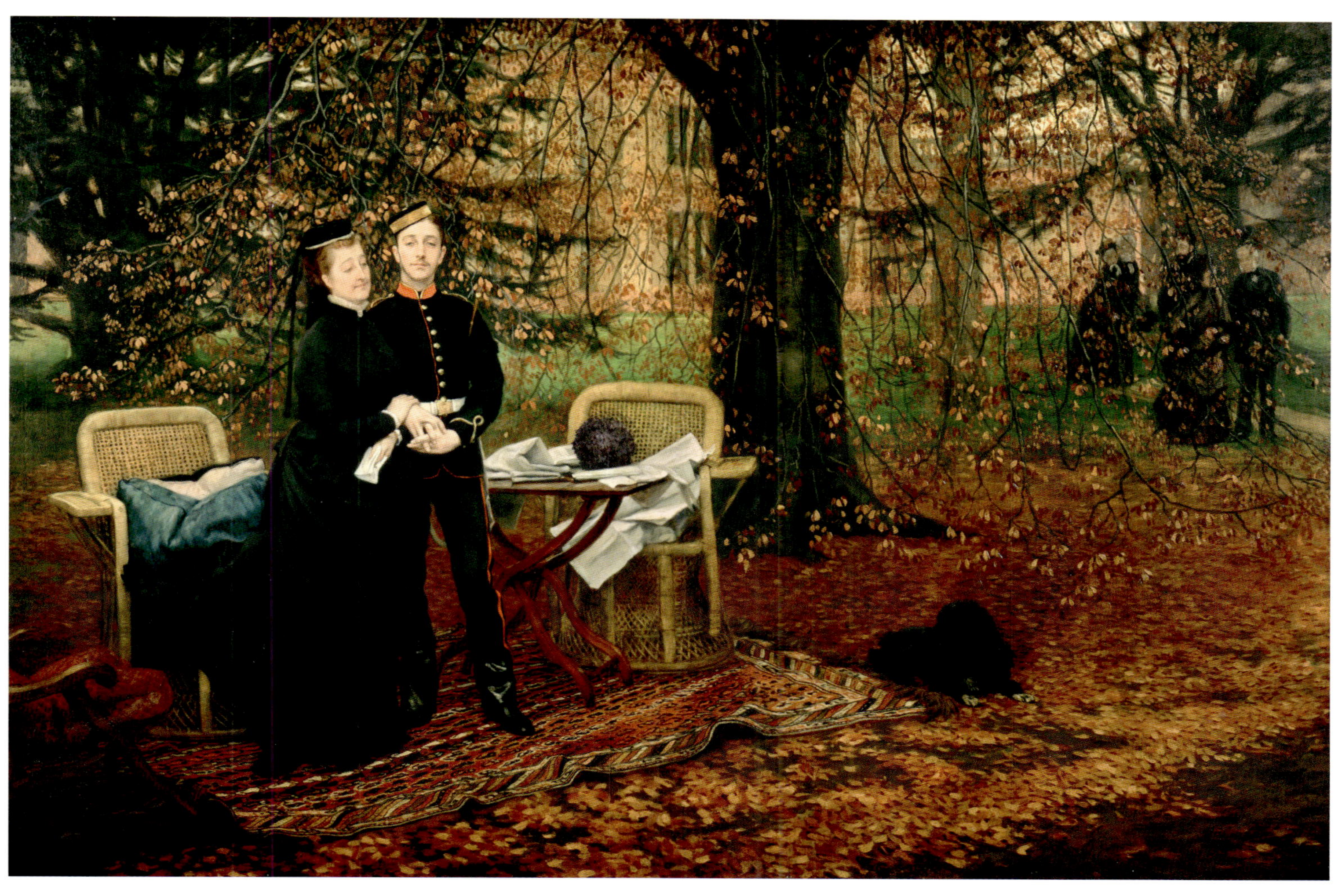

28

Empress Eugénie and the Prince Imperial in the Grounds of Camden Place, Chislehurst, 1874–1875

Oil on canvas, 42 × 60 in. (106.6 × 152.4 cm)
Musée National du Palais de Compiègne, France, Purchased in 1934

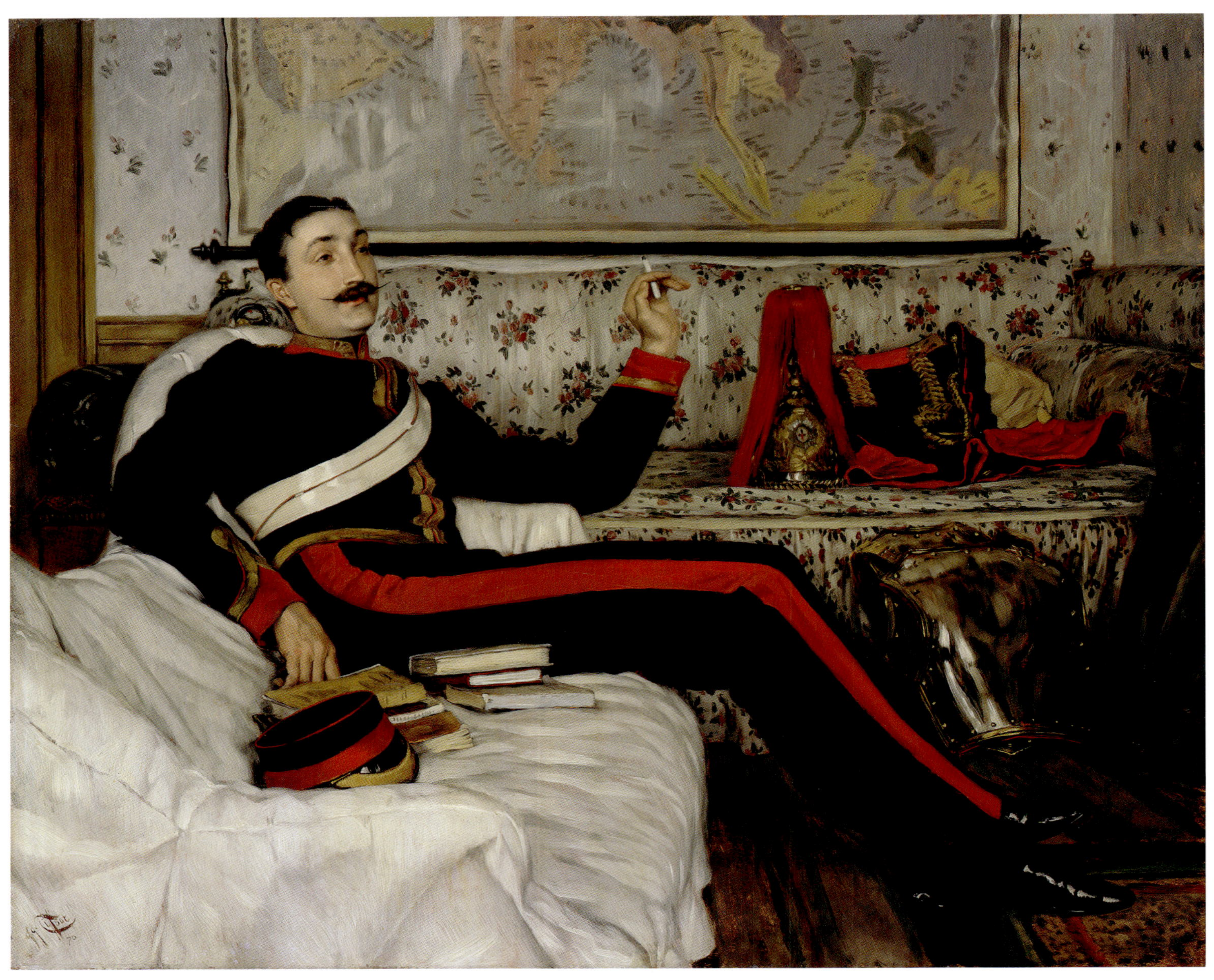

29

Portrait of Captain *** [Frederick Burnaby], 1870

Oil on wood panel, 19⅝ × 24 in. (50 × 61 cm)

National Portrait Gallery, London, Purchased, 1933, NPG 2642

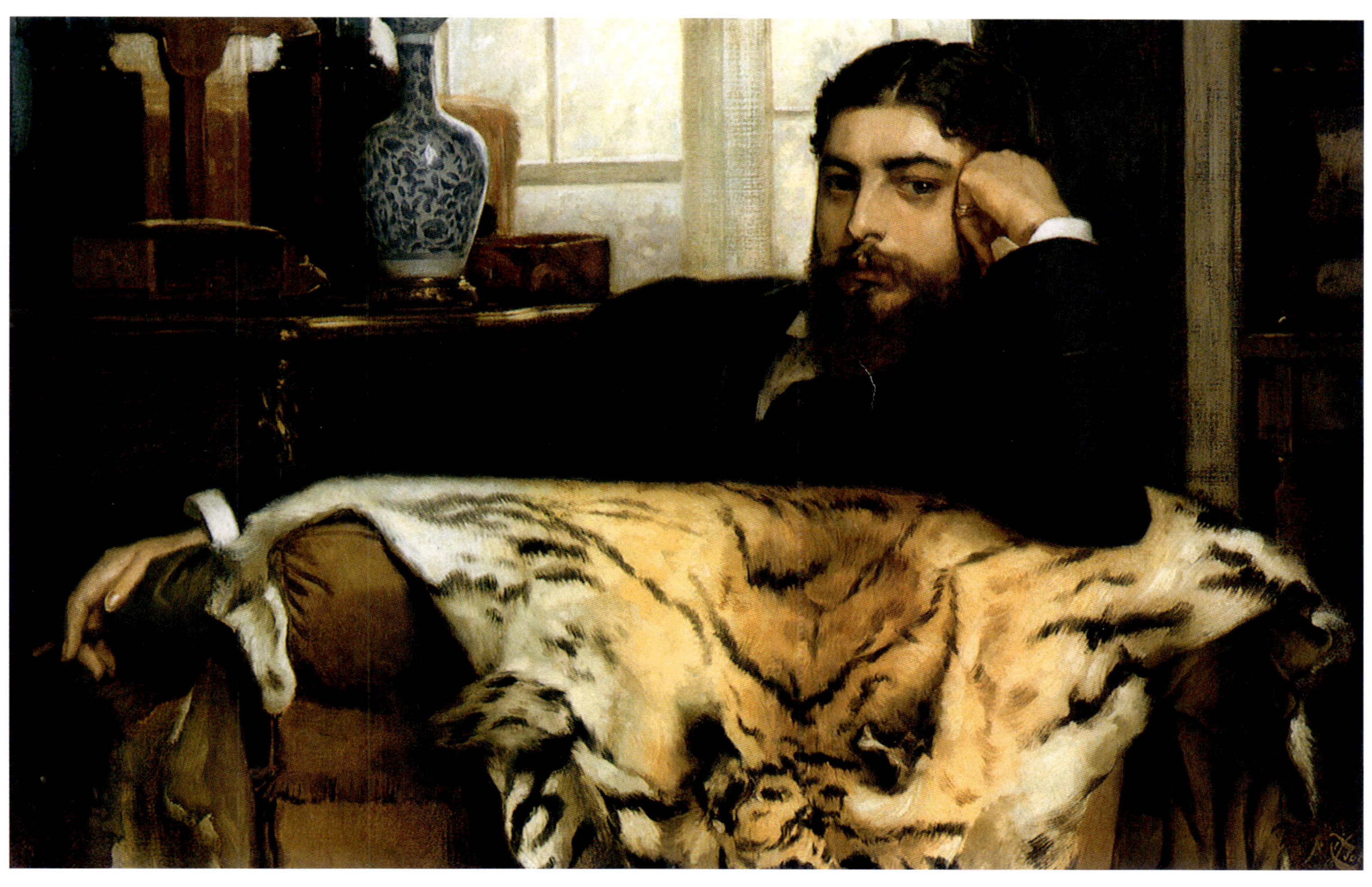

30

PORTRAIT OF ALGERNON MOSES MARSDEN, 1877

Oil on canvas, 19½ × 29 in. (49.5 × 73.7 cm)

Private collection, courtesy of Grant Ford Ltd.

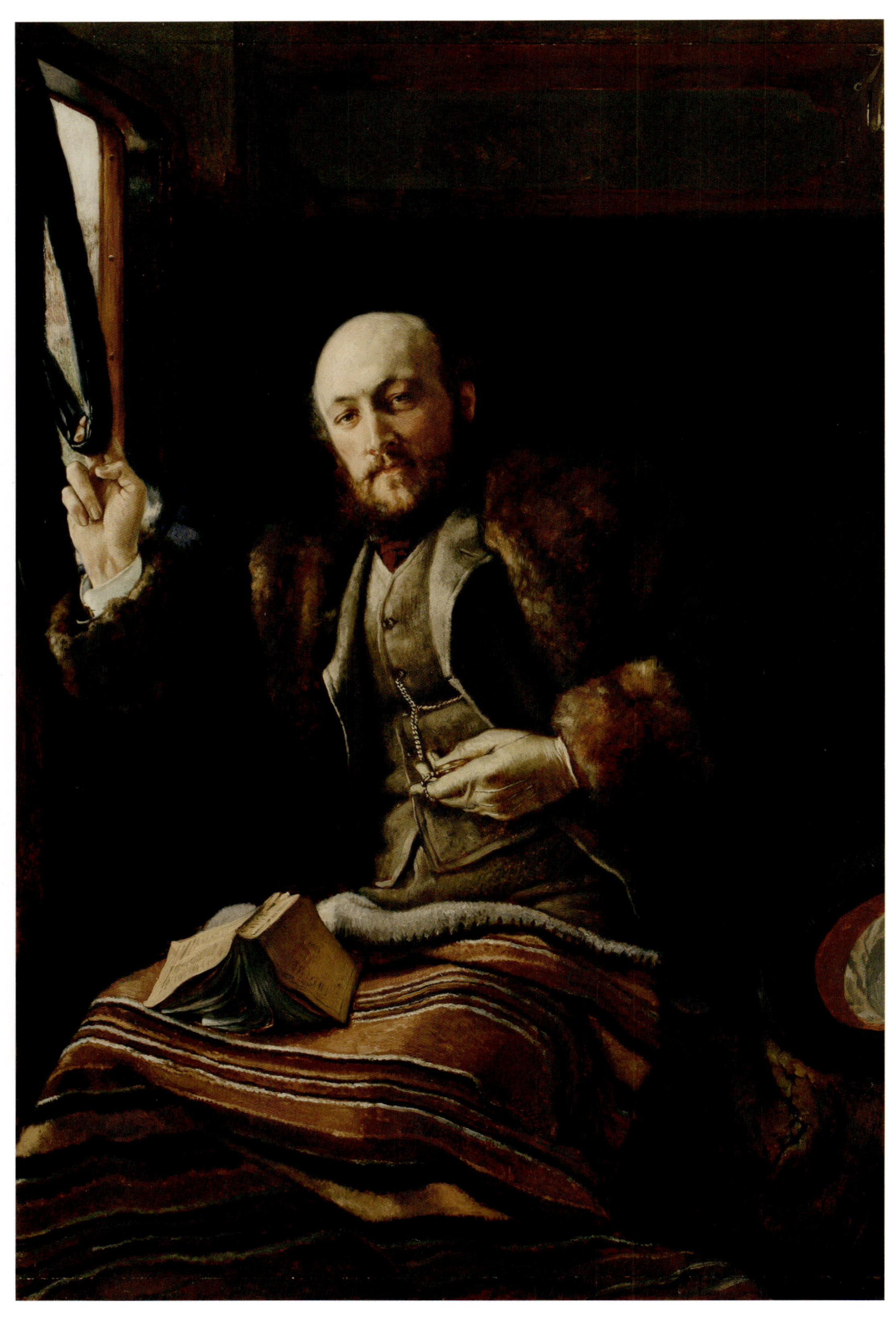

31

Portrait of Colonel *** [Longley], ca. 1872–1876
also known as **Gentleman in a Railway Carriage**

Oil on wood panel, 24⅞ × 16⅞ in. (63.3 × 43 cm)
Worcester Art Museum, Massachusetts, Alexander and Caroline Murdock De Witt Fund, 1965.16

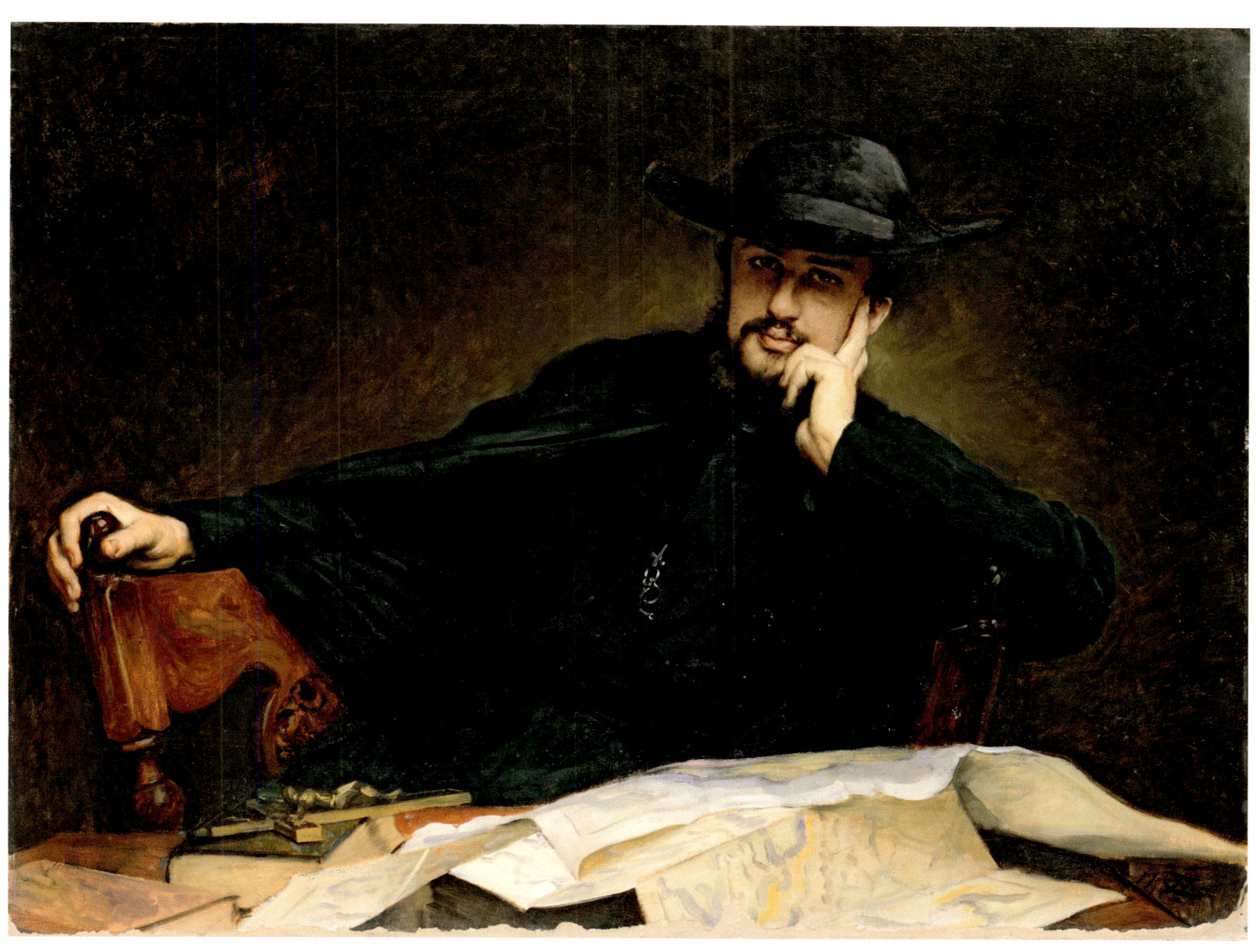

32

PORTRAIT OF REVEREND PÈRE B... [BICHET],
MISSIONARY OF GABON, CA. 1884–1885

Oil on canvas, 34⅝ × 46½ in. (88.1 × 117.7 cm)
Musée d'Arts de Nantes, Albert Bichet Bequest, 1920, Inv. 1978

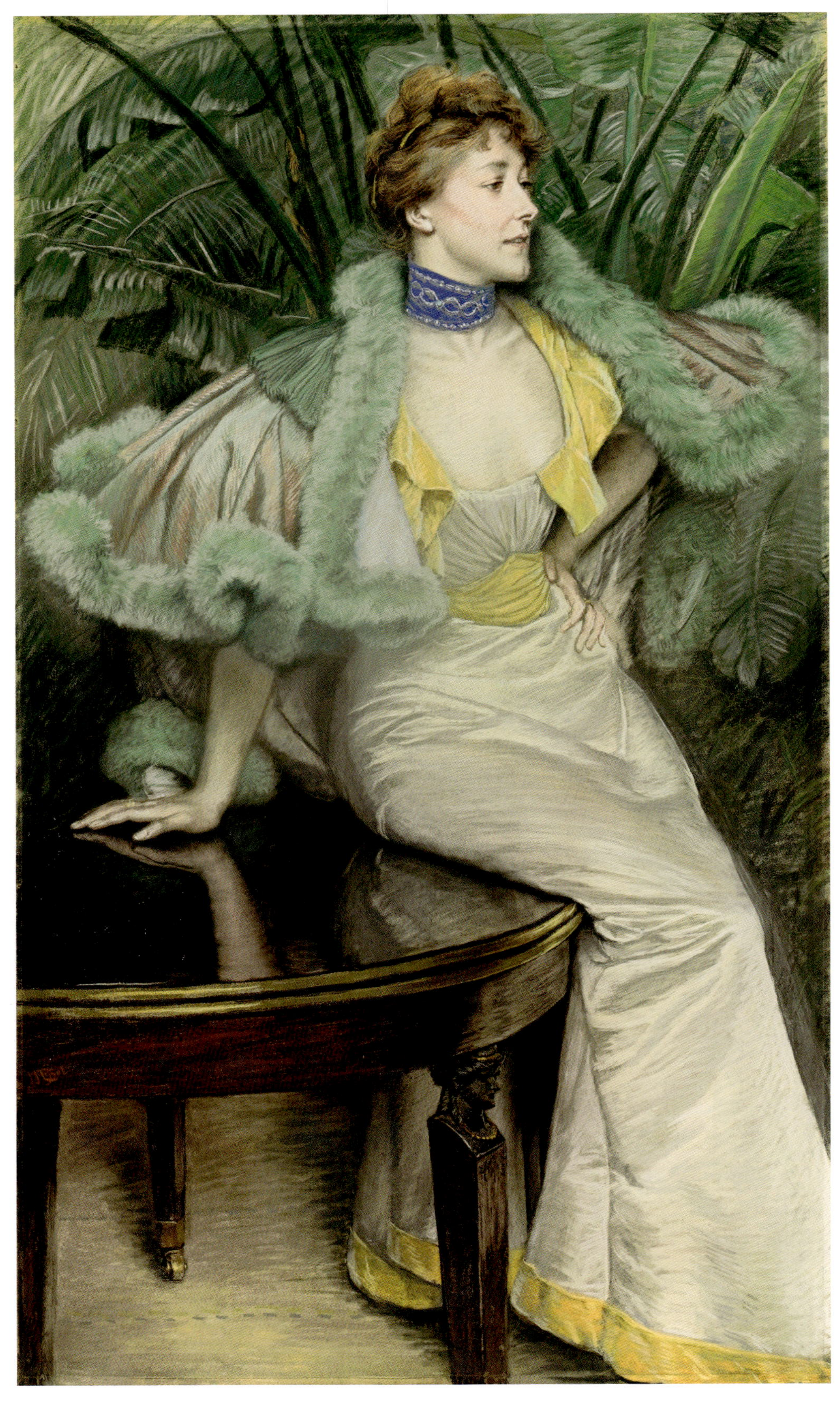

33

Portrait of the Princesse de Broglie, ca. 1895

Pastel on linen, 66⅛ × 38⅛ in. (168 × 96.8 cm)
Private collection

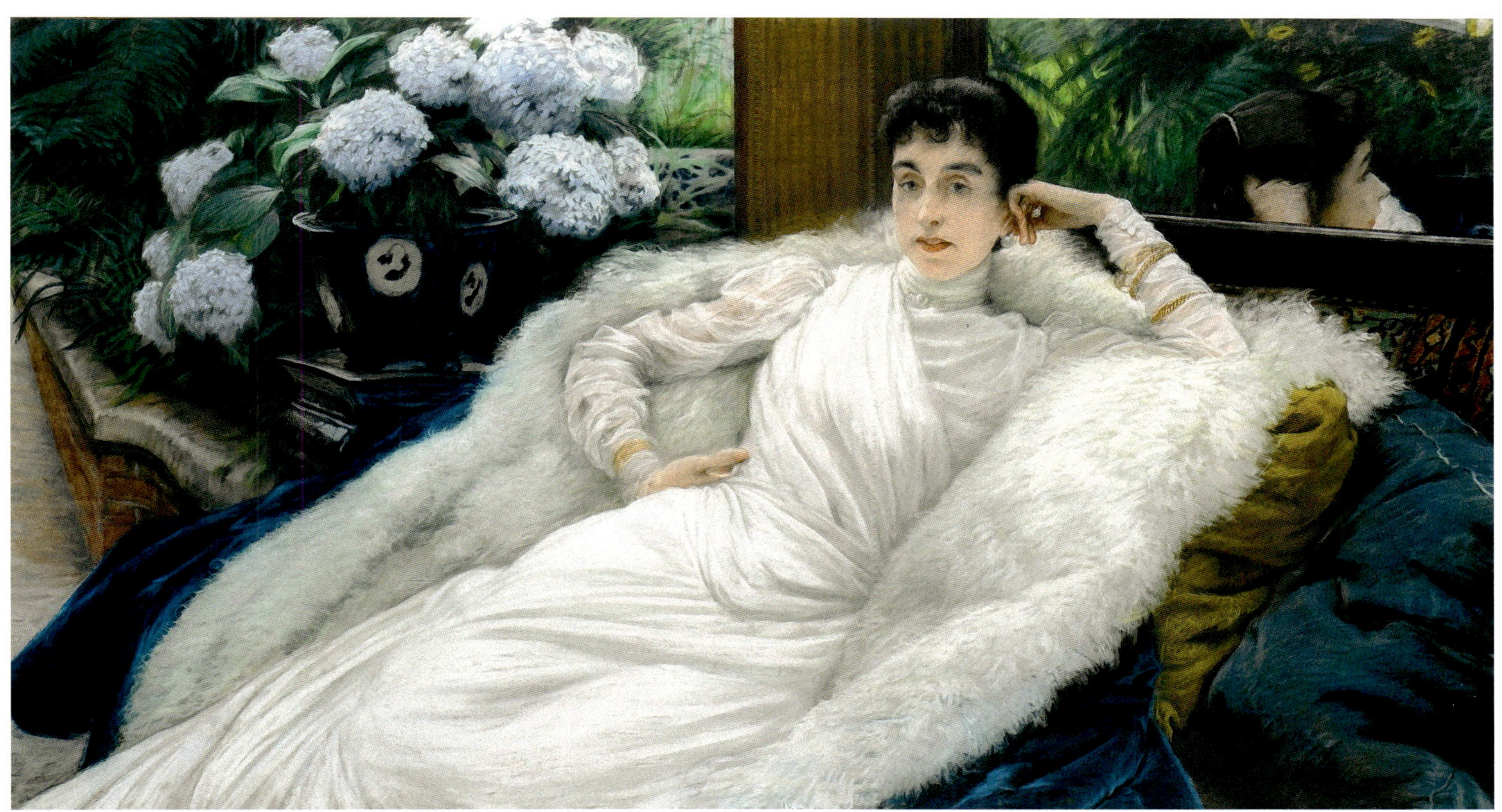

34

Portrait of Clotilde Briatte, Comtesse Pillet-Will, 1890s

Pastel on paper laid down on canvas, 35⅞ × 63¼ in. (91 × 160.5 cm)

Private collection

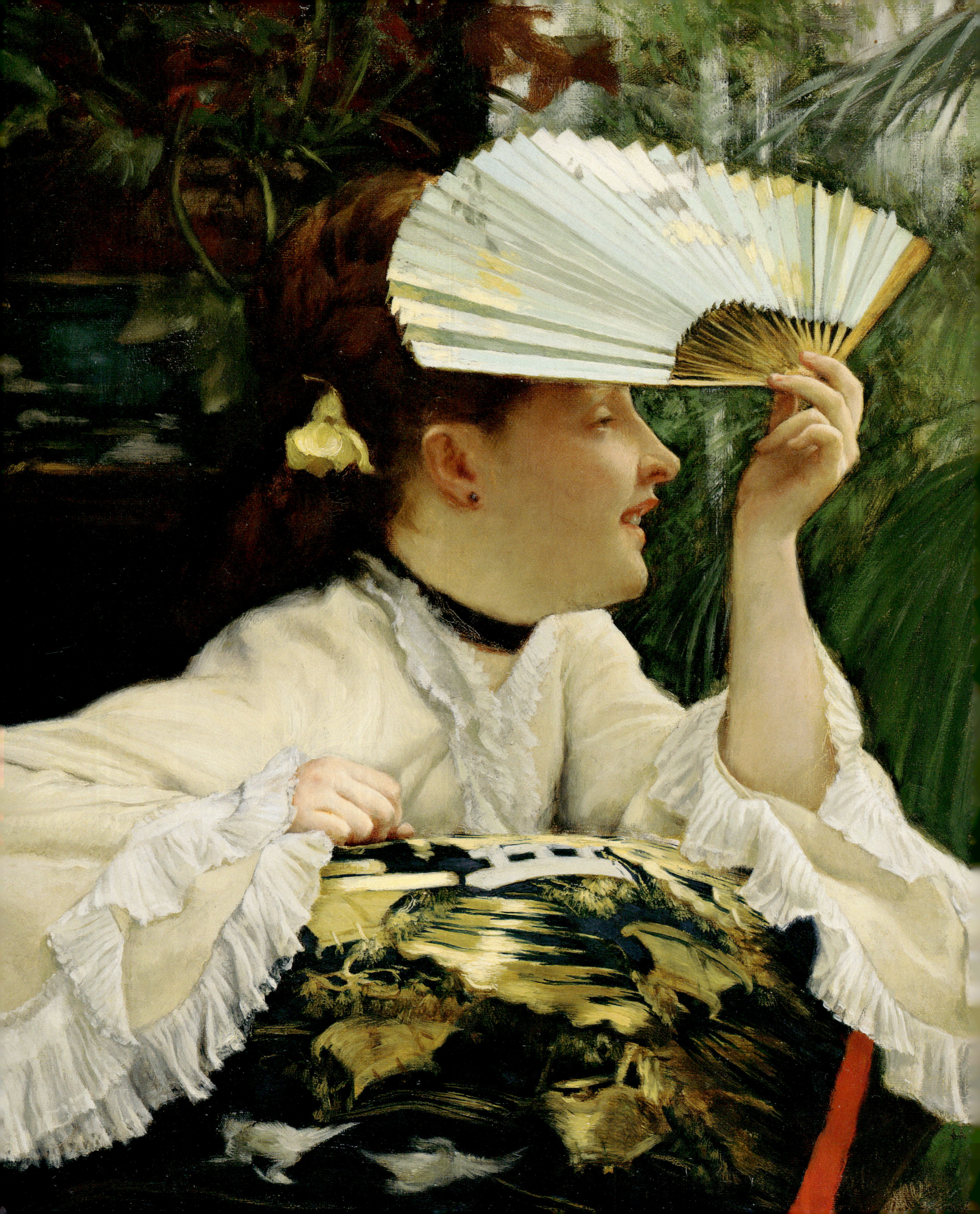

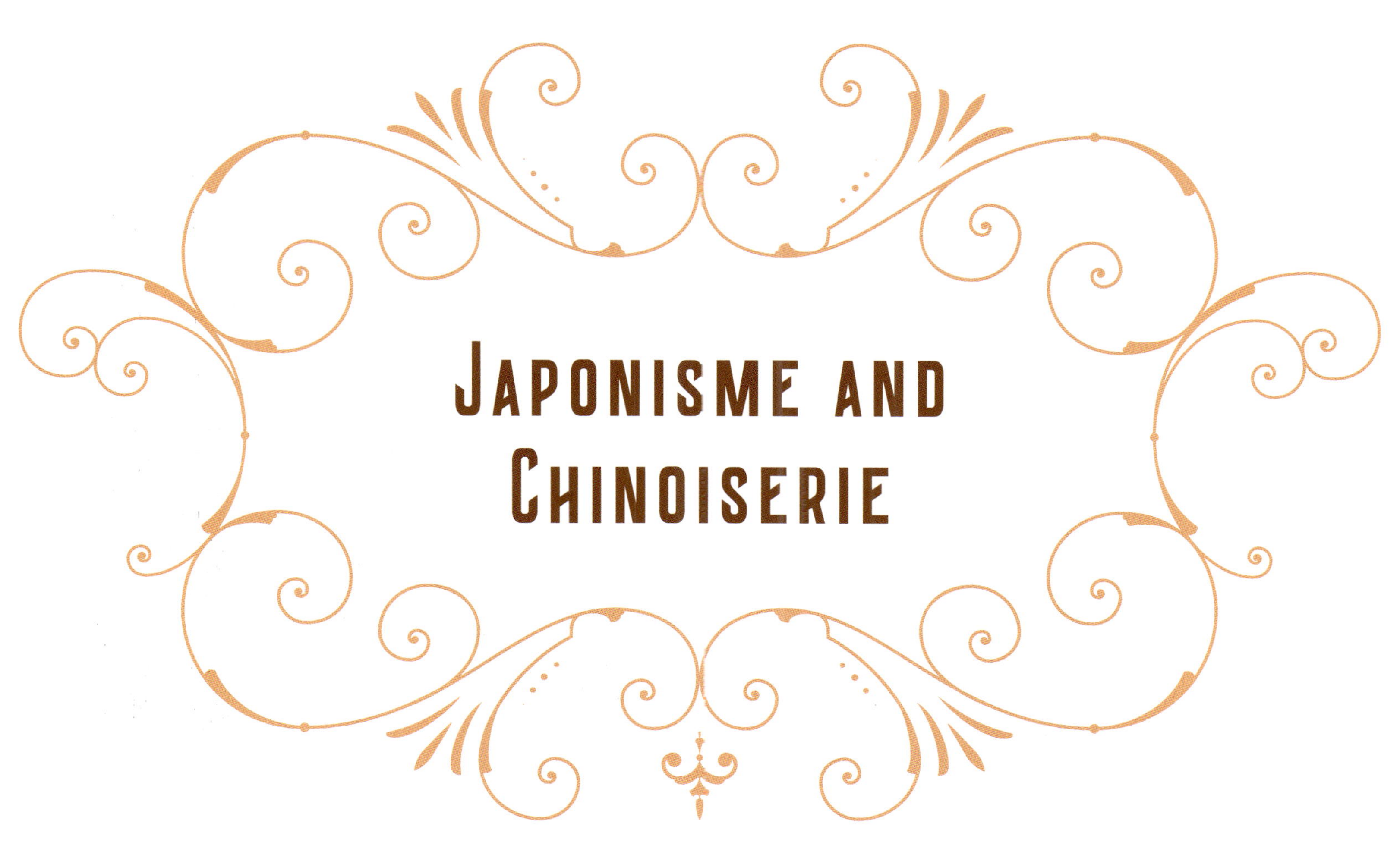

Japonisme and Chinoiserie

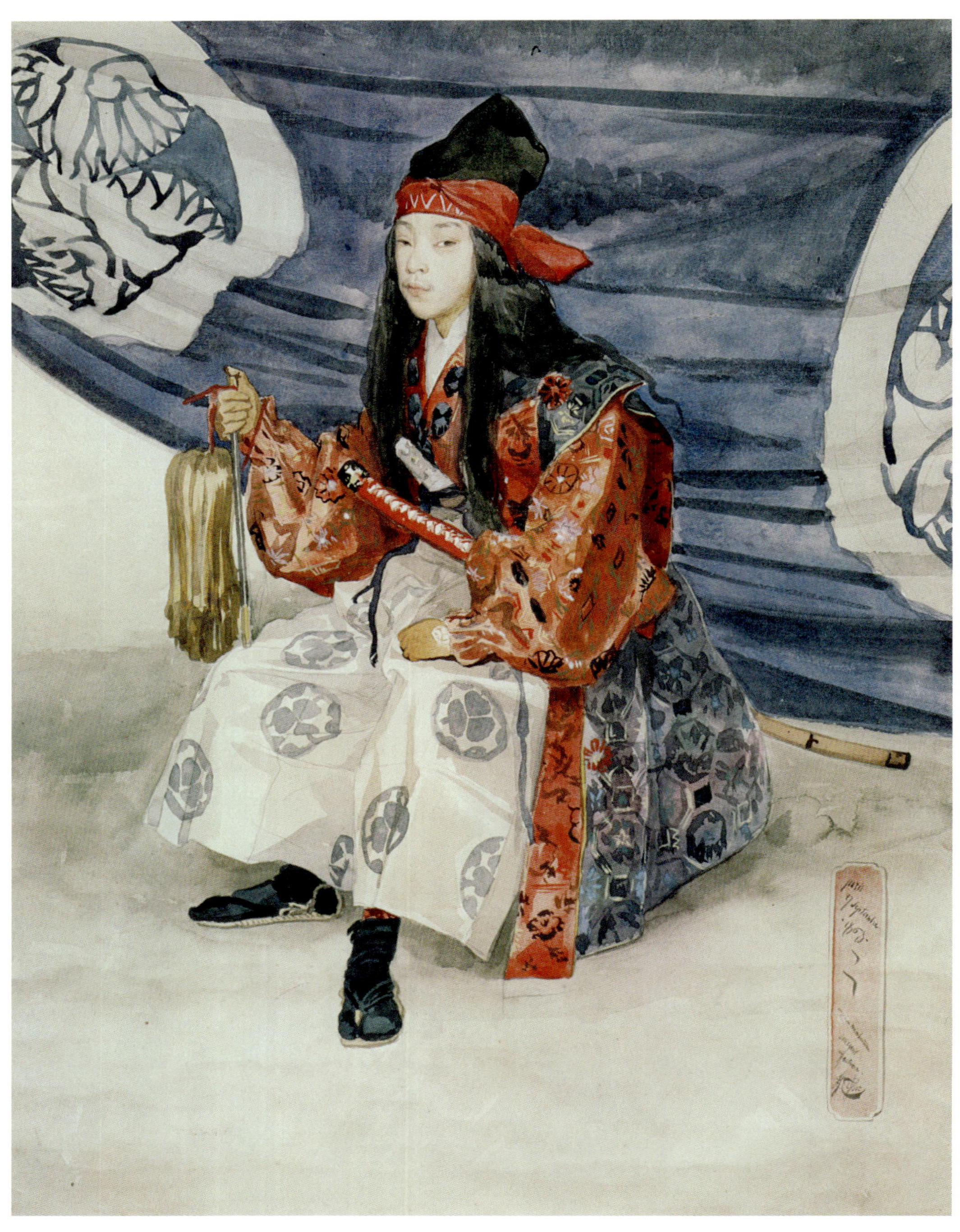

35

Portrait of Prince Akitake Tokugawa, 1868

Watercolor mounted in a hanging scroll, 24 × 18¾ in. (60.9 × 47.6 cm)
Historical Museum of the Tokugawa Family, Mito, Japan

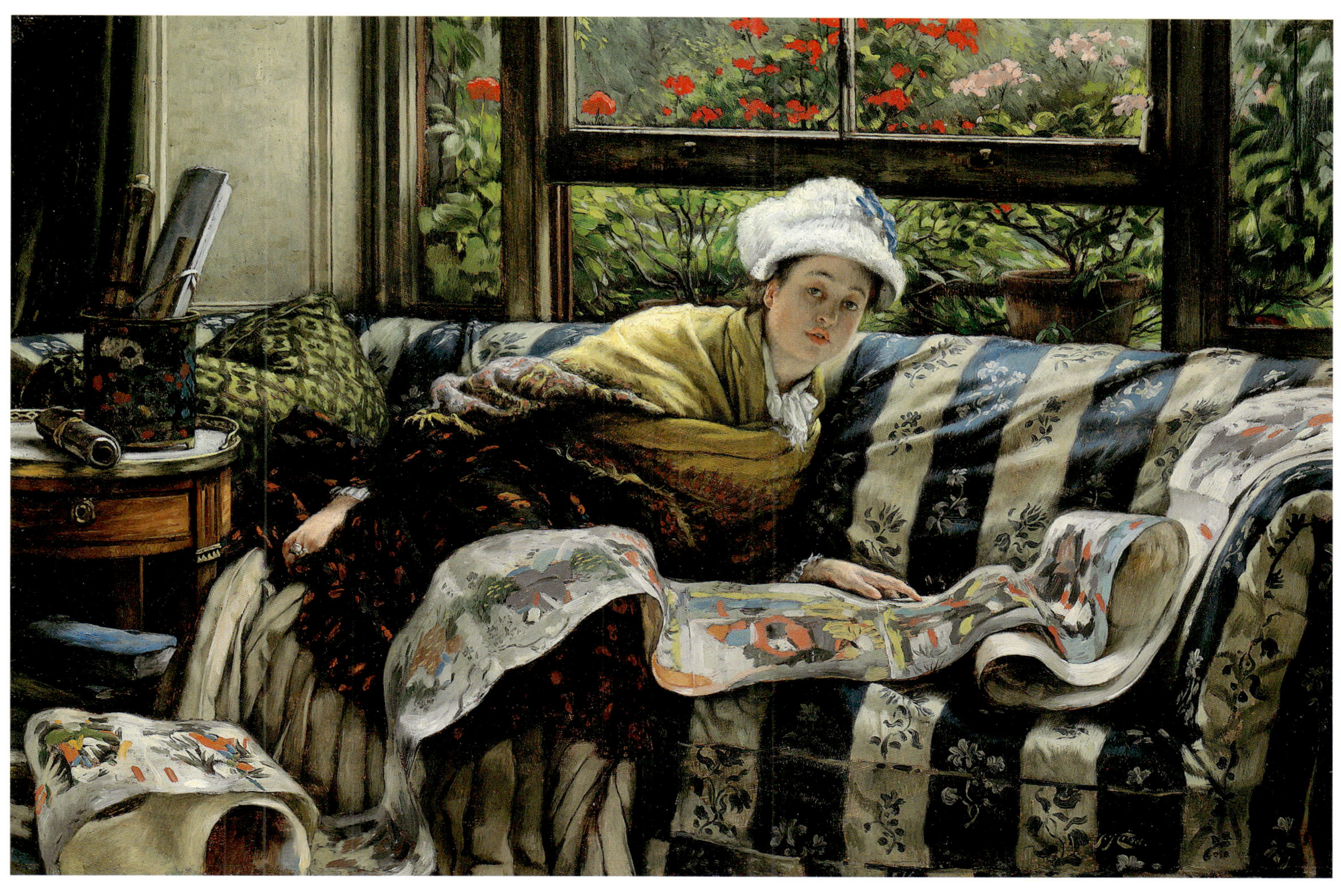

36

THE JAPANESE SCROLL, 1872–1873

Oil on wood panel, 15¼ × 22½ in. (38.7 × 57.2 cm)

Private collection

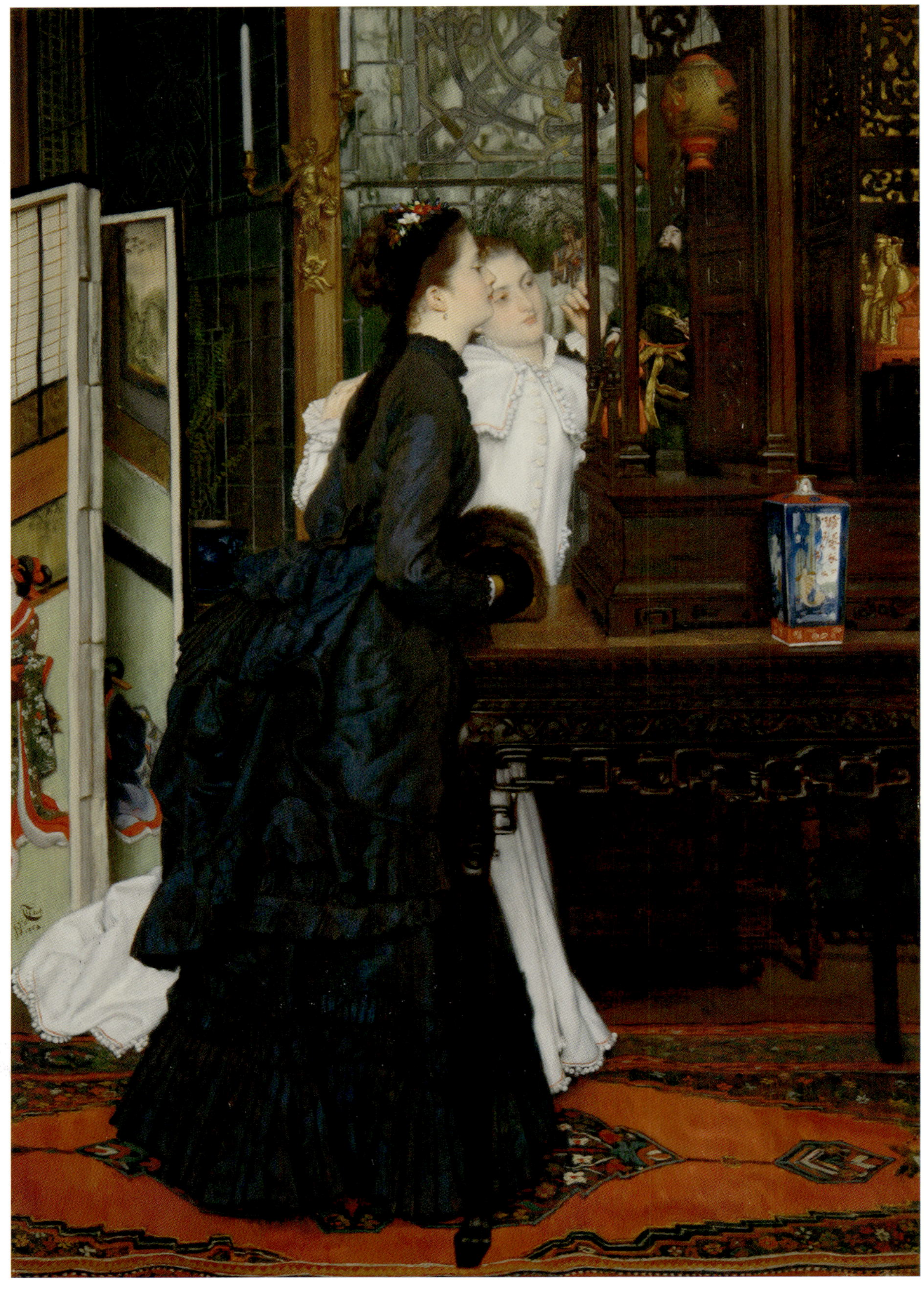

37

Young Women Looking at the Chinese Temple, 1869

Oil on canvas, 22 × 15½ in. (55.9 × 39.4 cm)

Private collection

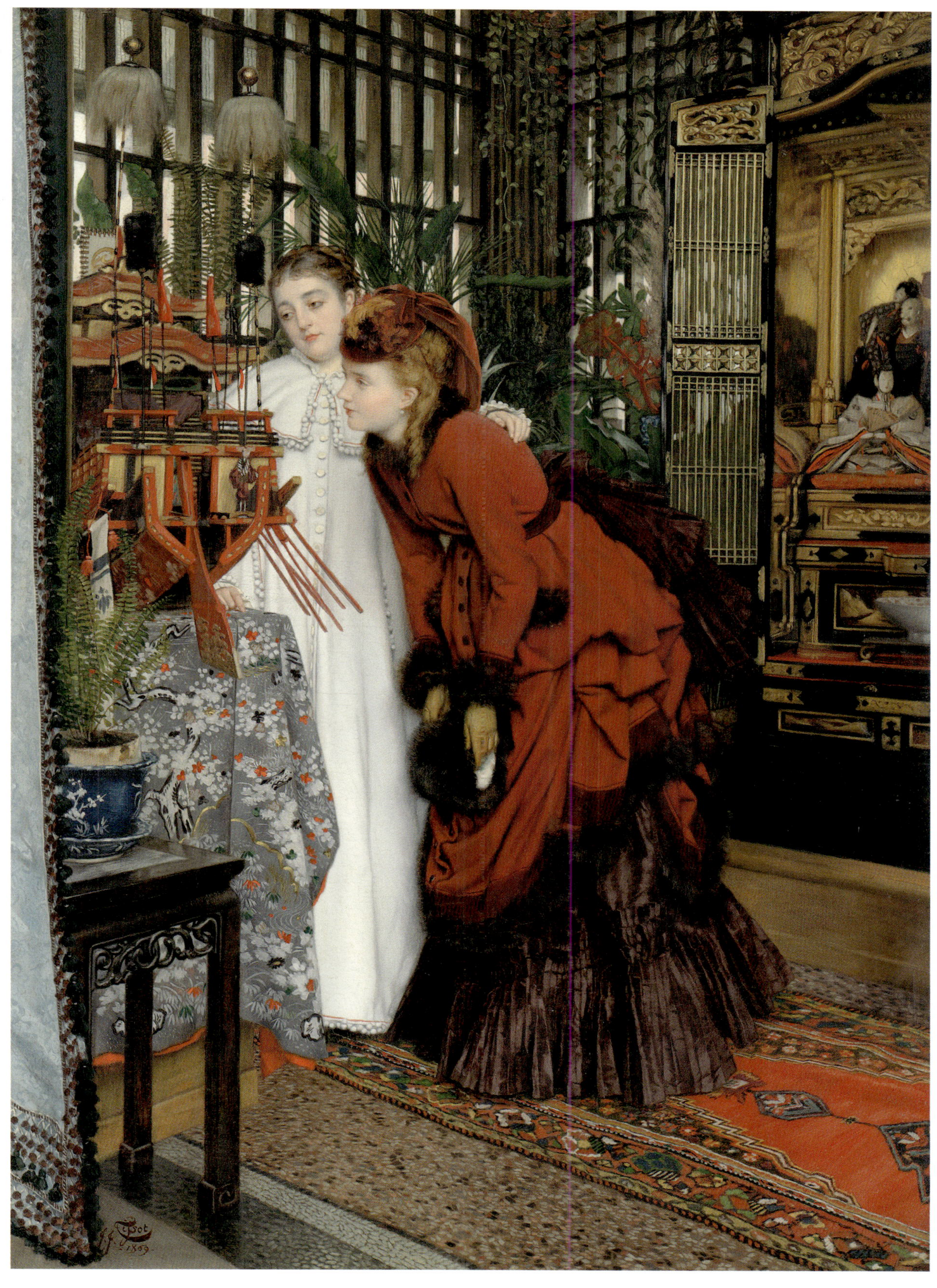

38

YOUNG WOMEN LOOKING AT JAPANESE OBJECTS, 1869

Oil on canvas, 27¾ × 19¾ in. (70.5 × 50.2 cm)

Cincinnati Art Museum, Gift of Henry M. Goodyear, M.D., 1984.217

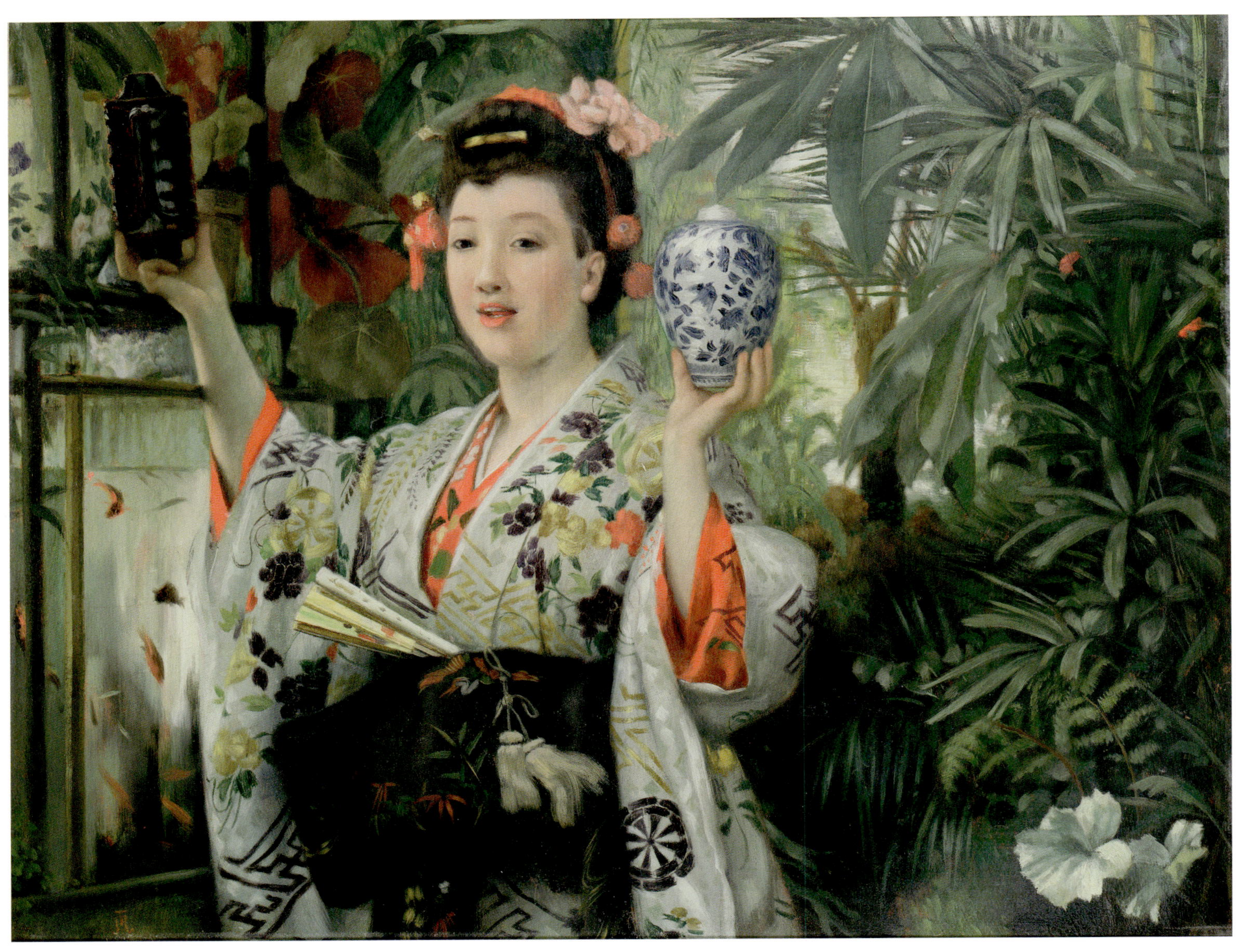

39

THE JAPANESE VASE, CA. 1870

Oil on canvas, 24 × 35 in. (61 × 89 cm)

Private collection

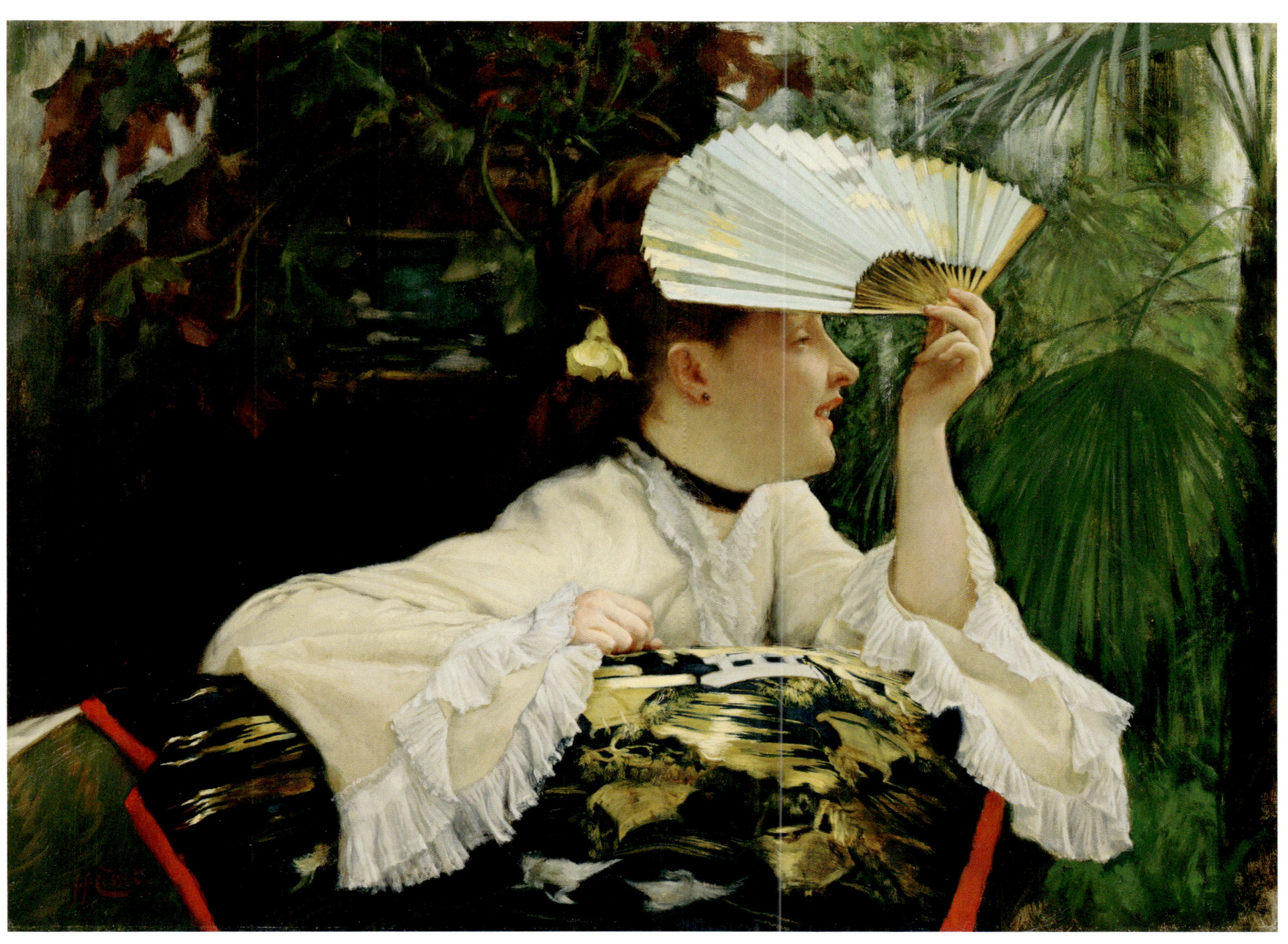

40

THE FAN, 1875

Oil on canvas, 15 ¼ × 20 ½ in. (38.7 × 52.1 cm)
Wadsworth Atheneum Museum of Art, Hartford, Connecticut,
The Ella Gallup Sumner and Mary Catlin Sumner Collection Fund, 1982.158

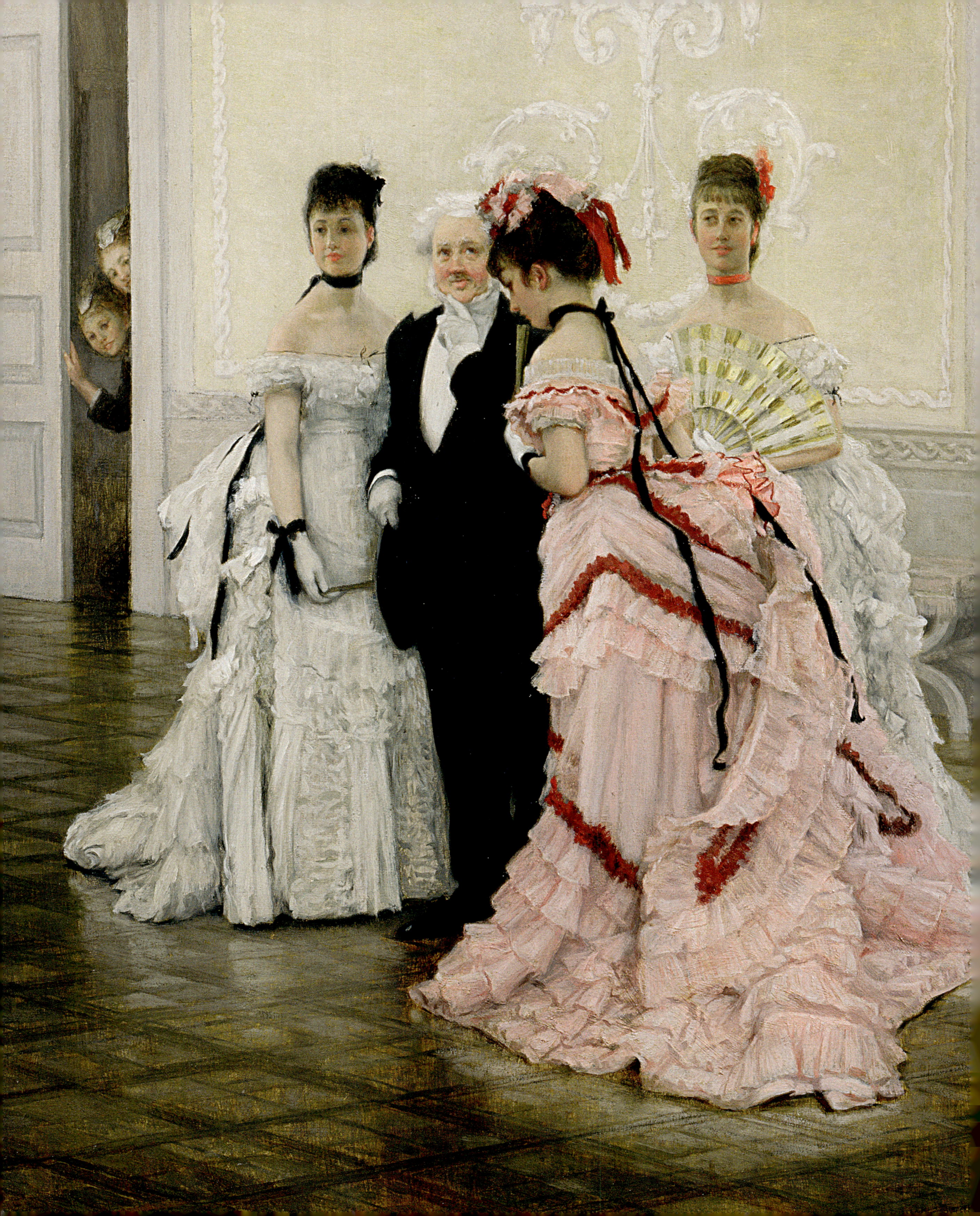

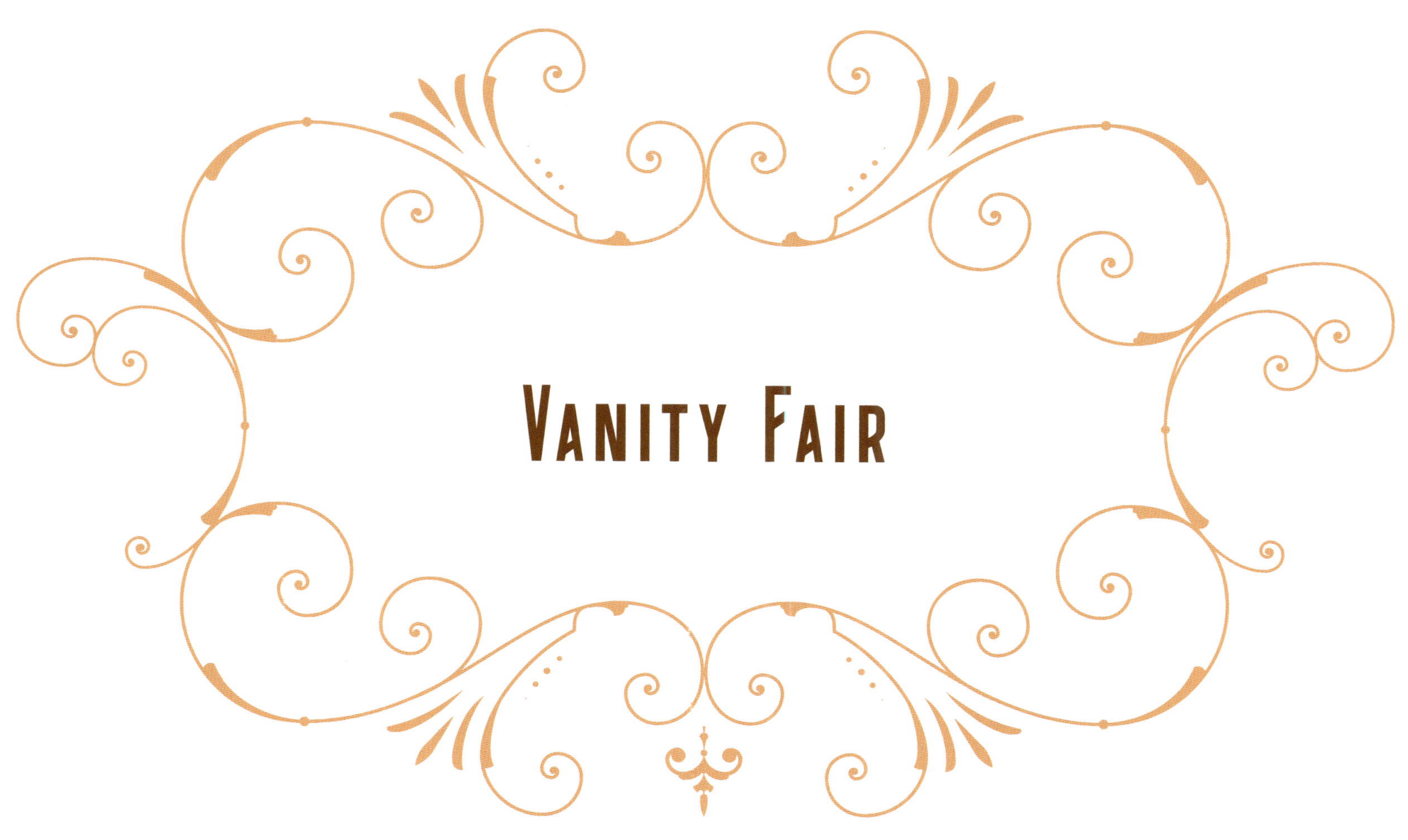

Vanity Fair

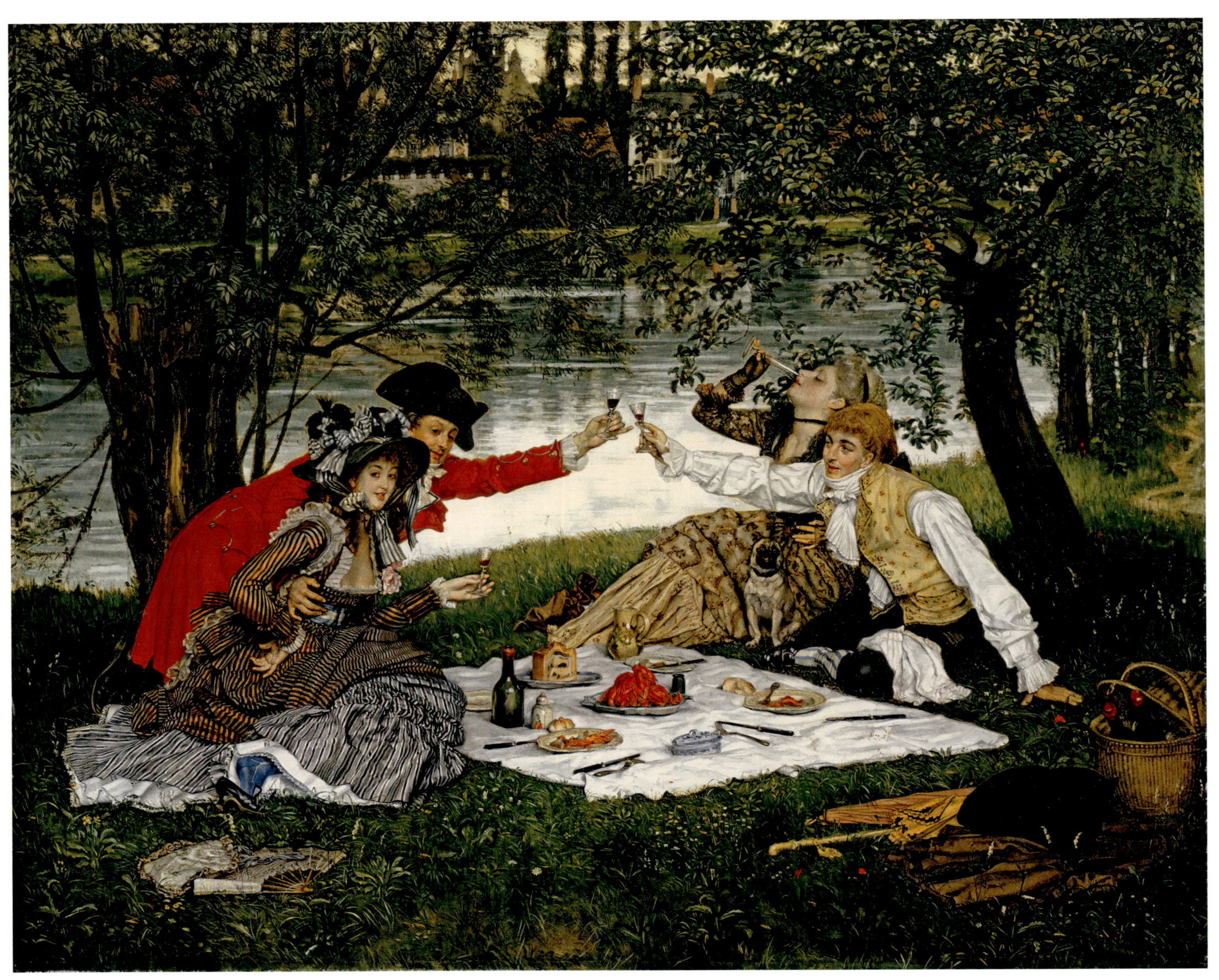

41

The Partie Carrée, 1870

Oil on canvas, 47 × 56 in. (114.3 × 142.2 cm)
National Gallery of Canada, Ottawa, Purchased 2018

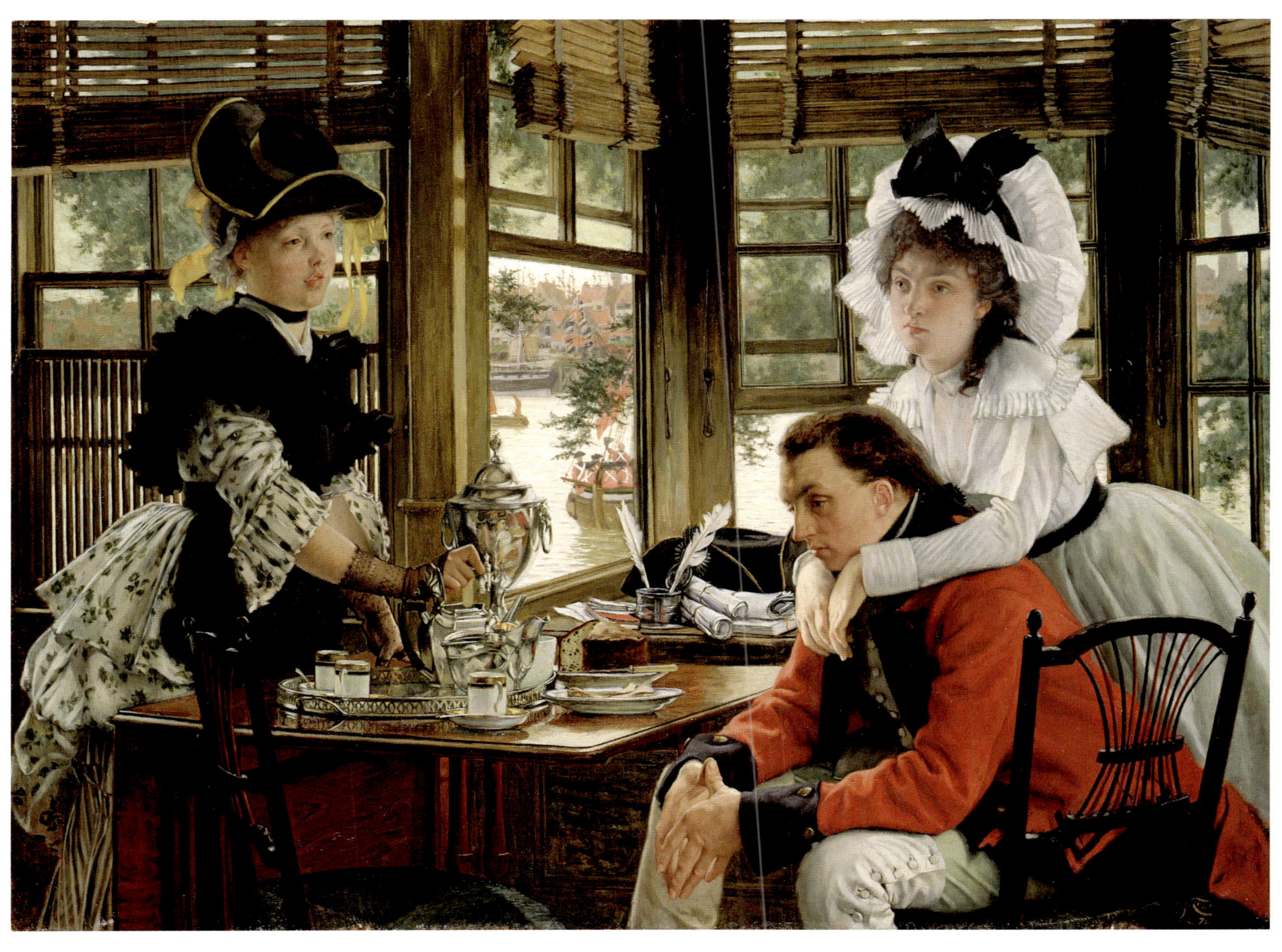

42

Before the Departure or The Parting, 1872

Oil on canvas, 27 × 36 in. (68.6 × 91.4 cm)
National Museum Wales, Cardiff, Bequeathed by William Menelaus, 1882, NMW A 184

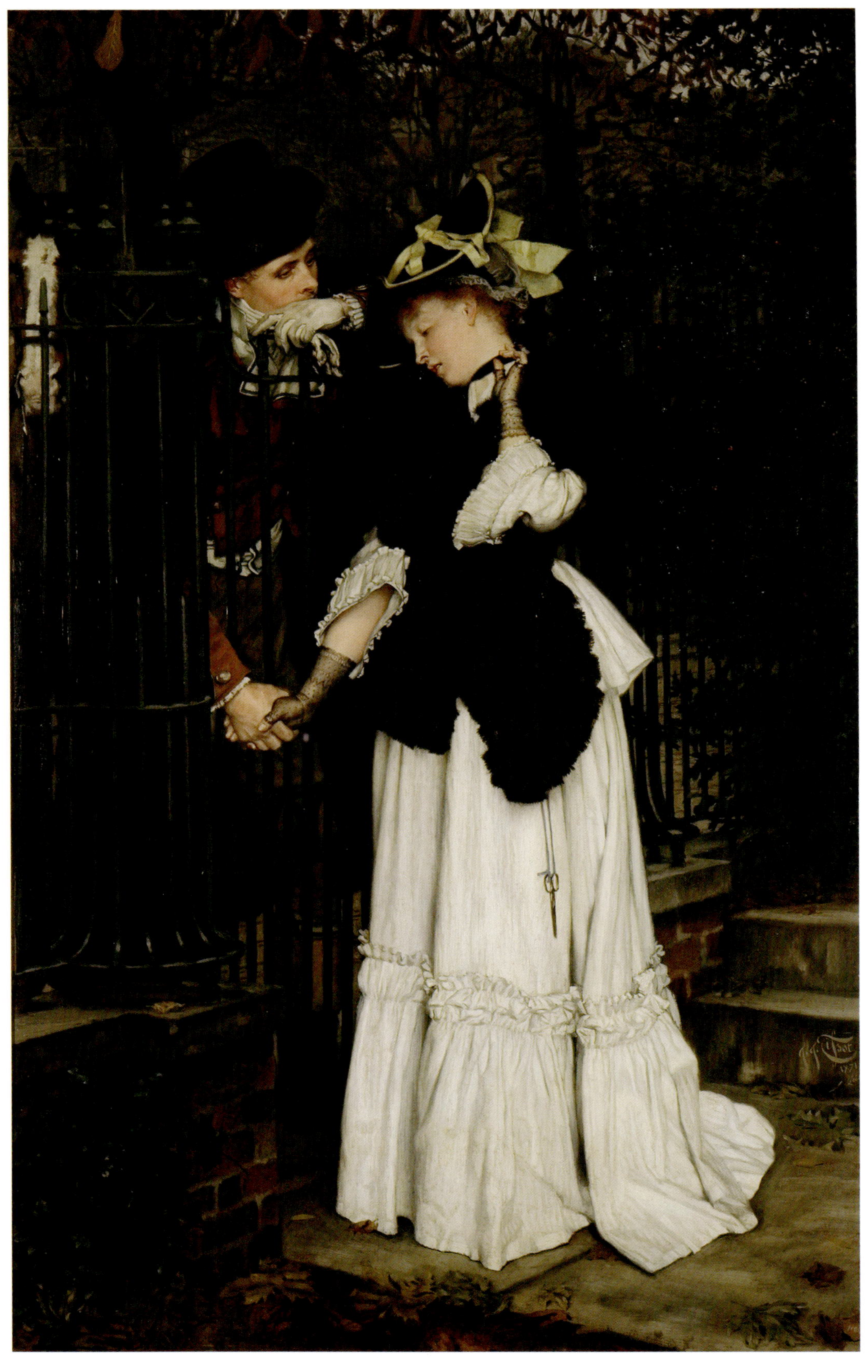

43

THE FAREWELLS, 1871

Oil on canvas, 39½ × 24⅝ in. (100.3 × 62.6 cm)
Bristol Museums and Art Gallery, Purchased 1955, K2432

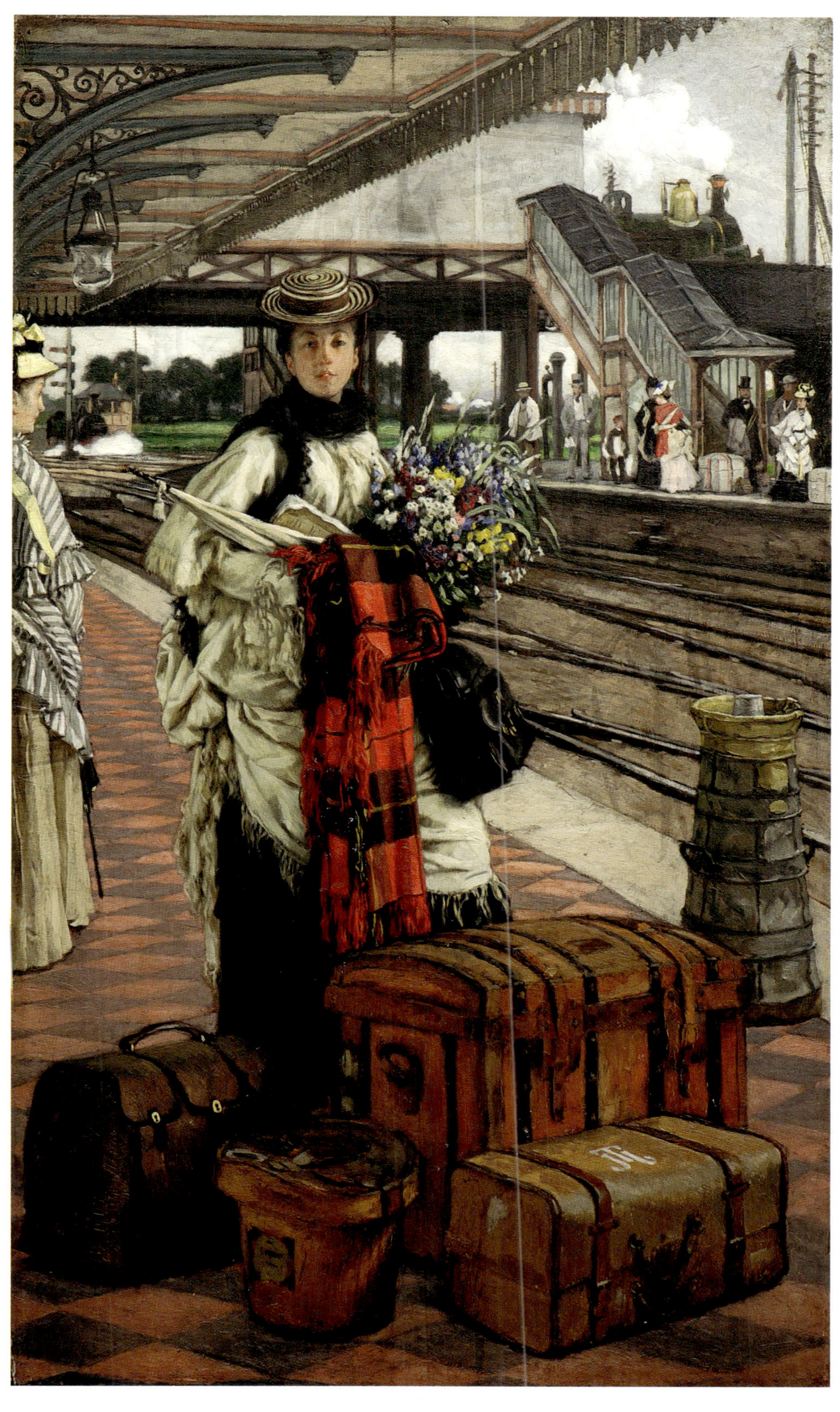

44

Railway Station, 1873

also known as Waiting for the Train (Willesden Junction)

Oil on canvas, 23 ½ × 13 ½ in. (59.7 × 34.2 cm)
Dunedin Public Art Gallery, New Zealand,
Purchased 1921 with funds from the Thomas Brown Fund, 1-1921

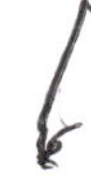

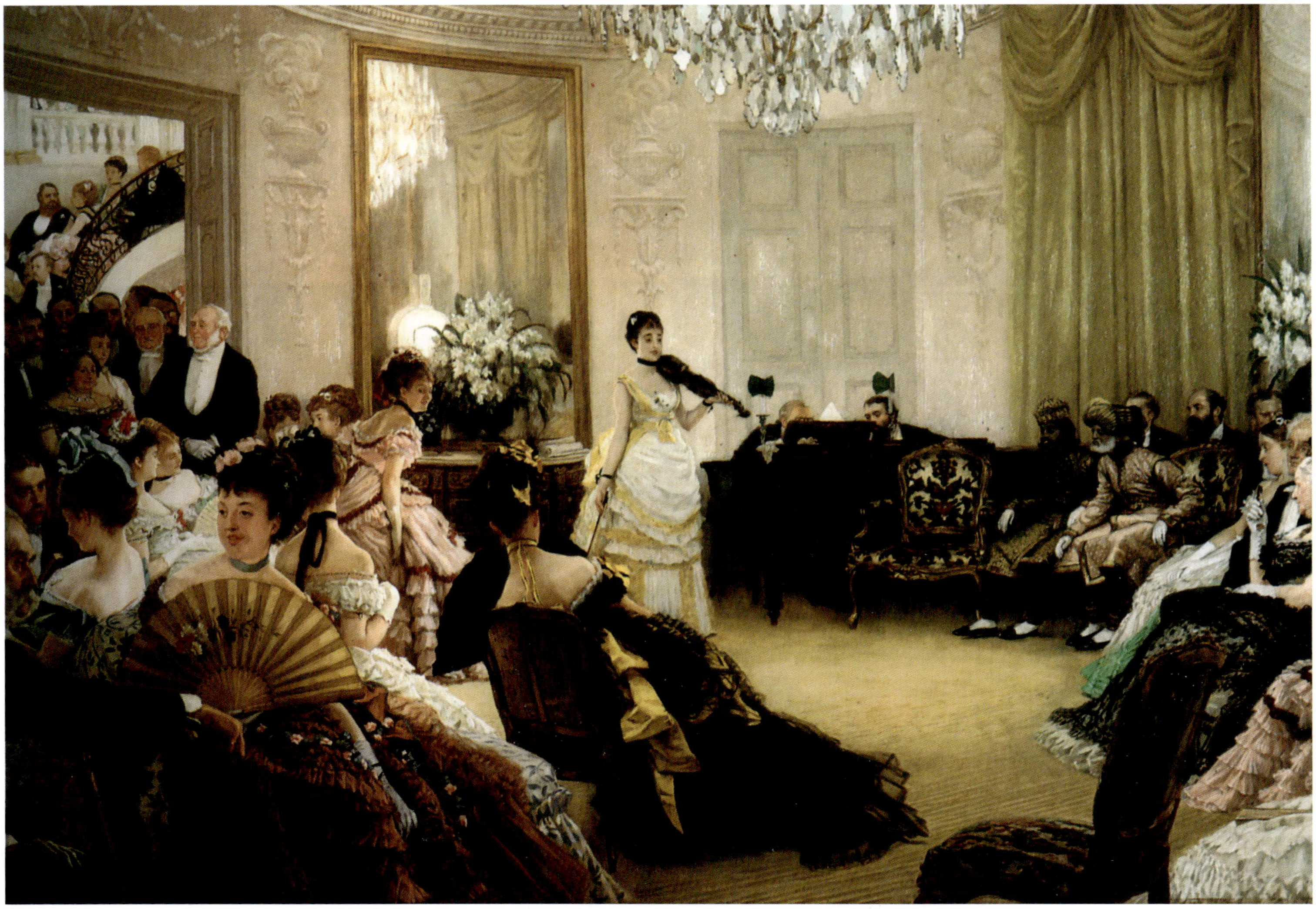

45

THE CONCERT or HUSH!, 1874

Oil on canvas, 29 × 44 in. (73.7 × 111.8 cm)
Manchester Art Gallery, Purchased 1933, 1933.56

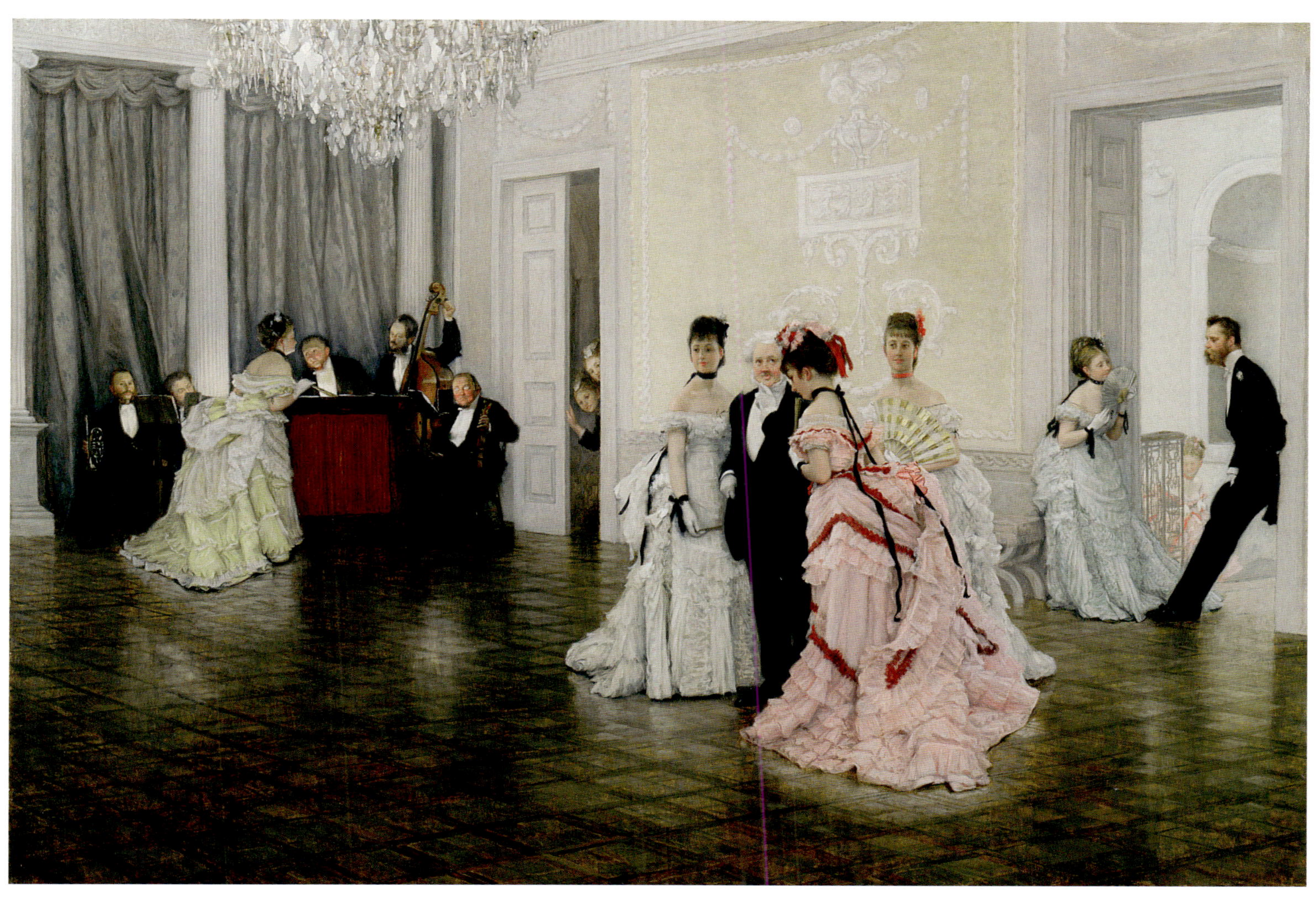

46

Too Early, 1873

Oil on canvas, 28 × 40⅛ in. (71 × 102 cm)
Guildhall Art Gallery, London, Bequeathed by Charles Gassiot, 1902, 738

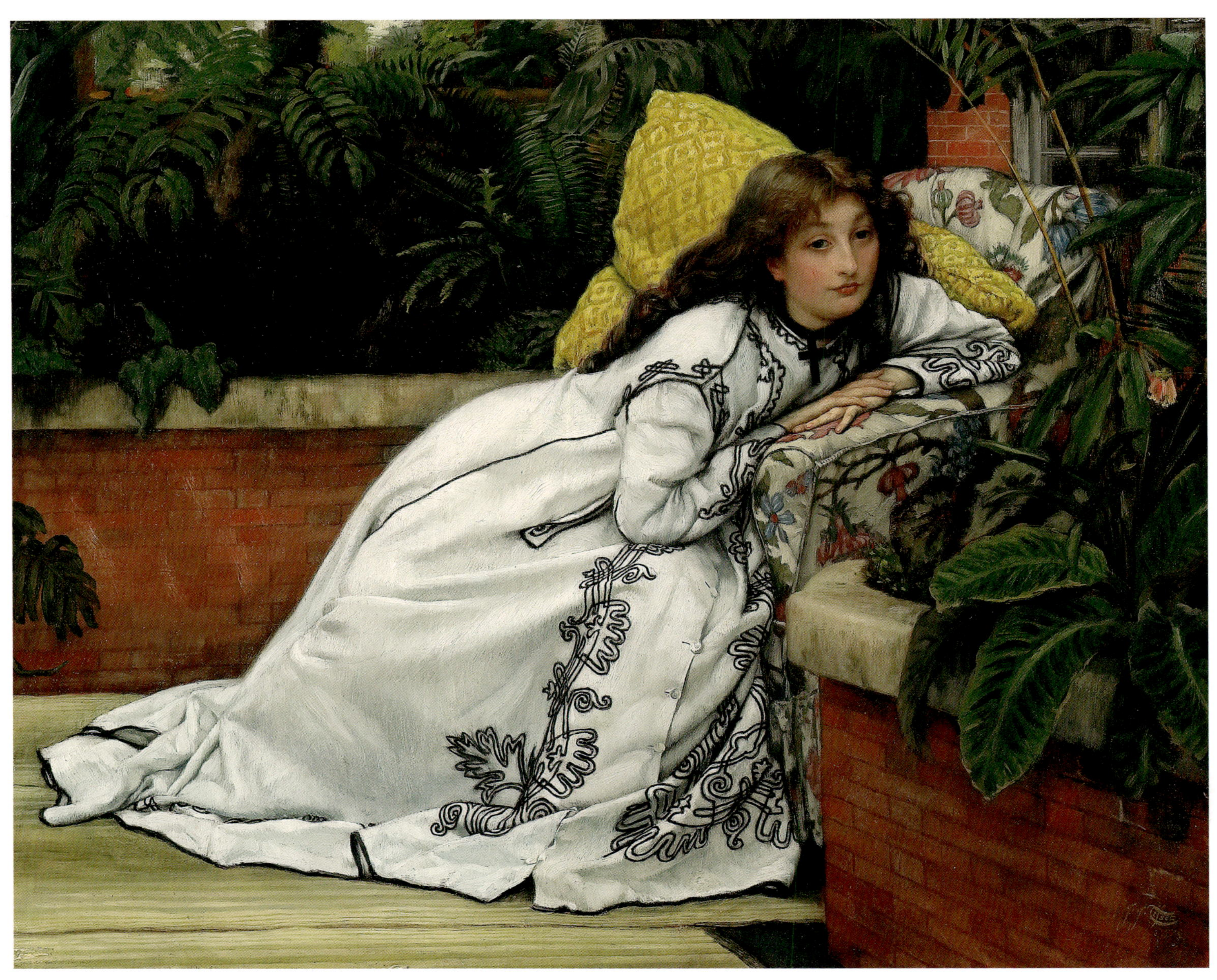

47

THE CONVALESCENT (GIRL IN AN ARMCHAIR), 1872

Oil on wood panel, 14¾ × 18 in. (37.5 × 45.7 cm)

Art Gallery of Ontario, Toronto, Gift of R.B.F. Barr, Esq., Q.C., 1966, 65/28

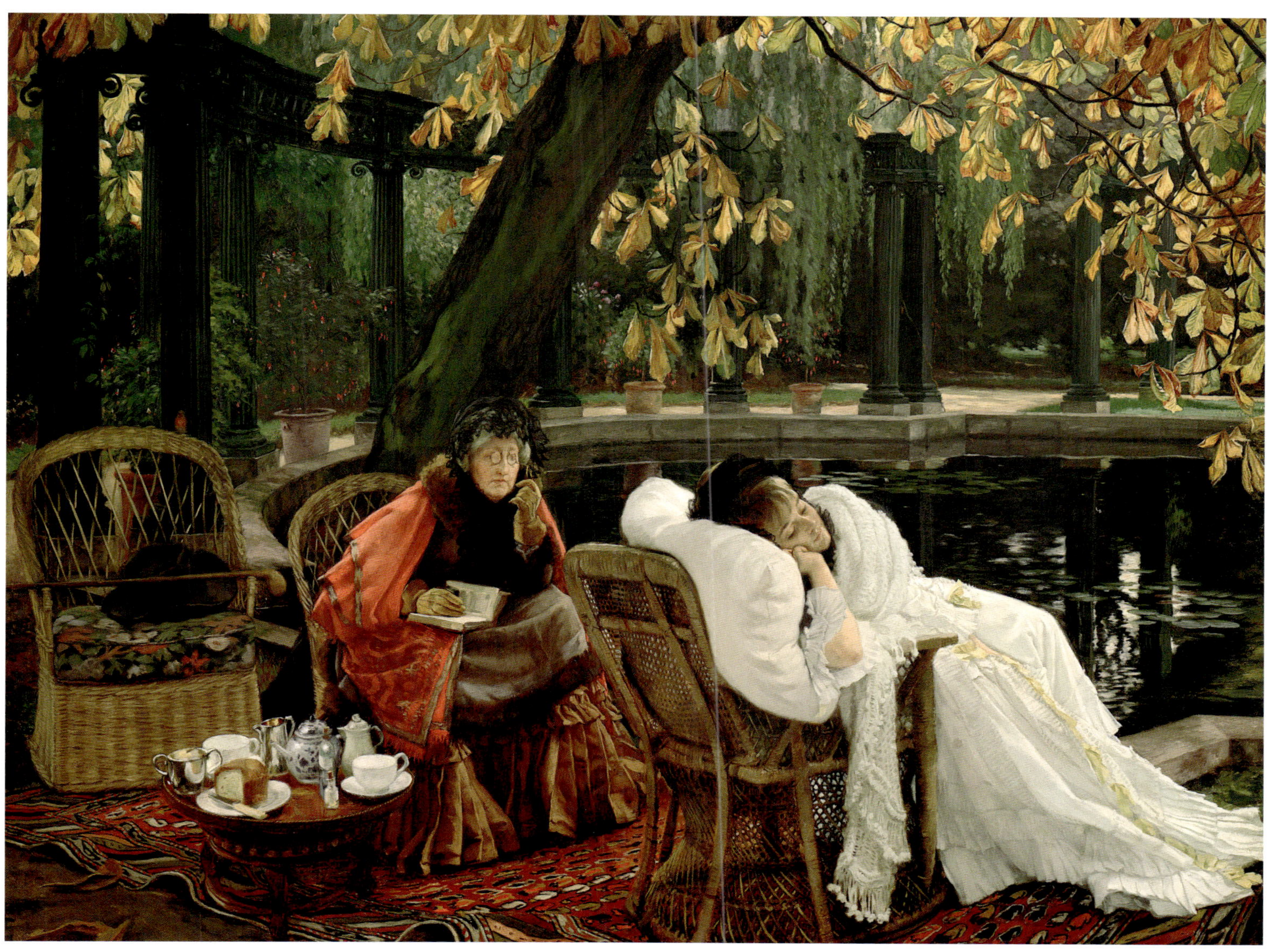

43

The Convalescent, 1875

Oil on canvas, 29¾ × 38¾ in. (75.4 × 98.4 cm)
Museums Sheffield, England. Purchased, 1949, VIS.2213

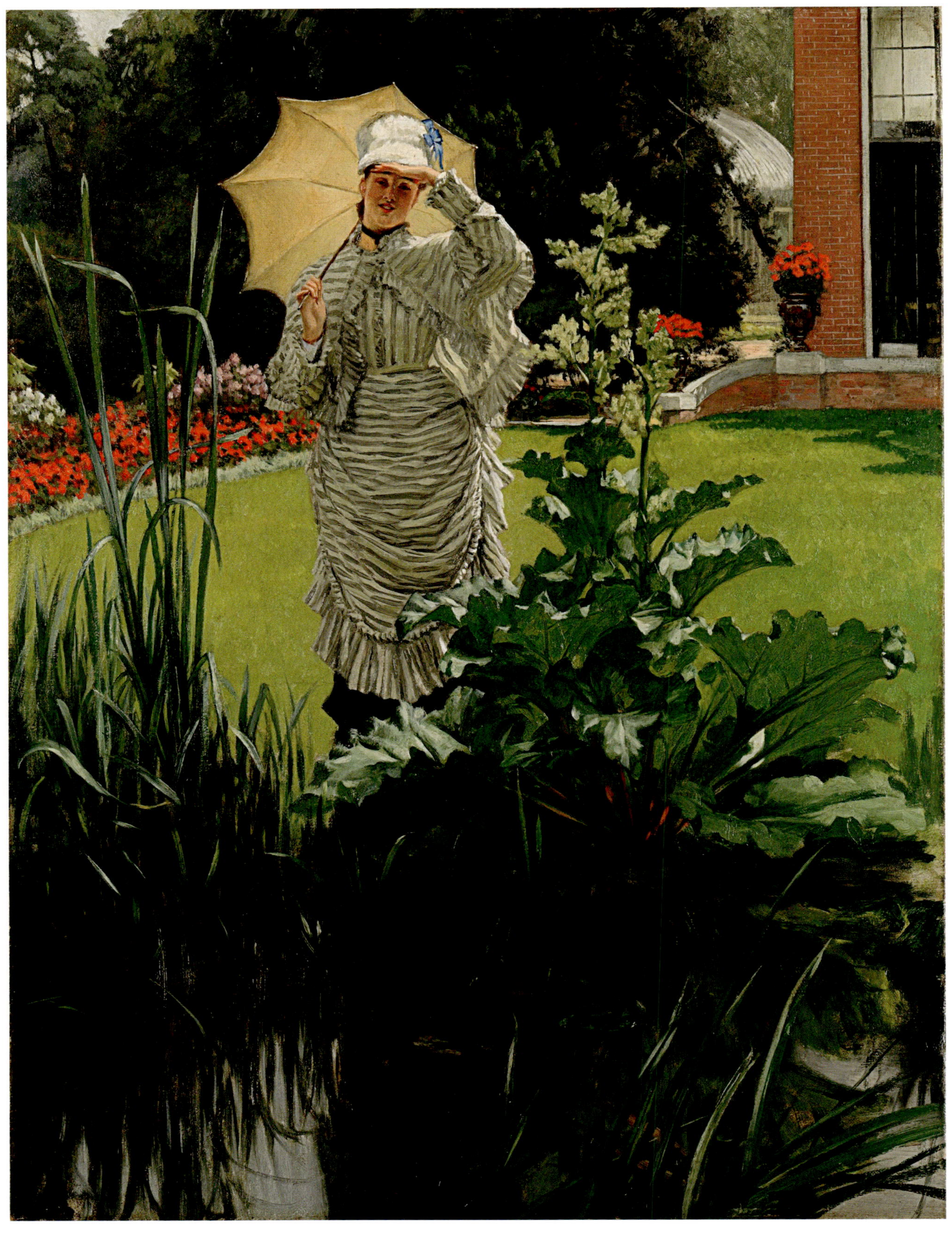

49

SPRING MORNING, 1875

Oil on canvas, 22 × 16¾ in. (55.9 × 42.5 cm)

The Metropolitan Museum of Art, New York, Gift of Mrs. Charles Wrightsman, 2009, 2009.359

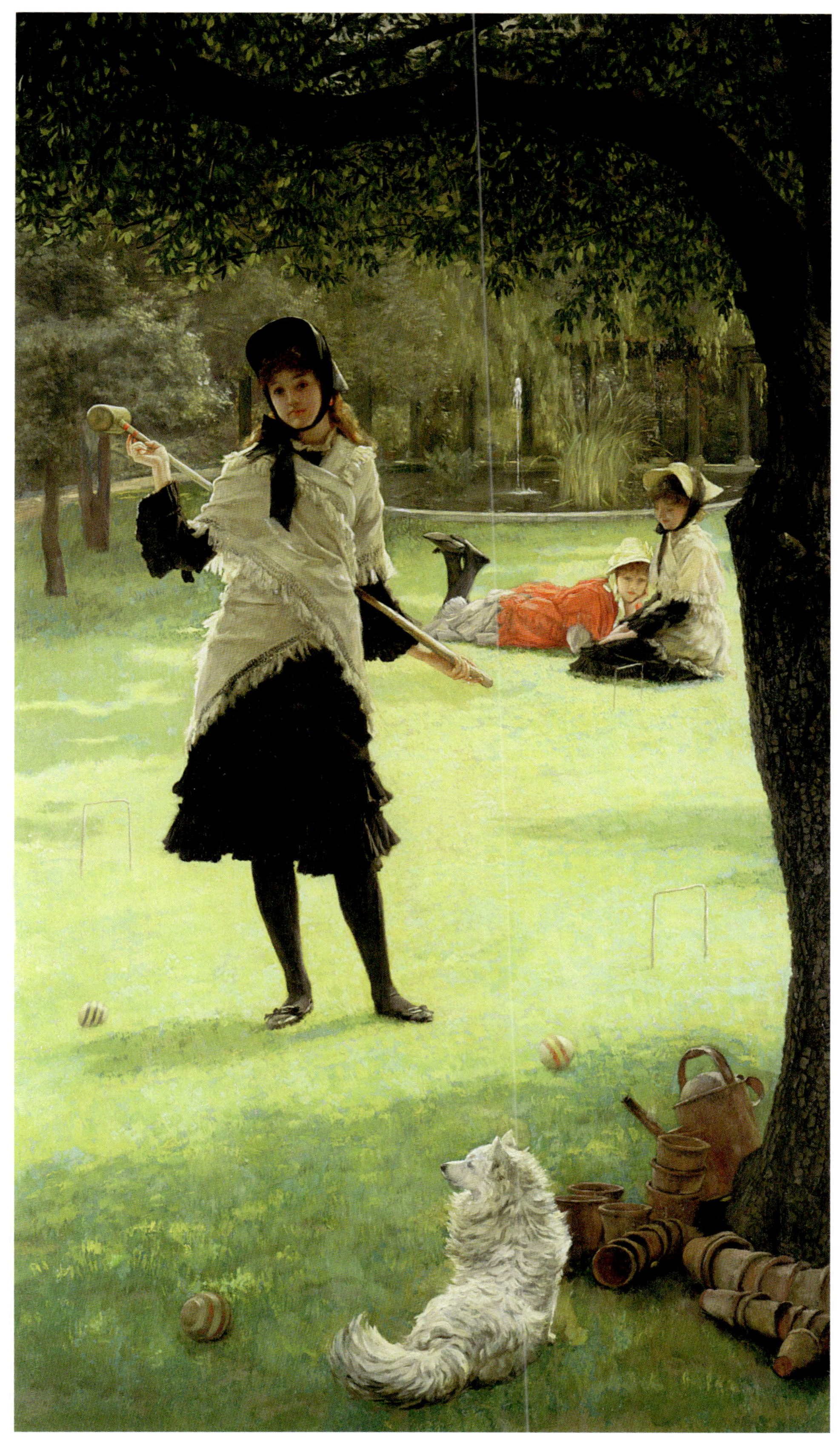

50

CROQUET, 1877–1878

Oil on canvas, 35 3/8 × 20 in. (90 × 50.8 cm)
Art Gallery of Hamilton, Ontario, Gift of Dr. and Mrs. Basil Bowman in memory of their daughter, Suzanne, 1965, 65.112.V

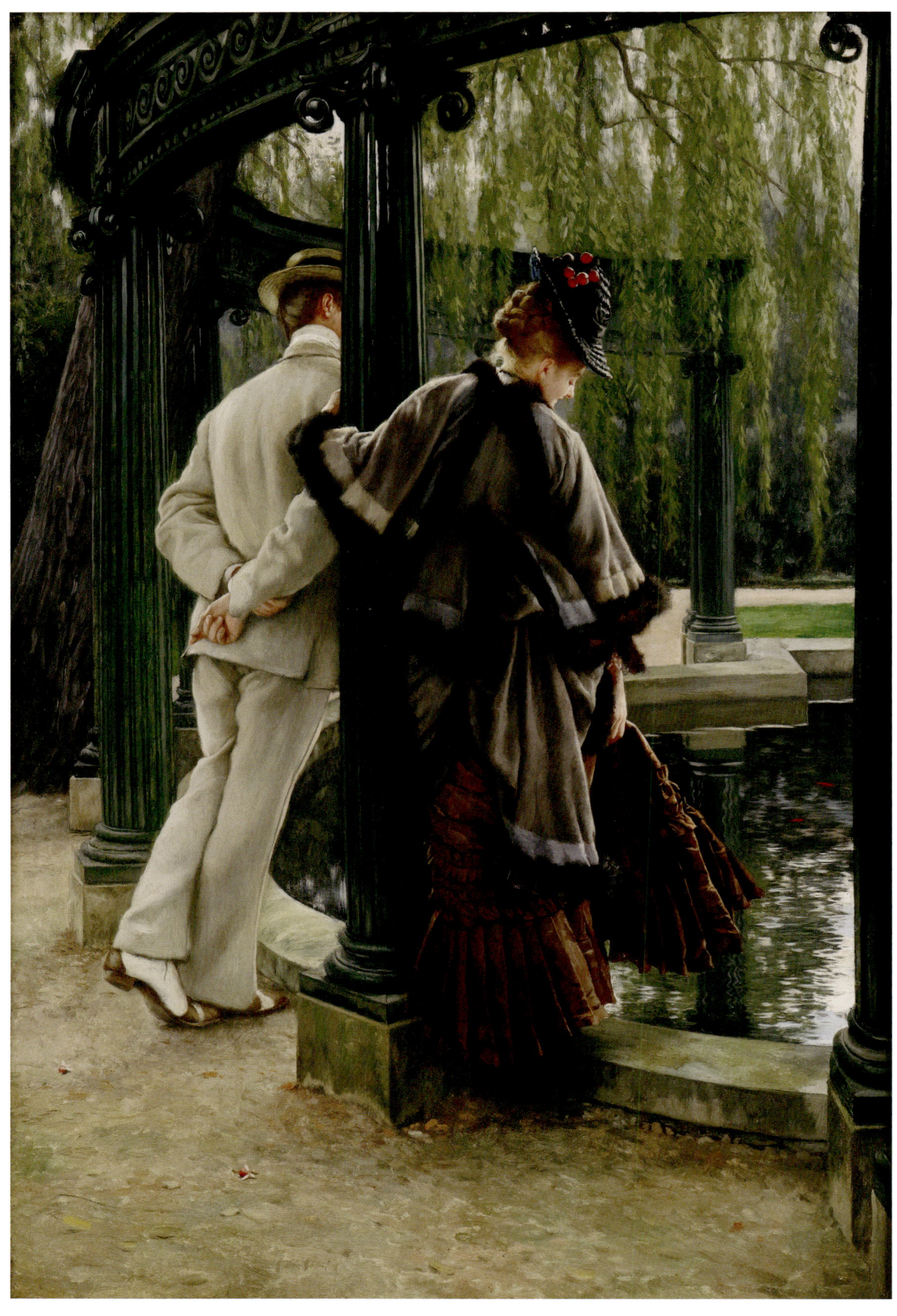

51

QUARRELLING, 1875–1876

Oil on canvas, 28½ × 19 in. (72.4 × 48.2 cm)
Private collection, courtesy of Grant Ford Ltd.

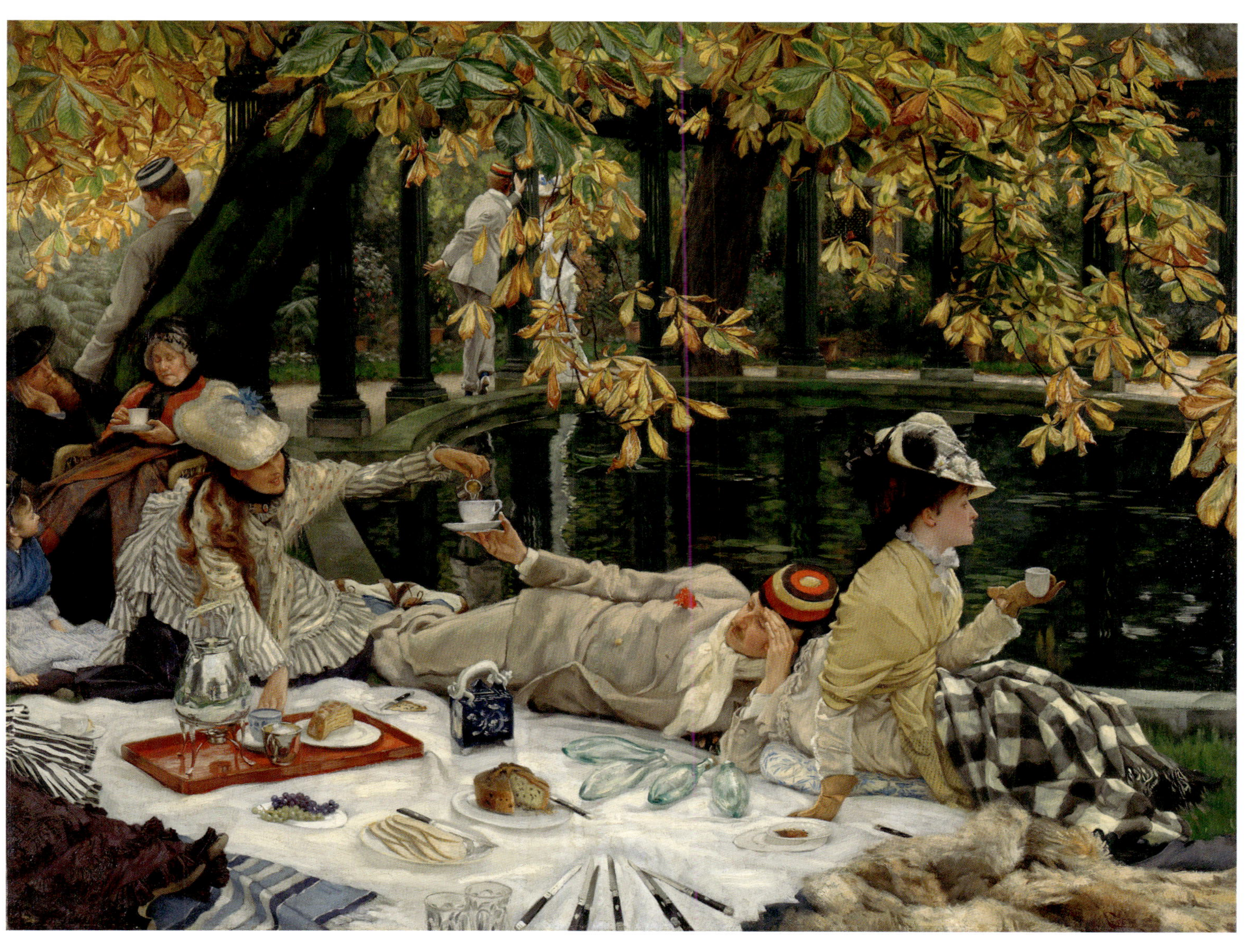

52

Holyday, 1876

Oil on canvas, 30 × 39 in. (76.2 × 99.4 cm)
Tate, London, Purchased 1928, N04413

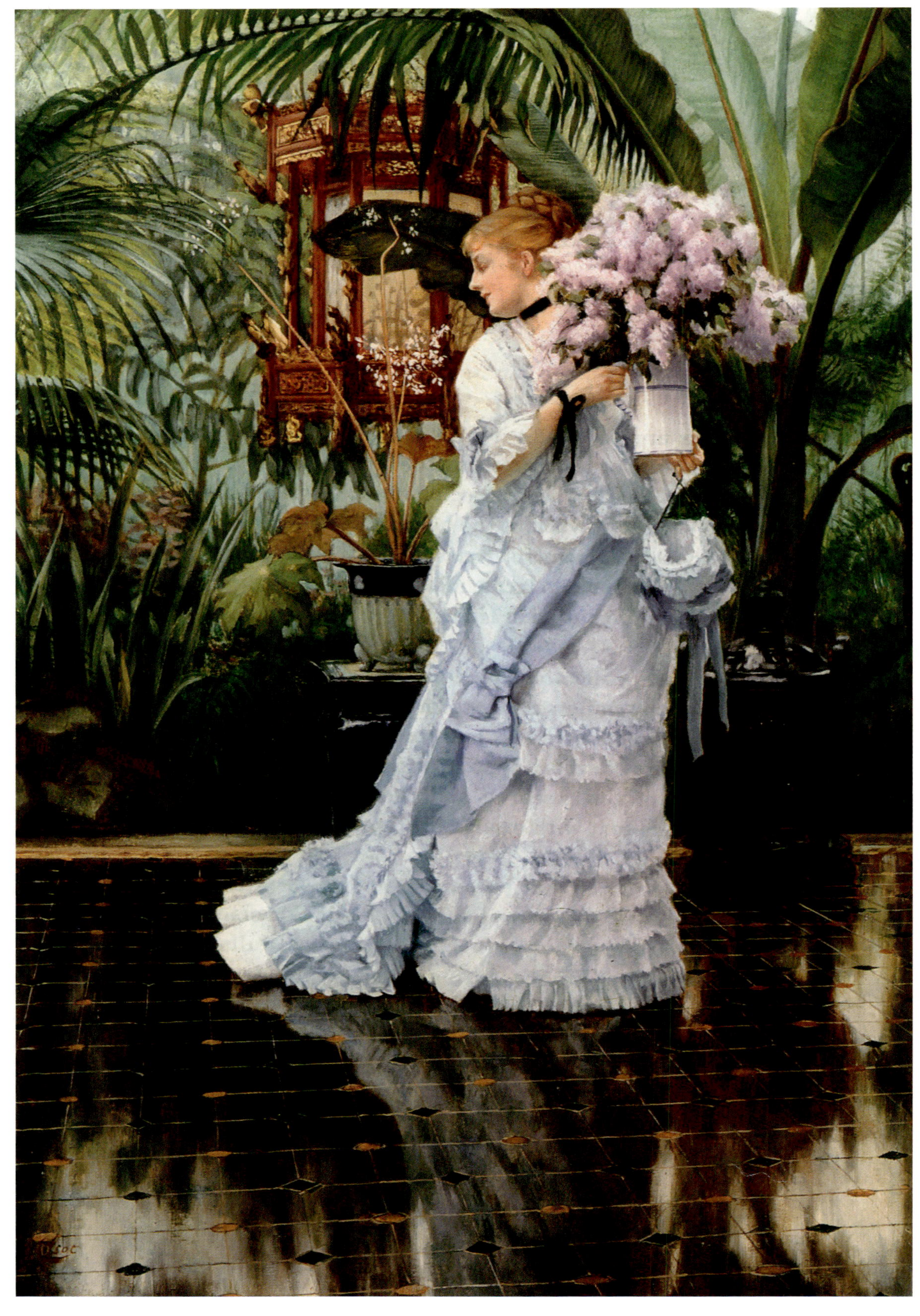

53

The Bouquet of Lilacs, 1874

Oil on canvas, 20 × 14 in. (50.8 × 35.6 cm)
Private collection

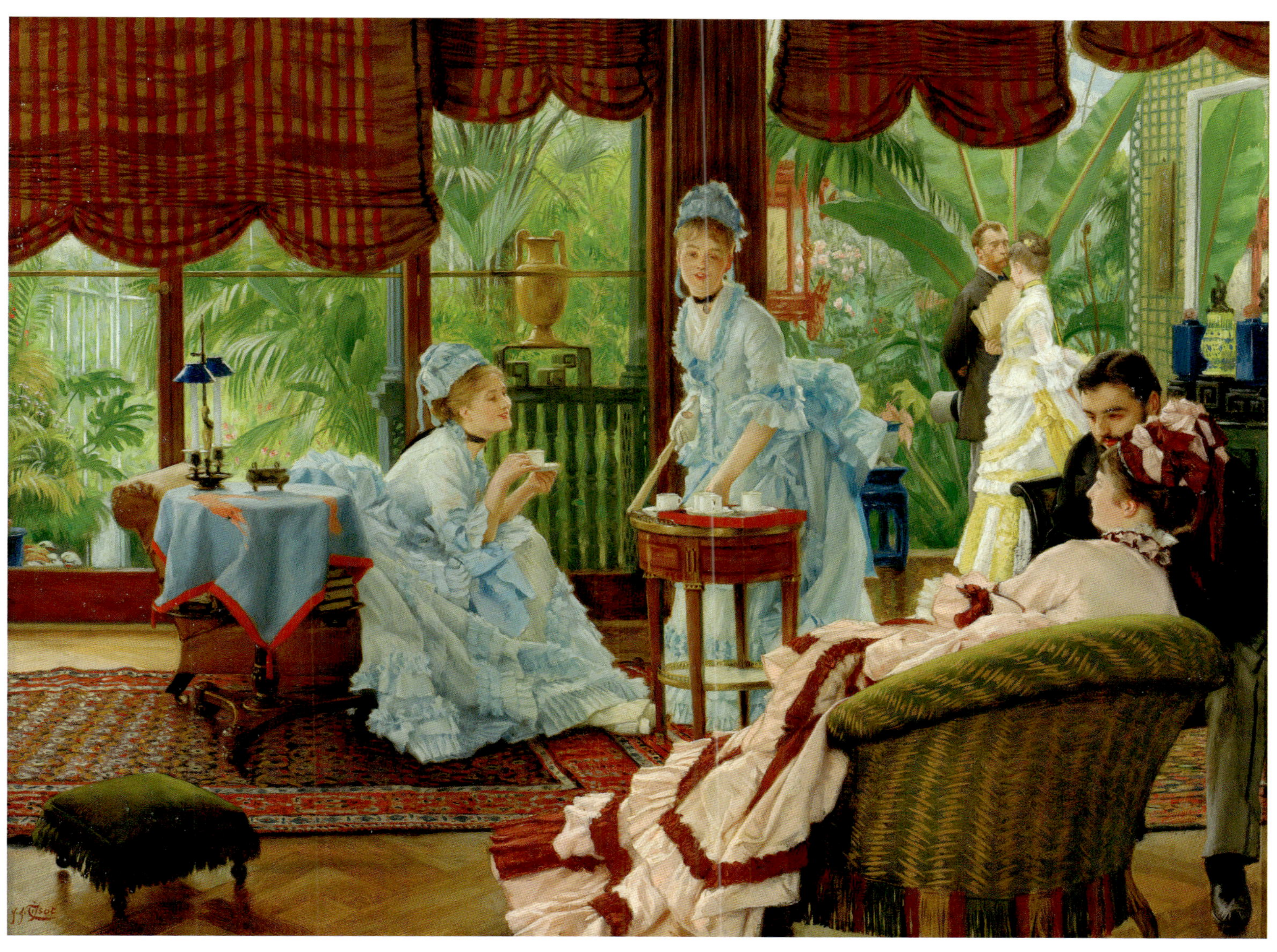

54

AFTERNOON TEA, 1874

also known as IN THE CONSERVATORY

Oil on canvas, 15⅛ × 20⅛ in. (38.4 × 51.1 cm)
Collection of Diane B. Wilsey, San Francisco

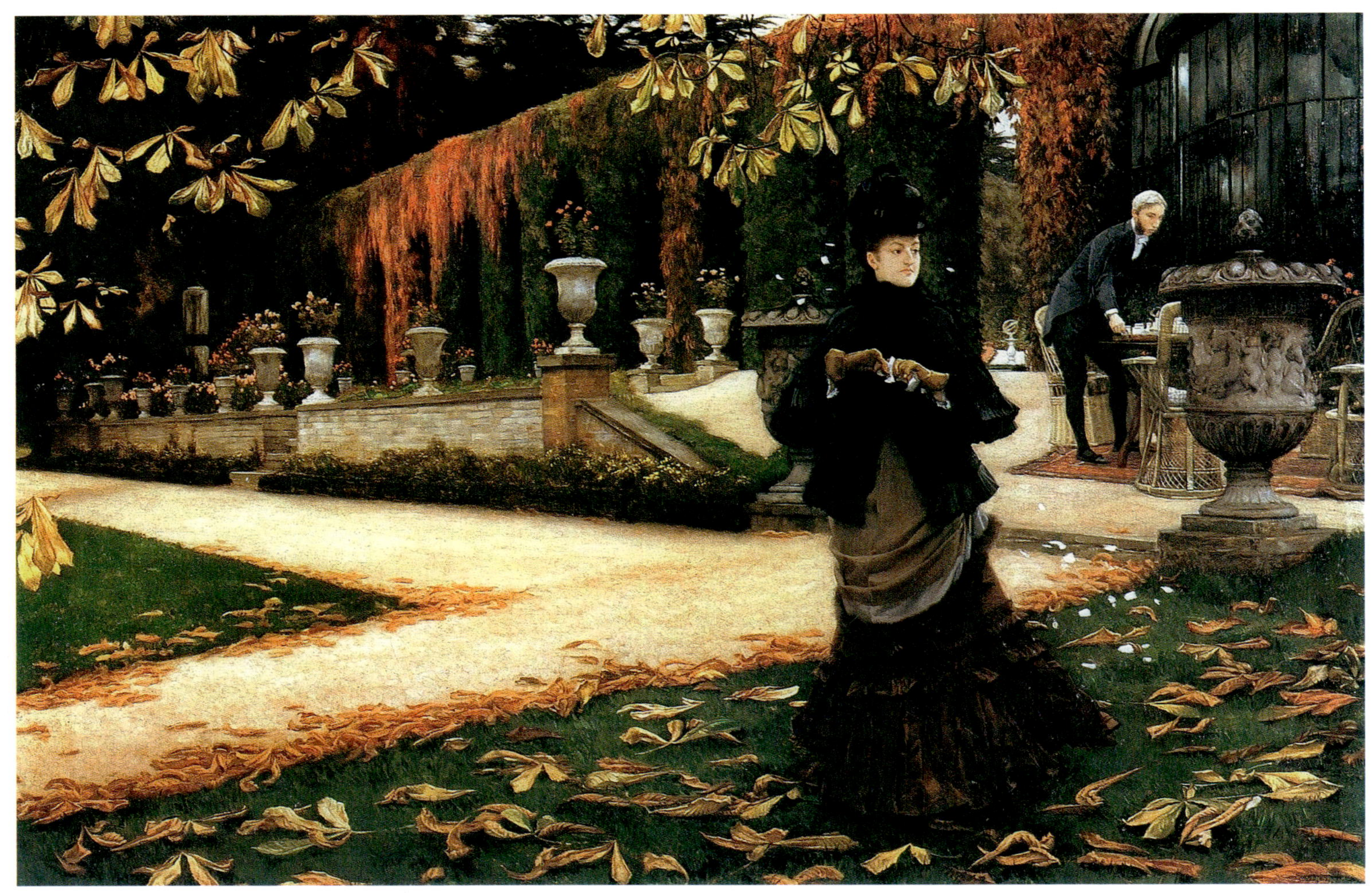

55

THE REPLY, 1874

also known as THE LETTER

Oil on canvas, 28¼ × 42¼ in. (71.4 × 107.1 cm)

National Gallery of Canada, Ottawa, Purchased 1964, 15191

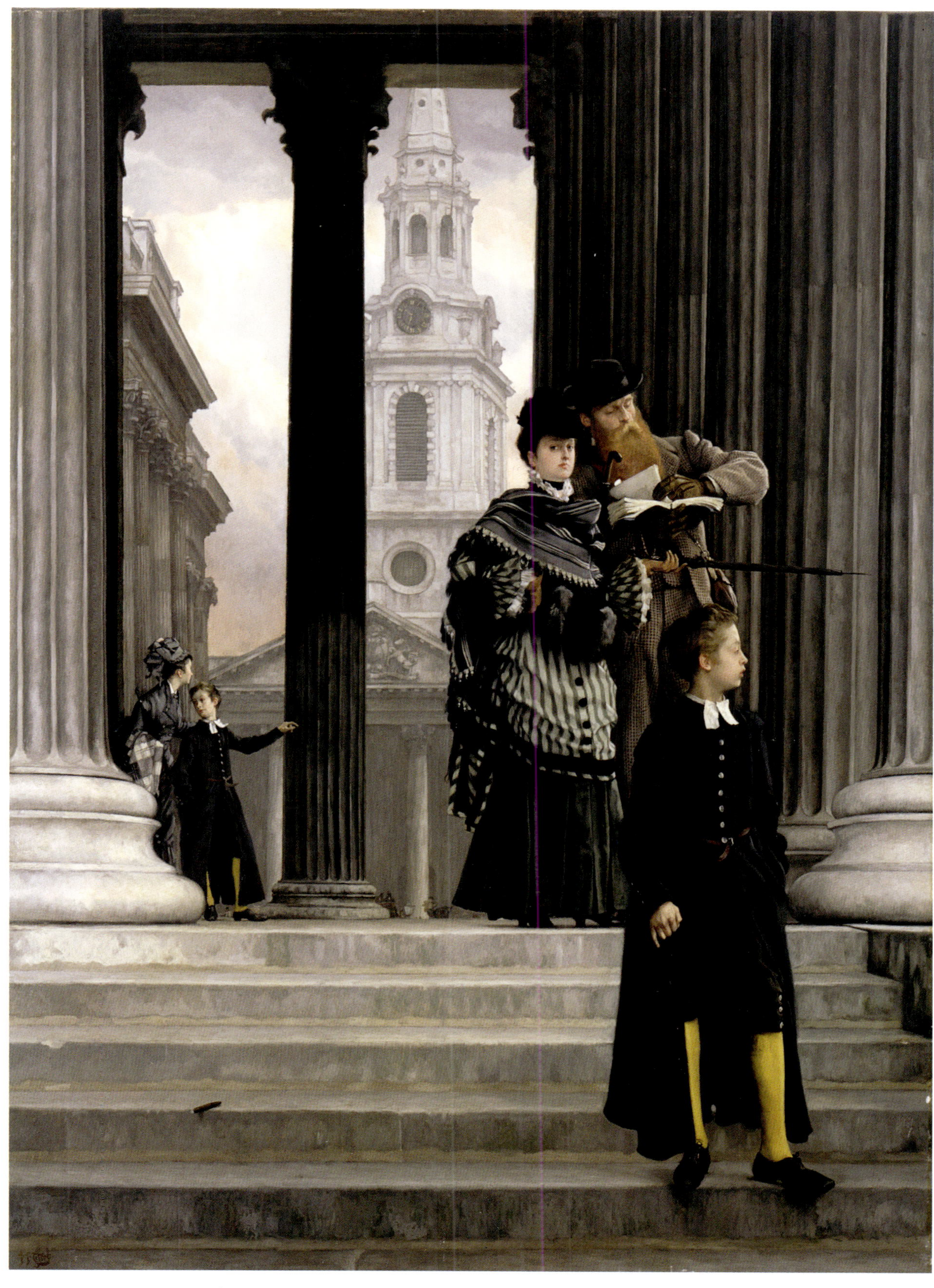

56

LONDON VISITORS, 1873–1874

Oil on canvas, 63 × 45 in. (160 × 114.2 cm)
Toledo Museum of Art, Ohio, Purchased with funds from the Libbey Endowment,
Gift of Edward Drummond Libbey, 1951.409

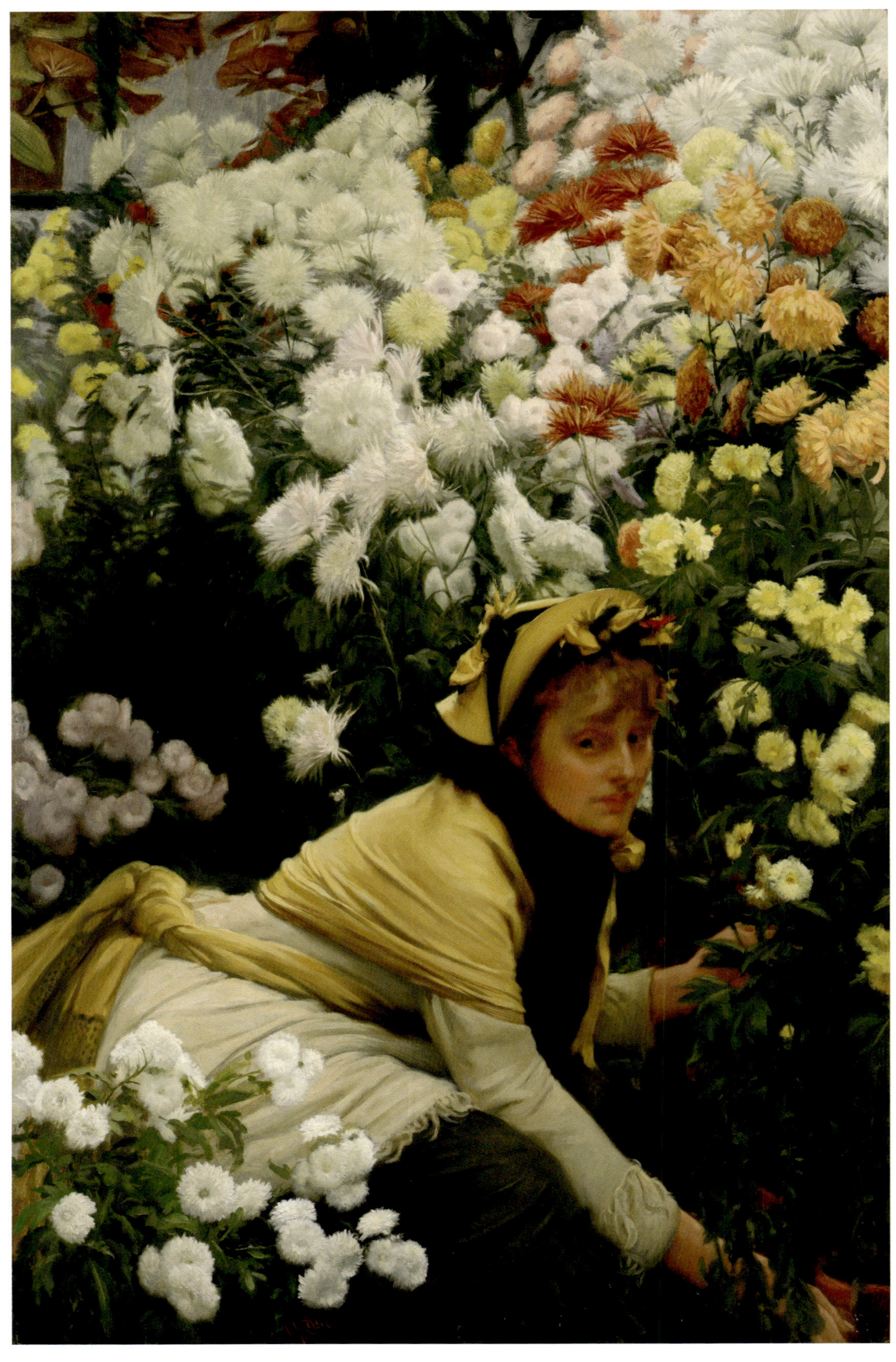

57

CHRYSANTHEMUMS, CA. 1876

Oil on canvas, 46⅝ × 30 in. (118.4 × 76.2 cm)
Sterling and Francine Clark Art Institute, Williamstown, Massachusetts,
Acquired in honor of David S. Brooke (Institute Director, 1977–1994), 1994, 1994.2

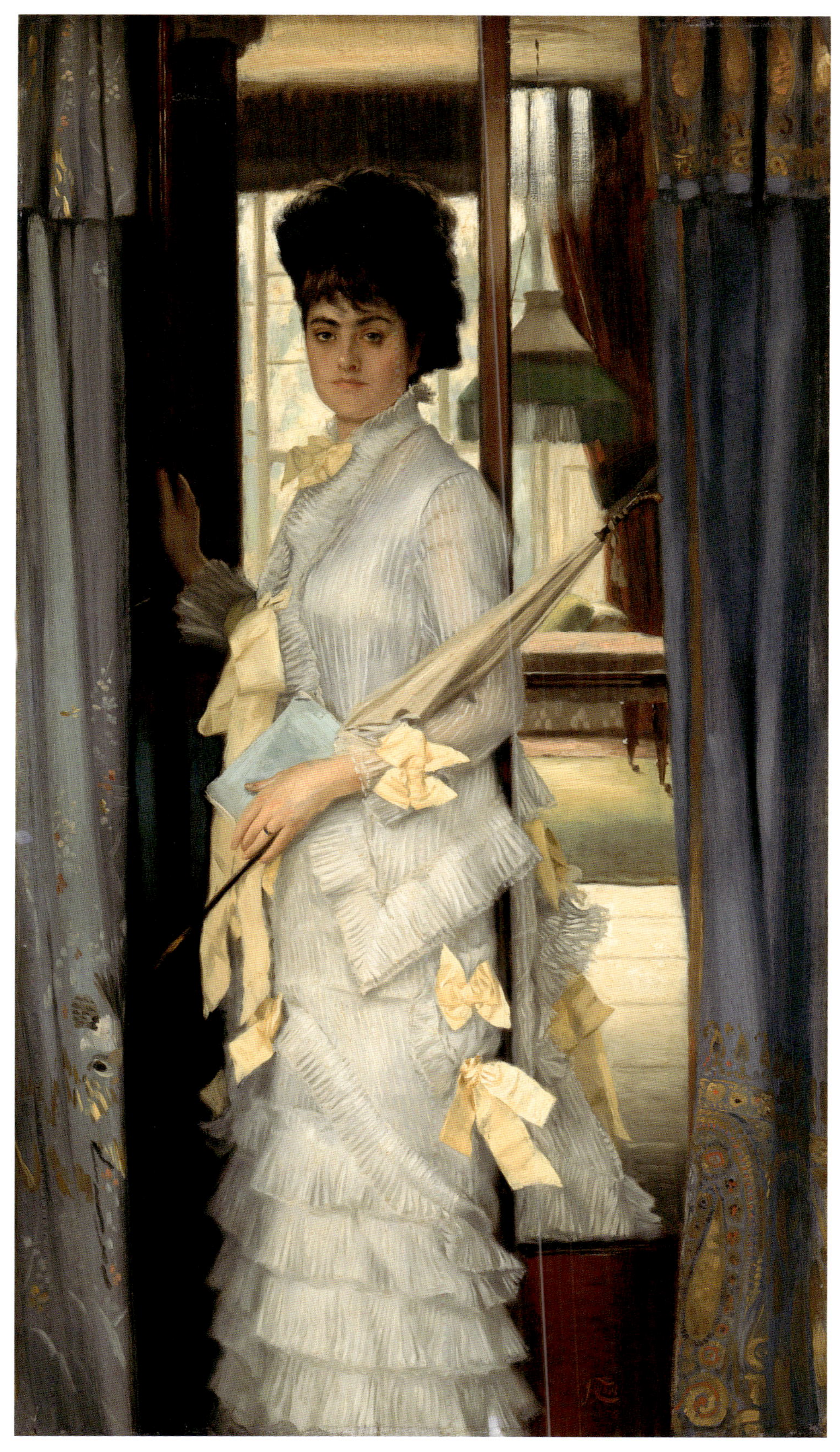

58

SUMMER, 1876

Oil on canvas, 36 × 20⅜ in. (91.4 × 51.8 cm)
Tate, London, Purchased from Mrs. Isa van Wisselingh (Clarke Fund), 1927, N04271

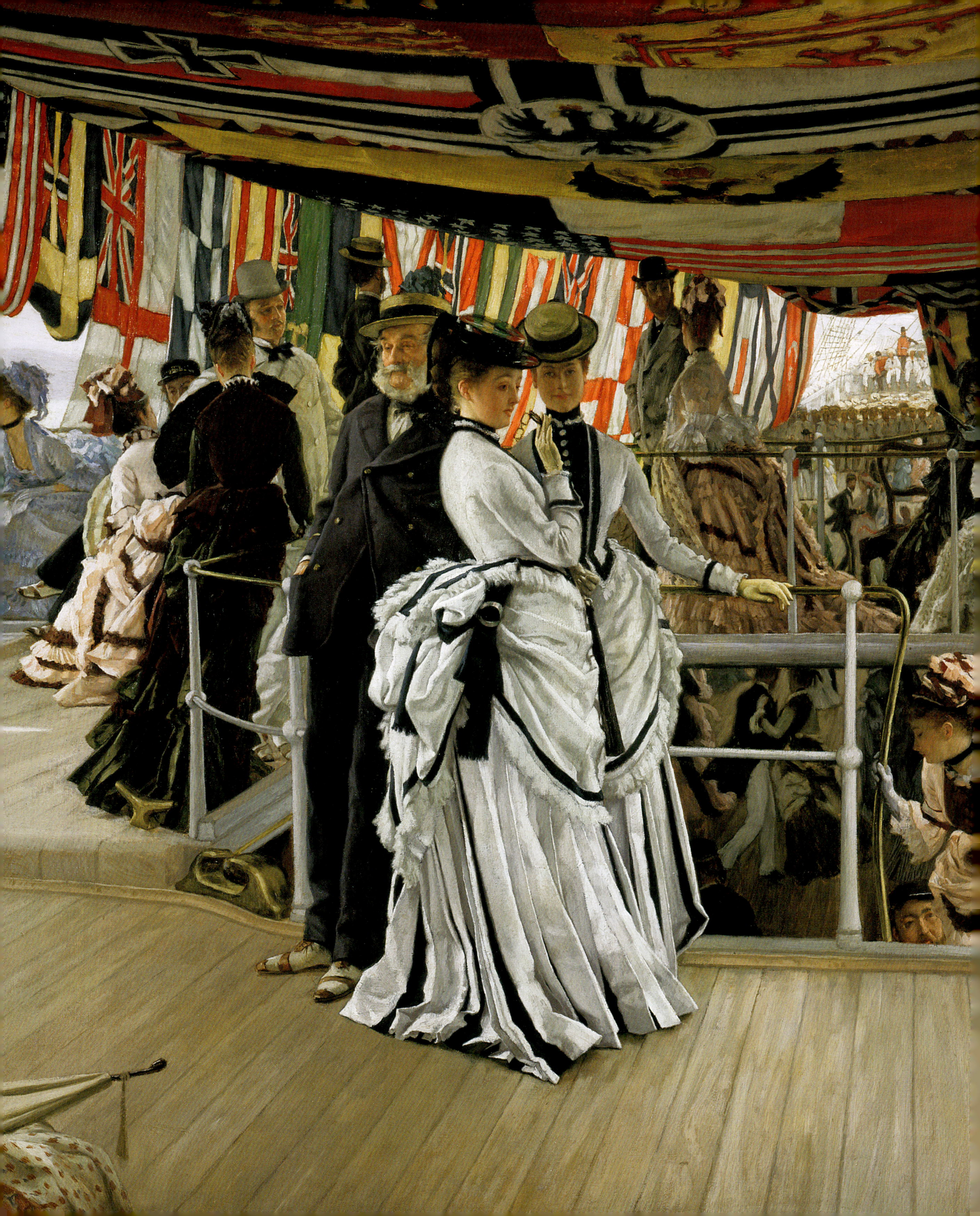

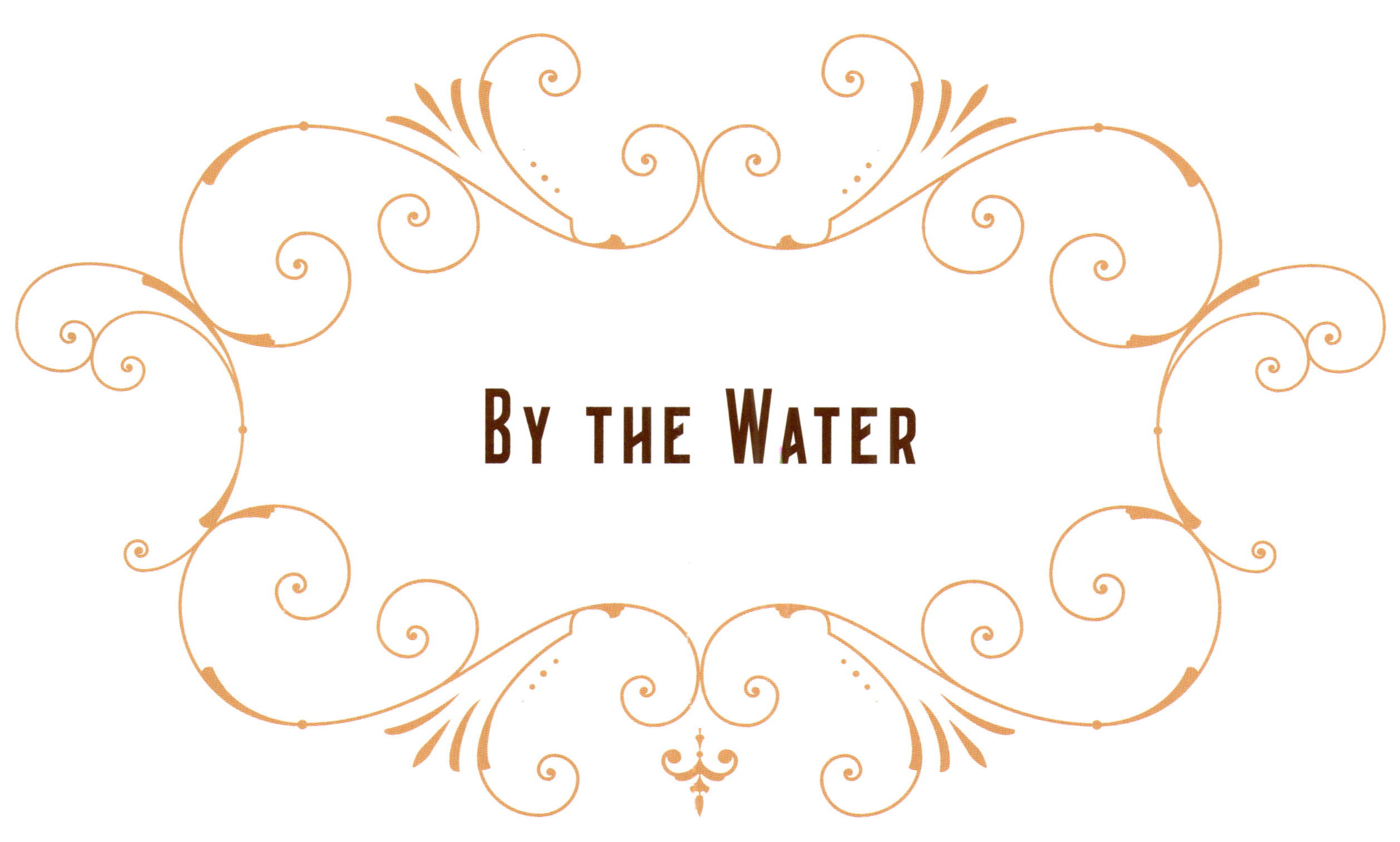

By the Water

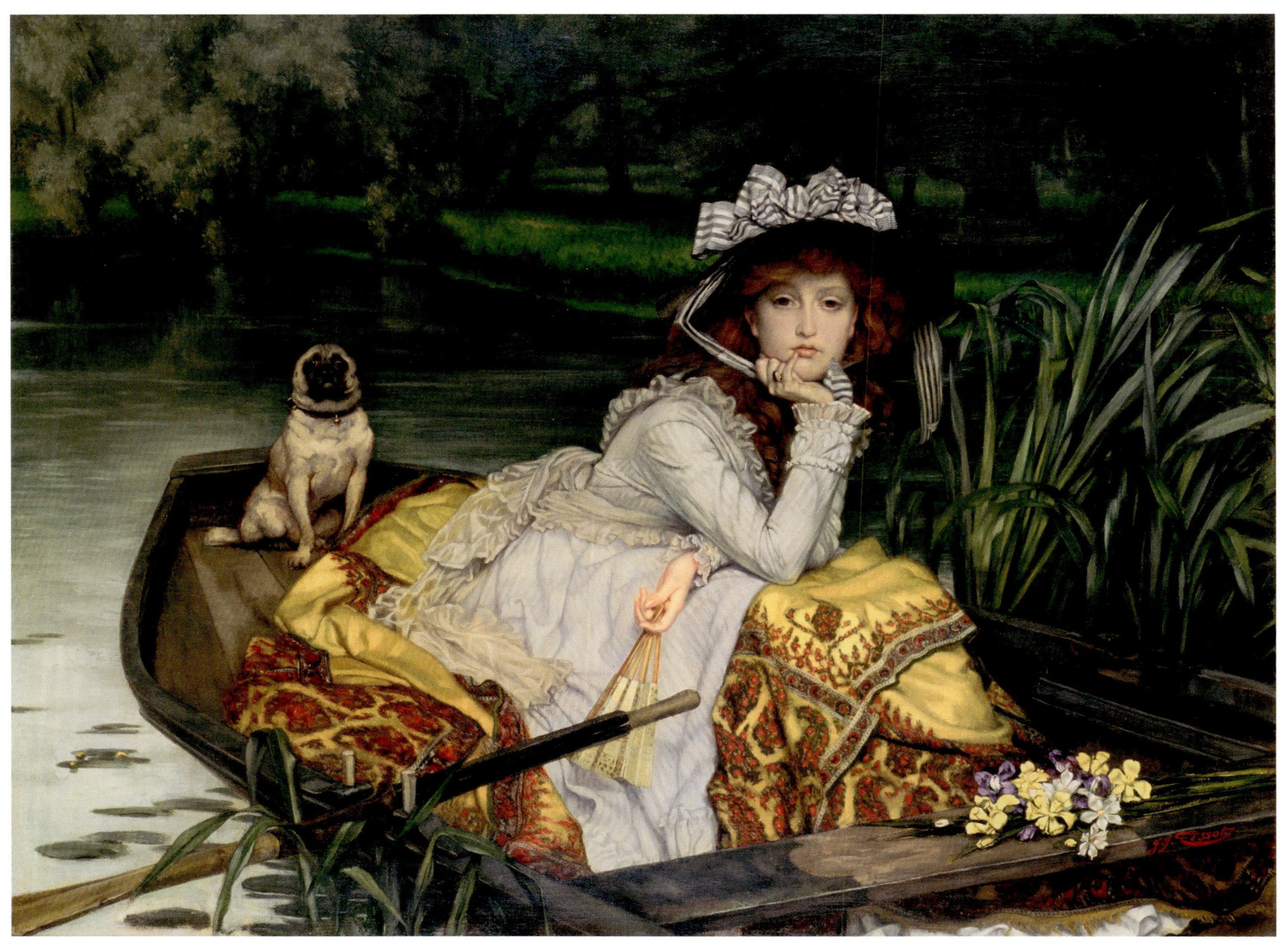

59

Young Lady in a Boat, 1869–1870

Oil on canvas, 19 × 25 in. (48.3 × 63.5 cm)

Private collection

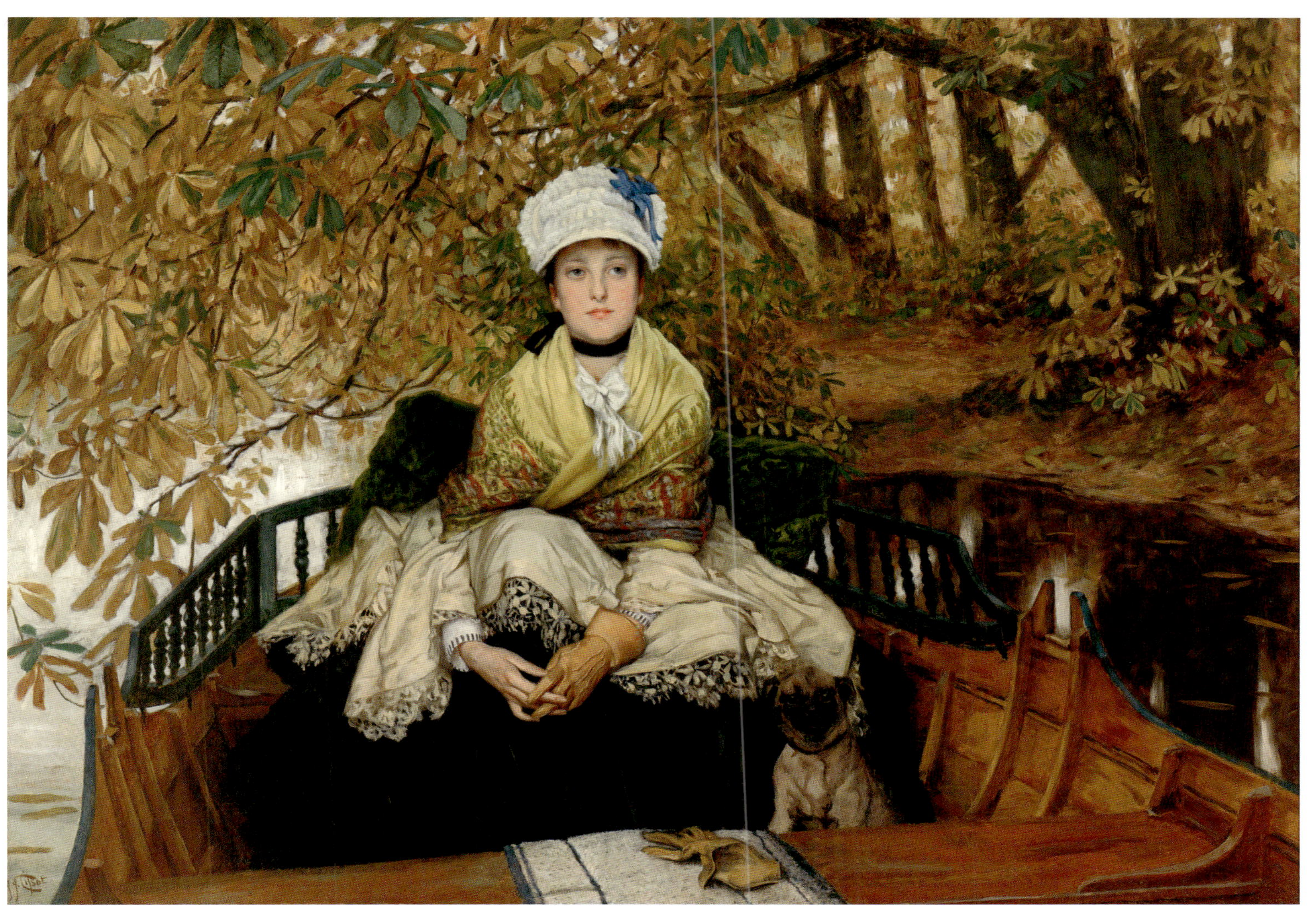

60

WAITING, 1873

also known as IN THE SHALLOWS

Oil on canvas, 22 × 31 in. (55.9 × 78.8 cm)

Collection of Diane B. Wilsey, San Francisco

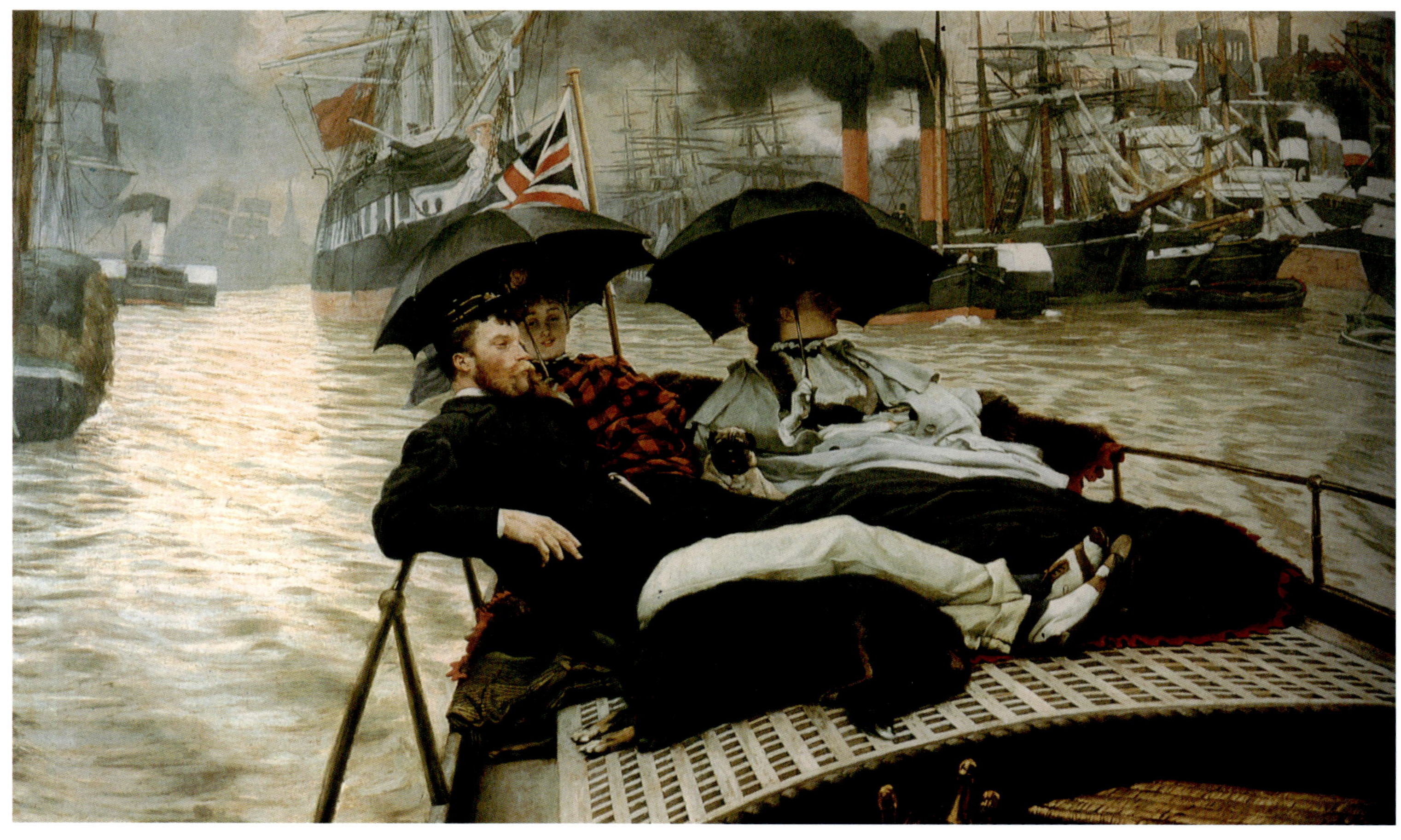

61

The Thames, 1875

Oil on canvas, $29\frac{1}{2} \times 46\frac{1}{2}$ in. (74.8×118 cm)
The Hepworth Wakefield, England, Purchased 1938

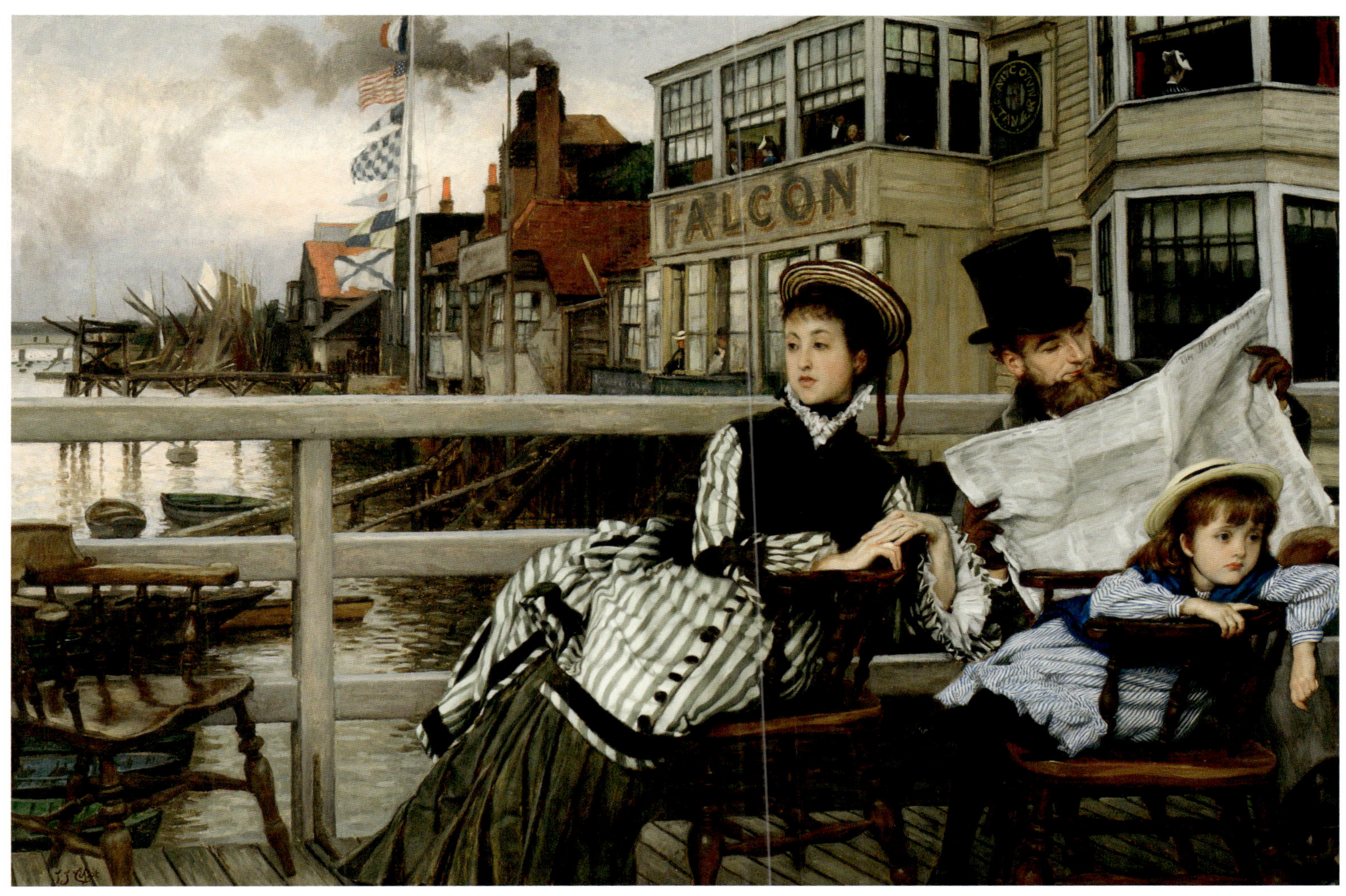

62

GRAVESEND, 1873

also known as WAITING FOR THE FERRY AT THE FALCON TAVERN

Oil on canvas, 26¼ × 38¼ in. (66.7 × 97 cm)

The Speed Art Museum, Louisville, Gift of Mrs. Blakemore Wheeler, 1963.41

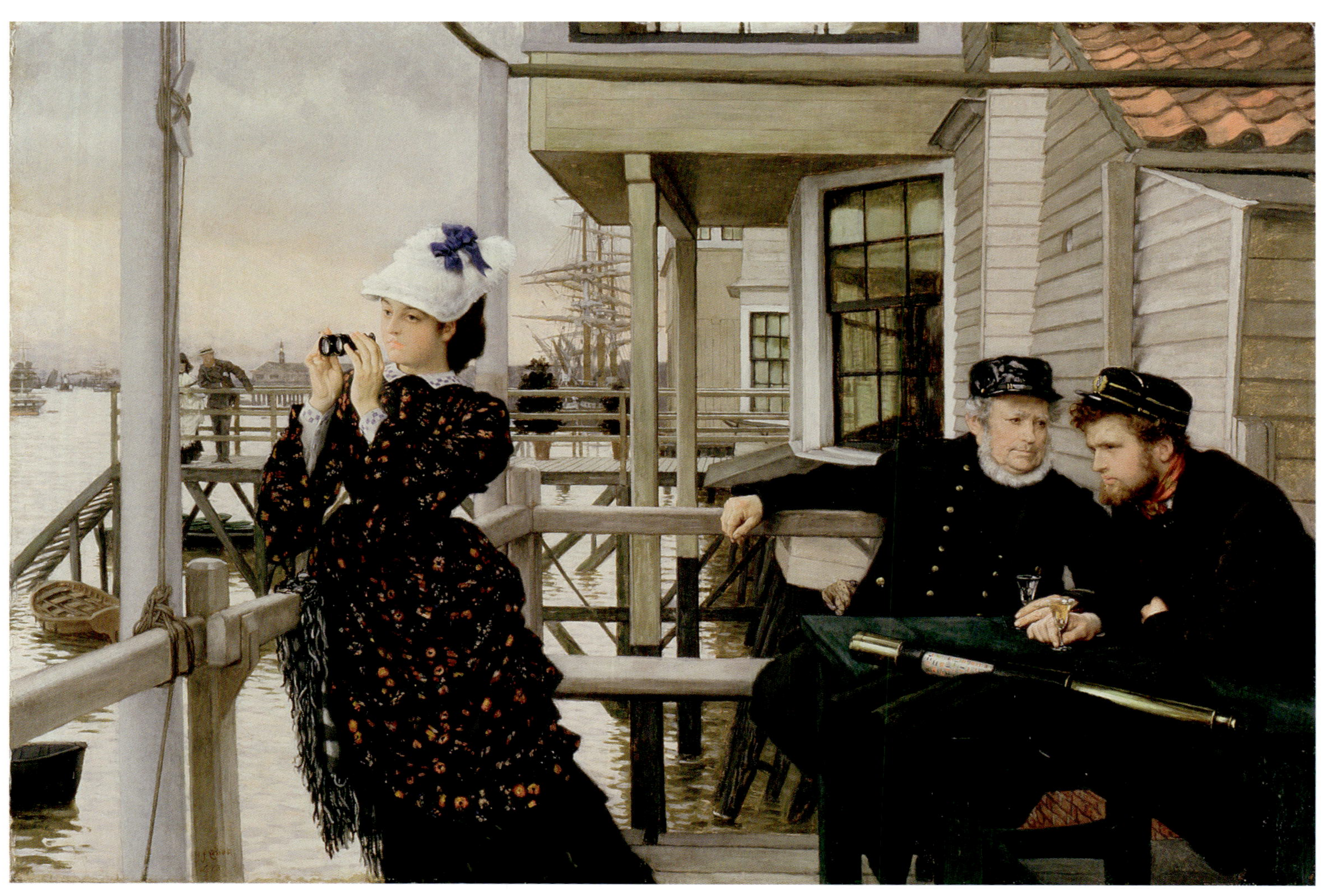

63

THE CAPTAIN'S DAUGHTER, 1873

Oil on canvas, 28½ × 41¼ in. (72.3 × 104.8 cm)
Southampton City Art Gallery, England, Purchased 1934 through the Frederick Smith Bequest Fund, SOTAG: 580

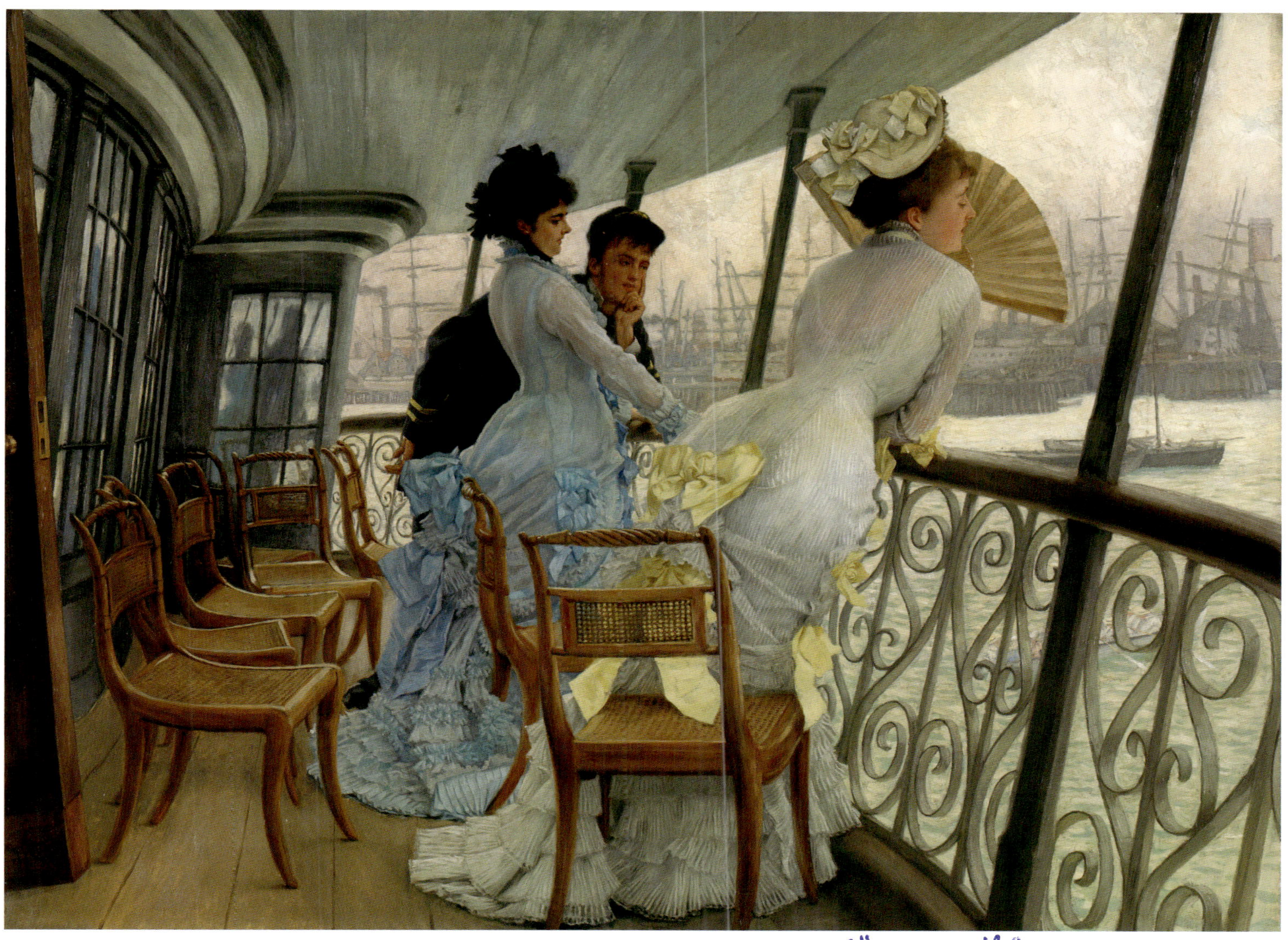

64

THE GALLERY OF HMS "CALCUTTA" (PORTSMOUTH), CA. 1876

Oil on canvas, 27 × 36⅛ in. (68.6 × 91.8 cm)

Tate, London, Presented by Samuel Courtauld, 1936, N04847

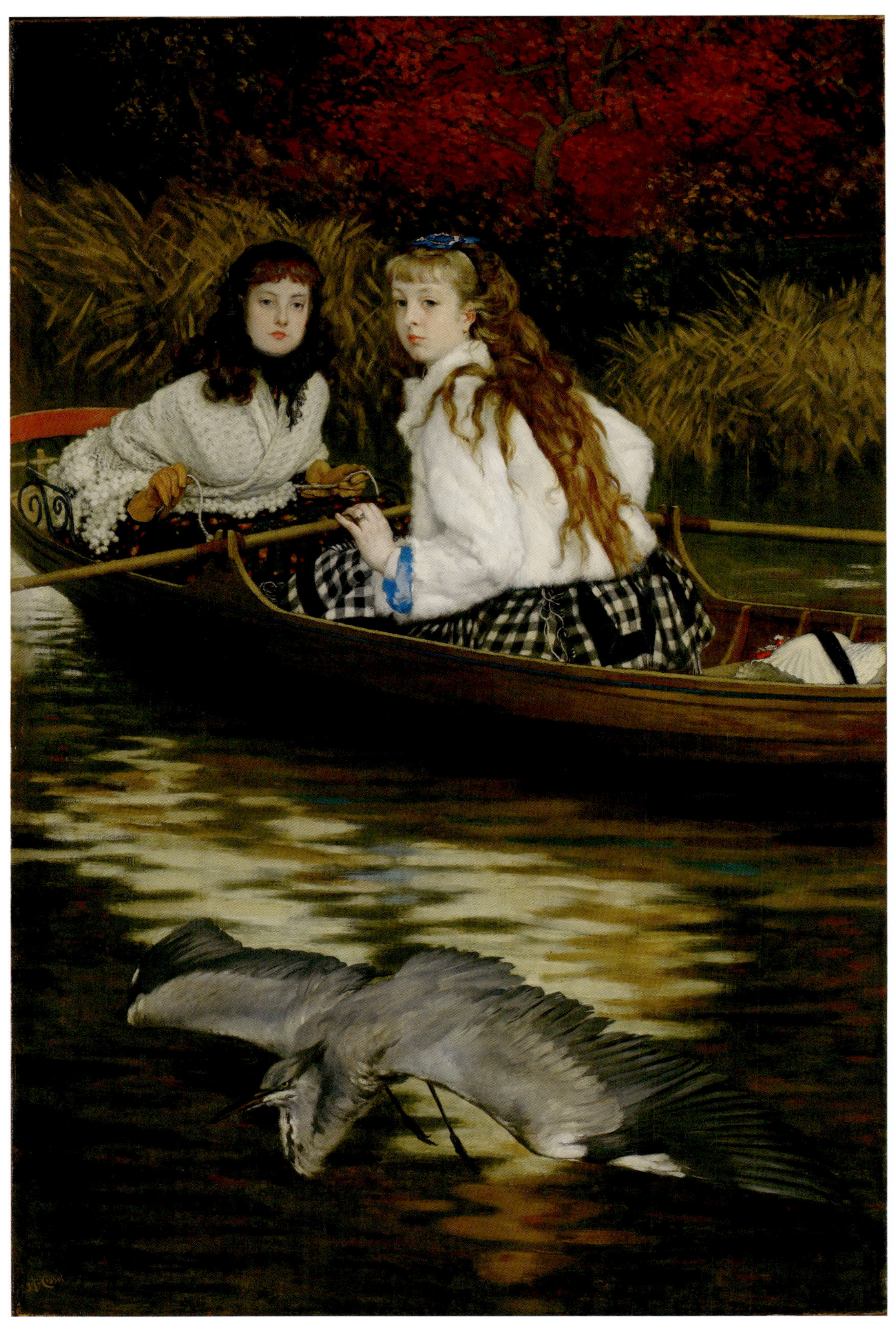

65

On the Thames, A Heron, ca. 1871–1872

Oil on canvas, 36½ × 23¾ in. (92.7 × 60.3 cm)

Minneapolis Institute of Art, Gift of Mrs. Patrick Butler, by exchange, 75.7

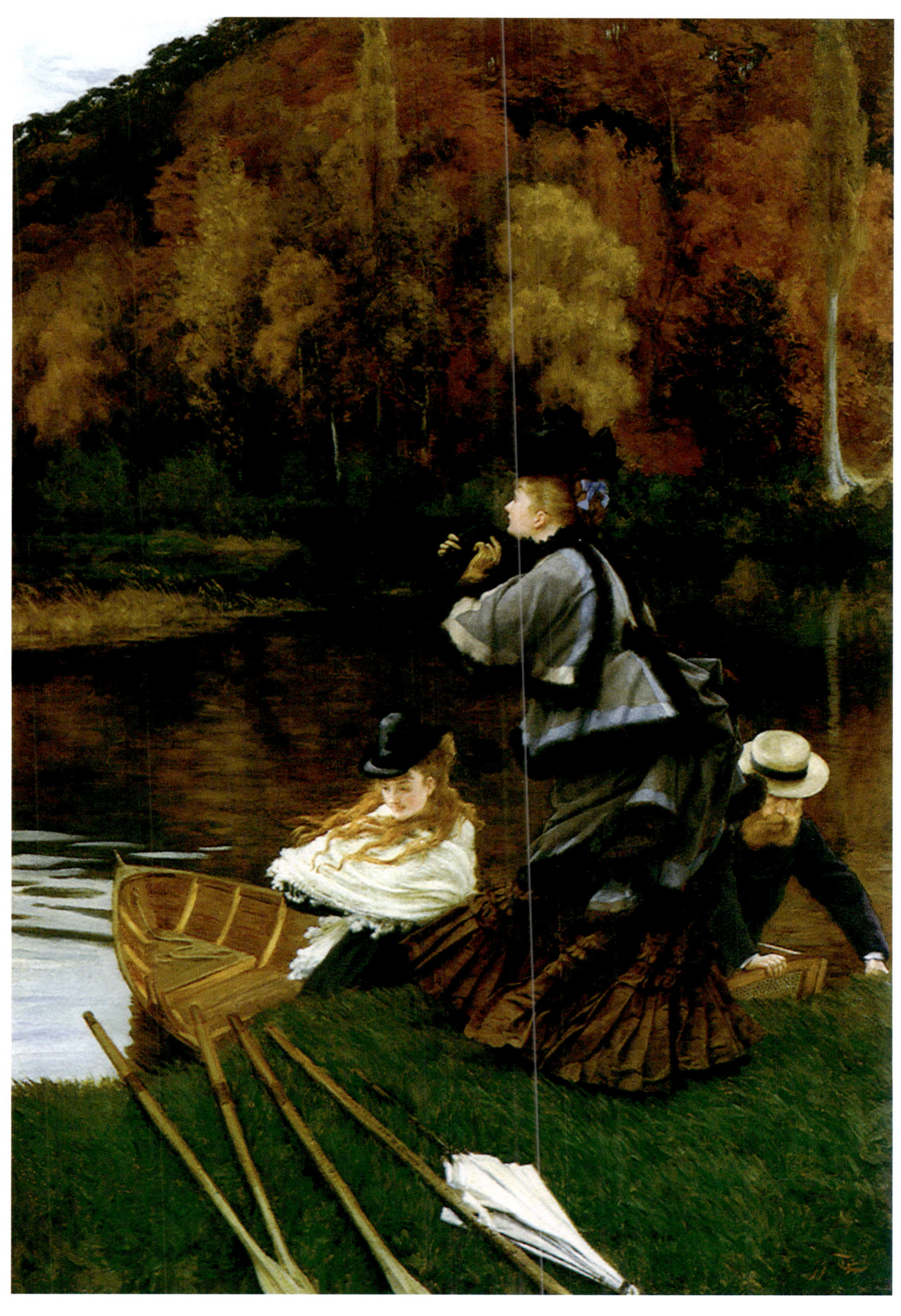

65
A WINDY DAY, 1874–1875
also known as AUTUMN ON THE THAMES (NUNEHAM COURTNEY)
Oil on wood panel, 29¼ × 19¼ in. (74.3 × 48.9 cm)
Private collection

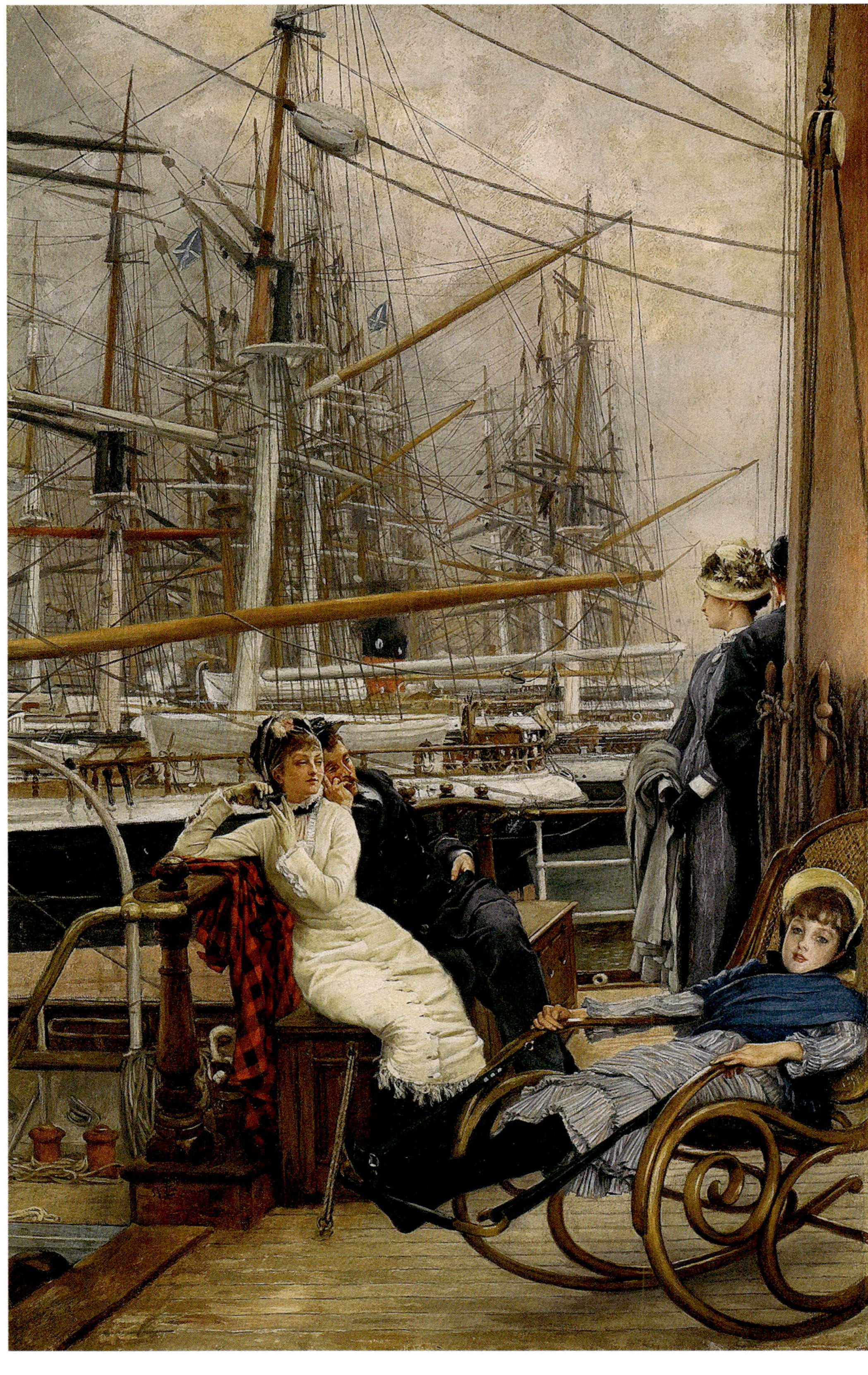

67

Docks, 1877–1878

also known as **A Visit to the Yacht**

Oil on canvas, 34 × 21 ¼ in. (86.5 × 54 cm)

Private collection

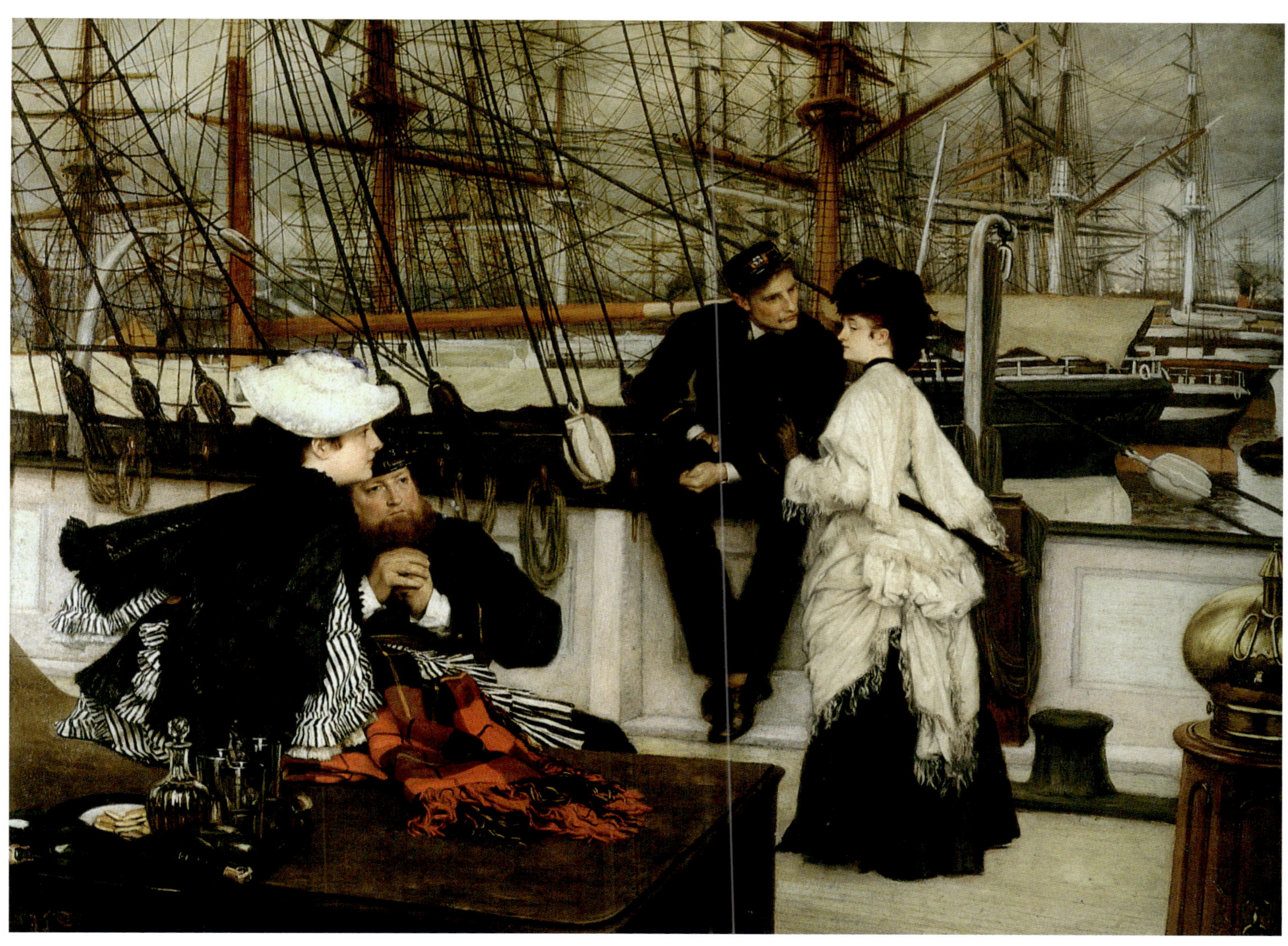

68

In the Docks, 1873

also known as The Captain and the Mate

Oil on wood panel, 21 × 30 in. (53.3 × 76.2 cm)

Private collection

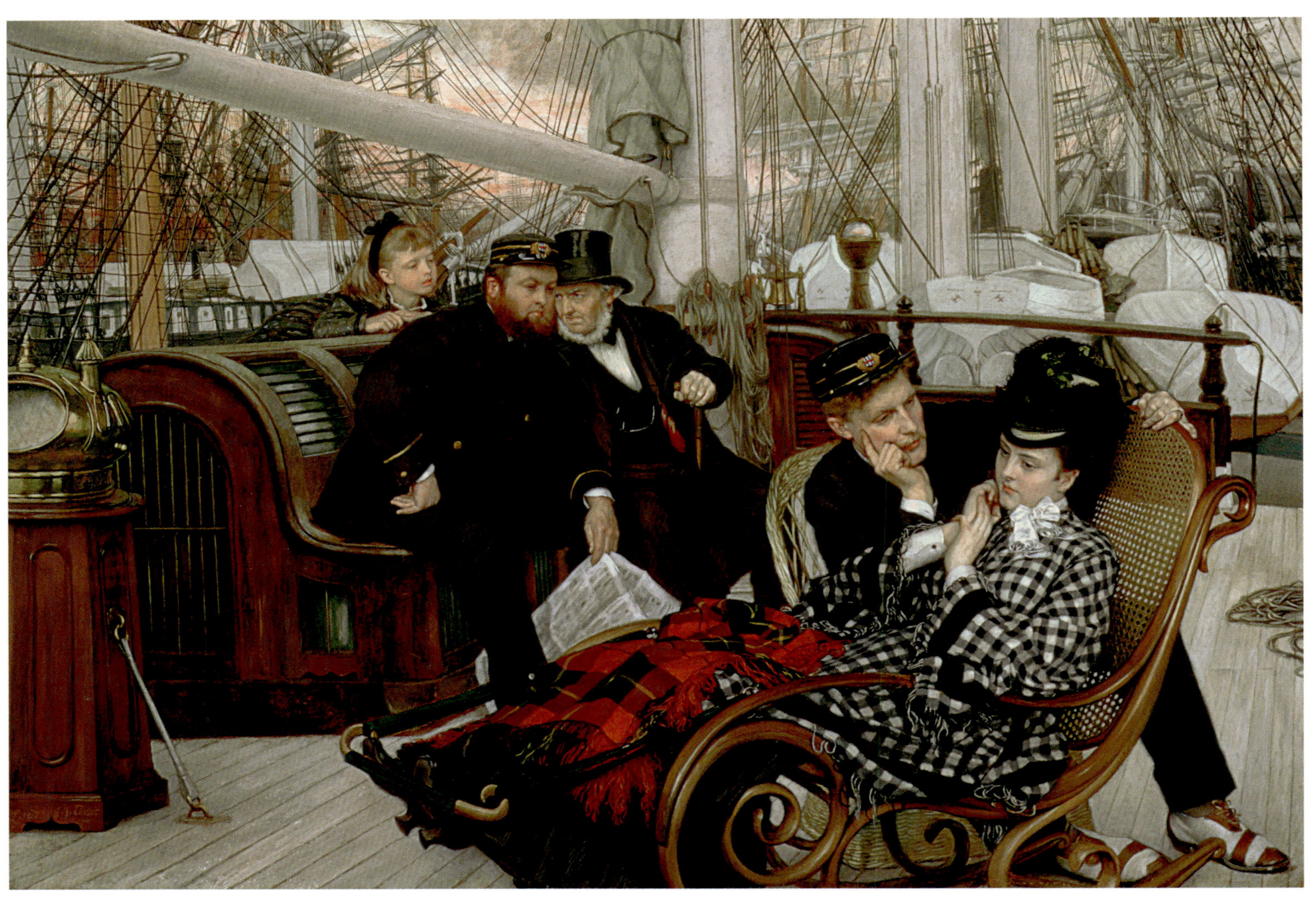

69

THE LAST EVENING, 1873

Oil on canvas, 28⅜ × 40½ in. (72 × 103 cm)

Guildhall Art Gallery, London, Bequeathed by Charles Gassiot, 1902, 737

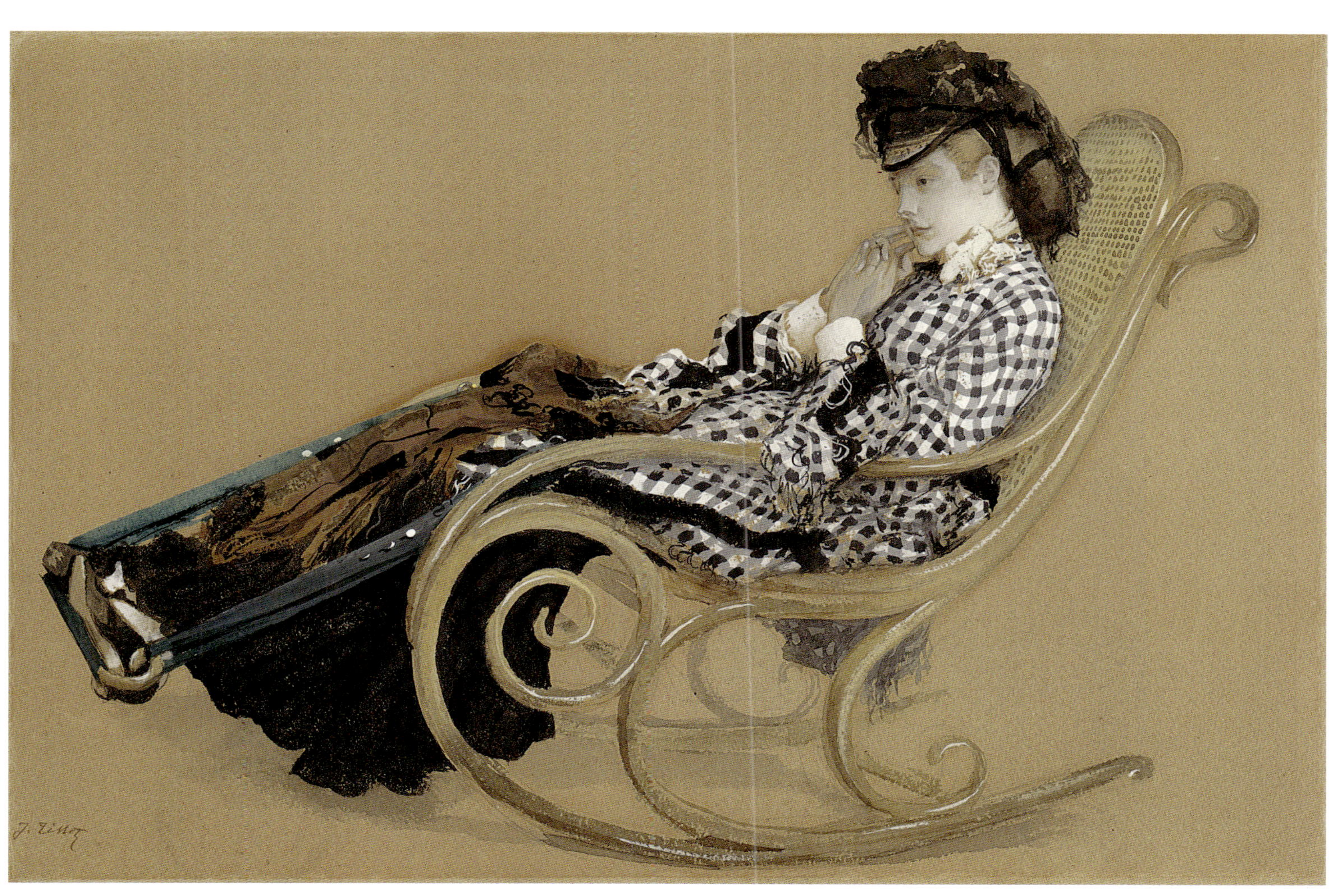

70

YOUNG WOMAN IN A ROCKING CHAIR,
variant of STUDY FOR "THE LAST EVENING," 1872

Brush and brown ink with opaque watercolor and watercolor over graphite on blue paper, 11¼ × 17 in. (28.7 × 43.2 cm)
The J. Paul Getty Museum, Los Angeles, 2002.30

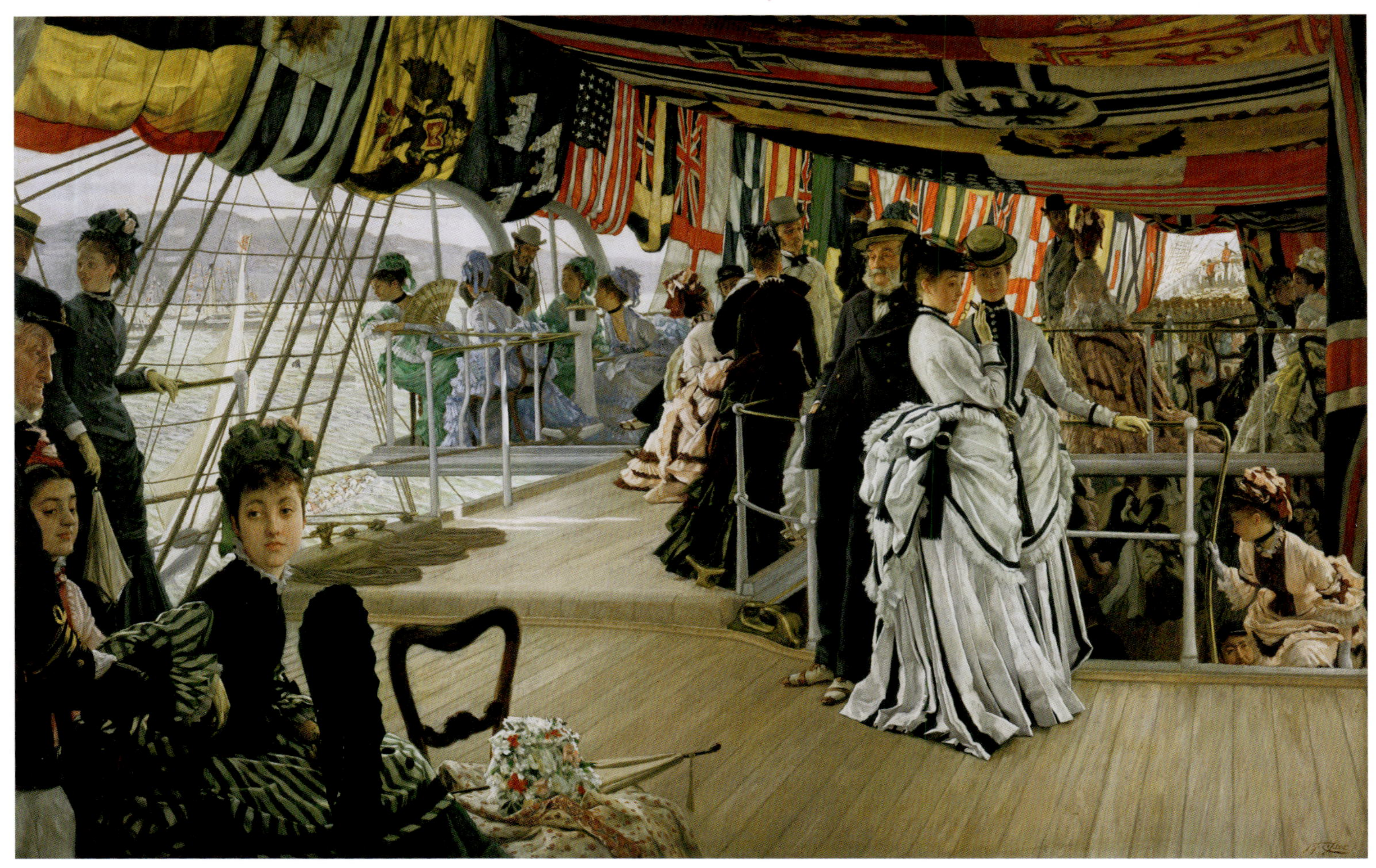

71

The Ball on Shipboard, ca. 1874

Oil on canvas, 33⅛ × 51 in. (84.1 × 129.5 cm)
Tate, London, Presented by the Trustees of the Chantrey Bequest, 1937, N04892

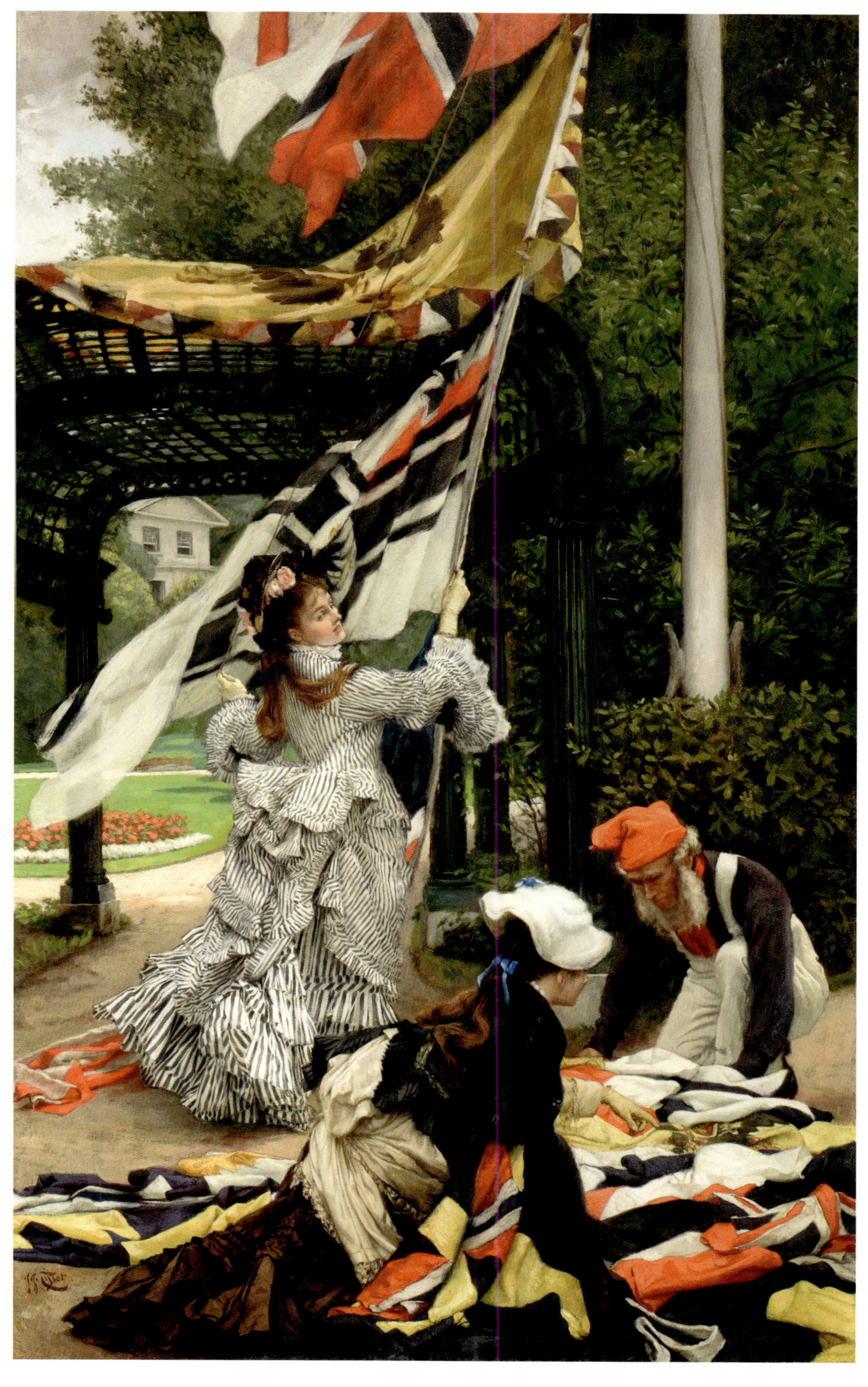

72

THE HOLIDAY, 1874–1875

also known as STILL ON TOP

Oil on canvas, 34½ × 21 in. (87.6 × 53.3 cm)

Auckland Art Gallery Toi o Tāmaki, Gift of Viscount Leverhulme, 1921, 1921/2

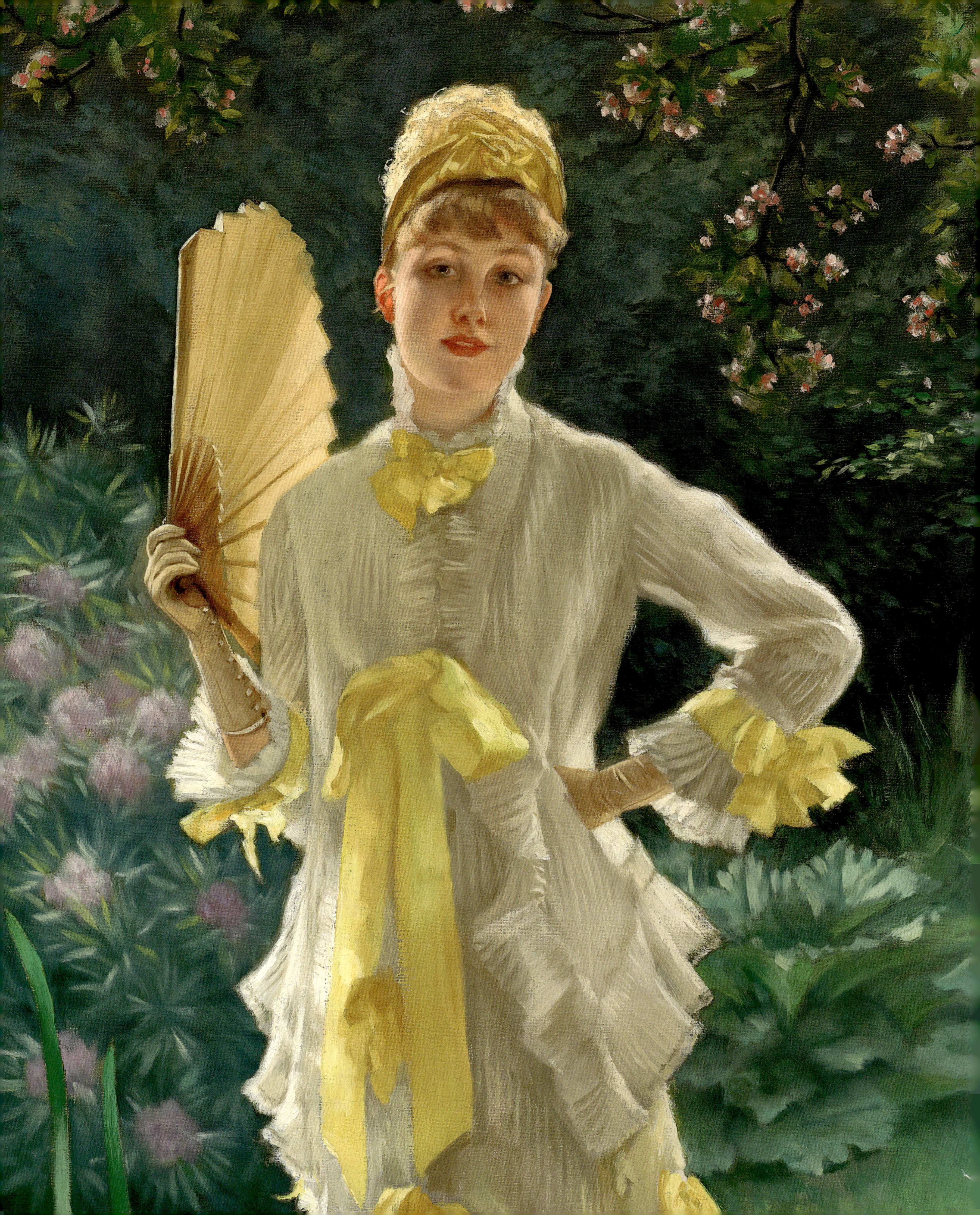

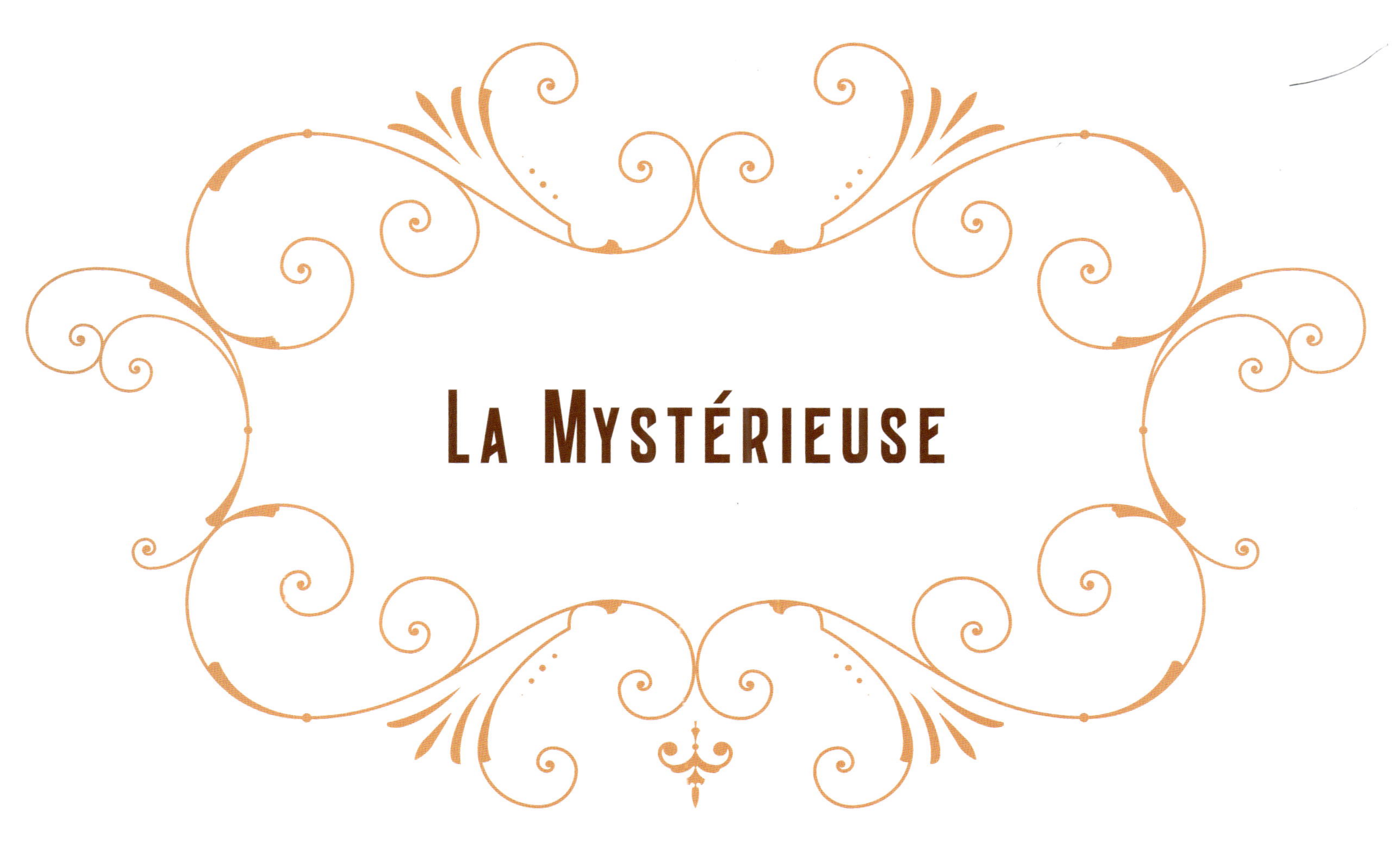

LA MYSTÉRIEUSE

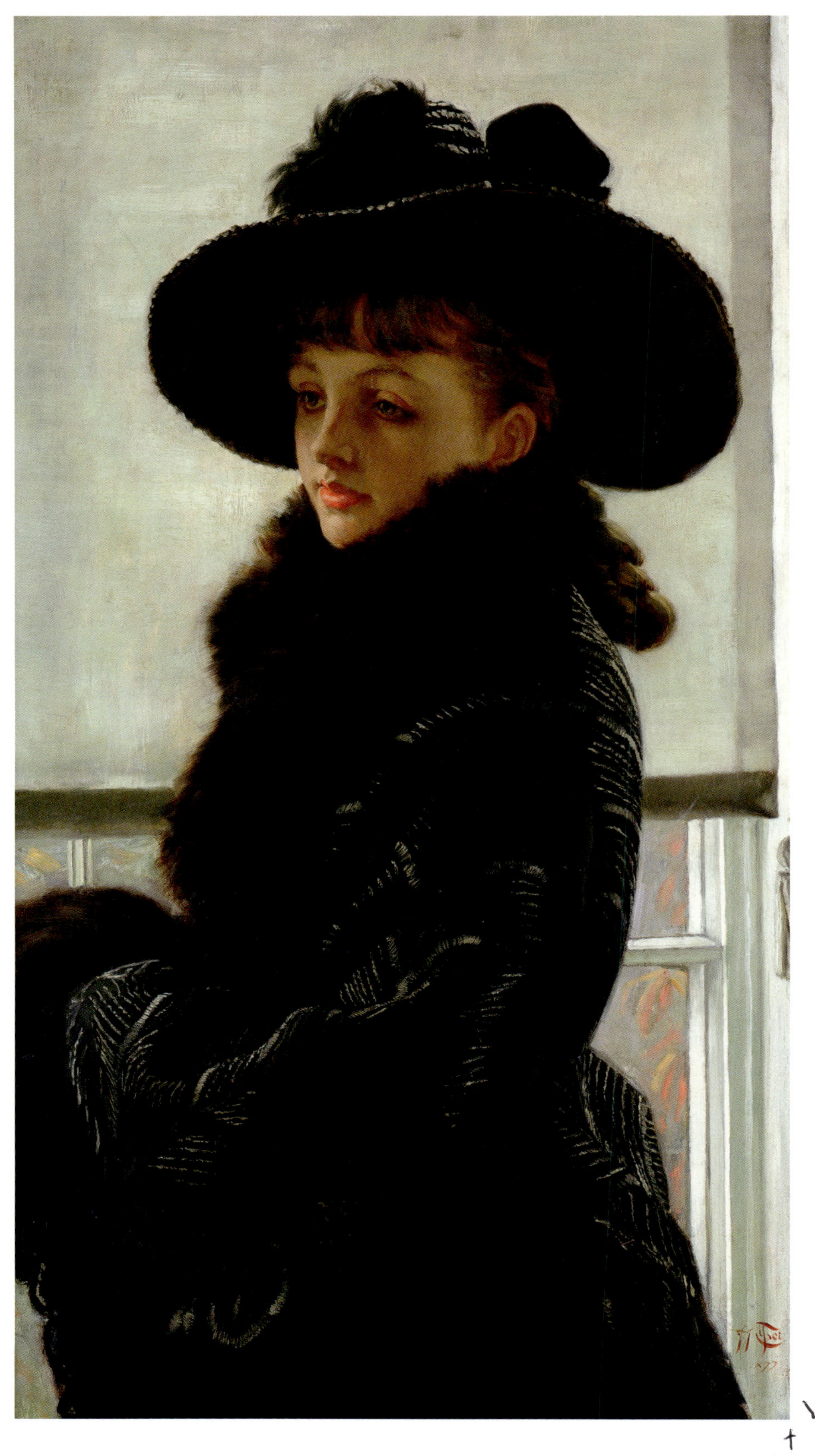

73

Winter or Mavourneen, 1877
also known as Portrait of Kathleen Newton

Oil on canvas, 34 ¾ × 20 in. (88.2 × 50.8 cm)
Private collection

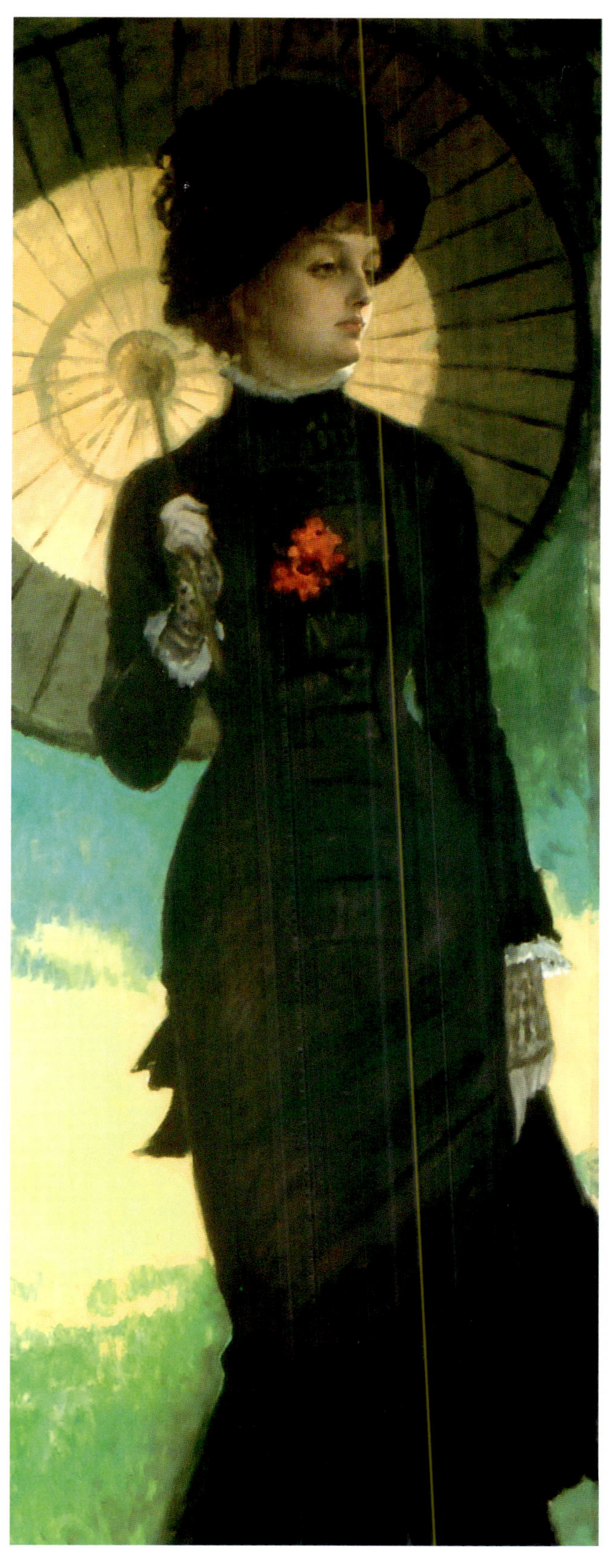

74

MRS. NEWTON WITH A PARASOL, CA. 1878

Oil on canvas, 56 × 18¾ in (142.2 × 47.6 cm)
Musée Baron Martin, Gray, France, Pigalle Bequest, GR-93-723

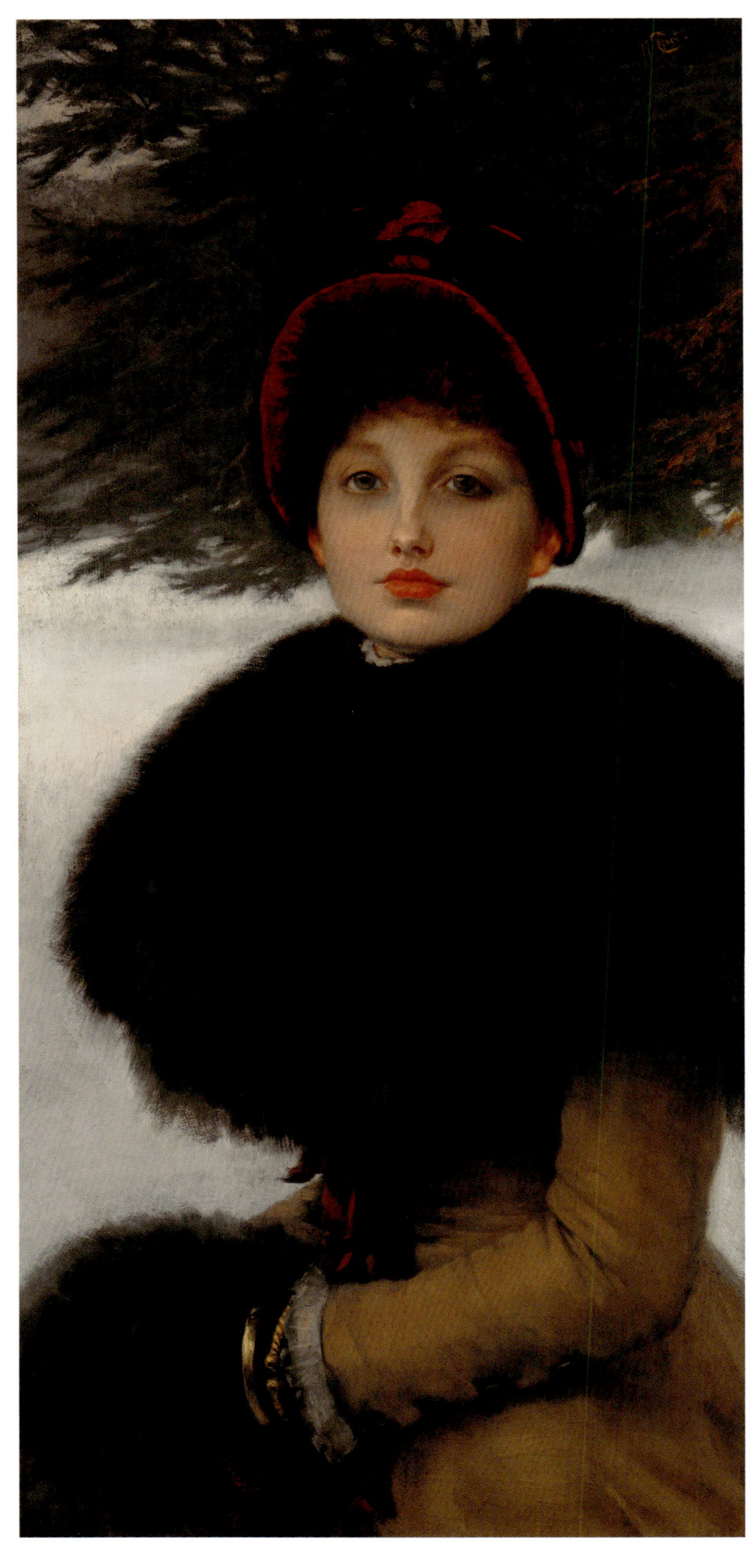

75

A Winter Walk, 1880

Oil on wood panel, 31⅛ × 14⅝ in. (79 × 37 cm)
Private collection

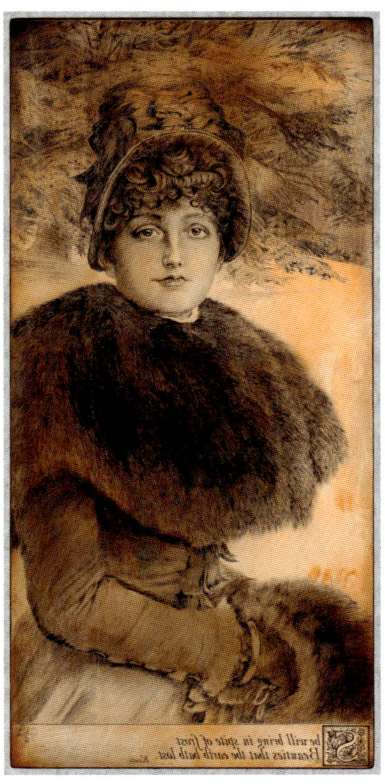

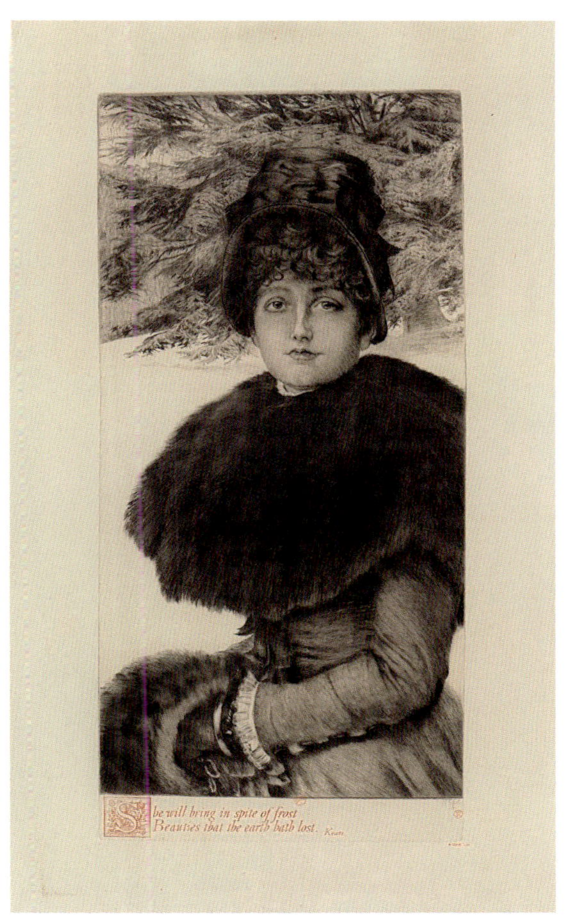

76

A Winter Walk, 1880

Copper plate, 22$\frac{1}{2}$ × 10$\frac{5}{8}$ in. (57.2 × 27 cm)
Bibliothèque Nationale de France, Paris

77

A Winter Walk, 1880

Etching and drypoint, second state, with text printed in red, 22$\frac{3}{8}$ × 10$\frac{3}{8}$ in. (56.7 × 26.4 cm)
Bibliothèque Nationale de France, Paris

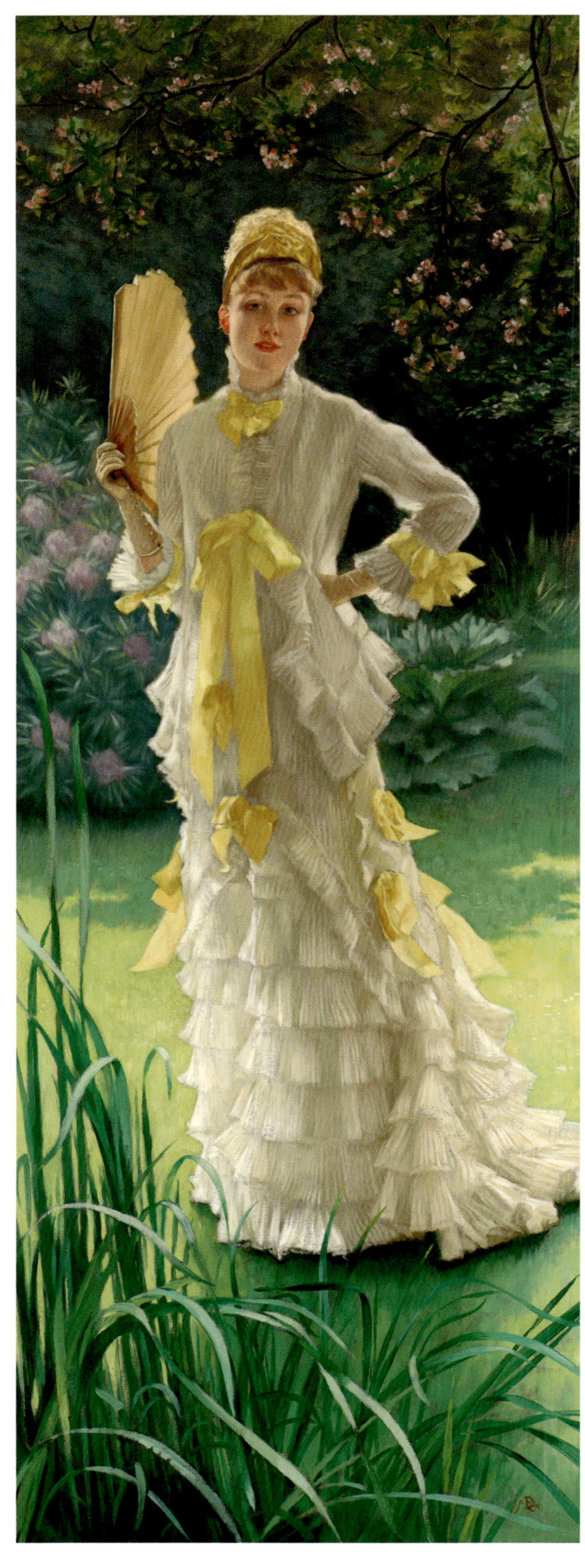

78

SPRING (SPECIMEN OF A PORTRAIT), 1877

Oil on canvas, 55¾ × 21 in. (141.5 × 53.3 cm)
Collection of Diane B. Wilsey, San Francisco

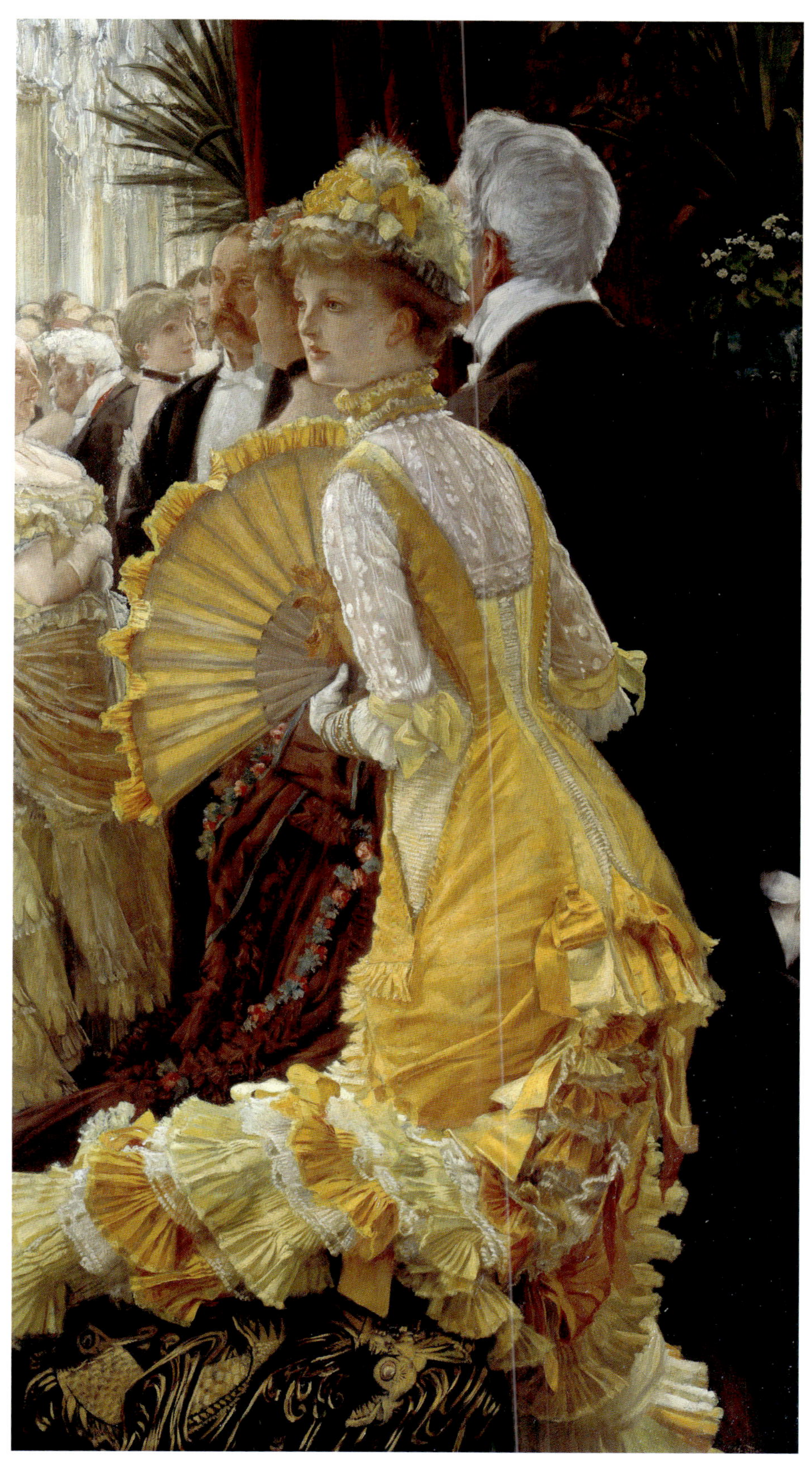

79

EVENING, 1878

also known as THE BALL

Oil on canvas, 35⅞ × 20⅛ in. (91 × 51 cm)
Musée d'Orsay, Paris, RF 2253

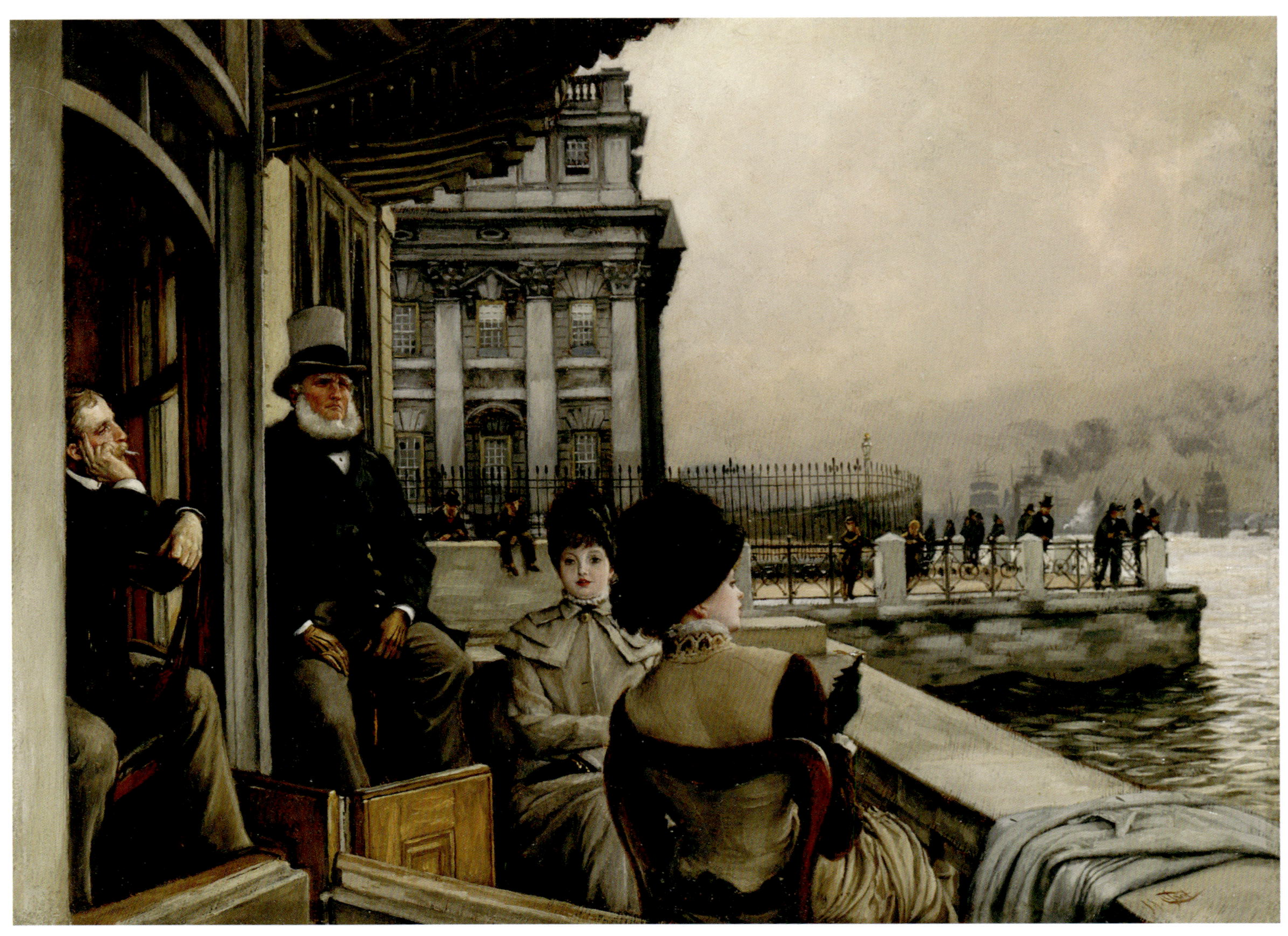

80

TRAFALGAR TAVERN (GREENWICH), 1879–1880

Oil on wood panel, 10⅝ × 14½ in. (27 × 36.8 cm)

New Orleans Museum of Art

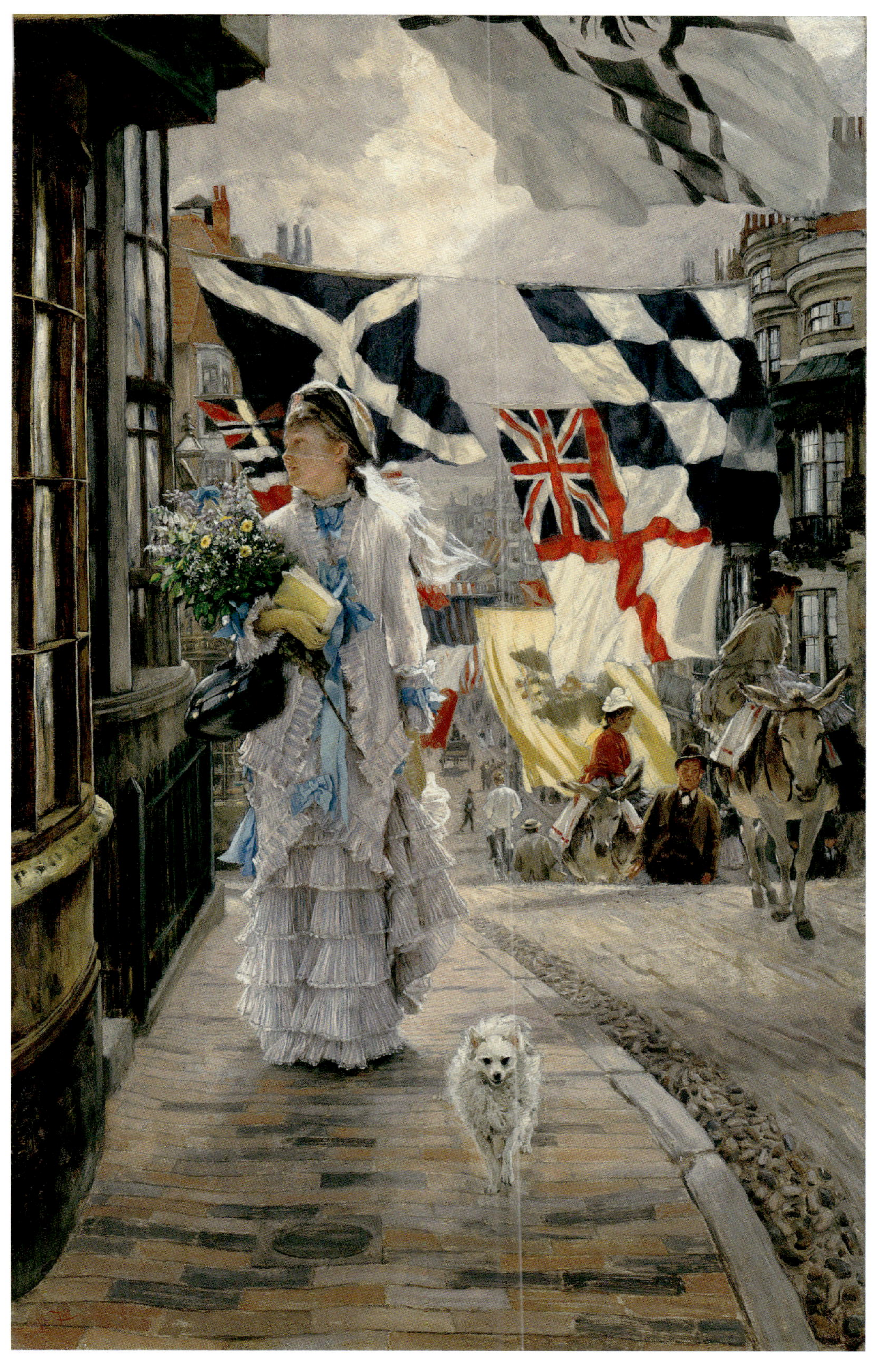

81

THE GALA DAY—SEASIDE, 1877–1878

also known as *A FÊTE DAY AT BRIGHTON*

Oil on canvas, $34 \times 21\frac{3}{4}$ in. (86.4×55.2 cm)

Private col ection, USA

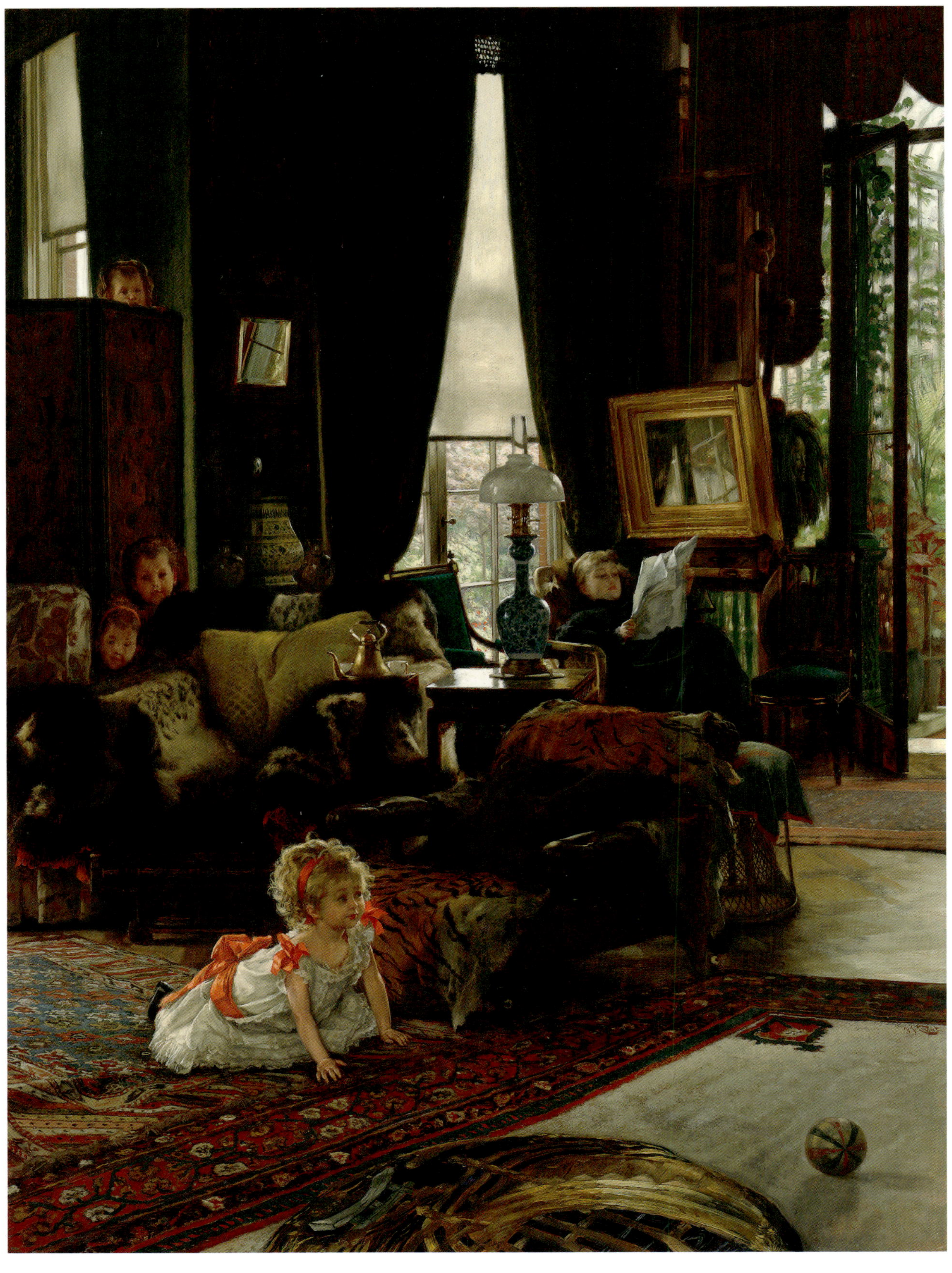

82

Hide and Seek, ca. 1877

Oil on wood panel, $28\frac{7}{8} \times 21\frac{1}{4}$ in. (73.4 × 53.9 cm)
National Gallery of Art, Washington, DC, Chester Dale Fund, 1978.47.1

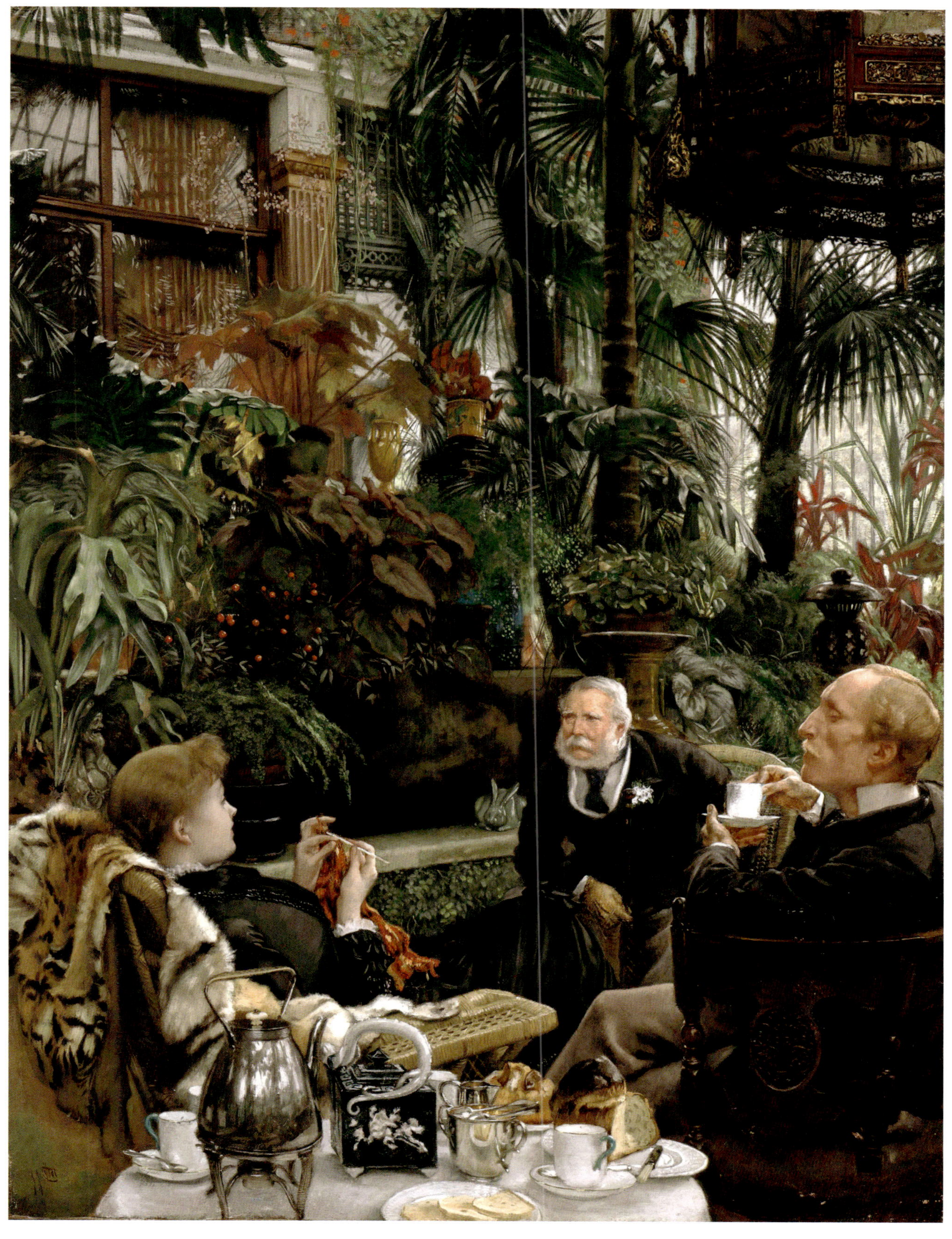

83

Rivals 1878–1879

Oil on canvas, 36¼ × 26¾ in. (92 × 68 cm)
The Marlene and Spencer Hays Collection

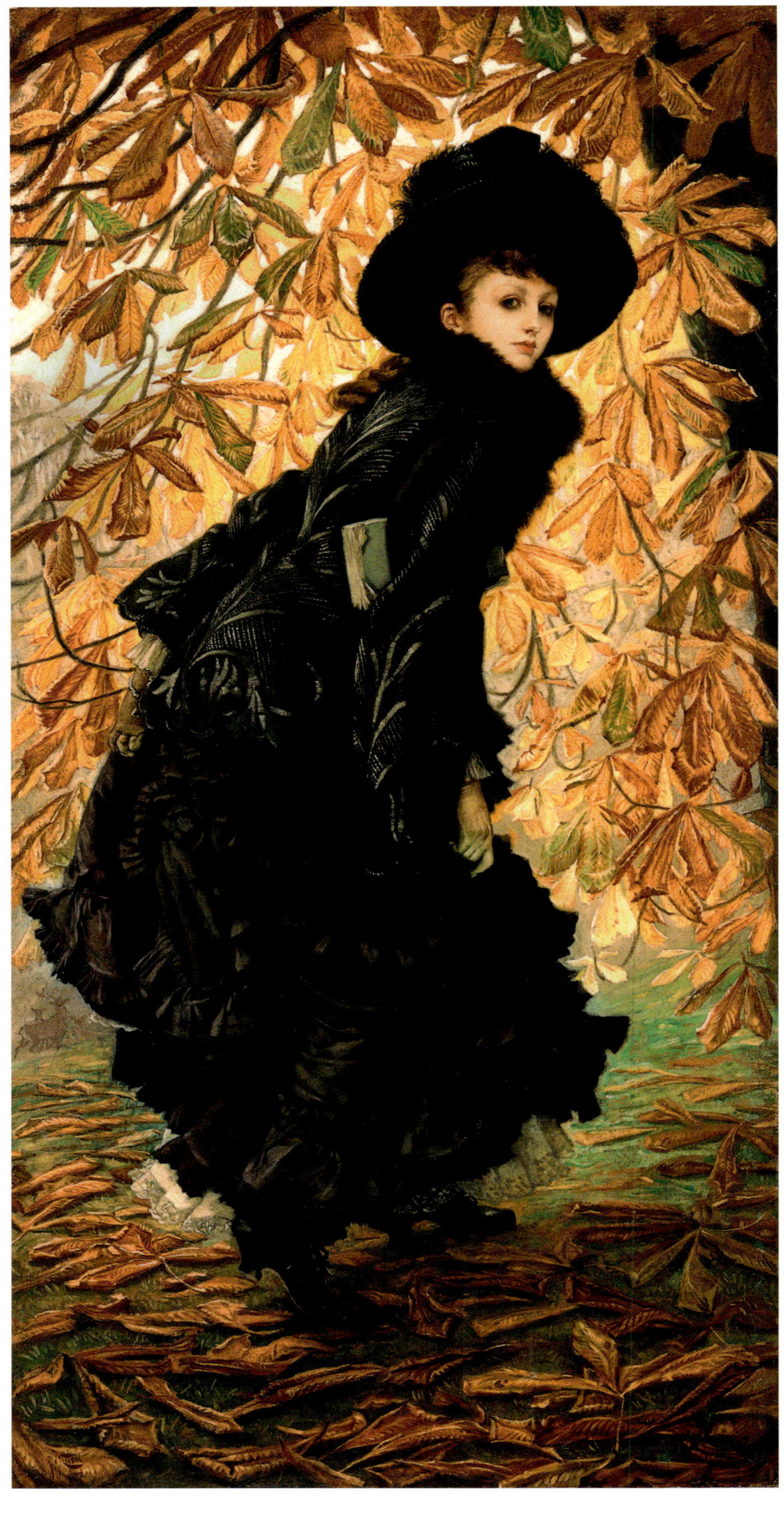

84

October, 1877

Oil on canvas, 85 × 42¾ in. (216 × 108.7 cm)

The Montreal Museum of Fine Arts, Gift of Lord Strathcona and family, inv. 1927.410

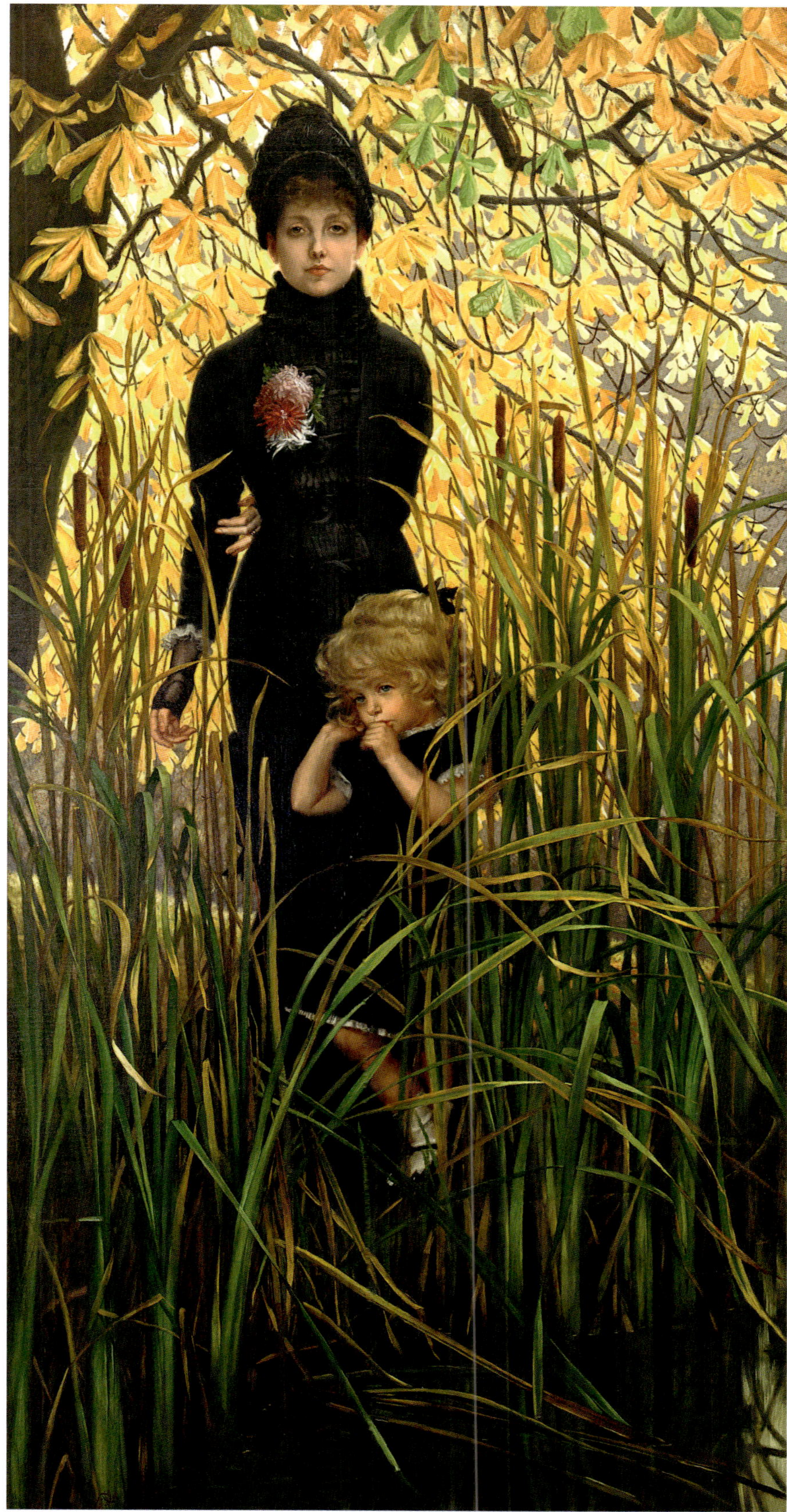

85

ORPHANS, 1878–1879

Oil on canvas, 85 × 43 in. (216 × 109.2 cm)

Private collection

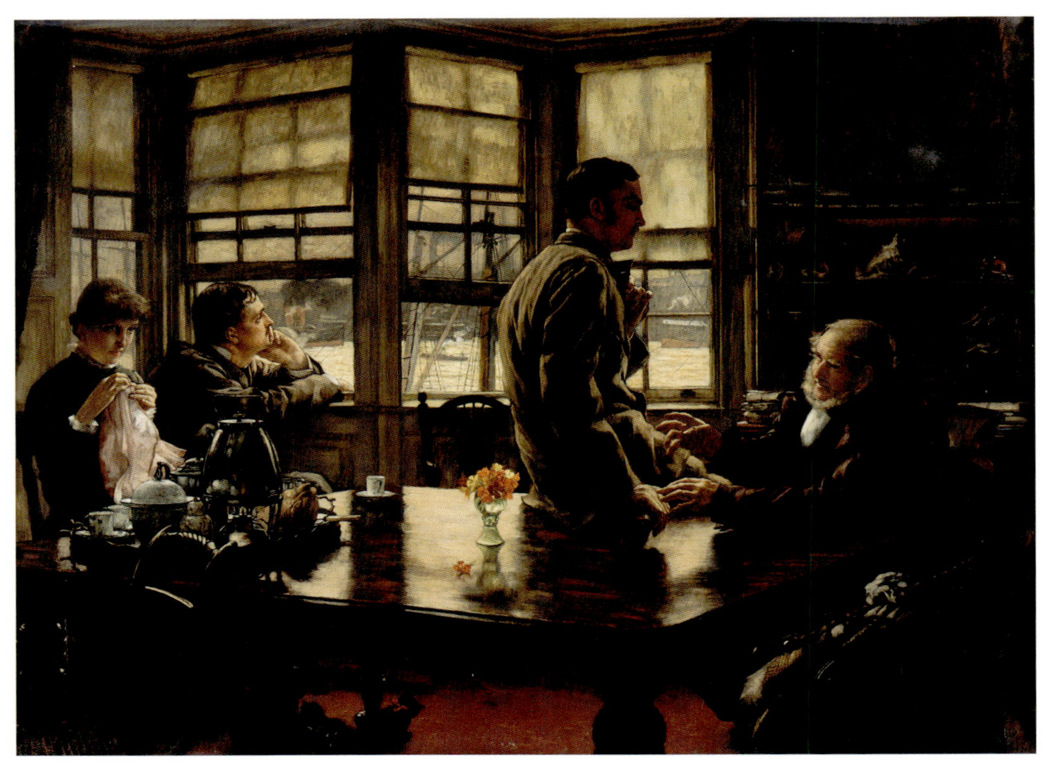

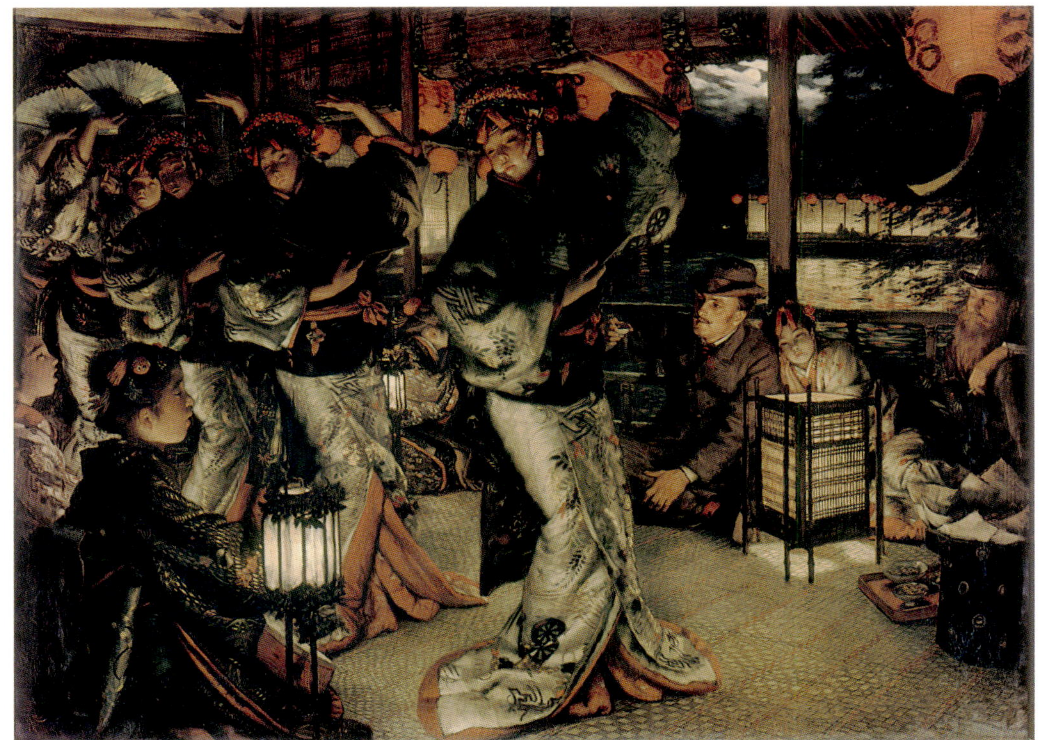

86

THE PRODIGAL SON IN MODERN LIFE: THE DEPARTURE, 1880

Oil on canvas, 39⅜ × 51⅛ in. (100 × 130 cm)
Musée d'Arts de Nantes, James Tissot Bequest, 1904, Inv. 1945

87

THE PRODIGAL SON IN MODERN LIFE: IN FOREIGN CLIMES, 1880

Oil on canvas, 39⅜ × 51⅛ in. (100 × 130 cm)
Musée d'Arts de Nantes, James Tissot Bequest, 1904, Inv. 1946

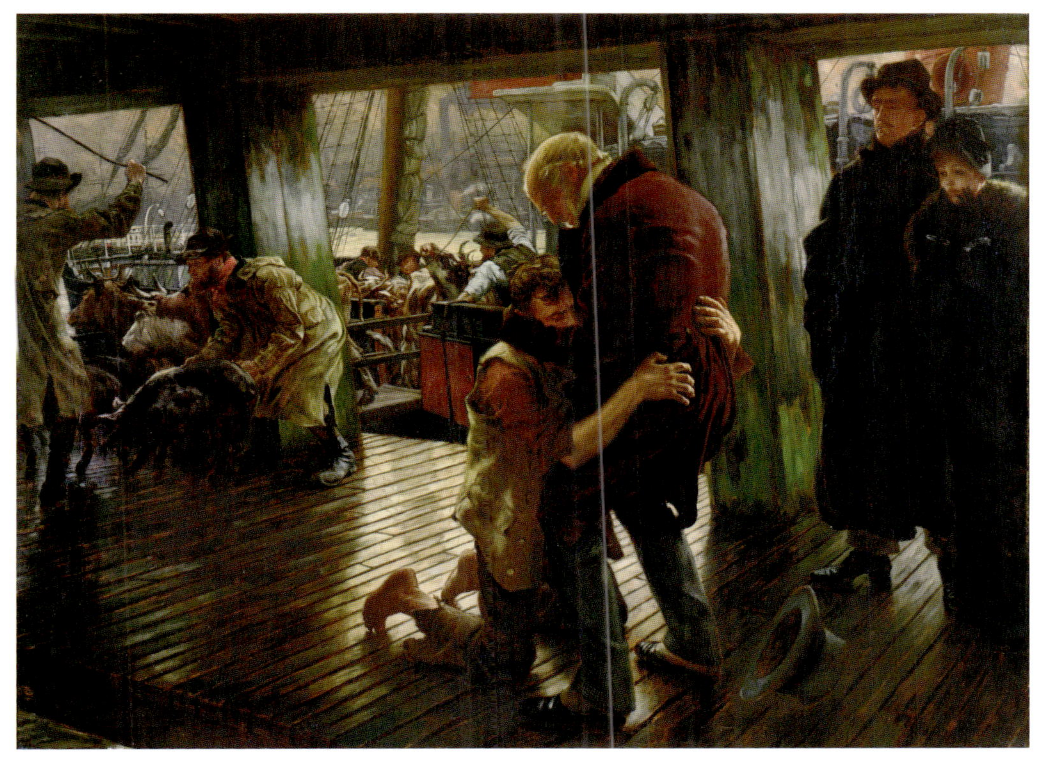

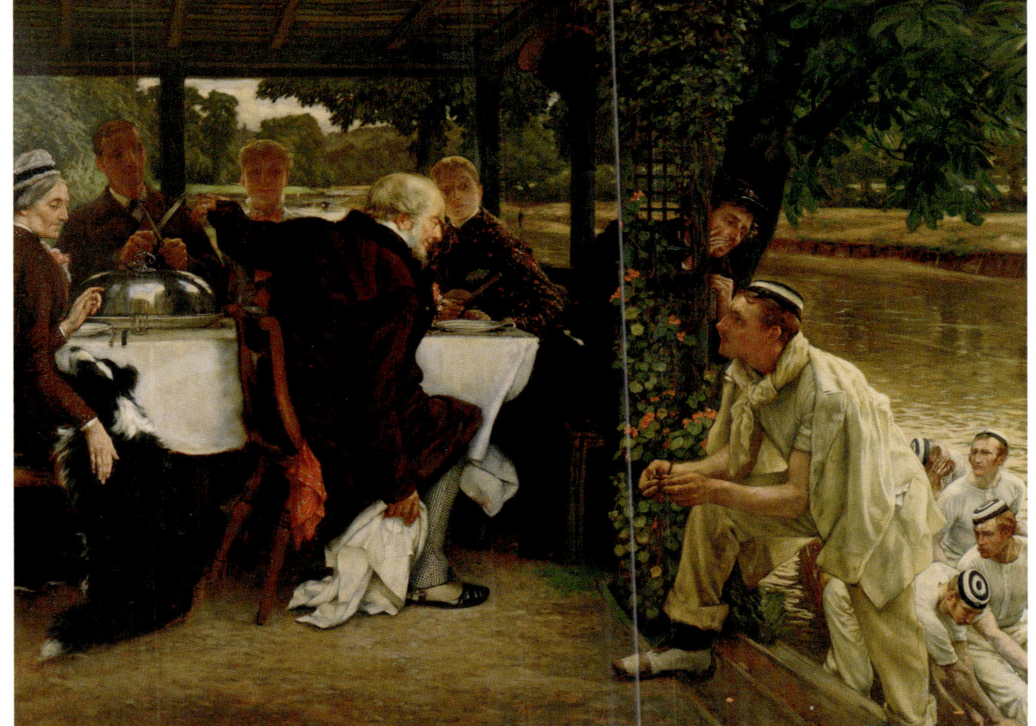

88

The Prodigal Son in Modern Life: The Return, 1880

Oil on canvas, 39 3/8 × 51 1/8 in. (100 × 130 cm)

Musée d'Arts de Nantes, James Tissot Bequest, 1904, Inv. 1947

89

The Prodigal Son in Modern Life: The Fatted Calf, 1880

Oil on canvas, 39 3/8 × 51 1/8 in. (100 × 130 cm)

Musée d'Arts de Nantes, James Tissot Bequest, 1904, Inv. 1948

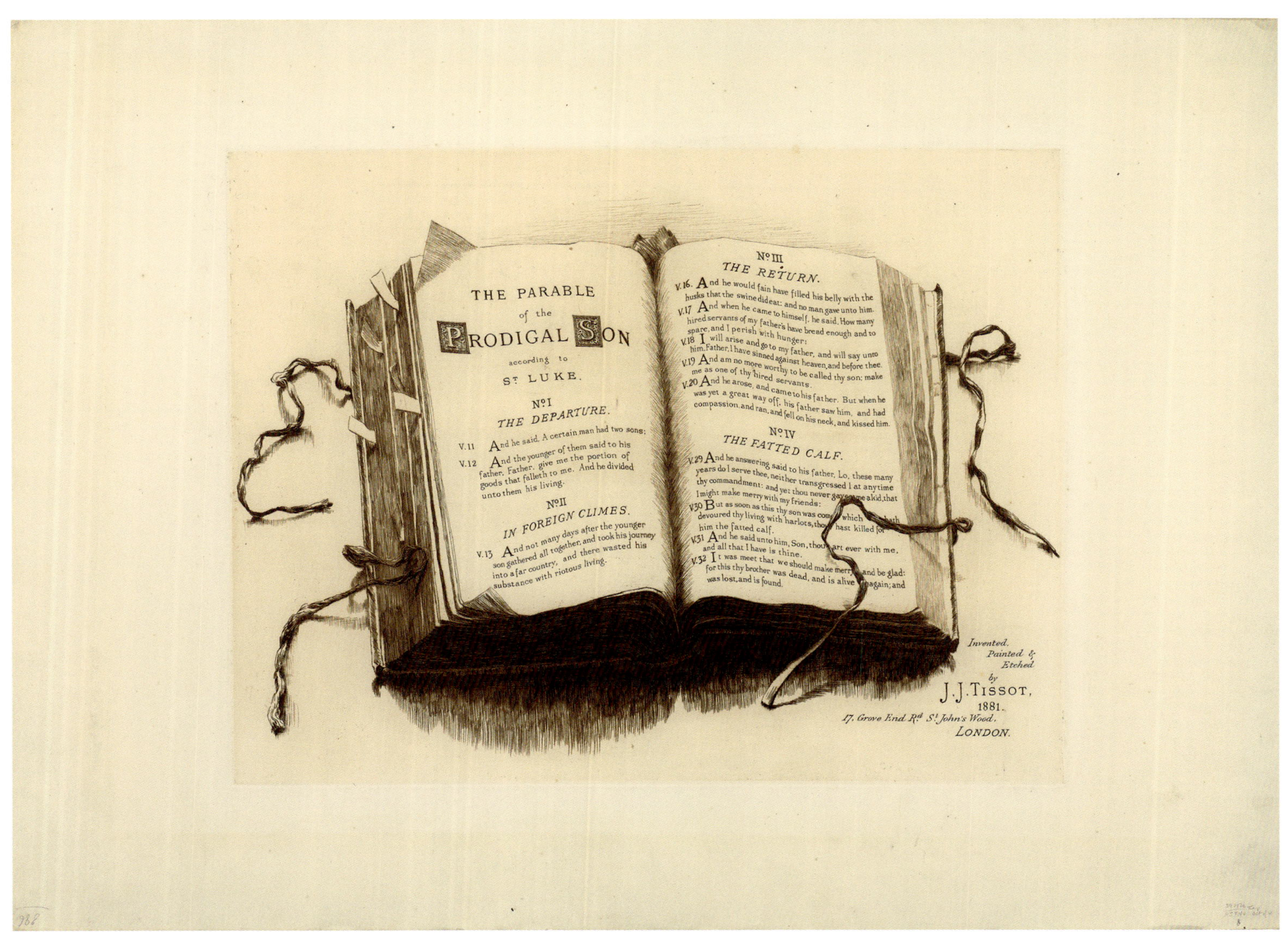

90

Frontispiece to "THE PRODIGAL SON," 1881

Etching and drypoint, 13⅞ × 17⅝ in. (35.2 × 44.9 cm)
Fine Arts Museums of San Francisco,
Achenbach Foundation for Graphic Arts, 1963.30.1395.1

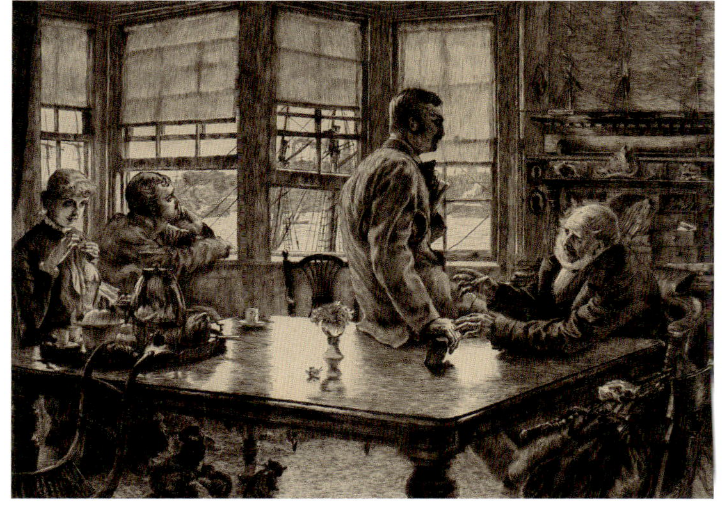
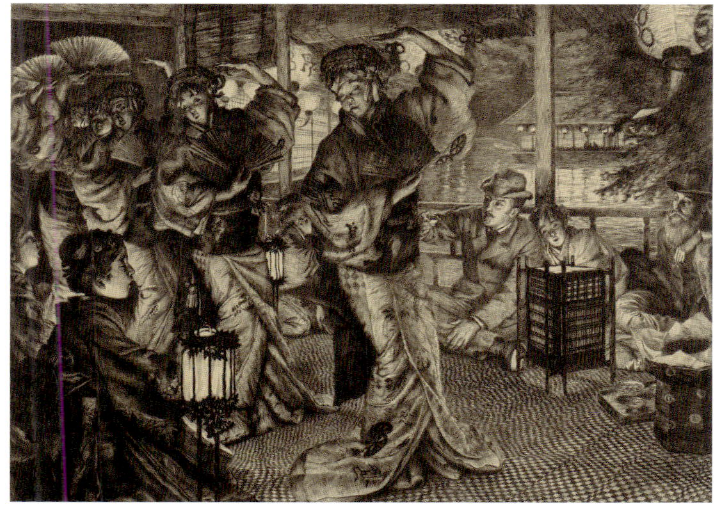
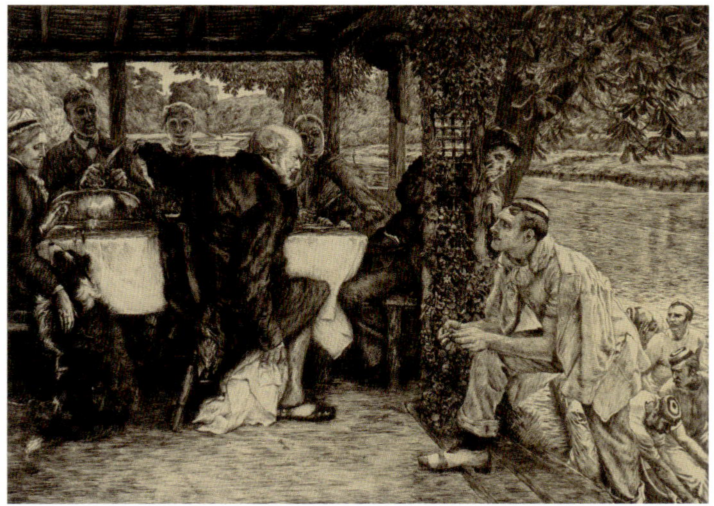
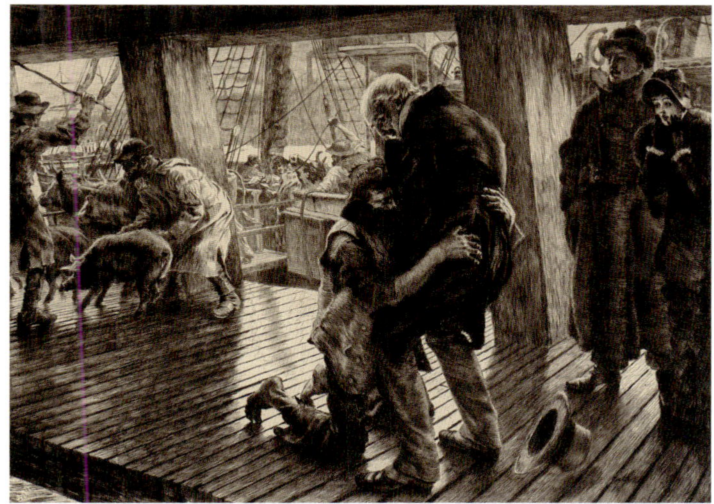

91–94 (clockwise from top left)

The Prodigal Son—The Departure, In Foreign Climes, The Return, The Fatted Calf, 1881

Etching and drypoint, 12¼ × 14¾ in. (31 × 37.3 cm)
Fine Arts Museums of San Francisco, Achenbach Foundation for Graphic Arts, 1963.30.1395.2, 1963.30.1395.3, 1963.30.1395.4, 1963.30.1395.5

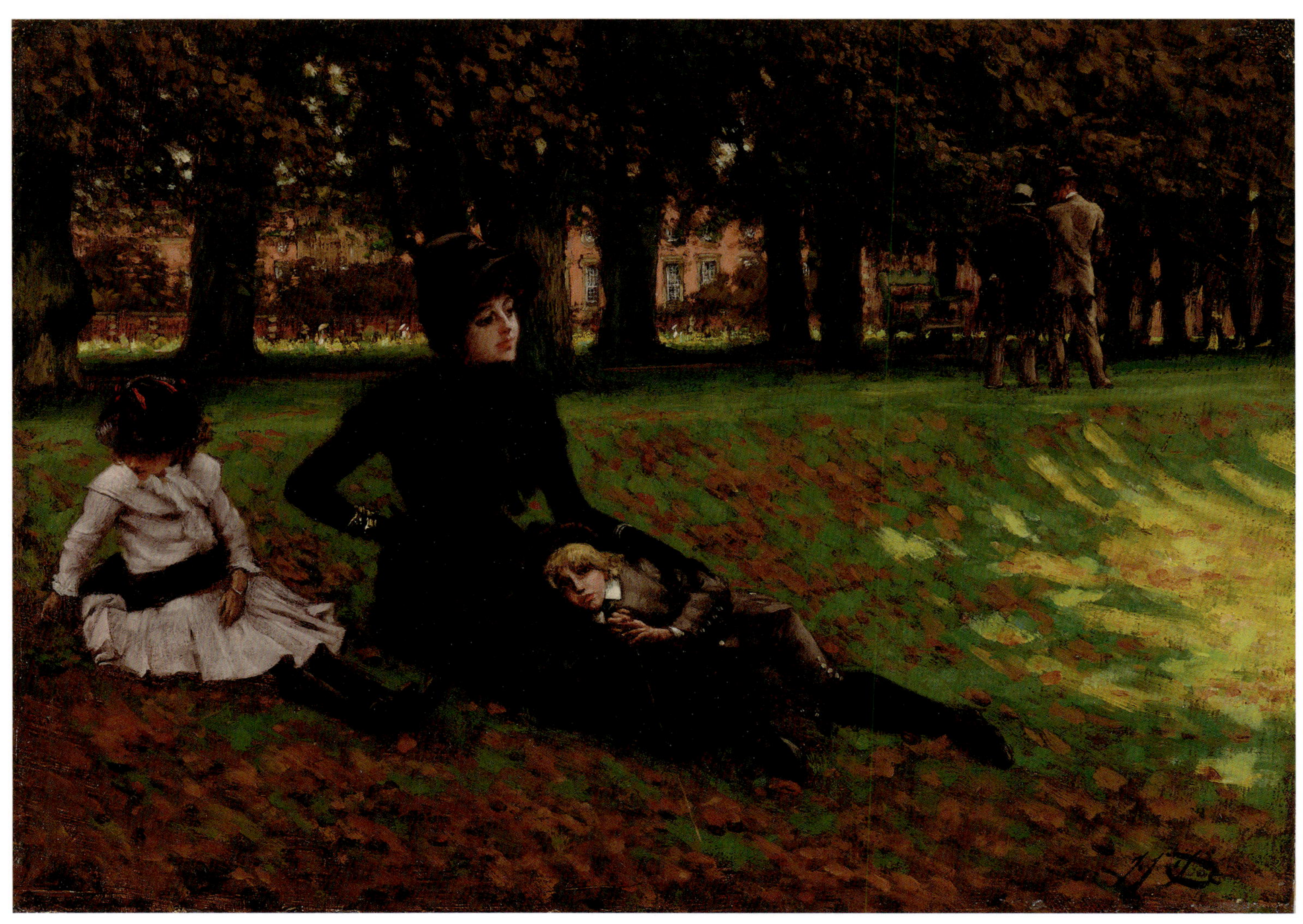

95

HAMPTON COURT, CA. 1882

also known as A VISIT TO THE PARK

Oil on wood panel, 9¼ × 13 in. (23.5 × 33 cm)

Collection of Ann and Gordon Getty

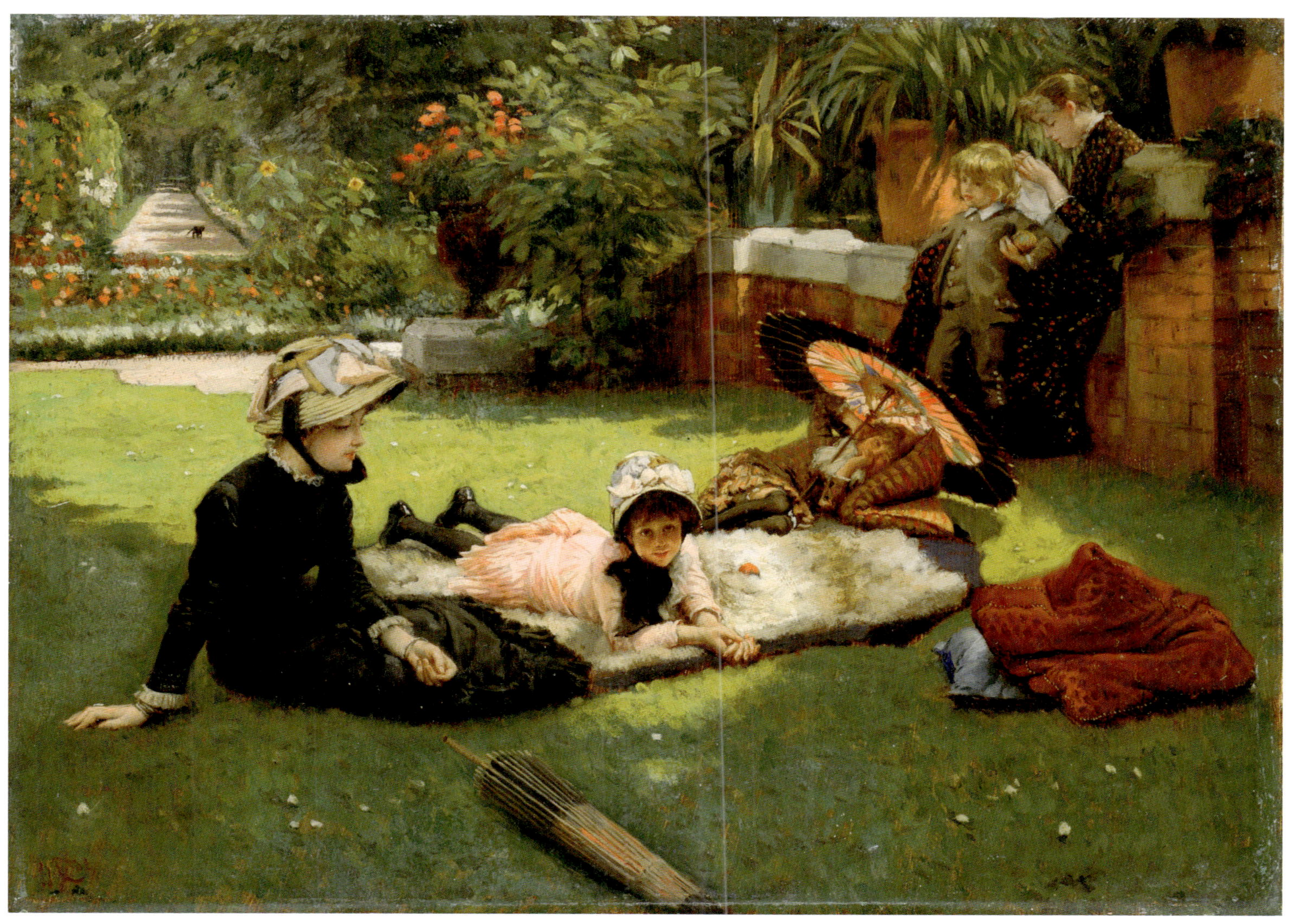

96

In Full Sunlight, 1881

Oil on wood panel, 9¾ × 13⅞ in. (24.8 × 35.2 cm)
The Metropolitan Museum of Art, New York, Gift of Mrs. Charles Wrightsman, 2006, 2006.278

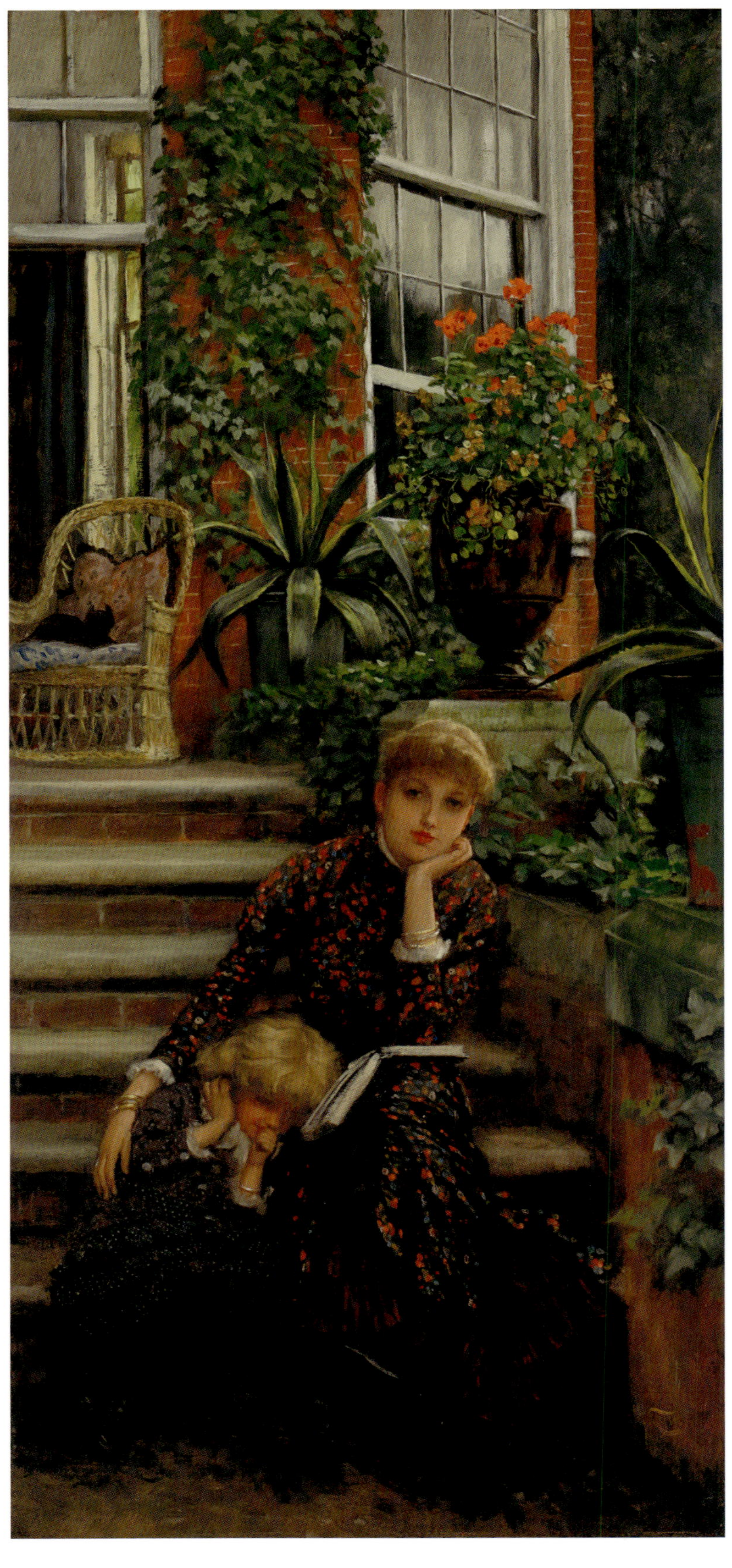

97

THE ELDER SISTER, CA. 1879–1880

Oil on wood panel, 17½ × 7⅞ in. (44.5 × 20 cm)
Private collection

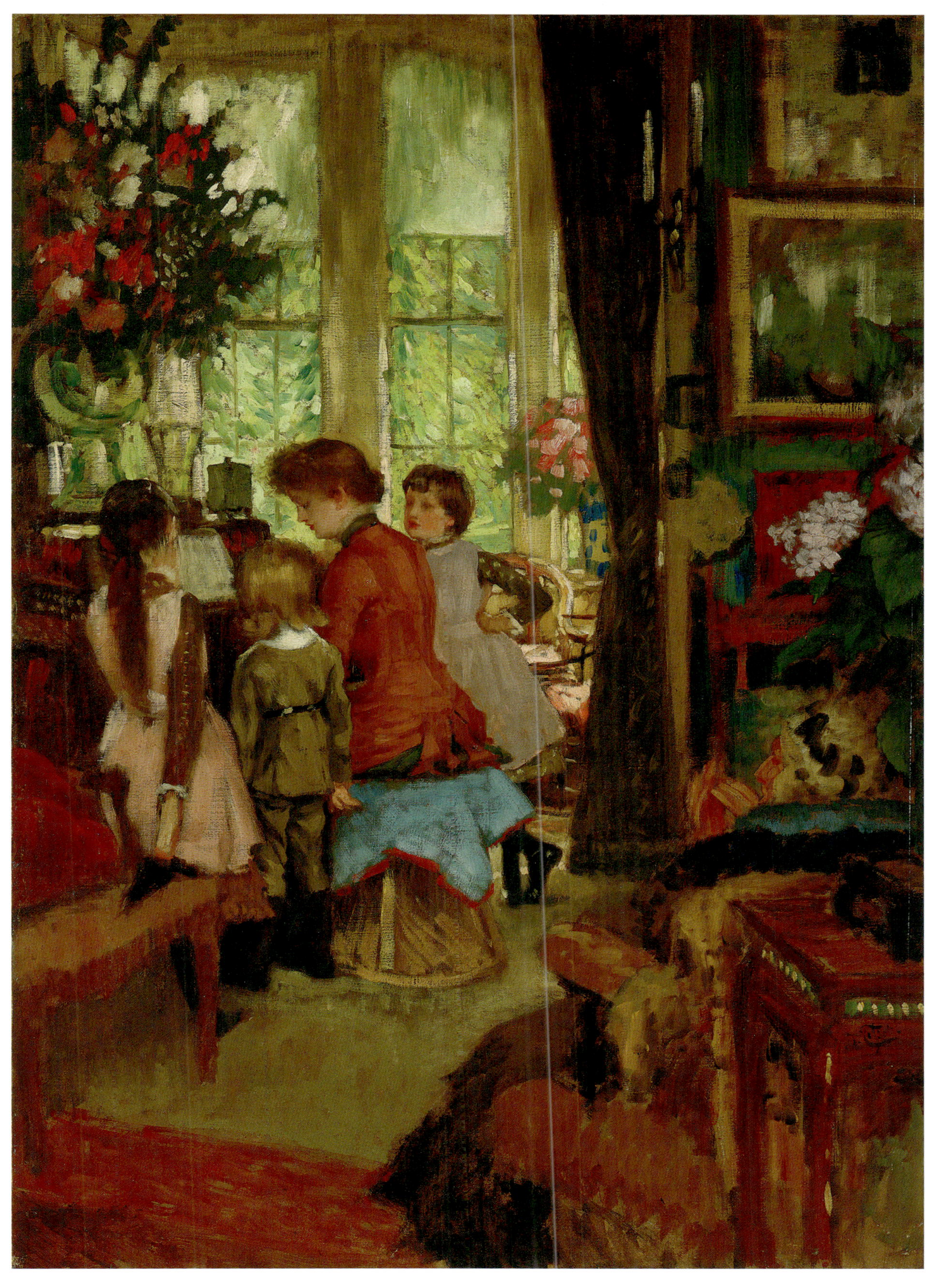

93

KATHLEEN NEWTON AT THE PIANO, CA. 1880–1881

Oil on canvas, 44 × 30½ in. (111.8 × 77.5 cm)
Collection of Ann and Gordon Getty

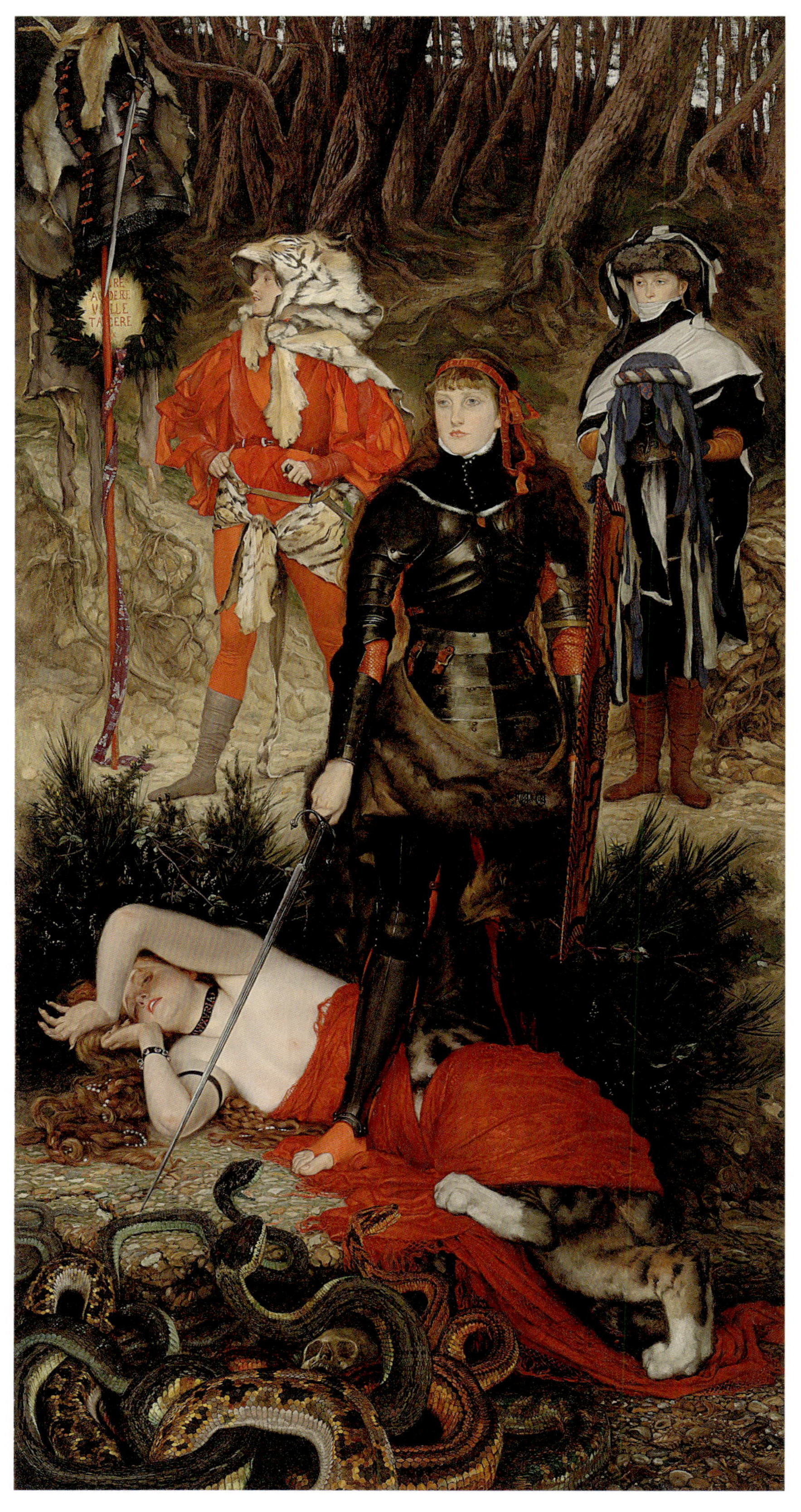

99

THE TRIUMPH OF WILL (POEM IN FIVE PARTS): I. THE CHALLENGE, CA. 1876–1877

Oil on canvas, 85 × 43 in. (215.9 × 109.2 cm)

Private collection

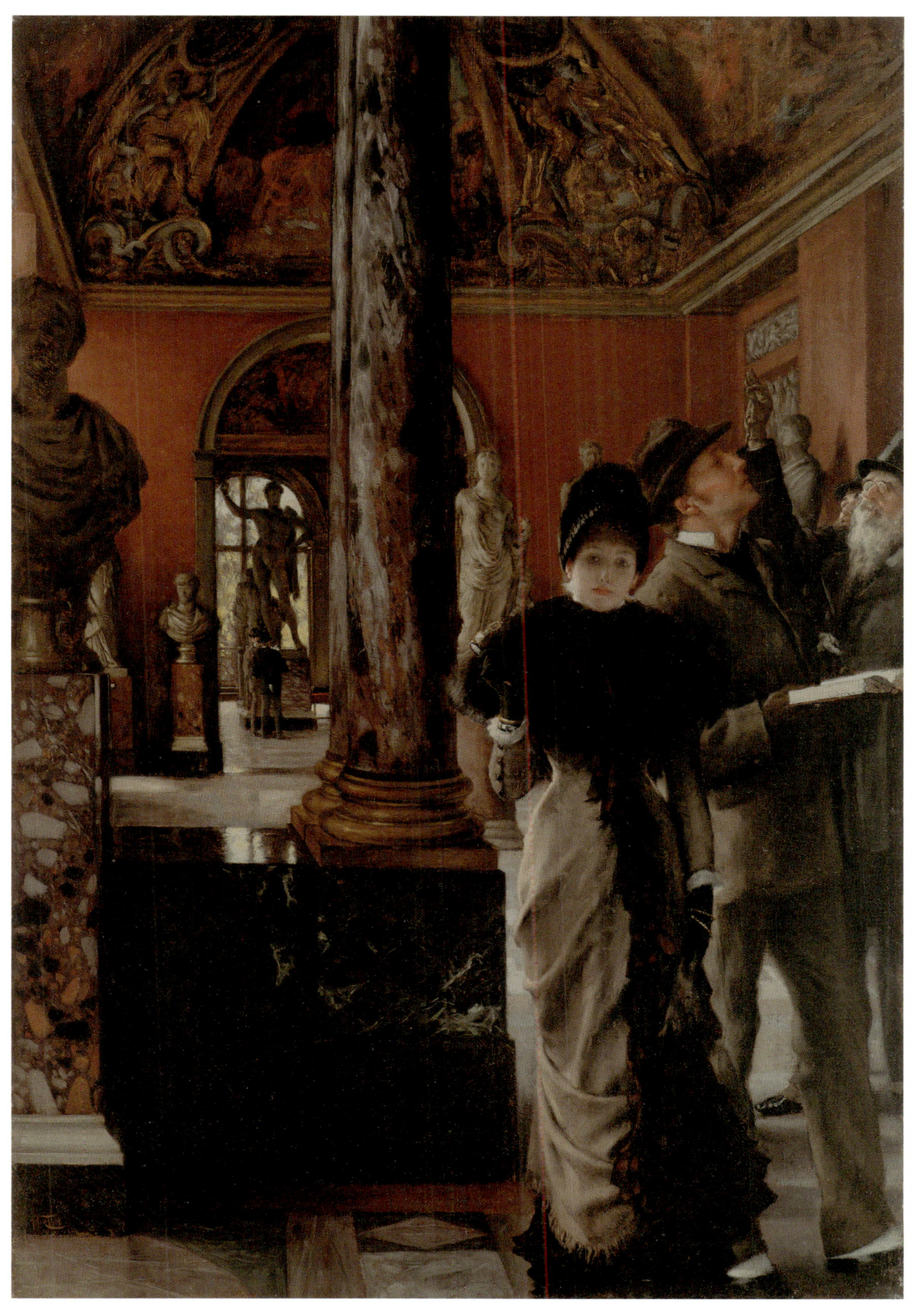

100

VISITING THE LOUVRE, 1879–1880

also known as FOREIGN VISITORS AT THE LOUVRE

Oil on wood panel, 29 × 19½ in. (73.7 × 49.5 cm)

Santa Barbara Museum of Art, SBMA, Gift of The Estate of Barbara Darlington Dupee, 2015.32.1

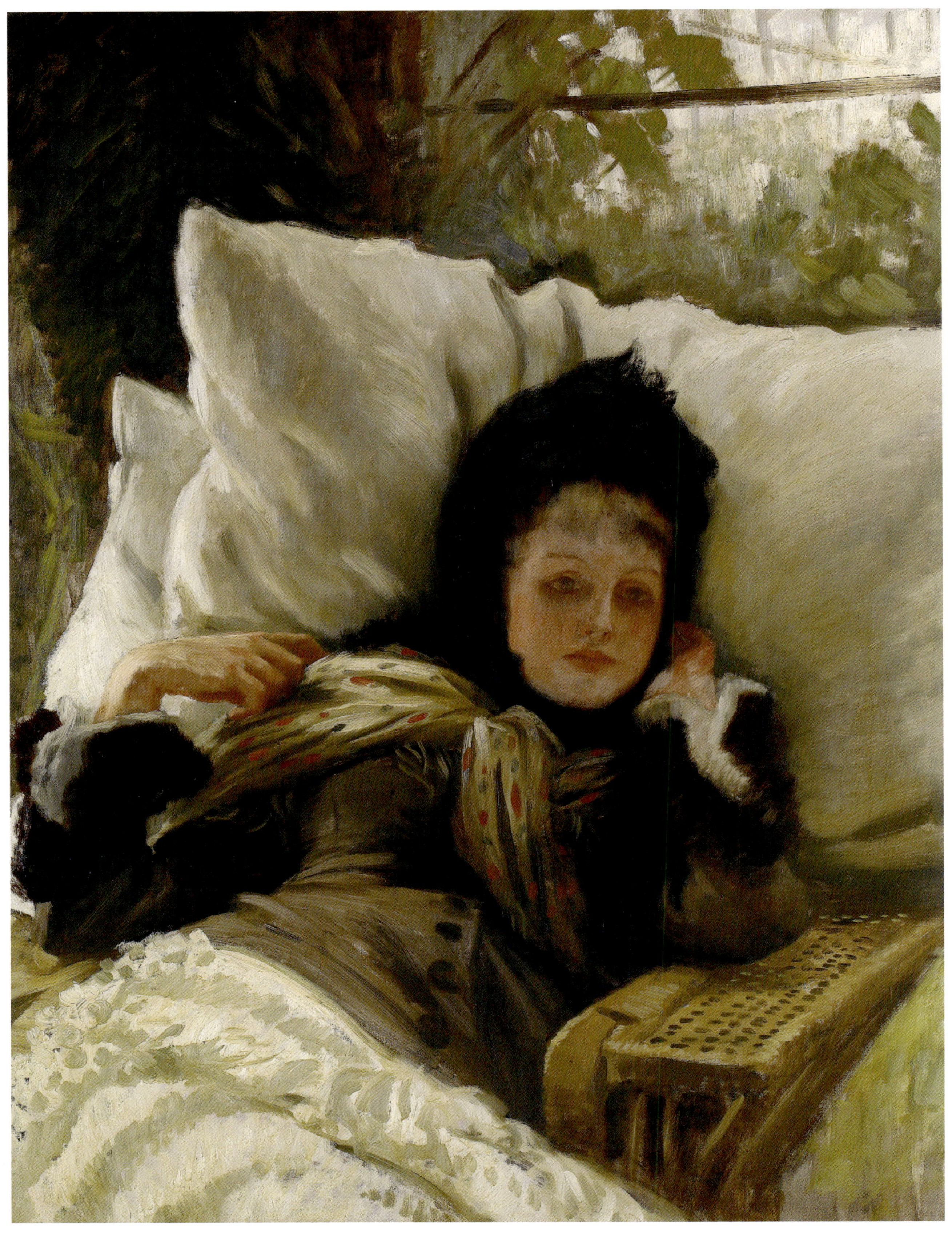

101

Mrs. Newton Resting on a Chaise Lounge, ca. 1881–1882

Oil on canvas, 35 ½ × 26 ⅞ in. (90.2 × 68.3 cm)
Musée Baron Martin, Gray, France, Pigalle Bequest

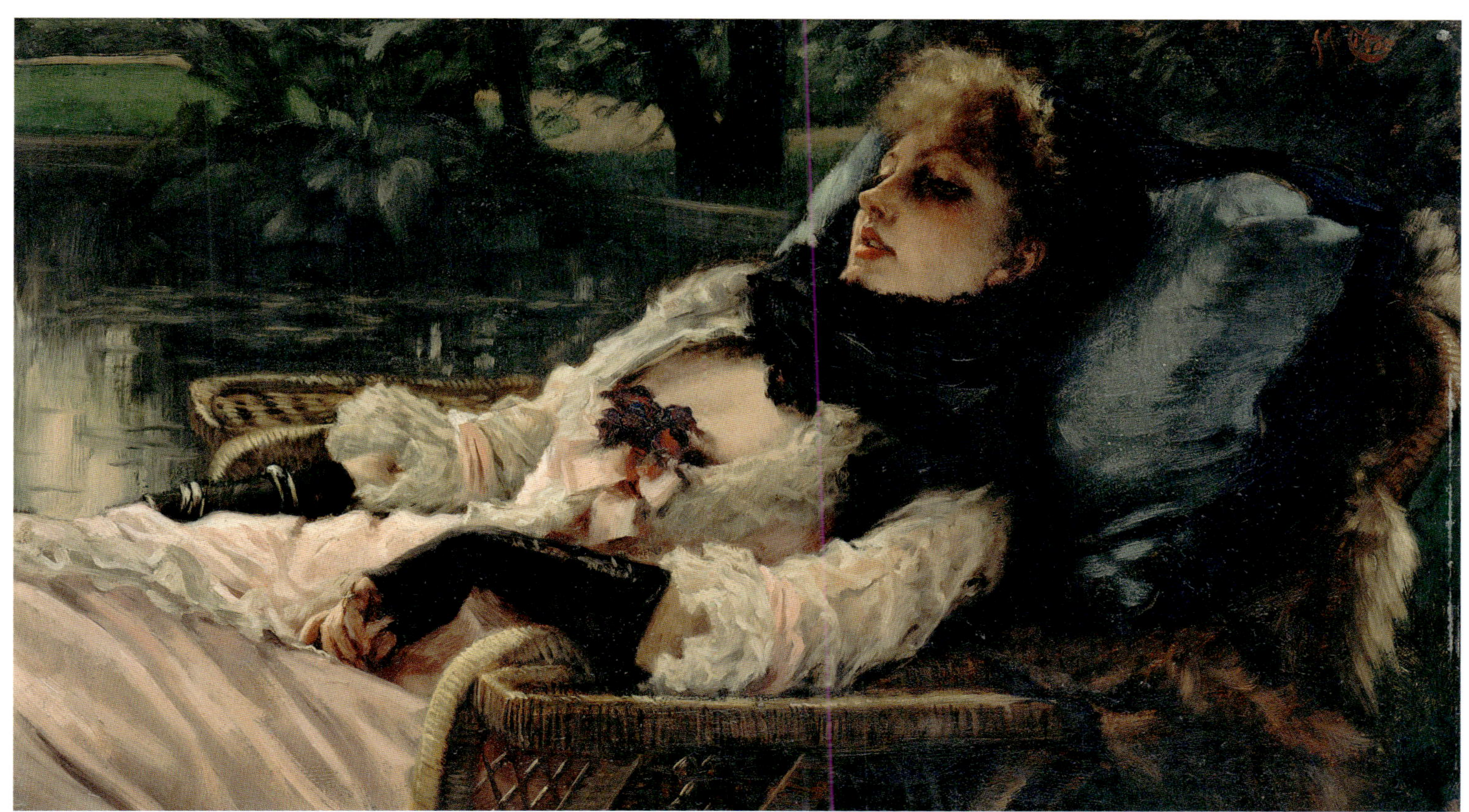

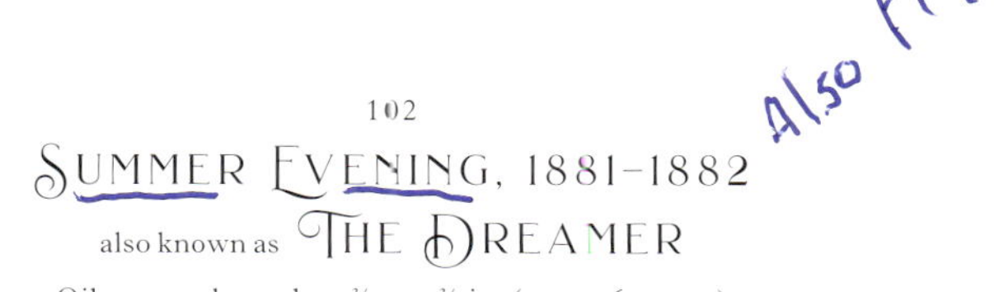

102

SUMMER EVENING, 1881–1882

also known as THE DREAMER

Oil on wood panel, 13 ¾ × 23 ¾ in. (34.9 × 60.3 cm)

Musée d'Orsay, Paris, Bequest of William Vaughan, 1919, RF 2254

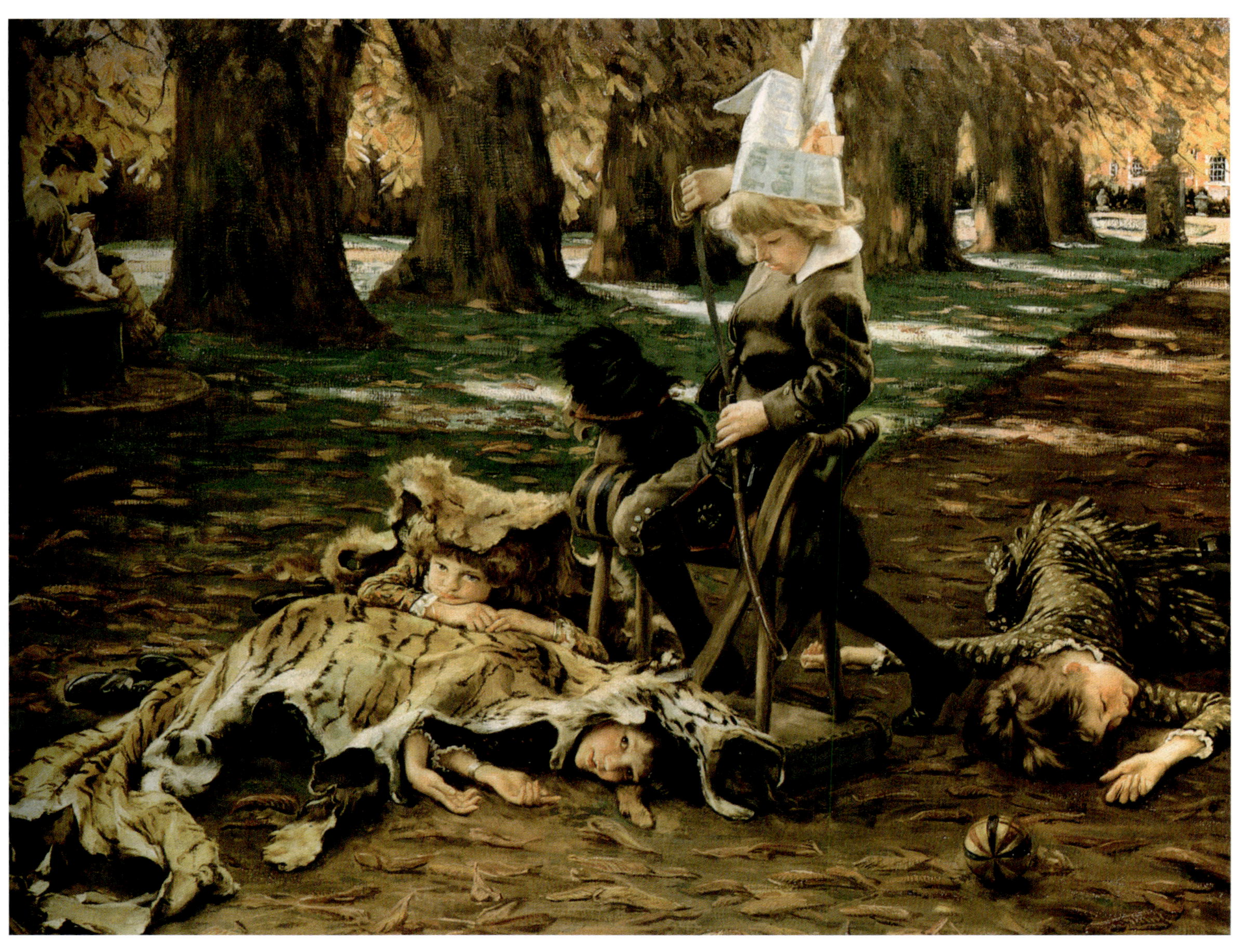

103

A Nimrod, ca. 1882–1883

also known as The Little Nimrod

Oil on canvas, $43^{1}/_{8} \times 55^{1}/_{8}$ in. (109.5 × 140 cm)

Musée des Beaux-Arts et d'Archéologie de Besançon, France, inv. 906.7.1

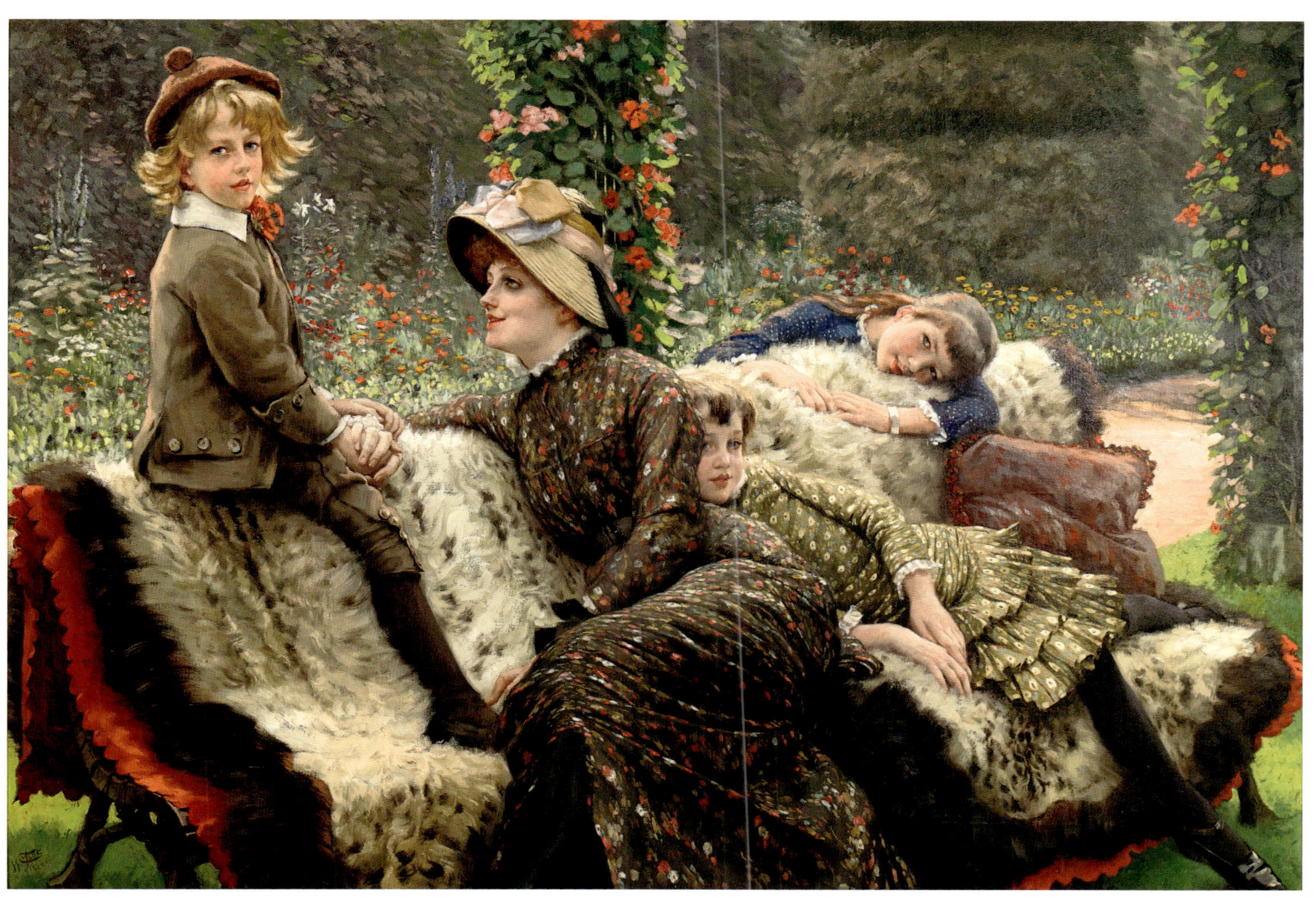

104

THE GARDEN BENCH, 1882

Oil on canvas, 39 × 56 in. (99.1 × 142.2 cm)
Private collection

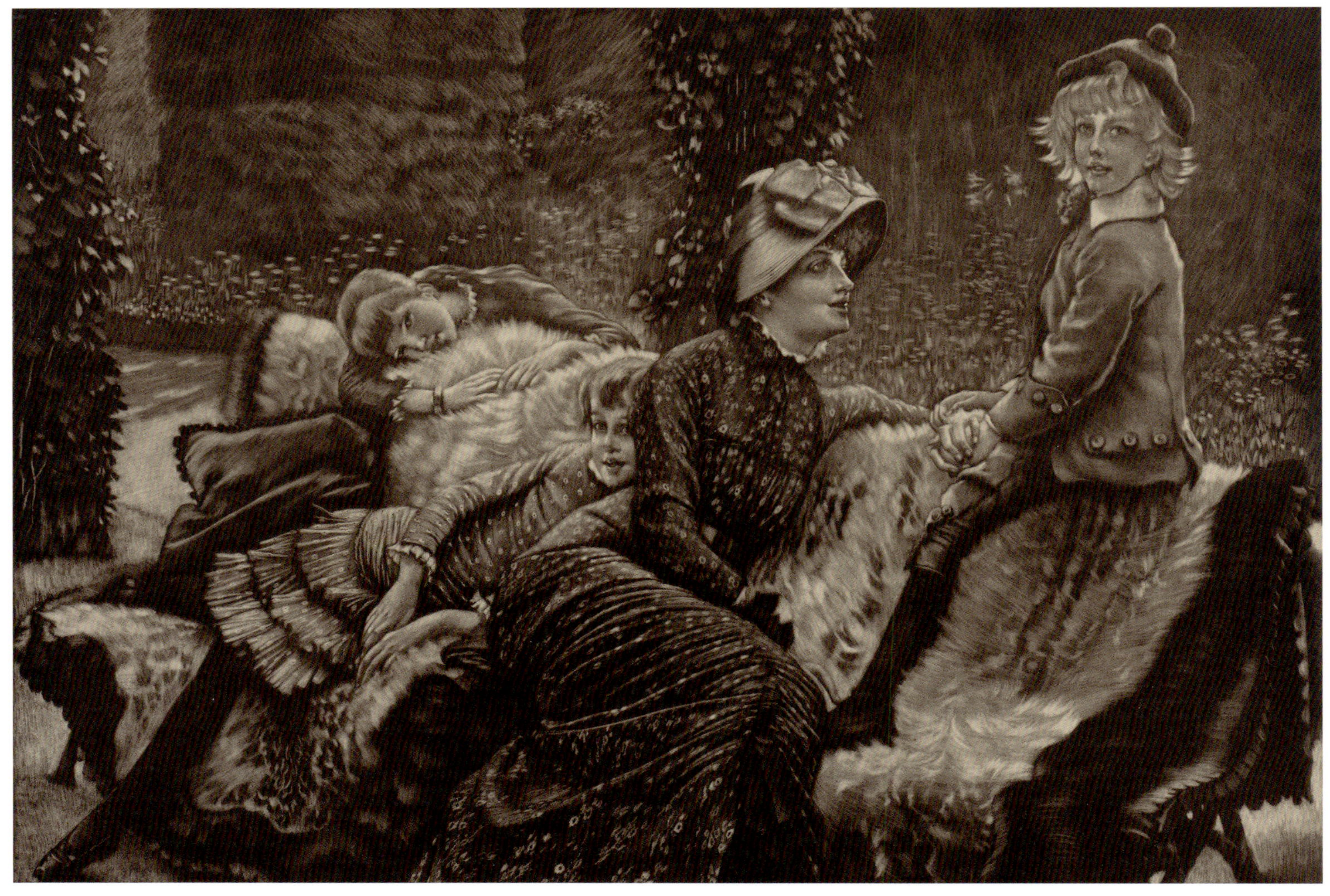

105

The Garden Bench, 1883

Mezzotint and drypoint, printed *chine collé*, 16¼ × 21 in. (41.4 × 53.4 cm)
Fine Arts Museums of San Francisco, Achenbach Foundation for Graphic Arts,
Gift of Edward Tyler Nahem, 2003.151.68

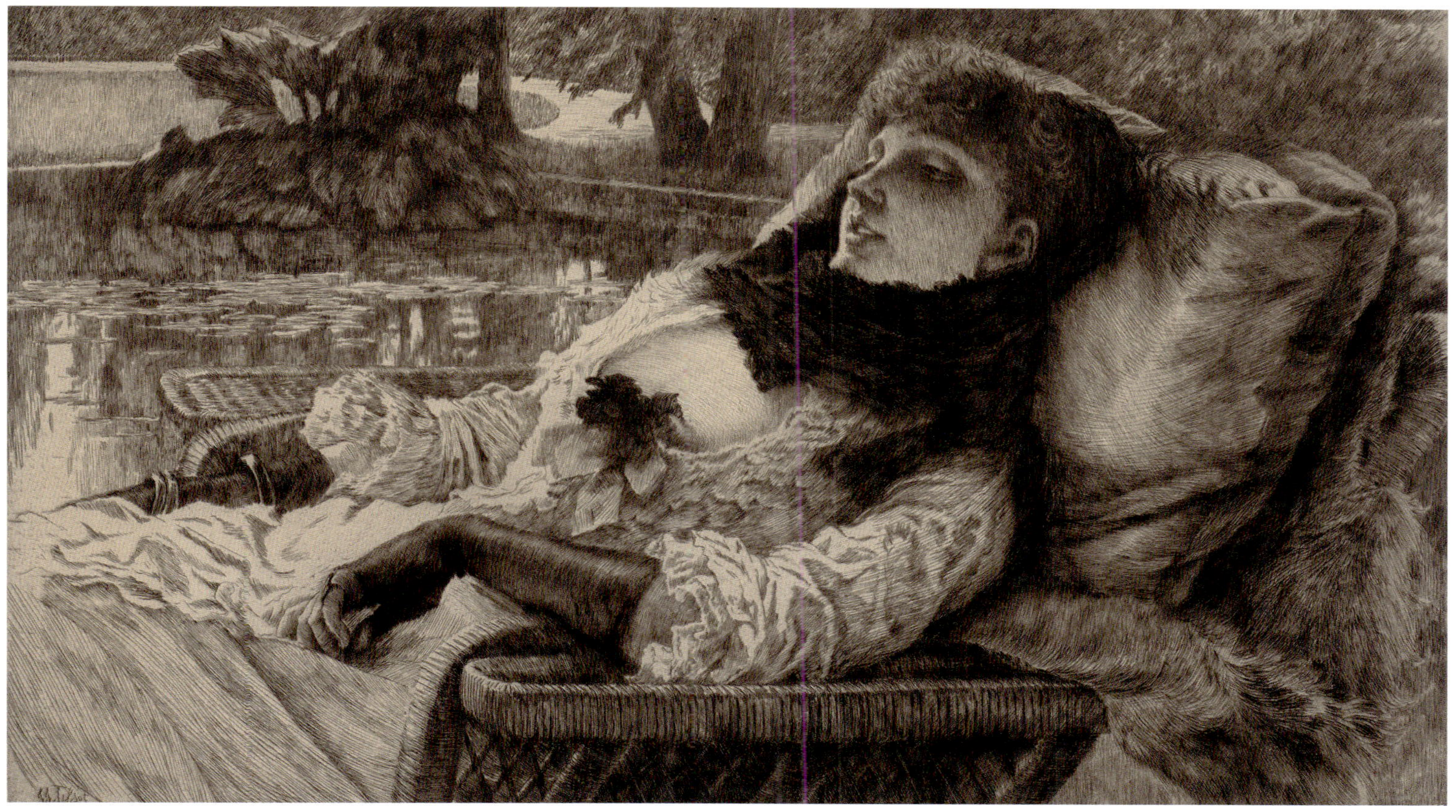

106

SUMMER EVENING, 1881

Drypoint and etching, 9 × 15⅝ in. (23 × 39.7 cm)
Fine Arts Museums of San Francisco,
Achenbach Foundation for Graphic Arts, 1963.30.1392

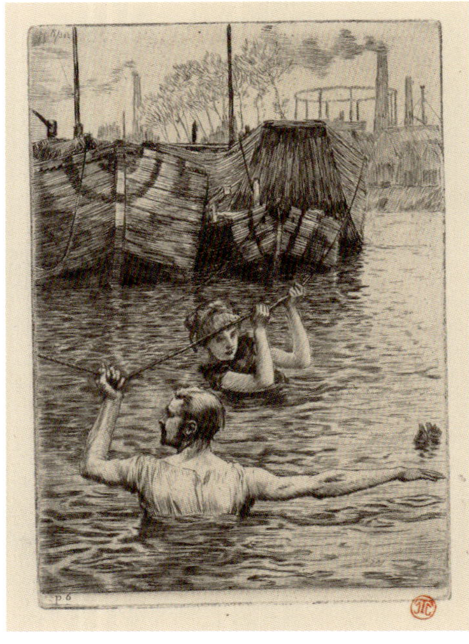

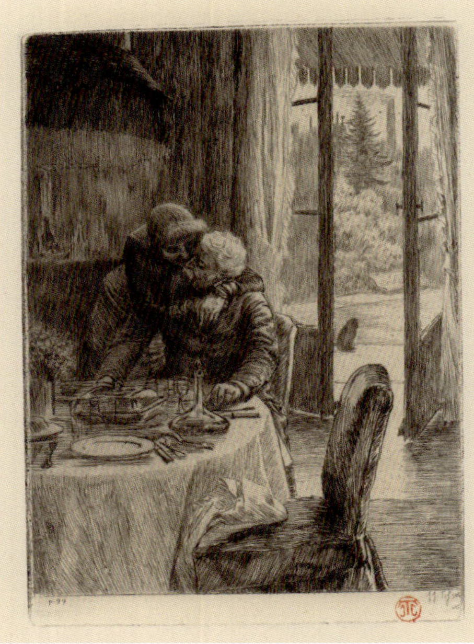

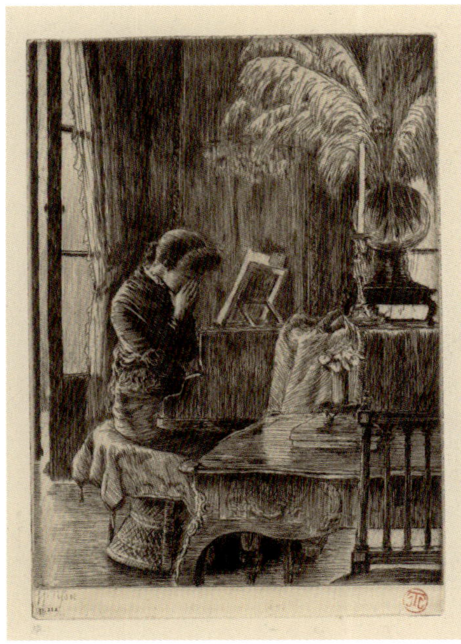

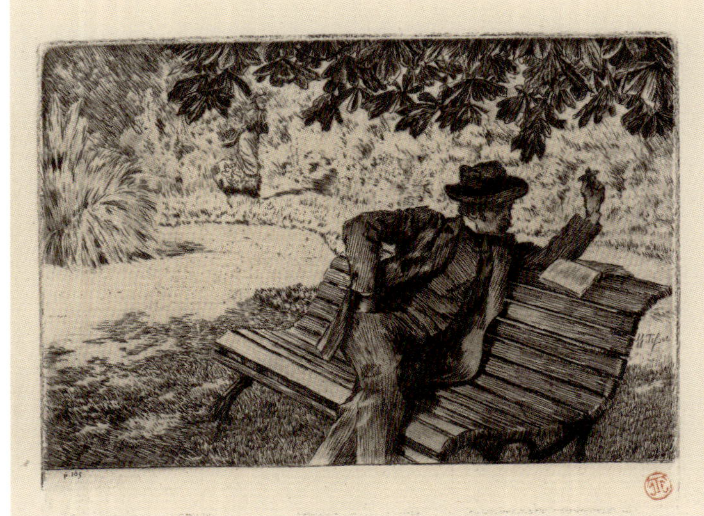

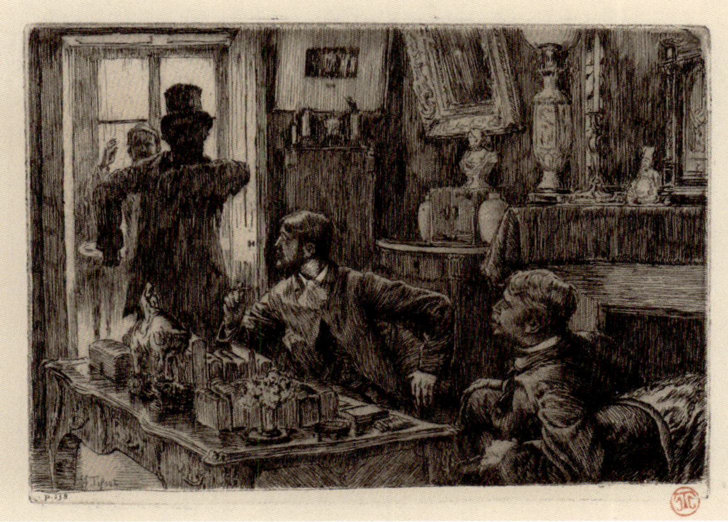

107–111 (clockwise from top left)

On the Seine, The Morning Kiss, At the Piano, In the Anteroom, Denoisel Reading in the Garden, 1882

Illustrations for *Renée Mauperin*, 1884
Authors: Edmond and Jules de Goncourt
Publisher: G. Charpentier & Cie, Paris
Etchings, 5⅝ × 3⅞ in. (14.3 × 9.9 cm), 5¾ × 4 in. (14.7 × 10 cm), 5½ × 3⅞ in. (14.1 × 9.7 cm), 4 × 5½ in. (10.1 × 14 cm), 4¼ × 5⅝ in. (10.9 × 14.2 cm)
Fine Arts Museums of San Francisco, Museum purchase,
Mrs. Alexander de Bretteville Fund, 1984.1.88.1, 1984.1.88.2, 1984.1.88.11, 1984.1.88.5, 1984.1.88.3

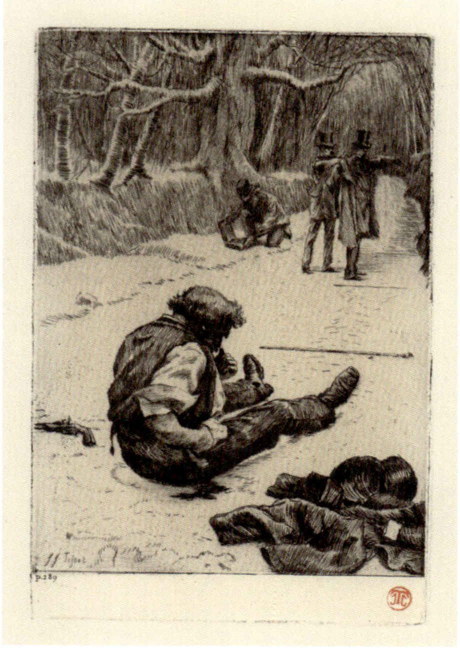

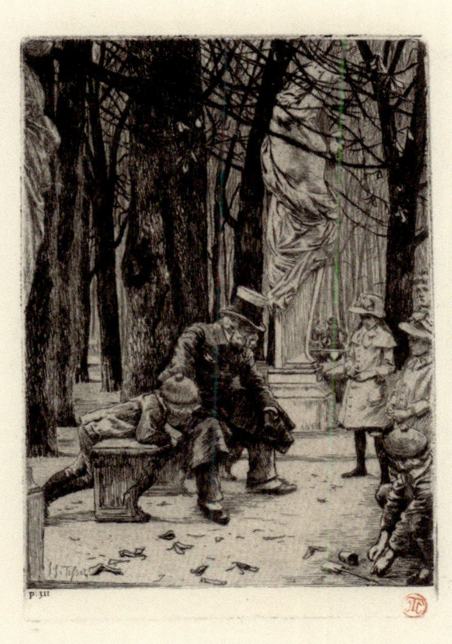

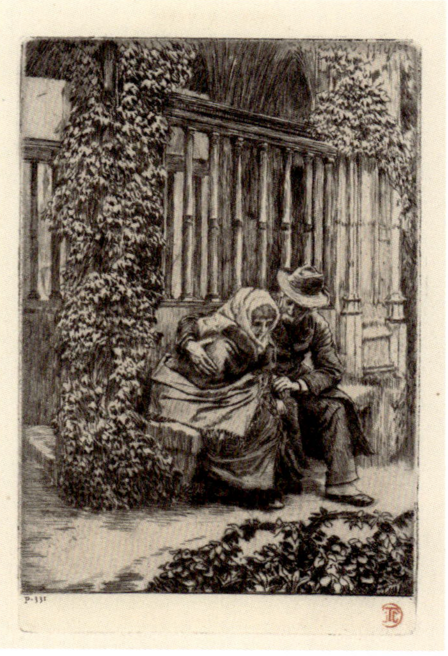

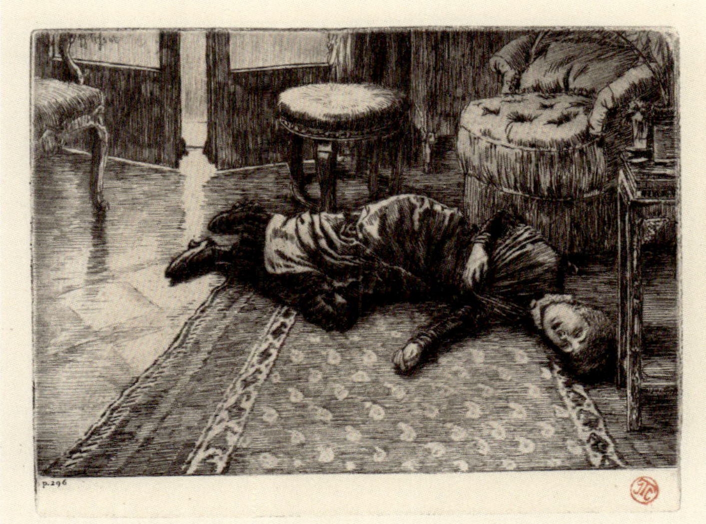

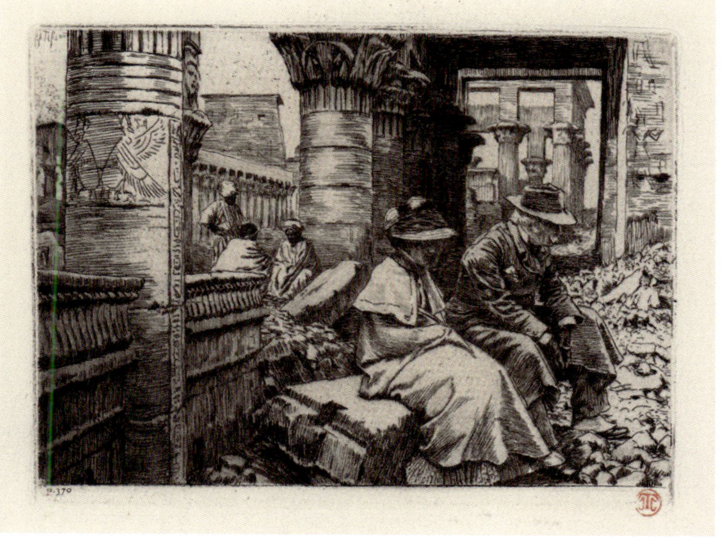

112–116 (clockwise from top left)

After the Duel, In the Public Gardens, Renée and Her Father at Morimond, In the Egyptian Ruins, Renée Fainting, 1882

Illustrations for *Renée Mauperin*, 1884
Authors: Edmond and Jules de Goncourt
Publisher: G. Charpentier & Cie, Paris
Etchings, 6 × 3⅞ in. (15.3 × 9.9 cm), 5¾ × 3⅞ in. (14.7 × 9.9 cm), 6 × 3⅞ in. (15.1 × 9.7 cm), 4¼ × 5⅝ in. (10.9 × 14.2 cm), 4¼ × 5⅝ in. (10.9 × 14.2 cm)
Fine Arts Museums of San Francisco, Museum purchase,
Mrs. Alexander de Bretteville Fund, 1984.1.88.6, 1984.1.88.8, 1984.1.88.9, 1984.1.88.10, 1984.1.88.7

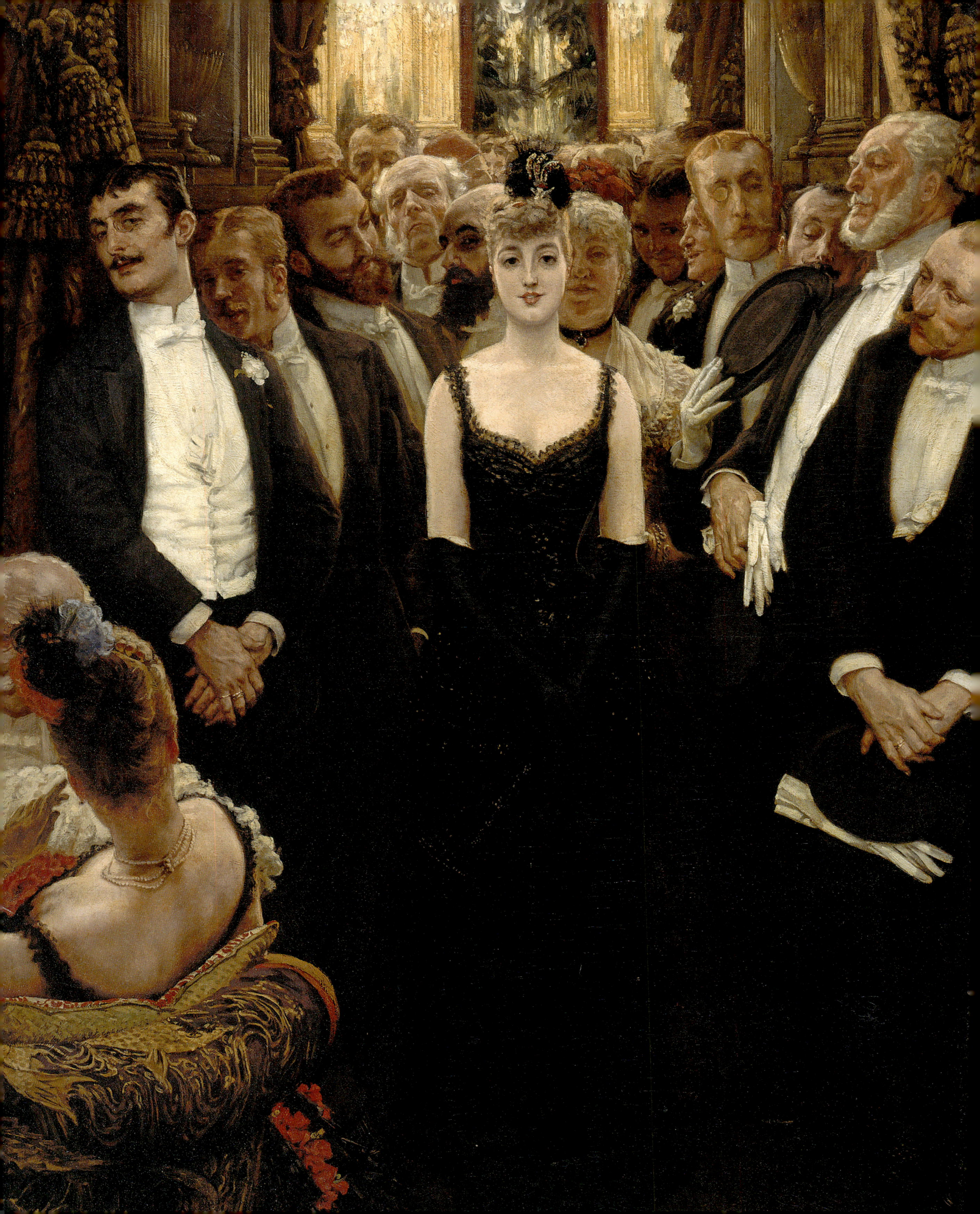

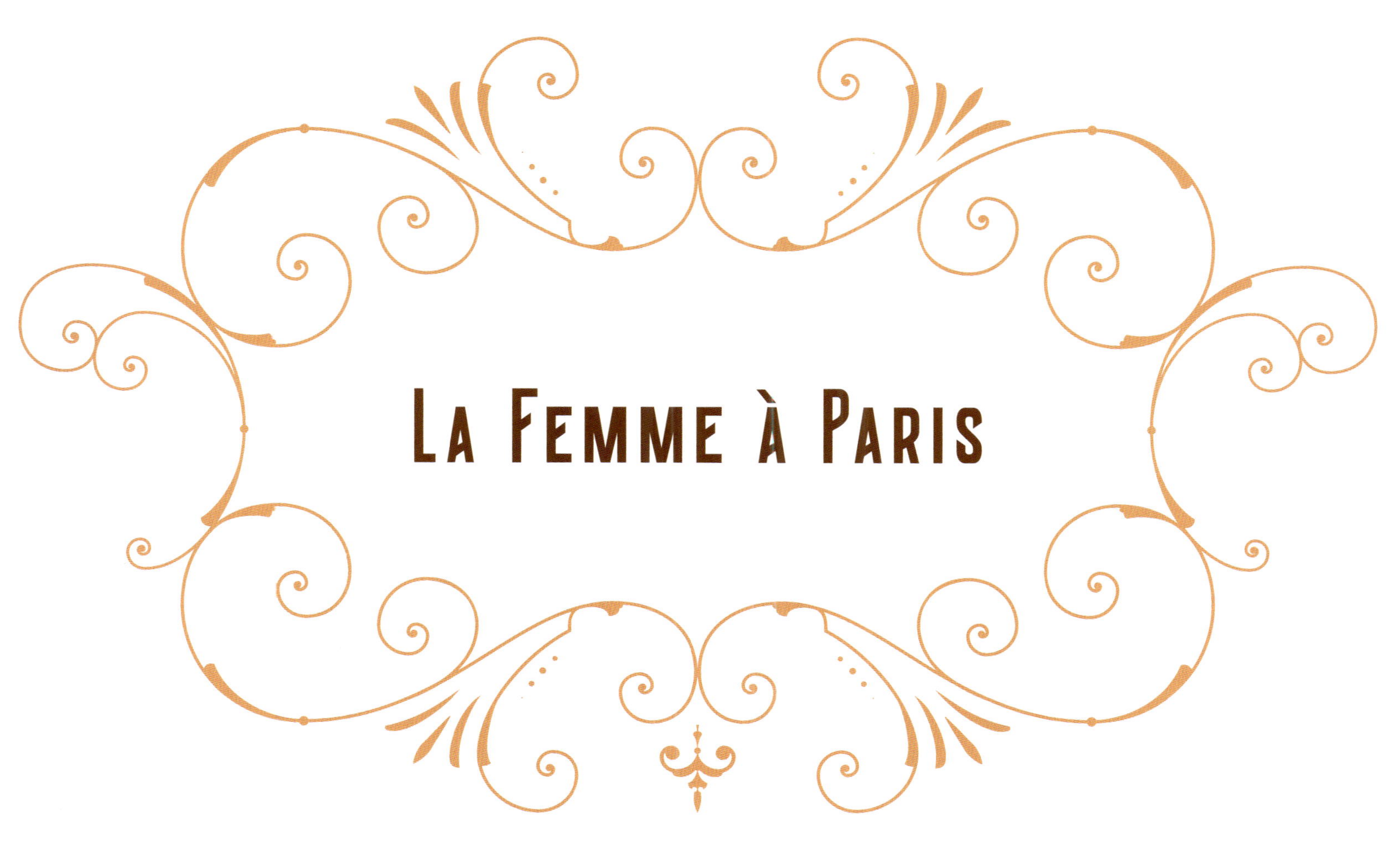

La Femme à Paris

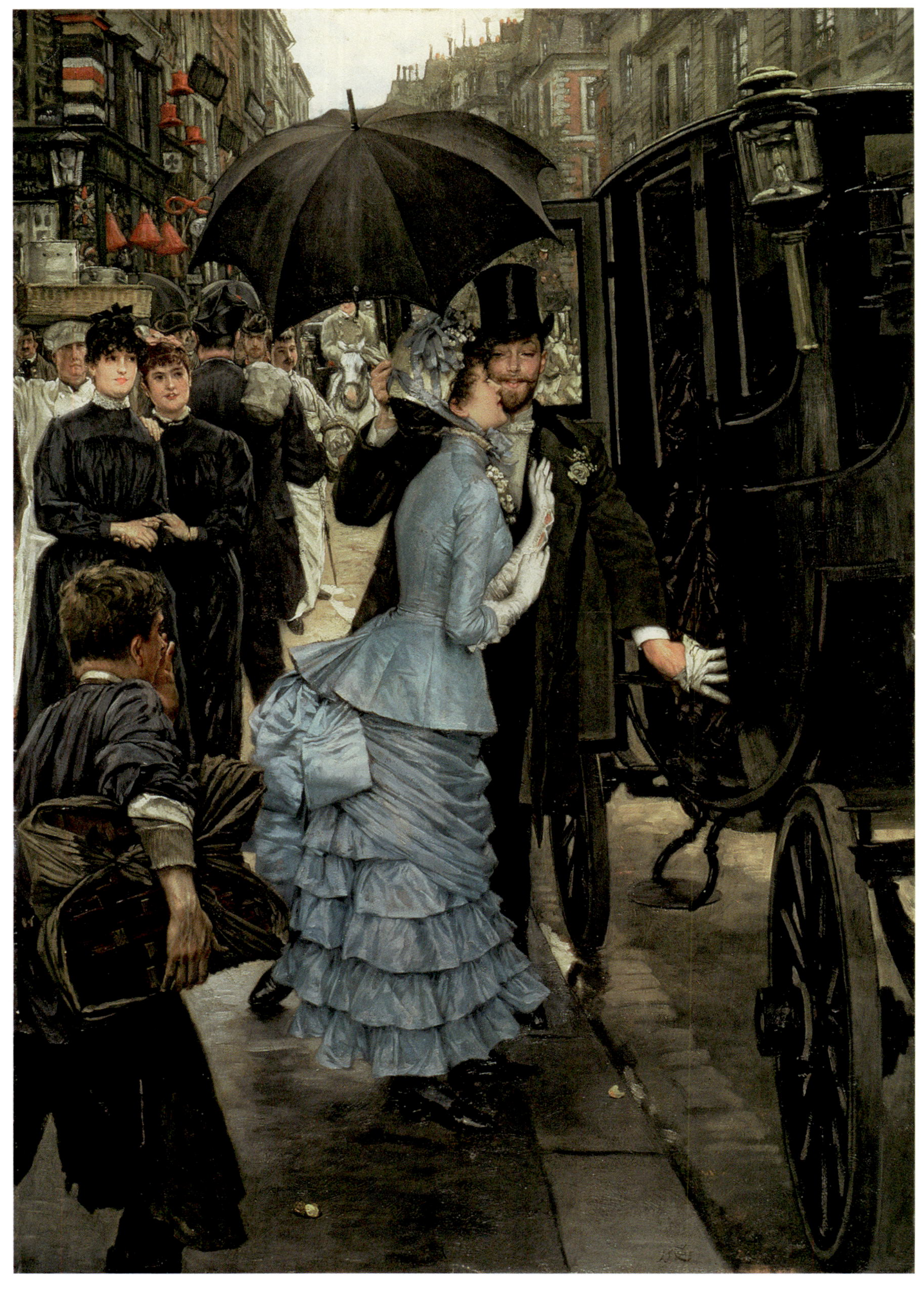

117

THE BRIDESMAID, CA. 1883–1885

Oil on canvas, 58 × 40 in. (147.3 × 101.6 cm)

Leeds Museums and Galleries, Gift from R. R. King, 1897, LEEAG.PA.1897.0015

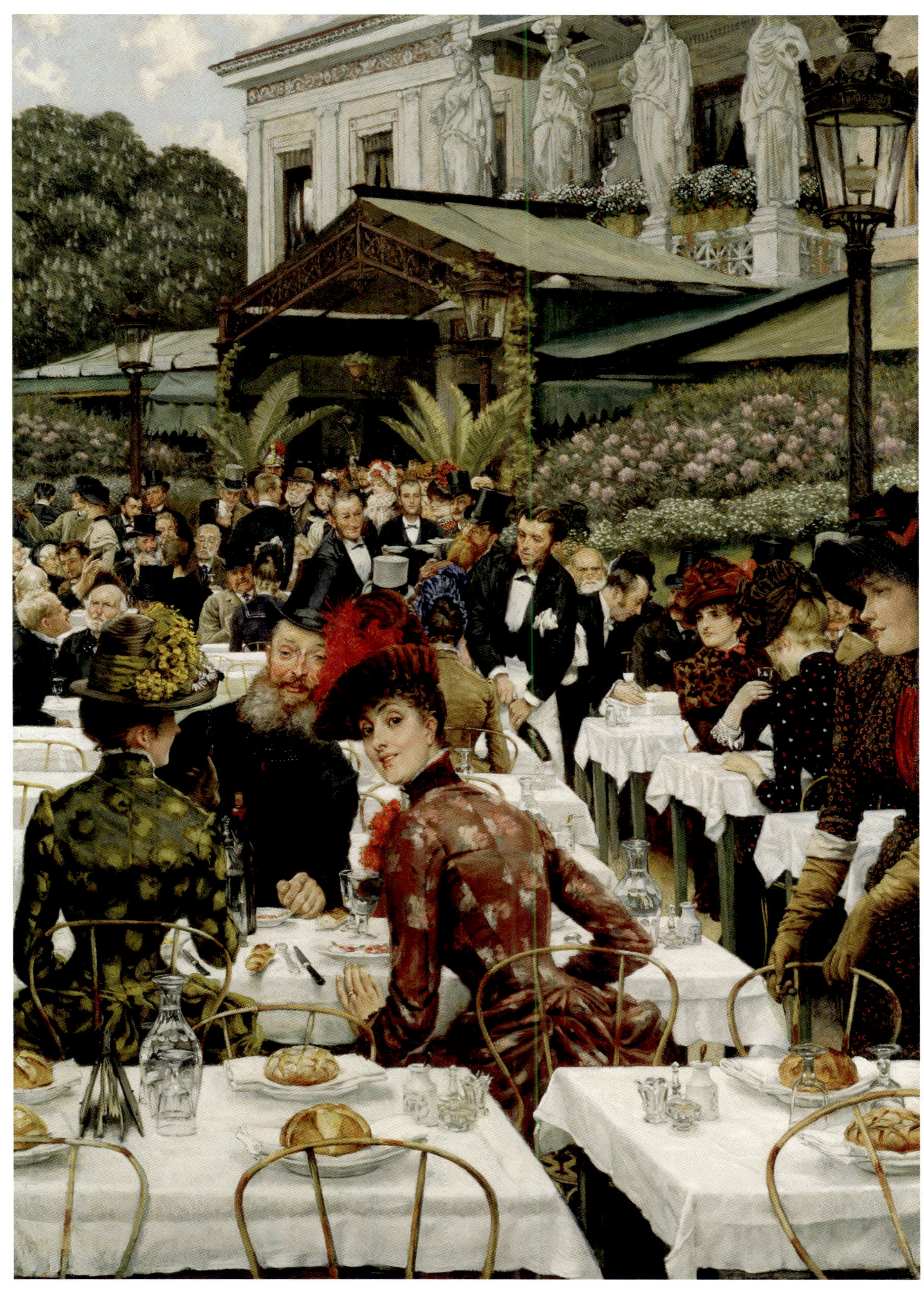

118

PAINTERS AND THEIR WIVES, CA. 1883–1885

also known as THE ARTISTS' WIVES

Oil on canvas, 57½ × 40 in. (146.1 × 101.6 cm)

Chrysler Museum of Art, Norfolk, Virginia, Gift of Walter P. Chrysler, Jr., and The Grandy Fund, Landmark Communications Fund, and "An Affair to Remember" 1982, 81.153

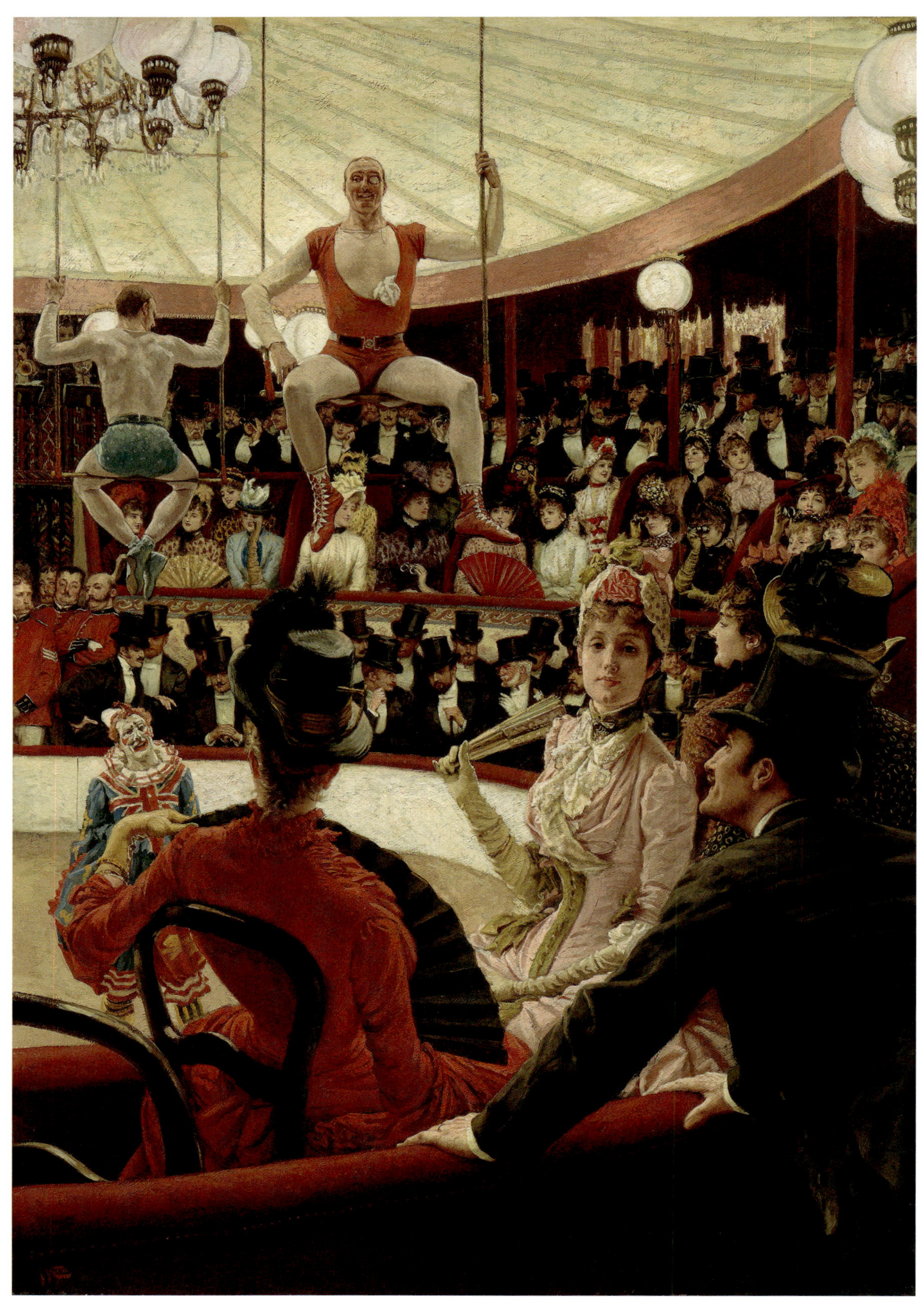

119

THE AMATEUR CIRCUS, CA. 1883–1885

also known as THE CIRCUS LOVER

Oil on canvas, 58 × 40 in. (147.3 × 101.6 cm)

Museum of Fine Arts, Boston, Juliana Cheney Edwards Collection, 58.45

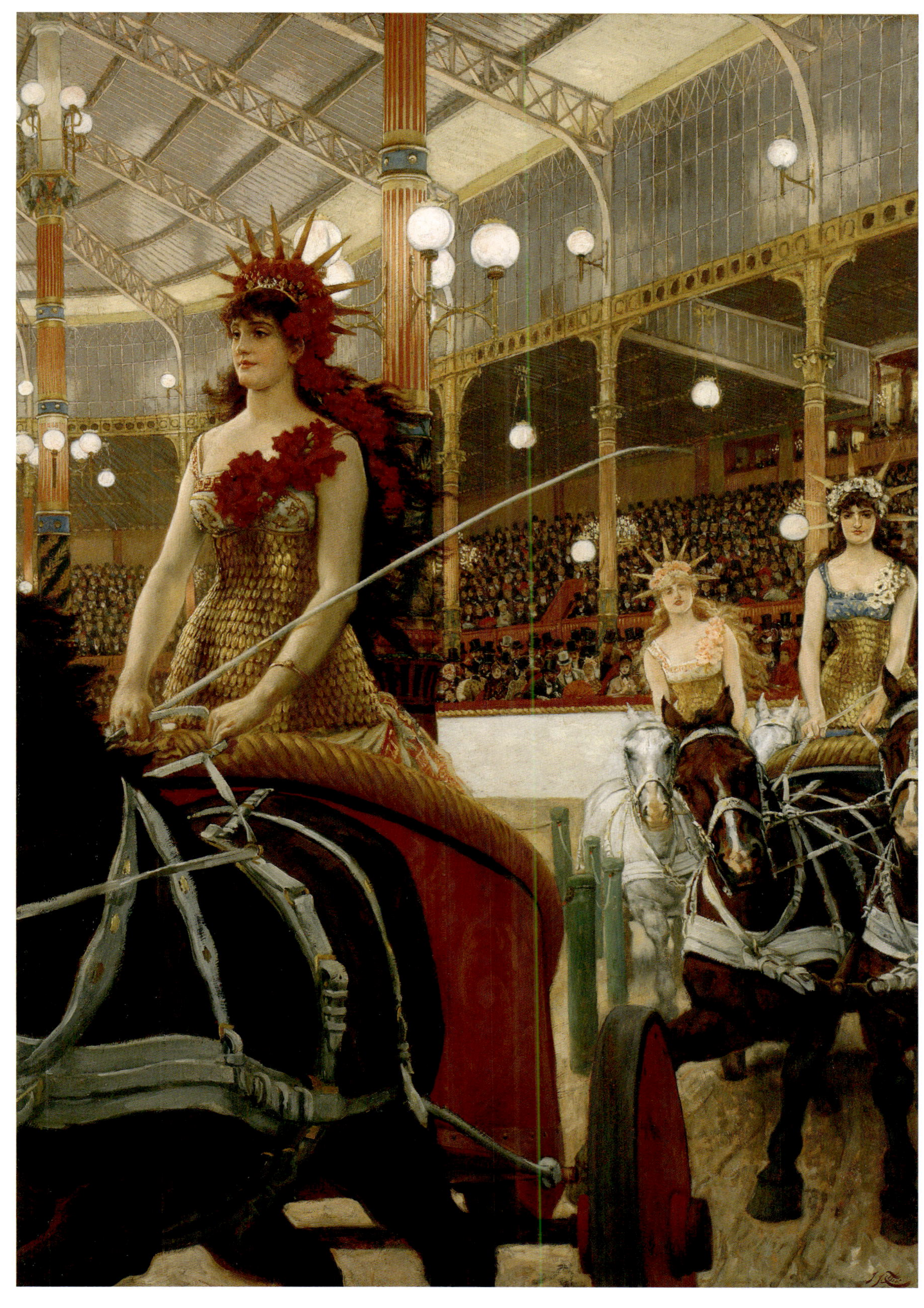

120

THE LADIES OF THE CARS, CA. 1883–1885
also known as THE LADIES OF THE CHARIOTS

Oil on canvas, 57½ × 39⅝ in. (146.1 × 100.7 cm)
Museum of Art, Rhode Island School of Design, Providence, Gift of Mr. Walter Lowry, 58.186

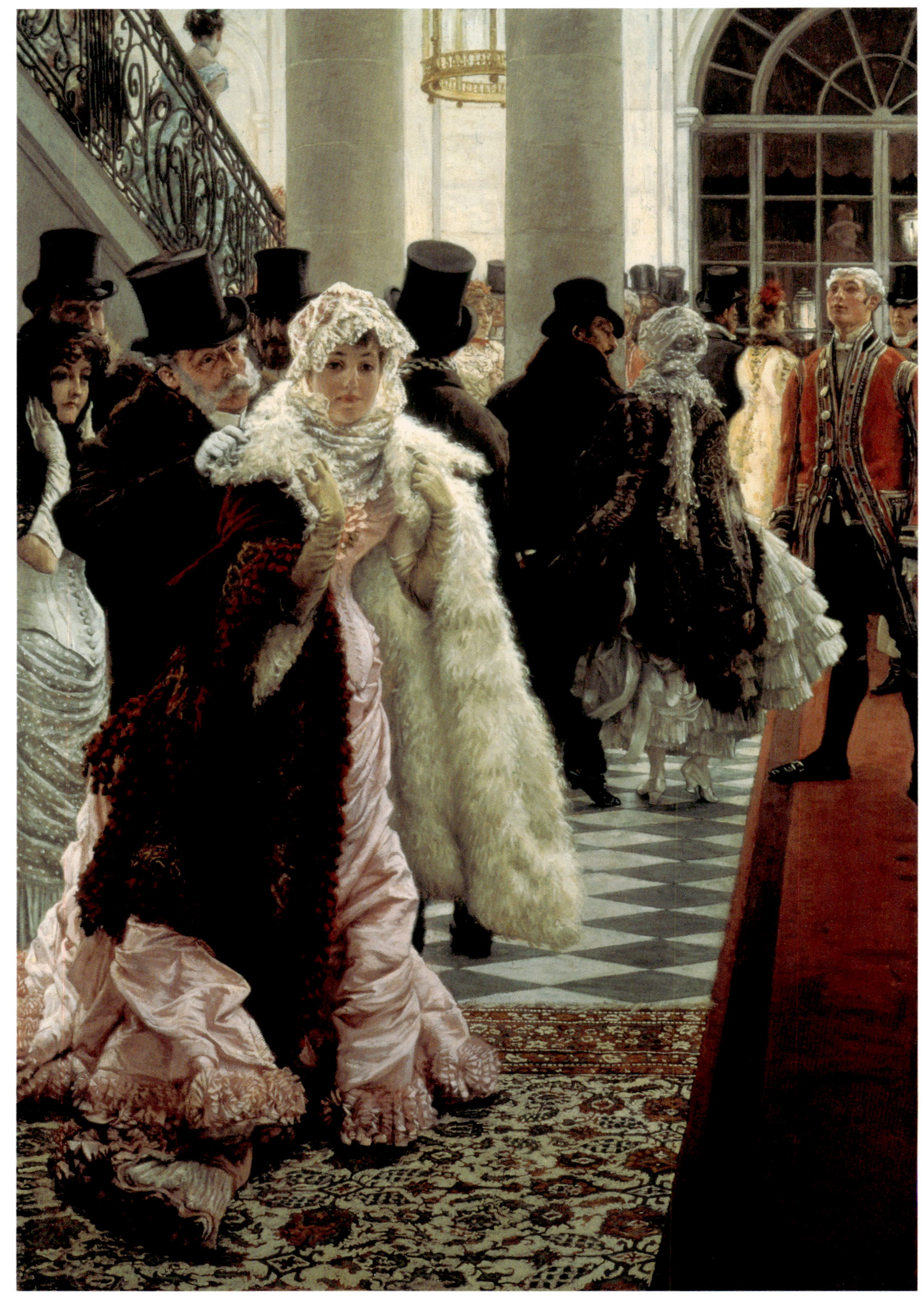

121

THE WOMAN OF FASHION, CA. 1883–1885

Oil on canvas, 57 × 39 in. (148.3 × 103 cm)
Private collection

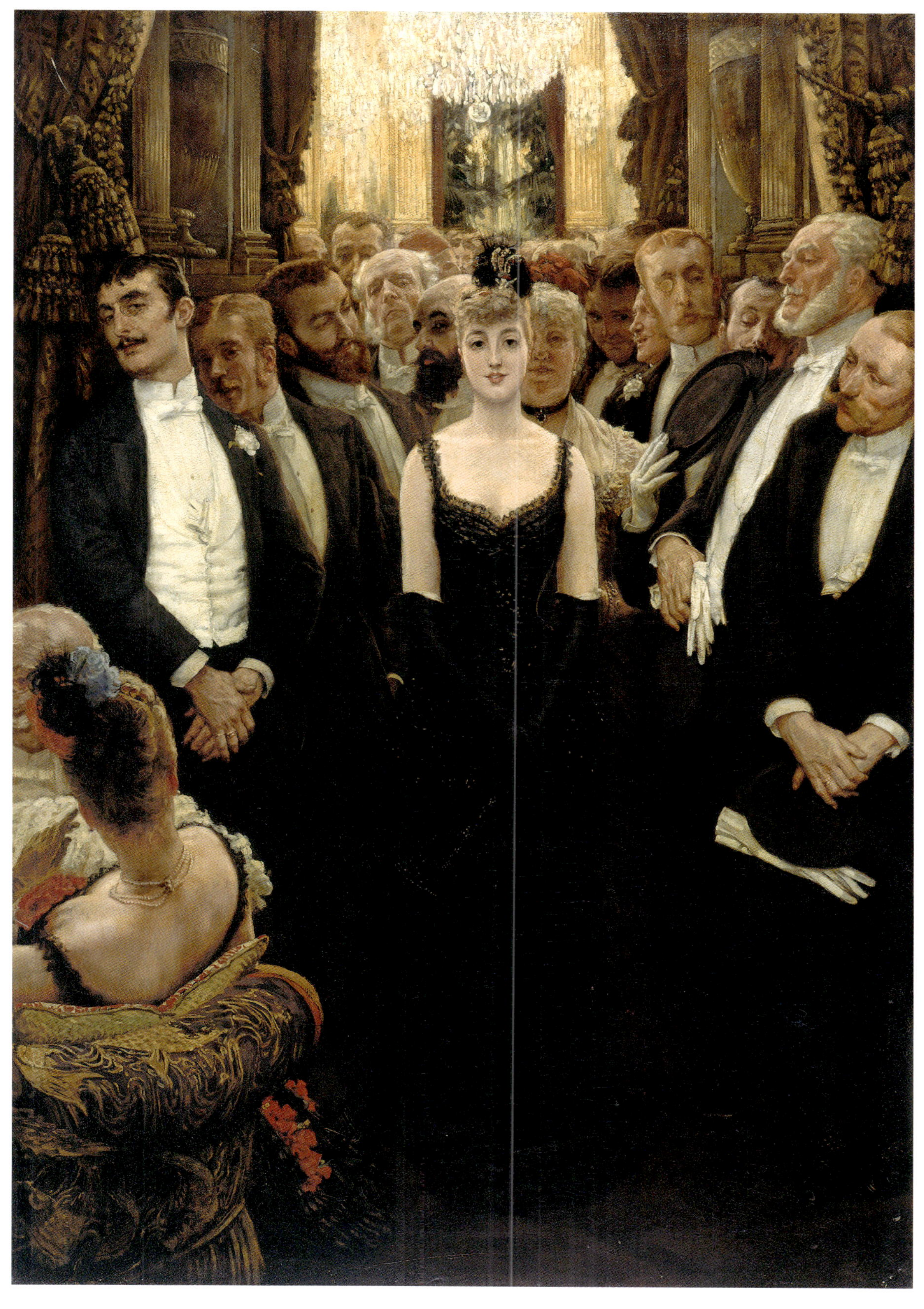

122

THE FASHIONABLE BEAUTY, CA. 1883–1885

Oil on canvas, 57⅝ × 40 in. (146.3 × 101.6 cm)

Musée d'Art et d'Histoire de Genève, inv. BA.1998.239

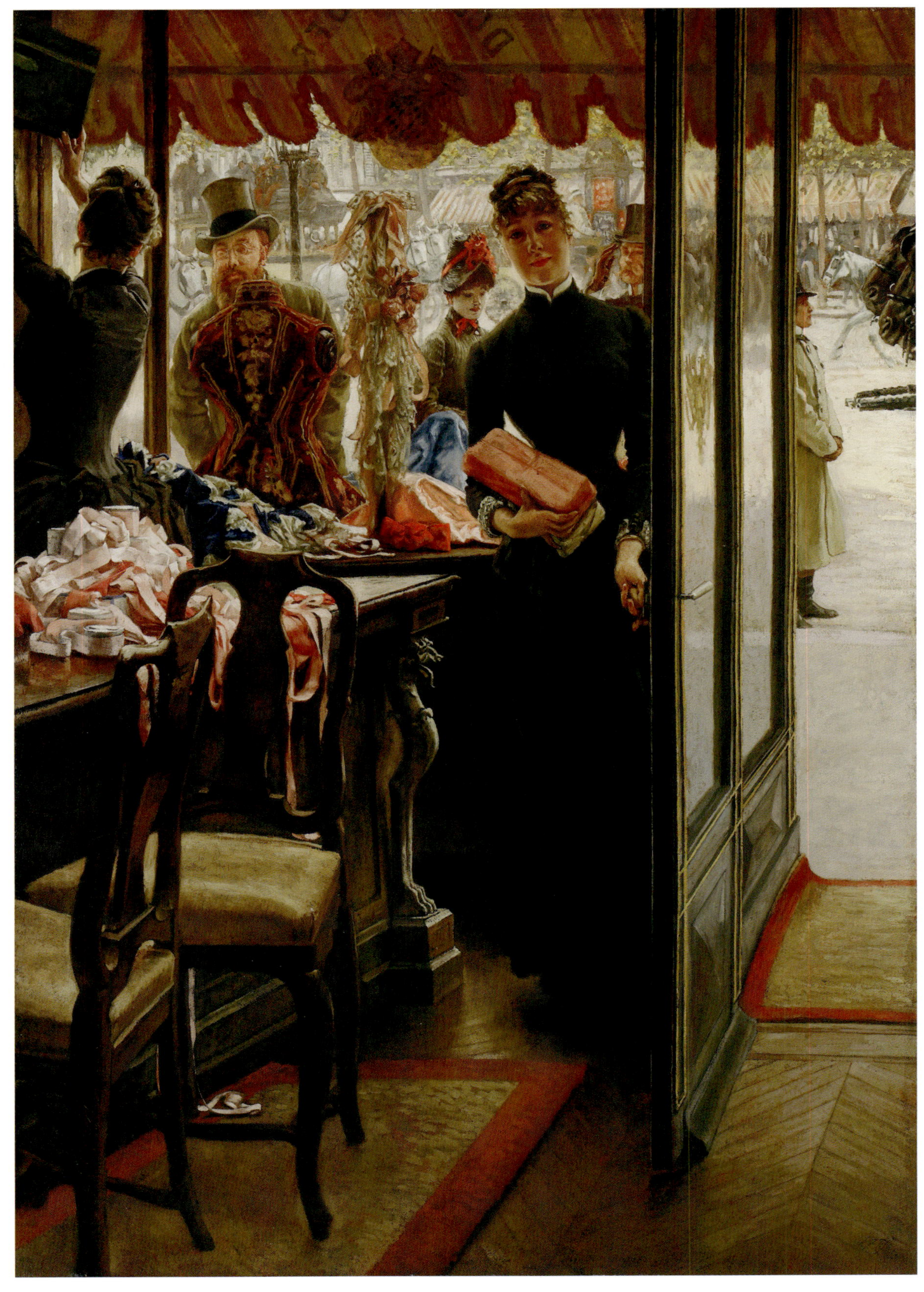

123

THE "YOUNG LADY" OF THE SHOP, CA. 1883–1885

Oil on canvas, 57½ × 40 in. (146.1 × 101.6 cm)

Art Gallery of Ontario, Toronto, Gift from Corporations' Subscription Fund, 1968, 67/55

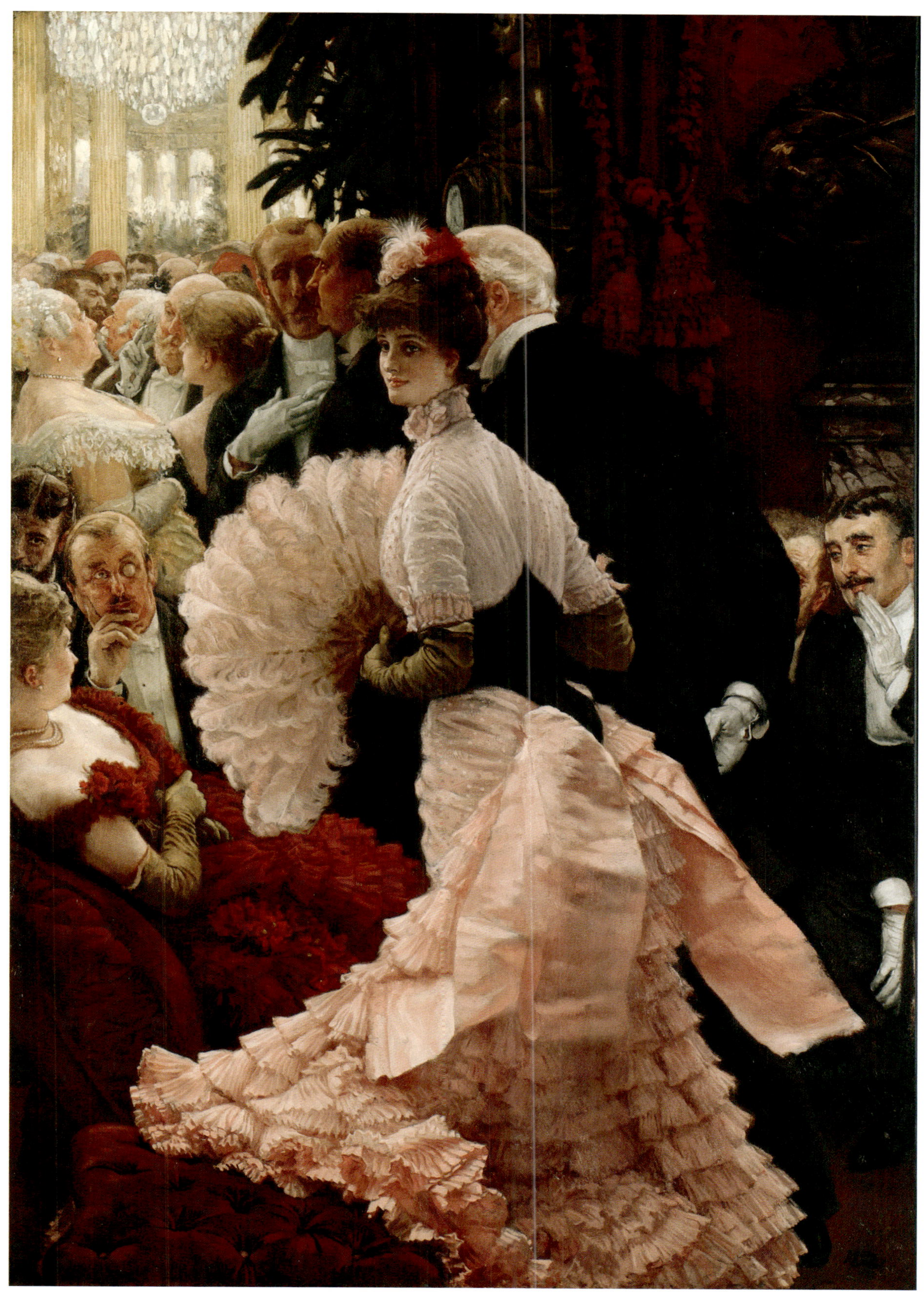

124

POLITICAL WOMAN, CA. 1883–1885

Oil on canvas, 56 × 40 in. (142.2 × 101.6 cm)

Albright-Knox Art Gallery, Buffalo, Gift of William M. Chase, 1909, 1909:10

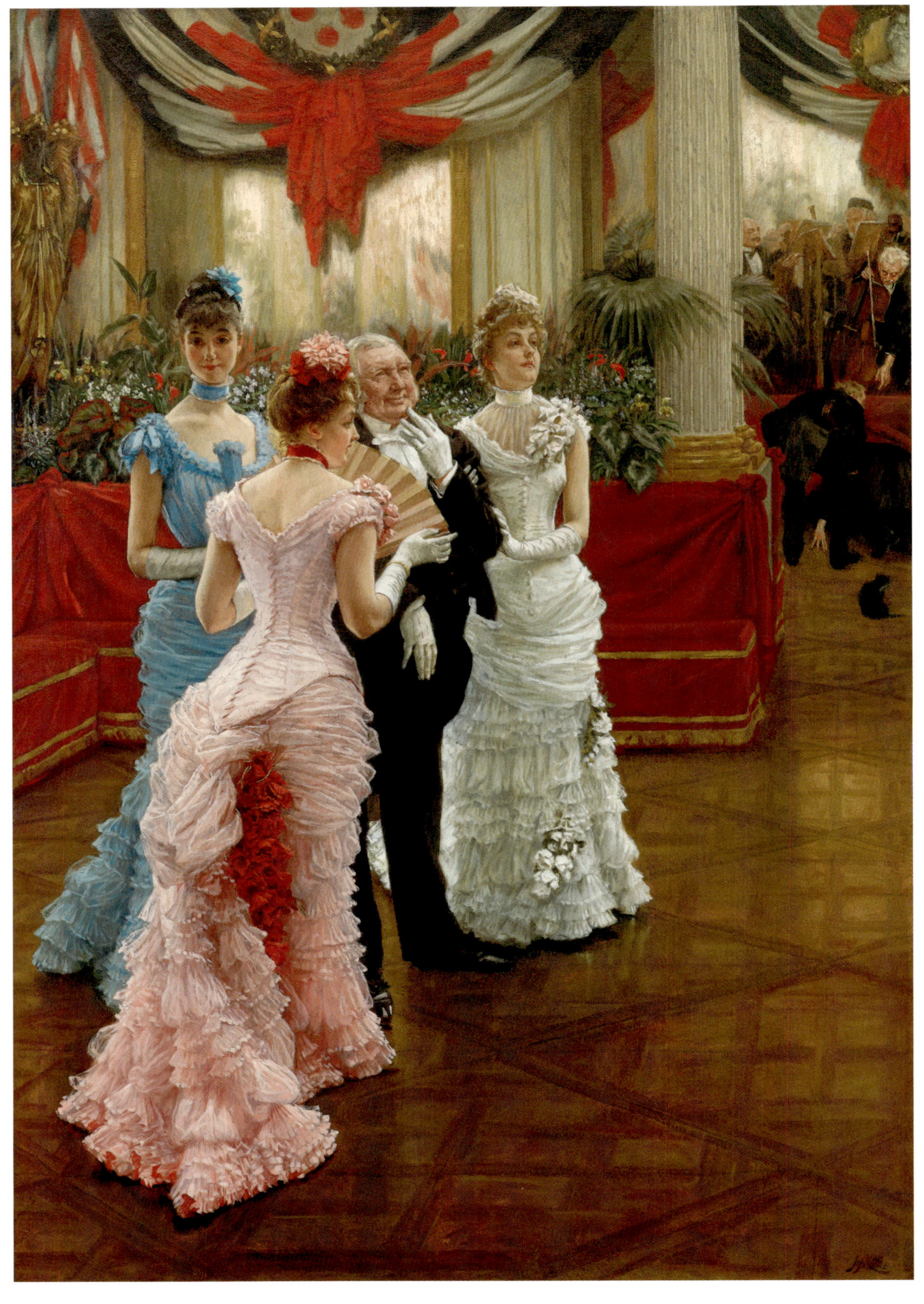

125

PROVINCIAL WOMAN, CA. 1883–1885

Oil on canvas, 58 × 40¼ in. (147.3 × 102.2 cm)

Collection of Diane B. Wilsey, San Francisco

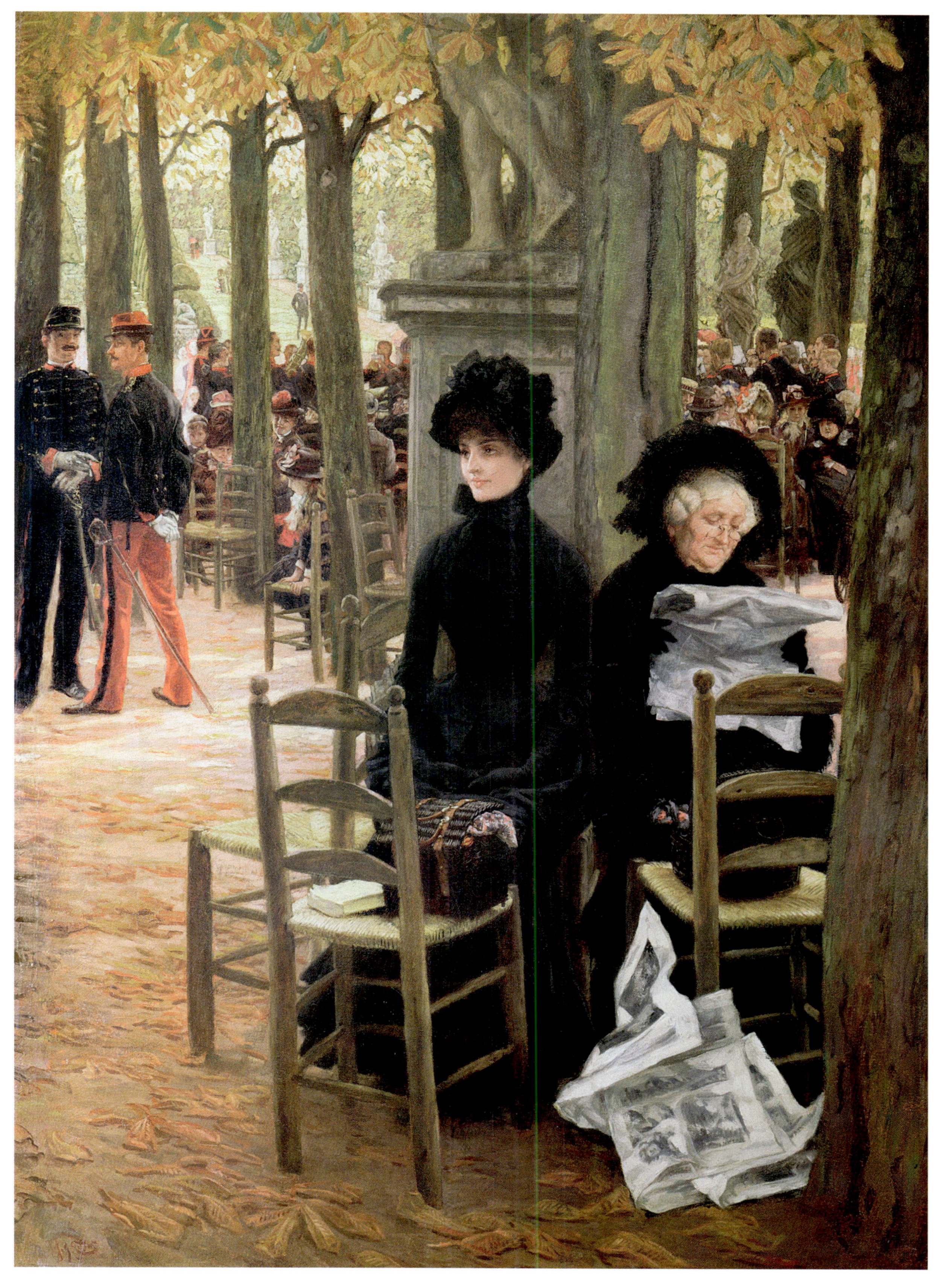

126

WITHOUT DOWRY, CA. 1883–1885

Oil on canvas, 58 × 40 in. (147.3 × 101.6 cm)

Private collection

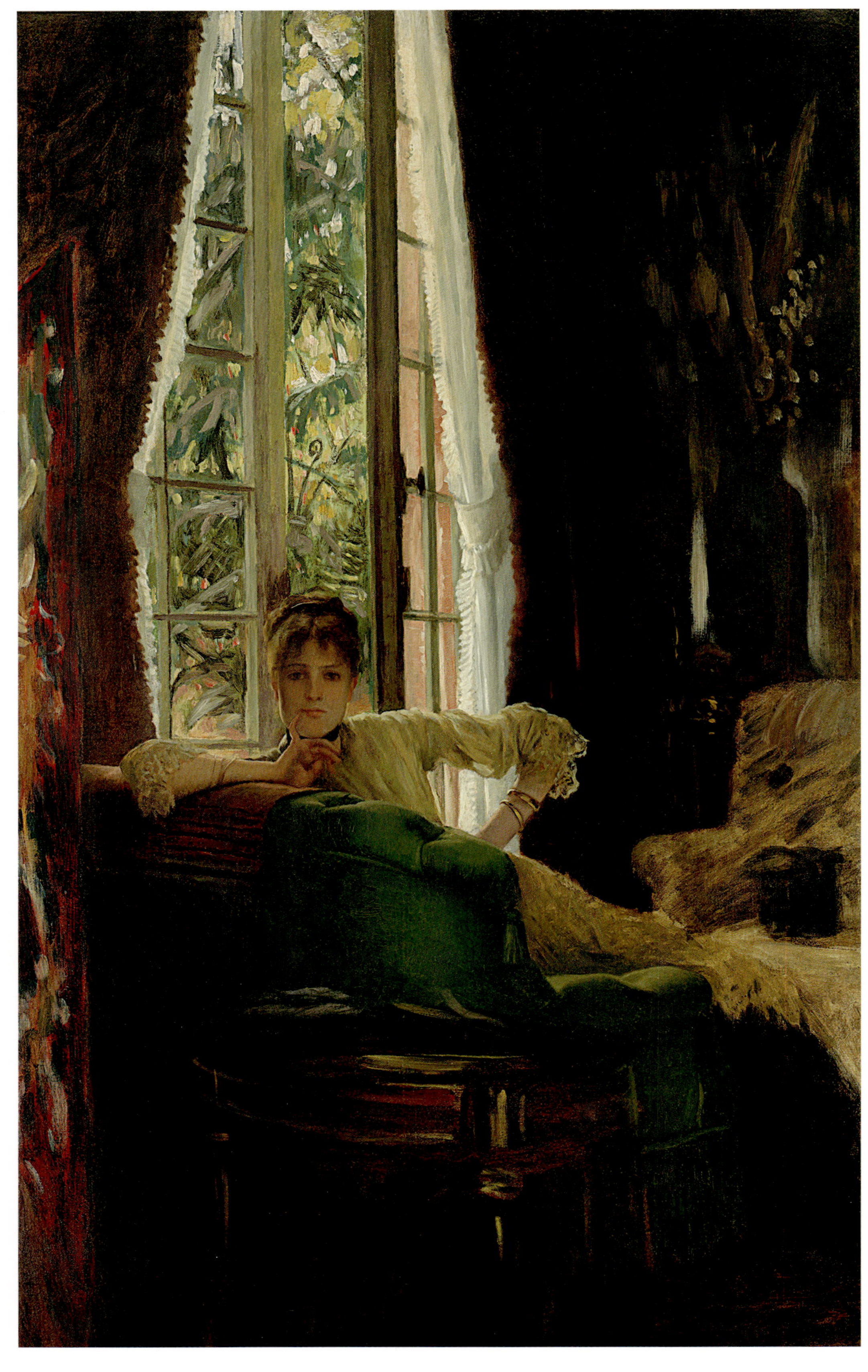

127

STUDY FOR "THE SPHINX" (WOMAN IN AN INTERIOR), CA. 1883–1885

Oil on wood panel, 43¾ × 27 in. (111.1 × 68.6 cm)

Private collection

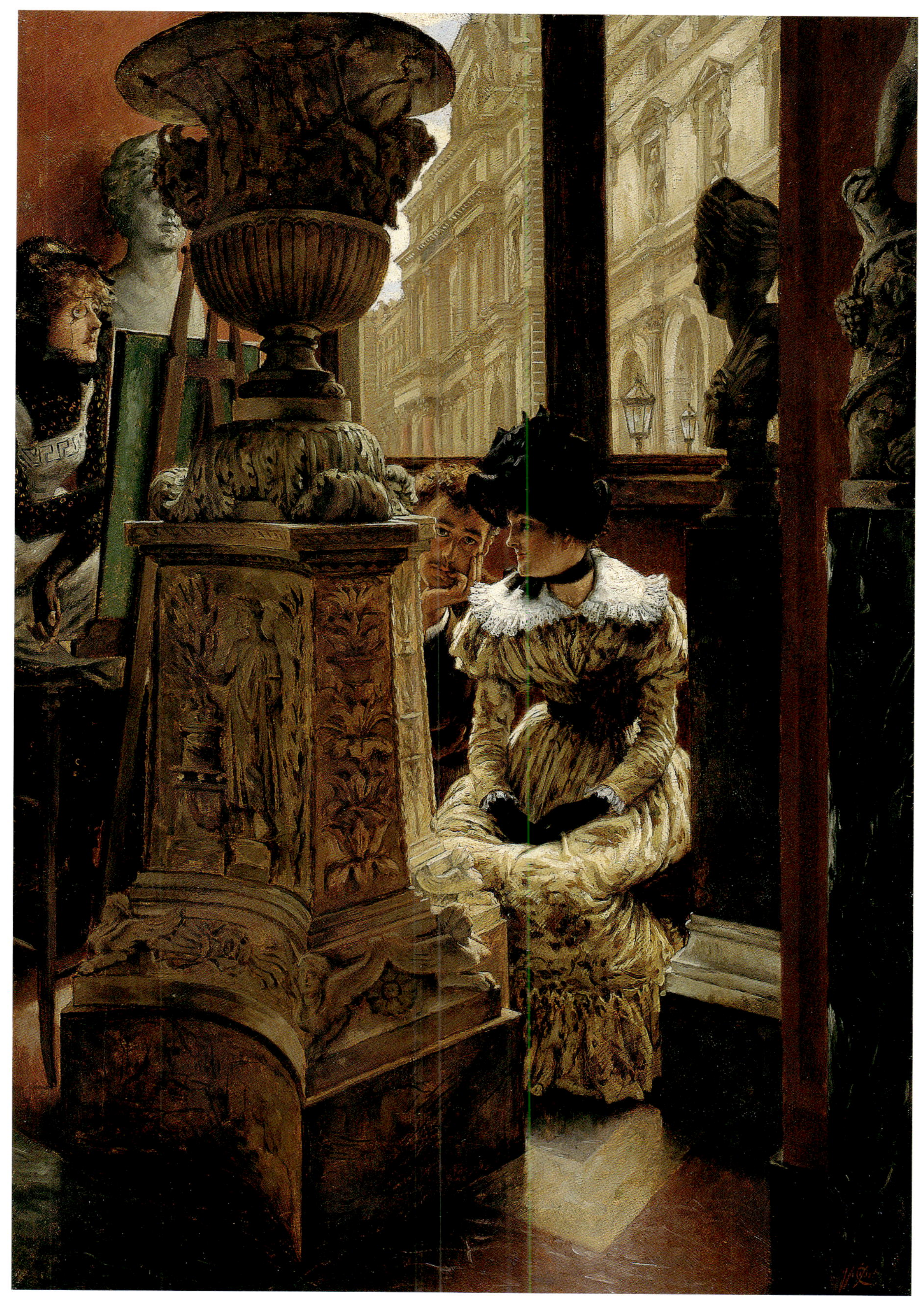

128

Aesthetic Woman, ca. 1883–1885

Oil on canvas, 25½ × 17½ in. (64.8 × 44.5 cm)
Colección Pérez Simón, Mexico City

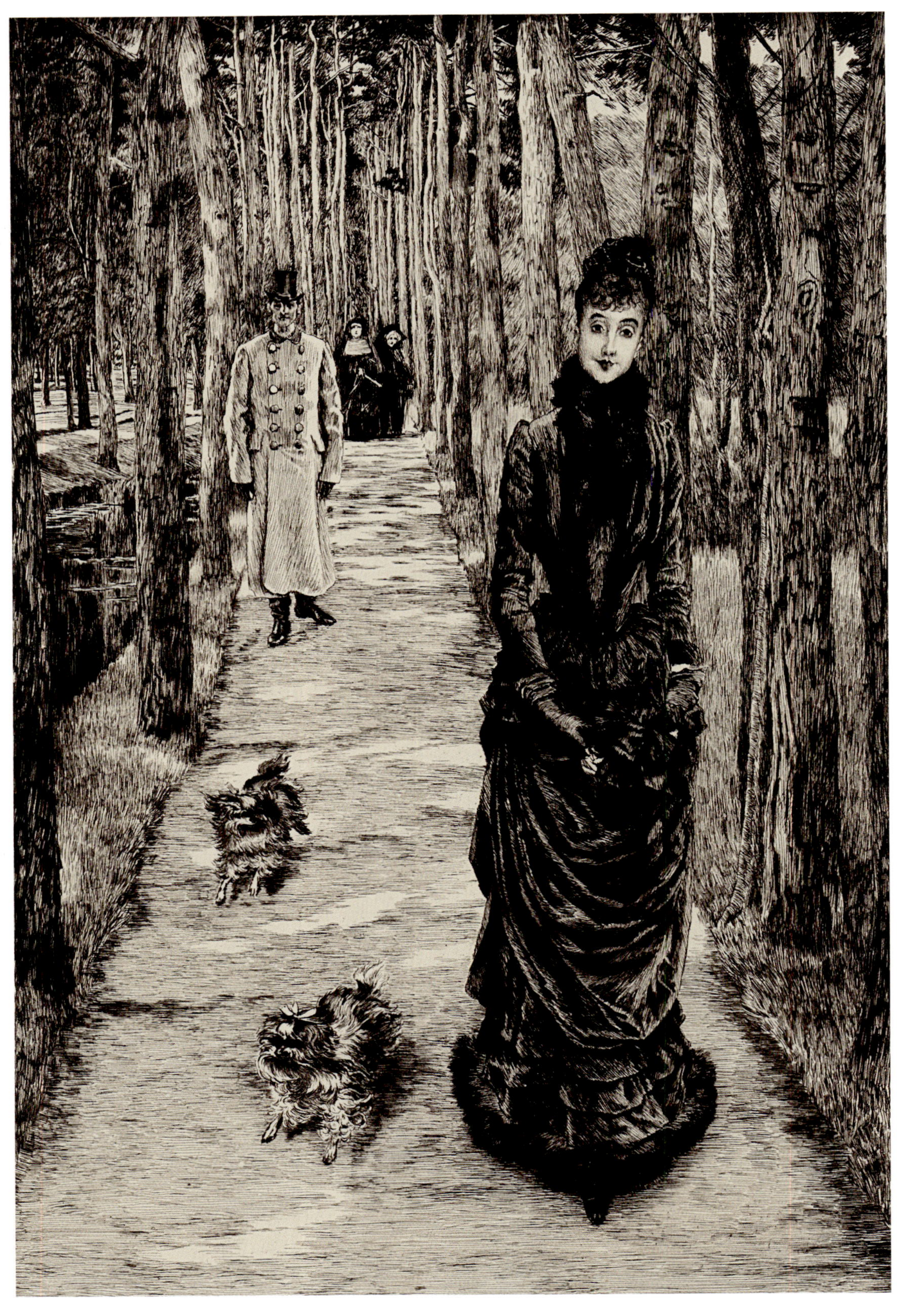

129

THE MYSTERY, CA. 1885

Etching and drypoint, 22¼ × 14¾ in. (56.5 × 37.5 cm)
Cantor Arts Center, Stanford University, Mortimer C. Leventritt Fund, 1972.43

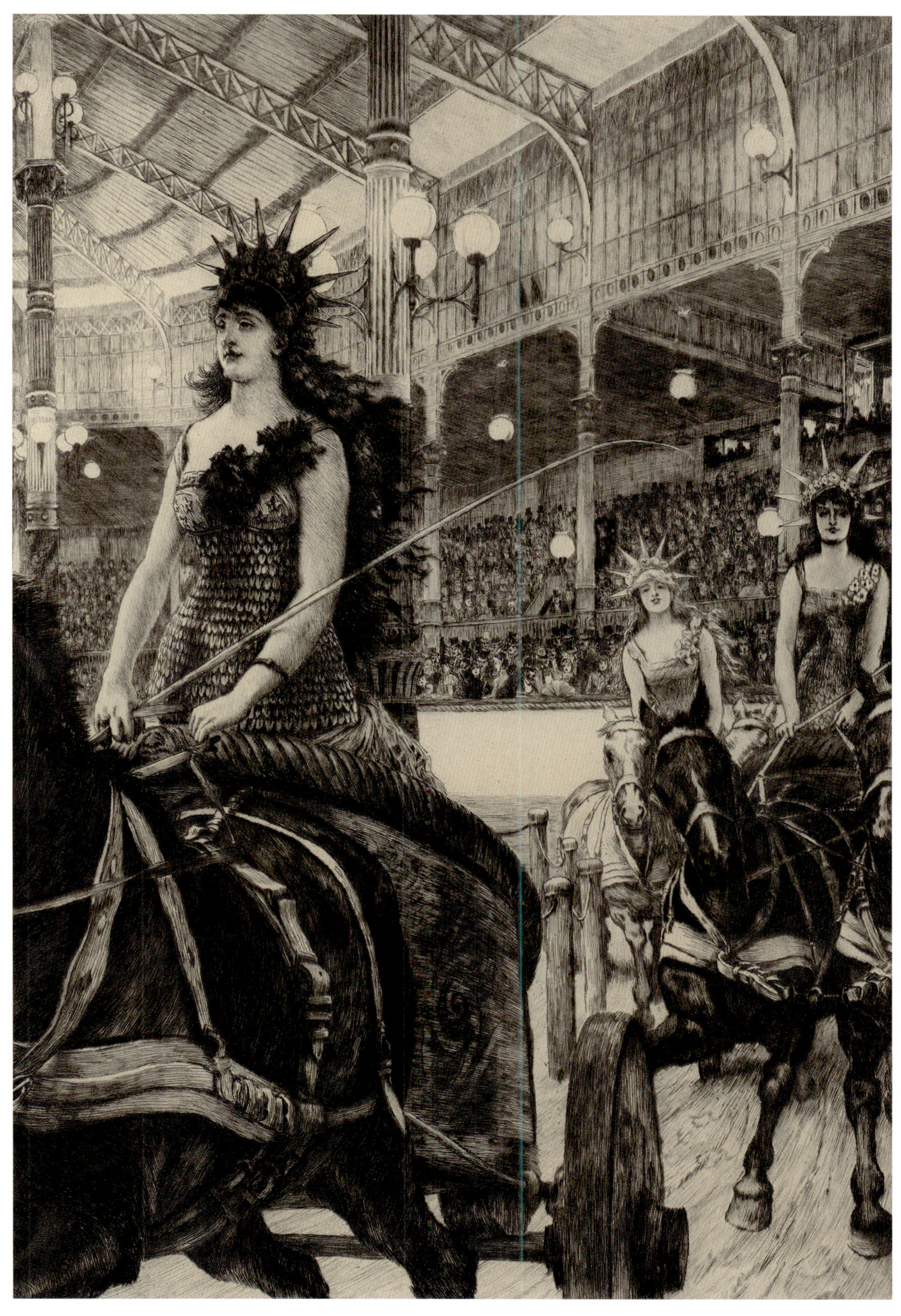

130

THE LADIES OF THE CARS, CA. 1885

also known as THE LADIES OF THE CHARIOTS

Etching and drypoint, 15 ¾ × 10 in. (40 × 25.4 cm)

Fine Arts Museums of San Francisco, Museum purchase, Achenbach Foundation for Graphic Arts Endowment Fund, 1982.1.18

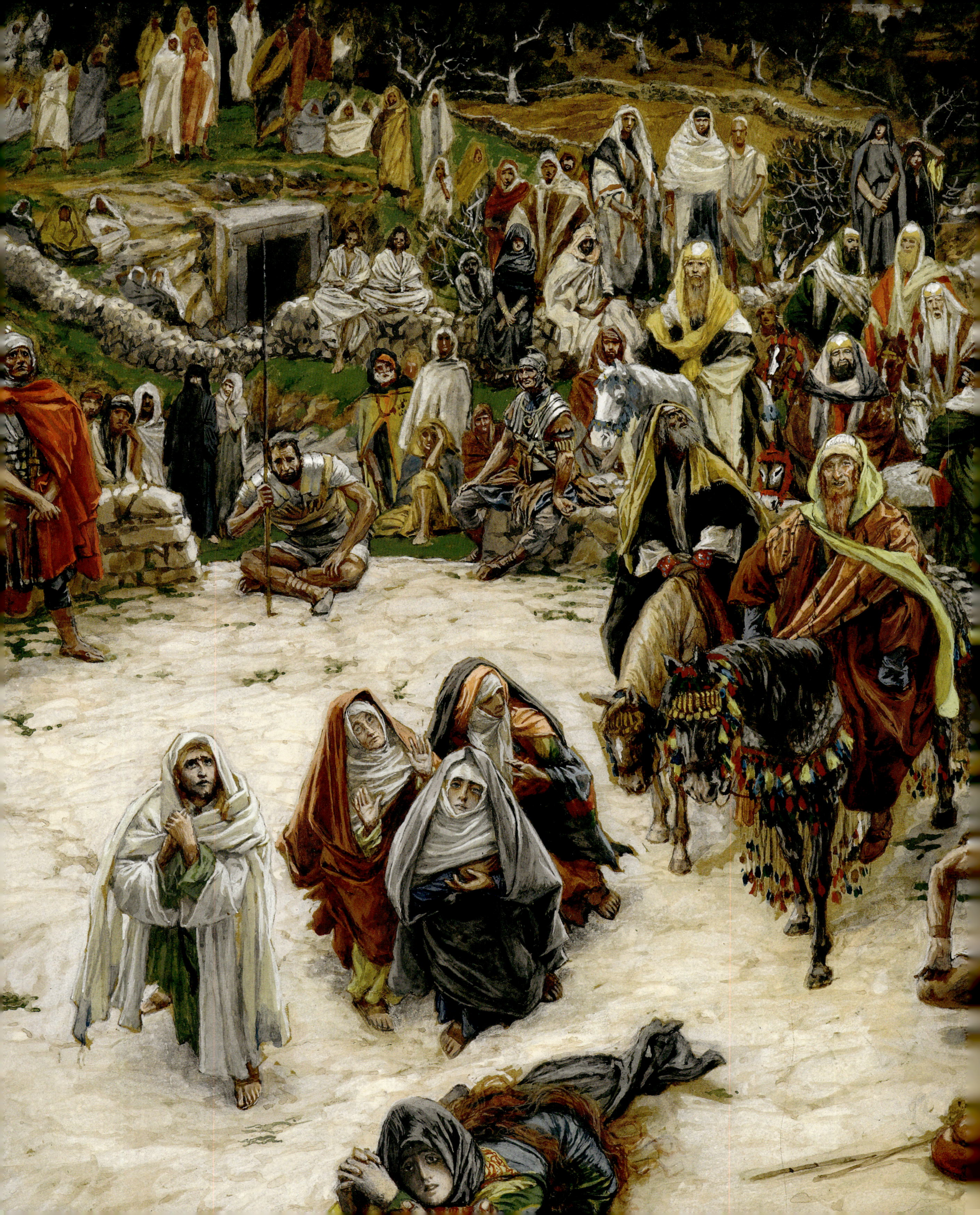

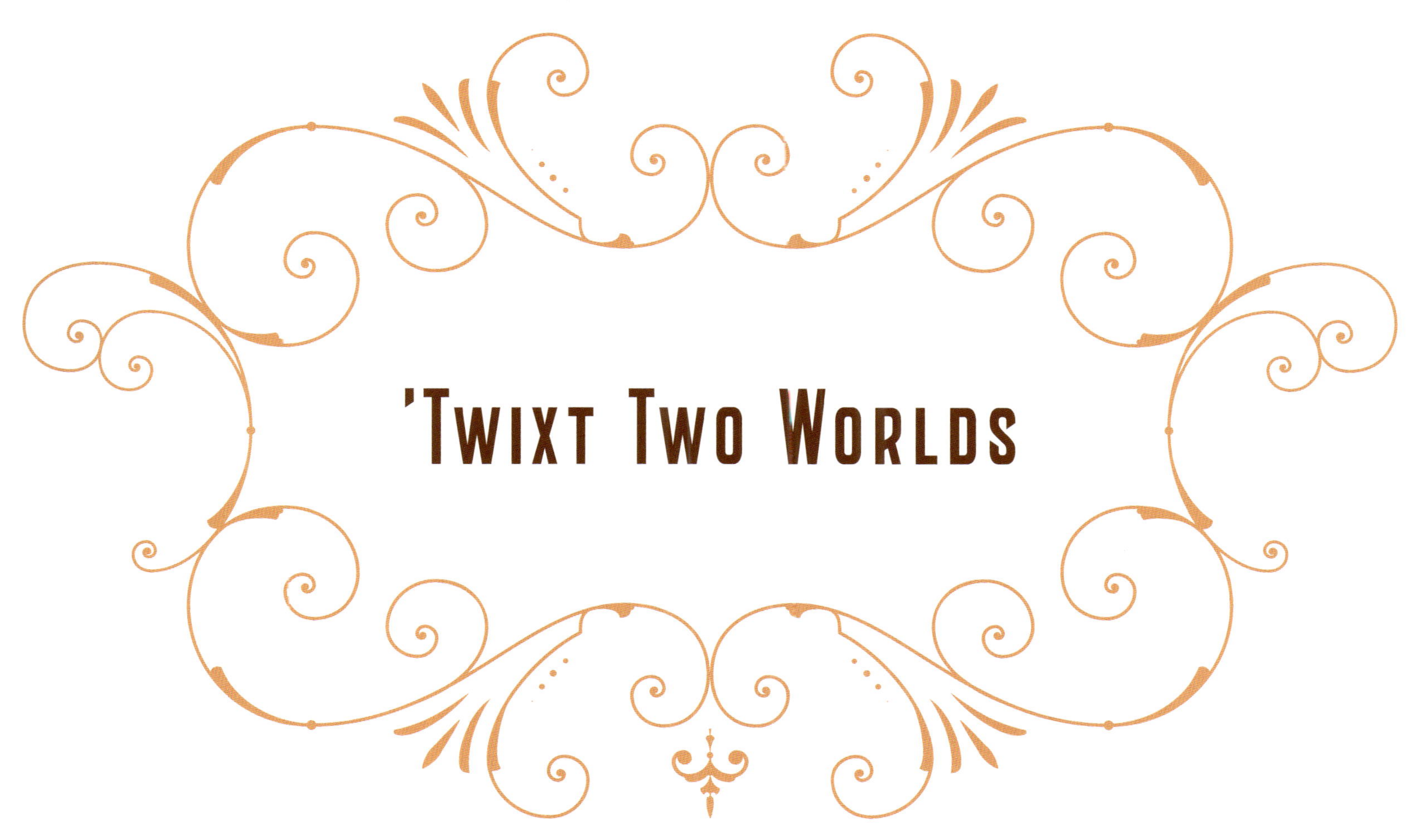

'Twixt Two Worlds

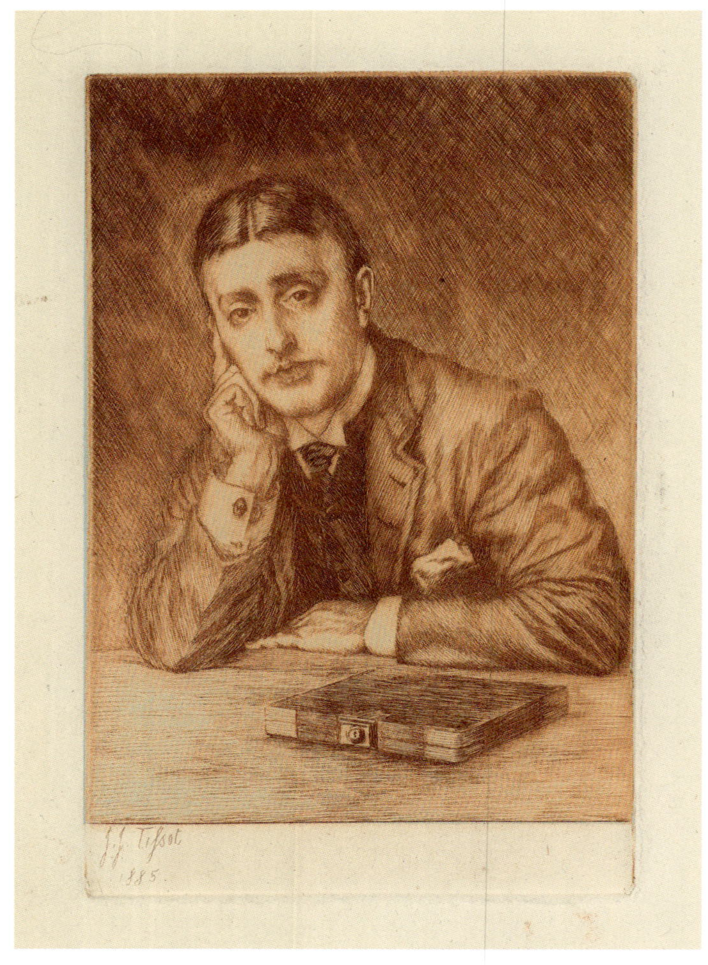

131

Portrait of William Eglinton, 1885

Etching printed in red, 15½ × 10 in. (39.4 × 25.4 cm)
Fine Arts Museums of San Francisco, Gift of John Gutmann, 1986.1.205

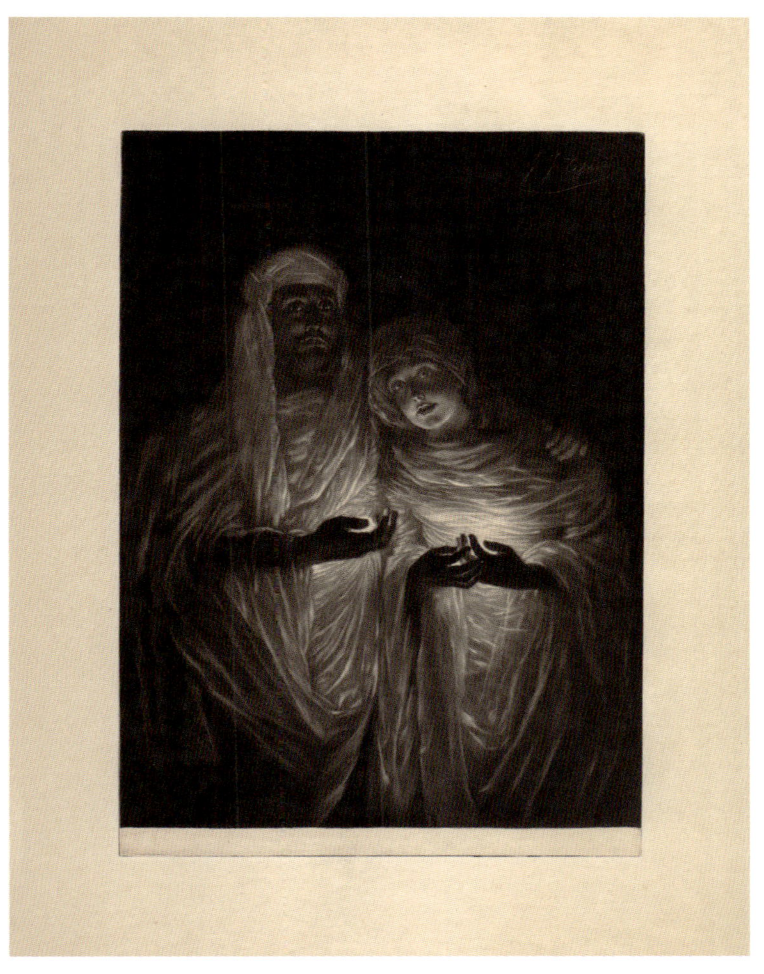

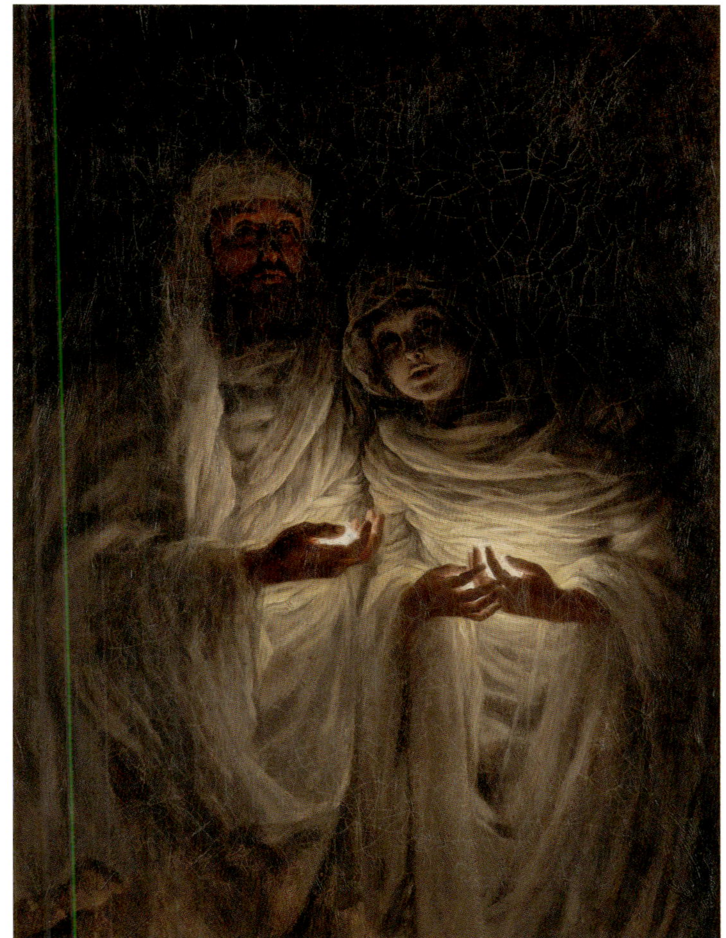

132

The Apparition, 1885

Mezzotint, 25 3/8 × 19 3/8 in. (64.5 × 49.2 cm)
Fine Arts Museums of San Francisco, Museum purchase,
Gift of the Graphic Arts Council, 2001.26

133

The Apparition, 1885

also known as **The Mediumistic Apparition**

Oil on canvas, 29 1/8 × 21 1/4 in. (74 × 54 cm)
Private collection

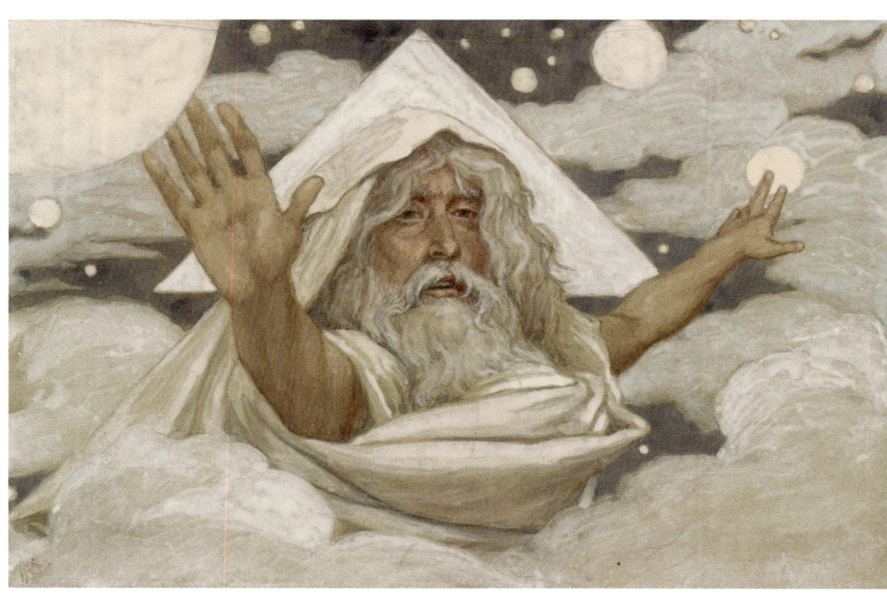

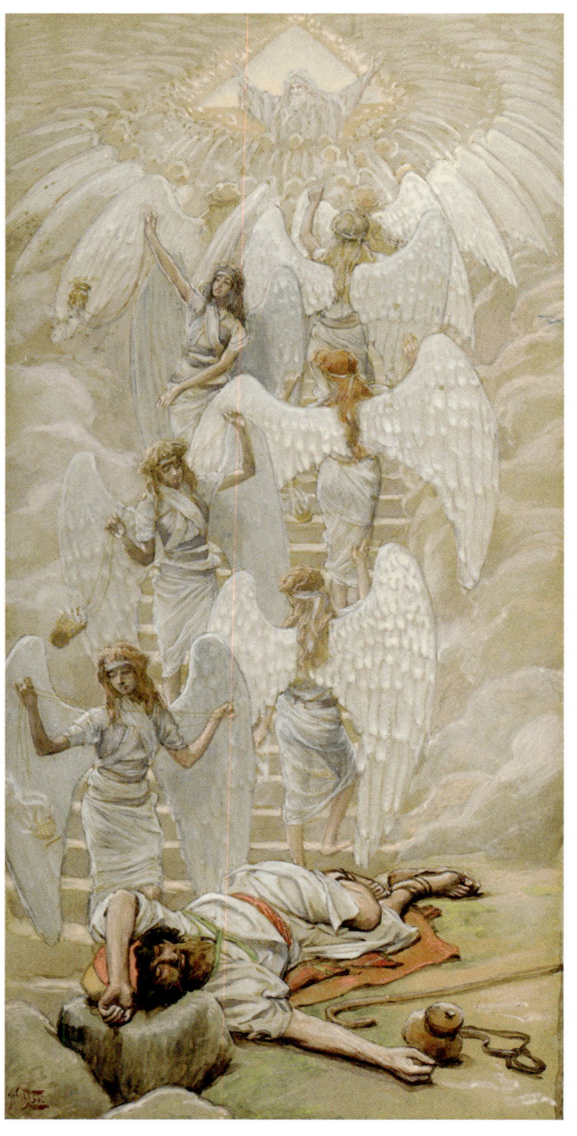

134

God Creating the World, ca. 1900–1902

Opaque watercolor on board, 5¼ × 7¾ in. (13.5 × 20.1 cm)
The Morgan Library and Museum, New York, Morgan Family Collection, 1976.22:1

135

Jacob's Dream, ca. 1896–1902

Opaque watercolor on board, 12¼ × 5⅞ in. (31 × 15 cm)
The Jewish Museum, New York, Gift of the heirs of Jacob Schiff, X1952-113

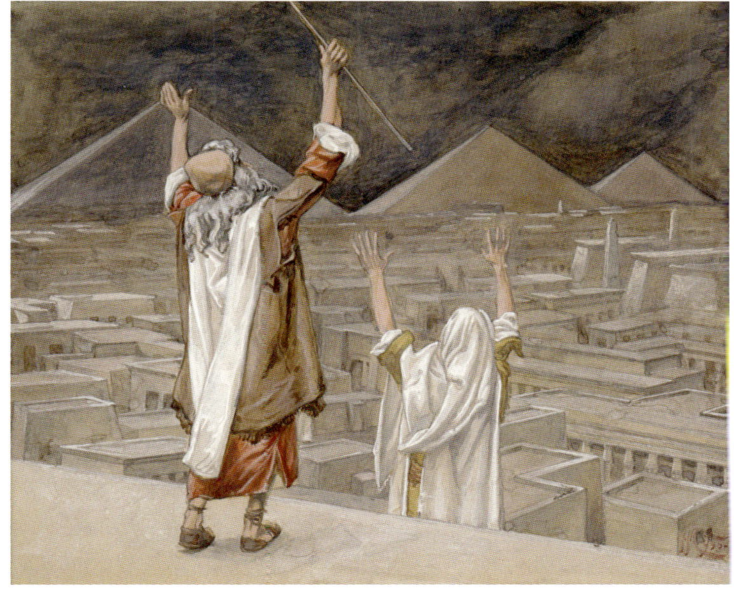

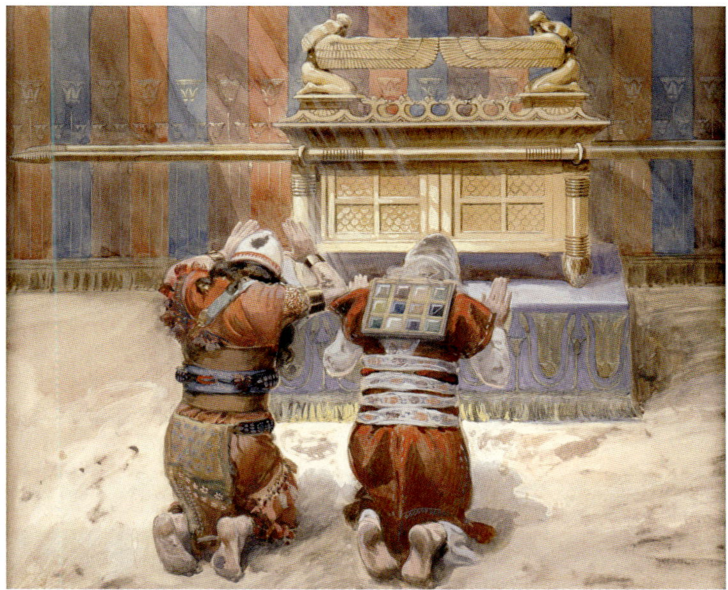

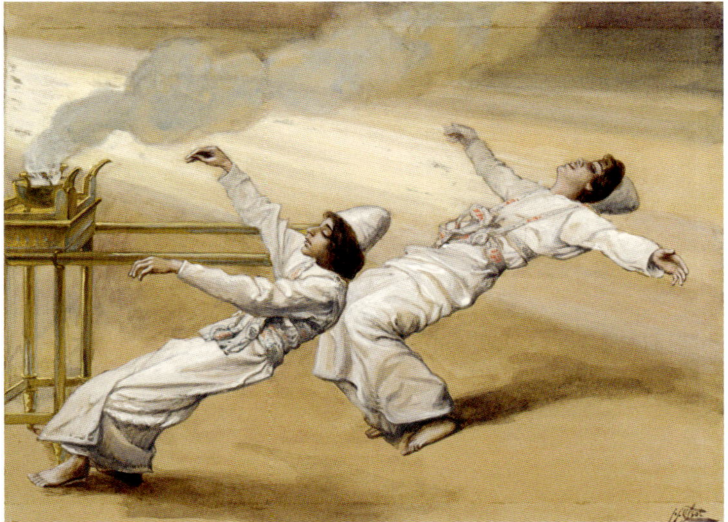

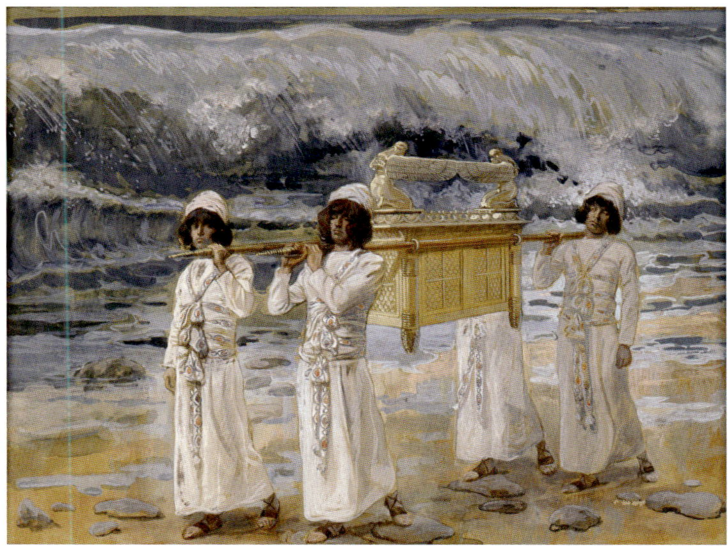

136–139 (clockwise from top left)

THE PLAGUE OF LOCUSTS, MOSES AND JOSHUA IN THE TABERNACLE, THE ARK PASSES OVER THE JORDAN, THE TWO PRIESTS ARE DESTROYED, CA. 1896–1902

Opaque watercolor on board, 7 3/4 × 9 3/8 in. (19.8 × 23.9 cm), 7 3/8 × 8 7/8 in. (18.7 × 22.5 cm), 8 3/8 × 10 7/8 in. (21.4 × 27.6 cm), 7 3/8 × 10 3/4 in. (18.7 × 27.3 cm)
The Jewish Museum, New York, Gift of the heirs of Jacob Schiff,
X1952-164, X1952-208, X1952-214, X1952-191

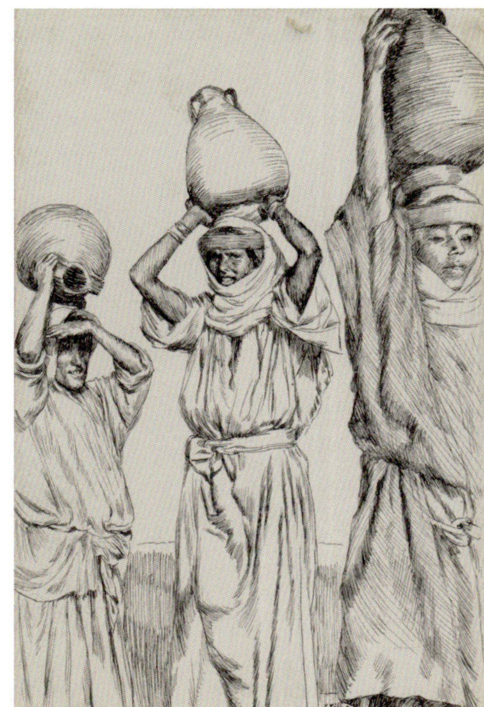

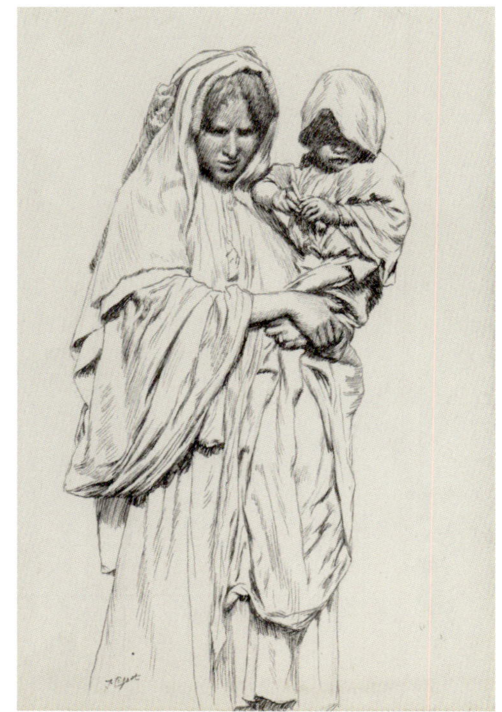

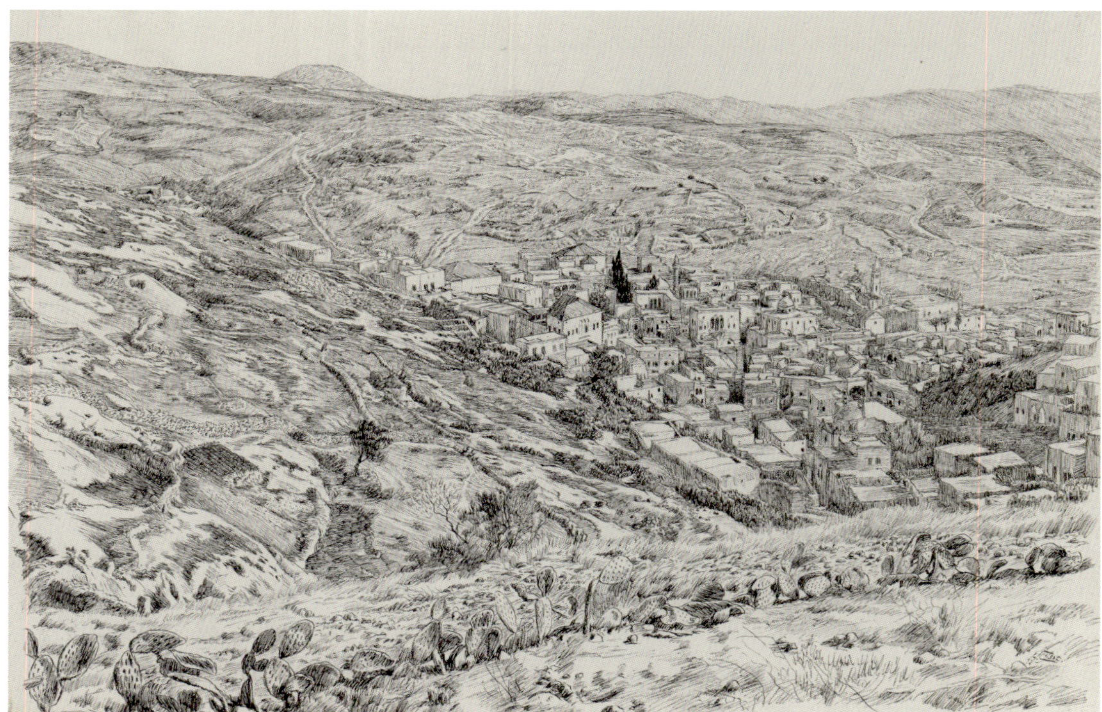

140

WOMEN OF GEBA, SAMARIA, 1886–1887 or 1888–1889

Pen and black ink on paper, 7¼ × 4¾ in. (18.4 × 11.9 cm)
Brooklyn Museum, Purchased by public subscription, 00.159.407

141

WOMAN AND CHILD OF JERICHO, 1886–1887 or 1888–1889

Pen and black ink on paper, 7 × 4¾ in. (17.9 × 11.9 cm)
Brooklyn Museum, Purchased by public subscription, 00.159.394

142

VIEW OF NAZARETH, 1886–1887 or 1888–1889

Pen and black ink on paper, 7 × 10½ in. (17.9 × 26.7 cm)
Brooklyn Museum, Purchased by public subscription, 00.159.361

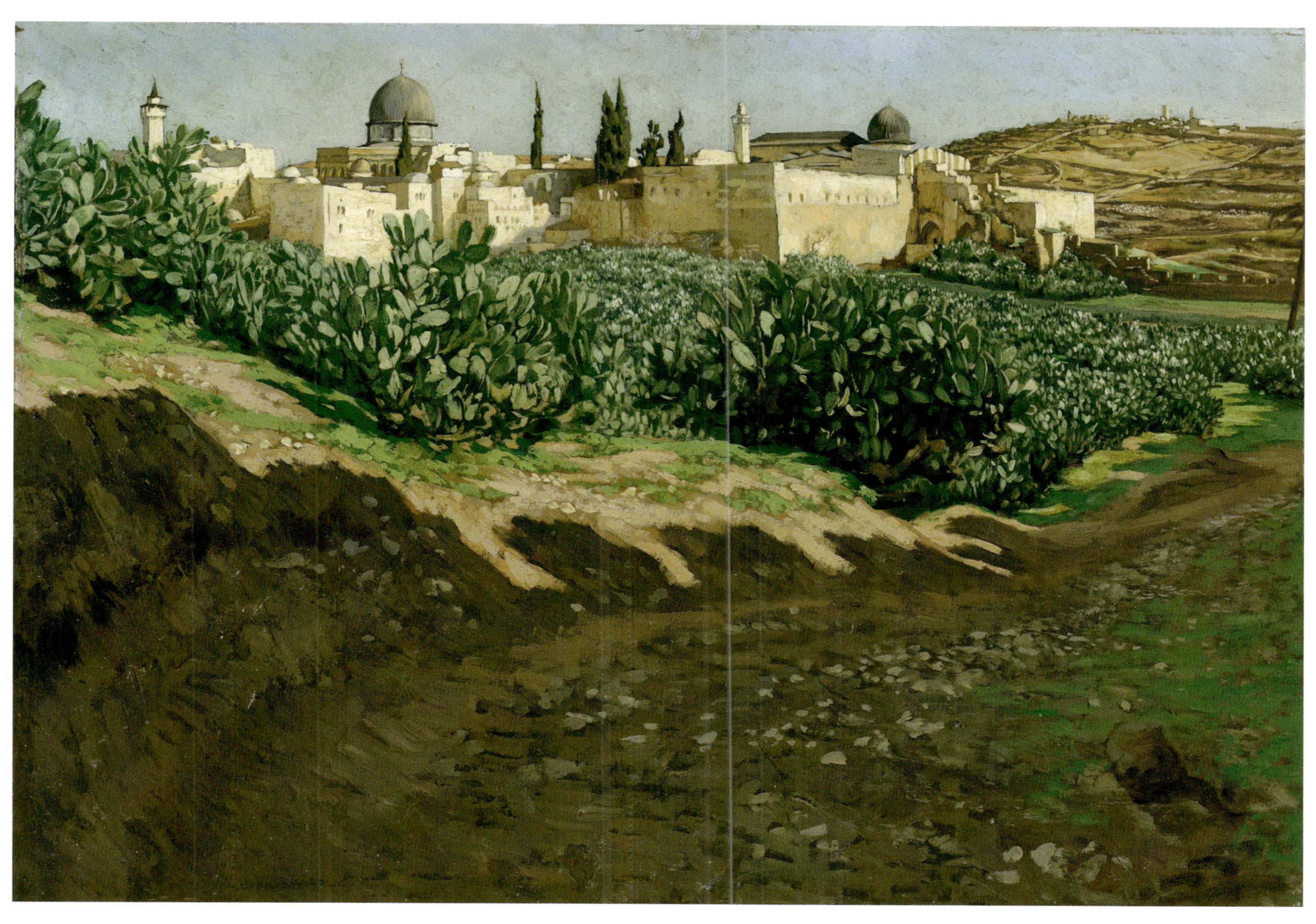

143

South-West Angle of the Haram on the Site of the Temple, Taken from the Gate of the Mugarabees, ca. 1886–1894

Oil on board, 14½ × 20¼ in. (36.7 × 51.4 cm)

Brooklyn Museum, Purchased by public subscription, 00.159.3

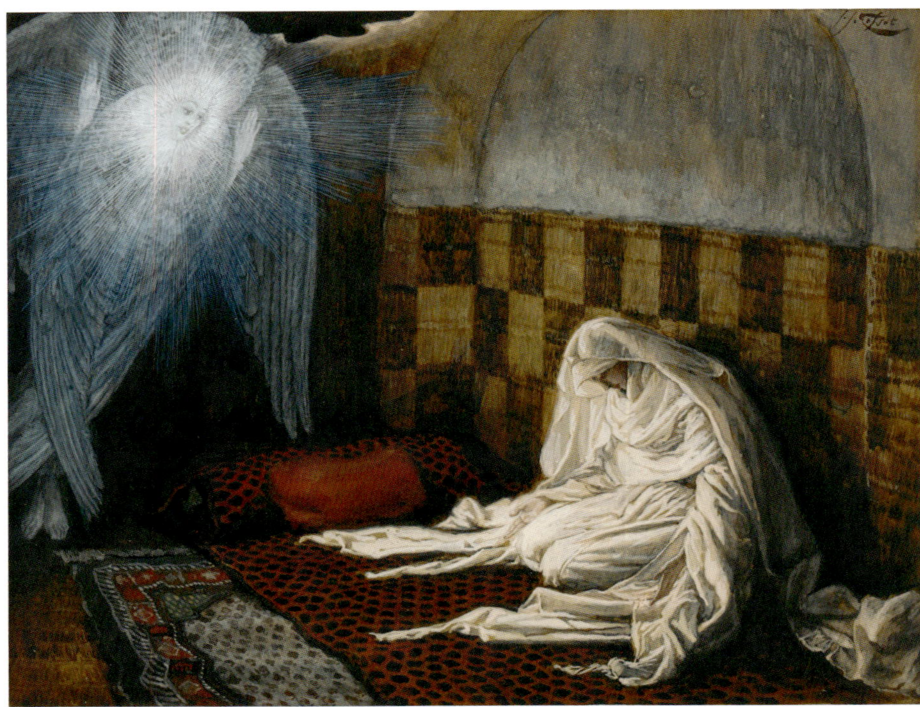

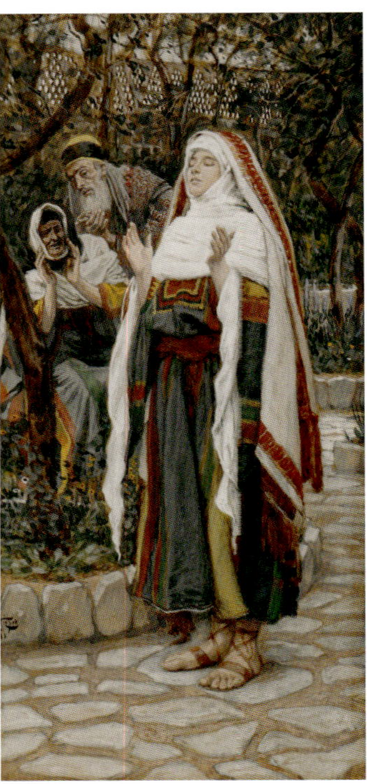

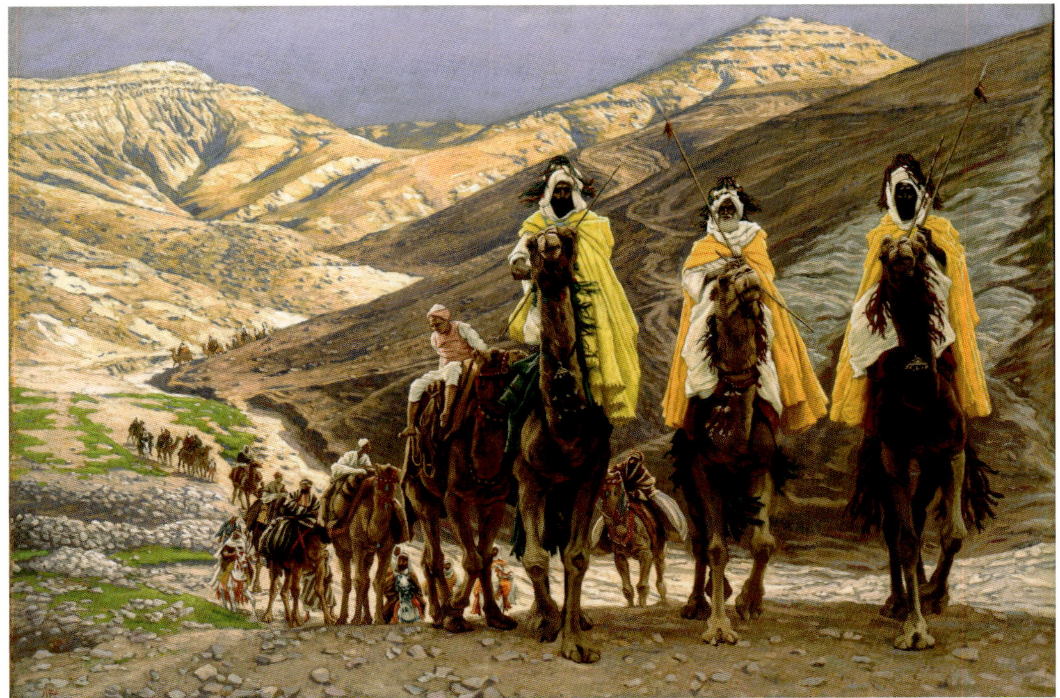

144

The Annunciation, ca. 1886–1894

Opaque watercolor over graphite on gray wove paper, 6¾ × 8½ in. (17 × 21.7 cm)
Brooklyn Museum, Purchased by public subscription, 00.159.16

145

The "Magnificat," ca. 1886–1894

Opaque watercolor over graphite on gray wove paper, 9⅞ × 4⅝ in. (25.2 × 11.7 cm)
Brooklyn Museum, Purchased by public subscription, 00.159.19

146

The Magi on Their Way to Bethlehem, ca. 1886–1894

Opaque watercolor over graphite on gray wove paper, 8 × 11½ in. (20.3 × 29.2 cm)
Brooklyn Museum, Purchased by public subscription, 00.159.30

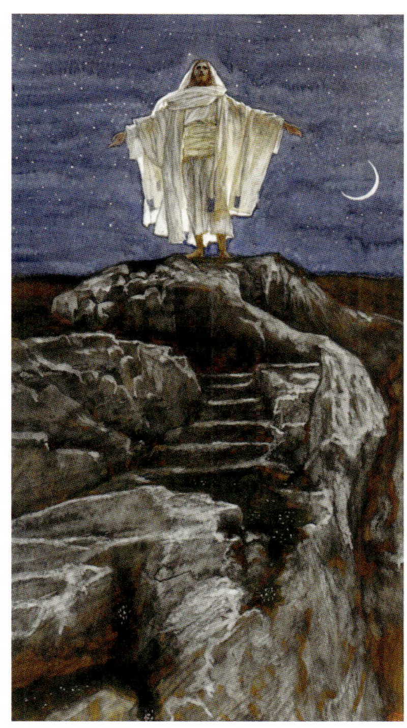

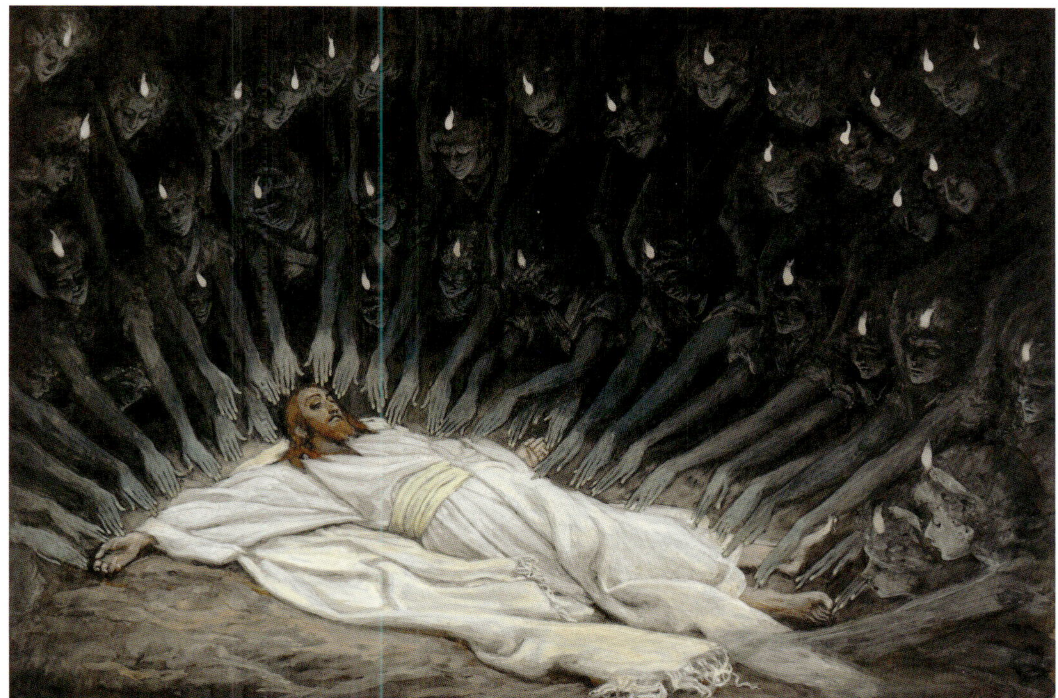

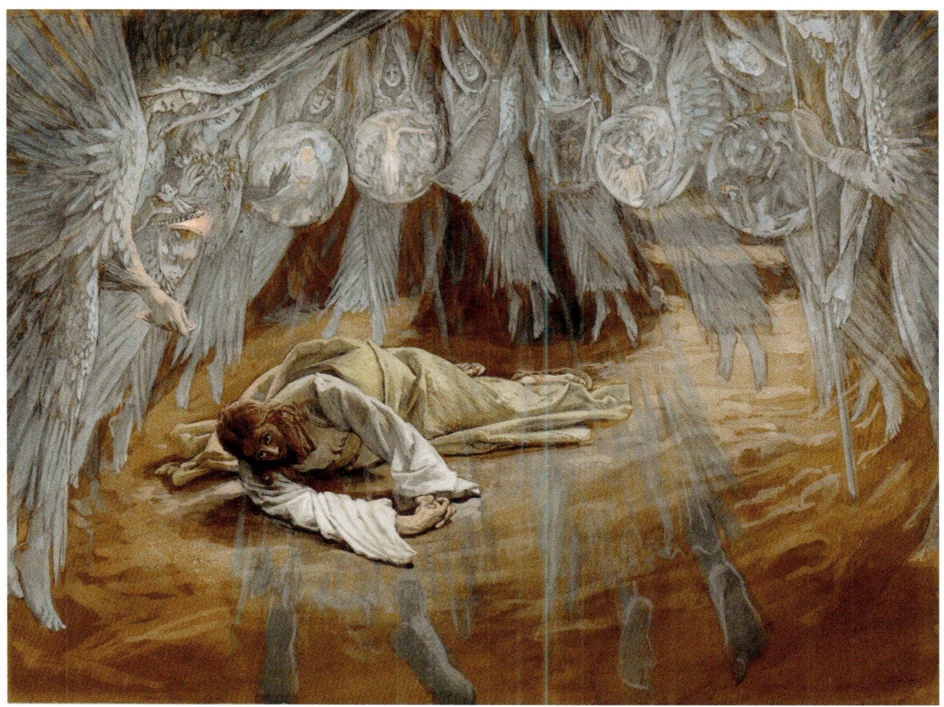

147

Jesus Going Up into a Mountain to Pray, ca. 1886–1894

Opaque watercolor over graphite on gray wove paper, 11⅜ × 6¼ in. (28.9 × 15.9 cm)
Brooklyn Museum, Purchased by public subscription, 00.159.137

148

Jesus Ministered to by Angels, ca. 1886–1894

Opaque watercolor over graphite on gray wove paper, 6¾ × 9¾ in. (17 × 24.8 cm)
Brooklyn Museum, Purchased by public subscription, 00.159.54

149

The Agony in the Garden, ca. 1886–1894

Opaque watercolor over graphite on dark brown wove paper, 11 × 14½ in. (28.1 × 36.7 cm)
Brooklyn Museum, Purchased by public subscription, 00.159.231

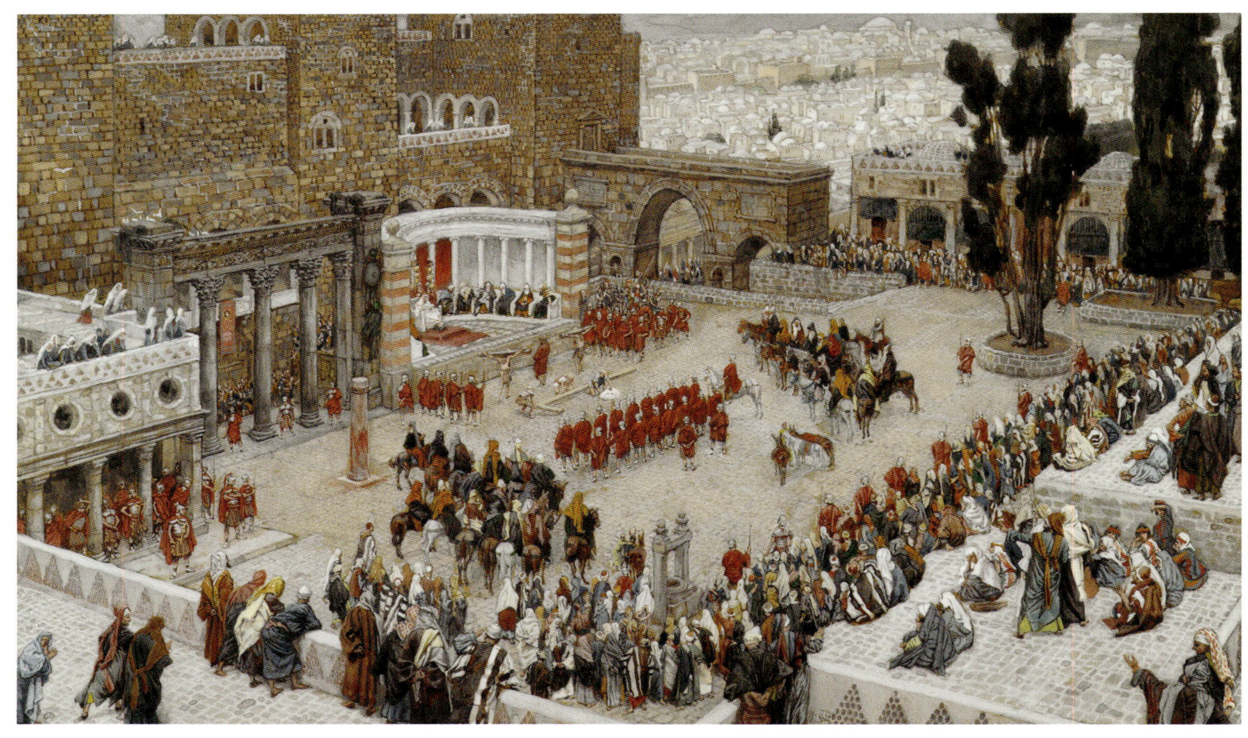

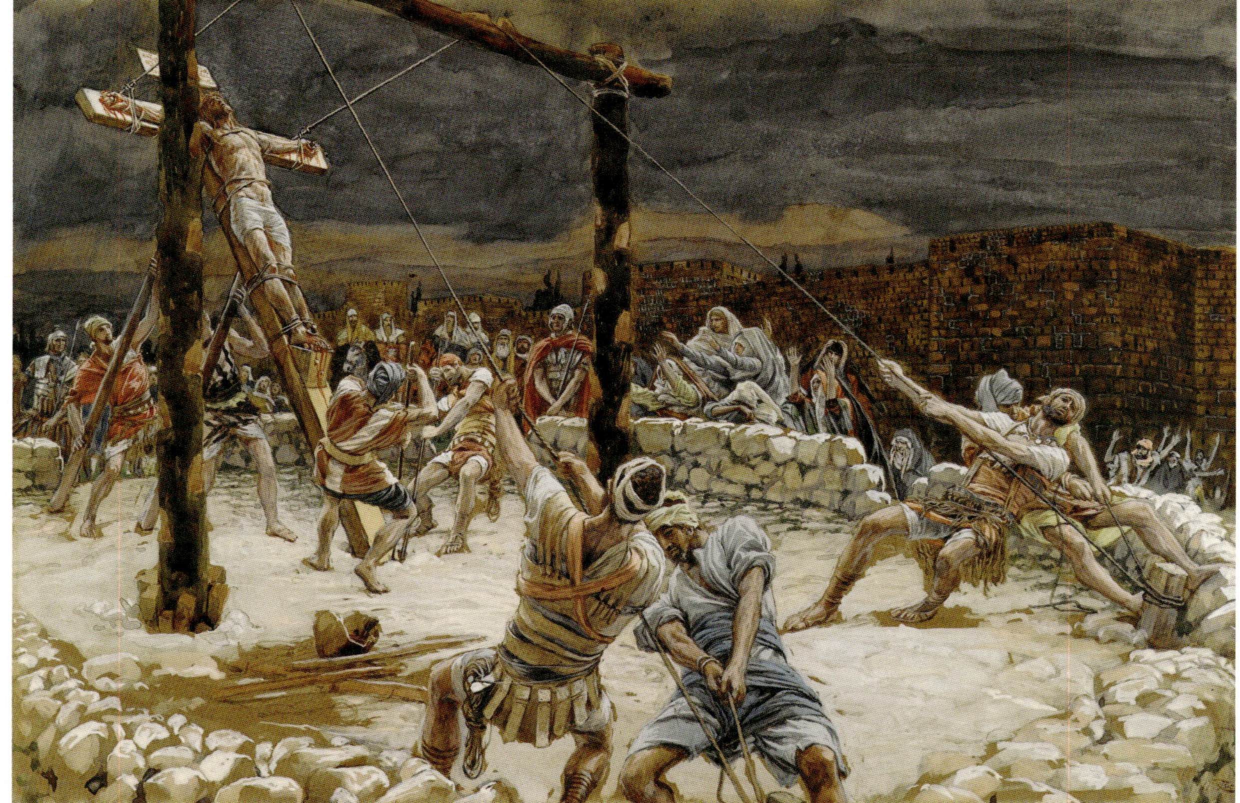

150

Bird's-Eye View of the Forum, ca. 1886–1894

Opaque watercolor over graphite on gray wove paper, 6⅞ × 11⅝ in. (17.6 × 29.4 cm)
Brooklyn Museum, Purchased by public subscription, 00.159.274

151

The Elevation of the Cross, ca. 1886–1894

Opaque watercolor over graphite on gray wove paper, 9⅞ × 14⅝ in. (25.2 × 37 cm)
Brooklyn Museum, Purchased by public subscription, 00.159.294

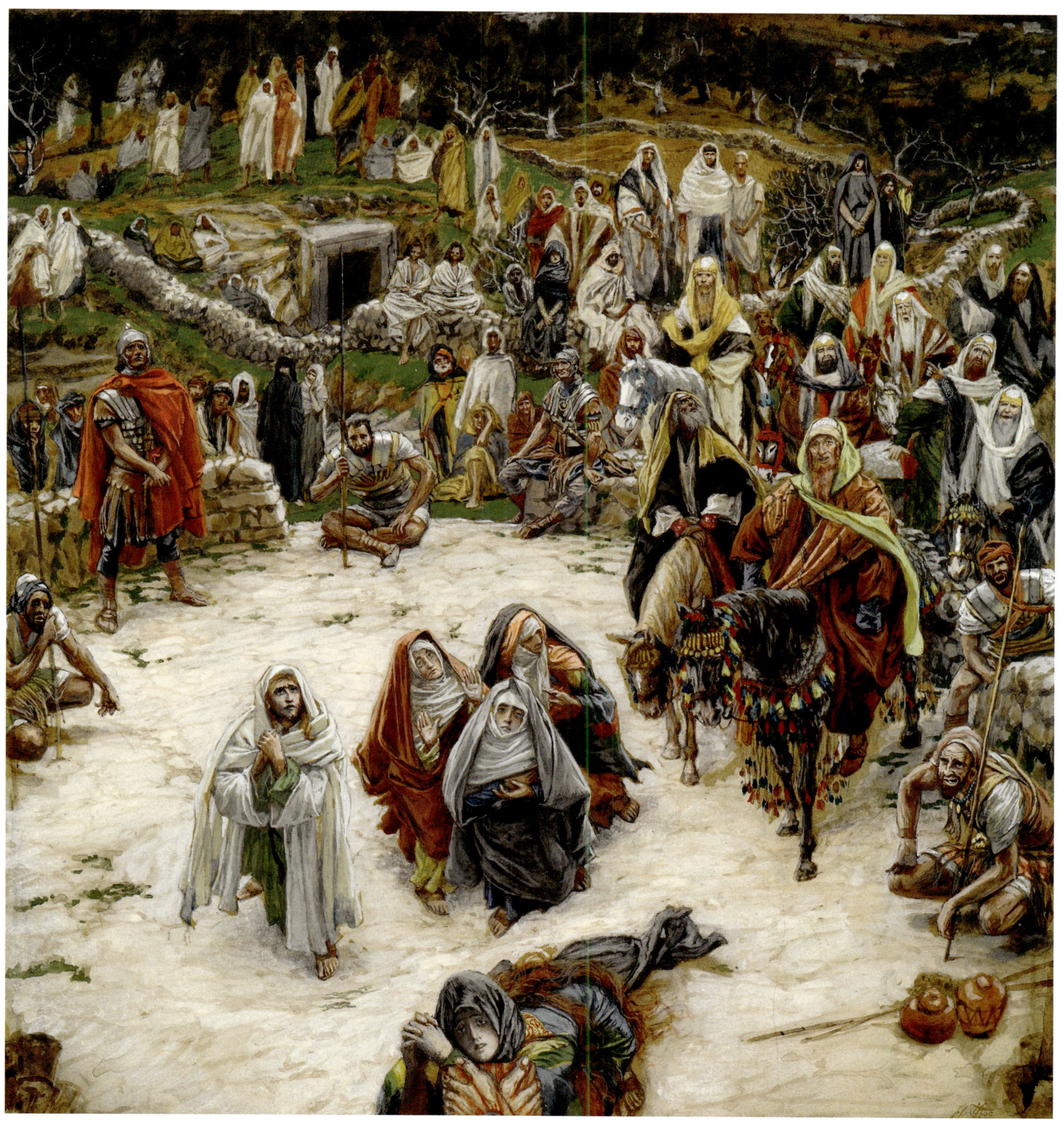

152

What Our Saviour Saw from the Cross, ca. 1886–1894

Opaque watercolor over graphite on gray-green wove paper, $9\frac{3}{4} \times 9$ in. (24.8 × 23 cm)
Brooklyn Museum, Purchased by public subscription, 00.159.299

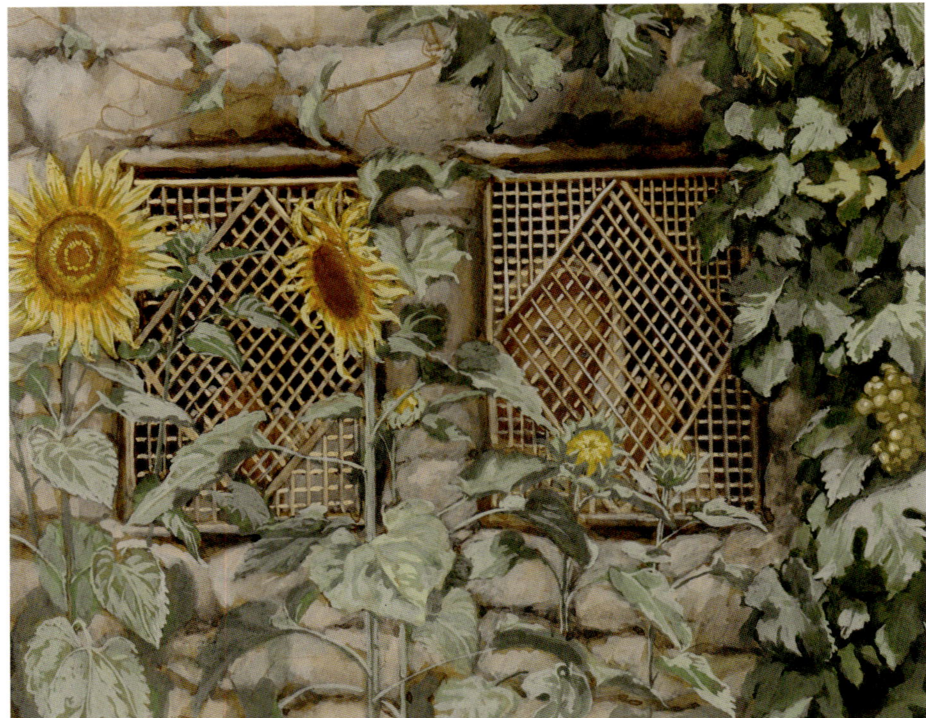

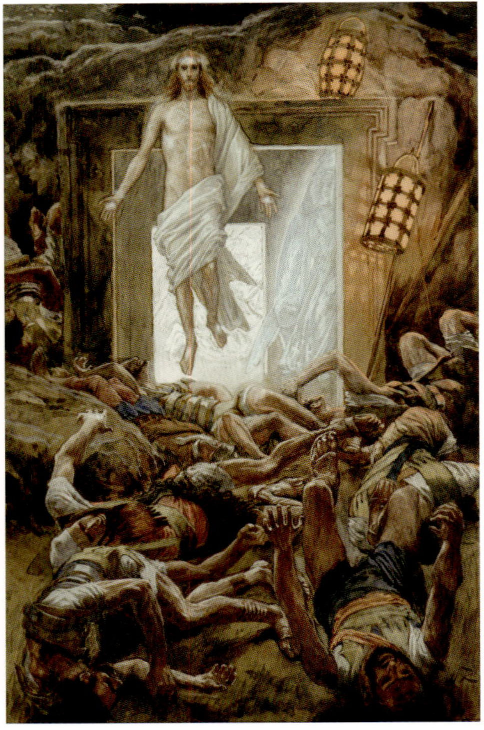

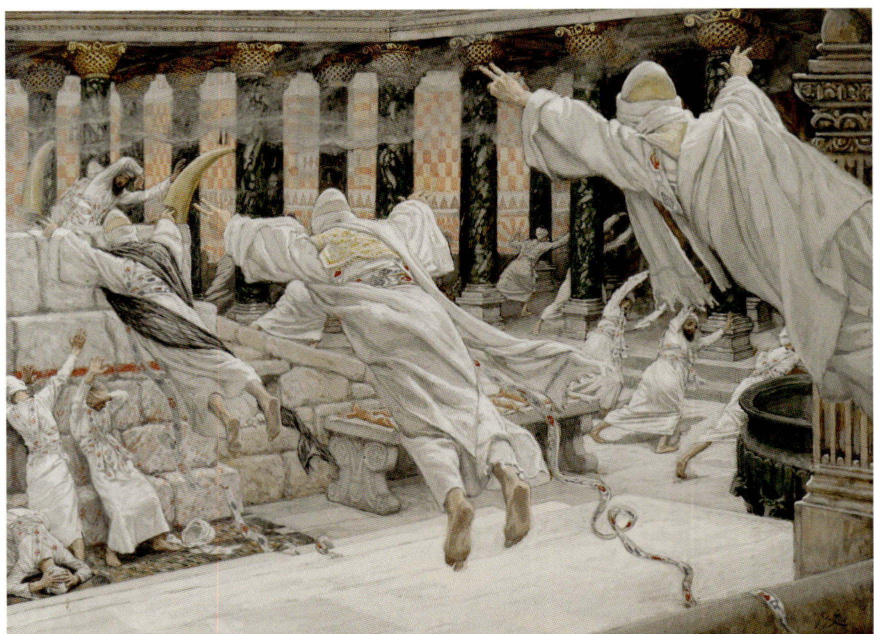

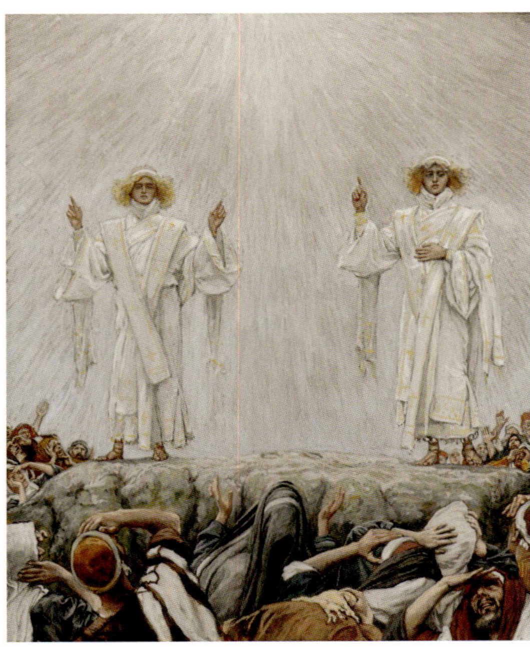

153–156 (clockwise from top left)

Jesus Looking through a Lattice, The Resurrection, The Ascension As Seen from Below, The Dead Appear in the Temple, ca. 1886–1894

Opaque watercolor over graphite on gray wove paper, 5⅝ × 6⅞ in. (14.4 × 17.6 cm), 12¾ × 8¼ in. (32.5 × 21.1 cm), 7½ × 6⅛ in. (19.2 × 15.7 cm), 8⅜ × 11⅛ in. (21.4 × 28.4 cm)
Brooklyn Museum, Purchased by public subscription, 00.159.11, 00.159.328, 00.159.349, 00.159.311

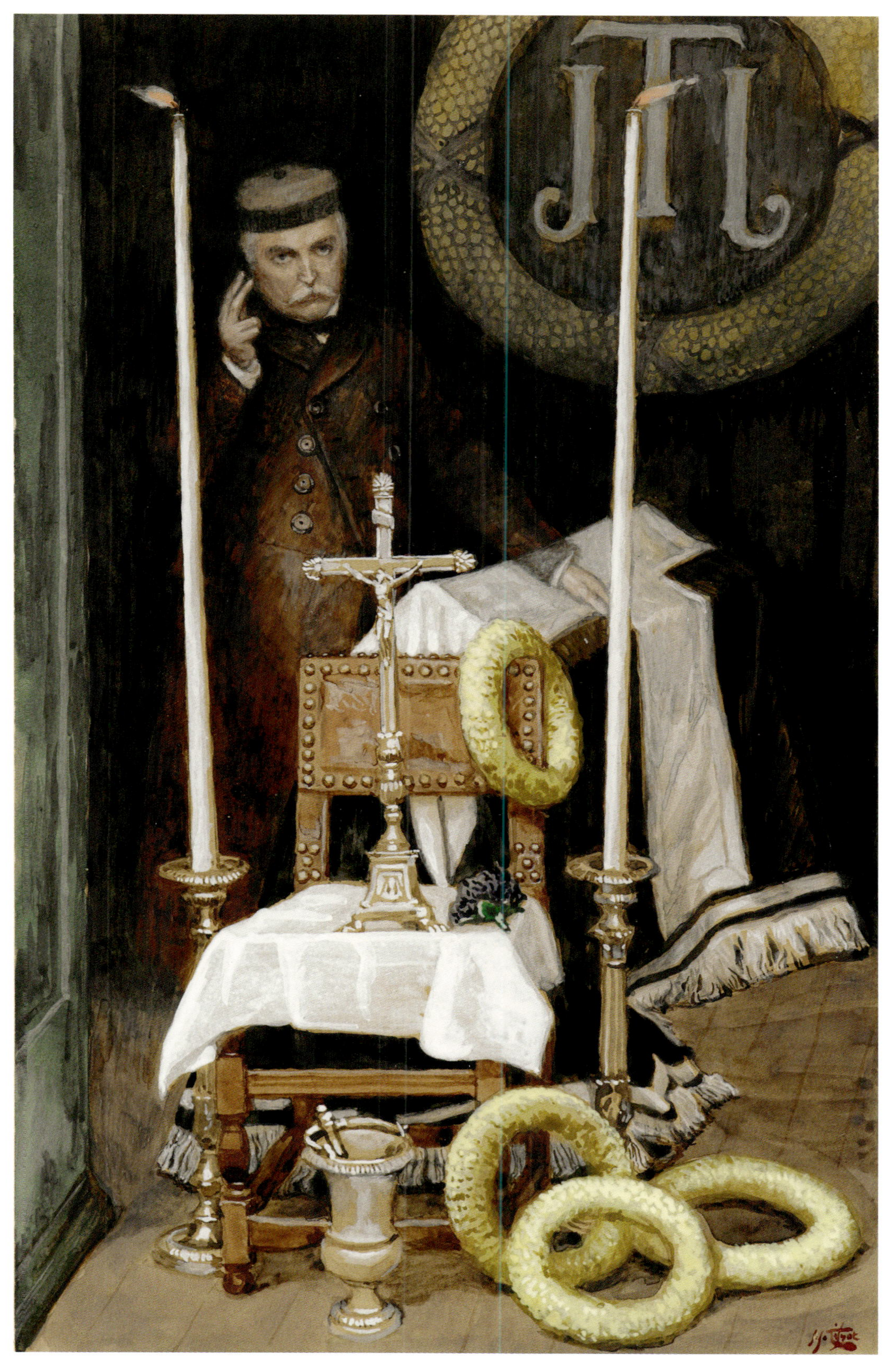

157

Portrait of the Pilgrim, ca. 1886–1894

also known as Self-Portrait

Opaque watercolor over graphite on gray wove paper, 9 × 5⅝ in. (23 × 14.3 cm)

Brooklyn Museum, Gift of Thomas E. Kirby, 06.39

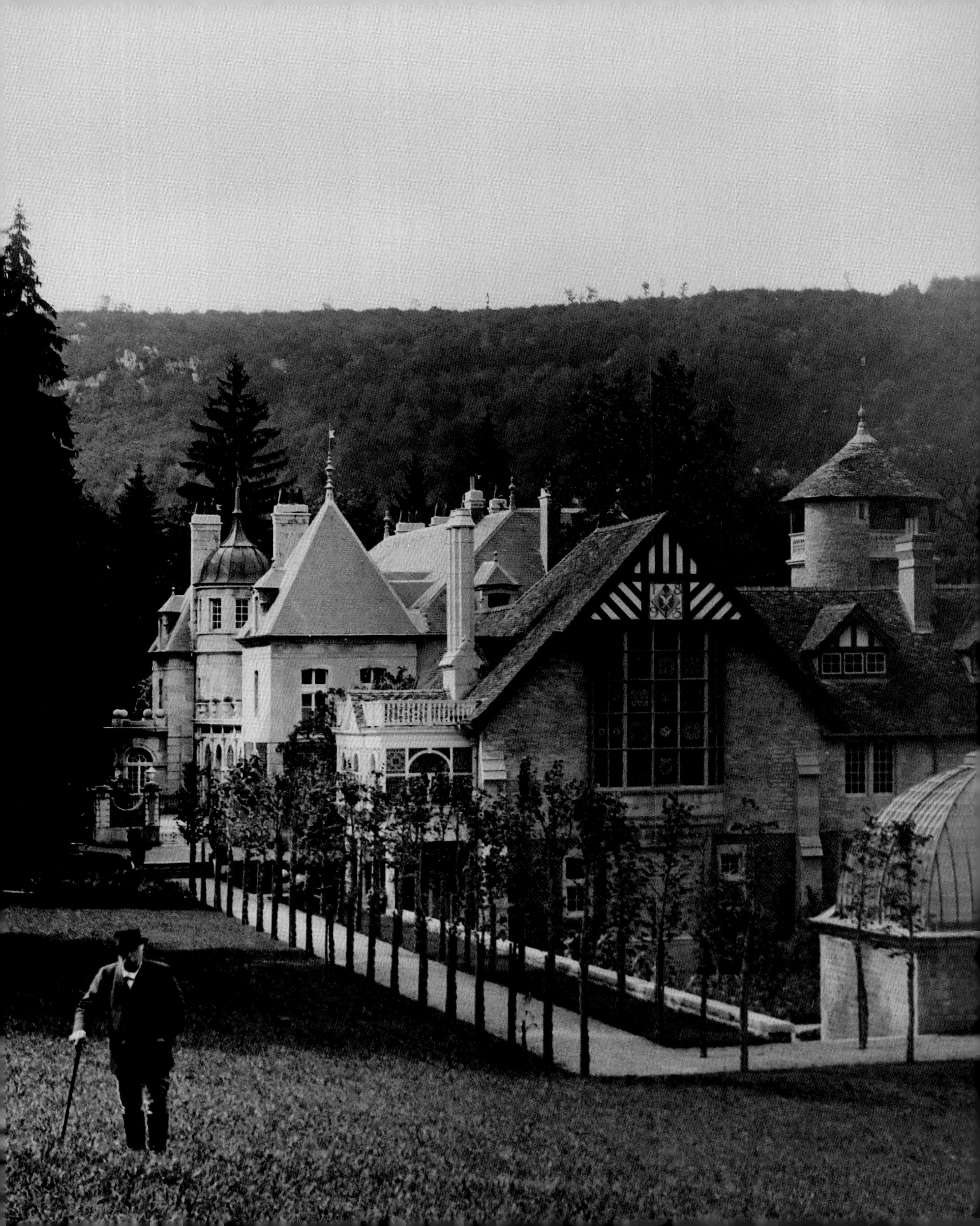

APPENDICES

"ALL ARE CLEVER, SEVERAL ARE HIDEOUS": TISSOT AND HIS PRINTS IN LONDON

DONATO ESPOSITO

Tissot's career as a printmaker was forged in parallel with his career as a painter, and there was much crossover. He never exhibited any of the promising etchings made in Paris during his first period of printmaking, 1860–1861. However, after moving to London from Paris in 1871, he resumed etching in 1875 and began to routinely submit prints for the first time to a variety of exhibitions. The rise of art criticism in Great Britain during the nineteenth century, which grew to encompass detailed reviews of print exhibitions, allows for a vivid reconstruction of the contemporary reception of Tissot's etchings.

Making prints provided Tissot the opportunity to reach audiences in several cities simultaneously. He must have felt confident enough with his new etchings, for in 1876, he chose to display a selection of them on both sides of the English Channel. This move signaled his public arrival into printmaking circles and capitalized on the burgeoning public interest in drypoint and etching. These two related print techniques, produced by scoring lines onto a copper plate with a sharp point, had long been popular with artists, since they require comparatively little technical skill or training. Drypoint is produced by directly scoring a metal plate, which is then inked for printing. For the etching process, the plate is covered with an acid-resistant ground before being scored and then dipped in an acid bath to accentuate the lines and to add variety and texture. The two mediums—often used in combination—date back to the sixteenth century, but they had lately fallen into abeyance. Tissot played a part in their revival in the second half of the nineteenth century.

Tissot's auspicious debut into printmaking exhibitions in 1876 heralded growing column inches and praise for his etchings in London and Paris. To the Royal Academy in London, he sent two recently completed works, his most technically complex to date: *Quarrelling* (1876; Wentworth 18) and *The Thames* (1876; Wentworth 20). Both prints demonstrate a skillful combination of drypoint and etching that captures the varied textures and complex physical details of their subjects' outdoor settings, even in such a restrictively monochromatic medium. In *Quarrelling*, which portrays an arguing couple, Tissot seems to have particularly delighted in the detailed drypoint of the woman's fur-trimmed coat. *The Thames* depicts a trio of figures on a moving boat; the backdrop shows the busy river life of London, illustrated through densely worked black areas set against unworked lighter areas. Billowing smoke, rippling water, and ships' masts are differentiated with subtle clarity. The carefully chosen titles of these prints complement their slightly ambiguous narratives, serving to either reveal (*Quarrelling*) or conceal (*The Thames*) the circumstances of the protagonists and the exact meaning of the scenarios. Many of Tissot's etchings were takes on his own works, usually paintings, and were often made around the same time. The painting *The Thames* (pl. 61) was included in the Royal Academy exhibition at the same time as its etching. Aside from

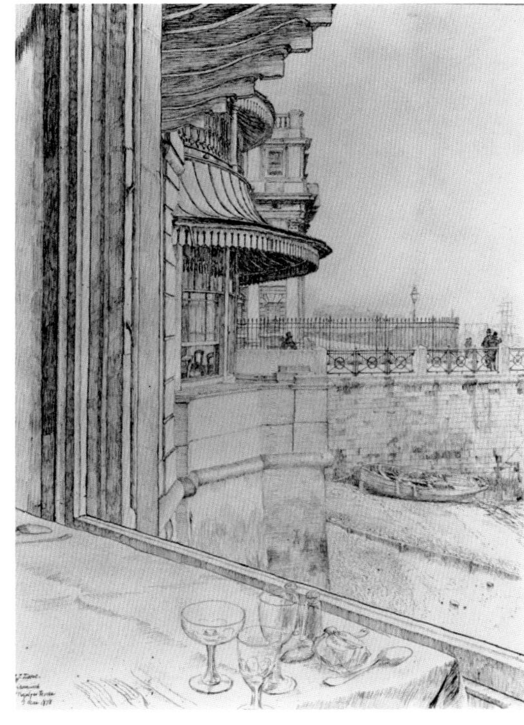

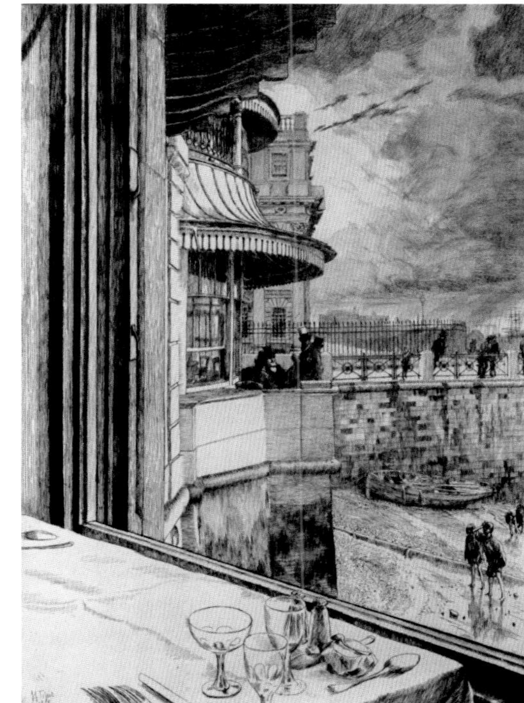

FIGURE 70
James Tissot, *From Trafalgar Tavern, Greenwich*, 1878. Black ink on off-white wove paper, 14 × 9⅞ in. (35.5 × 25 cm). Harvard Art Museums, Cambridge, Massachusetts, Bequest of Evert J. Wendell, 1919.565

FIGURE 71
James Tissot, *Trafalgar Tavern, Greenwich*, 1878. Etching with grayish-blue wash on cream wove paper, 21¼ × 14⅞ in. (54 × 37.8 cm). Harvard Art Museums, Cambridge, Massachusetts, Bequest of Evert J. Wendell to Harvard University, M934

the use of color, both renditions are virtually identical, allowing Tissot to showcase a successful composition using different media.

Tissot sent these same two prints to the Paris Salon in 1876. His other Parisian showing that year was of seven etchings, at an exhibition dedicated to black-and-white works on paper at the Galerie Durand-Ruel.[1] This commercial showing in Paris was briefly noted in the British press, including in the *Illustrated London News*.[2] Tissot also sent three prints to a relatively new venture at the London-based Dudley Gallery, which would become the primary venue for his prints until his return to Paris, in 1882. The Dudley Gallery was an artist-led institution, formed in 1865, that specialized in small paintings and watercolors. It was housed in the Egyptian Hall on Piccadilly, diagonally opposite the Royal Academy. In 1872, the gallery had added a new offering to its roster of exhibitions, *Exhibition of Works of Art in Black and White*, which focused on monochrome works on paper.[3] Tissot showed three etchings at the fourth of these exhibitions—there was no exhibition in 1873—which opened on June 12, 1876: *By the Window* (1875; Wentworth 9), *Souvenir de 1870* (two prints in one frame: *Bastien Pradel* [1875; Wentworth 15] and *Sylvain Perier* [1875; Wentworth 16]), and *Spring Morning* (1875; Wentworth 13). At 10 pounds and 10 shillings, *Spring Morning* was the second most expensive print in the exhibition, which featured about fifty artists.

Critics reviewing Tissot's submissions were divided. A reviewer from *The Builder* regarded *By the Window* as "one of the cleverest and most original things in the room," executed in a "very free sketchy style," yet wondered how "the artist who can do this can so often content himself with mere commonplace figures."[4] By contrast, that same critic scoffed at the "odious girl" who directly gazed at the viewer in *Spring Morning*.[5] *The Athenaeum* considered *Spring Morning* "intensely vulgar," an adjective that dogged the critical reception of Tissot's unfolding British career.[6] The Pre-Raphaelite critic William Michael Rossetti was more measured in his response, conceding that the etching was "unreasonably black and blurred, yet done with a cunning hand."[7]

Despite the criticism, in 1877, Tissot exhibited three more prints at the Dudley Gallery: *Portrait of Miss L…* or *A Door Must Be Either Open or Shut* (1876; Wentworth 23), *Portrait of Mrs. N…* (1876; Wentworth 26), and *The Widower* (1877; Wentworth 28). *Portrait of Mrs. N…*—a depiction of the artist's companion, Kathleen Newton—is among the most elaborate of Tissot's prints, characterized by densely worked areas rendered with tremendous precision using the etching needle, seen in the fur-lined cloak and feathered hat. The critic for *The Graphic* was not impressed:

> M. Tissot's powers as an etcher, though distinctly shown in the reproduction of his own picture of *The Widower*, in which there is a great deal of very dexterous dry point, can hardly be said to be adequately represented by this plate and the portrait of Madame N— nestling in her furs.[8]

The Widower, a reworking of an 1876 painting of the same name,[9] was admired by *The Times* for its technical qualities; the critic considered it a "very powerful etching . . . noticeable [too] for the power of its dry point."[10] The other etching shown at the Dudley in 1877, *Portrait of Miss L…*, was a reworking of a painting simultaneously exhibited only a short distance away, at the Grosvenor Gallery, as *Summer* (pl. 58). This stumped the critic for *The Athenaeum*, who did not know that the painting was on view at that time elsewhere in London: "To M. Tissot's *Portrait of Miss L—* (507) we turned with some curiosity, in search of an original of one of the damsels he so frequently paints; we found nothing of the sort, but a capital study."[11]

The Dudley Gallery's *Black and White* exhibitions were eagerly reviewed in the wider press outside of London. In 1878, at the sixth of these exhibitions, Tissot contributed four more etchings: *An Encampment—Siege of Paris—Parc d'Issy* (pl. 20); *How Happy Could I Be with Either* (1877; Wentworth 30); *My Garden at Saint John's Wood* (fig. 49), exhibited as

FIGURE 72
James Tissot, *Emigrants*, 1880. Etching and drypoint, trial proof, 13¾ × 6¼ in. (34.9 × 15.9 cm). Museum of Fine Arts, Boston, Frederick Keppel Memorial Bequest, M23433

FIGURE 73
James Tissot, *Emigrants*, 1880. Etching and drypoint, trial proof, 13¾ × 6¼ in. (34.9 × 15.9 cm). Museum of Fine Arts, Boston, Frederick Keppel Memorial Bequest, M23434

FIGURE 74
James Tissot, *Emigrants*, 1880. Etching and drypoint, trial proof, 13¾ × 6¼ in. (34.9 × 15.9 cm). Museum of Fine Arts, Boston, Frederick Keppel Memorial Bequest, M23435

FIGURE 75
James Tissot, *Emigrants*, 1880. Etching and drypoint, trial proof, 13¾ × 6¼ in. (34.9 × 15.9 cm). Museum of Fine Arts, Boston, Frederick Keppel Memorial Bequest, M23436

FIGURE 76
James Tissot, *Emigrants*, 1880. Etching and drypoint, 15¼ × 7⅝ in. (38.8 × 19.4 cm). Art Gallery of New South Wales, Sydney, 3420

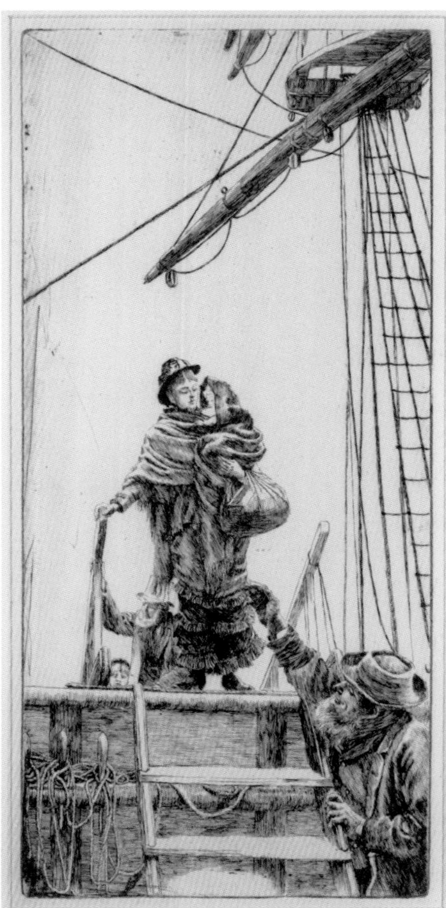

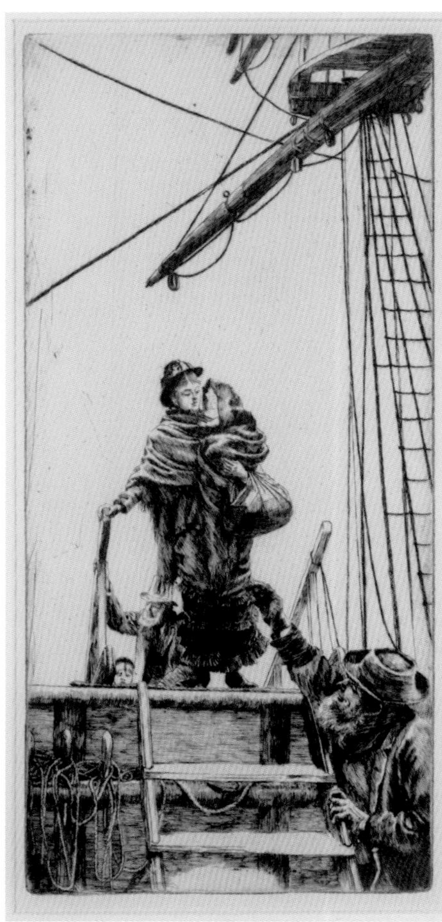

A Colonnade; and *The Organ Grinder* (1878; Wentworth 38). Of *How Happy Could I Be with Either*—a reworking of the painting *Portsmouth Dockyard* (ca. 1877; Tate, London), which Tissot had shown the year before at the Grosvenor Gallery—a reviewer for Edinburgh's *The Scotsman* said, "M. Tissot sends a skillful but rather vulgar etching."[12] At the same Dudley Gallery exhibition, Tissot also showed a pen-and-ink drawing, *From Trafalgar Tavern, Greenwich* (fig. 70), which depicted the window view from a dining table at a riverside London tavern.[13] The drawing was priced at 27 pounds and 6 shillings.

The following year, to the same venue, he sent an etching made after this intricate drawing, titled *Trafalgar Tavern, Greenwich* (1878; Wentworth 36), which at 5 pounds and 5 shillings was priced more reasonably than the drawing (fig. 71). At comparable dimensions and composed from the same perspective, the etching hews closely to its related drawing, but one is a subtle translation of the other. For the etching, Tissot added children playing on the shore, and a dramatic cloudy sky. Printmaking provided a means for adapting and evolving compositions. Showing both renditions in successive exhibitions at the same gallery helped demonstrate the artist's technical prowess and thought process. *The Athenaeum* enthused over the "remarkable piece of draughtsmanship, the foreshortening of the old balcony being excellent."[14]

In addition to *Trafalgar Tavern, Greenwich*, in 1879, Tissot also sent the Dudley Gallery *Croquet* (1878; Wentworth 37), *October* (1878; Wentworth 33), *The Portico of the National Gallery, London* (1878; Wentworth 40), and *Summer* (1878; Wentworth 43). To the Grosvenor Gallery he contributed *My Garden at Saint John's Wood* (as *A Garden*); *The Portico of the National Gallery, London*; *Summer*; and *Trafalgar Tavern, Greenwich*. Thus, Tissot had three etchings—*The Portico of the National Gallery, London*; *Summer*; and *Trafalgar Tavern, Greenwich*—simultaneously at two venues in London, where he could appeal to two contrasting audiences: the lofty New Bond Street clientele of the Grosvenor, and the humbler, more diverse crowd that gathered at the Dudley Gallery.

In 1880, one of Tissot's submissions to the Dudley Gallery, *Emigrants* (1880; Wentworth 45), received unanimous praise. The print, which shows a woman boarding a ship with her infant, was one of the artist's rare forays into pressing social issues. *The Athenaeum* contended that the Frenchman handled with "rare good fortune the intricacies of the rigging of many ships seen against the sky, and, although with needless excess of blackness, the solidity and force of the figure."[15] The dense web of etched lines that make up the rigging behind the central figure of the woman was a calculated success on the part of Tissot. To complete the elaborate print, he worked up the nonfigurative elements in successive stages, or states, each one printed after lines had been added to the metal plate (figs. 72–76). Tissot carefully checked the progress of these additions by pulling impressions of the print as he worked, producing a series of proofs—never intended for public viewing—that ensured the process went according to plan. Though Tissot must have produced such proofs for most of his prints, the series showing the successive states of *Emigrants* is one of the

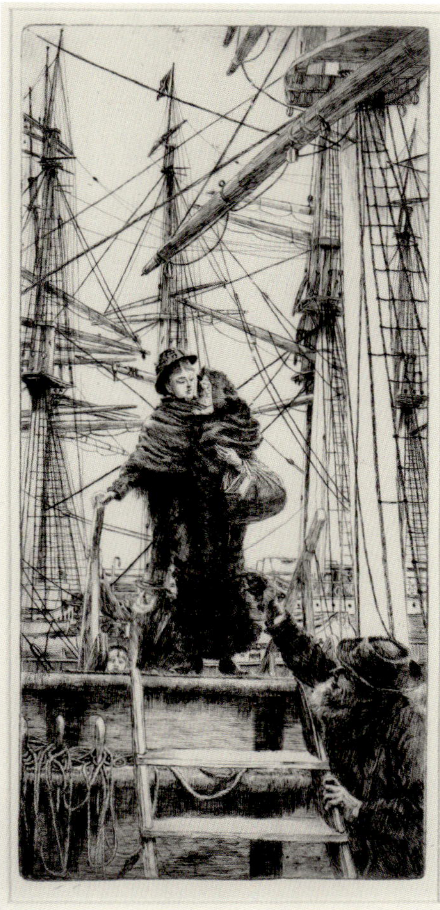

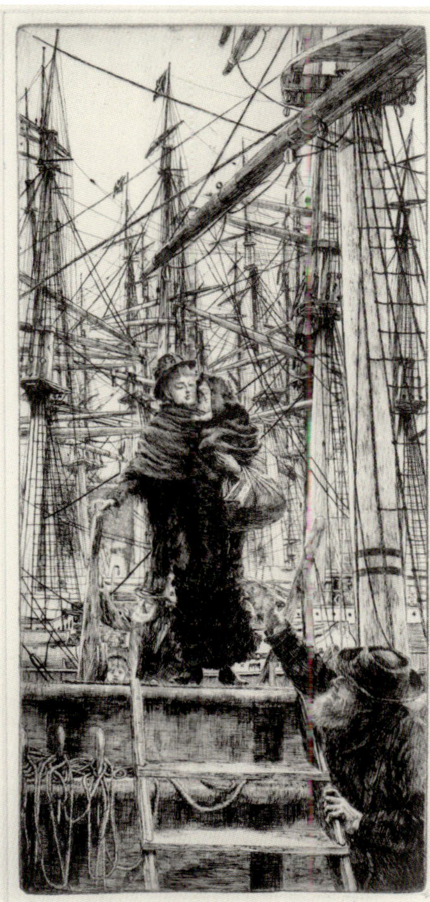

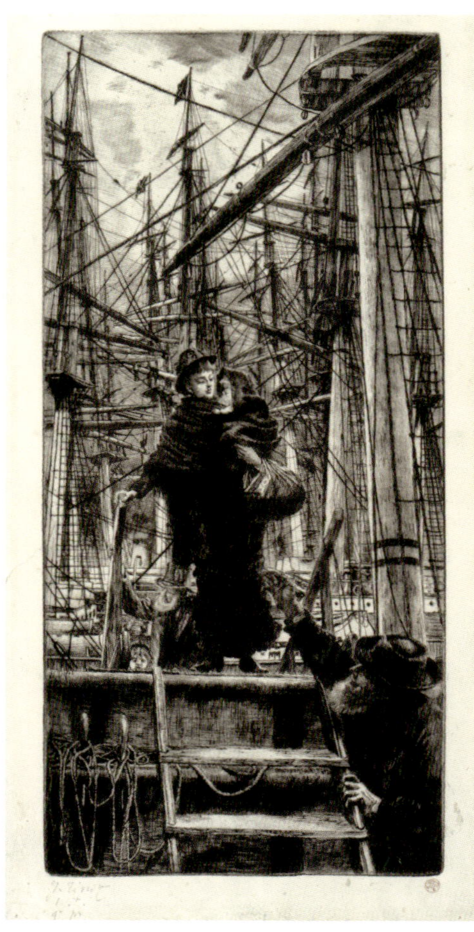

few surviving examples. The *Daily News* praised the final work as a "good drawing of rigging and shipping, and a clever arrangement of light and shade."[16] Indeed, some reviewers thought the translation of the painting of the same name into black and white was "perhaps, even better than the picture."[17] Tissot also chose, appropriately, to send *Emigrants* to the port city of Glasgow, where there, too, in the inaugural *Black and White* exhibition at the Glasgow Institute of the Fine Arts in 1880, it generated positive remarks in the contemporary press. The critic of the *Glasgow Herald* remarked, "*Emigrants* (864) is a network of masts and rigging by J. Tissot, whose artistic faculty is manifest in the lines through which he has carried the details of the vessels. This etching has great artistic merits."[18]

Tissot's other submissions in London that same year were not passed over. *The Hammock* (fig. 77), also shown at the Dudley, was a "spirited etching . . . very dainty and delicate," contended the *Morning Post*.[19] Elsewhere, at the Fine Art Society on New Bond Street, Tissot featured in a commercial group show and drew favorable comparisons to the seventeenth-century Bohemian Wenceslaus Hollar, whose brilliant etchings had long been celebrated:

> M. Tissot has some wonderfully clever transcripts of his own works, in which many of their objectionable qualities have evaporated. The rendering of the textures of fur and woollen is almost worthy of old Hollar himself, who seems to have afforded the text M. Tissot has striven to follow.[20]

It seemed several reviewers even preferred Tissot's etched translations over his colorful paintings. The monochromatic prints appeased the sometimes critical distaste for color, which could be interpreted as garish, and proved attractive to wider tastes. In fact, Dowdeswell & Dowdeswells, an influential gallery in London, included Tissot in a list incorporating the "finest stock of modern etchings in London" (fig. 78).[21]

The income Tissot generated from print sales increased from 1876 onward. The years 1880 and 1881 were his most lucrative, with sales amounting to more than 1,000 pounds each year.[22] However, the rise of competition from the Society of Painter-Etchers and Engravers (later the Royal Society of Painter-Etchers and Engravers), which Tissot helped found in 1880, appears to have negatively impacted the *Black and White* shows at the Dudley Gallery.[23] The ninth of these, in 1881 (fig. 79), was the last, and to this final showing Tissot sent five of his recent etchings: *A Children's Garden Party* (1880; Wentworth 49), *His First Breeches* (1880; Wentworth 51), *On the Grass* (1880; Wentworth 50), *Reverie* (as *Deep in Thought*) (1881; Wentworth 52), and *A Winter Walk* (pl. 77). Tissot took up the new opportunity to exhibit with the Society of Painter-Etchers and Engravers, which opened its first exhibition on April 4, 1881, at the Hanover Gallery in London. He included a previously exhibited etching, *The Portico of the National Gallery, London*, of which *The Standard* wrote:

> Mr. Tissot is a dashing painter, much of whose best labour is in etching . . . , [which demonstrates] a rare combination of elegance and realism. The scene is, our grey London, but somehow rightly beautified—the lines of its architecture delicately seen and skillfully made the most of.[24]

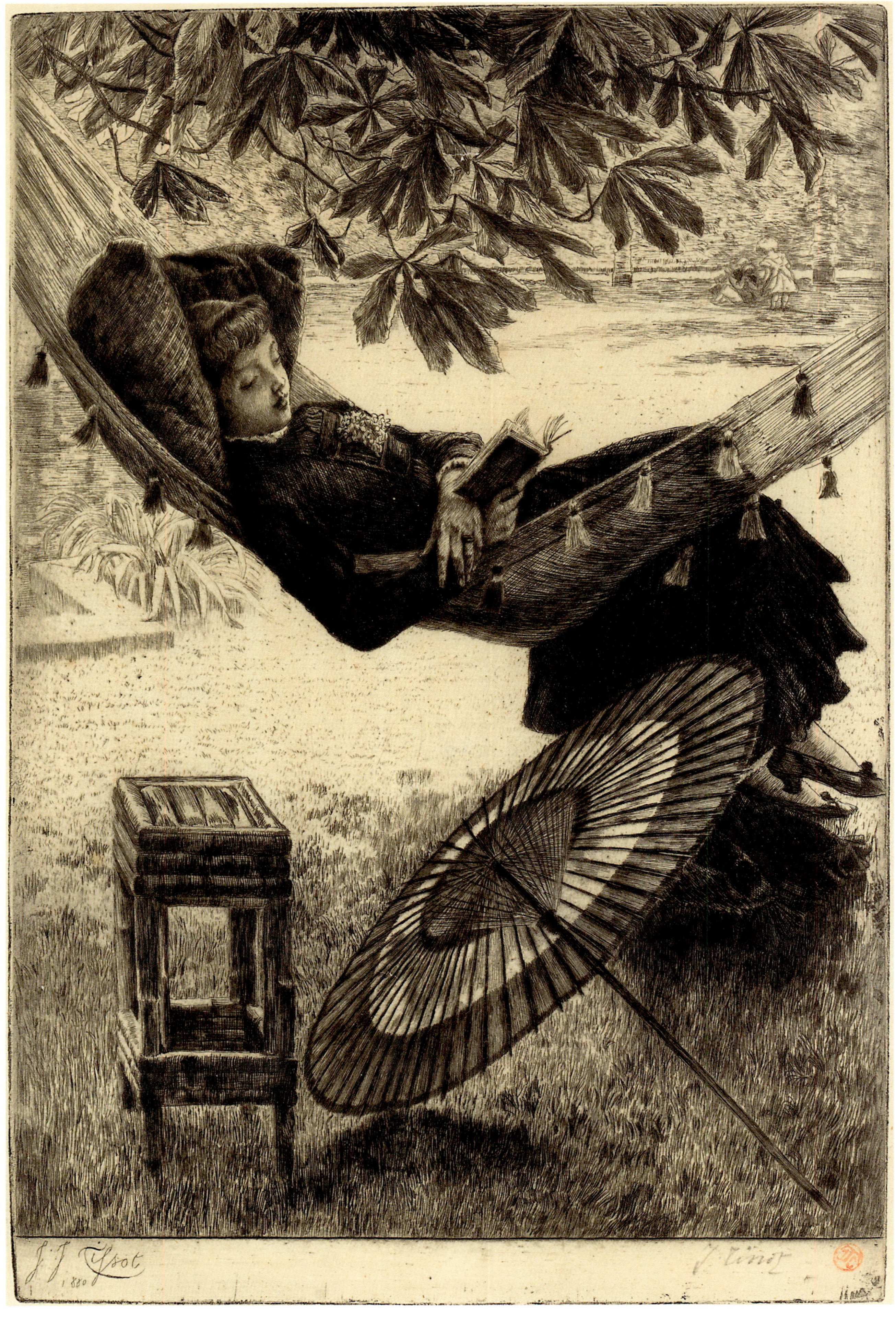

In 1882, Tissot was the subject of the solo exhibition *An Exhibition of Modern Art* at the Dudley Gallery. The show was composed of more than fifty etchings and a dozen paintings, amounting to a mini retrospective of his print work. Reviews were mixed, with one critic contending, "All are clever, several are hideous, most are not to our taste."[25] Tissot's etchings are "curiously unequal in execution; some are hairy, dirty, and muddled; others surprisingly bright and spirited," quipped another.[26] Nonetheless, the print of *Trafalgar Tavern, Greenwich*, drew praise from the *Morning Post* for its "accuracy of drawing and the texture of the stone wall abutting on the river."[27]

Following his permanent relocation to Paris, Tissot's etchings continued to be exhibited in London and throughout Britain, but his printmaking activity declined rapidly, and he exhibited this type of work less and less. Despite engaging with other new print techniques, such as mezzotint, pressing preoccupations took over his attention and time, not least his series of religious watercolors *The Life of Christ* (see Buron, this volume). This dramatic shift of his artistic attention left behind him a brief but fascinating and productive encounter with etching.

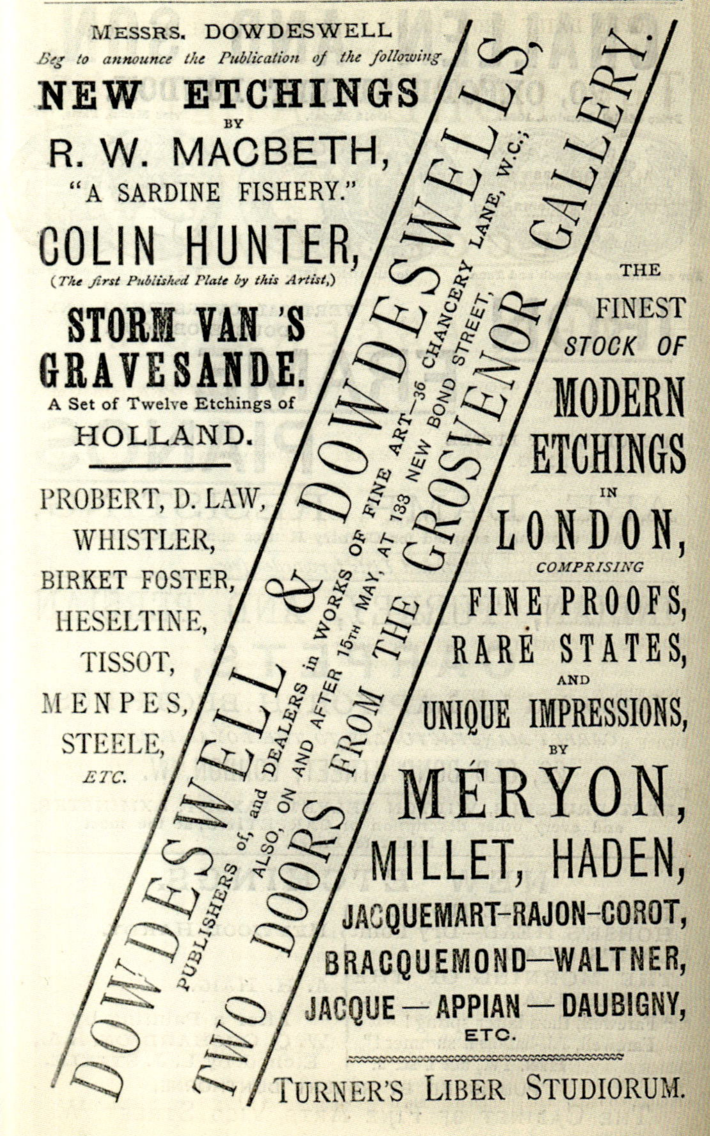

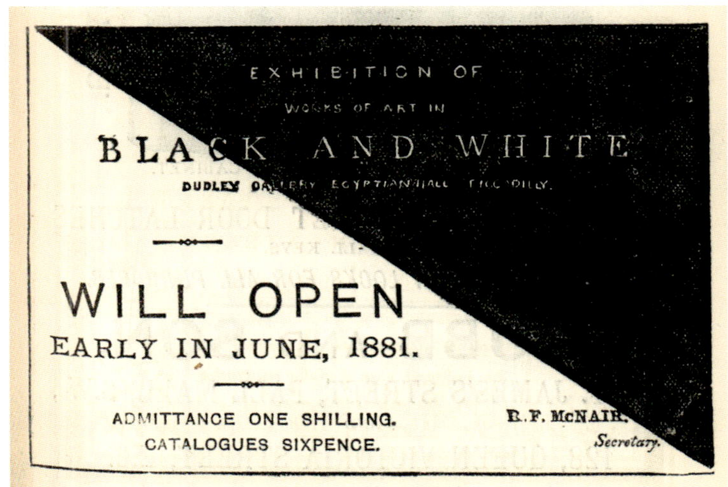

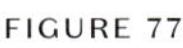

FIGURE 77
James Tissot, *The Hammock*, 1880. Etching and drypoint, 11 × 7¼ in. (27.8 x 18.4 cm). National Gallery of Art, Washington, DC, Ailsa Mellon Bruce Fund, 1972.26.2

FIGURE 78
Advertisement for Dowdeswell & Dowdeswells, 1880, from Henry Blackburn's *Grosvenor Notes, 1880*. Published by Chatto and Windus, London. Courtauld Institute of Art Library, London

FIGURE 79
Advertisement for Dudley Gallery, 1881, from Henry Blackburn's *Grosvenor Notes, 1881*. Published by Chatto and Windus, London. Courtauld Institute of Art Library, London

"ALWAYS IN SEARCH OF THE EXQUISITE IN ART": TISSOT'S CLOISONNÉ ENAMELS

KRYSTYNA MATYJASZKIEWICZ

Included in James Tissot's one-man exhibition at London's Dudley Gallery in May 1882 was a group of recently made pieces in cloisonné enamel, "hitherto regarded as an almost exclusively Japanese art," noted the *Leeds Mercury*, admiring the "patience and ingenuity" with which Tissot had so proficiently mastered the craft, little known in Europe. Of one work, titled *Fortune* (fig. 80), the newspaper said, "Mr. Tissot goes a step further, and shows his power as a modeler, as a bronze worker, and as an author of a work of modern art which, both for originality of design and boldness of execution, is perhaps unique."[1]

Tissot had a long-standing interest in Asian art, and a trendsetting personal collection of Chinese and Japanese art and artifacts, some of which he may have brought from Paris to London, where he moved in 1871, and others he acquired while living there over the next decade. Displays of Japanese cloisonné at the International Exhibitions in 1862, 1867, and 1878, had led to enthusiasm among art lovers in Britain, France, and the United States for owning such artifacts, and to a burgeoning export trade from Japan. At the 1878 Paris exhibition, craftspeople demonstrated the manufacture of cloisonné, and seeing new French-made pieces on view there may have inspired Tissot to try making his own.[2]

How and when Tissot learned the laborious craft is uncertain; no instruction manuals had been published yet, and he would have had to study pieces in his collection, and experiment through trial and error. He owned a large sixteenth-century Chinese gilt-bronze and cloisonné enamel jardinière, on which he based two of his own creations: *Jardinière with Square Panels—The Cave and the Pool* (fig. 81) and *An Oval Jardinière—Lake and Sea* (fig. 82).[3] For his jardinières, Tissot transformed the gilt-bronze lions of the Chinese piece's handles into dragon heads, which support kneeling women whose nude bodies are almost completely covered by their flowing long hair. He also made cloisonné teapots, faithfully copying the shape of Japanese nineteenth-century examples, like one bought at the 1867 Paris exhibition (where Tissot might also have acquired pieces) by what is now the Victoria and Albert Museum.[4] Similarly, his vases *en gaine* (figs. 83–84),[5] one of which includes scenes based on his own paintings (see pl. 50), replicate the shape of a cloisonné vase in his collection, seen in the background of *Young Women at a Screen* (1869–1870; location unknown).[6] Copies of the original forms were made by shaping and welding sheet copper to use as the base for cloisonné decoration.

To make his cloisonné pieces, Tissot fixed copper wire onto the copper base, creating compartments, or *cloisons*, which would hold different-colored enamels and keep the colors from melting into one another. Finely powdered glass was then mixed with metal oxides and water, or gum, to create a paste, which was applied thinly to the copper base. Firing in a furnace heated to about 1,472 degrees Fahrenheit caused the glass to "fuse," creating enamel. The color could vary, depending on the oxide used. Some

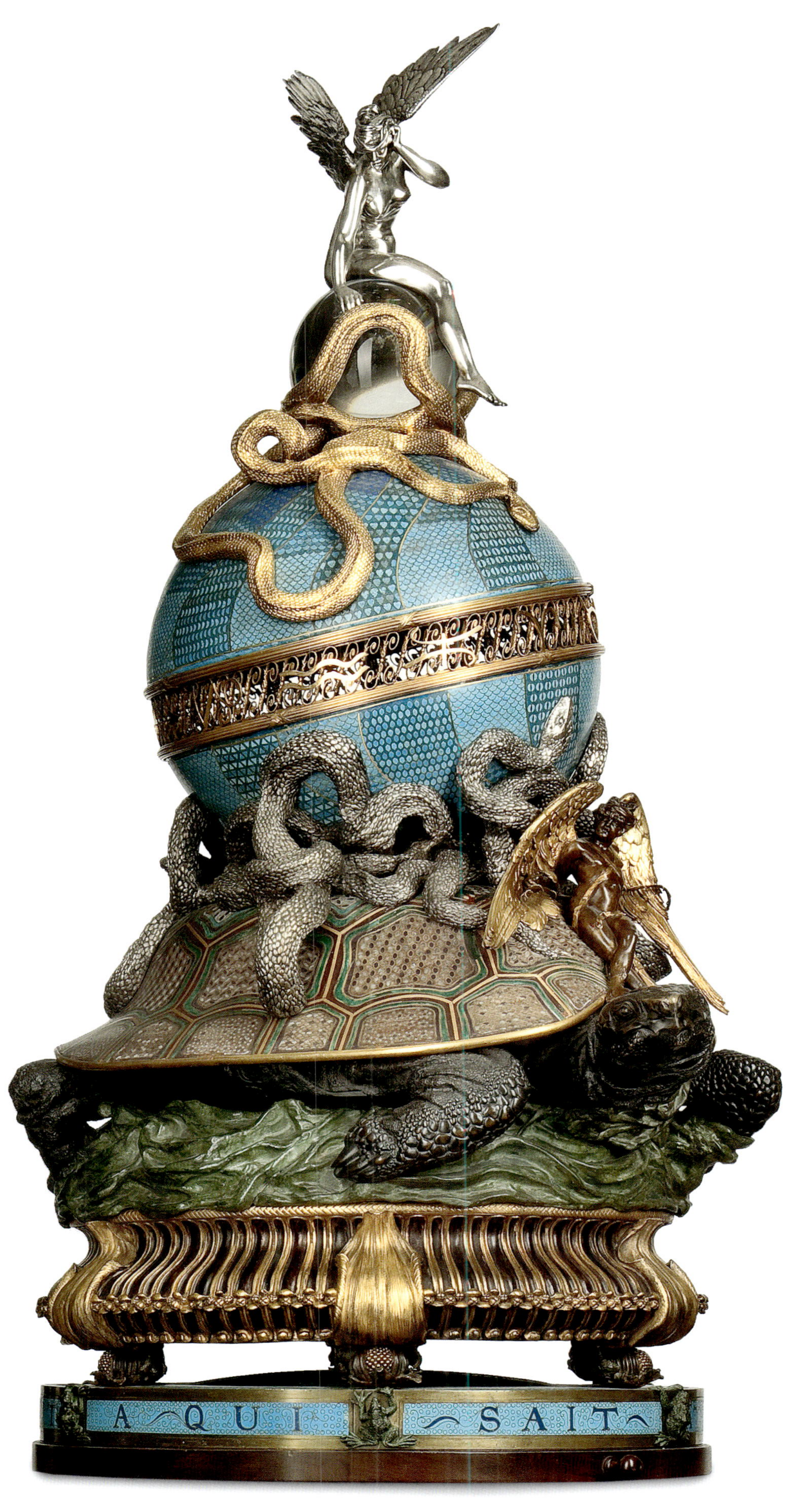
A QUI SAIT

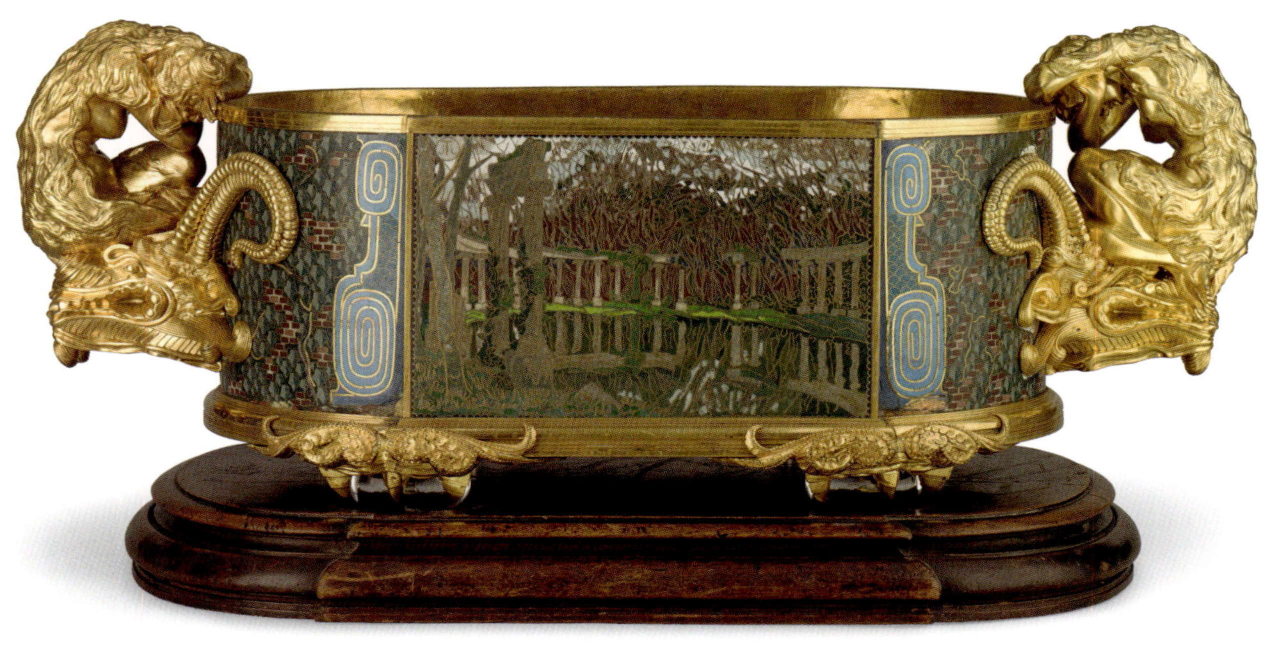

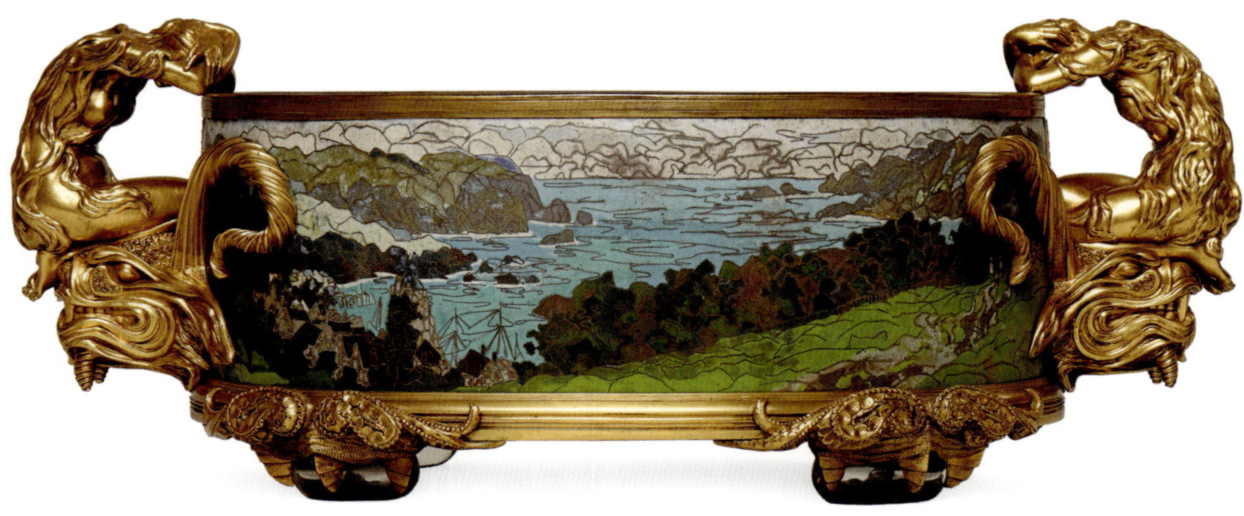

PREVIOUS PAGE, FIGURE 80
James Tissot, *Fortune*, ca. 1878–1882. Cloisonné enamel on copper, silvered bronze, gilt bronze, silver, and glass on walnut base, 50 × 25⅝ in. (127 × 65 cm). Musée des Arts Décoratifs, Paris, Gift of Albert Bichet, 1908, 14755

FIGURE 81
James Tissot, *Jardinière with Square Panels—The Cave and the Pool*, ca. 1880–1882. Cloisonné enamel on copper, mounted on gilt-bronze base with feet of rock crystal, 11 × 29⅛ in. (28 × 74 cm). Musée d'Orsay, Paris, RF MO OAO 2017 3

FIGURE 82
James Tissot, *An Oval Jardinière—Lake and Sea*, ca. 1880–1882. Cloisonné enamel on copper, mounted on gilt-bronze base with feet of rock crystal, 9½ × 24⅜ in. (24 × 62 cm). The Royal Pavilion, Art Gallery and Museums, Brighton, England, DA300613

colors were temperamental and would burn if subjected to excessive heat. Red and yellow were especially difficult to get right, and Tissot could be justifiably proud to announce in the Dudley Gallery exhibition catalogue his "trial-piece in the new sealing-wax red and turquoise-blue," decorated with his monogram (fig. 85).[7]

Fused enamel takes up less space than the original paste, leaving small gaps, so that more paste has to be added and the piece refired. Once the compartments are almost full of enamel, the piece must be filed and polished to a smooth surface. Any air bubbles leave tiny holes; close inspection reveals such pinholes in Tissot's enamel. They demonstrate that he followed the Chinese method, starting with an initial layer of white (or other stable color) enamel, followed by one, or more usually two, layers of color, each time with a separate firing.[8] The initial layer acts as a buffer for colors that change when fired directly on metal; it also makes some colors appear brighter, in the same way that oil colors on a white ground—a technique used by Tissot as well as the Impressionists and the Pre-Raphaelites—reflect more light and appear brighter.[9] Tissot was able to achieve particularly fine effects of color in his cloisonné, using his painter's eye to give dynamism through contrasting hues, just as he had enlivened his 1860s portraits with complementary touches of color (see pls. 21–22).

Cloisonné is a painstaking technique, but offers an opportunity for control—and creativity—at each stage. Tissot, notes Erika Speel, "mastered the art of cloisonné to an astonishing degree of excellence for one who apparently devoted only a limited number of years to this art."[10] Such manual labor, alongside painting and etching, may have been a welcome escape for Tissot from worry about his beloved Kathleen Newton's deteriorating health. Drawing designs onto the copper base, attaching the *cloisons*, enameling, and firing were things Tissot could do at home, sitting beside Newton, or in his garden studio. Most likely, he owned a small furnace. These were used by many craftsmen at this time, and were easily installed.[11] He probably employed help for grinding glass or quartz before paste mixing, and for the time-consuming work of filing down the enamel—done using a foot-operated lathe—as well as final surface polishing. Professional metalworkers likely made the copper bases, especially the complex orb and tortoiseshell forms of *Fortune*; the sculpture's gilt-bronze and patinated figures would have been cast and finished by specialist craftsmen, such as Hatfield's in London, or Maison Barbedienne in Paris.[12] Unlike many artists, Tissot was wealthy enough to pay for bronze casting without having a funded commission. The only documentary evidence discovered so far that gives insight into Tissot's bronze-sculpting techniques is his purchase in August 1881 of modeling wax, tools, and a stand from the London-based art supplier Charles Roberson & Co.[13] This discovery suggests that Tissot modeled at least some elements himself in wax, from which a founder made molds for casting in bronze.

Fortune developed themes from Tissot's planned series *The Triumph of Will*, of which only the first painting is known to have been completed (see pl. 99). Around the sculpture's base are the phrases "Tout vient à point à qui sait attendre" (Patience brings all things about) and, in various languages, "Wait and win."[14] The Dudley Gallery catalogue describes the winged goddess Fortune atop the sculpture as "seated at ease upon

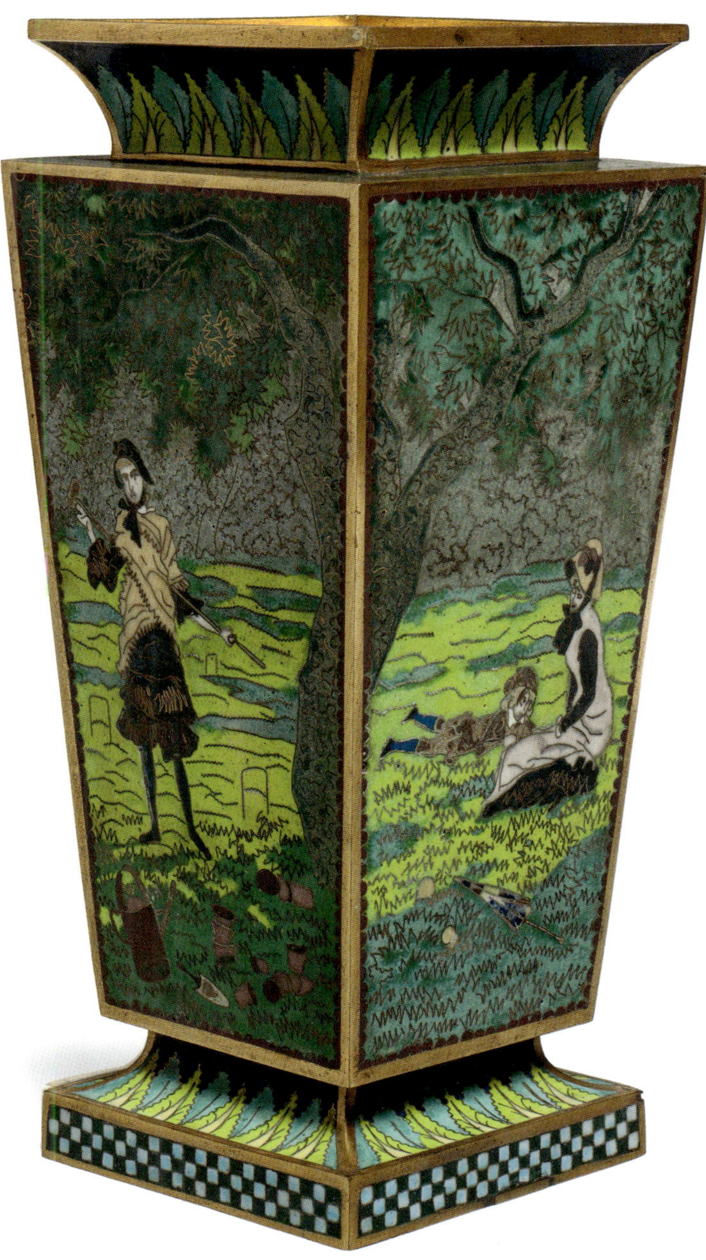

FIGURE 83
James Tissot, *Vase "en Gaine"—Children in a Garden*, ca. 1880–1882. Cloisonné enamel on copper, 9⅞ × 4 in. (25 × 10 cm). Musée des Arts Décoratifs, Paris, Purchased in 1903, 10645.A

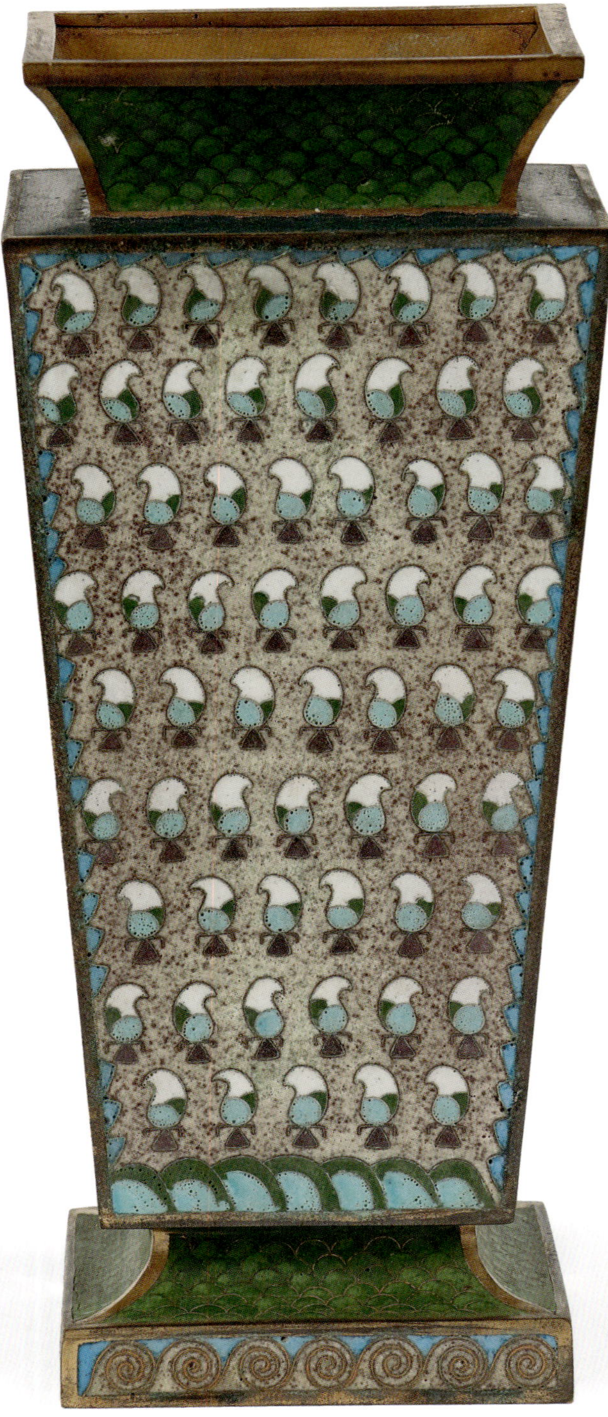

FIGURE 84
James Tissot, *Vase "en Gaine,"* ca. 1880–1882. Cloisonné enamel on copper, 9⅞ × 4¼ in. (25 × 10.7 cm). Musée des Arts Décoratifs, Paris, Purchased in 1903, 10645.B

FIGURE 85
James Tissot, plaque with artist's monogram, ca. 1880–1882. Cloisonné enamel on copper, 6¾ × 5⅜ × ½ in. (17.2 × 13.7 × 1.2 cm). Private collection

FIGURE 86
James Tissot, plaque, 1890s. Cloisonné enamel on copper, 6⅛ × 35⅛ (15.5 × 89.1 cm). Private collection

our globe." Around the large orb, symbols of the Zodiac represent Time flying by, and below, the figures of Love and Ambition cling to a large tortoise, which represents Patience.[15] Allegory is central to many works by Edward Burne-Jones, whom Tissot was considered to be emulating in *The Triumph of Will* (see Marshall, this volume). Having abandoned the allegorical paintings, Tissot was instead exploring similar themes through the three-dimensional form.

Fortune's seductively modeled nude figurines recall bronzes made by French contemporaries such as Antonin Mercié as well as earlier sculptors, in particular James Pradier.[16] This modeling style characterizes Britain's soon-to-emerge New Sculpture movement, which incorporated mythical subject matter and symbolism.[17] Alfred Gilbert's small bronze *Perseus Arming* (1882; Tate, London), exhibited at London's Grosvenor Gallery in 1882, heralded the New Sculpture movement. Gilbert had studied in Paris before moving to Rome in September 1878, and he, too, would have been familiar with the sculpture of Mercié. Tissot's cloisonné work also chimed with the general movement in France toward blurring the boundaries between fine and decorative art, most notably championed by the Central Union of Decorative Arts (L'union centrale des arts décoratifs), through which Tissot exhibited his cloisonné enamels in 1883.[18] Reviewing the display, Alfred de Lostalot said that the work "charmed everyone." Tissot, Lostalot said, was "always in search of the exquisite in art."[19]

According to the Dudley Gallery catalogue, Tissot intended to adapt *Fortune* into "a life size monument or fountain."[20] Had he pursued official sculpture commissions in Paris or collaborated with manufactories, as other artists did, his work might have taken a different direction. But Tissot's cloisonné enamels were not a commercial proposition. It is not certain they were for sale (prices of exhibited works were available on application and there is no indication whether this included enamels); as the pieces involved many hours of work, they could not be priced to compete with contemporary Japanese mass-produced cloisonné. Rather, their presence in Tissot's solo exhibitions served to demonstrate his remarkable versatility across media. Tissot was an artist who enjoyed a challenge, which work in cloisonné entailed.

Though his foray into the medium was brief, cloisonné seems to have held significant meaning for Tissot; he added personal touches to his enamel pieces not seen elsewhere in his work. Lawrence Alma-Tadema's daughter Anna recalled a trip to Paris with her parents and sister in the early 1890s during which they had visited Tissot, who showed them "an enormous *cloisonné* mantelpiece which he was constructing, decorated with Arabic verses and the names of his English friends, among which Alma-Tadema was moved to find his own."[21] A similar plaque—the monogram-emblazoned one Tissot so proudly touted in the Dudley Gallery catalogue—has matching firebrands and a turquoise background, and so was also intended for the mantelpiece. His largest known plaque is a panel in matching turquoise (fig. 86) bearing a Latin inscription, which strikes an intimate tone:

> So long as, by a flame, (heart) strings restore tired bodies with new vigour,
> With new strength and ardour they blaze, as friends are distant.[22]

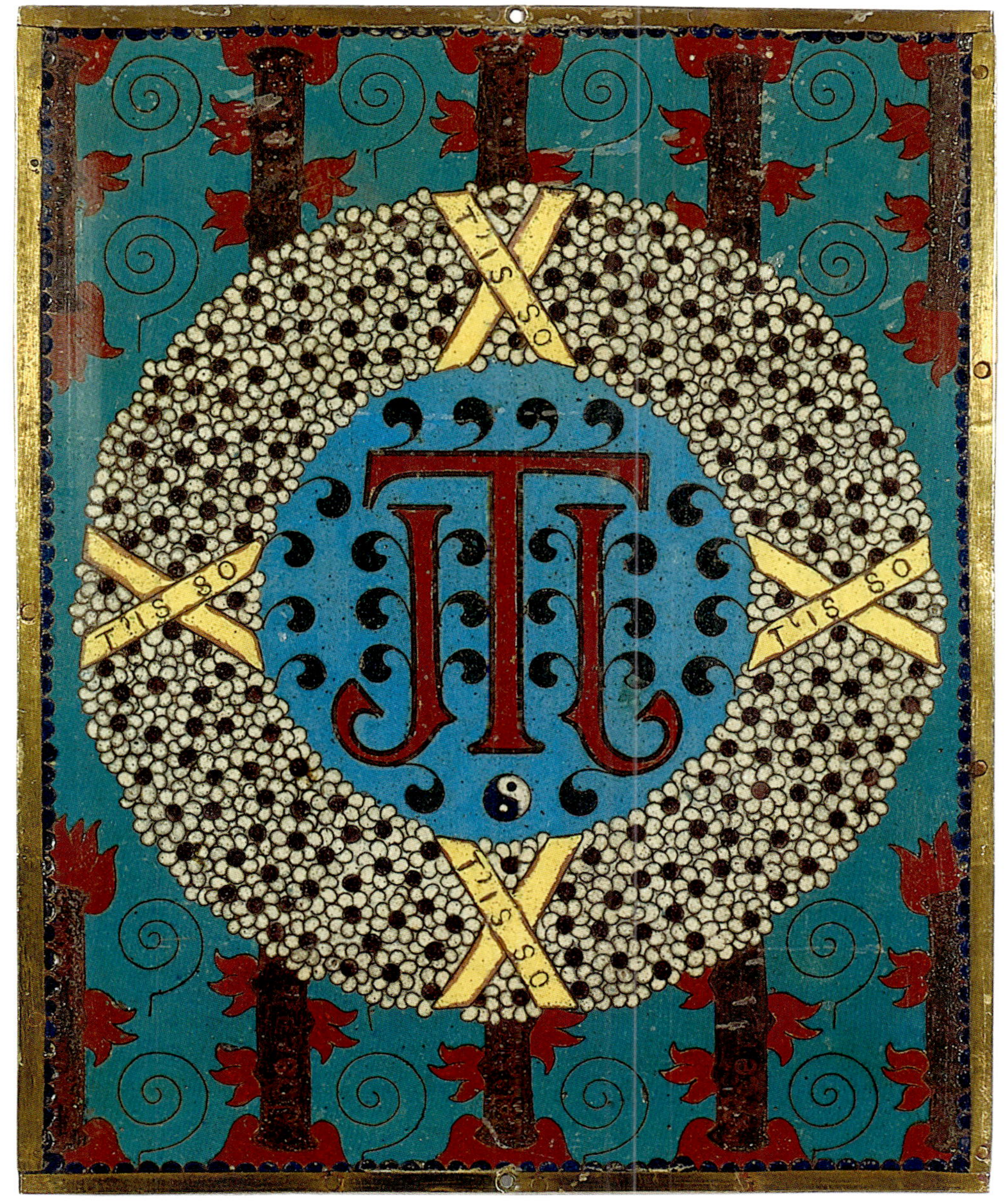
T·IS SO
T·IS SO
T·IS SO
T·IS SO

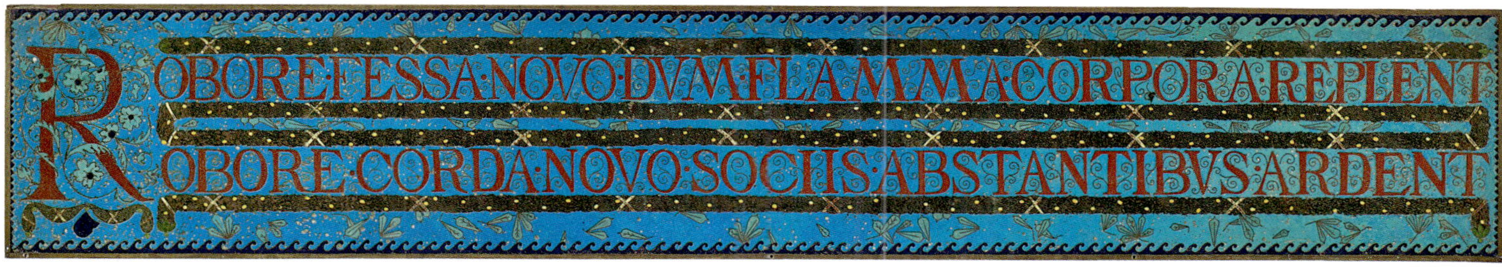
ROBORE·FESSA·NOVO·DVM·FLAMMA·CORPORA·REPLENT
ROBORE·CORDA·NOVO·SOCIIS·ABSTANTIBVS·ARDENT

TISSOT'S PAINTING TECHNIQUES

SARAH KLEINER

James Tissot was financially successful as an artist and documented his career from its early stages, devotedly logging his sales in an account book from 1857 to 1890 (see "Tissot's Sales Notebook," this volume) and compiling photographic albums of his own work (see figs. 15–22). Although primarily known as a painter, he was skilled across multiple mediums, including drawing and printmaking; he also experimented with enamels and photography. Trained in the nineteenth-century French Academic painting tradition, Tissot studied under Hippolyte Flandrin and Louis Lamothe in Paris while in his twenties.[1] As an academically trained artist, Tissot would have learned a formalized methodology for creating preparatory sketches (*esquisse* and *étude*) and working up paintings through regimented layers (*ébauche*) comprising lights, shadows, and halftones.[2] At first glance, many of his paintings appear to conform to the smooth surfaces and high degree of finish characteristic of Academic painters but, in fact, Tissot's style was multifaceted and demonstrates a variety of methods. Research into his materials and techniques helps highlight some of his unique practices—allowing for deeper appreciation of his work and providing information that may prove useful when dating paintings and considering questions of attribution.

Existing scholarship on Tissot's artistic methods is limited. In 1982, Willard Misfeldt published three of Tissot's albums, accompanied by an introduction to the artist's experiments with photography.[3] Misfeldt also authored *J.J. Tissot: Prints from the Gotlieb Collection* (1991), which includes his observations on Tissot's printmaking.[4] More recently, Mary Kisler and Sarah Hillary carried out an in-depth study of a single painting, *Still on Top* (ca. 1873; Auckland Art Gallery Toi o Tāmaki), published in 2001.[5] No major investigation into Tissot's painting materials and working methods has been published, although relevant comparative information lends some insight, including studies of materials and suppliers available to Impressionist and Barbizon painters working around the same time; British treatises and techniques; and the practices of artists who were part of Tissot's circle of friends, such as Edgar Degas and James McNeill Whistler.[6]

This essay outlines the preliminary findings of ongoing research into Tissot's painting methods that was conducted through three tiers of examination. The most in-depth level was the study of five paintings using advanced analytical techniques, such as *in-situ* macro X-ray fluorescence scanning and reflectance imaging spectroscopy.[7] The next tier encompassed seventeen paintings from both museum and private collections, which were researched through X-radiographs, documentary evidence shared by colleagues in the form of condition reports, and access to unframed works *in situ*. Finally, approximately ten additional Tissot paintings were closely observed in visible and raking light at the Parisian institutions the Musée d'Orsay and the Petit Palais, Musée des Beaux-Arts de la Ville de Paris. Access was also granted to the Château de Buillon, Tissot's former estate, where part of his studio and some of his art materials have been preserved, along with important documentary records.[8]

While research was limited to select works, certain patterns in Tissot's painting techniques did emerge. Initial studies reveal that he combined traditional methods with idiosyncratic tendencies and incorporated aspects of modern innovation into his studio practice. As a financially successful artist, Tissot often selected high-quality materials, which may have increased the appeal of his paintings to collectors. As his style matured, he found ways to expedite his painting process without sacrificing the quality of his workmanship.

SUPPORTS

For French painters in the mid-nineteenth century, the annual Paris Salon was the most important showcase for their work.[9] In fact, after Tissot began regularly appearing at the Salon—he debuted there in 1859—the prices of his paintings immediately increased (see Saint-Raymond, this volume, and "Tissot's Sales Notebook," this volume). During this time, commercial art dealers were emerging as a primary outlet for artists selling smaller, domestic-scaled compositions.[10] Krystyna Matyjaszkiewicz notes that many of Tissot's paintings from around the late 1860s to the early 1880s, with the exception of those intended for exhibition, are a maximum thirty-six inches tall or wide—ideal for residential walls and thus more marketable (see Matyjaszkiewicz, "Tissot's 'Genius' Picture-Selling in Britain," this volume).

When painting on panel, Tissot favored mahogany, a wood that provides a rigid support well suited to smaller works. Pre-primed wood panels were offered in four types: white wood (*bois blanc*), thin mahogany (*acajou mince*), thick mahogany (*acajou épais*), and cradled mahogany (*acajou parqueté*).[11] White wood and thin mahogany panels were comparable in price, while cradled mahogany was significantly more expensive.[12] The majority of panels analyzed in this study are thick mahogany, but cradled mahogany was also found. At least half of the panels retain their original stamps and labels, variants indicating the British manufacturer George Rowney & Co. and the Parisian retailer Deforge-Carpentier.[13] These suppliers appear to have been Tissot's preference, as pre-primed, ready-made mahogany panels were also commercially available from the London-based art supplier Winsor & Newton, where he often purchased canvases.[14]

Tissot's 1864 painting *Promenade on the Ramparts* (pl. 8), the earliest panel examined in this study, has the most straightforward construction; it is approximately five-eighths of an inch thick and has beveled edges on all four sides of the reverse. The painting retains a flat, even surface more than 150 years later, which speaks to the integrity of the wood. *Melancholy* (pl. 13) and *Self-Portrait* (pl. 1) were found to have a different preparation, with blunt edges and an auxiliary cradle support, characteristic of an *acajou parqueté*. Several clues suggest that these two works were originally part of a single piece of wood, most likely sold as a long cradled panel that Tissot cut into two pieces prior to painting. *Melancholy* is coarsely trimmed on the left side, and under high-powered magnification the original paint layer is visible going over the chipped edge of the wood.

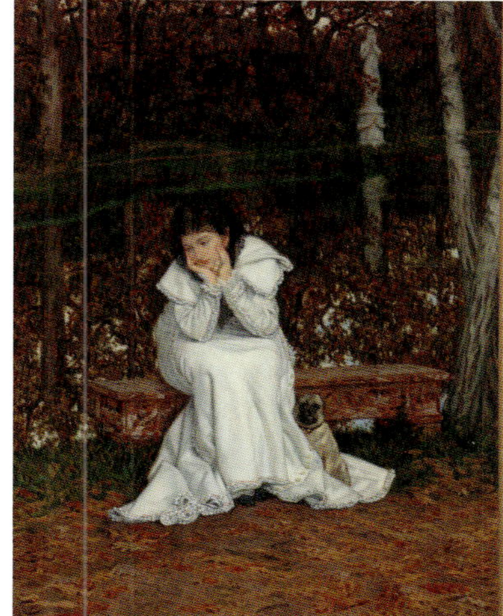

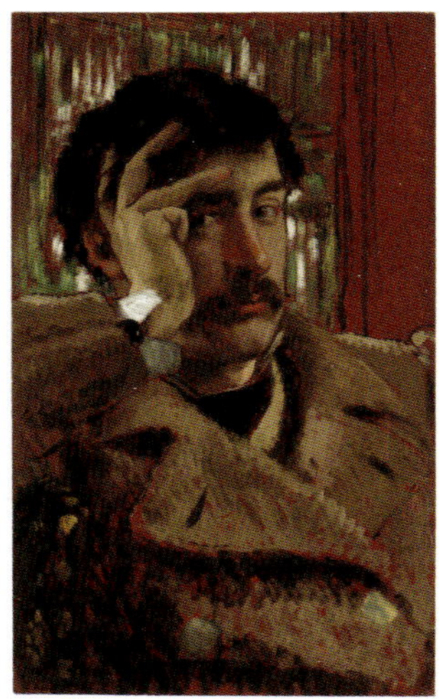

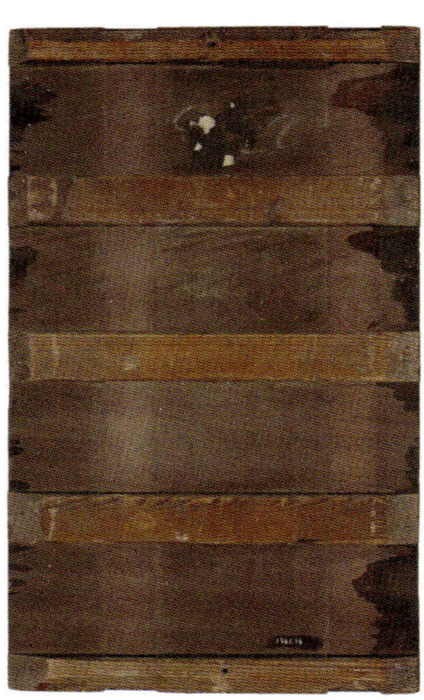

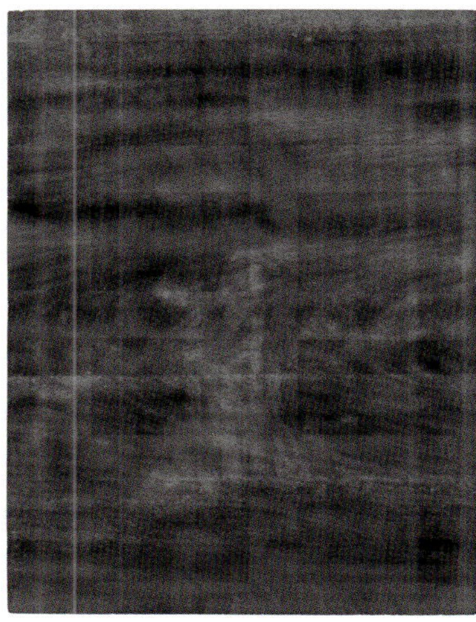

FIGURES 87–88 (top, left to right)
Melancholy (pl. 13) and *Self-Portrait* (pl. 1)

FIGURES 89–90 (center, left to right)
Reverse of *Melancholy* and *Self-Portrait*, showing original cradled backing. The vertical sliding cross-battens on *Self-Portrait* are missing.

FIGURES 91–92 (bottom, left to right)
X-radiographs of *Melancholy* and *Self-Portrait*. The horizontal wood grain aligns, showing that these two works were originally part of a single panel.

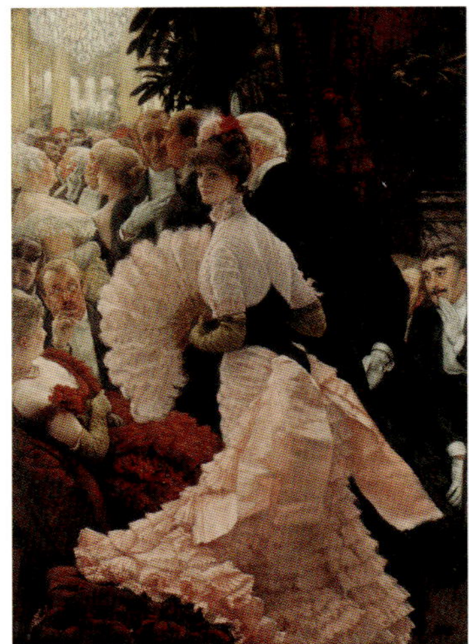

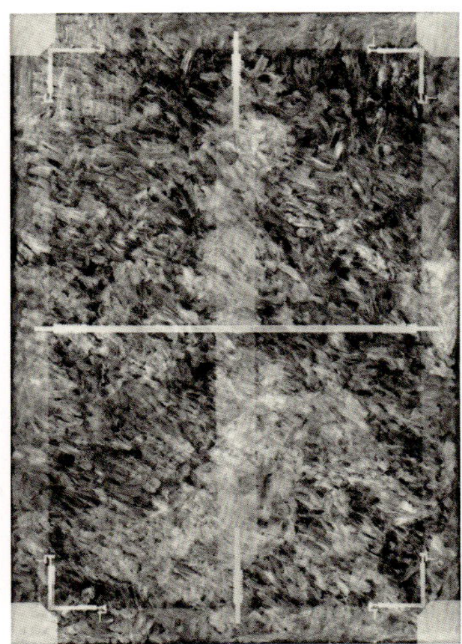

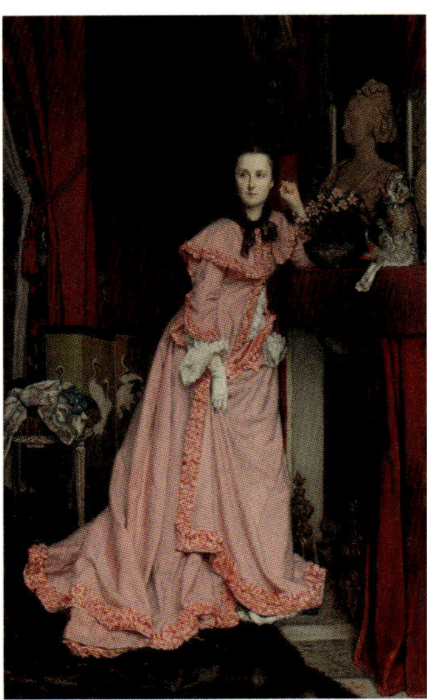

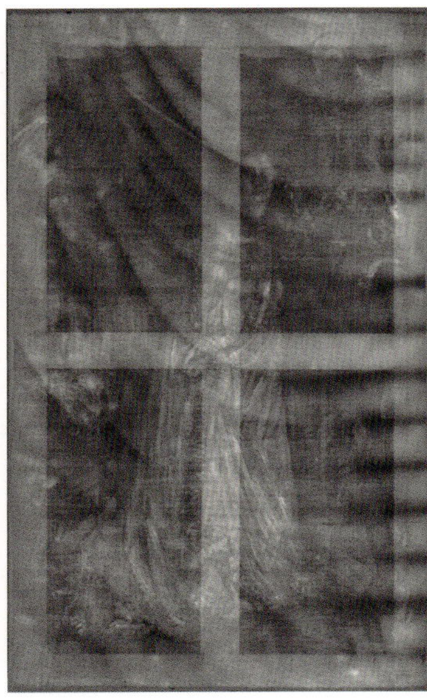

FIGURE 93 (top left)
Political Woman (pl. 124)

FIGURE 94 (top right)
X-radiograph of *Political Woman*, showing the artist-applied ground layer vigorously painted with a brush

FIGURE 95 (bottom left)
Portrait of the Marquise de Miramon, née Thérèse Feuillant (pl. 24)

FIGURE 96 (bottom right)
X-radiograph of *Portrait of the Marquise de Miramon, née Thérèse Feuillant*, showing the commercially applied ground layer

Self-Portrait is narrowed on the right side with the back beveled edge of the cradle having been roughly reconstructed. X-radiography reveals that the wood grain on both panels runs in the horizontal direction and aligns when the paintings are adjacent (figs. 87–92). In addition, fine toolmarks, likely from a mechanical thickness planer, are visible on the reverse of both panels in visible light and in their X-radiographs.[15] Because cradles typically have symmetrical configurations, the dimensions of the original panel can be calculated to 19¾ × 29 inches, which matches a more standard format for the time.[16]

Four panel paintings in this study dating between 1877 and 1882—*The Elder Sister* (pl. 97), *Hampton Court* (also known as *A Visit to the Park*, pl. 95), *Hide and Seek* (pl. 82), and *In Full Sunlight* (pl. 96)—have beveled edges on the reverse and a double coating composed of gray over white paint, extra levels of finish selected by Tissot. Three of these four supports were also reformatted, with the bevel removed on one or two sides, suggesting the panels were cut from larger pieces or reduced in size. These changes were likely made before or during Tissot's painting process, as conservator Charlotte Hale observed on *In Full Sunlight*, rather than as part of later restoration.[17] Interestingly, Tissot's modification of his supports while painting does not appear to be limited to wood panel. *Portrait of the Marquise de Miramon, née Thérèse Feuillant* (pl. 24), a work on canvas, was also cut down on both the left and right sides during painting, but retains the original tacking margin along the top and bottom edges.[18] Tissot's propensity to alter the sizes of his supports is a notable characteristic of his technique. These types of tendencies can potentially help scholars link previously unrelated paintings or aid in the dating of his work.

GROUNDS

Tissot often purchased pre-primed canvas or panel supports with white or light-colored grounds that he further modified in color and texture.[19] The underlayers of *Melancholy*, dated around 1869, appear to be consistent with his Academic training: a smooth white or light-colored ground beneath locally applied transparent layers of earth-colored pigments, used to establish tonal ranges between compositional elements—indicative of an *ébauche* design layer. In other cases, Tissot modified the white/light ground with an overall toning layer, using a semitransparent reddish-brown paint applied in a striated or brushed fashion.[20] Dark-brown or red-brown grounds were popular among seventeenth- and eighteenth-century artists, but less common in the nineteenth century, when the overall tonal key of paintings was moving toward lighter and brighter, as seen in Pre-Raphaelite and Impressionist works.[21] Whether using the localized color of the *ébauche* or the overall application of a toning layer, Tissot typically allowed these underlayers to serve as the mid-tone in his paintings. This traditional use of colored grounds expedited the process; by adding lights and darks, an artist could quickly articulate a sense of form.[22]

While Tissot's ground colors were traditional, many of his paintings have dynamic brushwork visible on the surface that does not correspond to the uppermost paint layers, emblematic of a more modern aesthetic.

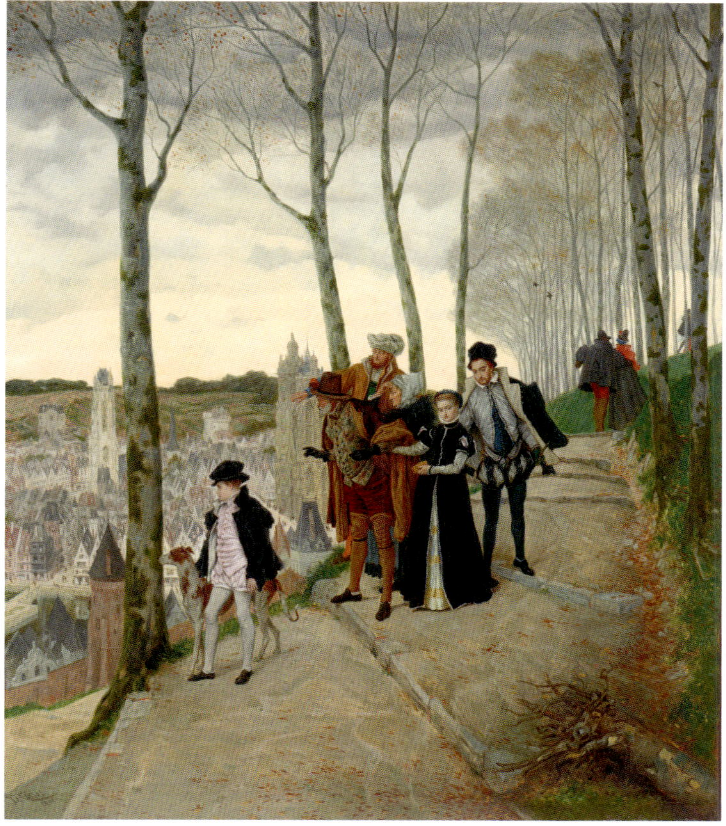

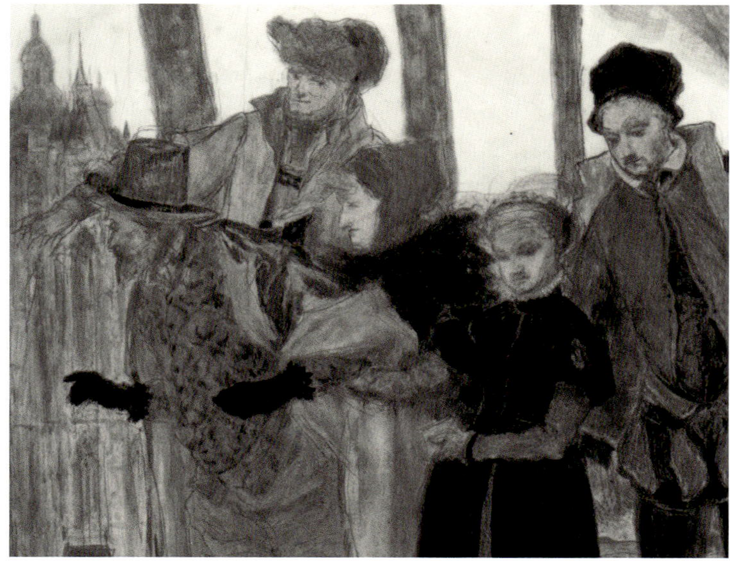

FIGURE 97
Promenade on the Ramparts (pl. 8)

FIGURE 98
Infrared reflectogram of *Promenade on the Ramparts*, detail showing the pencil underdrawing beneath the paint layers

For a strictly Academic painter, whose ultimate aim would be to have a porcelainlike finish, such texture would have been perceived as a hindrance.[23] In Tissot's work, the heavily textured underlayer enlivens the final surface, giving the appearance of a more complex paint structure. One of the most extreme examples of this technique is the vigorous, brush-applied ground he used in *Political Woman* (pl. 124). An X-radiograph of this painting shows the radio-opaque, artist-applied ground, which is in sharp contrast to the smooth contours of the commercially applied ground layer he had selected for *Portrait of the Marquise de Miramon, née Thérèse Feuillant* (figs. 93–96). Although not present on all of Tissot's paintings, this combination of a textured ground with a reddish-brown toning layer is a frequent hallmark of his work.

COMPOSITION

Tissot was a skilled draftsman; his numerous sketches as a soldier during the Franco-Prussian War demonstrate how important drawing was to the way he processed his surroundings (see figs. 1–10). Infrared reflectography, a noninvasive imaging technique, was used in this study to look beneath the surface of paintings in order to see carbon-based underdrawing, revealing aspects of Tissot's creative process and how he made adjustments while working. An infrared reflectogram of *Promenade on the Ramparts* shows detailed pencil underdrawing; minor shifts, such as the positions of hats and hands, illustrate the painter's search to find exact contours of form (figs. 97–98). More typical of Tissot's style, however, are brush-applied outlines in transparent blackish-brown paint that sometimes peek through the final paint layers, as highlighted in the detail from *Self-Portrait* (fig. 99) and the infrared reflectogram of *Melancholy* (fig. 100). This "sauce"—traditionally reddish-brown paint thinned with turpentine—was used by academically trained artists to lay in their compositions.[24]

Often, Tissot used photography—a technology that underwent significant developments during the nineteenth century—as a compositional aid. He had a dedicated photography studio at the Château de Buillon, and evidence reveals that he used the medium to capture poses or other compositional elements. For example, the staging of the figures in the painting *Waiting for the Ferry* (ca. 1878; private collection) directly correlates to one of his photos, now held at the Fine Arts Museums of San Francisco (accession number 1988.3.6). Photographs and gelatin-bromide glass negatives found in the artist's studio after he died show models posed for his biblical watercolor illustrations, which he began working on in the 1880s (see figs. 13–14, and Buron, this volume).[25] No specific evidence emerged through this study showing that Tissot used any direct transfer methods from photograph to canvas.

PIGMENTS

The pigment analysis conducted as part of this research focused on a group of five paintings brought into the Fine Arts Museums of San Francisco for in-depth examination (see "Pigment Analysis," this volume).[26] In the early nineteenth century, barely a dozen pigments were available to artists. Brilliant yellow and green pigments were rare, and blue ultramarine was very expensive.[27] Further into the nineteenth century,

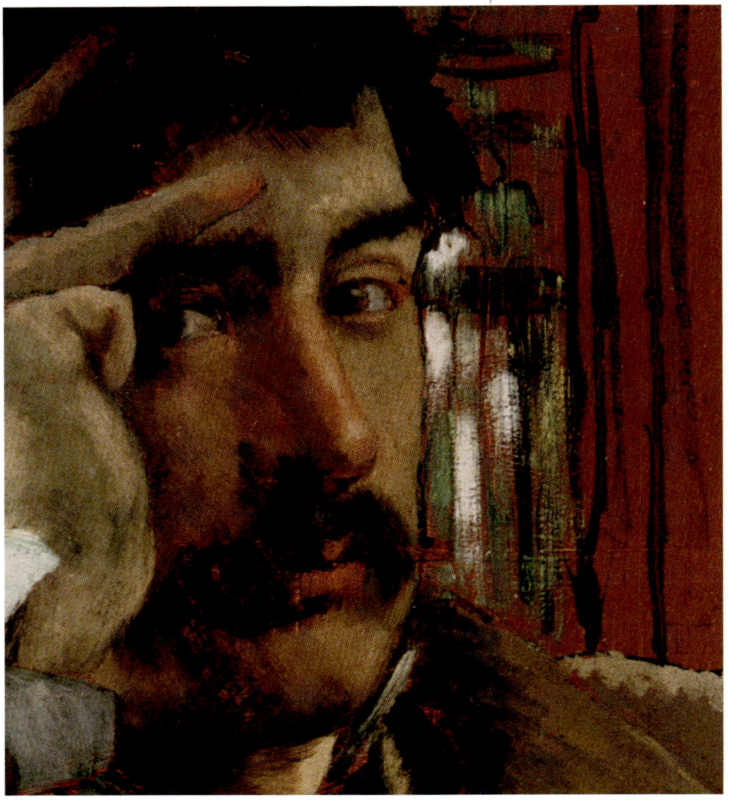

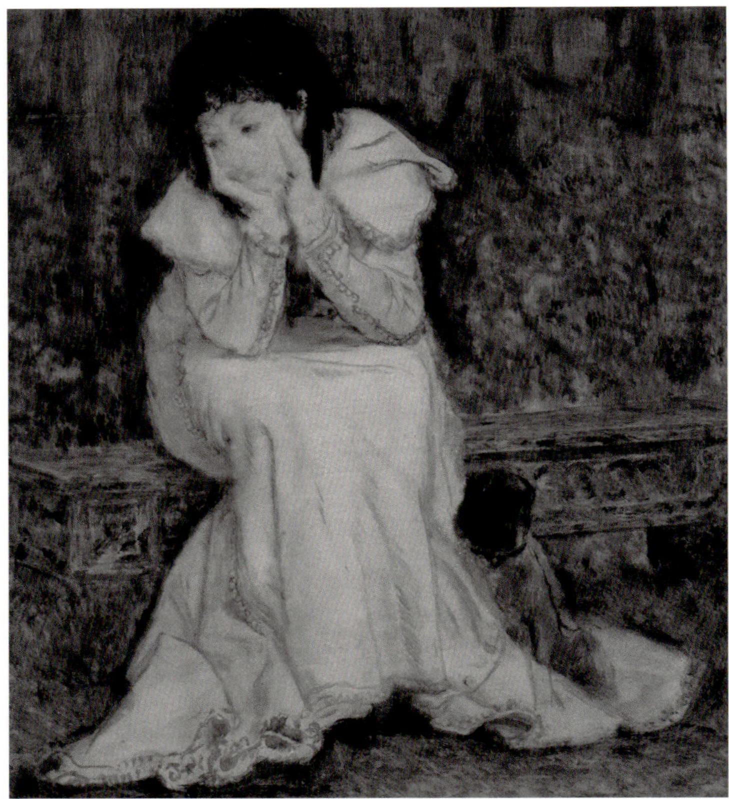

FIGURE 99
Detail of *Self-Portrait*, showing thin, dark-brown undermodeling, or "sauce," peeking through the final paint layer

FIGURE 100
Infrared reflectogram of *Melancholy*, detail showing undermodeling beneath the paint layers

systematic research in the fields of chemistry and mineralogy led to the development of many new pigments, particularly for yellows, greens, blues, and whites.[28] As with his grounds, Tissot's color palette reflects a mix of traditional and modern choices. His use of bone black, burnt umber, vermilion, iron oxide, and lead white align with the traditional pigments available in the early part of the century, but he also took advantage of more contemporary options.

In 1883, a catalogue from the Parisian art supplier LeFranc listed a range of greens at the following prices, per 100 grams: emerald green at 2 francs, chrome oxide green at 4 francs, cobalt green at 10 francs, and viridian at 15 francs.[29] Tissot had used the low-cost, brilliantly colored emerald green for his *Variant of a "Ball on Shipboard"* (ca. 1878–1886; private collection) but chose the more expensive cobalt green for *Kathleen Newton at the Piano* (pl. 98) and *Hampton Court*.[30] Both of these latter paintings also include cadmium yellow, which was four times as expensive as chromium-based yellow and was known to be more stable and likely to retain its brightness. In *Kathleen Newton at the Piano*, Tissot fully exploited these bold colors, along with strontium and zinc yellows, to highlight the contour of Newton's face against a vivid shock of green leaves. Despite the range of blue hues visible throughout the five paintings analyzed, only cobalt blue was detected, sometimes mixed with other pigments—such as zinc white—to modify the tint.[31]

CONCLUSION

Acquiring a deep understanding of an artist's techniques and materials is essential for exploring questions of attribution. Currently, at the Fine Arts Museums of San Francisco, exhibition curator Melissa E. Buron is revisiting a theory originally put forth by Richard Thomson in 1988 that *The Impresario* (fig. 101), a piece in the museum's collection currently attributed to Edgar Degas, was actually painted by James Tissot.[32] Noting the similarities between the pose of the slightly bent man in *The Impresario* and the men who stand behind the central figures in Tissot's paintings *Evening* (also known as *The Ball*, pl. 79) and *Political Woman*, Thomson posited the oil sketch as a study for those works.[33] Several factors indicate that this is a worthy exploration. The dimensions of *The Impresario* are comparable to a variety of studies that Tissot painted, such as *A Study for "By Water"* (ca. 1879–1880; Wimpole Hall, Cambridgeshire, England), *Study for "Seaside"* (also known as *Room Overlooking the Harbour*, ca. 1879; Musée Magnin, Dijon, France), and *Study of Kathleen Newton* (fig. 102).[34] The backgrounds of these three studies as well as that of *The Impresario* have the highly characteristic striated or brushed reddish-brown toning layer favored by Tissot.[35] The undermodeling of the figure in *The Impresario* shares the fluid line quality and transparent blackish-brown color indicative of Tissot's "sauce" used for underdrawing, particularly along the hairline, where the parallel clipped lines peek through the upper layers of light and shadow, similar to Tissot's hairline in *Self-Portrait*. Furthermore, as with a number of works by Tissot, the format of *The Impresario* has been altered; remnants of a pencil line used to demarcate the location of the cut are visible under high-powered magnification, and the tip of the man's nose was clipped off and later retouched.[36] How the initial findings of this study might affect the attribution of *The Impresario* requires further research—including analysis of and comparison to Degas's own techniques—but the potential to contribute to discussions of this nature highlights the value of technical analysis and the importance of carrying out these kinds of in-depth examinations.

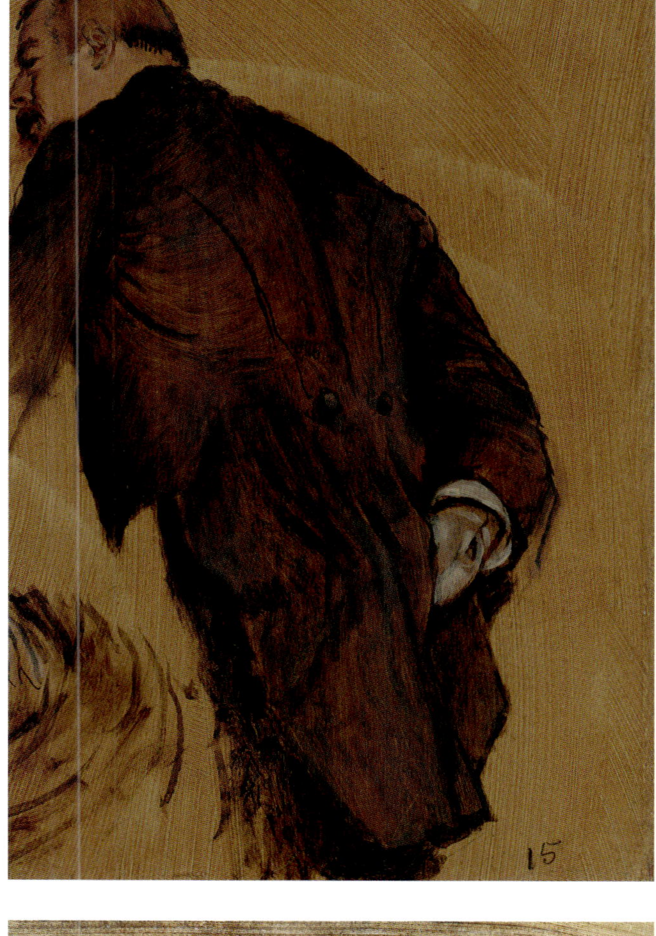

FIGURE 101
Attributed to Edgar Degas (French, 1834–1917), *The Impresario*, ca. 1877. Oil on pressed paper board, 15 × 10 in. (38.1 × 25.4 cm). Fine Arts Museums of San Francisco, Gift of Mr. and Mrs. Louis A. Benoist, 1956.72. Museum curators are currently exploring whether this work should be reattributed to James Tissot.

FIGURE 102
James Tissot, *Study of Kathleen Newton*, ca. 1879. Oil on cardboard, 12⅜ × 8⅝ in. (31.5 × 22 cm). Fondation Custodia / Collection Frits Lugt, Paris, Acquired in 1953; inv. 6585. The background of this study has a striated reddish-brown toning layer similar to that of *The Impresario*.

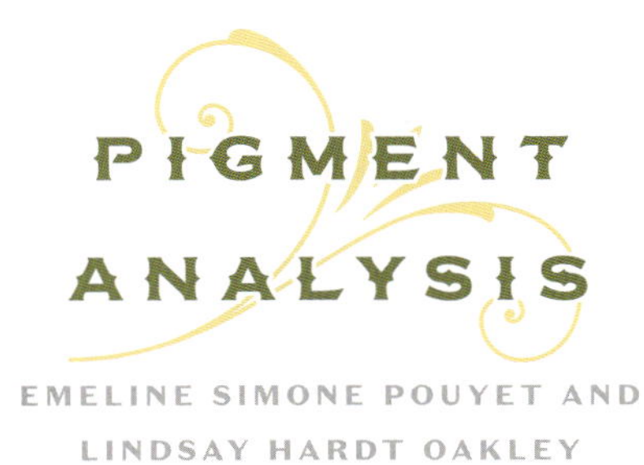

PIGMENT ANALYSIS

EMELINE SIMONE POUYET AND
LINDSAY HARDT OAKLEY

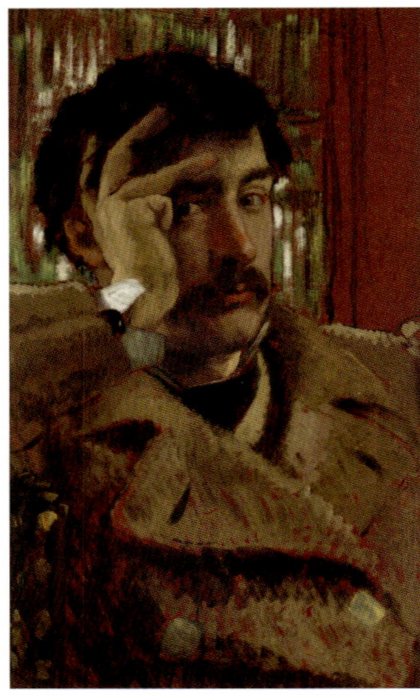

SELF-PORTRAIT, CA. 1865
(PL. 1)
Oil on wood panel, 19⅝ × 11⅞ in. (49.8 × 30.2 cm)
Fine Arts Museums of San Francisco

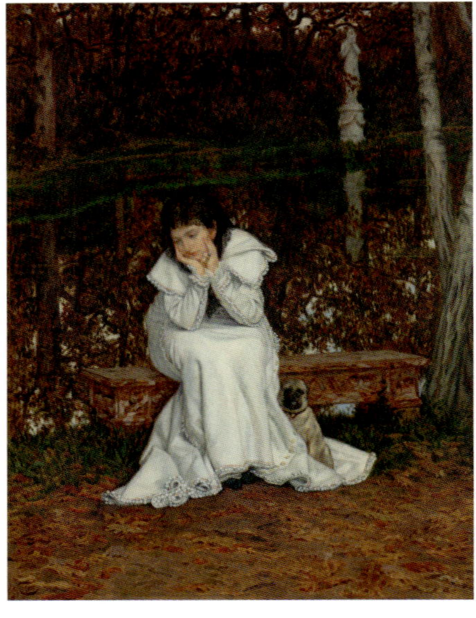

MELANCHOLY, CA. 1869
(PL. 13)
Oil on wood panel, 19½ × 14¾ in. (49.5 × 37.5 cm)
Collection of Ann and Gordon Getty

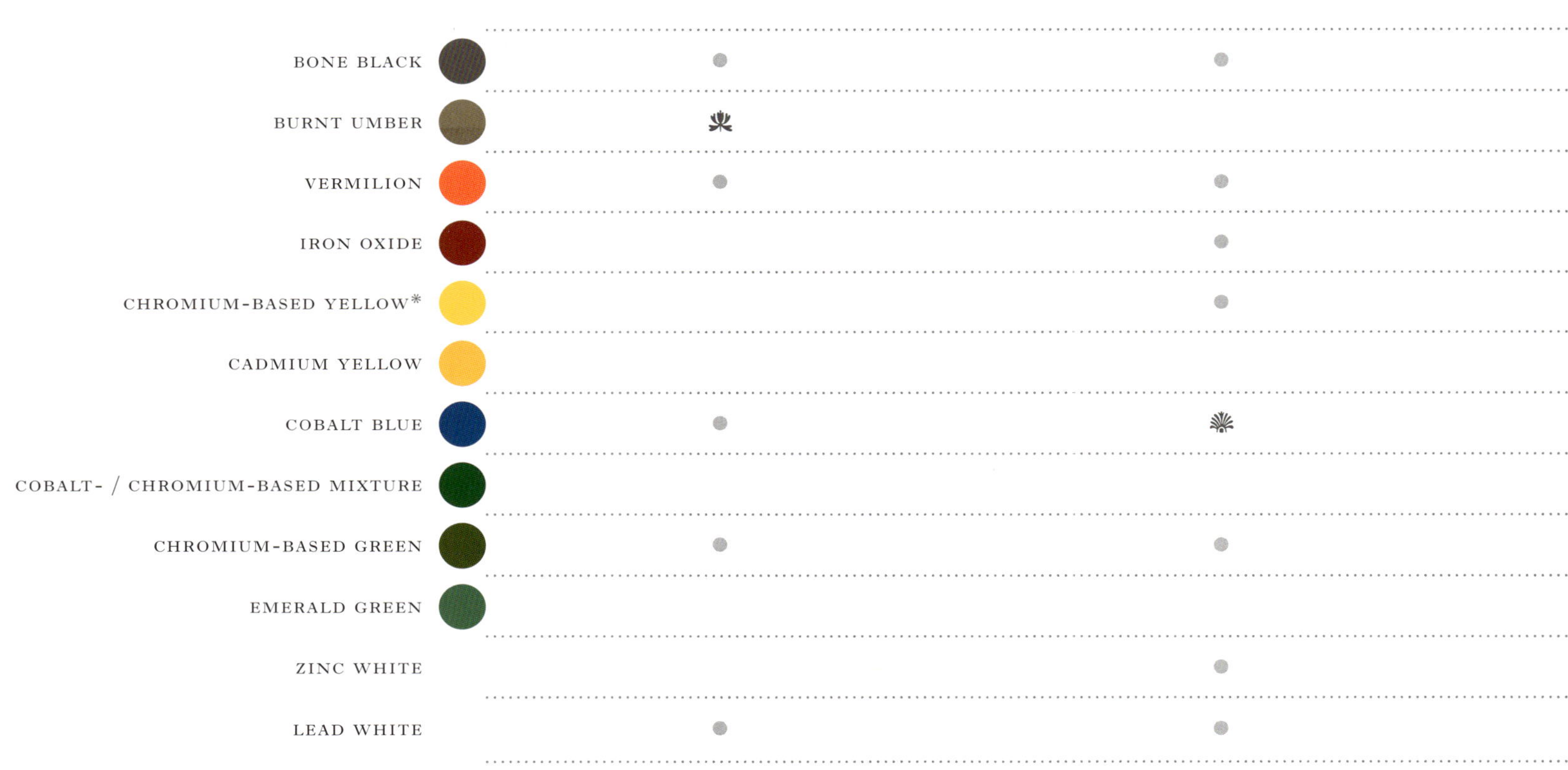

Pigment	Self-Portrait, ca. 1865	Melancholy, ca. 1869
BONE BLACK	●	●
BURNT UMBER	✻	
VERMILION	●	●
IRON OXIDE		●
CHROMIUM-BASED YELLOW*		●
CADMIUM YELLOW		
COBALT BLUE	●	✺
COBALT- / CHROMIUM-BASED MIXTURE		
CHROMIUM-BASED GREEN	●	●
EMERALD GREEN		
ZINC WHITE		●
LEAD WHITE	●	●

NOTE

The material analysis of five James Tissot paintings was conducted by the Center for Scientific Studies in the Arts. The table represents results obtained using *in-situ* macro-scanning X-ray fluorescence, a noninvasive analytical technique that provides maps of the chemical elements characteristic of pigments present in different paint layers. First, the painting is excited by an X-ray beam measuring approximately 1 mm in diameter, generating emission of X-ray fluorescence radiation. The energy of the recorded radiation is used to identify elements, which can be characteristic of certain types of pigments. The beam is then moved relative to the painting in order to scan its surface. Elemental distribution images reveal the spatial positions of various pigments on or beneath the surface of the painting.

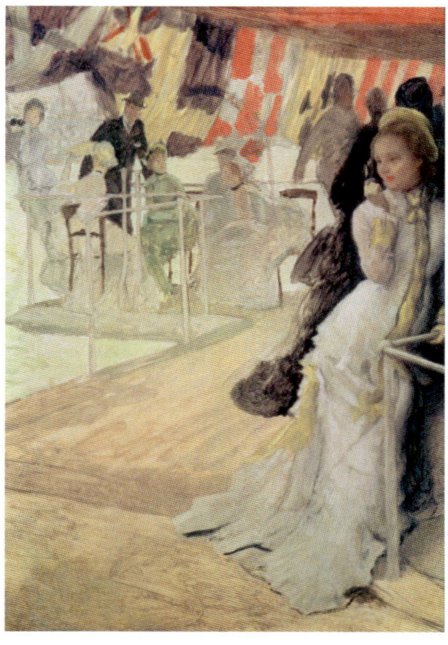

VARIANT OF A "BALL ON SHIPBOARD," CA. 1878–1886
Oil on canvas, 37¼ × 26½ in. (94.6 × 67.3 cm)
Private collection

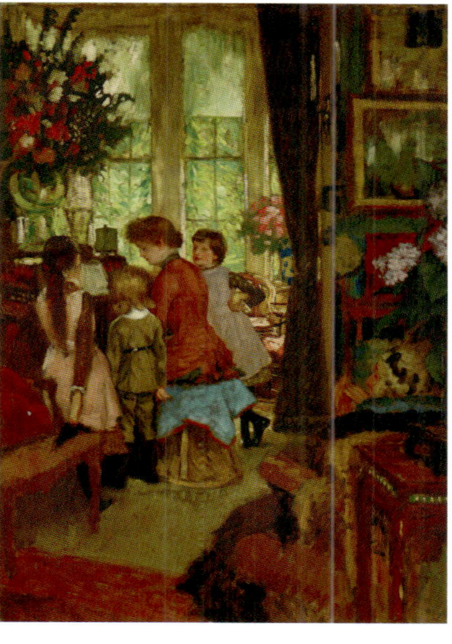

KATHLEEN NEWTON AT THE PIANO, CA. 1880–1881
(PL. 98)
Oil on canvas, 44 × 30½ in. (111.8 × 77.5 cm)
Collection of Ann and Gordon Getty

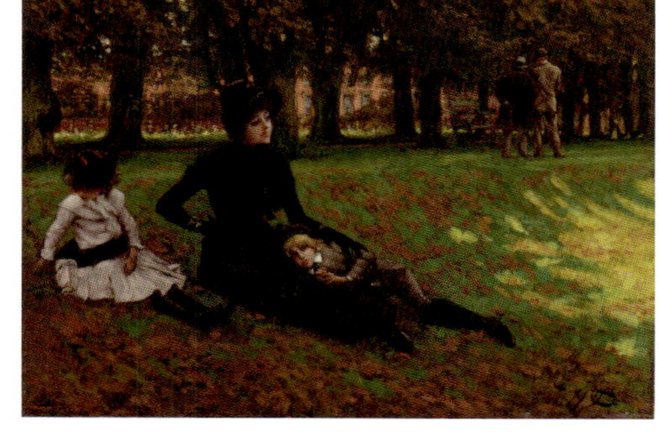

HAMPTON COURT (ALSO KNOWN AS A VISIT TO THE PARK), CA. 1882
(PL. 95)
Oil on wood panel, 9¼ × 13 in. (23.5 × 33 cm)
Collection of Ann and Gordon Getty

Variant of a "Ball on Shipboard"	Kathleen Newton at the Piano	Hampton Court
	●	●
	✾	✾
●	☼	●
	●	●
●	●	
	✳	✳
●	✺	
	✢	✢
	●	●
●		
	●	
●	●	●

KEY

✾ Presence of umber indicated by detection of iron and manganese.

☼ Mixed with zinc white in light-vermilion areas.

✳ Barium-based pigment also detected in these areas—barium white proposed.

✺ Mixed with zinc white in light-blue areas.

✢ Presence of cobalt green proposed based on the correlation of zinc and cobalt distribution. However, it cannot be excluded that other zinc and cobalt-based pigment(s) may be present.

* Type(s) of chromium-based yellow pigment(s) proposed: lead chromate, strontium chromate, and/or zinc yellow.

TISSOT AND DEGAS: CONTOURS OF A FRIENDSHIP

MARINE KISIEL

Edgar Degas's great portrait of James Tissot, which hangs in the Metropolitan Museum of Art, New York, sets an ambiguous and intriguing scene for the friendship between the two painters (fig. 103). Today, in the history of art, Degas's position is more prominent than Tissot's, and a lack of sources has complicated the understanding of their relationship. The openness and substance of their epistolary exchanges, however, revealed in the few letters from their youth that have survived, disclose the contours of their friendship and of the beginnings of their careers.

It is common, when discussing Degas's friendships, to begin with the endings. The estrangement between Degas and Tissot has long been dated to the Franco-Prussian War, when both men served as members of the National Guard in the winter of 1870–1871. Reportedly, Tissot showed Degas a sketch of the fallen body of their friend the sculptor Joseph Cuvelier, who had perished in combat, whereupon Degas indignantly pushed away the image, retorting that Tissot would have done better to have retrieved the body.[1] But this would most certainly not have prompted a definitive break. It has also been suggested that Degas broke with Tissot "upon learning that he had gone over to the Communards."[2] But recent documentary proof of Tissot's efforts to ensure, while in London in 1872, that he was not compromised in France because of his activities in Paris during the Commune (see Tillier, this volume), as well as a certain sympathy that Degas seems to have had for the Communards in the 1870s, indicates that it was not this that caused Degas to distance himself from Tissot.[3] Eight letters from Degas to Tissot, dating from 1871 to 1875, now housed in the Bibliothèque nationale de France, Paris,[4] testify to a closeness between the two men that is clearly untroubled by the events of the "Terrible Year" (*L'année terrible*).[5]

This closeness emerges in the letters exchanged between the two men after Tissot's move to London, in the summer of 1871. The earliest letter's opening suggests the resumption of an interrupted conversation: On September 30, 1871, from Paris, Degas begins, "Tissot, why the devil did you not send me a line? They tell me you are earning a lot of money. Do give me some figures."[6] This direct and lively tone sheds light on the nature of the two men's relationship in the early 1870s; every letter demonstrates familiarity and genuine attachment but also the energy that both artists were exerting to succeed and the friendly rivalry that bound them. This is more marked in Degas's correspondence, partly because more of his letters survive to establish it, and partly because of Degas's still-insecure place in the art world at the time. Thus, even while Degas, in late 1872 and early 1873, haphazardly demands that Tissot write to him at length, describes the dreadful troubles his eyes are giving him, and sketches out his feelings about family—"A good family: it is really a good thing to be married, to have good children, to be free of the need of

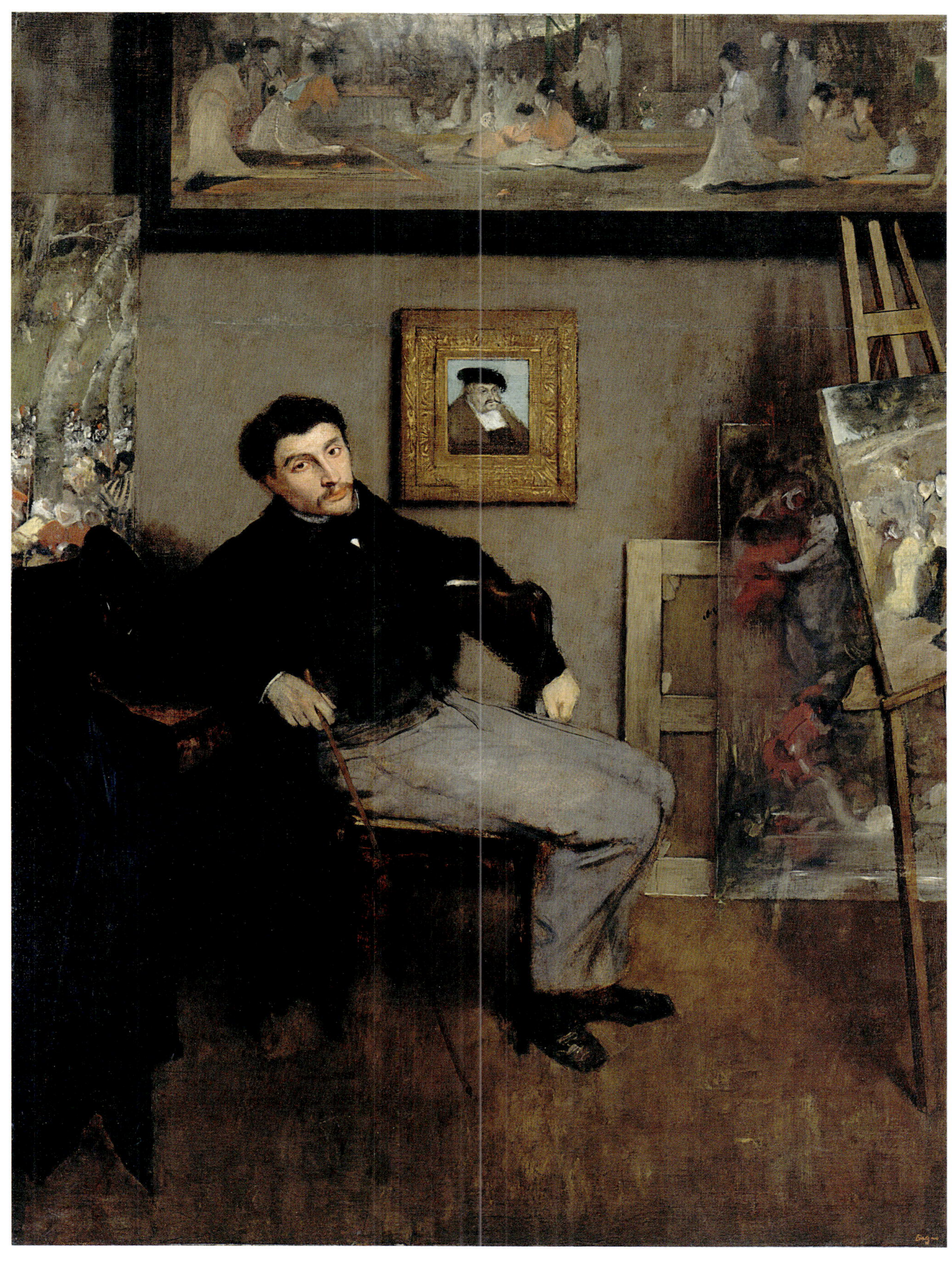

FIGURE 103
Edgar Degas (French, 1834–1917), *James-Jacques-Joseph Tissot*, ca. 1867–1868. Oil on canvas, 59⅝ × 44 in. (151.4 × 111.8 cm). The Metropolitan Museum of Art, New York, Rogers Fund, 1939, 39.161

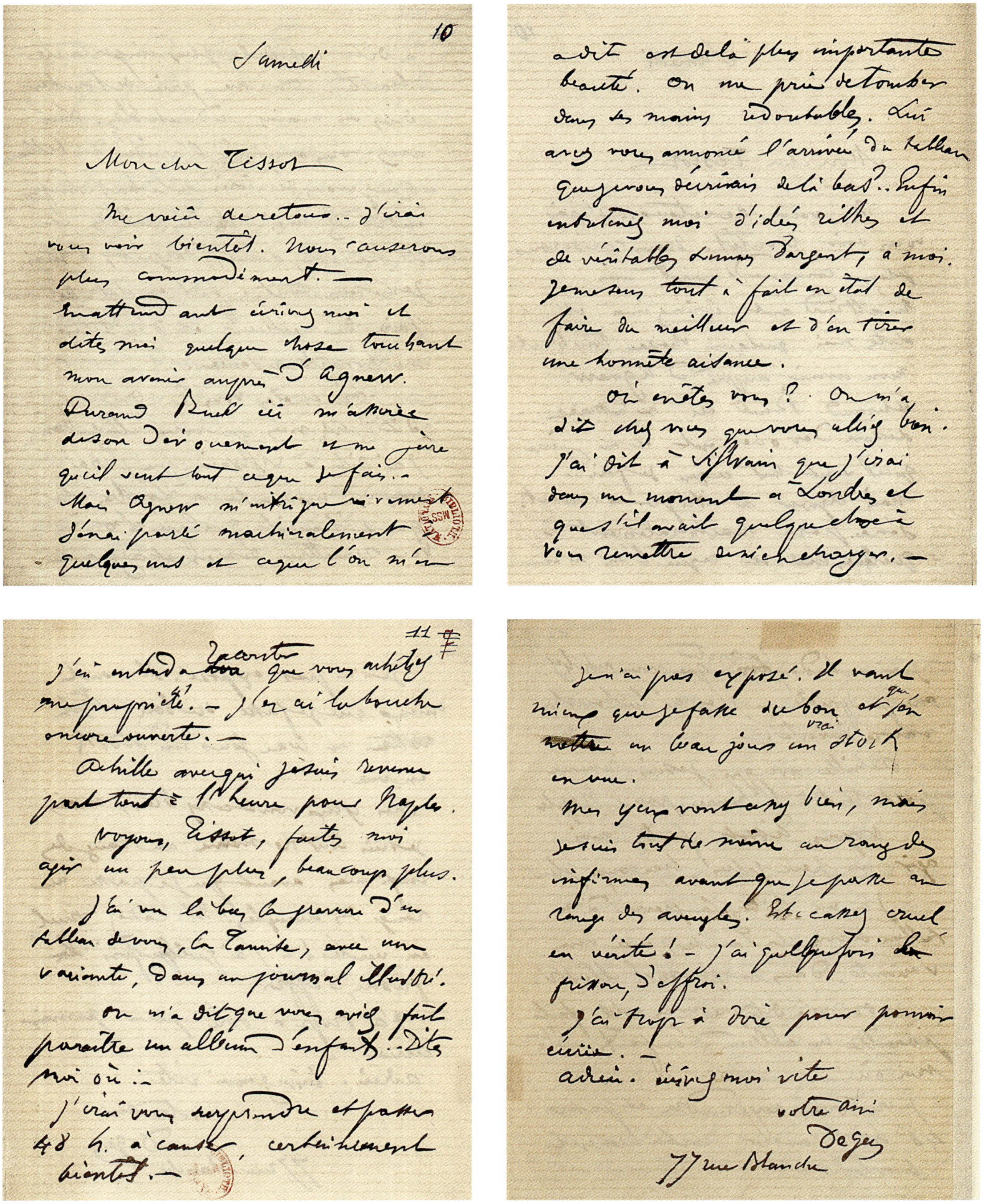

10

Samedi

Mon cher Tissot

Me voici de retour. – J'irai vous voir bientôt. Nous causerons plus commodément. –

En attendant écrivez moi et dites moi quelque chose touchant mon avenir auprès d'Agnew. Durand Ruel ici m'assure de son dévouement et me jure qu'il veut tout ce que je fais. – Mais Agnew m'intrigue vivement. J'en ai parlé naturellement à quelques uns et ce que l'on m'en a dit est de la plus importante beauté. On me prie de tomber dans ses mains redoutables. Lui avez vous annoncé l'arrivée du tableau que je vous écrivais de là bas? – Enfin entretenez moi d'idées riches et de véritables donneurs d'argent, à moi. Je me sens tout à fait en état de faire du meilleur et d'en tirer une honnête aisance.

Où en êtes vous? On m'a dit chez vous que vous alliez bien. J'ai dit à Sylvain que j'irai dans un moment à Londres et que s'il avait quelque chose à vous remettre je m'en chargerais. –

11

J'ai entendu Lacoste que vous achetiez une propriété? – J'en ai la bouche encore ouverte. –

Achille avec qui je suis revenu part tout à l'heure pour Naples.

Voyons, Tissot, faites moi agir un peu plus, beaucoup plus.

J'ai vu là bas la gravure d'un tableau de vous, La Tamise, avec une variante, dans un journal illustré.

On m'a dit que vous aviez fait paraître un album d'enfants. – Dites moi où.

J'irai vous surprendre et passer 48 h. à causer, certainement bientôt. –

Je n'ai pas exposé. Il vaut mieux que je fasse du bon et que j'en mette un beau jour un vrai stock en vue.

Mes yeux vont assez bien, mais je suis tout de même au rang des infirmes avant que je passe au rang des aveugles. Est-ce assez cruel en vérité! – J'ai quelquefois des frissons d'effroi.

J'ai trop à dire pour pouvoir écrire.

Adieu. Écrivez moi vite

votre ami

Degas

77 rue Blanche

FIGURE 104
Letter from Edgar Degas to James Tissot, April 1873. Manuscripts Department, Bibliothèque Nationale de France, Paris, NAF 13005

being gallant. Ye gods, it is really time one thought about it"[7]—all while being amused by his own constantly changing thoughts—"My puppy mind is still what's best about me"[8]—financial competition and commercial strategies are still central.

Besides the brief updates the two men exchange about their artist friends—Henri Fantin-Latour, Édouard Manet, Alfred Stevens, and James McNeill Whistler, among others—and the paintings they discuss in passing, the main theme of their correspondence can be summed up in three words: Tissot was selling.[9] Degas, having just arrived in America in October 1872, proudly writes, just below his brother's cotton-business letterhead: "My dear Tissot, what do you say to the heading? It is the paper of the firm. Here one speaks of nothing but cotton and exchange."[10] He does not hide his admiration for the successes that Tissot has apparently previously related: "And you, what news is there since the 700 pounds? You with your terrible activity would be capable of drawing money out of this crowd of cotton brokers and cotton dealers, etc."[11] Shortly later, he writes: "You are getting on like a house on fire! 900 pounds, but that's a fortune!"[12] Finally, Degas admits, "Here I have acquired the taste for money, and once back I shall know how to earn some I promise you."[13]

These comments are indicative of Tissot's accomplishments. The evidence is further contained in Tissot's sales notebook, published in this volume, which records sums even larger than those that so impressed Degas. In 1872 alone, Tissot logs earnings of 4,085 pounds in total receipts; and in 1873, more than 8,000 pounds. And then there was Tissot's lifestyle, manifested, in 1873, by the purchase of a house in Saint John's Wood, London, to which Degas humorously responds: "I hear that you have bought a house. My mouth is still open" (fig. 104).[14] Was Tissot being guarded about the reasons for his success? Nothing suggests that he would have kept the keys to his achievements to himself. One letter seems to prove it: to Degas, who was preparing to go to London,[15] a disappointed Tissot replies that he will not be there—"How I wish I could be with you and serve as your guide"[16]—but tells him who is the best person to give him the lay of the land, the etcher Alphonse Legros, an important intermediary between French artists and the London market.[17] In the absence of further replies to Degas, we cannot assess Tissot's subsequent support of his friend, although Degas frequently solicits him: for general advice ("Give me some idea how I too could gain some profit from England"[18]); for a favor with the manager of the London branch of Paul Durand-Ruel's gallery ("Go at once to [Charles] Deschamps. If he still has the *Danseuses* and if Durand-Ruel gives his permission and if there is still time get him to send them to the Paris exhibition, before the 20 March"[19]); and for Tissot's help in working with an English gallery rather than with Durand-Ruel ("[T]ell me something about my future with [Thomas] Agnew"[20]).

Did Tissot find this tiresome? Again, nothing suggests it, though it is known that Tissot refused the March 1874 invitation from Degas—no doubt pleased to finally reciprocate—to show at the first exhibition of the soon-to-be-named Impressionists. The tone is very friendly: "Look here, my dear Tissot, no hesitations, no escape. You positively must exhibit at the Boulevard. It will do you good, you (for it is a means of showing yourself in Paris from which people said you were running away) and us too."[21] Yet, the closing suggests the emergence of a diverging point of view, with Degas now declaring himself more interested in the progress of his art than in financial success: "There must be a salon of realists. . . . So forget the money side for a moment. Exhibit. Be of your country and with your friends."[22] Tissot's choice to ignore the exhibition on the Boulevard des Capucines—to commit to an "official" strategy in England rather than to a French avant-garde whose future was by no means assured—may have wounded Degas, who was now, ironically, acting unconcerned about money, a subject he had hitherto written Tissot about incessantly. A letter to Deschamps the following year, anyway, shows Degas determined to break into the English market without the help of Tissot, whose support he no longer seeks. On August 22, 1875, writing to inform the dealer that he is sending him works for an exhibition, Degas says: "Now is the time to do whatever I must to get ahead in England. . . . However late in the day, I'll show Tissot that I can use my own means to my own advantage."[23]

Was this the end point of a fifteen-year friendship? The evidence suggests traces of distance rather than a rupture. The time of conversations and confidences seemed nevertheless far away: the time when Louis Lamothe—a student of Hippolyte Flandrin, from whom he had inherited his Ingresque heritage—guided the two young painters' early careers in Paris from his private studio (where Degas studied around 1855, and Tissot around 1856–1857); to their stints at the École des Beaux-Arts (infrequently attended by both—Degas in 1855–1856, Tissot in 1857–1858[24]), though we cannot be sure the two young men met during this period;[25] to the time of Italy, where Degas traveled from summer 1856 to spring 1859, and where Tissot went in late summer 1862, writing of his discoveries; to the time, finally, of close friendship and discreet references to romances. But although it is not known exactly when the two painters met (it was probably in the early 1860s, perhaps through Élie Delaunay, who came from Tissot's hometown of Nantes, and whom Degas had met in Rome[26]), a long letter from Tissot to Degas recounts all of this with animation. Dated September 18, 1862, and mailed from Venice, it reveals an obvious and immediate intimacy and a genuine pleasure in its burgeoning, possibly recent, as Degas is described as "an acquaintance." Tissot writes: "I hasten to tell you . . . how touched I was by the amiable kindness you showed me lately when I was ill, and by your farewell. . . . I am more thankful than ever to have made an acquaintance like you."[27] He adds—a rare mention of Degas's love life—"And Pauline? what is happening with her. How far have you gotten by now. Is this pent-up ardor spent only on Semiramis?"[28] Mostly, Tissot talks about painting, revealing his affinity with a host of young artists—Degas, Jean-Jacques Henner, Gustave Moreau—whose trajectories were destined to diverge, as the evolution of their careers would demonstrate, but who were, in their youth, united by a common love for the Italian "primitives" that had much to do with the Ingresque heritage fostered at the Villa Medici—which they all attended, as recipients of the Prix de Rome or as visitors—by the director of the institution, Victor Schnetz.[29]

A few years after Degas—with his father's blessing and inspired by Moreau[30]—became interested in the Italian Renaissance painter Vittore

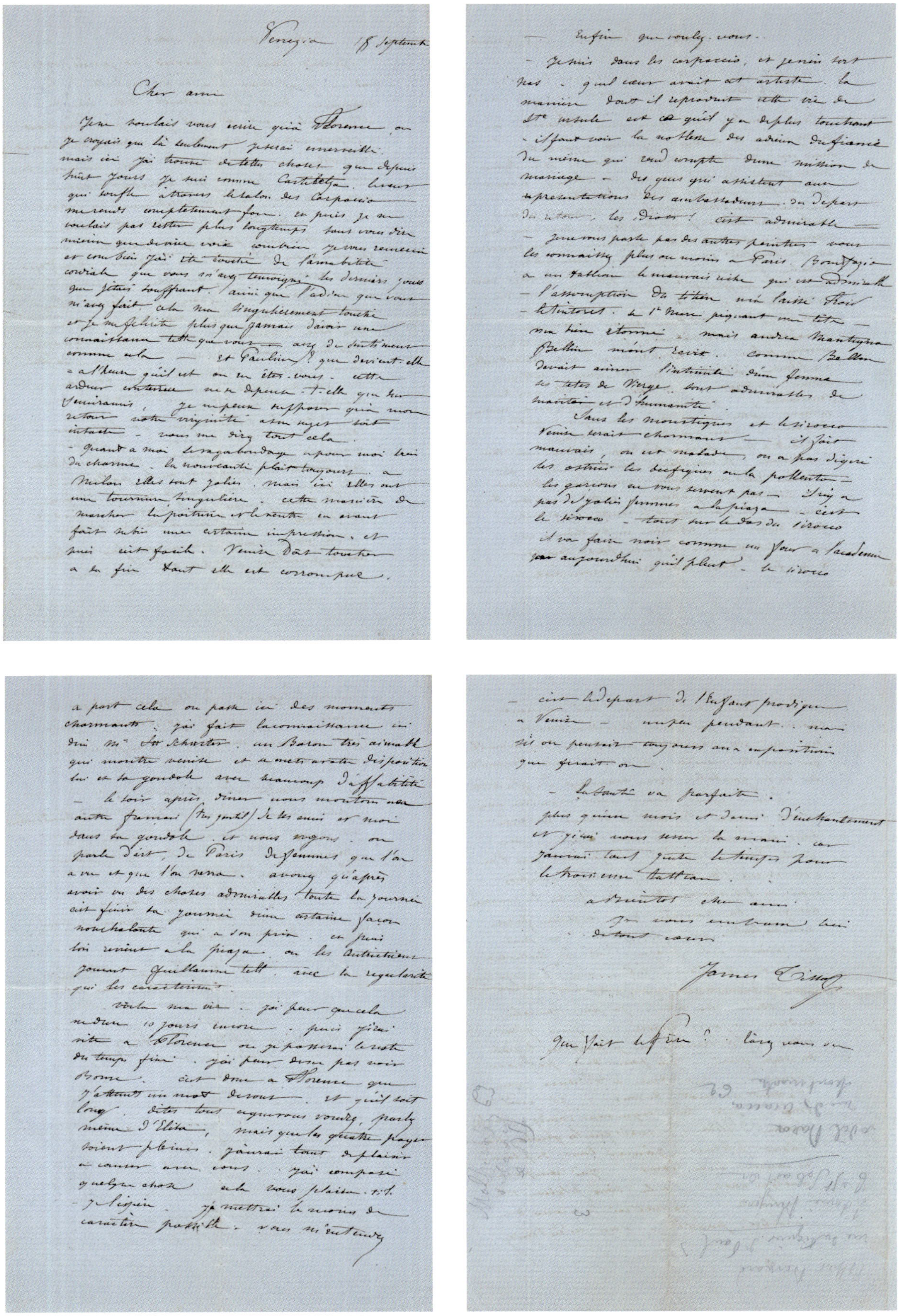

FIGURE 105

Letter from James Tissot to Edgar Degas, September 18, 1862. Fonds Nepveu-Degas, Musée d'Orsay, Paris, ODO 2008-1-2

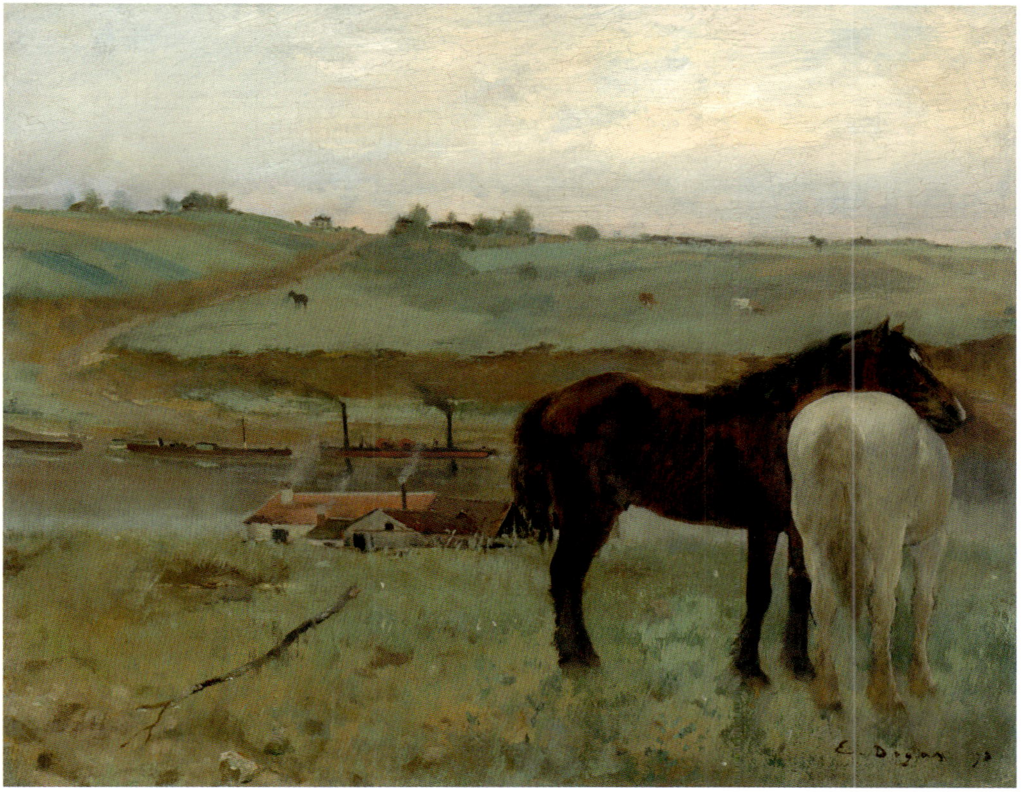

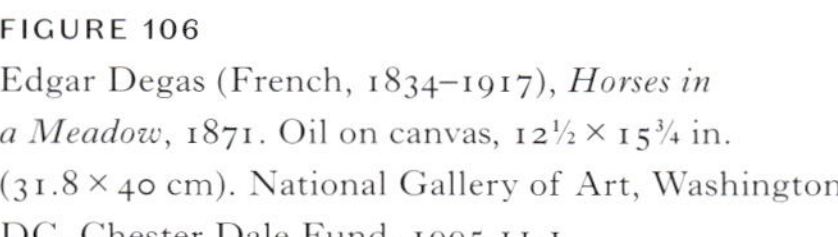

FIGURE 106
Edgar Degas (French, 1834–1917), *Horses in a Meadow*, 1871. Oil on canvas, 12½ × 15¾ in. (31.8 × 40 cm). National Gallery of Art, Washington, DC, Chester Dale Fund, 1995.11.1

Carpaccio, whose "revival" had begun in the late 1850s,[31] Tissot reports his own enthusiasms: "The wind blowing through the Carpaccio gallery drives me utterly mad."; "I'm among the Carpaccios, and here I'll stay. What heart that artist had. The way in which he conveyed this life of Saint Ursula is the most moving thing in the world."[32] Tissot notes, in an expression of his—truly—Pre-Raphaelite taste: "Titian's Assumption left me cold," immediately adding in contrast, "Andrea Mantegna [and] Bellini thrilled me. How Bellini must have loved intimacy with a woman his Virgins' heads are wonderful in their sweetness and humanity" (fig. 105).[33] Unfortunately, there is no record of Degas's reply to these revealing reflections.

A few years later, around 1867–1868, the great portrait of Tissot could take its place. Conveying the image of a friendship, between the passions of youth and the anxieties of blossoming careers, the painting may represent a moment of equilibrium in the two artists' trajectories. The large-format work is replete with artistic references indirectly revealed: the significance to Tissot of early German painting, demonstrated by Lucas Cranach the Elder's portrait of Frederick III the Wise; Tissot's taste for Japanese art, signaled by the long makimono; and the crucial importance of *plein-air* representation of modern life to a painter in the 1860s, indicated by the paintings surrounding Tissot. As such, the portrait emphasizes the figure of Tissot as much as Degas's mastery of portraiture, and endows both with grandeur. Yet, it shows a fragile balance: while Tissot, in bourgeois garb, enjoys the comfort of the studio of the fashionable artist he already is—a setting invented, most likely, by Degas's own hand—Degas identifies the sources of Tissot's inspiration, emphasizing their diversity, and portraying his friend as a man in a hurry, neither really seated nor exactly rising. Wavering between friendly tribute and commentary on the manufacture of popular success, the work is fascinatingly ambiguous, a quality intensified by a previously unacknowledged fact: the portrait was found in Degas's studio after he died, in 1917. Did Tissot ever own it, or had he parted with it? Might Degas have bought it back, perhaps at the sales (unfortunately uncatalogued) following Tissot's death, in 1902, or even before then? If so, it would be particularly meaningful, for then, given Degas's legendary detestation of those who sold works he had given them, the moment of his symbolic break with Tissot could be dated to the 1890s, when Tissot parted with his Degases. In 1890, Tissot sold *Horses in a Meadow* (fig. 106) to Durand-Ruel's gallery, then, in 1897, also to Durand-Ruel, *Woman with Binoculars* (ca. 1875–1876; Galerie Neue Meister, Dresden)—both gifts from Degas, who lambasted him for it.

Degas clearly acknowledged the amateur's right to sell anything he had bought—"Tissot, that old friend, whom I went through so much with, with such jollity, such closeness, he bought several paintings from me and he resold them, that's his business"—but he balked at his gifts being sold.[34] Having spotted, the month following the sale, *Woman with Binoculars* at Durand-Ruel, Degas railed, in his way, against Tissot: "I was going to write him a furious letter. What's the use? I'll collect a few drawings he once gave me. I'll return them without a word. He'll understand." Then Degas envisions retaliating in pencil: "Oh, I could get revenge, I'd make a caricature of Tissot, and Christ, behind him, whipping him, and below: *Christ chasing the man who sold him from the temple.* Oh, my God!"[35] What a pity that such a potentially delicious work was never carried out . . .

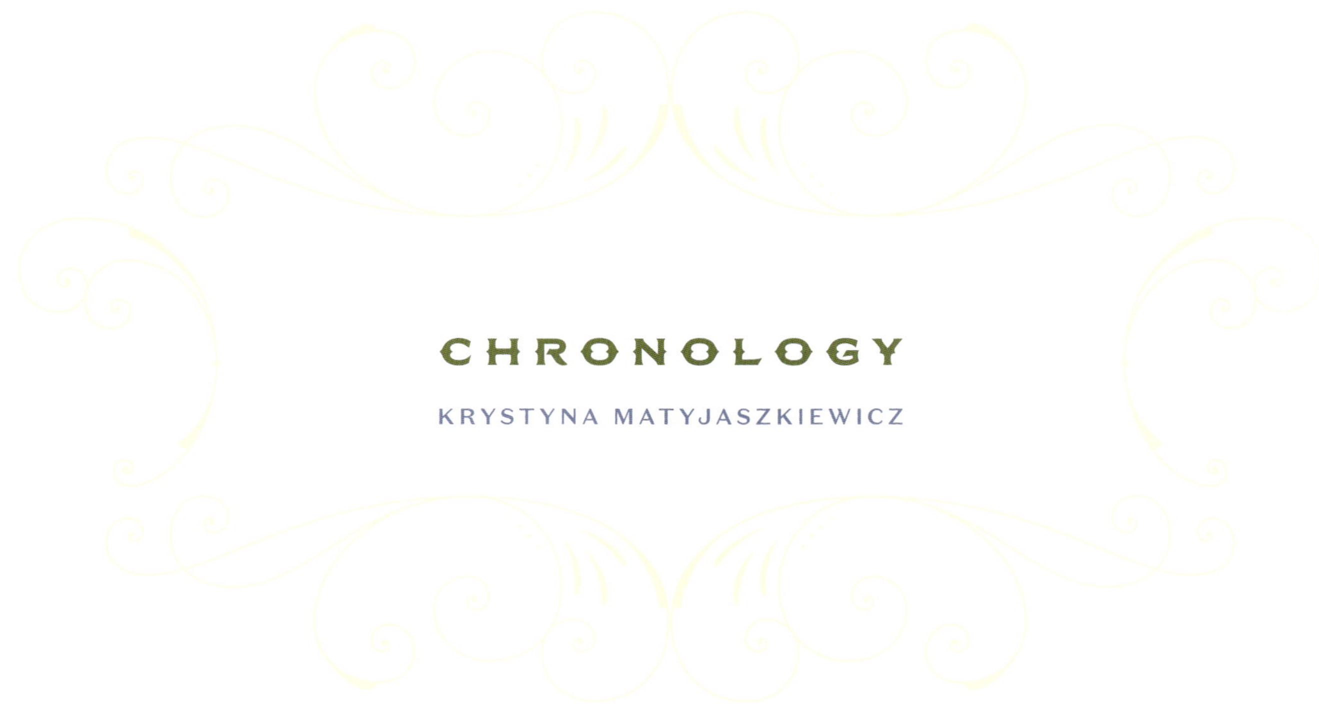

CHRONOLOGY

KRYSTYNA MATYJASZKIEWICZ

1836

October 15: Jacques-Joseph Tissot (fig. 107) born in Nantes, the fourth son of Marcel-Théodore Tissot and his wife, Marie, née Durand, who runs a Nantes hat shop.[1]

1845

Marcel-Théodore buys Château de Buillon, an estate built on Cistercian abbey ruins, near Besançon, Doubs, in southeast France.[2]

1848

Tissot sent to Jesuit college in Brugelette, Belgium, as Catholic secondary teaching has been banned in France.[3]

1850

New law in France allows Roman Catholic Church to open its own secondary schools. Tissot attends one of the first Jesuit colleges established, in the medieval port city of Vannes, Brittany, before moving to another school in Dole, near Besançon.[4]

1855

Arrives in Paris the year of the Exposition Universelle; studies art in the studios of Hippolyte Flandrin and Louis Lamothe, both former students of Jean-Auguste-Dominique Ingres. Among Lamothe's pupils during this year is Edgar Degas, who becomes a close friend of Tissot.[5] ⁂ Enlists in Parisian military reserve, Garde Nationale de la Seine, alongside artist Paul Flandrin, brother of Hippolyte.[6]

1857

January 26: Registers at the Louvre, with permission to copy, using address 41, rue Monsieur-le-Prince, Paris.[7] ⁂ March 9: With recommendation from Lamothe, gains place at École des Beaux-Arts; takes classes with Hippolyte Flandrin.[8] ⁂ Meets James McNeill Whistler at Musée du Luxembourg while both are copying Ingres's *Roger Freeing Angelica* (1819; Musée du Louvre, Paris).[9] ⁂ Begins recording art sales in a notebook.[10]

1858

April 13: Registers at the Louvre, with permission to copy, using address 10, rue Racine, Paris.[11] ⁂ Places fifteenth in first round of the École des beaux-arts Prix de Rome award with *Jesus in the Garden of Olives* (1858; location unknown), but does not make it through to final round.[12] ⁂ October 16: Registers at the Louvre Cabinet des Estampes, with permission to copy, as a pupil of Lamothe and Flandrin, using address 60, rue Saint-Louis (now rue Saint-Louis-en-Île), Paris.[13]

1859

April: Five works accepted for the Paris Salon: two sets of patron saints painted in beeswax and resin, similar to Flandrin's mural paintings (1859;

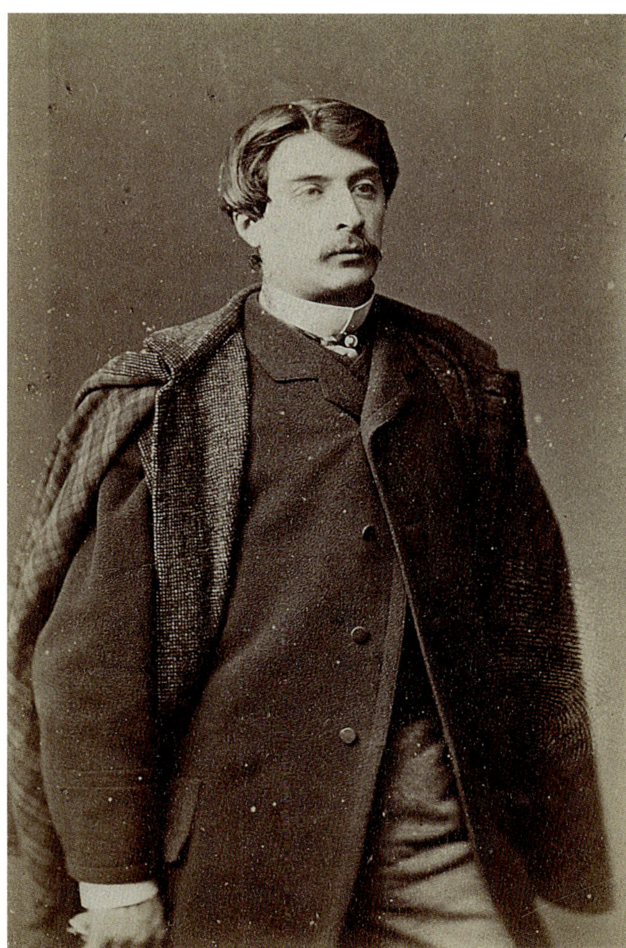

location unknown); a historical-dress picture titled *Walk in the Snow* (1858; private collection), inspired by Henri Leys; and portraits of Madame T… (probably his mother) and Mademoiselle H. de S… (both ca. 1859; location unknown). Arranges to have these paintings photographed, thus beginning habit of keeping photographic albums of his work.[14] ❦ Travels to Flanders, Belgium, Switzerland, and Germany to see works by Old Masters. In Antwerp, meets Leys and, possibly, Leys's pupil Lawrence Alma-Tadema.[15]

1860

Sells three pictures to Parisian art dealers Maison Goupil.[16] ❦ French state buys *Meeting of Faust and Marguerite* (pl. 3).

1861

Living at 39, rue Bonaparte, in a room above writer Alphonse Daudet.[17] ❦ Six paintings accepted for the Paris Salon: *During the Service* (also known as *Martin Luther's Doubts*, pl. 5), *Faust and Marguerite in the Garden* (fig. 30), *Marguerite at the Service* (1861; location unknown), *Meeting of Faust and Marguerite* (pl. 3), *Portrait of Mlle M. P…* (ca. 1861; location unknown), and *Way of Flowers, Way of Tears* or *Dance of Death* (pl. 7).[18] Photographs and prints of the non-portraits sold worldwide, popularizing Tissot's work.[19] ❦ May 4: Tissot's mother dies at Château de Buillon, and is buried in the estate's private chapel.[20]

1862

London International Exhibition includes *Walk in the Snow*, lent by art collector Émile Péreire. ❦ September: Visits Venice and Florence.[21]

1863

February 14: Registers as an independent artist at the Louvre, with permission to copy.[22] ❦ April: London's French Gallery, established by art dealer Ernest Gambart, buys *During the Service* and exhibits it as *Young Luther in Church*, together with *Dance of Death* and *Faust and Marguerite in the Garden*. ❦ *Departure of the Betrothed* (1862–1863; location unknown),[23] *Departure of the Prodigal Son* (pl. 9) and *Return of the Prodigal Son* (pl. 10) exhibited at the Paris Salon; rejected works by other artists displayed in separate Salon des refusés. ❦ October: Exhibits *Marguerite in Church* at Liverpool Institution of Fine Arts.[24] ❦ Commissioned by Tom Taylor to illustrate his translation of *Ballads and Songs of Brittany* (fig. 108).

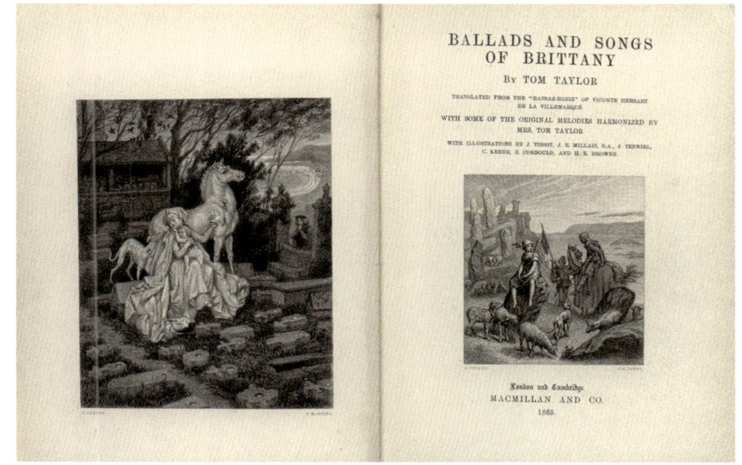

1864

The Elopement (1861; location unknown) and *Return of the Prodigal Son* exhibited at London's Society of British Artists. *At the Break of Day* (ca. 1861; location unknown) accepted for London's Royal Academy exhibition.[25] Tissot gives Paris address along with 7 Saint Philip's Terrace, Kensington (home of the artist John Watkins Chapman). ❦ Visits London, probably to attend exhibition.[26] ❦ Shows two modern-life paintings at the Paris Salon: *Portrait of Mlle L. L…* (pl. 22) and *The Two Sisters; Portrait* (pl. 21). ❦ August: *Marguerite in the Garden* and *Dance of Death* shown at Franco-Spanish exhibition in Bayonne, France. ❦ October: *The Elopement* and *Return of the Prodigal Son* exhibited at Liverpool Institution of Fine Arts. ❦ *At the Break of Day* (under the title *The Duel*) and *Departure of the Betrothed* (as *Departure of a Betrothed Soldier*) appear at Royal Manchester Institution.

FIGURE 107
James Tissot, 1866. Collection Frédéric Mantion

FIGURE 108
Frontispiece with engravings after illustrations by James Tissot, from Tom Taylor's *Ballads and Songs of Brittany*, 1865. Published by Macmillan and Co., London. British Museum, London

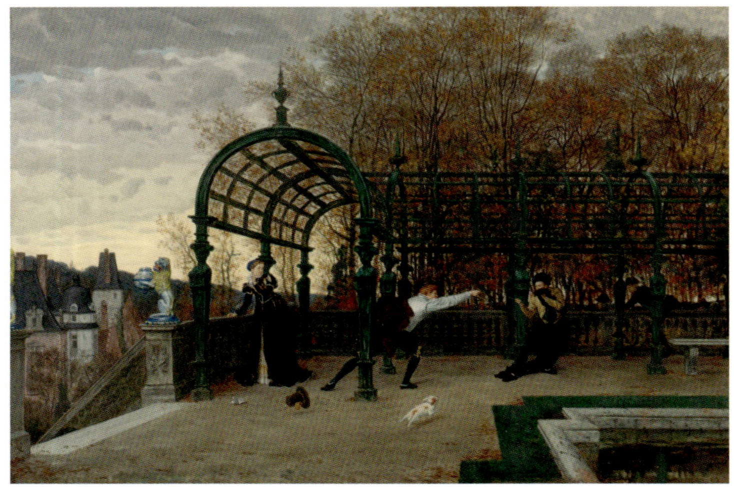

1865

At the Paris Salon, exhibits *Attempted Abduction* (fig. 109) and *Spring* (pl. 15). *Faust and Marguerite in the Garden* and *Marguerite at the Fountain* (fig. 31) exhibited by art dealers Knoedler and Avery in New York.[27] ⁂ Paints family portrait of Marquis de Miramon's family (pl. 23). ⁂ August 22: Registers as an artist at the Louvre, with permission to copy.[28]

1866

Buys plot at 64, avenue de l'Impératrice, Paris, in order to build a house there. ⁂ At the Paris Salon, exhibits *The Confessional* (1865; Southampton City Art Gallery, England) and *Young Woman in a Church* (1865; Hermitage Museum and Gardens, Norfolk, VA); wins a Salon medal.[29] ⁂ *Spring* exhibited at London's French Gallery; family portrait of the Miramons at Paris's Circle of the Artistic Union (Cercle de l'union artistique); and *Departure of the Betrothed* (as *Faust and Marguerite*) at Adolphe Goupil's New York gallery. ⁂ Paints *Portrait of the Marquise de Miramon* (pl. 24) and receives advance payment for *The Circle of the Rue Royale* (pl. 27), completed in 1868. ⁂ December–January: *Spring* and *Dance of Death* displayed in the *Second Annual Exhibition of French Paintings* at Fine Arts Gallery, New York, organized by French Etching Club president Alfred Cadart.[30]

1867

At the Paris Salon, shows *The Secret* (also known as *The Confession*, fig. 41) and *Young Woman Singing in the Choir* (ca. 1867; location unknown), bought by Goupil, who sells the latter to London's French Gallery, where it is exhibited as *Holy Prayer*.[31] ⁂ Exposition Universelle in Paris includes Tissot's *Portrait of the Marquise de Miramon* and *The Rendez-vous* (ca. 1867; location unknown).[32] ⁂ Moves into new house on avenue de l'Impératrice (fig. 110).

FIGURE 109
James Tissot, *Attempted Abduction*, 1865. Oil on wood panel, 26¾ × 38 in. (67.9 × 96.5 cm). Private collection

FIGURE 110
Exterior of Tissot's home in Paris, 64, avenue de l'Impératrice (now avenue Foch), 1890s. Collection Frédéric Mantion

1868

March–October: Employed to teach drawing to Japanese prince Akitake Tokugawa (see pl. 35). ⁂ Exhibits *Beating the Retreat in the Tuileries Gardens* (1867; private collection), *A Luncheon* (ca. 1868; location unknown), and two watercolors at the Paris Salon.[33]

1869

Sends five paintings to Vienna Künstlerhaus for Austrian Artists' Society's First Great International Art Exhibition.[34] ⁂ *Young Women Looking at Japanese Objects* (pl. 38) and *A Widow* (1868; location unknown) shown at the Paris Salon.[35] ⁂ Commissioned by Thomas Gibson Bowles, editor of *Vanity Fair*, to draw caricatures for the magazine under pseudonym "Coïdé."[36] ⁂ Exhibits *The Circle of the Rue Royale* and two paintings of actors at Circle of the Artistic Union.[37]

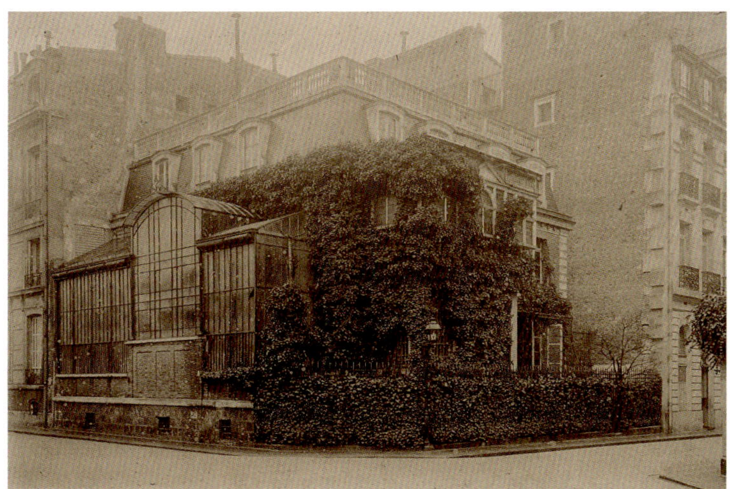

1870

Shows *The Penitent* at Austrian Artists' Society's Second Great International Art Exhibition.[38] ⁂ At the Paris Salon, displays *Young Lady in a Boat* (pl. 59), lent by W. H. Stewart, and *The Partie Carrée* (pl. 41). ⁂ September 20: As the Franco-Prussian War (begun in July) continues, Versailles surrenders and Prussians lay siege to Paris. ⁂ September 30: Joins National Guard; abandons his house and relocates to shared lodgings with Bowles, who is in Paris as a war correspondent for the *Morning Post*.[39] ⁂ October 21: Tissot's battalion takes part in an unsuccessful sortie at Malmaison. Among the fatalities is friend Joseph Cuvelier, a sculptor, whose fallen body Tissot sketches.[40]

1871

January 5: Caricature of King of Prussia published in *Vanity Fair* on same day monthlong bombardment of Paris begins. ⁂ January 27–29: Armistice declared and an assembly elected. Prussians march into forts surrounding Paris. Troops having been dismissed, Tissot returns home, and Bowles soon returns to London. ⁂ March: Submits *Long Live the Republic! 1793* to Austrian Artists' Society for Third Great International Art Exhibition.[41] ⁂ March 18: Government troops try unsuccessfully to reclaim Montmartre cannon from the National Guard; army and government withdraw, and

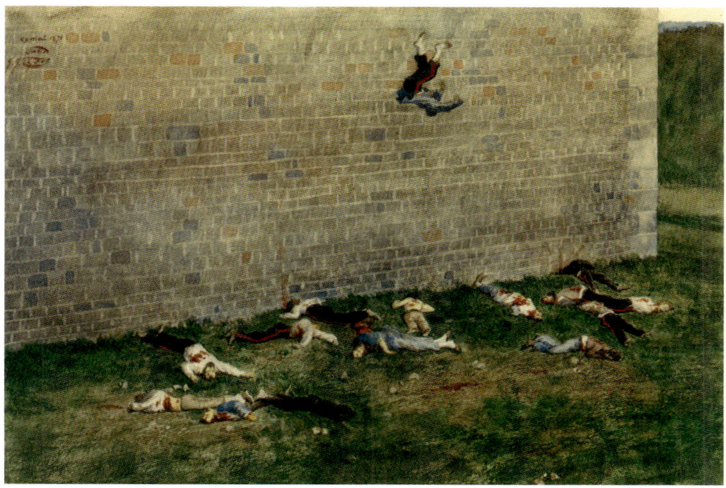

National Guard committee takes charge. March 28: New revolutionary leadership, the Commune, installed. Government troops bombard Champs-Élysées and other parts of Paris, and heavy fighting ensues at Neuilly, with a truce reached on April 25 in order to evacuate casualties.

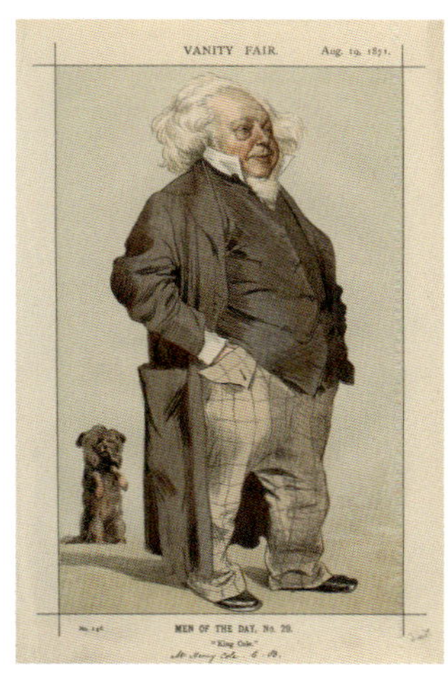

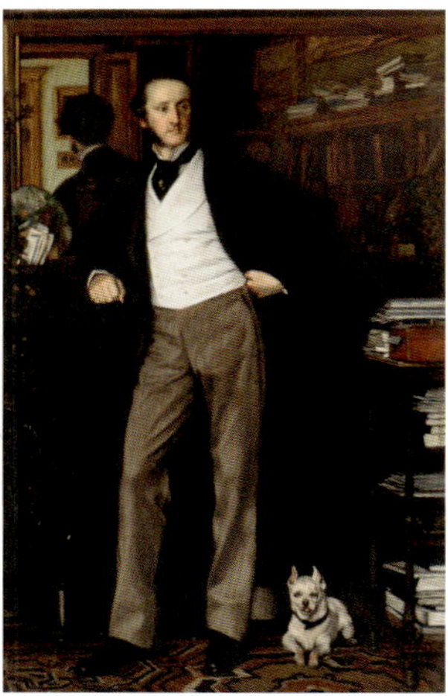

Tissot volunteers as a Red Cross stretcher-bearer, taking wounded to an American medical station on avenue de l'Impératrice. His *laissez-passer* for "citoyen James Tissot" is dated April 21, 1871, overwritten May.[42] ⁂ May 25: Execution of Communards on rue Saint-Germain-l'Auxerrois, which Tissot witnesses and records.[43] May 26: Communards execute more than fifty prisoners, including the Jesuit priest Pierre Olivaint, professor of history at Brugelette when Tissot was a pupil. ⁂ May 28–29: After French army gains upper hand and the Commune is declared over, witnesses execution of two hundred members of National Guard accused of participating in the Commune; makes rapid sketch from which he paints a watercolor (fig. 111). ⁂ June 19: Official French contribution to International Exhibition opens in London, and includes preliminary version of *Dance of Death*, exhibited as *A Picture of Life*.[44] Brings war sketches to London, several of which are used as illustrations for Bowles's *The Defence of Paris: Narrated as It Was Seen* (1871).[45] ⁂ August: Reported in newspapers that Tissot is *Vanity Fair* caricaturist; drawings appear weekly until December 30 (fig. 112). ⁂ Paints portraits of Bowles, President of the Board of Trade Chichester Parkinson-Fortescue (fig. 113), and his wife, Lady Waldegrave.[46] ⁂ August–November: Stays with Bowles at Palace Chambers, 88 Saint James's Street, London. ⁂ Late November/early December: Moves to 73 Springfield Road, Saint John's Wood, London.

FIGURE 111
James Tissot, *The Execution of Communards by French Government Forces at Fortifications in the Bois de Boulogne*, 1871. Watercolor on paper, 7½ × 11⅛ in. (19 × 28.3 cm). Private collection

FIGURE 112
James Tissot, *Men of the Day No. 29: "King Cole,"* from *Vanity Fair*, August 19, 1871. Color lithograph, 14⅛ × 9½ in. (35.9 × 24.2 cm). National Portrait Gallery, London, NPG D43497

FIGURE 113
James Tissot, *Portrait of Chichester Fortescue, Later Lord Carlingford*, 1871. Oil on canvas, 74½ × 47½ in. (189.2 × 120.7 cm). University of Oxford, Oxford Portraits, Gift from Francis Fortescue Urquhart, of Urquhart, ca. 1904

1872

Corresponds with officials in Paris to determine that he is not listed as a Communard (see Tillier, this volume). ⁂ March: *The Farewells* (pl. 43) and *An Interesting Story* (fig. 47) accepted for exhibition at Royal Academy. ⁂ April: Shows *Bad News* (fig. 15), *Portrait of Captain *** [Frederick Burnaby]* (pl. 29), *Portrait of Colonel *** [Longley]* (pl. 31), and *The Thames* (fig. 17) in French section of London International Exhibition.[47] ⁂ May: London art dealer Thomas Agnew starts buying and handling work by Tissot.

1873

Arranges for Italian painter Giuseppe de Nittis to live in his Paris house.[48] ⁂ Buys house at 17 (now 44) Grove End Road, Saint John's Wood, London. ⁂ March 24: Nominated for membership of the Arts Club. ⁂ April: *The Captain's Daughter* (pl. 63), *The Last Evening* (pl. 69), and *Too Early* (pl. 46) accepted for Royal Academy exhibition. *The Crack Shot* (pl. 16) exhibited as *Safe to Win* at London's French Gallery. ⁂ May: Steel engraving of *The Farewells* published by Pilgeram & Lefèvre. ⁂ August: Steel engraving of *News of Our Marriage* (fig. 16) published by Pilgeram & Lefèvre.[49]

1874

Amid anti-Communard clampdown and widespread rumors of Commune involvement, visits Paris to clear name of Communard involvement, receiving documentary proof.[50] ⁂ March: *The Ball on Shipboard* (pl. 71) and *London Visitors* (pl. 56) displayed in Tissot's studio before successful submission to Royal Academy with *Waiting* (pl. 60). ⁂ April: *Société Anonyme des Artistes* exhibition takes place at 35, boulevard des Capucines (later known as first Impressionist exhibition) without participation by Tissot, who had been invited by Degas to join.[51] ⁂ May: New Grove End Road studio described and illustrated in *Building News* (fig. 114). ⁂ December: Empress Eugénie visits Tissot's studio to see progress on her portrait (pl. 28).

1875

March: French ambassador visits studio to view portrait of Empress Eugénie. Newspapers report its submission to Royal Academy with *Hush!* (pl. 45), *The Coming Storm* (1874; Beaverbrook Art Gallery, Fredericton, New Brunswick), and "Two warmer lovers, also in a room overlooking the water."[52] ❧ April: *Hush!* and *The Bouquet of Lilacs* (pl. 53) accepted for Royal Academy exhibition and other works rejected. ❧ Takes up etching in earnest. Ceases working with Agnew, selling instead to other dealers.[53] ❧ May: Visits Paris; buys Édouard Manet's *The Grand Canal, Venice*.[54]

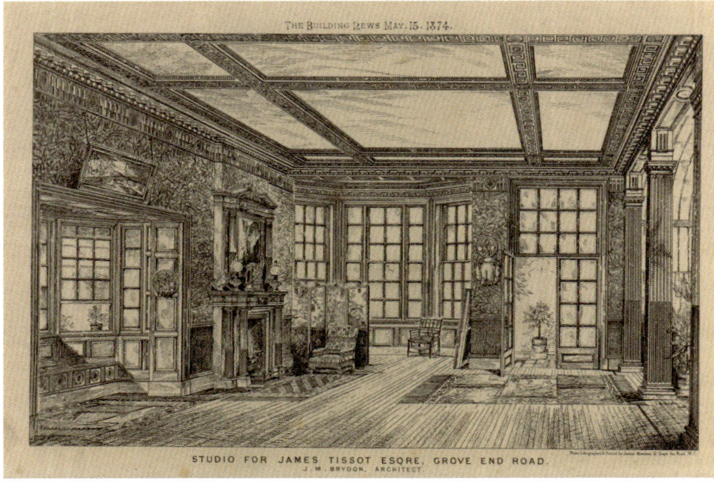

1876

January: *Glasgow Herald* lists Tissot and Whistler as among "the leaders of new thought . . . likely to be rejected as being too extreme" in forthcoming Royal Academy elections of six new associate members; Alma-Tadema and Edwin Long are appointed.[55] ❧ Successfully submits to Royal Academy *The Convalescent* (pl. 48) and *The Thames* (pl. 61) as well as etchings of *Quarrelling* (1876; Wentworth 18) and *The Thames* (1876; Wentworth 20). ❧ Four etchings at London-based Dudley Gallery's *Black and White* exhibition; seven in Paris's *Black and White* exhibition organized by Durand-Ruel. ❧ October–November: Kathleen Newton, a young divorcée, first sits for Tissot, resulting in etched *Portrait of Mrs. N...* (1876; Wentworth 26), made too late for inclusion in Tissot's *Ten Etchings* (fig. 115), a portfolio published in December.

1877

April: Fifteen etchings in spring exhibition at Brighton Pavilion. ❧ Spring/summer: Newton moves into Grove End Road house (figs. 116–117). Her children remain with their cousins and nanny nearby, at 6 Hill Road. ❧ May: Ten oil paintings at opening exhibition of London's Grosvenor Gallery, including *Chrysanthemums* (pl. 57), *The Gallery of HMS "Calcutta" (Portsmouth)* (pl. 64), *Holyday* (pl. 52), *Summer* (pl. 58), *The Triumph of Will (Poem in Five Parts): I. The Challenge* (pl. 99), and *Winter* (pl. 73).[56] John Ruskin praises Tissot's "dexterity and brilliance" but summarizes his pictures as "unhappily, mere coloured photographs of vulgar [ordinary] society." In same review, Ruskin accuses Whistler of "Cockney impudence" for asking "two hundred guineas for flinging a pot of paint in the public's face."[57] Whistler instructs his solicitor to sue Ruskin for libel. ❧ Etchings exhibited in Glasgow at Edward Fox White's North British Galleries, and at Dudley Gallery's *Black and White* exhibition. ❧ July 25: Brother Marcel-African dies at Rigney, France, after falling from a horse; Tissot signs death certificate.[58] ❧ December 15: *The Graphic* publishes an engraving after Tissot's Grosvenor Gallery picture *Winter* (pl. 73).

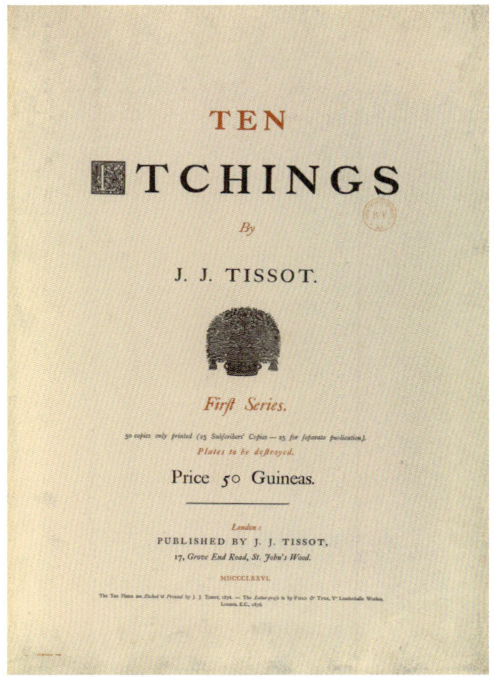
TEN
ETCHINGS
By
J. J. TISSOT.
First Series.
Plates to be destroyed.
Price 50 Guineas.
London:
PUBLISHED BY J. J. TISSOT,
17, Grove End Road, St. John's Wood.
MDCCCLXXVI.

1878

May: Four etchings and five oil paintings displayed at Grosvenor Gallery, including *Croquet* (pl. 50), *Evening* (pl. 79), *July (Specimen of a Portrait)* (fig. 58), and *Spring (Specimen of a Portrait)* (pl. 78). ❧ May 3: Fish supper of Grosvenor Gallery exhibitors at Trafalgar Tavern, where Tissot makes a drawing (fig. 70), shown with four etchings in Dudley Gallery's *Black and White* exhibition in June. ❧ May–July: Visits Paris Exposition Universelle. Decides to organize one-man exhibition in Paris for February/March 1879; asks Léon Boussod at Goupil gallery and Paris art dealer Georges Petit for advice.[59] ❧ September–December: Exhibits work at the Walker Art Gallery, Liverpool; the Royal Manchester Institution; and Dudley Gallery's Winter Exhibition.[60] ❧ November: Subpoenas served to Tissot and others to appear as witnesses on behalf of Whistler in libel case against Ruskin. Tissot pleads illness, and Whistler says he will leave Tissot in peace. Whistler wins case but is awarded only a farthing in damages and has to pay legal costs; he files for bankruptcy in May 1879.

FIGURE 114
James Akerman, "Studio for James Tissot Esqre, Grove End Road: J. M. Brydon, Architect," from *Building News*, May 15, 1874. Private collection

FIGURE 115
Frontispiece from *Ten Etchings by J. J. Tissot*, 1876. Published by J. J. Tissot, London. Bibliothèque Nationale de France, Paris

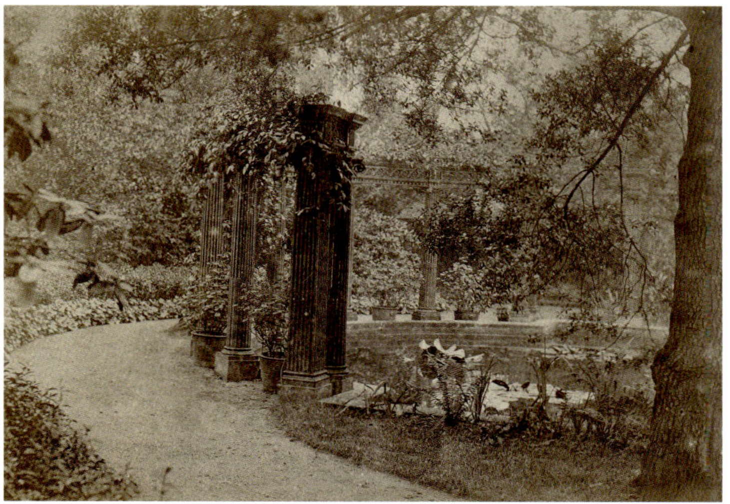

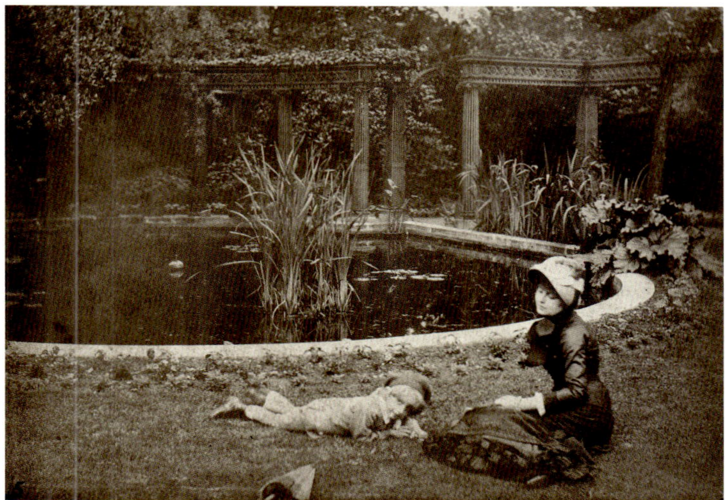

1879

February: Sends works on approval to Georges Petit; returned in March for London exhibition. ❧ April: Sends other works to Petit.[61] May: Visits Paris with Newton. ❧ Eight oils at Grosvenor Gallery, including *The Hammock* (fig. 118), *Orphans* (pl. 85 or smaller version), and *Rivals* (pl. 83), plus four etchings, including *Trafalgar Tavern, Greenwich* (fig. 71).[62] ❧ Etchings at Dudley Gallery's *Black and White* exhibition, and other work at Royal Manchester Institution; Walker Art Gallery, Liverpool; and Dudley Gallery's Winter Exhibition.[63] ❧ Embarks on *The Prodigal Son in Modern Life* series (pls. 86–89). ❧ October: Back in Paris, sketching at the Louvre.

1880

Portrait of Newton (1880; location unknown) among commissions from *The Graphic* for *Types of Beauty*, exhibited in London and Glasgow, and published October 1881. ❧ Work exhibited in Glasgow and Southport.[64] Not invited to exhibit at Grosvenor Gallery.[65] ❧ May: New York art dealer Samuel Avery in London and invited to Tissot's studio.[66] ❧ June: Three etchings in Dudley Gallery's *Black and White* exhibition; other work in Leeds. ❧ July 31: Meeting at house of Francis Seymour Haden resolves to establish Society of Painter-Etchers; Tissot, a founding Fellow, elected to provisional Council.[67] ❧ September–November: Shows work in Birmingham and Liverpool.[68] ❧ November: Invited by Fine Art Society, London, as one of "the Elite of Etchers" to show work in an exhibition originally planned to showcase Whistler's Venice etchings. ❧ November–December: *Prodigal Son* oils shown in Tissot's studio to newspaper critics.[69]

FIGURE 116
The garden pond and colonnade at Tissot's Grove End Road property, London, ca. 1881. The painter used these elements as a backdrop in compositions such as *The Convalescent* (pl. 48), *Croquet* (pl. 50), *Holyday* (pl. 52), and *Quarrelling* (pl. 51). Collection Frédéric Mantion

FIGURE 117
Kathleen Newton and her son Cecil George in the garden of the Grove End Road property, London, ca. 1881. Collection Frédéric Mantion

1881

January: At Society of Painter-Etchers meeting, Tissot listed as secretary for foreign correspondence; translates society's prospectus and canvases potential French exhibitors. ❧ February–March: Exhibits work in London, Southport, and Glasgow.[70] April: *Quiet* (ca. 1881; private collection) and *Goodbye: On the Mersey* (ca. 1881; location unknown) accepted for Royal Academy exhibition. ❧ Census lists Tissot as having two domestic servants as well as a gardener and his wife; Newton continues to live at Grove End Road (fig. 119), although registers at the house of her sister. ❧ June: Work in *Le Salon à Londres* exhibition of French artists at Royal Panorama Galleries, London, the first time since 1872 he has aligned himself with French artists.[71] Shows etchings at Dudley Gallery's *Black and White* exhibition, with others for sale in Glasgow and New York. ❧ August–December: Works on cloisonné enamels (fig. 120).

1882

March–April: Work exhibited in Southport and Birmingham.[72] ❧ May–June: One-man exhibition at Dudley Gallery, London; Duchess of Edinburgh among visitors. Work exhibited in Leeds and Newcastle.[73] ❧ Elected to Société des aquarellistes français.[74] ❧ May 28: Visits Edmond de Goncourt in Paris to discuss illustration of Edmond and Jules de Goncourt's novel *Renée Mauperin*. ❧ June: In response to letter from Degas, arranges for Durand-Ruel representative to meet Edward Fox White, Tissot's dealer. Durand-Ruel stages exhibition in July with work by Degas and other Impressionists at White's former gallery space at 13 King Street, Saint James's, London.[75] ❧ September–October: Exhibits work in Liverpool, Glasgow, and Manchester.[76] ❧ November 9: Newton dies of tuberculosis at Tissot's London house; her sister Mary Pauline registers the death. ❧ November 14: Newton's funeral at Church of Our Lady, Lisson Grove, Saint John's Wood, followed by burial in Saint Mary's Roman Catholic Cemetery, Kensal Green. ❧ November 15: Edmond de Goncourt records Tissot's arrival in Paris.

1883

Société des aquarellistes publishes illustrated descriptions of members, including biography of Tissot by Alfred de Lostalot.[77] ❧ January:

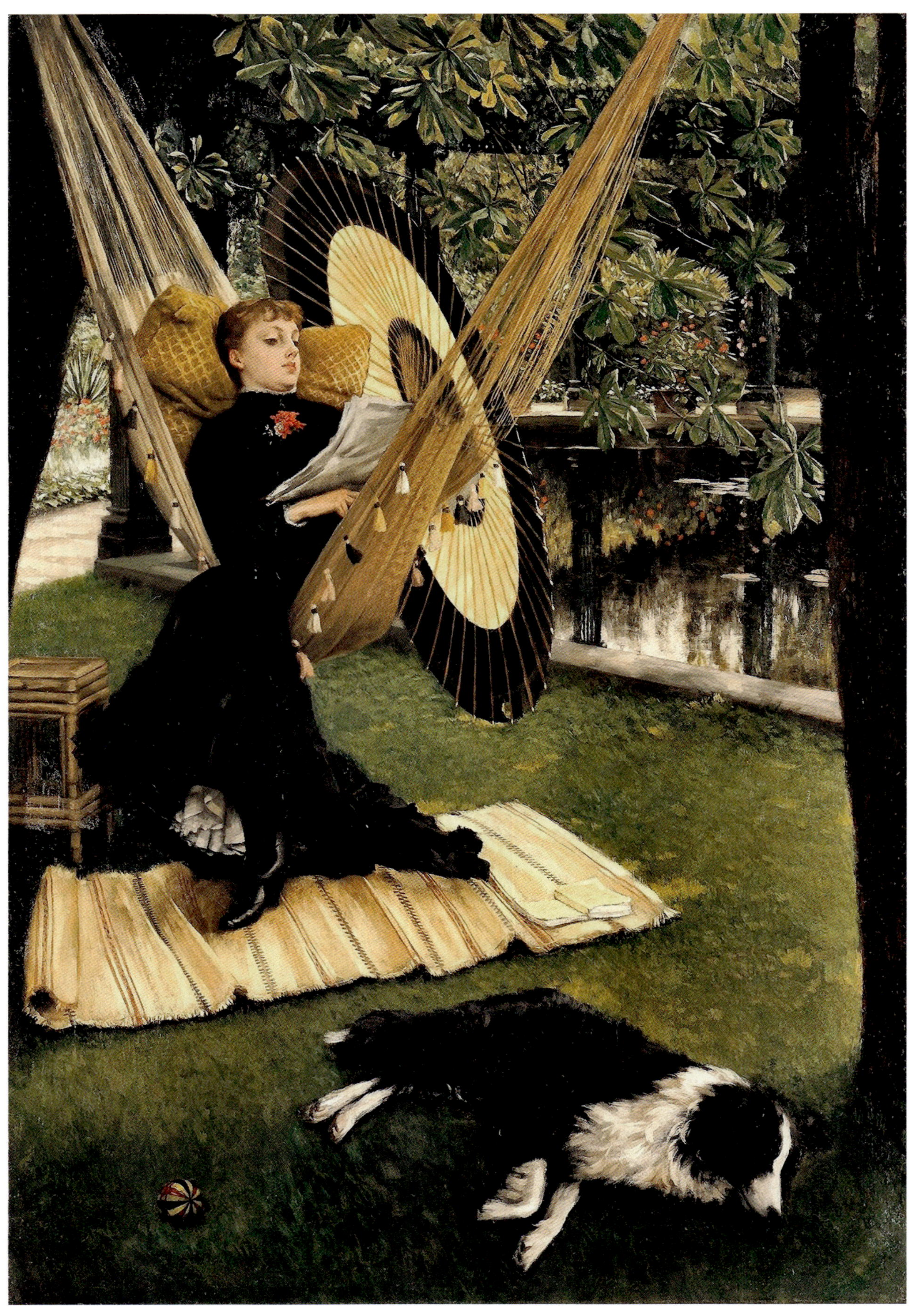

FIGURE 118
James Tissot, *The Hammock*, ca. 1878–1879. Oil on canvas, 50 × 30 in. (127 × 76.2 cm). Private collection

Discussions with dealer Georges Petit to exhibit all of Tissot's work at Petit's rue de Seze gallery, possibly in combination with Japanese art.[78] January to mid-February: Works on paintings to decorate dining-room walls of Henry Oppenheim's London house.[79] ⁂ February: Seven watercolors and twelve etchings in Société des aquarellistes exhibition at Galerie Georges Petit. ⁂ March: One-man exhibition at L'union centrale des arts décoratifs, Palais de l'Industrie, Paris, including oils, pastels, watercolors, etchings, and cloisonné enamels. ⁂ April: Grove End Road house advertised for sale with immediate possession. ⁂ May: Visits London and attends séance with medium Henry Slade at home of Albert Besnard, who records the supposed "spirit apparition" (fig. 121), later exposed as Besnard's red-haired model Annie Jones.[80] ⁂ After sharing with Daudet ideas for a series of etchings and stories about modern women, approaches potential publishing collaborator who declines; goes ahead with self-publication.[81] ⁂ July 27: Auction of London house; bought then or subsequently by Alma-Tadema. ⁂ October: *Prodigal Son* paintings in Exposition nationale des Beaux-Arts, Paris. ⁂ December: Copies available of the Goncourts' *Renée Mauperin* with ten etched illustrations by Tissot, published 1884 by Charpentier.

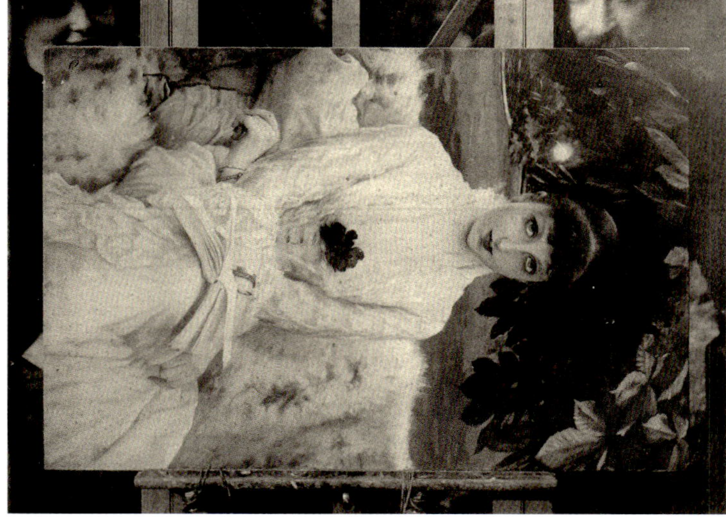

1884

Works on paintings and etchings of modern woman in Paris. ⁂ February: Four pastel portraits and ten *Renée Mauperin* etchings in Société des aquarellistes exhibition at Galerie Georges Petit, Paris.

1885

January: Edmond de Goncourt records that during dinner Aurélien Scholl

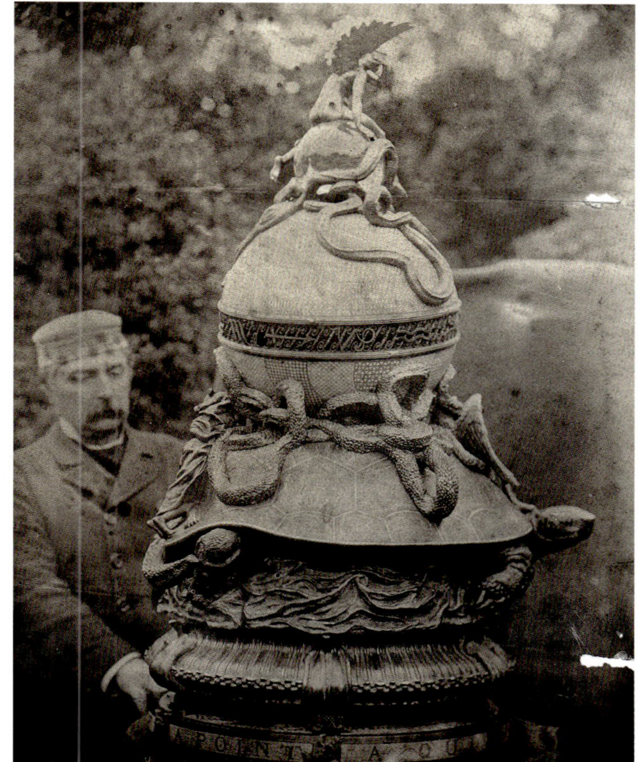

talked about a tightrope dancer both he and Tissot were courting.[82] ⁂ February: Meets spiritualist medium William Eglinton in Paris, after which they have several séances.[83] ⁂ April: Four works in exhibition of new Société des pastellistes at Galerie Georges Petit. ⁂ April–June: One-man exhibition of fifteen *La Femme à Paris* paintings, alongside other work, at Galerie Sedelmeyer, Paris (fig. 122). ⁂ May 20: Séance in London with Eglinton, at which Tissot claims to see Newton appear; subsequently records event in *The Apparition* (pls. 132–133).[84] ⁂ October: Goncourt records that, through Madame Daudet's matchmaking, Tissot had been engaged to Louise Riesener and had added a floor to his house in anticipation of marriage, but that Riesener changed her mind.[85]

1886

Makes cloisonné enamel plaques with names of friends for proposed mantelpiece.[86] ⁂ February: Shows five watercolors and two prints, including *The Apparition*, at Société des aquarellistes exhibition. ⁂ May–October: One-man exhibition *Pictures of Parisian Life*, comprising sixteen paintings and thirty-six etchings, at Tooth's gallery, London. ⁂ October 15: Sets out for Holy Land on occasion of fiftieth birthday (see fig. 123).

1887

March: Returns to Paris from Jerusalem; works for rest of year on illustrations for *The Life of Christ*. ⁂ October: Etchings in *Exposition des Graveurs du Siècle* at Galerie Georges Petit.

1888

Renée Mauperin with Tissot illustrations published in English by Vizetelly. ⁂ March 13: Tissot's father dies in Paris.[87] ⁂ May–September: Completes ninety drawings for *The Life of Christ*.[88] ⁂ Late October: Leaves Paris for Jerusalem via Marseille, to return April 1889.

FIGURE 119
Kathleen Newton (left) and Tissot (right) behind the painting *Reading in the Park* (ca. 1881; Musée des Beaux-Arts, Dijon, France), ca. 1881–1882. Collection Frédéric Mantion

FIGURE 120
Tissot with his sculpture *Fortune* (fig. 80) in the garden of his Grove End Road property, London, ca. 1882. Collection Frédéric Mantion

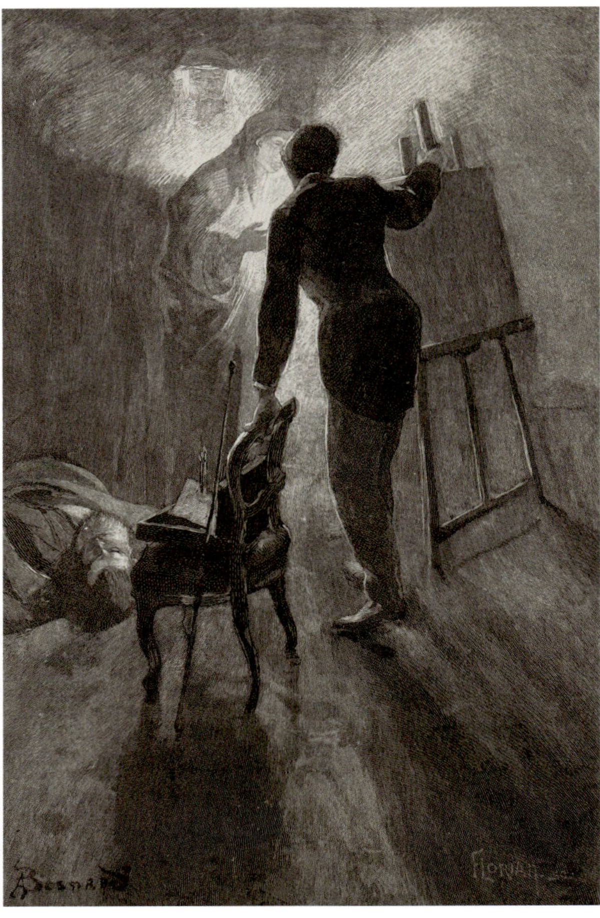

1889

January–February: Sends work to first exhibition of Société des peintres-graveurs at Galerie Durand-Ruel, Paris.[89] ❧ April: Returns to Paris from Jerusalem; completes fifty more illustrations for *The Life of Christ* by end of year, despite illness with fever.[90] ❧ As part of Paris's Exposition Universelle, shows *Marguerite at the Service* (lent by Monsieur Léon Say) and four etchings in *Exposition Centennale de l'Art Français*; and four *Prodigal Son* paintings (pls. 86–89) and *Portrait of Reverend Père B... [Bichet]* (pl. 32) in *Exposition Décennale*, where awarded Gold Medal. ❧ August: Press reports *Life of Christ* illustrations to be reproduced in black and white, probably wood engravings, and published in book form by Firmin-Didot, Paris.[91]

1890

January: Edmond de Goncourt records Tissot's intention to buy a small mountain near Jerusalem for 7,000 francs and build a studio there, to become a center for religious art and a French place of influence in the Holy Land.[92] ❧ February 1: Goncourt and the Daudets visit Tissot's studio to view *Life of Christ* illustrations as well as a "toy theatre" with little models Tissot uses to aid composition.[93] ❧ March: Tissot sells Degas's *Horses in a Meadow* (fig. 106) and Manet's *The Grand Canal, Venice* to

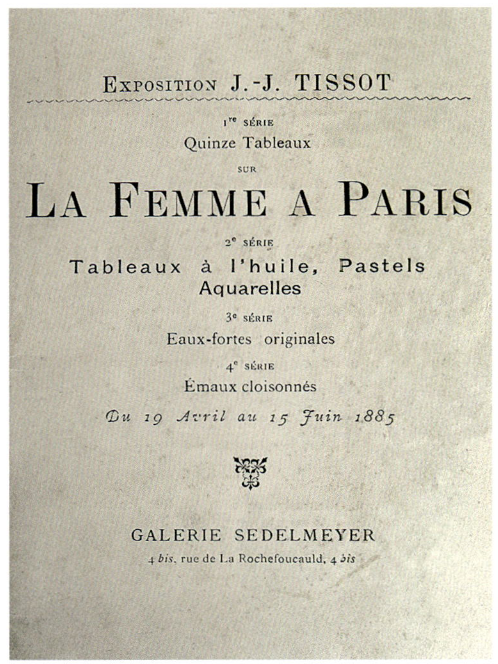

EXPOSITION J.-J. TISSOT

1re SÉRIE
Quinze Tableaux
SUR

LA FEMME A PARIS

2e SÉRIE
Tableaux à l'huile, Pastels
Aquarelles

3e SÉRIE
Eaux-fortes originales

4e SÉRIE
Émaux cloisonnés

Du 19 Avril au 15 Juin 1885

GALERIE SEDELMEYER
4 bis, rue de La Rochefoucauld, 4 bis

Durand-Ruel.[94] ❧ May: Japanese color woodcuts exhibited at École des Beaux-Arts, Paris; Mary Cassatt reports to Berthe Morisot that she saw Tissot, "who also is occupied with the problems of making color prints."[95] ❧ Completes another eighty watercolors for *The Life of Christ*.[96]

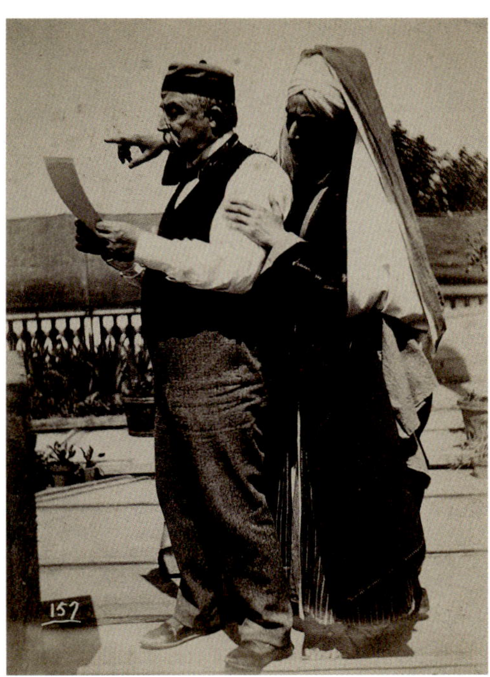

FIGURE 121
Frédéric Florian (Swiss, 1858–1926), wood engraving after wash drawing by Albert Besnard (French, 1849–1934), 1887, from Yveling Rambaud's *Force psychique*, 1889. Published by Ludovic Baschet, Paris. In the book, the accompanying text reads: *En la voyant, il s'écria* (When he saw her, he cried).

FIGURE 122
Catalogue title page for *La Femme à Paris* exhibition at Galerie Sedelmeyer, Paris, 1885. Collection Frédéric Mantion

FIGURE 123
Photograph of Tissot during one of his three trips to the Holy Land, 1886–1887, 1888–1889, or 1896. Collection Frédéric Mantion

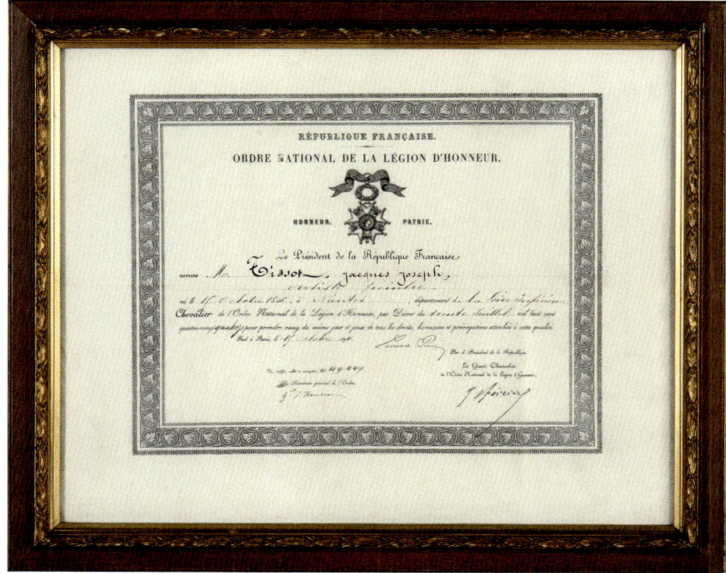
RÉPUBLIQUE FRANÇAISE.
ORDRE NATIONAL DE LA LÉGION D'HONNEUR.
HONNEUR. PATRIE.

1891

Last year listed as a member of Société des aquarellistes.

1892

Pastel portrait in Société des pastellistes français exhibition.

1893

May: *Prodigal Son* paintings and etchings shown in World's Columbian Exposition, Chicago, together with pastel portrait; another portrait shown in Société des pastellistes exhibition, Paris. ❦ December 20: According to Edmond de Goncourt, Tissot has three hundred compositions for *The Life of Christ* to exhibit at Champs-Élysées the following April but has not yet found a book publisher in France, although he is confident of finding one in America.[97]

1894

January: Edith Coues (later O'Shaughnessy) tries to interest American publisher Century in Tissot's book proposal.[98] ❦ April 25: *Société nationale des Beaux-Arts* exhibition opens at Palais du Champ-de-Mars, Paris, with two rooms devoted to pastels and watercolors, including 270 *Life of Christ* illustrations and the painting *Inner Voices* or *Christ the Comforter* (also known as *The Ruins*, fig. 32). ❦ Tissot awarded Légion d'Honneur (fig. 124). ❦ July: *The Times* reports that *Life of Christ* illustrations are to be reproduced in large photogravures by Catholic publishing firm Alfred Mame et fils, of Tours.[99] ❦ Mame comes to arrangement with art publishers Lemercier & Co. of Paris for Lemercier to reproduce Tissot's watercolors as color lithographs (fig. 125).[100]

FIGURE 124
Certificate of Tissot's Légion d'Honneur award. Collection Frédéric Mantion

FIGURE 125
Frontispiece from *La Vie de Notre Seigneur Jésus Christ*, vol. 1, 1896. Published by Alfred Mame et Fils, Tours, France. Collection Frédéric Mantion

1895

Work taking place over next few years at Château de Buillon, inherited in 1888 from Tissot's father. Modifications include construction of new studio as well as landscaping and archaeological digging.[101] ❦ Paints reception of Cardinal Langénieux as apostolic legate in Jerusalem.[102] ❦ 1895–1897: Designs for a *Museum of James Tissot Works* by Henri Paul Nénot (figs. 62–63) submitted unsuccessfully to competition for Exposition Universelle 1900 pavilions.[103]

1896

February/March: Tissot returns to Jerusalem. ❦ March 26: Exhibition of *The Life of Christ* opens in London's former Doré Gallery, New Bond Street, renamed Lemercier Gallery; admission 1 shilling. Remains on view until mid-1898, when packed for transport to America.[104] ❦ November: Just returned from the Holy Land, visits Lemercier Gallery exhibition.[105] Stays in London a week; visits Alma-Tadema, who shows him changes made to Grove End Road property.

1897

Works on colossal Christ Pantocrator for Dominican church apse in Paris (fig. 126).[106] January: Sells Degas's *Woman with Binoculars* (ca. 1875–1876; Galerie Neue Meister, Dresden) to Durand-Ruel. ❦ February:

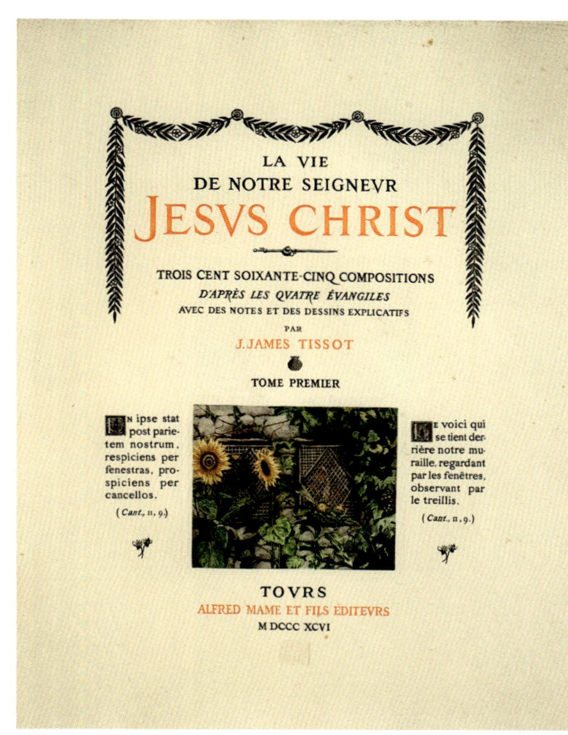
LA VIE
DE NOTRE SEIGNEVR
JESVS CHRIST
TROIS CENT SOIXANTE-CINQ COMPOSITIONS
D'APRÈS LES QVATRE ÉVANGILES
AVEC DES NOTES ET DES DESSINS EXPLICATIFS
PAR
J. JAMES TISSOT
TOME PREMIER

En ipse stat post parietem nostrum, respiciens per fenestras, prospiciens per cancellos.
(Cant., II, 9.)

Le voici qui se tient derrière notre muraille, regardant par les fenêtres, observant par le treillis.
(Cant., II, 9.)

TOVRS
ALFRED MAME ET FILS ÉDITEVRS
M DCCC XCVI

Daniel Halévy records anger of Degas at Tissot's sale of Degas's *Horses in a Meadow* and *Woman with Binoculars*, which had both been gifts from the artist.[107] ❦ April: Tissot's painting of Cardinal Langénieux in *Société nationale des Beaux-Arts* exhibition, Champ-de-Mars, Paris.[108] ❦ May 5: Paris exhibition of chromolithographic prints faithfully reproducing *Life of Christ* illustrations opens at Galerie Georges Petit.[109] ❦ June 25: Royal party visit Lemercier Gallery, London, to view *Life of Christ* illustrations.[110] ❦ September: Archbishop of Tours writes letter of endorsement published

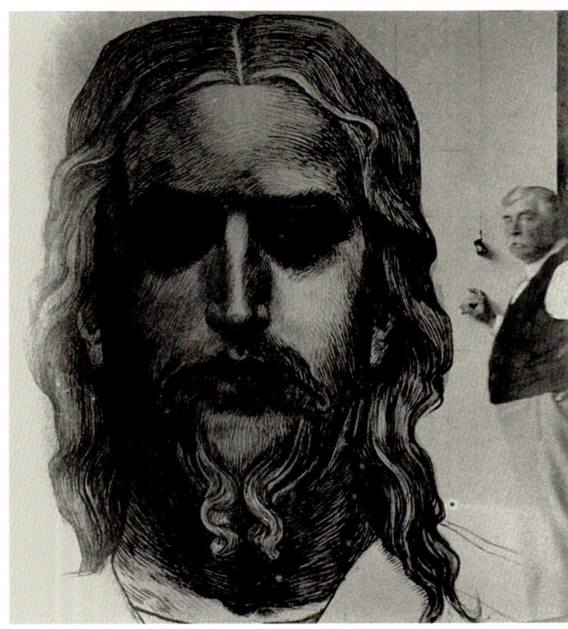

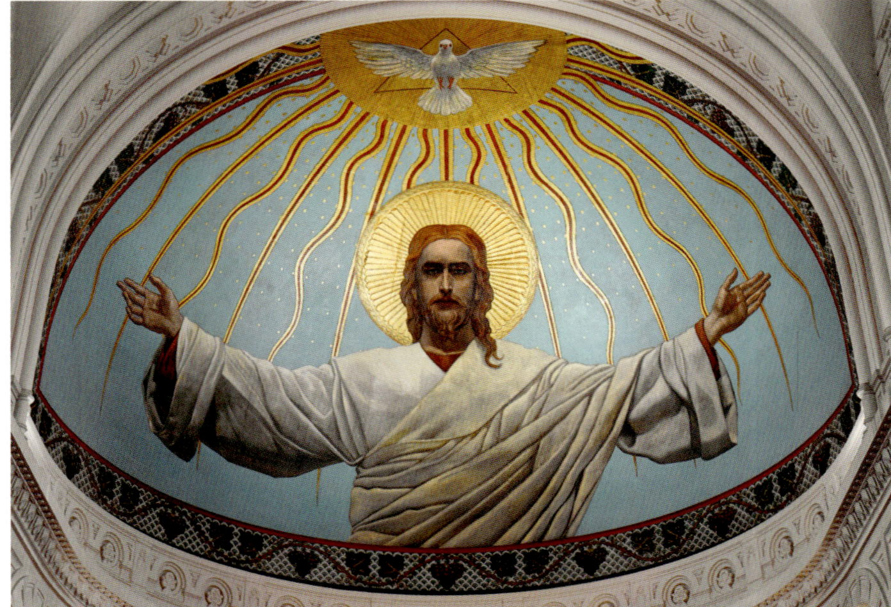

as preface to Mame's *Life of Christ: Edition Nationale*. Prime Minister William Ewart Gladstone accepts dedication of English-language edition, to be published by Sampson Low & Co. under arrangement with Mame and Lemercier.[111] ❧ December 3: Tissot's Christ Pantocrator consecrated (fig. 127).[112]

1898

January: Draws up will before traveling to New York. ❧ February: In New York to make arrangements for North American tour of *The Life of Christ*.[113] ❧ HRH Duke of York visits Lemercier Gallery to see *Life of Christ* illustrations.[114] ❧ June: *Exhibition of French Paintings* opens at Guildhall Art Gallery, City of London, including Tissot's *The Last Evening* (pl. 69) and *Too Early* (pl. 46), lent by Charles Gassiot. ❧ July 25: Reception and dance given by Corporation of City of London attended by Tissot and French dignitaries.[115] ❧ September: Lemercier sends *Life of Christ* illustrations to New York. ❧ October: Tissot travels to America with his friend, engineer Maurice De Brunhoff. ❧ November 15: *Life of Christ* exhibition opens at American Art Association galleries, Manhattan; Tissot attends opening. ❧ November 19: Reported "bruised and shaken up in an attempt to board a Madison Avenue bus" after visiting Archbishop Corrigan.[116] *Life of Christ* exhibition subsequently travels to Brooklyn, Chicago, Philadelphia, Boston, Saint Louis, and Toronto, before returning to Brooklyn in 1900.[117] ❧ December 17: Arrives in Liverpool from New York with De Brunhoff.[118]

FIGURE 126
Tissot working on Christ Pantocrator, 1897. Collection Frédéric Mantion

FIGURE 127
James Tissot, Christ Pantocrator, 1897. Oil on canvas pasted on wall. Convent of the Annunciation, Paris

FIGURE 128
Tissot's funeral procession circling the park of the Château de Buillon, 1902. Collection Frédéric Mantion

1899

With help of De Brunhoff, American edition of *The Life of Christ* published in four volumes by McClure-Tissot Company, New York, established for the purpose. Sends personal letters to potential subscribers in America.[119] ❧ Working on Old Testament illustrations; by August has sketched 430 compositions.[120]

1900

January: Trustees of Brooklyn Institute of Arts and Sciences decide to purchase *Life of Christ* illustrations for 60,000 dollars by public subscription. Tissot offers to come to America to design special galleries and paint a large Christ as focal point.[121] ❧ April–May: *The Life of Christ* exhibited in Brooklyn then at National Academy of Design, Manhattan, where delegates to Ecumenical Conference invited to view.[122]

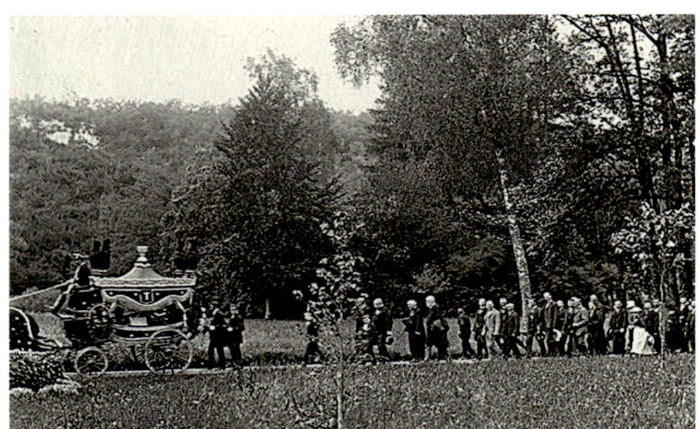

1901

April: Two rooms at *Société nationale des Beaux-Arts* exhibition, Champ-de-Mars, Paris, display ninety-five Tissot illustrations of the Old Testament book of Genesis. ❧ May: *The Life of Christ* watercolors, newly gold-mounted and reframed, go on display in new purpose-built galleries at Brooklyn Museum, remaining on view until 1930s.[123]

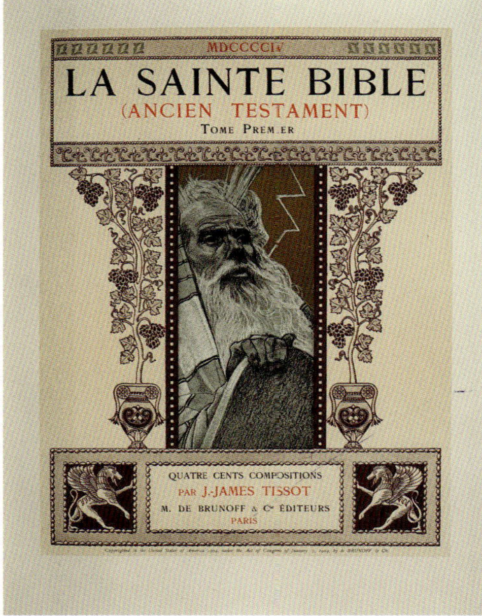

1902

August 8: James Tissot dies of fever at age sixty-six, at the Château de Buillon (fig. 128). ✻ De Brunhoff arranges for completion, publication, and exhibition of Old Testament illustrations. ✻ Tissot's nephew and nieces inherit his homes and contents. Muriel Violet Mary and Cecil George Newton, children of Kathleen Newton, are bequeathed 1,000 francs each.[124]

1903

Auction sale of Tissot's Paris studio contents at Hôtel Drouot, Paris.[125]

1904

Publication by De Brunhoff of *Old Testament* with chromolithographs of 373 illustrations by or after Tissot (fig. 129). Watercolor originals exhibited in America under auspices of American Tissot Society, touring to Brooklyn, Manhattan, Cincinnati, Chicago, Kansas, Washington, and Detroit until 1908.[126]

1909

American Tissot Society has to sell Old Testament drawings; philanthropist Jacob H. Schiff buys and gives them to the New York Public Library, transferring them in 1952 to the Jewish Museum.

1933

Leicester Galleries, London, *James Tissot Exhibition* brings together for the first time paintings made in England and hitherto dispersed.

FIGURE 129
Frontispiece from *La Sainte Bible (Ancien Testament)*, vol. 1, 1904. Published by M. De Brunhoff & Cie, Paris. Collection Frédéric Mantion

FIGURE 130
Auction sale of the contents of the Château de Buillon, 1964. Bibliothèque Municipale de Besançon, France, Ph2255 2

1936

James Laver's biography of Tissot, *"Vulgar Society": The Romantic Career of James Tissot, 1836–1902*, published by Constable.

1946

Newton's niece Lilian Hervey contacts journalist Marita Ross in response to her article about Tissot's mysterious muse, identifying Newton.[127]

1955

Graves Art Gallery, Sheffield, exhibition of work spanning Tissot's career (but not including items or information from France).

1964

Auction sale of Château de Buillon contents, following death of Tissot's last surviving niece, Jeanne Marie (fig. 130).[128]

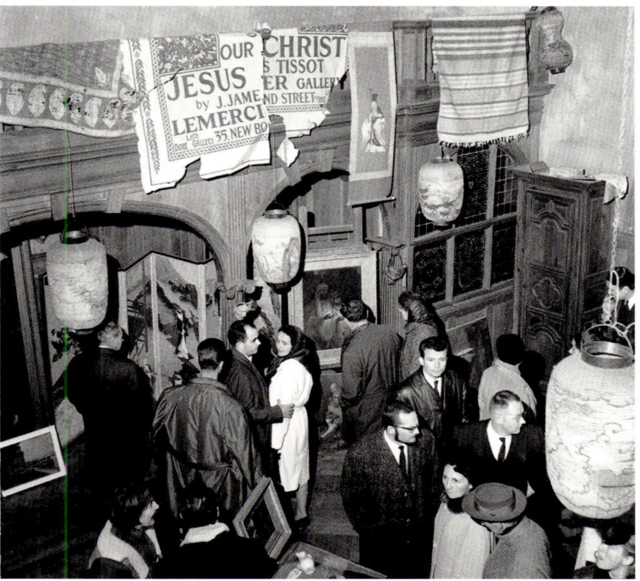

1968

James Jacques Joseph Tissot, first retrospective exhibition in America, at Museum of Art, Rhode Island School of Design, Providence, and Art Gallery of Ontario, Toronto.

1984–1985

James Tissot, first retrospective exhibition in Europe, at Barbican Art Gallery, London; Whitworth Art Gallery, Manchester; and Musée du Petit Palais, Paris.

1999–2000

James Tissot: Victorian Life / Modern Love exhibition at Yale Center for British Art, New Haven; Musée du Québec, Québec City; and Albright-Knox Art Gallery, Buffalo.

2019–2020

James Tissot: Fashion and Faith, first major North American West Coast exhibition, opens at the Legion of Honor, San Francisco, then travels to become first monographic exhibition presented at the Musée d'Orsay, Paris.

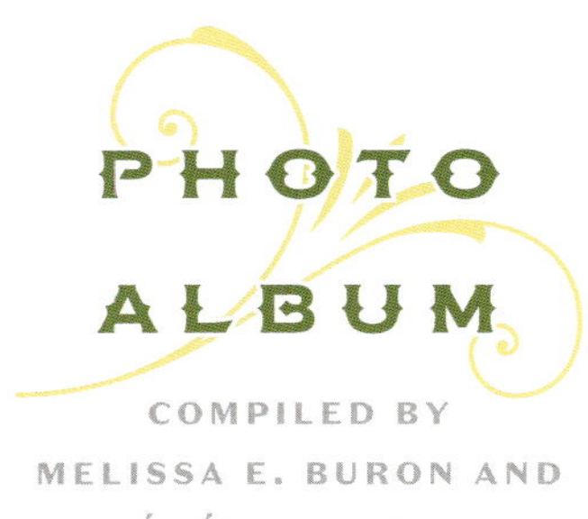

PHOTO ALBUM

COMPILED BY MELISSA E. BURON AND FRÉDÉRIC MANTION

In the course of research for this exhibition, hundreds of photographs and numerous glass-plate negatives once belonging to Tissot were discovered, originating from the contents of his estate in eastern France, the Château de Buillon, where he spent much of his time in his final years. These images—many of which have never been published—provide a glimpse into Tissot's private world and the carefully cultivated environment of his estate, to which he made many modifications after inheriting it in 1888, following his father's death. Such changes included additions to the château, which sits at the center of the estate's extensive grounds, as well as the construction of a studio inside a neighboring *abbatiale* that in the twelfth century housed the monks who founded Buillon. It was in this studio that Tissot painted many of his biblical illustrations; he also installed a photography room there. "Hundreds of years ago godly men chose this place for a monastery," Tissot said of Buillon, "and on the ruins of their building I have made my home for contemplation."[1]

All photos Collection Frédéric Mantion; photographers unknown

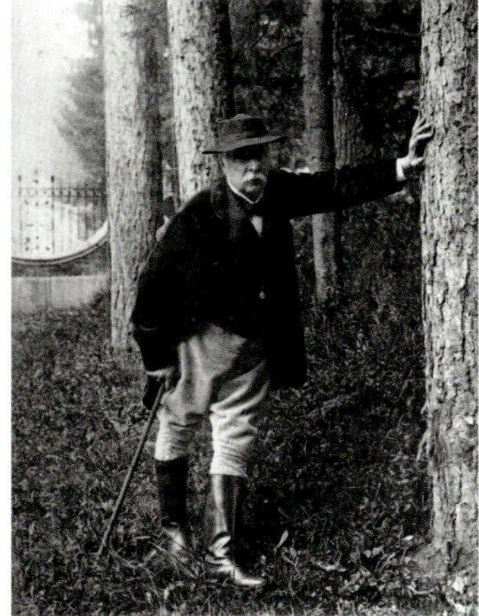

Tissot on the grounds behind the Château de Buillon, ca. 1898. The painter copied this pose for his *Self-Portrait, June 1898* (pl. 2).

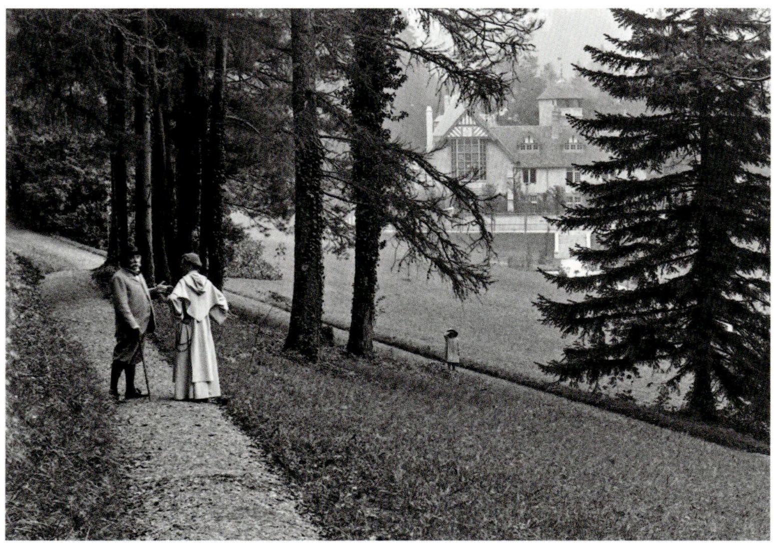

Tissot and Antonin-Gilbert Sertillanges, O.P., a Dominican priest, in the forested park of the château, with the studio building in the background, ca. 1898. In December 1897, Sertillanges had delivered an address at the inauguration of Tissot's Christ Pantocrator in Paris's Convent of the Annunciation church (fig. 127).

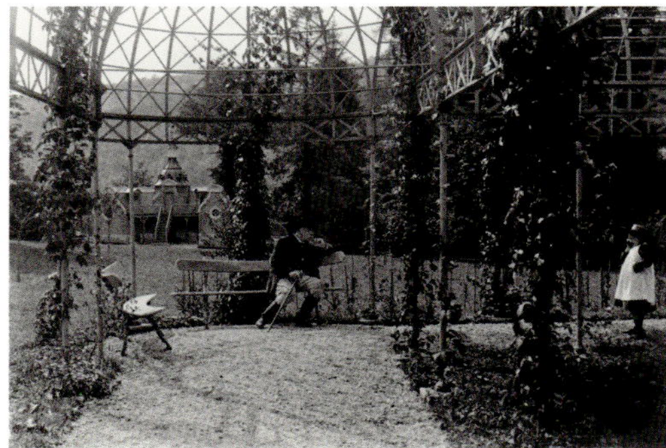

Tissot and his grand-niece Simone (later Madame Jean de Gournay of Paris) under the trellis in the garden behind the château, ca. 1898. The *volaillerie*, where the artist raised birds, can be seen in the left background.

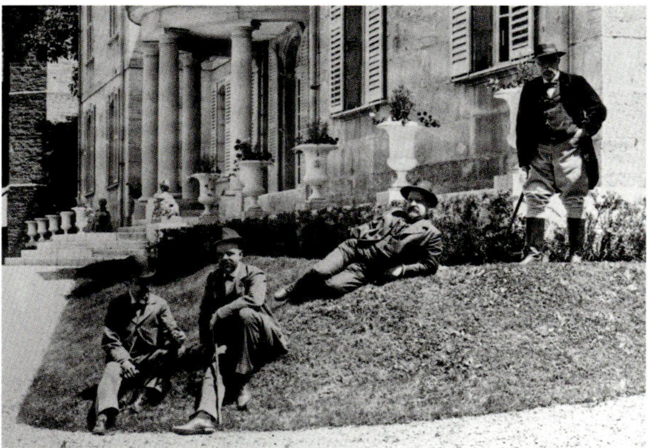

Tissot (standing far right); the publisher of his Old Testament series of watercolors, Maurice de Brunhoff (second from left); and two unidentified men in front of the château, ca. 1898.

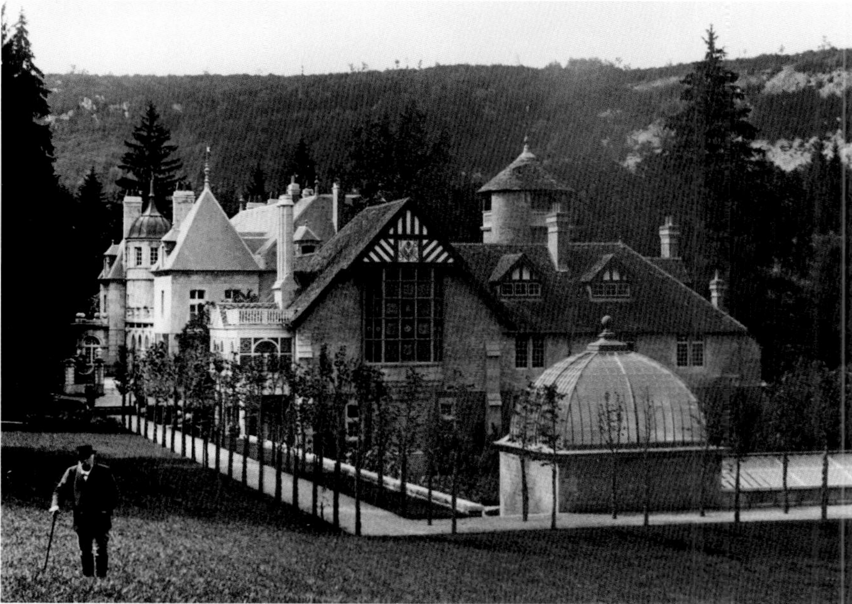

Tissot walking on the grounds of the estate, ca. 1895. The old *abbatiale* that Tissot turned into his studio building is shown from the southeast, with the château just behind it. The panels of the studio's large stained-glass window were designed and installed by Tissot in 1894.

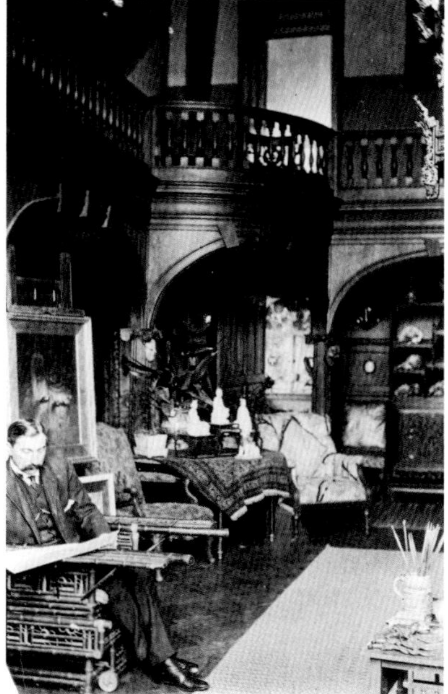

Possibly Tissot's nephew Henri Marcel-African, seated in Tissot's studio, ca. 1898–1901. *The Apparition* (pl. 133) is propped on an easel behind him. A table in the left background displays pieces from Tissot's collection of Asian artifacts. In the right foreground is a mug holding the artist's paintbrushes on a small red table, which still sits in the studio today.

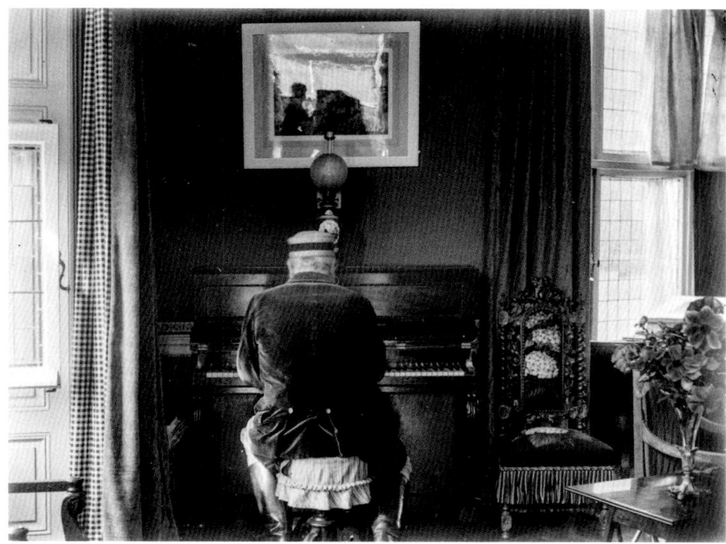

Tissot playing piano in the large salon of the English-style mill that he built in the 1880s on the banks of the Loue River, which runs through property, ca. 1898–1901.

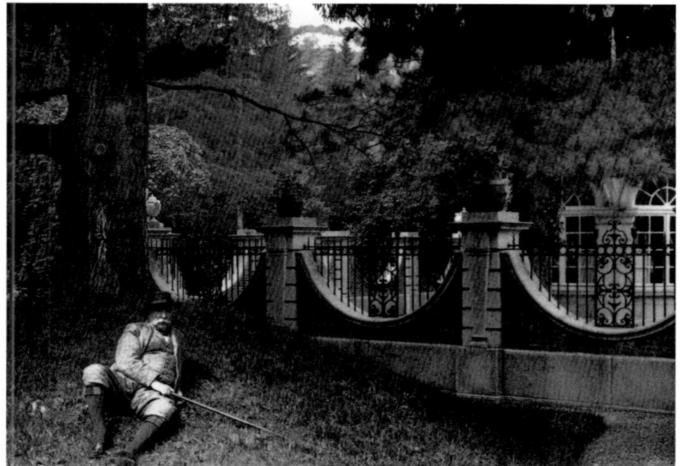

Tissot reclining on the grounds of his estate behind the château, ca. 1898–1901.

= 1866 =

Après Vêpres (sur les remparts) 3,000 fs

(Goupil

tableau de 12 portraits

M. de la Tour Maubourg
du Lau d'Allemans
de Rochechouart
Vansittart
de Miramon
Hottinguer
de Ganay Maurice
id Etienne
de St Maurice
de Polignac Edmond
de Galliffet
Ch. Haas

6,000

portrait de madame de Miramon 3,000
id de Mr aimé Seillière 2,000
id du jeune J. de Montbriton 2,000

16,000

TISSOT'S SALES NOTEBOOK (CARNET DE VENTES)

TRANSCRIPTION AND INTRODUCTION BY
KRYSTYNA MATYJASZKIEWICZ

From 1857, while still an art student in Paris, until 1890, in the midst of a successful career, James Tissot recorded sales of his work in a small notebook, a copy of which was recently rediscovered at his former estate, the Château de Buillon in France.[1] The document allows for an unprecedented glimpse into the artist's output and earnings, giving shape to the trajectory of his career. In the notebook, sales of works are listed by year, followed by their prices; annual totals are calculated at the bottom. Beginning in 1866, purchasers—often art dealers—are noted in the right-hand column, where Tissot also recorded resales of which he was aware, tracking some paintings over several years. The entries are scrawled in a sloping cursive, frequently using shorthand. This transcription aims to preserve the graphic layout of the text as well as its idiosyncrasies: abbreviations, strikeouts, and spelling errors are retained, with references clarified in the endnotes.

The sales notebook is not a comprehensive record of Tissot's output. It does not include, for example, works that Tissot gave as gifts or kept for himself, nor those that remained unsold and were among his property when he died. Many paintings appear in the numerous photograph albums Tissot compiled of his work—used for his own reference or to show potential clients—that are not listed in the notebook.[2] Among those omitted are several of his most well-known pictures, such as the portrait of Frederick Burnaby (pl. 29), owned by *Vanity Fair* editor Thomas Gibson Bowles—a mutual friend of Burnaby and Tissot—which was probably a gift, and *The Gallery of HMS "Calcutta" (Portsmouth)* (pl. 64), owned by the artist John Robertson Reid, possibly a gift in exchange. *The Triumph of Will (Poem in Five Parts): I. The Challenge* (pl. 99) and *The Two Sisters; Portrait* (pl. 21), both large-scale paintings, were either kept by Tissot or unsold; they appeared in 1903 at the posthumous sale of the contents of Tissot's Paris house, but are not in the notebook.

The sale also included many sketches, such as Tissot's *Self-Portrait* (pl. 1), none of which have notebook entries. *Summer* (pl. 58), lent to the 1877 Grosvenor Gallery exhibition by art dealer Edward Fox White and described in the catalogue as "from a series of the Four Seasons," is not listed, nor is another painting from that series, mounted in the same album.[3] Perhaps, Tissot did not log consigned works, for which payment was deferred until sale, and neglected to note any eventual receipts. Also missing from the notebook are paintings apparently given by Tissot as payment, such as *July* (1871; location unknown), consigned to Christie's, London, in May 1883 by the solicitors Pyke and Minchin, who were agents for the sale of Tissot's London house at 17 Grove End Road. *Evening* (also known as *The Ball*, pl. 79), recorded in the stock books of the art dealer Arthur Tooth & Sons in 1879 as bought from Tissot, is not included by the artist among sales to Tooth, and may also have been exchanged for services.

Although Tissot's sales notebook contains only a selection of his entire output, it is a crucially important document and a useful asset for scholars. It lists early works never before mentioned; gives names of sitters for portraits, which can then be matched up with photographs in Tissot's albums and used to identify models (see Perrin, this volume); notes which pictures are replicas; and details the payments Tissot received as well as the collectors or dealers to whom he sold. When comparing the notebook with surviving records of stock books for the Paris-based art dealers Goupil & Cie, the British-based Arthur Tooth & Sons and Thomas Agnew & Sons, and the New York dealer M. Knoedler & Co., who all recorded considerable profits from sales of Tissot's work, it is easy to understand why Tissot was "vowing vengeance against the dealers" at early meetings of the Society of Painter-Etchers.[4] The artist records limited sales from 1860 to 1867, possibly attributed to the high prices he sought early in his career (see Matyjaszkiewicz, "Tissot's 'Genius' Picture-Selling in Britain," this volume). Once Tissot achieved recognition at the 1867 Exposition Universelle in Paris, dealers responded to the increased interest in his work among collectors in Europe and the United States. The notebook reveals previously unrecorded buyers, including private individuals such as French economist Léon Say and Glasgow merchant Alexander Kay, and dealers, most notably the highly successful, Paris-based Frédéric Reitlinger and the lesser-known, Liverpool-based William Herbert.

The sales notebook shines an interesting light on the question of Tissot's picture titles. In 1882, the painter stated to Alfred de Lostalot, who had asked about works made during Tissot's eleven-year stint in London, that "it would be a monotonous list of two hundred and fifty titles, which are not intended to express anything, for I avoid titles intended for effect as much as possible."[5] This might have been true of the multiple works called *Holiday* or *Seaside*, but not of such titles as *The Eve of Departure*, *An Interesting Conversation*, *The Last Guest*, *Storm Brewing*, or *Uninteresting Story*, which seem to point viewers in a certain interpretative direction. A comparison of the titles Tissot recorded in his notebook with those entered in dealers' stock books suggests that dealers chose, or developed with Tissot, catchy or evocative titles in order to stimulate sales and distinguish between similar pictures. Agnew, for example, recorded the first of Tissot's *Portico of the National Gallery* versions as *The Portico (Country Cousins)*, subsequently referring to it as *Country Cousins*, and the second version as *London Visitors* (pl. 56). Tooth changed *The Last Guest* to *Waiting for the Fourth*; the dealer P. L. Everard exhibited the copy of Colonel Longley's portrait (pl. 31) as *Time Is Money*. For Tissot's 1872 exhibition pictures, British dealers or artist friends familiar with their native audience likely proposed *Bad News* instead of *Swoon*, and *An Interesting Story* instead of *An Interesting Conversation*.

Furthermore, the notebook reveals the ratio of Tissot's portraits to his subject pictures and still lifes over a period of almost forty years. At first, the artist kept a running total of the number of paintings, portraits, and drawings he created, ceasing the cumulative analysis in 1868, when sales filled his notebook page. The turmoil of 1875, when Tissot's portrait of ex-empress Eugénie (pl. 28) was rejected from the Royal Academy with at least two other Tissot submissions, is reflected in scribbled strikeouts, as are two failed sales of *The Thames* (pl. 61). Income from etching, which Tissot returned to in earnest in 1875, is recorded separately beginning in 1876. These sales accounted for 40 percent of Tissot's art-related earnings in 1880 and 1881. Payments are noted in pounds from 1871 to 1886, initially within entries, then from 1876 in a separate column alongside their equivalent amounts in francs. More orderly bookkeeping for 1878 to 1880 evidences the secretarial help of Charles Buckingham, whom Tissot took on in 1880, and who tidied the accounts retrospectively.

In 1881, Tissot calculated his cumulative earnings over the preceding twenty-five years, and comparative earnings for every five years, logged in the final page of the notebook. Subsequently, before voyaging to the Holy Land in 1886, Tissot calculated his total earnings over thirty years, which exceeded 1.4 million francs. His record year for painting sales was 1873, a total of 208,141 francs, a leap from 1872—his first year in London—when he earned 94,515, more than twice the 39,000 total of his best previous year, 1869 in Paris. He had begun in 1857 with an annual total of 680 francs. When he ceased keeping records in 1890, Tissot was focused on illustrating *The Life of Christ*, a project so successful that it alone would eventually bring earnings equivalent to his previous thirty years' work as an artist.

1857

portrait de Mr Daldin ainé[6]	40 [frs]
Copie d'un portrait Louis XV[7]	200
portrait d'une jeune fille[8]	30
id id id[9]	30
Cartons de Vitraux (Le Mans)[10]	350
portrait de Madame Maton	30
	680

~~45~~ Tableaux ~~ou~~ dessins 1[11]

1 copie

1858

Copie d'un portrait Louis XVI[12]	150 [frs]
id id id Louis XV[13]	150
id d'un General de l'Empire[14]	100
portrait de la petite fille de M Maton[15]	30
id	60
Copie de l'Enfant Jesus de M[gneur] de Segur[16]	200
portrait pour Du Cleuziou	100
S[t] Francois de Sales (M[g[?]] de Segur)[17]	100
	890

2 tableaux 6 copies

total 6 tableaux

tous portraits[18]

1859

Esquisse de la danse Macabre[19] (vendu a Basset)	750 [fr]	en 1868 chez un Marchand rue Notre dame de Lorette	1,500 [fr]
		en Janv. 1870 id .... pres le Nouvel Opera[20]	4,000
		vendu a l'exposition internationale a Londres en Aout 1871[21]	7,000
promenade dans la Neige[22] (appartient a Mr Pereire)[23]	500	Vendu a l'hotel du Ventes en fevr. 1872[24]	2,750
2 portraits des 2 enfants de Mr Anatole de Segur[25]	400		
portraits de M[r] et Madame Bourgeois	400		
	2050		

6 tableaux

total 12 tableaux

dont 10 portraits[26]

1860

Marguerite a la fenêtre[27]	1,500 fr		
(en Russie) (Vendu a Goupil)[28]			
Marguerite a L'Eglise (a Genoux)[29]	1,500	en 1861 appartient a Mr Portalès	
(Goupil)[30]		id 1862 id . . . M. Mayer de Vienne[31]	
id reduction Partielle[35]	500	id 1868 vendu a l'hotel des Ventes a Mr	
	3,500	Vurtemberg[32]	2,480 fr
		id 1871 Hotel des Ventes	4,500[33]
		chez Goupil en mai 1879. en demande	10,000 fr[34]

3 tableaux
total 15 tableaux
dont 10 portraits

1861

Marguerite a l'Eglise (assise)[36]	
(vendu a Mr Leon Say)[37]	2,500 frs

1 tableau
total 16 tableaux
dont 10 portraits

1862

pas d'exposition cette année-la[38]

1863

Rencontre de Faust et de Marguerite[39]	5,000 fr	vu au Palais de St Cloud en 1869[40]
(Musée de Luxembourg)		vu au musée du Luxembourg en 1872[41]
Jeune homme a L'Eglise[42]	2,500 fr	appartient a Mr Charles Waring a Londres[43]
(Gambart)[44]		
2 Dessins	1,000 fr	
(pour les Contes Bretons de)	8,500 fr	
Londres		
tom Taylor[45]		

2 tableaux
total 18 tableaux 3 dessins
dont 10 portraits

1864

Portrait de Madame Derome[46]	300 fr	
id id id Ladrocat[47]	600 fr	
Marguerite au Rempart[48]	2,000	
(Limoges)		
Portrait de Me[?] Vausanges[49]	400	
Melancolie (manteau jaune)[50]	2,000	a philadelphie?
(Amerique) (Goupil)[51]	5,300	

5 tableaux
total 23 tableaux 3 dessins
dont 13 portraits

1865

tentative d'Enlèvement[52]	3,000 fr
(Goupil)[53] amerique	
Portrait du Mquis de Miramon	
sa femme et ses 2 Enfants[54]	5,000
Faust et Marguerite au Jardin[55]	
(Goupil)[56] amerique	2,000
depart du fiancé[57]	2,500
(Goupil)[58]	12,500

4 tableaux
total 27 tableaux 3 dessins
dont 17 portraits

1866

Apres Vêpres (sur les Remparts)[59]		3,000 fr	vendu a l'hotel Drouot 7,000fr mai 1875.[60] Reiltinger appartient a Mr Fould (a Christie le 3 juillet 1875 (£315 (7,875fr). Nelson[62]
(Goupil)[61] tableau de 12 Portraits[63]	Mr de la tour Maubourg[64] du Lau d'allemans[65] de Rochechouart[66] Vansitarte[67] de Miramon[68] Hottinguer[69] de Ganay Maurice[71] id Etienne[72] de St Maurice[73] de Polignac Edmond[74] de Gallifet[75] Ch. Haas[76]	6,000[70]	appartient a Mr Hottinguer
portrait de Madame de Miramon[77]		3,000	
id de Mr Aimé Seillière[78]		2,000	
id de Jeune J. de Montbrison[79]		2,000	
		16,000	

1866

a reporter[80]	16,000fr	
Le Confessional[81]	3,000fr	(Goupil)[82] Amerique
id aquarelle (petite)[83]	250fr	~~Lucas~~ ~~id~~ (fils Goupil)[84]
depart du fiancé (aquarelle)[85]	250fr	(fils Goupil)[86]
	19,500fr	

6 tableaux 2 dessins ou aquarelles
total 33 tableaux 5 dessins ou aquarelles
dont 32 portraits[87]

1867

Confidence[88]	4,000fr	(Goupil)[89] Amerique a Christie juin 1875 £375[92]
Jeunes femme Chantant dans une tribune[90]	4,000	(Goupil) achete par Wallis de Londres[91]
aquarelle du Confessional[93]	250	Lucas (amerique)[94]
portrait de Mr Coppens de Fontenay[95]	1,000	
le Printemps[96]	1,800	Vendu a Cadart 2,500fr[97] (amerique)
portrait de Mr Buquet[98]	1,500	
portrait de Mlle Cottin	3,000	
	15,550	

6 tableaux 1 aquarelle
total 39 tableaux 6 dessins ou aquarelles
dont 32 portraits[99]

1868

Depart de l'Enfant prodigue[100]	2,000fr	a Mr de londre[101] (both)
Retour de l'Enfant prodigue[102]	4,000fr	
portraits des 2 garcons de Monsieur Kanh[103]	5,000fr	
3me Comedien[104]	1,000	a Petit[105] / puis repris pour mon compte[106] (both)
4me Comedien[107]	1,000	
Portrait charge de Mr de Lambertye	300fr	
id id du Cercle des patineurs 35 pts[108]	1,400	
le Déjeuner[109]	4,500	vendu a Mr Michel Heine
2 esquisses[110]	400	id a Cartier
Leçons du dessin au prince Mumboutason Tagoukaua[111]	2,220	
portrait de ce prince Japonais (aquarelle)[112]	1,000	
portrait des 4 enfants de Mr Gaillard[113]	6,000	
5 petites têtes sur marbres id[114]	2,000	
les tambours aux tuilleries[115]	7,000	princesse Mathilde[116]
	37,820fr	

1869

Patineuse[117]	2,000 fr	(Goupil)[118]
Melancolie (l'étang)[119]	1,800	(Goupil)[120] Angleterre
femmes regardant le temple Chinois[121]	2,000	Goupil[122] ~~amerique~~ a Mr Springer (Vienne)
Une Veuve[123]	3,000	Goupil[124] Amerique
femmes regardant un navire Japonais[125]	3,000	id[126] id
reduction du dejeuner[127]	2,000	a un membre du Tribunal de Commerce[128]
1re Comedien[129]	1,000	à Gustave Rotschile[130]
Nature Morte (le petit lare)[131]	800	a Mr Springer (Vienne)
portrait du chien de Madame Somoïtoff[132]	500	
le Rendez-vous[133]	2,000	a Mr Ch. Poirson
5me Comedien[134]	600	(Goupil)[135]
le toast[136]	5,000	a Kaïser de Vienne
Jeune femme sur un Divan[137]	1,800	Goupil[138]
le Confessional (robe verte)[139]	2,600	Goupil[140] (amerique)
le tête a tête[141]	2,300	Goupil[142]
	30,400 fr	

1869

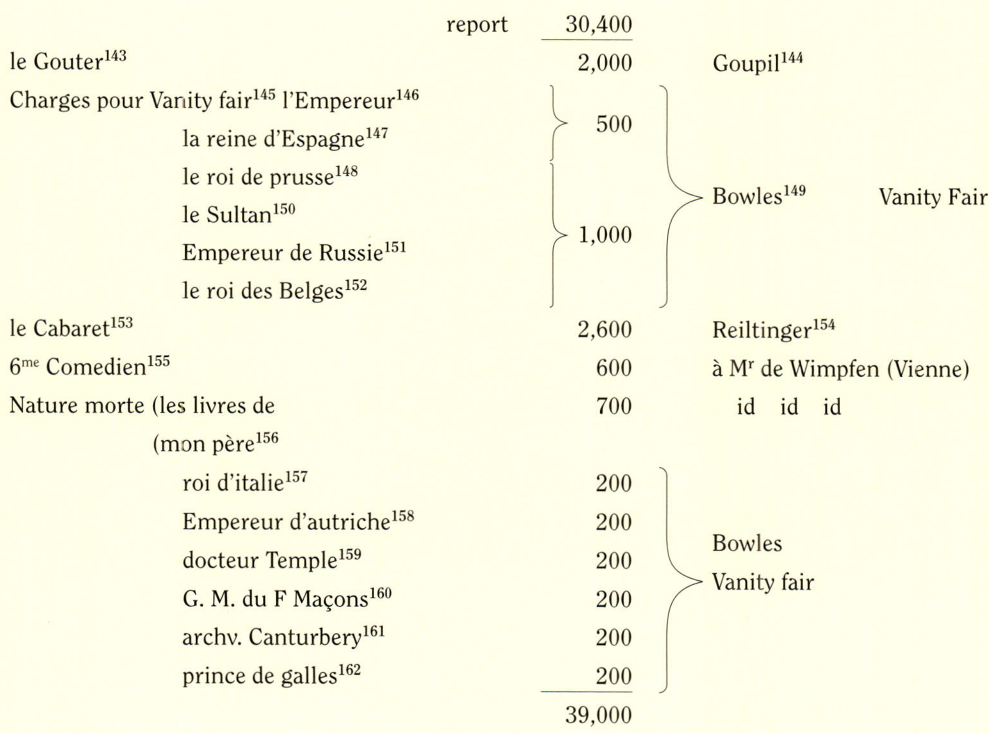

report	30,400	
le Gouter[143]	2,000	Goupil[144]
Charges pour Vanity fair[145] l'Empereur[146], la reine d'Espagne[147]	500	Bowles[149] Vanity Fair
le roi de prusse[148], le Sultan[150], Empereur de Russie[151], le roi des Belges[152]	1,000	Bowles[149] Vanity Fair
le Cabaret[153]	2,600	Reiltinger[154]
6me Comedien[155]	600	à Mr de Wimpfen (Vienne)
Nature morte (les livres de (mon père[156]	700	id id id
roi d'italie[157]	200	Bowles Vanity fair
Empereur d'autriche[158]	200	Bowles Vanity fair
docteur Temple[159]	200	Bowles Vanity fair
G. M. du F Maçons[160]	200	Bowles Vanity fair
archv. Canturbery[161]	200	Bowles Vanity fair
prince de galles[162]	200	Bowles Vanity fair
	39,000	

1870

La femme en Bateau[163]	3,300 fr	Reitlinger, a Mr Stewart. H. V.[164] Amerique a Glasgow par pilgeram en 1875
femmes au paravent[165]	3,000	id
Melancolie / manteau jaune / aquarelle[166] /	200	id
le pape[167] Emile Olivier[168] Rochefort[169]	600	Bowles Vanity fair
Sur le port[170]	1,500	Mr Caroline Levy
3me Comedien[171]	600	Reitlinger
Danse Macabre[172]	2,000	id. (Amerique)
J. femme se chauffant (Louis XVI)[173]	2,300	id. (Amerique)
les Stalles[174]	2,500	id. (Amerique)
Enlevement[175]	3,800	id. (Amerique)
Partie Carée[176]	8,000	id. a Madame Martinet / Claude Lafontaine[177]
Bismarck[178] le prince de prussie[179] General Trochu[180]	600	Bowles Vanity fair
	28,400 fr	

1871 (LONDRES)

5me Comedien	550	a Mr Sauvage
portrait de Th. G. Bowles[182]	800	
id de Mr Chicester fortescue[183] (300£)	7,500	
id de Lady Waldegraves (150G.)[184]	3,936	
La Marguerite a la Bouche (250 G.)[185]	6,550	a Mr Charles Waring. Londres (pilgeram l'achete Ca vend a agnew. qui la vend a Mr[186])
~~portrait de Madame Desoye~~[187]	~~1,500~~	Paris
	20,836[188]	
21 portraits charges a 200[189]	4,200	Bowles Vanity fair
	25,036[190]	

1872

Les adieux[191] 300£	7,500 fr	Pilgeram. à Charles Waring (gravé)[192]
la conversation interessante[193] 400£	10,000 fr	a Charles Waring
portrait de Lt Colonnel Longley[194] 200£	5,000 fr	
le balcon[195] 400£	10,000 fr	puis a Agnew[196]
2 Jeunes filles en bateau[197] 300£	7,500 fr	
la Gazette[198] 300£	7,500 fr	vendus a Pilgeram
l'Eventail[200] 150£	3,750 fr	gravé par Simmons[199]
la paresseuse[201] 100£	2,500 fr	
la Veille du Depart[202] 600£	15,000 fr	vendus a Agnew[203]
le thé[204] 200£	5,000 fr	
La Tamise[205] 400£	10,000 fr	id[206] gravé dans le Graphic[207]
Evanouie[208] 200£	5,000 fr	id[209]
1 dessin gouache Etude de la femme dans le fauteuil du (Last Evening)[210] 30£	750 fr	id[211]
id id[212]	750 fr	id[213]
1 dessin gouache femme debout[214] 25£	625 fr	id[215]
1 id id id id[216]	625 fr	id[217]
1 id id id id[218]	625 fr	id[219]
	92,115	

1872

a reporter	92,115	
6 portraits charges a 400fr[220]	2,400	
	94,515 fr	

1873

last Evening[221] 700£	17,500 fr	vendus a Agnew. W. A. Gasciott. Mr[222]
la fille du Capitaine[223] 700£	17,500	
le pistolet[224] 280£	7,000 fr	a Pilgeram. Wallis
to Early[225] 800£	20,000	a Pilgeram. Agnew 1000£. a Gasciott 1,400[226]
Japonaise dans une serre[227] 120£	3,000	a Pilgeram[228]
la visite au navire[229] 650	16,250	
les Docks[230] 650	16,250	Agnew
le pont de taplow[231] 400	10,000	
3 dessins esquisses. la femme rose £25 de too Early[232]	625	
S d g. J. f. pour les Docks[233] 20£	500	Ch. Waring
Esq… J. Femme du bateau a vapeur[234] 20£	500	
	109,125 fr	

1873 (SUITE)

a reporter	109,125 fr	
esquisse peinte d'après nature		
du pont de taplow sans figure[235] 100£	2,500	Agnew[236]
la Station[237] £550	13,750	id[238]
le bateau (chale jaune)[239] £550	13,750	id[240]
falcon hotel[241] £800	20,000	id[242]
le portique de National Gallery[243] £800	20,000	id[244]
4 portraits charges[245] 52£	1,100	Bowles, Vanity fair
1 portrait charge[246] 16 guineas	416	id id
le rouleau Japonais[247] (400£)	10,000	Pilgeram
	190,641	
La convalescente[248] £700	17,500	
	208,141	

1874

Bal on Shipboard[249] 1400£	35,000	}
le portique de National Gallery		}
en grand[250] £1000	25,000	} Agnew
Concert[251] £1200	30,000	}
Reponse a la lettre[252] £800	20,000	}
J. femme en blanc dans le		
vestibule de ma maison de Paris[253] 200£	5,000	Pilgeram
tea party[254] 700£	17,500	Pilgeram
Storm Browing[255] 900£	22,500	Agnew[256]
le Bouquet de Lilas[257] 400£	10,000	Agnew
francs	165,000	

1875

la femme et l'invalide		
Blanc et Bleu[258] 800£	20,000 francs	Agnew[259]
the Last guest[260] 735£	18,375	tooth[261]
the Hollyday (la plus grand)[262]		
Simon (10%)[263] £550	13,750	tooth[264]
~~la tamise (the private steamer)~~[265]		
~~10% Simon) 900 guineas~~	~~23,525~~	~~Thom. Gilbert~~[266] [
le coup de vent[267] ~~l'Eventail~~ 450 guineas	11,250	Tooth (le coup de vent)[268]
l'éventail[269] ~~coup de vent~~ 250 guineas	6,250	Tooth (l'éventail)[270]
the Hollyday (le long)[271] 10% Simon £500	12,500	Murrieta (Mariano)[272]
~~La tamise (private lunch) £800~~[273] [	~~20,000~~	}
La convalescente (en blanc)		}
l'automne[274] £600	15,000	} Marsden[275]
le portrait de l'imperatrice		}
Eugenie et le prince imperial[276] £700	17,500	}
Matinée d'été[277] £350	8,750	} de la Penha[278]
frs	123,375	

1876

La tamise	£ 800	20,000	Marsden
(private steamer)[279]			
Quarelling[280]			
commission 10% Wallace[281]	525	13,125	Alexander Kay[282]
Captain's Balcony[283]	600	15,000	J. J. White[284]
le portrait de Longley[285]	120	3,000	Everard[286]
last pic-nic[287]	650	16,250	Tailor par White[288]
replica de Capt[s] Balc[289]	300	7,500	White[290]
	2,995	74,875	
Vanity fair[291]	120	3,000	
Etchings[292]	82	2,050	
	3,197	79,925	

1877

Le Veuf[293]	£ 420	10,500 fr	J. Davies Esq[r 294]
les Chrysanthemes[295]	325	8,125	Hermon M. P.[296]
Uninteresting Story n[r] 2[297]	315	7,875	MacLean[298]
port de la fille de M[c]Lean[299]	105	2,625	"
" de Marsden[300]	50	1,250	Marsden
La Meditation ancien tableau[301]	400	10,000	Sir Richard Wallace[302]
Portsmouth dockyard			
(the Highlander)[303]	300	7,500	G. W. Herbert[304]
dessin a l'essence du Crocket[305]	100	2,500	" " "
spring (du long)[306]	300	7,500	E. F. White[307]
port. de M[rs] gill et ses 2 enfants[308]	472	11,800	
	2,787	69,675	
Vanity fair[309]	20	500	
Etchings	361	9,025	
	£ 3,168	79,200	

1878

		francs	
Hid & Sicke[310]	£ 400	10,000	Herbert
Croquet[311]	180	4,500	E. White. vendu au Grosvenor gallery
Docks (en hauteur[?])[312]	380	9,500	id.
Sea Side (Drapeaux)[313]	290	7,250	id.
Dessin (replica de Spring.)[314]	50	1,250	id.
Replica d'October[315]	250	6,250	MacLean
portrait de Lumley[316]	52	1,300	
October[317]	425	10,625	MacLean. M[r] Lee[318]
port de M[rs] M[c]Laren[319]	300	7,500	
Summer[320]	220	5,500	Goupil[321]
Nowty book[322]	100	2,500	Herbert
	£ 2,647 =	66,175	
Etchings[323]	£ 464 =	11,600	
	£ 3,111 =	77,775f.[324]	

1879

	£	fr.	
Replica "Orphans"[325]	£ 275	6,875	McLean
id. Widower. petit[326]	60	1,500	tooth[327]
id. Fenetre petit[328]	60	1,500	tooth[329]
id. Hansome. petit[330]	60	1,500	tooth[331]
Portico. petit[332]	80	2,000	White
(les Docks) Emigrants[333]	250	6,250	McLean
Reverie le petit tableau brune[334]	90	2,250	"
replica le petit "Evening"[335]	70	1,750	"
(Albion hot. Ramsgate) Sea-side[336]	80	2,000	"
(falcon) Gravesend[337]	80	2,000	"
replica "hammock" Under the Chestnut[338]	65	1,625	"
Crossing the Channel[339]	65	1,625	"
Kew gardens[340]	80	2,000	tooth[341]
Richmond Bridge[342]	80	2,000	McLean
July[343]	140	3,500	Knoedler[344]
id. dessin essence[345]	23	575	"[346]
(Blackfriars) Steamboat[347]	65	1,625	McLean
	£ 1,623	40,575	

1879

	£		fr.	
report	£ 1,623		40,575	
Mavourneen[348]	130		3,250	McLean
"piano"[349] "Lily"[350]	80		2,000	tooth[351]
Orphans[352]	500		12,500	Grosvenor gallery
Going to Business[353]	225		5,625	" "
Quiet afternoon[354]	300		7,500	Agnew (Grosven. Gall.)[355]
tête de femme (avec les capucines)[356]	150		3,750	Graphic[357]
port. de Lawson. Dessin[358]	17		425	Reynolds
replica Emigrants[359]	80		2,000	McLean
" "[360]	75		1,875	"
Organ grinder[361]	70		1,750	Liverpool[362]
	£ 3,250	=	81,250 fr.	
Etchings	£ 852.12.8.	=	21,315 fr.	
	£ 4,102.12.8	=	102,565 fr.	

1880

	£	fr.	
the Warior's Daughter[363]	£ 100	2,500 fr.	White
Rivals[364]	270	6,750	White
La Lettre[365]	125	3,125	McLean
petit replica robe bleue / sur le sofa[366]	80	2,000	McLean = Georges Trist[367]
petit replica Good Bye[368]	84	2,100	Georges Trist[369]
Winter Walk[370]	180	4,500	Rhodes[371]
Eldest Sister[372]	80	2,000	Boussaton[373]
Le Louvre (Salle des Saisons)[374]	300	7,500	} Knoedler[376]
Sur les Marches[375]	70	1,750	}
le Hammock[377]	150	3,750	G. Trist[378]
Trafalgar tavern (le Duncan)[379]	150	3,750	Newcastle[380]
Quiet[381]	80	2,000	id
Gardening[382]	70	4,250	id
replica Salle des Saisons Louvre[383]	85	2,125	Liverpool[384]
	£ 1,924 =	48,100 fr.	
Etchings	£ 1,289 =	32,225	
	£ 3,213 =	80,325	

1881

	£	fr.	
By Land[385] } oil paint			
By Water[386] }	£ 300	7,500 fr.	G. Trist[387]
le g^d^ Hammock avec le chien[388]	160	4,500	Donkin Newcastle[389]
the Eldest Sister oil[390]	300	7,500	W. Waughan[391] — Chislehurst
By Land[392] } wat. col.			
By Water[393] }	300	7,500	G. Petit[394] Paris
Children pic-nic oil[395]	150	4,250	G. Trist[396]
the Eldest Sister (wat col.)[397]	120	3,000	G. Petit Paris
Richmond (the Castle Hotel)[398]	100	2,500	} Knoedler[400]
On the Sun[399]	100	2,500	}
	1,530	39,250	
Etchings	1,120	27,500	
	2,650	66,750	

1882

	£	fr.	
Summer Evening[401]	£ 150	3,750	Mr Vaugham[402]
Quiet. aquarelle[403]	50	1,250	Mr Green
decoration Salle a Manger[404]	100	2,500	Mr Openheim[405]
	£ 300	7,500	
Etchings	£ 125.18.7.	3,147	
	£ 425.18.7	10,647	

1883

Hampton Ct.[406]	£ 120	3,000	G. Petit
aquar. Visiteurs au Louvre[407]	80	2,000	G. Petit
a compte sur la Salle a Manger[408]	140	3,500	Openheim
......	80	2,000	G. Petit[409]
port. de Me Laure Hayman[410]	120	3,000	Cte Lafond
La reste de la decoration de la salle a manger[411]	110	2,750	Openheim
port de Mad. Serebriany[?]	120	3,000	Marin[?]
port. Me Marie Beckman[?]	80	2,000	Sacelmans[?]
le Banc de jardin aquar.[412]	100	2,500	Marzocordato[?]
	£ 950 =	23,750	

1883—SUITE

	950	23,750	
dessin plume le petit Nemrod[413]	80	2,000	Goupil
port d'une petite americaine (morte)[414]	80	2,000	Goupil[415]
	£ 1,110	27,750	
Etchings	222	5,554	
	£ 1,332	33,304	

1884

port. Me Bega[?]	£ 60	1,500	
Etchings	171.16.0	4,295	
	£ 231.16.0	5,795	

1885

(Trop tot) dessin Figaro[416]	£ 48	1,200	
replica Sedelmeyer (l'Esthetique)[417]	£ 80	2,000	
port de Mlle Faulchier[?]	£ 80	2,000	acheté par Petit
port. de Mlle Gaulomier[?]	£ 80	2,000	
	£ 288	6,200	
Etchings	267.5.7	6,557	
	£ 555.5.7	13,757	

1886

Tooth & Sons 15 tableaux			
de la Femme a Paris[418]	£ 2,436	69,000	Tooth & Sons
Aquarelles falcon hotel[419]	40	1,000	Beaugniet[421]
id. l'auberge des 3 corbeaux[420]	40	1,000	
id le dejeuner du Matin[422]	32	800	
2e port. de Mlle Faulchier	80	2,000	
port de Mad^{e} May[423]	120	3,000	
port de Mlle Miette	40	1,000	
le piano[424]	40	1,000	J. Bulla[425]
Vis. au Louvre			
Salle des Saisons[426]	40	1,000	
	2,868	79,800	
Etchings	96.2.6	2,403	
	2,964.2.6	82,203	

1887

Gravesend. Aquarelle[427]		625	MacLean
Sur la tamise[428]		2,500	Georges Petit
		3,125	
Etchings	Kroshar[?]	660	
	Abley[?]	362	
	tooth	450	
	Mayer	237	
		1,709	

1888

port. d'homme. Baroura[?] Double	500
id id.	500
Second voyage a Jerusalem[429]	1,000

1889

Dessins. Julien.		400
Me Lailliere[?] port.		1,000
		1,400
Etchings	Dumont[430]	300
id.	Knoecler	2,816
	Dumont	300
		3,416
		1,400
		4,816

1890

port. de Me Groult[431]	1,000
le jeune Seillière port.[432]	600
Mlle Marianne Pichou port.	2,000
Mr de Fontenay port[433]	2,000
une esquisse Arthur Meyer[434]	200
recu de Arthur Meyer[435]	4,900
	10,700

le port de Me[?] Jacquemart	2500	
promenade du Matin[436]	1500	
~~Mlle Christine Seilliere port.~~		~~2,000~~
Etchings Dumont		300
l'apparit. Medi.[437]		50
" Knoedler		450
		800
		10,700
		11,500
port. Mlle Christ. Seillière[438]		2,000
		13,500

	an	par 5 ans	par 10 ans
1857	680		
1858	890		
1859	2,050	9,620	
1860	3,500		
1861	2,500		55,420
1862	0,000		
1863	8,500		
1864	5,300	45,800	
1865	12,500		
1866	19,500		
1867	15,550		
1868	37,820	55,420 /prem 10 années	
1869	39,000	145,806	
1870	28,400	201,226 /1res 15 années	
1871	25,036[440]		
1872	94,515		
1873	208,141		
1874	165,000	670,956fr	

1875	123,375	872,182fr les 20 1re années
1876	79,925	
1877	79,125	
1878	77,525	
1879	102,800	406,300
1880	80,100	
1881	66,750	1,278,482fr en 25 ans
1882	10,647	
1883	33,300	
1884	5,795	145,702fr
1885	13,757	
1886	82,203	1,424,184fr les 30 années[439]
1887		
1888		
1889		
1890		
1891		
1892		

a Londres
en 11 ans 1,102,292[441]

(goupil)

(goupil) angleterre.

goupil (~~amerique~~ a Mr Springer (Vienne)

goupil, amerique.

id id

a un membre du Tribunal de Commerce

à Gustave Rotschild

a Mr Springer (Vienne)

a Mr Ch. Poirson

(goupil)

a Kaëser de Vienne

goupil

goupil (amerique)

goupil

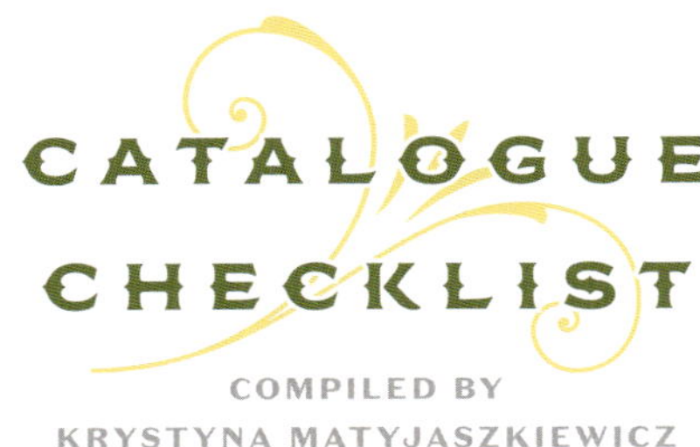

CATALOGUE CHECKLIST

COMPILED BY
KRYSTYNA MATYJASZKIEWICZ

A NOTE TO THE READER

The titles used in this checklist are the ones used for each artwork upon first exhibition, recorded sale, or publication. When two titles were originally used interchangeably, both are given. The title is also listed in French (in blue) when a French title was used for first exhibition, recorded sale, or publication. Original French titles have been translated into English. If the work is now widely known by a different title, that title is also included. Other titles from exhibition, publication, or sales records are included in relevant category sections.

Entries include information regarding provenance; exhibition, publication, and bibliographical history; and artist signatures, when available. For abbreviations used in the Provenance sections, see the key at the end of the checklist. For abbreviations used in the Exhibitions sections, see "Exhibition Abbreviations," this volume. For abbreviations used in the Bibliography sections, see "Bibliography," this volume. Artworks included in the San Francisco exhibition are indicated by a * symbol. This checklist reflects the most complete information available at the time of publication.

1

*SELF-PORTRAIT, CA. 1865

Oil on wood panel, 19⅝ × 11⅞ in. (49.8 × 30.2 cm)
Signed l. r.: *James Tissot*
Fine Arts Museums of San Francisco, Museum purchase, Mildred Anna Williams Collection, 1961.16
Prov.: Tissot studio sale, Paris, 1903, bt. Xavier Desparmet-Fitz-Gérald; Mildred Anna Williams Collection; purchased 1961.
Exh.: Providence and Toronto 1968; Yale 1999; Rome 2015.
Bibl.: *Art Quarterly* 1961, 302, 310; Misfeldt 1971, 67–68, fig. 31; London and Manchester 1984–1985, fig. 3; Wentworth 1984, 59, pl. 36; Paris 1985, fig. 3; Wood 1986, fig. 3; Arscott 1999, 66, fig. 25; New Haven, Québec, and Buffalo 1999–2000, 52–53; Nash, Orr, and Stewart 1999, 127; *Gazette des Beaux-Arts* 2000, fig. 11; London and Paris 2017–2018, 81, 83 (illus.).

2

*SELF-PORTRAIT, JUNE 1898, BUILLON, 1898

Opaque watercolor on silk, 44⅛ × 20⅛ in. (112 × 51 cm)
Signed, dated, and inscribed u. r.: *J. J. Tissot / Son portrait par lui même / juin 1898 / Buillon*
Collection Frédéric Mantion
Prov.: Tissot sale, Besançon, 1964.
Exh.: London and Manchester 1984–1985.
Bibl.: Misfeldt 1982, pl. IV-58; Treble 1984, 182; Wood 1986, 151–153, fig. 163.

3

*MEETING OF FAUST AND MARGUERITE, 1860

RENCONTRE DE FAUST ET DE MARGUERITE

Oil on wood panel, 30¾ × 46⅛ in. (78 × 117 cm)
Signed and dated l. l.: *JAMES TISSOT / 1860*
Musée d'Orsay, Paris, Acquired in 1860, RF 1983.93
Prov.: Bought from Tissot by the French state for the Musée du Luxembourg, Paris, July 17, 1860, and delivered to the Dépôt de l'État, July 25, 1863, when Tissot received payment of 5,000FF (Notebook); transferred to Ministry of the Interior, 1907; then Dépôt de l'État; Mairie of Chambon-Feugerolles (Loire), 1960; Musée d'Orsay, 1982 (attribution of FNAC, 1983).
Exh.: Paris Salon 1861 as *Rencontre de Faust et de Marguerite*, with quote "FAUST: Ma belle demoiselle, oserai-je vous offrir mon bras et ma conduite? (Faust. GOETHE)"; Palais de Saint-Cloud 1869 (Notebook); Musée du Luxembourg 1872 (Notebook); Paris 1889; Paris 1974; Paris 1985; Paris-Bruxelles 1997; Copenhagen 2000; Saint-Antoine-L'Abbaye 2004; Nantes 2005; Rome 2015; Paris 2016; Munich 2018.
Publ.: Photograph by Robert Bingham published August 1, 1862 (legal deposit BNF, July 19, 1862, no. 1256); photograph by Maison Braun published by Braun & Co., 1896 (inv. Braun 13.322).
Bibl.: Lagrange 1861, 346; Foucher 1881, illus. facing 179; Strahan 1882, 49–51; Musée National du Luxembourg 1884, 1887, 1892, 73 (illus.); Bénédite 1909, 146 (illus.), 148; Saunier 1911, vol. 2, 175 (illus.); Providence and Toronto 1968; Zerner 1968, 22; Misfeldt 1971, 36, 39, fig. 6; Misfeldt 1982, pl. I-15; London and Manchester 1984–1985, 88, fig. 40; Wentworth 1984, 22, 28, 31–32, 57, 199, pl. 2; Paris 1985, 135, pl. III; Wood 1986, 23–25, fig. 9; New Haven, Quebec, and Buffalo 1999–2000, 26; Nantes 2005–2006, 15–16.

4

*MARGUERITE IN CHURCH, CA. 1860–1865

Oil on canvas, 19¾ × 29½ in. (50 × 75 cm)
Signed l. l. in monogram: *JT*
National Gallery of Ireland, Dublin, Presented, Sir Alfred Chester Beatty, 1950, NGI.4280
Prov.: Probably sold by Mme Antoinette Moisset, divorced wife of M. Egbert Abadie, Hôtel Drouot, Paris, December 12–13, 1899 (21), as *Marguerite à l'eglise*, oil on canvas, 19¾ × 29½ in. (50 × 75 cm), signed with monogram, 780FF, bt. C. Blanc; Sir Alfred Chester Beatty; presented by him, 1950.
Exh.: London and Manchester 1984–1985 as *Marguerite à l'eglise*; Paris 1985; Yale 1999; Nantes 2005.
Bibl.: Misfeldt 1971, 40, fig. 12; Wentworth 1978, 36, fig. 1f; National Gallery of Ireland 1981, 164 (4280 CB); Misfeldt 1982, pl. I-21; London and Manchester 1984–1985, 98; Wentworth 1984, 28, 32–33, 136, pl. 7; Paris 1985, 139; New Haven, Québec, and Buffalo 1999–2000, 26–27; Dolkart, ed. 2009, 13–14, fig. 5.

5

DURING THE SERVICE, 1860

also known as **MARTIN LUTHER'S DOUBTS**

PENDANT L'OFFICE

Oil on wood panel, 34¾ × 26¾ in. (88.3 × 68 cm)
Signed and dated l. l.: *JAMES TISSOT / 1860*
Colección Pérez Simón, Mexico City
Prov.: Sold by Tissot in 1863 as *Jeune homme à l'eglise* [Young Man in Church] for 2,500FF to Gambart (Notebook), whose French Gallery in London had been managed since 1861 by Henry Wallis with the support of Jean Pilgeram and Léon Lefèvre; Charles Waring, London, by 1868; consigned to Christie's, London, May 8, 1886 (87) as *Luther's Misgivings*, 1860, £84, bt. in; Margaret E. Galbreaith, Hamilton, Ontario; sold by her executors, Christie's, New York, May 21, 1986 (118); sold Christie's, New York, February 15, 1994 (44).
Exh.: Paris Salon 1861 as *Pendant l'office*; Limoges 1862 as *Les vêpres* [Vespers]; French Gallery, London, 1863, as *Young Luther in Church*; Leeds 1868 as *Young Luther in Church*, lent by Charles Waring; Hamilton 1949–1985, on loan from Bequest of Margaret Galbreaith; Providence and Toronto 1968; London and Manchester 1984–1985 as *Pendant l'office*; Paris 1985; Yale 1999.
Publ.: Photograph by Robert Bingham published December 1, 1861, as *Les vêpres* [Vespers] (legal deposit BNF, February 22, 1862, no. 354).
Bibl.: Misfeldt 1971, 44, 47–50, fig. 20; Misfeldt 1982, pl. I-13; Warner 1982, 2 (illus.); London and Manchester 1984–1985, 98; Thomson 1984, 89; Wentworth 1984, 35, 199, pl. 10; Paris 1985, 136; Wood 1986, 27, fig. 12; New Haven, Québec, and Buffalo 1999–2000, 22, 24–25.

6

MARGUERITE ON THE RAMPARTS, 1861

MARGUERITE AU REMPART

Oil on canvas, 43¼ × 34 in. (109.9 × 86.4 cm)
Signed and dated l. r.: *J. Tissot / 1861*
Colección Pérez Simón, Mexico City
Prov.: Sold by Tissot in 1864 at Limoges for 2,000FF (Notebook); sold Sotheby's, Monaco, December 2, 1988 (693); sold Sotheby's, New York, May 23, 1989 (79); sold Christie's, London, November 29, 1991 (52); sold by a Southern private collector, Sotheby's, New York, October 2, 1994 (79).

Exh.: Probably Limoges 1864.
Publ.: Photograph published by Goupil & Cie, October 1, 1862 (legal deposit BNF, December 13, 1862, no. 2423); etching by Charles Courtry (exhibited Paris Salon 1870 [5135b]) published with text by René Ménard in *Le musée universel* (Paris: Goupil & Cie, 1868 and 1870; Paris: Librairie Renouard, 1888), and in *Art Gems* (London, Paris, and Frankfurt: Henry Sotheran, Joseph Baer and Co., 1873).
Bibl.: Ménard 1868, 1870, 1888; Thiébault-Sisson 1902, cover (illus.); Providence and Toronto 1968; Misfeldt 1971, 39, fig. 10; Misfeldt 1982, pl. I-17; London and Manchester 1984–1985, 98–99; Wentworth 1984, 22, 28, 33, pl. 8; Paris 1985, 139, fig. 33; Wood 1986, 23.

7

*WAY OF FLOWERS, WAY OF TEARS or DANCE OF DEATH, 1860

VOIE DES FLEURS, VOIE DES PLEURS or DANSE MACABRE

Oil on canvas, 14⅝ × 48¼ in. (37.2 × 122.4 cm)
Signed and dated l. l.: *JACOBUS TISSOT. PINXIT. 1860*
Museum of Art, Rhode Island School of Design, Providence, Jesse Metcalf Fund, Georgianna Sayles Aldrich Fund, Mary B. Jackson Fund and Edgar J. Lownes Fund, 54.172
Prov.: Sold by Tissot in 1870 as *Danse macabre* [Dance of Death] for 2,000FF to Reitlinger, who sold it to an American buyer (Notebook); Mr. T. A. Dolan, Philadelphia, by 1879; Private collection, Philadelphia; purchased from Julius Weitzner, New York, September 28, 1954.
Exh.: Paris Salon 1861 as *Voie des fleurs, voie des pleurs*, with description *Penetrantes in interiora mortis*; French Gallery, London, 1862, as *Dance of Death*; Bayonne 1864 as *Penetrantes in Interiora Mortis*; New York 1866–1867 as *Danse macabre*; Vienna 1869 as *Todten-Tanz* [Dance of Death], price 3,000FF; Providence and Toronto 1968.
Publ.: Etching in reverse by Gustave Greux, printed by Delâtre, Paris, published as *Voie des fleurs, voie des pleurs* in *L'artiste*, April 15, 1862, following 184.
Bibl.: Du Camp 1861, 102–103; Gautier 1861, 338–342; Lagrange 1861, 346; Merson 1861, 266–268; *L'artiste* 1862, 184; *Times* 1863, 3; *Daily News* 1864, 2; Paletta 1866, 136; Strahan 1879, 23, 39, illus. 23 as "*Penetrantes in Interiora Mortis*, fac-simile of a sketch from the original painting by James Tissot, collection Mr. T. A. Dolan"; Gourley 1964, fig. 1; Misfeldt 1971, 44–46, fig. 16; Reff 1976, I, 96 and II, 109, Nb18; Rosenfeld 1981, 92–94, no. 31; Cohen 1982, 40; Misfeldt 1982, pl. I-11; London and Manchester 1984–1985, 14, 29, 86, 88, fig. 39; Wentworth 1984, 36–39, pl. 12; Wood 1986, 27, fig. 13 (1859 version); Lochnan 1999, 3–4; Saddlemyer 1999, 157, fig. 63 (1859 version).

8

*PROMENADE ON THE RAMPARTS, 1864

PROMENADE SUR LES REMPARTS

Oil on wood panel, 20½ × 17½ in. (52.1 × 44.5 cm)
Signed and dated l. l.: *J. J. Tissot / 1864*
Cantor Arts Center, Stanford University, California, Gift of Mr. Robert Sumpf, 1968.107
Prov.: Robert Sumpf, Pasadena, by 1968; given by him to Stanford University, 1968.
Exh.: Providence and Toronto 1968, lent by Robert Sumpf, Pasadena; Japan 1988.
Publ.: Photograph (probably of another version) published by Goupil & Cie, 1864 (legal deposit BNF, September 22, 1866, no. 1514); photogravure of Goupil photograph published by Goupil & Cie, 1883.
Bibl.: Lostalot 1883, 377 (illus. as *Excursion on the Ramparts*, from Goupil photograph); Misfeldt 1971, 44, fig. 14; Misfeldt 1982, pl. I-33 (Cantor or Goupil version); Wentworth 1984, 42, 73, pl. 18; Wood 1986, fig. 15; Nantes 2005–2006, 18.

9

*DEPARTURE OF THE PRODIGAL SON, 1863

DÉPART DE L'ENFANT PRODIGUE

Oil on canvas, 42⅛ × 89 in. (107 × 226 cm)
Signed and dated l. r.: *J. James Tissot. 1863*
Petit Palais, Musée des Beaux-Arts de la Ville de Paris, Purchased, 1985, PDUT1453
Prov.: Sold by Tissot in 1868 for 2,000FF to M. de Londre [Delondre] (Notebook); consigned by Delondre, Hôtel Drouot, Paris, May 12, 1896 (70) as *Le départ de l'enfant prodigue*, 1863, bt. in; sold by executors of Louis Paul Delondre, Hôtel Drouot, Paris, May 27–28, 1898 (5) 430FF, bt. Sohier; consigned to Christie's, London, June 21, 1985 (103) but withdrawn; purchased by Musée du Petit Palais, 1985 Inv. PDUT 1453.
Exh.: Paris Salon 1863 as *Départ* [Departure]; Rome 2015.
Publ.: Photograph by Robert Bingham published May 1, 1863 (legal deposit BNF, June 6, 1863, no. 1201).
Bibl.: Wentworth 1978, 245, fig. 57b; Misfeldt 1982, pl. I-24; London and Manchester 1984–1985, 65, 98; Wentworth 1984, 40–41, pl. 16; Wood 1986, 28–29, fig. 16; Tokyo, Osaka, Mie, Tochigi, and Yokohama 1988, 128 (illus.); *Revue du Louvre* 1993, no. 49; New Haven, Québec, and Buffalo 1999–2000, 163; Nantes 2005–2006, 20.

10

*RETURN OF THE PRODIGAL SON, 1862

RETOUR DE L'ENFANT PRODIGUE

Oil on canvas, 45¼ × 81⅛ in. (115 × 206 cm)
Signed and dated l. l.: *James Tissot 1862*
Petit Palais, Musée des Beaux-Arts de la Ville de Paris, Purchased, 1992, PPP4856
Prov.: Sold by Tissot in 1868 for 4,000FF to M. de Londre [Delondre] (Notebook); sold by Delondre, Hôtel Drouot, Paris, May 12, 1896 (71) as *Le retour de l'enfant prodigue*, 1862, 750FF, bt. Delondre; sold by executors of Louis Paul Delondre, Hôtel Drouot, Paris, May 27–28, 1898 (6), 2,150FF, bt. Bernheim Jeune; Private collection, Toulouse; Mr. and Mrs. Joseph M. Tanenbaum, Toronto; sold Sotheby Parke Bernet, New York, May 1982 (49); Manney collection; sold Christie's, London, June 12, 1992 (117); purchased by Musée du Petit Palais, 1992, Inv. PPP 4856.
Exh.: Paris Salon 1863 as *Retour de l'enfant prodigue*; London 1864; Liverpool 1864 as *The Prodigal Son*; London and Manchester 1984–1985; Paris 1985; Japan 1988; Nantes 2005.
Publ.: Photograph by Robert Bingham published May 1, 1863 (legal deposit BNF, June 6, 1863, no. 1201).
Bibl.: *Era* 1864, 15; *Art Journal* 1864, 151; Misfeldt 1971, 44–47, 52, 55–56, fig. 18; Wentworth 1978, 245, fig. 57a (incorrectly titled à Venise); Misfeldt 1982, pl. I-22; London and Manchester 1984–1985, 64–65, fig. 25, col. pl. 2; Wentworth 1984, 39–40, 199, pl. 14; Paris 1985, 141; Wood 1986, 28, fig. 14; *Revue du Louvre* 1993, "Acquisitions," no. 48; *Gazette des Beaux-Arts* 1994, fig. 84; New Haven, Québec, and Buffalo 1999–2000, 163; Nantes 2005–2006, 19 (illus.), 20, 22.

11

STUDY FOR "DEPARTURE OF THE PRODIGAL SON," 1862–1863

Brush and brown ink, brush and brown wash, over graphite (recto); graphite (verso), 6 × 13 in. (15.2 × 32.9 cm)
The Metropolitan Museum of Art, New York, Rogers Fund, 1970, 1970.114.2
Prov.: With P. & D. Colnaghi & Co., London, April 1970; purchased from Colnaghi, 1970.
Exh.: London 1970; New York 1972; Paris 1973–1974; New York 1989.
Bibl.: Roberts 1970, 327, 322 (illus.), fig. 66; New York 1972; Wentworth 1984, 41.

12

STUDIES FOR "DEPARTURE OF THE PRODIGAL SON," 1862–1863

Graphite, heightened with white, on pink paper, 9½ × 12 in. (24.1 × 30.6 cm)
The Metropolitan Museum of Art, New York, Rogers Fund, 1970, 1970.114.1
Prov.: With P. & D. Colnaghi & Co., London, April 1970; purchased from Colnaghi, 1970.
Exh.: London 1970; New York 1972; Paris 1973–1974; New York 1989; New York 2009.
Bibl.: *Burlington Magazine* 1970b; Roberts 1970, 327; New York 1972; London and Manchester 1984–1985, 98; Wentworth 1984, 41.

13

*MELANCHOLY, CA. 1869

MÉLANCOLIE

Oil on wood panel, 19½ × 14¾ in. (49.5 × 37.5 cm)
Signed l. l.: *J J Tissot*
Collection of Ann and Gordon Getty
Prov.: Sold by Tissot in 1869 as *Melancolie (l'étang)* [Melancholy (The Pond)] for 1,800FF to Goupil (Notebook), Goupil recording receipt April 29, 1869; sold by Goupil, July 7, 1869, for 2,500FF to M. Couthrie, 27 Bruton St., London; sold Sotheby's, London, March 15, 1967 (103) as *Chagrin d'amour*; Property of a Gentleman, sold Sotheby's, London, June 7, 1995 (113).
Publ.: Photograph published by Goupil & Cie, 1869 (legal deposits BNF, October 30, 1869, Galerie photographique, no. 1237, and December 16, 1871, Musée Goupil, no. 1067).
Bibl.: Misfeldt 1971, 90, fig. 46; Misfeldt 1982, pl. I-62; London and Manchester 1984–1985, 69, 96n19; 96n19; Wentworth 1984, 67; Paris 1985, 89, 111n19, *Apollo* 1995b.

14

*THE STAIRCASE, 1869

Oil on canvas, 22 × 15 in. (55.9 × 38.1 cm)
Signed and dated l. l.: *J. J. Tissot / 1869*
Colección Pérez Simón, Mexico City
Prov.: Perhaps *Jeune femme en blanc dans le vestibule de ma maison de Paris* [Young Woman in White in the Vestibule of My House in Paris], sold by Tissot in 1874 for £200 or 5,000FF to Pilgeram (Notebook); sold by Mrs Woosman, Christie's, London, May 17, 1923 (143) as *The Staircase*, 20 × 14 in. (50.8 × 35.6 cm), 14gns, bt. Nicol; with M. Newman Gallery, London, November 1962; James Coats, New York; Mr. and Mrs. Joseph M. Tanenbaum, Toronto, by 1968; with Frederick Koch, New York, 1990; sold Sotheby's, New York, May 26, 1993 (111).
Exh.: Providence and Toronto 1968; Ottawa 1978; London and Manchester 1984–1985; Rome 2015.

Bibl.: *Connoisseur* 1962; Misfeldt 1971, 90–91, fig. 43; *Art Bulletin* 1972, J. M. Tanenbaum Collection, Toronto, fig. 22; Reff 1976, 231–232, 331, fig. 154; Misfeldt 1982, pl. I-80; Wentworth 1984, 20–30, 67–68, 95, 104, 162, pl. 52; Paris 1985, 88, fig. 36; Wood 1986, 44–45, fig. 35; Silver 1999, 132, fig. 49.

15
*SPRING, 1865
LE PRINTEMPS

Oil on canvas, 36 × 50 in. (91.4 × 127 cm)
Signed and indistinctly dated l. r.: *Tissot 1865*
Colección Pérez Simón, Mexico City
Prov.: Sold by Tissot in 1867 for 1,800FF (to Cadart?), and at Cadart's exhibition for 2,500FF to an American buyer (Notebook); Private collection, Sweden; sold Christie's, London, November 30, 1984 (93) as *Le printemps*, bt. Stair Sainty Fine Art Inc.; sold Sotheby's, New York, May 24, 1995 (229).
Exh.: Paris Salon 1865 as *Printemps*; French Gallery, London, 1866 as *Spring*; New York 1866–1867 as *Spring*; Madrid 2010; Rome 2015.
Bibl.: Mantz 1865, 12, 19; Paletta 1866, 136; "Salon de 1865" in Thoré 1870, 2:200; Maas 1975, 191; Misfeldt 1982, pl. I-32; London and Manchester 1984–1985, 100; Wentworth 1984, 41–42, 46, 53, 91, 199, pl. 30; Wood 1986, 33, fig. 20.

16
*SAFE TO WIN, 1869
also known as THE CRACK SHOT or AT THE RIFLE RANGE

Oil on canvas, 26⅝ × 18¼ in. (67.3 × 46.4 cm)
Signed and dated l. l.: *Tissot* [*69* below signature visible on photograph in Tissot's photo albums]
Wimpole Hall, Cambridgeshire, England, National Trust Collections (The Bambridge Collection), NT 207841
Prov.: Sold by Tissot in 1873 as *Le pistolet* [The Pistol] for £280 or 7,000FF to Pilgeram, who sold it to Wallis [French Gallery] (Notebook); consigned by Adriano de Murrieta, Marqués de Santurce, Christie's, London, April 7, 1883 (151) as *The Crack Shot*, £220.10s, bt. in; sold by Joseph Beausire of Wethersfield, Christie's, London, April 13, 1934 (76) as *The Rifle Range*, £52.10s, bt. Tooth; with Leicester Galleries, London, by 1936; bt. from Leicester Galleries by Captain George Bambridge, 1937; thence to his widow, Elsie Kipling, Mrs Bambridge, by whom left to the National Trust with Wimpole Hall and all its contents on her death in 1976.
Exh.: French Gallery, London, 1873 as *Safe to Win*; Leicester Galleries 1937 as *At the Rifle Range*; London and Manchester 1984–1985; National Gallery, London, 1995 as *The Crack Shot*; Barletta 2006.
Bibl.: Laver 1936, 73, 75, pl. V; Misfeldt 1982, pl. I-78; Wentworth 1984, 111, pl. 96; Paris 1985, fig. 40; Wood 1986, 42, fig. 33.

17
STUDY FOR "FOYER OF THE COMÉDIE-FRANÇAISE DURING THE SIEGE OF PARIS," 1870

Graphite, heightened white opaque watercolor, and wash on paper laminated on cardboard, 19½ × 12½ in. (49.6 × 31.6 cm)
Musée d'Arts de Nantes, Bought in 2014, 14.2.1.D
Prov.: Purchased 2014.
Bibl.: Rome 2015–2016, 41, fig. 2.

18
*FOYER OF THE COMÉDIE-FRANÇAISE DURING THE SIEGE OF PARIS, 1877
LE FOYER DE LA COMÉDIE-FRANÇAISE PENDANT LE SIÈGE DE PARIS

Etching, 15 × 10⅞ in. (38.1 × 27.6 cm)
Fine Arts Museums of San Francisco, Museum purchase, Achenbach Foundation for Graphic Arts Endowment Fund, 1978.1.32
Prov.: Purchased 1978.
Publ.: Published by Tissot as *Le foyer de la Comédie-Française pendant le siège de Paris*, 1877 (Wentworth 27).
Bibl.: Béraldi 1892, no. 20; Providence and Toronto 1968; Wentworth 1978, 126–129; London and Manchester 1984–1985, 105; Paris 1985, 188; Misfeldt 1991, 70; New Haven, Québec, and Buffalo 1999–2000, 48; Saddlemyer 1999, 141, fig. 51; Bedford 2002, no. 6; Rome 2015–2016, 41, fig. 3; London and Paris 2017–2018, 34.

19
*THE WOUNDED SOLDIER, CA. 1870

Watercolor on paper, 13⅞ × 9⅞ in. (35.3 × 25.2 cm)
Tate, London, Purchased 2016, T14636
Prov.: Tissot sale, Besançon, 1964 (62); sold Renoud-Grappin, Besançon, April 21, 2013 (11) as *Le jeune soldat*; purchased 2016.
Exh.: London and Paris 2017.
Bibl.: London and Paris 2017–2018, 34.

20
*AN ENCAMPMENT—SIEGE OF PARIS—PARC D'ISSY, 1878
LE CAMPEMENT, PARC D'ISSY (SOUVENIR DU SIÈGE DE PARIS)

Etching and drypoint, 6⅝ × 9⅛ in. (16.8 × 23.2 cm)
Fine Arts Museums of San Francisco, Museum purchase, Achenbach Foundation for Graphic Arts Endowment Fund, 1980.1.26
Prov.: Purchased 1980.
Publ.: Published by Tissot as *Le campement, parc d'Issy (Souvenir du siège de Paris)*, 1878 (Wentworth 41).
Bibl.: Béraldi 1892, no. 33; Providence and Toronto 1968; Wentworth 1978, 182–183; London and Manchester 1984–1985, 105–106, no. 38; Wentworth 1984, 79; Paris 1985, 194; Misfeldt 1991, 96.

21
*THE TWO SISTERS; PORTRAIT, 1863
LES DEUX SŒURS; PORTRAIT

Oil on canvas, 82⅝ × 53½ in. (210 × 135.5 cm)
Signed and dated l. r.: *J. J. Tissot / 1863*
Musée d'Orsay, Paris, Gift of Albert Bichet, RF 2788
Prov.: Tissot studio sale, Paris, 1903, as *Grand tableau. Jeune fille dans un parc avec sa mère*, bt. Albert Bichet; given by Bichet to Musée du Luxembourg, Paris, 1904; transferred to Musée du Louvre, Paris, 1929; transferred to Musée d'Orsay, 1982.
Exh.: Paris Salon 1864 as *Les deux soeurs; portrait*; Madrid 1918; Paris 1922; London and Manchester 1984–1985; Paris 1985; Yale 1999; Bremen 2005; Paris 2012; Fort Worth 2014; Milan 2017.
Bibl.: Misfeldt 1971, 61–63, fig. 21; *Connoisseur* 1978, 272 (illus. as *Portraits dans un parc*); Misfeldt 1982, pl. I-29; London and Manchester 1984–1985, 100, fig. 14; Wentworth 1984, 47, 49–54, 56, 59, 106, 116, 199, pl. 29; Paris 1985, 142, col. pl. IV; Wood 1986, 32–33, fig. 19; New Haven, Québec, and Buffalo 1999–2000, 38–39; Nantes 2005–2006, fig. 10; Chicago, New York, and Paris 2012–2013, 148, 281; Rome 2015–2016, fig. 1.

22
*PORTRAIT OF MLLE L. L..., 1864
PORTRAIT DE MLLE L. L...

Oil on canvas, 48⅞ × 39⅛ in. (123.5 × 99 cm)
Signed and dated l. r.: *James Tissot fév. 1864*
Musée d'Orsay, Paris, Acquired at the Thiébault-Sisson Sale, 1907, RF 2698
Prov.: Mme. Thiébault-Sisson sale, Hôtel Drouot, Paris, November 23, 1907 (101) as *Jeune femme dans un intérieur*; acquired by the French state for the Musée du Luxembourg, Paris; transferred to Musée du Louvre, Paris, 1929; Musée d'Orsay, Paris, 1986.
Exh.: Paris Salon 1864 as *Portrait de Mlle L. L...*; Paris 1946; Providence and Toronto 1968; Paris 1978; Berlin-Prague 1982; London and Manchester 1984–1985; Paris 1985; Paris 1994; Paris-Bruxelles 1997; Yale 1999; La Haye 2002; Bremen 2005; Moscow 2006; San Francisco 2010; Paris 2012; Rome 2015; Paris 2016; Zurich 2017.
Bibl.: About 1864, 3; Castagnary 1864, 3; Chesneau 1864, 3; Gautier 1864, 1; Lagrange 1864, 525–526; Saint-Victor 1864, 2; Misfeldt 1971, 59–62, fig. 22; Wentworth 1978, 46, fig. 4a; Misfeldt 1982, pl. I-28; London and Manchester 1984–1985, 100, pl. 24; Wentworth 1984, 46–49, 59, 199, pl. 26; Paris 1985, 143–144, pl. VI; Wood 1986, 32–33, fig. 18; Lochnan, ed. 1999, pl. XIX; Maeder 1999, 83; New Haven, Québec, and Buffalo 1999–2000, 34, 40–41; Nantes 2005–2006, 27, 29, fig. 3; Barletta 2006, 66, 68 (illus.); Chicago, New York, and Paris 2012–2013, 148, 281; Mancoff 2012, 24–25; Ribeiro 2016, 324, pl. 242; London and Paris 2017–2018, 82.

23
*PORTRAIT OF THE MARQUIS AND MARQUISE DE MIRAMON AND THEIR CHILDREN, 1865
PORTRAIT DE FAMILLE DE MARQUIS DE M.

Oil on canvas, 69¾ × 85⅜ in. (177 × 217 cm)
Signed and dated l. l.: *J. J. Tissot / 1865*
Musée d'Orsay, Paris, Acquired in 2006, RF 2006.22
Prov.: Commissioned by René de Cassagne de Beaufort, Marquis de Miramon, from Tissot, who was paid 5,000FF in 1865 (Notebook); by descent; acquired from the family through Cabinet Blondeau-Breton by the Musée d'Orsay, 2006.
Exh.: Paris 1866 as *Portrait de famille de Marquis de M.*; Paris 2012; Tokyo 2014; Madrid 2015; Paris 2016.
Bibl.: Lagrange 1866, 400; Misfeldt 1971, 70–71; Misfeldt 1982, pl. I-36; London and Manchester 1984–1985, 100; Wentworth 1984, 59–60, pl. 38; Des Cars 2007; Chicago, New York, and Paris 2012–2013, 149; London and Paris 2017–2018, 82.

24
*PORTRAIT OF THE MARQUISE DE MIRAMON, NÉE THÉRÈSE FEUILLANT, 1866
PORTRAIT DE MME LA MARQUISE DE M.

Oil on canvas, 50½ × 30⅜ in. (128.3 × 77.2 cm)
Signed and dated l. r.: *J. J. Tissot / 1866*
The J. Paul Getty Museum, Los Angeles, 2007.7
Prov.: Commissioned by René de Cassagne de Beaufort, Marquis de Miramon, from Tissot, who was paid 3,000FF in 1866 (Notebook); consigned by a descendant of the sitter,

Christie's, New York, October 12, 1993 (42); acquired from a descendant through Cabinet Blondeau-Breton by the Getty Museum, 2006.
Exh.: Paris 1867 as *Portrait de Mme la marquise de M.*; Paris 2012.
Bibl.: Misfeldt 1982, pl. I-141; London and Manchester 1984–1985, 100; Wentworth 1984, 62–63, 207, pl. 40.

25

PORTRAIT OF AIMÉ SEILLIÈRE, 1866

Oil on canvas, 50⅜ × 28 in. (128 × 71 cm)
Signed and dated c. r.: *J. J. Tissot / 1866*
Staatliche Kunsthalle Karlsruhe, Germany, Inv. 2826
Prov.: Commissioned from Tissot, who was paid 2,000FF in 1866 (Notebook); sold Audap-Godeau-Solanet, Hôtel Drouot, Paris, June 14, 1988 (39) as *Portrait d'homme*; with Hazlitt, Gooden & Fox Ltd., London, from whom acquired by the Staatliche Kunsthalle Karlsruhe, 1989.
Bibl.: Misfeldt 1982, pl. I-39; *Jahrbuch der Staatlichen Kunstsammlungen in Baden-Württemberg* 1990, 149–150.

26

PORTRAIT OF EUGÈNE COPPENS DE FONTENAY, 1867

Oil on canvas, 27½ × 15⅜ in. (69.8 × 39.1 cm)
Signed and dated l. r.: *J. J. Tissot avril 1867*
Philadelphia Museum of Art, Purchased with the W. P. Wilstach Fund, 1972, W1972-2-1
Prov.: Commissioned from Tissot, who was paid 1,000FF in 1867 (Notebook); sold Christie's, London, March 5, 1971 (71), bt. Holstein; with H. Shickman Gallery, New York, by October 1971; purchased by Philadelphia Museum of Art for the Wilstach collection, March 14, 1972.
Bibl.: *Art Quarterly* 1972; Misfeldt 1982, pl. I-49; Wentworth 1984, 63, pl. 41; Wood 1986, 36, fig. 24; Chicago, New York, and Paris 2012–2013, 151, fig. 3; London and Paris 2017–2018, 82.

27

THE CIRCLE OF THE RUE ROYALE, 1866–1868

LE CERCLE DE LA RUE ROYALE

Oil on canvas, 68⅞ × 110⅝ in. (175 × 281 cm)
Signed and dated l. r.: *J. J. Tissot 1868*
Musée d'Orsay, Paris, Purchased, 2011, RF 2011.53
Prov.: Commissioned from Tissot, who was paid 6,000FF by the twelve sitters in 1866 (Notebook); lots drawn for ownership of the painting won by Baron Hottinguer, Paris; by descent; declared a historic monument of France, September 3, 1998; purchased by the French state for the Musée d'Orsay, 2011.
Exh.: Paris 1869 as *Le cercle de la rue Royale*; Paris 1922; Wildenstein 1955; Paris 1957; Vichy 1961; Paris 1965; Providence and Toronto 1968; Paris 2012; Paris 2014; Paris 2016.
Bibl.: Burty 1868, 62; Proust 1923; Laver 1936, 15; Proust 1955–1956, 200; Misfeldt 1971, 70–72, fig. 34; Misfeldt 1982, pl. I-37; New York 1982, 20–21 (illus.); London and Manchester 1984–1985, 100; Wentworth 1984, 60–62, 88, pl. 39; Paris 1985, 144, fig. 54; Wood 1986, 35–36, fig. 23; Garb 1999, 106–107, fig. 43; Lochnan, ed. 1999, pl. XV; Luckhurst 2000, 113, 120; Duby 2008; Karpeles 2008, 236–237 (illus.); Rey 2011; Chicago, New York, and Paris 2012–2013, 146–151; London and Paris 2017–2018, 82.

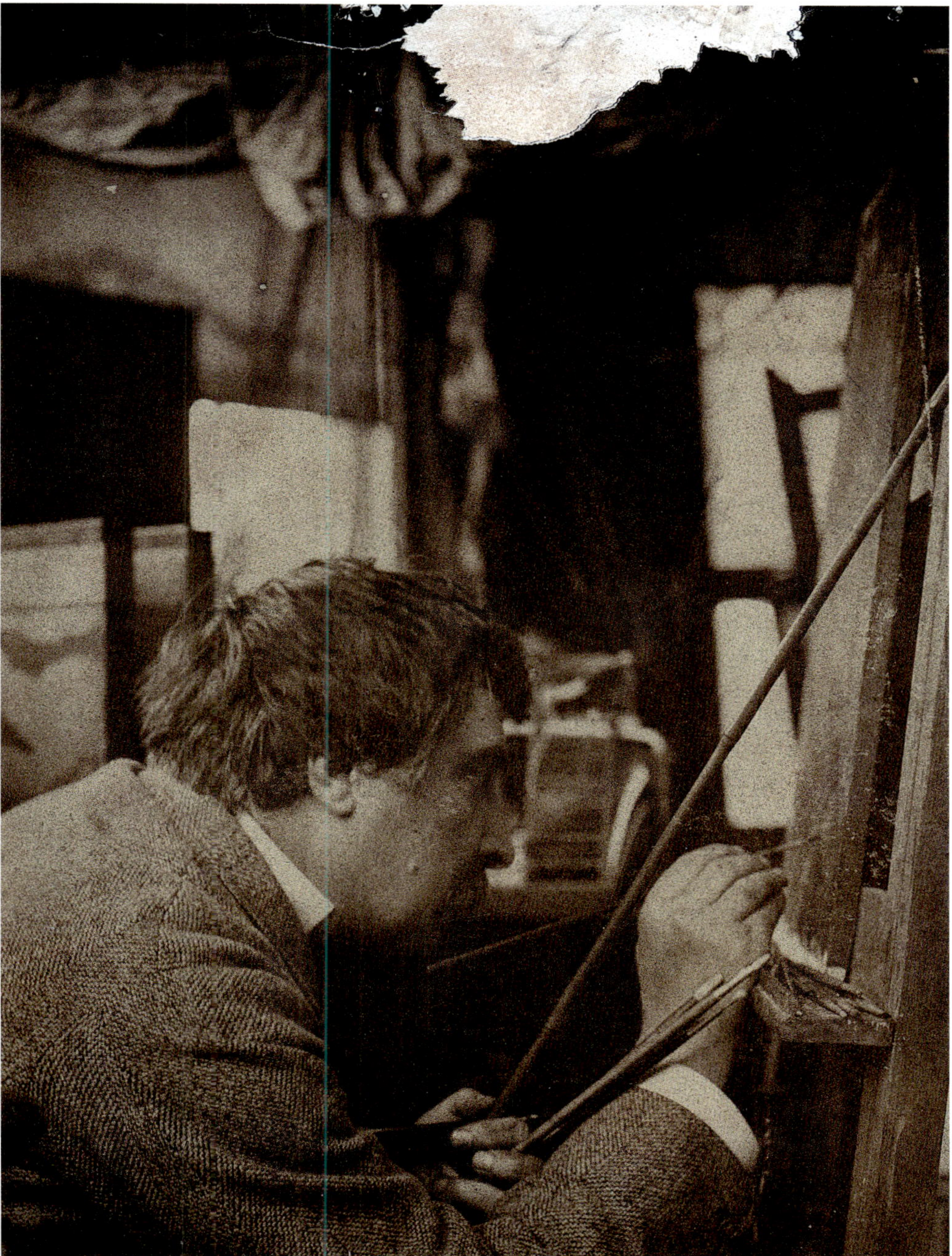

FIGURE 131
James Tissot at his easel, ca. 1870s

28

EMPRESS EUGÉNIE AND THE PRINCE IMPERIAL IN THE GROUNDS OF CAMDEN PLACE, CHISLEHURST, 1874–1875

Oil on canvas, 42 × 60 in. (106.6 × 152.4 cm)
Signed l. r.: *J. J. Tissot*
Musée National du Palais de Compiègne, France, Purchased in 1934
Prov.: Sold by Tissot in 1875 as *Le Portrait de l'Impératrice Eugénie et le prince impérial* for £700 or 17,500FF to Marsden (Notebook); probably sold by Marsden to Kaye Knowles; sold by executors of Kaye Knowles, Esq., late of Warrington Crescent, Christie's, London, May 14, 1887 (150) as *Chislehurst*, 1874, 40¼ × 60 in. (102.2 × 152.4 cm), £54.12s, bt. Tooth on behalf of Morris, recording sale for £57.6s; with Fosters, Pall Mall; with Leicester Galleries, 1933; acquired from them by Musée du Louvre, Paris, 1934.
Exh.: Submitted to Royal Academy 1875, but rejected; Leicester Galleries 1933 as *The Empress Eugénie and the Prince Imperial in the grounds of Camden House, Chislehurst, 1877*; London and Manchester 1984–1985; Paris 1985; Nantes 2005; Rome 2015; Paris 2016; London and Paris 2017.
Bibl.: Tissot 1871–1878, 35; *Freeman's Journal* 1874, 6; Domino 1874, 1; *Morning Post* 1875, 5; *Observer* 1875, 5; *Graphic* 1875, 319; *Illustrated London News* 1875a, 318; Laver 1936, 35–36, pl. XV; Misfeldt 1971, 155–156, fig. 82; London and Manchester 1984–1985, 112; Wentworth 1984, 119–120, pl. 112; Paris 1985, 175, pl. XVII; Wood 1986, 78, 80, fig. 78; Maeder 1999, 81, fig. 33; Nantes 2005–2006, 87 (illus.); London and Paris 2017–2018, 84, 92–93; Matyjaszkiewicz, ed. 2019a.

29

*PORTRAIT OF CAPTAIN *** [FREDERICK BURNABY], 1870

Oil on wood panel, 19⅝ × 24 in. (50 × 61 cm)
Signed and dated l. l.: *J. J. Tissot / 70*
National Portrait Gallery, London, Purchased, 1933, NPG 2642
Prov.: Thomas Gibson Bowles; by descent to his son, George F. S. Bowles (godson of the sitter); purchased from the latter, 1933.
Exh.: London International Exhibition 1872 as *Portrait of Captain* ***; Providence and Toronto 1968; *Vanity Fair* 1976; London and Manchester 1984–1985 as *Colonel Frederick Gustavus Burnaby*; Paris 1985; Tate 1992; Japan 1995; Yale 1999; Bedford 2002; Washington 2007; V&A 2011; Paris 2012; Rome 2015; London and Paris 2017.
Bibl.: Tissot 1871–1878, 1; Claretie 1873, 374; *Country Life* 1936, 678 (illus.); Laver 1936, 17–18, pl. III; Betjeman 1938, illus. as *The Ouida Guardsman*; Naylor 1965, illus. facing 33; Wentworth 1978, 82, 85, fig. 15d; Wentworth 1979–1980, 8, fig. 1; National Portrait Gallery 1981, 80; Warner 1982, 8 (illus.); London and Manchester 1984–1985, 104, pl. 11; Wentworth 1984, 89–91, 100, 142, 207, pl. 71; Paris 1985, 154–155; Wood 1986, 56, fig. 44; New Haven, Québec, and Buffalo 1999–2000, 50, 54–55; Barletta 2006, 35–36 (illus.); *Times* 2008, 1; London and Paris 2017–2018, 83, 88–89; Jan Marsh, extended catalogue entry for Frederick Burnaby, NPG 3428, National Portrait Gallery, London, npg.org.uk/collections/search/portraitExtended/mw00933/Frederick-Burnaby.

30

*PORTRAIT OF ALGERNON MOSES MARSDEN, 1877

Oil on canvas, 19½ × 29 in. (49.5 × 73.7 cm)
Signed and dated l. r.: *J. J. Tissot / 1877*
Private collection, courtesy of Grant Ford Ltd.
Prov.: Commissioned from Tissot, who was paid £50 or 1,250FF in 1877 (Notebook); sold Sotheby's, London, February 17, 1971 (59); sold Sotheby's, London, November 25, 1983 (64).
Exh.: London and Manchester 1984–1985; Yale 1999; V&A 2011.
Bibl.: Wentworth 1979–1980, 10, fig. 4; Wentworth 1984, 142–143, pl. 128; Wood 1986, 101, fig. 99; New Haven, Québec, and Buffalo 1999–2000, 58–59; Barletta 2006, 35–38, 37 (illus.); London, Paris, and San Francisco 2011–2012, pl. 9; London and Paris 2017–2018, 83; Matyjaszkiewicz, ed. 2019a.

31

PORTRAIT OF COLONEL *** [LONGLEY], CA. 1872–1876

also known as GENTLEMAN IN A RAILWAY CARRIAGE

Oil on wood panel, 24⅞ × 16⅞ in. (63.3 × 43 cm)
Signed u. l.: *J. J. Tissot*
Worcester Art Museum, Massachusetts, Alexander and Caroline Murdock De Witt Fund, 1965.16
Prov.: Probably *Le portrait de Longley* [The Portrait of Longley] sold by Tissot for £120 or 3,000FF to the dealer Everard in 1876 (Notebook), and sold by Everard, Christie's, London, December 13, 1879 (69) as *Time Is Money*, £78.15, bt. Greig, then sold by W. Dallas O. Grieg Esq., Christie's, London, June 14, 1884 (112), £39.18s, bt. Adams; perhaps the painting sold by Doig, Wilson and Wheatley (Edinburgh), Christie's, London, June 4, 1928 (145) as *La première classe*, oil on panel, 23½ × 17 in. (59.7 × 43.2 cm), £8.8s, bt. Waters; New York art market; Gropper Art Galleries, Cambridge, Mass., 1964; purchased from Gropper Art Galleries, 1965.
Exh.: 1872 version at London International Exhibition 1872 as *Portrait of Colonel* ***; probably Everard 1877–1879 as *Time Is Money*; Gropper 1964; Providence and Toronto 1968; Yale 1999 as *M. le capitaine *** (Gentleman in a Railway Carriage)*; Liverpool 2008.
Bibl.: Tissot 1871–1878, 6 (photograph of 1872 version); *Graphic* 1877b, 523; Pattison 1913, 109; Worcester Art Museum 1965, as *Gentleman in a Coach*; Wentworth 1979–1980, 9–27; Wentworth 1984, 89–90, 100, 207, pl. 72; Wood 1986, 56, fig. 50; New Haven, Québec, and Buffalo 1999–2000, 56–57; Kansas City and Liverpool 2008–2009, 107, 109, 111 (illus.).

32

*PORTRAIT OF REVEREND PÈRE B... [BICHET], MISSIONARY OF GABON, CA. 1884–1885

PORTRAIT DU RÉVÉREND PÈRE B..., MISSIONNAIRE AU GABON

Oil on canvas, 34⅝ × 46½ in. (88.1 × 117.7 cm)
Signed l. r.: *J. J. Tissot* and inscribed *à Claire*
Musée d'Arts de Nantes, Albert Bichet Bequest, 1920, Inv. 1978
Prov.: Given by Tissot to his sister-in-law, Claire Tissot, née Bichet; bequest of Albert Bichet, 1920.
Exh.: Paris 1885 as *Portrait du Révérend Père B..., missionnaire au Gabon*; Paris 1889 as *Portrait du R. P. B.*; Japan 1988; Nantes 2005; Rome 2015.
Bibl.: Misfeldt 1971, 219; Misfeldt 1982, pl. III-66; Wentworth 1984, 172, 207; Nantes 2005–2006, 42–43 (illus.).

33

PORTRAIT OF THE PRINCESSE DE BROGLIE, CA. 1895

Pastel on linen, 66⅛ × 38⅛ in. (168 × 96.8 cm)
Signed l. l.: *J. J. Tissot*
Private collection
Prov.: Family of Princesse de Broglie; Mr. and Mrs. Joseph M. Tanenbaum, Toronto; sold Sotheby's, New York, October 24, 1989 (113); sold from the collections of Lily and Edmond J. Safra, Sotheby's, New York, October 18, 2011 (789).
Exh.: Japan 1988.
Bibl.: Misfeldt 1982, pl. IV-29; Wentworth 1984, 156–158, col. pl. V; Wood 1986, 127, 129, fig. 133.

34

PORTRAIT OF CLOTILDE BRIATTE, COMTESSE PILLET-WILL, 1890S

Pastel on paper laid down on canvas, 35⅞ × 63¼ in. (91 × 160.5 cm)
Private collection
Prov.: Comtesse Pillet-Will; by descent; sold Xavier de la Perraudière, Saumur, December 1, 2012 (119); sold Sotheby's, New York, May 9, 2013 (27).
Bibl.: Misfeldt 1982, pl. IV-25.

35

PORTRAIT OF PRINCE AKITAKE TOKUGAWA, 1868

Watercolor mounted in a hanging scroll, 24 × 18¾ in. (60.9 × 47.6 cm)
Signed, dated, and inscribed b. r.: *Paris / 27 Septembre / 1868 / au Prince Mimboutaiua / Souvenir / affecteux / J. J. Tissot*
Historical Museum of the Tokugawa Family, Mito, Japan
Prov.: Commissioned from Tissot, who was paid 1,000FF for the portrait in 1868 (Notebook).
Bibl.: Ikegami 1980, 147–155; London and Manchester 1984–1985, 65; Wentworth 1984, 68, pl. 54; Paris 1985, 86; Wood 1986, 38–40, fig. 29; Ikegami 1988, fig. 4; Nantes 2005–2006, 49 (illus.), 56–58; Barletta 2006, 72.

36

*THE JAPANESE SCROLL, 1872–1873

Oil on wood panel, 15¼ × 22½ in. (38.7 × 57.2 cm)
Signed l. r.: *J J Tissot*
Private collection
Prov.: Sold by Tissot in 1873 as *Le rouleau japonais* [The Japanese Scroll] for £400 or 10,000FF to Pilgeram (Notebook); probably Isaac Smith, Esq., JP, of Field House, Daisy Hill, Bradford, and sold by his executors, Christie's, London, May 15, 1911 (105) as *A Question of Colour*, oil on panel, 14½ × 21¾ in. (36.8 × 55.3 cm), £15.15s, bt. Gaunt; with Leicester Galleries, London, from whom acquired by the father of the seller at Sotheby's, London, June 18, 1985 (78); with Paul Rosenberg, New York; consigned to Christie's, New York, October 22, 2008 (132), bt. in; sold Christie's, New York, June 4, 2009 (113).
Exh.: San Diego 2006.
Bibl.: Tissot 1871–1878, 21; Misfeldt 1971, 93, fig. 52 as *Looking at the Surimono*; San Diego 2006, 67 (illus.), 81; London and Paris 2017–2018, 98–99 (illus.).

37

*YOUNG WOMEN LOOKING AT THE CHINESE TEMPLE, 1869

FEMMES REGARDENT LE TEMPLE CHINOIS

Oil on canvas, 22 × 15½ in. (55.9 × 39.4 cm)
Signed and dated l. l.: *J. J. Tissot / 1869*
Private collection
Prov.: Sold by Tissot in 1869 as *Femmes regardant le temple chinois* [Women Looking at the Chinese Temple] for 2,000FF to Goupil (Notebook), Goupil recording receipt as *Le temple japonais*, February 8, 1869; sold by Goupil "at the Boulevard," February 28, 1869, for 3,000FF; with M. Springer, Vienna (Notebook); purchased ca. 1900 by the grandfather of the seller, a European private collector, Sotheby's, New York, May 5, 1999 (285); anonymous sale, Sotheby's, New York, October 24, 2006 (148).
Publ.: Photograph published by Goupil & Cie, 1869, as *Chinoiseries* (legal deposits BNF, June 11, 1870, Galerie photographique, no. 669; December 16, 1871, Musée Goupil, no. 1067; carte-de-visite format, May 18, 1872, no. 342); wood engraving by Henri Bogaerts and (?) Walter published by Henri Bogaerts and Marcelin la Garde in *L'illustration* (Brussels), ca. 1870, as *Les bibelots*.
Bibl.: Misfeldt 1971, 93–95, fig. 48; Misfeldt 1982, pl. I-63; Wentworth 1984, col. pl. II, facing 75; Wood 1986, 37–38, fig. 28; Arscott 1999, 55, fig. 21; Nantes 2005–2006, 58, 95 (illus. Goupil photo).

38

*YOUNG WOMEN LOOKING AT JAPANESE OBJECTS, 1869

JEUNES FEMMES REGARDANT DES OBJETS JAPONAIS

Oil on canvas, $27\frac{3}{4} \times 19\frac{3}{4}$ in. (70.5 × 50.2 cm)

Signed and dated l. l.: *J. J. Tissot / 1869*

Cincinnati Art Museum, Gift of Henry M. Goodyear, M.D., 1984.217

Prov.: Sold by Tissot in 1869 as *Femmes regardant un navire japonais* [Women Looking at a Japanese Ship] for 3,000FF to Goupil (Notebook), Goupil recording receipt as *Les curiosités japonaises* [The Japanese Curiosities], March 30, 1869, for 3,000FF with a note stating "*Partage de bénéfice au . . . de 4,000FF suivant l'exposition*" [Share of profits from 4,000FF after the exhibition]; sold by Goupil, December 31, 1869, for 4,000FF to M. Knoedler, New York; Knoedler had already sold the painting October 29, 1869, as *Chinese Cabinet* for 1,325 dollars to Boston art dealers Williams & Everett; bought 1930s by Dr. Goodyear from a Cincinnati interior decoration warehouse with paintings, probably as a gift for Mrs. Goodyear; gift of Dr. Henry M. Goodyear, 1984.

Exh.: Paris Salon 1869 as *Jeunes femmes regardant des objets japonais*; Yale 1999; V&A 2011.

Bibl.: Ménard 1868, 1870, 1888; Providence and Toronto 1968, no. 12; Misfeldt 1971, 93–95, fig. 49; Misfeldt 1982, pl. I-65; New Haven, Québec, and Buffalo 1999–2000, 10, 44–45; Nantes 2005–2006, 58; Barletta 2006, 43 (illus.); London, Paris, and San Francisco 2011–2012, pl. 75; London and Paris 2017–2018, 82.

39

THE JAPANESE VASE, CA. 1870

Oil on canvas, 24 × 35 in. (61 × 89 cm)

Signed l. l. with monogram: *JTJ*

Private collection

Prov.: Probably *Portrait de Madame Desoye*, listed but deleted by Tissot under 1871 sales (Notebook); with Peter Nahum at the Leicester Galleries.

Bibl.: Providence and Toronto 1968, no. 12; Misfeldt 1971, 93, fig.51; Weisberg 1975, 3–4, 16nn23–28; Misfeldt 1982, pl. I-79; Wood 1986, 37; Darby 1999, 179–180, fig. 72; Kirk 2008, 116–119.

40

*THE FAN, 1875

Oil on canvas, $15\frac{1}{4} \times 20\frac{1}{2}$ in. (38.7 × 52.1 cm)

Signed l. l.: *J. J. Tissot*

Wadsworth Atheneum Museum of Art, Hartford, Connecticut, The Ella Gallup Sumner and Mary Catlin Sumner Collection Fund, 1982.158

Prov.: Sold by Tissot in 1875 as *L'éventail* [The Fan] for 250gns or 6,250FF to Tooth (Notebook), Tooth recording receipt as *The Fan*, May 7, 1875, 20 × 15 in. (50.8 × 38.1 cm), cost £210; sold by Tooth, May 24, 1875, for £330 to José Murrieta Esq.; sold Sotheby Parke Bernet, London, June 15, 1982 (69), bt. Charles Jerdein, London; purchased from Jerdein, 1982.

Exh.: Yale 1999; V&A 2011.

Bibl.: Tissot 1871–1878, 32; New Haven, Québec, and Buffalo 1999–2000, 100; Serafini 2015, 45, fig. 1.

41

*THE PARTIE CARRÉE, 1870

Oil on canvas, 47 × 56 in. (114.3 × 142.2 cm)

Signed l. r.: *J. J. Tissot*

National Gallery of Canada, Ottawa, Purchased 2018

Prov.: Sold by Tissot in 1870 for 8,000FF to Reitlinger, who sold it to Madame Martinet (Claude La Fontaine) (Notebook); sold by executors of Mme. L. M.[artinet], Hôtel Drouot, Paris, June 3, 1893 (71) as *Partie carrée, costumes de directoire*, 2,100FF, bt. [Henri] Haro; sold by Mme Moreau, Paris, June 25–26, 1923, as *La partie carrée*, 800FF; sold Sotheby's, London, March 25, 1964 (225) as *A Picnic by the River*, bt. Williams & Son, London; with Kaplan Gallery, London, by November 1964; private collection, Zurich, by 1968; offered at Sotheby's, London, November 3, 1993 (246), bt. in; sold Sotheby's, New York, May 24, 1995 (241); private collection, West Coast, by 2001; sold Christie's, New York, May 2, 2001 (44), bt. by a private collector, from whom acquired by National Gallery of Canada, 2018.

Exh.: Paris Salon 1870 as *Partie carrée*; Providence and Toronto 1968.

Publ.: Photograph by Robert Bingham published as *Partie carrée*, 1870; photograph published by Lecadre, 1878 (legal deposit BNF, February 9, 1878, album format, no. 244).

Bibl.: *Connoisseur* 1964; Misfeldt 1971, 99, 101, fig. 52; Misfeldt 1982, pl. I-73; London and Manchester 1984–1985, 66, fig. 27; Wentworth 1984, 74, 75, 102, 200, pl. 61; Paris 1985, 86, fig. 35; Wood 1986, 47, fig. 38; Maeder 1999, 79–80, 84–85, 89, fig. 31; London and Paris 2017–2018, 82.

42

BEFORE THE DEPARTURE or THE PARTING, 1872

Oil on canvas, 27 × 36 in. (68.6 × 91.4 cm)

Signed and dated l. r.: *J. J. Tissot / L.72*

National Museum Wales, Cardiff, Bequeathed by William Menelaus, 1882, NMW A 134

Prov.: Sale recorded by Tissot in 1872 as *La veille du départ* [The Evening before Departure] for £600 or 15,000FF to Agnew (Notebook), who was acting for Lord Dunmore, to whom Agnew recorded sale for £840 on July 26, 1872, the same day received as *Before the Departure*; consigned by Lord Powerscourt, the Earl of Dunmore, Christie's, London, March 14, 1874 (134) as *Avant le départ*, £945, bt. in; acquired from Lord Dunmore by Agnew, June 3, 1875, as *Avant le départ*; offered as Manley Hall Art Union Prize, August 1875; sold by Agnew, November 10, 1875, for £1,050 to Alexander Bannatyne Stewart, Glasgow; sold by A. B. Stewart, Christie's, London, May 9, 1881 (134) as *The Parting*, 1872, 27 × 36 in. (68.6 × 91.4 cm), £378, bt. Agnew on behalf of William Menelaus; bequeathed by William Menelaus to Cardiff Museum, 1882.

Exh.: Glasgow 1876 as *Before the Departure*, lent by A. B. Stewart, Esq.; Glasgow 1878 as *The Parting*, lent by A. B. Stewart; Sheffield 1955; Arts Council 1955; London and Manchester 1984–1985 as *Bad News (The Parting)*; Paris 1985; Nantes 2005 as *Mauvaises nouvelles*.

Bibl.: Tissot 1871–1878, 9 Laver 1936, 33; Providence and Toronto 1968, nos. 16, 50, fig. 6; Brooke 1968, 22–26 (illus.); Misfeldt 1971, 138, fig. 71; London and Manchester 1984–1985, 20, 68, 107, 128, pl. 26; Wentworth 1984, 100, 103, 207, pl. 78; Paris 1985, 162–163, pl. XI; Wood 1986, 60, fig. 54; Maeder 1999, 85; Fahy, ed. 2005, 401–402, fig. 1; Nantes 2005–2006, 25–26 (illus.); Barletta 2006, 84; London and Paris 2017–2018, 84.

43

THE FAREWELLS, 1871

LES ADIEUX

Oil on canvas, $39\frac{1}{2} \times 24\frac{5}{8}$ in. (100.3 × 62.6 cm)

Signed and dated l. r. on step: *J. J. Tissot / 1871 Londres*

Bristol Museums and Art Gallery, Purchased 1955, K2432

Prov.: Sold by Tissot in 1872 as *Les adieux* for £300 or 7,500FF to Pilgeram, who sold it on to Charles Waring (Notebook); label on back of frame gives Tissot's address as 73 Springfield Road; with Grundy and Smith, Manchester, December 1872; Charles Waring; sold by his executors, Christie's, London, April 28, 1888 (17) as *Les adieux*, £231, bt. F. Walker; purchased from F. Walker's son, Lt. Col. P. L. E. Walker, 1955.

Exh.: Royal Academy 1872 as *Les adieux*; Manchester 1872; Sheffield 1955, lent by Lt. Col. Lionel Walker; Arts Council 1955, lent by Lt. Col. Lionel Walker; London and Manchester 1984–1985; Paris 1985; Yale 1999; Bedford 2002; London and Paris 2017.

Publ.: Steel engraving by Joel (John) Ballin published by Pilgeram & Lefèvre, London, May 30, 1873, and by William Schaus, USA.

Bibl.: Tissot 1871–1878, 5; *Manchester Evening News* 1872, 4; Laver 1936, 27; Bell 1959, 727 (illus.), 728; Providence and Toronto 1968, no. 49; Misfeldt 1971, 136, 138–140, fig. 69; Bristol 1975, 18; Wentworth 1978, 349; Warner 1982, 6 (illus.); Wentworth 1984, 101–102, 106, 201, pl. 76; Wood 1986, 57–58, fig. 52; Lochnan 1999, 14, fig. 6; Maeder 1999, 85; New Haven, Québec, and Buffalo 1999–2000, 30–31; Prelinger 1999, 186–187; Barletta 2006, 45–46 (illus.); London and Paris 2017–2018, 84, 90–91.

44

RAILWAY STATION, 1873

also known as WAITING FOR THE TRAIN (WILLESDEN JUNCTION)

Oil on canvas, $23\frac{1}{2} \times 13\frac{1}{2}$ in. (59.7 × 34.2 cm)

Signed l. l.: *J. J. Tissot* and on the trunk with monogram *JTJ*

Dunedin Public Art Gallery, New Zealand, Purchased 1921 with funds from the Thomas Brown Fund, 1-1921

Prov.: Sold by Tissot in 1873 as *La station* [The Station] for £550 or 13,750FF to Agnew (Notebook), Agnew recording receipt as *Railway Station*, August 19, 1873; sold by Agnew, October 28, 1873, for £650 to James Hall; returned by James Hall to Agnew, March 3, 1874; with Agnew, Manchester, July 23, 1875; consigned by Agnew, Christie's, London, April 29, 1876 (43), bt. in; sold by Agnew, June 4, 1877, for £575 to Everard; with Everard's Continental Gallery, London, 1877–1879; consigned by Everard, Christie's, London, January 31, 1880, as *Waiting for the Train*, bt. in; with Leggatt Gallery, London, 1911; purchased for Dunedin Public Art Gallery through the Thomas Brown Bequest, 1921.

Exh.: Everard 1877–1879; Japan 1988.

Bibl.: Tissot 1871–1878, 20; *Graphic* 1877b; Wentworth 1979–1980, 19–20, fig. 10; London and Manchester 1984–1985, 73, 76, 110; Wentworth 1984, 90, 111, 134, pl. 98; Kansas City and Liverpool 2008–2009, 107, 109, col. illus. 110; Ribeiro 2016, 546.

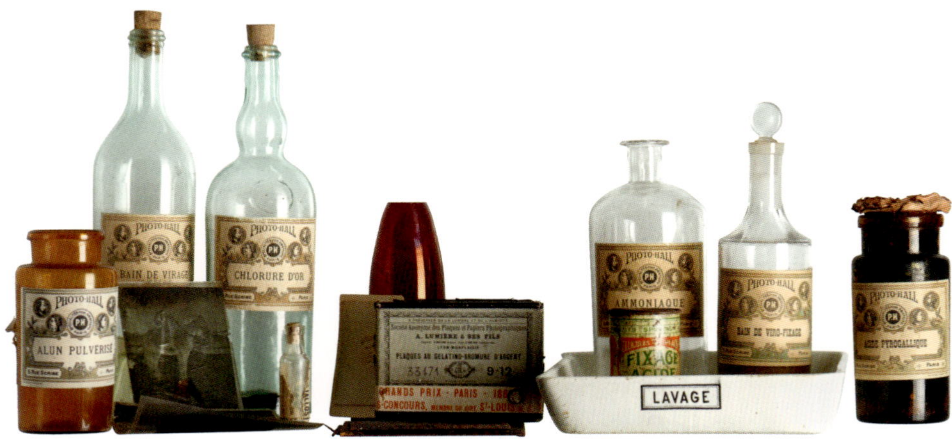

FIGURE 132
Photography chemicals and glass plates found in Tissot's Château de Buillon studio after his death

45
THE CONCERT or HUSH!, 1874

Oil on canvas, 29 × 44 in. (73.7 × 111.8 cm)
Signed l. r.: *J. J. Tissot*
Manchester Art Gallery, Purchased 1933, 1933.56
Prov.: Sold by Tissot in 1874 as *Concert* for £1,200 or 30,000FF to Agnew (Notebook); Agnew recorded receipt as *The Concert (Hush!)*, June 24, 1874, sale price £1,500; with Agnew, Manchester, as *The Concert*, January 6, 1875, and again July 23, 1875; sent by Agnew to Liverpool, August 11, 1876, price £1,260; with Agnew, Manchester, April 20, 1877, price £1,260; with Agnew, London, 1878, price £1,575; still with Agnew, London, 1889; sold by Agnew, January 12, 1898, for £150 to Charles Gasquet; with Leicester Galleries, London, 1933; purchased by Manchester City Art Gallery, 1933.
Exh.: Royal Academy 1875 as *Hush!*; Manchester 1877 as *The Concert*; Whitechapel 1889, lent by Agnew; Leicester Galleries 1933 as *The Concert*; Sheffield 1955; Arts Council 1955; London and Manchester 1984–1985 as *Hush! (The Concert)*; Paris 1985; Japan 1988; Yale 1999; Barletta 2006; London and Paris 2017.
Bibl.: Tissot 1871–1878, 25; *Saturday Review* 1875, 756–757; *Manchester Weekly Times* 1877; Laver 1936, 33–34, pl. XIV; Reynolds 1953, pl. 99; Misfeldt 1971, 144–145, 152–155, fig. 79; Wood 1976, 30–31, fig. 18; Warner 1982, 13 (illus.); Manchester City Art Gallery 1983; London and Manchester 1984–1985, 9, 28, 37, 41, 45, 76, 111–112, pl. 6; Wentworth 1984, 16, 88, 114–119, 144, 201, pl. 103; Paris 1985, 178, pl. XVIII; Wood 1986, 69, 71, fig. 67; Arscott 1999, 70–71; Darby 1999, 167; Lochnan 1999, 9; Lochnan, ed. 1999, pl. XIII; New Haven, Québec, and Buffalo 1999–2000, 96–99; Saddlemyer 1999, 145; Silver 1999, 130–132; Barletta 2006, 38, 47, 65, 82; London and Paris 2017–2018, 83, 84, 95; Matyjaszkiewicz, ed. 2019a.

46
*TOO EARLY, 1873

Oil on canvas, 28 × 40⅛ in. (71 × 102 cm)
Signed and dated l. l.: *J. Tissot 1873*
Guildhall Art Gallery, London, Bequeathed by Charles Gassiot, 1902, 738
Prov.: Sold by Tissot in 1873 for £800 or 20,000FF to Pilgeram, who sold it on to Agnew for £1,000, thence to Gassiot for £1,400 (Notebook), although the latter sum is incorrect as Agnew recorded sale to Gassiot for £1,155, March 26, 1873, with receipt of the painting from Tissot (rather than Pilgeram) as *The Ball*, March 28, 1873; bequeathed by Charles Gassiot, 1902.
Exh.: Royal Academy 1873; Sheffield 1955; Arts Council 1955; Providence and Toronto 1968; London and Manchester 1984–1985; Paris 1985; Barletta 2006; Rome 2015; London and Paris 2017.
Bibl.: Tissot 1871–1878, 15; *Builder* 1873, 340; *Graphic* 1873, 539; Jopling 1925, 60; Laver 1936, 29, 31, pl. VI; Reynolds 1953, pl. 98; Misfeldt 1971, 143–144, fig. 77; Wood 1976, 28, 30, pl. 17; Warner 1982, 12 (illus.); London 1984a, no. 41; London and Manchester 1984–1985, 9, 28, 37, 76, 109, 111, pl. 7; Wentworth 1984, 96, 103, 113–117, 163, 201, pl. 101; Paris 1985, 171–172, pl. XIV; Wood 1986, 66, fig. 64; Arscott 1999, 63–65, 69–70, 72; Darby 1999, 167; Lochnan 1999, 1, 7, 9; Lochnan, ed. 1999, pl. I; Maeder 1999, 85; New Haven, Québec, and Buffalo 1999–2000, 12–13; Prelinger 1999, 186; Saddlemyer 1999, 145; Silver 1999, 130–131; Barletta 2006, 47, 65–66, 69; Mancoff 2012, 32–33; London and Paris 2017–2018, 84, 94; Matyjaszkiewicz, ed. 2019a.

47
*THE CONVALESCENT (GIRL IN AN ARMCHAIR), 1872

Oil on wood panel, 14¾ × 18 in. (37.5 × 45.7 cm)
Signed and dated l. r.: *J. J. Tissot / 1870 or 1872*
Art Gallery of Ontario, Toronto, Gift of R. B. F. Barr, Esq., Q.C., 1966, 65/28
Prov.: Probably *La paresseuse* [The Idle One] sold by Tissot in 1872 for £100 or 2,500FF to Pilgeram (Notebook); with Ferrers Gallery, London, August 1962; donated by R. B. F. Barr, Esq., QC, 1966.
Exh.: Providence and Toronto 1968; London and Manchester 1984–1985 as *A Girl in an Armchair (The Convalescent)*; Paris 1985.
Bibl.: *Apollo* 1962; Misfeldt 1982, pl. I-76; London and Manchester 1984–1985, 103; Wentworth 1984, 112, pl. 99; Paris 1985, 154; Wood 1986, fig. 42; Darby 1999, 169; Maeder 1999, 86–87, fig. 35; Mancoff 2012, 14 (illus.), 15.

48
*THE CONVALESCENT, 1875

Oil on canvas, 29¾ × 38¾ in. (75.4 × 98.4 cm)
Signed l. l.: *J. J. Tissot*
Museums Sheffield, England, Purchased, 1949, VIS.2213
Prov.: Sold by Tissot in 1875 as *La Convalescente (en blanc) l'automne* [The Convalescent (in white) Autumn] for £600 or 15,000FF to Marsden (Notebook); probably bought from Marsden by a member of the Knowles family, thence by descent; sold by Lt. Col. Andrew Knowles, Christie's, London, January 21, 1949, as *The Convalescent*, 29½ × 38½ in. (74.9 × 97.8 cm), £241.10s, bt. Fine Art Society, London; purchased by Sheffield City Art Galleries, 1949.
Exh.: Royal Academy 1876; Sheffield 1955, lent by Sheffield City Art Galleries; Arts Council 1955; London and Manchester 1984–1985; Paris 1985; Japan 1988; Barletta 2006; Rome 2015.
Publ.: A drypoint and etching three-quarters view in reverse of the convalescent, with pool and chestnut leaves, was made by Tissot in 1875 (Wentworth 6; only known impression Bibliothèque Nationale de France, Paris).
Bibl.: Tissot 1871–1878, 40; Providence and Toronto 1968, no. 26; Misfeldt 1971, 160–161; Wentworth 1978, 52, 54, fig. 6a; London and Manchester 1984–1985, 57, 73, 115–117, 120, pl. 19; Wentworth 1984, 94, 112, 120, 128, 130, 139, 162, 167, 201, pl. 113; Paris 1985, 180, pl. XIX; Wood 1986, 76, fig. 73; Arscott 1999, 69; Darby 1999, 169; Lochnan, ed. 1999, pl. XVI; London and Paris 2017–2018, 85.

49
SPRING MORNING, 1875

Oil on canvas, 22 × 16¾ in. (55.9 × 42.5 cm)
The Metropolitan Museum of Art, New York, Gift of Mrs. Charles Wrightsman, 2009, 2009.359
Prov.: Probably sold by Tissot in 1875 as *Matinée d'été* [Summer Morning] for £350 or 8,750FF to [Diaz?] de la Penha (Notebook); with Thomas McLean (label on reverse); with Goupil, London (label on reverse); receipt or sale, "WD / 638B / 13/2/20" (inscription on reverse); sold Sotheby's, Belgravia, March 23, 1981 (67) as *Matinée de printemps*; Mr. and Mrs. Charles Wrightsman, New York, 1981–1986; Mrs. Charles Wrightsman; given by her in 2009.
Publ.: Large drypoint in reverse by Tissot of the figure and rhubarb plant, *Spring Morning*, dated 1875 (Wentworth 13).
Bibl.: Tissot 1871–1878, 37; Wentworth 1978, 76–79; London 1981, no. 1; London and Manchester 1984–1985, 56–57, 60, 89, 116, fig. 23; Wentworth 1984, 138; Paris 1985, 76, 179, fig. 27; Misfeldt 1991, 42; Fahy, ed. 2005, 404–405, no. 115.

50
*CROQUET, 1877–1878

Oil on canvas, 35⅜ × 20 in. (90 × 50.8 cm)
Art Gallery of Hamilton, Ontario, Gift of Dr. and Mrs. Basil Bowman in memory of their daughter, Suzanne, 1965, 65.112.V
Prov.: Sold by Tissot in 1878 for £180 or 4,500FF to E. F. White, who sold it at the Grosvenor Gallery (Notebook); Laing Galleries, Toronto, Ontario; donated by Dr. and Mrs. Basil Bowman in memory of their daughter, Suzanne, 1965.

Exh.: Grosvenor Gallery 1878; Providence and Toronto 1968; London and Manchester 1984–1985; Paris 1985; Japan 1988; Yale 1999.
Publ.: Etching and drypoint by Tissot dated 1878 (Wentworth 37).
Bibl.: Tissot 1871–1878, 55; Brooke 1968, 58 (illus.); Misfeldt 1971, 187–188, fig. 99; Wentworth 1978, 168, 170, fig. 37a; Warner 1982, 16 (illus.); London and Manchester 1984–1985, 60, 79, 123, 135; Wentworth 1984, 147, 151, 165, 202, pl. 142; Paris 1985, 204; Wood 1986, 105, fig. 105; Misfeldt 1991, 88; Arscott 1999, 68, fig. 27; New Haven, Québec, and Buffalo 1999–2000, 114–115; Saddlemyer 1999, 148–149; London and Paris 2017–2018, 84.

51

*QUARRELLING, 1875–1876

Oil on canvas, 28½ × 19 in. (72.4 × 48.2 cm)

Private collection, courtesy of Grant Ford Ltd.
Prov.: Sold by Tissot in 1876 for £525 or 13,125FF to Alexander Kay, commission 10 percent to "Wallace" [Wallis?] (Notebook); with Hammer Galleries, New York, March 1955, as *In the Garden (St John's Wood)*; sold Charpentier, Paris, June 1956 (82) as *The Garden at St. John's Wood*.
Exh.: Yale 1999.
Publ.: Etching by Tissot dated 1876 (Wentworth 18) published by Tissot in *Ten Etchings by J. J. Tissot*. Tissot 1876.
Bibl.: Tissot 1871–1878, 38; *Connoisseur* 1955; Providence and Toronto 1968, no. 63; Misfeldt 1971, 159, fig. 85; Wentworth 1978, 90, fig. 18b; London and Manchester 1984–1985, 116; Wentworth 1984, 111, 121, pl. 97; Paris 1985, 186; Wood 1986, 76–77, fig. 74; Misfeldt 1991, 52; New Haven, Québec, and Buffalo 1999–2000, 105–107; Saddlemyer 1999, 147, 151, fig. 54; Silver 1999, 132.

52

*HOLYDAY, 1876

Oil on canvas, 30 × 39 in. (76.2 × 99.4 cm)

Signed l. r.: *J. J. Tissot*
Tate, London, Purchased 1928, N04413
Prov.: Sold by Tissot in 1876 as *Last Pic-nic* for £650 or 16,250FF to Tailor [Taylor] through [E. F.] White (Notebook); James Taylor; Thomas McLean Ltd., from whom purchased by the Tate Gallery through the Clarke Fund, 1928.
Exh.: Grosvenor Gallery 1877 as *Holyday*, lent by James Taylor Esq.; Sheffield 1955 as *The Picnic*; Arts Council 1955; Providence and Toronto 1968; London and Manchester 1984–1985; Paris 1985; Yale 1999; Barletta 2006; London and Paris 2017.
Bibl.: Tissot 1871–1878, 43; Colvin 1877, 830; Wilde 1877, 125–126; Laver 1936, pl. XXXIII as *The Picnic*; Rothenstein 1947, pl. 23; Peacock 1949, pl. 58; Misfeldt 1971, 171–172, fig. 91; Wood 1976, 179, pl. 191; Alley 1981, 722–723; Warner 1982, 17 (illus.); London and Manchester 1984–1985, 73, 116–117; Wentworth 1984, 120, 130, 139, 202, pl. 123; Paris 1985, 186–187; Wood 1986, 100, fig. 98; Misfeldt 1991, 42, fig. 10; New Haven, Québec, and Buffalo 1999–2000, 104–105, 110–111; Nantes 2005–2006, fig. 12; Barletta 2006, 40 (illus.), 49, 66; Dolkart, ed. 2009, 14, fig. 6; Rome 2015–2016, fig. 5; London and Paris 2017–2018, 202–203 (illus.); Matyjaszkiewicz, ed. 2019a.

53

THE BOUQUET OF LILACS, 1874

Oil on canvas, 20 × 14 in. (50.8 × 35.6 cm)

Signed l. l.: *J. J. Tissot*
Private collection
Prov.: Sold by Tissot in 1874 as *Le bouquet de lilas* [The Bouquet of Lilacs] for £400 or 10,000FF to Agnew (Notebook), Agnew recording receipt as *Bouquet of Lilacs*, September 16, 1874; with Agnew, Manchester, as *Lady Holding Flowers*, November 16, 1874; sold by Agnew, March 13, 1875, for £577.10s to Albert Grant; sold by Albert Grant, Christie's, London, April 28, 1877 (127) as *Lilacs, a Lady*, £346.10s, bt. Agnew; sold by Agnew, May 15, 1877, to H. R. Willis, 5 percent; consigned by H. R. Willis of The Shrubbery, Wolverley, Kidderminster, Christie's, London, April 2, 1881 (227) as *Lilacs*, bt. in; consigned by H. R. Willis of Brockencote Hall, Chaddesley Corbett, Worcestershire, Christie's, London, February 26, 1887 (129) as *The Bunch of Lilacs*, bt. in; Henry Preen; sold Christie's, London, December 7, 1895 (65) as *Lilacs*, bt. Agnew, and sold by Agnew, December 9, 1895, for £50.18 to H. R. Willis; sold by H. R. Willis to Agnew, February 27, 1897; sold by Agnew, January 11, 1898, for £52.10s to W. W. Galloway; sold Christie's, London, July 25, 1975 (40), bt. Richard Green; sold Christie's, London, March 26, 1982 (127).
Exh.: Royal Academy 1875 as *The Bunch of Lilacs*; Birmingham 1882 as *The Lilacs*.
Bibl.: Tissot 1871–1878, 27; Laver 1936, 67; *Revue du Louvre* 1982; Wentworth 1984, 119, 142, 201, pl. 107; Wood 1986, 74, 106, pl. 1; Darby 1999, 178–180; Lochnan, ed. 1999, pl. IX; Fahy, ed. 2005, 408, fig. 2.

54

*AFTERNOON TEA, 1874

also known as **IN THE CONSERVATORY**

Oil on canvas, 15⅛ × 20⅛ in. (38.4 × 51.1 cm)

Signed l. l.: *J. J. Tissot*
Collection of Diane B. Wilsey, San Francisco
Prov.: Sold by Tissot in 1874 as *Tea Party* for £700 or 17,500FF to Pilgeram (Notebook); sold by executors of Kaye Knowles, Esq., late of Warrington Crescent, Christie's, London, May 14, 1887 (149) as *Afternoon Tea*, 14½ × 20 in. (36.8 × 50.8 cm), £52.10s, bt. Agnew on behalf of Andrew Knowles, 5 percent terms; Robert Knowles; Mrs. Mary Grant by 1936; sold by J. E. Grant, Esq., and Mrs. P. M. Mackay Scobie, Christie's, London, October 16, 1981 (84) as *Rivals*; Richard Green Gallery, from whom bought by Mr. and Mrs. Charles Wrightsman; Mr. and Mrs. Wrightsman, 1981–1986; Mrs. Charles Wrightsman, by whom gifted to the Metropolitan Museum of Art, New York, 2009; sold by the Metropolitan Museum of Art, Christie's, New York, October 28, 2013 (42) as *In the Conservatory (Rivals)*.
Exh.: Leicester Galleries 1937 as *In the Conservatory*, lent by Mrs. Grant; Sheffield 1955, lent by Mrs. M. Grant; Arts Council 1955, lent by Mrs. M. Grant.
Bibl.: Tissot 1871–1878, 26 Laver 1936, 70, front cover wrapper; Reynolds 1953, 36, 39, fig. 101 as *In the Conservatory*; Misfeldt 1971, 162, fig. 83 as *The Rivals*; *Burlington Magazine* 1981; Wentworth 1984, 6, 141–142, 145, pl. 137; Wood 1986, 105, fig. 107; *Country Life* 1987, fig. 3 as *The Rivals*; Darby 1999, 163, 177–178; Lochnan 1999, 11; Lochnan, ed. 1999, pl. VII; Silver 1999, 128–129; Fahy, ed. 2005, 406–409; Barletta 2006, 68, 70 (illus.); Matyjaszkiewicz, ed. 2019a.

55

*THE REPLY, 1874

also known as **THE LETTER**

Oil on canvas, 28¼ × 42¼ in. (71.4 × 107.1 cm)

Signed and indistinctly dated on base of urn: *J. J. Tissot 18[7?]*
National Gallery of Canada, Ottawa, Purchased 1964, 15191
Prov.: Sold by Tissot in 1874 as *Réponse à la lettre* [Reply to the Letter] for £800 or 20,000FF to Agnew (Notebook), Agnew recording receipt as *The Reply*, October 8, 1874; with Agnew, Manchester, as *The Answer*, October 1874, thence sent to Hay and Sons, Newcastle, November 9, 1874; sold by Agnew as *The Reply*, December 15, 1874, for £1,312.10s to W. J. Houldsworth; consigned by Colonel Holdsworth [*sic*], Christie's, London, April 30, 1881 (77), £787.10s, bt. in; returned by W. J. Houldsworth to Agnew, Manchester, July 25, 1881, thence to Agnew, London, August 8, sale price £892.10s; with Agnew, April 17, 1882; sold by Agnew, March 6, 1894, for £105 to W. W. Galloway; with Hon. Mrs. Basil Ionides by 1955; sold by Mrs. Nellie Ionides, Sotheby's, London, May 29, 1963 (170) as *The Letter*, bt. P. Claas; James Coats, New York, from whom purchased by National Gallery of Canada, 1964.
Exh.: Manchester 1886, probably lent by Agnew; Sheffield 1955 as *The Letter*, lent by Hon. Mrs. Ionides; Providence and Toronto 1968; London and Manchester 1984–1985; Paris 1985; Yale 1999.
Bibl.: Tissot 1871–1878, 28; Reynolds 1953, 99, pl. 100; London and Manchester 1984–1985, 117, 137, pl. 18; Wentworth 1984, 20, 111, 130, 139, 141, pl. 114; Paris 1985, 188, pl. XXI; Wood 1986, 105–106, fig. 106; Arscott 1999, 67; Lochnan, ed. 1999, pl. XVII; New Haven, Québec, and Buffalo 1999–2000, 108–109; Silver 1999, 128, 132–134; Matyjaszkiewicz, ed. 2019a.

56

*LONDON VISITORS, 1873–1874

Oil on canvas, 63 × 45 in. (160 × 114.2 cm)

Signed l. l.: *J. J. Tissot*
Toledo Museum of Art, Ohio, Purchased with funds from the Libbey Endowment, Gift of Edward Drummond Libbey, 1951.409
Prov.: Sale recorded by Tissot in 1874 as *Le portique de National Galerie en grand* [The Portico of the National Gallery, large size] for £1,000 or 25,000FF to Agnew (Notebook), who was acting for collector Hilton Philipson, to whom Agnew recorded sale as *London Visitors*, April 1, 1874, with *Ball on Shipboard* (pl. 71), for £3,150, and receipt of the painting, April 1, 1874; by descent to Philipson's daughter, Mrs. Bannister; with M. Bernard, London, June 1951; Robert Frank, London; gift of Edward Drummond Libbey, 1951.
Exh.: Royal Academy 1874; Leicester Galleries 1937, lent by Mrs. Bannister; Ottawa 1965; Providence and Toronto 1968; Washington 1997; Yale 1999.
Bibl.: Tissot 1871–1878, 23; Laver 1936, 67; *Connoisseur* 1951; Reynolds 1953, fig. 102; Flaizik 1960, 41 (illus.), 44–45; Wittmann 1962, 1663; Clarke 1963; Rosenblum 1965, 140, fig. 6; Misfeldt 1971, 146–149, fig. 80; Wentworth 1984, 7, 75, 94, 106, 117, 119, 133, 155, 156, 162, 201, pl. 106; Wood 1986, 69, fig. 66; London 1987a, 173; Misfeldt 1991, 94; Lochnan, ed. 1999, pl. XVIII; Marshall 1999, 27–28; New Haven, Québec, and Buffalo 1999–2000, 16–17, 70–75; Prelinger 1999, 189; Silver 1999, 130; Barletta 2006, 38–39 (illus.); London and Paris 2017–2018, 108; Matyjaszkiewicz, ed., 2019a.

57

*CHRYSANTHEMUMS, CA. 1876

Oil on canvas, 46⅝ × 30 in. (118.4 × 76.2 cm)
Signed l. c.: *J. J. Tissot*
Sterling and Francine Clark Art Institute, Williamstown, Massachusetts, Acquired in honor of David S. Brooke (Institute Director, 1977–1994), 1994, 1994.2
Prov.: Sold by Tissot in 1877 for £325 or 8,125FF to [Edward] Hermon M. P. (Notebook); sold by executors of Edward Hermon Esq., M.P., Christie's, London, May 13, 1882 (80), 46 × 30 in. (116.8 × 76.2 cm), £273, bt. Tooth; sold by Tooth, November 18, 1882, to Lovatt; perhaps (if size recorded incorrectly) bought by Tooth from W. Lawson, November 1, 1883, as *Chrysanthemums*, 60 × 40 in. (and 60 × 36 in.), for £210, and sold by Tooth, May 30, 1884, to Oakshott; Surgeon-Major John Ewart Martin of Liverpool and Edinburgh, who settled in South Africa; by descent to the mother of the consignor for sale, Phillips, London, December 14, 1993 (67), bt. in; purchased after the sale by Christopher Wood and Richard Green for £250,000; bought by the Clark Institute in honor of David S. Brooke, 1994.
Exh.: Grosvenor Gallery 1877, lent by E. Hermon Esq., M.P.; London 1994.
Bibl.: Tissot 1871–1878, 41; *Aberdeen Press and Journal* 1877, 5; *Art Journal* 1877, 64; Laver 1936, 73; Wentworth 1984, 202; *Apollo* 1995c; *Burlington Magazine* 2005, fig. XVIII; Serafini 2015, 46, fig. 3; Matyjaszkiewicz, ed. 2019a.

58

SUMMER, 1876

Oil on canvas, 36 × 20⅜ in. (91.4 × 51.8 cm)
Signed and dated l. r.: *J. J. Tissot / 1876*
Tate, London, Purchased from Mrs. Isa van Wisselingh (Clarke Fund), 1927, N04271
Prov.: Consigned or sold by Tissot to E. F. White by 1877; sold by executors of John Polson, of Thornley and Tranent, Christie's, London, July 21, 1911 (43) as *An Afternoon Call*, 1876, 35 × 19 in. (88.9 × 48.3 cm), £42, bt. Van Wisselingh; purchased from Mrs. Ida van Wisselingh by Tate Gallery, 1927.
Exh.: Grosvenor Gallery 1877, lent by E. F. White, Esq.; Sheffield 1955 as *The Visit*; Arts Council 1955 as *The Visit*; Barletta 2006 as *Portrait (Miss Lloyd)*; Paris 2012 as *Portrait*; Rome 2015 as *Ritratto di Mrs L.*; London and Paris 2017 as *Summer*.
Publ.: Drypoint by Tissot dated 1876 (Wentworth 23) published by Tissot as *Portrait of Miss L...* in *Ten Etchings by J. J. Tissot*. Tissot 1876.
Bibl.: Tissot 1871–1878, 52; *Aberdeen Press and Journal* 1876, 5; Carr 1877, 273 (illus. Tissot's drypoint as *Summer*); Laver 1936, pl. XIII; Misfeldt 1971, 171; Wentworth 1978, 110, 112, fig. 23a; Alley 1981, 720; London and Manchester 1984–1985, 112–113, fig. 15; Wentworth 1984, 135, 142, 202; Paris 1985, 182, fig. 17; Wood 1986, 95, 98, fig. 94; Misfeldt 1991, 62; Saddlemyer 1999, 144–145, 147–148, 151; Silver 1999, 127; Barletta 2006, 58 (illus.), 66, 71; Ribeiro 2016, 546; London and Paris 2017–2018, 84, 110, 111 (illus.); Matyjaszkiewicz, ed. 2019b.

59

YOUNG LADY IN A BOAT, 1869–1870
JEUNE FEMME EN BATEAU

Oil on canvas, 19 × 25 in. (48.3 × 63.5 cm)
Signed l. r.: *J. J. Tissot*
Private collection
Prov.: Sold by Tissot in 1870 as *La femme en bateau* [The Woman in a Boat] for 3,300FF to Reitlinger, who sold it to Mr H. V. [William H.] Stewart of America (Notebook); bought from Mr. Stewart by Goupil as *Promenade sur l'eau* [Promenade on the Water], November 3, 1873, for 6,500FF including frame; sold by Goupil, December 22, 1873, for 10,000FF to M. Maison of London; sold in Glasgow by Pilgeram, 1875 (Notebook); Mrs. Moyes; T. H. Farr, Esq.; with Newman Galleries, London, December 1958, as *Reflections*; acquired from Newman Galleries by the late owner, whose executors sold at Sotheby's, London, June 18, 1985 (75) as *Jeune femme en bateau*.
Exh.: Paris Salon 1870 as *Jeune femme en bateau*, lent by Mr. W. H. Stewart; Yale 1999.
Publ.: Photograph by Robert Bingham published 1870, as *À la dérive* [Adrift].
Bibl.: *Athenaeum* 1870a, vol. 1, 779; *Connoisseur* 1958; Misfeldt 1971, 98–99, fig. 45; Wentworth 1975, 36, 39, fig. 2 (Bingham photograph); Wentworth 1978, fig. 20c; Misfeldt 1982, pl. I-74; Wentworth 1984, 74, 111, pl. 67; Wood 1986, 48, fig. 41; Lochnan 1999, 11; Lochnan, ed. 1999, pl. XIV; Maeder 1999, 86; New Haven, Québec, and Buffalo 1999–2000, 28–29.

60

*WAITING, 1873
also known as IN THE SHALLOWS

Oil on canvas, 22 × 31 in. (55.9 × 78.8 cm)
Signed l. l.: *J. J. Tissot*
Collection of Diane B. Wilsey, San Francisco
Prov.: Sold by Tissot in 1873 as *Le bateau (chale jaune)* [The Boat (Yellow Shawl)] for £550 or 13,750FF to Agnew (Notebook), Agnew recording receipt as *Waiting*, November 22, 1873; sold by Agnew, January 23, 1874, for £800 to E. Levita; returned by Levita to Agnew, February 17, 1874, and sold April 1, 1874, for £770 to James Houldsworth; returned by James Houldsworth to Agnew, June 5, 1875, and sold June 2, 1875 for £800 to Colonel Hargreaves, London; sold by executors of Colonel John Hargreaves, Christie's, London, May 2, 1896 (122), bt. Sampson; sold Christie's, London, June 17, 2014 (14).
Exh.: Royal Academy 1874; perhaps Newcastle 1878 as *A Reverie*, described as "fair maiden sits day-dreaming in a punt upon a quiet inland stream"; Reading 1882, lent by John Hargreaves, of Maiden Erlegh, Berkshire.
Bibl.: Tissot 1871–1878, 18; *Graphic* 1874, 474; *Birmingham Daily Post* 1882, 7; Misfeldt 1971, 146; Wentworth 1975, 49; Wentworth 1984, 201.

61

*THE THAMES, 1875

Oil on canvas, 29½ × 46½ in. (74.8 × 118 cm)
Signed l. r.: *J. J. Tissot*
The Hepworth Wakefield, England, Purchased 1938
Prov.: Sold by Tissot in 1876 as *La Tamise (private steamer)* for £800 or 20,000FF to Marsden (Notebook), probably acting on behalf of Kaye Knowles; sold by executors of Kaye Knowles, Christie's, London, May 14, 1887 (147) as *A Picnic on the Thames*, 29 × 46 in. (73.7 × 116.8 cm), £69.6s., bt. Polak; perhaps Mrs. Roland Philipson by 1937 as *On the Thames*; Stella Mary Newton, London, from whom purchased by the Wakefield Corporation, September 1938.
Exh.: Royal Academy 1876; perhaps Leicester Galleries 1937 as *On the Thames*, ca. 1879, lent by Mrs. Roland Philipson; Sheffield 1955 as *"How Happy Could I Be with Either" or "On the Thames"*; Arts Council 1955; Greenwich 1977; London and Manchester 1984–1985; Washington 1997; Yale 1999; Bedford 2002; Wakefield 2013; Rome 2015; London and Paris 2017.
Publ.: Etching by Tissot dated 1876 (Wentworth 20) published by Tissot in *Ten Etchings by J. J. Tissot*. Tissot 1876.
Bibl.: Tissot 1871–1878, 39; Providence and Toronto 1968, no. 64; Misfeldt 1971, 158–159, 161–162, fig. 83; Wentworth 1978, 98–101, fig. 20b; London 1981, no. 3; Thomson 1982, 329, fig. 4; London and Manchester 1984–1985, 60, 111, 114, pl. 15; Wentworth 1984, 88, 94, 107–109, 120, 131, 134, 141, 201, pl. 115; Paris 1985, 185, fig. 30; Wood 1986, 83, fig. 79; Misfeldt 1991, 56; New Haven, Québec, and Buffalo 1999–2000, 8, 66–67; Saddlemyer 1999, 147, 177, fig. 71; Thomson 2000, fig. 2; London and Paris 2017–2018, 84, 220 (illus.).

62

GRAVESEND, 1873
also known as WAITING FOR THE FERRY AT THE FALCON TAVERN

Oil on canvas, 26¼ × 38¼ in. (66.7 × 97 cm)
Signed l. l.: *J. J. Tissot*
The Speed Art Museum, Louisville, Gift of Mrs. Blakemore Wheeler, 1963.41
Prov.: Sold by Tissot in 1873 as *Falcon Hotel* for £800 or 20,000FF to Agnew (Notebook), Agnew recording receipt as *Gravesend*, January 8, 1874; sold by Agnew in Liverpool, March 3, 1874, for £1,155 to James Hall; Wilfred Hall, Newcastle; Mrs. Edward Reeves, Winchester; bequeathed by Mrs. Blakemore Wheeler, 1963.
Exh.: Newcastle 1887, Fine Arts Section, Loan Collection; Louisville 1964; Louisville 2002–2003.
Bibl.: Tissot 1871–1878, 22; *J. B. Speed Art Museum Bulletin* 1964, n.p., illus.; Misfeldt 1971, 149, fig. 81; Martin, ed. 1973, 145; Bennett, ed. 1983, 155; London and Manchester 1984–1985, 120; Wentworth 1984, 119, 131, pl. 111; Paris 1985, 201; Wood 1986, 78, fig. 75.

63

*THE CAPTAIN'S DAUGHTER, 1873

Oil on canvas, 28½ × 41¼ in. (72.3 × 104.8 cm)
Signed and dated l. l.: *J. J. Tissot / L. 73*
Southampton City Art Gallery, England, Purchased 1934 through the Frederick Smith Bequest Fund, SOTAG: 580
Prov.: Sold by Tissot in 1873 as *La fille du capitaine* [The Captain's Daughter] for £700 or 17,500FF to Agnew (Notebook), Agnew recording receipt, March 26, 1873; sold by Agnew in Liverpool, March 31, 1873, for £1,050 to Benson Rathbone; "disposed of ... in exchange for other pictures from a dealer in Liverpool" (son, George Rathbone, in letter to James Laver, 1937); with Messrs. Bradley, Pass & Co., June 1885 (*Liverpool Mercury*); sold Branch & Leete, September 24, 1903 (190), £183.15s; with French Gallery, London; with Leicester Galleries, London, by 1933; bought from Leicester Galleries through the Smith Fund, 1934.
Exh.: Royal Academy 1873; Darwen 1879; London and Manchester 1984–1985; Paris 1985; Yale 1999; Nantes 2005; Barletta 2006; Rome 2015.

Bibl.: Tissot 1871–1878, 13; Laver 1936, 29, pl. IX; Brooke 1968, 26; Misfeldt 1971, 140–142, fig. 73; Wentworth 1978, 134, 139, fig. 29b; London and Manchester 1984–1985, 9, 109, 111, pl. 8; Wentworth 1984, 95, 103–106, 113, 131, 147, 201, pl. 81; Paris 1985, 168; Wood 1986, 62, fig. 58; Misfeldt 1991, 104; Arscott 1999, 54; Lochnan 1999, 9; Lochnan, ed. 1999, pl. V; New Haven, Québec, and Buffalo 1999–2000, 60–63; Nantes 2005–2006, 68–69 (illus.), 79 (illus.); Barletta 2006, 49, 69; London and Paris 2017–2018, 84; Matyjaszkiewicz, ed. 2019a.

64

*THE GALLERY OF HMS "CALCUTTA" (PORTSMOUTH), CA. 1876

Oil on canvas, 27 × 36⅛ in. (68.6 × 91.8 cm)

Signed l. l.: *J. J. Tissot*

Tate, London, Presented by Samuel Courtauld, 1936, N04847

Prov.: John Robertson Reid by 1877; sold by executors of art dealer E. F. White, Christie's, London, March 24, 1900 (144) as *A Visit to the Training Ship*, 27 × 35 in. (68.6 × 88.9 cm), £31.10s; sold by executors of Henry Trengrouse, Teddington, at Puttick and Simpson, London, February 27, 1929 (107); with Leicester Galleries by 1933; presented by Samuel Courtauld, 1936.

Exh.: Grosvenor Gallery 1877, lent by J. Robertson Reid Esq.; Glasgow 1878 as *Gallery of H.M.S. Calcutta*; Leicester Galleries 1933 as *Officer and Ladies on Board HMS Calcutta*; Sheffield 1955; Arts Council 1955; Yale 1999; Rome 2015; London and Paris 2017.

Publ.: Etching by Tissot dated 1876 (Wentworth 25) published by Tissot in *Ten Etchings by J. J. Tissot*. Tissot 1876. Wood engraving by an unknown artist published as a supplement to *The Graphic*, August 18, 1877.

Bibl.: Tissot 1871–1878, 42; *Graphic* 1877a, 150; Laver 1936, 37; Misfeldt 1971, 172–175, fig. 95; Wentworth 1978, 118, fig. 25a; London and Manchester 1984–1985, 114, fig. 51; Wentworth 1984, 6, 108, 135, 139–141, 202, pl. 124; Paris 1985, 184, fig. 11; Wood 1986, 98–99, fig. 95; Misfeldt 1991, 62, 66; Lochnan 1999, 9; Lochnan, ed. 1999, pl. X; Maeder 1999, 88; New Haven, Québec, and Buffalo 1999–2000, 84–87; Silver 1999, 122; Thomson 2000, fig. 1; Barletta 2006, 66, 67 (illus.); Ribeiro 2016, 365, pls. 226, 275; London and Paris 2017–2018, 84, 112 (illus.); Matyjaszkiewicz, ed. 2019a.

65

ON THE THAMES, A HERON, CA. 1871–1872

Oil on canvas, 36½ × 23¾ in. (92.7 × 60.3 cm)

Signed l. l.: *J. J. Tissot*

Minneapolis Institute of Art, Gift of Mrs. Patrick Butler, by exchange, 75.7

Prov.: Sold by Tissot in 1872 as *2 Jeunes filles en bateau* [Two Young Women in a Boat] for £300 or 7,500FF to Pilgeram (Notebook); sold by José de Murrieta, Christie's, London, May 24, 1873 (315) as *On the Thames: the Frightened Heron*, 570gns, bt. in; sold by José de Murrieta, Marqués de Santurce, Christie's, London, June 16, 1883 (164) as *On the Thames / Frightened Heron*, £273, bt. Higgs; sold through Robinson and Fisher at Willis's Rooms, London, July 1, 1892 (132) as *On the River—The Heron Alarmed*; with Mrs. Stuart-Black by 1937; with Wildenstein Arte, S.A., Buenos Aires, 1948; sold Sotheby Parke-Bernet, Los Angeles, April 8–9, 1973 (208), bt. H. Shickman Gallery, New York; gift of Mrs. Patrick Butler by exchange to Minneapolis Institute of Arts, 1975.

Exh.: Leicester Galleries 1937, lent by Mrs. Stuart-Black.

Bibl.: Tissot 1871–1878, 11; Laver 1936, 33; Wentworth 1975, 35–49; *Gazette des Beaux-Arts* 1977, 59, no. 245; Wentworth 1984, 110–111, pl. 90; Wood 1986, 72, fig. 69.

66

A WINDY DAY, 1874–1875

also known as **AUTUMN ON THE THAMES (NUNEHAM COURTNEY)**

Oil on wood panel, 29¼ × 19¼ in. (74.3 × 48.9 cm)

Signed l. r.: *J. J. Tissot*

Private collection

Prov.: Sold by Tissot in 1875 as *Le Coup de vent* [The Gust of Wind] for 450gns or 11,250FF to Tooth (Notebook), Tooth recording receipt as *A Windy Day*, May 7, 1875, 28 × 20 in. (78.1 × 50.8 cm), cost £525; sold by Tooth, May 15, 1875, for £600 to James Rhodes Esq.; The Rt. Hon. Malcolm MacDonald, M.P., by 1933; with Ernest Brown & Phillips Ltd., London; Wildenstein Arte, S. A., Buenos Aires, from whom purchased in 1961 by Mr. and Mrs. George W. Murphy, Columbus, Georgia; sold by them, Sotheby's, New York, October 19, 1984 (147); Richard Green Galleries, London, December 1984; Sotheby's, New York, May 26, 1994 (144) as *Autumn on the Thames (Nuneham Courtney)*.

Exh.: Leicester Galleries 1933 as *Autumn on the River*, lent by Malcolm MacDonald, Esq., M.P.; Yale 1999.

Bibl.: Tissot 1871–1878, 31; Laver 1936, pl. XI; Wentworth 1975, 39, fig. 5; Thomson 1979, 55–56; Wentworth 1984, 111, pl. 93; Wood 1986, 72–73, fig. 69; New Haven, Québec, and Buffalo 1999–2000, 61, 64–65; London and Paris 2017–2018, 84.

67

DOCKS, 1877–1878

also known as **A VISIT TO THE YACHT**

Oil on canvas, 34 × 21¼ in. (86.5 × 54 cm)

Signed l. l.: *J. J. Tissot*

Private collection

Prov.: Sold by Tissot in 1878 as *Docks (en hauteur[?])* [up high?] for £380 or 9,500FF to E. [F.] White (Notebook); sold by executors of E. F. White, Christie's, London, March 24, 1900 (145) as *A Visit to the Yacht*, 33 × 20 in. (83.8 × 50.8 cm), £30.9s, bt. Gooden; sold by Vicars Brothers at Christie's, London, April 3, 1922 (75); with Leicester Galleries, London, by 1933; bought from Leicester Galleries by William Hulme Lever, 2nd Lord Leverhulme, in 1933; thence by descent; sold from the Leverhulme Collection at Sotheby's, London, December 4, 2013 (47).

Exh.: Perhaps Glasgow 1888 as *Visit to Ship in the Docks*, lent by the artist; Leicester Galleries 1933; Port Sunlight 1948; Christie's 2000.

Bibl.: Tissot 1871–1878, 57; Laver 1936, 45–46, pl. XXIV; Wentworth 1984, 106.

68

IN THE DOCKS, 1873

also known as **THE CAPTAIN AND THE MATE**

Oil on wood panel, 21 × 30 in. (53.3 × 76.2 cm)

Signed and dated l. l.: *J. J. Tissot / L.1873*

Private collection

Prov.: Sale recorded by Tissot in 1873 as *Les Docks* [The Docks] for £650 or 16,250FF to Agnew (Notebook), who was acting for collector Andrew Knowles, to whom Agnew recorded sale on June 16, 1873, for £924, and receipt of painting from Tissot as *In the Docks*, June 18, 1873; returned by Andrew Knowles to Agnew, March 29, 1877; with Agnew, Manchester, April 20, 1877, price £892.10s; sold by Agnew to J. Broadhead, May 14, 1877, for £700; perhaps with Tissot, 1888; sold by executors of Abraham Farrar, Esq., late of Leeds and Harrogate, Christie's, London, March 27, 1909 (68) as *In the Docks*, 1873, oil on panel, 21 × 29½ in. (53.3 × 74.9 cm), £31.10s, bt. Vicars; sold Christie's, London, February 17, 1922, as *The Captain and the Mate*, bt. Sampson; with R. Skinner by 1933.

Exh.: Perhaps Glasgow 1888 as *Visit to Ship in the Docks*, lent by the artist; Leicester Galleries 1933, lent by R. Skinner, Esq.; London and Manchester 1984–1985; Paris 1985; Royal Academy 2003.

Bibl.: Tissot 1871–1878, 17; Laver 1936, 29–30, pl. VII; London and Manchester 1984–1985, 73, 109–110, pl. 13; Wentworth 1984, 31, 105–107, col. pl. III; Paris 1985, 169–171, pl. XIII; Wood 1986, 63–64, 89, fig. 61; Marshall 2003, 173–177; Ribeiro 2016, 546.

69

*THE LAST EVENING, 1873

Oil on canvas, 28⅜ × 40½ in. (72 × 103 cm)

Signed and dated l. l.: *L.1873 J. J. Tissot*

Guildhall Art Gallery, London, Bequeathed by Charles Gassiot, 1902, 737

Prov.: Sale recorded by Tissot in 1873 for £700 or 17,500FF to Agnew (Notebook), who was acting for collector Charles Gassiot, to whom Agnew recorded sale on February 10, 1873, for £1,000, and receipt of painting March 11, 1873; bequeathed by Charles Gassiot, 1902.

Exh.: Royal Academy 1873; Guildhall 1898; Leicester Galleries 1933; Sheffield 1955; Arts Council 1955; Barbican 1984; Paris 1985; Nantes 2005.

Bibl.: Tissot 1871–1878, 14; Laver 1936, 29–30, pl. VIII; Providence and Toronto 1968; Misfeldt 1971, 140–143, fig. 74; Wentworth 1979–1980, 23, fig. 74; London and Manchester 1984–1985, 9, 10, 14, 73, 109–111, 128, pl. 14; Wentworth 1984, 102–103, 105–106, 113, 147, 201, pl. 84; Paris 1985, 166–167, pl. XII; Wood 1986, 62–63, fig. 60; Misfeldt 1991, 104; New Haven, Québec, and Buffalo 1999–2000, 63, fig. 14; Nantes 2005–2006, 77 (illus.); Ribeiro 2016, 546; London and Paris 2017–2018, 84; Matyjaszkiewicz, ed. 2019a.

70

YOUNG WOMAN IN A ROCKING CHAIR,

variant of **STUDY FOR "THE LAST EVENING," 1872**

Brush and brown ink with opaque watercolor and watercolor over graphite on blue paper, 11¼ × 17 in. (28.7 × 43.2 cm)

Signed l. l.: *J. Tissot*

The J. Paul Getty Museum, Los Angeles, 2002.30

Prov.: Sold by Tissot in 1872 as *Dessin gouache, étude de la femme dans le fauteuil du Last Evening* [Gouache drawing, Study of the Woman in the Armchair of The Last Evening] for £30 or 750FF to Agnew (Notebook); perhaps one of two drawings, *Study, 11 x 17*, recorded as received November 26, 1872, one of which was sold the same day for £47.5s to Sir Joseph Heron, bought back from him on June 16, 1873, and sold with other drawings on June 24 to Ja[me]s H. White; the second was sold by Agnew in Liverpool, November 23, 1874, for £42 to J. G. Sowerby; Christie's, London, November 28, 2001 (22).

71
*THE BALL ON SHIPBOARD, CA. 1874

Oil on canvas, 33⅛ × 51 in. (84.1 × 129.5 cm)
Signed l. l.: *J. J. Tissot*
Tate, London, Presented by the Trustees of the Chantrey Bequest, 1937, N04892
Prov.: Sale recorded by Tissot in 1874 for £1,400 or 35,000FF to Agnew (Notebook), who was acting for collector Hilton Philipson, to whom Agnew recorded sale as *Ball on Shipboard*, April 1, 1874, with *London Visitors* (pl. 56), for £3,150, and receipt of painting the same day; recorded in Agnew's London Daybooks as received (after Royal Academy exhibition) October 8, 1874, as *The Ariadne Ball*; by descent to Hilton Philipson's son, Roland Philipson; Mrs. Roland Philipson; purchased for the Nation through the Chantrey Bequest (via the offices of Royal Academy President, Sir Alfred Munnings) from the Leicester Galleries, London, June 1937.
Exh.: Royal Academy 1874; Leicester Galleries 1937 as *The Ball on Shipboard, Cowes*, lent by Mrs. Roland Philipson; Royal Academy Jubilee Exhibition 1937; Glasgow 1937; London and Manchester 1984–1985; Paris 1985; Washington 1997; Yale 1999; Paris 2012; London and Paris 2017.
Bibl.: Tissot 1871–1878, 24; *Leeds Mercury* 1874, 5; *Times* 1874, 5; Sitwell 1937, 92–93, 118, pl. 129; Misfeldt 1971, 144–147, 149–151, fig. 78; Wood 1976, 30–31, col. pl. 18; Misfeldt 1978, no. 66, fig. 5; Wentworth 1978, 118, fig. 25b; Alley 1981, 719–720; Warner 1982, 14, col. pl.; Thomson 1982, 328, fig. 1; London and Manchester 1984–1985, 9, 28, 34, 36, 73, 76, 109–112, 120, pl. 25; Wentworth 1984, 4–5, 31, 50, 96, 106, 109, 114–116, 118–119, 139, 141–142, 201, pl. 102; Paris 1985, 174, pls. I, XV; Wood 1986, fig. 65, endpapers; Darby 1999, 177; Lochnan 1999, 5; Lochnan, ed. 1999, pl. XII; New Haven, Québec, and Buffalo 1999–2000, 2, 80–83; Prelinger 1999, 186, 201; Saddlemyer 1999, 145; Silver 1999, 128–129, 131; Fahy, ed. 2005, 408, fig. 1; Nantes 2005–2006, fig. 2; Barletta 2006, 61 (illus.), 65, 66; Chicago, New York, and Paris 2012–2013, 175, 177, 178, 288; Mancoff 2012, 34–35 (illus.); Rome 2015–2016, fig. 7; London and Paris 2017–2018, 84, 196–197 (illus.); Matyjaszkiewicz, ed. 2019a.

72
THE HOLIDAY, 1874–1875
also known as **STILL ON TOP**

Oil on canvas, 34½ × 21 in. (87.6 × 53.3 cm)
Signed l. l.: *J. J. Tissot*
Auckland Art Gallery Toi o Tāmaki, Gift of Viscount Leverhulme, 1921, 1921/2
Prov.: Sold by Tissot in 1875 as *The Holiday (la plus grand)* [the larger], for £550 or 13,750 to Tooth, "10% Simon" (Notebook); Tooth recorded receipt as *The Holiday*, 34 × 20 in. (86.4 × 50.8 cm), cost £525, August 30, 1875; sold by Tooth, November 23, 1875, for £630 to E. Simon; Lord Leverhulme, by whom presented to Auckland City Art Gallery, 1921.
Exh.: Providence and Toronto 1968 as *Still on Top*; Japan 1988.
Bibl.: Tissot 1871–1878, 34; *Auckland City Art Gallery Quarterly* 1956, 3; Auckland 1962, pl. 8; Misfeldt 1971, 172, fig. 93; Wentworth 1984, 4, 119, pl. 109; Wood 1986, 78, fig. 77; Maeder 1999, 80, 85–86, fig. 32.

73
*WINTER or MAVOURNEEN, 1877
also known as **PORTRAIT OF KATHLEEN NEWTON**

Oil on canvas, 34¾ × 20 in. (88.2 × 50.8 cm)
Signed and dated l. r.: *J J Tissot / 1877*
Private collection
Prov.: This or a replica sold by Tissot in 1879 as *Mavourneen* for £130 or 3,250FF to McLean (Notebook); Private collection, Australia; sold in conjunction with Theodore Bruce, Adelaide, at Christie's, London, November 30, 1984 (100) as *Portrait of Mrs Kathleen Newton (Mavourneen)*; with Owen Edgar Gallery, London, 1985; sold Christie's, New York, May 25, 1995 (99) as *Mavourneen, Portrait of Kathleen Newton*; sold Sotheby's, New York, October 24, 2006 (210).
Exh.: Grosvenor Gallery 1877, catalogued as *A Portrait* then as *Winter*; probably Manchester 1878 as *Wintertime*, price £250.
Publ.: Etching by Tissot dated 1877 (Wentworth 31) titled *Mavourneen*; wood engraving published as *In Winter Time* in *The Graphic*, December 15, 1877, 568–569.
Bibl.: Tissot 1871–1878, 48; *Aberdeen Press and Journal* 1877, 5; *Graphic* 1877c, 558; *Pall Mall* 1877, 12; Wentworth 1978, 142; London and Manchester 1984–1985, 117; Wentworth 1984, 143; Paris 1985, 193; Wood 1986, 105, fig. 104; Misfeldt 1991, 78; *Apollo* 1995a; Matyjaszkiewicz, ed. 2019b.

74
*MRS. NEWTON WITH A PARASOL, CA. 1878

Oil on canvas, 56 × 18¾ in. (142.2 × 47.6 cm)
Musée Baron Martin, Gray, France, Pigalle Bequest, GR-93-723
Prov.: Probably Tissot studio sale, Paris, 1903 (13) as *Femme à l'ombrelle*; bequeathed by Edmond Pigalle to Musée Baron Martin, Gray, 1921.
Exh.: Japan 1979; Gray 1983; London and Manchester 1984–1985; Paris 1985; Nantes 2005; Barletta 2006; Rome 2015.
Bibl.: Wentworth 1978, 186, 188, fig. 43a; London and Manchester 1984–1985, 118, 119, pl. 17; Wentworth 1984, 147, pl. 140; Paris 1985, 196, pl. XXIII; Wood 1986, 113, fig. 113; Misfeldt 1991, 100–101 (re. *Summer*); Nantes 2005–2006, 64 (illus.); Barletta 2006, 71, 82, 84; London and Paris 2017–2018, 84, 85 (illus.).

75
A WINTER WALK, 1880

Oil on wood panel, 31⅛ × 14⅝ in. (79 × 37 cm)
Signed u.r.: *J. J. Tissot*
Private collection
Prov.: Sold by Tissot in 1880 as *Winter Walk* for £180 or 4,500FF to Rhodes (Notebook); sold Christie's, London, February 25, 1888 (144) as *A Winter Walk*; J. C. Haslam; sold by his executors, Christie's, London, March 12, 1900 (113) as *A Winter Walk / "She will bring in spite of frost / Beauties that the earth has lost"*, oil on panel, 30 × 14 in. (76.2 × 35.6 cm), £27.6s, bt. Tooth on behalf of Philips, to whom sold by Tooth for £28.13s on March 12; Mrs. Bannister by 1937; H. Talbot de Vere Clifton, Lytham Hall, Lancashire, by 1955; Christie's, London, January 22, 1965 (54) as *Portrait of a Lady*; with Leger Galleries, London, 1965; Sotheby's, London, June 5, 1996 (134) as *Promenade dans la neige (A Winter's Walk)*; Sotheby's, London, December 16, 2010 (9) as *A Winter's Walk (Promenade dans la neige)*.
Exh.: Leicester Galleries 1937, lent by Mrs. Bannister; Preston 1955–1956 as *Lady with Muff*, lent by H. Talbot de Vere Clifton Collection.
Publ.: Etching by Tissot dated 1880 (Wentworth 48).
Bibl.: Laver 1936, 44–45; *Apollo* 1965; Wentworth 1978, 212, fig. 48f; London and Manchester 1984–1985, 122; Paris 1985, 210; Misfeldt 1991, 110; New Haven, Québec, and Buffalo 1999–2000, 126; Nantes 2005–2006, no. 53.

76
A WINTER WALK, 1880
PROMENADE DANS LA NEIGE

Copper plate, 22½ × 10⅝ in. (57.2 × 27 cm)
Bibliothèque Nationale de France, Paris
Bibl.: Wentworth 1978, 204.

77
A WINTER WALK, 1880
PROMENADE DANS LA NEIGE

Etching and drypoint, second state, with text printed in red, 22⅜ × 10⅜ in. (56.7 × 26.4 cm)
Signed and dated l. r.: *J. J. Tissot / 1880*
Bibliothèque Nationale de France, Paris
Exh.: a first state exhibited London and Manchester 1984–1985 and Paris 1985.
Bibl.: Wentworth 1978, 204–213; London 1981, no. 11; London and Manchester 1984–1985, 122; Paris 1985, 210; Misfeldt 1991, 110–111; New Haven, Québec, and Buffalo 1999–2000, 126–127; Nantes 2005–2006, no. 53; Rome 2015–2016, 107, no. 36.

78
*SPRING (SPECIMEN OF A PORTRAIT), 1877

Oil on canvas, 55¾ × 21 in. (141.5 × 53.3 cm)
Signed l. r.: *J. J. Tissot*
Collection of Diane B. Wilsey, San Francisco
Prov.: Sold by Tissot in 1877 as *Spring (du long)* [full-length] for £300 or 7,500FF to E. F. White (Notebook); consigned by E. F. White, Christie's, London, March 7, 1891 (314), bt. in; sold by executors of E. F. White, Christie's, London, March 24, 1900 (143), bt. Mitchell; C. R. Gresnier; anonymous sale, Christie's, London, May 27, 1949 (133); anonymous sale, Christie's, London, November 26, 2003 (21).
Exh.: Grosvenor Gallery 1878 as *Spring (Specimen of a Portrait)*.
Publ.: Etching by Tissot (1878; Wentworth 34).
Bibl.: Tissot 1871–1878, 54; Misfeldt 1971, 178; Wentworth 1978, 154–157; London and Manchester 1984–1985, 60, 76, 118; Wentworth 1984, 138, 142–144, 202; Wood 1986, 101; Misfeldt 1991, 84; New Haven, Québec, and Buffalo 1999–2000, 121, 123; Ribeiro 2016, 546; Matyjaszkiewicz, ed. 2019b.

79
*EVENING, 1878
also known as **THE BALL**

Oil on canvas, 35⅞ × 20⅛ in. (91 × 51 cm)
Signed l. r.: *J. J. Tissot*
Musée d'Orsay, Paris, RF 2253
Prov.: Acquired from Tissot on March 27, 1879, by Tooth, who recorded receipt as *The Ball Room*, 36 × 20 in., cost £150 (not listed by Tissot in Notebook); sold by Tooth, April 19, 1879, to James Rhodes; William Vaughan; offer

by Vaughan as bequest to National Gallery, London, 2002 (NG Archive) declined; bequeathed to the Musée du Luxembourg, 1919; with Ministère des Affaires Étrangères, 1920 to 1948; with Musée National d'Art Moderne, Paris, 1948 to 1977; allocated to Musée du Louvre, Paris, 1977; transferred to Musée d'Orsay, 1977.
Exh.: Grosvenor Gallery 1878 as *Evening*; Manchester 1878, price £430; London and Manchester 1984–1985; Paris 1985; Taipei 1997; Atlanta 2002; National Gallery, London, 2002 as *The Ball*; Melbourne 2004; Nantes 2005 as *Le bal*; Barletta 2006; Seoul 2007; Tokyo 2010; Paris 2012; Tokyo 2016; Milan 2017.
Bibl.: Tissot 1871–1878, 60; Misfeldt 1971, 178, 185–187; London and Manchester 1984–1985, 119; Wentworth 1984, 143, 162, 202; Paris 1985, 198; London 2002, 138, 141–142, 145, 146, 202, fig. 105; Nantes 2005–2006, 28–29 (illus.); Barletta 2006, 68–69, 71.

80

TRAFALGAR TAVERN (GREENWICH), 1879–1880

Oil on wood panel, 10⅝ × 14½ in. (27 × 36.8 cm)
Signed l. r.: *J. J. Tissot*
New Orleans Museum of Art
Prov.: Recorded by Tissot as *Trafalgar Tavern (le Duncan)*, sold in 1880 for £150 or 3,750FF from exhibition in Newcastle (Notebook); label on back of canvas inscribed "No. 1 Trafalgar Tavern / (Greenwich) / oil painting / James Tissot / 17 Grove End Road / St John's Wood / London / N. W."; sold by Sir Thomas Wilson, Bt., Sotheby's Belgravia, May 20, 1970 (72), bt. Richard Green; sold as the property of a Lady of Title, Christie's, London, November 5, 1993 (160).
Exh.: Newcastle 1880.
Bibl.: Wentworth 1978, 162, fig. 36d; Misfeldt 1982, pl. III-16; London and Manchester 1984–1985, 121; Wentworth 1984, 131, pl. 121; Paris 1985, 203; London and Paris 2017–2018, 106.

81

THE GALA DAY—SEASIDE, 1877–1878
also known as **A FÊTE DAY AT BRIGHTON**

Oil on canvas, 34 × 21¾ in. (86.4 × 55.2 cm)
Signed l. l.: *J. J. Tissot*
Private collection, USA
Prov.: Sold by Tissot in 1878 as *Sea Side (drapeaux)* [flags] for £290 or 7,250 to E. [F.] White (Notebook); P. H. Bonner, Esq.; with M. Newman Galleries Ltd., London; with M. Knoedler & Co., New York; with Hirschl and Adler, New York, 1965; Lilian Bostwick Phipps; anonymous sale, Sotheby's, New York, May 24, 1988 (68); with Richard Green, London, from whom acquired by the consignor to Christie's, New York, October 26, 2005 (142).
Exh.: Glasgow 1879 as *The Gala Day—Seaside*; McLean's 1880 as *A Bank Holiday at Brighton*; Leicester Galleries 1933 as *A Fête Day, Brighton*.
Bibl.: Tissot 1871–1878, 53; Laver 1936, pl. XVIII; Misfeldt 1971, 172, fig. 92; Wentworth 1984, 119, pl. 110; Wood 1986, 78, fig. 76; Brighton 1995, col. illus. back cover; New Haven, Québec, and Buffalo 1999–2000, 102.

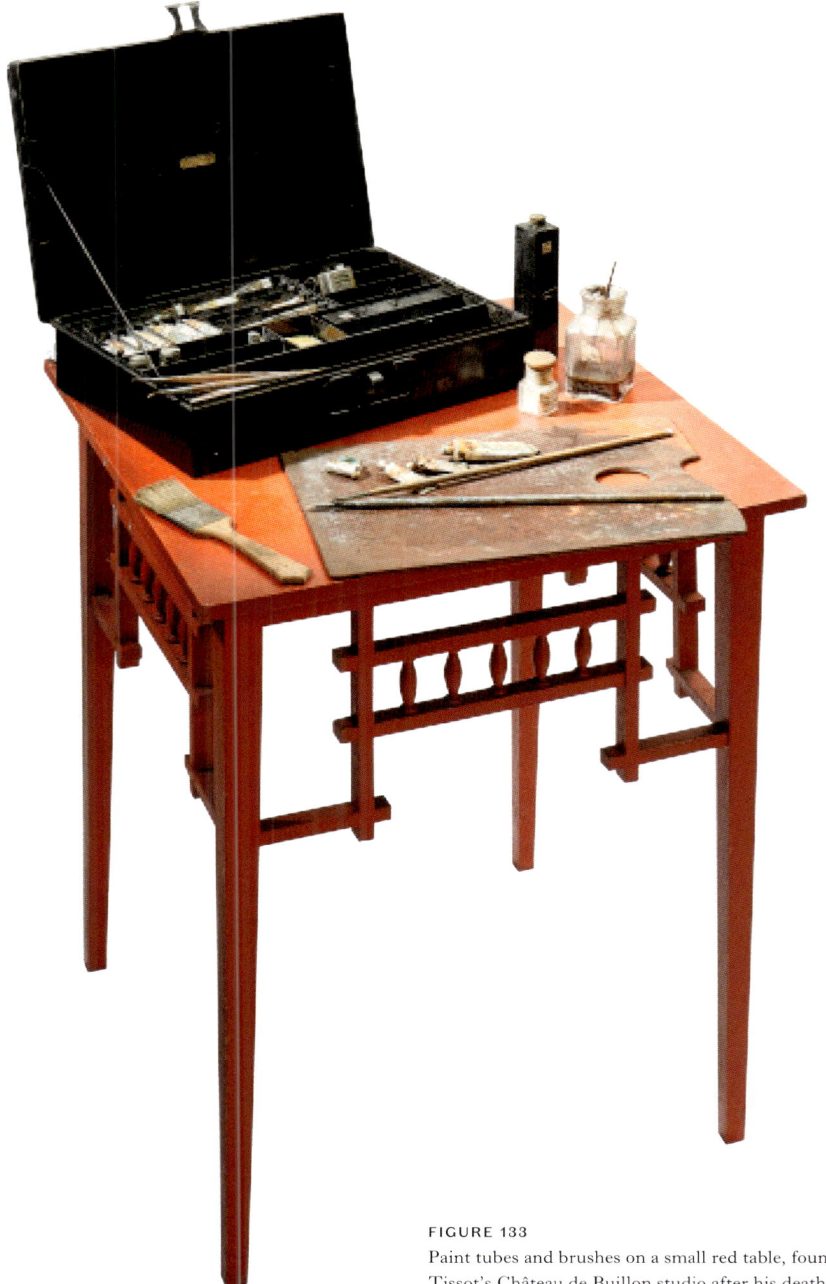

FIGURE 133
Paint tubes and brushes on a small red table, found in Tissot's Château de Buillon studio after his death

82

*HIDE AND SEEK, CA. 1877

Oil on wood panel, 28⅞ × 21¼ in. (73.4 × 53.9 cm)
Signed l. r.: *J. J. Tissot*
National Gallery of Art, Washington, DC, Chester Dale Fund, 1978.47.1
Prov.: Sold by Tissot in 1878 for £400 or 10,000FF to Herbert (Notebook); sold by J. R. Ormrod, Esq., Christie's, London, February 22, 1957 (43), 850 guineas, bt. Fine Art Society; sold Sotheby's, London, March 20, 1963 (140), £2,200, bt. Mrs. C. Behr; sold from collection of Julian Spiro, Esq., Christie's, London, October 15, 1976 (43), £22,000, bt. H. Schickman Gallery, New York; acquired by the National Gallery of Art, Washington, through the Chester Dale Fund, 1978.
Exh.: Yale 1999.
Bibl.: Tissot 1871–1878, 56; Misfeldt 1971, 191–192, fig. 108; London and Manchester 1984–1985, 113; Wentworth 1984, 151, pl. 160; Wood 1986, 113, fig. 117; Darby 1999, 174–175, 178, fig. 68; New Haven, Québec, and Buffalo 1999–2000, 134–135; Prelinger 1999, 201.

83

RIVALS, 1878–1879

Oil on canvas, 36¼ × 26¾ in. (92 × 68 cm)
Signed l. l.: *J. J. Tissot*
The Marlene and Spencer Hays Collection
Prov.: Sold by Tissot in 1880 for £270 or 6,750FF to [E. F.] White (Notebook); sold by executors of John Polson, of Tranent and Thornly, Christie's, London, July 21, 1911 (44), bt. Lindlas; sold by executors of Sir Edward J. Harland, Baroda House, London, Christie's, London, May 31, 1912; Ingegnoli Collection, Milan; sold by executors of Ingegnoli, Galleria Pesaro, Milan, May 1933; Private collection, Milan; sold Pandolfini Casa d'Aste, Florence, October 28, 2014 (35) as *I Rivali*; Stair Sainty Fine Art, London.
Exh.: Grosvenor Gallery 1879; Manchester 1879, price £400; Milan 1957.
Bibl.: *Times* 1879a, 3; Misfeldt 1971, 162–163, 191; Misfeldt 1982, pl. III-2; Wentworth 1984, 88, 119, 141, 145–147, 151, 203, pl. 159; Wood 1986, 106; Darby 1999, 163, 166, 180–181, fig. 73; Saddlemyer 1999, 150–151; Matyjaszkiewicz 2014, 14–21; Rome 2015–2016, 104–105.

84

*OCTOBER, 1877

Oil on canvas, 85 × 42¾ in. (216 × 108.7 cm)
Signed and dated l. l.: *J. J. Tissot / 1877*
The Montreal Museum of Fine Arts, Gift of Lord Strathcona and family, inv. 1927.410
Prov.: Sold by Tissot in 1878 for £425 or 10,625FF to McLean, who sold it to Mr Lee (Notebook); sold by William Lee, Christie's, London, June 22–23, 1888 (426) as *Autumn*, 83 × 42 in. (210.8 × 106.7 cm), £168, bt. Koekkoek, Holland, on behalf of Donal Smith; Lord Strathcona (Donal Smith), Montreal, to 1914; donated to Montreal Museum of Fine Arts by Lord Strathcona and family, 1927.
Exh.: This or the replica exhibited McLean's 1878; Providence and Toronto 1968; London and Manchester 1984–1985; New York 1990.
Publ.: Etching by Tissot dated 1878 (Wentworth 33).
Bibl.: Tissot 1871–1878, 61; Misfeldt 1971, fig. 100; Wentworth 1978, 150, 152, fig. 33a; London and Manchester 1984–1985, 118, frontispiece col. illus.; Wentworth 1984, 143–144; Paris 1985, 38–39, fig. 2; Wood 1986, 93, 101, 105, 113, fig. 101; Misfeldt 1991, 82; Marshall 1999, 26; New Haven, Québec, and Buffalo 1999–2000, 122; Matyjaszkiewicz, ed. 2019b.

85

ORPHANS, 1878–1879

Oil on canvas, 85 × 43 in. (216 × 109.2 cm)
Signed l. l.: *J. J. Tissot*
Private collection
Prov.: Sold by Tissot at the Grosvenor Gallery in 1879 for £500 or 12,500FF (Notebook); Christie's, London, February 12, 1955 (101); Agnew's, until 1984; acquired 1993.
Exh.: Grosvenor Gallery 1879; Royal Academy 2003.
Publ.: Etching by Tissot (ca. 1879; Wentworth 44).
Bibl.: *Times* 1879a, 3; Blackburn 1879, 31; Wentworth 1978, 190, fig. 44d; Misfeldt 1982, pl. III-3; London and Manchester 1984–1985, 123; Wentworth 1984, 66, 113, 138, 145–147, 203, pl. 138; Paris 1985, 208–209; Wood 1986, 108, 111, 113, pl. 111; Misfeldt 1991, 102; Marshall 1999, 26; Saddlemyer 1999, 151; Marshall 2003, 172, 174, 307.

86

*THE PRODIGAL SON IN MODERN LIFE: THE DEPARTURE, 1880

Oil on canvas, 39⅜ × 51⅛ in. (100 × 130 cm)
Musée d'Arts de Nantes, James Tissot Bequest, 1904, Inv. 1945
Prov.: Tissot bequest to the French state, 1904; deposited by Musée du Luxembourg, Paris, with Musée des Beaux-Arts de Nantes, 1914; Musée d'Orsay, Paris, deposited with Musée des Beaux-Arts de Nantes.
Exh.: Dudley Gallery 1882; Paris 1883; Paris 1885; Paris 1889; Chicago 1893; Nantes 2005; Rome 2015.
Publ.: Etching by Tissot dated 1881 (Wentworth 58).
Bibl.: Providence and Toronto 1968, no. 75; Misfeldt 1971, 200–204, fig. 126; Wentworth 1978, 244–245, 248, fig. 58a; Misfeldt 1982, pl. IV-31; London and Manchester 1984–1985, 133–134; Wentworth 1984, 148–149, 208; Paris 1985, 230; Wood 1986, 113, 115, fig. 118; Misfeldt 1991, 128–129; New Haven, Québec, and Buffalo 1999–2000, 163, 165–166; Nantes 2005–2006, 20 (illus.); Dolkart, ed. 2009, 14–15, fig. 7; Rome 2015–2016, 122–123 (illus.), 126.

87

*THE PRODIGAL SON IN MODERN LIFE: IN FOREIGN CLIMES, 1880

Oil on canvas, 39⅜ × 51⅛ in. (100 × 130 cm)
Signed l. l.: *J. J. Tissot*
Musée d'Arts de Nantes, James Tissot Bequest, 1904, Inv. 1946
Prov.: Tissot bequest to the French state, 1904; deposited by Musée du Luxembourg with Musée des Beaux-Arts de Nantes, 1914; Musée d'Orsay, Paris, deposited with Musée des Beaux-Arts de Nantes.
Exh.: Dudley Gallery 1882; Paris 1883; Paris 1885; Paris 1889; Chicago 1893; Paris 1985; Nantes 2005; Rome 2015.
Publ.: Etching by Tissot dated 1881 (Wentworth 59).
Bibl.: Wentworth 1978, 244–245, 250, fig. 59a; Misfeldt 1982, pl. IV-32; London and Manchester 1984–1985, 133–134; Wentworth 1984, 148–149, 208; Paris 1985, 228–230; Wood 1986, 113, 115, fig. 119; Misfeldt 1991, 128–129; New Haven, Québec, and Buffalo 1999–2000, 163, 165–166; Nantes 2005–2006, 20–21 (illus.), 22; Dolkart, ed. 2009, 14–15, fig. 8; Rome 2015–2016, 122, 124 (illus.), 126.

88

*THE PRODIGAL SON IN MODERN LIFE: THE RETURN, 1880

Oil on canvas, 39⅜ × 51⅛ in. (100 × 130 cm)
Signed and dated l. l.: *J. J. Tissot / 1880*
Musée d'Arts de Nantes, James Tissot Bequest, 1904, Inv. 1947
Prov.: Tissot bequest to the French state, 1904; deposited by Musée du Luxembourg with Musée des Beaux-Arts de Nantes, 1914; Musée d'Orsay, Paris, deposited with Musée des Beaux-Arts de Nantes.
Exh.: Dudley Gallery 1882; Paris 1883; Paris 1885; Paris 1889; Chicago 1893; Paris 1985; Nantes 2005; Rome 2015.
Publ.: Etching by Tissot dated 1881 (Wentworth 60).
Bibl.: Thiébault-Sisson 1902, repr. 3; Wentworth 1978, 244–245, 252, fig. 60a; Misfeldt 1982, pl. IV-33; London and Manchester 1984–1985, 133–134; Wentworth 1984, 148–149, 208; Paris 1985, 229–230; Wood 1986, 113, 115, fig. 120; Misfeldt 1991, 128–129; New Haven, Québec, and Buffalo 1999–2000, 163, 165, 168; Nantes 2005–2006, 22 (illus.); Dolkart, ed. 2009, 14–15, fig. 9; Rome 2015–2016, 122, 125 (illus.), 126; London and Paris 2017–2018, 85 (illus.).

89

*THE PRODIGAL SON IN MODERN LIFE: THE FATTED CALF, 1880

Oil on canvas, 39⅜ × 51⅛ in. (100 × 130 cm)
Signed l. r.: *J. J. Tissot*
Musée d'Arts de Nantes, James Tissot Bequest, 1904, Inv. 1948
Prov.: Tissot bequest to the French state, 1904; deposited by Musée du Luxembourg, Paris, with Musée des Beaux-Arts de Nantes, 1914; Musée d'Orsay, Paris, deposited with Musée des Beaux-Arts de Nantes.
Exh.: Dudley Gallery 1882; Paris 1883; Paris, Exposition Nationale, 1883; Paris 1885; Paris 1889; Chicago 1893; Nantes 2005; Rome 2015.
Publ.: Etching by Tissot dated 1881 (Wentworth 61).
Bibl.: Wentworth 1978, 244–245, 254, fig. 61a; Misfeldt 1982, pl. IV-34; London and Manchester 1984–1985, 133–134; Wentworth 1984, 148–149, 208; Paris 1985, 230; Wood 1986, 113, 116, fig. 121; Misfeldt 1991, 128–129; New Haven, Québec, and Buffalo 1999–2000, 163, 165, 168; Nantes 2005–2006, 22–23 (illus.); Dolkart, ed. 2009, 14–15, fig. 10; Rome 2015–2016, 122, 126, 127 (illus.).

90

*Frontispiece to

"THE PRODIGAL SON," 1881

Etching and drypoint, 13⅞ × 17⅝ in. (35.2 × 44.9 cm)
Fine Arts Museums of San Francisco, Achenbach Foundation for Graphic Arts, 1963.30.1395.1
Prov.: Purchased through the Achenbach Foundation for the Arts, 1963.
Publ.: 1881 (Wentworth 57).
Bibl.: Wentworth 1978, 246–247; London 1981, no. 12; London and Manchester 1984–1985, 133; Paris 1985, 229; Misfeldt 1991, 130–131; Rome 2015–2016, 118, no. 45.

91

*THE PRODIGAL SON— THE DEPARTURE, 1881

Etching and drypoint, 12¼ × 14¾ in. (31 × 37.3 cm)
Fine Arts Museums of San Francisco, Achenbach Foundation for Graphic Arts, 1963.30.1395.2
Prov.: Purchased through the Achenbach Foundation for the Arts, 1963.
Publ.: 1881 (Wentworth 58).
Bibl.: Wentworth 1978, 248–249; London and Manchester 1984–1985, 133–134; Wentworth 1984, 148–149, 208, pl. 154; Paris 1985, 230; Misfeldt 1991, 132–133; New Haven, Québec, and Buffalo 1999–2000, 163, 165–167; Rome 2015–2016, 120, no. 48.

92

*THE PRODIGAL SON—IN FOREIGN CLIMES, 1881

Etching and drypoint, 12¼ × 14¾ in. (31 × 37.3 cm)
Fine Arts Museums of San Francisco, Achenbach Foundation for Graphic Arts, 1963.30.1395.3
Prov.: Purchased through the Achenbach Foundation for the Arts, 1963.
Publ.: 1881 (Wentworth 59).
Bibl.: Wentworth 1978, 250–251; London and Manchester 1984–1985, 133–134; Wentworth 1984, 148–149, 208, pl. 155; Paris 1985, 230; Misfeldt 1991, 132–133; New Haven, Québec, and Buffalo 1999–2000, 163, 165–167; Rome 2015–2016, 121, no. 49.

93

*THE PRODIGAL SON—THE RETURN, 1881

Etching and drypoint, 12¼ × 14¾ in. (31 × 37.3 cm)
Fine Arts Museums of San Francisco, Achenbach Foundation for Graphic Arts, 1963.30.1395.4
Prov.: Purchased through the Achenbach Foundation for the Arts, 1963.
Publ.: 1881 (Wentworth 60).
Bibl.: Wentworth 1978, 252–253; London and Manchester 1984–1985, 133–134; Wentworth 1984, 148–149, 208, pl. 156; Paris 1985, 230; Misfeldt 1991, 134–135; New Haven, Québec, and Buffalo 1999–2000, 163, 165, 168–169; Rome 2015–2016, 119, no. 46.

94

*THE PRODIGAL SON—THE FATTED CALF, 1881

Etching and drypoint, 12¼ × 14¾ in. (31 × 37.3 cm)
Fine Arts Museums of San Francisco, Achenbach Foundation for Graphic Arts, 1963.30.1395.5
Prov.: Purchased through the Achenbach Foundation for the Arts, 1963.
Publ.: 1881 (Wentworth 61).

Bibl.: Wentworth 1978, 254–255; London and Manchester 1984–1985, 133–134; Wentworth 1984, 148–149, 208, pl. 157; Paris 1985, 230; Misfeldt 1991, 134–135; New Haven, Québec, and Buffalo 1999–2000, 163, 165, 168–169; Rome 2015–2016, 120, no. 47.

95

*HAMPTON COURT, CA. 1882

also known as **A VISIT TO THE PARK**

Oil on wood panel, 9¼ × 13 in. (23.5 × 33 cm)
Signed l. r.: *J. J. Tissot*
Collection of Ann and Gordon Getty
Prov.: Sold by Tissot in 1883 as *Hampton Court* for £120 or 3,000FF to Georges Petit (Notebook); M. Newman Ltd., London; Sotheby's, New York, May 23, 1996 (289) as *Le repos dans un parc* (A Visit to the Park).
Bibl.: Wentworth 1978, 221, fig. 50a; Misfeldt 1982, pl. III-34; London and Manchester 1984–1985, 132; Wentworth 1984, 152, pl. 167; Paris 1985, 227.

96

IN FULL SUNLIGHT, 1881

Oil on wood panel, 9¾ × 13⅞ in. (24.8 × 35.2 cm)
Signed l. l.: *J. J. Tissot*
The Metropolitan Museum of Art, New York, Gift of Mrs. Charles Wrightsman, 2006, 2006.278
Prov.: Sold by Tissot in 1881 as *On the Sun* for £100 or 2,500FF to Knoedler (Notebook), Knoedler recording receipt November 14, 1881, price £100; sold by Knoedler, April 17, 1882, as *Richmond*, 900 dollars to George C. Cooper, New York; Thomas Lenz, Milwaukee, by 1976; sold by him March 31, 1976, to Williams and Son, London, from whom bought by Guy Stair Sainty; sold by Stair Sainty to Marquis of Bristol; Marquis of Bristol, 1976–1983; sold to Stair Sainty, from whom bought by Wrightsman; Mr. and Mrs. Charles Wrightsman, 1983–1986; Mrs. Wrightsman; gift from her, 2006.
Exh.: New York 1983.
Publ.: Etching by Tissot dated 1881 (Wentworth 54) made for and published in Palmer, ed. 1881.
Bibl.: Wentworth 1978, 234; Misfeldt 1982, pl. III-31; Matthiesen ca. 1983, 22 (color illus.); London and Manchester 1984–1985, 126; Wentworth 1984, 151, 152, 153, pl. IV; Paris 1985, 125; Wood 1986, 89, fig. 86; Misfeldt 1991, 122, fig. 32; Marshall 1999, 24; New Haven, Québec, and Buffalo 1999–2000, 136; Fahy, ed. 2005, 409–411; London and Paris 2017–2018, 84, 100–101.

97

*THE ELDER SISTER, CA. 1879–1880

Oil on wood panel, 17½ × 7⅞ in. (44.5 × 20 cm)
Signed l. r.: *J. J. Tissot*
Private collection
Prov.: Sold by Tissot in 1880 as *Sur les marches* [On the Steps] for £70 or 1,750FF to Knoedler (Notebook); Knoedler recorded receipt as *La terrasse*, September 14, 1880, from Bulla Frères et Jouy, acting as agents for Knoedler, price 2,000FF; sold by Knoedler, October 20, 1880, as *Mother and Child "Terrace"* for $700 to F. G. Avery, Buffalo, New York; Parke-Bernet, New York, October 5, 1961 (51); Sotheby's, Belgravia, June 20, 1972 (96); Carpenter-Deforge, Paris; Sotheby's, London, November 22, 1983 (60); Stair Sainty Fine Art, Inc., New York, until 1984; D. C. Dueck; Sotheby's, London, December 11, 2007 (12).
Exh.: London and Manchester 1984–1985.
Bibl.: Wentworth 1978, 230, 233, fig. 53c; Misfeldt 1982, pl. III-22; London and Manchester 1984–1985, 124, pl. 12; Wentworth 1984, 152, pl. 163; Paris 1985, fig. 79; Galinou 1989, 120–123, fig. 6; New Haven, Québec, and Buffalo 1999–2000, 138.

98

✓*KATHLEEN NEWTON AT THE PIANO, CA. 1880–1881

Oil on canvas, 44 × 30½ in. (111.8 × 77.5 cm)
Collection of Ann and Gordon Getty
Prov.: Perhaps *Le piano* [The Piano], sold by Tissot in 1886 for 1,000 francs or £40 to Paris art dealer J. Bulla (Notebook); sold Étude Couturier Nicolay at Hôtel Drouot, Paris, December 12, 1984 (12) as *La leçon de piano*; consigned to Sotheby's, London, November 26, 1985 (66) as *Woman at the Piano*, bt. in; sold Sotheby's, New York, October 24, 1996 (190) as *Kathleen Newton at the Piano*.
Bibl.: *Antiques Trade Gazette* 1985, 36; Paris 1985, 225.

99

THE TRIUMPH OF WILL (POEM IN FIVE PARTS): I. THE CHALLENGE, CA. 1876–1877

Oil on canvas, 85 × 43 in. (215.9 × 109.2 cm)
Signed l. r.: *J J Tissot*
Private collection
Prov.: Tissot studio sale, Paris, 1903 (2) as *La Volonté vainqueur de la Volupté* [Will Conquering Voluptuousness]; Tissot sale, Besançon, 1964; Private collection, Besançon; sold Christie's, Monaco, June 15, 1986 (119); Private collection; sold Sotheby's, London, June 8, 1993 (25); sold Sotheby's, New York, February 1994 (117); with Kurt E. Schon Fine Art, New Orleans, August 1994; Private collection, Detroit; sold Christie's, New York, October 31, 2018 (24).
Exh.: Grosvenor Gallery 1877, lent by the artist.
Bibl.: Tissot 1871–1878, 49; *Ipswich Journal* 1877, 2; *Times* 1877a, 4; Ruskin 1877, 161; Laver 1936, 37–38, 69; Misfeldt 1971, 168–170; London and Manchester 1984–1985, 29, 96, 115, 141; Wentworth 1984, 136–138, 140–141, 175, 202; Paris 1985, 57, 112, 190–192, 232–233; Wood 1986, 95.

100

*VISITING THE LOUVRE, 1879–1880

also known as **FOREIGN VISITORS AT THE LOUVRE**

Oil on wood panel, 29 × 19½ in. (73.7 × 49.5 cm)
Santa Barbara Museum of Art, SBMA, Gift of The Estate of Barbara Darlington Dupee, 2015.32.1
Prov.: Sold by Tissot in 1880 as *Le Louvre (Salle des saisons)* [The Louvre (Room of the Seasons)] for £300 or 7,500FF to Knoedler (Notebook), Knoedler recording receipt on August 16, 1880 as *Louvre* from Bulla Frères et Jouy, acting on behalf of Tissot, price 6,750FF (the difference probably being Bulla's handling fee); sold by Knoedler, March 4, 1884, for $2,000 to Mrs. Mary J. Morgan, New York; sold by executors of the late Mrs. Mary J. Morgan, American Art Association, Chickering Hall, March 5, 1886 (lot 178) as *In the Louvre*, 28 x 18 in. (71.1 x 45.7 cm), $1,600.
Bibl.: Misfeldt 1982, pl. III-21; London and Manchester 1984, 122; Wentworth 1984, 163; Paris 1985, 207–208; Wood 1986, 139 and 141; Marshall 1999, 26–27, 30–31.

101

*MRS. NEWTON RESTING ON A CHAISE LONGUE, CA. 1881–1882

Oil on canvas, 35½ × 26⅞ in. (90.2 × 68.3 cm)
Musée Baron Martin, Gray, France, Pigalle Bequest
Prov.: Bequeathed to Musée Baron Martin, Gray, by Edmond Pigalle, 1921.
Exh.: Gray 1983; London and Manchester 1984–1985; Paris 1985; Rome 2015.
Bibl.: Misfeldt 1971, 197, fig. 116; Wentworth 1978, 240, 243, fig. 56b; London and Manchester 1984–1985, 127; Wentworth 1984, 153, pl. 171; Paris 1985, 220; Marshall 1999, 24, fig. 10; London and Paris 2017–2018, 85.

102

*SUMMER EVENING, 1881–1882

also known as **THE DREAMER**

Oil on wood panel, 13¾ × 23¾ in. (34.9 × 60.3 cm)
Signed u. r.: *J. J. Tissot*
Musée d'Orsay, Paris, Bequest of William Vaughan, 1919, RF 2254
Prov.: Sold by Tissot in 1882 as *Summer Evening* for £150 or 3,750FF to William Vaughan (Notebook); offer by Vaughan as bequest to National Gallery, London, 2002 (NG Archive) declined; bequeathed to the Musée du Luxembourg, Paris, 1919; Ministère des Affaires étrangères, 1922; Musée du Louvre, Paris, 1929; deposited at Musée de Metz, 1929; Musée du Louvre, Paris, 1970; Musée d'Orsay, Paris, 1981.
Exh.: Dudley Gallery 1882; Paris 1985; Barletta 2006.
Publ.: Etching by Tissot dated 1881 (Wentworth 56).
Bibl.: Misfeldt 1971, 196–197, fig. 115; Wentworth 1978, 240, fig. 56a; Misfeldt 1982, pl. III-29; London and Manchester 1984–1985, 127, fig. 60; Wentworth 1984, 153, 204, pl. 170; Paris 1985, 223; Misfeldt 1991, 126, fig. 36.

103

*A NIMROD, CA. 1882–1883

also known as **THE LITTLE NIMROD**

UN NEMROD

Oil on canvas, 43⅛ × 55⅛ in. (109.5 × 140 cm)
Signed l. l.: *J. J. Tissot*
Musée des Beaux-Arts et d'Archéologie de Besançon, France, inv. 906.7.1
Prov.: Tissot studio sale, Paris, 1903 (4) as *Le petit nemrod*, probably bt. Albert Bichet; bequeathed by Albert Bichet to Musée des Beaux-Arts et d'Archéologie, Besançon, 1920.
Exh.: Paris 1883 as *Un nemrod*; Paris 1885; Gray 1983; London and Manchester 1984–1985; Besançon 1985; Paris 1985; Japan 1988; Nantes 2005; Rome 2015.
Publ.: Mezzotint by Tissot (1886; Wentworth 83).
Bibl.: Wentworth 1978, 330; London and Manchester 1984–1985, 132, pl. 23; Besançon 1985, n.p. (illus.); Wood 1986, 123, fig. 127; Misfeldt 1991, 174; Lochnan 1999, 16; New Haven, Québec, and Buffalo 1999–2000, 118–119, 142; Prelinger 1999, 201, fig. 89; Nantes 2005–2006, 90–91 (illus.), 94 (illus.).

104

THE GARDEN BENCH, 1882

LE BANC DE JARDIN

Oil on canvas, 39 × 56 in. (99.1 × 142.2 cm)
Signed and dated l. r.: *J. J. Tissot / 1882*
Private collection
Prov.: Tissot studio sale, Paris, 1903 (5) as *Le banc de jardin*; Tissot sale, Besançon, 1964; sold Christie's, London, June 24, 1983 (103), bt. Christopher Wood; acquired 1994.

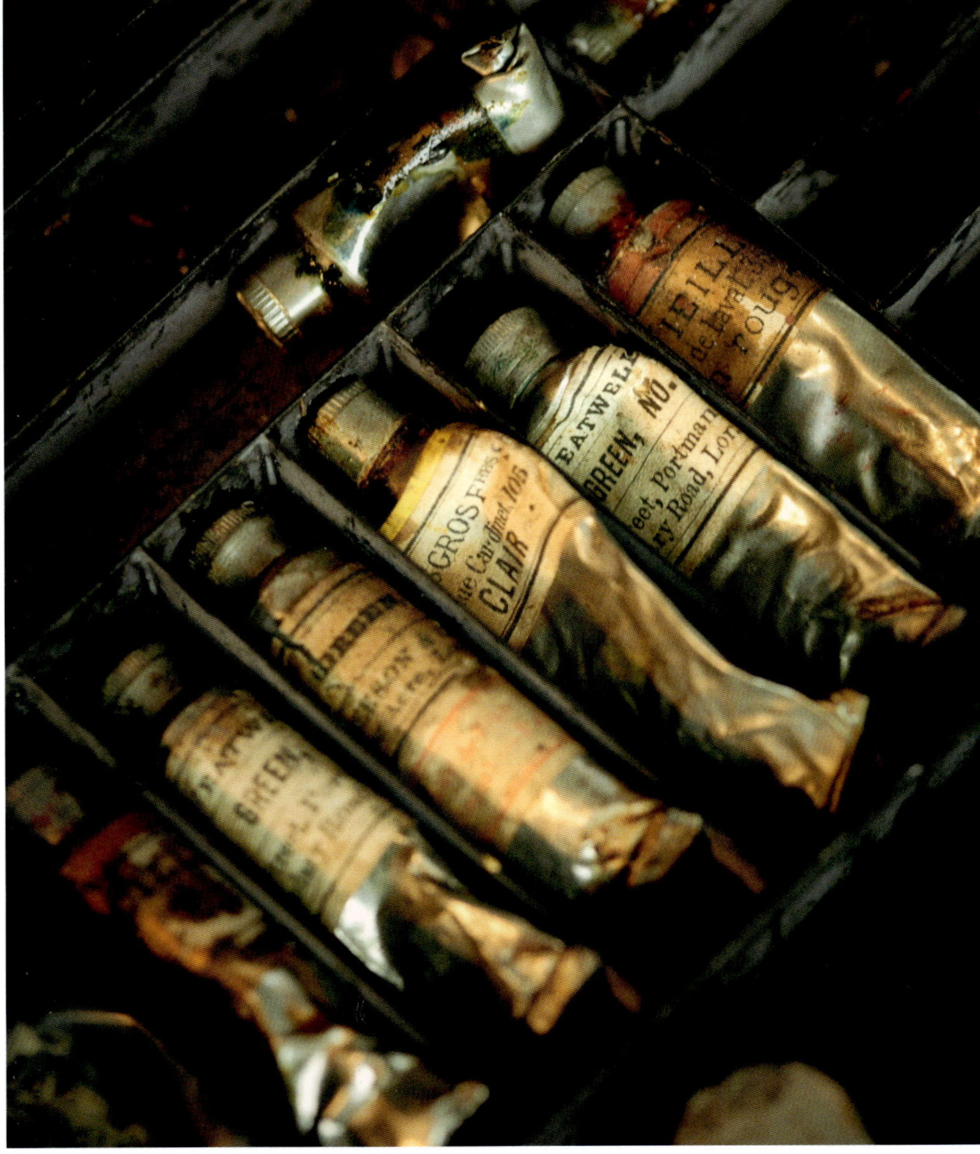

FIGURE 134
Paint tubes found in Tissot's Château de Buillon studio after his death

Exh.: Paris 1883 as *Le banc de jardin*; Paris 1885; London 1983; London and Manchester 1984–1985; Paris 1985; Royal Academy 2003.
Publ.: Mezzotint by Tissot (Wentworth 75).
Bibl.: Wentworth 1978, 290–293; Christie's 1983; London and Manchester 1984–1985, 132–133, pl. 22; Wood 1986, 123, fig. 126; Marshall 1999, 26; Marshall 2003, 174–175, 307.

105
*THE GARDEN BENCH, 1883
LE BANC DE JARDIN

Mezzotint and drypoint, printed *chine collé*, 16¼ × 21 in. (41.4 × 53.4 cm)
Fine Arts Museums of San Francisco, Achenbach Foundation for Graphic Arts, Gift of Edward Tyler Nahem, 2003.151.68
Prov.: Given to Fine Arts Museums of San Francisco by Edward Tyler Nahem, 2003.
Publ.: 1883 (Wentworth 75).
Bibl.: Providence and Toronto 1968, no. 81; Wentworth 1978, 290–293; London and Manchester 1984–1985, 132–133; Wentworth 1984, 152, pl. 168; Misfeldt 1991, 154–155, 157, 174; Lochnan 1999, 16; New Haven, Québec, and Buffalo 1999–2000, 142–143; Prelinger 1999, 193, fig. 79; Marshall 2003, 307.

106
*SUMMER EVENING, 1881
SOIRÉE D'ÉTÉ

Drypoint and etching, 9 × 15⅝ in. (23 × 39.7 cm)
Fine Arts Museums of San Francisco, Achenbach Foundation for Graphic Arts, 1963.30.1392
Prov.: Purchased through the Achenbach Foundation for Graphic Arts, 1963.
Publ.: 1881 (Wentworth 56).
Bibl.: Wentworth 1978, 240–243; Wood 1986, 120, fig. 122; Misfeldt 1991, 126–127; Marshall 1999, 24–25; Prelinger 1999, 193, fig. 80; Rome 2015–2016, 103, no. 33.

107–116
ILLUSTRATIONS FOR EDMOND AND JULES DE GONCOURT'S *RENÉE MAUPERIN* (1884)

Prov.: Purchased through Mrs. Alexander de Bretteville Fund, 1984.
Bibl.: Wentworth 1978, 256–257; London and Manchester 1984–1985, 129–130; Preston 1984, 442–444; Paris 1985, 226–227; Misfeldt 1991, 136–137; Prelinger 1999, 205, 209; Silver 1999, 122; Nantes 2005–2006, 103, 180–189; London and Paris 2017–2018, 85.

107
ON THE SEINE, 1882

Etching, 5⅝ × 3⅞ in. (14.3 × 9.9 cm)
Fine Arts Museums of San Francisco, Museum purchase, Mrs. Alexander de Bretteville Fund, 1984.1.88.1
Publ.: 1884 (Wentworth 62).
Bibl.: Wentworth 1978, 258–259; Misfeldt 1991, 137–138; Nantes 2005–2006, 180.

108
THE MORNING KISS, 1882

Etching, 5¾ × 4 in. (14.7 × 10 cm)
Fine Arts Museums of San Francisco, Museum purchase, Mrs. Alexander de Bretteville Fund, 1984.1.88.2
Publ.: 1884 (Wentworth 63).
Bibl.: Wentworth 1978, 260–261; Misfeldt 1991, 137, 139; Nantes 2005–2006, 180–181.

109
AT THE PIANO, 1882

Etching, 5½ × 3⅞ in. (14.1 × 9.7 cm)
Fine Arts Museums of San Francisco, Museum purchase, Mrs. Alexander de Bretteville Fund, 1984.1.88.11
Publ.: 1884 (Wentworth 65).
Bibl.: Wentworth 1978, 264–265; Misfeldt 1991, 137, 141; Nantes 2005–2006, 183.

110
IN THE ANTEROOM, 1882

Etching, 4 × 5½ in. (10.1 × 14 cm)
Fine Arts Museums of San Francisco, Museum purchase, Mrs. Alexander de Bretteville Fund, 1984.1.88.5
Publ.: 1884 (Wentworth 66).
Bibl.: Wentworth 1978, 266–267; Misfeldt 1991, 137, 142; Nantes 2005–2006, 184.

111
*DENOISEL READING IN THE GARDEN, 1882

Etching, 4¼ × 5⅝ in. (10.9 × 14.2 cm)
Fine Arts Museums of San Francisco, Museum purchase, Mrs. Alexander de Bretteville Fund, 1984.1.88.3
Publ.: 1884 (Wentworth 64).
Bibl.: Wentworth 1978, 262–263; Misfeldt 1991, 137, 140; Nantes 2005–2006, 182.

112
AFTER THE DUEL, 1882

Etching, 6 × 3⅞ in. (15.3 × 9.9 cm)
Fine Arts Museums of San Francisco, Museum purchase, Mrs. Alexander de Bretteville Fund, 1984.1.88.6
Publ.: 1884 (Wentworth 67).
Bibl.: Wentworth 1978, 268–269; Misfeldt 1991, 137, 143; Nantes 2005–2006, 184–185.

113

IN THE PUBLIC GARDENS, 1882

Etching, 5¾ × 3⅞ in. (14.7 × 9.9 cm)

Fine Arts Museums of San Francisco, Museum purchase, Mrs. Alexander de Bretteville Fund, 1984.1.88.8

Publ.: 1884 (Wentworth 69).

Bibl.: Wentworth 1978, 272–273; Misfeldt 1991, 137, 145; Nantes 2005–2006, 186–187.

114

RENÉE AND HER FATHER AT MORIMOND, 1882

Etching, 6 × 3⅞ in. (15.1 × 9.7 cm)

Fine Arts Museums of San Francisco, Museum purchase, Mrs. Alexander de Bretteville Fund, 1984.1.88.9

Publ.: 1884 (Wentworth 70).

Bibl.: Wentworth 1978, 274–275; Wood 1986, 122, fig. 124; Misfeldt 1991, 137, 146; Nantes 2005–2006, 188.

115

IN THE EGYPTIAN RUINS, 1882

Etching, 4¼ × 5⅝ in. (10.9 × 14.2 cm)

Fine Arts Museums of San Francisco, Museum purchase, Mrs. Alexander de Bretteville Fund, 1984.1.88.10

Publ.: 1884 (Wentworth 71).

Bibl.: Wentworth 1978, 276–277; London and Manchester 1984–1985, 129–130; Paris 1985, 226, fig. 94; Misfeldt 1991, 137, 147; Nantes 2005–2006, 188–189.

116

RENÉE FAINTING, 1882

Etching, 4¼ × 5⅝ in. (10.9 × 14.2 cm)

Fine Arts Museums of San Francisco, Museum purchase, Mrs. Alexander de Bretteville Fund, 1984.1.88.7

Publ.: 1884 (Wentworth 68).

Bibl.: Wentworth 1978, 270–271; Misfeldt 1991, 137, 144; Nantes 2005–2006, 186.

117–130

LA FEMME À PARIS

Prov.: Fifteen canvases sold by Tissot in 1886 for £2,436 or 69,000FF to Tooth (Notebook), these excluding *Musique sacrée* (Paris 1885, cat. no. 15) but including *L'esthétique* (Paris 1885, cat. no. 21).

Exh.: Paris 1885; Tooth 1886.

Bibl.: Dargenty 1885, 200; *New York Times* 1885; *Daily News* 1886, 2; *Liverpool Mercury* 1886, 7; *Times* 1886, 9; Misfeldt 1971, 218–236; London and Manchester 1984–1985, 136–139; Wentworth 1984, 154–173, 205; Paris 1985, 237–242; Wood 1986, 129–141; Misfeldt 1991, 161; Garb 1999, 95–120; New Haven, Québec, and Buffalo 1999–2000, 147.

117

***THE BRIDESMAID, CA. 1883–1885**

LA DEMOISELLE D'HONNEUR

Oil on canvas, 58 × 40 in. (147.3 × 101.6 cm)

Signed l. r.: *J. J. Tissot*

Leeds Museums and Galleries, Gift from R. R. King, 1897, LEEAG.PA.1897.0015

Prov.: Bought from Tissot by Tooth, 1886, recorded December 31, 58 × 40 in. (147.3 × 101.6 cm), cost price £100; sold by Tooth, Christie's, London, March 30, 1889 (140), £69.6s; given by R. R. King to Leeds City Art Gallery, 1897.

Exh.: Paris 1885 as *La Demoiselle d'honneur*; Tooth 1886; Leeds 1888; Southport 1892; Sheffield 1955; London and Manchester 1984–1985; Paris 1985; Yale 1999.

Bibl.: Providence and Toronto 1968, no. 35; Misfeldt 1971, fig. 140; Budge 1982, no. 91, 28–30; Misfeldt 1982, pl. III-61; Warner 1982, 22, col. illus.; Wright 1982, 25; London and Manchester 1984–1985, 138; Wentworth 1984, 162, 164–167, 169, 205, pl. 191; Paris 1985, 238–239; Wood 1986, 138–139, fig. 149; Garb 1999, 104, fig. 42; New Haven, Québec, and Buffalo 1999–2000, 156–157; Prelinger 1999, 201–202.

118

***PAINTERS AND THEIR WIVES, CA. 1883–1885**

also known as **THE ARTISTS' WIVES**

LES FEMMES D'ARTISTE

Oil on canvas, 57½ × 40 in. (146.1 × 101.6 cm)

Signed l. l.: *J. J. Tissot*

Chrysler Museum of Art, Norfolk, Virginia, Gift of Walter P. Chrysler, Jr., and The Grandy Fund, Landmark Communications Fund, and "An Affair to Remember" 1982, 81.153

Prov.: Bought from Tissot by Tooth, 1886, recorded December 30, 58 × 40 in. (147.3 × 101.6 cm), cost price £100; sold by Tooth, Christie's, London, March 30, 1889 (134), £78.15s, and reacquired by Tooth from Mr. Day as *Artists and their Wives*, April 1, for same price; sold by Tooth, July 25, 1891, for £55 to [Charles Field] Haseltine; Art Association of the Union League of Philadelphia by 1894; M. Knoedler and Co., New York, 1981; Gift of Walter P. Chrysler, Jr., and The Grandy Fund, Landmark Communications Fund, and "An Affair to Remember," 1982.

Exh.: Paris 1885 as *Les femmes d'artiste*; Tooth 1886; Providence and Toronto 1968, lent by the Union League of Philadephia; Atlanta 1983; Rome 2015.

Bibl.: Union League of Philadelphia 1908, 27; Union League of Philadelphia 1940, 26; Providence and Toronto 1968, no. 35; Misfeldt 1971, fig. 135; Whiteman 1978, 98, 90 (illus. as *The Café Royal, Paris*); Chrysler Museum 1982, cover illus.; Misfeldt 1982, pl. III-60; Wentworth 1984, 162, 167, 169, 205, pl. 187; Wood 1986, 137, fig. 145; Garb 1999, 103, 112–115, fig. 38; Maeder 1999, 88; Silver 1999, 125–126.

119

THE AMATEUR CIRCUS, CA. 1883–1885

also known as **THE CIRCUS LOVER**

LES FEMMES DE SPORT

Oil on canvas, 58 × 40 in. (147.3 × 101.6 cm)

Signed l. l.: *J. J. Tissot*

Museum of Fine Arts, Boston, Juliana Cheney Edwards Collection, 58.45

Prov.: Bought from Tissot by Tooth, 1886, recorded December 30, 58 × 40 in. (147.3 × 101.6 cm), cost price £100; anonymous sale (E. Simon for Tooth), Christie's, London, March 30, 1889 (143), £61.19s, bt. King; with William Marchant and Co., The Goupil Gallery, London (label on stretcher, date unknown); with Hollander & Cremetti, Hanover Gallery, London, May 1893, as *The Cirque Molière, Paris*; The Hon. Mrs. Arthur Henniker; with Gerald M. Fitzgerald by 1955; sold by Fitzgerald, Christie's, London, July 26, 1957 (100), bt. Marlborough Fine Art Ltd., from whom bought by Museum of Fine Arts for $5,000, February 13, 1958.

Exh.: Paris 1885 as *Les femmes de sport*; Tooth 1886; Newcastle 1887; Hanover 1893 as *The Cirque Molière, Paris*; Sheffield 1955, lent by Mr. G. M. Fitzgerald; Marlborough 1957; San Francisco 1959; Providence and Toronto 1968 as *L'acrobate (The Amateur Circus)*; Yale 1999; Paris 2012.

Bibl.: *Newcastle Courant* 1887; *Manchester Guardian* 1893, 5; *Illustrated London News* 1955, 1151; Gourley 1964, fig. 7; Wagner 1965, fig. 1; Providence and Toronto 1968, no. 35; Misfeldt 1971, fig. 137; Misfeldt 1982, pl. III-55; Wentworth 1984, 159, 162, 164, 168, 205, pl. 183; Wood 1986, 132, fig. 139; Arscott 1999, 71; Darby 1999, 161; Garb 1999, 106–119; Lochnan, ed. 1999, pl. XXIII; New Haven, Québec, and Buffalo 1999–2000, 20, 152–153; Prelinger 1999, 203.

120

***THE LADIES OF THE CARS, CA. 1883–1885**

also known as **THE LADIES OF THE CHARIOTS**

CES DAMES DES CHARS

Oil on canvas, 57½ × 39⅝ in. (146.1 × 100.7 cm)

Signed l. r.: *J. J. Tissot*

Museum of Art, Rhode Island School of Design, Providence, Gift of Mr. Walter Lowry, 58.186

Prov.: Bought from Tissot by Tooth, 1886, recorded December 30 as *Ladies of the Cars*, 58 × 40 in. (147.3 × 101.6 cm), cost price £100; sold by Tooth, Christie's, London, March 30, 1889 (141) as *The Ladies of the Bar*, £42; given to Rhode Island School of Design by Mr. Walter Lowry, 1958.

Exh.: Paris 1885 as *Ces dames des chars*; Tooth 1886 as *The Ladies of the Cars*; Newcastle 1887; San Francisco 1964–1965.

Publ.: Etching by Tissot (1885; Wentworth 78).

Bibl.: *Newcastle Courant* 1887; Gourley 1964, fig. 6; Providence and Toronto 1968, no. 35; Misfeldt 1971, 226, fig. 136; Wentworth 1978, 308, 310, fig. 78d; Misfeldt 1982, pl. III-54; London and Manchester 1984–1985, 136–137; Wentworth 1984, 162, 165–166, 168, 170, 205, pl. 179; Paris 1985, 241–242; Wood 1986, 132, fig. 138; Misfeldt 1991, 164; Garb 1999, 103–104, 109–110, fig. 39; New Haven, Québec, Buffalo 1999–2000, 159; Prelinger 1999, 203; Silver 1999, 121, 122–123; Nantes 2005–2006, 96, 176.

121

THE WOMAN OF FASHION, CA. 1883–1885

LA MONDAINE

Oil on canvas, 57 × 39 in. (148.3 × 103 cm)

Signed l. r.: *J. J. Tissot*

Private collection

Prov.: Bought from Tissot by Tooth, 1886, cost price recorded as £300; sold by Tooth, July 14, 1886, to F[rederic] Layton; Benjamin Goldberg, Royal Oak, Michigan; with Detroit Institute of Art in 1968; Jerome Eisenberg, New York; by January 1970 with H. Shickman Gallery, New York, from whom purchased in November 1970 by Mr. and Mrs. Joseph M. Tanenbaum, Toronto; consigned as property of a Gentleman and a Lady, Christie's, London, November 25, 1983 (99); sold from the Joey and Toby Tanenbaum Collection, Sotheby's, New York, February 17, 1993 (52).

Exh.: Paris 1885 as *La mondaine*; Tooth 1886; H. Shickman 1970; Ottawa 1978; London and Manchester 1984–1985.

Bibl.: Providence and Toronto 1968, no. 35; *Burlington Magazine* 1970a; Misfeldt 1971, fig. 141; Misfeldt 1982, pl. III-57; London and Manchester 1984–1985, 137–138; Wentworth 1984, 31, 162, 164, 166, 168, 169, 205, pl. 185; Paris 1985, 92–93, fig. 42; Wood 1986, 131–132, fig. 135; Weisberg 1993, 21; Prelinger 1999, 203–204, fig. 90; Serafini 2015, 47, fig. 5.

122

THE FASHIONABLE BEAUTY, CA. 1883–1885

LA PLUS JOLIE FEMME DE PARIS

Oil on canvas, 57⅝ × 40 in. (146.3 × 101.6 cm)

Signed l. r.: *J. J. Tissot*

Musée d'Art et d'Histoire de Genève, inv. BA.1998.239

Prov.: Bought from Tissot by Tooth, 1886, recorded December 30 with amended title *The Aesthetic Beauty*, 58 × 40 in. (147.3 × 101.6 cm), cost price £150; sold by Tooth, Christie's, London, March 30, 1889 (136) as *The Aesthetic Lady*, £78.15s, and reacquired by Tooth from Weir, April 1, for same price; sold by Tooth, July 25, 1891, for £55 to [Charles Field] Haseltine; probably sold by Haseltine to George I. Seney, then reacquired by Haseltine; sold by Haseltine at Haseltine Galleries, Philadephia, March 21–31, 1894 (708) as *The Soiree*, "from the collection of the late Geo. I. Seney, from whom Mr. Haseltine purchased . . . originally formed part of the special Tissot Exhibition in London"; Private collection, Switzerland; acquired 1998.

Exh.: Paris 1885 as *La plus jolie femme de Paris*; Tooth 1886; Rome 2015.

Publ.: Etching by Tissot (1885; Wentworth 81).

Bibl.: Providence and Toronto 1968, no. 35; Misfeldt 1971, 221, fig. 138; Wentworth 1978, 322–325, fig. 81c; Misfeldt 1982, pl. III-59; London and Manchester 1984–1985, 137; Wentworth 1984, 31, 162, 164, 166–168, 171, 205, pl. 182; Paris 1985, 240–241; Wood 1986, 132, fig. 136; Misfeldt 1991, 170; Garb 1999, 100–103, fig. 37; New Haven, Québec, and Buffalo 1999–2000, 158; Prelinger 1999, 203; Nantes 2005–2006, 191.

123

***THE "YOUNG LADY" OF THE SHOP, CA. 1883–1885**

LA DEMOISELLE DE MAGASIN

Oil on canvas, 57½ × 40 in. (146.1 × 101.6 cm)

Signed l. r.: *J. J. Tissot*

Art Gallery of Ontario, Toronto, Gift from Corporations' Subscription Fund, 1968, 67/55

Prov.: Bought from Tissot by Tooth, 1886, recorded December 30, 58 × 40 in. (147.3 × 101.6 cm), cost price £100; sold by Tooth, Christie's, London, March 30, 1889 (139) as *The Young Lady of the Shop*, £52.10s, bt. King; with Leicester Galleries, London, by 1936; Henry Talbot de Vere Clifton of Lytham Hall by 1955; sold Christie's, London, January 22, 1965 (55) as *The Milliner's Shop*, bt. Leger Galleries, London; given to Art Gallery of Ontario through Corporation's Subscription Fund, 1968.

Exh.: Paris 1885 as *La demoiselle de magasin*; Tooth 1886; Whitechapel 1887, lent by Tooth; Leeds 1888 as *On the Boulevards*; Leicester Galleries 1937 as *L'article de Paris*; Preston 1955, lent by H. de Vere Clifton; Leger 1967; Providence and Toronto 1968; London and Manchester 1984–1985; Paris 1985; Yale 1999; Paris 2012.

Bibl.: *Leeds Mercury* 1888; Laver 1936, pl. XXIX; *Burlington Magazine* 1967, pl. XXVI as *L'article de Paris*, The Leger Galleries Ltd., London; Providence and Toronto 1968, no. 35; Misfeldt 1971, fig. 134; Misfeldt 1982, pl. III-62; London and Manchester 1984–1985, 138; Wentworth 1984, 163, 166, 169, 205, pl. 191; Paris 1985, 239; Wood 1986, 133, fig. 140; Misfeldt 1991, 44; Garb 1999, 103, 110–112; Lochnan 1999, 4; Lochnan, ed. 1999, pl. XXI; Maeder 1999, 91; New Haven, Québec, and Buffalo 1999–2000, 146, 154–155; Prelinger 1999, 204, 205–207; Saddlemyer 1999, 148; Silver 1999, 125; Dolkart, ed. 2009, 11, fig. 2; Ribeiro 2016, 396, pl. 300.

124

POLITICAL WOMAN, CA. 1883–1885

L'AMBITIEUSE

Oil on canvas, 56 × 40 in. (142.2 × 101.6 cm)

Signed l. r.: *J. Tissot*

Albright-Knox Art Gallery, Buffalo, Gift of William M. Chase, 1909, 1909:10

Prov.: Bought from Tissot by Tooth, 1886, recorded as *At the Reception*, cost price £300; sold by Tooth, October 6, 1886, to American collector George L. Seney; sold by Charles Haseltine at Haseltine Galleries, Philadephia, March 21–31, 1894 (709) as *The Reception*, 58 × 40 in. (147.3 × 101.6 cm), "from the collection of the late Geo. I. Seney, from whom Mr. Haseltine purchased ... originally formed part of the special Tissot Exhibition in London"; given to Albright-Knox Art Gallery by William M. Chase, 1909.

Exh.: Paris 1885 as *L'ambitieuse*; Tooth 1886; Brooklyn 1887 as *At the Reception*; London and Manchester 1984–1985; Paris 1985; Yale 1999.

Publ.: Etching by Tissot (1885; Wentworth 77).

Bibl.: Providence and Toronto 1968, no. 35; Misfeldt 1971, fig. 139; Wentworth 1978, 302–304, fig. 77g; Misfeldt 1982, pl. III-56; London and Manchester 1984–1985, 136; Wentworth 1984, 162, 165–166, 168, 205, pl. 178; Paris 1985, 239–240; Wood 1986, 130–131, fig. 128; Misfeldt 1991, 162, fig. 47; Arscott 1999, 71–72; Garb 1999, 95–96, 115; Lochnan 1999, 1, 4, 13; Lochnan, ed. 1999, pl. XXII; Maeder 1999, 82; New Haven, Québec, and Buffalo 1999–2000, 150–151; Nantes 2005–2006, 168; Dolkart, ed. 2009, 11, fig. 1.

125

***PROVINCIAL WOMAN, CA. 1883–1885**

LES DEMOISELLES DE PROVINCE

Oil on canvas, 58 × 40¼ in. (147.3 × 102.2 cm)

Signed l. r.: *J J Tissot*

Collection of Diane B. Wilsey, San Francisco

Prov.: Bought from Tissot by Tooth, 1886, recorded as 50 × 40 in. (127 × 101.6 cm), cost price £300; sold by Tooth for £320, May 22, 1886, to Baker; bought back from Baker by Tooth, December 28, 1886, for £320; title amended by Tooth to *Provincial Women* in 1887, and cost to £150 in 1888; anonymous sale (E. Simon for Tooth), Christie's, London, March 30, 1889 (135) as *Provincial Ladies*, £141.15s, bt. Tooth, recorded as 58 × 40 in. (147.3 × 101.6 cm), sold the same day for £148.17s to Nusely; anonymous sale (Lefèvre & Sons), Christie's, London, April 15, 1905 (140) as *Early Arrivals*, bt. in.

Exh.: Paris 1885 as *Les demoiselles de province*; Tooth 1886.

Bibl.: Providence and Toronto 1968, no. 35; Misfeldt 1982, pl. III-63; Wentworth 1984, 163, 169, 205, pl. 189; Wood 1986, 137, fig. 144; Arscott 1999, 72–73, fig. 30; Prelinger 1999, 203; Serafini 2015, 47, fig. 4.

126

WITHOUT DOWRY, CA. 1883–1885

SANS DOT

Oil on canvas, 58 × 40 in. (147.3 × 101.6 cm)

Signed l. l.: *J. J. Tissot*

Private collection

Prov.: Bought from Tissot by Tooth, 1886, cost price recorded as £300; sold by Tooth, August 17, 1886, to American collector George I. Seney; sold by executors of the late George I. Seney, Chickering Hall, Fifth Avenue, New York, February 8, 1894 (210) as *A Parisian Afternoon*, 58 × 40 in. (147.3 × 101.6 cm), $510, bt. J. M. Brown; sold Christie's, London, October 4, 1973 (231) as *Sunday in the Luxembourg Gardens*; with H. Shickman Gallery, New York, from whom acquired in 1975 by Mr. and Mrs. Joseph M. Tanenbaum; sold from the Joey and Toby Tanenbaum Collection, Sotheby's, New York, February 17, 1993 (60); sold October 31, 2000.

Exh.: Paris 1885 as *Sans dot*; Tooth 1886; Brooklyn 1887 as *In Versailles*; Ottawa 1978; London and Manchester 1984–1985.

Publ.: Etching by Tissot (Wentworth 79).

Bibl.: Providence and Toronto 1968, no. 35; Wentworth 1978, 314–317, fig. 79d; Misfeldt 1982, pl. III-58; London and Manchester 1984–1985, 137; Wentworth 1984, 66, 162, 166, 168, 171, 205, pl. 180; Paris 1985, 240, fig. 100; Wood 1986, 137–138, fig. 146; Misfeldt 1991, 166; Garb 1999, 104, fig. 41; Saddlemyer 1999, 148; Silver 1999, 122; Nantes 2005–2006, 173.

127

***STUDY FOR "THE SPHINX" (WOMAN IN AN INTERIOR), CA. 1883–1885**

Oil on wood panel, 43¾ × 27 in. (111.1 × 68.6 cm)

Private collection

Prov.: Given by Tissot to Léonce Bénédite, Director of the Musée du Luxembourg, Paris, ca. 1885; by descent to Bénédite family, Paris; with Ferrers, London, July 1972, as *Portrait of Mlle Reisener*; H. Shickman Gallery, New York, from whom acquired in 1973 by Mr. and Mrs. Joseph M. Tanenbaum, Toronto; sold from the Joey and Toby Tanenbaum Collection, Sotheby's, New York, February 17, 1993 (55) as *Study for "Le Sphinx" (Woman in an Interior)*; sold Sotheby's, New York, October 31, 2000 (103).

Exh.: Ottawa 1978.

Bibl.: *Apollo* 1972; Misfeldt 1978, 192; Wentworth 1984, 160, 163, 166–167, 169, 205, pl. 190; Wood 1986, fig. 142; Darby 1999, 176; Garb 1999, 104–105; Prelinger 1999, 186, 202–203.

128

***AESTHETIC WOMAN, CA. 1883–1885**

L'ESTHÉTIQUE

Oil on canvas, 25½ × 17½ in. (64.8 × 44.5 cm)

Signed l. l.: *J. J. Tissot*

Colección Pérez Simón, Mexico City

Prov.: Painted for art dealer Charles Sedelmeyer, who paid Tissot £80 or 2,000FF in 1885 (Notebook); estate sale of Charles Sedelmeyer, Paris, 1907 (100); either this or the larger version with Charles A. Green, Rochester, New York, by 1913; Owen Edgar Gallery, London, by 1984; sold Sotheby's, New York, May 26, 1993 (108).

Exh.: Paris 1900; London and Manchester 1984–1985; Rome 2015.

Bibl.: Pattison 1913, 108–109, repr. 103 as *Corner of the Louvre*; London and Manchester 1984–1985, 138, pl. 27; Wentworth 1984, 163, 206, pl. 193; Paris 1985, 93, fig. 41; Wood 1986, 139, 140, fig. 150.

129

*THE MYSTERY, CA. 1885

LA MYSTÉRIEUSE

Etching and drypoint, 22¼ × 14¼ in. (56.5 × 37.5 cm)
Cantor Arts Center, Stanford University, Mortimer C. Leventritt Fund, 1972.43
Prov.: Purchased 1972.
Bibl.: Wentworth 1978, 318–321; Wentworth 1984, 134, 162, 166, 168, 170, 205, pl. 181; Misfeldt 1991, 168–169; Garb 1999, 104; New Haven, Québec, and Buffalo 1999–2000, 160–161; Silver 1999, 123–124; Nantes 2005–2006, 172; Rome 2015–2016, 109, no. 38.

130

THE LADIES OF THE CARS, CA. 1885

also known as **THE LADIES OF THE CHARIOTS**

CES DAMES DES CHARS

Etching and drypoint, 15¾ × 10 in. (40 × 25.4 cm)
Fine Arts Museums of San Francisco, Museum purchase, Achenbach Foundation for Graphic Arts Endowment Fund, 1982.1.18
Prov.: Purchased through the Achenbach Foundation for Graphic Arts Endowment Fund, 1982.
Bibl.: Wentworth 1978, 308–313; London and Manchester 1984–1985, 136–137; Paris 1985, 241–242; Misfeldt 1991, 164–165; New Haven, Québec, and Buffalo 1999–2000, 159; Nantes 2005–2006, 176; Rome 2015–2016, 137, no. 59.

131

*PORTRAIT OF WILLIAM EGLINTON, 1885

Etching printed in red, 15½ × 10 in. (39.4 × 25.4 cm)
Fine Arts Museums of San Francisco, Gift of John Gutmann, 1986.1.205
Prov.: Given to Fine Arts Museums of San Francisco by John Gutmann, 1986.
Bibl.: Wentworth 1978, 334–337; London 1981, no. 21; London and Manchester 1984–1985, 133; Wentworth 1984, 176; Paris 1985, 237; Wood 1986, 145–146, fig. 155; Misfeldt 1991, 176–177; Keshavjee 1999, 219–220; Lochnan, ed. 1999, pl. XXV; Saddlemyer 1999, 154–156, fig. 61; Nantes 2005–2006, 190.

132

*THE APPARITION, 1885

L'APPARITION MÉDIUNIMIQUE

Mezzotint, 25⅜ × 19⅜ in. (64.5 × 49.2 cm)
Fine Arts Museums of San Francisco, Museum purchase, Gift of the Graphic Arts Council, 2001.26
Prov.: Gift of the Graphic Arts Council, 2001.
Bibl.: Wentworth 1978, 294–299 Wood 1986, 146–147, fig. 156; Misfeldt 1991, 156–159; Keshavjee 1999, 213–214, 220–221; Lochnan 1999, 16; Lochnan, ed. 1999, pl. XXIV; Marshall 1999, 46; New Haven, Québec, and Buffalo 1999–2000, 144–145; Prelinger 1999, 198; Saddlemyer 1999, 155–156, fig. 62; Nantes 2005–2006, 178–179; Dolkart, ed. 2009, 22–23, fig. 24.

133

*THE APPARITION, 1885

also known as **THE MEDIUMISTIC APPARITION**

L'APPARITION MÉDIUNIMIQUE

Oil on canvas, 29⅛ × 21¼ in. (74 × 54 cm)
Private collection
Prov.: Tissot sale, Besançon, 1964.
Publ.: Mezzotint by Tissot dated 1885 (76).
Bibl.: Wentworth 1978, 294–298; London and Manchester 1984–1985, 133; Wentworth 1984, 177–178, 186, 196; Paris 1985, 236–237; Misfeldt 1991, 156–157; New Haven, Québec, and Buffalo 1999–2000, 144; Nantes 2005–2006, 178; Dolkart, ed. 2009, 23.

134–139

OLD TESTAMENT ILLUSTRATIONS, CA. 1896–1902

Prov.: Following a tour of the United States under the auspices of the American Tissot Society, 373 watercolors purchased by Jacob H. Schiff and given to the New York Public Library; transferred by the Schiff heirs to the Jewish Museum, New York, in 1952.
Exh.: Paris 1901 (95 watercolor illustrations); Jewish Museum 1982.
Publ.: Color lithographs after Tissot's watercolors published by Maurice de Brunhoff in *The Old Testament: Three Hundred and Ninety-Six Compositions Illustrating the Old Testament*, 1904.
Bibl.: New York 1982; London and Manchester 1984–1985, 141; Thomson 1984, 93; Wentworth 1984, 193–195; Paris 1985, 248–249; New Haven, Québec, and Buffalo 1999–2000, 163–164, 188–194.

134

GOD CREATING THE WORLD, CA. 1900–1902

Opaque watercolor on board, 5¼ × 7¾ in. (13.5 × 20.1 cm)
Signed l. l.: *J. J. Tissot*
The Morgan Library and Museum, New York, Morgan Family Collection, 1976.22:1

135

*JACOB'S DREAM, CA. 1896–1902

Opaque watercolor on board, 12¼ × 5⅞ in. (31 × 15 cm)
Signed l. l.: *J. J. Tissot*
The Jewish Museum, New York, Gift of the heirs of Jacob Schiff, X1952-113
Exh.: Jewish Museum 1982; London and Manchester 1984–1985; Paris 1985.
Bibl.: Wood 1986, 154, fig 170.

136

*THE PLAGUE OF LOCUSTS, CA. 1896–1902

Opaque watercolor on board, 7¾ × 9⅜ in. (19.8 × 23.9 cm)
Signed l. r.: *J. J. Tissot*
The Jewish Museum, New York, Gift of the heirs of Jacob Schiff, X1952-164
Exh.: Jewish Museum 1982; London and Manchester 1984–1985; Paris 1985; Yale 1999.
Bibl.: New York 1982, 37 (illus.); Wood 1986, 154, fig. 168; New Haven, Québec, and Buffalo 1999–2000, 194.

137

*MOSES AND JOSHUA IN THE TABERNACLE, CA. 1896–1902

Opaque watercolor on board, 7⅜ × 8 ⅞ in. (18.7 × 22.5 cm)
The Jewish Museum, New York, Gift of the heirs of Jacob Schiff, X1952-208
Exh.: Jewish Museum 1982.

138

*THE ARK PASSES OVER THE JORDAN, CA. 1896–1902

Opaque watercolor on board, 8⅜ × 10 ⅞ in. (21.4 × 27.6 cm)
The Jewish Museum, New York, Gift of the heirs of Jacob Schiff, X1952-214
Exh.: Jewish Museum 1982.
Bibl.: New York 1982, 15 (color illus.).

139

*THE TWO PRIESTS ARE DESTROYED, CA. 1896–1902

Opaque watercolor on board, 7⅜ × 10¾ in. (18.7 × 27.3 cm)
Signed l. r.: *J. J. Tissot*
The Jewish Museum, New York, Gift of the heirs of Jacob Schiff, X1952-191
Exh.: Jewish Museum 1982.

140–156

THE LIFE OF CHRIST ILLUSTRATIONS, CA. 1886–1894

Prov.: Purchased by public subscription for the Brooklyn Museum, New York, 1900, following tour of the United States.
Exh.: Paris 1894 (270 watercolors); Lemercier 1896–1898; American Art Association 1900; Brooklyn Museum 1901–1930s; Brooklyn Museum 2009.
Publ.: Color lithographs after Tissot's watercolors, printed by Lemercier et Cie, and wood engravings after Tissot's drawings, published as *The Life of Our Lord Jesus Christ* by Mame et Cie, of Tours, 1896–1897; Sampson Low, Marston & Co., London, 1897–1898; Doubleday & McClure, 1898; McClure-Tissot Company, 1899.
Bibl.: *Daily News* 1894, 5; *Times* 1894a, 4; *New York Times* 1894; *Times* 1896, 8; Providence and Toronto 1968, nos. 56–59; Misfeldt 1971, 246–279, figs. 145–153; Wentworth 1978, 347; Leeds, Leicestershire, Bristol, and London 1978, no. 58; New York 1982, 6–7, 19, 23–30; Warner 1982, 24; London and Manchester 1984–1985, 140–141; Thomson 1984, 91–93; Wentworth 1984, 36, 136, 148–149, 157–158, 174–197, pls. 198, 200–204; Paris 1985, 246–247; Wood 1986, 147–151, 153; Keshavjee 1999, 220–221; Lochnan 1999, 17; New Haven, Québec, and Buffalo 1999–2000, 163–164, 170–187; Dolkart, ed. 2009.

140

*WOMEN OF GEBA, SAMARIA, 1886–1887 or 1888–1889

Pen and black ink on paper, 7¼ × 4¾ in. (18.4 × 11.9 cm)
Brooklyn Museum, Purchased by public subscription, 00.159.407
Publ.: Reproduced as a wood engraving within the text (London 1897–1898 edition, Vol. 2, 23).

141

*WOMAN AND CHILD OF JERICHO, 1886–1887 or 1888–1889

Pen and black ink on paper, 7 × 4¾ in. (17.9 × 11.9 cm)
Signed l. l.: *J. Tissot*
Brooklyn Museum, Purchased by public subscription, 00.159.394
Publ.: Reproduced as a wood engraving within the text (London 1897–1898 edition, Vol. 1, 203).

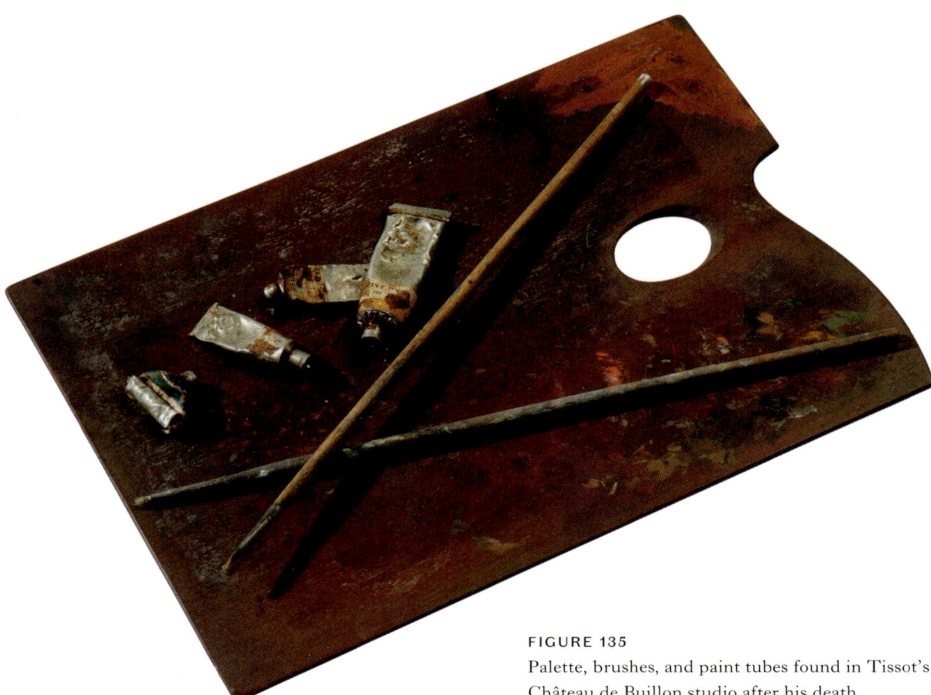

FIGURE 135
Palette, brushes, and paint tubes found in Tissot's Château de Buillon studio after his death

142
*VIEW OF NAZARETH, 1886–1887 or 1888–1889

Pen and black ink on paper, 7 × 10½ in. (17.9 × 26.7 cm)
Brooklyn Museum, Purchased by public subscription, 00.159.361
Publ.: Reproduced as a wood engraving within the text (London 1897–1898 edition, Vol. 1, 15).

143
*SOUTH-WEST ANGLE OF THE HARAM ON THE SITE OF THE TEMPLE, TAKEN FROM THE GATE OF THE MUGARABEES, CA. 1886–1894

Oil on board, 14½ × 20¼ in. (36.7 × 51.4 cm)
Brooklyn Museum, Purchased by public subscription, 00.159.3
Publ.: Reproduced as a wood engraving within the text, with careful modulation of lines to imitate the painting (London 1897–1898 edition, 71).
Bibl.: Dolkart, ed. 2009, 202 (illus.).

144
*THE ANNUNCIATION, CA. 1886–1894
L'ANNONCIATION

Opaque watercolor over graphite on gray wove paper, 6¾ × 8½ in. (17 × 21.7 cm)
Brooklyn Museum, Purchased by public subscription, 00.159.16
Publ.: Reproduced as a color lithograph within the text (London 1897–1898 edition, 8).
Bibl.: New Haven, Québec, and Buffalo 1999–2000, 172–173; Saddlemyer 1999, 151, fig. 60; Dolkart, ed. 2009, 72–73 (illus.), 78 (illus.).

145
*THE "MAGNIFICAT," CA. 1886–1894
LE MAGNIFICAT

Opaque watercolor over graphite on gray wove paper, 9⅞ × 4⅝ in. (25.2 × 11.7 cm)
Signed l. l.: *J. J. Tissot*
Brooklyn Museum, Purchased by public subscription, 00.159.19
Exh.: Paris 1985; Brooklyn Museum 2009.
Publ.: Reproduced as a full-page color lithograph (London 1897–1898 edition, opp. 10).
Bibl.: Thiébault-Sisson 1902, 8 (illus.); Paris 1985, 246; Dolkart, ed. 2009, fig. 5, 80 (illus.).

146
*THE MAGI ON THEIR WAY TO BETHLEHEM, CA. 1886–1894
LES ROIS MAGES EN VOYAGE

Opaque watercolor over graphite on gray wove paper, 8 × 11½ in. (20.3 × 29.2 cm)
Brooklyn Museum, Purchased by public subscription, 00.159.30
Publ.: Reproduced as a monochrome lithograph within the text (London 1897–1898 edition, 28).
Bibl.: Wood 1986, 149–150; New Haven, Québec, and Buffalo 1999–2000, 186–187; Dolkart, ed. 2009, 86 (illus.).

147
*JESUS GOING UP INTO A MOUNTAIN TO PRAY, CA. 1886–1894
JÉSUS MONTE SEUL SUR UNE MONTAGNE POUR PRIER

Opaque watercolor over graphite on gray wove paper, 11⅜ × 6¼ in. (28.9 × 15.9 cm)
Signed l. r.: *J. J. Tissot*
Brooklyn Museum, Purchased by public subscription, 00.159.137
Publ.: Reproduced as a monochrome lithograph within the text (London 1897–1898 edition, 176).
Bibl.: Dolkart, ed. 2009, 150 (illus.).

148
JESUS MINISTERED TO BY ANGELS, CA. 1886–1894
JÉSUS ASSISTÉ PAR LES ANGES

Opaque watercolor over graphite on gray wove paper, 6¾ × 9¾ in. (17 × 24.8 cm)
Signed l. r.: *J. J. Tissot*
Brooklyn Museum, Purchased by public subscription, 00.159.54
Publ.: Reproduced as a color lithograph within the text (London 1897–1898 edition, 68).
Bibl.: Dolkart, ed. 2009, 104 (illus.).

149
*THE AGONY IN THE GARDEN, CA. 1886–1894
LA GROTTE DE L'AGONIE

Opaque watercolor over graphite on dark brown wove paper, 11 × 14½ in. (28.1 × 36.7 cm)
Brooklyn Museum, Purchased by public subscription, 00.159.231
Publ.: Reproduced as a monochrome lithograph within the text (London 1897–1898 edition, 96).
Bibl.: Dolkart, ed. 2009, 212 (illus.).

150
*BIRD'S-EYE VIEW OF THE FORUM, CA. 1886–1894
LE FORUM "VU À VOL D'OISEAU" or JÉSUS ENTEND SA CONDAMNATION À MORT

Opaque watercolor over graphite on gray wove paper, 6⅞ × 11⅝ in. (17.6 × 29.4 cm)
Brooklyn Museum, Purchased by public subscription, 00.159.274
Publ.: Reproduced as a color lithograph within the text (London 1897–1898 edition, Vol. 2, 149).
Bibl.: Dolkart, ed. 2009, 68–69 (illus.), 237 (illus.).

151
*THE ELEVATION OF THE CROSS, CA. 1886–1894
L'ÉLÉVATION DE LA CROIX

Opaque watercolor over graphite on gray wove paper, 9⅞ × 14⅝ in. (25.2 × 37 cm)
Signed l. r.: *J. J. Tissot*
Brooklyn Museum, Purchased by public subscription, 00.159.294
Publ.: Reproduced as a monochrome lithograph within the text (London 1897–1898 edition, 184).
Bibl.: Dolkart, ed. 2009, 198–199 (illus.), 201, 249 (illus.).

152
*WHAT OUR SAVIOUR SAW FROM THE CROSS, CA. 1886–1894
CE QUE VOYAIT NOTRE-SEIGNEUR SUR LA CROIX

Opaque watercolor over graphite on gray-green wove paper, 9¾ × 9 in. (24.8 × 23 cm)
Signed l. r.: *J. J. Tissot*
Brooklyn Museum, Purchased by public subscription, 00.159.299
Publ.: Reproduced as a full-page color lithograph (London 1897–1898 edition, opp. 190).
Bibl.: Wood 1986, 150, fig. 162; New Haven, Québec, and Buffalo 1999–2000, 180–181; Thomson 2000, fig. 3; Dolkart, ed. 2009, 201, 252 (illus.).

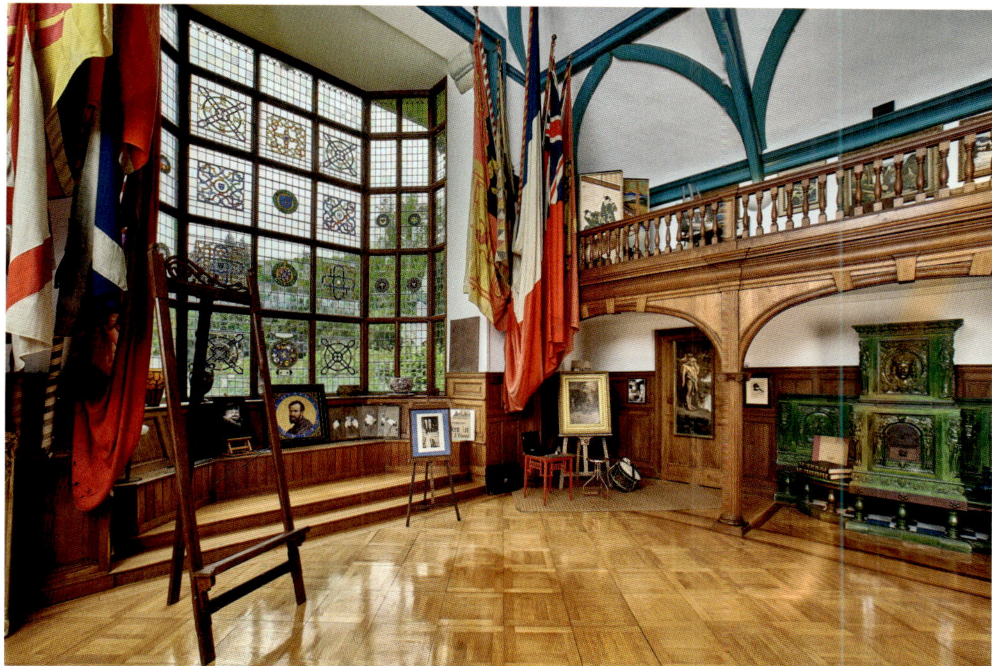

FIGURE 136
Tissot's Château de Buillon studio today, 2019

153

***JESUS LOOKING THROUGH A LATTICE, CA. 1886–1894**

JÉSUS REGARDANT À TRAVERS LE TREILLIS

Opaque watercolor over graphite on gray wove paper, $5^{5}/_{8} \times 6^{7}/_{8}$ in. (14.4 × 17.6 cm)

Signed l. l.: *J. J. Tissot*

Brooklyn Museum, Purchased by public subscription, 00.159.11

Exh.: Providence and Toronto 1968; Yale 1999.

Publ.: Reproduced as a color lithograph within the text (London 1897–1898 edition, Vol. 1, title page).

Bibl.: New Haven, Québec, and Buffalo 1999–2000, 170–171; Dolkart, ed. 2009, 4 (illus.), 94–95 (illus.).

154

***THE RESURRECTION, CA. 1886–1894**

LA RÉSURRECTION

Opaque watercolor over graphite on gray wove paper, $12^{3}/_{4} \times 8^{1}/_{4}$ in. (32.5 × 21.1 cm)

Signed l. r.: *J. J. Tissot*

Brooklyn Museum, Purchased by public subscription, 00.159.328

Publ.: Reproduced as a full-page color lithograph (London 1897–1898 edition, opp. 238).

Bibl.: Dolkart, ed. 2009, 272 (illus.).

155

***THE ASCENSION AS SEEN FROM BELOW, CA. 1886–1894**

L'ASCENSION

Opaque watercolor over graphite on gray wove paper, $7^{1}/_{2} \times 6^{1}/_{8}$ in. (19.2 × 15.7 cm)

Signed u. r.: *J. J. Tissot*

Brooklyn Museum, Purchased by public subscription, 00.159.349

Publ.: Reproduced as a monochrome lithograph within the text (London 1897–1898 edition, 269).

Bibl.: Dolkart, ed. 2009, 262–263, 284 (illus.).

156

***THE DEAD APPEAR IN THE TEMPLE, CA. 1886–1894**

LES MORTS APPARAISSENT DANS LE TEMPLE

Opaque watercolor over graphite on gray wove paper, $8^{3}/_{8} \times 11^{1}/_{8}$ in. (21.4 × 28.4 cm)

Signed l. r.: *J. J. Tissot*

Brooklyn Museum, Purchased by public subscription, 00.159.311

Publ.: Reproduced as a color lithograph within the text (London 1897–1898 edition, 205).

Bibl.: New Haven, Québec, and Buffalo 1999–2000, 182–183; Dolkart, ed. 2009, fig. 13, 259 (illus.), 288–289 (illus.).

157

***PORTRAIT OF THE PILGRIM, CA. 1886–1894**

also known as **SELF-PORTRAIT**

PORTRAIT DU PÈLERIN

Opaque watercolor over graphite on gray wove paper, $9 \times 5^{5}/_{8}$ in (23 × 14.3 cm)

Signed l. r.: *J. J. Tissot*

Brooklyn Museum, Gift of Thomas E. Kirby, 06.39

Exh.: Paris 1894; Providence and Toronto 1968; Yale 1999; Brooklyn Museum 2009.

Publ.: Reproduced as a monochrome lithograph within the text (London 1897–1898 edition, 272).

Bibl.: Wood 1986, 150, fig. 152; New Haven, Québec, and Buffalo 1999–2000, 184–185; Dolkart, ed. 2009, fig. 25, 287 (illus.).

KEY

Prov.: Provenance
Exh.: Exhibitions
Publ.: Published as an engraving, etching, lithograph, photograph, etc.
Bibl.: Bibliography

Signature and date locations:
u. l.: upper left
u. r.: upper right
c. r.: center right
l. c.: lower center
l. l.: lower left
l. r.: lower right

Provenance abbreviations:
Auction lot numbers are given in parentheses.

Agnew: Thomas Agnew & Sons Ltd., art dealers, London and Manchester.
bt. in: Bought in (whereby a work consigned to auction fails to reach its reserve price).
Christie's: British auctioneers.
Everard: P. L. Everard, art dealer, director of the Gallery of Continental Pictures, New Coventry Street, London.
FF: French francs.
gns: Guineas (one pound and one shilling or twenty-one shillings).
Gambart: Ernest Gambart, art dealer and publisher, and director of the French Gallery, London.
Goupil: Adolphe Goupil, director of Goupil & Cie, art dealers and publishers, with a gallery in Place de l'Opéra and premises at Boulevard Montmartre, Paris, as well as a gallery in London.
Herbert: William Greene Herbert, art dealer based in Lancashire, England.
Knoedler: Roland Knoedler, head of M. Knoedler & Co. beginning in 1878. M. Knoedler & Co., a successor to the New York branch of Goupil & Cie, was established in 1857.
Marsden: Algernon Moses Marsden, art dealer, director of the Conduit Street Gallery, London, then the King Street Galleries, London.
Notebook: See "Tissot's Sales Notebook," this volume.
Pilgeram: Jean Pilgeram, who—with Léon Lefèvre—supported Henry Wallis in management of the French Gallery, London, from 1861.
Reitlinger: Frédéric Reitlinger, art dealer based in Paris.
Rhodes: James Rhodes, art dealer based in Bradford, England.
Tissot sale, Besançon, 1964: Sale following the death of Tissot's last surviving niece, Jeanne Tissot, at the Château de Buillon, France, November 8–9, 14–15, and 21–22, 1964.
Tissot studio sale, Paris, 1903: "L'atelier de J. James Tissot," sale at Hôtel Drouot, Paris, July 9–10, 1903.
Tooth: Arthur Tooth & Sons, art dealer, London.
Wallis: Henry Wallis, appointed manager of the French Gallery, London, in 1861 by Ernest Gambart.
White, E. F.: Edward Fox White, art dealer, with galleries in London and Glasgow.

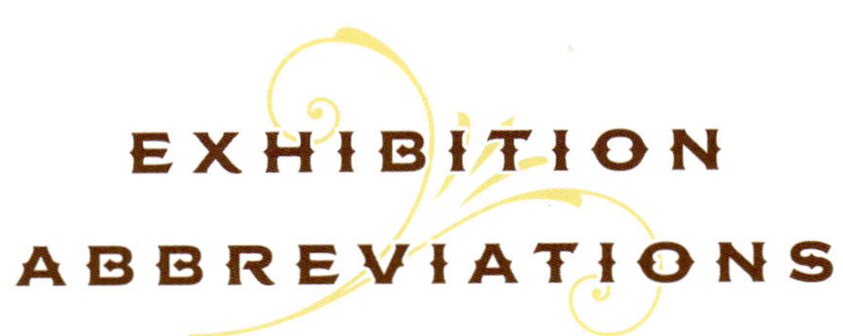

EXHIBITION ABBREVIATIONS

Agnew 1974: *Paintings by Old Masters*, an exhibition within the Fine Art an Antiques Festival, Thomas Agnew & Sons Ltd., London, 1974.

American Art Association 1900: American Art Association galleries, Manhattan, traveling to Chicago, Philadelphia, Boston, Saint Louis, Toronto, and Brooklyn, 1900.

Arts Council 1955: *Paintings, Drawings and Etchings by James Tissot 1836–1902*, selected from an exhibition arranged by the Graves Art Gallery, The Arts Council, Sheffield, England, 1955.

Atlanta 1983: *French Salon Paintings from Southern Collections*, High Museum of Art, Atlanta; Chrysler Museum, Norfolk, Virginia; North Carolina Museum of Art, Raleigh; and The John and Mable Ringling Museum of Art, Sarasota, Florida, 1983.

Atlanta 2002: *Paris in the Age of Impressionism: Masterworks from the Musée d'Orsay*, High Museum of Art, Atlanta; and the Museum of Fine Arts, Houston, 2002.

Barbican 1984: *The City's Pictures: A Selection of Paintings from the Collection of the Corporation of London*, Barbican Art Gallery, London, 1984.

Barletta 2006: *De Nittis e Tissot: Pittori della vita moderna*, Pinacoteca G. De Nittis, Barletta, Italy, 2006.

Bayonne 1864: Franco-Spanish exhibition, Bayonne, France, 1864.

Bedford 2002: *J. J. Tissot and his London Circle*, Cecil Higgins Art Gallery, Bedford, England, 2002–2003.

Berlin and Prague 1982: *Von Courbet bis Cézanne*, Nationalgalerie, Staatliche Museen zu Berlin; and Národní Gallery, Prague, 1982.

Besançon 1985: *James Tissot 1836–1902*, Musée des Beaux-Arts, Besançon, France, 1985.

Birmingham 1882: *Worcestershire Exhibition*, Birmingham, England, 1882.

Bremen 2005: *Monet und Camille: Frauenportraits im Impressionismus*, Kunsthalle Bremen, Germany, 2005–2006.

Brooklyn 1887: *Mr. George Seney's Collection of Paintings on Exhibition at the Gallery of the Brooklyn Art Association*, Brooklyn, 1887.

Brooklyn Museum 1901–1930s: *The Life of Christ*, Tissot Gallery, Brooklyn Museum, 1901–1930s.

Brooklyn Museum 2009: *James Tissot: "The Life of Christ,"* Brooklyn Museum, 2009–2010.

Chicago 1893: *World's Columbian Exposition*, Chicago, 1893.

Christie's 2000: *Treasures of the North*, Christie's, London, 2000.

Copenhagen 2000: *Gloria Victis! Tradition og nybrud i fransk kunst 1848–1910*, Ny Carlsberg Glyptotek, Copenhagen, 2000.

Darwen 1879: Darwen Art Treasures exhibition, 1879.

Dudley Gallery 1882: *An Exhibition of Modern Art by J. J. Tissot*, Dudley Gallery, London, 1882.

Everard 1877–1879: Everard's Continental Gallery, London, 1877–1879.

Fort Worth 2014: *Faces of Impressionism: Portraits from the Musée d'Orsay*, Kimbell Art Museum, Fort Worth, Texas, 2014.

French Gallery, London: Changing exhibitions of work for sale, French Gallery, London.

Glasgow 1876: Annual Exhibition of the Royal Glasgow Institute of the Fine Arts, 1876.

Glasgow 1878: *Fine Art Loan Exhibition*, Glasgow Royal Infirmary benefit, Corporation Galleries, Glasgow, 1878.

Glasgow 1879: Annual Exhibition of the Royal Glasgow Institute of the Fine Arts, 1879.

Glasgow 1888: International Exhibition, Glasgow, 1888.

Glasgow 1937: Annual Exhibition of the Royal Glasgow Institute of the Fine Arts, 1937.

Gray 1983: *Peinture et Société 1870–1914: À travers des collections des Musées de Franche-Comté*, organized by L'Association des Conservateurs de Franche-Comté, Gray, France, and touring to other venues, 1983–1984.

Greenwich 1977: *London and the Thames: Paintings of Three Centuries*, selected and catalogued by Harley Preston, National Maritime Museum, Greenwich, London, 1977.

Gropper 1964: *Tenth Anniversary Exhibition*, Gropper Art Galleries, Cambridge, Massachusetts, 1964.

Grosvenor Gallery: Summer exhibitions, The Grosvenor Gallery, London, 1877–1879.

Guildhall 1898: *Loan Exhibition of French Paintings*, Guildhall Art Gallery, London, 1898.

H. Shickman 1970: *The Neglected 19th Century: An Exhibition of French Paintings*, H. Shickman Gallery, New York, 1970.

Hamilton 1949–1985: Works on loan from Bequest of Margaret Galbreaith, Art Gallery of Hamilton, Ontario, 1949–1985.

Hanover 1893: Hanover Gallery, London, 1893.

Japan 1979: *Japonisme in Art*, traveling to Tokyo, Osaka, and Fukuoka, Japan, 1979–1980.

Japan 1988: *James Tissot*, exhibition coordinated by Brain Trust Inc., traveling to Isetan Museum of Art, Tokyo; Daimaru Museum, Osaka Umeda; Mie Prefectural Museum, Japan; Tochigi Prefectural Museum of Fine Arts, Japan; and Yokohama Takashimaya Gallery, 1988.

Japan 1995: *Treasures from the National Portrait Gallery*, traveling exhibition, Japan, 1995–1996.

Jewish Museum 1982: *J. James Tissot: Biblical Paintings*, The Jewish Museum, New York, 1982.

La Haye 2002: *De tijd van Degas*, Gemeentemuseum, The Hague, 2002.

Leeds 1868: *Leeds Art Treasures Exhibition*, Leeds General Infirmary, England, 1868.

Leeds 1888: Leeds City Art Gallery Inaugural Exhibition, England, 1888.

Leger 1967: Leger Galleries, London, 1967.

Leicester Galleries 1933: *In the Seventies: An Exhibition of Paintings by James Tissot*, The Leicester Galleries, London, 1933.

Leicester Galleries 1937: *The Second James Tissot Exhibition*, The Leicester Galleries, London, 1937.

Lemercier 1896–1898: Lemercier Gallery, London, 1896–1898.

Limoges 1862: Société des amis des arts du Limousin, Limoges, France, 1862.

Limoges 1864: Société des amis des arts du Limousin, Limoges, France, 1864.

Liverpool 1864: Liverpool Institution of Arts, 1864.

Liverpool 1880: *Annual Exhibition*, Walker Art Gallery, Liverpool, 1880.

Liverpool 2008: *Art in the Age of Steam: Europe, America and the Railway, 1830–1970*, Walker Art Gallery, Liverpool; and Nelson-Atkins Museum of Art, Kansas City, Missouri, 2008–2009.

London 1864: *Society of British Artists Exhibition*, Suffolk Street, London, 1864.

London 1872: London International Exhibition, 1872.

London 1970: *Exhibition of Nineteenth Century Drawings by European Artists*, P. & D. Colnaghi & Co., London, 1970.

London 1983: *Victorian Fanfare: Important Acquisitions for 1983*, Christopher Wood Gallery, London, 1983.

London 1994: *Elegant Ladies*, Christopher Wood Gallery, London, 1994.

London and Manchester 1984–1985: *James Tissot*, Barbican Art Gallery, London; and Whitworth Art Gallery, Manchester, 1984–1985.

London and Paris 2017: *Impressionists in London: French Artists in Exile 1870–1904*, Tate, London; and Petit Palais, Musée des Beaux-Arts de la ville de Paris, 2017–2018.

Louisville 1964: J. B. Speed Art Museum, Bequest of Mrs. Blakemore Wheeler, Louisville, 1964.

Louisville 2002–2003: *Corot to Picasso*, The Speed Art Museum, Louisville, 2002–2003.

Madrid 1918: *Pintura Francesa Contemporánea 1870–1914*, Ministerio de Instrucción Pública y Bellas Artes, Madrid, 1918.

Madrid 2010: *Jardines impresionistas*, Museo Nacional Thyssen-Bornemisza, Fundación Caja Madrid, 2010–2011.

Madrid 2015: *El canto del cisne: Pinturas académicas del Salón de Paris: Colecciones Musée d'Orsay*, Fundación Mapfre, Madrid, 2015.

Manchester 1872: Grundy and Smith, Manchester, 1872.

Manchester 1877: Agnew's Annual Exhibition, Manchester, 1877.

Manchester 1878: Royal Manchester Institution, 1878.

Manchester 1879: Royal Manchester Institution, 1879.

Manchester 1886: Royal Institution Autumn Exhibition, Manchester Art Gallery, 1886.

Marlborough 1957: *XIX and XX Century European Masters*, Marlborough Fine Art Limited, London, 1957.

McLean's 1878: Thomas McLean's Gallery, London, 1878.

McLean's 1880: Thomas McLean's Gallery, London, 1880.

Melbourne 2004: *The Impressionists—Masterpieces from the Musée d'Orsay*, National Gallery of Victoria, Melbourne, 2004.

Milan 1957: *La Mostra Nazionale di Pittura. "L'arte e il convito,"* Palazzo della Permanente, Milan, 1957.

Milan 2017: *Manet e la Parigi moderna*, Palazzo Reale, Milan, 2017.

Moscow 2006: *Chefs-d'œuvre du musée d'Orsay pour le 150e anniversaire de la galerie Tretyakov*, Tretyakov Gallery, Moscow, 2006.

Munich 2018: *Du bist Faust: Goethes Drama in der Kunst*, Kunsthalle München, Germany, 2018.

Nantes 2005: *James Tissot et ses maîtres*, Musée des Beaux-Arts de Nantes, 2005–2006.

National Gallery, London, 1995: *In Trust for the Nation: Paintings from National Trust Houses*, National Gallery, London, 1995–1996.

National Gallery, London, 2002: *Fabric of Vision: Dress and Drapery in Painting*, National Gallery, London, 2002.

New York 1866–1867: *Second Annual Exhibition of French Paintings*, organized by the French Etching Club, Fine Arts Gallery (or Derby Gallery), New York, 1866–1867.

New York 1972: *Drawings Recently Acquired. 1969–1971*, The Metropolitan Museum of Art, New York, 1972.

New York 1983: *Old Master and Nineteenth-Century Paintings, Drawings and Sculpture*, Stair Sainty Matthiesen, New York, 1983.

New York 1989: *Drawings, Prints and Photographs: A Selection*, The Metropolitan Museum of Art, New York, 1989.

New York 1990: *Pierre Bonnard: The Graphic Art*, The Metropolitan Museum of Art, New York, 1990.

New York 2009: *Drawings and Prints: Selections from the Permanent Collection*, The Metropolitan Museum of Art, New York, 2009.

Newcastle 1878: Newcastle Arts Association exhibition, Newcastle-upon-Tyne, England, 1878.

Newcastle 1880: Newcastle Arts Association exhibition, Newcastle-upon-Tyne, England, 1880.

Newcastle 1887: *Royal Jubilee Exhibition*, Newcastle-upon-Tyne, England, 1887.

Ottawa 1965: *Victorian Artists in England*, National Gallery of Canada, Ottawa, 1965.

Ottawa 1978: *The Other Nineteenth Century: Paintings and Sculpture in the Collection of Mr. and Mrs. Joseph M. Tanenbaum*, National Gallery of Canada, Ottawa, 1978.

Palais de Saint-Cloud 1869: Palais de Saint-Cloud, Paris, 1869.

Paris 1866: Cercle de l'union artistique, Paris, 1866.

Paris 1867: Exposition Universelle, Paris, 1867.

Paris 1883: *Exposition des Oeuvres de M. J. J. Tissot*, organized by L'union centrale des arts décoratifs, Palais de l'Industrie, Paris, 1883.

Paris 1885: *Exposition J. J. Tissot: 1re série quinze tableaux sur la Femme à Paris; 2e série tableaux à l'huile, pastels, aquarelles, 3e série eaux-fortes originales, 4e série émaux cloisonnés*, Galerie Sedelmeyer, Paris, 1885.

Paris 1889: *L'exposition Décennale*, Exposition Universelle, Palais des Beaux-Arts, Paris, 1889.

Paris 1894: Société des Beaux-Arts, Champ-de-Mars, Paris, 1894.

Paris 1900: *Exposition rétrospective de la ville de Paris*, Exposition Universelle, Paris, 1900.

Paris 1901: Société des Beaux-Arts, Champ-de-Mars, Paris, 1901.

Paris 1922: *Le décor de la vie sous le Second Empire*, Musée des Arts Décoratifs, Paris, 1922.

Paris 1946: *Les Goncourt et leur temps*, Les Musées Nationaux, Paris, 1946.

Paris 1957: *Le Second Empire*, Musée Jacquemart-André, Paris, 1957.

Paris 1965: *Marcel Proust*, Bibliothèque Nationale de France, Paris, 1965.

Paris 1973–1974: *Dessins français du Metropolitan Museum of Art, New York, de David à Picasso*, Musée du Louvre, Paris, 1973–1974.

Paris 1974: *Le Musée du Luxembourg en 1874*, Galeries nationales du Grand Palais, Paris, 1974.

Paris 1978: *Autour de quelques œuvres du Second Empire*, Paris, 1978.

Paris 1985: *James Tissot*, Petit Palais, Musée des Beaux-Arts de la ville de Paris, 1985.

Paris 1994: *Origins of Impressionism*, Galeries nationales du Grand Palais, Paris; and The Metropolitan Museum of Art, New York, 1994–1995

Paris 2012: *Impressionism, Fashion, and Modernity*, Musée d'Orsay, Paris; The Metropolitan Museum of Art, New York; and Art Institute of Chicago, 2012–2013.

Paris 2014: *7 ans de réflexion: Dernières acquisitions du Musée d'Orsay, 2008–2014*, Musée d'Orsay, Paris, 2014.

Paris 2016: *Spectaculaire Second Empire, 1852–1870*, Musée d'Orsay, Paris, 2016–2017.

Paris-Bruxelles 1997: *Paris-Bruxelles / Bruxelles-Paris*, Galeries nationales du Grand Palais, Paris; and Musée des Beaux Arts de Gand, Ghent, Belgium, 1997.

Paris, Exposition Nationale, 1883: Exposition Nationale, Paris, 1883.

Paris Salon: Paris exhibitions, Palais des Champs-Élysées, 1860–1861, 1863–1865, 1869–1870.

Port Sunlight 1948: *The Pre-Raphaelites—Their Friends and Followers—Centenary Exhibition*, Liverpool Museums, Lady Lever Art Gallery, Port Sunlight, England, 1948.

Preston 1955: *Paintings from Lytham Hall*, Harris Museum and Art Gallery, Preston, England, 1955.

Preston 1955–1956: Harris Museum and Art Gallery, Preston, England, 1955–1956.

Providence and Toronto 1968: *James Jacques Joseph Tissot, 1836–1902, A Retrospective Exhibition*, Museum of Art, Rhode Island School of Design, Providence and Art Gallery of Ontario, Toronto, 1968.

Reading 1882: Reading Museum, England, 1882.

Rome 2015: *James Tissot*, Chiostro del Bramante, Rome, 2015–2016.

Royal Academy: Annual exhibitions, Royal Academy of Arts, London.

Royal Academy 2003: *Pre-Raphaelite and Other Masters: The Andrew Lloyd Webber Collection*, Royal Academy, London, 2003.

Saint-Antoine-L'Abbaye 2004: *Regards sur le Moyen-Age, le XIXe siècle de Viollet-le-Duc*, Saint-Antoine-L'Abbaye, France, 2004.

San Francisco 1959: *All About the Circus*, Legion of Honor, San Francisco, 1959.

San Francisco 1964–1965: *Man, Glory, Jest, and Riddle*, Legion of Honor, San Francisco, 1964–1965.

San Francisco 2010: *Birth of Impressionism: Masterpieces from the Musée d'Orsay*, de Young, San Francisco; and Frist Art Museum, Nashville, 2010.

San Diego 2006: *Personal Views: Regarding Private Collections in San Diego*, San Diego Museum of Art, 2006–2007.

Seoul 2007: *De Millet à Bonnard: La Création Picturale dans les Collections du Musée d'Orsay (1848–1914)*, Hangaram Art Museum, Seoul, 2007.

Sheffield 1955: *James Tissot (1836–1902): An Exhibition of Paintings, Drawings and Etchings*, Graves Art Gallery, Sheffield, England, 1955.

Southport 1892: *Centenary Exhibition of Art Treasures*, Southport, England, 1892.

Taipei 1997: *L'âge d'or de l'impressionnisme—Chefs-d'œuvre du Musée d'Orsay*, National Museum of History, Taipei, Taiwan, 1997.

Tate 1992: *The Swagger Portrait*, Tate, London, 1992–1993.

Tokyo 2010: *Manet et le Paris moderne*, Mitsubishi Ichigokan Museum, Tokyo, 2010.

Tokyo 2014: *Naissance de l'impressionnisme*, National Art Center, Tokyo, 2014.

Tokyo 2016: *Renoir: Chefs-d'œuvre des Musées d'Orsay et de l'Orangerie*, National Art Center / Nikkei Inc., Tokyo, 2016.

Tooth 1886: *Pictures of Parisian Life by J. J. Tissot*, Arthur Tooth & Sons Gallery, London, 1886.

V&A 2011: *The Cult of Beauty: The Aesthetic Movement 1860–1900*, Victoria and Albert Museum, London; Musée d'Orsay, Paris; and de Young, San Francisco, 2011–2012.

***Vanity Fair* 1976**: Vanity Fair, *An Exhibition of Original Cartoons*, National Portrait Gallery, London, 1976.

Vichy 1961: *Exposition d'Ingres à Renoir*, Vichy, 1961.

Vienna 1869: *First Great International Art Exhibition*, Vienna Künstlerhaus, 1869.

Wakefield 2013: *James Tissot: Painting the Victorian Woman*, The Hepworth Wakefield, England, 2013.

Washington 1997: *The Victorians. British Painting 1837–1901*, National Gallery of Art, Washington, DC, 1997.

Washington 2007: *Great Britons, National Portrait Gallery*, Smithsonian Institution, Washington, DC, 2007.

Whitechapel 1887: *St. Jude's Art Exhibition*, Whitechapel Art Gallery, London, 1887.

Whitechapel 1889: *St. Jude's Art Exhibition*, Whitechapel Art Gallery, London, 1889.

Wildenstein 1955: *Marcel Proust*, Wildenstein Gallery, London, 1955.

Yale 1999: *James Tissot: Victorian Life / Modern Love*, touring exhibition organized by the American Federation of Arts and Yale Center for British Art, traveling to Yale Center for British Art, New Haven, Connecticut; Musée du Québec, Québec City; Albright-Knox Art Gallery, Buffalo, New York, 1999–2000.

Zurich 2017: *Gefeiert und verspottet: französische Malerei 1820–1880*, Kunsthaus Zürich, 2017.

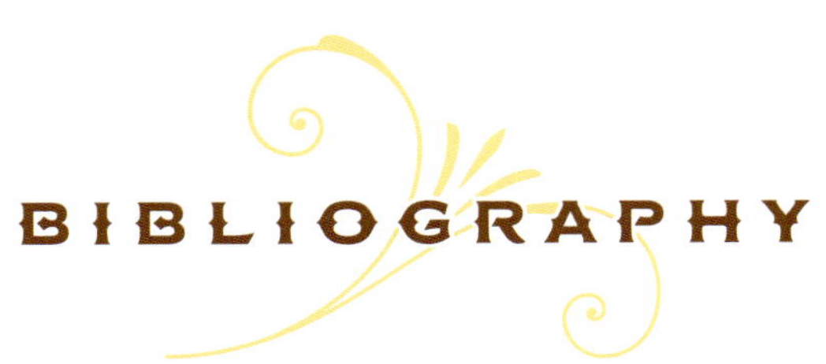

BIBLIOGRAPHY

ABDY 1984 Jane Abdy. "Tissot: His London Friends and Visitors." In *James Tissot*, 40–52. Exh. cat. Barbican Art Gallery, London; and Whitworth Art Gallery, Manchester, 1984–1985. Edited by Krystyna Matyjaszkiewicz. Oxford: Phaidon Press; London: Barbican Art Gallery, 1984.

ABERDEEN PRESS AND JOURNAL 1876 "The Grosvenor Gallery." *Aberdeen Press and Journal*, June 2, 1876, 5.

ABERDEEN PRESS AND JOURNAL 1877 "The Grosvenor Gallery." *Aberdeen Press and Journal*, June 2, 1877, 5.

ABOUT 1864 Edmond About. "Salon de 1864." *Le Petit Journal*, July 6, 1864, 3.

ACADEMY 1877 "Fine Art: The Grosvenor Gallery." *The Academy*, May 5, 1877, 396–397.

ADBURGHAM 1975 Alison Adburgham. *Liberty's: A Biography of a Shop*. London: George Allen & Unwin, 1975.

ALLANIC 1902 Jean Allanic. "Histoire du Collège de Vannes." *Annales de Bretagne et des pays de l'Œest* 18, no. 1 (1902): 59–105.

ALLEY 1981 Ronald Alley. *Catalogue of the Tate Gallery's Collection of Modern Art Other than Works by British Artists*. London: Tate Gallery in association with Sotheby Parke Bernet, 1981.

ANTIQUES TRADE GAZETTE 1985 "Tissot ladies." *Antiques Trade Gazette*, January 19, 1985, 36.

APOLLO 1962 Ferrers advertisement. Clipping, Witt Library, Courtauld Institute of Art, London. *Apollo* (August 1962).

APOLLO 1965 Leger Galleries advertisement. Clipping, Witt Library, Courtauld Institute of Art, London. *Apollo* (August 1965).

APOLLO 1972 Ferrers advertisement. Clipping, Witt Library, Courtauld Institute of Art, London. *Apollo* (July 1972).

APOLLO 1995A Christie's advertisement. Clipping, Witt Library, Courtauld Institute of Art, London. *Apollo* (May 1995).

APOLLO 1995B Sotheby's sale advertisement. Clipping, Witt Library, Courtauld Institute of Art, London. *Apollo* (June 1995).

APOLLO 1995C Phillips sale advertisement. Clipping, Witt Library, Courtauld Institute of Art, London. *Apollo* (September 1995).

ARSCOTT 1999 Caroline Arscott. "The Invisible and the Blind in Tissot's Social Recitals." In *Seductive Surfaces: The Art of Tissot*, 53–76. Edited by Katharine Lochnan. New Haven: Yale University Press, 1999.

ART BULLETIN 1972 Article title unknown. *Art Bulletin*, September 1972.

ARTIST 1882 "The Art of M. Tissot." *The Artist*, August 1, 1882, 235–236.

ART JOURNAL 1864 "Society of British Artists, Suffolk Street: The Forty-First Annual Exhibition." *Art Journal* (May 1864): 150–153.

ART JOURNAL 1868 "French and Flemish Gallery: Fifteenth Exhibition." *Art Journal* (May 1868): 86–87.

ART JOURNAL 1877 "Notes." *Art Journal*, New Series 3 (1877): 64.

ART QUARTERLY 1961 "Accessions of American and Canadian Museums, April–June, 1961." *Art Quarterly* (Autumn 1961): 302, 310.

ART QUARTERLY 1972. Article title unknown. Clipping, Witt Library, Courtauld Institute of Art, London. *Art Quarterly* (1972).

ASTRUC 1859 Zacharie Astruc. *Les 14 stations du Salon: 1859*. Paris: Poulet-Malassis et de Broisé, 1859.

ATHENAEUM 1860 C. [pseud.]. "Belgian Exhibition of Pictures." *The Athenaeum*, September 1, 1860, 291.

ATHENAEUM 1863 "The French Gallery." *The Athenaeum*, April 18, 1863, 527–528.

ATHENAEUM 1864A "Society of British Artists." *The Athenaeum*, April 9, 1864, 513.

ATHENAEUM 1864B "The Royal Academy." *The Athenaeum*, May 14, 1864, 682–684.

ATHENAEUM 1866 "The French Art-Exhibition of 1866." *The Athenaeum*, July 7, 1866, 22–23.

ATHENAEUM 1870A "Fine Arts / The Salon, Paris, 1870 / (Fifth Notice)." *The Athenaeum*, June 11, 1870, 778–780.

ATHENAEUM 1870B "The British Museum." *The Athenaeum*, June 25, 1870, 838.

ATHENAEUM 1873 "The Royal Academy: Second Notice." *The Athenaeum*, May 10, 1873, 603–605.

ATHENAEUM 1874 "Royal Academy (Fourth Notice)." *The Athenaeum*, May 30, 1874, 738.

ATHENAEUM 1876 "Exhibition of Works of Art in Black and White—Dudley Gallery." *The Athenaeum*, June 17, 1876, 836–837.

ATHENAEUM 1877 "The Exhibition of 'Black and White,' Dudley Gallery." *The Athenaeum*, June 16, 1877, 773.

ATHENAEUM 1879A "The Grosvenor Gallery Exhibition." *The Athenaeum*, May 10, 1879, 607.

ATHENAEUM 1879B "Fine Arts: Exhibition of Works in Black and White." *The Athenaeum*, June 14, 1879, 768.

ATHENAEUM 1880 "Exhibition of Works in Black and White, Dudley Gallery." *The Athenaeum*, June 19, 1880, 797–798.

ATHENAEUM 1898 "Minor Exhibitions." *The Athenaeum*, April 2, 1898, 444–445.

AUCKLAND 1962 *British Taste in the Nineteenth Century*. Exh. cat. Auckland City Art Gallery, 1962. Auckland: Auckland City Art Gallery, 1962.

AUCKLAND AND DUNEDIN 2001–2002 *Tissot: Still on Top*. Exh. cat. Auckland Art Gallery Toi o Tāmaki; and Dunedin Public Art Gallery, 2001–2002. Catalogue by Mary Kisler and Sarah Hillary. Auckland: Auckland Art Gallery, 2001.

AUCKLAND CITY ART GALLERY QUARTERLY 1956 *Auckland City Art Gallery Quarterly* 1 (Winter 1956): 3.

BAEDEKER 1881 Karl Baedeker. *Paris and its Environs*. London: Dulau and Co., 1881.

BAETENS 2016 Jan Dirk Baetens. "Alma-Tadema in Antwerp: The Legacy of Henri Leys." In *Lawrence Alma-Tadema: At Home in Antiquity*, 38–47. Exh cat. Fries Museum, Leeuwarden, Holland; Belvedere, Vienna; and Leighton House Museum, London, 2016–2017. Edited by Elizabeth Prettejohn and Peter Trippi. Leeuwarden, The Netherlands: Fries Museum; Munich: Prestel, 2016.

BARLETTA 2006 *De Nittis e Tissot: Pittori della vita moderna*. Exh. cat. Pinacoteca G. De Nittis, Barletta, Italy, 2006. Edited by Emanuela Angiuli and Katy Spurrell. Milan: Skira, 2006.

BARRINGTON 1878 E. I. Barrington. "Is a Great School of Art Possible in the Present Day?" *Nineteenth Century* (April 1878): 714–732.

BASTARD 1906 Georges Bastard. "Nos Peintres. James Tissot. Notes intimes." *Revue de Bretagne et de Vendée*, 2nd series, no. 36 (November 1906): 253–278.

BAUDELAIRE (1863) 1964 Charles Baudelaire. "Le peintre de la vie moderne." Reprinted in *The Painter of Modern Life and other Essays*. Translated by Jonathan Mayne. London: Phaidon Press, 1964.

BEATTIE 1983 Susan Beattie. *The New Sculpture*. New Haven and London: Yale University Press, 1983.

BEDFORD 2002 *J. J. Tissot and His London Circle*. Exh. cat. Cecil Higgins Art Gallery, Bedford, England, 2002. Catalogue by James McGregor. Bedford, England: Cecil Higgins Art Gallery, 2002.

BELL 1959 Quentin Bell. "Forgotten Galleries—VIII: Bristol." *The Listener*, October 29, 1959, 727–728.

BELL'S LIFE 1882 "The Tatler." *Bell's Life in London*, May 13, 1882, 7.

BÉNÉDITE 1909 Léonce Bénédite. *La Peinture au XIXe siècle*. Paris: E. Flammarion, 1909.

BENNETT 1932 Arnold Bennett. *The Journal of Arnold Bennett, 1896–1910*. New York: Viking Press, Inc., 1932.

BENNETT, ED. 1983 Allis Eaton Bennett, ed. *J. B. Speed Art Museum Handbook*. Louisville: J. B. Speed Art Museum, 1983.

BÉRALDI 1892 Henri Béraldi. *Les graveurs du xixe siècle: Guide de l'amateur d'estampes modernes*, vol. XII. Paris: Librairie L. Conquet, 1892.

BESANÇON 1985 *James Tissot, 1836–1902*. Exh. cat. Musée des Beaux-Arts, Besançon, France, 1985. Besançon, France: Musée des Beaux-Arts, 1985.

BETJEMAN 1938 John Betjeman. “Best & Worst of Ouida / A Victorian Eccentric.” *Sunday Times*, June 19, 1938, 9.

BIRMINGHAM DAILY POST 1882 “Gleanings.” *Birmingham Daily Post*, July 28, 1882, 7.

BLACKBURN 1879 Henry Blackburn. *Grosvenor Notes, 1879*. London: Chatto and Windus, 1879.

BLACKBURN 1880 Henry Blackburn. *Grosvenor Notes 1880: No. III*. London: Chatto & Windus, 1880.

BLANC 1859 Charles Blanc. “Considérations sur le costume.” *Gazette des Beaux-Arts* 2 (1859): 542–557.

BLANC 1874A Charles Blanc. “Costumes historiques des XVIe, XVIIe et XVIIIe siècles.” *Gazette des Beaux-Arts* 10 (1874): 542–557.

BLANC 1874B Charles Blanc. *Grammar of Painting and Engraving (Grammaire des Arts du Dessin)*. Translated by Kate Newell Doggett. New York: Hurd and Houghton; Cambridge, MA: Riverside Press, 1874.

BLANCHE 1938 Jacques-Émile Blanche. *Portraits of a Lifetime, The Late Victorian Era, The Edwardian Pageant, 1870–1914*. New York: Coward-McCann Inc., 1938.

BOASE 1893 George Clement Boase. “Charles Thomas Longley.” In *Dictionary of National Biography, 1885–1900*, vol. 34. Edited by Sidney Lee. New York: Macmillan & Co.; London: Smith, Elder & Co., 1893.

BOILLAT 2007 Alain Boillat. *Du bonimenteur à la voix-over: Voix-attraction et voix-narration au cinéma*. Lausanne: Antipodes, 2007.

BOIME 1971 Albert Boime. *The Academy & French Painting in the Nineteenth Century*. London: Phaidon Press, 1971.

BOLTER AND GRUSIN 1999 Jay David Bolter and Richard Grusin. *Remediation: Understanding New Media*. Cambridge, MA: MIT Press, 1999.

BOMFORD 2004 David Bomford, with contributions from Jo Kirby and Ashok Roy. “Degas at Work.” In *Art in the Making: Degas*, 20–43. Exh. cat. National Gallery, London, 2004. Edited by David Bomford. London: National Gallery; New Haven: Yale University Press, 2004.

BORDERLAND 1897 “The Gospel in Pictures by a Spiritualist.” *Borderland: A Quarterly Review and Index* 4 (1897): 178.

BOWLES 1871 Thomas Gibson Bowles. *The Defence of Paris; Narrated as It Was Seen*. London: Sampson Low, Son and Marston, 1871.

BRADFORD OBSERVER 1875 “The Yorkshire Fine Art Galleries.” *Bradford Observer*, June 17 1875, 8.

BRIGHTON 1995 *Brighton Revealed Through Artists' Eyes c. 1760–c. 1960*. Exh. cat. Royal Pavilion Art Gallery and Museums, Brighton, England, 1995. Edited by David Beevers. Brighton, England: Royal Pavilion Art Gallery and Museums, 1995.

BRISTOL 1975 *An Anthology of Victorian and Edwardian Paintings*. Bristol: Bristol Art Gallery, 1975.

BRITISH ARCHITECT 1880 “The Black-and-White at the Dudley Gallery.” *British Architect*, June 18, 1880, 293.

BROOKE 1968 David S. Brooke. “James Tissot and the ‘Ravissante Irlandaise’: Reflections on an Exhibition at the Art Gallery of Ontario.” *The Connoisseur* (May 1968): 55–59.

BROOKE 1969 David S. Brooke. “Tissot's ‘The Parting’.” *Amgueddfa: Bulletin of the National Museum of Wales* 2 (Summer–Autumn 1969): 22–26.

BROOME 1875 F. N. Broome. “Literature and Art in London at the Present Day.” *Evening Hours* 2 (1875): 766–775.

BRUSSELS 1860 *Exposition générale des Beaux-Arts à Bruxelles: Le Salon de 1860*. Exh. cat. Catalogue by Max Sulzberger. Brussels: 1860.

BRUSSELS AND AMSTERDAM 2009–2010 *Alfred Stevens, Brussels–Paris 1823–1906*. Exh. cat. Musées royaux des Beaux-Arts de Belgique, Mercatorfonds, Brussels; and Van Gogh Museum, Amsterdam, 2009–2010. Brussels: Musées royaux des Beaux-Arts de Belgique; Amsterdam: Van Gogh Museum, 2009.

BUDGE 1982 Adrian Budge. “A Note on *The Bridesmaid* by James J. Tissot.” *Leeds Arts Calendar* 91 (1982): 28–30.

BUILDER 1873 “Architecture at the Royal Academy.” *The Builder*, May 3, 1873, 340.

BUILDER 1876 “Works in Black and White.” *The Builder*, June 17, 1876, 587.

BUILDER 1895 “Illustrations / Studio, Château de Buillon.” *The Builder*, June 15, 1895, 452–453.

BUILDER 1897 “Illustrations / Château de Buillon.” *The Builder*, May 1, 1897, 400–401.

BUILDING NEWS 1874 “The interior of the studio, a part of the additions recently completed at the house of M. Tissot—the well-known French artist . . . under the superintendence of Mr J. M. Brydon.” *Building News*, May 1874, 526.

BURLINGTON MAGAZINE 1967 “Notable Works of Art Now on the Market.” *Burlington Magazine* 109, no. 771 (June 1967).

BURLINGTON MAGAZINE 1970A H. Shickman Gallery advertisement. Clipping, Witt Library, Courtauld Institute of Art, London. *Burlington Magazine* 112, no. 803 (February 1970).

BURLINGTON MAGAZINE 1970B Colnaghi advertisement. Clipping, Witt Library, Courtauld Institute of Art, London. *Burlington Magazine* 112, no. 805 (April 1970).

BURLINGTON MAGAZINE 1981 Christie's advertisement. *Burlington Magazine* 123, no. 945 (December 1981).

BURLINGTON MAGAZINE 2005 *Burlington Magazine* 147, no. 1225 (April 2005).

BURNE-JONES 1904 Georgiana Burne-Jones. *Memorials of Edward Burne-Jones, I*. London: Macmillan & Co., 1904.

BURTY 1868 Philippe Burty. “Exposition de la Royal Academy.” *Gazette des Beaux-Arts* 25 (1868): 62.

BUSER 2002 Thomas Buser. *Religious Art in the Nineteenth Century in Europe and America*. Lewiston, NY: Edwin Mellen Press, 2002.

CALLEN 2000 Anthea Callen. *The Art of Impressionism: Painting Technique and the Making of Modernity*. New Haven and London: Yale University Press, 2000.

CALLEN 2019 Anthea Callen. “*L'Impresario*: Degas—or Tissot?” *Fine Arts* (Fall 2019).

CARLYLE 2001 Leslie Carlyle. *The Artist's Assistant: Oil Painting Instruction Manuals and Handbooks in Britain 1800–1900, with Reference to Selected Eighteenth-Century Sources*. London: Archetype Publications, 2001.

CARR 1877 Joseph Comyns Carr. “La Saison d'Art à Londres / II / La ‘Grosvenor Gallery.’” *L'art* 2 (1877): 273.

CARR 1908 J. Comyns Carr. *Some Eminent Victorians: A Personal Recollection of the World of Letters*. London: Duckworth & Co., 1908.

CASTAGNARY 1864 Jules Castagnary. “Salon de 1864.” *Le Grand Journal*, June 12, 1864, 3.

CASSATT 1984 *Cassatt and Her Circle: Selected Letters*. Edited by Nancy Mowll Mathews. New York: Abbeville Press, 1984.

CHARON ET AL. 2018 Philippe Charon et al. *Commerce atlantique, traite et esclavage (1700–1848)*. Rennes: Presses universitaires de Rennes, 2018.

CHESNEAU 1864 Ernest Chesneau. “Salon de 1864.” *Le constitutionnel*, June 14, 1864, 3.

CHICAGO, NEW YORK, AND PARIS 2012–2013 *Impressionism, Fashion, and Modernity*. Exh. cat. Art Institute of Chicago; Metropolitan Museum of Art, New York; and Musée d'Orsay, Paris, 2012–2013. Edited by Gloria Groom. New Haven: Yale University Press, 2012.

CHRISTIE'S 1983 *Christie's Review of the Season, 1983*. Edited by John Herbert. Oxford: Phaidon Press, 1983.

CHRYSLER MUSEUM 1982 *The Chrysler Museum: Selections from The Permanent Collection*. Norfolk, VA: Chrysler Museum, 1982.

CLARETIE 1873 Jules Claretie. “Etudes artistiques, M. James Tissot.” In *Peintres et sculpteurs contemporains*. Paris: Charpentier & Cie, 1873.

CLARKE 1963 A. G. Clarke. “But were these Londoners' Guides?” *The Blue* 90, no. 2 (April 1963).

CLÉMENT 1864 Charles Clément. “Exposition de 1864.” *Journal des débats*, May 12, 1864, 2.

COATS 1968 Alice M. Coats. *Flowers and Their Histories*. London: Black, 1968.

COLVIN 1877 Sidney Colvin. “The Grosvenor Gallery.” *Fortnightly Review*, June 1, 1877, 820–833.

COMMUNE DE PARIS 1997 *Journal officiel de la Commune de Paris*. 3 vols. Cœuvres-et-Valsery, France: Éditions Ressouvenances, 1997.

CONNOISSEUR 1951 M. Bernard advertisement. Clipping, Witt Library, Courtauld Institute of Art, London. *Connoisseur*, June 1951.

CONNOISSEUR 1955 Hammer Galleries advertisement. Clipping, Witt Library, Courtauld Institute of Art, London. *Connoisseur*, March 1955.

CONNOISSEUR 1958 Newman Galleries advertisement. Clipping, Witt Library, Courtauld Institute of Art, London. *Connoisseur*, December 1958.

CONNOISSEUR 1962 M. Newman Gallery advertisement. Clipping, Witt Library, Courtauld Institute of Art, London. *Connoisseur*, November 1962.

CONNOISSEUR 1964 Kaplan Gallery advertisement. Clipping, Witt Library, Courtauld Institute of Art, London. *Connoisseur*, November 1964.

CONNOISSEUR 1978 Article title unknown. *Connoisseur*, December 1978, 272.

CONSTANTIN 2001 Stéphanie Constantin. "The Barbizon Painters: A Guide to Their Suppliers." *Studies in Conservation* 46 (2001): 49–67.

CONZELMAN 2002 Adrienne Ruger Conzelman. *After the Hunt: The Art Collection of William B. Ruger.* Mechanicsburg, PA: Stackpole Press, 2002.

COUNTRY LIFE 1936 Article title unknown. *Country Life*, December 26, 1936.

COUNTRY LIFE 1987 "A Celebration of the Summer House." *Country Life*, July 9, 1987, 97.

DAILY NEWS 1864 "The Bayonne Exhibition." *Daily News*, September 20, 1864, 2.

DAILY NEWS 1876 "Art at the Mansion House." *Daily News*, June 12, 1876, 3.

DAILY NEWS 1880 "The Exhibition of Works in Black and White." *Daily News*, July 1, 1880, 3.

DAILY NEWS 1882 "Modern Art." *Daily News*, May 18, 1882, 6.

DAILY NEWS 1886 "Pictures of Parisian Life." *Daily News*, May 24, 1886, 2.

DAILY NEWS 1894 "The Champ de Mars Salon." *Daily News*, April 24, 1894, 5.

DAILY TELEGRAPH 1879 "The Grosvenor Gallery, Second Notice." *Daily Telegraph*, May 10, 1879, 3.

DARBY 1999 Margaret Flanders Darby. "The Conservatory in St. John's Wood." In *Seductive Surfaces: The Art of Tissot*, 160–184. Edited by Katharine Lochnan. New Haven: Yale University Press, 1999.

DARCEL 1871 Alfred Darcel. "Les musées, les arts et les artistes pendant la Commune." *Gazette des Beaux-Arts* 4 (1871): 285–306, 414–429.

DARGENTY 1885 G. Dargenty. "Exposition de J. J. Tissot." *Courier de l'art*, April 24, 1885, 200.

DE YOUNG 2012A Justine De Young. "Fashion and Intimate Portraits." In *Impressionism, Fashion, and Modernity*, 106–123. Exh. cat. Art Institute of Chicago; Metropolitan Museum of Art, New York; and Musée d'Orsay, Paris, 2012–2013. Edited by Gloria Groom. New Haven: Yale University Press, 2012.

DE YOUNG 2012B Justine De Young. "Fashion and the Press." In *Impressionism, Fashion, and Modernity*, 232–243. Exh. cat. Art Institute of Chicago; Metropolitan Museum of Art, New York; and Musée d'Orsay, Paris, 2012–2013. Edited by Gloria Groom. New Haven: Yale University Press, 2012.

DEGAS 1947 Edgar Degas. *Degas: Letters*. Edited by Marcel Guérin. Translated by Marguerite Kay. Oxford: Bruno Cassirer, 1947.

DES CARS 2007 Laurence des Cars. "Portrait du marquis et de la marquise de Miramon et de leurs enfants." *48/14 La revue du Musée d'Orsay*, no. 25 (Autumn 2007): 43.

DICKENS 1885 Charles Dickens. *Dictionary of Oxford and Cambridge.* London: Macmillan & Co., 1885.

DOLKART 2009A Judith F. Dolkart. "James Tissot, Prodigal Son." In *James Tissot: "The Life of Christ,"* 11–33. Edited by Judith F. Dolkart. London: Merrell Publishers; New York: Brooklyn Museum, 2009.

DOLKART 2009B Judith F. Dolkart. *"The Life of Christ* Comes to the 'Acropolis of Brooklyn.'" In *James Tissot: "The Life of Christ,"* 35–47. Edited by Judith F. Dolkart. London: Merrell Publishers; New York: Brooklyn Museum, 2009.

DOMINO 1874 Un Domino. "Échos de Paris." *Le Gaulois*, December 14, 1874, 1.

DONNELLY 1999 Max Donnelly. "Daniel Cottier, Pioneer of Aestheticism." *Decorative Arts Society Journal* 23 (1999): 32–51.

DROTH, EDWARDS, AND HATT, EDS. 2014 Martina Droth, Jason Edwards, and Michael Hatt, eds. *Sculpture Victorious: Art in an Age of Invention, 1837–1901*. New Haven and London: Yale University Press, 2014.

DRUMMOND 2006 Kent Drummond. "Culture Club: Marketing and Consuming *The Da Vinci Code*." In *Consuming Books: The Marketing and Consumption of Literature*, 60–72. Edited by Stephen Brown. London: Routledge, 2006.

DUBY 2008 Georges Duby, with Guy Lobrichon. *L'histoire de Paris par la peinture*. Paris: Editions Citadelles & Mazenod, 2008.

DU CAMP 1861 Maxime Du Camp. *Le Salon de 1861*. Paris: Librairie Nouvelle, 1861.

DU CAMP 1878 (1883) Maxime Du Camp. *Les Convulsions de Paris* (1878). 4 vols. Paris: Hachette, 1883.

DU MAURIER 1890–1891 George du Maurier. *"Society" Pictures from* Punch. 3 vols. London: Bradbury, Agnew & Co., ca. 1890–1891.

DUPUY 2010 Roger Dupuy. *La Garde nationale: 1789–1872.* Paris: Gallimard, 2010.

EGLINTON 1886 William Eglinton. "The 'Apparition Mediunimique.'" *The Medium and Daybreak* 17, no. 831 (March 5, 1886): 153.

EMMERICH 2003 Anne Catherine Emmerich. *The Dolorous Passion of Our Lord Jesus Christ: According to the Meditations of Anne Catherine Emmerich*. Edited and translated by Klemens Maria Brentano. El Sobrante, CA: North Bay Books, 2003.

ENDICOTT 1965 Vivian Endicott. "Gentleman in a Coach." *Worcester Art Museum, News Bulletin and Calendar*, October 1965, n.p.

ERA 1864 "Society of British Artists." *The Era*, April 3, 1864, 15.

ERA 1874 "Royal Academy Exhibition, No. II: Comedy." *The Era,* May 17, 1874, 12.

EVERYBODY'S WEEKLY 1946 "The Truth about Tissot." *Everybody's Weekly*, June 15, 1946, 6–7.

EXAMINER 1880 "Stray Leaves." *The Examiner*, February 21 1880, 249.

EYRE 1913 Alan Montgomery Eyre. *Saint John's Wood: Its History, Its Houses, Its Haunts and Its Celebrities*. London: Chapman and Hall, 1913.

FAHY, ED. 2005 Everett Fahy, ed. *The Wrightsman Pictures*. New York: Metropolitan Museum of Art, 2005.

FARMER 1890 John Stephen Farmer. *'Twixt Two Worlds: A Narrative of the Life and Work of William Eglinton*. 2nd ed. London: E. W. Allen, 1890.

FLAUBERT AND DU CAMP 1881 Gustave Flaubert and Maxime Du Camp. *Par les champs et par les grèves*. Paris: Charpentier & Cie, 1881.

FILM INDEX 1910 "Vitagraph Notes." *Film Index* 5, no. 4 (January 22, 1910): 10.

FLAIZIK 1960 John N. Flaizik. "Pictorial Literature." *Toledo Museum News*, no. 3 (Spring 1960): 41–45.

FORD 1896 Ford Madox Ford. *Ford Madox Brown: A Record of His Life and Work*. London, New York, and Bombay: Longmans, Green, and Co., 1896.

FOSTER 1998 Gwendolyn Audrey Foster. "Performativity and Gender in Alice Guy's *La Vie du Christ*." *Film Criticism* 23, no. 1 (Fall 1998): 6–17.

FOUCHER 1881 Foucher. "Art Contemporain, Tissot." In *Les Chefs-d'œuvre d'art au Luxembourg*. Paris: L. Baschet, 1881.

FOURNIER 2007 Eric Fournier. *Paris en ruines: Du Paris haussmannien au Paris communard*. Paris: Imago, 2007.

FRASER'S 1863 "The Royal Academy Exhibition." *Fraser's*, June 1863, 783–795.

FREEMAN'S JOURNAL 1874 "Fashion and Varieties." *Freeman's Journal*, December 12, 1874, 6.

GALINOU 1989 Mireille Galinou. "Green-Finger Painting." *Country Life*, July 13, 1989, 120–123.

GALLISSOT 2005 Nathalie Gallissot. "Le Japon rêvé de James Tissot." In *James Tissot et ses Maîtres*, 47–67. Exh. cat. Musée des Beaux-Arts de Nantes, 2005–2006. Catalogue by Cyrille Sciama. Paris: Somogy, 2005.

GARB 1999 Tamar Garb. "Painting the 'Parisienne': James Tissot and the Making of the Modern Woman." In *Seductive Surfaces: The Art of Tissot*, 95–120. Edited by Katharine Lochnan. New Haven: Yale University Press, 1999.

GAUTIER 1855 Théophile Gautier. *Les Beaux-Arts en Europe*. Paris: Michel Lévy Frères, 1855.

GAUTIER (1858) 2015 Théophile Gautier. *De la mode*. Reprinted with an introduction by Ulrich Lehmann and translated by Richard George Elliott. *Art in Translation* 7, no. 2 (2015): 205–211.

GAUTIER 1861 Théophile Gautier. *Abécédaire de Salon de 1861*. Paris: E. Dentu, 1861.

GAUTIER 1864 Théophile Gautier. "Salon de 1864." *Le Moniteur Universel* 169 (June 17, 1864): 1.

GAUTIER 1905 *The Works of Théophile Gautier*. 24 vols. Edited and translated by Frederick C. de Sumichrast. Cambridge, MA: The Jenson Society, 1905.

GAZETTE DES BEAUX-ARTS 1977 "La chronique des arts / Principales acquisitions des musées en 1975." *Gazette des Beaux-Arts* 89, no. 1298 (supplément) (March 1977), 59.

GAZETTE DES BEAUX-ARTS 1994 "La chronique des arts / Principales acquisitions des musées en 1993." *Gazette des Beaux-Arts* 123, no. 1502 (supplément) (March 1994), 21.

GAZETTE DES BEAUX-ARTS 2000 "La chronique des arts / Musées, monuments historiques, expositions." *Gazette des Beaux-Arts* 1754, no. 1573 (February 2000), 6–7.

GERE 2010 Charlotte Gere. *Artistic Circles, Design and Decoration in the Aesthetic Movement*. London: V&A Publishing, 2010.

GIBSON 1989 Ralph Gibson. *A Social History of French Catholicism 1789–1914*. London and New York: Routledge, 1989.

GLASGOW HERALD 1876 "The Royal Academy and Its Honours / Sunday Evening." *Glasgow Herald*, January 3, 1876, 5.

GLASGOW HERALD 1880 "The Black and White Exhibition: Concluding Notice." *Glasgow Herald*, September 28, 1880, 3.

GLASGOW HERALD 1889 "'The Life of Christ' / Illustrated by James Tissot." *Glasgow Herald*, August 17, 1889, 4.

GOETHE (1808) 1962 Johann Wolfgang von Goethe. *Faust: Part 1*. Translated by Peter Salm. New York: Bantam Books, 1962.

GONCOURT 1855 Edmond de Goncourt and Jules de Goncourt. *La Peinture à l'exposition de 1855*. Paris: E. Dentu, 1855.

GONCOURT 1884 Edmond de Goncourt and Jules de Goncourt. *Renée Mauperin: édition ornée de dix compositions à l'eau-forte par James Tissot*. Paris: Charpentier, 1884.

GONCOURT 1895 Edmond and Jules de Goncourt. *Journal: Mémoires de la vie littéraire*. 8 vols. Paris: G. Charpentier, 1895.

GONCOURT 1896 Edmond and Jules de Goncourt. *Journal: Mémoires de la vie littéraire*. 8 vols. Paris: G. Charpentier & E. Fasquelle, 1896.

GONCOURT 1959 Edmond and Jules de Goncourt. *Journal: Mémoires de la vie littéraire*. 3 vols. Edited by Robert Ricatte. Paris: Robert Laffont, 1959.

GONCOURT 1989 Edmond and Jules de Goncourt. *Journal: Mémoires de la vie littéraire*. 3 vols. Edited by Robert Ricatte. Paris: Robert Laffont, 1989.

GONCOURT 2014 Edmond and Jules de Goncourt. *Journal: Mémoires de la vie littéraire*. 3 vols. Edited by Robert Ricatte. Paris: Robert Laffont, 1989. Reprinted 2014.

GOURLEY 1964 Hugh Gourley. "Tissots in the Museum's Collection." *Museum Notes, Bulletin of the Museum of Art, Rhode Island School of Design* (March 1964): 1–11.

GRAPHIC 1873 "The Royal Academy / II." *The Graphic*, June 7, 1873, 539.

GRAPHIC 1874 "Fine Arts / II / Royal Academy." *The Graphic*, May 16, 1874, 474.

GRAPHIC 1875 "Royal Academy Anticipations / II." *The Graphic*, April 3, 1875, 319.

GRAPHIC 1876 "Exhibition of the Royal Academy V." *The Graphic*, May 27, 1876, 523.

GRAPHIC 1877A "Our Illustrations / *The Gallery of H.M.S. 'Calcutta' at Portsmouth*." *The Graphic*, August 18, 1877.

GRAPHIC 1877B "Fine Arts / Continental Gallery." *The Graphic*, December 1, 1877, 523.

GRAPHIC 1877C "Our Illustrations / *In Winter Time*." *The Graphic*, December 15, 1877, 558.

GRAVES 1905–1906 Algernon Graves. *The Royal Academy of Arts: A Complete Dictionary of Contributors and Their Work from Its Foundation in 1769 to 1904*. 8 vols. London: H. Graves and Co. and George Bell and Sons, 1905–1906.

GUIFFAN, BARREAU, AND LITERS 2008 Jean Guiffan, Joël Barreau, and Jean-Louis Liters. *Le lycée Clemenceau à Nantes: 200 ans d'histoire*. Nantes: Librairie Coiffard, 2008.

GUY BLACHÉ 1986 Alice Guy Blaché. *The Memoirs of Alice Guy Blaché*. Edited by Anthony Slide. Translated by Roberta and Simone Blaché. Metuchen, NJ: Scarecrow Press, 1986.

HALÉVY 1964 Daniel Halévy. *My Friend Degas*. Middletown, CT: Wesleyan University Press, 1964.

HALÉVY 1995 Daniel Halévy. *Degas parle*. Paris: Fallois, 1995.

HAMERTON 1869 Philip Gilbert Hamerton. *Painting in France, after the Decline of Classicism. An Essay*. London: Seeley, Jackson, and Halliday, 1869.

HARRIS 1999 Ruth Harris *Lourdes: Body and Spirit in the Secular Age*. New York: Viking, 1999.

HARVARD 1885 Henry Harvard. "Chronique." *Le Siècle*, April 21, 1885, 2.

HOPKINSON 1999 Martin Hopkinson. *No Day Without a Line: The History of the Royal Society of Painter-Etchers 1880–1999*. Oxford: Ashmolean Museum, 1999.

HOPKINSON 2012 Martin Hopkinson. "The Dudley Gallery's 'Black and White' Exhibitions 1872–81." *Print Quarterly* 29, no. 4 (December 2012): 379–395.

HOUSE 1997 John House. *Pierre-Auguste Renoir: La Promenade*. Los Angeles: J. Paul Getty Museum, 1997.

HOUSSAIS 2004 Laurent Houssais. "Les Goncourt et le japonisme." *Cahiers Edmond et Jules de Goncourt* 11 (2004): 59–78.

HUNGERFORD 1993 Constance Cain Hungerford. "'Les choses importantes': Meissonier et la peinture d'histoire." In *Ernest Meissonier*, 162–176. Exh. cat. Musée des Beaux-Arts de Lyon, 1993. Paris: Réunion des musées nationaux, 1993.

HYMANS 1854 Louis Hymans. "Exposition des Beaux-Arts à Bruxelles." *L'Illustration* 12 (July–December 1854): 199–202.

IKEGAMI 1980 Chuji Ikegami. "James Tissot, 'Drawing Master' to Tokugawa Akitake." In *Japonisme in Art: An International Symposium*, 147–155. Edited by Chisaburo Yamada. Tokyo: Committee for the Year 2001, 1980.

IKEGAMI 1988 Chuji Ikegami. "Notes éparses sur Tissot." [In Japanese.] In *James Tissot*, 33–37. Exh. cat. Isetan Museum of Art, Tokyo; Daimaru Museum, Osaka; Mie Prefectural Museum, Japan; Tochigi Prefectural Museum of Fine Arts, Japan; and Yokohama Takashimaya Gallery, 1988. Catalogue by Krystyna Matyjaszkiewicz. Tokyo: Brain Trust Inc., 1988.

ILLUSTRATED LONDON NEWS 1863 "The Exhibition at the French Gallery." *Illustrated London News*, April 18, 1863, 439.

ILLUSTRATED LONDON NEWS 1867 "Exhibition of the French and Flemish Schools." *Illustrated London News*, April 13, 1867, 371.

ILLUSTRATED LONDON NEWS 1874 "Fine Arts. Exhibition of the Royal Academy, Third Notice." *Illustrated London News*, May 16, 1874, 470.

ILLUSTRATED LONDON NEWS 1875A "Works for the Royal Academy Exhibition." *Illustrated London News*, April 3, 1875, 318.

ILLUSTRATED LONDON NEWS 1875B "Royal Academy Exhibition / Fourth Notice." *Illustrated London News*, May 22, 1875, 486.

ILLUSTRATED LONDON NEWS 1876 "Fine Arts: Black and White Exhibition at Paris." *Illustrated London News*, September 9, 1876, 251.

ILLUSTRATED LONDON NEWS 1896 "M. Tissot's Pictures." *Illustrated London News*, April 11, 1896, 474.

ILLUSTRATED LONDON NEWS 1955 "Other Times, Other Customs." *Illustrated London News*, June 25, 1955, 1151.

IPSWICH JOURNAL 1877 "London Notes / (By Our Special Correspondent)." *Ipswich Journal*, May 1, 1877, 2.

IRVINE 2006 Gregory Irvine. *Japanese Cloisonné: The Seven Treasures*. London: V&A Publishing, 2006.

JACKSON 1912 Rev. W. H. Jackson. "*The Life of Christ* (Kalem)." *Moving Picture World* 14, no. 2 (October 12, 1912): 121–124.

JAHRBUCH DER STAATLICHEN KUNSTSAMMLUNGEN IN BADEN-WÜRTTEMBERG 1990 *Jahrbuch der Staatlichen Kunstsammlungen in Baden-Württemberg*, Band 27/1990. Munich and Berlin: Deutscher Kunstverlag, 1990.

JAMES (1877) 1956 Henry James. "The Picture Season in London, 1877." *The Galaxy* (August 1877). Reprinted in *The Painter's Eye: Notes and Essays on the Pictorial Arts by Henry James*. Edited by John L. Sweeney. Cambridge, MA: Harvard University Press, 1956.

J. B. SPEED ART MUSEUM BULLETIN 1964 "Bequest of Mrs. Blakemore Wheeler." *Bulletin of the J. B. Speed Art Museum* 25 (October 1964): n.p.

JONES 2014 Claire Jones. *Sculptors and Design Reform in France, 1848 to 1895: Sculpture and the Decorative Arts*. Abingdon, England; New York: Routledge, 2014.

JOPLING 1925 Louise Jopling. *Twenty Years of My Life, 1867–1887*. London: John Lane The Bodley Head Limited, 1925.

KANSAS CITY AND LIVERPOOL 2008–2009 *The Railway: Art in the Age of Steam*. Exh. cat. Nelson-Atkins Museum of Art, Kansas City, MO; and Walker Art Gallery, National Museums Liverpool, 2008–2009. Catalogue by Ian Kennedy and Julian Treuherz. Kansas City, MO: Nelson-Atkins Museum of Art; Liverpool: National Museums Liverpool, 2008.

KARPELES 2008 Eric Karpeles. *Paintings in Proust*. London: Thames and Hudson, 2008.

KEIL 1992 Charles Keil. *"From the Manger to the Cross*: The New Testament Narrative and the Question of Stylistic Retardation." In *An Invention of the Devil? Religion and Early Cinema*, 112–120. Edited by Roland Cosandey, André Gaudreault, and Tom Gunning. Sainte-Foy, Québec: Presses de l'Université Laval; Lausanne: Payot, 1992.

KESHAVJEE 1999 Serena Keshavjee. "The 'Scientization' of Spirituality." In *Seductive Surfaces: The Art of Tissot*, 213–244. Edited by Katharine Lochnan. New Haven: Yale University Press, 1999.

KIRK 2008 Anna Marie Kirk. "Japonisme and Femininity: A Study of Japanese Dress in British and French Art and Society, c. 1860–c. 1899." *Costume* 42, no. 1 (Spring 2008): 111–129.

KLEINE 1905 *Complete Illustrated Catalog of Moving Picture Machines, Stereopticons, Slides, Films*. Chicago: Kleine Optical Company, 1905.

KONTOU AND WILLBURN, EDS. 2012 Tatiana Kontou and Sarah Willburn, eds. *The Ashgate Research Companion to Nineteenth-Century Spiritualism and the Occult*. Burlington, England: Ashgate, 2012.

LABOURDETTE 2005 Anne Labourdette. "James Tissot et la photographie." In *James Tissot et ses maîtres*, 91–107. Exh. cat. Musée des Beaux-Arts de Nantes, 2005–2006. Catalogue by Cyrille Sciama. Paris: Somogy, 2005.

LACASSE 2000 Germain Lacasse. *Le Bonimenteur de vues animées: Le cinéma "muet" entre tradition et modernité*. Québec City and Paris: Nota Bene / Méridiens Klincksieck, 2000.

LACHAPELLE 2011 Sofie Lachapelle. *Investigating the Supernatural: From Spiritism and Occultism to Psychical Research and Metapsychics in France, 1853–1931*. Baltimore: Johns Hopkins University Press, 2011.

LAGRANGE 1861 Léon Lagrange. "Salon de 1861." *Gazette des Beaux-Arts* 10 (June 1861): 321–347.

LAGRANGE 1864 Léon Lagrange. "Le Salon de 1864." *Gazette des Beaux-Arts* 16 (1864): 501–536.

LAGRANGE 1866 Léon Lagrange. "Exposition de l'union artistique." *Gazette des Beaux-Arts* 20 (1866): 398–400.

LA LIBRE PAROLE 1897 "L'œuvre de J. Tissot." *La Libre Parole*, May 24, 1897, 1.

LANIGAN 2003 Dennis Lanigan. "The Dudley Gallery: Water Colour Drawings Exhibitions 1865–1882." *Journal of Pre-Raphaelite Studies* 12 (Spring 2003): 74–96.

LA PRESSE 1898 "Salle Windsor. Tableau de la Passion." *La Presse*, April 5, 1898, 8.

LA PRESSE 1899 "Chronique des théâtres. Tableaux de Tissot." *La Presse*, October 27, 1899, 3.

L'ARTISTE 1862 "Gravures du numéro / Voie des fleurs, voie des pleurs." *L'artiste* (April 1862): 184–186.

LAVER 1936 James Laver. *"Vulgar Society": The Romantic Career of James Tissot, 1836–1902*. London: Constable & Co., 1936.

LA VIE PARISIENNE 1885 "La Femme à Paris, exposition Tissot." *La Vie Parisienne* 23, no. 18 (May 2, 1885): 255.

LEARD 1997 Lindsay Leard. "The Société des Peintres-Graveurs Français in 1889–97." *Print Quarterly* 14, no. 4 (December 1997): 355–363.

LECAILLON 2016 Jean-François Lecaillon. *Les peintres français et la guerre de 1870*. Paris: Bernard Giovanangeli / Éditions des Paraiges, 2016.

LEEDS, LEICESTERSHIRE, BRISTOL, AND LONDON 1978 *Great Victorian Pictures: Their Paths to Fame*. Exh. cat. Leeds City Art Gallery; Leicestershire Museum and Art Gallery, England; Bristol City Art Gallery; and Royal Academy of Arts, London, 1978. London: Arts Council of Great Britain, 1978.

LEEDS MERCURY 1874 "Special Correspondence / (By Private Telegraph) / London, Monday Night." *Leeds Mercury*, March 10, 1874, 5.

LEEDS MERCURY 1882 "The Dudley Gallery." *Leeds Mercury*, May 18, 1882, 7.

LEEDS MERCURY 1888 "Leeds Fine Art Gallery / Vestibule and Queen's Room—II." *Leeds Mercury*, October 24, 1888.

LEMOISNE 1946–1949 Paul-André Lemoisne. *Degas et son œuvre*. 4 vols. Paris: Paul Brame et C. M. de Hauke, 1946–1949.

LE TEMPS 1885 "Au jour le jour." *Le temps*, no. 8754 (April 18, 1885): 2.

LEVY 1898 Clifton Harby Levy. "James Tissot and His Work." *Outlook* 60, no. 16 (December 17, 1898): 954.

LÉVY, ED. 2017 Sophie Lévy, ed. *Musée d'arts de Nantes: le guide des collections*. Ghent: Snoeck, 2017.

LEWANDOWSKI 2018 Hélène Lewandowski. *La face cachée de la Commune*. Paris: Éditions du Cerf, 2018.

LISSAGARAY (1876) 1990 Prosper-Olivier Lissagaray. *Histoire de la Commune de 1871*. Paris: La Découverte, 1990.

LIVERPOOL MERCURY 1886 "Pictures of the London Season." *Liverpool Mercury*, July 13, 1886, 7.

LOCHNAN 1999 Katharine Lochnan. "The Medium and the Message: Popular Prints and the Work of James Tissot." In *Seductive Surfaces: The Art of Tissot*, 1–22. Edited by Katharine Lochnan. New Haven: Yale University Press, 1999.

LOCHNAN, ED. 1999 Katharine Lochnan, ed. *Seductive Surfaces: The Art of Tissot*. New Haven: Yale University Press, 1999.

LONDON 1882 *An Exhibition of Modern Art by J. J. Tissot*. Exh. cat. Dudley Gallery, London, 1882. Catalogue by James Tissot. London: Dudley Gallery, 1882.

LONDON 1896 *The Life of Our Lord Jesus Christ: 365 Pictures Taken from the Four Gospels, Supplemented by Paintings & Pen & Ink Drawings. Landscape & Figures, Studies Made in Palestine by J. James Tissot*. Exh. cat. Lemercier Gallery, London, 1896. Catalogue by James Tissot. London: Lemercier Gallery, 1896.

LONDON 1933 *In the Seventies: An Exhibition of Paintings by James Tissot, 1836–1902.* Exh. cat. Leicester Galleries, London, 1933. Introduction by Edward Knoblock. London: Ernest Brown & Phillips Ltd., The Leicester Galleries, 1933.

LONDON 1937 *The Second James Tissot Exhibition.* Exh. cat. Leicester Galleries, London, 1937. London: Ernest Brown & Phillips Ltd., The Leicester Galleries, 1937.

LONDON 1955 *Paintings, Drawings and Etchings by James Tissot 1836–1902.* Exh. cat. Arts Council of Great Britain, London, 1955. Introduction by James Laver. London: Arts Council of Great Britain, 1955.

LONDON 1981 *J. J. Tissot: Etchings, Drypoints and Mezzotints*. Exh. cat. Bury Street Gallery, London, 1981. Catalogue by Jane Abdy. London: Frederick Mulder, 1981.

LONDON 1984A *The City's Pictures: A Selection of Paintings from the Collection of the Corporation of London*. Exh. cat. Barbican Art Gallery, London, 1984. London: Barbican Art Gallery, 1984.

LONDON 1984B *The Pre-Raphaelites*. Exh cat. Tate Gallery, London, 1984. Edited by Leslie Parris. London: Tate Gallery / Penguin Books, 1984.

LONDON 1987A *The Image of London: Views by Travellers and Emigrés 1550–1920*. Exh. cat. Barbican Art Gallery, London, 1987. Edited by Malcolm Warner. London: Trefoil Publications in association with Barbican Art Gallery, 1987.

LONDON 1987B *The Private Degas*. Exh. cat. Arts Council of Great Britain, London, 1987. Catalogue by Richard Thomson. New York: Thames and Hudson, 1987.

LONDON 2002 *Fabric of Vision: Dress and Drapery in Painting*. Exh. cat. National Gallery, London, 2002. Catalogue by Anne Hollander. London: National Gallery, 2002.

LONDON AND MANCHESTER 1984–1985 *James Tissot.* Exh. cat. Barbican Art Gallery, London; and Whitworth Art Gallery, Manchester, 1984–1985. Edited by Krystyna Matyjaszkiewicz. Oxford: Phaidon Press; London: Barbican Art Gallery, 1984.

LONDON AND PARIS 2017–2018 *Impressionists in London: French Artists in Exile 1870–1904*. Exh. cat. Tate, London; and Petit Palais, Musée des Beaux-Arts de la ville de Paris, 2017–2018. Edited by Caroline Corbeau-Parsons. London: Tate Publishing, 2017.

LONDON, PARIS, AND SAN FRANCISCO 2011–2012 *The Cult of Beauty: The Aesthetic Movement, 1860–1900.* Exh. cat. Victoria and Albert Museum, London; Musée d'Orsay, Paris; and de Young Museum, San Francisco, 2011–2012. Edited by Stephen Calloway and Lynn Federle Orr. London: V&A Publishing, 2011.

LONDON QUARTERLY REVIEW 1865 "Art. V.1. Ballads and Songs of Brittany." *London Quarterly Review* (July 1865): 406–431.

LONDON REVIEW 1863 "The French and Flemish Exhibition." *London Review*, April 18, 1863, 405–406.

LOSTALOT 1883A Alfred de Lostalot. "James Tissot." In *Société d'aquarellistes français*, 369–384. Paris: Goupil & Cie, 1883.

LOSTALOT 1883B Alfred de Lostalot. "Le musée des arts décoratifs: exposition de MM. Le Comte Lepic et James Tissot." *Gazette des Beaux-Arts* 2, no. 27 (1883): 445–456.

LOYRETTE 1991 Henri Loyrette. *Degas*. Paris: Fayard, 1991.

LOYRETTE 1994 Henri Loyrette. "Portraits and Figures." In *Origins of Impressionism*, 183–231. Exh. cat. Galeries nationales du Grand Palais, Paris; and Metropolitan Museum of Art, New York, 1994–1995. Edited by Henri Loyrette and Gary Tinterow. New York: Metropolitan Museum of Art, 1994.

LUCKHURST 2000 Nicola Luckhurst. *Science and Structure in Proust's À la Recherche du Temps Perdu*. Oxford: Clarendon, 2000.

LUGT 1938–1987 Frits Lugt. *Répertoire des catalogues de ventes publiques intéressant l'art ou la curiosité*. 4 vols. The Hague: Nijhoff, 1938–1987.

LYON 1993 *Ernest Meissonier*. Exh. cat. Musée des Beaux-Arts de Lyon, 1993. Paris: Réunion des musées nationaux, 1993.

MAAS 1975 Jeremy Maas. *Gambart: Prince of the Victorian Art World*. London: Barrie and Jenkins, 1975.

MAEDER 1999 Edward Maeder. "Decent Exposure: Status, Excess, the World of Haute Couture, and Tissot." In *Seductive Surfaces: The Art of Tissot*, 77–93. Edited by Katharine Lochnan. New Haven: Yale University Press, 1999.

MAGAZINE OF ART 1878 "The Grosvenor Gallery." *Magazine of Art* (January 1878): 81–82.

MANCHESTER CITY ART GALLERY 1983 *A Century of Collecting: A Guide to the Manchester Art Galleries, 1882–1982*. Manchester: Manchester City Art Gallery, 1983.

MANCHESTER COURIER 1880 "The Winter Exhibitions: No. II, Woodcuts and Etchings: Fine Art Society (From Our Own Correspondent)." *Manchester Courier and Lancashire General Advertiser*, November 9, 1880, 6.

MANCHESTER EVENING NEWS 1872 "Art, Literature, and Music / Local Notices." *Manchester Evening News*, December 16, 1872, 4.

MANCHESTER GUARDIAN 1864 "The Exhibition of Pictures at the Royal Institution." *Manchester Guardian*, October 18, 1864, 6.

MANCHESTER GUARDIAN 1875 "From our London correspondent." *Manchester Guardian*, February 11 1875, 5.

MANCHESTER GUARDIAN 1893 Article title unknown. *Manchester Guardian*, May 8, 1893, 5.

MANCHESTER WEEKLY TIMES 1877 "Messrs. Agnew's Exhibition." *Manchester Weekly Times*, February 24, 1877.

MANCOFF 2012 Debra N. Mancoff. *Fashion in Impressionist Paris*. London and New York: Merrell, 2012.

MANTZ 1865 P. Mantz. "Salon de 1865." *Gazette des Beaux-Arts* 19 (July 1865): 5–42.

MARSHALL 1999 Nancy Rose Marshall. "Image or Identity: Kathleen Newton and the London Pictures of James Tissot." In *Seductive Surfaces: The Art of Tissot*, 31–41. Edited by Katharine Lochnan. New Haven: Yale University Press, 1999.

MARSHALL 2003 Nancy Rose Marshall. "James Joseph Tissot." In *Pre-Raphaelite and Other Masters: The Andrew Lloyd Webber Collection*, 172–183 and 307. Exh. cat. Royal Academy of Arts, London, 2003. London: Royal Academy of Arts, 2003.

MARTIN 1983 Floyd W. Martin. "D. W. Griffith's *Intolerance*: A Note on Additional Visual Sources." *Art Journal* 43, no. 3 (Fall 1983): 231–233.

MARTIN, ED. 1973 John F. Martin, ed. *J. B. Speed Art Museum Handbook*. Louisville: J. B. Speed Art Museum, 1973.

MATHIEU 1976 Pierre-Louis Mathieu. *Gustave Moreau: Sa vie, son œuvre. Catalogue raisonné de l'œuvre achevé*. Paris: Bibliothèque des Arts, 1976.

MATTHIESEN CA. 1983 Stair Sainty Matthiesen. *Old Master and Nineteenth Century Paintings, Drawings and Sculpture*. New York: Matthiesen, n.d. (ca. 1983).

MATYJASZKIEWICZ 1984 Krystyna Matyjaszkiewicz. "Costume in Tissot's Pictures." In *James Tissot*, 64–77. Exh. cat. Barbican Art Gallery, London; and Whitworth Art Gallery, Manchester, 1984–1985. Edited by Krystyna Matyjaszkiewicz. Oxford: Phaidon Press; London: Barbican Art Gallery, 1984.

MATYJASZKIEWICZ 2011 Krystyna Matyjaszkiewicz. "Tissot, Jacques Joseph [*known as* James Tissot] (1836–1902)." Oxford Dictionary of National Biography, May 19, 2011, doi-org.ezproxy2.londonlibrary.co.uk/10.1093/ref:odnb/68966.

MATYJASZKIEWICZ 2014 Krystyna Matyjaszkiewicz. "I Rivali." In *Un Capolavoro di Tissot in Italia*, 14–21. Florence: Pandolfini Casa d'Aste, 2014.

MATYJASZKIEWICZ, ED. 2019A Krystyna Matyjaszkiewicz, ed. *In Focus:* The Ball on Shipboard, *1874 by James Tissot*. London: Tate Research Publication, 2019.

MATYJASZKIEWICZ, ED. 2019B Krystyna Matyjaszkiewicz, ed. *In Focus:* Summer, *1876 by James Tissot*. London: Tate Research Publication, 2019.

MATYJASZKIEWICZ, ED. 2020 Krystyna Matyjaszkiewicz, ed. *In Focus*: Portsmouth Dockyard, *1877 by James Tissot*. London: Tate Research Publication, 2020.

MATYJASZKIEWICZ 2020 Krystyna Matyjaszkiewicz. "Creating and Meeting Demand: James Tissot's London Replicas." In *Nineteenth-Century British Artists' Autograph Replicas: Auras, Aesthetics and Economics*. Edited by Julie Codell. New York: Taylor & Francis and Routledge, 2020.

MAYER AND MYERS 2013 Lance Mayer and Gay Myers. *American Painters on Technique: 1860–1945*. Los Angeles: J. Paul Getty Museum, 2013.

MEISSONIER 1897 Jean-Louis-Ernest Meissonier. *Ses souvenirs, ses entretiens*. Edited by M. O. Gréard. Paris: Librairie Hachette, 1897.

MÉNARD 1868, 1870, 1888 René Ménard. "Marguerite au rempart d'après Tissot." In *Le Musée universel*. Paris: Goupil, 1868 and 1870; Paris: Librairie Renouard, 1888, unpublished.

MERSON 1861 Olivier Merson. *Exposition de 1861: La Peinture en France*. Paris: E. Dentu, Librairie de la société des gens de lettres, 1861.

MISFELDT 1971 Willard Erwin Misfeldt. "James Jacques Joseph Tissot: A Bio-Critical Study." PhD dissertation, Washington University, 1971.

MISFELDT 1978 Willard Erwin Misfeldt. "James Tissot." In *The Other Nineteenth Century: Paintings and Sculpture in the Collection of Mr. and Mrs. Joseph M. Tanenbaum*, 184–187. Exh. cat. National Gallery of Canada, Ottawa, 1978. Ottawa: National Gallery of Canada, 1978.

MISFELDT 1982 Willard E. Misfeldt. *The Albums of James Tissot*. Bowling Green, OH: Bowling Green University Popular Press, 1982.

MISFELDT 1984 Willard E. Misfeldt. "James Tissot's Abbaye de Buillon." *Apollo* (January 1984): 24–29.

MISFELDT 1986 Willard E. Misfeldt. "James Tissot and Alphonse Daudet: Friends and Collaborators." *Apollo* (February 1986): 110.

MISFELDT 1988 Willard E. Misfeldt. "Lettres de James Tissot." In *Archives de l'art français, publiées par la société de l'histoire de l'art français: nouvelle période, tome XXIX*, 163–168. Paris: Librairie de la société de l'histoire de l'art français, 1988.

MISFELDT 1991 Willard E. Misfeldt. *J.J. Prints from the Gotlieb Collection*. Alexandria, VA: Art Services International, 1991.

MOFFETT 1899 Cleveland Moffett. "J. J. Tissot and His Paintings of the Life of Christ." *McClure's* 12, no. 5 (March 1899): 386–396.

MONGEAU 2017 Gilles Mongeau. "French Culture and Mysticism, 1850–1950." In *Mystical Landscapes: From Vincent Van Gogh to Emily Carr*, 57–66. Exh. cat. Art Gallery of Ontario, Toronto; and Musée d'Orsay, Paris, 2016–2017. Edited by Katharine Lochnan. Munich: DelMonico Books Prestel, 2017.

MONNIER 1995 Gérard Monnier. *L'art et ses institutions en France de la révolution à nos jours*. Paris: Gallimard, 1995.

MONROE 2008 John Warner Monroe. *Laboratories of Faith: Mesmerism, Spiritism, and Occultism in Modern France*. Ithaca: Cornell University Press, 2008.

MONTRÉAL 1897 *Catalogue des œuvres de J. James Tissot: La vie de Notre Seigneur Jésus-Christ*. Exh. cat. Windsor Hall, Montréal, 1897. Toronto: George N. Morang & Cie, 1897.

MOORE 1902 *W. B. Moore's Illustrated and Descriptive Catalogue and Price List of Stereopticons, Lantern Slides, Moving Picture Machines, Accessories for Projection*. Chicago: W. B. Moore, 1902.

MOREAU 1984 Gustave Moreau. *L'assembleur de rêves: Écrits complets*. Edited by Pierre-Louis Mathieu. Fontfroide-le-Haut, France: Fata Morgana, 1984.

MORGAN 2009 David Morgan. "American Holy Land: Tissot's Bible in the National Context." In *James Tissot: "The Life of Christ,"* 49–66. Edited by Judith F. Dolkart.

London: Merrell Publishers; New York: Brooklyn Museum, 2009.

MORISOT 1950 *Correspondance de Berthe Morisot avec sa famille et ses amis: Manet, Puvis de Chavannes, Degas, Monet, Renoir et Mallarmé: documents réunis et présentés*. Edited by Denis Rouart. Paris: Quatre Chemins-Éditart, 1950.

MORISOT 1987 *Berthe Morisot: The Correspondence with Her Family and Her Friends*. Edited by Denis Rouart. Translated by Betty W. Hubbard. Mount Kisco, NY: Moyer Bell, 1987.

MORNING POST 1875 "Fashionable World." *Morning Post*, March 4, 1875, 5.

MORNING POST 1880 "Dudley Gallery." *Morning Post*, June 14, 1880, 6.

MORNING POST 1882 "The Dudley Gallery." *Morning Post*, June 29, 1882, 3.

MOROWITZ 2009 Laura Morowitz. "A Passion for Business: Wanamaker's, Munkácsy, and the Depiction of Christ." *Art Bulletin* 91, no. 2 (June 2009): 184–206.

MORRIS 2009 Michael Morris. *Reel Religion: A Century of the Bible and Film*. New York: Museum of Biblical Art, 2009.

MOSCATIELLO 2008 Manuela Moscatiello. "Léontine e Giuseppe De Nittis: lettere inedite a Edmond de Goncourt e a Jules Jacquemart." *Saggi e Memorie di storia dell'arte*, no. 32 (2008): 269–301.

MOVING PICTURE WORLD 1912 Advertisement for the Tissot Picture Society—"Tissot's World Famous Bible Pictures in Lantern Slides." *Moving Picture World* 14, no. 10 (December 7, 1912): 1024.

MUSÉE NATIONAL DU LUXEMBOURG 1884, 1887, 1892 *Catalogue illustré du musée du Luxembourg*. Paris: L. Baschet, 1884. Reprinted 1887 and 1892.

NANTES 2005–2006 *James Tissot et ses maîtres*. Exh. cat. Musée des Beaux-Arts de Nantes, 2005–2006. Catalogue by Cyrille Sciama. Paris: Somogy, 2005.

NASH, ORR, AND STEWART 1999 S. A. Nash, L. Federle Orr, and M. C. Stewart. *Masterworks of European Painting in the California Palace of the Legion of Honor*. San Francisco: Fine Arts Museums of San Francisco, 1999.

NATIONAL GALLERY OF IRELAND 1981 *Illustrated Summary Catalogue of Paintings*. Dublin: National Gallery of Ireland, 1981.

NATIONAL PORTRAIT GALLERY 1981 *Complete Illustrated Catalogue 1856–1979*. Edited by K. K. Yung. London: National Portrait Gallery, 1981.

NAYLOR 1965 Leonard Naylor. *The Irrepressible Victorian: The Story of Thomas Gibson Bowles*. London: Macdonald, 1965.

NEWCASTLE COURANT 1887 "Royal Jubilee Exhibition / The Art Section." *Newcastle Courant*, April 29, 1887.

NEW HAVEN, QUÉBEC, AND BUFFALO 1999–2000 *James Tissot: Victorian Life / Modern Love*. Exh. cat. Yale Center for British Art, New Haven; Musée du Québec, Québec City; and Albright-Knox Art Gallery, Buffalo, 1999–2000. Catalogue by Nancy Rose Marshall and Malcolm Warner. New Haven and London: Yale University Press, 1999.

NEW PATH 1865 "Notes Here and There." *New Path* 2 (October 1865): 168.

NEW QUARTERLY MAGAZINE 1879 "The Poetic Phase in Modern English Art." *New Quarterly Magazine* (July 1879): 150–165.

NEW YORK 1972 *Drawings Recently Acquired, 1969–1971*. Exh. cat. Metropolitan Museum of Art, New York, 1972. Catalogue by Jacob Bean. New York: Metropolitan Museum of Art, 1972.

NEW YORK 1982 *J. James Tissot: Biblical Paintings*. Exh. cat. Jewish Museum, New York. New York: Jewish Museum, 1982.

NEW YORK DAILY TRIBUNE 1906 "Summer Amusements." *New York Daily Tribune*, July 29, 1906, 5.

NEW YORK TIMES 1885 "Tissot's Novel Art Work / Sketches He Has Made of Women in Paris." *New York Times*, May 10, 1885, 10.

NEW YORK TIMES 1894 "The Champ de Mars Salon / James Tissot's Life of Christ / A Marvellous Series." *New York Times*, June 10, 1894.

NEW YORK TIMES 1898A "The Week in the Art World / Sales and Exhibitions—Tissot's Work—Notes from Europe." *New York Times*, February 26, 1898.

NEW YORK TIMES 1898B "Accident to J. James Tissot / French Artist Bruised and Shaken Up in an Attempt to Board a Madison Avenue Car." *New York Times*, November 19, 1898.

NEW YORK TIMES 1900A "To Buy Tissot's Paintings / Brooklyn Institute Secures an Option on the Collection Illustrating the Life of Christ." *New York Times*, January 25, 1900, 7.

NEW YORK TIMES 1900B "Tissot Paintings on View." *New York Times*, April 21, 1900.

NEW YORK TIMES 1900C "Delegates to See Tissot Pictures." *New York Times*, April 22, 1900.

NEW YORK TRIBUNE 1899 Wanamaker's advertisement for Tissot's *The Life of Christ*. *New York Tribune*, October 27, 1899, 6.

NIBLO 1925 Fred Niblo. "Difficulties Encountered in Making *Ben-Hur*." *Film Daily* 32, no. 58 (June 7, 1925): 23.

NICKELODEON 1911 "Recent Films Reviewed. The Deluge—Vitagraph." *Nickelodeon* 5, no. 7 (February 18, 1911): 195–196.

NINETEENTH CENTURY 1878 "A Familiar Colloquy." *Nineteenth Century* (August 1878): 289–302.

OBSERVER 1875 "Royal Academy / Works of Art Intended for Exhibition." *The Observer*, March 28, 1875, 5.

OBSERVER 1880 "M. Tissot's New Pictures." *The Observer*, November 28, 1880, 1.

OPPENHEIM 1985 Janet Oppenheim. *The Other World: Spiritualism and Psychical Research in England, 1850–1914*. Cambridge, MA: Cambridge University Press, 1985.

PAJOT 2011 Stéphane Pajot. *Nantes: Vieux cafés et commerces*. Saint-Sébastien-sur-Loire, France: Éditions d'Orbestier, 2011.

PALETTA 1866 Paletta. "Art Matters." *American Art Journal* 6, no. 9 (December 22, 1866): 136–137.

PALL MALL 1877 "The Grosvenor Gallery (Second Article)." *Pall Mall Gazette*, May 15, 1877, 12.

PALMER, ED. 1881 John Williamson Palmer, ed. *A Portfolio of Autograph Etchings*. Boston: James R. Osgood, 1881.

PARIS (1861) 1977 *Paris Salon de 1861*. Exh. cat. New York and London: Garland Publishing, Inc., 1977.

PARIS 1883 *Exposition des Œuvres de M. J. J. Tissot*. Exh. cat. Palais de l'industrie, Paris, 1883. Paris: Palais de l'industrie, 1883.

PARIS 1885 *Exposition J. J. Tissot: 1re série quinze tableaux sur la Femme à Paris; 2e série tableaux à l'huile, pastels, aquarelles; 3e série eaux-fortes originales; 4e série émaux cloisonnés*. Exh. cat. Galerie Sedelmeyer, Paris, 1885. Paris: Galerie Sedelmeyer, 1885.

PARIS 1985 *James Tissot*. Exh. cat. Petit Palais, Musée des Beaux-Arts de la ville de Paris, 1985. Edited by Krystyna Matyjaszkiewicz. Paris: Petit Palais, Musée des Beaux-Arts de la ville de Paris, 1985.

PARIS 1988 *Degas inédit. Actes du colloque Degas*. Exh. cat. Musée d'Orsay and École du Louvre, Paris, 1988. Edited by Henri Loyrette. Paris: La documentation française, 1989.

PARIS 1990 *Polyptyques: Le tableau multiple du moyen âge au XXe siècle*. Exh. cat. Musée du Louvre, Paris, 1990. Paris: Réunion des musées nationaux, 1990.

PARRY, ED. 1996 Linda Parry, ed. *William Morris*. London: Philip Wilson for the Victoria and Albert Museum, 1996.

PATTISON 1913 James William Pattison. "An Art Lover's Collection." *Fine Arts Journal* 38, no. 2 (February 1913): 97–111.

PEACOCK 1949 Carlos Peacock. *Painters and Writers: An Anthology*. London: Tate Gallery, 1949.

PEARSALL 2004 Ronald Pearsall. *The Table-Rappers: The Victorians and the Occult*. Stroud, England: Sutton Publishing, 2004.

PENNELL 1902 Elizabeth and Joseph Pennell. *The Life of James McNeill Whistler*. 2 vols. London: William Heinemann, 1902.

PENOT 2017 Agnès Penot. *La maison Goupil: Galerie d'art internationale au XIXe siècle*. Paris: Mare et Martin, 2017.

PERRIER 1855 Charles Perrier. "Exposition universelle des Beaux-Arts. Écoles belge et hollandaise." *L'artiste* 25 (1855): 213–216.

POWELL 2004 Margaret Powell. *Master of the Sea: Charles Napier Hemy RA, RWS*. Penzance, UK: Alison Hodge, 2004.

PRELINGER 1999 Elizabeth Prelinger. "Tissot as Symbolist and Fetishist? A Surmise." In *Seductive Surfaces: The Art of Tissot*, 185–211. Edited by Katharine Lochnan. New Haven: Yale University Press, 1999.

PRESTON 1984 Harley Preston. "Tissot and *Renée Mauperin*." *Apollo* (June 1984): 442–444.

PROUST 1923 Marcel Proust. *À la recherche du temps perdu: La prisonnière*. Paris: Nouvelle revue française, 1923.

PROUST 1955–1956 Marcel Proust. *À la recherche du temps perdu: Le côté de Guermantes*. Paris: La Pléiade, 1955–1956.

PROVIDENCE AND TORONTO 1968 *James Jacques Joseph Tissot: A Retrospective Exhibition*. Exh. cat. Museum of Art, Rhode Island School of Design, Providence; and Art Gallery of Ontario, Toronto, 1968. Catalogue by David Brooke, Michael Wentworth, and Henri Zerner. Providence: Museum of Art, Rhode Island School of Design, 1968.

RANDALL 1979 Lilian M. C. Randall. *The Diary of George A. Lucas: An American Art Agent in Paris, 1857–1909*. Princeton, NJ: Princeton University Press, 1979.

REACH 1850 Angus B. Reach. "Town Talk and Table Talk." *Illustrated London News*, May 4, 1850, 306.

READER 1864 "Exhibition of French and Flemish Pictures." *The Reader*, June 11, 1864, 756.

REFF 1964 Theodore Reff. "Copyists in the Louvre, 1850–1870." *Art Bulletin* 46 (December 1964): 557–558.

REFF 1968A Theodore Reff. "The Pictures within Degas's Pictures." *Metropolitan Museum Journal* 1 (1968): 125–166.

REFF 1968B Theodore Reff. "Some Unpublished Letters of Degas." *Art Bulletin* 50, no. 1 (March 1968): 87–94.

REFF 1976 Theodore Reff. *Degas: The Artist's Mind.* New York: Metropolitan Museum of Art, 1976.

RÉPUBLIQUE FRANÇAISE 1870 "Faits divers." *Journal officiel de la République française*, October 28, 1870, 1667.

REVUE DU LOUVRE 1982 Christie's sale advertisement. Clipping, Witt Library, Courtauld Institute of Art, London. *Revue du Louvre* 4 (1982).

REVUE DU LOUVRE 1993 "Acquisitions." Clipping, Witt Library, Courtauld Institute of Art, London. *Revue du Louvre* 4 (October 1993).

REWALD 1973 John Rewald. *The History of Impressionism*. 4th ed. New York: Museum of Modern Art, 1973.

REY 2011 Xavier Rey. "Le Cercle de la rue Royale (1868) de James Tissot." *La revue des musées de France. Revue du Louvre* 5 (2011): 21–22.

REYNOLDS 1953 Graham Reynolds. *Painters of the Victorian Scene*. London: B. T. Batsford, 1953.

REYNOLDS 1992 Herbert Reynolds. "From the Palette to the Screen: The Tissot Bible as Sourcebook for *From the Manger to the Cross*." In *An Invention of the Devil? Religion and Early Cinema*, 275–310. Edited by Roland Cosandey, André Gaudreault, and Tom Gunning. Sainte-Foy, Canada: Presses de l'Université Laval; Lausanne: Payot, 1992.

RIBEIRO 2016 Aileen Ribeiro. *Clothing Art: The Visual Culture of Fashion, 1600–1914*. New Haven: Yale University Press, 2016.

RIZZI 2006 Mariella Rizzi. "Tissot e l'arte della moda." In *De Nittis e Tissot: Pittori della vita moderna*, 59–73. Exh. cat. Pinacoteca G. De Nittis, Barletta, Italy, 2006. Edited by Emanuela Angiuli and Katy Spurrell. Milan: Skira, 2006.

ROBAUT 1905 Alfred Robaut, with Étienne Moreau-Nélaton. *L'œuvre de Corot par Alfred Robaut: Catalogue raisonné et illustré*. 4 vols. Paris: H. Floury, 1905.

ROBERT 2008 Valentine Robert. "Regards croisés sur la crucifixion: les points de vue du cinéma." *Études de Lettres* 280 (2008/2): 29–52.

ROBERT 2015 Valentine Robert. "La Sainte Face interdite de toile. Apparitions et disparitions du visage du Christ au cinéma." In *Sainte Face, visage de Dieu, visage de l'homme dans l'art contemporain (XIXe-XXe siècles)*, 211–228. Edited by Paul-Louis Rinuy and Isabelle Saint-Martin. Paris: Presses Universitaires de Paris-Ouest, 2015.

ROBERTS 1970 Keith Roberts. "Current and Forthcoming Exhibitions: London." *Burlington Magazine*, May 1970, 323–327.

ROME 2015–2016 *James Tissot*. Exh. cat. Chiostro del Bramante, Rome, 2015–2016. Catalogue by Cyrille Sciama. Milan: Skira, 2015.

ROSENBLUM 1965 Robert Rosenblum. "Victorian Art in Ottawa." *Art Journal* 25, no. 2 (Winter 1965): 140.

ROSENFELD, ED. 1981 Daniel Rosenfeld, ed. *European Painting and Sculpture, ca. 1770–1937, in the Museum of Art, Rhode Island School of Design*. Providence: Museum of Art, Rhode Island School of Design, 1981.

ROSS 1946 Marita Ross. "The Truth about Tissot." *Everybody's*, June 15, 1946, 6–7.

ROSSETTI 1876 William Michael Rossetti. "Fine Art: The Black-and-White Exhibition." *The Academy*, June 17, 1876, 592–593.

ROTHENSTEIN 1947 John Rothenstein. *Modern Foreign Pictures in the Tate Gallery*. London: Tate Gallery, 1947.

ROUGE 1877 Talon Rouge. "The Social Week." *Vanity Fair*, March 3, 1877, 137–138.

ROY 1869 Élie Roy. "Salon de 1869." *L'artiste* 40 (July 1869): 82.

RUSKIN 1903–1912 John Ruskin. *The Works of John Ruskin*. 39 vols. Edited by E.T. Cook and Alexander Wedderburn. London: George Allen and Unwin, 1903–1912.

RUTHERFORD 1984 Jessica Rutherford. "Tissot's Cloisonné Enamels." In *James Tissot*, 78–85 and 96. Exh. cat. Barbican Art Gallery, London; and Whitworth Art Gallery, Manchester, 1984–1985. Edited by Krystyna Matyjaszkiewicz. Oxford: Phaidon Press; London: Barbican Art Gallery, 1984.

SACHS 1965 Murray Sachs. *The Career of Alphonse Daudet: A Critical Study.* Cambridge, MA: Harvard University Press, 1965.

SADDLEMYER 1999 Ann Saddlemyer. "Spirits in Space: Theatricality and the Occult in Tissot's Life and Art." In *Seductive Surfaces: The Art of Tissot*, 139–159. Edited by Katharine Lochnan. New Haven: Yale University Press, 1999.

SAINT-DENIS 2002 *Paris incendié, 21–28 mai 1871*. Exh. cat. Musée d'art et d'histoire, Saint-Denis, France, 2002. Catalogue by Laurence Goux. Saint-Denis, France: Musée d'art et d'histoire, 2002.

SAINT-RAYMOND 2016 Léa Saint-Raymond. "How to Get Rich as an Artist: The Case of Félix Ziem. Evidence from His Account Book from 1850 through 1883." *Nineteenth-Century Art Worldwide* 15, no. 1 (Spring 2016).

SAINT-RAYMOND 2018A Léa Saint-Raymond. "Alberto Pasini, un orientalista italiano al Salon." In *Pasini e l'Oriente*, 43–49. Edited by Paolo Serafini and Stefano Roffi. Milan: Silvana Editoriale, 2018.

SAINT-RAYMOND 2018B Léa Saint-Raymond. *Le pari des enchères: le lancement de nouveaux marchés artistiques à Paris entre les années 1830 et 1939*. PhD dissertation, Université Paris-Nanterre, 2018.

SAINT-RAYMOND 2018C Léa Saint-Raymond. "Les ventes aux enchères de tableaux, arts graphiques et sculptures à Paris (1831–1925): artistes, prix et adjudicataires." Harvard Dataverse, 2018. doi:10.7910/dvn/nmwg23.

SAINT-RAYMOND 2018D Léa Saint-Raymond. "Les ventes de tableaux, arts graphiques et sculptures à Paris en 1831, 1850, 1875, 1900 et 1925: Données pour l'analyse économétrique du prix d'adjudication." Harvard Dataverse, 2018. doi:10.7910/dvn/qpuwi0.

SAINT-RAYMOND 2019A Léa Saint-Raymond. "Artworks by James Tissot, Sold at Auction in Paris During the Artist's Lifetime." Harvard Dataverse, 2019. doi:10.7910/dvn/g5aivc.

SAINT-RAYMOND 2019B Léa Saint-Raymond. "Revisiting Harrison and Cynthia White: Academic vs. Dealer-Critic System." *Arts* (forthcoming, 2019).

SAINT-VICTOR 1864 Paul de Saint-Victor. Article title unknown. *La Presse*, May 26, 1864, 2.

SAN DIEGO 2006 *Personal Views: Regarding Private Collections in San Diego*. Exh. cat. San Diego Museum of Art, 2006. San Diego: San Diego Museum of Art, 2006.

SÁNCHEZ 1997 Gonzalo J. Sánchez. *Organizing Independence: The Artists Federation of the Paris Commune and Its Legacy, 1871–1889*. Lincoln: University of Nebraska Press, 1997.

SATURDAY REVIEW 1863 "The French and Flemish Gallery." *Saturday Review*, May 2, 1863, 567–568.

SATURDAY REVIEW 1866 "Pictures of the Year: VI." *Saturday Review*, July 7, 1866, 16–17.

SATURDAY REVIEW 1867 "Pictures of the Year." *Saturday Review*, March 9, 1867, 302–304.

SATURDAY REVIEW 1875 Article title unknown. *Saturday Review*, June 12, 1875, 756–757.

SATURDAY REVIEW 1877 "Royal Academy IV." *Saturday Review*, June 2, 1877, 671.

SAUNIER 1911 Charles Saunier. *Anthologie d'art français: La peinture XIXe siècle*, vol. 2. Paris: Bibliothèque Larousse, 1911.

SCHAEFER, SAINT-GEORGE, AND LEWERENTZ 2008 Iris Schaefer, Caroline von Saint-George, and Katja Lewerentz. "What Did Impressionists Paint With?" In

Painting Light: The Hidden Techniques of the Impressionists, 40–67. Milan: Skira, 2008.

SCHIFF 1982 Gert Schiff. "Tissot's Illustrations for the Hebrew Bible." In *J. James Tissot: Biblical Paintings*, 19–50. Exh. cat. Jewish Museum, New York, 1982. New York: Jewish Museum, 1982.

SCIAMA 2017 Cyrille Sciama. *Le beau bizarre: Les peintures du XIXe siècle du musée d'arts de Nantes*. Paris: Le Passage, 2017.

SCOTSMAN 1878 "Black and White Exhibition, London." *The Scotsman* (Edinburgh), June 15, 1878, 7.

SÉNÉCHAL AND BARBILLON, EDS. 2011 Philippe Sénéchal and Claire Barbillon, eds. *Dictionnaire critique des historiens de l'art actifs en France de la Révolution à la première guerre mondiale*. Paris: Institut national d'histoire de l'art, 2011.

SERAFINI 2015 Paolo Serafini. "Bought and Sold: Tissot e la Arthur Tooth & Sons Gallery di Londra." In *James Tissot*, 44–49. Exh. cat. Chiostro del Bramante, Rome, 2015–2016. Catalogue by Cyrille Sciama. Milan: Skira, 2015.

SHAW 1895 Albert Shaw. "This Year's Passion Play at Höritz, and Kindred Spectacles." In *Review of Reviews and World's Work: January–June 1895*, 671–674. New York: Review of Reviews, 1895.

SHEPHERD 2013 David J. Shepherd. *The Bible on Silent Film*. New York: Cambridge University Press, 2013.

SHEPHERD 2016 David J. Shepherd. "La naissance, la vie et la mort du Christ (Gaumont, 1906): The Gospel According to Alice Guy." In *The Silents of Jesus in the Cinema (1897–1927)*, 60–77. Edited by David J. Shepherd. New York and London: Routledge, 2016.

SHERARD 1895 Robert H. Sherard. "James Tissot and His *Life of Christ*." *Magazine of Art* 18 (1895): 1–2.

SILVER 1999 Carole G. Silver. "Tissot's Victorian Narratives: Allusion and Invention." In *Seductive Surfaces: The Art of Tissot*, 121–137. Edited by Katharine Lochnan. New Haven: Yale University Press, 1999.

SITAR 2009 Amy Sitar. "The Passion." In *James Tissot: "The Life of Christ,"* 200–201. Edited by Judith F. Dolkart. London: Merrell Publishers; New York: Brooklyn Museum, 2009.

SONTAG 2013 Susan Sontag. *Essays of the 1960s & 1970s*. Edited by David Rieff. New York: Literary Classics of the United States, Inc., 2013.

SPECTATOR 1874 "The Royal Academy (Third Notice)." *The Spectator*, May 30, 1874, 692.

SPECTATOR 1877 "Art. The Grosvenor Gallery (Second Notice)." *The Spectator*, May 26, 1877, 664–665.

SPECTATOR 1878 "Art. The Grosvenor Gallery, Second Notice." *The Spectator*, May 18, 1878, 636–637.

SPECTATOR 1879 "Review of the Grosvenor Gallery Exhibition." *The Spectator*, May 31, 1879, 691.

SPECTOR 1967 Jack Spector. *The Murals of Eugène Delacroix at Saint-Sulpice.* New York: College Art Association of America, 1967.

SPEEL 1986 Erika Speel. "Cloisonné Enamels Made in Europe in the 19th century." *Glass on Metal* 5, no. 3 (June 1986): 37–39.

STALEY 2013 Jeffrey L. Staley. "From the Manger to the Cross." In *Bible and Cinema: Fifty Key Films*, 98–103. Edited by Adele Reinhartz. London and New York: Routledge, 2013.

STANDARD 1881 "The Society of Painter-Etchers." *The Standard*, April 4, 1881, 2.

STEAD 1897 William Thomas Stead. "The Gospel in Pictures by a Spiritualist." *Borderland: A Quarterly Review and Index* 4 (1897): 178.

STENDHAL 1838 Stendhal. *Mémoires d'un touriste*. 2 vols. Paris: Ambroise Dupont, 1838.

STOREY 1899 George Adolphus Storey. *Sketches from Memory*. London: Chatto and Windus, 1899.

STRAHAN, ED. 1879 Edward Strahan, ed. *The Art Treasures of America*. 3 vols. Philadelphia: George Barrie, 1879.

STRAHAN 1882 Edward Strahan. "Tissot and the Medievalists." In *Études in Modern French Art*, 49–64. New York: Richard Worthington, 1882.

STRASDIN 2017 Kate Strasdin. *Inside the Royal Wardrobe: A Dress History of Queen Alexandra*. New York: Bloomsbury Academic, 2017.

SUTTON 1986 Denys Sutton. *Edgar Degas: Life and Work*. New York: Rizzoli, 1986.

SWANSON 1990 Vern G. Swanson. *The Biography and Catalogue Raisonné of the Paintings of Sir Lawrence Alma-Tadema.* London: Garton & Co., 1990.

TAYLOR 1877 Tom Taylor. "Exhibition in Black and White." *The Graphic*, June 23, 1877, 594.

TÉTART-VITTU 2012 Françoise Tétart-Vittu. "The Parisienne." In *Impressionism, Fashion, and Modernity*, 78–83. Exh. cat. Musée d'Orsay, Paris; Metropolitan Museum of Art, New York; and Art Institute of Chicago, 2012–2013. Edited by Gloria Groom. New Haven: Yale University Press, 2012.

THIÉBAULT-SISSON 1902 François Thiébault-Sisson. "J. James Tissot." *Les Arts* 9 (October 1902): 1–8 and cover.

THOMSON 1979 Ian Thomson. "Tissot and Oxford." *Oxford Art Journal* 2 (April 1979): 53–56.

THOMSON 1982 Ian Thomson. "A Study in Leisure: James Tissot's Paintings." *Country Life*, July 29, 1982, 328–329.

THOMSON 1984 Ian Thomson. "Tissot as a Religious Artist." In *James Tissot*, 86–93. Exh. cat. Barbican Art Gallery, London; and Whitworth Art Gallery, Manchester, 1984–1985. Edited by Krystyna Matyjaszkiewicz. Oxford: Phaidon Press; London: Barbican Art Gallery, 1984.

THOMSON 1985–1986 Richard Thomson. "Degas Literature: The Class of 1984." *Master Drawings* 23/24, no. 4 (1985–1986): 551–563.

THOMSON 1988 Richard Thomson. "Book Review of Denys Sutton's *Edgar Degas: Life and Work*." *Burlington Magazine*, March 1988, 239.

THOMSON 2000 Richard Thomson. "James Tissot: Victorian Life, Modern Love." *Apollo* 152 (463) (September 2000): 45–46.

THORÉ 1870 Théophile Thoré (W. Bürger). *Salons de W. Bürger, 1861 à 1868*. 2 vols. Paris: Ve Renouard, 1870.

TILLIER 2004 Bertrand Tillier. *La Commune de Paris: Révolution sans images? Politique et représentations dans la France républicaine (1871–1914).* Seyssel, France: Champ Vallon, 2004.

TILLIER 2017 Bertrand Tillier. "Painters Tested by the Terrible Year, 1870–1." In *Impressionists in London: French Artists in Exile, 1870–1904*, 23–27. Tate, London; and Petit Palais, Musée des Beaux-Arts de la ville de Paris, 2017–2018. Edited by Caroline Corbeau-Parsons. London: Tate Publishing, 2017.

TIMES 1863 "The French and Flemish Schools." *The Times* (London), April 15, 1863, 3.

TIMES 1872 "Exhibition at the Royal Academy." *The Times* (London), May 21, 1872, 7.

TIMES 1874 "Royal Academy / Third Notice." *The Times* (London), July 1, 1874, 5.

TIMES 1877A "The Grosvenor Gallery." *The Times* (London), March 12, 1877, 4.

TIMES 1877B "'Black and White.'" *The Times* (London), June 12, 1877, 4.

TIMES 1878 "The Grosvenor Gallery." *The Times* (London), May 2, 1878, 7.

TIMES 1879A "The Grosvenor Gallery." *The Times* (London), May 2, 1879, 3.

TIMES 1879B "The Grosvenor Gallery." *The Times* (London), May 7, 1879, 3.

TIMES 1886 "M. Tissot's Parisian Pictures." *The Times* (London), May 24, 1886, 9.

TIMES 1894A "The Champ de Mars Salon." *The Times* (London), April 27, 1894, 4.

TIMES 1894B "France / Paris, July 13." *The Times* (London), July 14, 1894, 7.

TIMES 1896 "M. Tissot's 'Life of Christ.'" *The Times* (London), March 26, 1896, 8.

TIMES 1897 "Court Circular." *The Times* (London), June 25, 1897, 10.

TIMES 2008 "The model chosen for a prince's birthday portrait." *The Times* (London), November 14, 2008, 1.

TISSOT 1865 Marcel Tissot. *Le manoir et le monastère: histoire franc-comtoise du quatorzième siècle*. Paris: Ch. Blériot, 1865.

TISSOT 1871–1878 James Tissot. "London from 1871 to 1878." Unpublished album of photographs. Digital copy courtesy of Frédéric Mantion.

TISSOT 1876 James Tissot. *Ten Etchings by J. J. Tissot*. London: J. J. Tissot, 1876.

TISSOT 1899 J. James Tissot. *The Life of Our Saviour Jesus Christ: Three Hundred and Sixty-five Compositions from the Four Gospels with Notes and Explanatory Drawings*. 4 vols. New York: McClure-Tissot Company, 1899.

TISSOT 2009 James Tissot. *The Life of Christ. The Complete Set of 350 Watercolors.* Edited by Judith F. Dolkart. London: Merrell Publishers; New York: Brooklyn Museum, 2009.

TOKYO, OSAKA, MIE, TOCHIGI, AND YOKOHAMA 1988 *James Tissot.* Exh. cat. Isetan Museum of Art, Tokyo; Daimaru Museum, Osaka; Mie Prefectural Museum, Japan; Tochigi Prefectural Museum of Fine Arts, Japan; and Yokohama Takashimaya Gallery, 1988. Catalogue by Krystyna Matyjaszkiewicz. Tokyo: Brain Trust Inc., 1988.

TREBLE 1984 Rosemary Treble. "James Tissot." *Burlington Magazine*, February 1984, 181–182.

UNION LEAGUE OF PHILADELPHIA 1908 *Catalogue of the Works of Art in the Union League of Philadelphia.* Philadelphia: J. B. Lippincott, 1908, 27.

UNION LEAGUE OF PHILADELPHIA 1940 *Catalogue of the Collection of Paintings Belonging to the Union League of Philadelphia.* Philadelphia: Union League of Philadelphia, 1940.

UNIVERSITY MAGAZINE 1879 "A Gossip on the Grosvenor Gallery." *University Magazine*, 1879, 66–70.

VALVERDE 2005 María Fernanda Valverde. *Photographic Negatives: Nature and Evolution of Processes.* 2nd edition. Rochester, NY: Advanced Residency Program in Photograph Conservation, 2005.

VARTIER CA. 1964 J. Vartier. "Derniers 'meubles' à quitter le château de Buillon. Les 5,000 volumes de la bibliothèque de James Tissot." Unknown publication, ca. 1964.

VEGESACK 1997 Alexander von Vegesack. *Thonet: Classic Furniture in Bent Wood and Tubular Steel.* New York: Rizzoli, 1997.

WAGNER 1965 Geoffrey Wagner. 'Art and the Circus." *Apollo* 82, no. 42 (August 1965): 134–136.

WALKLEY 1994 Giles Walkley. *Artists' Houses in London 1764–1914.* Aldershot, England: Scolar Press, 1994.

WARD 1920 Leslie Ward. *Forty Years of "Spy."* London: Chatto & Windus, 1920.

WARNER 1982 Malcolm Warner. *Tissot.* London: The Medici Society Ltd, 1982.

WARNER 1984 Malcolm Warner. "Comic and Aesthetic: James Tissot in the Context of British Art and Taste." In *James Tissot*, 28–37. Exh. cat. Barbican Art Gallery, London; and Whitworth Art Gallery, Manchester, 1984–1985. Edited by Krystyna Matyjaszkiewicz. Oxford: Phaidon Press; London: Barbican Art Gallery, 1984.

WARNER 1999 Malcolm Warner. "The Painter of Modern Love." In *James Tissot: Victorian Life / Modern Love*, 9–21. Exh. cat. Yale Center for British Art, New Haven; Musée du Québec, Québec City; and Albright-Knox Art Gallery, Buffalo, 1999–2000. Catalogue by Nancy Rose Marshall and Malcolm Warner. New Haven and London: Yale University Press, 1999.

WEISBERG 1975 Gabriel P. Weisberg. "Japonisme: Early Sources and the French Printmaker 1854–1882." In *Japonisme: Japanese Influence on French Art 1854–1910.* Exh. cat. Cleveland Museum of Art; Rutgers University Art Gallery, New Brunswick, NJ; and Walters Art Gallery, Baltimore, 1975. Cleveland and Rutgers: Cleveland: Cleveland Museum of Art; New Brunswick, NJ: Rutgers University, 1975.

WEISBERG 1993 Gabriel Weisberg. "Women of Fashion." *Sotheby's Preview*, January 1993, 21.

WENTWORTH 1975 Michael Wentworth. "Tissot's *On the Thames, a Heron.*" *Minneapolis Institute of Arts Bulletin* 62 (1975): 35-49.

WENTWORTH 1978 Michael Justin Wentworth. *James Tissot: Catalogue Raisonné of His Prints.* Minneapolis: Minneapolis Institute of Arts, 1978.

WENTWORTH 1979–1980 Michael Wentworth. "Energized Punctuality: James Tissot's *Gentleman in a Railway Carriage.*" *Worcester Art Museum Journal* 3 (1979–1980): 9–27.

WENTWORTH 1980 Michael Justin Wentworth. "Tissot and Japonisme." In *Japonisme in Art: An International Symposium*, 127–146. Edited by Yamada Chisaburo. Tokyo: Committee for the Year 2001, 1980.

WENTWORTH 1984 Michael Wentworth. *James Tissot.* Oxford: Clarendon Press, 1984.

WENTWORTH 1985 Michael Wentworth. "James Tissot: 'cet être complexe.'" [In French.] In *James Tissot 1836–1902*, 43–53. Exh. cat. Petit Palais, Musée des Beaux-Arts de la ville de Paris, 1985. Edited by Krystyna Matyjaszkiewicz. Paris: Petit Palais, Musée des Beaux-Arts de la ville de Paris, 1985.

WHITE AND WHITE 1965 Harrison C. White and Cynthia A. White. *Canvases and Careers: Institutional Change in the French Painting World.* New York: John Wiley and Sons, 1965.

WHITEMAN 1978 Maxwell Whiteman. *Paintings and Sculpture at the Union League of Philadelphia.* Philadelphia: Union League of Philadelphia, 1978.

WILDE 1877 Oscar Wilde. "The Grosvenor Gallery." *Dublin University Magazine* 90 (July 1877): 125–126.

WILSON-BAREAU 1989 Juliet Wilson-Bareau. "L'année impressioniste de Manet: Argenteuil et Venise en 1874." *Revue de l'art* 86 (1989): 28–34.

WITTMANN 1962 O. Wittmann. "Unchanged View of London." *Country Life* 32, no. 3434 (December 27, 1962): 1663.

WOOD 1976 Christopher Wood. *Victorian Panorama: Paintings of Victorian Life.* London: Faber and Faber, 1976.

WOOD 1986 Christopher Wood. *Tissot: The Life and Work of Jacques Joseph Tissot, 1836–1902.* London: Weidenfeld and Nicolson, 1986.

WOOD 1994 Christopher Wood. *The Pre-Raphaelites.* New York: Crescent Books, 1994.

WOODCOCK 1996 Sally Woodcock. "The Roberson Archive: Content and Significance." In *Historical Painting Techniques: History, Materials, and Studio Practice*, 30–37. Preprints of a Symposium, University of Leiden, the Netherlands, June 26–29, 1995. Edited by Arie Wallert, Erma Hermens, and Marja Peek. Marina del Rey, CA: Getty Conservation Institute, 1996.

WORTH 1928 Jean-Philippe Worth. *A Century of Fashion.* Translated by Ruth Scott Miller. Boston: Little, Brown, and Company, 1928.

WRIGHT 1982 Christopher Wright. "Renoir and Tissot: A Neglected Masterpiece and a Masterpiece to Neglect." *Art and Artists* (November 1982): 25.

ZERNER 1968 Henri Zerner. "James Tissot, De l'Angleterre victorienne au Paris de Marcel Proust." *L'oeil*, April 1968, 22.

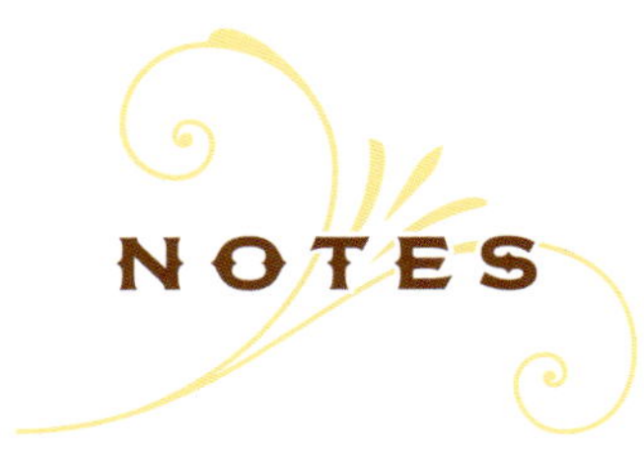

NOTES

THE MYSTERIOUS WORLD OF JAMES TISSOT

MELISSA E. BURON

Epigraph: Blanche 1938, 25. Blanche expresses his personal admiration for Tissot but surmises, "My readers probably know very little about Tissot, that mysterious forgotten figure, ill-judged for complex reasons . . . there seemed a mystery about his disconcerting personality."

1 Excellent secondary sources for more biographical information about Tissot are Misfeldt 1971 and Wentworth 1984.

2 In March 1874, Degas wrote to Tissot: "Look here, my dear Tissot, no hesitations, no escape. You positively must exhibit at the Boulevard. It will do you good, you (for it is a means of showing yourself in Paris from which people said you were running away) and us too. . . . Exhibit. Be of your country and with your friends." (Voyons, mon cher Tissot, pas d'hésitation, ni d'échappée. Il faut que vous exposiez au boulevard. Cela vous fera du bien à vous (c'est une manière de vous faire voir à Paris que des gens vous disent fuir) et à nous aussi. . . . Exposez. Restez de votre pays et avec vos amis.) Degas to Tissot, March 1874, Manuscripts Department, Bibliothèque nationale de France, Paris, NAF 13005, fol. 14r. English translation taken from Degas 1947.

3 The building that Tissot lived in has since been demolished.

4 The anecdote was recounted by the artist Jean-Louis Forain, quoted in Halévy 1995, 157.

5 It is sometimes suggested that Tissot was the father of Newton's second child, Cecil George Newton, however, this claim is less likely than the probability that Newton's children shared the same father. See Wentworth 1984, 126–127, esp. n4; Wood 1986, 86.

6 The complete set of Old and New Testament watercolors totals nearly eight hundred, however, Tissot had not finished the paintings for the Old Testament when he died, so some of these works were completed by other, unidentified artists. Scholars generally accept the signed Old Testament watercolors as autograph.

7 Ward 1920, 102. "Tissot had a strong personality, and from the psychological point of view his story is extraordinary. The woman to whom he was devoted (and who figured so frequently in his pictures) died, and Tissot, overcome with grief, perhaps with remorse, left England and went to the East to seek distraction in foreign travel. . . . He became at first extremely religious, and then the victim of religious mania. Later, he surprised his world by becoming a monk, driven by his devotion to the memory of the dead woman to the extremities which often arise when a strong character is suddenly disrupted by great sorrow. Finally, he entered a monastery, where he eventually lost his reason and died." Louise Jopling also incorrectly claims that after Tissot left London "he went to Rome, and joined the Society of Trappist monks." Jopling 1925, 61. See also Laver 1936, 62–63; Ross 1946, 7.

8 Misfeldt 1982. The three original albums are held in the Michael Wentworth Collection, Ryerson & Burnham Library, Art Institute of Chicago.

9 The exception is a catalogue for prints: Wentworth 1978.

10 Thomson 1985–1986, 561; Thomson 1988, 239.

11 In addition to *Evening* and *Political Woman* Tissot made at least two other variants of this composition. One is in a sketchbook of designs for a series of modern women (ca. 1868–1869; private collection, with copies in the Michael Wentworth Collection, box.ff 3.9), and another is a more finished oil painting of the same composition (private collection). Thanks to Krystyna Matyjaszkiewicz for sharing the latter image. Matyjaszkiewicz, email to author, May 23, 2019.

12 An article authored by Anthea Callen in the September 2019 *Fine Arts* magazine addresses this reattribution from a technical standpoint, with a focus on Tissot's techniques and materials. Callen 2019. This reattribution has also been supported in the author's recent correspondences with other scholars, including Richard Kendall, along with new correspondences with Richard Thomson and Kimberly A. Jones.

13 The private collection includes an actual branding tool with the "JTJ" monogram that features in many architectural details, furnishings and accessories, and works of art found at the château.

14 "Hier, Duplessis me racontait que Tissot, ce peintre plagiaire, avait le plus grand succès en Angleterre. N'a-t-il inventé, cet ingénieux exploiteur de la bêtise anglaise, d'avoir un atelier précédé d'une antichambre, où il se trouve, en tout temps, du champagne frappé à la disposition des visiteurs, et autour de son atelier, un jardin où l'on voit, toute la journée, un domestique en bas de soie occupé à brosser et à faire reluire les feuilles des arbustes?" Edmond de Goncourt, journal entry dated November 3, 1874, quoted in Wentworth 1984, 122.

15 The three albums in the 1982 publication contain black-and-white reproductions of photographs that Tissot used to document his oeuvre. A set of three volumes was exhibited in 1882 at the Dudley Gallery, London, however, the albums in the Wentworth Collection may be a duplicate set created from the originals. Misfeldt 1982, 2. Some images in these albums are the only record of works by Tissot that are now unlocated.

JAMES TISSOT'S YOUTH IN NANTES

CYRILLE SCIAMA

This essay was translated from the original French into English by Rose Vekony.

1 "So, he arrived in London without preparation, without recommendation and without knowing the language of the country, with *one hundred* francs in his pocket. To live, he began by characterizing famous men in an illustrated newspaper with the title: *Vanity Fair*, in other words: Exhibition of Vanities." (Il arriva donc à Londres sans préparation, sans recommandation et ne sachant pas la langue du pays, avec *cent* francs dans sa poche. Pour vivre, il commença par faire la charge des hommes célèbres dans un journal illustré, ayant pour titre: *Vanity Fair*, autrement dit: Foire aux Vanités.) Bastard 1906, 262.

2 See, for example, *Meeting of Faust and Marguerite* (pl. 3), *The Last Evening* (pl. 69), *The Two Sisters; Portrait* (pl. 21), and *Young Women Looking at Japanese Objects* (pl. 38).

3 Tissot may have arrived in Paris in late 1855, as he registered in the Paris National Guard as a resident that year. Misfeldt 1991, 46. In his biographical piece on the artist, Georges Bastard lists Tissot's arrival date as around 1856. Bastard 1906, 257.

4 Lostalot 1883a; Bastard 1906.

5 Some of the research for this essay was conducted at the Archives de Nantes. Specific documents are cited below.

6 Marriage certificate between Marcel-Théodore Tissot and Marie Durand (1E568), Archives de Nantes.

7 Birth certificate of Jacques-Joseph Tissot (1E602), Archives de Nantes. Tissot's three brothers were Marcel-African, born in 1835; Albert, born in 1838; and Olivier, born in 1840.

8 There is no Marcel-Théodore Tissot listed as a merchant on the electoral rolls 1849–1850 (1K3) or 1851–1856 (1K5), Archives de Nantes. Also see *Étrennes nantaises*, 1823–1859, Archives de Nantes.

9 *Étrennes nantaises*, 1823–1859.

10 Nineteenth-century *marchands de nouveautés* typically sold clothes, furniture, housewares, and porcelain. Pajot 2011. According to Bastard, Marie Durand exported hats to the Lesser Antilles. Bastard 1906, 254.

11 On the electoral rolls of Nantes between 1849 and 1850, Marcel-Théodore Tissot is listed as a hat seller living at 1, rue Lamartine, in the Canclaux quarter, a rather bourgeois neighborhood in Nantes. Between 1851 and 1856, a Marcel Tissot, still listed as a hat seller, resides at 1, rue d'Orléans (now Cours des Cinquante-Otages), in the center of Nantes. Electoral rolls 1849–1850 (1K3); electoral rolls 1851–1856 (1K5), Archives de Nantes.

12 "Du haut de la cathédrale, pourtant, on découvre un horizon qui vous récompense de vous être essoufflé à grimper les escaliers: en bas, à pic, les maisons se pressent et tassent leurs toits comme les chapeaux pointus d'une foule qui se serre aux épaules; à gauche, une large prairie se mouille au bord du fleuve large et gris qui se divise et fait un coude, tandis que les deux cours de l'Erdre et de la Sèvre, multipliant leurs bras et leurs îles, découpent la campagne en grandes lignes grises." Flaubert and Du Camp 1881, 78.

13 "Le bonheur de Nantes, c'est qu'elle est située en partie sur un coteau qui, prenant naissance au bord de la Loire, sur la rive droite et au nord, s'en éloigne de plus en plus en formant avec le fleuve un angle de trente degrés peut-être. Les chantiers où je suis occupent la première petite plaine qui se trouve entre la Loire et le coteau. Mais cette Loire n'est point large comme le Rhône à Lyon; Nantes est placée sur un bras fort étroit: ce fleuve, là comme ailleurs, est toujours gâté par des îles. Vis-à-vis des chantiers, ce bras de la Loire est rejoint par un autre beaucoup plus large." Stendhal 1838, 2:11.

14 On the transatlantic slave trade in Nantes, see Charon et al. 2018.

15 Bastard 1906; Lostalot 1883a/b.

16 Jesuit schools were known for their strict education and were mostly attended by children from wealthy families. Allanic 1902.

17 Bastard 1906, 257.

18 Guiffan, Barreau, and Liters 2008.

19 Pajot 2011.

20 The sculpture was commissioned by the duke and duchess's daughter, Anne of Brittany, queen of France, and was sculpted by Michel Colombe

21 These are *The Denial of Saint Peter*, *The Dream of Saint Joseph*, and *The Hurdy-Gurdy Player*. Information about the collections of the Musée des Beaux-Arts comes from Lévy, ed. 2017.

22 Bastard 1906, 256.

23 Sciama 2017, 113–114.

24 Nantes 2005–2006.

25 Bastard 1906, 258.

26 Ibid., 260. This assertion, however, is not supported by amounts recorded in Tissot's sales notebook, published in this volume. According to this ledger, Tissot records earnings of 12,500 francs in 1865, and 19,500 francs in 1866. It is not until 1872 that he nears—in fact, exceeds—70,000 francs a year; he records earnings of 94,515 francs that year.

"ONE GRAM OF HENRI LEYS, TWO GRAMS OF TALENT, ZERO GRAMS OF GENIUS": TISSOT'S EARLY PAINTINGS

JAN DIRK BAETENS

1 Brussels 1860, 119.

2 Tissot made multiple paintings titled *Marguerite in Church*. This painting was most likely one of two owned by the art dealer Goupil & Cie; the exhibition lists Goupil's location on rue Chaptal, Paris, as Tissot's address. In 1860, Goupil bought two works named *Marguerite in Church* from Tissot, one of which was published by Goupil as a photograph in October 1860 (see Wentworth 1984, pl. 6), and the other a reduced-size replica, listed as "réduction partielle" in Tissot's sales notebook in 1860 and recorded in Goupil's stock books on April 9, 1861, as "Marguerite à l'Église / réduction." Both of these pieces are currently unlocated. See "Tissot's Sales Notebook," this volume; Goupil & Cie / Boussod, Valadon & Co. Stock Books, 1846–1919, Getty Research Institute, Los Angeles, getty.edu/research/tools/digital_collections/goupil_cie/books.html.

3 Tissot mentions this trip in an unpublished letter to John Williamson Palmer. Tissot to Palmer, August 31, 1881, John Williamson Palmer Papers, Clifton Waller Barrett Library, accession 8099-a, University of Virginia Library, Charlottesville. Thank you to Krystyna Matyjaszkiewicz for generously sharing this reference. See also Lostalot 1883a, 338–340.

4 Ford 1896, 15–25. See also Powell 2004, 30–32. While there is no evidence that Tissot actually studied with Leys, his voyage was clearly prompted by his enthusiasm for the older artist's work. After the meeting, Tissot continued on to Germany and Switzerland to study paintings by Albrecht Dürer, Hans Holbein, and other fifteenth- and sixteenth-century northern painters to whom Leys's work is so much indebted. Tissot to Palmer, August 31, 1881, Palmer Papers.

5 Wentworth 1984, 24ff.

6 Ibid., 27.

7 See, for example, Gautier 1855, 211.

8 "Tissot, cet être complexe, mâtiné de mysticisme et de roublardise, cet intelligent laborieux en dépit de son crâne inintelligent et de ses yeux de merlan cuit, ce passionné, trouvant tous les deux ou trois ans un nouvel appassionnement, avec lequel il contracte un nouveau petit bail de sa vie." Edmond de Goncourt, journal entry dated January 26, 1890, quoted in Wentworth 1985, 47.

9 London and Manchester 1984–1985.

10 Warner 1984; Warner 1999, 11ff.

11 Goncourt 1855, 28–31.

12 See, for example, Hymans 1854, 199–200.

13 Perrier 1855, 214.

14 Gallissot 2005; Wentworth 1980.

15 Labourdette 2005, esp. 99–105; Wentworth 1980, 138.

16 The portrait has been read in different ways. See Loyrette 1994, 222–223; New Haven, Québec, and Buffalo 1999–2000, 53; Reff 1968a, 133–140; Wentworth 1980, 127–128. For more on this portrait, see Kisiel, this volume.

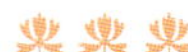

"LOVE, ERROR, AND REPENTANCE": THE FAUST AND MARGUERITE PAINTINGS

MARGARETTA S. FREDERICK

1 Related works include *Marguerite at the Fountain* (fig. 31); *Marguerite at the Window* (1860; location unknown); *Marguerite in Church* (pl. 4); a second painting titled *Marguerite in Church* (1860; location unknown) and a reduced version of this work (1860; location unknown); *Marguerite on the Ramparts* (pl. 6); and *Young Woman in a Church* (1865; Hermitage Museum and Gardens, Norfolk, VA). A small work titled *Faust and Marguerite* (ca. 1858; location unknown) predates these. Two additional unlocated paintings, *At the Break of Day* (ca. 1861) and *The Elopement* (1861), may also reference Goethe's drama; in photographic albums that Tissot kept of his work, they are included in close proximity to the other *Faust* subjects, suggesting a similar time period of creation. See Misfeldt 1982, pls. I-7, I-8, I-19.

2 Also see, for example, Leys's *Faust and Marguerite* (1856; Philadelphia Museum of Art).

3 Between 1848 and 1860, twenty-one paintings referencing *Faust* themes were exhibited at the Salon by eighteen different artists. For a comprehensive list of Salon exhibitions, see Salons et expositions de groupes: 1673–1914, Musée d'Orsay / Institut national d'histoire de l'art, Paris, salons.musee-orsay.fr.

4 While there is no documented evidence of Tissot's having seen Gounod's opera, its immense popular appeal would surely have recommended it to the young artist, newly arrived to the city. In addition, according to a review in the *New York Times* of Tissot's *La Femme à Paris* series, Tissot identified Gounod as his chosen author to write the literary accompaniment to the etching of *Sacred Music*, for a project that was abandoned. *Sacred Music* was listed as no. 15 in the Galerie Sedelmeyer 1885 exhibition catalogue, but perhaps was never completed, as it does not appear in Tissot's albums. Krystyna Matyjaszkiewicz, email to author, March 5, 2019; *New York Times* 1885; Wentworth 1984, 168–169. It is also possible that Tissot may have met Gounod in London, where the latter lived from 1870 to 1874.

5 "M. Tissot illustrated the legend of Marguerite in three paintings that summarize it: *The Meeting of Faust and Marguerite*, *Faust and Marguerite in the Garden*, *Marguerite at the Service*. Is it not, in fact, the whole story of poor Gretchen? Love, error, and repentance." (M. Tissot a illustré la légende de Marguerite en trois tableaux qui la résument: *La Rencontre de Faust et Marguerite*, *Faust et Marguerite au jardin*, *Marguerite à l'office*. N'est-ce pas, en effet, toute l'histoire de la pauvre Gretchen? L'amour, la faute et le repentir.) In Goethe's *Faust*, the character of Margarete (Marguerite) is also known as Gretchen. Gautier 1861, 341. English translation by Rose Vekony.

6 "We recall the beautiful paintings that M. Leys had sent from Belgium to the Exposition Universelle in 1855. They were, with highly distinguished qualities, a rather meticulous pastiche of the naive masters, corrected by modern impasto. These paintings caused a great sensation, and it is natural that a young artist would have tried to imitate them." (On se souvient des beaux tableaux que M. Leys avait envoyés de Belgique à l'exposition universelle de 1855. C'était, avec de très-éminentes qualités, un pastiche un peu minutieux des maîtres naïfs, corrigé par l'empâtement modern. Ces tableaux firent une grande sensation, et il est naturel qu'un jeune artiste ait tenté les imiter.) Du Camp 1861, 97. English translation by Rose Vekony.

7 "I don't believe that Goethe's *Faust* can, given its main character, fall into the domain of visual arts; the creation of *Faust* is purely psychological, and no matter how talented the painter, I doubt he could ever translate the poet's work by his brush." (Je ne crois pas que le *Faust* de Goethe puisse, par son personnage principal, tomber dans le domaine des arts plastiques; la création de *Faust* est pûrement psychologique et, quel que soit le talent d'un peintre, je doute qu'il puisse jamais traduire par son pinceau l'œuvre du poète.) Ibid., 100.

8 The French version of this phrase printed in the Salon catalogue was: "Ma belle demoiselle, oserai-je vous offrir mon bras et ma conduite?" Paris (1861) 1977, 362. It is likely that Tissot read the 1828 French translation of *Faust* by Gérard de Nerval. Nerval's translation was very popular and appeared regularly in new editions throughout the nineteenth century. The original German for this quote is "Mein schönes Fräulein, darf ich wagen, / Meinen Arm und Geleit Ihr anzutragen?" German quotations of *Faust* as well as the English translations are taken from Goethe (1808) 1962.

9 In this scene, titled "A Street" in Goethe's drama, we learn that Marguerite has just come from confession. Mephistopheles explains, "She only left her priest just now / who absolved her soul from every sin." (Sie kam von ihrem Pfaffen, / Der sprach sie aller Sünden frei.) It is not until later, at their meeting in the garden, that Faust asks Marguerite's forgiveness for the earlier intrusion: "Will you forgive the liberty I took, / the impertinence and my brazen words, / when you were coming out of church?" (Und du verzeihst die Freiheit, die ich nahm? / Was sich die Frechheit unterfangen, / Als du jüngst aus dem Dom gegangen?)

10 "Er liebt mich–liebt mich nicht." Mephistopheles refers to flowers as symbols of virginal females, noting in response to Faust's lecherous enchantment with Marguerite: "You talk like Jack the Libertine, / who craves each lovely blossom for himself. / He fancies that all gifts and favors / are free and ready for the plucking; but there are times without successes." (Du sprichst ja wie Hans Liederlich, / Der begehrt jede liebe Blum' für sich, / Und dünkelt ihm, es wär' kein' Ehr' / Und Gunst, die nicht zu pflücken wär'; / Geht aber doch nicht immer an.)

11 In Goethe's scene, Marguerite says, "How once I felt so high and mighty / when some poor girl would go astray; / a stream of words flowed from my busy tongue / to rail at someone else's sins. / When it seemed black, I blackened it some more. / I could never make it black enough, / and blessed myself with head held high, / and now it's me who's steeped in sin."

12 See, for example, Eugène Delacroix, *Marguerite in Church* (ca. 1850; Kunstmuseum Basel, Switzerland).

13 Tissot first met Daudet around 1859/1860, when he rented a studio in the same building as the author on rue Bonaparte, in Paris. Wentworth 1984, 17.

14 Daudet's *chroniques* have been described as "a succession of individual scenes, each colorfully detailed in itself, and calculated at the same time to advance the story one more step." Sachs 1965, 34.

TISSOT AND THE TRAUMAS OF THE "TERRIBLE YEAR"

BERTRAND TILLIER

This essay was translated from the original French into English by Rose Vekony.

1 In 1872, Hugo published his collection of poems about the Franco-Prussian War and its aftermath, titled *L'année terrible*.

2 "Je trouve saisissant son tableau des *Ruines de la Cour des Comptes*. Deux malheureux, presque idiots de douleur et de misère, sont là, l'homme et la femme. L'invisible Christ s'est approché d'eux, il est radieusement couvert d'une chape d'or, mais il l'entr'ouvre devant les misérables . . . et comme pour les consoler, les encourager à souffrir et à supporter, il leur montre son corps ensanglanté de divin martyr." Meissonier 1897, 166.

3 Montréal 1897, 11.

4 Levy 1898.

5 "*Tissot* a de nobles rêves, c'est un épris d'idéal. Il est tout aux sujets religieux maintenant, il va et vient en Palestine, sur les lieux mêmes des faits mémorables." Meissonier 1897, 166.

6 "Colossal effondrement" is Meissonier's phrase, quoted in Hungerford 1993, 175. The Tuileries Palace was the French royal residence until it was burned down by the Paris Commune in 1871.

7 "J'ai voulu faire une espèce de symphonie héroïque de la France." Lyon 1993, 7–8.

8 Saint-Denis 2002, 58–60.

9 Fournier 2007; Lewandowski 2018; Tillier 2004, 341–363.

10 Rouard's series of six oil paintings is titled *Interior Views of the Ruins of the Cour des Comptes* (1888; Musée Carnavalet–Histoire de Paris).

11 "On éprouve devant ces ruines si promptement faites une sensation étrange. Il me semble que deux mille ans aient passé en une nuit et que la rêverie du poète se soit réalisée lorsqu'il se représente Paris à l'état de ville morte et reconnaissable seulement à quelques débris semés sur les bords de la Seine déserte: la colonne couchée dans l'herbe et pareille 'Au clairon monstrueux d'un Titan disparu.'" From *Tableaux de siège (Paris, 1870–1871)*, in Gautier 1905, 20:336.

12 Robaut 1905, 1:249.

13 Tillier 2004, 267.

14 Moreau 1984, 125, 128. Also see Mathieu 1976, 115.

15 The drawing is in the Musée Gustave Moreau, Paris (des. 5871). Paris 1990, 171–173.

16 "J'ai appris à Paris que plusieurs personnes (entre autres Gustave Moreau, le peintre) étaient affectées de la même maladie que moi, c'est-à-dire *l'insupportation* de la foule; c'est une affection commune depuis nos désastres, à ce qu'il paraît." Flaubert to his niece Caroline, Croisset, France, August 22, 1872, flaubert.univ-rouen.fr/correspondance/conard/outils/1872.htm.

17 Edmond and Jules de Goncourt, journal entry dated November 15, 1882, reprinted in Goncourt 1989, 2:966.

18 "It was a dark fury, a frightful bad dream, enraged beings shaking a rain of fire on the dying city." (C'était une furie sombre, un mauvais rêve effrayant, des êtres fous de rage secouant une pluie de feu sur la cité agonisante.) Émile Zola, letter to the newspaper *Le Sémaphore de Marseille*, May 25, 1871.

19 Tillier 2004, ch. 19.

20 Du Camp 1878 (1883).

21 Tillier 2004, 90.

22 Tillier 2017, 23–27.

23 "Paris est vide et se videra encore. . . . De peintres et d'artistes, c'est à croire, à Paris, qu'il n'y en a jamais eu." Quoted in Rewald 1973, 260.

24 Lecaillon 2016.

25 Certificate of enlistment in the National Defense Volunteer Corps (Acte d'engagement dans le corps des volontaires de la défense nationale), Paris, September 30, 1870, Collection Frédéric Mantion.

26 Darcel 1871, 425.

27 Note on letterhead for the First Company of the Tirailleurs de la Seine, October 9, 1870, Collection Frédéric Mantion.

28 In a letter addressed to Tissot, a certain Albert Perrot asks if his brother Jules Perrot, another combatant in the Tirailleurs de la Seine, for whom he provides a photographic portrait, was among the victims of that sortie, which resulted in many fatalities. Perrot to Tissot, October 24, 1870, Collection Frédéric Mantion.

29 *République française* 1870, 1667.

30 Berthe Morisot, letter dated October [18?], 1870, reprinted in Morisot 1987, 56.

31 "C'était pendant la guerre . . . 1870 . . Tissot, James Tissot, celui qui a illustré les Évangiles pour Hachette ; l'a rencontré, lui a dit que Cuvelier [. . .] avait été grièvement blessé au Bourget [*sic*], qu'il l'avait vu. Et Tissot ajoute: 'J'ai fait un dessin, tenez, regardez . . .' Degas étend le bras, la main, écarte son papier, refuse de le voir. 'Vous auriez mieux fait de le ramasser.'" Quoted in Halévy 1995, 157.

32 "J'ai lu avec grand plaisir les détails que vous avez bien voulu me donner sur ce qui a été votre but pendant la Commune." Serionne to Tissot, January 13, 1872 [erroneously dated 1871], Collection Frédéric Mantion. I thank the staff of the Musée d'Orsay, who provided the rich and abundant documentation for this study—in particular Lionel Britten (head of documentation services), Marie-Liesse Boquien (documentalist), and Marine Kisiel and Paul Perrin (curators).

33 M. Mausat-Laroche (on letterhead of the Ministry of Justice) to Tissot, n.d. [spring 1872?], Collection Frédéric Mantion.

34 Dupuy 2010.

35 Bastard 1906, 262–263.

36 " … absent de Paris dans la crainte d'être compromis comme ayant pris part à la Commune." Serionne to Tissot, October 28, 1871, Collection Frédéric Mantion. The Circle of the Mirlitons (Cercle des mirlitons de la place Vendôme), also called the Circle of the Artistic Union (Cercle de l'union artistique), was created in 1860 by the Count d'Osmond (Charles Eustache Gabriel, known as Rainulphe d'Osmond).

37 "On a dit qu'un graveur de Paris avait reçu de vous une lettre qui l'invitait à faire partie d'une Commission nommée par la Commune pour désigner les objets qu'il fallait fondre ou conserver comme étant artistiques. Le graveur aurait montré cette lettre signée *Tis . . . Président de la Commission*. Bref, certains amis ou confrères n'ont pas manqué de vous accuser de participation et d'accord dans les communards et je pourrais vous citer des noms qui n'ont pas été indulgents pour vous." Serionne to Tissot, October 28, 1871.

38 Sánchez 1997; Tillier 2004, 104–112.

39 *Journal officiel de la Commune de Paris* entries May 11, 1871, and May 13, 1871, reprinted in *Commune de Paris* 1997, 3:525, 3:548, respectively.

40 Serionne to Tissot, January 13, 1872 [erroneously dated 1871], Collection Frédéric Mantion.

41 Mausat-Laroche to Tissot, n.d. [spring 1872?]; M. [Sermet?] to Tissot, June 14, 1872, Collection Frédéric Mantion.

42 In French, the phrase is "la plus espionnée." Lissagaray (1876) 1990, 441.

43 "Tissot se fit adopter par les Anglais." Ibid., 440.

44 "La nouvelle génération de peintres gagneurs d'argent et à cheval sur Paris et Londres." Edmond and Jules de Goncourt, journal entry dated February 23, 1878, reprinted in Goncourt 1989.

45 "Tissot, pourquoi diable ne m'avez-vous pas écrit un mot? On m'a dit que vous gagniez beaucoup d'argent. Donnez-moi donc des chiffres." Degas to Tissot, September 30, 1871, reprinted in Paris 1988, 358. English translations of Degas's letters are taken from Degas 1947.

46 Bowles 1871.

47 This print is often interpreted as being inspired by the death of Joseph Cuvelier.

48 "Voyons, mon cher Tissot, pas d'hésitation, ni d'échappée. Il faut que vous exposiez au boulevard. Cela vous fera du bien à vous (c'est une manière de vous faire voir à Paris que des gens vous disent fuir) et à nous aussi. . . . Exposez. Restez de votre pays et avec vos amis." Degas to Tissot, March 1874, reprinted in Paris 1988, 364–365.

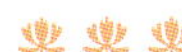

TISSOT AND THE FRENCH MARKET

LÉA SAINT-RAYMOND

I am grateful to Krystyna Matyjaszkiewicz for helping to identify Tissot's artworks sold at Parisian auction.

1 The Paris Salon was a biennial exhibition from 1853 through 1863, then became annual beginning in 1864. Monnier 1995, 124. In 1857, Tissot began logging his sales in an account book (see "Tissot's Sales Notebook," this volume).

2 Wentworth 1984, ch. 6.

3 For comprehensive information and data about the sale of Tissot's artworks at Parisian auction during his lifetime, including results in the minutes of the sales (name of the seller, name of the purchaser, and hammer price), see Saint-Raymond 2019a. In this essay, reference to the sales is given using their Lugt number. Frits Lugt was an art collector and scholar who used his extensive collection of auction catalogues to create a four-volume finding aid for art sales catalogues from the period 1600 to 1925. Lugt 1938–1987.

4 On the connection between the Paris Salon and artistic success, see White and White 1965, 84–92. Other artists that demonstrate this effect are Alberto Pasini and Félix Ziem. Saint-Raymond 2016; Saint-Raymond 2018a.

5 At the Péreire sale (March 6, 1872), a painting titled *The Promenade on the Ramparts* was sold at auction (lot 52, Lugt no. 32968). This was *Walk in the Snow*. Krystyna Matyjaszkiewicz, email to author, February 14, 2019.

6 Salons et expositions de groupes: 1673–1914, Musée d'Orsay / Institut national d'histoire de l'art, Paris, salons.musee-orsay.fr.

7 On Goupil's career, see Penot 2017.

8 See London and Manchester 1984–1985, 98, cat. 1. This now unlocated painting sold at Christie's, London, on June 25, 1998 (lot 333).

9 Lot 63, Lugt no. 29090. This price includes the buyer fee.

10 Lot 15, Lugt no. 32756. This price includes the buyer fee.

11 Once an artist gained recognition at the Salon, he or she was considered *hors concours* (out of competition), and therefore exempt from jury trial.

12 Goupil & Cie / Boussod, Valadon & Co. Stock Books, 1846–1919, Getty Research Institute, Los Angeles, getty.edu/research/tools/digital_collections/goupil_cie/books.html. In 1865, 4,000 francs was the equivalent of about 22,000 dollars in 2018. Historical currency conversions used in this essay were performed at Portal for Historical Statistics, historicalstatistics.org.

13 Lot 65, Lugt no. 35668. This price excludes the buyer fee. This painting appears to be a larger version of *Promenade on the Ramparts* (pl. 8). Krystyna Matyjaszkiewicz, email to author, February 14, 2019.

14 In 1875, the most valued living artists at Parisian auction, based on hammer price, were (in descending order): William-Adolphe Bouguereau, Jules Dupré, Alphonse de Neuville, Narcisse Diaz de la Peña, Eugène Fromentin, Alfred Stevens, Gustave Courbet, Jules Lefebvre, James Tissot, and Félix Ziem. Saint-Raymond 2018b/c.

15 The larger version of *Promenade on the Ramparts* (see n13) appeared in the Fould sale (May 14–15, 1875; lot 65, Lugt no. 35668).

16 After its purchase by Malinet in 1871, the painting *Marguerite in Church* appeared in the auction sale after the death of Hermann Oppenheim (April 23, 1877) and was repurchased for 4,150 francs by Oppenheim's widow (lot 53, Lugt no. 33370).

17 Saint-Raymond 2019a. Also see London and Manchester 1984–1985, 99. For Leys's influence on Tissot, see Baetens, this volume.

18 Tissot stopped participating in the Salon from 1871 to 1883, apart from exhibiting two etchings, *Quarrelling* (1876; Wentworth 18) and *The Thames* (1876; Wentworth 20), in 1876. He returned in 1883, showing the *Prodigal Son* series (pls. 86–89) at the *Exposition nationale des Beaux-Arts*. Afterward, he exhibited work with the Société des pastellistes, the Société des peintres-graveurs, and the Société des aquarellistes rather than the Salon until the 1890s. In 1894, he exhibited at the Salon 270 watercolors from his series of biblical watercolors, *The Life of Christ* (pls. 144–156), and in 1897, *The Reception in Jerusalem of the Apostolic Legate from the Holy See, S. E. Mgr. Cardinal Langénieux by the Patriarch S. B. Mgr. Piavi* (1897; formerly Reims Cathedral, destroyed in World War I). Salons et expositions de groupes: 1673–1914.

19 Tissot did exhibit fifteen modern female portraits at the prominent Galerie Sedelmeyer in Paris from April through June 1885. Wentworth 1984, 205–206.

20 Goupil & Cie / Boussod, 1846–1919; "Tissot's Sales Notebook," this volume.

21 Saint-Raymond 2019a.

22 Lot 10, Lugt no. 37266. This price excludes the buyer fee. According to the auction catalogue, the seller was the painter Ferdinand Roybet, but according to the minute, the sale combined artworks from two sellers: Roybet and Brame. Procès-verbal, D48E3 66, Archives de Paris.

23 After purchasing this painting in 1871, Malinet most likely then sold the artwork to Oppenheim in the 1870s. During the 1877 Oppenheim sale is when his widow repurchased the painting for 4,150 francs (lot 53, Lugt no. 37370). This price excludes the buyer fee.

24 Lots 70 and 71, Lugt no. 54434.

25 Lots 5 and 6, Lugt no. 56377. This price excludes the buyer fee.

26 Saint-Raymond 2018d.

27 According to Gibbs family records, Goupil sold the painting to Gibbs in 1879 for 315 pounds (7,957 francs). London and Manchester 1984–1985, 98. However, Goupil's stock book records the sale of a "Marguerite" in 1879 for 6,125 francs. Goupil & Cie / Boussod, 1846–1919, record no. G-20739.

28 The exact identity of this work is not certain. It may be the painting Tissot listed as *The Confessional (green dress)* (see "Tissot's Sales Notebook," this volume), sold to Goupil in 1869 and recorded in Goupil's books as *La Penitente*, then sold on to Vincent van Gogh in 1871 before Goupil bought it back in 1880, recording it as *Confessional*. Or it may be a replica of this 1869 painting.

29 Goupil & Cie / Boussod, 1846–1919, record nos. G-21763, G-22871, G-24708, G-24845.

30 M. Knoedler & Co. records, ca. 1848–1971, Knoedler Gallery Archive, Getty Research Institute, Los Angeles, getty.edu/research/special_collections/notable/knoedler.html; "Tissot's Sales Notebook," this volume.

31 Ibid., record no. K-6172.

32 Lot 27, Lugt no. 40713. At the sale, this painting was listed as *A Luncheon Before Leaving*.

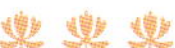

LOOKING BEYOND PARIS: TISSOT'S RECEPTION IN ENGLAND DURING THE 1860S

PETER TRIPPI

1 Even Tissot's appearances at small venues were mentioned; on March 9, 1867, for example, the *Saturday Review* noted that he was participating in the winter exhibition of Paris's Circle of the Artistic Union (Cercle de l'union artistique). *Saturday Review* 1867, 302.

2 "Leys has, to a very great extent, really done in relation to the Netherlandish painters of the fifteenth and sixteenth centuries, what, from their name, we might have expected from, but has not been attempted by, the modern pre-Raphaelites in relation to the early Italian painters." *Illustrated London News* 1863.

3 *Athenaeum* 1860. Margaret (in French, "Marguerite") is a character in Goethe's two-part tragic play *Faust* (1808).

4 *Walk in the Snow* was no. 197 at the 1862 International Exhibition, and was lent by the financier and art collector Émile Péreire. See Wentworth 1984, pl. 1.

5 Although the official publication year of *Ballads and Songs of Brittany* is listed as 1865, an advertisement in the December 24, 1864, issue of *The Athenaeum* indicates that the publisher, Macmillan & Co., made copies available on that day. The book features Taylor's translations of the

Barsaz-Breis collection of Breton popular songs formed by Vicomte Hersart de la Villemarqué.

6 Tissot's frontispiece depicts "The Murdered Lady, Child, Hound, and Horse, in a Breton Cemetery," while his title page shows a mounted knight with his page and a shepherdess with her flock near a seaside castle. For the frontispiece, he reused the pose from his paintings *Marguerite in Church* (pl. 4) and *Marguerite on the Ramparts* (pl. 6). See London and Manchester 1984–1985, 99, cat. 6. Tissot was paid 1,000 francs for the two drawings, engraved by an unknown artist for publication. See "Tissot's Sales Notebook," this volume.

7 "Rossetti was deeply impressed by the present work, writing to his friend Alexander Macmillan: 'I have seen the frontispiece & vignette to Tom Taylor's Breton Ballads designed by Tissot, which are admirable things. Could you as their publisher let me have a proof of each separate from the work?' Macmillan responded with the gift of a drawing, possibly the present one." Archived catalogue entry for Tissot's drawing of "The Crusader's Wife," prepared by Peter Nahum at the Leicester Galleries, leicestergalleries.com/19th-20th-century-paintings/d/the-crusaders-wife-from-breton-ballad/15190. Nahum cites Lona Mosk Packer, ed., *The Rossetti–Macmillan Letters* (1963), 41, letter no. 33, February 3, 1865. The current location of this drawing is unknown.

8 In 1861, Gambart had handed over management of the French Gallery to Henry Wallis, with support for French and Belgian material from Léon Lefèvre and Jean Pilgeram. Krystyna Matyjaszkiewicz, email to author, February 19, 2019.

9 Reviews of these three submissions were mixed. First shown at the 1861 Salon, *During the Service* (also known as *Martin Luther's Doubts*, pl. 5) was exhibited at the French Gallery in 1863 as *Young Luther in Church*. The work was described by the *Saturday Review* as a "laboured attempt to produce effect by mere costume and detail." *Saturday Review* 1863, 568. Of *Faust and Marguerite in the Garden* (fig. 30), the *London Review* said it was "repulsive in colour." *London Review* 1863, 406. Tissot's third submission was another holdover from the 1861 Salon, *Way of Flowers, Way of Tears*, exhibited at the French Gallery as *Dance of Death* (pl. 7), which *The Athenaeum* called "a subject in which the old German masters took grim delight." *Athenaeum* 1863, 528.

10 Baetens 2016, 46–47.

11 Gambart was initially impressed by Alma-Tadema's Leysian *Coming out of Church*, also known as *Leaving Church in the Fifteenth Century* (ca. 1864; La Colección Pérez Simón, Mexico City). Alma-Tadema's *Birthday Presents in the Sixteenth Century* (1865; location unknown) was commissioned by Gambart in 1865, and was exhibited at the French Gallery that year. The Roman scene *Returning Home from Market* (1865; location unknown), also commissioned in 1865, appeared at the French Gallery in 1866. Swanson 1990, 133. For evidence of Tissot's sales to other dealers, see "Tissot's Sales Notebook," this volume.

12 Exhibited at the Royal Manchester Institution as *The Departure of the Betrothed Soldier*, this work earned mixed reviews in *The Reader* and the *Manchester Guardian*. *Manchester Guardian* 1864; *Reader* 1864. Also see Wentworth 1984, pl. 13. A year earlier, in 1863, Tissot also exhibited a work titled *Margaret in the Church* at the Liverpool Institution. Krystyna Matyjaszkiewicz, email to author, February 19, 2019.

13 *At the Break of Day*, exhibited later that year at the Royal Manchester Institution as *The Duel*, was described by *The Athenaeum* as "a snow-scene in a mediaeval town. . . . In the mid-distance of the vista lies the body of a man at the foot of a crucifix . . . in the front, a passenger retreats in fear. . . . The effect is veiled moonlight." *Athenaeum* 1864b, 684. See Misfeldt 1982, pl. I-18.

14 Few critics mentioned Tissot's other submission to the 1864 Society of British Artists exhibition, *The Elopement* (1861; location unknown), although *The Athenaeum* described it as an "exceedingly effective study of night, with thin snow on the ground." *Athenaeum* 1864a. See Misfeldt 1982, pl. I-19.

15 *Art Journal* 1864, 151. The critic also noted that "a picture has no right to pretend to be an archaeological curiosity."

16 Reach 1850.

17 *Illustrated London News* 1867. This was a review of the 1867 French and Flemish Exhibition, to which Tissot had submitted *Holy Prayer*. My thanks to Krystyna Matyjaszkiewicz, who notes that this is probably the medievalizing painting that Tissot exhibited at the 1866 Paris Salon as *Young Woman in a Church* (1865; Hermitage Museum and Gardens, Norfolk, VA). Krystyna Matyjaszkiewicz, email to author, February 19, 2019.

18 Tissot's Faustian pictures did not disappear altogether, however. His first version of *Dance of Death* (1859; location unknown), for example, was exhibited at the 1871 London International Exhibition and sold for 7,000 francs (see "Tissot's Sales Notebook," this volume).

19 This painting was no. 298 at the Royal Academy. The difficult process of selling it is described in the catalogue for the exhibition *The Pre-Raphaelites* (Tate Gallery, London, 1984). London 1984b, 173. In the catalogue, the gallery curators also cite Millais's *Leisure Hours* (1864; Detroit Institute of Arts), which he premiered at the Royal Academy in 1864 (no. 289), as an example of his "strange solemnity." Ibid., 203.

20 The June 1866 issue of the journal *London Society* reproduced this painting as *Leaving the Confessional*. In 1866, it was sold by Tissot to the art dealer Adolphe Goupil, but appears to have subsequently been owned by the British collector Humphrey Roberts. "Tissot's Sales Notebook," this volume.

21 *Saturday Review* 1866, 17.

22 *Athenaeum* 1866, 23.

23 This was the sequel to Hamerton's book *Contemporary French Painters* (1867).

24 Hamerton 1869, 55.

25 Wentworth 1984, 54. Wentworth specifies Courbet's *Young Ladies on the Banks of the Seine (Summer)* (1857; Petit Palais, Musée des Beaux-Arts de la ville de Paris) as an example.

26 Ibid.

27 See Wentworth 1984, pl. 35.

28 *Art Journal* 1868, 87.

29 *London Quarterly Review* 1865, 410.

30 Made in 1860–1861, three of these were unpublished. For *Louise* (1861; Wentworth 3), only six impressions are known, and there are only two known impressions of *Portrait of Edgar Degas* (ca. 1860–1861; Wentworth 5). See London and Manchester 1984–1985, 100, cat. 12.

31 *Athenaeum* 1870b.

32 This work was purchased from the French art critic Philippe Burty in 1865. Catalogue entry for *Louise*, no. 1865,0114.87, British Museum, London, britishmuseum.org.

33 In August 1871, newspapers reported that *Vanity Fair*'s previous caricaturist, Carlo Pellegrini, whose pseudonym was "Ape," would officially be replaced by James Tissot. Krystyna Matyjaszkiewicz, email to author, February 19, 2019.

34 *Fraser's* 1863, 784.

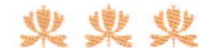

TISSOT'S BRITISH MODERN-LIFE PAINTINGS

NANCY ROSE MARSHALL

1 Palmer, ed. 1881, 18.

2 "La modernité, c'est le transitoire, le fugitif, le contingent, la moitié de l'art, dont l'autre moitié est l'éternel et l'immuable." Baudelaire (1863) 1964, 12.

3 *Illustrated London News* 1896; Wentworth 1984, 85–86. According to Tissot's sales notebook, printed in this volume, he earned more than 7,680 pounds in 1873, 6,600 pounds in 1874, and 4,935 pounds in 1875 (the equivalent of about 567,000 dollars in 2019). Currency conversion was performed using the Bank of England's inflation calculator, bankofengland.co.uk/monetary-policy/inflation/inflation-calculator.

4 *Daily News* 1876; Walkley 1994, 126–128.

5 A pupil at the École des Beaux-Arts and regular exhibitor at the Paris Salon, Tissot demonstrated the career strategies of someone seeking acceptance by the elite academic institutions of Paris, yet he also kept company with avant-garde artists like Edgar Degas. For more on the subject, see London and Manchester 1984–1985; Wentworth 1984; Wood 1986.

6 Degas to Tissot, February/March 1874. Degas 1947, 38–40.

7 For example, Tissot often depicted nasturtiums (in French, "capucines") in his paintings, including in the first and last scenes of *The Prodigal Son in Modern Life*—on the table and in the arbor trellis, respectively. Degas had initially proposed that the not-yet-named Impressionists be known as the Capucines, after the boulevard on which they held their first exhibitions, Boulevard des Capucines. Sutton 1986, 105.

8 *Magazine of Art* 1878, 82.

9 *New Quarterly Magazine* 1879, 163.

10 Ibid.

11 Ibid.

12 *Academy* 1877, 396.

13 James (1877) 1956, 155.

14 *Era* 1874.

15 "[Tissot's] latest efforts can only please those blasé with Mr. Frith's *Road to Ruin*." *Daily News* 1882. "These works will compare very favourably with the well remembered series by Mr. Frith illustrating the same subject. Both artists have a purely modern version of the story to tell, but the Frenchman tells his in the language of art, whilst our native painter violates his art to point a moral." *Artist* 1882, 236.

16 *Leeds Mercury* 1882.

17 The Bullingdon Club identification appears in *Daily News* 1882. Whether or not Tissot was intentionally referring to the infamously dissolute Bullingdon Club is unclear. Charles Dickens's *Dictionary of Oxford and Cambridge* (1885) identified the club's colors as "sky-blue and white stripes," suggesting a lighter blue than is represented in Tissot's painting, as indeed it is today. Dickens 1885, 34. Tissot includes similar striped caps in other pictures, such as *Holyday* (pl. 52), in which they are more likely those of cricket teams; in both instances, however, they suggest the elite "clubbability" of the portrayed men.

18 "The prodigal has by this time become so moral, and so physically flourishing, that he is not to be distinguished from the brother who was moral and wore a frock coat ab initio. The prodigal son or the other one is just stepping out of a boat. . . . The other one, or the prodigal son, is sharpening a carving knife." The brother's wife "looks . . . as if she couldn't for the life of her tell which of the brothers was which, and as though she might be quite happy with either." *Artist* 1882, 236. "Might be quite happy with either" is a reference to both a popular song and to another Tissot painting, *Portsmouth Dockyard* (ca. 1877; Tate, London)—exhibited as an etching at London's Dudley Gallery in 1878 as *How Happy Could I Be with Either*—in which a soldier flirts with two ladies.

19 The parable is itself somewhat morally surprising, suggesting that the petty jealousy of the good son is misplaced, and that the principle of forgiveness trumps that of virtuous living.

20 As an instance of the Victorian tendency to read pictures like novels, one reviewer understood the invalid taking in sunshine under the concerned oversight of an elderly chaperone in Tissot's painting *The Convalescent* (pl. 48) as suffering from a "case of love-sickness." *Graphic* 1876.

21 Barrington 1878, 724. Russell & Allen was an establishment for high-end fashions.

22 *Athenaeum* 1873, 605; *Illustrated London News* 1874.

23 Consider, for instance, the famous dissociation between reflection and "reality" in Édouard Manet's *Bar at the Folies-Bergère* (1882; Courtauld Gallery, London).

24 In 1873, Tissot sold *The Captain's Daughter* through the art dealer Thomas Agnew for 700 pounds, and in 1874, he sold through Agnew *The Ball on Shipboard* for 1,400 pounds. See "Tissot's Sales Notebook," this volume.

25 "Je sentais les hauteurs où il planait et la matérialité où je luttais alors de plus en plus." Tissot to Georgiana Burne-Jones, January 1899, reprinted in Burne-Jones 1904, 282. He added, "This all discouraged me so much that I no longer saw him." (Tous cela m'intimida tellement que je n'allais plus le voir.) With thanks to Marie-Agathe Simonetti for suggestions as to the English translation.

26 "I could see that his mind was deeply exercised by the impression the English painter had made upon him." Carr gets the chronology wrong, however, as he claims that Tissot observed the "lighter essays of his hung in close juxtaposition with the widely different work of Burne-Jones" at the Grosvenor and vowed to change his style. In actuality, *The Triumph of Will* appeared at the first Grosvenor Gallery show, in 1877. Carr 1908, 268. The Grosvenor Gallery was a relatively new exhibition space (founded in 1877) that aimed to provide an alternative to what many in the art world saw as the crassly commercial aspects of the Royal Academy.

27 *The Spectator* called *The Triumph of Will* "unintelligible." *Spectator* 1877, 665. A critic for the *Saturday Review* described it as "a performance of considerable humour." *Saturday Review* 1877. "M. Tissot has very seriously mistaken his talent," commented another. *Pall Mall* 1877.

28 "Potage une dame avec un serpent!" Carr 1908, 269.

29 *Nineteenth Century* 1878, 297; *Spectator* 1878, 637. Another journalist, recounting a visit to Burne-Jones's studio in the year prior to the exhibition of *Laus Veneris*, described the painting as "sensuous and unhealthy." Rouge 1877, 137. Similarly, Tissot's *Evening* presents a salient contrast with Burne-Jones's allegorical *Night* (1870; Harvard Art Museums, Cambridge, Massachusetts), exhibited at the Grosvenor in 1878.

30 See, for example, Wood 1986, 85–124; Wentworth 1984, 125–153. Newton was the model for Tissot's *October*; *Orphans*; the first, third, and fourth paintings of *The Prodigal Son in Modern Life* series; *Rivals*; and numerous other works. She is the sole female figure in the eight paintings and four etchings that Tissot submitted to the Grosvenor in 1879, so he was clearly preoccupied with rendering her form and features.

31 In 1874, Edmond de Goncourt even went so far as to dismiss Tissot as "that plagiarist painter" for his tendency to pick up other artists' styles. Edmond and Jules de Goncourt, journal entry dated November 3, 1874, quoted in Wentworth 1984, 122.

32 Most of Tissot's viewers would not have known the identity of the models, so our current tendency to map biography onto the paintings and to cite them as indications of Tissot's blissful household arrangements or of his despair at Newton's deteriorating health would have been, in Tissot's day, an interpretation available only to those in his inner circle. There were some figures in the art world who had privileged knowledge of Tissot's homelife—those who, as one reviewer acknowledged, "possess occult knowledge of the lady . . . and maintain that she is much prettier than she is painted." These viewers, this review recounts, also recognized Lilian Hervey, Newton's niece, as the model for *Orphans*: "Do look at [the] dear little girl in 'Orphans;' that's exactly like her: she's always got her finger in her mouth." *University Magazine* 1879, 67. Most nineteenth-century viewers, however, would not have had access to the biographical details that now inform more recent descriptions of Tissot's art from this period. See, for example, Conzelman 2002; London and Manchester 1984–1985; Wentworth 1984; Wood 1986.

33 After Newton's death, Tissot sought comfort from the medium William Eglinton (see pl. 131) in séances that became renowned in Spiritualist circles for their success. *Borderland* 1897.

TISSOT'S "GENIUS" PICTURE-SELLING IN BRITAIN

KRYSTYNA MATYJASZKIEWICZ

1 Blanche to James Laver, June 12, 1936, Laver Papers, MS Laver B39, University of Glasgow Special Collections. Blanche first met Tissot while still a child, when visiting London with his family in 1874, and he regularly called on the artist during trips from 1880 onward. He wrote about his Tissot memories in response to a request from the art critic and curator James Laver, who was writing a biography on Tissot, *"Vulgar Society": The Romantic Career of James Tissot, 1836–1902* (1936).

2 Tissot to an unknown recipient, undated, but most likely dated before July 17, 1860, when *Meeting of Faust and Marguerite* was bought by the French state. This letter is archived at the Musée Baron Martin, Gray, France, no. 2204. For Tissot's eventual sales prices, see "Tissot's Sales Notebook," this volume.

3 "Tissot's Sales Notebook," this volume.

4 For example, several paintings that Maison Goupil purchased directly from Tissot—including *The Confessional* (1865; Southampton City Art Gallery, England), purchased in 1866; *The Secret* (fig. 41), purchased in 1867; and *The Conversation* (1869; location unknown), *The Sofa* (1869; location unknown), *A Widow* (1868; private collection), and *Young Women Looking at Japanese Objects* (pl. 38), all purchased in 1869—were sold by Goupil to the New York–based art dealer Roland Knoedler. "Tissot's Sales Notebook," this volume.

5 Most of Tissot's paintings from around 1867 to 1882 are approximately twenty to thirty—at maximum thirty-six—inches tall or wide. Some pictures intended for exhibition were larger, but even at four or five feet, these works could be accommodated on residential walls if collectors lacked dedicated gallery spaces.

6 Although he praised the "dexterity" and "conscientiousness" of Tissot's works, Ruskin also bewailed, "Most of them are, unhappily, mere coloured photographs of vulgar [ordinary] society," except for *The Triumph of Will (Poem in Five Parts): I. The Challenge* (pl. 99), which he admired. "Fors Clavigera: Letters to the Workmen and Labourers of Great Britain," letter dated June 18, 1877, in Ruskin 1903–1912, 27:161.

7 "Vous seriez capable, avec votre terrible activité, de faire sortir de l'argent de cette foule de cotton brokers, cotton dealers, etc." Edgar Degas, letter to James Tissot, November 19, [1872], in Paris 1988, 359. Manuscripts Department, Bibliothèque nationale de France, Paris, NAF 13005, fol. 6r. Translations from the French are my own.

8 See, for example, Degas's *Out of the Paddock (Racehorses)* (ca. 1871–1872, reworked ca. 1874–1878; private collection) and *Scene from the Steeplechase: The Fallen Jockey* (1866, reworked 1880–1881 and ca. 1897; National Gallery of Art, Washington, DC). David Bomford writes, "As well as revising and correcting his paintings as he initially developed them, Degas would also habitually

return to paintings made years before and rework them." Bomford 2004, 24.

9 This taste was reflected in contemporary ceramics and furniture, like the pieces we see in Tissot's pictures; elements of fashion at that time—in particular, hats and complete gowns, such as is worn by Mrs. Clara Bischoffsheim in her portrait by John Everett Millais (1873; Tate, London); and paintings such as George Adolphus Storey's *The Old Soldier* (1869; Hamburger Kunsthalle).

10 Records from the Thomas Agnew & Sons archives show receipt from Tissot of *Tea* (as *Le Thé*) on September 19, 1872, and the subsequent sale to John K[ynaston] Cross on November 5, 1872, for 330 pounds by W[illiam] A[gnew] [in Manchester]. Thomas Agnew & Sons Ltd Archive, NGA 27, National Gallery, London.

11 The drawing, which is now held in a private collection, is inscribed: "À mon ami Degas / J. Tissot / Londres." See London and Manchester 1984–1985, 48, no. 45.

12 *Graphic* 1873.

13 *Builder* 1873.

14 See "Tissot's Sales Notebook," this volume.

15 *Illustrated London News* 1875b.

16 Lostalot 1883a, 381. Tissot's work was only included in Grosvenor Gallery exhibitions from 1877 to 1879. At least two major Tissot paintings, *The Coming Storm* (1874; Beaverbrook Art Gallery, Fredericton, New Brunswick) and the portrait *Empress Eugénie and the Prince Imperial in the Grounds of Camden Place, Chislehurst* (pl. 28), had been rejected when submitted for exhibition at the Royal Academy in 1875. Matyjaszkiewicz, ed. 2019a. In 1876, there were changes among the Royal Academicians on the Council and Hanging Committee, resulting in more artists who were favorable to Tissot, and two of his paintings were subsequently accepted. Matyjaszkiewicz, ed. 2020. The year of 1880 passed without a major showing. In 1881, Tissot was persuaded by fellow members of the new Society of Painter-Etchers, who were also Royal Academicians, to submit work there, and two paintings were selected. In 1882, Tissot organized his own one-man exhibition in London.

17 Matyjaszkiewicz, ed. 2019a. Although Tissot counted Royal Academicians and Grosvenor Gallery regulars Lawrence Alma-Tadema, Frederic Leighton, and Millais among his friends, there were other artists who were less friendly. Indeed, some—most notably, Francis Grant and John Callcott Horsley—were hostile. Alma-Tadema had been made a British citizen by Queen Victoria in 1873, so no longer counted as a "foreigner," like Tissot. According to a *Glasgow Herald* correspondent writing about the Royal Academy's imminent appointment of six new associate members in January 1876: "The names most generally put forward as representing the various schools of painting now in the ascendant, are unfortunately not those of men likely to find favour with the elderly gentlemen of an old and worn-out school in whom the decision is vested. Such names are those of Mr Whistler in the first rank, Mr [Luke] Fildes, Mr Tissot, and Mr Marcus Stone. But as the leaders of the new thought are likely to be rejected as being too extreme, a 'conciliations list' has, I am told, been prepared which will be composed of the names of Mr Alma Tadema, Mr [Edwin] Long . . ." *Glasgow Herald* 1876. Alma-Tadema and Long were elected associate members on January 26, 1876. Whistler's friendship with Tissot, which became stronger after Tissot's Royal Academy rejection in 1875, cooled after Tissot was unable to testify as a witness for Whistler in the latter's 1878 libel case against Ruskin.

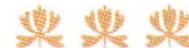

TISSOT'S HOUSES IN SAINT JOHN'S WOOD, LONDON

CHARLOTTE GERE

My interest in James Tissot and his residence in London dates back to my long friendship with Jane, Lady Abdy, who played a pioneering role in Tissot's rediscovery in the 1970s, and it is to her that I owe much of my knowledge of his work and homes. My understanding of Saint John's Wood and its artist residents was greatly enhanced by researching Lawrence Alma-Tadema's houses, first with Julian Treuherz in 1996, and more recently with Elizabeth Prettejohn and Peter Trippi in 2016–2017. Max Donnelly has given generously of his information on Daniel Cottier and his associates. I am indebted to Kate Hay, specialist in Victorian garden furniture at the Victoria and Albert Museum, for providing information about the Chinese rattan garden chairs and hammocks.

1 London and Manchester 1984–1985. Tissot arranged to let his house to de Nittis in early 1873. In a letter dated February 1, 1873, de Nittis uses the address of Tissot's Paris house as his home address and includes it in his 1873 Salon submissions. Krystyna Matyjaszkiewicz, email to author, March 18, 2019.

2 For accounts of Saint John's Wood as an artists' colony, see Eyre 1913; Gere 2010, ch. 4.

3 Du Maurier 1890–1891.

4 In 1875, Whistler's friend Arthur Lasenby Liberty set up his eponymous store in Regent Street, and Tissot may also have patronized this new outlet for Japanese art. Alma-Tadema was an early customer of Liberty's shop as well. Tissot's rival for kimonos at Madame Desoye's in Paris, Dante Gabriel Rossetti, favored Murray Marks in Oxford Street, where Tissot may also have shopped. Adburgham 1975.

5 These items appear in *Before the Departure* or *The Parting* (pl. 42) and *An Interesting Story* (fig. 47), the latter exhibited at the Royal Academy in 1872. In a review of this exhibition, *The Times* referred to Tissot's pictures of "pretty maidens" in the "dainty, though quaint costume of some hundred years ago." *Times* 1872.

6 The ebonized chairs, also known as "Rossettis," were designed by Dante Gabriel Rossetti around 1862, and Rossetti owned a set himself. Similar French country chairs can be seen in the home of Claude Monet, at Giverny, in Normandy. Parry, ed. 1996, 176, cat. J24. Michael Thonet, of Vienna, was particularly known for the manufacture of bentwood furniture, for which he had developed the first industrial-scale production processes. The bentwood rocking chair was created in 1860. Vegesack 1997.

7 The property address is now 44 Grove End Road. Tissot was surrounded by artists at Grove End Road, his immediate neighbors being Guido Bach at number 15, and Philip Hermogenes Calderon at number 16. Philip Morris rented a studio and glasshouse at 1 Grove End Place in 1876. Grove End Place disappeared, and the studio, now listed at 33 Saint John's Wood Road, was named Acer House. In nearby Kensington were Louise Jopling and her husband, Joseph; Sir Francis Seymour Haden, founding member—along with Tissot and Whistler—of the Society of Painter-Etchers; and Clara Montalba. Hemy lived in the eighteenth-century Myrtle Lodge at North End in Hampstead; du Maurier at Grove Lodge; and Macbeth had a purpose-built studio at 62 Park Road, Haverstock Hill, also in Hampstead. In 1873, Tissot's election to the Arts Club in Hanover Square, in London's West End, was ensured by his friends among the founding members, including Sir Julius Benedict (who posed as the pianist in *The Concert* or *Hush!* [pl. 45]), du Maurier, and Whistler. Ferdinand Heilbuth was already a member; once Macbeth, Morris, and de Nittis (who was painting and exhibiting in London) joined the club, it provided a rendezvous for this intimate group. Abdy 1984. For the occupation dates and addresses of Tissot's artist friends, see Graves 1905–1906; Walkley 1994.

8 Tissot's prints, particularly the ten illustrations he contributed to Edmond and Jules de Goncourt's *Renée Mauperin* (1884) (pls. 107–116), in which Tissot deployed his French eighteenth-century furniture for verisimilitude, allowed a wider public access to the furnishing and decoration of his house. The Grove End Road property's conservatory and garden were also both extensively recorded in this medium.

9 The designer-decorator Daniel Cottier, a fellow member of the Arts Club (elected 1870), may have suggested his then little-known business partner, Brydon, as Tissot's architect. Both of them were committed to the Design Reform Movement, and Cottier admired Japanese decorative art and Oriental rugs. Cottier was also Tissot's neighbor, living around this time at 3 Saint James's Terrace, Regent's Park. Donnelly 1999, 32–51; Max Donnelly, private communication with author, October 2018.

10 *Building News* 1874.

11 See, for example, the etching *An Uninteresting Story* (1878; Wentworth 32).

12 Tissot's 1877 portrait of his then dealer, Algernon Moses Marsden (pl. 30), is also set in the Grove End Road studio.

13 Chrysanthemums were a relatively recent introduction to England. The plant hunter Robert Fortune introduced the first Japanese cultivars into the country in 1862. Several London nurseries specialized in their cultivation and sale by the time Tissot took up raising them in his conservatory. Coats 1968.

14 *Times* 1878.

15 *Times* 1879b.

16 See *Quarrelling* (pl. 51), *The Convalescent* (pl. 48), and *Holyday* (pl. 52).

17 See, for example, *The Picnic* (ca. 1881–1882; Musée des Beaux-Arts de Dijon, France), *Quiet* (ca. 1881; private collection), or *A Quiet Afternoon* (ca. 1879; private collection).

18 The trellis pillars are shown in two 1868 paintings, *A Luncheon* (fig. 48) and *A Widow* (private collection). See Wentworth 1984, pls. 51 and 60. The trellis pillars do not show in *My Garden at Saint John's Wood* or *Quarrelling*. The trellis pillars shown in the London paintings may have been copied from the Paris pictures.

19 The carpet bedding is clearly shown in *The Gardener* (ca. 1879–1880; location unknown) and *A Quiet Afternoon*. See Laver 1936, pl. XXII; Wentworth 1984, pls. 139 and 144.

20 The Renaissance poet Torquato Tasso described the enchanted garden created by Armida for meetings with her lover, Rinaldo, in *Gerusalemme Liberata* (1581).

21 *Daily Telegraph* 1879.

22 The Japanesque Worcester porcelain "dragon" teakettle seen in *Holyday* was a novelty item very recently introduced. It must have been available by 1875–1876, when Tissot was painting this work, although most ceramics historians date it to 1878. Tissot includes it in *Rivals* (pl. 83) as well. According to the Museum of Royal Worcester collections website, the date of introduction is unknown. Museum of Royal Worcester, England, museumofroyalworcester.org.

23 *Spectator* 1879. The hammock paintings exhibited at the Grosvenor Gallery in 1879 attracted extensive press commentary, much of it in the same vein of moral disapproval. The criticism is unjust; hammocks, usually associated in nineteenth-century art with women, were often acquired for those in poor health and depicted in subjects associated with illness. Newton can be seen reclining in a hammock on the right side of *A Quiet Afternoon*.

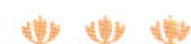

THE CAREER OF A PORTRAIT PAINTER

PAUL PERRIN

This essay was translated from the original French into English by Alexandra Bonfante-Warren.

The author thanks Philippe Guegan, Margaret Fowler, Justine Gain, and David Cornillon for their valuable assistance in the research for this essay.

1 In 2006, the Musée d'Orsay, Paris, added to its collections *Portrait of the Marquis and Marquise de Miramon and Their Children* (pl. 23) and, in 2011, *The Circle of the Rue Royale*. The acquisitions gave "a new impetus to the reassessment of Tissot" and reawoke interest in a genre that was more important than it might seem in the painter's career. Des Cars 2007, 43.

2 This album, which resides in a private collection, contains photographic reproductions of sixty-four paintings executed by Tissot in London between 1871 and 1878. In 1982, Willard Misfeldt published the content of three other albums compiled by Tissot that are now in the Michael Wentworth Archives, collection of the Ryerson and Burnham Archives of the Art Institute of Chicago. Misfeldt 1982.

3 Thank you to the Collection Frédéric Mantion for sharing the sales notebook.

4 Not all of Tissot's known portraits are recorded in the sales notebook; some of them may have been not sold but given to the sitters, as in the case of Frederick Burnaby.

5 That is, 146,756 francs out of a total of 1,384,750 francs.

6 "James Tissot s'était beaucoup épris également de Holbein, d'Albert Dürer et de l'école des Flandres, mais comme l'art ne nourrissait point son homme, ce débutant dut brosser, au prix de 40 francs, des portraits des *bonnes* et de *maîtresses d'hôtel*." Bastard 1906, 258.

7 These are titled *Pierre de Ségur* (1859; private collection) and *Henri de Ségur* (1859; private collection). "Tissot's Sales Notebook," this volume.

8 Ibid. Thank you to Krystyna Matyjaszkiewicz for pointing out this information.

9 Ibid.

10 The dates for these two portraits are unknown, as are their current whereabouts. *Portrait of Mme T...* may be a depiction of the artist's mother.

11 "M. Tissot s'amuse à faire des peintures d'élève pour les placer ensuite dans des cadres de maître. Ses deux petits portraits de femme et de jeune fille n'ont aucun caractère spécial. Ils dérivent—on le voit de suite—de MM. Flandrin et Robert Fleury." Astruc 1859, 22.

12 "Les deux portraits exposés par M. Tissot sont de véritables tableaux, et ce sont de bons tableaux dont le premier mérite consiste dans la sincérité du sentiment moderne." Lagrange 1864, 525.

13 "M. Tissot . . . a peint cette année deux tableaux que nous rangerons parmi les portraits, quoiqu'on puisse aussi bien, à cause de l'importance donnée aux accessoires, les faire rentrer dans le genre." Clément 1864, 2.

14 Rey 2011.

15 The painting is reproduced in Misfeldt 1982, pl. I-42, with the title *Portrait of an Unidentified Boy*. In 1866, Tissot's sales notebook lists a "portrait of the young J. de Montbrison," sold for 2,000 francs. "Tissot's Sales Notebook," this volume.

16 The painting is reproduced in Misfeldt 1982, pl. I-58, with the title *Portrait of Unidentified Children*.

17 Tissot also painted "five small heads painted on marble" for Émile Gaillard in 1868—probably portraits of Gaillard's children and wife. "Tissot's Sales Notebook," this volume.

18 In 1868, Tissot noted in his account book a first "portrait of Monsieur de Lambertye" and a caricature of the "cercle des patineurs," followed by the entry "35 p[or]t[rait]s." Ibid.

19 This portrait is recorded in Tissot's sales notebook under 1871; location unknown. "Tissot's Sales Notebook," this volume.

20 *Portrait of Mrs B...* (1876; Wentworth 21). Bowles and Jessica's elder daughter was Sydney Bowles, wife of David Freeman-Mitford and mother of the famous Mitford sisters.

21 Parkinson-Fortescue, twice in the government and Secretary for Ireland in the 1860s, also appeared in a *Vanity Fair* caricature—drawn by Carlo Pellegrini, under the pseudonym "Ape"—on August 14, 1869. He was president of the Board of Trade in the early 1870s. Thomson 1979.

22 Boase 1893, 122.

23 "The Empress Eugénie has just commissioned her portrait and that of the Prince Imperial from a greatly talented French artist, M. Tissot. The prince will be represented in the uniform of the cadets of Woolwich Military Academy. No doubt, photography will soon enable us to see the two portraits, which are spoken of very highly." (L'impératrice Eugénie vient de commander à un artiste français de grand talent, M. Tissot, son portrait, ainsi que celui du Prince impérial. Le Prince sera représenté avec l'uniforme des élèves de l'École militaire de Woolwich. Il est probable que la photographie ne tardera pas à nous faire connaître ces deux portraits, dont on dit le plus grand bien.) Domino 1874, 1.

24 It is interesting to observe that Tissot's genre scenes consistently sold better than his portraits, even the more important portraits. For example, in 1874, the painter sold to Hilton Philipson through the art dealer Thomas Agnew the iconic *The Ball on Shipboard* (pl. 71) for the stunning sum of 35,000 francs.

25 Matyjaszkiewicz, ed. 2019a.

26 Comte Lafond paid 3,000 francs for the "portrait of Madame Laure Hayman." "Tissot's Sales Notebook," this volume. A comparison with photographs of the model suggests that it may be she who is depicted in *Portrait of an Unidentified Lady*. See Misfeldt 1982, pl. III-43. The model for *Portrait of an Actress in Eighteenth-Century Dress* (ca. 1883; private collection) may also be Laure Hayman. Just as Charles Haas, on the right in *The Circle of the Rue Royale*, was Marcel Proust's model for the character of Swann in, *In Search of Lost Time* (*À la recherche du temps perdu*, 1913–1927), Hayman would provide Proust with certain aspects of the courtesan Odette de Crécy, whom Swann falls in love with.

27 *Portrait of Madame de Bonnières* (1890; private collection).

28 *Portrait of Madame Ernest May, née Marie-Héloise Jeanne Ferré* (1886; private collection).

29 *La Vicomtesse de Montmorand (Geneviève de Miramon)* (1889; private collection); *La Vicomtesse de Montmorand (Geneviève de Miramon)*. See Misfeldt 1982, pl. IV-13.

30 In 1890, Tissot noted in his account book the portraits of "young Seillière" for 600 francs, and "Mlle Christ[ine] Seillière" for 2,000 francs. The portrait of fifteen-year-old René Bordères-Seillière may be *Portrait of an Unidentified Boy*. See Misfeldt 1982, pl. IV-21. The portrait of Christine Bordères-Seillière has not been identified. "Tissot's Sales Notebook," this volume.

31 Marie Say was the cousin of Léon Say, one of the first to appreciate Tissot, whose painting *Marguerite in Church* he bought at the end of the 1861 Salon. See Misfeldt 1982, pl. I-12, or Wentworth 1984, pl. 5.

32 *The Comtesse d'Yanville and Her Children* (1893; Minneapolis Institute of Art). In 1893, at the *Exposition des portraits des écrivains et journalistes du siècle (1793–1893)* at Galerie Georges Petit, Tissot also showed a portrait of the writer Julia Allard (Madame Alphonse Daudet), painted on the cover of one of her works. This copy of the book *Enfants et mères* (1889) belonged to Edmond de Goncourt. Goncourt 2014, 1056.

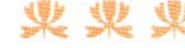

TISSOT AND FASHION

JUSTINE DE YOUNG

English translations are the author's, unless otherwise indicated.

1 Wentworth 1984, 9–10.

2 De Young 2012a.

3 For an extensive discussion of Tissot's use of historic dress and his repetitions, see London and Manchester 1984–1985.

4 *Illustrated London News* 1874.

5 "[L]a jeune femme est un modèle d'élégance, de noblesse et de simplicité . . . dans une pose modeste et digne. . . . [N]ous sommes loin des portraits à la mode, avec leurs airs prétentieux et leurs brillants atours!" Thoré 1870, 101–102.

6 De Young 2012b, 235.

7 "It is also a sort of portrait of a woman, but in a small sitting room, sitting negligently on the edge of her work table, near a chair cluttered with books and notebooks." (C'est aussi une espèce de portrait de femme, mais dans l'intérieur d'un petit salon, assise négligemment sur le bord de sa table à ouvrage, près d'une chaise encombrée de livres et de cahiers.) Thoré 1870, 101–102. "The portrait of Mme L. L. represents a young woman in a red zouave and black taffeta skirt, sitting negligently in a small sitting room cluttered with fashionable trivialities." (Le portrait de Mme L. L. représente une jeune fille en zouave rouge, en jupe de taffetas noir, assise négligemment dans un petit salon encombré des futilités à la mode.) Gautier 1864.

8 "[C]es accessoires si bien traités, ces meubles de fantaisie, cet intérieur élégant, n'exhalent plus le parfum sain de la famille." Lagrange 1864, 525.

9 "Nos créations industrielles et artistiques peuvent périr, nos mœurs et nos costumes peuvent tomber dans l'oubli, un tableau de M. Tissot suffira aux archéologues de l'avenir pour reconstituer notre époque." Roy 1869.

10 *Athenaeum* 1874.

11 *Illustrated London News* 1874.

12 *Tablet*, June 27, 1874, 810, quoted in New Haven, Québec, and Buffalo 1999–2000, 82.

13 New Haven, Québec, and Buffalo 1999–2000, 15, 87.

14 Ibid., 150–151; London and Manchester 1984–1985, 76.

15 Strasdin 2017. Krystyna Matyjaszkiewicz further explores the sisters' like-dressing and argues that they may have inspired the white-clad women in the right foreground in *The Ball on Shipboard*, which, if true, would highlight how subjective critics' interpretations of the class of women based on their dress could be. Matyjaszkiewicz, ed. 2019.

16 For example, one critic noted the models' "lanky faces, crane necks, and falling shoulders," while another noted the "sameness in his models of young ladies." *Illustrated London News* 1874; *Spectator* 1874.

17 *Athenaeum* 1879a. On the narratives critics tended to construct, see Marshall 1999.

18 "La femme qu'il peint est une femme des bords de la Tamise. Elle n'a point encore la grâce et l'élégance de la vraie Parisienne." *Le Temps* 1885. *La Vie Parisienne* was unsparing in its assessment: "Of the Parisienne, not at all, the painter has simply given us fourteen more or less successful English genre pictures for which a bar maid has been the only model." (De la Parisienne, il n'en est pas question, le peintre nous met simplement sous les yeux une série de quatorze tableaux de genre plus ou moins réussis de la vie anglaise où le Bar's maid a été son seul modèle.) *La Vie Parisienne* 1885. For *Le Siècle*, Henry Harvard wrote, "They dress themselves in London." (Elles se font habiller à Londres.) Harvard 1885.

19 The dress has sometimes been attributed by scholars to the couturier Charles Frederick Worth, but there is no evidence to support such a claim. For example, Edward Maeder wrote, "Dresses of the kind that Worth made famous can be found in numerous paintings by Tissot, the most spectacular example being the pink confection worn by *The Political Lady*, 1883-5." Maeder 1999, 82.

20 "[E]lle n'a pas l'ambition d'être citée comme élégante, avec une de ces robes roses qu'on veut toujours finir et qu'on ne finit jamais, d'une coupe surannée, sans aucune tournure, mais avec une ceinture noire à pointe, comme on en a porté il y a vingt ans." *La Vie Parisienne* 1885.

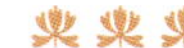

A SUMMER DRESS WITH YELLOW RIBBONS

FRANÇOISE TÉTART-VITTU

This essay was translated from the original French into English by Rose Vekony.

1 In 1858, Gautier wrote: "If [artists] went into society more, and were willing to cast off their studio prejudices for an evening, they would see that ball wear has what it takes to overcome the most stubborn preconceptions, and that a painter who depicted this clothing in the historical manner, applying his own individual style but without ceasing to be exact, would achieve astonishing effects of beauty, elegance, and color." (Si [les artistes] allaient plus souvent dans le monde et voulaient se dépouiller de leurs préjugés d'atelier pendant une soirée, ils verraient que les toilettes de bal ont de quoi satisfaire les plus difficiles, et que le peintre qui les traiterait d'une façon historique, en y appliquant le style, sans cesser pour cela d'être exact, arriverait à des effets de beauté, d'élégance et de couleur dont on serait étonné.) Gautier (1858) 2015. In 1862, Gautier became chairman of the Société nationale des Beaux-Arts, founded by Louis Martinet and other painters who wanted to be independent of the Paris Salon, including Gustave Courbet, Édouard Manet, and Jean-François Millet.

2 "[I]l est beaucoup plus commode de déclarer que tout est absolument laid dans l'habit d'une époque, que de s'appliquer à en extraire la beauté mystérieuse qui y peut être contenue, si minime ou si légère qu'elle soit. La modernité, c'est le transitoire, le fugitif, le contingent, la moitié de l'art, dont l'autre moitié est l'éternel et l'immuable." Baudelaire (1863) 1964, 13.

3 The Salon des refusés ("exhibition of rejects") was an 1863 exhibition of artists whose works had been rejected from the official Paris Salon.

4 The exhibitions *De Nittis e Tissot: Pittori della vita moderna* (Barletta, Italy, 2006) and *Impressionism, Fashion, and Modernity* (Musée d'Orsay, Paris; Metropolitan Museum of Art, New York; Art Institute of Chicago, 2012–2013) have underlined the importance of these works. See also De Young 2012; Rizzi 2006; Tétart-Vittu 2012.

5 Painters such as Louis Leloir, Ferdinand Roybet, and Jules Worms exemplified this trend. Leloir bought seventeenth-century costumes in Nuremberg in 1870. Roybet specialized in "Flemish" painting, with costumes re-created for him by Henri Clootens. Worms painted Spanish scenes using his large collection of costumes. Painters could also refer to photographs of costumed actors that were sold for their use. Blanc 1874a. Tissot was also deeply influenced by the historical paintings of the Belgian painter Henri Leys, who received a medal of honor at the Exposition Universelle in Paris in 1855. Inspired by Leys, Tissot drew on themes from Johann Wolfgang von Goethe's *Faust* (1808) for several of his works, including for two paintings he presented at the 1861 Salon: *Faust and Marguerite in the Garden* (fig. 30) and *Meeting of Faust and Marguerite* (pl. 3), the latter purchased by the French government on July 17 of the same year for the Musée du Luxembourg. See Baetens and Frederick, this volume.

6 Brussels and Amsterdam 2009–2010.

7 Tissot socialized with Alfred Stevens and his wife, who regularly received guests such as Manet and Berthe Morisot. Reff 1976, 226–227. Several of Tissot's works from the mid-1860s show a strong influence by Stevens. Wentworth 1984, 53–56. The critic W. Bürger (Théophile Thoré) remarked on the Belgian painter's influence on the subjects presented by Tissot at the Salon of 1866. Thoré 1870, 1:49. Tissot's drawing was more precise, while Stevens played more with color and light, but both were interested in photography's contribution to the creation of their painted works. Labourdette 2005.

8 Worth often imposed bright colors on his customers, even the Empress Eugénie, who typically preferred soft colors like lilac, white, or gray. He dressed a lot of women thought of as cocottes, due to their conspicuous and expensive dresses, such as Rosalie Léon, for whom Worth created a yellow dress with green ribbons that unleashed the indignation of his wife. Worth 1928.

9 "Il est naturel, en effet, que l'homme, après avoir pris l'habitude d'attacher certaines idées à un habit, ne puisse plus le revêtir sans se pénétrer des idées que cet habit représente." Blanc 1859, 557, Sénéchal and Barbillon, eds. 2011, s.v. Charles Blanc.

10 Ross 1946.

THE VISIONS OF TISSOT

MELISSA E. BURON

Research for this essay was drawn from my forthcoming PhD thesis, *'Twixt Two Worlds: The Visions of James Tissot* (Birkbeck, University of London). I wish to thank Nancy Rose Marshall, Krystyna Matyjaszkiewicz, and Jason Rosenfeld, who read early versions of this essay and provided generous and helpful feedback. English translations are mine, unless otherwise indicated.

1 The New Testament series precedes the Old Testament. For bibliographic information on the American, English, and French editions, see Misfeldt 1971, 272n21.

2 Newton was born Kathleen Irene Kelly in 1854. I am grateful to Krystyna Matyjaszkiewicz for suggesting that "Tissot, raised in Brittany with a Breton Catholic mother, would not have had any difficulty reconciling Catholicism with Spiritualism." Krystyna Matyjaszkiewicz, email to author, March 27, 2019. "Breton Catholicism . . . was characterized by a taste for the mystical and the irrational . . . the world of the dead was an integral part of that of the living." Gibson 1989, 176.

3 The Anglicized term "Spiritualism" is used in this essay since Tissot's known Spiritualist activity occurred under the guidance of an English medium, William Eglinton. On Spiritualism and Spiritism, see Kontou and Willburn, eds.

2012; Lachapelle 2011; Monroe 2008; Oppenheim 1985; Pearsall 2004. See also Keshavjee 1999.

4 Although these practices were not sanctioned by the Catholic Church, many nineteenth-century Catholics were drawn to Spiritualism and Spiritism because they provided "consoling dialogue" with the souls of the dead. Monroe 2008, 12–13.

5 The exact date of Tissot's vision in Saint-Sulpice is unknown, but it likely occurred the same year as *Inner Voices* was painted: 1885. Willard Misfeldt suggests that "the séance at which Kathleen's spirit materialized seems to have taken place after the mystic revelation at Saint-Sulpice." Misfeldt 1971, 238. However, the séance likely occurred first.

6 Michael Wentworth declares, "It is difficult to believe that these overworked little pictures ever aroused particular interest: that they were met with hushed reverence and immense popularity on two continents is nearly incomprehensible." Wentworth 1984, 174. He further adds, "For modern taste, this 'monographie réaliste de Jésus' is acceptable only in small doses. To spend an afternoon turning the pages of the Tissot Bible is a disheartening task, although now and again a little work . . . attracts by its genre approach and ornamental treatment." Ibid., 188. Misfeldt wrote, "To modern eyes James Tissot's religious paintings are his least interesting and his least rewarding either from the standpoint of visual interest or from the standpoint of their being documents revelatory of the beliefs and passions of an individual or of the tastes and activities in a limited sense of a particular social stratum at a particular time." Misfeldt 1971, 247.

7 Ross 1946, 7. Following her funeral on November 14, 1882, at the Church of Our Lady, Lisson Grove, Saint John's Wood, London, Newton was buried on consecrated ground in Saint Mary's Roman Catholic Cemetery, Kensal Green. Anna Humphrey, Superintendent, Saint Mary's Cemetery, email to author, December 15, 2015.

8 "Tissot . . . arrived in the night from England and . . . is very affected by the death of the English Mauperin [Newton], who, already very ill, he had used as the model for the illustration to my book." (Visite, ce matin, de Tissot arrivé dans la nuit d'Angleterre et qui me dit, dans la conversation, être très affecté de la mort de la Mauperin anglaise, qui, déjà bien souffrante, lui avait servi de modèle pour l'illustration pour mon livre.) Goncourt 1959, 3:204–205. See Tissot's illustrations to Edmond and Jules de Goncourt's 1884 novel *Renée Mauperin* (pls. 107–116).

9 Consumption is also referred to as the white plague, wasting disease, and phthisis. Susan Sontag wrote, "TB is disintegration, febrilisation, dematerialisation; it is a disease of liquids—the body turning to phlegm and mucus and sputum and, finally, blood—and of air, of the need for better air." Sontag 2013, 681.

10 Jopling 1925, 60–61. Jopling misstates that Newton was married while involved with Tissot. In fact, Newton was divorced by *decree nisi* on July 20, 1872. Georges Bastard, who wrote a biographical article on Tissot, suggested that it was the 1877 death of Tissot's brother Marcel-African that first precipitated the artist's interest in mysticism and the occult. Bastard 1906, 264.

11 Farmer 1890, 187. Eglinton was suspected and accused of fraud, although he is not known to have spent time in prison.

12 Eglinton claims that he came to Tissot's attention in late 1884 and that they first met in Paris, where he found the artist to be "a keenly intellectual and sympathetic man, ready to be convinced of the great facts of Spiritualism, if sufficient evidence were forthcoming . . . and the séances which I gave him during my brief visit sufficiently aroused a desire on his part to know more." Eglinton 1886, 153.

13 Ibid.

14 A painting titled *L'apparition* appears in Tissot's posthumous estate-sale catalogue; the description, however, refers to *Inner Voices*: "Christ clothed in the priesthood, amid the ruins of the Cour des Comptes, comes to the aid of the unfortunately mistreated of the Commune." (Le Christ revêtu sacerdotaux, au milieu des ruines de la Cour des Comptes, vient au secours d'un malheureux abusé de la Commune.) Hôtel Drouot, Paris, *L'Atelier de J. James Tissot* (July 9–10, 1903), Bibliothèque nationale de France, Paris, 3. According to Bastard, the painting was not in the artist's studio after his death. Bastard 1906, 278. Wentworth "supposes" that Tissot destroyed it. Cited in Misfeldt 1971, 157. Photographs taken during Tissot's lifetime and in 1964 at the Château de Buillon after Tissot's death document this painting as being there.

15 A double slate, which Eglinton used to allegedly communicate with spirits, sits on the table in the composition's foreground. A related drawing was found among Tissot's papers at the Château de Buillon after his death. Frédéric Mantion, email to author, March 20, 2019. See Misfeldt 1991, pl. 54.

16 Collection Frédéric Mantion. The volumes found at Tissot's estate date from around October 1882 to July 1884. Tissot signed his name on the front page of each volume.

17 "Il avait un faible pour les ectoplasmes, les tables tournantes, l'ésotérisme et le spiritisme. Plusieures centaines de volumes sont rassemblés traitant de ces matières ainsi que de la sorcellerie et des artifices du démon. Certains d'etre eux remontent au XVII et au XVIII siècles, tels a L'histoire des imaginations extravagantes et le Traité de Jean Boduc de la démonomaine contre les sorciers. Parmi les guéridons tripodes de style Empire qui se vendirent si cher, certains ont sans doute servi à l'invocation des esprits. On sent que James Tissot avait ramené de son long séjour en Angleterre un goût marqué pour les phénomènes de l'au-de-là et les fantômes hantant les châteaux romantiques." Vartier ca. 1964.

18 "The apparitions are near each other; the spirit and Kitty [Newton] are a reddish tone, strangely contrasting with Kitty's diaphanous head, lit as if by electric rays that emerge from their hands." (Les apparitions sont l'une près de l'autre; l'esprit et Kitty est d'un ton rougeâtre, contrastant singulièrement avec la tête vaporeuse de Kitty, éclairée comme par des rayons électriques qui se dégagent de leurs mains.) Bastard 1906, 265–266.

19 "Et dans le crépuscule, se refusant à chercher des allumettes, avec une voix qui se fait tout à fait mystérieuse et des yeux vagues, il nous montre une boule en cristal de roche et un plateau d'émail, qui servent à des évocations, où l'on entend, assure-t-il, des voix qui se disputent. Il tire d'une commode des cahiers, où il nous montre des pages entières, contenant l'historique de ces évocations, et nous montre enfin un tableau représentant une femme aux mains lumineuses, qu'il dit être venue l'embrasser et dont il a senti sur sa joue ses lèvres, des lèvres pareilles à des lèvres de feu." Goncourt 1959, 3:1118. English translation from New Haven, Québec, and Buffalo 1999–2000, 199.

20 I am grateful to Krystyna Matyjaszkiewicz for this suggestion.

21 I wish to acknowledge colleagues in the Ancient Art and Interpretation Department at the Fine Arts Museums of San Francisco, Renée Dreyfus, Curator in Charge, and Louise Chu, Associate Curator, for helping me decode these symbols.

22 Appropriating a variety of complex symbols in cloisonné may already have been on the artist's mind when he created *Fortune* (fig. 80), a model for an unrealized fountain, which included zodiac symbols in bronze around a blue enameled globe flanked with writhing serpents and angels. See Matyjaszkiewicz, "'Always in Search of the Exquisite in Art': Tissot's Cloisonné Enamels," this volume.

23 Farmer 1890, 187.

24 The lettering on *The Apparition* mezzotint reads: "Dark seance d'Eglinton / du 20 May 1885 / Londres." In 1893, Tissot gave Newton's niece Isabelle Hervey an impression of this print for her wedding, suggesting the personal resonance the image held for him. Misfeldt 1971, 156n5.

25 "The mezzotint is more suitable than any other style of engraving to represent phantoms, incantations, artificial lights like those of the lamp, torches, fire, all the drama of conflagrations, all the effects of night." Blanc 1874b, 281. The creation of a mezzotint starts with a metal plate that is treated to catch ink. The printed image is then revealed by burnishing away surface areas that will not hold ink and will print white. Tissot often made his own plates for his prints. He only made five mezzotints, four of which include Newton.

26 Tissot 1899, x–xi.

27 Ibid.

28 There is no proof that Tissot ever abandoned religion. The years that he lived with Newton out of wedlock challenged his acceptance in polite society and within the Catholic Church, but this does not prove that either Tissot or Newton were without faith. It is interesting that Tissot's Saint John's Wood house was very near one of the few Roman Catholic churches in London, the Roman Catholic Church of Our Lady.

29 Baedeker 1881, 247. Saint-Sulpice also houses Eugène Delacroix's murals, which decorate the Chapel of the Holy Angels. On Delacroix's murals, see Spector 1967.

30 The 1884 Parisian debut of Jules Massenet's opera *Manon* occurred around the time of Tissot's Saint-Sulpice vision. The reunion between the opera's hero, the Chevalier des Grieux, with his former love, Manon Lescaut, may have reminded Tissot of his desire to reunite with Kathleen Newton. Saint-Sulpice is also a central location in Honoré de Balzac's *The Atheist's Mass* (*La messe de l'athée*, 1836), part of the author's collection of intertwined novels about nineteenth-century French society, *The Human Comedy* (*La comédie humaine*).

31 Despite their ecclesiastic function, elements in the left arm of the church's transept (a meridian line and an astronomical gnomon) foment persistent theories about the church, reaching a feverous pitch with the publication of Dan Brown's novel *The Da Vinci Code* (2003), which includes a pivotal scene inside Saint-Sulpice. These

theories became so prevalent that a response was posted in the church: "Contrary to fanciful allegations in a recent best-selling novel, this is not a vestige of a pagan temple. No such temple ever existed in this place. . . . No mystical notion can be derived from this instrument of astronomy except to acknowledge that God the Creator is the master of time." Drummond 2006, 71.

32 Saint-Sulpice features in Joris-Karl Huysmans's novel about Satanism in nineteenth-century France, *The Damned* (*Là-Bas*, 1891).

33 It is not known if Tissot actually ever made this painting; there is no image of it in Tissot's photographic albums of his art. Misfeldt 1982, 8. According to Misfeldt, "It was the custom in Paris at that time for fashionable women, mainly opera singers, to perform at mass. The painting entitled *Musique Sacrée* depicted a prima donna and a nun rehearsing a duet in an organ loft with another nun accompanying them at the organ." Misfeldt 1971, 236.

34 Levy 1898, 954, 956.

35 In his introduction to *The Life of Christ*, Tissot wrote, "I also consulted Catherine Emmerich, whose visions, generally so precise, impressed me greatly." Tissot 1899, xi. Emmerich's visions were first published in German in 1833, with the French translation published in 1854. Emmerich 2003. A notebook found at the Château de Buillon contains Tissot's notes on the gospels and on Emmerich's corresponding visions. Collection Frédéric Mantion.

36 Cleveland Moffett recounted that Tissot "had gone with the pilgrims to Lourdes to ask a benediction on his effort." Moffett 1899, 390. For more on Lourdes, see Harris 1999. See also Mongeau 2017. Tissot also reportedly planned an unrealized series about another seer of visions, Joan of Arc. Bastard 1906, 277–278.

37 Stead 1897, 178.

38 Sherard 1895.

39 Shaw 1895.

40 Tissot 2009, 39. Tissot earned 100,000 dollars from the United States tour admission fees alone.

41 This amounts to approximately 1,800,000 dollars in 2019. The acquisition of these works was heralded by the president of the Brooklyn Museum's board of trustees, A. Augustus Healy, as so important that "the popular interest in them will be permanent and that the galleries . . . which will contain them, will be the most crowded of the building." Tissot 2009, 37, 39. The museum later acquired a sketchbook for *The Life of Christ* series (accession number: 1992.20), which reveals how Tissot worked out his ideas in squares that he painted over in red when completed.

42 New York 1982. Tissot writes about this process to Maurice de Brunhoff, publisher of the Old Testament series; the letters are held in the Fondation Custodia / Collection Frits Lugt, Paris.

43 Collection Frédéric Mantion.

44 I wish to thank Krystyna Matyjaszkiewicz, who first brought these designs to my attention. Matyjaszkiewicz suggests that auditorium seating and a stage on the lower level could have been for dioramas or lantern-slide presentations. Krystyna Matyjaszkiewicz, email to author, October 12, 2015. Bastard wrote that Tissot wanted to make a giant panorama for the 1900 exposition, but that this ambition remained unrealized. Bastard 1906, 277–278.

45 Jopling 1925, 61.

46 The portrait is accompanied by the text: "Ye who have read these volumes written for your benefit and have perhaps been moved by what they contain . . . say a prayer for their author: Oh God, have mercy on the soul of him who wrote this book, cause Thy light go shine upon him and grant to him eternal rest." Tissot 1899, 272.

47 Nancy Rose Marshall observes of this image that Tissot's left hand seems transparent, as if he is a dematerializing or materializing spirit, giving the impression that "he seems to hover in space, as though this were a portrait of his ghost rather than his living body, like the spirit of Kathleen Newton in *The Apparition*." New Haven, Québec, and Buffalo 1999–2000, 184.

48 Moffett 1899, 387.

49 Misfeldt 1971, 238.

50 Cited in Laver 1936, 48–49. Tissot is also mentioned in Bennett's April 9, 1905, diary entry. Bennett 1932, 214.

51 Thomson 1984, 92.

52 Wentworth 1984, 196.

53 "J'ai ressenti la même émotion dans Jérusalem, au saint Sepulcre, le lieu même, les vieux souvenirs, tout sur la foi, on entre certainment là dans un état d'âme spécial, on sent, ou plutôt je sens une certaine présence autour de soi que nous pénêtre particulièrement, l'intuition se développe certainement on se dématerialise, on s'attendrit sans cesse." Tissot to Brunhoff, Jerusalem, April 6, 1896, record ID: 116297, Morgan Library and Museum, New York. Brunhoff was the publisher of Tissot's series of Old Testament illustrations.

THE RESURRECTION OF PAINTING: TISSOT AND CINEMA

VALENTINE ROBERT

This essay was translated from the original French into English by Rose Vekony.

1 For more on Tissot's *The Life of Christ*, see Tissot 2009.

2 The term comes from Bolter and Grusin 1999.

3 Beginning in 1906, newspapers announced the projection of biblical films "according to the French artist J. J. Tissot"; *New York Daily Tribune* 1906. Vitagraph Studios indicated that it had consulted the painter's work to prepare the sets for *The Life of Moses* (J. Stuart Blackton, 1909); *Film Index* 1910. "The touch of [Tissot's] master hand" was said to be evident in *The Deluge* (J. Stuart Blackton, 1911); *Nickelodeon* 1911, 196. Also, the director Fred Niblo stated that the casting of the Virgin Mary for his production of *Ben-Hur* (1925) was based on Tissot's drawings; Niblo 1925, 23.

4 Cyrille Sciama, interviewed in the documentary *First Passion* (*Première Passion*, Philippe Baron, 2010).

5 Herbert Reynolds documents these references in detail in Reynolds 1992.

6 Staley 2013, 99.

7 In her memoirs and interviews, Guy-Blaché elucidates the influence of Tissot on her work, an aspect studied in particular by Gwendolyn Audrey Foster in Foster 1998. Also see Staley 2013; Shepherd 2016. With regard to *Christus*—a film celebrated for its many tableaux vivants inspired by diverse art-historical sources—no one has previously remarked on the importance of Tissot's influence, even though nearly a dozen of the film's tableaux vivants are clearly based on his work.

8 In *Intolerance*, the scene of the adulteress is a strict imitation of Tissot's *The Adulterous Woman* (ca. 1886–1894; Brooklyn Museum), but the composition is reversed, which possibly indicates that Griffith knew the composition as recorded on the engraving plate or had seen it projected in reverse during a lantern-slide lecture. In *Redemption*, the painter's influence can be specifically noted in the scene of Mary Magdalene anointing Jesus's feet, a direct reenactment of Tissot's composition of the same event, *The Ointment of the Magdalene* (ca. 1886–1894; Brooklyn Museum). A still of this scene from *Redemption* can be found in the undated and unpaginated "Publicité artistique" collection of promotional pictures and posters for the film, published by Gaumont-concessionnaire, and conserved at the Cinémathèque française in Paris. In *Ben-Hur*, Wyler explores the cinematic potential of one of the most innovative images of the Passion offered by Tissot: *Bird's-Eye View of the Forum* (pl. 150), which depicts the scene when Jesus is told his death sentence. This reference is identified in Morris 2009, 23. The scale and width of the composition is perfectly adapted to the CinemaScope format. The chromatic balance—in particular, the dialectic of red and white that surrounds Jesus's silhouette—gives the director the opportunity to enhance the Technicolor possibilities. The perspective from above, which de-dramatizes this moment using distance and order while also giving it its right collective and historical measure, blends perfectly with the framing aesthetics of Wyler's film, in which Christ is depicted as only a silhouette, without a face. For more about the ban on film depictions of Christ's face, see Robert 2015.

9 Buser 2002, 429.

10 Sitar 2009, 200.

11 Alice Guy-Blaché's sets were replicas; she explicitly asked her set decorator, Henri Ménessier, to construct twenty-five sets after Tissot's Bible. Foster 1998, 10.

12 David J. Shepherd even claims that Tissot "effectively anticipated the cinematic cut-in shot." Shepherd 2016, 71.

13 Jackson 1912, 121.

14 See Robert 2008.

15 Reynolds 1992, 285 n5, 277.

16 Keil 1992, 117.

17 Shepherd 2013, 145.

18 The full English title of the Tissot Bible was *The Life of Our Lord Jesus Christ: Three Hundred and Sixty-Five Compositions from the Four Gospels with Notes and Explanatory Drawings by James Tissot*. On Tissot's scientific context and the "illusion" of his historical accuracy, see Schiff 1982.

19 Guy-Blaché 1986, 42.

20 The intertitle that quotes John 2:1 to announce the episode of the marriage at Cana in Galilee contains a footnote

specifying, "The ceremony according to [Archibald] Sayce, [James] Hastings, [Francis] Brown, and Tissot." On the use of Tissot's work as visual documentation for *Intolerance*, see Martin 1983.

21 Dolkart 2009a, 27.

22 On these promotional exhibitions, which took place in spring 1897—or perhaps as early as 1896—at the Galerie Georges Petit in Paris, see ibid., 27, 33n72.

23 Dolkart 2009b, 45.

24 The projection plates reproducing the works of Tissot's *The Life of Christ* have an exceptional status in most magic-lantern catalogues in terms of both quantity (they could be sold in series comprising more than two hundred items) and quality (they sometimes cost more than average and were praised for their precise reproduction technique). See in particular Kleine 1905, 164–166; Moore 1902, 153, 431–434.

25 The first films about Jesus had already appeared by 1898, but the development of cinema in no way diminished the success of Tissot's still projections; in fact, the opposite is true. Series of his plates remained popular in catalogues up to the 1920s. The success of Olcott's *From the Manger to the Cross* even became a selling point; an advertisement in *Moving Picture World* urged readers to go see the still projections of the paintings, which were "the basis of the Kalem Co.'s famous production." *Moving Picture World* 1912.

26 Tissot personally selected the images to project for a lecture given at Plymouth Church in Brooklyn on November 29, 1899, some months before the Brooklyn Museum acquired his work. Morgan 2009, 65n28.

27 The Goncourt brothers, who attended this event at Tissot's home, describe it in a February 1, 1890, entry in their journal. Goncourt 1895, 130. Early films existed only as live film shows; an exhibitor would buy the films and then present many of them in one touring show, replete with additional accompaniments, such as a narrator-showman speaking next to the screen and live music. On the central role played in early film screenings by this narrator (*bonimenteur*), see Boillat 2007; Lacasse 2000. In their account, the Goncourts use the term "boniment" to describe Tissot's performance.

28 In Montreal, for example, the "Famous Tissot Paintings" were shown in 1899 at Windsor Hall—the same place where *The Passion Play of Oberammergau*, produced by the Edison Co. had been screened the year before. *La Presse* 1898; *La Presse* 1899. In 1899, the New York–based department store Wanamaker's anointed a "Tissot Gallery" on its fifth floor in order to display the painter's religious watercolors and sell the Tissot Bible. *New York Tribune* 1899. Some twelve years later, Olcott's *From the Manger to the Cross* would premiere in that same gallery. Morowitz 2009, 199.

FINAL YEARS AT THE BUILLON ESTATE

FRÉDÉRIC MANTION

This essay was translated from the original French into English by Rose Vekony.

1 Tissot 1865.

2 Misfeldt 1984, 25.

3 Ibid., 24–25.

4 Ibid., 24.

5 Misfeldt 1971, 328.

6 Misfeldt 1984, 25–26.

7 Ibid., 24.

"ALL ARE CLEVER, SEVERAL ARE HIDEOUS": TISSOT AND HIS PRINTS IN LONDON

DONATO ESPOSITO

The author thanks Rachel Sloan at the Courtauld Institute of Art Library, London, for her assistance with obtaining images used in this essay.

1 Misfeldt 1991, 182.

2 *Illustrated London News* 1876.

3 Hopkinson 2012; Lanigan 2003.

4 *Builder* 1876, also quoted in Hopkinson 2012, 388.

5 Ibid.

6 *Athenaeum* 1876, 837.

7 Rossetti 1876, 592.

8 Taylor 1877.

9 *The Widower* (1876; Art Gallery of New South Wales, Sydney).

10 *Times* 1877b.

11 *Athenaeum* 1877. The etching's catalogue number was 507.

12 *Scotsman* 1878. The etching was Tissot's most expensive submission that year, priced at 9 pounds and 9 shillings.

13 Also see the painting *Trafalgar Tavern (Greenwich)* (pl. 80).

14 *Athenaeum* 1879b.

15 *Athenaeum* 1880, 798.

16 *Daily News* 1880.

17 *British Architect* 1880. The large version of the painting *Emigrants* is dated 1873 (location unknown), and Tissot painted at least two small replicas as well. Either the 1873 picture or one of the smaller versions—it is not known which—was exhibited at the Grosvenor Gallery in 1879. See "Tissot's Sales Notebook," this volume.

18 *Glasgow Herald* 1880. The etching's catalogue number was 864.

19 *Morning Post* 1880.

20 *Manchester Courier* 1880.

21 Blackburn 1880, ii.

22 Tissot records earnings from etchings totaling 1,289 pounds in 1880, and 1,120 pounds in 1881. Misfeldt 1991, 21; "Tissot's Sales Notebook," this volume.

23 On the founding of the Royal Society of Painter-Etchers and Engravers, see Hopkinson 1999.

24 *Standard* 1881.

25 *Daily News* 1882.

26 *Bell's Life* 1882.

27 *Morning Post* 1882.

"ALWAYS IN SEARCH OF THE EXQUISITE IN ART": TISSOT'S CLOISONNÉ ENAMELS

KRYSTYNA MATYJASZKIEWICZ

1 *Leeds Mercury* 1882.

2 French manufacturers, notably Ferdinand Barbedienne and Christofle & Cie, had shown new cloisonné enamel pieces at the 1878 Exposition Universelle in Paris. No independent artists outside of these manufactories, however, were attempting to make cloisonné enamels at the time Tissot was developing his creations, which was most likely from around 1878. Tissot continued making cloisonné enamels until at least 1888, the year of his latest-dated plaque. His pieces were larger and more technically difficult than the cloisonné bracelets for which the French jeweler Lucien Falize became famous.

3 The Chinese jardinière that Tissot owned is pictured in Rutherford 1984, 81, fig. 36.

4 Irvine 2006, 29, pl. 25.

5 Tissot's description for the vases, "en gaine," is difficult to translate into English, and his precise intended meaning is unknown. In nineteenth-century French, "gaine" meant "scabbard" or "sheath," but could also mean "case." The term was also used in architecture to denote a terminal, while in naval speak it referred to a canvas edging.

6 See Matyjaszkiewicz 1988, 53, pl. 16.

7 Dudley Gallery 1882 exhibition catalogue, quoted in Rutherford 1984, 85.

8 Information on Chinese and European methods as well as Tissot's were kindly shared with me by Erika Speel after her close-up viewing of Tissot's cloisonné enamels at the Barbican Art Gallery, London. Erika Speel, correspondence with author, January 1985.

9 Speel 1986, 38.

10 Ibid., 37, 39.

11 No small furnace has ever been found on the Grove End Road property in Saint John's Wood, where Tissot spent the bulk of his London years. The only known reference to Tissot's cloisonné materials being at the house is a recollection by Lawrence Alma-Tadema's daughter Anna, stated to the Tissot biographer James Laver, of "the basement" of the property being "full of pots containing colours." Laver 1936, 50.

12 No bronze-founder's marks have yet been identified on Tissot's pieces. Further research is needed to determine who cast and finished his bronze sculptures. Barbedienne was the leading Paris founder at the time. Hatfield's specialized in bronze figure and ormolu manufacture. "British Bronze Sculpture Founders and Plaster Figure Makers, 1800–1980," National Portrait Gallery, London, npg.org.uk/research/programmes/british-bronze-founders-and-plaster-figure-makers-1800-1980-1/british-bronze-founders-and-plaster-figure-makers-1800-1980-h.

13 Tissot's 1881 purchases from Roberson include four pounds of red modeling wax, modeling tools, and sealing wax on August 3; eight pounds of red modeling wax and a secondhand modeling stand on August 12; eight pounds of hard red modeling wax on August 24; four and a half pounds of hard red modeling wax and one pound of ordinary "ditto" on August 27; twelve pounds of dark-red wax plus eleven pounds of red wax on August 30; two steel modeling tools on September 21; and six small steel modeling tools on November 3. On March 23, 1882, he also purchased an additional modeling stand. Roberson Archive, Hamilton Kerr Institute, Fitzwilliam Museum, Cambridge, England.

14 The phrase "wait and win" appears in Arabic, English, French, German, Hebrew, Latin, and Russian.

15 Dudley Gallery 1882 exhibition catalogue, quoted in Rutherford 1984, 85.

16 Several of Tissot's painted compositions echo sculptures by Pradier. For example, the languorous woman in Tissot's oil painting *Sweet Idleness* (*Dolce far niente*) (ca. 1880–1882; location unknown) recalls the supine figure in a small edition of Pradier's erotic bronze *Il dolce far niente* (1840s; location unknown).

17 Mercié's *David with the Head of Goliath* (1872; Musée d'Orsay, Paris) and *Gloria Victis* (1874; Musée d'Orsay, Paris) were exhibited at the 1878 Exposition Universelle, where Tissot would also have seen them. For influences on and emergence of the New Sculpture movement, see Beattie 1983, 135–158.

18 Paris 1883. For more on the Central Union of Decorative Arts (L'union centrale des arts décoratifs) and the blurring of boundaries between fine and decorative art, see Jones 2014. On how Victorian sculptors in Britain also debated and explored the blurring of boundaries, see Droth, Edwards, and Hatt, eds. 2014, ch. 8.

19 Lostalot 1883b, 454.

20 Dudley Gallery 1882 exhibition catalogue, quoted in Rutherford 1984, 85.

21 Laver 1936, 60. The plaque with Alma-Tadema's name is illustrated in Rutherford 1984, 84, fig. 38.

22 "Robore fessa novo dum flamma corpora replent / Robore corda novo sociis abstantibus ardent." "Corda" can mean "heart" or (instrument) "strings." I'm very grateful to Dr. Frederick Jones, University of Liverpool (through the kind offices of his colleague Dr. Zofia Archibald), for the translation.

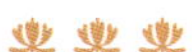

TISSOT'S PAINTING TECHNIQUES

SARAH KLEINER

I am indebted to Melissa E. Buron, whose passion for Tissot served as the catalyst for this research. Our scientific capabilities were greatly enhanced by the expertise of Emeline Simone Pouyet, who also furthered important international collaborations, and Lindsay Hardt Oakley. I owe a special thanks to Ann and Gordon Getty, Deborah Hatch, Maria Santangelo, Susan Roberts-Manganelli, Carole McNeil, and Sue and Bob O'Donnell, for providing access to privately held works by Tissot. From the outset, Devi Ormond guided me through nineteenth-century artist materials; she was an important partner throughout the project, along with Catherine Patterson. I am deeply grateful to Charlotte Hale and Alan Miller for sharing their expertise on the technical aspects of this essay. Frédéric Mantion and Ysabel and Frédéric Monnier kindly shared the magic of Tissot's former estate, the Château de Buillon, with me. Finally, thank you to my talented and patient colleagues at the Fine Arts Museums of San Francisco: Elise Effmann Clifford, who edited many drafts of this essay, and Tricia O'Regan and Natasa Morovic, whose work in the department made time for this research.

1 Warner 1999, 9–21.

2 An *esquisse* is a preliminary sketch used to work out the basic compositional elements of a design. An *étude* is a study of a detail, like drapery, hands, etc. An *ébauche* is undermodeling used to rough in a design and establish tonal relationships onto a prepared surface prior to painting the final composition. It is usually carried out in thin layers of earth colors. Boime 1971.

3 Misfeldt 1982.

4 Misfeldt 1991.

5 Auckland and Dunedin 2001–2002.

6 On nineteenth-century painting materials in Paris and London, see Callen 2000; Constantin 2001; Schaefer, Saint-George, Lewerentz 2008. See also Carlyle 2001.

7 The Fine Arts Museums of San Francisco received a 2018 grant from the Northwestern University / Art Institute of Chicago Center for Scientific Studies in the Arts, made possible by the generous support of the Andrew W. Mellon Foundation. The grant allowed for scientific analysis of five Tissot works using primarily noninvasive technologies, namely *in-situ* macro X-ray fluorescence and reflectance imaging spectroscopy (in the UV-visible and near-infrared ranges), together with microanalyses of microsamples. Key partners of the team included Emeline Simone Pouyet, research associate, and Lindsay Hardt Oakley, postdoctoral fellow.

8 Thank you to Frédéric Mantion for providing this access.

9 House 1997, 5.

10 House 1997, 20.

11 These wood types are identified in an 1888 sales list from Bourgeois Ainé. Schaefer, Saint-George, and Lewerentz 2008, 55.

12 Ibid., 53–56. Lower-priced options included unprimed softwood panels sold by the dozen to fit artists' travel cases, and cigar box lids, sometimes used for studies.

13 These include *Beating the Retreat in the Tuileries Gardens* (1867; private collection), *The Elder Sister* (pl. 97), *Hide and Seek* (pl. 82), *In Full Sunlight* (pl. 96), and *Promenade on the Ramparts* (pl. 8). Similar labels and stamps were found on *An Interesting Story* (fig. 47) and *Railway Station* (also known as *Waiting for the Train [Willesden Junction]*, pl. 44).

14 Mayer and Myers 2013, 25–26. Other Tissot paintings—such as *The Apparition* (also known as *The Mediumistic Apparition*, pl. 133), *Mary Magdalene at the Feet of Jesus* (ca. 1886–1894; private collection), and *Spring (Specimen of a Portrait)* (pl. 78)—have stamps from Winsor & Newton, sometimes on both canvas and stretcher. Tissot also bought canvases from William Badger, also listed as "W. BADGER / LATE EATWELL"; two examples are *Kathleen Newton at the Piano* (pl. 98) and *Reading in the Park* (ca. 1881; Musée des Beaux-Arts, Dijon, France).

15 Alan Miller, Associate Conservator, Metropolitan Museum of Art, correspondence with author regarding toolmarks, September 20, 2018. The toolmarks on the front of both panels are visible in the X-radiographs due to the radio-opaque ground.

16 Approximately 3 inches from the center of the panel is missing. The section may have gotten damaged when the single panel was coarsely cut into two pieces. In the nineteenth century, both panels and canvases were available in standard sizes. Special-order purchases or nonstandard sizes were costlier. The sales records of the British art materials supplier Charles Roberson & Co. include four entries for Tissot dating between 1873 and 1883. His purchases included plain-weave canvases in standard sizes, sometimes ordered on the "best" stretchers, and prepared panels cut to nonstandard sizes. In general, Tissot's use of standard and nonstandard sizes warrants further analysis. Roberson Archive, Fitzwilliam Museum, Cambridge, England, HKI MS. 109-1993 581, HKI MS. 248-1993 52, HKI MS. 250-1993 38. With gratitude to Rupert Featherstone, Director, Hamilton Kerr Institute and Assistant Director (Conservation), for providing access to the archive. See also Woodcock 1996.

17 Hale found that the panel for *In Full Sunlight* was scored and cut along the right edge likely during the painting process; the original green of the grass traverses and fills part of the score line. Charlotte Hale, correspondence with author, November 1, 2018.

18 Devi Ormond, Associate Paintings Conservator, J. Paul Getty Museum, Los Angeles, is currently undertaking a full technical study of this painting.

19 A note on the examination of the ground layers: many of the paintings in this study came from private collections, and sampling was not possible. Instead, conclusions about the ground layers came from careful observation under high-powered magnification and observations through X-radiography. A second phase of this research will include cross sections from a few select paintings to further characterize the ground and paint layers. A 2017 study of Tissot's *The Gallery of HMS "Calcutta" (Portsmouth)* (pl. 64), *Holyday* (pl. 52), and *Summer* (pl. 58) found thin, pale-gray primings of lead white with significant amounts of chalk and trace amounts of bone black. Two of the paintings had a double-gray priming; the other was from a fragmented cross section. Joyce Townsend has suggested that the unusually large amount of chalk could signify that the paintings had an absorbent priming conducive to Tissot's rapid working method. Dr. Joyce Townsend, Senior Conservation Scientist, unpublished conservation records, Tate, London, record nos. N04413, N04271, N04847.

20 Distinguishing between the varied tones of the *ébauche* or an overall *imprimatura* layer can be challenging, even with the aid of a microscope. This topic warrants further study through cross-sectional analysis.

21 Callen 2000, 63.

22 Ibid.

23 Callen 2000, 59.

24 Boime 1971, 37.

25 At the Château de Buillon is a list of keys for all of the rooms and buildings on the property in a thin, hand-bound book with a soft canvas cover. Key number "123" was for the "laboratoire photographie.' Also among the items found in Tissot's studio are numerous boxes of glass-plate negatives labeled "plaques au gelatino-bromure d'argent," from "A. Lumière & Ses Fils" in Lyon-Monplaisir. Other brands in the collection include an orange-label box from Guilleminot & Cie, 6, rue Choron, Paris, of gelatin-bromide plates targeted to portraits and moving subjects; and "plaques ultra-rapides" from E. Grieshaber & Cie. Other photographic materials found in the studio that likely belonged to Tissot include items labeled "Bain de Virage," "Chlorure d'Or," "Alun Pulvérisé," "Ammoniaque," and "Bain d'Alun," purchased from Photo-Hall at 5, rue Scribe, Paris.

26 The pigment analysis was carried out by scientists Emeline Simone Pouyet and Lindsay Hardt Oakley from the Center for Scientific Studies in the Arts using *in-situ* macro-scanning X-ray fluorescence, a noninvasive analytical technique.

27 Schaefer, Saint-George, and Lewerentz 2008, 59–62.

28 Ibid.

29 Callen 2000, 146–147.

30 The presence of cobalt green was proposed based on the correlation of zinc and cobalt distribution, however, it cannot be excluded that other zinc and cobalt-based pigment(s) may be present. Further analysis is needed to confirm. Joyce Townsend identified cobalt green on three other Tissot paintings, all ca. 1876. Dr. Joyce Townsend, Senior Conservation Scientist, unpublished conservation records, Tate, London, record nos. N04413, N04271, N04847. Additional pigment information on *Spring* can be found in an unpublished analysis by Libby Sheldon, who examined the painting using cross sections and polarized-light microscopy. Libby Sheldon, Report F1690, December 2002, for Victorian Pictures Christie's, History of Art Department, University College London, additionally cited by Krystyna Matyjaszkiewicz in the catalogue note for *Spring*, November 26, 2003, lot 21, Christie's, London, 90.

31 The analytical tools used to identify the blue pigment were not sensitive to low atomic number elements, such as those found in ultramarine. Supplementary analysis is underway to further explore the pigments and binders used by Tissot.

32 Thomson 1988, 239. Also see Callen 2019.

33 Ibid.

34 *The Impresario* is executed on pressed paper board that has been inset into a wooden cradle and varnished, likely in a later restoration.

35 Another example of the reddish-brown, striated, brush-applied toning layer can be found on Tissot's oil painting *Uncle Fred*, noted in the unpublished report C658, UCL Painting Analysis LTD, History of Art Department, University College London. Special thanks to Krystyna Matyjaszkiewicz for the reference.

36 When these formatting changes occurred and by whose hand cannot be determined from the current evidence. The other three sides of the sketch may also have undergone formatting changes.

TISSOT AND DEGAS: CONTOURS OF A FRIENDSHIP

MARINE KISIEL

This essay was translated from the original French into English by Alexandra Bonfante-Warren.

1 Wentworth 1978, 94, based on Halévy 1964, 118, and Lemoisne 1946–1949, 1:67.

2 Henri Loyrette noted, "It is often said that Degas broke with [Tissot] upon learning that he had gone over to the Communards: but the letters he wrote to him between 1871 and 1874 prove that he did not." (On a beaucoup dit que Degas rompit avec [Tissot] lorsqu'il apprit qu'il s'était rangé du côté des communards: mais les lettres qu'il lui écrivit entre 1871 et 1874 prouvent qu'il n'en est rien.) Paris 1988, 130, quoted in Reff 1968b, 89.

3 On June 5, 1871, Marie Cornélie Morisot wrote to her daughter, the painter Berthe Morisot, that Degas and Édouard Manet were both sympathetic to the Paris Commune and "critical of the repression's energetic ways" (blâment les moyens énergiques de la repression). Morisot 1950, 58. Degas, in a letter from August 1875, goes out of his way to advocate for Jules Dalou with the London dealer Charles Deschamps, manager of the Durand-Ruel gallery in London, expressing the hope "that there may be no political obstacle" (qu'il n'y ait pas d'empêchement politique) to his exhibiting work by the Communard sculptor, who was exiled in London. Degas to Deschamps, August 1875, reprinted in Reff 1968b, 89.

4 Manuscripts Department, Bibliothèque nationale de France, Paris, NAF 13005. These letters were published in Paris 1988, 357–366.

5 In 1872, Victor Hugo published his collection of poems about the Franco-Prussian War and its aftermath, titled *L'année terrible* (*The Terrible Year*).

6 "Tissot, pourquoi diable ne m'avez-vous pas écrit un mot? On m'a dit que vous gagniez beaucoup d'argent. Donnez-moi donc des chiffres." Degas to Tissot, September 30, 1871, Manuscripts Department, Bibliothèque nationale de France, Paris, NAF 13005, fol. 1r. English translations of Degas's letters are taken from Degas 1947, unless otherwise indicated.

7 "Bonne famille! C'est quelque chose de vraiment bon d'être marié, d'avoir de bons enfants et la tête délivrée du besoin de galanterie. Il est temps, grands dieux, d'y réfléchir." Degas to Tissot, November 19, 1872, Manuscripts Department, Bibliothèque nationale de France, Paris, NAF 13005, fol. 6v.

8 "C'est encore ce que je possède de meilleur que ma tête de jeune chien." Degas to Tissot, February 18, 1873, Manuscripts Department, Bibliothèque nationale de France, Paris, NAF 13005, fol. 9r. English translation by Alexandra Bonfante-Warren.

9 Over the course of their correspondence, Degas refers to seven of his paintings (L 186, L 281, L 295, L 298, L 309, L 320, L 321) as well as to family portraits and a print by Tissot "of a painting by you, the Thames, with a variant" (d'un tableau de vous, la Tamise, avec une variante). Manuscripts Department, Bibliothèque nationale de France, Paris, NAF 13005; Wentworth 1978, 349. L numbers refer to Paul-André Lemoisne's catalogue; Lemoisne 1946–1949.

10 "De Gas Brothers, New Orleans. / Tissot, que dites-vous de cet en-tête? C'est le papier de la maison. Ici on ne parle que coton et change." Degas to Tissot, November 19, 1872, fol. 6r.

11 "Et vous, qu'y a-t-il de nouveau depuis les 700 livres? Vous seriez capable, avec votre terrible activité, de faire sortir de l'argent de cette foule de cotton brokers, cotton dealers, etc." Degas to Tissot, November 19, 1872, fol. 6r.

12 "Comme vous y allez! 900 livres, mais c'est une fortune!" Degas to Tissot, February 18, 1873, fol. 8v.

13 "J'ai pris ici le goût de l'argent, et une fois de retour j'en saurai gagner, je vous le jure." Degas to Tissot, November 19, 1872, fol. 6r.

14 "J'ai entendu raconter que vous achetiez une propriété. J'en ai la bouche encore ouverte." Degas to Tissot, April 1873, Manuscripts Department, Bibliothèque nationale de France, Paris, NAF 13005, fol. 11r.

15 This may be a response to a letter dated September 30, 1871, in which Degas writes: "Within the next few days I may possibly make a flying visit to London with Achille. But it is not yet certain. In the meanwhile honour me with a few details." (Il se peut que j'aille à Londres ces jours-ci avec Achille pour un moment. Mais c'est incertain. En attendant honorez-moi de quelques écrits.) Degas to Tissot, September 30, 1871, fol. 1r. Achille was Degas's younger brother.

16 "Que je voudrais moi-même être avec vous et vous servir de guide." Tissot to Degas, Fonds Nepveu-Degas, Musée d'Orsay, Paris, ODO 2008-1-2. I suggest dating this letter to around October 1871, since Degas appears to be unfamiliar with London and to require advice of every kind concerning his stay; indeed, Degas, writing from London, describes himself thus to the etcher Alphonse Legros in a letter dated October 1871, most probably after receiving Tissot's advice to do so. Reff 1968b, 89. The fact remains that Tissot, in this letter, asks Degas to send his regards to Legros, Jean Louis Prévost, and Whistler, all of whom live in London. Would he have done so if he had only just recently left the city he lived in?

17 London and Paris 2017–2018.

18 "Donnez-moi quelque idée de la manière dont je pourrais tirer moi aussi quelque avantage de l'Angleterre." Degas to Tissot, September 30, 1871, fol. 2r.

19 "Allez tout de suite trouver Deschamps. S'il a encore les *Danseuses* . . . , qu'il les envoie à l'Exposition de Paris avant le 20 mars." Degas to Tissot, February 18, 1873, fol. 8r.

20 "Dites-moi quelque chose touchant mon avenir auprès d'Agnew." Degas to Tissot, April 1873, fol. 10r.

21 "Voyons, mon cher Tissot, pas d'hésitation, ni d'échappée. Il faut que vous exposiez au boulevard. Cela vous fera du bien à vous (c'est une manière de vous faire voir à Paris que des gens vous disent fuir) et à nous aussi." Degas to Tissot, March 1874, Manuscripts Department, Bibliothèque nationale de France, Paris, NAF 13005, fol. 14r.

22 "Il doit y avoir un Salon réaliste. . . . Laissez donc, un instant, la question d'argent. Exposez. Restez de votre pays et avec vos amis." Ibid.

23 "C'est le moment pour moi de faire flèche en Angleterre. . . . Que Tissot apprenne, bien que tard, à me voir me servir moi-même d'une de mes armes." Degas to Deschamps, August 22, 1875, reprinted in Reff 1968b, 89.

24 The archives of the École des Beaux-Arts record, albeit very concisely, Degas's and Tissot's entries and brief stays at the institution. Degas competed for a place in March 1856, and Tissot in March 1857. AJ 52 76, 235, and 272, Archives Nationales, Pierrefitte-sur-Seine, France.

25 In Henri Loyrette's view, "If Degas crossed paths with [Tissot], then it was only in passing at their common master's studio: the notebooks from this period do not name Tissot, and Degas never mentioned him during his three years in Rome." (Si Degas le croise alors [Tissot], ce n'est que très rapidement chez leur maître commun: les carnets de cette époque ne citent pas le nom de Tissot et Degas ne le mentionne jamais durant les trois années de son séjour italien.) Paris 1988, 130. I concur with this interpretation—it is difficult to see how Tissot could have met Degas at Lamothe's in 1858, as stated in Paris 1985, 129; Degas was in Italy for three years (1856–1859, then March–April 1860), with only short visits to Paris.

26 Paris 1988, 130; Wentworth 1984, 16.

27 "Je ne voulais pas rester plus longtemps sans vous dire . . . combien j'ai été touché de l'amabilité cordiale que vous m'avez témoigné les derniers jours que j'étais souffrant, ainsi que de l'adieu que vous m'avez fait. . . . Je me félicite plus que jamais d'avoir une connaissance telle que vous." Tissot to Degas, September 18, 1862, Fonds Nepveu-Degas, Musée d'Orsay, Paris, ODO 2008-1-2.

28 "Et Pauline? que devient-elle. À l'heure qu'il est où en êtes-vous. Cette ardeur contenue ne se dépense-t-elle que sur Sémiramis?" Ibid. "Semiramis" refers to Degas's *Semiramis Building Babylon* (ca. 1860–1862; Musée d'Orsay, Paris).

29 Loyrette 1991, 98–99.

30 On this subject, see ibid., 81 and esp. 141.

31 Ibid., 81, 137.

32 "Le vent qui souffle à travers le salon des Carpaccio me rend complètement fou."; "Je suis dans les Carpaccio, et je n'en sors pas. Quel cœur avait cet artiste. La manière dont il reproduit cette vie de Ste Ursule est ce qu'il y a de plus touchant." Tissot to Degas, September 18, 1862, Fonds Nepveu-Degas.

33 "L'assomption du Titien [l]'a laissé froid."; "Andrea Mantegna [et] Bellini m'ont ravi. Comme Bellini devait aimer l'intimité d'une femme ses têtes de Vierge sont admirables de suavité et d'humanité." Ibid.

34 "Tissot, ce vieil ami, avec qui j'ai tant vécu, si gaiement, si familièrement, il avait acheté plusieurs tableaux de moi, il les a revendus, c'est son affaire." Degas's comments are recalled by Daniel Halévy in Halévy 1995, 162.

35 "J'ai été sur le point de lui écrire une lettre terrible. À quoi bon? Je vais réunir quelques dessins qu'il m'avait donnés autrefois. Je les lui renverrai sans un mot. Il comprendra"; "Ah, je pourrais me venger, je ferais une caricature de Tissot, et le Christ, derrière lui, le fouettant, et dessous: *Le Christ chassant son vendeur du temple*. Ah, mon Dieu!" Ibid.

CHRONOLOGY

KRYSTYNA MATYJASZKIEWICZ

1 Sciama, this volume.

2 Misfeldt 1971, 14–15.

3 Bastard 1906, 255; Gibson 1989, 123. The Jesuit school at Brugelette had students from England, where Roman Catholic practice had been banned until 1829.

4 Bastard 1906, 255.

5 According to Bastard, Tissot's mother recommended him to Nantes-born painter Jules-Élie Delaunay. Bastard 1906, 257. Delaunay left for Italy in 1856, having won the École des Beaux-Arts Prix de Rome award, and probably directed Tissot to the two artists under whom Delaunay had studied, Lamothe and Flandrin. Tissot is stated to be a pupil of Lamothe and Flandrin in his 1858 registration to copy at the Cabinet des Estampes, and in the 1859 and 1861 Paris Salon catalogues. Degas enrolled at the École des beaux-arts on April 6, 1855, as a pupil of Lamothe; he traveled around France in July–September 1855, including Lyon, and was in Italy from October 1856 to March 1859, meeting Delaunay in Rome. London 1987b, 136.

6 Misfeldt 1991, 46. Tissot is already calling himself "James" by 1855.

7 Reff 1964, 557.

8 Nantes 2005–2006, 14, 44.

9 Meeting recorded in Pennell 1902, 1:73. Whistler's copy of the painting (private collection) is dated 1857; the location of Tissot's copy is unknown.

10 "Tissot's Sales Notebook," this volume.

11 Reff 1964, 557.

12 Nantes 2005, 14, 44. An oil-on-canvas *Saint John the Baptist* (sold Hôtel Drouot, Paris [June 7, 2006; lot 120]; location unknown) was described in the sale catalogue as relating to the Prix de Rome competition.

13 Reff 1964, 558.

14 On Tissot's photograph albums, see introduction to "Tissot's Sales Notebook," this volume. For the patron saint works, *Saint James the Great and Saint Bernard* and *Saint Marcel and Saint Olivier*, see Misfeldt 1982, pls. I-3 and I-4; *Walk in the Snow*, see Wentworth 1984, pl. 1; *Portrait of Mme T. . .*, see Misfeldt 1991, pl. I-1; *Portrait of Mlle H. de S. . .* (Ségur?), probably Misfeldt 1991, pl. I-2. The patron saints and *Walk in the Snow* are signed with Tissot's name in Latin, *Jacobus Tissot*.

15 Tissot to John Williamson Palmer, August 31, 1881, John Williamson Palmer Papers, Clifton Waller Barrett Library, accession 8099-a, University of Virginia Library, Charlottesville.

16 *Marguerite at the Window*, *Marguerite in Church*, and a partial replica of the latter. "Tissot's Sales Notebook," this volume.

17 Misfeldt 1986, 110.

18 For *Marguerite at the Service*, see Wentworth 1984, pl. 5; *Portrait of Mlle M. P...* is probably the painting dated 1861 (Northampton Art Gallery, England), illustrated in Wentworth 1984, pl. 24.

19 For photographs of Tissot paintings published by Goupil, Bingham, and Braun, see Nantes 2005, 107, 117–118.

20 Misfeldt 1971, 289, 328.

21 Tissot to Edgar Degas, September 18, 1862, Fonds Nepveu-Degas, Musée d'Orsay, Paris, ODO 2008-1-2, reprinted in Lemoisne 1946–1949, 1:230–231.

22 Reff 1964, 558.

23 See Wentworth 1984, pl. 13.

24 It is not known which version of *Marguerite in Church* this was.

25 For *The Elopement* and *At the Break of Day*, see Misfeldt 1982, pls. I-19, I-18; sold Elstob & Elstob, Bedale Hall (March 24, 2019; lot 564); location unknown.

26 A small portrait of "Two Sisters" (collection of Lady Sophia Topley) is inscribed verso on the stretcher "London 1864" (perhaps in another hand). Exhibited Rome 2015–2016, no. 12.

27 *Faust and Marguerite in the Garden* was exhibited at Knoedler's gallery, and *Marguerite at the Fountain* at S. P. Avery's rooms, also in New York. *New Path* 1865.

28 Reff 1964, 558.

29 *The Confessional* is illustrated in Wentworth 1984, pl. 32; *Young Woman in a Church* in Misfeldt 1982, pl. I-38.

30 Paletta 1866, 136.

31 *Young Woman Singing in the Choir* is illustrated in Wentworth 1984, pl. 35.

32 *The Rendez-vous* is illustrated in Misfeldt 1982, pl. I-47.

33 *Beating the Retreat* is illustrated in Wentworth 1984, pl. 45; *A Luncheon*, in Wentworth 1984, pl. 60; and a replica of the latter, with slight variations, is illustrated as *A Luncheon* (fig. 48) in this volume. The two watercolors, titled *Melancholy* and *Portrait*, are unidentified; *Melancholy* may be a replica of the oil painting *Melancholy* (pl. 13) or, if the same work as the watercolor *Melancholy* sold in 1870, may be a replica of *Marguerite at the Fountain* (fig. 31), as both the latter and the 1870 watercolor are described in Tissot's sales notebook as "Melancholy (yellow cloak)." "Tissot's Sales Notebook," this volume.

34 *Dance of Death* (probably pl. 7), priced 3,000 francs; *From the Life of a Libertine*, *The Rendez-vous*, priced 2,000 francs, likely to be the painting illlustrated in Misfeldt 1982, pl. I-67 (1869; location unknown); *From the Life of a Libertine, Married*, priced 2,000 francs, likely to be Misfeldt 1982, pl. I-72 (ca. 1869; location unknown); *The Widow*, priced 5,000 francs, may be a replica of the Paris Salon picture (whose exhibition overlaps) or a different, unidentified work; *The Abduction* or *The Elopement*, priced at 7,000 francs, is probably the painting now in the collection of Musée d'arts de Nantes, illustrated in Rome 2015–2016, 58–59, cat. 4.

35 *A Widow* is illustrated in Wentworth 1984, pl. 51.

36 Tissot's caricatures of Napoleon III (fig. 35) and Queen of Spain Isabella II appeared in September 1869 under "Coïdé"; Leopold II King of Belgians, Alexander II Emperor

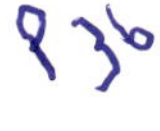

of Russia, and Abdul Aziz Sultan of Turkey in October; Reverend Temple, Bishop Designate of Exeter in November; and Earl of Zetland in December 1869. Drawings of Pope Pius IX, Émile Ollivier, Henri Rochefort, and Victor Emanuel I were published in January 1870; General Trochu and Crown Prince of Prussia in September 1870; and Count von Bismarck in October 1870.

37 Tissot painted six small pictures of single actors (*comédiens*), illustrated in Misfeldt 1982, pls. I-50–I-55.

38 *The Penitent* may be the painting that Tissot sold to Goupil in 1869 as *The Confessional (green dress)*, a work corresponding to the photograph illustrated in Misfeldt 1982, pl. I-71; the latter, or a replica, sold at Sotheby's, London (July 14, 2016; lot 30); location unknown.

39 Bowles 1871, 93.

40 Tissot's sketch of Cuvelier's dead body was made in one of his pocket sketchbooks, now held in a private collection.

41 Louis XVI and Queen Marie Antoinette were executed at the guillotine by French revolutionaries in 1793. Tissot's choice of title likely reflects his political opinions following French defeat in 1871. The painting, which was priced at 3,500 francs, is probably a replica of *Le Toast*, illustrated in Misfeldt 1982, and bought in 1869 by the Kaiser of Vienna for 5,000 francs; one of these versions is in the Museum and Picture Gallery, Baroda, India.

42 Willard Misfeldt, letter to author, 1989; Misfeldt had seen the *laissez-passer*.

43 Watercolor recording execution of two Communards inscribed *rue Saint Germain l'Auxerrois, 25 mai 1871*, sold through Thierry de Maigret, Paris (March 17, 2004; lot 102); location unknown.

44 "Tissot's Sales Notebook," this volume.

45 Tissot inscribed and gave a drawing of a soldier to Mrs. Millais on June 19, 1871 (London and Manchester 1984–1985, 104).

46 "Tissot's Sales Notebook," this volume.

47 *The Thames* was listed in the first edition of the 1872 exhibition catalogue as *Before the Departure*, subsequently amended.

48 De Nittis had bought a house near Tissot's the day war was declared with Prussia in 1870 and had returned to it after fleeing to Italy, but was having difficulties meeting mortgage repayments. Tissot may have offered his Paris house to de Nittis for peppercorn rent; he was about to buy a house in London. De Nittis gives the same address as Tissot's house (64, avenue Uhrich, the new name for avenue de l'Impératrice since 1871) in a letter dated February 1, 1873, to Telemaco Signorini, and subsequently continues using it (avenue Uhrich becoming avenue du Bois de Boulogne in 1875) until sometime around March to September 1880. In January 1880, de Nittis finalized payment on building of a new house at 3, bis rue Viette, in the Monceau district of Paris, where he moved with his family later that year. Letters quoted in Moscatiello 2008.

49 London and Manchester 1984–1985, 107, no. 48.

50 Georges Bastard says this took place in 1874. Bastard 1906, 263. However, recently uncovered documentary evidence shows that Tissot had already cleared his name in 1872. See Tillier, this volume.

51 Degas to Tissot, March 1874, Manuscripts Department, Bibliothèque nationale de France, Paris, NAF 13005, fol. 14r. Reprinted in Paris 1988, 364–365.

52 The picture of "Two warmer lovers" is unidentified but may be the oil version of the etching *Ramsgate* (Wentworth 22).

53 "Tissot's Sales Notebook," this volume.

54 Manet's *The Grand Canal, Venice* (1874; Shelburne Museum, Vermont) resulted from an extended autumn–winter 1874 sojourn in the Italian city by Manet and his wife, and was bought by Tissot in Paris on May 24, 1875, for 2,500 francs. Wilson-Bareau 1989. Mistaken dating of Manet's visit to Venice has led earlier authors to suggest, erroneously, that Tissot accompanied him.

55 *Glasgow Herald* 1876. Alma-Tadema and Edwin Long were appointed Associates of the Royal Academy on January 26, 1876; Marcus Stone and Peter Graham on January 24, 1877; Edward Boehm and Alfred Waterhouse on January 16, 1878.

56 Other paintings shown by Tissot at the 1877 Grosvenor Gallery exhibition were *Gossiping* (1865; location unknown), *Meditation* (1865; location unknown), *Portsmouth Dockyard* (ca. 1877; Tate, London), and *The Widower* (1876; Art Gallery of New South Wales, Sydney).

57 "Fors Clavigera: Letters to the Workmen and Labourers of Great Britain," letter dated June 18, 1877, in Ruskin 1903–1912, 27:161.

58 Misfeldt 1971, 328; Misfeldt, letter to author, 2003.

59 Tissot to Petit, August 9, 1878. Fondation Custodia / Collection Frits Lugt, Paris, 1992-A.908.

60 *July* exhibited in Liverpool, *Evening* and *Winter* (as *Wintertime*) in Manchester, and *Reverie* (1878; location unknown) at the Dudley Gallery.

61 Tissot to Petit, March 4, 1879, March 12, 1879, and April 1, 1879. Fondation Custodia / Collection Frits Lugt, Paris, 1992-A.909-910; 1992-A.911.

62 Other paintings shown by Tissot at the 1879 Grosvenor Gallery exhibition were *Emigrants* (one of several known versions, ca. 1878–1879; Speed Art Museum, Louisville, and location unknown) and *Under the Chestnut Tree*, *A Quiet Afternoon*, *Going to Business*, and *Crossing the Channel* (all ca. 1878–1879; location unknown).

63 *Rivals* and *The Hammock* exhibited in Manchester, *The Organ Grinder* (ca. 1878–1879; location unknown) in Liverpool, and *The Warrior's Daughter* (ca. 1878–1879; Manchester Art Gallery) and *Quiet* (ca. 1878–1879; private collection) at the Dudley Gallery.

64 *Uncle Fred* (ca. 1879; private collection) and *The Hammock* were exhibited in Glasgow, and *The Gardener* (as *Gardening*, ca. 1879–1880; location unknown) at Southport.

65 Lostalot 1883a, 381.

66 Tissot to Avery, May 21, 1880, Samuel Putnam Avery Papers, 14869/301, Metropolitan Museum of Art, New York.

67 Hopkinson 1999, 11; records of the Royal Society of Painter-Printmakers, London, NRA 38876, The National Archives, London.

68 *The Tale* (ca. 1880; private collection) in Birmingham; *Visiting the Louvre* (ca. 1880; location unknown) and *Uncle Fred* in Liverpool.

69 A critic for *The Observer* described "a translation into nineteenth-century English of the biblical narrative of the Prodigal Son." The same critic declared that Tissot's "intense belief in the artistic possibilities of modern life is shown in its greatest strength" in the series, and that "M. Tissot's freedom from conventionalism makes his treatment extremely interesting." *Observer* 1880.

70 At the Hanover Gallery, London, Tissot showed the watercolor *Do-re-mi-fa-sol-la-si-do* (ca. 1880), described as a lady seated at a piano practicing, which is probably the watercolor now at the Museum of Art, Rhode Island School of Design, Providence. At the Atkinson Art Gallery, Southport, he exhibited *Visiting the Louvre* (ca. 1880; location unknown) and *Uncle Fred*; and at the Glasgow Institute of Fine Arts, the oils *Do, re, mi, fa, sol, la, te, do!* (ca. 1880–1881; location unknown) and *Meditation* (ca. 1881; probably the painting now known as *Reading in the Park*, Musée des Beaux-Arts, Dijon, see fig. 119), plus a watercolor *Good-Bye!—On the Mersey* (ca. 1880–1881; probably the watercolor in the Walker Art Gallery, Liverpool).

71 *Le Salon à Londres* at the Royal Panorama Galleries, Leicester Square, London, was advertised in June 1881 newspapers, with Tissot listed among exhibiting artists; no details of Tissot's exhibits are known.

72 Oil of *Goodbye: On the Mersey* (ca. 1881; location unknown) exhibited at Southport; watercolors of *Goodbye (on the Mersey?)* and *Quiet* (ca. 1881; location unknown) exhibited at Royal Society of Artists, Birmingham, together with four etchings.

73 *An Exhibition of Modern Art by J. J. Tissot* opened on May 15, 1882, at the Dudley Gallery, with private views on May 12 and 13. It included "The Prodigal Son in Modern Life; Paintings, Etchings and Émaux Cloisonnés." The Duchess of Edinburgh visited the exhibition on May 22. Tissot's exhibits at the Yorkshire Fine Arts Society, Leeds, and Newcastle Arts Association are unknown.

74 Jehan Georges Vibert, an artist friend in Paris, wrote to Tissot on May 17, 1882, to tell him that he had been elected. Misfeldt 1971, 210. On June 1, 1882, Tissot sent Georges Petit watercolors of *Summer Evening* and *Children's Picnic* by steamer for the next exhibition of the Société des aquarellistes français. Tissot to Petit, June 2 and June 10, 1882. Fondation Custodia / Collection Frits Lugt, Paris, 1992-A.912-913.

75 Degas to Tissot, June 8, 1882; postmarked June 9, 1882, introduces Mr. Marriott, coming on behalf of Durand-Ruel to organize a small exhibition in London. The July 1882 exhibition was the first organized by Durand-Ruel since 1874 of work by Impressionist artists. He returned in 1883 with a larger exhibition at different premises.

76 Watercolor versions of *The Prodigal Son* (ca. 1881; location unknown), an oil of *The Tale* (ca. 1881; private collection), and three etchings exhibited at Liverpool; four etchings in Glasgow; and unknown work in Manchester.

77 Lostalot 1883a.

78 Misfeldt 1988, 164–165.

79 "Tissot's Sales Notebook," this volume.

80 The artist Jacques-Émile Blanche, who also attended the séance, gave an account to Tissot's biographer James Laver. Blanche to Laver, June 12, 1936, Laver Papers, MS Laver B39, University of Glasgow Special Collections; Laver 1936, 51. Blanche thought the séance took place about 1885, but Besnard only lived in London until late 1883. The mention of 1885 has led to confusion of this séance with a different one on May 20, 1885, recorded in Tissot's mezzotint *The Apparition* (pl. 132).

81 Misfeldt 1988, 166–167.

82 Scholl was to write the story to accompany Tissot's proposed, but not executed, etching after his painting *The Tight-Rope Dancer* (ca. 1883–1885; location unknown) in the *La Femme à Paris* series.

83 Farmer 1890, 186–187.

84 Farmer 1890, 187.

85 Wentworth 1984, 160, 178.

86 Matyjaszkiewicz,"'Always in Search of the Exquisite in Art': Tissot's Cloisonné Enamels," this volume.

87 Misfeldt 1971, 328.

88 Tissot notes "mai 1888 / juin / juillet / août / sept / 70 [+] 20 [total] 90" and "Dessins / 1888–90" in his sketchbook of preparatory drawings for *The Life of Christ*. A. Augustus Healy Fund, Healy Purchase Fund B and the Alfred T. White Fund, Brooklyn Museum, 1992.20.

89 On this exhibition, see Leard 1997, 355–356. Tissot showed a watercolor titled *The Luncheon*, lent by A. M. Beugniet (probably *Morning Luncheon*, bought by Beugniet in 1886; see "Tissot's Sales Notebook," this volume); a watercolor titled *On the Thames* (probably Misfeldt 1982, pl. IV-4; location unknown); a watercolor titled *At the Louvre* (probably London and Manchester 1984–1985, 122, no. 118; location unknown); *The Little Maid*, described as a sketch (probably Misfeldt 1982, pl. III-70; location unknown); *Coldstream Guards Fifers*, two oil studies (location unknown; one of them formerly owned by Maurice de Brunhoff); and twenty etchings, of which eleven were lent by the publisher A. M. L. Dumont and were for sale.

90 Tissot to Ernest Meissonier, September 28, 1889, Correspondance de Meissonier, NUM 0424 (2, T), Fonds d'Archives Jean-Louis-Ernest Meissonier, Manuscrits de la Bibliothèque centrale des musées nationaux, Institut national d'histoire de l'art, Paris. Tissot writes that he cannot take up Meissonier's invitation as he has been ill with fever since returning from Jerusalem. A note that fifty drawings are completed is logged in Tissot's sketchbook for *The Life of Christ* (see n88).

91 *Glasgow Herald* 1889. This publication proposal fell through, and over the next few years Tissot was reported to be seeking a publisher. Not until the exhibition of 270 illustrations in 1894 was Tissot able to secure one: Alfred Mame et fils. Some of his drawings were made into wood engravings and included in the eventual publication (pls. 140–142).

92 Although Tissot did not build his planned studio, Père Marie-Joseph Lagrange, whom Tissot knew well and who wrote about the *Life of Christ* illustrations, founded in 1890 the École pratique des études bibliques within the Dominican Monastery of Saint Stephen, Jerusalem, where later scholars would be responsible for the Jerusalem Bible translated from original languages.

93 Use of such models was frequent among artists who had complex groupings or lighting to resolve.

94 Degas had sold the painting in 1872 to Durand-Ruel, who exhibited it in London, then sold it to Gabriel Faure in 1874. Faure gave it to Degas, who then gave it to Tissot, who subsequently sold the painting to Durand-Ruel on March 11, 1890. Tissot also owned *Woman with Binoculars* (ca. 1875–1876; Galerie Neue Meister, Dresden) by Degas. The Manet was bought from the artist by Tissot in 1875 and sold in March 1890 for 6,000 francs to Durand-Ruel, who sold it to Mr. Havemeyer in 1895. It is possible that the sales related to his Jerusalem building plans. The year 1890 is also the last that Tissot recorded sales in his sales notebook, and it appears he was wrapping up activity other than his religious illustration. "Tissot's Sales Notebook," this volume.

95 Mary Cassatt to Madame Manet [Berthe Morisot], Tuesday [April 1890], reprinted in Cassatt 1984, 214. Tissot's interest may have been in the context of Société des peintres-graveurs preoccupations, but he was also investigating possible ways of reproducing his *Life of Christ* illustrations.

96 Note in Tissot's sketchbook for *The Life of Christ* (see n88).

97 Goncourt 1896, 177–178.

98 Edith Coues to Mr. Johnson [Century Press], January 24, 1894, Century Company records, series I, General Correspondence, box 102, Manuscripts and Archives Division, New York Public Library.

99 *Times* 1894b.

100 Color lithography was a very new form of reproduction, requiring separate printing of each color using separate lithographic stones for each plate. It was reported that an estimated sixteen thousand working days had been spent on printing Tissot's plates, using between four thousand and five thousand lithographic stones, each of which required ten to twelve successive printings of different colors. Misfeldt 1971, 273.

101 Misfeldt 1984, 24–27; *Builder* 1895; *Builder* 1897.

102 Tissot to Cardinal Langénieux, January 29, 1895, regarding the pose of the legate in the painting Tissot is working on. Misfeldt 1971, 276.

103 There was a series of competitions for the Exposition Universelle 1900 master plan and buildings therein from late 1894 to 1897. Nénot's designs for Tissot incorporate a basement auditorium, perhaps for showing dioramas or lantern-slide projections, and may be linked to Tissot's unrealized idea to make "a gigantic panorama" for the 1900 Exposition Universelle. Bastard 1906, 277. I am grateful to Roselyne Hurel for bringing Nénot's designs to my attention in 1994.

104 Exhibition opened to the public Thursday March 26, 1896, with previews from March 23; reviews appeared in British newspapers from March 24, 1896, until at least December 12, 1897. Classified advertisements for the exhibition continued to appear until at least June 21, 1898. Watercolors were withdrawn periodically for copying as color lithographs.

105 This is mentioned in a brief news item at the bottom of a page in the *Daily News* on November 25, 1896: "M. James Tissot having just returned from the Holy Land paid a visit to the Lemercier Gallery yesterday to view his collection of drawings, 'The Life of Our Lord,' and was much pleased at the way they were arranged. We understand M. Tissot intends remaining in town during the week."

106 See Paris 1985, 250–251; the oil on canvas design for the Christ was deposited by the Bibliothèque du Sauchoir at the Petit Palais, Musée des Beaux-Arts de la ville de Paris.

107 Halévy 1964.

108 *The Reception in Jerusalem of the Apostolic Legate from the Holy See, S. E. Mgr. Cardinal Langénieux by the Patriarch S. B. Mgr. Piavi*, commissioned by M. le Comte Chaudon de Briailles, who gave it to the Cardinal, who in turn gave it to Reims Cathedral; destroyed in bombardment of Reims during the First World War. Engraving of it published in Paris 1985, 106, fig. 49. A study for it was sold through Mes. André Havard and Régis Bailleul, Hôtel des Ventes, Bayeaux, May 19, 1985; location unknown.

109 *La Libre Parole* 1897. The day before the exhibition opened, May 4, there was a terrible fire at the Bazar de la Charité, Paris, caused by ignited cinema film, with more than one hundred people killed, including many society ladies, among them the Duchesse d'Alençon.

110 "Her Royal Highness the Duchess of Saxe-Coburg and Gotha, their Royal Highnesses the Grand Duke and Grand Duchess of Hesse, and their Imperial Highnesses the Grand Duke and Grand Duchess Serge of Russia visited the Lemercier Gallery . . . yesterday, to inspect the collection of pictures of J. James Tissot illustrating the life of Our Lord Jesus Christ." *Times* 1897.

111 Sampson Low's English-language edition appeared in monthly installments from October 1897. Examples were available to view at the Lemercier Gallery, London, where from 1896 it was possible to subscribe to the whole two-volume French-language edition published by Mame (200 guineas for the first twenty copies, which all sold; 60 guineas for copies 21–1,000), or to order individual prints, ranging from 1 to 4 guineas each. Lemercier Gallery exhibition catalogue, 1896.

112 The inauguration was accompanied by a conference on Christian art.

113 *New York Times* 1898a.

114 A classified advertisement in *The Times* on March 1, 1898, read: "His Royal Highness the Duke of York honoured the Lemercier Gallery, 35, New Bond Street, W., with a visit on Saturday last to inspect the Collection of Pictures illustrating the 'Life of Our Lord Jesus Christ' by J. James Tissot."

115 Tissot had also received an invitation to the exhibition dinner given by the Lord Mayor at the Mansion House on July 23 but is not named among attendees; in a letter dated July 3, Buillon, to De Brunhoff, Tissot mentions the invitation and asks advice as to whether he should attend. Misfeldt 1971, 276–277.

116 *New York Times* 1898b.

117 Misfeldt 1971, 274; Tissot 2009, 28.

118 Tissot and De Brunhoff arrived aboard the *Campania*. UK Incoming Passenger Lists, findmypast.co.uk.

119 Addressees included William B. Allison, Iowa (University of Virginia Libraries, Clifton Waller Barrett Library, Charlottesville); Mr. H. C. Barnabee, New York,

and Mr. R. R. Bowker, New York (Manuscripts and Archives, New York Public Library); Luther A. Brewer, Cedar Rapids, and W. C. Crane, New York (private collections); Mr. P. Cummings, Brookline (Getty Research Institute Research Library, Los Angeles); and Charles E. Norton, Cambridge, Massachusetts (Houghton Library, Harvard, Cambridge, Massachusetts).

120 Tissot to Mr. Rowland Strong, Paris, August 9, 1899, Getty Research Institute Research Library, Los Angeles.

121 *New York Times* 1900a.

122 *New York Times* 1900b; *New York Times* 1900c.

123 Tissot 2009, 35–47.

124 Tissot's will is summarized in Misfeldt 1971, 325–327.

125 *L'atelier de J. James Tissot*, Hôtel Drouot, Paris, July 9–10, 1903. Many items included in the auction were not listed in the printed catalogue; some are noted in annotated copies.

126 Misfeldt 1971, 287.

127 Ross 1946.

128 Misfeldt 1971, 322–324.

PHOTO ALBUM

COMPILED BY MELISSA E. BURON AND FRÉDÉRIC MANTION

1 Misfeldt 1984.

TISSOT'S SALES NOTEBOOK (*CARNET DE VENTES*)

TRANSCRIPTION AND INTRODUCTION BY KRYSTYNA MATYJASZKIEWICZ

In these notes, text that directly transcribes or translates Tissot's entries is placed within quotation marks. Some liberties are taken with capitalization and punctuation for the sake of clarity. Dimensions of works are referenced only when essential to the identification of a work of which there may be nearly identical variants. In addition to bibliographical citations, some notes reference exhibitions in abbreviated form; refer to "Exhibition Abbreviations," this volume, for full listings.

1 The Tissot scholar Willard Misfeldt had access to the notebook, which he referred to as Tissot's *carnet*, and used its data for his published analysis of Tissot's print sales. Misfeldt 1991, 19–21.

2 Several of these albums, spanning Tissot's career, have been uncovered. Three of the albums were owned by the Tissot scholar Michael Wentworth and are now stored at the Ryerson and Burnham Archives, Ryerson and Burnham Libraries, Art Institute of Chicago (accession no. 2007.06). These albums include works made in Paris from 1857 to 1871, and in London and Paris from 1878 to about 1885 (with "1878 to 1882" on the spine, but including photographs of works made in 1885), and about 1882 to 1898. Among the last images is *Self-Portrait* (pl. 2), dated June 1898. These albums were published by Willard Misfeldt, with some of the images in the third album out of order. Misfeldt 1982. A copy of a fourth album, "London from 1871 to 1878," has recently been shared courtesy of Frédéric Mantion. Several photographs from this London album are reproduced in the present volume (figs. 15–22). Another Tissot album containing sixty-six photographs, including London paintings, was on the French art market in 2012, offered for sale by Christian Rebert (Librairie Comtoise, Vesoul, May 12, 2012, lot 330; location now unknown). All five of the known albums were at the Château de Buillon, Besançon, in 1964. At his 1882 one-man exhibition in London's Dudley Gallery, Tissot had three albums of photographs available to view: vol. I, 1859 to 1870; vol. II, 1870 to 1876; and vol. III, 1876 to 1882. It is possible that the first of these is the same as the first Wentworth album.

3 This is no. 51 in Tissot's photograph album labeled "London from 1871 to 1878." It is identified as part of the same "series of the Four Seasons" in Matyjaszkiewicz, ed. 2019a. It is known as *In the Conservatory* (private collection); sold through Christie's, New York, October 25, 2006 (lot 131) as *Dans la serre*.

4 Hopkinson 1999, 11, quoting Hubert von Herkomer's recollection of a meeting on July 31, 1880, to discuss formation of the society.

5 Lostalot 1883a, 376.

6 "Portrait of Mr. Daldin the elder" (ca. 1857; location unknown).

7 "Copy of a Louis XV[–era] portrait" (ca. 1857; location unknown).

8 "Portrait of a young girl" (ca. 1857; location unknown).

9 Tissot uses the abbreviation "id" (idem), which means "the same."

10 "Cartoons for Stained Glass (Le Mans)." It is not known for which church Tissot created these designs, or whether the stained glass was ever made and installed. According to Georges Bastard, early in Tissot's career, when he was living in the same building as Alphonse Daudet, he had received a commission for church stained glass. Bastard 1906, 259. These cartoons are not the pictures of saints exhibited at the 1859 Paris Salon and recorded in Tissot's photograph albums, which were painted in an encaustic medium used for wall paintings and lack the schematic arrangement of designs for stained glass (sold through Renoud-Grappin, Besançon, April 21, 2013 (lot 12); location unknown). For the 1859 saints, see Misfeldt 1982, pls. I-3 and I-4.

11 "4 Paintings, one drawing."

12 "Copy of a Louis XVI[–era] portrait" (ca. 1858; location unknown).

13 "[Copy of a] Louis XV[–era] [portrait]" (ca. 1858; location unknown).

14 "[Copy] of an Empire[–era] General" (ca. 1858; location unknown). Refers to the Napoleonic empire, early nineteenth-century.

15 "Portrait of the granddaughter of Mr. Maton" (ca. 1858; location unknown).

16 "Copy of Baby Jesus of Monseigneur de Segur" (ca. 1858; location unknown). Monseigneur de Ségur, based in Paris, was a leading champion of the loving vision of God being like a mother, with humanity as her infant, a philosophy promoted by Saint François de Sales. Gibson 1989, 183.

17 Monseigneur de Ségur founded the organization L'œuvre de Saint-François de Sales in 1857, aimed specifically at priestly ministry to the poor. The notebook title likely refers to "*Saint François de Sales, évèque et prince de Genève* by J. Tissot," engraved by R. Strang, printed as a soft-ground etching by Chardon Ainé, and published by the Catholic publisher August Wilhelm Schulgen, 25, rue Saint-Sulpice. Legal deposit of the engraving at the Bibliothèque nationale de France, Paris, was recorded on March 10, 1860 (no. 423). Legal deposit record: 28-05-2010, with compliments of *Image of France*, lib.uchicago.edu/efts/ARTFL/projects/mckee.

18 Tissot kept a cumulative record of paintings and portraits until 1867.

19 "Sketch of the Dance of Death." A finished preliminary version of pl. 7, dated 1859 and recorded in Tissot's photograph albums. See Misfeldt 1982, pl. I-8.

20 "In 1868 with a dealer in rue Notre Dame de Lorette, 1,500 francs; in January 1870 with a dealer near the new Opera, 4,000 [francs]." Tissot tracked resale of some of his works in the right-hand column, either from newspaper reports and hearsay, or from seeing them in the windows or galleries of dealers. Here the painting may have been sold by one dealer to another, or owned in the interim by a private collector.

21 "Sold at the London International Exhibition in August 1871." The painting was catalogued as no. 618, *L'image de la vie* (*The Image of Life*), with no lender named; perhaps Tissot came to an arrangement with the dealer who had it in 1870. Its subsequent history was unknown until it was sold at Christie's, London, on January 28, 1972 (lot 91) as *An Allegory of the Transience of Life* (1859; location unknown).

22 "Walk in the Snow" (1858; private collection). See Wentworth 1984, pl. 1.

23 "Belonging to Mr. [Émile] Pereire." Péreire was a wealthy Parisian financier and art collector.

24 "Sold at the Hôtel des Ventes in February 1872." Actually sold at the Péreire house, 26 boulevard des Italiens, Paris, on March 6, 1872 (lot 52) as *La Promenade aux remparts* (*The Walk on the Ramparts*) to the Comtesse Duchastel for 2,750 francs. Lugt 1938–1987.

25 "2 portraits of 2 children of / Mr. Anatole de Segur." *Portraits of Pierre and Henry de Ségur* (1859; private collection). Sold at Sotheby's, Paris, on June 16, 2016 (lot 78).

26 "Total 12 paintings / of which 10 [are] portraits."

27 "Marguerite at the window" (1860; location unknown). Sold at Sotheby's, London, June 18, 1995 (lot 72) as *Meditation*. This work was recorded in Tissot's photograph albums. See Misfeldt 1982, pl. I-9.

28 "(In Russia) (Sold to Goupil)." Tissot may have been mistaken, as the painting is not listed in Goupil stock books. Goupil & Cie / Boussod, Valadon & Co. Stock Books, 1846–1919, Getty Research Institute, Los Angeles, getty.edu/research/tools/digital_collections/goupil_cie/books.

29 "Marguerite in Church (Kneeling)" (1860; location unknown). See Wentworth 1984, pl. 4.

30 Goupil stock books record receipt of the painting from Tissot on May 20, 1860, for 1,500 francs, plus an additional 100 francs for the frame. The work was exchanged by

Goupil—with another dealer—for a painting by Henri Leys. Goupil & Cie / Boussod, 1846–1919.

31 "In 1861 belonged to Mr. Portalès [and] in 1862 [belonged to] Mr. Mayer [Meyer] of Vienna." See n32.

32 "In 1868 sold at the Hôtel des Ventes to Mr. Vurtemberg." This painting actually sold to M. Wertheimer, an art dealer, on April 27–28, 1866 (lot 63), at Hôtel Drouot, Paris, consigned by M. Meyer of Vienna. Lugt 1938–1987; Saint-Raymond 2019a.

33 "In 1871 Hôtel des Ventes . . . 4,500 [francs]." Actually sold at Hôtel Drouot, Paris, in December 7–8 by Wertheimer for 4,900 francs. Lugt 1938–1987; Saint-Raymond 2019a.

34 "With Goupil in May 1879, priced 10,000 francs." Sold by Goupil in London for 6,125 francs to Henry Martin Gibbs on May 9, 1879; Goupil's earlier purchase from Mme. Oppenheim was recorded as May 14, 1879, for 5,000 francs including frame. Goupil & Cie / Boussod, 1846–1919.

35 "Partial replica" of *Marguerite in Church* (1860; location unknown). Tissot does not list a buyer but Goupil recorded receipt of *Marguerite à l'église* (*reduction*) on April 9, 1861, for 500 francs; it was valued at 600 francs when exchanged with Parisian dealer Georges Petit for other work in 1861. Goupil & Cie / Boussod, 1846–1919.

36 "Marguerite in Church (sitting)" (1861; location unknown). This must be the painting exhibited in 1861 at the Paris Salon (no. 2971) as *Marguerite à l'office* (*Marguerite at the Service*). See Wentworth 1984, pl. 5.

37 "(Sold to Mr. Leon Say)." Léon Say was an economist and statesman, and he was also French Finance Minister in the 1870s. His family's wealth derived from sugar-refining in Nantes. See Perrin, this volume.

38 "No exhibition this year." In fact, Tissot exhibited work in Limoges, and his small *Walk in the Snow* (see n22) was shown in the London International Exhibition, lent by Émile Péreire.

39 "Meeting of Faust and Marguerite" (pl. 3).

40 "Seen at the Palace of St Cloud in 1869." The Château Saint-Cloud was one of the residences used by Emperor Napoleon III and Empress Eugénie.

41 "Seen at the Musée du Luxembourg in 1872." This is evidence that Tissot visited Paris that year.

42 "Young man in Church," known as *During the Service* (pl. 5).

43 "Belonging to Mr. Charles Waring in London."

44 Ernest Gambart was an art dealer who established the French Gallery in London, where this painting was exhibited in 1863 as *Young Luther in Church*. Given the titles that Tissot used for its exhibition at the Paris Salon and this notebook entry, it would appear that it was either Gambart or the French Gallery managers since 1861, Henry Wallis, with support from Jean Pilgeram and Léon Lefèvre, who gave the painting its new title, certain to prove attractive in Protestant England.

45 "2 Drawings / (for the Breton Tales of / London / tom Taylor." Refers to Taylor's *Ballads and Songs of Brittany* (1865, see fig. 108).

46 Possibly not Derome, but Derorne.

47 "[Portrait of Madame] Ladrocat."

48 "Marguerite on the Rampart" (pl. 6).

49 Possibly not Vausanges, but Vauganges.

50 "Melancholy (yellow cloak)."

51 Goupil recorded receipt from Tissot for 2,000 francs, on September 30, 1864, for *Jeune fille à la fontaine* (*Young Woman at the Fountain*); sold by Goupil to "M. Walters" on December 1, 1864, for 2,400 francs. This would be the American collector William Walters. By October 1865, it was with Samuel Avery, exhibited as *Margaret by the Fountain* (also known as *Marguerite at the Fountain*, fig. 31), which may be the same painting if Tissot was mistaken in his "yellow cloak" description, or may be another version of the same subject.

52 "Attempted Abduction" (fig. 109).

53 Goupil recorded receipt from Tissot for 3,000 francs including frame, May 6, 1865; sold for 4,000 francs through M. Knoedler, New York, according to Knoedler's note to Goupil dated May 29, 1866—Knoedler recording sale May 10, 1866, as *The Duel* for 1,200 dollars to William Beebe of Boston. M. Knoedler & Co. records, ca. 1848–1971, Knoedler Gallery Archive, Getty Research Institute, Los Angeles, getty.edu/research/special_collections/notable/knoedler.html.

54 "Portrait of the Marquis de Miramon / his wife and their 2 Children" (pl. 23).

55 "Faust and Marguerite in the Garden" (fig. 30).

56 Goupil recorded receipt from Tissot of *Faust and Marguerite* (*Le Jardin*) for 1,800 francs, plus 100 francs for the frame, July 4, 1865; sold for 2,900 francs through M. Knoedler, New York, according to Knoedler's letter to Goupil dated September 14, 1865, Knoedler recording sale September 17, 1865, as *Faust and Marguerite in the Garden* for 800 dollars to H. E. Maynard of Boston. M. Knoedler & Co. records, ca. 1848–1971.

57 "Departure of the betrothed" (1862; location unknown). See Wentworth 1984, pl. 13.

58 Goupil recorded receipt from Tissot for 2,500 francs including frame, November 14, 1865; sold June 29, 1871, for 2,500 francs to M. Avery, New York (the art dealer Samuel Avery). Goupil & Cie / Boussod, 1846–1919.

59 "After Vespers (on the Ramparts)" is another version of *Promenade on the Ramparts* (pl. 8).

60 "Sold [by executors of Adolphe Fould] at Hôtel Drouot, 7,000 francs, May [14–15] 1875" (lot 65) as *La Promenade en dehors des remparts*, oil on panel, 22⅞ x 18⅛ in. (58 x 46 cm), signed and dated 1864. Tissot records it as bought by Reitlinger (here spelled incorrectly as Reiltinger) but it was actually bought by another dealer, Hector Brame. Saint-Raymond 2019a. The note written below reads "belonging to Mr. Fould."

61 Goupil recorded receipt as *Promenade hors les murs* (*Promenade Outside the Walls*), January 31, 1866, for 3,000 francs including frame, and sale the same day for 4,000 francs to M. Turner, London; returned to Goupil by M. Turner, July 5, 1867, as *La Promenade sur les remparts* (*The Promenade on the Ramparts*) for 4,000 francs; sold by Goupil, May 1869, for 4,000 francs to M. A. Fould. Goupil & Cie / Boussod, 1846–1919.

62 "At Christie's [London, consigned by "Simon"] July 3 1875 [lot 105], 315 pounds (7,875 francs). [bt.] Nelson." In fact the painting was bought in: "Nelson" was one of several auctioneers' codes for works unsold, quoted in newspaper reports as buyers. Christie's Archive, London. Consigned by Brame, Hôtel Drouot, Paris, March 24, 1877 (lot 10) as *La Promenade à Anvers*, 22¼ x 19¾ in. (56.5 x 50 cm), 2,000 francs, bt. Brame. Saint-Raymond 2019a. Probably the version with Fine Art Society, London, 1972, as *Figures on a Path Leading to a Medieval Town*, 22⅜ x 19¼ in. (56.8 x 48.9 cm), signed and dated 1864 (location unknown).

63 "Painting of 12 / Portraits" (*The Circle of the Rue Royale*, pl. 27).

64 Comte Alfred de Fay de la Tour-Maubourg.

65 Alfred Thérèse Armand, Marquis du Lau d'Allemans.

66 Comte Julien de Rochechouart.

67 Captain Coleraine Robert Vansittart (Tissot misspelled the surname).

68 René de Cassagne de Beaufort, Marquis de Miramon.

69 Baron Rodolphe Hottinguer.

70 Tissot is reported to have been paid 1,000 francs per sitter, totaling 12,000. The 6,000 recorded in 1866 would, therefore, have been the initial payment but no further payment is recorded in the notebook. If Tissot received but overlooked recording the balancing payment, it would alter his earnings calculations. See final page of notebook and n440.

71 Maurice, Marquis de Ganay.

72 Étienne, Marquis de Ganay.

73 Gaston de Saint-Maurice.

74 Edmond Melchior Jean Marie, Prince de Polignac.

75 Gaston Auguste, Marquis de Galliffet.

76 Charles Haas.

77 "Portrait of Madame [Marquise] de Miramon" (pl. 24).

78 See pl. 25.

79 "Portrait of Young J[acques] de Montbrison" (fig. 50).

80 "Brought forward" (carried over from previous year).

81 "The Confessional" (1865; Southampton City Art Gallery, England). See Wentworth 1984, pl. 32.

82 Goupil recorded receipt from Tissot for 3,000 francs including frame, October 22, 1866; sold for 4,000 francs to M. Knoedler, New York, according to Knoedler's note to Goupil dated January 2, 1867, Knoedler recording sale December 14, 1866, as *Confessional* for 1,430 dollars to William Beebe of Boston. This painting is probably the untitled Tissot, 4,000 francs, returned by Knoedler to Goupil in April 1868 by steamer; there is an entry in Goupil's stock books corresponding to receipt of a Tissot from Knoedler in 1868. Goupil & Cie / Boussod, 1846–1919; M. Knoedler & Co. records, ca. 1848–1971. By 1876, *The Confessional* was in Britain, where it was lent that year to an exhibition in Wrexham by Humphrey Roberts, from whom it was bought in September 1880 by Agnew, who sold it in December to George C. Dobell, of Liverpool.

83 "[The Confessional] watercolor (small)" (ca. 1866; location unknown).

84 Refers to Goupil's son. Goupil's stock books for drawings are lost, so it is not possible to determine whether this was a private or business purchase, and, if the latter, its subsequent purchase history. Tissot recorded painting two watercolor replicas of *The Confessional*: this small version and one for Lucas, recorded in the 1867 notebook entry. Also see n94.

85 "Departure of the betrothed (watercolor)." Perhaps the watercolor (location unknown) sold at Sotheby's, New York, October 29, 2002 (lot 74).

86 Refers to Goupil's son. See n84.

87 "6 paintings 2 drawings or watercolors / total 33 paintings 5 drawings or watercolors / of which 32 [are] portraits."

88 "Secret" (fig. 41). Or see Wentworth 1984, pl. 31 (before the canvas was trimmed down).

89 Goupil recorded receipt from Tissot for 4,000 francs, February 4, 1867; sold for the same price through M. Knoedler, New York, according to Knoedler's note to Goupil dated June 2, 1868, Knoedler recording sale May 29, 1868, as *Confidence* for 1,300 dollars to De Vries, Ibarra & Co. of Boston (art dealers). M. Knoedler & Co. records, ca. 1848–1971.

90 "Young woman Singing in / an organ loft" (ca. 1867; location unknown). See Wentworth 1984, pl. 35.

91 "(Goupil) bought by Wallis of London." Goupil recorded receipt from Tissot for 4,000 francs, February 4, 1867, as *La tribune des orgues* (*The Organ Loft*); sold to M. Wallis (manager of the French Gallery), February 10, 1867, for 4,250 francs; exhibited at the French Gallery, London, in 1868 as *A Duet at High Mass*; consigned by Wallis to Fosters, London, May 12, 1869 (lot 56).

92 "At Christie's [London, sold by Samuel Barlow] June [19] 1875 375 pounds." Actually sold at 367 pounds and 10 shillings, or 350 guineas; bt. Mendoza (lot 135), as *The World and the Cloister*.

93 "Watercolor of the Confessional" (ca. 1866; Walters Art Museum, Baltimore).

94 George Lucas was acting as agent for William Walters and collected the watercolor from Tissot on February 19, 1867, recording in his diary payment to Tissot of 250 francs. Randall 1979, 2:234.

95 See pl. 26.

96 "Spring" (pl. 15).

97 "Sold to Cadart 2,500 francs." Alfred Cadart, president of the French Etching Club, was lead organizer of the *Second Annual Exhibition of French Paintings* at the Fine Arts Gallery (or Derby Gallery), 625 Broadway, New York, at the turn of 1866–1867, to which Tissot sent *Dance of Death* (pl. 7) and *Spring*, the latter of which must have sold from the exhibition, hence payment recorded by Tissot to Cadart. Paletta 1866.

98 Possibly Buguet, Bugnet, or Beugnier.

99 "Total 39 paintings 6 drawings or watercolors / of which 32 [are] portraits." This is the last cumulative tally of types of work recorded in the notebook.

100 See pl. 9.

101 Louis Paul Delondre.

102 See pl. 10.

103 "Portraits of the 2 sons of / Monsieur Kanh," perhaps Monsieur Kahn (1868; location unknown). See Misfeldt 1982, pl. I-58.

104 "3rd Actor" (ca. 1868; location unknown). Although *comédien* has often been translated as "comedian," the French word translates as "actor," and Tissot is portraying actors, as from the *Comédie-Française*. See Misfeldt 1982, pl. I-52.

105 "[Sold] to [art dealer Georges] Petit."

106 "Then taken back for my account [or profit]."

107 "4th Actor" (ca. 1868 location unknown). See Misfeldt 1982, pl. I-53.

108 "Caricature of Mr. de Lambertye / [caricatures] of the Skaters Circle / 35 portraits." One of these portrait caricatures can be seen in Wood 1986, fig. 45.

109 "Luncheon" (ca. 1868; location unknown). See Wentworth 1984, pl. 60.

110 "2 sketches," subjects unknown.

111 "Drawing lessons for prince / Mumboutason [Akitake] Tagoukaua [Tokugawa]."

112 "Portrait of this Japanese prince (watercolor)" (pl. 35).

113 "Portrait of the 4 children of Mr. Gaillard" (fig. 51).

114 "5 small heads on marble [for Mr. Gaillard]" (ca. 1868; location unknown).

115 "Drums in the tuileries,' also known as *Beating the Retreat in the Tuileries Gardens* (1867; private collection). See Wentworth 1984, pl. 45.

116 Princess Mathilde Bonaparte, who bought the painting from the 1868 Paris Salon; sold by her executors, Galerie Georges Petit, Paris, May 17–21, 1904 (lot 205).

117 "Skater" (1869; location unknown). See Misfeldt 1982, pl. I-64.

118 Goupil recorded receipt from Tissot for 1,900 francs as *Les patineuses* (*The Skaters*), April 29, 1869; sold to M. Springer (an art dealer in Vienna) for 2,400 francs, March 1870. Goupil & Cie / Boussod, 1846–1919.

119 "Melancholy (the pond)" (pl. 13).

120 Goupil recorded receipt from Tissot for 1,800 francs, April 29, 1869; sold for 2,500 to M. Couthrie, 27 Bruton Street, London, July 7, 1869. Goupil & Cie / Boussod, 1846–1919.

121 "Ladies looking at the Chinese temple," known as *Young Women Looking at the Chinese Temple* (pl. 37).

122 Goupil recorded receipt from Tissot for 2,000 francs as *Le temple japonais* (*The Japanese Temple*), February 8, 1869; sold "at the Boulevard" for 3,000 francs, February 28, 1869. Goupil & Cie / Boussod, 1846–1919.

123 "A Widow" (1869; location unknown). See Wentworth 1984, pl. 51.

124 Goupil recorded receipt from Tissot for 3,000 francs, March 30, 1869, with profit-sharing on 4,000 francs price after the (Paris Salon) exhibition; sold for 4,000 francs through M. Knoedler, New York, according to Knoedler's note to Goupil dated May 13, 1870 (no receipt of profit-share recorded by Tissot in the notebook). Knoedler recorded sale May 2, 1870, as *The Widow* for 1,000 dollars to H. N. Smith, "bill to Carver & Co.," with credit in November 1870 to Benjamin Carver "by return of picture by Tissot 1,000 [dollars]"; Knoedler informing Goupil by note dated May 27, 1870, and Goupil receiving the painting June 9, 1870; sold at Goupil's Place de l'Opéra gallery to a Mr. Collins, February 27, 1872. Goupil & Cie / Boussod, 1846–1919; M. Knoedler & Co. records, ca. 1848–1971.

125 "Ladies looking at a Japanese ship," known as *Young Women Looking at Japanese Objects* (pl. 38).

126 Goupil recorded receipt from Tissot for 3,000 francs as *Les curiosités japonaises* (*Japanese Curiosities*), March 30, 1869, with profit-sharing on 4,000 francs price after the (Paris Salon) exhibition; sold to M. Knoedler, New York, December 31, 1869, for 4,000 francs (no receipt of profit-share recorded by Tissot in the notebook). Knoedler recorded sale October 29, 1869, as *Chinese Cabinet* for 1,325 dollars to the art dealers Williams & Everett, Boston. M. Knoedler & Co. records, ca. 1848–1971.

127 "Replica of Luncheon" (fig. 48).

128 "[Sold by Tissot] to a member of the Tribunal de Commerce."

129 "1st Actor" (ca. 1868; location unknown). See Misfeldt 1982, pl. I-50.

130 "To Gustave Rothschild."

131 "Still Life (the little household god)" (ca. 1869; location unknown). See Misfeldt 1982, pl. I-70.

132 "Portrait of Madame Somoïtoff's dog." This may be the painting of a dog sold at Hôtel Drouot, Paris, November 13, 1876 (lot 119) as *Chien*, 101 francs, bt. M. de Chaumont. Saint-Raymond 2019a.

133 "The Rendezvous." This refers to either the painting exhibited in 1867 at the Paris International Exhibition as *Le rendezvous* (see Misfeldt 1982, pl. I-47) or to the painting exhibited in 1869 at the Vienna Künstlerhaus as *From the Life of a Libertine, The Rendezvous*, which was priced at 2,000 francs, and is probably Misfeldt 1982, pl. I-67.

134 "5th Actor" (ca. 1868; location unknown). See Misfeldt 1982, pl. I-54.

135 Goupil recorded receipt from Tissot for 600 francs as *Comédien, la politesse, No. 5* (Actor, Politeness, No. 5), March 22, 1869; sold to M. Knoedler for 700 francs, June 27, 1870. Goupil & Cie / Boussod, 1846–1919. Sold by Knoedler on November 23, 1870, as *A Comedian* for 250 dollars to the art dealer Charles F. Haseltine. M. Knoedler & Co. records, ca. 1848–1971.

136 "The Toast" (ca. 1869; perhaps the version in Baroda Museum and Picture Gallery, Vadodara, India); probably Misfeldt 1982, pl. I-69.

137 "Young lady on a Sofa" (1869; location unknown). See Wentworth 1984, pl. 50.

138 Goupil recorded receipt from Tissot for 1,600 francs as *Le divan* (*The Sofa*), September 29, 1869; sold for 1,800 francs through M. Knoedler, New York, according to Knoedler's note to Goupil dated May 24, 1871, Knoedler recording sale April 26, 1871, as *Contemplation* for 600 dollars to Henry C. Gibson of Philadelphia. Goupil & Cie / Boussod, 1846–1919; M. Knoedler & Co. records, ca. 1848–1971. Formerly in the collection of Pennsylvania Academy of the Fine Arts, Philadelphia.

139 "The Confessional (green dress)" (1869; location unknown). See Misfeldt 1982, pl. I-71.

140 Goupil recorded receipt from Tissot for 3,000 francs as *La pénitente* (*The Penitent*), November 18, 1869; sold for 3,500 francs to M. Van Gogh, Amsterdam, La Haye, March 21, 1871. However, Tissot thought it had gone to an American buyer. Goupil & Cie / Boussod, 1846–1919.

141 "The tête-à-tête" (ca. 1869; location unknown).

142 Goupil recorded receipt from Tissot for 2,400 francs as *La conversation* (*The Conversation*), September 29, 1869; sold for 2,800 francs through M. Knoedler, New York, according to Knoedler's note to Goupil dated November 1, 1871, Knoedler recording sale October 4, 1871, as *The Conversation* for 800 dollars to Williams & Everett. Goupil & Cie / Boussod, 1846–1919; M. Knoedler & Co. records, ca. 1848–1971. This may be the painting sold by the executors of Henry Hilton at the American Art Galleries, New York, February 13, 1900, as *Une partie de dames* (lot 75), 36 x 25 in. (91.4 x 63.5 cm), described as "four prettily dressed women in a setting of landscape with willow trees and a stream. Two are in a boat and two on the landing on the bank. One of the latter . . . bends over to speak to her friend who is sitting in the bow of the punt" (location unknown). Lugt 1938–1987.

143 "The Snack" (1869; location unknown). See Wentworth 1984, pl. 48.

144 Goupil recorded receipt from Tissot, September 29, 1869, as *Le lunch* for 1,800 francs; sold for 2,000 francs through M. Knoedler, according to Knoedler's note to Goupil dated May 24, 1871, Knoedler recording sale on May 10, 1871, as *The Wine Tasting* for 600 dollars to William H. Vanderbilt. Goupil & Cie / Boussod, 1846–1919; M. Knoedler & Co. records, ca. 1848–1971.

145 Caricatures for *Vanity Fair*, the weekly satirical magazine founded and edited by Thomas Gibson Bowles, published in London.

146 "The Emperor." Napoleon III; published September 4, 1869 (fig. 35).

147 "The Queen of Spain." Isabella II; published September 18, 1869.

148 "The King of Prussia." Published January 7, 1871.

149 Thomas Gibson Bowles (see n145).

150 "The Sultan." Abdul Aziz; published October 30, 1869. Now at the National Portrait Gallery, London.

151 "Emperor of Russia." Alexander II; published October 16, 1869. Now at the National Portrait Gallery, London;

152 "The King of the Belgians." Leopold II; published October 9, 1869.

153 "The Tavern (or The Tea-service)." The French word "cabaret" can mean either. The location of this painting is unknown.

154 A misspelling of Frédéric Reitlinger, Paris-based art dealer.

155 "6th Actor" (ca. 1868; location unknown). See Misfeldt 1982, pl. I-55.

156 "Still life (my father's books)" (ca. 1869; location unknown). See Misfeldt 1982, pl. I-48.

157 "King of Italy." Caricature for *Vanity Fair*; unpublished.

158 "Emperor of Austria." Caricature for *Vanity Fair*; unpublished.

159 "Doctor Temple." Reverend Frederick Temple, Bishop Designate of Exeter; caricature for *Vanity Fair*; published November 6, 1869.

160 "G[rand] M[aster] of Freemasons." Earl of Zetland; caricature for *Vanity Fair*; published December 4, 1869.

161 The *Vanity Fair* caricature of the Archbishop of Canterbury, published December 25, 1869, is signed "Ape," the pseudonym of Carlo Pellegrini. Tissot's version was perhaps an alternative image; unpublished.

162 "Prince of Wales." Caricature for *Vanity Fair*; Royal Collection; unpublished.

163 "The lady in a Boat," known as *Young Lady in a Boat* (pl. 59).

164 "[Sold by] Reitlinger, to Mr. Stewart. H. V." Actually William H. Stewart, a Philadelphian millionaire resident in Paris, who lent the painting to the 1870 Paris Salon; sold by Stewart to Goupil, November 3, 1873, for 6,500 francs including frame, and sold by Goupil to M. Maison of London, December 22, 1873, for 10,000 francs. Goupil & Cie / Boussod, 1846–1919.

165 "Ladies at a screen," known as *Young Women Looking at Japanese Objects* (ca. 1870; location unknown). See Tokyo, Osaka, Mie, Tochigi, and Yokahama 1988, no. 16.

166 "Melancholy / yellow cloak / watercolor." Probably the watercolor exhibited in the 1868 Paris Salon; perhaps a replica of *Marguerite at the Fountain* (see nn50–51), and therefore may be the watercolor in the Musée du Louvre, Paris.

167 "The pope." Pius IX; caricature for *Vanity Fair*; published January 1, 1870.

168 Caricature for *Vanity Fair*; published January 15, 1870.

169 "[Henri] Rochefort." Caricature for *Vanity Fair*; published January 22, 1870.

170 "In the port." Perhaps the painting recorded in Tissot's photograph albums, in which case dated 1864 (location unknown). See Misfeldt 1982, pl. I-31.

171 "3rd Actor" (ca. 1868; location unknown). See Misfeldt 1982, pl. I-52. Sold to Georges Petit in 1868 for 1,000 francs but taken back by Tissot.

172 "Dance of Death" (pl. 7).

173 "Young lady warming herself (Louis XVI[–era])," known as *La cheminée* (*The Fireside*) (ca. 1870; location unknown). See Wentworth 1984, pl. 64.

174 "The Pews" (1865; location unknown). Probably the painting exhibited in 1866 at the Paris Salon (no. 1843) as *Jeune femme dans une église* (*Young Woman in a Church*), and at the French Gallery, London, April 1867 (no. 178) as *Holy Prayer*; subsequently reacquired by Tissot (see nn301–302). See Misfeldt 1982, pl. I-38.

175 "Abduction." Probably the painting in the Musée d'Arts de Nantes.

176 Pl. 41. "Partie carrée" is a French term meaning a party of two men and two women.

177 "[Sold by Reitlinger] to Madame Martinet / Claude Lafontaine." The company Claude Lafontaine, Prévost, Martinet & Cie was a French bank, established in 1868.

178 "[Count] Bismarck." Caricature for *Vanity Fair*; published October 15, 1870.

179 "[Crown] Prince of Prussia." Caricature for *Vanity Fair*; published September 24, 1870.

180 Caricature for *Vanity Fair*; published September 17, 1870.

181 "5th Actor" (ca. 1868; location unknown). Tissot had sold *Fifth Actor* to Goupil in 1869 and perhaps meant here *Fourth Actor*, which he had sold to Georges Petit in 1868 but taken back. See Misfeldt 1982, pl. I-53.

182 "Portrait of Th[omas] G[ibson] Bowles" (ca. 1871; location unknown).

183 "[Portrait] of Mr. Chichester Fortescue" (fig. 113). Subscribed for and presented to the sitter's wife, Frances, Lady Waldegrave, who probably engineered the commission by a group of sixty-one Irish MPs, bishops, and peers to commemorate Fortescue's term of office as chief secretary for Ireland.

184 "[Portrait] of Lady Waldegraves [*sic*]." Sold by Earl Waldegrave, Christie's, London, February 10, 1900 (lot 70) as *Frances, Countess of Waldegrave*, "in pink and white dress, seated at a window," 50 x 37 in. (127 x 94 cm), bt. Sampson; location unknown.

185 "The Marguerite in the Mouth," known as *On the River* (1871; Government Art Collection, London). See Wentworth 1984, pl. 66.

186 Agnew recorded the purchase from Pilgeram of *Marguerite*, May 7, 1872 (Agnew's first purchase of a work by Tissot), and sold it June 14, 1872, for 404.50 pounds to John Heugh; sold by John Heugh, Christie's, London, April 25, 1874 (lot 156) as *Summer Time*, 1871, bt. Permain. Thomas Agnew & Sons Ltd Archive, The National Gallery, London; Christie's Archive, London.

187 This is probably the painting known as *The Japanese Vase* (pl. 39). Madame Desoye, with her husband, E. Desoye, opened a Paris shop in 1862 at 220, rue de Rivoli, selling "curiosities" that included goods from China and Japan. Tissot was one of their leading customers. E. Desoye had lived for some time in Japan and his wife may well have been of Japanese origin or dressed in Japanese fashion, like in Tissot's painting.

188 Tissot omitted to deduct the deleted sale of *Portrait of Madame Desoye* (1,500 francs), which would bring the subtotal to 19,336 francs.

189 "21 caricatures at 200 [francs]." Twenty-two caricatures by Tissot were published in *Vanity Fair* between August 5 and December 30, 1871.

190 With adjustment for deduction of the deleted portrait, this total should be 23,536 francs.

191 "The Farewells" (pl. 43).

192 "Engraved." Engraving by Joel Ballin, published by Pilgeram & Lefèvre, London, May 30, 1873.

193 "The interesting conversation," known as *An Interesting Story* (fig. 47).

194 "Portrait of Lt. Colonel Longley." The first version of pl. 31; shown by Tissot at the 1872 London International Exhibition.

195 "The balcony." See n196.

196 Agnew recorded purchase from Pilgeram & Lefèvre of *Les amoureux* (*The Lovers*), July 6, 1872; sold June 30, 1873, for 690 pounds to J. H. White, of New York. Thomas Agnew & Sons Ltd Archive. This is probably the painting for which an oil sketch is known, *The Tryst, Greenwich* (location unknown). See London and Manchester 1984–1985, fig. 49.

197 "2 Young ladies in a boat," known as *On the Thames, A Heron* (pl. 65).

198 "The Newspaper," known as *News of Our Marriage* (fig. 16), owned by H. W. F. Bolckow, MP, by 1874; his executors' sale, Christie's, London, June 18, 1892 (lot 148), 28 x 21 in. (71.1 x 53.3 cm), 67 pounds and 4 shillings, bt. King.

199 "Engraved by [William Henry] Simmons." Published as *News of Our Marriage* by Pilgeram & Lefèvre, November 5, 1873, and printed as a supplement to *The Graphic*, Christmas number, 1892, as *News of Our Wedding*, with permission of Pilgeram & Lefèvre; London and Manchester 1984–1985, no. 48.

200 "The Fan" (ca. 1870; location unknown). Purchased from Pilgeram by Agnew, July 6, 1872; sold in Bradford, December 24, 1872, to John Foster. Thomas Agnew & Sons Ltd Archive. See London and Manchester 1984–1985, no. 27.

201 "The idle one," known as *The Convalescent (Girl in an Armchair)* (pl. 47).

202 "The Eve of Departure," known as *Before the Departure* (pl. 42).

203 *Before the Departure* was bought from Tissot by Agnew on behalf of Lord Dunmore, July 26, 1872. After this, Agnew bought work from Tissot both speculatively and on behalf of clients. Thomas Agnew & Sons Ltd Archive.

204 "Tea" (1872; Metropolitan Museum of Art, New York). See Wentworth 1984, pl. 79. Agnew sold the painting on November 5, 1872, for 330 pounds to John Kynaston Cross, who owned cotton mills in Bolton. Thomas Agnew & Sons Ltd Archive.

205 "The Thames" (fig. 17).

206 Bought from Tissot by Agnew on behalf of Hilton Philipson, December 16, 1872, as *Greenwich*. Thomas Agnew & Sons Ltd Archive. Passed by descent to Philipson's daughter, Annie Bannister, who lent the painting to the Leicester Galleries, *Second James Tissot Exhibition* in 1937 (no. 17).

207 "Engraved in the Graphic." Engraving published in *The Graphic*, February 8, 1873. See Wentworth 1984, pl. 75.

208 "Swoon" (fig. 15). Shown by Tissot at the 1872 London International Exhibition as *Bad News* (no. 1181), and described in *The Times*, May 17, 1872, as "a woman has fainted on the floor after reading a letter."

209 Bought from Tissot by Agnew on behalf of Henry Thomas Morton, December 16, 1872. Thomas Agnew & Sons Ltd Archive. Sold by executors of H. T. Morton, Christie's, London, March 11, 1899 (lot 127) as *The Letter* (oil on panel, 12 x 20 in. [30.5 x 50.8 cm]; location unknown).

210 "1 gouache drawing Study of a woman in / the arm-chair of (Last Evening)." Either pl. 70 or the Smith College study (see n211).

211 Agnew recorded purchase of two drawings from Tissot on November 26, 1872, both titled *A Study*, 11 x 17 in. (28 x 43.1 cm); and three on June 16, 1873, all titled *Sketch* (no dimensions recorded). Agnew's 1872 dimensions match pl. 70; the second 1872 drawing may have been the study for *The Captain and the Mate*, bought by Agnew at the same time but entered under 1873 in the Painting stock book (see n214), or the second *Last Evening* study (Smith College Museum of Art, Northampton, MA), measured incorrectly. One of the 11 x 17 in. drawings was sold by Agnew to Jas. H. White, along with two of the other studies (see n214). Thomas Agnew & Sons Ltd Archive.

212 Two gouache studies are known for the woman in the rocking chair in *The Last Evening* (pl. 70 and Smith College, see n211).

213 See n211.

214 "1 gouache drawing woman standing." This could be one of five known drawings: the study of a standing woman for *The Captain and the Mate* (London and Manchester 1984–1985, no. 63; Ashmolean Museum, Oxford); a study for *The Return from the Boating Trip* (location unknown; painting illus. London and Manchester 1984–1985, col. pl. 4); a study for *The Captain's Daughter*, sold Christie's, New York, November 19, 1998 (lot 138); location unknown; the study of a young woman in blue dress for *Too Early*, sold Christie's, London, November 17, 2005 (lot 151); location unknown; and of the woman in white dress for *Too Early* (sold, property from the estate of Brooke Astor, Sotheby's, New York, September 24, 2012 [lot 94] as *Waiting Here [Study for Too Early]*). There may be other drawings not hitherto known: Waring bought three in 1873, one of which may be known.

215 See n211; Jas. H. White bought two of the sketches of standing women from Agnew.

216 See n214.

217 See n211.

218 See n214.

219 See n211.

220 "6 caricatures at 400 francs." Eight caricatures by Tissot were published in *Vanity Fair* between June 29 and December 7, 1872.

221 See pl. 69.

222 "Sold to Agnew. W. A. Gasciott. Mr." Tissot misspells the surname of Charles Gassiot. Agnew bought the painting on behalf of Gassiot, to whom Agnew recorded sale, February 10, 1873, with receipt of the painting from Tissot, March 11. Thomas Agnew & Sons Ltd Archive.

223 "The Captain's daughter" (pl. 63).

224 "The pistol," known as *Safe to Win* (pl. 16).

225 See pl. 46.

226 "To Pilgeram. Agnew 1000 pounds. To Gasciott 1,400 [pounds]." Agnew recorded selling the painting to Gassiot, March 26, 1873, for 1,155 pounds, with purchase and receipt of the painting from Tissot, rather than Pilgeram, March 28, 1873. Gassiot probably saw the painting in Tissot's studio; he was a good client of Agnew's, who would have come to an agreement with Pilgeram, to whom Tissot recorded sale.

227 "Japanese woman in a conservatory" (ca. 1873; private collection). Replica of the painting known as *The Japanese Vase* (pl. 39).

228 Pilgeram & Lefèvre sold *A Japanese Conservatory* at Christie's, London, June 22, 1878 (lot 107), 75 pounds and 12 shillings, bt. Polak (an art dealer); Tooth recorded purchase "from Christie's," June 25, 1878, 18 x 14½ in. (45.7 x 36.8 cm), 93 pounds and 2 shillings; shown at Tooth's Gallery, London, *Winter Exhibition*, November 1878 (no. 4) as *In the Conservatory*, displayed with Japanese art; cost price increased to 96 pounds in 1879 ledger; sold by Tooth, February 15, 1879, to W. G. Herbert (a Liverpool art dealer, see n303). Records of Arthur Tooth & Sons, Getty Research Institute Library, Los Angeles. See Wood 1986, fig. 26.

229 "The visit to the ship," known as *Boarding the Yacht* (1873; location unknown). Exhibited London and Manchester 1984–1985, no. 64 and col. pl. 9. Recorded by Agnew as *Visit to the Ship*, received June 18, 1873, and sold November 3, 1873, to David Jardine. Thomas Agnew & Sons Ltd Archive.

230 "The Docks," also known as *The Captain and the Mate* (pl. 68). Recorded by Agnew as *In the Docks*, received June 18, 1873, and sold November 3, 1873, to Andrew Knowles. Thomas Agnew & Sons Ltd Archive.

231 "Taplow bridge," known as *The Return from the Boating Trip* (1873; private collection). Exhibited London and Manchester 1984–1985, no. 60 and col. pl. 4; recorded by Agnew as *At Maidenhead*, bought from Tissot on behalf of collector R. M. Knowles, to whom Agnew sold the painting May 19, 1873, recording receipt from Tissot, June 18, 1873. Thomas Agnew & Sons Ltd Archive.

232 "3 drawings sketches. the woman in pink / of too Early" (ca. 1872–1873; location unknown).

233 Shorthand for "Signed lower left. Young woman for the Docks" (ca. 1872–1873; probably Ashmolean Museum, England). Probably the gouache study for the seated figure in *The Captain and the Mate*; exhibited London and Manchester 1984–1985, no. 62.

234 "Sketch . . . [Young] Woman from the steamboat" (ca. 1872–1873; location unknown). Probably a study for *Boarding the Yacht*.

235 "Sketch painted from nature / of the taplow bridge without figures" (ca. 1872–1873; location unknown).

236 Agnew recorded purchase from Tissot as *Maidenhead Bridge* on behalf of collector S. Lard, to whom Agnew sold the painting July 9, 1873, with receipt of it from Tissot, August 9, 1873. Thomas Agnew & Sons Ltd Archive. Sold Sotheby's, London, June 23, 1987 (lot 30); location unknown.

237 "The Station," known as *Railway Station* (pl. 44).

238 Agnew recorded receipt from Tissot as *Railway Station*, August 19, 1873. Thomas Agnew & Sons Ltd Archive.

239 "The boat (yellow shawl)," known as *Waiting* (pl. 60).

240 Agnew recorded receipt from Tissot as *Waiting*, November 22, 1873, and sold the painting January 23, 1874. Thomas Agnew & Sons Ltd Archive.

241 *Gravesend* (pl. 62).

242 Agnew recorded purchase from Tissot as *Gravesend*, January 8, 1874; sold in Liverpool, March 3, 1874, for 1,155 pounds to James Hall. Thomas Agnew & Sons Ltd Archive.

243 "The portico of [the] National Gallery," known as *London Visitors* (1873; Milwaukee Art Museum). See London and Paris 2017–2018, 108.

244 Agnew recorded purchase from Tissot, January 8, 1874, as *The Portico (Country Cousins)*, sold October 17, 1874, for 950 guineas to W. J. Houldsworth, from whom reacquired by Agnew, December 15, 1874, as *Our Country Cousins*, and sold June 30, 1877, to William Lee. Thomas Agnew & Sons Ltd Archive. Sold by William Lee, Christie's, London, June 23, 1888 (427) as *London Visitors*, bt. Tooth on behalf of Frederick Layton.

245 "4 caricatures." See n246.

246 "1 caricature." This makes a total of five *Vanity Fair* caricatures for which Tissot recorded receiving payment in 1873; nine caricatures by him were in fact published. Four of these, relating to Cowes Week, may have been made by Tissot in lieu of payment for Bowles's hospitality there.

247 "The Japanese scroll" (pl. 36).

248 "The convalescent." This is the painting known as *The Morning Ride*, sold at Sotheby's, New York, May 4, 2012 (lot 47). Its present location is unknown. Tissot does not list the buyer but Agnew recorded purchase from Tissot of *The Convalescent*, with receipt of the painting on November 22, 1873 (together with *Waiting*), and sale on December 8, 1873, for 1,260 pounds to R. H. Prance. See Wentworth 1984, pl. 100. Agnew took back the painting from Prance on February 9, 1875, in exchange for another work by a different artist, and sold it on May 16, 1877, for 687 pounds and 10 shillings to William Lee. Bought back from Lee by Agnew on May 8, 1878, it was sold on November 25, 1897, for 100 pounds to Thomas McLean. When exhibited at McLean's Gallery in 1898, the work was described as "a lady riding through a garden full of splendid flowers." *Athenaeum* 1898, 445.

249 See pl. 71.

250 "The portico of [the] National Gallery / in large size," known as *London Visitors* (pl. 56).

251 See pl. 45.

252 "Reply to the letter," known as *The Reply* (pl. 55).

253 "[Young] woman in white in the / entrance to my Paris house." Perhaps the painting known as *The Staircase* (pl. 14); or, more likely, the painting known as *Two Figures at the Door* (fig. 23).

254 Known subsequently as *Afternoon Tea* (also known as *In the Conservatory*, pl. 54).

255 "Storm Br[e]wing," known as *A Passing Storm* (1874; Beaverbrook Art Gallery, Fredericton, New Brunswick). See Wentworth 1984, pl. 116.

256 Agnew recorded purchase from Tissot, November 23, 1874, as *The Coming Storm*, sold February 5, 1875, to James Lund. Thomas Agnew & Sons Ltd Archive. Newspapers describing pictures being submitted to the 1875 Royal Academy exhibition included mention of Tissot's *A Coming Storm* (*The Manchester Guardian*, February 1) or *A Storm Brewing* (*Graphic* 1875; *Observer* 1875); it was one of at least three paintings submitted by Tissot in 1875 that were rejected.

257 "The Bouquet of Lilacs" (pl. 53).

258 "The woman and the invalid / White and Blue," known as *Reading the News* (ca. 1874; location unknown). Exhibited London and Manchester 1984–1985, no. 68 and col. pl. 1.

259 Agnew recorded payment to Tissot, February 11, 1875, for *White and Blue*, with receipt of the painting June 30, listed in stock books as *Blue and White*; sold by Agnew to William Ingram, M.P., November 11, 1880. Thomas Agnew & Sons Ltd Archive.

260 See fig. 18 and n261.

261 Tooth recorded purchase from Tissot for 735 pounds, May 3, 1875, as *The Fourth*, sold to James Rhodes (a Bradford-based art dealer), April 29, 1875, for 900 pounds; Tooth was therefore buying on behalf of Rhodes. Records of Arthur Tooth & Sons. It was exhibited at Rhodes's Yorkshire Fine Art Galleries, Bradford, where a reviewer in *The Bradford Observer* (June 17, 1875) described it: "M. Tissot's picture '*Waiting for the Fourth*' is a good example of this artist. It shows us a rather fresh-faced gentleman standing beside a table in a river-side hotel reading the *Times*, while two young ladies, fashionably attired, sit at the opposite ends of the table, talking of someone who is immediately expected. The table is set out for dinner, but there is a vacant chair, and whether the 'fourth' will come and fill it or not is a problem that the spectator will not be able readily to solve." *Waiting for the Fourth* was sold by executors of the late Lord Holden, Christie's, London, July 18, 1913.

262 "The Hollyday (the largest)" (pl. 72). See n264.

263 Simon was paid commission by Tissot for arranging sales of two paintings titled *The Holiday* in 1875; one, sold to Tooth in August, was bought from the dealer three months later by an "E. Simon," probably the same person. It is likely to be "*l'ami E. Simon*," to whom Tissot dedicated and gave *Seaside*, which is known as *July (Specimen of a Portrait)* (fig. 58). Another sale negotiated by Simon fell through (see n266). Simon also consigned *Promenade on the Ramparts* to Christie's in July 1875 on behalf of Paris-based dealer Hector Brame (see n62).

264 Tooth recorded purchase from Tissot, August 30, 1875, as *The Holiday*, 34 x 20 in. (86.4 x 50.8 cm) for 525 pounds (rather than the 550 pounds Tissot recorded); sold by Tooth, November 21, 1875, for 630 pounds to E. Simon. Records of Arthur Tooth & Sons. The size matches the painting known as *Still on Top* (pl. 72).

265 "The thames (the private steamer)," known as *The Thames* (pl. 61).

266 This third sale negotiated in 1875 by Simon, to whom Tissot was going to pay commission, fell through, as would another proposed sale of the same painting (see n273).

267 "The gust of wind," known as *A Windy Day* (pl. 66).

268 Tooth recorded purchase from Tissot, May 7, 1875, as *A Windy Day*, 28 x 20 in. (71.1 x 50.8 cm), for 525 pounds (more than the 450 guineas Tissot recorded, equating to 472 pounds and 5 shillings); sold by Tooth, May 15, 1875, for 600 pounds to Bradford-based dealer James Rhodes. Records of Arthur Tooth & Sons. There are strikeouts and swapped listings for *A Windy Day* and *The Fan* (pl. 66 and n270) in Tooth's stock book echoing those in Tissot's notebook.

269 "The fan" (pl. 40).

270 Tooth recorded purchase from Tissot, May 7, 1875, as *The Fan*, 20 x 15 in. (50.8 x 38.1 cm), for 210 pounds (less than the 250 guineas Tissot recorded, equating to 262 pounds and 5 shillings); sold by Tooth, May 25, 1875, for 330 pounds to José Murrieta. Records of Arthur Tooth & Sons.

271 "The Hollyday (full length)." Probably the painting known as *Preparing for the Gala*, sold Christie's, London, June 8, 2006 (lot 209); location unknown.

272 Mariano de Murrieta lent Tissot's *The Fête Day* to an 1886 exhibition at Whitechapel Art Gallery, London (no. 97), presumably the painting he bought from Tissot as *The Holiday* (see n271).

273 "The thames (private lunch [or launch])" (pl. 61). A proposed sale through Simon having fallen through (see n266), this second attempted sale, to dealer Algernon Moses Marsden, was also unsuccessful. Marsden would buy the painting in 1876, probably on behalf of the collector Kaye Knowles, who subsequently owned it.

274 "The convalescent (in white) / autumn" (pl. 48).

275 Algernon Moses Marsden, art dealer (see pl. 30).

276 "The portrait of Empress / Eugénie and the Prince Imperial" (pl. 28).

277 "Summer morning." Probably the painting known as *Spring Morning* (pl. 49).

278 Probably Tissot's artist friend, Diaz de la Penha.

279 "The thames / (private steamer)" (pl. 61). This third attempt at sale was probably successful because Marsden was acting on behalf of the collector Kaye Knowles, who had commissioned from the Paris-based Italian artist Giuseppe de Nittis a series of London street views, which Tissot's river view would complement.

280 See pl. 51.

281 Perhaps Sir Richard Wallace, whom Tissot would have known from Paris, and who was to buy one of the artist's paintings in 1877 (see n302); or this may be a misspelling of Wallis, manager of the French Gallery.

282 A wealthy Glasgow East India merchant and art patron. *Quarrelling* was probably a wedding gift for his daughter, Eliza, who married in August 1876.

283 *Captain's Balcony* may be the painting related to Tissot's etching *The Three Crows Inn* (1877; Wentworth 29).

284 This may have been a private collector but is more likely the art dealer Edward Fox White, listed by Tissot with incorrect initials.

285 *Portrait of Colonel *** [Longley]* (pl. 31). This is a replica of the portrait shown by Tissot at the 1872 London International Exhibition.

286 Art dealer P. L. Everard, of the Continental Gallery, London.

287 "Last pic-nic," known as *Holyday* (pl. 52).

288 *Holyday* was lent to the 1877 Grosvenor Gallery exhibition by James Taylor (misspelled here by Tissot); the sale having been made through recommendation or negotiation of White (most likely the dealer Edward Fox White).

289 "Replica of Captain's Balcony." See n283.

290 Probably Edward Fox White, who was to be a major buyer of Tissot's paintings and etchings; sold through White's galleries in London and Glasgow. Tissot painted White's portrait (fig. 20), not listed in Tissot's notebook; sold by a grandchild of White, Christie's, London, November 25, 1988 (lot 96) as *Portrait of Mr. Edward Fox-White* (location unknown).

291 Six caricatures by Tissot were published in *Vanity Fair* during 1876.

292 Tissot had taken up etching in earnest after his Royal Academy rejections in 1875, and recorded total income from etching sales every year from 1876.

293 "The Widower" (1876; Art Gallery of New South Wales, Sydney). See Wentworth 1984, pl. 122.

294 This is James Phineas Davis (Tissot misspelled the surname). *The Widower* was lent to the 1877 Grosvenor Gallery exhibition by J. P. Davis. He was a solicitor who lived at Loudon Hall, 20 Grove End Road, near Tissot's house, and had a practice at 15 Clifford Street, near Bond Street.

295 "The Chrysanthemums" (pl. 57).

296 Member of Parliament Edward Hermon.

297 It is unknown whether there was an earlier version, *Uninteresting Story No. 1*. Tissot's etched version of *Uninteresting Story* (1878; Wentworth 32) matches a painting recorded in Tissot 1871–1878, 50. This may be the painting sold by executors of A. S. Dixon, Esq., at Christie's, London, in 1918 as *Explaining the Chart*, 30 x 19 in. (76.2 x 48.3 cm), and sold by executors of Lord Leverhulme, Anderson Galleries, New York, February 17–19, 1926 (lot 264) as *Explaining the Chart*, 28 x 17½ in. (71.1 x 44.5 cm), "from the collection of A. S. Dixon, Esq., 1918" (location unknown).

298 Art dealer Thomas McLean, who had a gallery at 7 Haymarket, London.

299 "Portrait of McLean's daughter." Probably the painting *Miss Adah Maclean*, shown as no. 108 in the exhibition *Victorian Life* (Leicester Galleries, London, 1937), lent by Dr. A. Propert; location unknown.

300 "[Portrait] of [Algernon Moses] Marsden" (pl. 30). See n301.

301 "The Meditation, old picture." *Marguerite in Church* (1865)—exhibited at the 1866 Paris Salon as *Jeune femme dans une église* (*Young Woman in Church*). See Misfeldt 1982, pl. I-38. Likely sold by Tissot as *The Pews* to Reitlinger in 1870 (see n174); bought from Everard by Goupil, July 11, 1875, for 6,000 francs; sold by Goupil, Christie's, London, January 21–22, 1876 (lot 203), 315 pounds, bt. Marsden; probably part-exchanged for Marsden's portrait (pl. 30); lent by Tissot to the 1877 Grosvenor Gallery exhibition (no. 21) as *Meditation*.

302 Wallace recorded purchase from Tissot for 400 pounds, August 8, 1877; by descent to Sir John Murray Scott, residuary legatee of Lady Wallace, 1903; sold by Miss M. Scott, Christie's, London, June 17, 1927 (lot 95) as *Marguerite in Church* (1865), oil on panel, 20½ x 27½ in. (52.1 x 69.9 cm), 21 pounds, bt. Sloane (auctioneer's cross-reference to January 21, 1876 sale; Hermitage Museum and Gardens, Norfolk, VA).

303 Ca. 1877; Tate, London. Exhibited London and Manchester 1984–1985, no. 83 and col. pl. 16.

304 Actually W. G. (William Greene) Herbert, a Liverpool-based art dealer and younger brother of the Pre-Raphaelite artist John Rogers Herbert.

305 "Drawing in essence of Croquet." *Essence* is very diluted oil paint, favored for sketches by Edgar Degas as well as Tissot. An oil version of *Croquet* was sold by Tissot in 1878 (see n311 and pl. 50). There is a replica at the Museum of Art, Rhode Island School of Design, Providence, described as a gouache (opaque watercolor), which may be this drawing, or Tissot made another replica.

306 "Spring (full length)," known as *Spring (Specimen of a Portrait)* (pl. 78).

307 Sold by executors of Edward Fox White, Christie's, London, March 24, 1900 (lot 143) as *Spring*, 55 x 21 in. (139.7 x 53.3 cm), bt. Mitchell.

308 "Portrait of Mrs. gill and her 2 children," known as *Catherine Smith Gill and Two of her Children* (Walker Art Gallery, Liverpool). See Wentworth 1984, pl. 127. Catherine was the wife of Chapple Gill, a Liverpool cotton broker.

309 Only one *Vanity Fair* caricature by Tissot appeared in 1877: *Admiral Sir Hastings Reginald Yelverton GCB*, published June 23. This was the last caricature by Tissot published in the magazine.

310 "Hide & Seek" (pl. 82).

311 See pl. 50.

312 "Docks (up high[?])" (pl. 67).

313 "Sea Side (Flags)," known as *The Gala Day—Seaside* (pl. 81).

314 "Drawing (replica of Spring)." Probably the replica in oil on paper laid down on panel, exhibited London and Manchester 1984–1985, no. 101; location unknown.

315 "Replica of October." Sold Sotheby's, New York, February 16, 1995 (lot 144), 46 x 21 in. (116.8 x 53.3 cm); location unknown.

316 Perhaps a portrait of Lumley Kennedy, mariner and model for numerous shipboard pictures by Tissot.

317 See pl. 84.

318 Sold by William Lee, Christie's, London, June 22, 1888 (lot 426) as *Autumn*, 83 x 42 in. (210.8 x 106.9 cm), 168 pounds, bt. Koekkoek on behalf of Donald Smith (later Lord Strathcona).

319 "Portrait of Mrs. McLaren" (fig. 22). Mrs. McLaren, née Laura Pochin, had married Scottish barrister Charles McLaren, MP for Stafford and Bosworth, in 1877. Charles McLaren took over running his father-in-law Henry Pochin's vast industrial empire, and the couple lived at Bodnant, in north Wales. McLaren became 1st Lord Aberconway in 1911.

320 See fig. 39.

321 Goupil recorded purchase from Tissot for 5,500 francs, July 1878; exhibited Goupil Gallery, London, *Annual Exhibition of High Class Continental Pictures*, 1879 (no. 87); sold by Goupil, June 25, 1884, for 3,000 francs to Philadelphia art dealer, Charles Field Haseltine. Goupil & Cie / Boussod, 1846–1919. With John Francis Brice, Paris, by 1908/1909, by descent; sold Christie's, London, June 7, 2007 (lot 38).

322 "Naughty book." Probably erotic Indian miniatures. In a letter to another potential buyer, dated October 11, 1878, Tissot enclosed "the book of Indian paintings," for which he hoped there would be an admirer, priced 120 pounds including 20 pounds commission, adding "I'd ask you not to let it leave your house, if you'd be obliged." James Tissot Letters, 1878–1879, Getty Research Institute Research Library, Los Angeles.

323 This entry, written in a different and neater copperplate script, is probably the hand of Tissot's secretary, Charles Buckingham. Employed from 1880, it appears that Buckingham retrospectively tidied accounts for 1878–1879.

324 See n323.

325 Sold Christie's, London, November 4, 1994 (lot 101), 46 x 21½ in. (117.2 x 54.6 cm); location unknown.

326 "[Replica] Widower. small" (private collection).

327 Tooth recorded purchase from Tissot for 60 pounds, March 22, 1879, as *The Widower*, 14½ x 9½ in. (36.8 x 24.1 cm); sold May 31, 1879, to Pakinton. Records of Arthur Tooth & Sons.

328 "[Replica] Window, small" (location unknown). Probably a replica of *The Bow Window*. See Misfeldt 1982, pl. III-7.

329 Tooth recorded purchase from Tissot for 60 pounds, March 22, 1879, as *The Window*, 16 x 6½ in. (40.6 x 16.2 cm); sold March 27, 1879, to H. J. Turner. Records of Arthur Tooth & Sons.

330 "[Replica] Hansom. small." Replica of *Going to Business*. See n353.

331 Tooth recorded purchase from Tissot for 60 pounds, March 14, 1879, as *The Hansom Cab*, 17 x 7½ in. (43.2 x 19.1 cm); sold March 27, 1879, to Mr. H. J. Thauser (identified by Paolo Serafini in Rome 2015–2016, 45). Records of Arthur Tooth & Sons. Probably the oil on panel painting, 17¼ x 10 in. (43.8 x 25.4 cm), exhibited London and Manchester 1984–1985, no. 115; sold Sotheby's, New York, February 28, 1990 (lot 151) as *Going to Business*; location unknown.

332 "Portico. small." Probably a painting (location unknown) relating to Tissot's etching *The Portico of the National Gallery, London* (1878; Wentworth 40).

333 "(The Docks) Emigrants." Given the sale price, this is probably the large version dated 1873; location unknown. See Misfeldt 1982, pl. III-9. Sold by William Lee, Christie's, London, June 22, 1888 (lot 425) as *The Emigrant*, 45½ x 20½ in. (115.6 x 52.1 cm), bt. Koekkoek for Donald Smith, later Lord Strathcona; given by family of Lord Strathcona to the Montreal Museum of Fine Arts, 1927, where recorded as dated 1873; damaged and cut down (see Wentworth 1978, fig. 45e); sold 1945.

334 "Reverie the small brown picture" (1878; location unknown). See Misfeldt 1982, pl. III-8; oil on panel; sold Sotheby's, New York, October 1988 (lot 120).

335 "Replica the small 'Evening.'" A smaller-size copy of *Evening* (pl. 79); location unknown.

336 Probably the painting known as *Room Overlooking the Harbour*; private collection. See London and Manchester 1984–1985, no. 77 and col. pl. 21. The setting is a room in the Albion Hotel, Ramsgate, England (demolished for harbor improvements); 80 pounds is the price Tissot charged for other small oils of this size (10 x 13 in. [25.4 x 33 cm]).

337 "(Falcon) Gravesend." Probably the painting set outside the Falcon Tavern, Gravesend, Kent, England, known as *Waiting for the Ferry* (location unknown). See London and Manchester 1984–1985, no. 111 and col. pl. 20.

338 Replica of fig. 21; location unknown.

339 See Wentworth 1984, pl. 146; sold by Baron Cassel, Galerie Charpentier, Paris, December 2, 1954 (lot 50) as *Crossing the Channel*, oil on panel, 10¼ x 6¾ in. (26 x 17 cm), signed in monogram b. r.; location unknown.

340 See Misfeldt 1982, pl. III-6.

341 Tooth recorded purchase from Tissot for 80 pounds, June 25, 1879, as *Visitors at Kew*, 17 x 8 in. (43.2 x 20.3 cm); sold June 27, 1879, to W. Towne. Records of Arthur Tooth & Sons. Sold Christie's, New York, February 16, 1994 (lot 181) as *Kew Gardens*, 17 x 7½ in. (43.2 x 19.1 cm); location unknown.

342 Exhibited London and Manchester 1984–1985, no. 110 and col. pl. 5; location unknown.

343 Another version of fig. 58; probably the one at the Cleveland Museum of Art. See n344.

344 Knoedler recorded receipt, July 14, 1879, as *Femme au sofa*, from Bulla Frères et Jouy (acting as Knoedler's agents), price 3,250 francs (the 250 francs difference between this and Tissot's recorded price probably equating to Bulla's handling fee); sold by Knoedler, October 4, 1879, as *Summer Hours* for 1,400 dollars to Judge Henry Hilton, New York. M. Knoedler & Co. records, ca. 1848–1971. At Hilton's posthumous sale, American Art Galleries, New York, February 13, 1900, *Summer Hours* (lot 74) was described as showing "a lawn in sunlight" beyond the window, corresponding to a description of *July* exhibited in Liverpool, October 1878. It appears that, later, the view through the window was repainted and the hairstyle and face were also altered. Cf. fig. 58 and painting at the Cleveland Museum of Art.

345 "[July] drawing [in] essence," as in the publication titled *Essence*.

346 Knoedler recorded receipt as *Esquisse femme au sofa*, July 31, 1879, for 500 dollars, with sale December 11, 1879, for 450 dollars to William H. Vanderbilt; location unknown. M. Knoedler & Co. records, ca. 1848–1971.

347 See Wentworth 1984, pl. 145; Blackfriars Bridge is in the background. Sold from the estate of the late Captain R. S. De Q. Quincey, Christie's, London, June 11, 1993 (lot 100) as *The Ferry*; location unknown.

348 See pl. 73.

349 Probably Misfeldt 1982, pl. III-23; location unknown.

350 See Misfeldt 1982, pl. III-12; location unknown.

351 Tooth recorded receipt, July 22, 1879, as *Music*, 14½ x 10 in. (36.8 x 25.4 cm) for 80 pounds, and *Amusing Baby*, 14½ x 10½ in. (36.8 x 25.4 cm) for 80 pounds, indicating payment to Tissot was 160 pounds in total, not 80 pounds. Both were in Tooth's 1879 winter exhibition, where at least one reviewer confused titles and descriptions for the two. *Music* was sold May 1, 1880, for 85 pounds to Hartenout; bought back by Tooth, June 11, 1883, as *The Rehearsal*, 16 x 12 in. (40.6 x 30.5 cm), having already sold it June 9, 1883, to Higgie. A watercolor replica of *Music* (not listed in Tissot's notebook) was exhibited in 1881 at the Hanover Gallery, London, as *Do re mi fa sol la ti do* (probably the one now at the Museum of Art, Rhode Island School of Design, Providence).

352 See pl. 85.

353 See Misfeldt 1982, pl. III-4 (there are slight differences in the alignment of the lamps to the replica [see n330]); location unknown.

354 See Wentworth 1984, pl. 144; location unknown.

355 Agnew arranged the transaction with Tissot, May 18, 1879, on behalf of a private collector to whom the sale had been made on May 11, 1879. Thomas Agnew & Sons Ltd Archive. This was Tissot's first business dealing with Agnew since Tissot's Royal Academy rejections in 1875, and he would make no further transactions with Agnew after this one.

356 "Woman's head (with nasturtiums)." Misfeldt 1982, pl. III-20; sold by Graves, Christie's, London, March 12, 1881 (lot 306) as *Pensive Moments, Painted for the Beauty's Gallery*; sold Christie's, London, October 25, 1991 (lot 48) as *Type of Beauty: Portrait of Mrs. Kathleen Newton, in Red Dress and Black Bonnet*; location unknown.

357 The proprietors of *The Graphic* commissioned a number of artists "to paint each his particular idea of a beautiful woman. The result is the charming little gallery of female loveliness now being exhibited in Grafton Street" (*The Examiner*, February 21, 1880). Following their London exhibition, "The *Graphic* Beauties" were shown in Glasgow.

358 "Por[trait] of Lawson. Drawing." Probably Lionel Lawson, a caricature of whom Tissot had made earlier for *Vanity Fair*, published February 19, 1876; exhibited London and Paris 1984–1985, no. 72.

359 Two small versions are known of *Emigrants* (the large 1873 painting, formerly the Montreal Museum of Fine Arts [see n333]): 1. Oil on panel, 15½ x 7⅜ in. (39.4 x 18.6 cm), Speed Art Museum, Louisville, gift of Mr. and Mrs. W. Armin Willig, 1991 (sold Sotheby's, London, November 30, 1955 [lot 148], bt. M. Newman Ltd., London; with Stair-Murdock Fine Arts Ltd., New York, January 1981); and 2. Oil on panel, 15½ x 7 in. (39.4 x 17.8 cm), consigned to Sotheby's, New York, May 3, 2000 (lot 253), formerly owned by Robert Frank, London, from whom it was acquired June 18, 1958, by Mrs. John Hay Whitney; location unknown. One of these is probably the painting shown by Tissot at the 1879 Grosvenor Gallery exhibition, where it was described as one of Tissot's smaller pictures.

360 See n359.

361 Related to Tissot's etching *The Organ Grinder* (1878; Wentworth 38).

362 *Annual Exhibition*, Walker Art Gallery, Liverpool (no. 448), as *The Organ Grinder*, oil painting, priced 70 pounds.

363 "The Warrior's Daughter," formerly known as *The Convalescent*; Manchester Art Gallery. Exhibited London and Manchester 1984–1985, no. 107.

364 See pl. 83.

365 "The Letter." Probably the painting recorded in Tissot's albums; location unknown. See Misfeldt 1982, pl. III-19.

366 "Small replica blue dress / on the sofa." Probably a replica of the painting known as *La Lecture dans le parc* (*Reading in the Park*) (see fig. 119).

367 George Trist was the brother of wine merchant and collector John Hamilton Trist. Sold by executors of George Trist, late of Eliot Lodge, Sydenham Hill, and 62, Old Broad Street, City, Christie's, London, May 1, 1886 (lot 169) as *In the Garden*, 49 pounds and 7 shillings; location unknown.

368 "Small replica Good Bye." Small replica of *Goodbye, On the Mersey*. See Wentworth 1984, pl. 147.

369 Sold by executors of George Trist, Christie's, London, May 1, 1886 (lot 167) as *"Good-Bye," From the Royal Academy*, 1881 (probably incorrect, as the Royal Academy picture would have been the larger version not a smaller replica), 52 pounds and 10 shillings, bt. McLean; sold by executors of John Clark, late of Curling Hall, June 8, 1895 (lot 116) as *Farewell*, 18½ x 9 in. (47 x 22.9 cm). This is either the oil on panel, 13½ x 9 in. (34.3 x 22.9 cm), in a private collection, or another version, location unknown.

370 See pl. 75.

371 Bradford-based art dealer James Rhodes.

372 Reproduced in Tissot's photograph albums. See Misfeldt 1982, pl. III-24.

373 Paris auctioneer Jules Auguste Boussaton; sold by Boussaton, Galerie Georges Petit, Paris, May 5, 1891 (lot 80) as *The Eldest Sister*, 15¾ x 7⅛ in. (40 x 18 cm), 2,200 francs; property of a California private collector, sold Sotheby's, New York, February 24, 1987 (lot 79) as *La sœur ainée* (The Eldest Sister), oil on panel, 16 x 7 in. (40.6 x 17.8 cm); location unknown.

374 "The Louvre (Salle des Saisons)" (pl. 100).

375 "On the Steps." Probably the painting known as *The Elder Sister* (pl. 97).

376 Knoedler recorded receipt on September 14, 1880, as *La terrasse* from Bulla Frères et Jouy (acting as agents for Knoedler), price 2,000 francs; sold by Knoedler, October 22, 1880, as *Mother and Child "Terrace"* for 700 dollars to F. G. Avery, Buffalo. M. Knoedler & Co. records, ca. 1848–1971.

377 "The Hammock." Probably fig. 21.

378 Sold by executors of George Trist, May 1, 1886 (lot 164), 43 pounds and 1 shilling, bt. McLean; location unknown.

379 See pl. 80. "Le Duncan" refers to the top-hatted man, recognizable by his distinctive beard as James Duncan, the major Scottish collector of French art at this time. He is not known to have owned any paintings by Tissot but may have bought etchings.

380 Exhibition of the Newcastle Arts Association.

381 Either the painting exhibited London and Manchester 1984–1985, no. 134 (private collection), or a replica (location unknown).

382 See Misfeldt 1982, pl. III-10; location unknown.

383 "Replica Salle des Saisons Louvre." A smaller version of *Visiting the Louvre* (pl. 100).

384 Exhibited at *Annual Exhibition*, Walker Art Gallery, Liverpool, 1880 (no. 172) as *Visiting the Louvre*, priced 100 pounds (presumably including commission, hence Tissot recording income of 85 pounds from sale). Probably the version from the collection of H. Stewart Black, England; sold Sotheby's, New York, April 23, 2004 (lot 108) as *Visiteurs étrangers au Louvre*.

385 See Misfeldt 1982, pl. III-25.

386 See Misfeldt 1982, pl. III-26.

387 *By Land* was consigned by executors of George Trist, Christie's, London, May 1, 1886 (lot 165), bt. in; sold by executors of George Trist, Christie's, London, June 19, 1886 (lot 181), 52 pounds and 10 shillings, bt. McLean. *By Water* was sold by executors of George Trist, Christie's, London, May 1, 1886 (lot 166), 70 pounds and 7 shillings, bt. McLean. Both paintings were sold by executors of John Clark, of Curling Hall, Christie's, London, June 8, 1895 (lot 114) as *By Sea*, (lot 115) as *By Land*, "the companion"; both 22 x 12 in. (55.9 x 30.5 cm), 131 pounds and 5 shillings, bt. Lawrie; location unknown.

388 "The large Hammock with the dog" (fig. 118).

389 Probably George Donkin, of Donkin & Nichol, Newcastle, makers of steering gear for ships; sold Christie's, London, November 28, 2001 (lot 21) as *The Hammock*, oil on canvas, 50 x 30 in. (127 x 76.2 cm); location unknown.

390 Exhibited Paris 1985, no. 119 as *La sœur ainée* (*The Eldest Sister*); Musée de Cambrai, France.

391 William Vaughan offered to bequeath this painting and his other Tissots to the National Gallery, London, but was turned down; instead he bequeathed the works to French museums.

392 See Misfeldt 1982, pl. IV-36; sold Christie's, London, June 11, 2003 (lot 12) as *The Departure Platform, Victoria Station*; location unknown.

393 Probably the watercolor exhibited London and Manchester 1984, no. 138; location unknown.

394 Paris-based art dealer Georges Petit, to whom Tissot had last sold work in 1868, but with whom Tissot had corresponded since 1878.

395 See Misfeldt 1982, pl. III-28.

396 Sold by executors of George Trist, Christie's, London, May 1, 1886 (lot 168) as *The Picnic*, 28 pounds and 7 shillings, bt. Nathan; sold by executors of John Clark, Christie's, London, June 8, 1895 (lot 117) as *The Garden Party*, 10 x 15 in. (25.4 x 38.1 cm); 12 pounds, 1 shilling, and 6 pence; bt. Moody; on loan to Tate Gallery, London, when illustrated Laver 1936, pl. X, as *The Picnic*; exhibited Sheffield 1955 (no. 19); sold Sotheby's, New York, February 16, 1994 (lot 163) as *Children's Party*, oil on panel, 9½ x 12¾ in. (24.1 x 32.4 cm); location unknown.

397 Consigned to Christie's, London, July 13, 2016 (lot 135) as *La sœur ainée*; location unknown.

398 Receipt from Tissot recorded by Knoedler, November 14, 1881, as *On the Sun* (stock no. 3614), price 100 pounds; sold by Knoedler, April 18, 1882, as *On the Thames* (stock no. 3613) for 550 dollars to J. M. Vose, Providence. Knoedler appears to have confused the titles of the two paintings received together from Tissot, both priced 100 pounds, and changed the title of this one; for the second painting, see n400. M. Knoedler & Co. records, ca. 1848–1971. London's Castle Hotel, in Richmond (where the town hall now stands), had grounds extending to the Thames, near Richmond Bridge. See Misfeldt 1982, pl. III-30. Sold by executors of Thomas B. Holmes, of Hornsea, East Yorkshire, Christie's, London, December 5, 1913, as *On the Thames*; sold Christie's, New York, May 22, 1997 (lot 167) as *A Declaration of Love*; location unknown.

399 Known as *In the Sun* (pl. 96).

400 Knoedler recorded receipt from Tissot of two paintings on November 14, 1881: *Richmond* (stock no. 3613) and *On the Sun* (stock no. 3614), both priced 100 pounds. He sold 3614 as *On the Thames* (see n398). It would therefore appear that he did not make the link between the title *On the Sun* and Tissot's etching in reverse of the same composition, *In Full Sunlight*, and that the painting known as *In the Sun* was sold as *Richmond*, April 17, 1882, for 900 dollars to George C. Cooper, New York. M. Knoedler & Co. records, ca. 1848–1971.

401 See pl. 102.

402 See n391.

403 "Quiet. watercolor." Collection of A. Alfred Taubman, sold Sotheby's, New York, November 5, 2015 (lot 215T); location unknown.

404 "Decoration [of] Dining Room." Exhibited Galerie Sedelmeyer, Paris, in 1883 (no. 5) as *Le Jardin des Hespérides, panneaux décoratifs pour la salle à manger de M. H. Oppenheim, de Londres* (*The Garden of the Hesperides*, decorative panels for the dining room of Mr. H. Oppenheim, of London). See Misfeldt 1982, pls. IV-49–IV-57; location unknown.

405 Henry Oppenheim was a partner of Bank Oppenheim. In 1882, he bought a house at 16 Bruton Street, Berkeley Square, London; Tissot's dining room decorations were part of the refurbishment. The house was severely damaged during Second World War bombardment and subsequently was demolished.

406 See pl. 95.

407 "[Watercolor.] Visitors to the Louvre." It is not known whether this is a replica of a painting set in the Salle des Saisons, on the north stairs, or in another part of the Louvre.

408 "On account for the Dining Room." See nn404–405.

409 Tissot made a pastel portrait of Georges Petit's baby with its nurse (Misfeldt 1982, pl. III-40) in January–February 1883, and was also arranging with Petit to exhibit work with the Société des aquarellistes, and independently. Letters written by Tissot to Petit mention payment of 3,000 francs in January, and a request for the 2,000 francs balance remaining on an account of 4,000 francs. Misfeldt 1988, 163–165. The notebook lists receipt of just one payment of 2,000 francs on account.

410 See fig. 54 and Perrin, this volume.

411 "The balance for the decoration of the dining room." See nn404–405.

412 "The garden Bench [watercolor]." Watercolor replica of pl. 104; location unknown.

413 "Pen-and-ink drawing, the little Nimrod." Probably related to the oil painting *A Little Nimrod* (pl. 103); location unknown.

414 "Portrait of a little American girl (deceased)."

415 Goupil recorded receipt from Tissot, October 18, 1883, for 2,000 francs of *Portrait d'enfant* (*Portrait of a child*), 19¾ x 16⅛ in. (50 x 41 cm), sold the same day to Mr. Whitney, Hotel Meurice, for 2,500; location unknown. Goupil & Cie / Boussod, 1846–1919.

416 "(Too early) drawing [for] Figaro." Drawn for *Le Figaro*, this is probably the pen-and-ink drawing, with oil and gouache, of the principal group's head and shoulders in *Provincial Woman* (pl. 125), consigned to Neal Auction Company, New Orleans, April 5, 2003 (lot 193) as *Study for La Femme de Paris*; location unknown.

417 "Replica [for] Sedelmeyer (Aesthetic Woman)" (pl. 128).

418 *The Tissot Exhibition of Pictures of Life in Paris* at Arthur Tooth & Sons' Galleries, Haymarket, London, opened to the public on May 24, 1886, with a preview on May 22. Tooth recorded sale of one painting, *Provincial Woman* (pl. 125), at the preview, and another five during the exhibition or shortly thereafter. Cost prices recorded by Tooth were six at 300 pounds, one at 150 pounds, and eight at 100 pounds, totaling 2,750 pounds, rather than the 2,436 pounds that Tissot recorded; Tooth probably paid Tissot in francs, as that figure is a rounded sum of 69,000 in Tissot's notebook.

419 "Watercolors falcon hotel." Probably Misfeldt 1982, pl. IV-1; location unknown. Lent by Beugniet to the 1886 Société des aquarellistes exhibition as *L'Auberge du folçon à Gravesend* (*The Falcon Tavern at Gravesend*).

420 "[Watercolor] the 3 crows inn." Probably Misfeldt 1982, pl. IV-2; location unknown. Lent by Beugniet to the 1886 Société des aquarellistes exhibition as *La Tamise à Gravesend* (*The Thames at Gravesend*).

421 Paris-based art dealer Adolphe Beugniet.

422 "[Watercolor] Morning luncheon." Probably Misfeldt 1982, pl. IV-3; location unknown. Lent by Beugniet to the 1886 Société des aquarellistes exhibition as *Le déjeuner du matin* (*The Morning Luncheon*).

423 Pastel, recorded in Tissot's photograph albums. See Misfeldt 1982, pl. IV-8; sold Sotheby's, New York, May 5, 1999 (lot 344) as *Portrait of Marie-Héloise Jeanne Ferré May*; location unknown. May was married to Parisian stockbroker Ernest May, an important early collector of Impressionist art.

424 The sale price suggests that this was a watercolor. It may have been a replica of one of the oils sold by Tissot in 1879 (see nn349–351) or a composition similar to pls. 98 and 109.

425 J. Bulla was a partner of the Paris-based art dealers Bulla Frères et Jouy, who had handled Tissot works as agents for Knoedler in New York.

426 "Vis[itors] to the Louvre / Salle des Saisons." Probably Misfeldt 1982, pl. III-42; sold Christie's, London, November 22, 2006 (lot 211) as *Visiteurs étrangers au Louvre* (*Foreign Visitors at the Louvre*); location unknown.

427 "Gravesend. Watercolor." Perhaps another version of the *Three Crows Inn, Gravesend* (see n420), or of figures on the landing stage outside the inn (see pl. 62); location unknown.

428 "On the thames." Probably the painting known as *Return from Henley*. See Misfeldt 1982, pl. III-67; consigned from the collections of Lily & Edmond J. Safra, Sotheby's, New York, October 18, 2011 (lot 790) as *Sur la Tamise (Return from Henley)*; location unknown.

429 "Second voyage to Jerusalem." Tissot had visited the Holy Land from October 1886 to March 1887, and had been inspired to illustrate the life of Christ (see pls. 140–156). His second visit was from late October 1888 to April 1889.

430 Dumont was a publisher; he lent a group of Tissot etchings to the first exhibition of the Société des peintres-graveurs at Galerie Durand-Ruel, Paris, in January 1889, before Tissot's return from Jerusalem.

431 Groult was a neighbor of Tissot; this portrait of Mme. Groult (location unknown) may be Misfeldt 1982, pl. IV-37; a pencil drawing of the sitter is inscribed *1891 / James Tissot à mon / amical voisin C. Groult* (exhibited London and Manchester 1984–1985, no. 174; location unknown).

432 "Young Seillière port[rait]." Refers to René Seillière. See Perrin, this volume.

433 Tissot had painted a portrait of Eugène Coppens de Fontenay in 1867 (pl. 26).

434 "A sketch Arthur Meyer."

435 "Received from Arthur Meyer."

436 "Morning walk." Perhaps Misfeldt 1982, pl. III-39; location unknown.

437 See pl. 132.

438 "Port[rait] [of] Mlle. Christine Seillière." See Perrin, this volume.

439 Tissot's total income for thirty years includes the deleted payment in 1871 for the portrait of Madame Desoye (1,500 francs) but omits two payments recorded by Tooth in 1879 (see n441) and any balancing payment for the *Circle of the Rue Royale* (see n70). It is therefore not the exact sum.

440 Tissot's total for 1871 includes the deleted portrait of Madame Desoye (1,500 francs); when deducted the annual total is 23,036 francs.

441 In London, for the duration of eleven years (1872 to 1881); the total should be higher if Tooth correctly recorded in 1879 two payments to Tissot of 80 pounds (for *Piano* and *Lily*, Tissot recording only one [see n351]), and another of 150 pounds (for *Evening* [pl. 79], not recorded by Tissot).

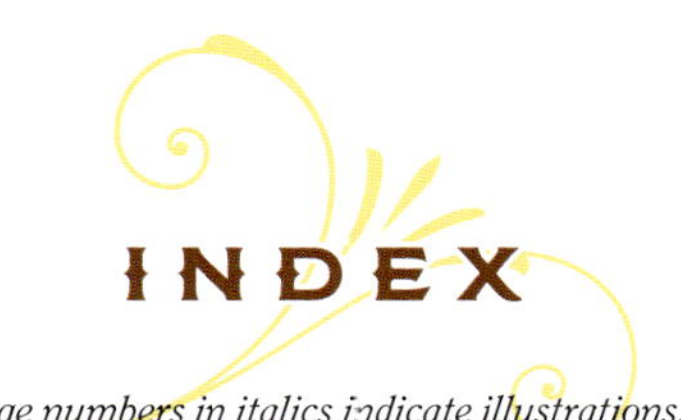

INDEX

Page numbers in italics indicate illustrations.

A

B

C

D

E

M

N

O

P

R

S

T

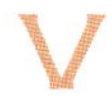

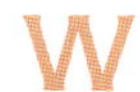

Z

ACKNOWLEDGMENTS

Narrowing the list of people to thank for their contributions during the preparation for this ambitious exhibition and its catalogue is as challenging as succinctly defining the multifaceted and often enigmatic James Tissot. There are many to whom much appreciation is owed, and this list represents only a fraction of the support our project received from national and international colleagues, donors, and friends. I extend sincere gratitude to all those who have made this journey and its exciting outcomes possible.

The Fine Arts Museums of San Francisco's presentation would not have been feasible without the extraordinary support of our generous donors: John A. and Cynthia Fry Gunn, Robert G. and Sue Douthit O'Donnell, Barbro and Bernard Osher, Denise Littlefield Sobel, Diane B. Wilsey, Gladyne Kenderdine Mitchell, Barbara A. Wolfe, The Diana Dollar Knowles Fund, Carole McNeil, Lucy Young Hamilton, and David A. Wollenberg. Additional support is provided by Sandra and Paul Bessières, Marion Moore Cope, George and Leslie Hume, Michael and Dorothy Leung, and Christina and Barry Ongerth. Scientific analyses were performed by Emeline Simone Pouyet and Lindsay Hardt Oakley at the Northwestern University / Art Institute of Chicago Center for Scientific Studies in the Arts and made possible by the generous support of the Andrew W. Mellon Foundation. The exhibition is also supported by an indemnity from the Federal Council on the Arts and the Humanities. This catalogue is published with the assistance of the Andrew W. Mellon Foundation Endowment for Publications. Additional research support is provided by the Paul Mellon Centre for Studies in British Art.

The presentation has been enhanced by the goodwill of the many lenders who have shared their knowledge and works of art with us. We extend our gratitude to: Shelley Falconer, Tobi Bruce, and Christine Braun at the Art Gallery of Hamilton, Ontario; Stephan Jost, Julian Cox, Caroline Shields, Maria Sullivan, Meaghan Monaghan, and Christine Fillion at the Art Gallery of Ontario, Toronto; Anne Pasternak, Lisa Small, and Shea Spiller at the Brooklyn Museum; Susan Dackerman, Shanna Dickson, and Susan Roberts-Manganelli at the Cantor Arts Center, Stanford University, California; Erik Neil at the Chrysler Museum of Art, Norfolk, Virginia; Cameron Kitchin and Peter Jonathan Bell at the Cincinnati Art Museum; Juan Antonio Pérez Simón, along with Roberto Fernández and Graciela Téllez Trevilla at the Colección Pérez Simón, Mexico City; Ann and Gordon Getty, along with Deborah Hatch, Maria Santangelo, and Nora McGovern at the Collection of Ann and Gordon Getty; David Bradbury, Jeremy Johnson, and Katherine Pearce at the Guildhall Art Gallery, London; Simon Wallis at The Hepworth Wakefield, England; Claudia Gould, Darsie Alexander, and Katherine Danalakis at The Jewish Museum, New York; James Cuno, Timothy Potts, Davide Gasparotto, Scott Allan, and Devi Ormond at The J. Paul Getty Museum, Los Angeles; Ralph and Terry Kovel; John Roles at

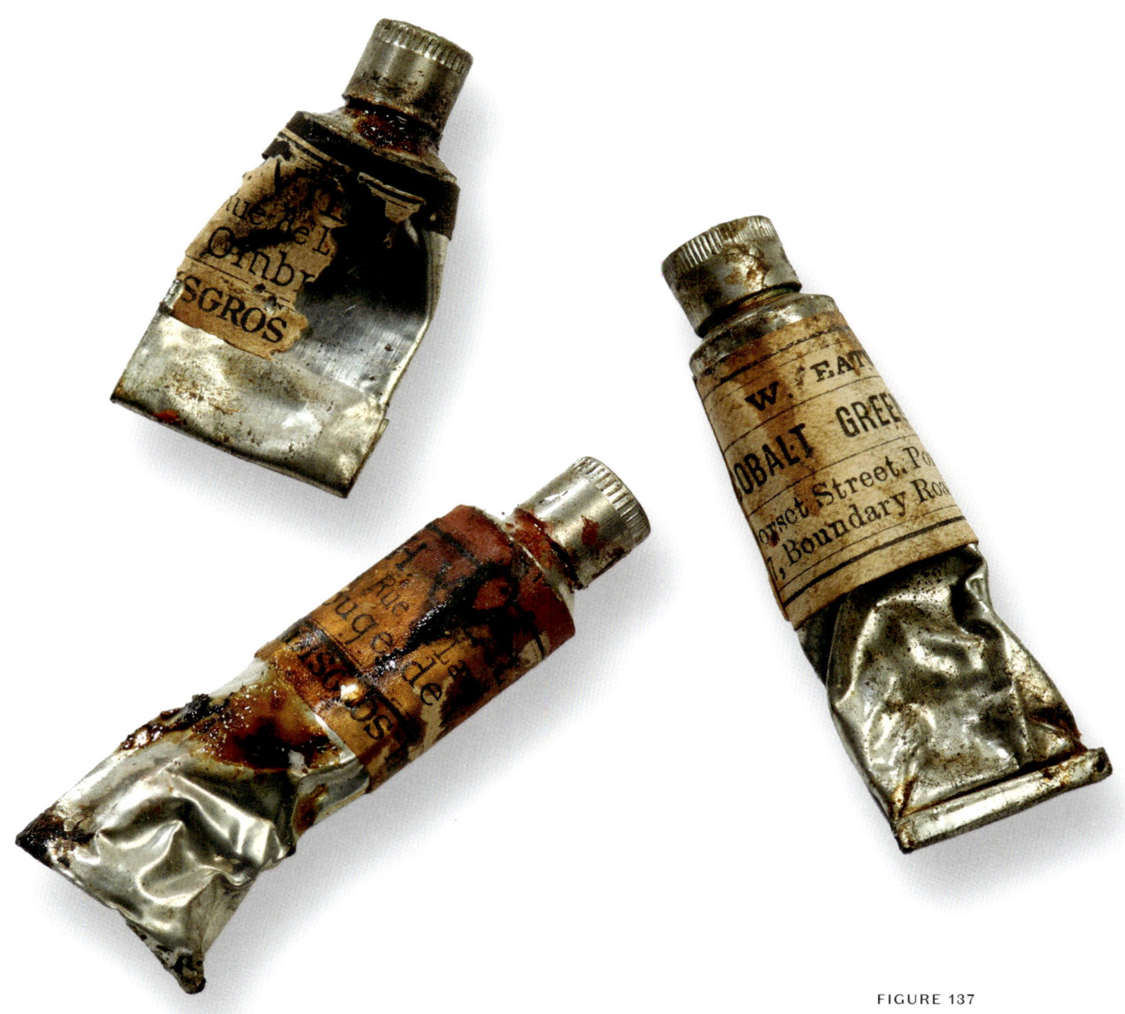

FIGURE 137
Paint tubes found in Tissot's Château de Buillon studio after his death

the Leeds Museums and Galleries; Frédéric Mantion; Nathalie Bondil and Anne Grace at the Montreal Museum of Fine Arts; Brigitte Olivier at the Musée Baron Martin Gray, France; Sophie Lévy and Cyrille Sciama at the Musée d'Arts de Nantes; Olivier Gabet, Audrey Gay-Mazuel, and Béatrice Quette at the Musée des Arts Décoratifs, Paris; Nicolas Surlapierre at the Musée des Beaux-Arts et d'Archéologie de Besançon, France; Laurence des Cars, Sylvie Patry, Marine Kisiel, Paul Perrin, and Stéphanie de Brabander at the Musée d'Orsay, Paris; John W. Smith and Maureen C. O'Brien at the Museum of Art, Rhode Island School of Design, Providence; Kim Streets at the Museums Sheffield, England; Earl "Rusty" Powell, Kaywin Feldman, Mary Morton, and Kimberley Jones at the National Gallery of Art, Washington, DC; Marc Mayer, Alexandra "Sasha" Suda, Paul Lang, Anabelle Kienle Poňka, and Christopher Etheridge at the National Gallery of Canada, Ottawa; Sean Rainbird at the National Gallery of Ireland, Dublin; Nicholas Cullinan and Alison Smith at the National Portrait Gallery, London; Christophe Leribault and Stéphanie Cantarutti at the Petit Palais, Musée des Beaux-Arts de la Ville de Paris; Janita Bagshawe at The Royal Pavilion, Art Gallery and Museums, Brighton, England; Larry J. Feinberg and Eik Kahng at the Santa Barbara Museum of Art; Tim Craven at the Southampton City Art Gallery, England; Pia Müller-Tamm and Leonie Beiersdorf at the Staatliche Kunsthalle Karlsruhe, Germany; Olivier Meslay and Esther Bell at the Sterling and Francine Clark Art Institute, Williamstown, Massachusetts; Maria Balshaw, Alex Farquharson, Caroline Corbeau-Parsons, Carol Jacobi, and Amy Concannon at Tate, London; Brian Kennedy, Lawrence W. Nichols, and Halona Westbrook at the Toledo Museum of Art, Ohio; Thomas J. Loughman and Oliver Tostmann at the Wadsworth Atheneum Museum of Art, Hartford, Connecticut; Diane B. Wilsey; Hilary McGrady at Wimpole Hall, Cambridgeshire, England; and additional private collectors who wish to remain anonymous. We are also appreciative of the various dealers who have helped us with loans: Peter Brown, James Hastie, and Ellanor Notides at Christie's; Grant Ford at Grant Ford Ltd.; Martin Beisly at Martin Beisly Fine Art; Benjamin Dollar and Jennifer Biederbeck at Sotheby's; Guy Stair Sainty at Stair Sainty Gallery; and Anthony Chriton-Stewart at Thos. Agnew & Sons Ltd.

Our exhibition has been organized under the guidance of Krista Brugnara, director of exhibitions, whose perceptive insights on matters from the evolution of the exhibition concept to details of the gallery layout have made this project possible. Moreover, our excellent exhibitions team at the Legion of Honor, Hilary Magowan, exhibitions manager, and Sarah Miller, exhibitions assistant, shepherded this project through various stages of preparation. Gratitude is given to Christopher Busch, senior exhibitions designer; Kate Agarwal, exhibition graphic designer; and Jesse Beckman, exhibition graphics preparator, for producing the elegant exhibition design and didactics. On the conservation team, we also wish to thank Elise Effmann Clifford, head of paintings conservation; Debra Evans, head of paper conservation; and Jane Williams, head of objects conservation, along with Victoria Binder, paper conservator, and Céline Chrétien, associate objects conservator. Special recognition is extended to Sarah Kleiner, associate paintings conservator, for leading the technical research for "Team Tissot." Her collaboration on this initiative added depth to our project's scope. Kimberley Montgomery, chief registrar, and Nadia Ghani, museum registrar, were key to organizing our indemnity application and the essential coordination of our registration efforts. Ryan Butterfield, chief preparator and his team are integral partners in the presentation of our installation. Two former recipients of the Joseph F. McCrindle Curatorial Internship in the Fine Arts Museums' European Paintings Department, Isabella Holland, curatorial assistant in European Paintings, and Lexi Paulson, administrative assistant to the director of the art division, were crucial allies in list-making, fact-checking, and Tissot-sleuthing; they established a foundation for so much of what this project required, and its success is indebted to their commitment, patience, and good humor.

We wish to thank each of the authors whose scholarship has added to the intellectual abundance of this catalogue, especially Krystyna Matyjaszkiewicz, whose expertise has been profoundly generous. Beyond Krystyna, this volume was realized due to the rich contributions from Donato Esposito, Marine Kisiel, Sarah Kleiner, Nancy Rose Marshall, Paul Perrin, Cyrille Sciama, and Bertrand Tillier, along with Jan Dirk Baetens, Justine De Young, Margaretta S. Frederick, Charlotte Gere, Frédéric Mantion, Valentine Robert, Léa Saint-Raymond, Françoise Tétart-Vittu, and Peter Trippi. This book was produced by the Fine Arts Museums, under the unparalleled guidance of Leslie Dutcher, director of publications. Nikki Bazar, editor, delivered dedicated precision and thoughtful care for the material, which has resulted in a book that rivals the beauty of Tissot's art. José Jovel was instrumental in gathering the images that illustrate these pages. Others in the Publications Department, including Trina Enriquez, editor; Victoria Gannon, editor; and Kate Bove, associate editor, assisted with various details to bring this catalogue to completion. New photography for this volume was made possible by Sue Grinols, director of photo services, and Randy Dodson, head photographer. Translations of the French texts were prepared by Alexandra Bonfante-Warren and Rose Vekony. Bob Aufuldish of Aufuldish & Warinner is responsible for the delightful design that draws cleverly from period motifs and details in the decorations at Tissot's château in Buillon, France. The lavish reproductions and the printing of this volume were done by Verona Libri, Italy, under the guidance of Sergio Brunelli, Fabio Ferrandini, Zeno Ferrandini, Nancy Freeman, Vanni Perbellini, and Mari Perina. The distribution of the book in the trade was managed by Mary DelMonico, publisher, at DelMonico Books • Prestel, who has shared her expertise and collegiality with us across so many wonderful titles; at Prestel, we also thank Karen Farquhar, Erica Haas, and Amelia Rina.

Our Board of Trustees, overseen by Jason Moment, president and chair of the Corporation of the Fine Arts Museums Board, and Diane B. Wilsey, chair emerita, has enthusiastically advocated for this presentation, as they do for all of our museum initiatives. We extend our sincere thanks to Thomas P. Campbell, our director and CEO, who has avidly supported the final stages of bringing the exhibition to fruition. We also recognize Colin B. Bailey, former director, and Max Hollein, former director and CEO, who each championed this project and its merits in its formative stages. The staff at the Museums has worked together to realize this project. We acknowledge Ed Prohaska, chief financial officer, and Jason Seifer, director of finance; and Megan Bourne, chief of staff, and Melissa Powers, manager of board relations and special projects. We are grateful to Sheila Pressley, director of education; Emily Jennings, director of school and family programs; Francesca D'Alessio, senior manager of public programs; and Emily Stoller-Patterson, education digital project manager. We thank Amanda Riley, director of development, along with Karen Huang, senior director of individual and major giving; Larissa Trociuk, director of individual and major giving; and Derek Lance, individual giving officer. We are appreciative of Linda Butler, director of marketing, communications, and visitor experience, as well as Amy Browne, director of graphic design; Miriam Newcomer, director of public relations; Wynter Martinez, associate director of marketing; Helena Nordstrom, international public relations manager; and Benjamin Shaykin, lead graphic designer. We also thank Stuart Hata, director of retail operations, and Tim Niedert, book and media manager.

Merci beaucoup to our partners in Paris and, in particular, to Laurence des Cars, president of the Musées d'Orsay et de l'Orangerie, for her confidence in this project. Merci encore to "Team Tissot," in France, especially curatorial colleagues Marine Kisiel and Paul Perrin, as well as Lionel Britten and Marie-Liesse Boquien. Our collaboration was supplemented by the expertise of Cyrille Sciama, directeur général, Musée des Impressionnismes Giverny. Gratitude is given in abundance to Annie Dufour, head of publications at the Orsay, for her help with our catalogue, and Hélène Flon and Stéphanie de Brabander on the Orsay's wonderful exhibitions team. We also wish to thank former Orsay colleagues Guy Cogeval and Xavier Rey, with whom our Museums first began to dialogue about this project.

Beyond the exhibition and this catalogue, my PhD thesis on Tissot has been steadfastly supervised by Lynda Nead, FBA, Pevsner Chair of the History of Art at Birkbeck, University of London. I am grateful for the many conversations in her office overlooking Gordon Square where my ideas have been enriched and refined. I also received critical encouragement through a Research Support Grant from the Paul Mellon Centre, London, where I extend thanks to Mark Hallett, director of studies; Sarah Victoria Turner, deputy director for research; and Martin Postle, deputy director for grants and publications. Participation at several conferences also developed my ideas with helpful feedback from fellow scholars at "The Arts and Feeling in Nineteenth-Century Literature and Culture" (Birkbeck, London, 2015); "Biblical Imagery in the Age of Spectacle" (College Art Association, New York, 2016); "Consuming [the] Victorians" (Cardiff University, Wales, 2016); and "Crossing the Channel: French Refugee Artists in London (1870–1904)" (Paul Mellon Centre, London, 2018). Special thanks are given to friends on "Holy Hill" in Berkeley who shared kindred research interests with me, including Fr. Christopher Renz, OP, who kindly made available various treasures from the Blackfriars Gallery at the Dominican School of Philosophy & Theology, Berkeley; Kate Barush, assistant professor of art history and religion at the Graduate Theological Union, Berkeley, and the Jesuit School of Theology of Santa Clara University; and the late Fr. Michael Morris, OP. Frédéric Mantion along with Fred and Ysabel Monnier are true friends and keepers of James Tissot's legacy—their genuine enthusiasm for the artist and their sincere hospitality is beyond measure. Memories of our time together on the "Tissot Trail" are meaningful beyond words. Finally, this project would not have been possible without the infinite encouragement of my family, especially my husband, Stephen G. Stock, who provided the essential elements for research and writing: inspiration, editing advice, and endless cups of tea. I also wholeheartedly thank my parents, O. Eileen and Col. William E. Buron, who first encouraged the pursuit of intellectual curiosity. My final thanks must be expressed to the brilliant James Tissot, himself. It has been a privilege to study his life and work, and it is my sincere hope that this project does him justice. I dedicate this book to his memory.

MELISSA E. BURON
Director of the Art Division
Fine Arts Museums of San Francisco

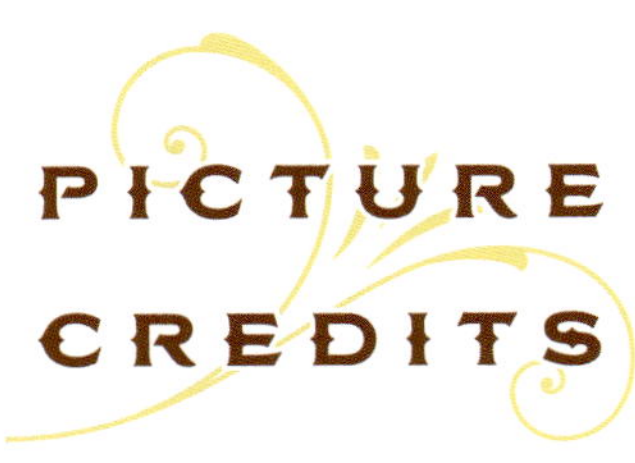

PLATE ILLUSTRATIONS

1, 18, 20, 90–94, 97, 105–116, 127, 130–132: Courtesy of the Fine Arts Museums of San Francisco; photograph by Randy Dodson. 2, 133: Courtesy of Frédéric Mantion; photograph by Eric Marin. 3, 21–23, 27: Musée d'Orsay, Paris / Bridgeman Images. 4: Photograph © National Gallery of Ireland, Dublin. 5–6, 14–15, 128: Courtesy of Colección Pérez Simón, México. 7, 120: Courtesy of the Museum of Art, Rhode Island School of Design (RISD), Providence. 8: Courtesy of the Cantor Arts Center, Stanford University, California; photograph by Randy Dodson. 9: © Stéphane Piera / Petit Palais / Roger-Viollet. 10: © Petit Palais / Roger-Viollet. 11–12, 49, 96: Courtesy of The Metropolitan Museum of Art, New York. 13, 95, 98: Courtesy of Ann and Gordon Getty; photograph by Randy Dodson. 16: Wimpole Hall, Cambridgeshire, England, The Bambridge Collection (National Trust), NT 207841 / Bridgeman Images. 17: Photograph by Cécile Clos / © Musée d'Arts de Nantes. 19, 58, 64: © Tate Images. 24, 37, 70: Courtesy of The J. Paul Getty Museum, Los Angeles. 25: bpk Bildagentur / Staatliche Kunsthalle Karlsruhe, Germany / Photograph: Annette Fischer / Heike Kohler. 26: Courtesy of the Philadelphia Museum of Art. 28: © RMN-Grand Palais / Art Resource, NY. 29: © National Portrait Gallery, London. 30: Universal Images Group North America LLC / Alamy Stock Photo. 31: Worcester Art Museum, Massachusetts, USA / Bridgeman Images. 32, 88–89: Musée d'Arts de Nantes, France / Bridgeman Images. 33: Photograph courtesy of Sotheby's, Inc. 34, 67: Painters / Alamy Stock Photo. 35: The Tokugawa Museum © The Tokugawa Museum Image Archives / DNPartcom. 36: Private Collection / Photograph © Christie's Images / Bridgeman Images. 38: Cincinnati Art Museum, Ohio, USA / Gift of Henry M. Goodyear, M.D. / Bridgeman Images. 39: Private Collection / Photograph © Peter Nahum at The Leicester Galleries, London / Bridgeman Images. 40: Allen Phillips / Wadsworth Atheneum Museum of Art, Hartford, Connecticut. 41, 80: Photograph © Christie's Images / Bridgeman Images. 42: National Museum Wales / Bridgeman Images. 43: Bristol Museums and Art Gallery, UK / Purchased, 1955 / Bridgeman Images. 44: Collection of the Dunedin Public Art Gallery. 45: Courtesy of the Manchester Art Gallery, UK. 46, 69: Guildhall Art Gallery, City of London / Bridgeman Images. 47, 123: Copyright © Art Gallery of Ontario, Toronto. 48: Sheffield Galleries and Museums Trust, UK / Photograph © Museums Sheffield / Bridgeman Images. 50: Art Gallery of Hamilton, Ontario, Canada / Bridgeman Images. 51: Private Collection, courtesy of Grant Ford Ltd. 52: © Tate Images 2019. 53, 68, 85, 104, 126: Private Collection. 54, 60, 78, 125: Courtesy of Diane B. Wilsey; photograph by Randy Dodson. 55: National Gallery of Canada, Ottawa, Ontario, Canada / Bridgeman Images. 56: Courtesy of the Toledo Museum of Art, Ohio. 57: Sterling and Francine Clark Art Institute, Williamstown, Massachusetts, USA / Bridgeman Images. 59: Private Collection / Bridgeman Images. 61: The Hepworth Wakefield, West Yorkshire, UK / Bridgeman Images. 62: Courtesy of the Speed Art Museum, Louisville, Kentucky. 63: Southampton City Art Gallery, Hampshire, UK / Bridgeman Images. 65: Minneapolis Institute of Art, Minnesota, USA / Gift of Mrs. Patrick Butler, by exchange / Bridgeman Images. 66: Picturenow / Contributor / Getty Images; Private Collection. 71: Tate, London, 2008. 72: Courtesy of the Auckland Art Gallery Toi o Tāmaki. 73: Private Collection / Photograph © Christie's Images / Bridgeman Images. 74: Musée Baron Martin, Gray, France / G. Dagli Orti / De Agostini Picture Library / Bridgeman Images. 75: Photograph courtesy of Sotheby's, Inc. © 2010. 76: Bibliothèque Nationale de France, Paris. Reserve Musée PL-72. 77: Bibliothèque Nationale de France, Paris. 79: Musée d'Orsay, Paris / Photograph © Photo Josse / Bridgeman Images. 81: © Christie's Images Limited. 82: Courtesy of the National Gallery of Art, Washington, DC. 83: Courtesy of The Marlene and Spencer Hays Collection. 84: Musée des Beaux-Arts de Montréal / The Montreal Museum of Fine Arts, Gift of Lord Strathcona and family, inv. 1927.410. 86: © RMN / Gérard Blot. 87: Musée d'Arts de Nantes, France. 99: Private Collection / Photograph © Christie's Images. 100: Courtesy of the Santa Barbara Museum of Art. 101: Baron Martin Museum Collection: GR-93-724; Studio shot Bernardot. 102: The Picture Art Collection / Alamy Stock Photo. 103: © Besançon, Musée des Beaux-Arts et d'Archéologie / Photograph C. Choffet. 117: Leeds Museums and Galleries (Leeds Art Gallery) UK / Bridgeman Images. 118: Courtesy of the Chrysler Museum of Art, Norfolk, Virginia. 119: Museum of Fine Arts, Boston, Massachusetts, USA / Juliana Cheney Edwards Collection / Bridgeman Images. 121: Snark / Art Resource, NY. 122: © Musée d'Art et d'Histoire, Ville de Genève / photograph: Bettina Jacot-Descombes. 124: Courtesy of the Albright-Knox Art Gallery, Buffalo. 129: Courtesy of the Iris & B. Gerald Cantor Center for Visual Arts at Stanford University, California; Mortimer C. Leventritt Fund. 134: Courtesy of The Morgan Library and Museum, New York. 135–139: Courtesy of The Jewish Museum, New York. 140–157: Courtesy of the Brooklyn Museum. A Note to the Reader: The order of the illustrations in the 1884 edition of *Renée Mauperin* (pls. 107–116) is as follows: *On the Seine* (pl. 107), *The Morning Kiss* (pl. 108), *Denoisel Reading in the Garden* (pl. 111), *At the Piano* (pl. 109), *In the Anteroom* (pl. 110), *After the Duel* (pl. 112), *Renée Fainting* (pl. 116), *In the Public Gardens* (pl. 113), *Renée and Her Father at Morimond* (pl. 114), and *In the Egyptian Ruins* (pl. 115).

FIGURE ILLUSTRATIONS

1–10: Courtesy of Malingue S.A., Paris. 11–12, 49, 87–90, 99, 101, 114: Courtesy of the Fine Arts Museums of San Francisco; photograph by Randy Dodson. 13: Courtesy of The Jewish Museum, New York. 14, 59, 85–86, Photo Album images (pp. 264–265), 131–137: Courtesy of Frédéric Mantion; photograph by Eric Marin. 15–22, 69, 107, 110, 116–117, 119–120, 122–126, 128–129, Tissot's Sales Notebook images (pp. 267 and 283): Courtesy of Frédéric Mantion. 23: Courtesy of Ralph and Terry Kovel; photograph by Julie Hahn. 24: © André Bocquel / Château des ducs de Bretagne—Musée d'Histoire de Nantes. 25: © RMN-Grand Palais / Art Resource, NY. 26–27: Photograph by Cécile Clos / © Musée d'Arts de Nantes. 28: Courtesy of the Royal Library of Belgium, Brussels. 29: Courtesy of The Museum of Fine Arts Ghent, Belgium, lukasweb.be; photograph by Michel Burez. 30: Private Collection / Bridgeman Images. 31: Private Collection; photograph by John Dean. 32: Courtesy of the Auer Collection, The State Heritage Museum, Saint Petersburg. 33: Musée d'Orsay, Paris / Bridgeman Images. 34: Musée de la Ville de Paris, Musée Carnavalet, Paris / Archives Charmet / Bridgeman Images. 35: Courtesy of The Cleveland Museum of Art. 36, 55, 104, 115: Bibliothèque Nationale de France, Paris. 37: Saint-Raymond 2019a. 38: Dealer Stock Books, Getty Research Institute, Los Angeles, piprod.getty.edu/starweb/stockbooks/servlet.starweb?path=stockbooks/stockbooks.web. 39: Private Collection / Photograph © Christie's Images / Bridgeman Images. 40: Lady Lever Art Gallery, Liverpool Museums / Bridgeman Images. 41, 57: Photograph © Christie's Images / Bridgeman Images. 42–43, 108: © The Trustees of the British Museum. 44: Courtesy of The Metropolitan Museum of Art, New York. 45, 48: Private Collection / Roy Miles Fine Paintings / Bridgeman Images. 46: Laing Art Gallery, Newcastle-upon-Tyne, UK / © Tyne & Wear Archives & Museums / Bridgeman Images. 47: National Gallery of Victoria, Melbourne, Australia / Bridgeman Images. 50: Michael Wentworth Collection, Ryerson and Burnham Archives, The Art Institute of Chicago; digital file # 200706_190410-001. 51: Photograph courtesy of Sotheby's, Inc. 52: Courtesy of Moyse's Hall Museum, West Suffolk Council, Bury Saint Edmunds, England. 53: © National Portrait Gallery, London. 54: Michael Wentworth Collection, Ryerson and Burnham Archives, The Art Institute of Chicago; digital file # 200706_190410-002. 56, 106: Courtesy of the National Gallery of Art, Washington. 58: Private Collection / Photo © Lefevre Fine Art Ltd., London / Bridgeman Images. 60, 64–65, 67: Courtesy of the Brooklyn Museum. 61: Courtesy of Blackfriars Gallery, Dominican School of Philosophy & Theology, Berkeley. 62–63: Archives Nationales, France; Rémi Champseit. 66: TCD / Prod.DB / Alamy Stock Photo. 68: Courtesy of Cohen Film Collection LLC. 70–71: Courtesy of the Harvard Art Museums / Fogg Museum, Cambridge, Massachusetts. 72–75: Courtesy of the Museum of Fine Arts, Boston. 76: Courtesy of the Art Gallery of New South Wales, Sydney; photograph by Jenni Carter, AGNSW 3420. 77: National Gallery of Art, Washington, DC; photo credit: Art Resource, NY. 78–79: Courtesy of the Courtauld Institute of Art Library, London. 80: 14755 / © MAD (Musée des Arts Décoratifs, Paris); photograph by Jean Tholance. 81: Musée d'Orsay, Paris; agence photo de la RMN-GP. 82: Courtesy of The Royal Pavilion, Art Gallery and Museums, Brighton and Hove, England; photograph by Tessa Hallmann. 83: 10645.A / © MAD (Musée des Arts Décoratifs, Paris); photograph by Jean Tholance. 84: 10645.B / © MAD (Musée des Arts Décoratifs, Paris); photograph by Jean Tholance. 91–92, 94, 96, 98, 100: Courtesy of the Paintings Conservation Department, Fine Arts Museums of San Francisco. 93: Courtesy of the Albright-Knox Art Gallery, Buffalo. 95: Courtesy of The J. Paul Getty Museum, Los Angeles. 97: Courtesy of the Iris & B. Gerald Cantor Center for Visual Arts at Stanford University, California; photograph by Randy Dodson. 102: Pascal Faligot 2009. 103: Image copyright © The Metropolitan Museum of Art, New York; image source: Art Resource, NY. 105: Fonds Nepveu-Degas, Musée d'Orsay, Paris, ODO 2008-1-2. 109: Fine Art Images / Heritage-Images. 111: © Tate, London 2019. 112: Courtesy of the National Portrait Gallery, London. 113: © Oxford University Images. 118: Painters / Alamy Stock Photo. 121: © The British Library Board. 127: The Picture Art Collection / Alamy Stock Photo. 130: Bibliothèque municipale de Besançon, Ph22552.

DECORATIVE ILLUSTRATIONS

Jacket: James Tissot, *Holyday*, 1876 (detail of pl. 52). p. 2: James Tissot, *October*, 1877 (detail of pl. 84). p. 6: James Tissot, *Self-Portrait*, ca. 1865 (detail of pl. 1). p. 8: James Tissot at his easel, ca. 1870s (detail of fig. 131). p. 10: James Tissot, *Young Women Looking at the Chinese Temple*, 1869 (detail of pl. 37). pp. 20–21: Detail of Tissot and his grand-niece Simone, ca. 1898 (p. 264). pp. 78–79: Detail of Tissot reclining on the grounds of his estate behind the Château de Buillon, ca. 1898–1901 (p. 265). p. 84: James Tissot, *Melancholy*, ca. 1869 (detail of pl. 13). p. 102: James Tissot, *Portrait of the Marquise de Miramon, née Thérèse Feuillant*, 1866 (detail of pl. 24). p. 118: James Tissot, *The Fan*, 1875 (detail of pl. 40). p. 126: James Tissot, *Too Early*, 1873 (detail of pl. 46). p. 146: James Tissot, *The Ball on Shipboard*, ca. 1874 (detail of pl. 71). p. 162: James Tissot, *Spring (Specimen of a Portrait)*, 1877 (detail of pl. 78). p. 194: James Tissot, *The Fashionable Beauty*, ca. 1883–1885 (detail of pl. 122). p. 210: James Tissot, *What Our Saviour Saw from the Cross*, ca. 1886–1894 (detail of pl. 152). pp. 224–225: Detail of Tissot walking on the grounds of his French estate, ca. 1895 (p. 265). p. 355: Detail of Tissot on the grounds behind the Château de Buillon, ca. 1898 (p. 264). End papers: Design by Bob Aufuldish, Aufuldish & Warinner.

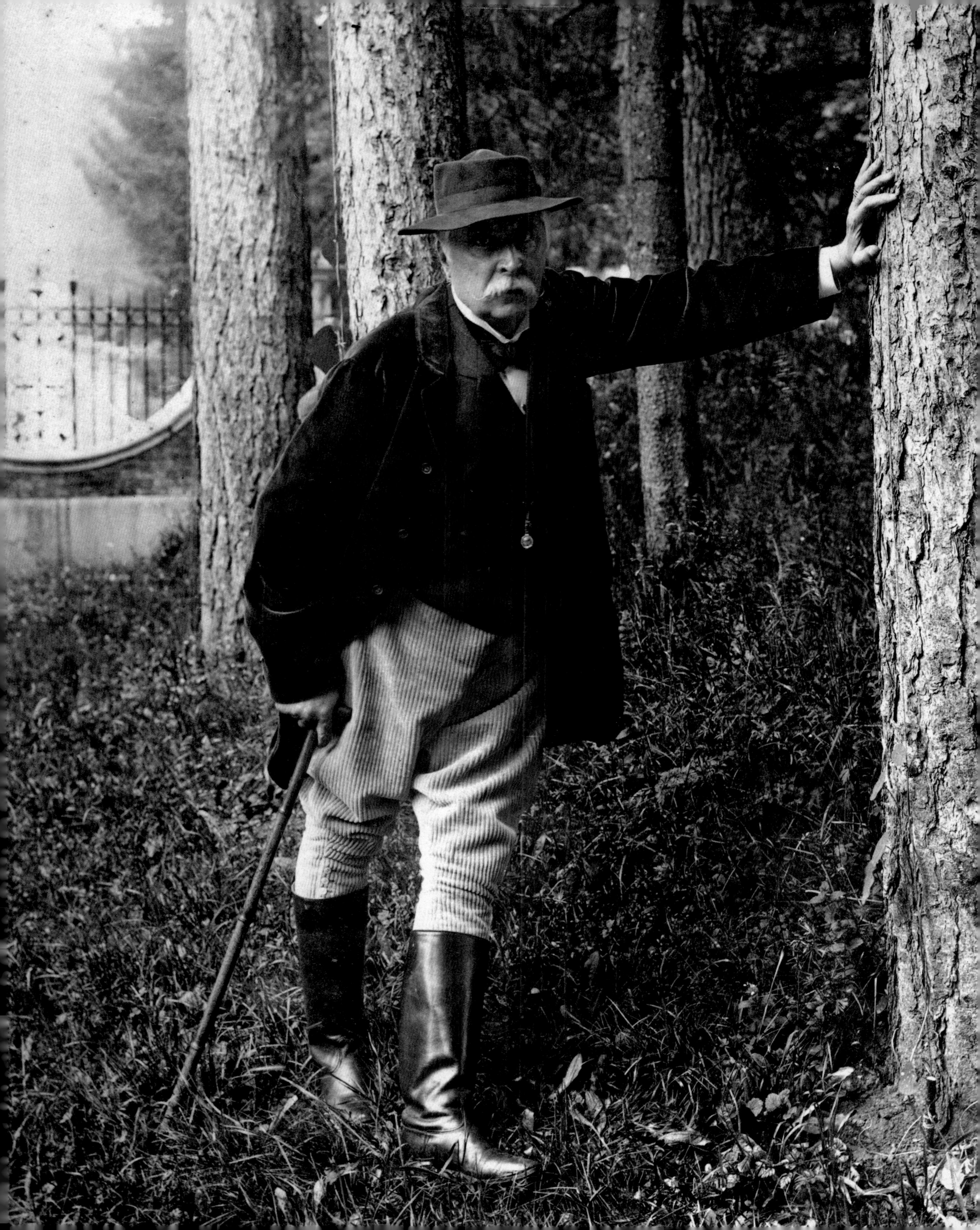

Published in 2019 by
the Fine Arts Museums of San Francisco and DelMonico Books • Prestel
on the occasion of the exhibition

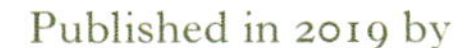

JAMES TISSOT
FASHION AND FAITH

at the Legion of Honor, San Francisco, from
October 12, 2019, to February 9, 2020,
and at the Musée d'Orsay, Paris, from
March 23 to July 19, 2020.

This exhibition is organized by
the Fine Arts Museums of San Francisco and
the Musées d'Orsay et de l'Orangerie, Paris.

de Young \ \ Legion of Honor fine arts museums of san francisco

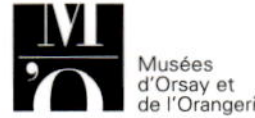

PRESENTING SPONSORS
John A. and Cynthia Fry Gunn
Robert G. and Sue Douthit O'Donnell
Barbro and Bernard Osher
Denise Littlefield Sobel
Diane B. Wilsey

MAJOR SUPPORT
Gladyne Kenderdine Mitchell
Barbara A. Wolfe

SIGNIFICANT SUPPORT
The Diana Dollar Knowles Fund
Carole McNeil

GENEROUS SUPPORT
Lucy Young Hamilton
David A. Wollenberg

ADDITIONAL SUPPORT IS PROVIDED BY
Sandra and Paul Bessières, Marion Moore Cope,
George and Leslie Hume, Michael and Dorothy Leung, and
Christina and Barry Ongerth.

Scientific analyses were performed by the Northwestern University / Art Institute of Chicago Center for Scientific Studies in the Arts and made possible by the generous support of the Andrew W. Mellon Foundation.

The exhibition is supported by an indemnity from the Federal Council on the Arts and the Humanities.

The catalogue is published with the assistance of the Andrew W. Mellon Foundation Endowment for Publications. Additional research support is provided by the Paul Mellon Centre for Studies in British Art.

Library of Congress Cataloguing in Publication Control Number: 2019025111

A CIP catalogue record for this book is available from the British Library.

ISBN: 978-3-7913-5919-9

Quotation from p. 7: "Nos créations industrielles et artistiques peuvent périr, nos moeurs et nos costumes peuvent tomber dans l'oubli, un tableau de M. Tissot suffira aux archéologues de l'avenir pour reconstituer notre époque." Roy 1869.

A NOTE TO THE READER
This volume provides catalogue raisonné numbers (in parentheses) for Tissot's works on paper, corresponding to Michael Justin Wentworth, *James Tissot: Catalogue Raisonné of his Prints* (Minneapolis: Minneapolis Institute of Arts, 1978).

Fine Arts Museums of San Francisco
de Young
Golden Gate Park
50 Hagiwara Tea Garden Drive
San Francisco, CA 94118-4502
www.famsf.org

Leslie Dutcher, Director of Publications
Nikki Bazar, Editor
Trina Enriquez, Editor
Victoria Gannon, Editor
Kate Bove, Associate Editor
José Jovel, Publications Assistant
Jennifer Melikian, Publications Intern

Edited and project managed by Nikki Bazar
Designed and typeset by Bob Aufuldish, Aufuldish & Warinner
Proofread by Susan Richmond with Kate Bove and Trina Enriquez
Catalogue Checklist edited by Victoria Gannon
Translations by Alexandra Bonfante-Warren and Rose Vekony
Index by Jane Friedman
Picture research by José Jovel
Color separations and printing by Verona Libri, Verona, Italy

DelMonico Books, an imprint of Prestel, a member of Verlagsgruppe Random House GmbH

Prestel Verlag
Neumarkter Strasse 28
81673 Munich

Prestel Publishing Ltd.
14–17 Wells Street
London W1T 3PD

Prestel Publishing
900 Broadway, Suite 603
New York, NY 10003

www.prestel.com

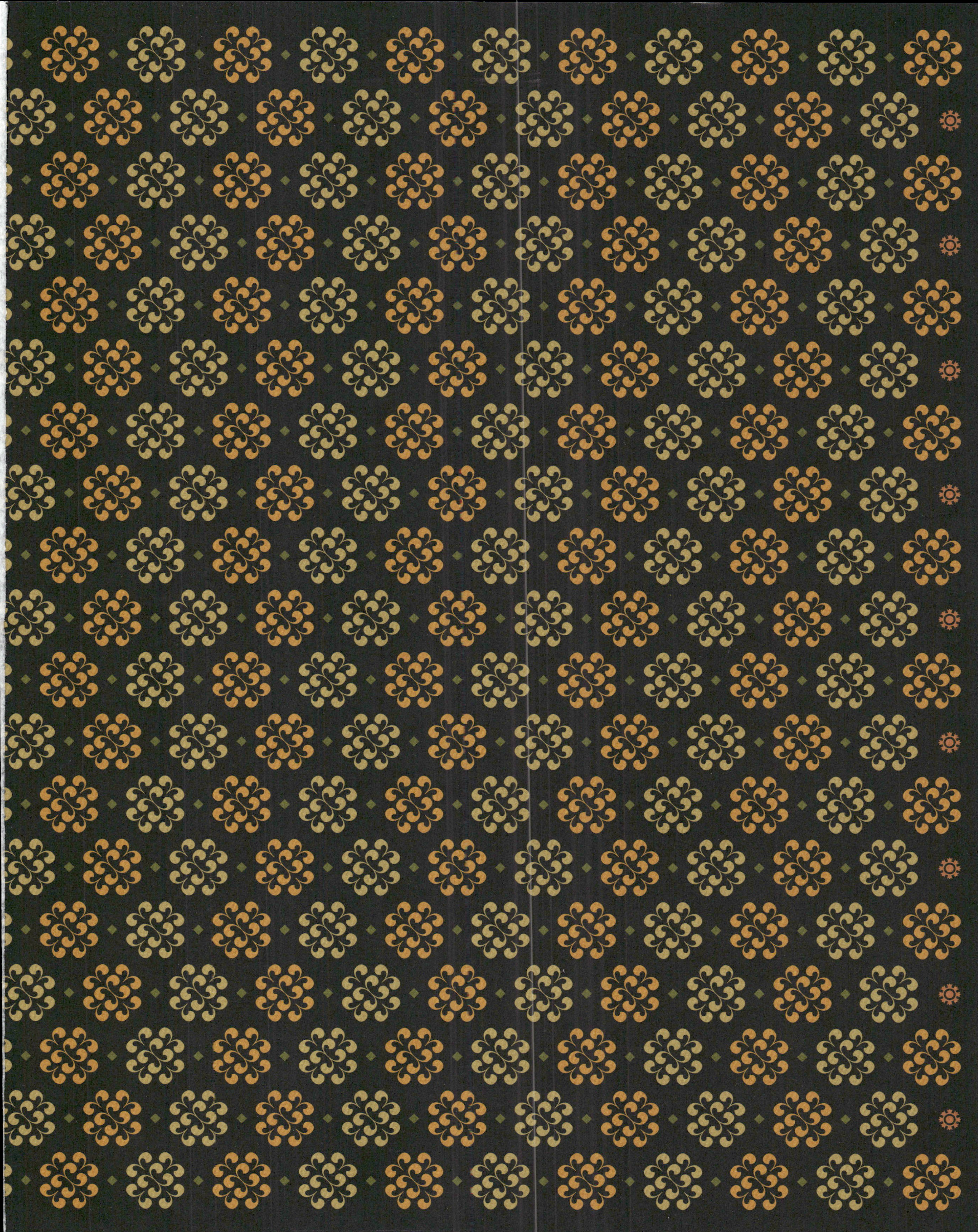

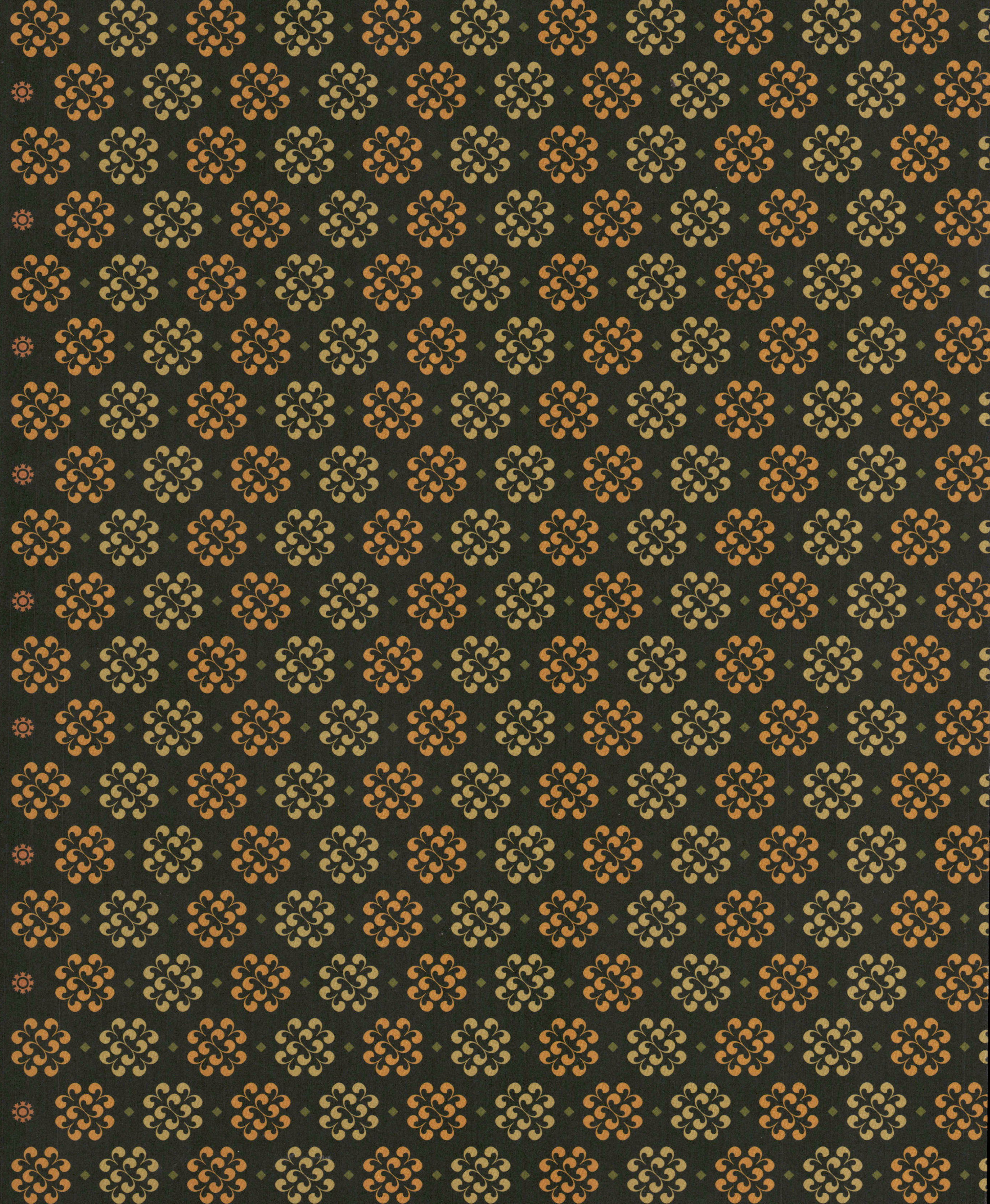